Psychology Themes & Variations

Custom Edition for Community College of Baltimore County

Wayne Weiten

CENGAGE
Learning·

Australia • Brazil • Japan • Korea • Mexico • Singapore • Spain • United Kingdom • United States

CENGAGE
Learning·

Psychology Themes & Variations

Psychology Themes & Variations, Briefer Version, Ninth Edition
Wayne Weiten
© 2014 Cengage Learning. All rights reserved.

Senior Project Development Manager:
Linda deStefano

Market Development Manager:
Heather Kramer

Senior Production/Manufacturing Manager:
Donna M. Brown

Production Editorial Manager:
Kim Fry

Sr. Rights Acquisition Account Manager:
Todd Osborne

For product information and technology assistance, contact us at
Cengage Learning Customer & Sales Support, 1-800-354-9706

For permission to use material from this text or product,
submit all requests online at **cengage.com/permissions**
Further permissions questions can be emailed to
permissionrequest@cengage.com

This book contains select works from existing Cengage Learning resources and was produced by Cengage Learning Custom Solutions for collegiate use. As such, those adopting and/or contributing to this work are responsible for editorial content accuracy, continuity and completeness.

Compilation © 2013 Cengage Learning

ISBN-13: 978-1-285-89418-8

ISBN-10: 1-285-89418-9

Cengage Learning
5191 Natorp Boulevard
Mason, Ohio 45040
USA
Cengage Learning is a leading provider of customized learning solutions with office locations around the globe, including Singapore, the United Kingdom, Australia, Mexico, Brazil, and Japan. Locate your local office at:
international.cengage.com/region.

Cengage Learning products are represented in Canada by Nelson Education, Ltd.
For your lifelong learning solutions, visit **www.cengage.com/custom.**
Visit our corporate website at **www.cengage.com.**

Printed in the United States of America

Common Course Outline
PSYC 101
Introduction to Psychology
3 credits

The Community College of Baltimore County

Description

PSYC 101 – 3 credits - Introduction to Psychology is a survey of the science of psychology. Topics addressed include research methods, biological bases of behavior, sensation and perception, states of consciousness, learning, memory, motivation and emotion, language, lifespan development, intelligence, stress and health, social behavior, personality, abnormal behavior and its treatment. Applications of psychology in a culturally diverse world are discussed.

3 credits
Prerequisites: ENGL 052, RDNG 052, and MATH 081

Overall Course Objectives

Upon completion of the course, students will be able to:

1. define the fundamental concepts associated with each of the course's major topics;
2. identify the advantages and disadvantages of the various research methods used to study animal and human behavior and mental processes;
3. apply major theoretical perspectives and/or data derived from psychological research to maximize self-management, self-improvement, and/or resolve personal, relational, social and/or workplace situations;
4. analyze psychological information found in print, information technology, film, television, radio, and other resources by evaluating the authenticity, timeliness, relevance and validity of that information;
5. explain the ethical considerations that govern psychological research with humans and animals and in conducting psychotherapy;
6. demonstrate the skills of accessing, evaluating, and communicating current research pertaining to psychology topics by engaging in class discussions, individual or collaborative presentations, and/or written assignments that are well organized, cohesive and logical;
7. explain how psychological data and theories have continually evolved and why that requires the ability to pursue lifelong learning;
8. analyze and evaluate the role of diverse cultural, international, and global perspectives in the formation of differences in behavior, attitudes, and perceptions; and
9. analyze and evaluate their strengths and weaknesses as learners.

Major Topics

I.	The evolution of modern psychology
II.	Research methods and ethical issues in psychology
III.	The sub-fields of psychology
IV.	Biological bases of behavior and mental processes
V.	Sensation and perception
VI.	States of consciousness
VII.	Basic principles of learning
VIII.	Memory
IX.	Cognition, language and intelligence
X.	Human development
XI.	Motivation and emotion
XII.	Personality theories and assessment
XIII.	Stress: its causes, effects and control
XIV.	Psychological disorders: their nature and causes
XV.	Prevention and treatment of mental disorders
XVI.	Social psychology
XVII.	The nature of cultural and gender diversity in the human experience

Course Requirements

Grading/exams: Grading procedures will be determined by the individual faculty member but will include the following:

A minimum of three exams with four or more recommended

Written Assignments: Students are required to submit one or more critical written assignment totaling at least 1000 words on a topic in Introduction to Psychology. These are assignments are to be based on psychological research articles and/or books, InfoTech sources, media, or service learning projects. The written assignments are to have students demonstrate an integration of psychological vocabulary, perspectives, and principles. Students are required to utilize appropriate academic resources. An accepted citation format must be used (preferably the format of the American Psychological Association).

In addition, students will also submit at least one additional assessment, such as: another written assignment, a class presentation, a collaborative learning assignment, a computer or laboratory activity pertaining to Introduction to Psychology.

Completion of a learning styles and/or study skills activities to provide students insight into their strengths and weaknesses as learners is recommended.

Other Course Information

This is an approved General Education Social and Behavioral Science course.

Revised 5/2012

T. J., this one is for you

About the Author

Wayne Weiten is a graduate of Bradley University and received his Ph.D. in social psychology from the University of Illinois, Chicago in 1981. He has taught at the College of DuPage and Santa Clara University and currently teaches at the University of Nevada, Las Vegas. He has received distinguished teaching awards from Division Two of the American Psychological Association (APA) and from the College of DuPage. He is a Fellow of Divisions 1 and 2 of the American Psychological Association and a Fellow of the Midwestern Psychological Association. In 1991 he helped chair the APA National Conference on Enhancing the Quality of Undergraduate Education in Psychology, and in 1996–1997 he served as president of the Society for the Teaching of Psychology. In 2006, one of the five national teaching awards given annually by the Society for the Teaching of Psychology was named in his honor. He currently is serving as president of the Rocky Mountain Psychological Association. Weiten has conducted research on a wide range of topics, including educational measurement, jury decision-making, attribution theory, pressure as a form of stress, cerebral specialization, and the technology of textbooks. He is also the author of *Psychology: Themes & Variations* (2013, 9th ed.) and a co-author of *Psychology Applied to Modern Life: Adjustment in the Twenty-First Century* (with Dana S. Dunn and Elizabeth Yost Hammer, 2012, 10th ed.). Weiten has also created an educational CD-ROM titled *PsykTrek: A Multimedia Introduction to Psychology*.

To the Instructor

Psychology is an exciting, dynamic discipline that has grown by leaps and bounds in recent decades. This progress has been reflected in the field's introductory texts, which have grown longer and longer. However, the length of the introductory psychology course generally has not changed. Hence, an increasing number of professors are reporting that they find it difficult to cover the wealth of material found in the typical introductory text. With this situation in mind, I decided to write a briefer version of *Psychology: Themes and Variations* to help meet the needs of those teachers who would like a challenging, but concise, introductory text.

If I had to sum up in a single sentence what I hope will distinguish this text, the sentence would be this: I have set out to create a *paradox* instead of a *compromise*.

Let me elaborate. An introductory psychology text must satisfy two disparate audiences: professors and students. Because of the tension between the divergent needs and preferences of these audiences, textbook authors usually indicate that they have attempted to strike a compromise between being theoretical versus practical, comprehensive versus comprehensible, research oriented versus applied, rigorous versus accessible, and so forth. However, I believe that many of these dichotomies are false. As Kurt Lewin once remarked, "What could be more practical than a good theory?" Similarly, is rigorous really the opposite of accessible? Not in my dictionary. I maintain that many of the antagonistic goals that we strive for in our textbooks only *seem* incompatible and that we may not need to make compromises as often as we assume.

In my estimation, a good introductory textbook is a paradox in that it integrates characteristics and goals that appear contradictory. With this in mind, I have endeavored to write a text that is paradoxical in three ways. First, in surveying psychology's broad range of content, I have tried to show that our interests are characterized by diversity *and* unity. Second, I have emphasized both research *and* application and how they work in harmony. Finally, I have aspired to write a book that is challenging to think about *and* easy to learn from. Let's take a closer look at these goals.

Goals

1. *To show both the unity and the diversity of psychology's subject matter.* Students entering an introductory psychology course are often unaware of the immense diversity of subjects studied by psychologists. I find this diversity to be part of psychology's charm, and throughout the book I highlight the enormous range of questions and issues addressed by psychology. Of course, our diversity proves disconcerting for some students, who see little continuity among such disparate areas of research as physiology, motivation, cognition, and abnormal behavior. Indeed, in this era of specialization, even some psychologists express concern about the fragmentation of the field.

However, I believe that there is considerable overlap among the subfields of psychology and that we should emphasize their common core by accenting the connections and similarities among them. Consequently, I portray psychology as an integrated whole rather than as a mosaic of loosely related parts. A principal goal of this text, then, is to highlight the unity in psychology's intellectual heritage (the themes), as well as the diversity of psychology's interests and uses (the variations).

2. *To illuminate the process of research and its intimate link to application.* For me, a research-oriented book is not one that bulges with summaries of many studies but one that enhances students' appreciation of the logic and excitement of empirical inquiry. I want students to appreciate the strengths of the empirical approach and to see scientific psychology as a creative effort to solve intriguing behavioral puzzles. For this reason, the text emphasizes not only *what* we know (and don't know) but *how* we attempt to find

out. It examines methods in some detail and encourages students to adopt the skeptical attitude of a scientist and to think critically about claims regarding behavior.

Learning the virtues of research should not mean that students cannot also satisfy their desire for concrete, personally useful information about the challenges of everyday life. Most researchers believe that psychology has a great deal to offer those outside the field and that psychologists should share the practical implications of their work. In this text, practical insights are carefully qualified and closely tied to data, so that students can see the interdependence of research and application. I find that students come to appreciate the science of psychology more when they see that worthwhile practical applications are derived from careful research and sound theory.

3. *To make the text challenging to think about and easy to learn from.* Perhaps most of all, I have sought to create a book of ideas rather than a compendium of studies. I consistently emphasize concepts and theories over facts, and I focus on major issues and tough questions that cut across the subfields of psychology (for example, the extent to which behavior is governed by nature, nurture, and their interaction), as opposed to parochial debates (such as the merits of averaging versus adding in impression formation). Challenging students to think also means urging them to confront the complexity and ambiguity of our knowledge. Thus, the text doesn't skirt gray areas, unresolved questions, and theoretical controversies. Instead, readers are encouraged to contemplate open-ended questions, to examine their assumptions about behavior, and to apply psychological concepts to their own lives. My goal is not simply to describe psychology but to stimulate students' intellectual growth.

However, students can grapple with "the big issues and tough questions" only if they first master the basic concepts and principles of psychology—ideally, with as little struggle as possible. In my writing, I never let myself forget that a textbook is a tool for teaching. Accordingly, I have taken great care to ensure that the book's content, organization, writing, illustrations, and pedagogical aids work in harmony to facilitate instruction and learning.

Admittedly, these goals are ambitious. If you're skeptical, you have every right to be. Let me explain how I have tried to realize the objectives I have outlined.

Special Features

This text has a variety of unusual features, each contributing in its own way to the book's paradoxical nature. These special features include unifying themes, Personal Application sections, Critical Thinking Application sections, Reality Checks, a didactic illustration program, an integrated running glossary, Concept Checks, Key Learning Goals, and Practice Tests.

UNIFYING THEMES

Chapter 1 introduces seven key ideas that serve as unifying themes throughout the text. The themes serve several purposes. First, they provide threads of continuity across chapters that help students see the connections among various areas of research in psychology. Second, as the themes evolve over the course of the book, they provide a forum for a relatively sophisticated discussion of enduring issues in psychology, thus helping to make this a "book of ideas." Third, the themes focus a spotlight on a number of basic insights about psychology and its subject matter that should leave lasting impressions on your students. In selecting the themes, the question I asked myself (and other professors) was, "What do I really want students to remember five years from now?" The resulting themes are grouped into two sets.

THEMES RELATED TO PSYCHOLOGY AS A FIELD OF STUDY

Theme 1: Psychology is empirical. This theme is used to enhance the student's appreciation of psychology's scientific nature and to demonstrate the advantages of empiricism over uncritical common sense and speculation. I also use this theme to encourage the reader to adopt a scientist's skeptical attitude and to engage in more critical thinking about information of all kinds.

Theme 2: Psychology is theoretically diverse. Students are often confused by psychology's theoretical pluralism and view it as a weakness. I don't downplay or apologize for our field's theoretical diversity because I honestly believe that it is one of our greatest strengths. Throughout the book, I provide concrete examples of how clashing theories have stimulated productive research, how converging on a question from several perspectives can yield increased understanding, and how competing theories are sometimes reconciled in the end.

Theme 3: Psychology evolves in a sociohistorical context. This theme emphasizes that psychology is embedded in the ebb and flow of everyday life. The text shows how the spirit of the times has often shaped psychology's evolution and how progress in psychology leaves its mark on our society.

THEMES RELATED TO PSYCHOLOGY'S SUBJECT MATTER

Theme 4: Behavior is determined by multiple causes. Throughout the book, I emphasize, and repeatedly illustrate, that behavioral processes are complex and that multifactorial causation is the rule. This theme is used to discourage simplistic, single-cause thinking and to encourage more critical reasoning.

Theme 5: People's behavior is shaped by their cultural heritage. This theme is intended to enhance students' appreciation of how cultural factors moderate psychological processes and how the viewpoint of one's own culture can distort one's interpretation of the behavior of people from other cultures. The discussions that elaborate on this theme do not simply celebrate diversity. They strike a careful balance: accurately reflecting the research in this area while highlighting both cultural variations and similarities in behavior.

Theme 6: Heredity and environment jointly influence behavior. Repeatedly discussing this theme permits me to explore the nature versus nurture issue in all its complexity. Over a series of chapters, students gradually learn how biology shapes behavior, how experience shapes behavior, and how scientists estimate the relative importance of each. Along the way, students will gain an in-depth appreciation of what we mean when we say that heredity and environment interact.

Theme 7: Our experience of the world is highly subjective. All of us tend to forget the extent to which we view the world through our own personal lens. This theme is used to explain the principles that underlie the subjectivity of human experience, to clarify its implications, and to repeatedly remind readers that their view of the world is not the only legitimate view.

After introducing all seven themes in Chapter 1, I discuss different sets of themes in each chapter as they are relevant to the subject matter. The connections between a chapter's content and the unifying themes are highlighted in a standard section near the end of the chapter, in which I reflect on the "lessons to be learned" from the chapter. The discussions of the unifying themes are largely confined to these sections, titled "Reflecting on the Chapter's Themes." I have not tried to make every chapter illustrate a certain number of themes. Rather, the themes were allowed to emerge naturally, and I found that two to five surfaced in any given chapter. The chart on the next page shows which themes are highlighted in each chapter. Color-coded icons near the beginning of each "Reflecting on the Chapter's Themes" section indicate the specific themes featured in each chapter.

PERSONAL APPLICATIONS

To reinforce the pragmatic implications of theory and research stressed throughout the text, each chapter includes a Personal Application section that highlights the practical side of psychology. Each Personal Application devotes two to three *pages* of text (rather

Unifying Themes Highlighted in Each Chapter

Chapter	1 Empiricism	2 Theoretical Diversity	3 Sociohistorical Context	4 Multifactorial Causation	5 Cultural Heritage	6 Heredity and Environment	7 Subjectivity of Experience
1. The Evolution of Psychology	✓	✓	✓	✓	✓	✓	✓
2. The Research Enterprise in Psychology	✓						✓
3. The Biological Bases of Behavior	✓			✓		✓	
4. Sensation and Perception		✓			✓		✓
5. Variations in Consciousness		✓	✓	✓	✓		✓
6. Learning			✓			✓	
7. Human Memory		✓		✓			✓
8. Cognition and Intelligence	✓		✓		✓	✓	✓
9. Motivation and Emotion		✓	✓	✓	✓	✓	
10. Human Development Across the Life Span		✓	✓	✓	✓	✓	
11. Personality		✓	✓		✓		
12. Social Behavior	✓			✓	✓		✓
13. Stress, Coping, and Health				✓			✓
14. Psychological Disorders			✓	✓	✓	✓	
15. Treatment of Psychological Disorders		✓			✓		

than the usual box) to a single issue that should be of special interest to many of your students. Although most of the Personal Application sections have a "how to" character, they continue to review studies and summarize data in much the same way as the main body of each chapter. Thus, they portray research and application not as incompatible polarities but as two sides of the same coin. Many of the Personal Applications—such as those on finding and reading journal articles, understanding art and illusion, and improving stress management—provide topical coverage unusual for an introductory text.

CRITICAL THINKING APPLICATIONS

A great deal of unusual coverage can also be found in the Critical Thinking Applications that follow the Personal Applications. Conceived by Diane Halpern (Claremont McKenna College), a leading authority on critical thinking, these applications are based on the assumption that critical thinking skills can be taught. They do not simply review research critically, as is typically the case in other introductory texts. Instead, they introduce and model a host of critical thinking skills, such as looking for contradictory evidence or alternative explanations; recognizing anecdotal evidence, circular reasoning, hindsight bias, reification, weak analogies, and false dichotomies; evaluating arguments systematically; and working with cumulative and conjunctive probabilities.

The specific skills discussed in the Critical Thinking Applications are listed in the accompanying table (see page x), where they are organized into five categories using a taxonomy developed by Halpern (1994). In each chapter, some of these skills are applied to topics and issues related to the chapter's content. For instance, in the chapter that covers drug abuse (Chapter 5), the concept of alcoholism is used to highlight the immense power of definitions and to illustrate how circular reasoning can seem so seductive. Skills that are particularly important may surface in more than one chapter, so students see them applied in a variety of contexts. For example, in Chapter 7 students learn how hindsight bias can contaminate memory, and in Chapter 11 they see how hindsight can distort analyses of personality. Repeated practice across chapters should help students spontaneously recognize the relevance of specific critical thinking skills when they encounter certain types of information. The skills approach taken to critical thinking and the content it has spawned are unprecedented for an introductory psychology text.

REALITY CHECKS

Each chapter includes three or four Reality Checks, which address common misconceptions related to psychology and provide direct refutations of the misinformation. These Reality Checks are sprinkled throughout the chapters, appearing adjacent to the relevant material. Examples of misconceptions that are dispelled include the myth that B. F. Skinner raised his daughter in a Skinner box, which led to her becoming severely disturbed (Chapter 1); the notion that people use only 10% of their brains (Chapter 3); the assumption that people who are color blind see the world in black and white (Chapter 4); and the idea that it is dangerous to awaken someone who is sleepwalking (Chapter 5).

Most of the misconceptions covered in these Reality Checks were addressed in previous editions, but not with direct refutations. In other words, accurate information was provided on the issues, but usually without explicitly stating the misconception and providing a rebuttal. Why the change in strategy? The impetus was a fascinating article in *Teaching of Psychology* by Patricia Kowalski and Annette Taylor (2009). This article summarized evidence that students typically come into introductory psychology with a variety of misconceptions and that, for the most part, they tend to leave the course with their misconceptions intact. To see if this problem could be ameliorated, they tested the impact of direct refutations on students' misconceptions in the introductory course. Their data suggested that explicit repudiations of erroneous ideas reduce students' misconceptions more effectively than the simple provision of correct information. With that evidence in mind, I decided to craft this new feature that explicitly confronts and disputes common fallacies that range from oversimplified to profoundly inaccurate. Because the Reality Checks mostly supplement the normal coverage in the text, I chose to keep them concise. For the most part, they can be found in the margins of the pages.

A DIDACTIC ILLUSTRATION PROGRAM

When I first outlined my plans for this text, I indicated that I wanted every aspect of the illustration program to have a genuine didactic purpose and that I wanted to be deeply involved in its development. In retrospect, I had no idea what I was getting myself into, but it has been a rewarding learning experience. In any event, I have been intimately involved in planning every detail of the illustration program. I have endeavored to create a program of figures, diagrams, photos, and tables that work hand in hand with the prose to strengthen and clarify the main points in the text.

The most obvious results of our didactic approach to illustration are the Illustrated Overviews that combine tabular information, photos, diagrams, and sketches to provide exciting overviews of key ideas in the areas of methods, sensation and perception, learning, personality theory, psychopathology, and psychotherapy. But I hope you will also notice the subtleties of the illustration program. For instance, diagrams of important

Taxonomy of Skills Covered in the Critical Thinking Applications

Verbal Reasoning Skills

Understanding the way definitions shape how people think about issues	Chapter 5
Identifying the source of definitions	Chapter 5
Avoiding the nominal fallacy in working with definitions and labels	Chapter 5
Recognizing and avoiding reification	Chapter 8

Argument/Persuasion Analysis Skills

Understanding the elements of an argument	Chapter 9
Recognizing and avoiding common fallacies, such as irrelevant reasons, circular reasoning, slippery slope reasoning, weak analogies, and false dichotomies	Chapters 9 and 10
Evaluating arguments systematically	Chapter 9
Recognizing and avoiding appeals to ignorance	Chapter 8
Understanding how Pavlovian conditioning can be used to manipulate emotions	Chapter 6
Developing the ability to detect conditioning procedures used in the media	Chapter 6
Recognizing social influence strategies	Chapter 12
Judging the credibility of an information source	Chapter 12

Skills in Thinking as Hypothesis Testing

Looking for alternative explanations for findings and events	Chapters 1, 8, and 10
Looking for contradictory evidence	Chapters 1, 3, and 8
Recognizing the limitations of anecdotal evidence	Chapters 2 and 15
Understanding the need to seek disconfirming evidence	Chapter 7
Understanding the limitations of correlational evidence	Chapters 10 and 13
Understanding the limitations of statistical significance	Chapter 13
Recognizing situations in which placebo effects might occur	Chapter 15

Skills in Working with Likelihood and Uncertainty

Utilizing base rates in making predictions and evaluating probabilities	Chapter 13
Understanding cumulative probabilities	Chapter 14
Understanding conjunctive probabilities	Chapter 14
Understanding the limitations of the representativeness heuristic	Chapter 14
Understanding the limitations of the availability heuristic	Chapter 14
Recognizing situations in which regression toward the mean may occur	Chapter 15
Understanding the limits of extrapolation	Chapter 3

Decision-Making and Problem-Solving Skills

Using evidence-based decision making	Chapter 2
Recognizing the bias in hindsight analysis	Chapters 7 and 11
Seeking information to reduce uncertainty	Chapter 13
Making risk-benefit assessments	Chapter 13
Generating and evaluating alternative courses of action	Chapter 13
Recognizing overconfidence in human cognition	Chapter 7
Understanding the limitations and fallibility of human memory	Chapter 7
Understanding how contrast effects can influence judgments and decisions	Chapter 4
Recognizing when extreme comparitors are being used	Chapter 4

concepts (conditioning, synaptic transmission, EEGs, experimental design, and so forth) are often repeated in several chapters (with variations) to highlight connections among research areas and to enhance students' mastery of key ideas. Numerous easy-to-understand graphs of research results underscore psychology's foundation in research, and photos and diagrams often bolster each other (for example, see the treatment of classical conditioning in Chapter 6). Color is used carefully as an organizational device, and visual schematics help simplify hard-to-visualize concepts (see, for instance, the figure explaining reaction range for intelligence in Chapter 8). All of these efforts have gone toward the service of one master: the desire to make this an inviting book that is easy to learn from.

INTEGRATED RUNNING GLOSSARY

An introductory text should place great emphasis on acquainting students with psychology's technical language—not for the sake of jargon, but because a great many of our key terms are also our cornerstone concepts (for example, *independent variable, reliability,* and *cognitive dissonance*). This text handles terminology with a running glossary embedded in the prose itself. The terms are set off in **blue boldface italics**, and the definitions follow in **blue, boldface roman** type. This approach retains the two advantages of a conventional running glossary: vocabulary items are made salient, and their definitions are readily accessible. However, it does so without interrupting the flow of discourse, while eliminating redundancy between text matter and marginal entries.

CONCEPT CHECKS

To help students assess their mastery of important ideas, Concept Checks are sprinkled throughout the book. In keeping with my goal of making this a book of ideas, the Concept Checks challenge students to apply ideas instead of testing rote memory. For example, in Chapter 6 the reader is asked to analyze realistic examples of conditioning and identify conditioned stimuli and responses, reinforcers, and schedules of reinforcement. Many of the Concept Checks require the reader to put together ideas introduced in different sections of the chapter. For instance, in Chapter 4 students are asked to identify parallels between vision and hearing. Some of the Concept Checks are quite challenging, but students find them engaging, and they report that the answers (available in Appendix A in the back of the book) are often illuminating.

KEY LEARNING GOALS AND REVIEWS OF KEY LEARNING GOALS

To help students organize, assimilate, and remember important ideas, each major section of every chapter begins with a succinct, numbered set of Key Learning Goals. The Key Learning Goals are found adjacent to the level-one headings that begin each major section. The Key Learning Goals are thought-provoking learning objectives that should help students focus on the key issues in each section. These learning goals provide the organization for the Review of Key Learning Goals found at the end of the chapter. This is a highly detailed summary of the chapter that addresses the issues posed in the Key Learning Goals. Where appropriate, the Reviews of Key Learning Goals also include figures, diagrams, and photos from the chapter to further reinforce important concepts and principles.

PRACTICE TESTS

In addition to the answers to the Concept Checks, Appendix A at the back of the book includes a Practice Test for each chapter in the text. These 12-item multiple-choice Practice Tests should give students realistic assessments of their mastery of specific chapters and valuable practice taking the type of test that many of them will face in the classroom (if the instructor uses the Test Bank). This feature grew out of some research that I conducted on students' use of textbook pedagogical devices (see Weiten, Guadagno, & Beck, 1996). This research indicated that students pay scant attention to some standard pedagogical devices. When I grilled my students to gain a better understanding of this finding, it quickly became apparent that students are very pragmatic about pedagogy. Essentially, their refrain was "We want study aids that will help us pass the next test." With this mandate in mind, I devised the Practice Tests. They should be useful, as I took most of the items from Test Banks for previous editions.

In addition to the special features just described, the text includes a variety of more conventional, "tried and true" features. The back of the book contains a standard *alphabetical glossary*. Opening *outlines* preview each chapter, I make frequent use of *italics for emphasis*, and I depend on *frequent headings* to maximize organizational clarity. The preface for students describes these pedagogical devices in more detail.

Content

The text is divided into 15 chapters, which follow a traditional ordering. The chapters are not grouped into sections or parts, primarily because such groupings can limit your options if you want to reorganize the order of topics. The chapters are written in a way that facilitates organizational flexibility, as I always assumed that some chapters might be omitted or presented in a different order.

The topical coverage in the text is relatively conventional, but there are some subtle departures from the norm. For instance, Chapter 1 presents a relatively "meaty" discussion of the evolution of ideas in psychology. This coverage of history lays the foundation for many of the crucial ideas emphasized in subsequent chapters. The historical perspective is also my way of reaching out to the students who find that psychology isn't what they expected it to be. If we want students to contemplate the mysteries of behavior, we must begin by clearing up the biggest mysteries of them all: "Where did these rats, statistics, synapses, and genes come from, what could they possibly have in common, and why doesn't this course bear any resemblance to what I anticipated?" I use history as a vehicle to explain how psychology evolved into its modern form and why misconceptions about its nature are so common.

I also devote an entire chapter (Chapter 2) to the scientific enterprise—not just the mechanics of research methods but the logic behind them. I believe that an appreciation of the nature of empirical evidence can contribute greatly to improving students' critical thinking skills. Ten years from now, many of the "facts" reported in this book will have changed, but an understanding of the methods of science will remain invaluable. An introductory psychology course, by itself, isn't going to make a student think like a scientist, but I can't think of a better place to start the process.

As its title indicates, this book is a condensed version of my introductory text, *Psychology: Themes and Variations*. I have reduced the word count of this book to 70% of the word count of the full-length version. How was this reduction accomplished? It required a great many difficult decisions, but fortunately, I had excellent advice from a team of professors who served as consultants. About 40% of the reduction came from deleting entire topics, such as psychophysics, intellectual disability, latent learning, and so forth. However, the bulk of the reduction was achieved by compressing and simplifying coverage throughout the book. I carefully scrutinized the parent book sentence by sentence and forced myself to justify the existence of every study, every example, every citation, every phrase. The result is a thoroughly *rewritten* text, rather than one that was *reassembled* through "cut and paste" techniques.

Changes in the Ninth Edition

A good textbook must evolve with the field of inquiry it covers. Although the professors and students who used the first eight editions of this book did not clamor for alterations, there are some changes. I have already described the Reality Checks, which are new to this edition. Another new element is that each chapter-opening spread includes a puzzling paradox related to the upcoming content of the chapter. These paradoxes are brief brain teasers that hopefully will provoke some thought and create a little intrigue as students embark on their reading of each chapter.

You may also notice that for the first time in nine editions, I have altered the order of the chapters. It is not a major reorganization. I have simply moved the chapter on Social Behavior up from Chapter 15 to Chapter 12. Why? Although some instructors juggle chapter order, most seem to assign the chapters in sequence. Many of us often fall behind our planned schedule and struggle to get through all the chapters we intended to cover. This reality means that the chapter on social psychology probably gets dropped more often than other chapters because it comes at the end of the book. I think that this is an unfortunate situation in that the chapter on social psychology includes some of the most inherently interesting and important material in the course. So, after mulling it over for years, I decided it should no longer suffer the fate of being the last chapter. Of course, that means that another chapter has to become the precarious, final chapter. As you will see, that fate now falls to the chapter on the Treatment of Psychological Disorders. Admittedly, this material is also important. But the text includes two chapters on clinical psychology—the chapter on disorders (14) and the one on treatment (15)—so even if the chapter on treatment gets dropped, students can have a healthy exposure to clinical psychology. This shift also means that the chapters on personality (11) and social psychology (12) fall together, which seems appropriate given the enormous overlap and historical kinship between these subfields.

You will also find a variety of other changes in this edition, including four new chapter-opening vignettes (in Chapters 3, 10, 12, and 14). The graphic design of the text has been refreshed and improved in a variety of ways. For instance, the beginning of each chapter features more dramatic illustrations. In the line art, we have increased the use of color-coded text, and wherever possible, we have replaced drawings of humans with actual photos that are integrated into our graphics and diagrams. And we have strived to make the photo program more engaging by adding a host of silhouetted images that are woven into the text columns, creating a more modern, magazine-style look. We have also refreshed the treatments of the level-one headings and the Concept Checks. Perhaps most dramatic, we have shifted from a two-column page design to one-column design, resulting in a simpler, cleaner, less-cluttered look. To help make room for the one-column design, we have removed the interim summaries that were sprinkled through the chapters and replaced them with one detailed summary, organized by Key Learning Goals, at the end of the chapter. And to accommodate this two-page Review of Key Learning Goals, we have moved the Practice Tests to Appendix A.

Of course, the book has been thoroughly updated to reflect recent advances in the field. One of the exciting things about psychology is that it is not a stagnant discipline. It continues to move forward at what seems a faster and faster pace. This progress has necessitated a host of specific content changes that you'll find sprinkled throughout the chapters. Also reflecting this progress, over 900 of the reference citations in the book are new to this edition. Following is a partial list of specific changes in each chapter of the ninth edition.

CHAPTER 1: THE EVOLUTION OF PSYCHOLOGY
- Introduction of new text feature called Reality Checks, which are sprinkled throughout the book
- New table highlighting popular myths about psychology
- Condensed coverage of psychology's history
- New coverage discussing Watson's expulsion from academia and his successful application of psychology to advertising
- New Reality Check on the rumor that Skinner's daughter was raised in a Skinner box and grew up to be highly dysfunctional
- New data on the rise of the cognitive and neuroscience perspectives since the 1950s
- New Reality Check on the notion that psychology has always been part of the mental health system

- New Reality Check on the oversimplification that psychology equals the study of the mind
- New Reality Check on the belief that psychology and psychiatry are largely the same
- Profiles of new research on the importance of study habits to college success
- Streamlined coverage of improving reading in the Personal Application

CHAPTER 2: THE RESEARCH ENTERPRISE IN PSYCHOLOGY

- New Reality Check on how often social scientists use random sampling
- New example of naturalistic observation research focusing on how drivers make decisions at yellow lights
- Additional example illustrating an innovative, new way to conduct naturalistic observation
- Added example of case study research focusing on assessing the effectiveness of a specific therapy
- Interesting, new example of survey research showing how the amount of time people watch TV relates to social class and their health
- New Reality Check on correlation and causation
- New discussion of the importance and value of meta-analysis
- New coverage of Arnett's (2008) critique of American psychology for its excessive reliance on American participants, thus ignoring 95% of the world's population
- Expanded analysis of placebo effects
- New Reality Check on the belief that placebo effects are weak effects
- New discussion of halo effects in making ratings in questionnaire research
- Critical Thinking Application discusses new research on the powerful influence of anecdotal evidence

CHAPTER 3: THE BIOLOGICAL BASES OF BEHAVIOR

- New Reality Check on the idea that neurons do all the information processing in the nervous system
- Streamlined discussion of neurotransmitters and behavior
- New research on endorphins and the "runner's high"
- New Reality Check on the myth that people use only 10% of their brains
- Revised take on the role of the cerebellum
- New discussion of the possible evolutionary significance of hemispheric specialization in the brain
- New research relating weak cerebral lateralization to lower IQ and vulnerability to schizophrenia
- New coverage of the role of oxytocin in pair bonding
- New research on oxytocin's influence on empathy and trust
- New coverage of recent findings in epigenetics
- Streamlined Personal Application on the significance of hemispheric specialization
- New research showing that musicians have more bilateral hemispheric organization than others
- New research suggesting that music training may be related to enhanced cognitive performance
- New Reality Check on the belief that people are either right-brained or left-brained
- New Reality Check explaining that playing classical music for children will not enhance their brain development

CHAPTER 4: SENSATION AND PERCEPTION

- New Reality Check on the myth that reading in the dark or sitting close to the TV will damage one's vision
- Expanded discussion of the evolutionary significance of face-detecting cells in the brain
- New Reality Check on the notion that people who are color blind see the world in black and white

- New theory on how exposure to colors can influence psychological functioning
- New research on how the color red undermines achievement strivings but enhances men's attraction to women
- New discussion of how 3D movies manipulate the perception of depth
- New research on how depth perception can be skewed by people's motivational states
- New discussion of how portable music players can cause hearing loss
- Revised coverage of pitch perception
- New Reality Check on the classic tongue map
- New discussion of the possibility that umami should be viewed as a fifth basic taste
- New research on humans' ability to track faint scents
- New research on how contextual factors modulate the experience of pain
- New Reality Check on the belief that humans have just five senses

CHAPTER 5: VARIATIONS IN CONSCIOUSNESS
- New research reporting the counter-intuitive finding that older adults may need less sleep than younger adults
- New data on whether growing older, by itself, leads to poor sleep in the elderly
- New research on ethnicity and sleep complaints
- New data linking REM sleep to neurogenesis
- New findings suggesting that REM sleep may enhance creativity
- New Reality Check on the notion that the effects of sleep deprivation are insignificant
- New Reality Check on the belief that it is dangerous to awaken sleepwalkers
- New Reality Check dispelling the idea that a shocking dream could be fatal
- Added distinction between focused attention and open monitoring approaches to meditation
- New findings suggesting that meditation can increase one's tolerance of pain
- New research suggesting that meditation has the potential to modify brain structure
- New Reality Check dispelling the myth that hypnotized individuals can perform feats that they could never perform otherwise
- New research on napping and performance

CHAPTER 6: LEARNING
- New Reality Check on the notion that Pavlov's demonstration of classical conditioning relied on a bell
- New section on evaluative conditioning as a form of classical conditioning
- New discussion of what happened to Little Albert in the aftermath of Watson and Rayner's landmark study, including new evidence on Little Albert's identity
- New discussion of the effects of delayed reinforcement
- New Reality Check explaining that rewarding a behavior every time is not the best way to ensure that it will last
- New Reality Check explaining that negative reinforcement and punishment are not the same thing
- New findings on the negative effects of corporal punishment in children
- Condensed discussion of biological constraints on conditioning
- New discussion of B. F. Skinner's theory of noncontingent reinforcement as an explanation for superstitious behavior
- New coverage of how superstitious behavior can be analyzed in terms of normal cognitive biases and errors that promote irrational reasoning
- Coverage of new research showing that supersitious beliefs can actually influence people's performance
- Added discussion of how exposure to media violence may desensitize people to the effects of aggression in the real world
- New research on how desensitization to aggression may undermine helping behavior

CHAPTER 7: HUMAN MEMORY

- New research on why cell phone conversations sap attention and impair driving
- New research on how the motivation to remember affects encoding
- New Reality Check questioning the conventional wisdom on the capacity of short-term memory
- New findings on the nature and significance of working memory capacity
- Expanded discussion of hypnosis and memory
- New Reality Check disputing the idea that hypnosis can enhance memory retrieval
- New research on the power of the misinformation effect
- New Reality Check explaining that memory is not like a mental videotape
- New Reality Check on the notion that forgetting is due to the decay of memory traces
- Streamlined coverage of the repressed memories controversy
- New work distinguishing two groups that report recovered memories of abuse that differ in the likelihood of corroboration
- Condensed coverage of the neural circuitry of memory
- Expanded discussion of how H.M.'s case contributed to the understanding of memory
- Increased coverage of the testing effect on memory

CHAPTER 8: COGNITION AND INTELLIGENCE

- New research on the incubation effect in problem solving
- Expanded coverage of cultural disparities in cognitive style
- Updated research on choice overload and its roots
- New Reality Check on the assumption that the more choices people have, the better
- Streamlined coverage of making choices about preferences
- New coverage of the deliberation-without-attention effect, showing that intuitive, unconscious decisions can yield greater post-decision satisfaction
- New Reality Check disputing the idea that good decision making depends on careful, systematic deliberation
- New evidence on the relationship between intelligence and vulnerability to cognitive bias and error, showing that even very bright people are not immune to irrational thinking
- Condensed discussion of evolutionary analyses of flaws in decision making
- New data on how students' self-perceptions of their abilities influence their academic performance
- Addition of Stanovich's criticism of how IQ tests do not assess rational thinking
- New Reality Check on the notion that IQ tests measure mental ability in a truly general sense
- New research on the correlation between IQ and the size of specific areas in the brain
- New research on the association between IQ and the volume of gray and white matter in the brain
- Compressed discussion of Sternberg's theory of intelligence
- New research on how people with higher intelligence tend to live longer
- New discussion of the possible mechanisms underlying the relationship between intelligence and mortality
- New research on how living abroad appears to enhance creativity

CHAPTER 9: MOTIVATION AND EMOTION

- Additional data on how the quantity of food available influences the amount eaten
- New findings on the effects of the presence of others on eating behavior
- New material on how food advertisements influence eating behavior
- New Reality Check on whether eating at night fosters weight gain
- New findings on gender disparities in orgasmic consistency and interest in sex
- New research on gender differences in interest in sex, as related to age

- New research on the developmental roots of sexual orientation
- New Reality Check on the notion that people high in the need for achievement tend to be big risk takers
- New coverage on the inaccuracy of affective forecasting
- Added coverage of a classic study of affective forecasting (Dunn, Wilson, & Gilbert, 2003)
- New Reality Check on the accuracy of lie detectors
- New research on whether emotional facial expressions are innate
- New coverage of classic study by Dutton and Aron (1974) on two-factor theory of emotion
- Revised discussion of the relationship between income and subjective well-being, including a recent study by Kahneman and Deaton (2010)
- New research on the connection between social activity and happiness

CHAPTER 10: HUMAN DEVELOPMENT ACROSS THE LIFE SPAN

- New chapter-opening vignette focusing on developmental transitions in the life of Angelina Jolie
- Revised statistics and terminology on the threshold of viability
- New Reality Check on the wisdom of social drinking during pregnancy
- Added coverage of the effects of maternal emotions during prenatal development
- Added coverage of the effects of environmental toxins during prenatal development
- New section on fetal origins of adult diseases, such as diabetes and heart disease
- New Reality Check on bonding at birth and later attachment
- New findings on how the search for identity often continues beyond adolescence
- New data on how self-esteem changes over the course of adulthood
- New Reality Check on the prevalence of the midlife crisis
- New data suggesting that cohabitation may no longer be a risk factor for marital dissolution
- New Reality Check on the arrival of children and marital satisfaction
- New data on how older adults tend to feel an average of 13 years younger than they are
- Revised coverage of protective factors for Alzheimer's disease
- New discussion of whether cognitive training programs can slow cognitive decline in the elderly
- New data on gender differences in math achievement
- New findings on how fetal testosterone levels relate to subsequent gender-typing
- New research on the developmental significance of father absence

CHAPTER 11: PERSONALITY

- Expanded description of the Big Five traits
- New Reality Check on the influence of the unconscious
- Added sublimation to the roster of defense mechanisms covered
- Condensed coverage of Jung and Adler
- Expanded critique of Freudian theory
- New Reality Check on the power of situational forces
- New discussion of a proposed revision of Maslow's hierarchy of needs
- Streamlined coverage of behavioral genetics research
- New Reality Check questioning the assumption that parents exert great influence over their children's personality
- Revised critique of biological models of personality
- Revised Illustrated Overview of personality theory now includes information on the assumptions of each approach
- New discussion of the history of narcissism as a personality trait
- New findings on the nature, correlates, and social consequences of narcissism
- New research on how levels of narcissism have increased in recent decades
- Streamlined coverage of terror management theory

CHAPTER 12 (FORMERLY 15): SOCIAL BEHAVIOR

- New introductory vignette focuses on how modern technology is altering the fabric of social relationships
- New research on effects of brains versus beauty as related to income
- New data on the accuracy of inferences about personality based on "thin slices of behavior"
- Compressed coverage of attribution processes
- New evidence on the matching hypothesis based on real-world behavior at HOTorNOT.com website
- New findings on how similarity affects friendship formation
- New Reality Check on whether opposites attract in romantic relationships
- Condensed discussion of the dynamics of interpersonal attraction
- New coverage of the use of a "scientific approach" to matching people based on compatibility at eHarmony.com and similar websites
- New coverage of research on the correlation between attitudes and actual behavior
- New Reality Check on how well attitudes predict behavior
- Introduces the distinction between implicit and explicit attitudes
- New coverage of how the Implicit Association Test (IAT) measures implicit attitudes
- New discussion of the correlates of implicit prejudice
- New coverage of the mere exposure effect
- New Reality Check on the notion that familiarity breeds contempt
- New coverage of Burger's recent partial replication of Milgram's study
- New discussion of the effects of modern technology on the evolving nature of groups
- New discussion of how dividing the world into ingroups versus outgroups contributes to prejudice

CHAPTER 13 (FORMERLY 12): STRESS, COPING, AND HEALTH

- Highlighted discussion of the distinction between primary and secondary appraisal of stress, with new graphic
- New data on pressure and heart disease
- New Reality Check on the idea that stress is always imposed on people from outside forces
- New research on how positive emotions predict greater longevity
- New graphic illustrating Selye's general adaptation syndrome
- New coverage of gender differences in stress reactions
- New Reality Check on the belief that stress is always harmful
- Report of new meta-analysis of the surprisingly strong association between social support and longevity
- New findings on cultural disparities in the type of social support people prefer
- Added coverage of the effects of second-hand smoke
- New Reality Check on the significance of failing in efforts to quit smoking
- New data on trends in exercise habits and the link between exercise and mortality
- Streamlined coverage of behavioral factors and AIDS
- New discussion of the importance of good sleep habits for minimizing physiological vulnerability to stress
- New discussion of the importance of considering base rates when evaluating claims about the value of medications and other treatments

CHAPTER 14 (FORMERLY 13): PSYCHOLOGICAL DISORDERS

- New introductory vignette focusing on contemporary celebrities with obsessive-compulsive disorder
- New discussion of the influence of stigmatizing labels on the mentally ill
- New Reality Check on the belief that people with psychological disorders typically exhibit extremely bizarre behavior

- New Reality Check on the belief that people with psychological disorders are often dangerous and violent
- Multiple previews of proposed changes for DSM-5
- Added coverage of the debate about categorical versus dimensional approaches to describing disorders
- New data on the most common types of phobic fears
- New graphic on the most common types of compulsions seen in OCD patients
- Concept of anhedonia introduced in discussion of major depression
- New coverage of chronic depression
- New Reality Check on the notion that schizophrenia refers to a split personality
- Updated coverage of neurochemical factors in the etiology of schizophrenia
- New research on whether cannabis use may help precipitate schizophrenia in young people who are vulnerable to the disorder
- New discussion of how schizophrenia may be caused by a disruption of neural connectivity
- New coverage of autism, including recent findings on the dramatic increase in its prevalence
- New discussion of the etiology of autistic disorders, including the autism-vaccination controversy
- New Reality Check on the belief that vaccinations can cause autism

CHAPTER 15 (FORMERLY 14): TREATMENT OF PSYCHOLOGICAL DISORDERS
- New findings on the extent to which drug therapy has become the dominant mode of treatment for psychological disorders
- New data on the demographics of who seeks treatment
- New Reality Check on the notion that seeking therapy is a sign of weakness
- Inclusion of marriage and family therapists in coverage of professions providing mental health services
- New table comparing the various mental health professions
- New Reality Check on the belief that the typical therapy patient lies on a couch and talks about the past
- New summary of the core features of modern psychodynamic therapies
- New discussion of couples/marital therapy
- New coverage of family therapy
- New discussion of exposure therapies for anxiety disorders
- New research on the value of antidepressants in relation to the severity of patients' depression
- New Reality Check on the belief that psychological disorders are chronic and incurable
- New findings on how often psychiatrists prescribe multiple medications to patients
- New discussion of the value of treating patients with multiple approaches
- New discussion of the rise of eclecticism in therapy
- New evidence on ethnic disparities in mental health care
- New data on declining expenditures on mental health care and emerging shortages of psychiatric beds

PsykTrek: A Multimedia Introduction to Psychology

PsykTrek is a multimedia supplement that provides students with new opportunities for active learning and reaches out to "visual learners" with greatly increased efficacy. *PsykTrek* is intended to give students a second pathway to learning much of the content of introductory psychology. Although it does not cover all of the content of the introductory course, I think you will see that a great many key concepts and principles can be explicated *more effectively* in an interactive audiovisual medium than in a textbook.

PsykTrek consists of four components. The main component is a set of 65 *Interactive Learning Modules* that present the core content of psychology in a whole new way. These tutorials include thousands of graphics, hundred of photos, hundreds of animations, approximately 4 hours of narration, 40 carefully selected videos, and about 160 uniquely visual concept checks and quizzes. The 10 *Simulations* allow students to explore complex psychological phenomena in depth. They are highly interactive, experiential demonstrations that will enhance students' appreciation of research methods. The *Multimedia Glossary* allows students to look up over 800 psychological terms, access hundreds of pronunciations of obscure words, and pull up hundreds of related diagrams, photos, and videos. The *Video Selector* permits students (or faculty) to directly access the video segments that are otherwise embedded in the Interactive Learning Modules.

The key strength of *PsykTrek* is its ability to give students new opportunities for active learning outside of the classroom. For example, students can run themselves through re-creations of classic experiments to see the complexities of data collection in action. Or they can play with visual illusions in ways that will make them doubt their own eyes. Or they can stack color filters to demonstrate the nature of subtractive color mixing. *PsykTrek* is intended to supplement and complement *Psychology: Themes & Variations*. For instance, after reading about operant conditioning in the text, a student could work through three interactive tutorials on operant principles, watch four videos (including historic footage of B. F. Skinner shaping a rat), and then try to shape Morphy, the virtual rat, in one of the simulations.

PsykTrek is also available in an online format that can make student access easier than ever. All of the Interactive Learning Modules include a multiple-choice test, as well as an interactive quiz. We have also incorporated unit-level multiple-choice exams to permit students to better assess their mastery of content. And each unit includes a critical thinking exercise, written by Jeffry Ricker (Scottsdale Community College).

Other Supplementary Materials

The teaching/learning package that has been developed to supplement *Psychology: Themes and Variations, Briefer Version* includes many other useful tools. The development of all its parts was carefully coordinated so that they are mutually supported.

INSTRUCTOR'S RESOURCE MANUAL (COORDINATED BY RANDOLPH A. SMITH AND BENJAMIN R. SMITH)

A talented roster of professors have contributed to the *Instructor's Resource Manual (IRM)* in their respective areas of expertise. The *IRM* was developed under the guidance of Randolph Smith, the former editor of the journal *Teaching of Psychology*, and Benjamin R. Smith. It contains a diverse array of materials designed to facilitate efforts to teach the introductory course and includes the following sections.

- The *Instructor's Manual*, by Randolph A. Smith (Lamar University) and Benjamin R. Smith, contains a wealth of detailed suggestions for lecture topics, class demonstrations, exercises, discussion questions, and suggested readings, organized around the content of each chapter in the text. It also highlights the connections between the text coverage and *PsykTrek* content and features an expanded collection of masters for class handouts.

- *Strategies for Effective Teaching*, by Joseph Lowman (University of North Carolina), discusses practical issues such as what to put in a course syllabus, how to handle the first class meeting, how to cope with large classes, and how to train and organize teaching assistants.

- *AV Media for Introductory Psychology*, by Russ Watson (College of DuPage), provides a comprehensive, up-to-date, critical overview of educational films relevant to the introductory course.

- *Introducing Writing in Introductory Psychology*, by Dana Dunn (Moravian College), discusses how to work toward enhancing students' writing skills in the context of the introductory course and provides suggestions and materials for specific writing assignments chapter by chapter.

- *Crossing Borders/Contrasting Behaviors: Using Cross-Cultural Comparisons to Enrich the Introductory Psychology Course,* by Ginny Zahn, Bill Hill, and Michael Reiner (Kennesaw State University), discusses the movement toward "internationalizing" the curriculum and provides suggestions for lectures, exercises, and assignments that can add a cross-cultural flavor to the introductory course.

TEST BANK (BY JEFF HOLMES)

A large, diversified, and carefully constructed *Test Bank* accompanies this text. The questions are closely tied to each chapter's Key Learning Goals. The items are categorized as (a) factual, (b) conceptual/applied, (c) integrative, or (d) critical thinking questions. Data on item difficulty are included for many questions. For this edition, Jeff Holmes of Ithaca College carefully scrutinized every item for quality before he even began the update to accommodate the revised content of the text. And to keep item quality high, we decided to reduce the items per chapter to a more manageable number. I maintain that it is quicker, easier, and more efficient to select test questions from a reasonable number of items than to have to work through hundreds and hundreds of items that inevitably include superficial variations on the same questions.

POWERLECTURE™

The fastest, easiest way to build powerful, customized media-rich lectures, PowerLecture provides a collection of book-specific PowerPoint lecture and class tools to enhance the educational experience. For classroom presentations, the CD-ROM includes Power-Point lecture outlines with key images from the text integrated, and a complete library of graphics and photos from the book. An electronic version of the entire Instructor's Resource Manual is also found on the CD, making it easy to print or distribute handouts or exercises from the manual. The CD also includes an electronic version of the Test Bank. The *ExamView* software is user-friendly and allows teachers to insert their own questions and to edit those provided.

PSYCHOLOGY COURSEMATE

Psychology CourseMate is an online learning resource for your students. It includes
- An interactive eBook
- Interactive teaching and learning tools, including:
  - quizzes
  - flashcards
  - concept charts
  - videos
  - and more
- Engagement Tracker, a first-of-its-kind tool that monitors student engagement in the course

WEBTUTOR™ ON BLACKBOARD® AND WEBCT™

Jumpstart your course with customizable, rich, text-specific content within your Course Management System.
- Jumpstart—Simply load a WebTutor cartridge into your Course Management System.
- Customizable—Easily blend, add, edit, reorganize, or delete content.
- Content-rich, text-specific content, quizzes, flashcards, concept charts, videos, and more

Whether you want to Web-enable your class or put an entire course online, WebTutor delivers. Visit webtutor.cengage.com to learn more.

VIDEO RESOURCES

A wealth of video materials relevant to teaching the introductory psychology course are available from Cengage Learning including the following.

ABC VIDEOS: INTRODUCTORY PSYCHOLOGY

These videos from the ABC television network feature short, high-interest clips about current studies and research in psychology. They are perfect for starting discussions or enriching lectures. Topics include brain damage, measuring IQ, sleep patterns, obsessive-compulsive disorder, obedience to authority, rules of attraction, and much more.
Volume I ISBN: 0-495-50306-1
Volume II ISBN: 0-495-59637-X
Volume III ISBN: 0-495-60490-9

INTRODUCTORY PSYCHOLOGY, BBC MOTION GALLERY VIDEO

Introductory Psychology, Vol. 1 drives home the relevance of course topics through short, provocative clips of current and historical events. Perfect for enriching lectures and engaging students in discussion, many of the segments on this volume have been gathered from BBC Motion Gallery. The 14 short (1–6 minutes) videos include topics such as emotional intelligence, attachment disorder, women and stress, and teen depression. Ask your Cengage Learning representative for a complete list of contents.
Vol. 1 ISBN: 978-1-111-35260-8

WADSWORTH PSYCHOLOGY: RESEARCH IN ACTION

The *Research in Action* videos feature the work of research psychologists to give students an opportunity to learn about cutting-edge research—not just who is doing it, but how it is done and how and where the results are being used. By taking students into the laboratories of both established and up-and-coming researchers, and by showing research results being applied outside of the laboratory, these videos offer insight into both the research process and the many ways in which real people's lives are affected by research in the fields of psychology and neuroscience. The 46 videos in this series feature interviews with many of the field's most prominent researchers, including David Barlow, Roy Baumeister, Sheldon Cohen, Larry Squire, Claude Steele, Elizabeth Loftus, and Mark Snyder.
Vol. 1 DVD ISBN: 0-495-59520-9
Vol. 2 DVD ISBN: 0-495-59813-5

REVEALING PSYCHOLOGY

The *Revealing Psychology* video (available on DVD) is ideal for both classroom presentation and online study. The clips include a refreshed and innovative Candid Camera–like segment depicting people in socially challenging situations, with a focus on applications of concepts and experimental variations; classic experiments in real-world context with a new look and feel; and personal profiles with interviews of real people talking about their lives in ways that illustrate social psychological concepts such as conformity, personal space, and group polarization.
ISBN: 0-547-01453-8

GUEST LECTURE SERIES

The *Guest Lecture Series* features many talented teachers sharing their teaching tips and best practices on a wide range of topics, including Rational Emotive Behavior Theory, Blogging as an Effective Tool, Demonstrations on Taste, Dramatizing Perspectives in Psychology, How to Teach Writing in Psychology, and more. This series focuses on the teaching-learning process and is intended to help faculty in their course preparation and planning.
ISBN: 0-547-00401-X

Acknowledgments

Creating an introductory psychology text is a complicated challenge, and a small army of people have contributed to the evolution of this book. Foremost among them are the psychology editors I have worked with—Claire Verduin, C. Deborah Laughton, Phil Curson, Eileen Murphy, Edith Beard Brady, Michele Sordi, Jon-David Hague, and Tim Matray—and the developmental editor for the first edition of this book, John Bergez. They have helped me immeasurably, and each has become a treasured friend along the way. I am especially indebted to Claire, who educated me in the intricacies of textbook publishing, and to John, who has left an enduring imprint on my writing.

The challenge of meeting a difficult schedule in producing this book was undertaken by a talented team of people coordinated by Joan Keyes, who did a superb job of pulling it all together. Credit for coordination of the text design goes to Vernon Boes, who was very creative in revamping the previous design. Terri Wright handled photo research with enthusiasm and efficiency, and Jackie Estrada did an outstanding job once again in copyediting the manuscript. Fred Harwin and Carol Zuber-Mallison made stellar contributions to the artwork.

A number of psychologists deserve thanks for the contributions they made to this book. I am grateful to Diane Halpern for her work on the Critical Thinking Applications; to Marky Lloyd for writing the online appendix on careers in psychology; to Susan Koger and Britain Scott for crafting a compelling appendix on sustainability; to Rick Stalling and Ron Wasden for their work on previous editions of the *Study Guide;* to Jeff Holmes for his revision of the *Test Bank;* to Randy Smith, Ben Smith, Joseph Lowman, Russ Watson, Dana Dunn, Ginny Zahn, Bill Hill, and Michael Reiner for their contributions to the *Instructor's Resource Manual;* to Jeffry Ricker for devising *PsykTrek's* critical thinking exercises; to Randy Smith, David Matsumoto, and Jeremy Houska for contributing ancillary books; to Jim Calhoun for providing item analysis data for the test items; to Harry Upshaw, Larry Wrightsman, Shari Diamond, Rick Stalling, and Claire Etaugh for their help and guidance over the years; and to the chapter consultants listed on page xxiv and the reviewers listed on pages xxv and xxvi, who provided insightful and constructive critiques of various portions of the manuscript.

Many other people have also contributed to this project, and I am grateful to all of them for their efforts. Bill Roberts, Tom Dorsaneo, Nancy Sjoberg, John Odam, Fiorella Ljunggren, Jim Brace-Thompson, Susan Badger, Sean Wakely, Eve Howard, Linda Rill, Joanne Terhaar, Marjorie Sanders, Kathryn Stewart, Lori Grebe, Dory Schaeffer, Margaret Parks, Kim Russell, Lauren Keyes, Sue Howard, and Jennie Redwitz helped with varied aspects of previous editions. At Wadsworth, Linda Ganster, Pat Waldo, Kristin Makarewycz, Liz Rhoden, Trina Tom, Lauren Moody, and Travis Holland made valuable contributions to the current edition. At the College of DuPage, where I taught until 1991, all of my colleagues in psychology provided support and information at one time or another, but I am especially indebted to Barb Lemme, Alan Lanning, Pat Puccio, and Don Green. I also want to thank my former colleagues at Santa Clara University (especially Tracey Kahan, Tom Plante, and Jerry Burger), and my current colleagues at UNLV who have been fertile sources of new ideas. And I am indebted to the many graduate students who I have worked with at UNLV, and to Kerri Schafer and Erica Noles, who helped complete the new reference entries.

My greatest debt is to my wife, Beth Traylor, who has been a steady source of emotional sustenance while enduring the rigors of her medical career, and to my son T. J., for making dad laugh all the time.

Wayne Weiten

CHAPTER CONSULTANTS

Chapter 1
David Baker
University of Akron
Charles L. Brewer
Furman University
C. James Goodwin
Wheeling Jesuit University
E. R. Hilgard
Stanford University
David Hothersall
Ohio State University
Michael G. Livingston
St. John's University

Chapter 2
Larry Christensen
Texas A & M University
Francis Durso
University of Oklahoma
Donald H. McBurney
University of Pittsburgh
Wendy Schweigert
Bradley University

Chapter 3
Nelson Freedman
Queen's University at Kingston
Michael W. Levine
University of Illinois, Chicago
Corinne L. McNamara
Kennesaw State University
James M. Murphy
Indiana University–Purdue University at Indianapolis
Paul Wellman
Texas A & M University

Chapter 4
Stephen Blessing
University of Tampa
Nelson Freedman
Queen's University at Kingston
Kevin Jordan
San Jose State University
Michael W. Levine
University of Illinois, Chicago

John Pittenger
University of Arkansas, Little Rock
Chrislyn E. Randell
Metropolitan State College of Denver
Lawrence Ward
University of British Columbia

Chapter 5
Frank Etscorn
New Mexico Institute of Mining and Technology
Tracey L. Kahan
Santa Clara University
Charles F. Levinthal
Hofstra University
Wilse Webb
University of Florida

Chapter 6
A. Charles Catania
University of Maryland
Michael Domjan
University of Texas, Austin
William C. Gordon
University of New Mexico
Russell A. Powell
Grant MacEwan College
Barry Schwartz
Swarthmore College
Deborah L. Stote
University of Texas, Austin

Chapter 7
Tracey L. Kahan
Santa Clara University
Ian Neath
Purdue University
Tom Pusateri
Loras College
Stephen K. Reed
San Diego State University
Patricia Tenpenny
Loyola University, Chicago

Chapter 8
John Best
Eastern Illinois University

David Carroll
University of Wisconsin, Superior
Charles Davidshofer
Colorado State University
Shalynn Ford
Teikyo Marycrest University
Richard J. Haier
University of California, Irvine
Tom Pusateri
Loras College
Stephen K. Reed
San Diego State University
Timothy Rogers
University of Calgary
Dennis Saccuzzo
San Diego State University

Chapter 9
Robert Franken
University of Calgary
Russell G. Geen
University of Missouri
Douglas Mook
University of Virginia
D. Louis Wood
University of Arkansas, Little Rock

Chapter 10
Ruth L. Ault
Davidson College
John C. Cavanaugh
University of Delaware
Claire Etaugh
Bradley University
Doug Friedrich
University of West Florida
Barbara Hansen Lemme
College of DuPage

Chapter 11
Susan Cloninger
Russel Sage College
Caroline Collins
University of Victoria
Howard S. Friedman
University of California, Riverside

Christopher F. Monte
Manhattanville College
Ken Olson
Fort Hays State University

Chapter 12
Jerry M. Burger
Santa Clara University
Donelson R. Forsyth
Virginia Commonwealth University
Stephen L. Franzoi
Marquette University
Cheryl Kaiser
Michigan State University

Chapter 13
Robin M. DiMatteo
University of California, Riverside
Jess Feist
McNeese State University
Regan A. R. Gurung
University of Wisconsin, Green Bay
Chris Kleinke
University of Alaska, Anchorage

Chapter 14
David A. F. Haaga
American University
Richard Halgin
University of Massachusetts, Amherst
Chris L. Kleinke
University of Alaska, Anchorage
Elliot A. Weiner
Pacific University

Chapter 15
Gerald Corey
California State University, Fullerton
Herbert Goldenberg
California State University, Los Angeles
Jane S. Halonen
Alverno College
Thomas G. Plante
Santa Clara University

Reviewers for Briefer Version

Marcelle Bartolo Abela
Southern New Hampshire University

Randy Allen
Trocaire College

Elizabeth S. Athens
Kennesaw State University

Bart Bare
Caldwell Community College

Mitchell Berman
University of Southern Mississippi

Chris A. Bjornsen
Longwood University

Charles B. Blose
MacMurray College

Frederick Bonato
Saint Peter's College

Edward Brady
Belleville Area College

Paula Brown-Weinstock
Fulton-Montgomery Community College

Kate Byerwalter
Grand Rapids Community College

James F. Calhoun
University of Georgia

Cheryl Camenzuli
Hofstra University

Elaine Cassel
Lord Fairfax Community College

Heather Chabot
New England College

Monica Chakravertti
Mary Washington College

Jennifer Clark
University of North Carolina

Elizabeth Coccia
Austin Community College

Thomas Collins
Mankato State University

Luis Cordon
Eastern Connecticut State University

Christopher Cronin
Saint Leo University

Robert DaPrato
Solano Community College

Peggy A. DeCooke
Purchase College SUNY

Delores Doench
Southwestern Community College

Joan Doolittle
Anne Arundel Community College

Kimberley Duff
Cerritos College

David Eckerman
University of North Carolina

Kenneth Elliott
University of Maine, Augusta

Meredyth Fellows
West Chester University

Bob Fletcher
Truckee Meadows Community College

Christina Frederick
Southern Utah University

Barry Fritz
Quinnipiac College

Ronald Gage-Mosher
Imperial Valley College

Cassandra Germain
Campbell University

Linda Gibbons
Westark College

Amber Gilewski
Burlington County College

Richard Griggs
University of Florida

Robert Guttentag
University of North Carolina, Greensboro

Cheryl Hale
Jefferson College

Jane Halonen
James Madison University

Kevin B. Handey
Germanna Community College

Paul Herrle
College of Southern Nevada

Patricia Hinton
Cumberland College

Jeremy Ashton Houska
Nevada State University

Stephen Hoyer
Pittsburgh State University

Allen I. Huffcutt
Bradley University

Nancy Jackson
Johnson & Wales University

Cindy Kamilar
Pikes Peak Community College

Margaret Karolyi
University of Akron

Sheila Kennison
Oklahoma State University

Mark Krause
University of Portland

Charles F. Levinthal
Hofstra University

Gary Levy
University of Wyoming

Laura Madson
New Mexico State University

Kathleen Malley-Morrison
Boston University

Deborah R. McDonald
New Mexico State University

Marisa McLeod
Santa Fe Community College

Le'Ann Milinder
New England College

Antoinette R. Miller
Clayton State University

Jack J. Mino
Holyoke Community College

Joel Morogovsky
Brookdale Community College

Dirk W. Mosig
University of Nebraska at Kearney

David R. Murphy
Waubonsee Community College

Bonnie J. Nichols
Mississippi County Community College

Bonnie Nicholson
University of Southern Mississippi

Susan Nolan
Seton Hall University

Caroline Olko
Nassau Community College

Gayle Pitman
Sacramento City College

Edward I. Pollack
West Chester University of Pennsylvania

Rose Preciado
Mount San Antonio College

Rebecca L. Rahschulte
Ivy Tech Community College

Bryan Raudenbush
Wheeling Jesuit University

Sean Reilley
Morehead State University

Elizabeth A. Rider
Elizabethtown College

Alysia Ritter
Murray State University

Vicki Ritts
St. Louis Community College, Meramec

James Rodgers
Hawkeye Community College

Jayne Rose
Augustana College

Lori Rosenthal
Lasell College

Eileen Roth
Glendale Community College

Ana Ruiz
Alvernia College

H. R. Schiffman
Rutgers University

Heide Sedwick
Mount Aloysius College

George Shardlow
City College of San Francisco

Randolph A. Smith
Ouachita Baptist University

Thomas Smith
Vincennes University

Rita Smith-Wade-El
Millersville University of Pennsylvania

James L. Spencer
West Virginia State College

Jutta M. Street
Campbell University

Tim Tomczak
Genesee Community College

Iva Trottier
Concordia College

Travis Tubre
University of Southern Mississippi

Jim Turcott
Kalamazoo Valley Community College

Mary Ann Valentino
Reedley College

Doris C. Vaughn
Alabama State University

Paul Vonnahme
New Mexico State University

Shelly Watkins
Modesto Junior College

Julia Watson
Lakeland Community College

Will Wattendorf
Adirondack Community College

Randall Wight
Ouachita Baptist University

Carol Winters-Smith
Bay Path College

Dawn Young
Bossier Parish Community College

Brief Contents

1

The Evolution of Psychology

© Camilo Morales/Glowimages/Corbis

1

2

The Research Enterprise in Psychology 30

© Holger Winkler/Corbis

3

The Biological Bases of Behavior   62

© Marc Phares/Photo Researchers, Inc.

4

Sensation and Perception 100

© Buena Vista Images/Getty Images

5

Variations in Consciousness

140

© Bloomimage/Corbis

6

Learning 176

© AKIRA/amanaimages/Corbis

7

Human Memory 214

© Masterfile RF

8

Cognition and Intelligence 248

© Science Source/Photo Researchers, Inc.

9

Motivation and Emotion 288

© Darryl Leniuk/Getty Images

10

Human Development Across the Life Span 322

© Getty Images

11

Personality 360

© Dimitri Vervitsiotis/Getty Images; insets, (Asian male) michaeljung/Shutterstock.com; (Hispanic female) Andy Dean Photography/Shutterstock.com; (African-American female), Brian Eichhorn/Shutterstock.com; (Arab), Elnur/Shutterstock.com

12

Social Behavior 396

© DreamPictures/Blend Images/Corbis

13

Stress, Coping, and Health   434

© Angela Coppola/Corbis

14

Psychological Disorders 466

15

Treatment of Psychological Disorders 502

© Sigrid Olsson/PhotoAlto/Corbis

To the Student

Welcome to your introductory psychology textbook. In most college courses, students spend more time with their textbooks than with their professors, so it helps if students *like* their textbooks. Making textbooks likable, however, is a tricky proposition. By its very nature, a textbook must introduce students to many complicated concepts, ideas, and theories. If it doesn't, it isn't much of a textbook, and instructors won't choose to use it. Nevertheless, in writing this book I've tried to make it as likable as possible without compromising the academic content that your instructor demands. I've especially tried to keep in mind your need for a clear, well-organized presentation that makes the important material stand out and yet is interesting to read. Above all else, I hope you find this book challenging to think about and easy to learn from. Before you plunge into your first chapter, let me introduce you to the book's key features. Becoming familiar with how the book works will help you to get more out of it.

Key Features

You're about to embark on a journey into a new domain of ideas. Your text includes some important features that are intended to highlight certain aspects of psychology's landscape.

UNIFYING THEMES

To help you make sense of a complex and diverse field of study, I introduce seven themes in Chapter 1 that reappear in a number of variations as we move from chapter to chapter. These unifying themes are meant to provoke thought about important issues and to highlight the connections among chapters. They are discussed at the end of each chapter in a section called "Reflecting on the Chapter's Themes." Icons for the specific themes covered in a chapter appear near the beginning of these sections to help make the book's thematic structure more prominent.

PERSONAL APPLICATIONS

Toward the end of each chapter you'll find a Personal Application section that shows how psychology is relevant to everyday life. Some of these sections provide concrete, practical advice that could be helpful to you in your educational endeavors, such as those on improving academic performance, improving everyday memory, and achieving self-control. So, you may want to jump ahead and read some of these Personal Applications early.

CRITICAL THINKING APPLICATIONS

Each Personal Application is always followed by a two-page Critical Thinking Application that teaches and models basic critical thinking skills. I think you will find that these sections are refreshing and interesting. Like the Personal Applications, they are part of the text's basic content and should be read unless you are told otherwise by your instructor. Although the "facts" of psychology will gradually change after you take this course (thanks to scientific progress), the critical thinking skills modeled in these sections should prove valuable for many years to come.

REALITY CHECKS

Students typically come into the introductory psychology course with a variety of misconceptions. To foster a more accurate picture of psychology, each chapter includes three or four Reality Checks, which address common misconceptions related to psychology and provide direct refutations of the misinformation. These Reality Checks are sprinkled throughout the chapters, appearing adjacent to the relevant material. Examples of popular misconceptions that are dispelled include the myth that B. F. Skinner raised his daughter in a Skinner box, which led to her becoming severely disturbed (Chapter 1); the notion that people use only 10% of their brains (Chapter 3); the assumption that people who are color blind see the world in black and white (Chapter 4); and the idea that it is dangerous to awaken someone who is sleepwalking (Chapter 5). This text feature is based on recent research suggesting that explicit repudiations of erroneous ideas reduce students' misconceptions more effectively than the simple provision of correct information (Kowalski & Taylor, 2009). For the most part, the Reality Checks can be found in the margins of the pages, but they are a critical component of the text's educational material.

Learning Aids

This text contains a great deal of information. A number of learning aids have been incorporated into the book to help you digest it all.

An *outline* at the beginning of each chapter provides you with an overview of the topics covered in that chapter. Think of the outlines as road maps, and bear in mind that it's easier to reach a destination if you know where you're going.

Headings serve as road signs in your journey through each chapter. Four levels of headings are used to make it easy to see the organization of each chapter.

Key Learning Goals, found at the beginning of major sections, can help you focus on the important issues in the material you are about to read.

Reviews of Key Learning Goals, found at the end of the chapters, are detailed summaries of each chapter's key ideas, organized around the Key Learning Goals. The numbered paragraphs in these reviews address the learning objectives outlined in the Key Learning Goals. It's wise to read over these review materials to make sure you've digested the information in the chapter.

Italics (without boldface) are used liberally throughout the text to emphasize crucial points.

Key terms are identified with ***italicized blue boldface*** type to alert you that these are important vocabulary items that are part of psychology's technical language.

An *integrated running glossary* provides an on-the-spot definition of each key term as it's introduced in the text. These formal definitions are printed in **blue boldface** type. Becoming familiar with psychology's terminology is an essential part of learning about the field. The integrated running glossary should make this learning process easier.

Concept Checks are sprinkled throughout the chapters to let you test your mastery of important ideas. Generally, they ask you to integrate or organize a number of key ideas, or to apply ideas to real-world situations. Although they're meant to be engaging and fun, they do check conceptual *understanding,* and some are challenging. But if you get stuck, don't worry; the answers (and explanations, where they're needed) are in the back of the book in Appendix A.

Illustrations in the text are important elements in your complete learning package. Some illustrations provide enlightening diagrams of complicated concepts; others furnish examples that help flesh out ideas or provide concise overviews of research results. Careful attention to the tables and figures in the book will help you understand the material discussed in the text.

A 12-item *Practice Test* is provided for each chapter that should give you a realistic assessment of your mastery of that chapter and valuable practice in taking multiple-choice tests. These Practice Tests are found in Appendix A.

An *alphabetical glossary* is provided in the back of the book. Most key terms are formally defined in the integrated running glossary only when they are first introduced. So if you run into a technical term a second time and can't remember its meaning, it may be easier to look it up in the alphabetical glossary.

A Few Footnotes

Psychology textbooks customarily identify the studies, theoretical treatises, books, and articles that information comes from. These *citations* occur (1) when names are followed by a date in parentheses, as in "Smith (2011) found that . . ." or (2) when names and dates are provided together within parentheses, as in "In one study (Burke, Martinez, & Jones, 1999), the researchers attempted to . . ." All of the cited publications are listed by author in the alphabetized *References* section in the back of the book. The citations and references are a necessary part of a book's scholarly and scientific foundation. Practically speaking, however, you'll probably want to glide right over them as you read. You definitely don't need to memorize the names and dates.

PsykTrek: A Multimedia Introduction to Psychology

Developed to accompany this textbook, *PsykTrek* is an enormously powerful multimedia learning tool—available online or on CD-ROM—that can enhance your understanding of many complex processes and theories, provide you with an alternative way to assimilate many crucial concepts, and add a little more fun to your journey through introductory psychology. *PsykTrek* has been designed to supplement and complement your textbook. I strongly encourage you to use it. The *PsykTrek* icons that you will see in many of the headings in the upcoming chapters refer to the content of *PsykTrek*. An icon indicates that the textbook topic referred to in the heading is covered in the Interactive Learning Modules or Simulations found on *PsykTrek*. The relevant simulations (Sim1, Sim2, and so forth) and the relevant Interactive Learning Modules (1a, 1b, 1c, and so forth) are listed on the right of the icons.

A Final Word

I'm pleased to be a part of your first journey into the world of psychology, and I sincerely hope that you'll find the book as thought provoking and as easy to learn from as I've tried to make it. If you have any comments or advice on the book, please write to me in care of the publisher (Wadsworth/Cengage Learning, 20 Davis Drive, Belmont, CA 94002). You can be sure I'll pay careful attention to your feedback. Finally, let me wish you good luck. I hope you enjoy your course and learn a great deal.

Wayne Weiten

1

The Evolution of Psychology

PARADOX

Psychology has a long past, but a short history.

© Camilo Morales/Glowimages/Corbis

What is psychology? Why is it worth your time to study? Let me approach these questions by sharing a couple of stories with you.

In 2005, Greg Hogan, a college sophomore, briefly achieved national notoriety when he was arrested for a crime. Greg wasn't anybody's idea of a likely criminal. He was the son of a Baptist minister and the president of his class. He played cello in the university orchestra. He even worked part-time in the chaplain's office. So it shocked everybody who knew Greg when police arrested him at his fraternity house for bank robbery.

It seems that Greg had faked having a gun and made away with over $2800 from a local bank. His reason? Over a period of months he had lost $5000 playing poker on the Internet. His lawyer said Greg's gambling habit had become "an addiction" (Dissell, 2005; McLoughlin & Paquet, 2005).

Greg eventually entered a clinic for treatment of his gambling problem. In a way, he was lucky—at least he got help. Moshe Pergament, a 19-year-old community college student in Long Island, New York, wasn't so fortunate. Moshe was shot to death after brandishing a gun at a police officer. The gun turned out to be plastic. On the front seat of his car was a note that began, "Officer, it was a plan. I'm sorry to get you involved. I just needed to die." Moshe had just lost $6000 betting on the World Series. His death was what people in law enforcement call "suicide by cop" (Lindsay & Lester, 2004).

These stories are at the extreme edge of a trend that concerns many public officials and mental health professionals: The popularity of gambling—from lotteries to sports betting to online poker—is booming, especially among the young (D. F. Jacobs, 2004). College students seem to be leading the way. To some observers, gambling on college campuses has become an "epidemic." Student bookies on some campuses make tens of thousands of dollars a year taking sports bets from other students. Television shows such as *The World Series of Poker* are marketed squarely at college-student audiences. Poker sites on the web invite students to win their tuition by gambling online.

© Fuse/ Getty Images

For most people, gambling is a relatively harmless—if sometimes expensive—pastime. However, estimates suggest that 5%−6% of teens and young adults develop serious problems with gambling—two to four times the rate for older adults (Jacobs, 2004; Petry, 2005; Winters et al., 2004). The enormous growth of pathological gambling among young people raises a number of questions. Is gambling dangerous? Can it really be addictive? What is an addiction, anyway? If pathological gamblers abuse drugs or commit crimes, is gambling the cause of their troubles, or is it a symptom of a deeper problem? Perhaps most critically of all, why do some people become pathological gamblers while the great majority do not? Every day millions of people in the United States play the lottery, bet on sports, or visit casinos without apparent harm. Yet others can't seem to stop gambling until they have lost everything—their savings, their jobs, their homes, and their self-respect. Why? What causes such perplexing, self-destructive behavior?

Psychology is about questions like these. More generally, psychology is about understanding *all* the things we do. All of us wonder sometimes about the reasons underlying people's behavior—why it's hard to diet, why we procrastinate about studying, why we fall in love with one person rather than another. We wonder why some people are outgoing while others are shy. We wonder why we sometimes do things that we know will bring us pain and anguish, whether it's clinging to a destructive relationship or losing our tuition money in a game of Texas Hold 'Em. The study of psychology is about all these things, and infinitely more.

Many of psychology's questions have implications for people's everyday lives. For me, this is one of the field's major attractions—*psychology is practical.* Consider the case of gambling. Pathological gamblers suffer all kinds of misery, yet they can't seem to stop. Listen to the anguish of a gambler named Steve: "Over the past two years I have lost literally thousands . . . I have attempted to give up time after time after time, but failed every time. . . . I have debts around my neck which are destroying mine and my family's life. . . . I just want a massive light to be turned on with a message saying, 'This way to your old life, Steve'" (SJB, 2006).

What is the best way to help someone like Steve? Should he join a group like Gamblers Anonymous? Would counseling work? Are there drugs that can help? By probing the whys and hows of human behavior, psychology can help us find answers to pressing questions like these, as well as better understand issues that affect each of us every day. You will see the practical side of psychology throughout this book, especially in the Personal Applications at the ends of chapters. These Applications focus on everyday problems, such as coping more effectively with stress, improving self-control, and dealing with sleep difficulties.

Beyond its practical value, psychology is worth studying because it provides a powerful *way of thinking*. All of us make judgments every day about why people do the things they do. For example, we might think that pathological gamblers are weak willed, or irrational, or just too dumb to understand that the odds are stacked against them. Or we might believe they are in the grip of an addiction that simply overpowers them. How do we decide which of these judgments—if any—are right?

Psychologists are committed to investigating questions about human behavior in a scientific way. This means that they seek to formulate precise questions about behavior and then test possible answers through systematic observation. This commitment to testing ideas means that psychology provides a means of building knowledge that is relatively accurate and dependable. It also provides a basis for assessing the assertions we hear every day about behavior, from friends and family, as well as in the popular media. Although most people probably don't think about it much, psychology is in the news all the time—in newspapers and magazines, on TV and radio, and on the Internet. Unfortunately, this coverage is often distorted or grossly oversimplified, so that misinformation is commonplace. Thus, many "truisms" about behavior come to be widely believed, when they really are misconceptions or myths. A small sampling of some popular myths related to psychology is shown in **Table 1.1**. This list of common misconceptions comes from an excellent book titled *50 Great Myths of Popular Psychology* (Lilienfeld et al., 2010). In the pages to come we'll touch upon a host of misconceptions about psychology and provide more accurate, science-based information on these matters. For example, in Chapter 3 you will learn that the idea that people only use 10% of their brains is utter nonsense. Recent research suggests that the best way to dispel students' misconceptions is to confront these beliefs head on and provide a direct refutation (Kowalski & Taylor, 2009). Hence, throughout this book you will find a feature called Reality Checks that will highlight common fallacies and counter them with more accurate, realistic information. The Reality Check features will be found adjacent to relevant material, supplementing the normal text by explicitly attacking naive, fallacious beliefs.

In the case of gambling, for example, researchers have designed careful studies to probe the relationship of gambling problems to any number of possible influences, from childhood experiences to membership in a college fraternity. They have compared the way slot machines are set to reward players with frequent small payoffs to the way rats and pigeons are taught to earn food rewards in the laboratory. They have used state-of-the-art brain-imaging techniques to study the brains of people performing tasks similar to placing bets. They have even looked at whether some people are predisposed by their genes to develop problems with gambling (Petry, 2005; Rockey et al., 2005; Szegedy-Maszak, 2005).

If there is one clear conclusion that emerges from these studies, it is that there is no simple answer to the mystery of pathological gambling. Instead, a full explanation of gambling problems will likely involve many influences that interact in complex ways

TABLE 1.1 Popular Myths Related to Psychology

Myth	Relevant Chapter
Most people use only 10% of their brain power.	Chapter 3
Playing Mozart's music to infants boosts their intelligence.	Chapter 3
Hypnosis is a unique "trance" state that differs in kind from wakefulness.	Chapter 5
Hypnosis is useful for retrieving memories of forgotten events.	Chapter 7
The polygraph ("lie detector") test is an accurate means of detecting dishonesty.	Chapter 10
Opposites attract: We are most romantically attracted to people who differ from us.	Chapter 13
People with schizophrenia have multiple personalities.	Chapter 15
A large portion of criminals successfully use the insanity defense.	Chapter 15

© Cengage Learning

SOURCE: Based on Lilienfeld, S. O., Lynn, S. J., Ruscio, J., & Beyerstein, B. L. (2010). *50 great myths of popular psychology: Shattering widespread misconceptions about human behavior.* Malden, MA: Wiley-Blackwell.

(Derevensky & Gupta, 2004; Petry, 2005). As you'll see throughout this course, the same is true of most aspects of behavior. In my opinion, this is yet another reason to study psychology: It teaches us a healthy respect for the *complexity* of behavior. In a world that could use more understanding—and compassion—this can be an invaluable lesson.

As you go through this course, I hope you'll come to share my enthusiasm for psychology as a fascinating and immensely practical field of study. Let's begin our exploration by seeing how psychology has evolved from early speculations about behavior to a modern science. By looking at this evolution, you'll better understand psychology as it is today, a sprawling, multifaceted science and profession. We'll conclude our introduction with a look at seven unifying themes that will serve as connecting threads in the chapters to come. The chapter's Personal Application reviews research that provides insights into how to be an effective student. Finally, the Critical Thinking Application discusses how critical thinking skills can be enhanced.

Psychology's Early History

KEY LEARNING GOALS

1.1 Summarize Wundt's contributions to psychology, and describe the chief tenets of structuralism and functionalism.

1.2 Articulate Freud's principal ideas and why they inspired controversy.

1.3 Trace the development of behaviorism, and assess Watson's impact on the evolution of psychology.

1.4 Summarize Skinner's key insights, and explain the emergence of humanism and its underlying philosophy.

Psychology's story is one of people groping toward a better understanding of themselves. As the discipline has evolved, its focus, methods, and explanatory models have changed. Let's look at how psychology has developed from philosophical speculations about the mind into a modern research-based science.

The term *psychology* comes from two Greek words, *psyche*, meaning the soul, and *logos*, referring to the study of a subject. These two Greek roots were first put together to define a topic of study in the 16th century, when *psyche* was used to refer to the soul, spirit, or mind, as distinguished from the body (Boring, 1966). Not until the early 18th century did the term *psychology* gain more than rare usage among scholars. By that time it had acquired its literal meaning, "the study of the mind."

Of course, people have always wondered about the mysteries of the mind. In that sense, psychology is as old as the human race. But it was only about 140 years ago that psychology emerged as a scientific discipline.

A New Science Is Born

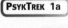

Psychology's intellectual parents were the disciplines of *philosophy* and *physiology*. By the 1870s a small number of scholars in both fields were actively exploring questions about the mind. How are bodily sensations turned into a mental awareness of the outside world? Are our perceptions of the world accurate reflections of reality? How do mind and body interact? The philosophers and physiologists who were interested in the mind viewed such questions as fascinating issues *within* their respective fields. It was a German professor, Wilhelm Wundt (1832−1920), who eventually changed this view. Wundt mounted a campaign to make psychology an independent discipline rather than a stepchild of philosophy or physiology.

In 1879 Wundt succeeded in establishing the first formal laboratory for research in psychology at the University of Leipzig. In recognition of this landmark event, historians have christened 1879 as psychology's "date of birth." Soon after, in 1881, Wundt established the first journal devoted to publishing research on psychology. All in all, Wundt's campaign was so successful that today he is widely characterized as the founder of psychology.

Wundt's conception of psychology dominated the field for two decades and was influential for several more. Borrowing from his training in physiology, Wundt (1874) declared that the new psychology should be a science modeled after fields such as physics and chemistry. What was the subject matter of the new science? According to Wundt, it was *consciousness*—the awareness of immediate experience. *Thus, psychology became*

Wilhelm Wundt

"Physiology informs us about those life phenomena that we perceive by our external senses. In psychology, the person looks upon himself as from within and tries to explain the interrelations of those processes that this internal observation discloses."

© Cengage Learning

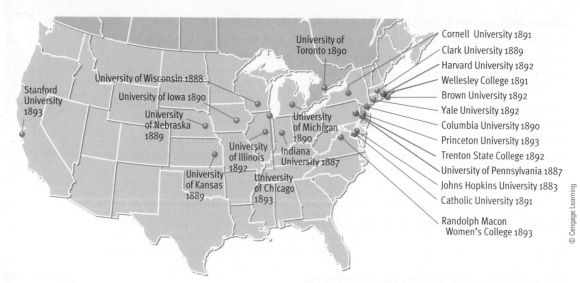

FIGURE 1.1

Early research laboratories in North America. This map highlights the location and year of founding for the first 23 psychological research labs established in North American colleges and universities. Many of these labs were founded by the students of Wilhelm Wundt. (Based on Benjamin, 2000)

University of Toronto 1890

University of Wisconsin 1888

Stanford University 1893

University of Iowa 1890

University of Nebraska 1889

University of Michigan 1890

University of Illinois 1892

Indiana University 1887

University of Kansas 1889

University of Chicago 1893

Cornell University 1891
Clark University 1889
Harvard University 1892
Wellesley College 1891
Brown University 1892
Yale University 1892
Columbia University 1890
Princeton University 1893
Trenton State College 1892
University of Pennsylvania 1887
Johns Hopkins University 1883
Catholic University 1891
Randolph Macon Women's College 1893

© Cengage Learning

the scientific study of conscious experience. This orientation kept psychology focused squarely on the mind. But it demanded that the methods used to investigate the mind be as scientific as those of chemists or physicists.

Many outstanding scholars came to Leipzig to study under Wundt and then fanned out around the world, establishing laboratories that formed the basis for the new science of psychology. The growth of this new field was particularly rapid in North America, where some 23 new psychological research labs sprang up between 1883 and 1893 at the universities shown in **Figure 1.1** (Benjamin, 2000). Although psychology was born in Germany, it blossomed into adolescence in North America.

The Battle of the "Schools" Begins: Structuralism Versus Functionalism

PSYKTREK 1a

Competing schools of thought exist in most scientific disciplines. Sometimes the disagreements among these schools are sharp. Such diversity in thought is natural and often stimulates enlightening debate. In psychology, the first two major schools of thought, *structuralism* and *functionalism,* were entangled in the first great intellectual battle in the field.

© infinity21/Shutterstock

Structuralism emerged through the leadership of Edward Titchener, an Englishman who emigrated to the United States in 1892. After training in Wundt's lab, he taught for decades at Cornell University. *Structuralism* **was based on the notion that the task of psychology is to analyze consciousness into its basic elements and investigate how these elements are related.** Just as physicists were studying how matter is made up of basic particles, the structuralists wanted to identify the fundamental components of conscious experience, such as sensations, feelings, and images.

Although the structuralists explored many questions, most of their work concerned sensation and perception in vision, hearing, and touch. To examine the contents of consciousness, the structuralists depended on the method of *introspection,* **or the careful, systematic self-observation of one's own conscious experience.** As practiced by the structuralists, introspection required training to make the *subject*—the person being studied—more objective and more aware. Once trained, participants were typically exposed to auditory tones, optical illusions, and visual stimuli such as pieces of fruit, and then they were asked to analyze what they experienced.

The functionalists, led by William James (1842–1910), a brilliant American scholar, took a different view of psychology's task. *Functionalism* **was based on the belief that psychology should investigate the function or purpose of consciousness, rather than its structure.** James argued that the structuralists' approach missed the real nature of conscious experience. Consciousness, he argued, consists of a continuous *flow* of thoughts. In analyzing consciousness into its "elements," the structuralists were looking at static points in that flow. James wanted to understand the flow itself, which he called the *stream of consciousness*. Today, people take this metaphorical description of mental life for granted, but at the time it was a revolutionary insight.

Whereas structuralists naturally gravitated to the lab, functionalists were more interested in how people adapt their behavior to the demands of the real world around them. Instead of focusing on sensation and perception, the functionalists began to investigate mental testing, patterns of development in children, the effectiveness of educational practices, and behavioral differences between the sexes. These new topics may have played a role in attracting the first women into the field of psychology (see **Figure 1.2**).

William James
"It is just this free water of consciousness that psychologists resolutely overlook."

**Mary Whiton Calkins
(1863–1930)**

Mary Calkins, who studied under William James, founded one of the first dozen psychology laboratories in America at Wellesley College in 1891, invented a widely used technique for studying memory, and became the first woman to serve as president of the American Psychological Association in 1905. Ironically, however, she never received her Ph.D. in psychology. Because she was a woman, Harvard University only reluctantly allowed her to take graduate classes as a "guest student." When she completed the requirements for her Ph.D., Harvard would only offer her a doctorate from its undergraduate sister school, Radcliffe. Calkins felt that this decision perpetuated unequal treatment of the sexes, so she refused the Radcliffe degree.

**Margaret Floy Washburn
(1871–1939)**

Margaret Washburn was the first woman to receive a Ph.D. in psychology. She wrote an influential book, *The Animal Mind* (1908), which served as an impetus to the subsequent emergence of behaviorism and was standard reading for several generations of psychologists. In 1921 she became the second woman to serve as president of the American Psychological Association. Washburn studied under James McKeen Cattell at Columbia University, but like Mary Calkins, she was only permitted to take graduate classes unofficially, as a "hearer." Hence, she transferred to Cornell University, which was more hospitable toward women, and completed her doctorate in 1894. Like Calkins, Washburn spent most of her career at a college for women (Vassar).

**Leta Stetter Hollingworth
(1886–1939)**

Leta Hollingworth did pioneering work on adolescent development, mental retardation, and gifted children. Indeed, she was the first person to use the term *gifted* to refer to youngsters who scored exceptionally high on intelligence tests. Hollingworth (1914, 1916) also played a major role in debunking popular theories of her era that purported to explain why women were "inferior" to men. For instance, she conducted a study refuting the myth that phases of the menstrual cycle are reliably associated with performance decrements in women. Her careful collection of objective data on gender differences forced other scientists to subject popular, untested beliefs about the sexes to skeptical, empirical inquiry.

FIGURE 1.2

Women pioneers in the history of psychology. Women have long made major contributions to the development of psychology (Milar, 2000; Russo & Denmark, 1987), and today nearly half of all psychologists are female. As in other fields, however, women have often been overlooked in histories of psychology (Furumoto & Scarborough, 1986). The three psychologists profiled here demonstrate that women have been making significant contributions to psychology almost from its beginning—despite formidable barriers to pursuing their academic careers.

The impassioned advocates of structuralism and functionalism saw themselves as fighting for high stakes: the definition and future direction of the new science of psychology. Their war of ideas continued energetically for many years. Who won? Most historians give the edge to functionalism. Both schools of thought gradually faded away. But the practical orientation of functionalism fostered the development of two important descendants—behaviorism and applied psychology (Green, 2009). We will discuss both momentarily.

Freud Brings the Unconscious into the Picture

Sigmund Freud
"The unconscious is the true physical reality; in its innermost nature it is as much unknown to us as the reality of the external world."

PSYKTREK 1a, 10a

Sigmund Freud (1856–1939) was an Austrian physician whose theories made him one of the most influential—and controversial—intellectual figures of modern times. Freud's (1900, 1933) approach to psychology grew out of his efforts to treat mental disorders. In his medical practice, Freud treated people troubled by psychological problems such as irrational fears, obsessions, and anxieties with an innovative procedure he called *psychoanalysis* (described in detail in Chapter 15). Decades of experience probing into his patients' lives provided much of the inspiration for Freud's theory.

His work with patients persuaded Freud of the existence of what he called the *unconscious*. According to Freud, **the *unconscious* contains thoughts, memories, and desires that are well below the surface of conscious awareness but that nonetheless exert great influence on behavior.** Freud based his concept of the unconscious on a variety of observations. For instance, he noticed that seemingly meaningless slips of the tongue (such as "I decided to take a summer school *curse*") often appeared to reveal a person's true feelings. He also noted that his patients' dreams often seemed to express important feelings that they were unaware of. Knitting these and other observations together, Freud eventually concluded that psychological disturbances are largely caused by personal conflicts existing at an unconscious level. More generally, his *psychoanalytic theory* attempts to

Concept Check 1.1

Understanding the Implications of Major Theories: Wundt, James, and Freud

Check your understanding of the implications of some of the major theories reviewed in this chapter by indicating who is likely to have made each of the statements quoted below. Choose from the following theorists: (a) Wilhelm Wundt, (b) William James, and (c) Sigmund Freud. You'll find the answers in Appendix A in the back of the book.

_____ 1. "He that has eyes to see and ears to hear may convince himself that no mortal can keep a secret. If the lips are silent, he chatters with his fingertips; betrayal oozes out of him at every pore. And thus the task of making conscious the most hidden recesses of the mind is one which it is quite possible to accomplish."

_____ 2. "The book which I present to the public is an attempt to mark out a new domain of science. . . . The new discipline rests upon anatomical and physiological foundations. . . . The experimental treatment of psychological problems must be pronounced from every point of view to be in its first beginnings."

_____ 3. "Consciousness, then, does not appear to itself chopped up in bits. Such words as 'chain' or 'train' do not describe it fitly. . . . It is nothing jointed; it flows. A 'river' or 'stream' are the metaphors by which it is most naturally described."

explain personality, motivation, and mental disorders by focusing on unconscious determinants of behavior.

Freud's concept of the unconscious was not entirely new, but he put it on the map for the general population and elaborated on it like never before (Lothane, 2006). It is important to emphasize that the concept of the unconscious was a major departure from the prevailing belief that people are fully aware of the forces affecting their behavior. In arguing that behavior is governed by unconscious forces, Freud made the disconcerting suggestion that people are not masters of their own minds. Other aspects of Freud's theory also stirred up debate. For instance, he proposed that behavior is greatly influenced by how people cope with their sexual urges. At a time when people were far less comfortable discussing sexual issues than they are today, even scientists were offended and scandalized by Freud's emphasis on sex. Small wonder, then, that Freud was soon engulfed in controversy.

In spite of its controversial nature, Freud's theory gradually won acceptance, attracting prominent followers such as Carl Jung and Alfred Adler. Important public recognition from psychology came in 1909, when G. Stanley Hall invited Freud to give a series of lectures at Clark University in Massachusetts. By the 1920s psychoanalytic theory was widely known around the world. Although psychoanalytic theory continued to generate heated debate, it survived to become an influential theoretical perspective. Today, many psychoanalytic concepts have filtered into the mainstream of psychology (Luborsky & Barrett, 2006; Pincus, 2006; Westen, Gabbard, & Ortigo, 2008).

Watson Alters Psychology's Course as Behaviorism Makes Its Debut

PSYKTREK 1a, 5b

In the early 1900s, another major school of thought appeared that dramatically altered the course of psychology. Founded by John B. Watson (1878–1958), *behaviorism* **is a theoretical orientation based on the premise that scientific psychology should study only observable behavior.** It is important to understand what a radical change this definition represents. Watson (1913, 1919) was proposing that psychologists *abandon the study of consciousness altogether* and focus exclusively on behaviors they could observe directly. In essence, he was redefining what scientific psychology should be about.

Why did Watson argue for such a fundamental shift in direction? Because to him, the power of the scientific method rested on the idea of *verifiability*. In principle, scientific claims can always be verified (or disproved) by anyone who is able and willing to make the required observations. However, this power depends on studying things that can be observed objectively. Otherwise, the advantage of using the scientific approach—replacing vague speculation and personal opinion with reliable, exact knowledge—is lost. In Watson's view, mental processes are not a proper subject for scientific study because they are ultimately private events. After all, no one can see or touch another's thoughts. Consequently, if psychology was to be a science, it would have to give up consciousness as its subject matter and become instead the *science of behavior.*

Behavior **refers to any overt (observable) response or activity by an organism.** Watson asserted that psychologists could study anything that people do or say—shopping, playing chess, eating, complimenting a friend. However, according to Watson they could *not* study scientifically the thoughts, wishes, and feelings that might accompany these behaviors.

Watson's radical reorientation of psychology did not end with his redefinition of its subject matter. He also took an extreme position on one of psychology's oldest and most fundamental questions: the issue of *nature versus nurture.* This age-old debate is concerned with whether behavior is determined mainly by genetic inheritance ("nature") or by environment and experience ("nurture"). To oversimplify, the question is this: Is a great concert pianist or a master criminal born, or made?

John B. Watson
"The time seems to have come when psychology must discard all references to consciousness."

© Cengage Learning

Watson argued that each is made, not born. He discounted the importance of heredity. He maintained that behavior is governed entirely by the environment. Indeed, he boldly claimed:

Give me a dozen healthy infants, well-formed, and my own special world to bring them up in and I'll guarantee to take any one at random and train him to become any type of specialist I might select—doctor, lawyer, artist, merchant-chief, and yes, even beggar-man and thief, regardless of his talents, penchants, tendencies, abilities, vocations and race of his ancestors. I am going beyond my facts and I admit it, but so have the advocates of the contrary and they have been doing it for many thousands of years. (1924, p. 82)

For obvious reasons, Watson's tongue-in-cheek challenge was never put to a test. Although this widely cited quote overstated and oversimplified Watson's views on the nature-nurture issue (Todd & Morris, 1992), his writings contributed to the environmental slant that became associated with behaviorism (Horowitz, 1992).

Behaviorism's approach contributed to the rise of animal research in psychology. Having deleted consciousness from their scope of concern, behaviorists no longer needed to study human subjects who could report on their mental processes. Many psychologists thought that animals would make better research subjects anyway. One key reason was that experimental research is often more productive if experimenters can exert considerable *control* over their subjects. Obviously, a researcher can exert much more control over a laboratory rat or pigeon than over a human subject. Thus, the discipline that had begun its life a few decades earlier as the study of the mind now found itself heavily involved in the study of simple responses made by lab animals.

Although Watson's views shaped the evolution of psychology for many decades, he ended up watching the field's progress from the sidelines. Because of a heavily publicized divorce scandal in 1920, Watson was forced to resign from Johns Hopkins University (Buckley, 1994). Bitterly disappointed, he left academia at the age of 42, never to return. Psychology's loss proved to be the business world's gain, as Watson went on to become an innovative, successful advertising executive (Brewer, 1991; Coon, 1994). The advertising industry was just emerging as a national force in the 1920s, and Watson quickly became one of its most prominent practitioners. He pioneered fear appeals, testimonials, selling the "prestige" of products, and the promotion of style over substance, all of which remain basic principles in modern marketing (Buckley, 1982). Moreover, "through an enormous output of books, magazine articles, and radio broadcasts he was able to establish himself as the public spokesman for the profession of psychology and an expert on subjects ranging from childrearing to economics. In effect, Watson became the first 'pop' psychologist" (Buckley, 1982, p. 217). So, ironically, Watson became the public face of the discipline that had banished him from its mainstream.

Skinner Questions Free Will as Behaviorism Flourishes

PsykTrek 1a, 10b

The advocates of behaviorism and psychoanalysis tangled frequently during the 1920s, 1930s, and 1940s. As psychoanalytic thought slowly gained a foothold within psychology, many psychologists softened their stance on the acceptability of studying internal mental events. However, this movement toward the consideration of internal states was dramatically reversed in the 1950s by a Harvard psychologist named B. F. Skinner (1904–1990).

Skinner did not deny the existence of internal mental events. However, he insisted that they could not be studied scientifically. Moreover, he maintained, there was no need to study them. According to Skinner, if the stimulus of food is followed by the response of eating, we can fully describe what is happening without making any guesses about

B. F. Skinner

"I submit that what we call the behavior of the human organism is no more free than its digestion."

whether the animal is experiencing hunger. Like Watson, Skinner also emphasized how environmental factors mold behavior.

The fundamental principle of behavior documented by Skinner is deceptively simple: *Organisms tend to repeat responses that lead to positive outcomes, and they tend not to repeat responses that lead to neutral or negative outcomes.* Despite its simplicity, this principle turns out to be quite powerful. Working with lab rats and pigeons in a small chamber called a Skinner box (see Chapter 6), Skinner showed that he could exert remarkable control over the behavior of animals by manipulating the outcomes of their responses. He was even able to train animals to perform unnatural behaviors. For example, he once trained some pigeons to play a respectable version of table tennis. They pecked a ball back and forth on a Ping Pong table (see the video found within *PsykTrek*). Skinner's followers eventually showed that the principles uncovered in their animal research could be applied to complex human behaviors as well. Behavioral principles are now widely used in factories, schools, prisons, mental hospitals, and a variety of other settings.

Skinner's ideas had repercussions that went far beyond the debate among psychologists about what they should study. Skinner spelled out the full implications of his findings in his book *Beyond Freedom and Dignity* (1971). There he asserted that all behavior is fully governed by external stimuli. In other words, your behavior is determined in predictable ways by lawful principles, just as the flight of an arrow is governed by the laws of physics. Thus, if you believe that your actions are the result of conscious decisions, you're wrong. According to Skinner, we are all controlled by our environment, not by ourselves. In short, Skinner arrived at the conclusion that *free will is an illusion.*

As you can readily imagine, such a disconcerting view of human nature was not universally acclaimed. Like Freud, Skinner was the target of harsh criticism. Much of this criticism stemmed from misinterpretations of his ideas reported in the popular press (Rutherford, 2000). For example, his analysis of free will was often misconstrued as an attack on the concept of a free society—which it was not. Somehow, a myth also emerged that Skinner raised his daughter in a version of a Skinner box and that this experience led her to be severely disturbed later in life. Despite the misinformation and controversy, however, behaviorism flourished as the dominant school of thought in psychology during the 1950s and 1960s (Gilgen, 1982).

The Humanists Revolt

PSYKTREK 1a, 10c

By the 1950s behaviorism and psychoanalytic theory had become the most influential schools of thought in psychology. However, many psychologists found these theoretical orientations unappealing. The principal charge hurled at both schools was that they were "dehumanizing." Psychoanalytic theory was attacked for its belief that behavior is dominated by primitive, sexual urges. Behaviorism was condemned for its preoccupation with the study of simple animal behavior. Both theories were criticized because they suggested that people are not masters of their own destinies. Above all, many people argued, both schools of thought failed to recognize the unique qualities of *human* behavior.

Beginning in the 1950s, the diverse opposition to behaviorism and psychoanalytic theory blended into a loose alliance that eventually became a new school of thought called "humanism" (Bühler & Allen, 1972). In psychology, **humanism** is a theoretical orientation that emphasizes the unique qualities of humans, especially their freedom and their potential for personal growth. Some of the key differences between the humanistic, psychoanalytic, and behavioral viewpoints are summarized in **Figure 1.3**. It compares six contemporary theoretical perspectives in psychology.

Humanists take an *optimistic* view of human nature. They maintain that people are not pawns of either their animal heritage or environmental circumstances. Further-

Perspective and Its Influential Period	Principal Contributors	Subject Matter	Basic Premise
Behavioral (1913–present)	John B. Watson Ivan Pavlov B. F. Skinner	Effects of environment on the overt behavior of humans and animals	Only observable events (stimulus-response relations) can be studied scientifically.
Psychoanalytic (1900–present)	Sigmund Freud Carl Jung Alfred Adler	Unconscious determinants of behavior	Unconscious motives and experiences in early childhood govern personality and mental disorders.
Humanistic (1950s–present)	Carl Rogers Abraham Maslow	Unique aspects of human experience	Humans are free, rational beings with the potential for personal growth, and they are fundamentally different from animals.
Cognitive (1950s–present)	Jean Piaget Noam Chomsky Herbert Simon	Thoughts; mental processes	Human behavior cannot be fully understood without examining how people acquire, store, and process information.
Biological (1950s–present)	James Olds Roger Sperry David Hubel Torsten Wiesel	Physiological bases of behavior in humans and animals	An organism's functioning can be explained in terms of the bodily structures and biochemical processes that underlie behavior.
Evolutionary (1980s–present)	David Buss Martin Daly Margo Wilson Leda Cosmides John Tooby	Evolutionary bases of behavior in humans and animals	Behavior patterns have evolved to solve adaptive problems; natural selection favors behaviors that enhance reproductive success.

© Vasiliy Koval/Shutterstock

© Franckreporter/IStockphoto

© Phil Date/Shutterstock

© Rafael Ramirez Lee/Shutterstock

© Dim Dimich/Shutterstock

© Eric Gevaert/Shutterstock

© Cengage Learning

FIGURE 1.3

Contemporary theoretical perspectives in psychology. The theoretical approaches outlined in this chart remain influential in modern psychology. As you can see, each theoretical perspective has its own take on what psychology should study.

more, these theorists say, because humans are fundamentally different from other animals, research on animals has little relevance to the understanding of human behavior. The most prominent architects of the humanistic movement have been Carl Rogers (1902–1987) and Abraham Maslow (1908–1970). Rogers (1951) argued that human behavior is governed primarily by each individual's sense of self, or "self-concept"—which animals presumably lack. Both he and Maslow (1954) maintained that to fully understand people's behavior, psychologists must take into account the human drive toward personal growth. They asserted that people have a basic need to continue to evolve as human beings and to fulfill their potentials.

Carl Rogers
"It seems to me that at bottom each person is asking, 'Who am I, really? How can I get in touch with this real self, underlying all my surface behavior? How can I become myself?'"

Concept Check   1.2

Understanding the Implications of Major Theories: Watson, Skinner, and Rogers

Check your understanding of the implications of some of the major theories reviewed in this chapter by indicating who is likely to have made each of the statements quoted below. Choose from the following: (a) John B. Watson, (b) B. F. Skinner, and (c) Carl Rogers. You'll find the answers in Appendix A at the back of the book.

_____ 1. "In the traditional view, a person is free. . . . He can therefore be held responsible for what he does and justly punished if he offends. That view, together with its associated practices, must be reexamined when a scientific analysis reveals unsuspected controlling relations between behavior and environment."

_____ 2. "I do not have a Pollyanna view of human nature. . . . Yet one of the most refreshing and invigorating parts of my experience is to work with [my clients] and to discover the strongly positive directional tendencies which exist in them, as in all of us, at the deepest levels."

_____ 3. "Our conclusion is that we have no real evidence of the inheritance of traits. I would feel perfectly confident in the ultimately favorable outcome of careful upbringing of a healthy, well-formed baby born of a long line of crooks, murderers and thieves, and prostitutes."

Psychology's Modern History

The principal storyline of psychology's early history was its gradual maturation into a research-based science. The seminal work of Wundt, James, Watson, Pavlov, Skinner, and a host of other pioneers served to establish psychology as a respected scientific discipline in the halls of academia. As you will learn momentarily, the principal storyline of psychology's modern history has been its remarkable growth into a multifaceted scientific and professional enterprise. In more recent decades psychology's story has been marked by expanding boundaries and broader interests.

Psychology Comes of Age as a Profession

PSYKTREK 1a

As you know, psychology is not all pure science. It has a highly practical side. Many psychologists provide a variety of professional services to the public. The first applied arm of psychology to achieve any prominence was *clinical psychology*. As practiced

KEY LEARNING GOALS

1.5 Discuss how historical events contributed to the emergence of psychology as a profession.

1.6 Describe two trends emerging in the 1950s–1960s that represented a return to psychology's intellectual roots.

1.7 Explain why Western psychology has shown an increased interest in cultural variables in recent decades.

1.8 Discuss the emergence and basic ideas of evolutionary psychology and positive psychology.

today, *clinical psychology* is the branch of psychology concerned with the diagnosis and treatment of psychological problems and disorders. In the early days, however, the emphasis was almost exclusively on psychological testing and adjustment problems in schoolchildren, and clinicians were a small minority in a field devoted primarily to research (Goldenberg, 1983).

That picture was about to change with dramatic swiftness. During World War II (1939–1945), many academic psychologists were pressed into service as clinicians. They were needed to screen military recruits and to treat soldiers suffering from trauma. Many of these psychologists (often to their surprise) found the clinical work to be challenging and rewarding, and a substantial portion continued to do clinical work after the war. More significantly, some 40,000 American veterans, many with severe psychological scars, returned to seek postwar treatment in Veterans Administration (VA) hospitals. With the demand for clinicians far greater than the supply, the VA stepped in to finance many new training programs in clinical psychology. Within a few years, about half of the new Ph.D.'s in psychology were specializing in clinical psychology (Goldenberg, 1983).

Since the 1950s, the professionalization of psychology has spread into additional areas of psychology. Today the broad umbrella of applied psychology covers a variety of professional specialties, including school psychology, industrial/organizational psychology, and counseling psychology (Benjamin & Baker, 2004).

Psychology Returns to Its Roots: Renewed Interest in Cognition and Physiology

PsykTrek 1a

While applied psychology has blossomed in recent years, scientific research has continued to progress. Ironically, two of the latest trends in research hark back more than a century to psychology's beginning, when psychologists were primarily interested in consciousness and physiology. Today psychologists are showing renewed interest in consciousness (now called "cognition") and the biological bases of behavior.

Cognition refers to the mental processes involved in acquiring knowledge. In other words, cognition involves thinking or conscious experience. For many decades, the dominance of behaviorism discouraged investigation of "unobservable" mental processes, and most psychologists showed little interest in cognition (Mandler, 2002). During the 1950s and 1960s, however, research on cognition slowly began to emerge (Miller, 2003). Major advances were made in the study of memory, language, and problem solving.

Cognitive theorists argue that psychology must include the study of internal mental events to fully understand human behavior (Gardner, 1985; Neisser, 1967). Advocates of the *cognitive perspective* point out that our mental processes surely influence how we behave. Consequently, focusing exclusively on overt behavior yields an incomplete picture of why we behave as we do. Equally important, psychologists investigating decision making, reasoning, and problem solving have shown that methods *can* be devised to study cognitive processes scientifically. Although the methods are different from those used in psychology's early days, recent research on the inner workings of the mind has put the *psyche* back in contemporary psychology. In fact, many observers maintain that the cognitive approach has become the dominant perspective in contemporary psychology. Some interesting data support this assertion, as can be seen in **Figure 1.4.** It plots estimates of the research productivity of four theoretical perspectives since 1950. As you can see, since 1975 the cognitive perspective has generated more published articles than any other perspective (Spear, 2007).

The 1950s and 1960s also saw many discoveries that highlighted the interrelations among mind, body, and behavior (Thompson & Zola, 2003). For example, researchers demonstrated that electrical stimulation of the brain could evoke emotional responses such as pleasure and rage in animals (Olds, 1956). Other work, which eventually earned a Nobel prize for Roger Sperry (in 1981), showed that the right and left halves of the brain are specialized to handle different types of mental tasks (Gazzaniga, Bogen, &

Sperry, 1965). These and many other findings stimulated an increase in research on the biological bases of behavior. Advocates of the *biological perspective* maintain that much of human and animal behavior can be explained in terms of the bodily structures and biochemical processes that allow organisms to behave. As you can see in **Figure 1.4**, the prominence of the neuroscience perspective has grown steadily since the 1950s (Spear, 2007). As you know, in the 19th century the young science of psychology had a heavy physiological emphasis. Thus, the renewed interest in the biological bases of behavior represents another return to psychology's heritage.

The cognitive and biological perspectives have become important theoretical orientations in modern psychology. They are increasingly influential viewpoints regarding what psychology should study and how. The cognitive and biological perspectives are compared to other contemporary theoretical perspectives in **Figure 1.3**.

Psychology Broadens Its Horizons: Increased Interest in Cultural Diversity

PsykTrek 1a

Throughout psychology's history, most researchers have worked under the assumption that they were seeking to identify general principles of behavior that would be applicable to all of humanity (Smith, Spillane, & Annus, 2006). In reality, however, psychology has largely been a Western (North American and European) enterprise with a rather provincial slant (Gergen et al. 1996; Norenzayan & Heine, 2005). Traditionally, Western psychologists have paid scant attention to how well their theories and research might apply to non-Western cultures, to ethnic minorities in Western societies, or even to women as opposed to men.

However, in recent years Western psychologists have begun to recognize that their neglect of cultural variables has diminished the value of their work. They are now devoting increased attention to culture as a determinant of behavior. What brought about this shift? The new interest in culture appears mainly attributable to two recent trends: (1) advances in communication, travel, and international trade have "shrunk" the world and increased global interdependence, bringing more and more Americans and Europeans into contact with people from non-Western cultures; and (2) the ethnic makeup of the Western world has become an increasingly diverse multicultural mosaic (Brislin, 1993; Hermans & Kempen, 1998; Mays et al., 1996).

These trends have prompted more and more Western psychologists to broaden their horizons and incorporate cultural factors into their theories and research (Lonner, 2009; Matsumoto & Yoo, 2006). These psychologists are striving to study previously underrepresented groups of subjects to test the generality of earlier findings and to catalog both the differences and similarities among cultural groups. These efforts to ask new questions and study new groups promise to enrich the discipline of psychology (Fowers & Davidov, 2006; Matsumoto, 2003; Sue, 2003).

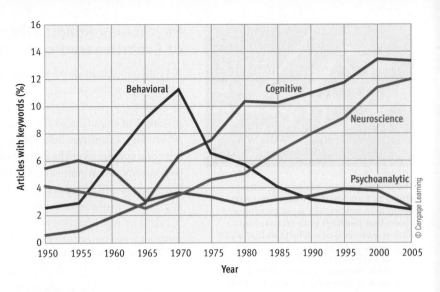

© Cengage Learning

FIGURE 1.4

The relative prominence of four major schools of thought in psychology. To estimate the relative productivity and influence of various theoretical orientations in recent decades, Joseph Spear (2007) conducted a keyword search of the psychological research literature indexed in PsycINFO to estimate the percentage of articles relevant to each school of thought. Obviously, his approach is just one of many ways one might gauge the prominence of various theoretical orientations in psychology. Nonetheless, the data are thought provoking. His findings suggest that the cognitive perspective surpassed the behavioral perspective in its influence on research sometime around 1975 and that it has continued as the leading perspective since then. As you can see, his data also demonstrate that the neuroscience perspective has grown steadily in influence since the 1950s.

SOURCE: Adapted from Spear, J. H. (2007). Prominent schools or other active specialties? A fresh look at some trends in psychology. *Review of General Psychology, 11*, 363-380. Copyright © 2007 by the American Psychological Association.

© Corbis Premium RF/Alamy

Psychology Adapts: The Emergence of Evolutionary Psychology

PsykTrek 1a

A relatively recent development in psychology has been the emergence of *evolutionary psychology,* a theoretical perspective that is likely to be influential in the years to come. Evolutionary psychologists assert that the patterns of behavior seen in a species are products of evolution in the same way that anatomical characteristics are. *Evolutionary psychology* **examines behavioral processes in terms of their adaptive value for members of a species over the course of many generations.** The basic premise of evolutionary psychology is that natural selection favors behaviors that enhance organisms' reproductive success—that is, passing on genes to the next generation. Thus, if a species is highly aggressive, evolutionary psychologists argue that it's because aggressiveness confers a survival or reproductive advantage for members of that species. Hence, genes that promote aggressiveness are more likely to be passed on to the next generation.

Evolutionary psychology began to emerge in the middle to late 1980s. A growing band of evolutionary psychologists (Buss, 1985, 1989; Cosmides & Tooby, 1989; Daly & Wilson, 1985) published widely cited studies on a broad range of topics. These topics included mating preferences, jealousy, aggression, sexual behavior, decision making, and development. By the mid-1990s, it became clear that psychology was witnessing the birth of its first major, new theoretical perspective since the cognitive revolution in the 1950s and 1960s.

Psychology Moves in a Positive Direction

PsykTrek 1a

Shortly after Martin Seligman was elected president of the American Psychological Association in 1997, he experienced a profound insight that he characterized as an "epiphany." This pivotal insight came from an unusual source—Seligman's 5-year-old daughter, Nikki. She scolded her overachieving, task-oriented father for being "grumpy" far too much of the time. Provoked by his daughter's criticism, Seligman suddenly realized that his approach to life *was* overly and unnecessarily negative. More important, he recognized that the same assessment could be made of the field of psychology—that, it too, was excessively and needlessly negative in its approach (Seligman, 2003). This revelation inspired Seligman to launch an influential new initiative within psychology that came to be known as the *positive psychology movement.*

Seligman went on to argue convincingly that the field of psychology had historically devoted too much attention to pathology, weakness, and damage, and ways to heal suffering. He acknowledged that this approach had yielded valuable insights and progress. But he argued that it also resulted in an unfortunate neglect of the forces that make life worth living. Seligman convened a series of informal meetings with influential psychologists and then more formal conferences to gradually outline the philosophy and goals of positive psychology. Like humanism before it, positive psychology seeks to shift the field's focus away from negative experiences. Thus, *positive psychology* **uses theory and research to better understand the positive, adaptive, creative, and fulfilling aspects of human existence.**

The emerging field of positive psychology has three areas of interest (Seligman, 2003). The first is the study of *positive subjective experiences,* or positive emotions, such as happiness, love, gratitude, contentment, and hope. The second focus is on *positive individual traits*—that is, personal strengths and virtues. Theorists are working to identify, classify, and analyze the origins of such positive traits as courage, perseverance, nurturance, tolerance, creativity, integrity, and kindness. The third area of interest is in *positive institutions and communities.* Here the focus is on how societies can foster civil discourse, strong families, healthful work environments, and supportive neighborhood communities.

Our review of psychology's past has shown how the field has evolved. We have seen psychology develop from philosophical speculation into a rigorous science committed

The praying mantis has an astonishing ability to blend in with its environment, along with remarkably acute hearing and vision that permit it to detect prey up to 60 feet away and powerful jaws that allow it to devour its prey. They are so deadly they will eat each other, which makes sex quite a challenge, but males have evolved a reflex module that allows them to copulate successfully while being eaten (even after decapitation)! These physical characteristics obviously represent adaptations that have been crafted by natural selection over the course of millions of generations. Evolutionary psychologists maintain that many patterns of behavior seen in various species are also adaptations that have been shaped by natural selection.

to research. We have seen how a highly visible professional arm involved in mental health services emerged from this science. We have seen how psychology's focus on physiology is rooted in its 19th-century origins. We have seen how and why psychologists began conducting research on lower animals. We have seen how psychology has evolved from the study of mind and body to the study of behavior, and how the investigation of mind and body has been welcomed back into the mainstream of modern psychology. We have seen how different theoretical schools have defined the scope and mission of psychology in different ways. We have seen how psychology's interests have expanded and become increasingly diverse. Above all else, we have seen that psychology is a growing, evolving intellectual enterprise.

Psychology's history is already rich, but its story has barely begun. The century or so that has elapsed since Wilhelm Wundt put psychology on a scientific footing is only an eyeblink of time in human history. What has been discovered during those years, and what remains unknown, is the subject of the rest of this book.

Psychology Today: Vigorous and Diversified

We began this chapter with an informal description of what psychology is about. Now that you have a feel for how psychology has developed, you can better appreciate a definition that does justice to the field's modern diversity: *Psychology* **is the science that studies behavior and the physiological and cognitive processes that underlie behavior, and it is the profession that applies the accumulated knowledge of this science to practical problems.**

Contemporary psychology is a thriving science and profession. Its growth has been remarkable. One simple index of this growth is the dramatic rise in membership in the American Psychological Association (APA), a national organization devoted to the advancement of psychology. The APA was founded by G. Stanley Hall in 1892 with just 26 members. Today, the APA has over 90,000 members. Moreover, as **Figure 1.5** shows, APA membership has increased ninefold since 1950. In the United States, psychology is the second most popular undergraduate major. The field accounts for nearly 10% of all doctoral degrees awarded in the sciences and humanities. Of course, psychology is an international enterprise. Today, over 2400 technical journals from all over the world publish research articles on psychology. Thus, by any standard of measurement—the

KEY LEARNING GOALS

1.9 Discuss the growth of psychology, and identify the most common work settings for contemporary psychologists.

1.10 List and describe the major research areas and professional specialties in psychology.

Reality Check

Misconception
Psychology is the study of the mind.

Reality
When the term was coined in the 16th century, *psychology* did refer to the study of the mind, but the term's original meaning is much too narrow today. Since the 19th century, scientific psychology has focused heavily on physiological processes, and the 20th century brought a new focus on overt behavior. Modern psychology encompasses the study of behavior and the mental and physiological processes that regulate behavior.

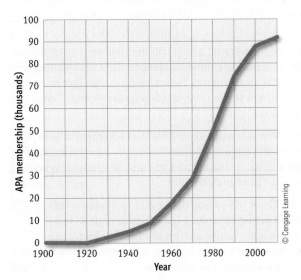

FIGURE 1.5

Membership in the American Psychological Association, 1900–2010. The steep rise in the number of psychologists in the APA since 1950 testifies to psychology's remarkable growth as a science and a profession. If graduate student members are also counted, the APA has over 150,000 members. (Adapted from data published by the American Psychological Association, by permission.)

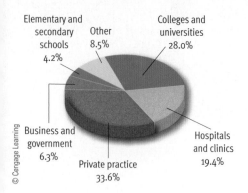

Elementary and
secondary
schools
4.2%

Other
8.5%

Colleges and
universities
28.0%

Business and
government
6.3%

Private practice
33.6%

Hospitals
and clinics
19.4%

FIGURE 1.6

Employment of psychologists by setting. The work settings in which psychologists are employed have become very diverse. Survey data on the primary employment setting of APA members indicates that one-third are in private practice (compared to 12% in 1976), while only 28% work in colleges and universities (compared to 47% in 1976). (Based on data published by the American Psychological Association)

number of people involved, the number of degrees granted, the number of studies conducted, the number of journals published—psychology is a healthy, growing field.

Psychology's vigorous presence in modern society is also demonstrated by the great variety of settings in which psychologists work. The distribution of psychologists employed in various categories of settings can be seen in **Figure 1.6**. They were once found almost exclusively in academia. However, today only about one-fourth of American psychologists work in colleges and universities. The remaining three-fourths work in hospitals, clinics, police departments, research institutes, government agencies, business and industry, schools, nursing homes, counseling centers, and private practice.

Clearly, contemporary psychology is a multifaceted field. This is especially apparent when we consider the many areas of specialization within psychology today. Let's look at the current areas of specialization in both the science and the profession of psychology.

Research Areas in Psychology

Most psychologists receive broad training that provides them with knowledge about many areas of psychology. However, they usually specialize when it comes to doing research. Such specialization is necessary because the subject matter of psychology has become so vast over the years. Today it is virtually impossible for anyone to stay abreast of the new research in all specialties. Specialization is also necessary because specific skills and training are required to do research in some areas.

The nine major research areas in modern psychology are (1) developmental psychology, (2) social psychology, (3) experimental psychology, (4) physiological psychology, (5) cognitive psychology, (6) personality, (7) psychometrics, (8) educational psychology, and (9) health psychology. **Figure 1.7** briefly describes each of these areas of inquiry.

Concept Check 1.3

Understanding the Major Research Areas in Contemporary Psychology

Check your understanding of the various research areas in psychology reviewed in this chapter by indicating which type of psychologist would be most likely to perform each of the investigations described below. Choose from the following: (a) physiological psychology, (b) cognitive psychology, (c) developmental psychology, (d) psychometrics, and (e) personality. You'll find the answers in Appendix A at the back of the book.

_____ 1. Researchers interviewed the parents of 141 children (all born in 1956) every few months throughout childhood. Questions dealt with various aspects of the children's temperaments. The conclusion was that most children fall into one of three temperamental categories: "easy," "difficult," or "slow to warm up."

_____ 2. It was discovered that rats will work extremely hard (pressing a lever, for instance) to earn small amounts of electrical stimulation directed to specific areas of their brains. Research indicates that the human brain may also contain similar "pleasure centers."

_____ 3. The Sensation Seeking Scale (SSS) was developed to measure individual differences in the extent to which people prefer high or low levels of sensory stimulation. People such as skydivers tend to score high on the SSS, while someone whose idea of a good time is settling down with a good book would tend to score low.

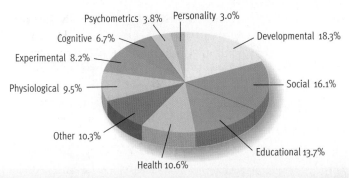

Psychometrics 3.8% Personality 3.0%

Cognitive 6.7%

Developmental 18.3%

Experimental 8.2%

Physiological 9.5%

Social 16.1%

Other 10.3%

Educational 13.7%

Health 10.6%

© Cengage Learning

FIGURE 1.7

Major research areas in contemporary psychology. Most research psychologists specialize in one of the nine broad areas described here. The figures in the pie chart reflect the percentage of academic and research psychologists belonging to APA who identify each area as their primary interest. (Based on data published by the American Psychological Association)

Area	Focus of research
Developmental psychology	Looks at human development across the life span. Developmental psychology once focused primarily on child development, but today devotes a great deal of research to adolescence, adulthood, and old age.
Social psychology	Focuses on interpersonal behavior and the role of social forces in governing behavior. Typical topics include attitude formation, attitude change, prejudice, conformity, attraction, aggression, intimate relationships, and behavior in groups.
Educational psychology	Studies how people learn and the best ways to teach them. Examines curriculum design, teacher training, achievement testing, student motivation, classroom diversity, and other aspects of the educational process.
Health psychology	Focuses on how psychological factors relate to the promotion and maintenance of physical health and the causation, prevention, and treatment of illness.
Physiological psychology	Examines the influence of genetic factors on behavior and the role of the brain, nervous system, endocrine system, and bodily chemicals in the regulation of behavior.
Experimental psychology	Encompasses the traditional core of topics that psychology focused on heavily in its first half-century as a science: sensation, perception, learning, conditioning, motivation, and emotion. The name experimental psychology is somewhat misleading, as this is not the only area in which experiments are done. Psychologists working in all the areas listed here conduct experiments.
Cognitive psychology	Focuses on "higher" mental processes, such as memory, reasoning, information processing, language, problem solving, decision making, and creativity.
Psychometrics	Is concerned with the measurement of behavior and capacities, usually through the development of psychological tests. Psychometrics is involved with the design of tests to assess personality, intelligence, and a wide range of abilities. It is also concerned with the development of new techniques for statistical analysis.
Personality	Is interested in describing and understanding individuals' consistency in behavior, which represents their personality. This area of interest is also concerned with the factors that shape personality and with personality assessment.

Professional Specialties in Psychology

Applied psychology consists of four well-established areas of specialization. The four main professional specialties are (1) clinical psychology, (2) counseling psychology, (3) school psychology, and (4) industrial/organizational psychology. Descriptions of these specialties can be found in **Figure 1.8** on the next page. Clinical psychology is currently the most widely practiced professional specialty.

Some people are confused about the difference between clinical psychology and psychiatry. The confusion is understandable, as both clinical psychologists and psychiatrists are involved in analyzing and treating psychological disorders. Although some overlap exists between the two professions, the training and educational requirements for the two are quite different. Clinical psychologists go to graduate school to earn one of several doctoral degrees (Ph.D., Ed.D., or Psy.D.) in order to enjoy full status in their

FIGURE 1.8

Principal professional specialties in contemporary psychology. Most psychologists who deliver professional services to the public specialize in one of the four areas described here. The figures in the pie chart reflect the percentage of APA members delivering professional services who identify each area as their chief specialty. (Based on data published by the American Psychological Association)

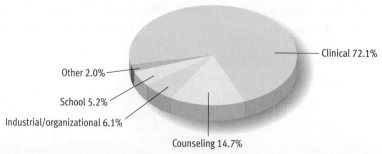

Clinical 72.1%
Other 2.0%
School 5.2%
Industrial/organizational 6.1%
Counseling 14.7%

Specialty	Focus of professional practice
Clinical psychology	Clinical psychologists are concerned with the evaluation, diagnosis, and treatment of individuals with psychological disorders, as well as treatment of less severe behavioral and emotional problems. Principal activities include interviewing clients, psychological testing, and providing group or individual psychotherapy.
Counseling psychology	Counseling psychology overlaps with clinical psychology in that specialists in both areas engage in similar activities—interviewing, testing, and providing therapy. However, counseling psychologists usually work with a somewhat different clientele, providing assistance to people struggling with everyday problems of moderate severity. Thus, they often specialize in family, marital, or career counseling.
Industrial and organizational psychology	Psychologists in this area perform a wide variety of tasks in the world of business and industry. These tasks include running human resources departments, working to improve staff morale and attitudes, striving to increase job satisfaction and productivity, examining organizational structures and procedures, and making recommendations for improvements.
School psychology	School psychologists strive to promote the cognitive, emotional, and social development of children in schools. They usually work in elementary or secondary schools, where they test and counsel children having difficulties in school and aid parents and teachers in solving school-related problems.

© Cengage Learning

Reality Check

Misconception

Psychology and psychiatry are largely the same.

Reality

Psychiatry is a branch of medicine that has focused almost exclusively on the treatment of mental disorders. Psychology is an academic field that is vastly broader in scope, focusing on learning, perception, human development, memory, intelligence and social behavior, although it does have a clinical arm concerned with mental disorders. Clinical psychologists and psychiatrists get very different kinds of training, earn different degrees, and tend to have different approaches to the treatment of mental illness (see Chapter 15).

KEY LEARNING GOALS

1.11 Understand the text's three unifying themes relating to psychology as a field of study.

1.12 Understand the text's four unifying themes relating to psychology's subject matter.

profession. Psychiatrists go to medical school for their postgraduate education, where they receive general training in medicine and earn an M.D. degree. They then specialize by completing residency training in psychiatry at a hospital. Clinical psychologists and psychiatrists also differ in the way they tend to approach the treatment of mental disorders, as we will see in Chapter 15. To summarize, *psychiatry* is a branch of medicine concerned with the diagnosis and treatment of psychological problems and disorders. In contrast, clinical psychology takes a nonmedical approach to such problems.

Seven Unifying Themes

The enormous breadth and diversity of psychology make it a challenging subject for the beginning student. In the pages ahead you will be introduced to many areas of research and a multitude of new ideas, concepts, and principles. Fortunately, not all ideas are created equal. Some are far more important than others. In this section, I will highlight seven fundamental themes that will reappear in a number of variations as we move from one area of psychology to another in this text. You have already met some of these key ideas in our review of psychology's past and present. Now we will isolate them and highlight their significance. In the remainder of the book these ideas serve as organizing themes to provide threads of continuity across chapters. They will also help you see the connections among the various areas of research in psychology.

In studying psychology, you are learning about both behavior and the scientific discipline that investigates it. Accordingly, our seven themes come in two sets. The first set consists of statements highlighting crucial aspects of psychology as a way of thinking and as a field of study. The second set consists of broad generalizations about psychology's subject matter: behavior and the cognitive and physiological processes that underlie it.

Themes Related to Psychology as a Field of Study

Looking at psychology as a field of study, we see three central ideas: (1) psychology is empirical, (2) psychology is theoretically diverse, and (3) psychology evolves in a socio-historical context. Let's look at each of these ideas in more detail.

THEME 1: PSYCHOLOGY IS EMPIRICAL

Everyone tries to understand behavior. Most of us have developed our own personal answers to such questions as why some people are hard workers, why some are overweight, and why others stay in demeaning relationships. If all of us are amateur psychologists, what makes scientific psychology any different or better? The critical difference is that psychology is *empirical.*

What do we mean by empirical? ***Empiricism* is the premise that knowledge should be acquired through observation.** This premise is crucial to the scientific method that psychology embraced in the late 19th century. To say that psychology is empirical means that its conclusions are based on direct observation rather than on reasoning, speculation, traditional beliefs, or common sense. Psychologists are not content with having ideas that sound plausible. They conduct research to test their ideas. Is intelligence higher on the average in some social classes than in others? Are men more aggressive than women? Psychologists find a way to make direct, objective, and precise observations to answer such questions.

The empirical approach requires a certain attitude—a healthy brand of skepticism. Empiricism is a tough taskmaster. It demands data and documentation. Psychologists' commitment to empiricism means that they must learn to think critically about generalizations concerning behavior. If someone asserts that people tend to get depressed around Christmas, a psychologist is likely to ask, "How many people get depressed? In what population? In comparison to what baseline rate of depression? How is depression defined and measured?" Their skeptical attitude means that psychologists are trained to ask, "Where's the evidence? How do you know?" If psychology's empirical orientation rubs off on you (and I hope it does), you will be asking similar questions by the time you finish this book.

THEME 2: PSYCHOLOGY IS THEORETICALLY DIVERSE

Although psychology is based on observation, a string of unrelated observations would not be terribly enlightening. Psychologists do not set out to collect isolated facts; they seek to explain and understand what they observe. To achieve these goals they must construct theories. **A *theory* is a system of interrelated ideas used to explain a set of observations.** In other words, a theory links apparently unrelated observations and tries to explain them. As an example, consider Sigmund Freud's observations about slips of the tongue, dreams, and psychological disturbances. On the surface, these observations appear unrelated. By devising the concept of the *unconscious,* Freud created a theory that links and explains these seemingly unrelated aspects of behavior.

Our review of psychology's past should have made one thing abundantly clear: Psychology is marked by theoretical diversity. Why do we have so many competing points of view? One reason is that no single theory can adequately explain everything that is known about behavior. Sometimes different theories focus on different aspects of behavior—that is, different collections of observations. Sometimes there is simply more than one way to look at something. Is the glass half empty or half full? Obviously, it is both. To take an example from another science, physicists wrestled for years with the nature of light. Is it a wave, or is it a particle? In the end, it proved useful to think of light sometimes as a wave and sometimes as a particle. Similarly, if a business executive

© Gregg Harris/Shutterstock

lashes out at her employees with stinging criticism, is she releasing pent-up aggressive urges (a psychoanalytic view)? Is she making a habitual response to the stimulus of incompetent work (a behavioral view)? Or is she scheming to motivate her employees with "mind games" (a cognitive view)? In some cases, all three of these explanations might have some validity. In short, it is an oversimplification to expect that one view has to be right while all others are wrong. Life is rarely that simple.

Students are often troubled by psychology's many conflicting theories. They tend to view this diversity as a weakness. *However, contemporary psychologists increasingly recognize that theoretical diversity is a strength rather than a weakness.* As we proceed through this text, you will learn how clashing theories have often stimulated productive research. You will also see how approaching a problem from several theoretical perspectives can often provide a more complete understanding than could be achieved by any one perspective alone.

THEME 3: PSYCHOLOGY EVOLVES IN A SOCIOHISTORICAL CONTEXT

Science is often seen as an "ivory tower" undertaking, isolated from the ebb and flow of everyday life. In reality, however, psychology and other sciences do not exist in a cultural vacuum. Dense interconnections exist between what happens in psychology and what happens in society at large (Altman, 1990; Danziger, 1990; Runyan, 2006). Trends, issues, and values in society influence psychology's evolution. Similarly, progress in psychology affects trends, issues, and values in society. To put it briefly, psychology develops in a *sociohistorical* (social and historical) context.

Psychology's past is filled with examples of how social trends have left their imprint on psychology. For example, Sigmund Freud's groundbreaking ideas emerged out of a specific sociohistorical context. Cultural values in Freud's era encouraged the suppression of sexuality. As a result, people tended to feel guilty about their sexual urges to a much greater extent than is common today. This situation clearly contributed to Freud's emphasis on unconscious sexual conflicts. As another example, consider how World War II sparked the rapid growth of psychology as a profession.

If we reverse our viewpoint, we can see that psychology has in turn left its mark on society. Consider, for instance, the pervasive role of mental testing in modern society. Your own career success may depend in part on how well you weave your way through a complex maze of intelligence and achievement tests made possible (to the regret of some) by research in psychology. As another example of psychology's impact on society, consider the influence that various theorists have had on parenting styles. Trends in childrearing practices have been shaped by the ideas of John B. Watson, Sigmund Freud, B. F. Skinner, and Carl Rogers—not to mention many more psychologists yet to be discussed. In short, society and psychology influence each other in complex ways. In the chapters to come, we will frequently have occasion to notice this dynamic relationship.

Themes Related to Psychology's Subject Matter

Looking at psychology's subject matter, we see four additional fundamental ideas: (4) behavior is determined by multiple causes, (5) behavior is shaped by cultural heritage, (6) heredity and environment jointly influence behavior; and (7) people's experience of the world is highly subjective.

THEME 4: BEHAVIOR IS DETERMINED BY MULTIPLE CAUSES

As psychology has matured, it has provided more and more information about the forces that govern behavior. This growing knowledge has led to a deeper appreciation of a simple but important fact: Behavior is exceedingly complex, and most aspects of behavior are determined by multiple causes.

Although the complexity of behavior may seem self-evident, people usually think in terms of single causes. Thus, they offer explanations such as "Andrea flunked out of school because she is lazy." Or they assert that "teenage pregnancies are increasing because of all the sex in the media." Single-cause explanations are sometimes accurate insofar as they go, but they are usually incomplete. In general, psychologists find that behavior is governed by a complex network of interacting factors. This idea is referred to as the *multifactorial causation of behavior.*

As a simple illustration, consider the multiple factors that might influence your performance in your introductory psychology course. Relevant personal factors might include your overall intelligence, your reading ability, your memory skills, your motivation, and your study skills. In addition, your grade could be affected by numerous situational factors, including whether you like your psychology professor, whether you like your assigned text, whether the class meets at a good time for you, whether your work schedule is light or heavy, and whether you're having any personal problems. As you proceed through this book, you will learn that complexity of causation is the rule rather than the exception. If we expect to understand behavior, we usually have to take into account multiple determinants.

THEME 5: BEHAVIOR IS SHAPED BY CULTURAL HERITAGE

Among the multiple determinants of human behavior, cultural factors are particularly prominent. Just as psychology evolves in a sociohistorical context, so, too, do individuals. Our cultural backgrounds exert considerable influence over our behavior. As Markus and Hamedani (2007) put it, "The option of being *a*social or *a*cultural—that is, living as a neutral being who is not bound to particular practices and socioculturally structured ways of behaving—is not available. People eat, sleep, work, and relate to one another in culture-specific ways" (p. 5). What is *culture?* Theorists have argued about the exact details of how to define culture for over a century, and the precise boundaries of the concept remain a little fuzzy (Matsumoto & Yoo, 2006). Broadly speaking, **culture refers to the widely shared customs, beliefs, values, norms, institutions, and other products of a community that are transmitted socially across generations.** Culture is a broad construct, encompassing everything from a society's legal system to its assumptions about family roles, from its dietary habits to its political ideals, from its technology to its attitudes about time, from its modes of dress to its spiritual beliefs, and from its art and music to its unspoken rules about sexual liaisons.

Much of our cultural heritage is invisible (Brislin, 2000). Assumptions, ideals, attitudes, beliefs, and unspoken rules exist in people's minds and may not be readily apparent to outsiders. Moreover, because our cultural background is widely shared, we feel little need to discuss it with others, and we often take it for granted. For example, you probably don't spend much time thinking about the importance of living in rectangular rooms, trying to minimize body odor, limiting yourself to one spouse at a time, or using credit cards to obtain material goods and services. We often fail to appreciate its influence, but our cultural heritage has a pervasive impact on our thoughts, feelings, and behavior (Matsumoto & Juang, 2008; Triandis, 2007).

Although the influence of culture is everywhere, generalizations about cultural groups must always be tempered by the realization that great diversity exists within any society or ethnic group (Markus & Hamedani, 2007). Researchers may be able to pinpoint genuinely useful insights about Ethiopian, Korean American, or Ukrainian culture, for example, but it would be foolish to assume that all Ethiopians, Korean Americans, or Ukrainians exhibit identical behavior. It is also important to realize that *both differences and similarities in behavior occur across cultures.* As we will see

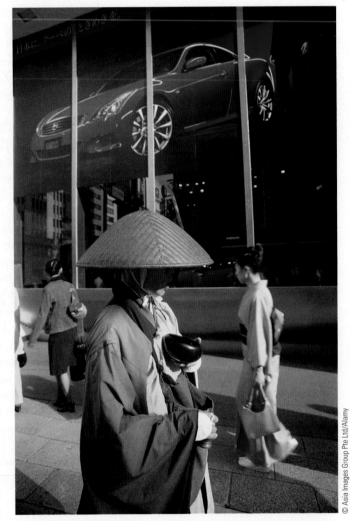

Cultural background has an enormous influence on people's behavior, shaping everything from modes of dress to sexual values and norms. Increased global interdependence brings more and more people into contact with cultures other than their own. This increased exposure to diverse cultures only serves to underscore the importance of cultural factors.

repeatedly, psychological processes are characterized by both cultural variance and invariance. Caveats aside, if we hope to achieve a sound understanding of human behavior, we need to consider cultural determinants.

THEME 6: HEREDITY AND ENVIRONMENT JOINTLY INFLUENCE BEHAVIOR

Are we who we are—athletic or artistic, quick-tempered or calm, shy or outgoing, energetic or laid back—because of our genetic inheritance or because of our upbringing? This question about the importance of nature versus nurture, or heredity versus environment, has been asked in one form or another since ancient times. Historically, the nature versus nurture question was framed as an all-or-none proposition. In other words, theorists argued that personal traits and abilities are governed entirely by heredity or entirely by environment. John B. Watson, for instance, asserted that personality and ability depend almost exclusively on an individual's environment. In contrast, Sir Francis Galton, a pioneer in mental testing, maintained that personality and ability depend almost entirely on genetic inheritance.

Today, most psychologists agree that heredity and environment are both important. A century of research has shown that genetics and experience jointly influence individuals' intelligence, temperament, personality, and susceptibility to many psychological disorders (Grigerenko & Sternberg, 2003; Plomin, 2004; Rutter, 2006). If we ask whether people are born or made, psychology's answer is "Both." This response does not mean that nature versus nurture is a dead issue. Lively debate about the *relative influence* of genetics and experience continues unabated. Furthermore, psychologists are actively seeking to understand the complex ways in which genetic inheritance and experience interact to mold behavior.

THEME 7: PEOPLE'S EXPERIENCE OF THE WORLD IS HIGHLY SUBJECTIVE

Our experience of the world is highly subjective. Even elementary perception—for example, of sights and sounds—is not a passive process. We actively process incoming stimulation, selectively focusing on some aspects of that stimulation while ignoring others. Moreover, we impose organization on the stimuli that we pay attention to. These tendencies combine to make perception personalized and subjective.

The subjectivity of perception was demonstrated nicely in a study by Hastorf and Cantril (1954). They showed students at Princeton and Dartmouth universities a film of a hotly contested football game between the two rival schools. The students were told to watch for rules infractions. Both groups saw the same film, but the Princeton students "saw" the Dartmouth players engage in twice as many infractions as the Dartmouth students "saw," and vice versa. The investigators concluded that the game "actually was many different games and that each version of the events that transpired was just as 'real' to a particular person as other versions were to other people" (Hastorf & Cantril, 1954). This study showed how people sometimes see what they *want* to see. Other studies have demonstrated that people also tend to see what they *expect* to see (Kelley, 1950).

Human subjectivity is precisely what the scientific method is designed to counteract. In using the scientific approach, psychologists strive to make their observations as objective as possible. Left to their own subjective experience, people might still believe that the earth is flat and that the sun revolves around it. Thus, psychologists are committed to the scientific approach because they believe it is the most reliable route to accurate knowledge.

Now that you have been introduced to the text's organizing themes, let's turn to an example of how psychological research can be applied to the challenges of everyday life. In our first Personal Application, we'll focus on a subject that should be highly relevant to you: how to be a successful student. In the Critical Thinking Application that follows it, we discuss the nature and importance of critical thinking skills.

Improving Academic Performance

1.13 Discuss some strategies for promoting adequate study, improving reading comprehension, and getting more out of lectures.

Answer the following "true" or "false."

____ **1** If you have a professor who delivers chaotic, hard-to-follow lectures, there is little point in attending class.

____ **2** Cramming the night before an exam is an efficient method of study.

____ **3** In taking lecture notes, you should try to be a "human tape recorder" (that is, write down everything your professor says).

____ **4** You should never change your answers to multiple-choice questions, because your first hunch is your best hunch.

All of the above statements are false. If you answered them all correctly, you may have already acquired the kinds of skills and habits that facilitate academic success. If so, however, you are not typical. Today, many students enter college with poor study skills and habits, and it's not entirely their fault. Our educational system generally provides minimal instruction on good study techniques. In this first Personal Application, I will try to remedy this situation to some extent by reviewing some insights that psychology offers on how to improve academic performance. We will discuss how to promote better study habits, how to enhance reading efforts, and how to get more out of lectures. You may also want to jump ahead and read the Personal Application for Chapter 7, which focuses on how to improve everyday memory.

Developing Sound Study Habits

People tend to assume that academic performance in college is largely determined by students' intelligence or general mental ability. This belief is supported by the fact that college admissions tests (the SAT and ACT), which basically assess general cognitive ability, predict college grades fairly well (Berry & Sackett, 2009; Kobrin et al., 2008). What is far less well known, however, is that measures of study skills, habits, and attitudes also predict college grades pretty well. In a large-scale review of 344 independent samples consisting of over 72,000 students, Crede and Kuncel (2008) reported that aggregate measures of study skills and habits predicted college grades almost as well as admissions tests, and that these factors accounted for variability in performance that the admissions tests could not account for. In other words, this massive review of evidence found that study habits are almost as influential as ability in determining college success. The practical meaning of this finding is that most students probably underestimate the importance of their study skills. And bear in mind that whereas most adults probably cannot increase their mental ability much, they can usually enhance their study habits considerably.

In any event, the first step toward effective study habits is to face up to the reality that studying usually involves hard work. You don't have to feel guilty if you don't look forward to studying. Most students don't. Once you accept the premise that studying doesn't come naturally, it should be apparent that you need to set up an organized program to promote adequate study. According to Siebert and Karr (2003), such a program should include the following considerations:

1. *Set up a schedule for studying.* If you wait until the urge to study strikes you, you may still be waiting when the exam rolls around. Thus, it is important to allocate definite times for studying. Review your various time obligations (work, chores, and so on) and figure out in advance when you can study. When allotting certain times to studying, keep in mind that you need to be wide awake and alert. Be realistic about how long you can study at one time before you wear down from fatigue. Allow time for study breaks—they can revive sagging concentration.

It's important to write down your study schedule. A written schedule serves as a reminder and increases your commitment to following it. You should begin by setting up a general schedule for the quarter or semester, like the one in **Figure 1.9** on the next page. Then, at the beginning of each week, plan the specific assignments that you intend to work on during each study session. This approach to scheduling should help you avoid cramming for exams at the last minute. Cramming is an ineffective study strategy for most students (Underwood, 1961; L. A. Wong, 2006; Zechmeister & Nyberg, 1982). It will strain your memorization capabilities, can tax your energy level, and may stoke the fires of test anxiety.

In planning your weekly schedule, try to avoid the tendency to put off working on major tasks such as term papers and reports. Time-management experts, such as Alan Lakein (1996), point out that many of us tend to tackle simple, routine tasks first, saving larger tasks for later when we supposedly will have more time. This common tendency leads many of us to repeatedly delay working on major assignments until it's too late to do a good job. You can avoid this trap by breaking major assignments down into smaller component tasks that can be scheduled individually.

2. *Find a place to study where you can concentrate.* Where you study is also important. The key is to find a place where distractions are likely to be minimal. Most people cannot study effectively while TV shows or music are playing or while other people are talking. Don't depend on will-

Weekly Activity Schedule							
	Monday	Tuesday	Wednesday	Thursday	Friday	Saturday	Sunday
8 A.M.						Work	
9 A.M.	History	Study	History	Study	History		
10 A.M.	Psychology	French ↓	Psychology	French ↓	Psychology	↓	
11 A.M.	Study		Study		Study		
Noon	Math	Study	Math	Study	Math	↓	Work
1 P.M.							
2 P.M.	Study	English	Study	English	Study		
3 P.M.	↓	↓	↓	↓	↓		↓
4 P.M.							
5 P.M.							
6 P.M.	Work	Study	Study	Work			Work
7 P.M.							
8 P.M.	↓	↓	↓	↓			↓
9 P.M.							
10 P.M.	↓			↓			

© Cengage Learning

FIGURE 1.9

One student's general activity schedule for a semester. Each week the student fills in the specific assignments to work on during each study period.

power to carry you through such distractions. It's much easier to plan ahead and avoid the distractions altogether.

3. *Reward your studying.* One reason it is so difficult to be motivated to study regularly is that the payoffs often lie in the distant future. The ultimate reward, a degree, may be years away. Even more short-term rewards, such as an A in the course, may be weeks or months away. To combat this problem, it helps to give yourself immediate, tangible rewards for studying, such as a snack, TV show, or phone call to a friend. Thus, you should set realistic study goals for yourself and then reward yourself when you meet them. The systematic manipulation of rewards involves harnessing the principles of behavior modification described by B. F. Skinner and other behavioral psychologists. These principles are covered in the Chapter 6 Personal Application.

Improving Your Reading

Much of your study time is spent reading and absorbing information. The keys to improving reading comprehension are to preview reading assignments section by section, work hard to actively process the meaning of the information, strive to identify the key ideas of each paragraph, and carefully review these key ideas after each section. Modern textbooks often contain a variety of learning aids that you can use to improve your reading. If a book provides a chapter outline, chapter summary, or learning objectives, don't ignore them. They can help you recognize the important points in the chapter. Graphic organizers (such as the Concept Charts available online for this text) can also enhance understanding of text material (Nist & Holschuh, 2000). A lot of effort and thought go into formulating these and other textbook learning aids. It is wise to take advantage of them.

Another important issue related to textbook reading is whether and how to mark up one's reading assignments. Many students deceive themselves into thinking that they are studying by running a marker through a few sentences here and there in their text. If they do so without thoughtful selectivity, they are simply turning a textbook into a coloring book. This situation probably explains why some professors are skeptical about the value of highlighting textbooks. Nonetheless, research suggests that highlighting textbook material *is* a useful strategy—if students are reasonably effective in focusing on the main ideas in the material and if they subsequently review what they have highlighted (Caverly, Orlando, & Mullen, 2000).

When executed effectively, highlighting can foster active reading, improve reading comprehension, and reduce the amount of material that one has to review later (Van Blerkom, 2006). The key to effective text marking is to identify (and highlight) only the main ideas, key supporting details, and technical terms (Daiek & Anter, 2004). Most textbooks are carefully crafted such that every paragraph has a purpose for being there. Try to find the sentence or two that best captures the purpose of each paragraph. Text marking is a delicate balancing act. If you highlight too little of the content, you are not identifying enough of the key ideas. But if you highlight too much of the content, you are not going to succeed in condensing what you have to review to a manageable size.

Getting More out of Lectures

Although lectures are sometimes boring and tedious, it is a simple fact that poor class attendance is associated with poor grades. For example, in one study, Lind-

© Don Bayley/iStockphoto

gren (1969) found that absences from class were much more common among "unsuccessful" students (grade average C− or below) than among "successful" students (grade average B or above). Even when you have an instructor who delivers hard-to-follow lectures, it is still important to go to class. If nothing else, you can get a feel for how the instructor thinks, which can help you anticipate the content of exams and respond in the manner expected by your professor.

Fortunately, most lectures are reasonably coherent. Studies indicate that attentive note taking *is* associated with enhanced learning and performance in college classes (Titsworth & Kiewra, 2004; Williams & Eggert, 2002). However, research also shows that many students' lecture notes are surprisingly incomplete, with the average student often recording less than 40% of the crucial ideas in a lecture (Armbruster, 2000). Thus, the key to getting more out of lectures is to stay motivated, stay attentive, and expend the effort to make your notes as complete as possible. Books on study skills (Longman & Atkinson, 2005; McWhorter, 2007) offer a number of suggestions on how to take good-quality lecture notes, some of which are summarized here:

• Extracting information from lectures requires *active listening*. Focus full attention on the speaker. Try to anticipate what's coming and search for deeper meanings.

• When course material is especially complex, it is a good idea to prepare for the lecture by *reading ahead* on the scheduled subject in your text. Then you have less new information to digest.

• You are not supposed to be a human tape recorder. Insofar as possible, try to write down the lecturer's thoughts *in your own words*. Doing so forces you to organize the ideas in a way that makes sense to you.

• In taking notes, *pay attention to clues* about what is most important. These clues may range from subtle hints, such as an instructor repeating a point, to not-so-subtle hints, such as an instructor saying "You'll run into this again."

• In delivering their lectures most professors follow an *organized outline,* which they may or may not share with the class (on the blackboard or via a presentation tool, such as PowerPoint). Insofar as you can decipher the outline of a lecture, try to organize your notes accordingly. When you go back to review your notes later, they will make more sense and it should be easier to identify the most important ideas.

• *Asking questions* during lectures can be helpful. Doing so keeps you actively involved in the lecture and allows you to clarify points that you may have misunderstood. Many students are more bashful about asking questions than they should be. They don't realize that most professors welcome questions.

In summary, sound study skills and habits are crucial to academic success. Intelligence alone won't do the job (although it certainly helps). Good academic skills do not develop overnight. They are acquired gradually, so be patient with yourself. Fortunately, tasks such as reading textbooks, writing papers, and taking tests get easier with practice. Ultimately, I think you'll find that the rewards—knowledge, a sense of accomplishment, and progress toward a degree—are worth the effort.

Developing Critical Thinking Skills: An Introduction

If you ask any group of professors, parents, employers, or politicians, "What is the most important outcome of an education?" the most popular answer is likely to be "the development of the ability to think critically." *Critical thinking* **is purposeful, reasoned, goal-directed thinking that involves solving problems, formulating inferences, working with probabilities, and making carefully thought-out decisions.** Critical thinking is the use of cognitive skills and strategies that increase the probability of a desirable outcome. Such outcomes would include good career choices, effective decisions in the workplace, wise investments, and so forth. In the long run, critical thinkers should have more desirable outcomes than people who are not skilled in critical thinking (Halpern, 1998, 2003). Here are some of the skills exhibited by critical thinkers:

• They understand and use the principles of scientific investigation. (How can the effectiveness of punishment as a disciplinary procedure be determined?)

• They apply the rules of formal and informal logic. (If most people disapprove of sex sites on the Internet, why are these sites so popular?)

• They think effectively in terms of probabilities. (What is the likelihood of being able to predict who will commit a violent crime?)

• They carefully evaluate the quality of information. (Can I trust the claims made by this politician?)

• They analyze arguments for the soundness of the conclusions. (Does the rise in drug use mean a stricter drug policy is needed?).

The topic of thinking has a long history in psychology. It dates back to Wilhelm Wundt in the 19th century. Modern cognitive psychologists have found that a useful model of critical thinking has at least two components: It consists of knowledge of the skills of critical thinking—the *cognitive component*—as well as the attitude or disposition of a critical thinker—the *emotional* or *affective component*. Both are needed for effective critical thinking.

The Skills and Attitudes of Critical Thinking

Instruction in critical thinking is based on two assumptions: (1) a set of skills or strategies exists that students can learn to recognize and apply in appropriate contexts, and (2) if the skills are applied appropriately, students will become more effective thinkers (Halpern, 2007). Critical thinking skills that would be useful in any context might include understanding how reasons and evidence support or refute conclusions; distinguishing among facts, opinions, and reasoned judgments; using principles of likelihood and uncertainty when thinking about probabilistic events; generating multiple solutions to problems and working systematically toward a desired goal; and understanding

how causation is determined. This list provides some typical examples of what is meant by the term *critical thinking skills*. Because these skills are useful in a wide variety of contexts, they are sometimes called *transcontextual skills*.

It is of little use to know the skills of critical thinking if you are unwilling to exert the hard mental work to use them or if you have a sloppy or careless attitude toward thinking. A critical thinker is willing to plan, flexible in thinking, persistent, able to admit mistakes and make corrections, and mindful of the thinking process. The use of the word *critical* represents the notion of a critique or evaluation of thinking processes and outcomes. It is not meant to be negative (as in a "critical person") but rather is intended to convey that critical thinkers are vigilant about their thinking (Riggio & Halpern, 2006).

The Need to Teach Critical Thinking

Decades of research on instruction in critical thinking have shown that the skills and attitudes of critical thinking need to be deliberately and consciously taught, because they often do not develop by themselves with standard instruction in a content area (Nisbett, 1993). For this reason, each chapter in this text ends with a "Critical Thinking Application." The material presented in each of these Critical Thinking Applications relates to the chapter topics, but the focus is on how to think about a particular issue, line of research, or controversy. Because the emphasis is on the thinking process, you may be asked to consider conflicting interpretations of data, judge the credibility of information sources, or generate your own testable hypotheses. The specific critical thinking skills highlighted in each Application are summarized in a table so that they are easily identified. Some of the skills will show up in multiple chapters. The goal is to help you spontaneously select the appropriate critical thinking skills when you encounter new information. Repeated practice with

NON SEQUITUR

selected skills across chapters should help you develop this ability.

An Example

As explained in the main body of the chapter, *evolutionary psychology* is emerging as an influential school of thought. To show you how critical thinking skills can be applied to psychological issues, let's examine the evolutionary explanation of gender differences in spatial talents and then use some critical thinking strategies to evaluate this explanation.

On the average, males tend to perform slightly better than females on most visual-spatial tasks, especially tasks involving mental rotation of images and navigation in space (Halpern, 2000; Silverman & Choi, 2005; see **Figure 1.10**). Irwin Silverman and his colleagues maintain that these gender differences originated in human evolution as a result of the sex-based division of labor in ancient hunting-and-gathering societies (Silverman & Phillips, 1998; Silverman et al., 2000). According to this analysis, males' superiority in mental rotation and navigation developed because the chore of *hunting* was largely assigned to men over the course of human history. These skills would have facilitated success on hunting trips (by helping men to traverse long distances, aim projectiles at prey, and so forth) and thus would have been favored by natural selection. In contrast, women in ancient societies generally had responsibility for *gathering* food rather than hunting it. This was an efficient division of labor because women spent much of their adult lives pregnant, nursing, or caring for the young. Therefore, they could not travel long distances. Thus, Silverman and Eals (1992) hypothesized that females ought to be superior to males on spatial skills that would have facilitated gathering, such as memory for locations. This is exactly what they

Can the set of blocks on the left be rotated to match the set at the right?

FIGURE 1.10

An example of a spatial task involving mental rotation. Spatial reasoning tasks can be divided into a variety of subtypes. Studies indicate that males perform slightly better than females on most, but not all, spatial tasks. The tasks on which males are superior often involve mentally rotating objects, such as in the problem shown here, for which the answer is no.

SOURCE: From Kalat, J. W. (2013). *Biological psychology* (11 ed.). Belmont, CA: Wadsworth. Reproduced by permission. www.cengage.com/permissions

found in a series of four studies. Thus, evolutionary psychologists explain gender differences in spatial ability—like other aspects of human behavior—in terms of how such abilities evolved to meet the adaptive pressures faced by our ancestors.

How can you critically evaluate these claims? If your first thought was that you need more information, good for you. You are already showing an aptitude for critical thinking. Some additional information about gender differences in cognitive abilities is presented in Chapter 10 of this text. You also need to develop the habit of asking good questions, such as, "Are there alternative explanations for these results? Are there contradictory data?" Let's briefly consider each of these questions.

Are there alternative explanations for gender differences in spatial skills? Well, there certainly are other explanations for males' superiority on most spatial tasks. For example, we could attribute this finding to the gender-typed activities that males are encouraged to engage in more than females, such as playing with building blocks, Lego sets, Lincoln Logs, and various types of construction sets, as well as a host of spatially oriented video

games. These gender-typed activities appear to provide boys with more practice than girls on most types of spatial tasks (Voyer, Nolan, & Voyer, 2000). Experience with spatial activities appears to enhance spatial skills (Lizarraga & Ganuza, 2003). For example, one study found that just 10 hours of playing an action video game could produce substantial gains in spatial ability (Feng, Spence, & Pratt, 2007). If we can explain gender differences in spatial abilities in terms of disparities in the everyday activities of males and females, we may have no need to appeal to natural selection.

Are there data that run counter to the evolutionary explanation for modern gender differences in spatial skills? Again, the answer is yes. Some scholars who have studied hunting-and-gathering societies suggest that women often traveled long distances to gather food and that women were often involved in hunting (Adler, 1993). In addition, women wove baskets and clothing and worked on other tasks that required spatial thinking (Halpern, 1997). Moreover—think about it—men on long hunting trips obviously needed to develop a good memory for locations or they might never have returned home. So, there is room for some argument about exactly what kinds of adaptive pressures males and females faced in ancient hunting-and-gathering societies.

Thus, you can see how considering alternative explanations and contradictory evidence weakens the evolutionary explanation of gender differences in spatial abilities. The questions we raised about alternative explanations and contradictory data are two generic critical thinking questions that can be asked in a wide variety of contexts. The answers to these questions do *not* prove that evolutionary psychologists are wrong in their explanation of gender differences in visual-spatial skills. They do, however, *weaken* the evolutionary explanation. In thinking critically about psychological issues, you will see that it makes more sense to talk about the *relative strength* of an argument, as opposed to whether an argument is right or wrong, because we will be dealing with complex issues that rarely lend themselves to being correct or incorrect.

TABLE 1.2 Critical Thinking Skills Discussed in This Application

Skill	Description
Looking for alternative explanations for findings and events	In evaluating explanations, the critical thinker explores whether there are other explanations that could also account for the findings or events under scrutiny.
Looking for contradictory evidence	In evaluating the evidence presented on an issue, the critical thinker attempts to look for contradictory evidence that may have been left out of the debate.

Chapter 1 — Review of Key Learning Goals

Psychology's Early History

1.1 Summarize Wundt's contributions to psychology, and describe the chief tenets of structuralism and functionalism.

Psychology became an independent discipline when Wilhelm Wundt established the first psychological research laboratory in 1879 at Leipzig, Germany. Wundt, who is widely characterized as the founder of psychology, viewed psychology as the scientific study of consciousness. The new discipline grew rapidly in North America in the late 19th century. The structuralists, led by Edward Titchener, believed that psychology should use introspection to analyze consciousness into its basic elements. The functionalists, inspired by the ideas of William James, believed that psychology should focus on the purpose and adaptive functions of consciousness. James argued that consciousness consists of a continuous flow of thoughts, which he called the stream of consciousness.

1.2 Articulate Freud's principal ideas and why they inspired controversy.

Sigmund Freud was an Austrian physician who invented psychoanalysis. His psychoanalytic theory emphasized the unconscious determinants of behavior and the importance of sexuality. Freud's ideas were controversial because he emphasized sexuality and suggested that people are not masters of their own minds. However, psychoanalytic concepts were gradually incorporated into mainstream psychology.

1.3 Trace the development of behaviorism, and assess Watson's impact on the evolution of psychology.

Behaviorists, led by John B. Watson, argued that psychology should study only observable behavior because science depends on observation. Thus, they campaigned to redefine psychology as the science of behavior. Watson emphasized the importance of the environment over heredity. Behaviorism's approach contributed to the rise of animal research in psychology. Ironically, Watson was banished from the mainstream of psychology but became its public face thanks to his popular writings.

Perspective and Its Influential Period	Subject Matter	Basic Premise
Behavioral (1913–present)	Effects of environment on the overt behavior of humans and animals	Only observable events (stimulus-response relations) can be studied scientifically.
Psychoanalytic (1900–present)	Unconscious determinants of behavior	Unconscious motives and experiences in early childhood govern personality and mental disorders.
Humanistic (1950s–present)	Unique aspects of human experience	Humans are free, rational beings with the potential for personal growth, and they are fundamentally different from animals.
Cognitive (1950s–present)	Thoughts; mental processes	Human behavior cannot be fully understood without examining how people acquire, store, and process information.
Biological (1950s–present)	Physiological bases of behavior in humans and animals	An organism's functioning can be explained in terms of the bodily structures and biochemical processes that underlie behavior.
Evolutionary (1980s–present)	Evolutionary bases of behavior in humans and animals	Behavior patterns have evolved to solve adaptive problems; natural selection favors behaviors that enhance reproductive success.

1.4 Summarize Skinner's key insights, and explain the emergence of humanism and its underlying philosophy.

Working with lab rats and pigeons, American behaviorist B. F. Skinner demonstrated that organisms tend to repeat responses that lead to positive consequences. Based on the belief that all behavior is fully governed by external stimuli, Skinner argued that free will is an illusion. His ideas were controversial and often misunderstood. Finding both behaviorism and psychoanalysis unsatisfactory, advocates of a new theoretical orientation called humanism became influential in the 1950s. Humanism, led by Abraham Maslow and Carl Rogers, emphasized the unique qualities of human behavior and humans' freedom and potential for personal growth.

Psychology's Modern History

1.5 Discuss how historical events contributed to the emergence of psychology as a profession.

Clinical psychology is the branch of psychology concerned with the diagnosis and treatment of psychological problems and disorders. Stimulated by the demands of World War II, clinical psychology grew rapidly in the 1950s. Thus, psychology became a profession as well as a science. This movement toward professionalization eventually spread to other areas in psychology, such as school psychology, industrial/organizational psychology, and counseling psychology.

1.6 Describe two trends emerging in the 1950s–1960s that represented a return to psychology's intellectual roots.

During the 1950s and 1960s advances in the study of cognition led to renewed interest in mental processes. Advocates of the cognitive perspective argue that human behavior cannot be fully understood without considering how people think. The 1950s and 1960s also saw advances in research on the physiological bases of behavior. Advocates of the biological perspective assert that human and animal behavior can be explained in terms of the bodily structures and biochemical processes that allow organisms to behave. The influence of both perspectives has grown steadily.

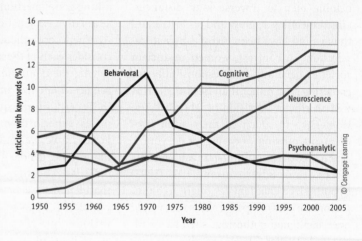

1.7 Explain why Western psychology has shown an increased interest in cultural variables in recent decades.

Traditionally, Western psychologists paid scant attention to how well their theories and research might apply to non-Western cultures. In the 1980s, however, Western psychologists developed a greater interest in how cultural factors influence behavior. This trend was sparked in large part by growing global interdependence and by increased cultural diversity in Western societies.

28 CHAPTER 1

1.8 Discuss the emergence and basic ideas of evolutionary psychology and positive psychology.

The 1990s witnessed the emergence of a new theoretical perspective called evolutionary psychology. The central premise of this new school of thought is that the patterns of behavior seen in a species are products of evolution in the same way that anatomical characteristics are. Around the beginning of the 21st century, the positive psychology movement became an influential force. Advocates of positive psychology argue that the field has historically devoted too much attention to pathology, weakness, and ways to heal suffering. Positive psychology seeks to better understand the adaptive, creative, and fulfilling aspects of human existence.

Psychology Today: Vigorous and Diversified

1.9 Discuss the growth of psychology, and identify the most common work settings for contemporary psychologists.

Psychology is the science that studies behavior and the physiological and cognitive processes that underlie behavior, and it is the profession that applies the accumulated knowledge of this science to practical problems. Contemporary psychology is a diversified science and profession that has grown rapidly in recent decades, as evidenced by the fact that APA membership has grown ninefold since 1950. The main work settings for contemporary psychologists are (1) private practice, (2) colleges and universities, (3) hospitals and clinics, and (4) business and government.

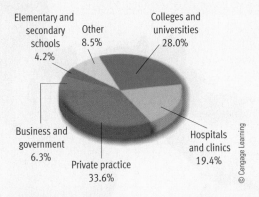

Elementary and secondary schools 4.2%
Other 8.5%
Colleges and universities 28.0%
Business and government 6.3%
Private practice 33.6%
Hospitals and clinics 19.4%

© Cengage Learning

1.10 List and describe the major research areas and professional specialties in psychology.

Major areas of research in modern psychology include developmental psychology (the study of development across the lifespan), social psychology (the study of interpersonal behavior), experimental psychology (the study of perception, learning, and motivation), physiological psychology (the study of the biological bases of behavior), cognitive psychology (the study of higher mental processes), personality (the study of personality traits), psychometrics (the study of testing and assessment), educational psychology (the study of classroom learning), and health psychology (the study of the psychosocial roots of health and illness). Applied psychology encompasses four professional specialties: clinical psychology (the diagnosis and treatment of psychological disorders), counseling psychology (the assessment and treatment of less severe problems), school psychology (the counseling and testing of schoolchildren), and industrial/organizational psychology (the application of psychological principles in the work environment).

Seven Unifying Themes

1.11 Understand the text's three unifying themes relating to psychology as a field of study.

Psychology is empirical because psychologists base their conclusions on observation through research rather than reasoning or common sense. Psychology is theoretically diverse, as there are many competing schools of thought in the field. This diversity has fueled progress and is a

strength rather than a weakness. Psychology also evolves in a sociohistorical context, as trends, issues, and values in society influence what goes on in psychology, and vice versa.

1.12 Understand the text's four unifying themes relating to psychology's subject matter.

Behavior is determined by multiple causes, as most aspects of behavior are influenced by complex networks of interacting factors. Although cultural heritage is often taken for granted, it has a pervasive impact on people's thoughts, feelings, and behavior. Lively debate about the relative importance of nature versus nurture continues, but it is clear that heredity and environment jointly influence behavior. People's experience of the world is highly subjective, as they sometimes see what they want to see or what they expect to see.

PERSONAL APPLICATION
Improving Academic Performance

1.13 Discuss some strategies for promoting adequate study, improving reading comprehension, and getting more out of lectures.

To foster sound study habits, you should devise a written study schedule, find a place to study where you can concentrate, and reward yourself for following your study schedule. To enhance reading, you should use active reading techniques to select the most important ideas from the material you read. Highlighting textbook material is a useful strategy—if students are reasonably effective in focusing on the main ideas and if they subsequently review what they have highlighted. The key to good note taking is to strive to make lecture notes as complete as possible. It's important to use active listening techniques and to record lecturers' ideas in your own words.

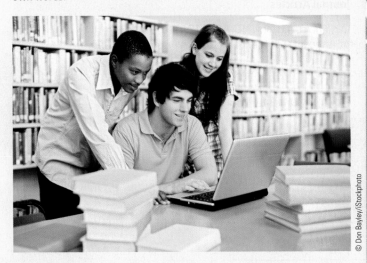

© Don Bayley/iStockphoto

CRITICAL THINKING APPLICATION
Developing Critical Thinking Skills: An Introduction

1.14 Explain the nature of critical thinking, and evaluate evolutionary explanations for gender differences in spatial abilities.

Critical thinking is the use of cognitive skills and strategies that increase the probability of a desirable outcome. A critical thinker is flexible, vigilant, able to admit mistakes, and mindful of the thinking process. Evolutionary psychologists attribute gender differences in spatial abilities to the sex-based division of labor in hunting-and-gathering societies. However, alternative explanations have been offered for these differences, focusing on the gender-typed activities that modern males and females engage in. There are also contradictory data regarding the adaptive pressures faced by females and males in hunting-and-gathering societies.

2 The Research Enterprise in Psychology

PARADOX

Coincidences have been the source of both great scientific discoveries and absurd conspiracy theories.

© Holger Winkler/Corbis

- Does sleeping less than 7 hours a day reduce how long you will live?
- Do violent video games make people more aggressive?
- Can you make better decisions by not deliberating about them?
- Can women judge men's testosterone level in just one quick glance?
- Do IQ scores predict how long people will live?

Questions, questions, questions—everyone has questions about behavior. Investigating these questions is what psychology is all about.

Some of these questions pop up in everyday life. Many a parent, for example, has wondered whether violent video games could have a harmful effect on their children's behavior. Other questions explored by psychologists might not occur to most people. For example, you may never have wondered what effects your sleeping habits or IQ could have on your life expectancy or whether women can judge men's testosterone levels. Of course, now that you've been exposed to these questions, you may be curious about the answers!

In the course of this book, you'll find out what psychologists have learned about the five questions asked above. Right now I want to call your attention to the most basic question of all—namely, how should we go about investigating questions like these? How do we find answers that are accurate and trustworthy?

As noted in Chapter 1, *psychology is empirical*. Psychologists are committed to addressing questions about behavior through formal, systematic observation. This commitment to the empirical method is what makes psychology a scientific endeavor. Many people may have beliefs about the effects of playing violent video games based on personal opinion, a feeling of aversion toward violence, a generally permissive attitude toward children's games, anecdotal reports from parents, or other sources. As scientists, however, psychologists withhold judgment on questions like these until they have objective evidence based on valid, reproducible studies.

In their scientific studies psychologists rely on a large toolkit of research methods because different kinds of questions call for different strategies of investigation. In this chapter, you'll learn about some of the principal methods used by psychologists in their research.

We'll begin our introduction to the research enterprise in psychology by examining the scientific approach to the study of behavior. From there we'll move to the specific research methods that psychologists use most frequently. Although scientific methods have stood the test of time, individual scientists are human and fallible. For this reason we'll conclude our discussion with a look at some common flaws in research. This section alone can make you a more skilled evaluator of claims that are said to be based on psychological studies. Then, in the Personal Application, you'll learn how to find and read journal articles that report on research. Finally, in the Critical Thinking Application, we'll examine the perils of a type of evidence people are exposed to all the time—anecdotal evidence.

Looking for Laws: The Scientific Approach to Behavior

KEY LEARNING GOALS

2.1 Describe the goals of the scientific enterprise, and clarify the relations between theory, hypotheses, and research.

2.2 Identify the steps in a scientific investigation, and list the advantages of the scientific approach.

Whether the object of study is gravitational forces or people's behavior under stress, *the scientific approach assumes that events are governed by some lawful order*. As scientists, psychologists assume that behavior is governed by laws or principles, just as the movement of the Earth around the sun is governed by the laws of gravity. The behavior of living creatures may not seem as lawful and predictable as the "behavior" of planets. However, the scientific enterprise is based on the belief that there are consistencies or laws that can be uncovered. Fortunately, the value of applying this fundamental assumption has been supported by the discovery of a great many such consistencies in behavior, some of which provide the subject matter for this text.

Goals of the Scientific Enterprise

Psychologists and other scientists share three sets of interrelated goals: measurement and description, understanding and prediction, and application and control.

1. *Measurement and description.* Science's commitment to observation requires that researchers figure out a way to measure the phenomenon under study. For example, a psychologist could not investigate whether men are more or less sociable than women without first developing some means of measuring sociability. Thus, the first goal of

psychology is to develop measurement techniques that make it possible to describe behavior clearly and precisely.

2. *Understanding and prediction.* A higher-level goal of science is understanding. Scientists believe that they understand events when they can explain the reasons for their occurrence. To evaluate such understanding, scientists make and test predictions called hypotheses. A *hypothesis* **is a tentative statement about the relationship between two or more variables.** *Variables* **are any measurable conditions, events, characteristics, or behaviors that are controlled or observed in a study.** If we predicted that putting people under time pressure would lower the accuracy of their time perception, the variables in our study would be time pressure and accuracy of time perception.

3. *Application and control.* Ultimately, most scientists hope that the information they gather will be of some practical value in helping to solve everyday problems. Once people understand a phenomenon, they can often exert more control over it. Today, the profession of psychology attempts to apply research findings to practical problems in schools, businesses, factories, and mental hospitals. For example, a school psychologist might use findings about the causes of math anxiety to devise a program to help students control their math phobias.

How do theories help scientists achieve their goals? As noted in Chapter 1, psychologists do not set out to just collect isolated facts about relationships between variables. To build toward a better understanding of behavior, they construct theories. A *theory* **is a system of interrelated ideas used to explain a set of observations.** For example, using a handful of concepts, such as natural selection and reproductive fitness, evolutionary theory (Buss, 1995, 1996) purports to explain a diverse array of known facts about mating preferences, jealousy, aggression, sexual behavior, and so forth (see Chapter 1). Thus, by integrating apparently unrelated facts and principles into a coherent whole, theories permit psychologists to make the leap from the *description* of behavior to the *understanding* of behavior. Moreover, the enhanced understanding afforded by theories guides future research by generating new predictions and suggesting new lines of inquiry (Fiske, 2004; Higgins, 2004).

A scientific theory must be testable. The cornerstone of science is its commitment to putting ideas to an empirical test. Most theories are too complex to be tested all at once. For example, it would be impossible to devise a single study that could test all the many aspects of evolutionary theory. Rather, in a typical study, investigators test one or two specific hypotheses derived from a theory. If their findings support the hypotheses, confidence in the theory grows. If their findings fail to support the hypotheses, confidence in the theory diminishes. The theory may then be revised or discarded. Thus, theory construction is a gradual, iterative process that is always subject to revision.

"IT MAY VERY WELL BRING ABOUT IMMORTALITY, BUT IT WILL TAKE FOREVER TO TEST IT."

Steps in a Scientific Investigation

Curiosity about a question provides the point of departure for any kind of investigation, scientific or otherwise. Scientific investigations, however, are *systematic.* They follow an orderly pattern, which is outlined in **Figure 2.1**. Let's look at how this standard series of steps was followed in a study of *naive realism* conducted by David Sherman, Leif Nelson, and Lee Ross (2003). Sherman and his colleagues wanted to investigate whether adversaries in political debates overestimate the gap between their views.

STEP 1: FORMULATE A TESTABLE HYPOTHESIS

The first step in a scientific investigation is to translate a theory or an intuitive idea into a testable hypothesis. Sherman et al. (2003) noted that in heated disputes people seem to assume that they see matters as they really are—that their perceptions are objective and accurate. And they assume that their opponents' views must be distorted by self-interest, ideology, or some other source of bias. The researchers call this belief in one's own objectivity and opponents' subjectivity "naive realism." Based on their concept of naive realism, Sherman and his colleagues speculated that in political debates people on both sides would tend to characterize their opponents as extremists and to overestimate the extent of their mutual disagreement. To explore this line of thinking, they chose to examine individuals' views on the contentious issue of affirmative action. Thus, they hypothesized that proponents of affirmative action would overestimate opponents' conservativism and that opponents of affirmative action would overestimate proponents' liberalism.

To be testable, scientific hypotheses must be formulated precisely, and the variables under study must be clearly defined. Researchers achieve these clear formulations by providing operational definitions of the relevant variables. **An** *operational definition* **describes the actions or operations that will be used to measure or control a variable.** Operational definitions—which may be quite different from dictionary definitions—establish precisely what is meant by each variable in the context of a study.

To illustrate, let's see how Sherman and his colleagues operationalized their variables. They decided that the issue of affirmative action is too complex and multifaceted to ask people about their views of affirmative action *in general*. Each person would be judging something different, based on his or her highly varied exposure to affirmative action initiatives. To circumvent this problem, they asked students to respond to a specific affirmative action program that supposedly had been proposed for their university. To get a precise measurement of participants' views, they asked the students to indicate their degree of support for the proposal on a 9-point scale anchored by the descriptions *definitely adopt* and *definitely reject*. Those checking 1 to 4 on the scale were designated as *supporters* of the proposal, while those checking 6 to 9 on the scale were designated as *rejectors* (those who checked the midpoint of 5 were classified as *neutral*).

STEP 2: SELECT THE RESEARCH METHOD AND DESIGN THE STUDY

The second step in a scientific investigation is to figure out how to put the hypothesis to an empirical test. The research method chosen depends to a large degree on the nature of the question under study. The various methods—experiments, case studies, surveys, naturalistic observation, and so forth—each have advantages and disadvantages. The researcher has to ponder the pros and cons, then select the strategy that appears to be the most appropriate and practical. In this case, Sherman and colleagues decided that their question called for *survey* research, which involves administering questionnaires or interviews to people.

Once researchers have chosen a general method, they must make detailed plans for executing their study. Thus, Sherman and associates had to decide how many people they needed to survey and where they would get their participants. *Participants,* **or** *subjects,* **are the persons or animals whose behavior is systematically observed in a study.** For their first study, Sherman et al. chose to use 78 undergraduates (45 women and 29 men) at Stanford University. Sherman and his colleagues also had to devise a plausible-sounding affirmative action proposal that students could evaluate. And they had to craft rating scales that would permit the assessment of subjects' political ideology and the subjects' perceptions of their opponents' political ideology.

STEP 3: COLLECT THE DATA

The third step in the research enterprise is to collect the data. Researchers use a variety of *data collection techniques,* **which are procedures for making empirical observations and measurements.** Commonly used techniques include direct observation, questionnaires, interviews, psychological tests, physiological recordings, and examination of archival records (see **Table 2.1**). The data collection techniques used in a study depend

Step 1 Formulate a hypothesis

Proponents of affirmative action will overestimate opponents' conservatism and opponents of affirmative action will overestimate proponents' liberalism.

Step 2 Design the study

Use survey method with undergraduate participants. Devise hypothetical affirmative action proposal and appropriate rating scales.

Step 3 Collect the data

Administer questionnaire to 78 students at Stanford University in exchange for small nonmonetary gift.

Step 4 Analyze the data and draw conclusions

Calculate average ratings of proposal by supporters and rejectors and compare to subjects' estimates of opponents' ratings. Data are consistent with the prediction that adversaries overestimate the gap between their views.

Step 5 Report the findings

Publish report of the study (and two companion studies) in a 2003 issue of the journal *Basic and Applied Social Psychology*.

© Cengage Learning

FIGURE 2.1

Flowchart of steps in a scientific investigation. As illustrated in the study by Sherman, Nelson, and Ross (2003), a scientific investigation consists of a sequence of carefully planned steps, beginning with the formulation of a testable hypothesis and ending with the publication of the study, if its results are worthy of examination by other researchers.

TABLE 2.1 Key Data Collection Techniques in Psychology

Technique	Description
Direct observation	Observers are trained to watch and record behavior as objectively and precisely as possible. They may use some instrumentation, such as a stopwatch or video recorder.
Questionnaire	Subjects are administered a series of written questions designed to obtain information about attitudes, opinions, and specific aspects of their behavior.
Interview	A face-to-face dialogue is conducted to obtain information about specific aspects of a subject's behavior.
Psychological test	Subjects are administered a standardized measure to obtain a sample of their behavior. Tests are usually used to assess mental abilities or personality traits.
Physiological recording	An instrument is used to monitor and record a specific physiological process in a subject. Examples include measures of blood pressure, heart rate, muscle tension, and brain activity.
Examination of archival records	The researcher analyzes existing institutional records (the archives), such as census, economic, medical, legal, educational, and business records.

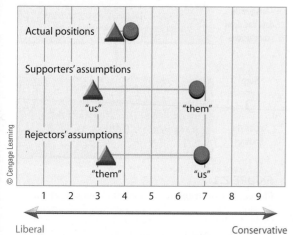

FIGURE 2.2

Results of the Sherman et al. (2003) study. As you can see, the actual positions of the supporters and rejectors of the affirmative action proposal were not all that far apart (top row). However, when supporters of the proposal were asked to estimate the political ideology of other supporters as well as of those who rejected the proposal, they assumed that there was a huge gap between the two groups (middle row). Similarly, when those who were against the proposal were asked to make the same estimates (bottom row), they also overestimated the disparity between the two groups.

SOURCE: Sherman, D. K., Nelson, L. D., & Ross, L. D. (2003). Naive realism and affirmative action: Adversaries are more similar than they think. *Basic and Applied Social Psychology, 25,* 275–289. Copyright © 2003 Lawrence Erlbaum Associates, Inc. Reprinted by permission.

largely on what is being investigated. For example, questionnaires are well suited for studying attitudes, psychological tests for studying personality, and physiological recordings for studying the biological bases of behavior. Depending on the nature and complexity of the study, data collection can often take months. It sometimes even requires years of work. One advantage of the survey method, however, is that data can often be collected quickly and easily, which was true in this case. Sherman and his colleagues simply had their subjects complete a carefully designed questionnaire in their dorm rooms in exchange for a small nonmonetary gift.

STEP 4: ANALYZE THE DATA AND DRAW CONCLUSIONS

The observations made in a study are usually converted into numbers, which constitute the raw data of the study. Researchers use *statistics* to analyze their data and to decide whether their hypotheses have been supported. Thus, statistics play an essential role in the scientific enterprise. Based on their statistical analyses, Sherman et al. (2003) concluded that their data supported their hypothesis. As predicted, they found that supporters of the affirmative action proposal greatly overestimated the conservatism of the rejectors of the proposal. Similarly, they found that the rejectors of the proposal greatly overestimated the liberalism of the supporters (see **Figure 2.2**). The data indicated that the actual (average) attitudes of the two groups really were not all that far apart. However, each group *assumed* that their opponents held very dissimilar views. Obviously, insofar as this may be true of political debates in general, it sheds light on (1) why it is often so difficult for opposing sides to bridge the (perceived) gap between them, and (2) why people often have such pervasively negative views of their adversaries.

STEP 5: REPORT THE FINDINGS

The publication of research results is a fundamental aspect of the scientific enterprise (Roberts, Brown, & Smith-Boydston, 2003). Scientific progress can be achieved only if researchers share their findings with one another and with the general public. Therefore, the final step in a scientific investigation is to write up a concise summary of the study and its findings. Typically, researchers prepare a report that is delivered at a scientific meeting and submitted to a journal for publication. **A *journal* is a periodical that publishes technical and scholarly material, usually in a narrowly defined area of inquiry.** The study by Sherman and his colleagues (2003) was published, along with two companion studies, in a journal called *Basic and Applied Social Psychology.*

The process of publishing scientific studies allows other experts to evaluate and critique new research findings. When articles are submitted to scientific journals, they go through a demanding *peer review process* that is summarized in **Figure 2.3**. Experts thoroughly scrutinize each submission. They carefully evaluate each study's methods, statistical analyses, and conclusions, as well as its contribution to knowledge and theory. The peer review process is so demanding, many top journals reject over 90% of submitted articles! The purpose of this process is to ensure that journals publish reliable findings based on high-quality research. The peer review process is a major strength of the scientific approach because it greatly reduces the likelihood of publishing erroneous findings.

Peer Review of Scientific Articles

Researcher or research team authors manuscript that describes the methods, findings, and implications of an empirical study or series of related studies.

Manuscript is submitted to the editor of a professional journal (such as *Journal of Abnormal Psychology* or *Psychological Science*) that seems appropriate given the topic of the research. A manuscript can be submitted to only one journal at a time.

The journal editor sends the manuscript to two to four experts in the relevant area of research who are asked to serve as reviewers. The reviewers provide their input anonymously and are not paid for their work.

The reviewers carefully critique the strengths, weaknesses, and theoretical significance of the research and make a recommendation as to whether it is worthy of publication in that specific journal. If the research has merit, the reviewers usually offer numerous suggestions for improving the clarity of the manuscript.

The editor reads the manuscript and expert reviews and decides whether the submission deserves publication. Most journals reject a substantial majority of submissions. The editorial decision, the reasoning behind it, and the expert reviews are sent to the author.

If the manuscript is accepted, the author may incorporate suggestions for improvement from the reviews, make final revisions, and resubmit the article to the journal editor.

If the manuscript is rejected, the author may (a) abandon the publication effort, or (b) use reviewers' suggestions to make revisions and then submit the article to another journal.

The article is published in a professional journal usually three to six months after final acceptance.

Following rejection, researchers sometimes give up on a line of research, but often they go back to the drawing board and attempt to design a better study.

© Cengage Learning

FIGURE 2.3

The peer review process for journal submissions. Scientists use an elaborate peer review process to determine whether studies merit publication in a technical journal. The goal of this process is to maximize the quality and reliability of published scientific findings.

Advantages of the Scientific Approach

Science is certainly not the only method that can be used to draw conclusions about behavior. We all use logic, casual observation, and good old-fashioned common sense. Because the scientific method requires painstaking effort, it seems reasonable to ask what advantages make it worth the trouble.

Basically, the scientific approach offers two major advantages. The first is its clarity and precision. Commonsense notions about behavior tend to be vague and ambiguous. Consider the old adage "Spare the rod and spoil the child." What exactly does this generalization about childrearing amount to? How severely should children be punished if parents are not to "spare the rod"? How do we assess whether a child qualifies as "spoiled"? A fundamental problem is that such statements have different meanings, depending on the person. In contrast, the scientific approach requires that people specify *exactly* what they are talking about when they formulate hypotheses. This clarity and precision enhance communication about important ideas.

The second and perhaps greatest advantage offered by the scientific approach is its relative intolerance of error. Scientists are trained to be skeptical. They subject their ideas to empirical tests. They also inspect one another's findings with a critical eye. They demand objective data and thorough documentation before they accept ideas. When the findings of two studies conflict, the scientist tries to figure out why, usually by conducting additional research. In contrast, commonsense analyses involve little effort to verify ideas or detect errors.

All this is not to say that science has an exclusive copyright on truth. However, the scientific approach does tend to yield more accurate and dependable information than casual analyses and armchair speculation do. Knowledge of scientific data can thus provide a useful benchmark against which to judge claims and information from other kinds of sources.

Now that we have had an overview of how the scientific enterprise works, we can focus on how specific research methods are used. **Research methods consist of differing approaches to the observation, measurement, manipulation, and control of variables in empirical studies.** In other words, they are general strategies for conducting studies. No single research method is ideal for all purposes and situations. Much of the ingenuity in research involves selecting and tailoring the method to the question at hand. The next two sections of this chapter discuss the two basic types of methods used in psychology: *experimental research methods* and *descriptive/correlational research methods*.

KEY LEARNING GOALS

2.3 Describe the experimental method, independent and dependent variables, and experimental and control groups.

2.4 Explain how experiments can vary in design, and evaluate the major advantages and disadvantages of the experimental method.

Looking for Causes: Experimental Research

Does misery love company? This question intrigued social psychologist Stanley Schachter. When people feel anxious, he wondered, do they want to be left alone, or do they prefer to have others around? Schachter's review of relevant theories suggested that in times of anxiety people would want others around to help them sort out their feelings. Thus, his hypothesis was that increases in anxiety would cause increases in the desire to be with others, which psychologists call the *need for affiliation*. To test this hypothesis, Schachter (1959) designed a clever experiment.

The *experiment* **is a research method in which the investigator manipulates a variable under carefully controlled conditions and observes whether any changes occur in a second variable as a result.** The experiment is a relatively powerful procedure that allows researchers to detect cause-and-effect relationships. Psychologists depend on this method more than any other. To see how an experiment is designed, let's use Schachter's study as an example.

Independent and Dependent Variables

PsykTrek SIM1, 1b

The purpose of an experiment is to find out whether changes in one variable (let's call it *X*) cause changes in another variable (let's call it *Y*). To put it more concisely, we want to find out *how X affects Y*. In this formulation, we refer to *X* as the *independent variable* and to *Y* as the *dependent variable*.

An *independent variable* **is a condition or event that an experimenter varies in order to see its impact on another variable.** The independent variable is the variable that the experimenter controls or manipulates. It is hypothesized to have some effect on the dependent variable. The experiment is conducted to verify this effect. **The *dependent variable* is the variable that is thought to be affected by manipulation of the independent variable.** In psychology studies, the dependent variable is usually a measurement of some aspect of the subjects' behavior. The independent variable is called *independent* because it is *free* to be varied by the experimenter. The dependent variable is called *dependent* because it is thought to *depend* (at least in part) on manipulations of the independent variable.

In Schachter's experiment, *the independent variable was the participants' anxiety level*. He manipulated anxiety level in a clever way. Subjects assembled in his lab were told by a "Dr. Zilstein" that they would be participating in a study on the physiological effects of electric shock. They were further informed that during the experiment they would receive a series of electric shocks from an intimidating-looking apparatus while their pulse and blood pressure were being monitored. Half of the participants were warned that the shocks would be very painful. They made up the *high-anxiety* group. The other half of the participants (the *low-anxiety* group) were told that the shocks would be mild and painless. In reality, there was no plan to shock anyone at any time. These orientation procedures were simply intended to evoke various levels of anxiety. After the orientation, the experimenter indicated that there would be a delay while he prepared the shock apparatus for use. The participants were asked whether they would prefer to wait alone or in the company of others. *The subjects' desire to be with others was the dependent variable.*

Experimental and Control Groups

PsykTrek SIM1, 1b

In an experiment the investigator typically assembles two groups of subjects who are treated differently with regard to the independent variable. These two groups are referred to as the *experimental group* and the *control group*. **The *experimental group* consists of the subjects who receive some special treatment in regard to the independent variable. The *control group* consists of similar subjects who do not receive the special treatment given to the experimental group.**

In the Schachter study, those in the high-anxiety condition constituted the experimental group. They received a special treatment designed to create an unusually high level of anxiety. The participants in the low-anxiety condition constituted the control group. They were not exposed to the special anxiety-arousing procedure.

It is crucial that the experimental and control groups in a study be very similar, except for the different treatment that they receive in regard to the independent variable. This stipulation brings us to the logic that underlies the experimental method. If the two groups are alike in all respects *except for the variation created by the manipulation of the independent variable*, then any differences between the two groups on the dependent variable *must be due to the manipulation of the independent variable*. In this way researchers isolate the effect of the independent variable on the dependent variable. Schachter, for example, isolated the impact of anxiety on the need for affiliation. As predicted, he found that increased anxiety led to increased affiliation. As **Figure 2.4** indicates, the percentage of participants in the high-anxiety group who wanted to wait with others was nearly twice that of the low-anxiety group.

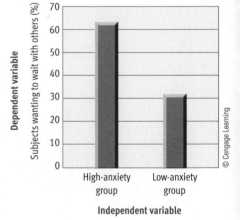

FIGURE 2.4

Results of Schachter's study of affiliation. The percentage of people wanting to wait with others was higher in the high-anxiety (experimental) group than in the low-anxiety (control) group, consistent with Schachter's hypothesis that anxiety would increase the desire for affiliation. The graphic portrayal of these results allows us to see at a glance the effects of the experimental manipulation on the dependent variable.

Extraneous Variables

As we have seen, the logic of the experimental method rests on the assumption that the experimental and control groups are alike except for their treatment in regard to the independent variable. Any other differences between the two groups can cloud the situation and make it difficult to draw conclusions about how the independent variable affects the dependent variable.

In practical terms, of course, it is impossible to ensure that two groups of subjects are exactly alike in *every* respect. The experimental and control groups have to be alike only on dimensions that are relevant to the dependent variable. Thus, Schachter did not need to worry about whether his two groups were similar in hair color, height, or interest in ballet. Obviously, these variables weren't likely to influence the dependent variable of affiliation behavior.

Instead, experimenters concentrate on making sure that the experimental and control groups are alike on a limited number of variables that could have a bearing on the results of the study. These variables are called extraneous, secondary, or nuisance variables. **Extraneous variables are any variables other than the independent variable that seem likely to influence the dependent variable in a specific study.**

In Schachter's study, one extraneous variable would have been the participants' tendency to be sociable. Why? Because subjects' sociability could affect their desire to be with others (the dependent variable).

Concept Check 2.1

Recognizing Independent and Dependent Variables

Check your understanding of the experimental method by identifying the independent variable (IV) and dependent variable (DV) in the following investigations. Note that one study has two IVs and another has two DVs. You'll find the answers in Appendix A in the back of the book.

1. A researcher is interested in how heart rate and blood pressure are affected by viewing a violent film sequence as opposed to a nonviolent film sequence.

   IV _____

   DV _____

2. An organizational psychologist develops a new training program to improve clerks' courtesy to customers in a large chain of retail stores. She conducts an experiment to see whether the training program leads to a reduction in the number of customer complaints.

   IV _____

   DV _____

3. A researcher wants to find out how stimulus complexity and stimulus contrast (light/dark variation) affect infants' attention to stimuli. He manipulates stimulus complexity and stimulus contrast and measures how long infants stare at various stimuli.

   IV _____

   DV _____

4. A social psychologist investigates the impact of group size on subjects' conformity in response to group pressure.

   IV _____

   DV _____

If the participants in one group had happened to be more sociable (on the average) than those in the other group, the variables of anxiety and sociability would have been confounded. **A *confounding of variables* occurs when two variables are linked in a way that makes it difficult to sort out their specific effects.** When an extraneous variable is confounded with an independent variable, a researcher cannot tell which is having what effect on the dependent variable.

Unanticipated confoundings of variables have wrecked innumerable experiments. That is why so much care, planning, and forethought must go into designing an experiment. A key quality that separates a talented experimenter from a mediocre one is the ability to foresee troublesome extraneous variables and control them to avoid confoundings.

Experimenters use a variety of safeguards to control for extraneous variables. For instance, subjects are usually assigned to the experimental and control groups randomly. ***Random assignment* of subjects occurs when all subjects have an equal chance of being assigned to any group or condition in the study.** When experimenters distribute subjects into groups through some random procedure, they can be reasonably confident that the groups will be similar in most ways.

To summarize the essentials of experimental design, **Figure 2.5** provides an overview of the elements in an experiment, using Schachter's study as an example.

Variations in Designing Experiments

$\boxed{\textsf{PsykTrek SIM1, 1b}}$

We have discussed the experiment in only its simplest format, with just one independent variable and one dependent variable. Actually, many variations are possible in conducting experiments. *Sometimes it is advantageous to use only one group of subjects who serve as their own control group.* The effects of the independent variable are evaluated by exposing this single group to two different conditions: an *experimental condition* and a *control condition*. For example, imagine that you wanted to study the effects of loud music on typing performance. You could have a group of participants work on a typing task while loud music was played (experimental condition) and in the absence of music (control condition). This approach would ensure that the participants in the experimental and control conditions would be alike on any extraneous variables involving their personal characteristics, such as motivation or typing skill (Davis & Bremner, 2006). After all, the same people would be studied in both conditions.

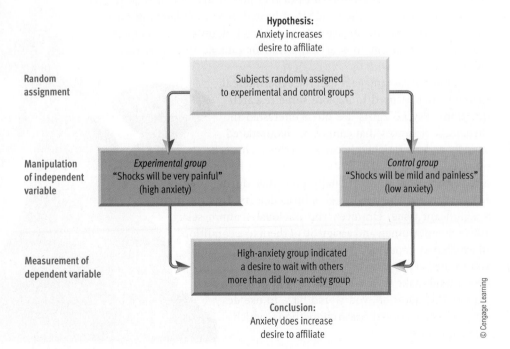

FIGURE 2.5

The basic elements of an experiment. As illustrated by the Schachter study, the logic of experimental design rests on treating the experimental and control groups exactly alike (to control for extraneous variables) except for the manipulation of the independent variable. In this way, the experimenter attempts to isolate the effects of the independent variable on the dependent variable.

© Cengage Learning

Distracting music

Present · Absent

Room temperature — Normal · High

FIGURE 2.6

Manipulation of two independent variables in an experiment. As this example shows, when two independent variables are manipulated in a single experiment, the researcher has to compare four groups of subjects (or conditions) instead of the usual two. The main advantage of this procedure is that it allows an experimenter to see whether two variables interact.

It is also possible to manipulate more than one independent variable or measure more than one dependent variable in a single experiment. For example, in another study of typing performance, you could vary both room temperature and the presence of distracting music as independent variables (see **Figure 2.6**), while measuring two aspects of typing performance (speed and accuracy) as dependent variables.

Advantages and Disadvantages of Experimental Research

The experiment is a powerful research method. Its principal advantage is that it permits conclusions about cause-and-effect relationships between variables. Researchers are able to draw these conclusions about causation because the precise control allows them to isolate the relationship between the independent variable and the dependent variable, while neutralizing the effects of extraneous variables. No other research method can duplicate this strength of the experiment. This advantage is why psychologists usually prefer to use the experimental method whenever possible.

For all its power, however, the experiment has limitations. One problem is that experiments are often artificial. Because experiments require great control over proceedings, researchers must often construct simple, contrived situations to test their hypotheses experimentally. For example, to investigate decision making in juries, psychologists have conducted many experiments in which participants read a brief summary of a trial and then record their individual "verdicts" of innocence or guilt. However, critics have pointed out that having a participant read a short case summary and make an individual decision is quite artificial in comparison to the complexities of real jury trials, which require group verdicts that are often the product of heated debates (Weiten & Diamond, 1979). When experiments are highly artificial, doubts arise about the applicability of findings to everyday behavior outside the experimental laboratory.

Another disadvantage is that the experimental method can't be used to explore some research questions. Psychologists are often interested in the effects of factors that cannot be manipulated as independent variables because of ethical concerns or practical realities. For instance, you might be interested in whether a nutritionally poor diet during pregnancy increases the likelihood of birth defects. This clearly is a significant issue. However, you obviously cannot select 100 pregnant women and assign 50 of them to a condition in which they consume an inadequate diet. The potential risk to the health of the women and their unborn children would make this research strategy unethical. To explore this question, you would have to use descriptive/correlational research methods, which we turn to next.

Looking for Links: Descriptive/Correlational Research

KEY LEARNING GOALS

2.5 Distinguish between positive and negative correlations, and discuss correlation in relation to prediction and causation.

2.6 Explain the role of naturalistic observation, case studies, and surveys in psychological research.

2.7 Evaluate the major advantages and disadvantages of descriptive/correlational research.

As we just noted, in some situations psychologists cannot exert experimental control over the variables they want to study. In such situations, investigators must rely on *descriptive/correlational research methods*. What distinguishes these methods is that the researcher cannot manipulate the variables under study. This lack of control means that these methods cannot be used to demonstrate a cause-effect relationship between variables. *Descriptive/correlational methods permit investigators to see only whether there is a link or association between the variables of interest.* Such an association is called a *correlation*, and the results of descriptive research are often summarized with a statistic called the *correlation coefficient*. In this section, we'll take a close look at the concept of correlation and then examine three specific approaches to descriptive research: naturalistic observation, case studies, and surveys.

The Concept of Correlation

PsykTrek 1d

In descriptive research, investigators often want to determine whether there is a correlation between two variables. **A *correlation* exists when two variables are related to each other.** A correlation may be either positive or negative, depending on the nature of the association between the variables measured. A *positive* correlation indicates that two variables co-vary (change together) in the *same* direction. This means that high scores on variable X are associated with high scores on variable Y and that low scores on variable X are associated with low scores on variable Y. For example, there is a positive correlation between high school grade point average (GPA) and subsequent college GPA. That is, people who do well in high school tend to do well in college. Likewise, those who perform poorly in high school tend to perform poorly in college (see **Figure 2.7**).

In contrast, a *negative* correlation indicates that two variables co-vary in the *opposite* direction. This means that people who score high on variable X tend to score low on variable Y, whereas those who score low on X tend to score high on Y. For example, in most college courses, there is a negative correlation between how frequently students are absent and how well they perform on exams. Students who have a high number of absences tend to get low exam scores, while students who have a low number of absences tend to earn higher exam scores (see **Figure 2.7**).

Positive correlation

High scores on *X* are associated with high scores on *Y*, and low scores on *X* are associated with low scores on *Y*.

X   Y   X   Y

High   College   High   College
school GPA   school GPA
GPA   GPA

Negative correlation

High scores on *X* are associated with low scores on *Y*, and low scores on *X* are associated with high scores on *Y*.

X   Y   X   Y

Absences Exam   Absences Exam
from class scores from class scores

FIGURE 2.7

Positive and negative correlation. Notice that the terms *positive* and *negative* refer to the direction of the relationship between two variables, not to its strength. Variables are positively correlated if they tend to increase and decrease together and are negatively correlated if one tends to increase when the other decreases.

© Cengage Learning

Negative correlation   **Positive correlation**

High   Moderate   Low   Low   Moderate   High

−1.00 −.90 −.80 −.70 −.60 −.50 −.40 −.30 −.20 −.10   0   .10   .20   .30   .40   .50   .60   .70   .80   .90   1.00

Strength of relationship

Increasing ⟵—————⟶ Increasing

FIGURE 2.8

Interpreting correlation coefficients. The magnitude of a correlation coefficient indicates the strength of the relationship between two variables. The sign (plus or minus) indicates whether the correlation is positive or negative. The closer the coefficient comes to +1.00 or −1.00, the stronger the relationship between the variables.

STRENGTH OF THE CORRELATION   PsykTrek 1d

The strength of an association between two variables can be measured with a statistic called the correlation coefficient. The *correlation coefficient* **is a numerical index of the degree of relationship between two variables.** This coefficient can vary between 0 and +1.00 (if the correlation is positive) or between 0 and −1.00 (if the correlation is negative). A coefficient near zero indicates no relationship between the variables. That is, high or low scores on variable X show no consistent relationship to high or low scores on variable Y. A coefficient of +1.00 or −1.00 indicates a perfect, one-to-one correspondence between the two variables. Most correlations fall between these extremes.

The closer the correlation is to either −1.00 or +1.00, the stronger the relationship (see **Figure 2.8**). Thus, a correlation of .90 represents a stronger tendency for variables to be associated than a correlation of .40. Likewise, a correlation of −.75 represents a stronger relationship than a correlation of −.45. Keep in mind that the *strength* of a correlation depends only on the *size of the coefficient*. The positive or negative sign simply indicates the direction of the relationship. Therefore, a correlation of −.60 reflects a stronger relationship than a correlation of +.30.

CORRELATION AND PREDICTION   PsykTrek 1d

You may recall that one of the key goals of scientific research is accurate *prediction*. A close link exists between the magnitude of a correlation and scientists' ability to make predictions. *As a correlation increases in strength (gets closer to either −1.00 or +1.00), the ability to predict one variable based on knowledge of the other variable increases.*

To illustrate, consider how college admissions tests (such as the SAT or ACT) are used to predict college performance. When students' admissions test scores and college GPA are correlated, researchers generally find moderate positive correlations in the .40s and .50s (Kobrin et al., 2008). Because of this relationship, college admissions committees can predict with modest accuracy how well prospective students will do in college. Admittedly, the predictive power of these admissions tests is far from perfect. But it's substantial enough to justify the use of the tests as one factor in making admissions decisions. However, if this correlation were much higher, say .90, admissions tests could predict with superb accuracy how students would perform. In contrast, if this correlation were much lower, say .20, the tests' prediction of college performance would be so poor that considering the test scores in admissions decisions would be unreasonable.

CORRELATION AND CAUSATION   PsykTrek 1d

Although a high correlation allows us to predict one variable on the basis of another, it does not tell us whether a cause-effect relationship exists between the two variables. The problem is that variables can be highly correlated even though they are not causally related.

Reality Check

Misconception

A strong correlation between variables suggests that one of those variables causes the other.

Reality

The magnitude of a correlation is not a useful guide to the likelihood of causation. Two variables could be highly correlated but both could be caused by a third variable. In contrast, a relatively low correlation might reflect a genuine, but weak causal effect.

DILBERT

SOMEONE SENT ME ANOTHER ANONYMOUS EMAIL WITH A LINK TO AN ARTICLE ABOUT THE WORLD'S WORST BOSSES.

I GET ONE OF THOSE EMAILS EVERY TIME I LEAVE YOUR CUBICLE. DID YOU THINK I WOULDN'T NOTICE THE CORRELATION?

CORRELATION DOES NOT IMPLY CAUSATION.

When we find that variables X and Y are correlated, we can safely conclude only that X and Y are related in some way. We do not know whether X causes Y or Y causes X, or whether both are caused by a third variable. For example, survey studies have found a positive correlation between smoking and the risk of experiencing a major depressive disorder (Johnson & Breslau, 2006; Kinnunen et al., 2006). It's clear that there is an association between smoking and depression. But it's hard to tell what's causing what. The investigators acknowledge that they don't know whether smoking makes people more vulnerable to depression or whether depression increases the tendency to smoke. Moreover, they note that they can't rule out the possibility that both are caused by a third variable (Z). Perhaps anxiety and neuroticism increase the likelihood of both taking up smoking and becoming depressed. The plausible causal relationships in this case are diagrammed in **Figure 2.9**. It illustrates the "third variable problem" in interpreting correlations. This is a common problem in research. You'll see this type of diagram again when we discuss other correlations. Thus, it is important to remember that *correlation is not equivalent to causation.*

FIGURE 2.9

Three possible causal relations between correlated variables. If variables X and Y are correlated, does X cause Y, does Y cause X, or does some hidden third variable, Z, account for the changes in both X and Y? As the relationship between smoking and depression illustrates, a correlation alone does not provide the answer. We will encounter this problem of interpreting the meaning of correlations frequently in this text.

Naturalistic Observation

What determines whether drivers stop or continue when they see a yellow light? Are there ethnic differences in sociability? These are just a couple examples of the kinds of questions that have been explored through naturalistic observation in recent studies. **In *naturalistic observation* a researcher engages in careful observation of behavior without intervening directly with the subjects.** This type of research is called *naturalistic* because behavior is allowed to unfold naturally (without interference) in its natural environment—that is, the setting in which it would normally occur. Of course, researchers have to make careful plans to ensure systematic, consistent observations (Angrosino, 2007). Let's look at two examples.

One recent study concerned with accident prevention used a system of three video cameras to record drivers' reactions to yellow lights at an intersection (Elmitiny et al., 2010). The cameras and other equipment allowed the researchers to gather information on the vehicles' place in the flow of traffic, speed, and distance from the light. They were then able relate these data to the drivers' on-the-fly decisions when the traffic light changed from green to yellow. The study provided some useful insights into the factors that lead people to inadvertently run red lights.

Another recent study (Ramirez-Esparza et al., 2007) examined ethnic differences in sociability using an innovative device called an electronically activated recorder

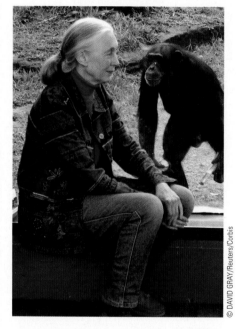

The method of naturalistic observation can be particularly useful in studying animals in their natural habitats. For example, Jane Goodall conducted ground-breaking research on the social lives of chimpanzees through years of painstaking naturalistic observation.

A creative use of naturalistic observation allowed researchers to gain new insights into ethnic differences in sociability.

(EAR). The EAR is an unobtrusive, portable audio recorder carried by participants that periodically records their conversations and other ambient sounds as they go about their normal daily activities (Mehl, 2007). Using this clever device, the researchers investigated an interesting paradox. Stereotypes suggest that Mexicans are outgoing and sociable, but when asked, Mexicans rate themselves as being less sociable than Americans. The study found that although Mexican participants rated themselves as less extraverted than American participants rated themselves, the EAR data on their actual daily behavior indicated they were *more* sociable than their American counterparts.

The major strength of naturalistic observation is that it allows researchers to study behavior under conditions that are less artificial than in experiments. Another plus is that engaging in naturalistic observation can be a good starting point when little is known about the behavior under study. And, unlike case studies and surveys, naturalistic observation can be used to study animal behavior. Many landmark studies of animal behavior, such as Jane Goodall's (1986, 1990) work on the social and family life of chimpanzees, have depended on naturalistic observation. More recent examples of naturalistic observation with animals include studies of communication in Australian sea lions (Charrier, Pitcher, & Harcourt, 2009), mating preferences in Eastern bluebirds (Liu et al., 2009), and tool use in wild spider monkeys (Lindshield & Rodrigues, 2009).

A major problem with this method is that researchers often have trouble making their observations unobtrusively so they don't affect their participants' behavior. *Reactivity occurs when a subject's behavior is altered by the presence of an observer.* Even animals may exhibit reactivity if observational efforts are readily apparent (Iredale, Nevill, & Lutz, 2010). Another disadvantage is that it often is difficult to translate naturalistic observations into numerical data that permit precise statistical analyses.

Concept Check 2.2

Understanding Correlation

Check your understanding of correlation by interpreting the meaning of the correlation in item 1 and by guessing the direction (positive or negative) of the correlations in item 2. You'll find the answers in Appendix A.

1. Researchers have found a substantial positive correlation between youngsters' self-esteem and their academic achievement (measured by grades in school). Check any acceptable conclusions based on this correlation.

    _____ a. Low grades cause low self-esteem.

    _____ b. There is an association between self-esteem and academic achievement.

    _____ c. High self-esteem causes high academic achievement.

    _____ d. High ability causes both high self-esteem and high academic achievement.

    _____ e. Youngsters who score low in self-esteem tend to get low grades, and those who score high in self-esteem tend to get high grades.

2. Indicate whether you would expect the following correlations to be positive or negative.

    _____ a. The correlation between age and visual acuity (among adults).

    _____ b. The correlation between years of education and income.

    _____ c. The correlation between shyness and the number of friends one has.

Case Studies

What portion of people who commit suicide suffer from psychological disorders? Which disorders are most common among victims of suicide? In health care visits during the final month of their lives, do people who commit suicide communicate their intent to do so? To investigate these kinds of questions, a research team in Finland studied the psychological characteristics of people who take their own lives (Henriksson et al., 1993; Isometsa et al., 1995). Other researchers had explored this issue, but the Finnish team planned a comprehensive, national study of unprecedented scope. Their initial sample consisted of all the known suicides in Finland for an entire year.

© Alain SHRODER/Getty Images

The research team decided that their question called for a case study approach. **A *case study* is an in-depth investigation of an individual subject.** When this method is applied to victims of suicide, the case studies are called *psychological autopsies*. A variety of data collection techniques can be used in case studies. In normal circumstances, when the subjects are not deceased, typical techniques include interviewing the subjects, interviewing people who are close to the subjects, direct observation of the participants, examination of records, and psychological testing. In this study, the investigators conducted thorough interviews with the families of the suicide victims and with the health care professionals who had treated them. The researchers also examined the suicide victims' medical, psychiatric, and social agency records, as well as relevant police investigations and forensic reports. Comprehensive case reports were then assembled for each person who committed suicide.

These case studies revealed that in 93% of the suicides the victim suffered from a significant psychological disorder (Henriksson et al., 1993). The most common diagnoses, by a large margin, were depression and alcohol dependence. In 571 cases, victims had a health care appointment during their final four weeks of life, but only 22% of these people discussed the possibility of suicide during their final visit (Isometsa et al., 1995). Even more surprising, the sample included 100 people who saw a health professional on the same day they killed themselves, yet only 21% of these individuals raised the issue of suicide. The investigators concluded that mental illness is a contributing factor in virtually all completed suicides and that the vast majority of suicidal people do not spontaneously reveal their intentions to health care professionals.

Clinical psychologists, who diagnose and treat psychological problems, routinely do case studies of their clients. When clinicians assemble a case study for diagnostic purposes, they generally are *not* conducting empirical research. Case study *research* typically involves investigators analyzing a collection of case studies to look for patterns that permit general conclusions. For example, one recent study (Arcelus et al., 2009) evaluated the efficacy of a treatment called *interpersonal psychotherapy* (IPT) for people suffering from bulimia (an eating disorder marked by out-of-control overeating followed by self-induced vomiting, fasting, and excessive exercise). Careful case assessments were made of 59 bulimic patients before, during, and after the 16-session course of IPT treatment. The results demonstrated that interpersonal therapy can be an effective treatment for bulimic disorders.

Case studies are particularly well suited for investigating certain phenomena, especially the roots of psychological disorders and the efficacy of selected therapeutic practices (Fishman, 2007). They can also provide compelling, real-life illustrations that bolster a hypothesis or theory. However, the main problem with case studies is that they are highly subjective. Information from several sources must be knit together in an impressionistic way. In this process, clinicians and researchers often focus selectively on information that fits with their expectations, which usually reflect their theoretical slant. Thus, it is relatively easy for investigators to see what they expect to see in case study research.

Surveys

Does the amount of time that people spend watching TV predict their physical health? Is social class related to people's TV viewing habits? These were the intriguing questions explored by a British research team that was interested in the health ramifications of sedentary behavior. Their study depended on survey data. **In a *survey* researchers use questionnaires or interviews to gather information about specific aspects of participants' background, attitudes, beliefs, or behavior.** In this case, Stamatakis and colleagues (2009) conducted household interviews with a representative sample of the adult population of Scotland. Almost 8000 participants were interviewed about how many hours per day they devote to television or other screen-based entertainment (including video games and material on computers). The participants were also questioned about their physical activity, general health, and cardiovascular health, as well as demographic characteristics (income, education, and other indicators of social class). Finally, subjects' height and weight were measured to permit the calculation of their body mass index (BMI), which is a widely used indicator of obesity.

What did the survey data reveal? They showed a clear association between the amount of time allocated to screen-based entertainment and impaired health. The more that people watched TV, the more likely they were to be obese or to report doctor-diagnosed diabetes or cardiovascular disease, and the less likely they were to report good general health (see **Figure 2.10**). The study also uncovered a rather strong link between social class and time devoted to screen-based entertainment: The people from lower socioeconomic strata spent considerably more time in front of TVs and other screens. These findings underscored the health ramifications of sedentary behavior and demonstrated that lower social class is a key risk factor for elevated sedentary behavior.

Surveys are often used to obtain information on aspects of behavior that are difficult to observe directly. Surveys also make it relatively easy to collect data on attitudes and opinions from large samples of participants. As Fife-Schaw (2006b) notes, "The humble questionnaire is probably the single most common research tool in the social sciences" (p. 212). However, potential participants' tendency to cooperate with surveys appears to have declined noticeably in recent decades (Tourangeau, 2004). The growing resentment of intrusive telemarketing and heightened concerns about privacy and identity theft seem to be the culprits underlying the reduced response rates for research surveys. The major weakness of surveys is that they depend on *self-report data*. As we'll discuss later, intentional deception, wishful thinking, memory lapses, and poorly worded questions can distort participants' verbal reports about their behavior (Krosnick, 1999).

Advantages and Disadvantages of Descriptive/Correlational Research

Descriptive/correlational research methods have advantages and disadvantages, which are compared with the strengths and weaknesses of experimental research in the Illustrated Overview of research methods on pages 48–49. As a whole, the foremost advantage of correlational methods is that they give researchers a way to explore questions they could not examine with experimental procedures. For example, after-the-fact analyses would be the only ethical way to investigate the possible link between poor maternal nutrition and birth defects in humans. In a similar vein, if researchers hope to learn how urban versus rural upbringing relates to people's values, they have to depend on descriptive methods, since they can't control where subjects grow up. Thus, *descriptive research broadens the scope of phenomena that psychologists are able to study.*

Unfortunately, descriptive methods have one significant disadvantage: Investigators cannot control events to isolate cause and effect. *Consequently, descriptive/correlational research cannot demonstrate conclusively that correlated variables are causally related.* Consider for instance, the correlation between time spent watching TV and poor health

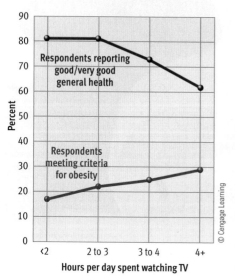

© Cengage Learning

FIGURE 2.10

TV viewing in relation to health indicators. In the survey by Stamatakis and colleagues (2009), participants provided information about their daily TV viewing habits, answered questions about their physical health, and had their height and weight measured to permit calculation of their body mass index (BMI), which is a standard index of obesity. The blue data line shows the percentage of people who reported being in good or very good general health in relation to TV viewing time. The red data line plots the percentage of participants who met the criteria of obesity in relation to TV watching. Clearly, as TV time increased, general health tended to decline and obesity to increase.

uncovered by Stamatakis and colleagues (2009). Their data do not permit us to conclude that sedentary behavior has a *causal* impact on health. Other factors might play a role in this association. For example, sedentary behavior could co-vary with some other factor, such as social class (which it did), that could be responsible for the observed differences in health.

Looking for Flaws: Evaluating Research

Scientific research is a more reliable source of information than casual observation or popular belief. However, it would be wrong to conclude that all published research is free of errors. Scientists are fallible human beings, and flawed studies do make their way into the body of scientific literature.

That is one of the reasons that scientists often try to replicate studies. **Replication is the repetition of a study to see whether the earlier results are duplicated.** The replication process helps science identify and purge inaccurate findings. Of course, the replication process sometimes leads to contradictory results. You'll see some examples in later chapters. Inconsistent findings on a research question can be frustrating and confusing for students. However, some inconsistency in results is to be expected, given science's commitment to replication.

Fortunately, one of the strengths of the empirical approach is that scientists work to reconcile or explain conflicting results. In their efforts to make sense of inconsistent research results, psychologists are increasingly depending on a technique called *meta-analysis,* which came into vogue in the 1980s (Cooper, 1990, 2010). *Meta-analysis* **combines the statistical results of many studies of the same question, yielding an estimate of the size and consistency of a variable's effects.** For example, Gentile and colleagues (2009) combined the results of 115 studies of gender differences in specific aspects of self-esteem. Among other things, they found that males tend to have somewhat higher self-esteem related to physical appearance and athletic ability, females score higher in self-esteem related to moral-ethical attributes, and gender differences in academic self-esteem are negligible. Meta-analysis allows researchers to test the generalizability of findings and the strength of a variable's effects across people, places, times, and variations in procedure in a relatively precise and objective way (Durlak, 2003; O'Sullivan, 2006).

As you will see in upcoming chapters, scientific advances often emerge out of efforts to double-check perplexing findings or to explain contradictory research results. Thus, like all sources of information, scientific studies need to be examined with a critical eye. This section describes a number of common methodological problems that often spoil studies. Being aware of these pitfalls will make you more skilled in evaluating research.

Sampling Bias

Empirical research always involves making statistical inferences about a population based on a sample (Sturgis, 2006). **A** *sample* **is the collection of subjects selected for observation in an empirical study.** In contrast, **the** *population* **is the much larger collection of animals or people (from which the sample is drawn) that researchers want to generalize about.** For example, when political pollsters attempt to predict elections, all of the voters in a jurisdiction represent the population. The voters who are actually surveyed constitute the sample. If researchers were interested in the ability of 6-year-old children to form concepts, those 6-year-olds actually studied would be the sample, and all similar 6-year-old children (perhaps those in modern, Western cultures) would be the population.

RESEARCH METHOD	DESCRIPTION	EXAMPLE APPLIED TO RESEARCH ON AGGRESSION

EXPERIMENT

Manipulation of an independent variable under carefully controlled conditions to see whether any changes occur in a dependent variable.

Example: Schachter's (1959) study of whether increased anxiety leads to increased affiliation.

Hypothesis: Anxiety increases affiliation

Random assignment → Subjects randomly assigned to experimental and control groups

Manipulation of independent variable: Experimental group "Shocks will be very painful" (high anxiety) | Control group "Shocks will be mild and painless" (low anxiety)

Measurement of dependent variable: High-anxiety group indicated a desire to wait with others more than did low-anxiety group

© Cengage Learning

Youngsters are randomly assigned to watch a violent or nonviolent film (manipulation of the independent variable), and some aspect of aggression (the dependent variable) is measured in a laboratory situation.

© T.M.O.Pictures/Alamy; (TV screen) © Andre Blais/Sh...

NATURALISTIC OBSERVATION

Careful, usually prolonged observation of behavior in its natural setting, without direct intervention.

Example: The Ramirez-Esparza et al. (2007) study comparing sociability in Mexican and American samples, using an electronically activated recorder (EAR).

© CREATISTA/Shutterstock

Youngsters' spontaneous acts of aggression during recreational activities on their playgound are recorded unobtrusively by a team of carefully trained observers.

© Laurence Mouton/Getty Images

CASE STUDIES

In-depth investigation of a single individual using direct interview, direct observation, review of records, interviews of those close to the person, and other data sources.

Example: The Isometsa et al. (1995) study of all known suicide cases in Finland for an entire year.

© Alain SHRODER/Getty Images

Detailed case histories are worked up for youngsters referred to counseling because of excessive aggressive behavior in school. The children are interviewed, as are their parents and teachers.

© Will & Deni McIntyre/CORBIS

SURVEYS

Use of questionnaires or interviews to gather information about specific aspects of participants' behavior, attitudes, and beliefs.

Example: The Stamatakis et al. (2009) study of sedentary behavior, which related hours per day devoted to TV viewing to social class and physical health.

© Gabe Palmer/Alamy

A large sample of youngsters are given a questionnaire describing hypothetical scenarios that might be expected to trigger aggressive behavior and are asked about how they think they would respond in the situations.

© David Grossman/Alamy

ADVANTAGES

DISADVANTAGES

Precise control over variables can eliminate alternative explanations for findings.

Researchers are able to draw conclusions about cause-and-effect relationships between variables.

Confounding of variables must be avoided.

Contrived laboratory situations are often artificial, making it risky to generalize findings to the real world.

Ethical concerns and practical realities preclude experiments on many important questions.

© Cengage Learning

Artificiality that can be a problem in laboratory studies is minimized.

It can be good place to start when little is known about the phenomena under study.

Unlike other descriptive/correlational methods, it can be used to study animal as well as human behavior.

© DAVID GRAY/Reuters/Corbis

It can be difficult to remain unobtrusive; even animal behavior may be altered by the observation process.

Researchers are unable to draw causal conclusions.

Observational data are often difficult to quantify for statistical analyses.

Case studies are well suited for study of psychological disorders and therapeutic practices.

Individual cases can provide compelling illustrations to support or undermine a theory.

Population

Unrepresentative sample

Subjectivity makes it easy to see what one expects to see based on one's theoretical slant.

Researchers are unable to draw causal conclusions.

Clinical samples are often unrepresentative and suffer from sampling bias.

© Cengage Learning

Data collection can be relatively easy, saving time and money.

Researchers can gather data on difficult-to-observe aspects of behavior.

Questionnaires are well suited for gathering data on attitudes, values, and beliefs from large samples.

Neuroticism

Smoking

Depression

Self-report data are often unreliable, due to intentional deception, social desirability bias, response sets, memory lapses, and poor wording of questions.

Researchers are unable to draw causal conclusions.

© Cengage Learning

The strategy of observing a limited sample in order to generalize about a much larger population rests on the assumption that the sample is reasonably *representative* of the population. A sample is representative if its composition (its demographic makeup in terms of age, sex, income, and so forth) is similar to the composition of the population (see **Figure 2.11**). *Sampling bias* **exists when a sample is not representative of the population from which it was drawn.** If a sample is not representative, generalizations about the population may be inaccurate. For instance, if a political pollster were to survey only people in posh shopping areas frequented by the wealthy, the pollster's generalizations about the voting public as a whole would be off the mark.

As we discussed in Chapter 1, American psychologists have historically tended to undersample ethnic minorities and people from non-Western cultures. In a recent analysis of this problem, Jeffrey Arnett (2008) reviewed the sample composition of studies published in six major APA-owned journals in recent years. He found that 68% of the samples came from the United States and another 27% from Europe or English-speaking countries, with only 5% coming from the remainder of the world. He asserts that the focus on American subjects is extremely disproportionate given that the United States accounts for less than 5% of the world's population. Moreover, Arnett notes that the vast majority of American samples were predominantly European American and that they depended much too heavily on white middle- and upper-class college students. He argues that this excessive reliance on American samples and college students is likely to distort findings in many research areas. In general, then, when you have concerns or doubts about the results of a study, the first thing to examine is the composition of the sample.

FIGURE 2.11

The relationship between the population and the sample. The process of drawing inferences about a population based on a sample works only if the sample is reasonably representative of the population. A sample is representative if its demographic makeup is similar to that of the population, as shown on the left. If some groups in the population are overrepresented or underrepresented in the sample, as shown on the right, inferences about the population may be skewed or inaccurate.

Placebo Effects

A *placebo* is a substance that resembles a drug but has no actual pharmacological effect. In studies that assess the effectiveness of medications, placebos are given to some participants to control for the effects of a treacherous extraneous variable: subjects' expectations. Placebos are used because researchers know that participants' expectations can influence their feelings, reactions, and behavior (Stewart-Williams, 2004). Thus, *placebo effects* **occur when participants' expectations lead them to experience some change even though they receive empty, fake, or ineffectual treatment.** In medicine, placebo effects are well documented (Benedetti, 2009). Many physicians tell of patients being "cured" by prescriptions of sugar pills. Similarly, psychologists have found that participants' expectations can be powerful determinants of their perceptions and behavior when they are under the microscope in an empirical study. For example, placebo effects have been seen in lab experiments on the effects of alcohol. In these studies, some of the participants are led to believe that they are drinking alcoholic beverages when in reality the drinks only appear to contain alcohol. Many of the subjects show effects of intoxication even though they haven't really consumed any alcohol (Assefi & Garry, 2003). If you know someone who shows signs of intoxication as soon as he or she starts drinking, before alcohol intake can have taken effect physiologically, you have seen placebo effects in action.

Placebo effects are attributable to people's expectations (Colagiuri & Boakes, 2010; Oken, 2008). However, recent studies have demonstrated

© karamysh/
Shutterstock

that mere expectations can have actual physiological effects. For example, studies of placebos given to subjects to reduce pain suggest that the placebos actually alter activity in brain circuits that are known to suppress pain (Wager, Scott, & Zubieta, 2007; Zubieta et al., 2005).

Researchers should guard against placebo effects whenever participants are likely to have expectations that a treatment will affect them in a certain way. The possible role of placebo effects can be assessed by including a fake version of the experimental treatment (a placebo condition) in a study.

Distortions in Self-Report Data

Research psychologists often work with *self-report data,* made up of participants' verbal accounts of their behavior. This is the case whenever questionnaires, interviews, or personality inventories are used to measure variables. Self-report methods can be quite useful. They take advantage of the fact that people have a unique opportunity to observe themselves full-time (Baldwin, 2000). However, self-reports can be plagued by several kinds of distortion.

One of the most problematic of these distortions is the *social desirability bias,* **which is a tendency to give socially approved answers to questions about oneself.** Subjects who are influenced by this bias work overtime trying to create a favorable impression, especially when they are asked about sensitive issues (Tourangeau & Yan, 2007). For example, many survey respondents will report that they voted in an election or gave to a charity when in fact it is possible to determine that they did not (Granberg & Holmberg, 1991; Hadaway, Marler, & Chaves, 1993). Interestingly, people who answer questions in socially desirable ways take slightly longer to respond to the questions. This tendency suggests that they are carefully "editing" their responses (Holtgraves, 2004).

Other problems can also produce distortions in self-report data (Krosnick, 1999; Schuman & Kalton, 1985). Respondents misunderstand questionnaire items surprisingly often, and the way questions are worded can shape participants' responses (Schwarz, 1999). Memory errors can also undermine the accuracy of verbal reports. Another source of distortion is that, in responding to certain kinds of scales, some people tend to agree with nearly all of the statements, while others tend to disagree with nearly everything (Krosnick & Fabrigar, 1998). An additional cause for concern is the *halo effect,* **which occurs when someone's overall evaluation of a person, object, or institution spills over to influence more specific ratings.** For example, a supervisor's global assessment of an employee's merit might sway specific ratings of the employee's dependability, initiative, communication, knowledge, and so forth. The crux of the problem is that a rater is unable to judge specific evaluative dimensions independently. Obviously, distortions like these can produce inaccurate results. Although researchers have devised ways to neutralize these problems, we should be especially cautious in drawing conclusions from self-report data (Schaeffer, 2000).

Experimenter Bias

As scientists, psychologists try to conduct their studies in an objective, unbiased way so that their own views will not influence the results. However, objectivity is a *goal* that scientists strive for, not an accomplished fact that can be taken for granted (MacCoun, 1998). In reality, most researchers have an emotional investment in the outcome of their research. Often they are testing hypotheses that they have developed themselves and that they would like to see supported by the data. It is understandable, then, that *experimenter bias* is a possible source of error in research.

Experimenter bias **occurs when a researcher's expectations or preferences about the outcome of a study influence the results obtained.** Experimenter bias can slip through to influence studies in many subtle ways. One problem is that researchers, like others, sometimes *see what they want to see.* For instance, when experimenters make apparently honest mistakes in recording subjects' responses, the mistakes tend to be heavily slanted in favor of supporting the hypothesis (O'Leary, Kent, & Kanowitz, 1975).

Research by Robert Rosenthal (1976) suggests that experimenter bias may lead researchers to unintentionally influence the behavior of their subjects. In one study, Rosenthal and Fode (1963) recruited undergraduate psychology students to serve as the "experimenters." The students were told that they would be collecting data for a study of how participants rated the success of people portrayed in photographs. In a pilot study, photos were selected that generated (on the average) neutral ratings on a scale extending from −10 (extreme failure) to +10 (extreme success). Rosenthal and Fode then manipulated the expectations of their experimenters by telling half of them that they would probably obtain average ratings of −5 and telling the other half to expect average ratings of +5. The experimenters were forbidden from conversing with their subjects except for reading some standardized instructions. Even though the photographs were exactly the same for both groups, the experimenters who *expected* positive ratings *obtained* significantly higher ratings than those who expected negative ones.

How could the experimenters have swayed the participants' ratings? According to Rosenthal, the experimenters unintentionally influenced their subjects by sending subtle nonverbal signals as the experiment progressed. Without realizing it, they sometimes smiled, nodded, or sent other positive cues when participants made ratings that were in line with their expectations. Thus, experimenter bias may influence both researchers' observations and their subjects' behavior (Rosenthal, 1994, 2002).

The problems associated with experimenter bias can be neutralized by using a double-blind procedure. **The *double-blind procedure* is a research strategy in which neither subjects nor experimenters know which subjects are in the experimental or control groups.** It's not particularly unusual for subjects to be "blind" about their treatment condition. However, the double-blind procedure keeps the experimenter in the dark as well. Of course, a member of the research team who isn't directly involved with subjects keeps track of who is in which group.

Looking at Ethics: Do the Ends Justify the Means?

KEY LEARNING GOALS

2.10 Discuss the controversies regarding deception in research and the use of animals in research.

Think back to Stanley Schachter's (1959) study on anxiety and affiliation. Imagine how you would have felt if you had been one of the participants in Schachter's high-anxiety group. You show up at a research lab, expecting to participate in a harmless experiment. The room you are sent to is full of unusual electronic equipment. An official-looking man in a lab coat announces that this equipment will be used to give you a series of painful electric shocks. His statement that the shocks will leave "no permanent tissue damage" is hardly reassuring. Surely, you think, there must be a mistake. All of a sudden, your venture into research has turned into a nightmare! Your stomach knots up in anxiety. The researcher explains that there will be a delay while he prepares his apparatus. He asks you to fill out a short questionnaire about whether you would prefer to wait alone or with others. Still reeling in dismay at the prospect of being shocked, you fill out the questionnaire. He takes it and then announces that you won't be shocked after all. It was all a hoax! Feelings of relief wash over you, but they're mixed with feelings of anger. You feel as though the experimenter has just made a fool out of you. You're embarrassed and resentful.

Should researchers be allowed to play with your feelings in this way? Should they be permitted to deceive participants in such a manner? Is this the cost that must be paid to advance scientific knowledge? As these questions indicate, the research enterprise sometimes presents scientists with difficult ethical dilemmas. *These dilemmas reflect concern about the possibility for inflicting harm on subjects.* In psychological research, the major ethical dilemmas center on the use of deception and the use of animals.

The Question of Deception

Elaborate deception, such as that seen in Schachter's study, has been fairly common in psychological research since the 1960s, especially in the area of social psychology (Epley & Huff, 1998; Korn, 1997). Over the years, psychologists have faked fights, thefts, muggings, faintings, epileptic seizures, rapes, and automobile breakdowns to explore a number of issues. Researchers have led subjects to believe that they (the subjects) were hurting others with electrical shocks, had homosexual tendencies, and were overhearing negative comments about themselves. Why have psychologists used so much deception in their research? Quite simply, they are trying to deal with the methodological problems discussed earlier. They often misinform participants about the purpose of a study to reduce problems resulting from placebo effects, the unreliability of self-reports, and other factors that can undermine the scientific value and validity of research (Berghmans, 2007).

Critics argue against the use of deception on several grounds (Baumrind, 1985; Kelman, 1982; Ortmann & Hertwig, 1997). First, they assert that deception is only a nice word for lying, which they see as inherently immoral. Second, they argue that by deceiving unsuspecting participants, psychologists may undermine many individuals' trust in others. Third, they point out that many deceptive studies produce distress for participants who were not forewarned about that possibility. Specifically, participants may experience great stress during a study or be made to feel foolish when the true nature of a study is explained.

Those who defend the use of deception in research maintain that many important issues could not be investigated if experimenters were not permitted to mislead subjects (Bröder, 1998). They argue that most research deceptions involve "white lies" that are not likely to harm participants. A review of the relevant research by Larry Christensen (1988) suggests that deception studies are *not* harmful to participants. Indeed, most subjects who participate in experiments involving deception report that they enjoyed the experience and that they didn't mind being misled. Moreover, the empirical evidence does not support the notions that deceptive research undermines subjects' trust in others or their respect for psychology or scientific research (Kimmel, 1996; Sharpe, Adair, & Roese, 1992). Finally, researchers who defend deception argue that the benefits—advances in knowledge that often improve human welfare—are worth the costs.

© Orange Line Media/Shutterstock

Concept Check **2.3**

Detecting Flaws in Research

Check your understanding of how to conduct sound research by looking for methodological flaws in the following studies. You'll find the answers in Appendix A.

Study 1. A researcher announces that he will be conducting an experiment to investigate the detrimental effects of sensory deprivation on perceptual-motor coordination. The first 40 students who sign up for the study are assigned to the experimental group, and the next 40 who sign up serve in the control group. The researcher supervises all aspects of the study's execution. Experimental subjects spend two hours in a sensory deprivation chamber, where sensory stimulation is minimal. Control subjects spend two hours in a waiting room that contains magazines and a TV. All subjects then perform ten 1-minute trials on a pursuit-rotor task that requires them to try to keep a stylus on a tiny rotating target. The dependent variable is their average score on the pursuit-rotor task.

Study 2. A researcher wants to know whether there is a relationship between age and racial prejudice. She designs a survey in which respondents are asked to rate their prejudice against six different ethnic groups. She distributes the survey to over 500 people of various ages who are approached at a shopping mall in a low-income, inner-city neighborhood.

Check the flaws that are apparent in each study.

Methodological flaw	Study 1	Study 2
Sampling bias	_____	_____
Placebo effects	_____	_____
Distortions in self-report	_____	_____
Confounding of variables	_____	_____
Experimenter bias	_____	_____

The Question of Animal Research

Psychology's other major ethics controversy concerns the use of animals in research. Psychologists use animals as research subjects for several reasons. Sometimes they simply want to know more about the behavior of a specific type of animal. In other instances, they want to identify general laws of behavior that apply to both humans and animals. Finally, in some cases psychologists use animals because they can expose them to treatments that clearly would be unacceptable with human participants. For example, most of the research on the relationship between deficient maternal nutrition during pregnancy and the incidence of birth defects has been done with animals.

It's this third reason for using animals that has generated most of the controversy. Some people maintain that it is wrong to subject animals to harm or pain for research purposes. Essentially, they argue that animals are entitled to the same rights as humans (Regan, 1997; Ryder, 2006). They accuse researchers of violating these rights by subjecting animals to unnecessary cruelty in many "trivial" studies (Bowd & Shapiro, 1993; Hollands, 1989). They also argue that most animal studies are a waste of time because the results may not even apply to humans (Millstone, 1989; Norton, 2005). Some of the more militant animal rights activists have broken into laboratories, destroyed scientists' equipment and research records, and stolen experimental animals.

In spite of the great furor, only 7%−8% of all psychological studies involve animals (mostly rodents and birds). Relatively few of these studies require subjecting the animals to painful or harmful manipulations (American Psychological Association, 1984). Psychologists who defend animal research point to the major advances attributable to psychological research on animals, which many people are unaware of (Baldwin, 1993; Compton, Dietrich, & Smith, 1995). Among them are advances in the treatment of mental disorders, neuromuscular disorders, strokes, brain injuries, visual defects, headaches, memory defects, high blood pressure, and problems with pain (Carroll & Overmier, 2001; Domjan & Purdy, 1995). To put the problem in context, Neal Miller (1985), a prominent psychologist who has done pioneering work in several areas, noted the following:

At least 20 million dogs and cats are abandoned each year in the United States; half of them are killed in pounds and shelters, and the rest are hit by cars or die of neglect. Less than 1/10,000 as many dogs and cats were used in psychological laboratories. . . . Is it worth sacrificing the lives of our children in order to stop experiments, most of which involve no pain, on a vastly smaller number of mice, rats, dogs, and cats? (p. 427)

As you can see, the manner in which animals can ethically be used for research is a highly charged controversy. Psychologists are becoming increasingly sensitive to this

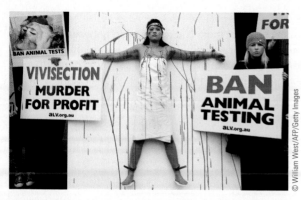

Many important scientific discoveries have been achieved through animal research, as the advertisement on the right notes. But many people remain vigorously opposed to animal research. The animal liberation activist shown above was covered in fake blood and strapped to a giant vivisection board as part of a protest against animal research in Melbourne, Australia. Clearly, the ethics of animal research is a highly charged controversy.

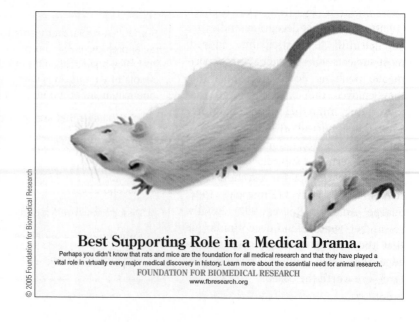

Best Supporting Role in a Medical Drama.

Perhaps you didn't know that rats and mice are the foundation for all medical research and that they have played a vital role in virtually every major medical discovery in history. Learn more about the essential need for animal research.

FOUNDATION FOR BIOMEDICAL RESEARCH
www.fbresearch.org

issue. Although animals continue to be used in research, strict regulations have been imposed that control nearly every detail of how laboratory animals can be used for research purposes (Ator, 2005; Garnett, 2005).

Ethical Principles in Research

The ethics issues that we have discussed in this section have led the APA to develop a set of ethical standards for researchers (American Psychological Association, 2002). Some of the most important guidelines for research with human participants include the following: (1) people's participation in research should always be voluntary and they should be allowed to withdraw from a study at any time; (2) participants should not be subjected to harmful or dangerous treatments; (3) if a study requires deception, participants should be debriefed (informed of the true nature and purpose of the research) as soon as possible; and (4) participants' right to privacy should never be compromised. Guidelines for research with animals include: (1) harmful or painful procedures cannot be justified unless the potential benefits of the research are substantial; and (2) research animals are entitled to decent living conditions.

Reflecting on the Chapter's Themes

KEY LEARNING GOALS

2.11 Identify the two unifying themes highlighted in this chapter.

 Empiricism

 Subjectivity of Experience

Two of our seven unifying themes have emerged strongly in this chapter. First, the entire chapter is a testimonial to the idea that psychology is empirical. Second, the discussion of methodological flaws in research provides numerous examples of how people's experience of the world can be highly subjective. Let's examine each of these points in more detail.

As explained in Chapter 1, the empirical approach entails testing ideas, basing conclusions on systematic observation, and relying on a healthy brand of skepticism. All of those features of the empirical approach have been apparent in this chapter. As you have seen, psychologists test their ideas by formulating clear hypotheses that involve predictions about relations between variables. They then use a variety of research methods to collect data, so they can see whether their predictions are supported. The data collection methods are designed to make researchers' observations systematic and precise. The entire venture is saturated with skepticism. In planning and executing their research, scientists are constantly on the lookout for methodological flaws. They publish their findings so that other experts can subject their methods and conclusions to critical scrutiny. Collectively, these procedures represent the essence of the empirical approach.

The subjectivity of personal experience became apparent in the discussion of methodological problems, especially placebo effects and experimenter bias. When research participants report beneficial effects from a fake treatment (the placebo), it's because they expected to see these effects. The studies showing that many subjects start feeling intoxicated just because they think that they have consumed alcohol are striking demonstrations of the enormous power of people's expectations. As pointed out in Chapter 1, psychologists and other scientists are not immune to the effects of subjective experience. Although they are trained to be objective, even scientists may see what they expect to see or what they want to see. This is one reason that the empirical approach emphasizes precise measurement and a skeptical attitude. The highly subjective nature of experience is exactly what the empirical approach attempts to neutralize.

The publication of empirical studies allows us to apply our skepticism to the research enterprise. However, you cannot critically analyze studies unless you know where and how to find them. In the upcoming Personal Application, we will discuss where studies are published, how to find studies on specific topics, and how to read research reports. In the subsequent Critical Thinking Application, we'll analyze the shortcomings of anecdotal evidence, which should help you appreciate the value of empirical evidence.

Finding and Reading Journal Articles

2.12 Explain the nature of technical journals, and describe how to use PsycINFO to search the research literature.

2.13 Describe the standard organization of journal articles reporting on empirical research.

Answer the following "yes" or "no."

___ 1 I have read about scientific studies in newspapers and magazines and sometimes wondered, "How did they come to those conclusions?"

___ 2 When I go to the library, I often have difficulty figuring out how to find information based on research.

___ 3 I have tried to read scientific reports and found them to be too technical and difficult to understand.

If you responded "yes" to any of the above statements, you have struggled with the information explosion in the sciences. We live in a research-oriented society. The number of studies conducted in most sciences is growing at a dizzying pace.

This Personal Application is intended to help you cope with the information explosion in psychology. It assumes that there may come a time when you need to examine original psychological research. Perhaps it will be in your role as a student (working on a term paper, for instance), in another role (parent, teacher, nurse, administrator), or merely out of curiosity. In any case, this Application explains the nature of technical journals and discusses how to find and read articles in them.

The Nature of Technical Journals   PSYKTREK 1e

As you will recall from earlier in the chapter, a *journal* is a periodical that publishes technical and scholarly material, usually in a narrowly defined area of inquiry. Journal articles represent the core of intellectual activity in any academic discipline. Although they are periodicals, you generally will not find technical journals at your local newsstand. Even public libraries carry relatively few professional journals. Academic libraries and professors account for the vast majority of subscriptions to technical journals.

In psychology, most journal articles are reports that describe original empirical studies. These reports permit researchers to communicate their findings to the scientific community. Another common type of article is the review article. *Review articles* summarize and reconcile the findings of a large number of studies on a specific issue. Some psychology journals also publish comments or critiques of previously published research, book reviews, theoretical treatises, and descriptions of methodological innovations.

Finding Journal Articles   PSYKTREK 1e

Reports of psychological research are commonly mentioned in newspapers and popular magazines. These summaries can be helpful to readers, but they often embrace the most sensational conclusions that might be drawn from the research. They also tend to include many oversimplifications and factual errors. Thus, if a study mentioned in the press is of interest to you, you may want to track down the original article to ensure that you get accurate information.

Most discussions of research in the popular press do not mention where you can locate the original technical article. However, there is a way to find out. A computerized database called PsycINFO makes it possible to locate journal articles by specific researchers or scholarly work on specific topics. This huge online database, which is updated constantly, contains brief summaries, or *abstracts,* of journal articles, books, and chapters in edited books, reporting, reviewing, or theorizing about psychological research. Over 2400 journals are checked regularly to select items for inclusion. The abstracts are concise—about 75 to 175 words. They briefly describe the hypotheses, methods, results, and conclusions of the studies. Each abstract should allow you to determine whether an article is relevant to your interests. If it is, you should be able to find the article in your library (or to order it) because a complete bibliographic reference is provided. The PsycINFO database can be accessed online through most academic libraries or directly via the Internet.

Although news accounts of research rarely mention where a study was published, they often mention the name of the researcher. If you have this information, the easiest way to find a specific article is to search PsycINFO for materials published by that researcher. For example, let's say you read a magazine article about a study that found that men were more sexually attracted to women who wore the color red. Let's assume that the news report mentioned the name of Andrew Elliot as the lead author and indicated that the article was published in 2008. To track down the original article, you would search for journal articles published by Andrew Elliot in 2008. If you conducted this search, you would turn up a list of 7 articles, and the relevant article, titled "Romantic red: Red enhances men's attraction to women" (Elliot & Niesta, 2008) would be obvious. **Figure 2.12** shows what you would see if you clicked to obtain the Abstract and Citation for this article. As you can see, the abstract shows that the original report was published in the November 2008 issue of the *Journal of Personality and Social Psychology*. Armed with this information, you could obtain the article easily.

You can also search PsycINFO for research literature on particular topics, such as achievement motivation, aggressive behavior, alcoholism, appetite disorders, or artistic ability. These computerized literature searches can be much more powerful, precise, and thorough than traditional, manual searches in a library. PsycINFO can sift through a few million articles in a matter of seconds to identify *all* the articles on a subject, such as alcoholism. Obviously, there is no way you can match this efficiency stumbling around in the stacks at your library. Moreover, the computer allows you to pair up topics to swiftly narrow your search to exactly those issues that interest you. For example, if you were preparing a term paper on whether marijuana affects memory, you could quickly identify all the articles dealing with marijuana *and* memory, which would be invaluable.

Reading Journal Articles

Once you find the journal articles you want to examine, you need to know how to decipher them. You can process the information in such articles more efficiently if you understand how they are organized. Depending on your needs and purpose, you may want to simply skim through some of the sections. Journal articles follow a fairly standard organization, which includes the following sections and features.

ABSTRACT

Most journals print a concise summary at the beginning of each article. This abstract allows readers scanning the journal to quickly decide whether articles are relevant to their interests.

INTRODUCTION

The introduction presents an overview of the problem studied in the research. It mentions relevant theories and quickly reviews previous research that bears on the problem, usually citing shortcomings in previous research that necessitate the current study. This review of the state of knowledge on the topic usually progresses to a specific and precise statement regarding the hypotheses under investigation.

METHOD

The next section provides a thorough description of the research methods used in the study. Information is provided on the subjects used, the procedures followed, and the data collection techniques employed. This description is made detailed enough to permit another researcher to attempt to replicate the study.

© Wayne Weiten 2000

RESULTS

The data obtained in the study are reported in the results section. This section often creates problems for novice readers because it includes complex statistical analyses, figures, tables, and graphs. This section does not include any inferences based on the data, as such conclusions are supposed to follow in the next section. Instead, it simply contains a concise summary of the raw data and the statistical analyses.

DISCUSSION

In the discussion section you will find the conclusions drawn by the author(s). In contrast to the results section, which is a straightforward summary of empirical observations, the discussion section allows for interpretation and evaluation of the data. Implications for theory and factual knowledge in the discipline are discussed. Conclusions are usually qualified carefully. Any limitations in the study may be acknowledged. This section may also include suggestions for future research on the issue.

REFERENCES

At the end of each article is a list of bibliographic references for any studies cited. This list permits the reader to examine firsthand other relevant studies mentioned in the article. The references list is often a rich source of leads about other articles that are germane to the topic that you are looking into.

FIGURE 2.12

Example of a PsycINFO abstract. This information is what you would see if you clicked to see the abstract of the study by Elliot and Niesta (2008), which reported that the color red increases men's attraction to women. It is a typical abstract from the online PsycINFO database. Each abstract in PsycINFO provides a summary of a specific journal article, book, or chapter in an edited book, and complete bibliographical information.

The Perils of Anecdotal Evidence: "I Have a Friend Who . . ."

KEY LEARNING GOALS

2.14 Recognize anecdotal evidence, and understand why it is unreliable.

Here's a tough problem. Suppose you are the judge in a family law court. As you look over the cases that will come before you today, you see that one divorcing couple have managed to settle almost all of the important decisions with minimal conflict. They have worked out who gets the house, who gets the car and the dog, and who pays which bills. However, there is one crucial issue left: Each parent wants custody of the children. Because they could not reach an agreement on their own, the case is now in your court. You will need the wisdom of the legendary King Solomon for this decision. How can you determine what is in the best interests of the children?

Child custody decisions have major consequences for all of the parties involved. As you review the case records, you see that both parents are loving and competent. So, there are no obvious reasons for selecting one parent over the other as the primary caretaker. In considering various alternatives, you mull over the possibility of awarding *joint custody.* In this arrangement, children spend half their time with each parent instead of the more usual situation where one parent has primary custody and the other has visitation rights. Joint custody seems to have some obvious benefits. But you are not sure how well these arrangements actually work. Will the children feel more attached to both parents if the parents share custody equally? Or will the children feel hassled by always moving around, perhaps spending half the week at one parent's home and half at the other parent's home? Can parents who are already feuding over child custody issues make these complicated arrangements work? Or is joint custody just too disruptive to everyone's life? You really don't know the answer to any of these vexing questions.

One of the lawyers involved in the case knows that you are thinking about the possibility of joint custody. She also understands that you want more information about how well joint custody tends to work before you make a decision. To help you make up your mind, she tells you about a divorced couple who have had a joint custody arrangement for many years. She offers to have them appear in court to describe their experiences "firsthand." They and their children can answer any questions you might have about the pros and cons of joint custody. They should be in the best position to know how well joint custody works because they are living it. Sounds like a reasonable plan. What do you think?

I hope you said, "No, no, no!" What's wrong with asking someone who's been there how well joint custody works? The crux of the problem is that the evidence a single family brings to the question of joint custody is **anecdotal evidence, which consists of personal stories about specific incidents and experiences.** Anecdotal evidence can be seductive. For example, one study found that psychology majors' choices of future courses to enroll in were influenced more by a couple of students' brief anecdotes than by extensive statistics on many other students' ratings of the courses from the previous term (Borgida & Nisbett, 1977). The power of anecdotes was also apparent in a more recent study that explored how to persuade people to take a personal health risk (for hepatitis B infection) more seriously. The researchers found that anecdotal accounts had more persuasive impact than sound factual and statistical evidence (de Wit, Das, & Vet, 2008). Anecdotes readily sway people because they are often concrete, vivid, and memorable. Many politicians are keenly aware of the power of anecdotes, and they frequently rely on a single vivid story rather than on solid data to sway voters' views. However, anecdotal evidence is fundamentally flawed (Ruscio, 2006; Stanovich, 2004).

Let's use some of the concepts introduced in the main body of the chapter to analyze the shortcomings of anecdotal evidence. First, in the language of research designs, the anecdotal experiences of one family resemble a single *case study.* The story they tell about their experiences with joint custody may be quite interesting, but their experiences—good or bad—cannot be used to generalize to other couples. Why not? Because they are only one family. They may be unusual in some way that affects how well they manage joint custody. To draw general conclusions based on the case study ap-

An abundance of anecdotal reports suggest that an association exists between the full moon and strange, erratic behavior. These reports often sound compelling, but as the text explains, anecdotal evidence is flawed in many ways. When researchers have examined the issue systematically, they have consistently found no association between lunar phases and the incidence of psychiatric emergencies, domestic violence, suicide, and so forth (Biermann et al., 2005; Chudler, 2007; Dowling, 2005; Kung & Mrazek, 2005; Lilienfeld & Arkowitz, 2009; McLay, Daylo, & Hammer, 2006).

DILBERT

WHAT CAN I DO TO AVOID GETTING COMPUTER VIRUSES?

GIVE YOUR POWER CORD A SPINAL ADJUSTMENT ONCE A WEEK TO PREVENT DISEASE.

I WAS SKEPTICAL UNTIL HE SAID THERE'S ANECDOTAL EVIDENCE THAT IT WORKS!

proach, you need a systematic series of case studies. Then you can look for threads of consistency. A single family is a sample size of one, which surely is not large enough to derive broad principles that would apply to other families.

Second, anecdotal evidence is similar to *self-report data,* which can be distorted for a variety of reasons, such as people's tendency to give socially approved information about themselves (the *social desirability bias*). When researchers use tests and surveys to gather self-report data, they can take steps to reduce or assess the impact of distortions in their data. But there are no comparable safeguards with anecdotal evidence. Thus, the family that appears in your courtroom may be eager to make a good impression and unknowingly slant their story accordingly.

Anecdotes are often inaccurate and riddled with embellishments. We will see in Chapter 7 that memories of personal experiences are far less accurate and reliable than widely assumed (Loftus, 2004; Schacter, 2001). And, although it would not be an issue in this case, in other situations *anecdotal evidence often consists of stories that people have heard about oth-*

ers' experiences. Hearsay evidence is not accepted in courtrooms for good reason. As stories are passed on from one person to another, they often become increasingly distorted and inaccurate.

Can you think of any other reasons for being wary of anecdotal evidence? After reading the chapter, perhaps you thought about the possibility of *sampling bias.* Do you think that the lawyer will pick a couple at random from all those who have been awarded joint custody? It seems highly unlikely. If she wants you to award joint custody, she will find a couple for whom this arrangement has worked very well. However, if she wants you to award sole custody to her client, she will find a couple whose inability to make joint custody work had dire consequences for their children. One reason people love to work with anecdotal evidence is that it is so readily manipulated. They can usually find an anecdote or two to support their position, whether or not the anecdotes are representative of most people's experiences.

If the testimony of one family cannot be used in making this critical custody decision, what sort of evidence should you be looking for? One goal of effective

critical thinking is to make decisions based on solid evidence. This process is called *evidence-based decision making.* In this case, you would need to consider the overall experiences of a large sample of families who have tried joint custody arrangements. In general, across many different families, did the children in joint custody develop well? Did the children or the parents experience an exceptionally high rate of emotional problems or other signs of stress? Did a higher percentage of families return to court at a later date to change their joint custody arrangements than did families with other types of custody arrangements? You can probably think of additional information that you would want to collect regarding the outcomes of various custody arrangements.

In examining research reports, many people recognize the need to evaluate the evidence by looking for the types of flaws described in the main body of the chapter (sampling bias, experimenter bias, and so forth). Curiously, though, many of the same people then fail to apply the same principles of good evidence to their personal decisions in everyday life. The tendency to rely on the anecdotal experiences of a small number of people is sometimes called the *"I have a friend who . . ." syndrome,* because no matter what the topic is, it seems that someone will provide a personal story about a friend as evidence for his or her particular point of view. In short, when you hear people support their assertions with personal stories, a little skepticism is in order.

TABLE 2.2 Critical Thinking Skills Discussed in This Application

Skill	Description
Recognizing the limitations of anecdotal evidence	The critical thinker is wary of anecdotal evidence, which consists of personal stories used to support one's assertions. Anecdotal evidence tends to be unrepresentative, inaccurate, and unreliable.
Using evidence-based decision making	The critical thinker understands the need to seek sound evidence to guide decisions in everyday life.

© Cengage Learning

Chapter 2 — Review of Key Learning Goals

Looking for Laws: The Scientific Approach to Behavior

2.1 Describe the goals of the scientific enterprise, and clarify the relations between theory, hypotheses, and research.

The scientific approach assumes that there are laws of behavior that can be discovered through empirical research. The goals of the science of psychology include (1) the measurement and description of behavior, (2) the understanding and prediction of behavior, and (3) the application of this knowledge to the task of controlling behavior. A hypothesis is a tentative statement about the relationship between two or more variables. A theory is a system of interrelated ideas used to explain a set of observations. By integrating apparently unrelated facts into a coherent whole, theories permit psychologists to make the leap from the description of behavior to the understanding of behavior. But theories must be testable. Confidence in a theory increases when hypotheses derived from it are supported by research.

2.2 Identify the steps in a scientific investigation, and list the advantages of the scientific approach.

A scientific investigation follows a systematic pattern that includes five steps: (1) formulate a testable hypothesis, (2) select the research method and design the study, (3) collect the data, (4) analyze the data and draw conclusions, and (5) report the findings. One major advantage of the scientific approach is its clarity in communication, which is promoted by its use of operational definitions. Operational definitions precisely describe the actions or operations that will be used to measure or control variables. Another key advantage of the scientific approach is its relative intolerance of error, which is promoted by scientists' constant testing of hypotheses and skeptical scrutiny of research findings.

Looking for Causes: Experimental Research

2.3 Describe the experimental method, independent and dependent variables, and experimental and control groups.

Experimental research involves the manipulation of an independent variable to determine its effect on a dependent variable. The independent variable is the variable that the experimenter controls or manipulates. The dependent variable is the variable that is thought to be affected by manipulation of the independent variable. The experimental group consists of the subjects who receive some special treatment in regard to the independent variable. The control group consists of similar subjects who do not receive the special treatment given to the experimental group. Any differences between the groups in the dependent variable ought to be the result of manipulation of the independent variable, as long as there are no significant problems with uncontrolled extraneous variables.

2.4 Explain how experiments can vary in design, and evaluate the major advantages and disadvantages of the experimental method.

Experimental designs may vary. For example, sometimes it is advantageous to use only one group of subjects who serve as their own control group. In this situation one compares performance in the experimental condition versus the control condition. And many experiments have more than one independent variable or more than one dependent variable. The chief advantage of the experiment is that it is a powerful research method that permits conclusions about cause-and-effect relationships between variables. However, the experimental method is often not usable for a specific problem, and many experiments tend to be artificial.

Looking for Links: Descriptive/Correlational Research

2.5 Distinguish between positive and negative correlations, and discuss correlation in relation to prediction and causation.

Correlations may be either positive (when two variables co-vary in the same direction) or negative (when two variables co-vary in the opposite direction). The correlation coefficient is a numerical index of the degree of relationship between two variables. The closer a correlation coefficient is to either +1.00 or −1.00, the stronger the association is. As a correlation increases in strength, the ability to predict one variable based on knowledge of the other variable increases. However, a correlation is no assurance of causation. When variables are correlated, we do not know whether X causes Y, Y causes X, or a third variable causes both.

2.6 Explain the role of naturalistic observation, case studies, and surveys in psychological research.

Naturalistic observation involves careful, prolonged observation of behavior in its natural setting without any intervention. Naturalistic observation allows researchers to study behavior under conditions that are less artificial than in experiments. Clinical research depends heavily on case studies, which involve in-depth investigations of individuals. In a survey, researchers interview participants or administer questionnaires to gather information on specific aspects of attitudes or behavior. Surveys are often used to obtain information on types of behavior that are difficult to observe directly. Each approach has its unique strengths and weaknesses.

2.7 Evaluate the major advantages and disadvantages of descriptive/correlational research.

Descriptive/correlational research methods allow psychologists to explore issues that might not be open to experimental investigation because the variables of interest cannot be manipulated for practical or ethical reasons. However, these research methods cannot demonstrate cause-effect relationships.

Looking for Flaws: Evaluating Research

2.8 Understand the importance of replication and meta-analysis in research.

Scientists often try to replicate research findings to double-check their validity. Although this process leads to some contradictory findings, science works toward reconciling inconsistent results. A useful tool in this effort is meta-analysis, which combines the statistical results of many studies of the same question, yielding an estimate of the size and consistency of a variable's effects.

2.9 Recognize common flaws in the design and execution of research.

Sampling bias occurs when a sample is not representative of the population of interest. American psychologists have historically tended to undersample ethnic minorities and people from non-Western cultures. Placebo effects occur when participants' expectations cause them to change their behavior in response to a fake treatment. Distortions in self-reports, such as response sets and the social desirability bias, are a source of concern whenever questionnaires and personality inventories are used to collect data. Experimenter bias occurs when researchers' expectations and desires distort their observations or unintentionally influence their subjects' behavior.

Population

Representative sample

Unrepresentative sample

© Cengage Learning

Looking at Ethics: Do the Ends Justify the Means?

2.10 Discuss the controversies regarding deception in research and the use of animals in research.

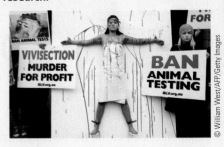

© William West/AFP/Getty Images

Critics argue that deception in research is unethical because it is inherently immoral, may undermine participants' trust in others, and may expose them to high levels of stress. Those who defend deception in research argue that many important issues could not be investigated without misleading subjects and that the negative effects of deception on participants have been overestimated. Critics of animal research argue that it violates animals' rights and that the findings of animal studies may not generalize to humans. Psychologists who defend animal research point out that only a small minority of studies involve animals, which are mostly rodents and birds. They also argue that animal research has brought major advances that are worth the costs.

Reflecting on the Chapter's Themes

2.11 Identify the two unifying themes highlighted in this chapter.

The empirical nature of psychology was elucidated throughout this chapter. Empiricism involves testing hypotheses, basing conclusions on systematic observation, and taking a skeptical approach. The chapter also showed repeatedly that people's experience of the world is highly subjective.

PERSONAL APPLICATION
Finding and Reading Journal Articles

2.12 Explain the nature of technical journals, and describe how to use PsycINFO to search the research literature.

Journals publish technical and scholarly material. In psychology, most journal articles are reports of original research. Subscriptions to journals are mostly held at academic libraries. PsycINFO is a computerized database that contains brief summaries of newly published journal articles, books, and chapters in edited books. Works on specific topics and publications by specific authors can be found by using the search mechanisms built into the database. Computerized literature searches can be much more powerful and precise than manual searches.

2.13 Describe the standard organization of journal articles reporting on empirical research.

Journal articles are easier to understand if one is familiar with the standard format. Most articles include six elements: abstract, introduction, method, results, discussion, and references. The results section does not include any inferences based on the data, as such conclusions are supposed to be limited to the discussion section.

CRITICAL THINKING APPLICATION
The Perils of Anecdotal Evidence: " I Have a Friend Who . . ."

2.14 Recognize anecdotal evidence and understand why it is unreliable.

Anecdotal evidence consists of personal stories about specific incidents and experiences. Anecdotal evidence can be very influential even thought it is fundamentally flawed. Anecdotal evidence is usually based on the equivalent of a single case study, which is not an adequate sample, and there are no safeguards to reduce the distortions often found in self-report data. Many anecdotes are inaccurate, second-hand reports of others' experiences.

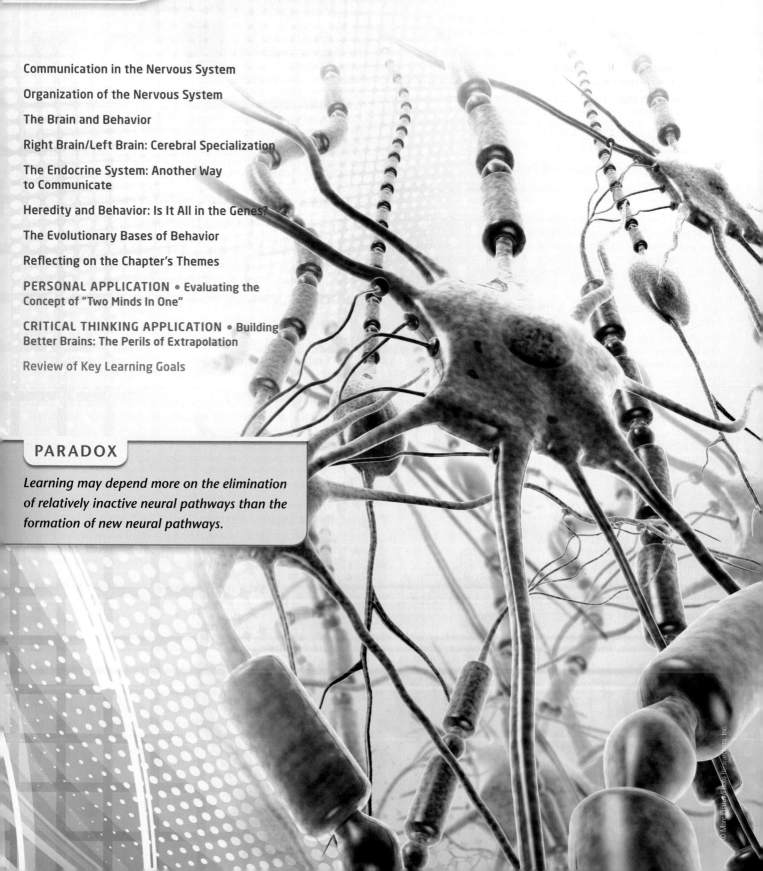

3

The Biological Bases of Behavior

PARADOX

Learning may depend more on the elimination of relatively inactive neural pathways than the formation of new neural pathways.

An ordinary-looking, 30-year old mother of three is walking down the street in a seedy neighborhood around 10:00 p.m. when she encounters a drugged-out man who presses a knife to her throat and threatens to kill her. Remarkably, the woman shows no signs of fear. Her heart rate doesn't quicken, her breathing doesn't change, she doesn't get nervous. Her completely calm, unruffled response to her attacker so unnerves *him* that he lets her go! Meet the woman who knows no fear.

The woman in this story, known by her initials, SM, has attracted interest from scientists who are intrigued by her apparent inability to experience fear. In a recent study designed to investigate SM's fearlessness, researchers exposed her to a variety of situations that would trigger fear in most people (Feinstein et al., 2011). For ethical reasons they chose fear-inducing stimuli that posed relatively little risk of actual harm. For example, they took her to an exotic pet store where they exposed her to snakes and spiders. What was her reaction? Instead of being scared, SM was fascinated and repeatedly asked to touch large snakes and a tarantula that were not safe to handle. Next, the scientists took SM to a famous haunted house. While others patrons screamed in fright, SM giggled and poked one of the monsters in the head—again scaring *him*. Taking yet another tack, the researchers showed SM clips from well-known scary movies, such as *The Ring*. She found the clips entertaining, but she experienced no fear. Finally, the researchers used a variety of methods to determine whether SM experiences other emotions. Their results revealed that she exhibits all the other basic emotions—anger, sadness, disgust, happiness, surprise—much like anyone else. Other tests demonstrated that SM scores normally on measures of intelligence, language, and memory.

Why is this woman absolutely fearless, yet she experiences other emotions? What could cause such a bizarre, exquisitely specific emotional deficit? It turns out that in childhood SM suffered an extremely rare disease that destroyed a small structure called the *amygdala* in both the right and left halves of her brain. Many studies, mostly with animals, have suggested that the amygdala is a crucial control center for the experience of fear. SM's case provides compelling, new *human* evidence that the amygdala has a unique role in the regulation of fear. By the way, if you are thinking that being fearless sounds appealing, think again. The research on SM has shown that she is fundamentally lacking when it comes to detecting when she's in danger, which is why she has a long history of getting herself into perilous situations.

SM's unusual case provides a dramatic demonstration that behavioral functioning is ultimately controlled by the brain. The fact that SM feels all the other emotions except fear shows just how precise the biological bases of behavior can be. The human brain is so complex, no computer has ever come remotely close to duplicating it. Your nervous system contains as many cells busily integrating and relaying information as there are stars in our galaxy. Whether you are scratching your nose or composing an essay, the activity of those cells underlies what you do. It is little wonder, then, that many psychologists have dedicated themselves to exploring the biological bases of behavior.

Communication in the Nervous System

KEY LEARNING GOALS

3.1 Identify the various parts of the neuron and the main functions of glial cells.

3.2 Describe the neural impulse, and explain how neurons communicate at chemical synapses.

3.3 Discuss some of the functions of acetylcholine, the monoamine neurotransmitters, GABA, and endorphins.

Imagine that you are watching a scary movie. As the tension mounts, your palms sweat and your heart beats faster. You begin shoveling popcorn into your mouth, carelessly spilling some in your lap. If someone were to ask you what you are doing at this moment, you would probably say, "Nothing—just watching the movie." Yet some highly complex processes are occurring without your thinking about them. A stimulus (the light from the screen) is striking your eye. Almost instantaneously, your brain is interpreting the light stimulus and signals are flashing to other parts of your body, leading to a flurry of activity. Your sweat glands are releasing perspiration, your heartbeat is quickening, and muscular movements are enabling your hand to find the popcorn and, more or less successfully, lift it to your mouth.

Even in this simple example, you can see that behavior depends on rapid information processing. Information travels immediately from your eye to your brain, from your brain to the muscles of your arm and hand, and from your palms back to your brain. In essence, your nervous system is a complex communication network in which signals are constantly being received, integrated, and transmitted. The nervous system handles information, just as the circulatory system handles blood. In this section, we take a close look at communication in the nervous system.

Nervous Tissue: The Basic Hardware

PsykTrek 2a

Your nervous system is living tissue composed of cells. The cells in the nervous system fall into two major categories: *glia* and *neurons*. Let's look at neurons first.

NEURONS

PsykTrek 2a

Neurons **are individual cells in the nervous system that receive, integrate, and transmit information.** They are the basic links that permit communication within the nervous system. The vast majority of them communicate only with other neurons. However, a small minority receive signals from outside the nervous system (from sensory organs) or carry messages from the nervous system to the muscles that move the body.

A highly simplified drawing of two "typical" neurons is shown in **Figure 3.1.** The *soma,* **or cell body, contains the cell nucleus and much of the chemical machinery common to most cells** (*soma* is Greek for "body"). The rest of the neuron is devoted exclusively to handling information. The neurons in **Figure 3.1** have a number of branched, feelerlike structures called *dendritic trees* (*dendrite* is a Greek word for "tree"). Each individual branch is a *dendrite. Dendrites* **are the parts of a neuron that are specialized to receive information.** Most neurons receive information from many other cells—sometimes thousands of others—and so have extensive dendritic trees.

From the many dendrites, information flows into the cell body, then travels away from the soma along the *axon* (from the Greek for "axle"). **The *axon* is a long, thin fiber that transmits signals away from the soma to other neurons or to muscles or glands.** Axons may be quite long (sometimes several feet), and they may branch off to communicate with a number of other cells.

In humans, many axons are wrapped in cells with a high concentration of a white, fatty substance called *myelin.* **The *myelin sheath* is insulating material that encases some axons.** It functions to speed up the transmission of signals that move along axons (Zorumski, Isenberg, & Mennerick, 2009). If an axon's myelin sheath deteriorates, signals may not be transmitted effectively. The loss of muscle control seen with the disease *multiple sclerosis* is due to a degeneration of myelin sheaths (Joffe, 2009).

The axon ends in a cluster of *terminal buttons,* **which are small knobs that secrete chemicals called neurotransmitters.** These chemicals serve as messengers that may activate neighboring neurons. The points at which neurons interconnect are called *synapses. A synapse* **is a junction where information is transmitted from one neuron**

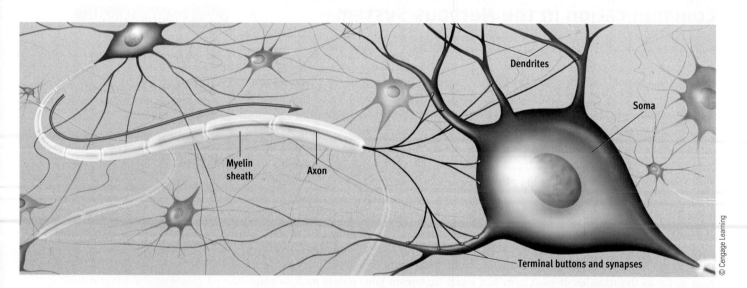

© Cengage Learning

FIGURE 3.1

Structure of the neuron. Neurons are the communication links of the nervous system. This diagram highlights the key parts of a neuron, including specialized receptor areas (dendrites), the cell body (soma), the axon fiber along which impulses are transmitted, and the terminal buttons, which release chemical messengers that carry signals to other neurons. Neurons vary considerably in size and shape and are usually densely interconnected.

to another (*synapse* is from the Greek for "junction"). To summarize, information is received at the dendrites, is passed through the soma and along the axon, and is transmitted to the dendrites of other cells at meeting points called synapses.

GLIA

PSYKTREK 2a

Glia **are cells found throughout the nervous system that provide various types of support for neurons.** Glia (literally "glue") tend to be much smaller than neurons, but they outnumber neurons by about 10 to 1. Hence, glial cells appear to account for over 50% of the brain's volume. Glial cells serve many functions. For example, they supply nourishment to neurons, help remove neurons' waste products, and provide insulation around many axons. The myelin sheaths that encase some axons are derived from special types of glial cells. Glia also play a complicated role in the development of the nervous system in the human embryo.

These functions, which have been known for many years, made glial cells the unsung heroes of the nervous system. Until recently, it was thought that the "glamorous" work in the nervous system—the transmission and integration of informational signals—was the exclusive province of the neurons. New research, however, suggests that glia may also send and receive chemical signals (Deitmer & Rose, 2010; Fields, 2004). Some types of glia can detect neural impulses and send signals to other glial cells. Surprised by this discovery, neuroscientists are now trying to figure out how this signaling system interfaces with the neural communication system. Some of the preliminary findings and theorizing have proven very interesting. For example, research suggests that glial cells may play an important role in memory formation (Bains & Oliet, 2007) and that gradual deterioration of glial tissue might contribute to Alzheimer's disease (Streit, 2005). Research also suggests that glial cells play a crucial role in the experience of chronic pain (Milligan & Watkins, 2009).

Although glia may contribute to information processing in the nervous system, the bulk of this crucial work is handled by the neurons. Thus, we need to examine the process of neural activity in more detail.

The Neural Impulse:
Using Energy to Send Information

PSYKTREK 2a

What happens when a neuron is stimulated? What is the nature of the signal—the *neural impulse*—that moves through the neuron? These were the questions that Alan Hodgkin and Andrew Huxley set out to answer in their groundbreaking experiments with axons removed from squid. Why did they choose to work with squid axons? Because squid have a pair of "giant" axons that are about a hundred times larger than those in humans (which still makes them only about as thick as a human hair). This large size permitted Hodgkin and Huxley to insert fine wires called *microelectrodes* into the axons. By using the microelectrodes to record the electrical activity in individual neurons, Hodgkin and Huxley were able to unravel the mystery of the neural impulse.

THE NEURON AT REST: A TINY BATTERY

PSYKTREK 2a

Hodgkin and Huxley (1952) learned that the neural impulse is a complex electrochemical reaction. Both inside and outside the neuron are fluids containing electrically charged atoms and molecules called *ions*. Positively charged sodium and potassium ions and negatively charged chloride ions flow back and forth across the cell membrane, but they do not cross at the same rate. The difference in flow rates leads to a slightly higher concentration of negatively charged ions inside the cell. The resulting voltage means that the neuron at rest is a tiny battery, a store of potential energy. The *resting potential* of a **neuron is its stable, negative charge when the cell is inactive.** As shown in **Figure 3.2(a)** on the next page, this charge is about −70 millivolts, roughly one-twentieth of the voltage of a flashlight battery.

Reality Check

Misconception
Neurons are responsible for all the information processing in the nervous system.

Reality
Until recently, it *was* thought that the transmission and integration of informational signals was the exclusive role of the neurons. However, newer research has demonstrated that glial cells also play an important role in information processing.

FIGURE 3.2

The neural impulse. The electrochemical properties of the neuron allow it to transmit signals. The electric charge of a neuron can be measured with a pair of electrodes connected to an oscilloscope, as Hodgkin and Huxley showed with a squid axon. Because of its exceptionally thick axons, the squid has frequently been used by scientists studying the neural impulse. **(a)** At rest, the neuron's voltage hovers around −70 millivolts. **(b)** When the axon is stimulated, there is a brief jump in a neuron's voltage, resulting in a spike on the oscilloscope recording of the neuron's electrical activity. This change in voltage, called an action potential, travels along the axon like a spark traveling along a trail of gunpowder.

THE ACTION POTENTIAL [PSYKTREK 2a]

As long as the voltage of a neuron remains constant, the cell is quiet, and no messages are being sent. When the neuron is stimulated, channels in its cell membrane open, briefly allowing positively charged sodium ions to rush in. For an instant, the neuron's charge is less negative and eventually positive, creating an action potential (McCormick, 2008). **An *action potential* is a very brief shift in a neuron's electrical charge that travels along an axon.** The firing of an action potential is reflected in the voltage spike shown in **Figure 3.2(b)**. Like a spark traveling along a trail of gunpowder, the voltage change races down the axon.

After the firing of an action potential, the channels in the cell membrane that opened to let in sodium close up. Some time is needed before they are ready to open again, and until that time the neuron cannot fire. **The *absolute refractory period* is the minimum length of time after an action potential during which another action potential cannot begin.** This "down time" isn't very long, only 1 or 2 milliseconds.

THE ALL-OR-NONE LAW [PSYKTREK 2a]

The neural impulse is an all-or-none proposition, like firing a gun. You can't half-fire a gun. The same is true of the neuron's firing of action potentials. Either the neuron fires or it doesn't, and its action potentials are all the same size (Kandel, 2000). That is, weaker stimuli do not produce smaller action potentials and stronger stimuli do not evoke larger action potentials.

Even though the action potential is an all-or-nothing event, neurons *can* convey information about the strength of a stimulus. They do so by varying the *rate* at which they fire action potentials. In general, a stronger stimulus will cause a cell to fire a more rapid volley of neural impulses than a weaker stimulus will. For example, a dim light might trigger 5 action potentials per second in a visual cell, whereas brighter lights might trigger 100 or 200 impulses per second (Burkhardt, 2010).

The Synapse: Where Neurons Meet [PSYKTREK 2b]

In the nervous system, the neural impulse functions as a signal. For that signal to have any meaning for the system as a whole, it must be transmitted from the neuron to other cells. As noted earlier, this transmission takes place at special junctions called *synapses,* which depend on *chemical* messengers.

SENDING SIGNALS: CHEMICALS AS COURIERS [PSYKTREK 2b]

A "typical" synapse is shown in **Figure 3.3**. The first thing that you should notice is that the two neurons don't actually touch. They are separated by the *synaptic cleft,* **a microscopic gap between the terminal button of one neuron and the cell membrane of another neuron.** Signals have to cross this gap to permit neurons to communicate. In this situation, the neuron that sends a signal across the gap is called the *presynaptic neuron,* and the neuron that receives the signal is called the *postsynaptic neuron.*

How do messages travel across the gaps between neurons? As mentioned earlier, the arrival of an action potential at an axon's terminal buttons triggers the release of *neuro-transmitters*—chemicals that transmit information from one neuron to another. Within the buttons, most of these chemicals are stored in small sacs, called *synaptic vesicles*. The neurotransmitters are released when a vesicle fuses with the membrane of the presynaptic cell and its contents spill into the synaptic cleft (Schwarz, 2008). After their release, neurotransmitters diffuse across the synaptic cleft to the membrane of the

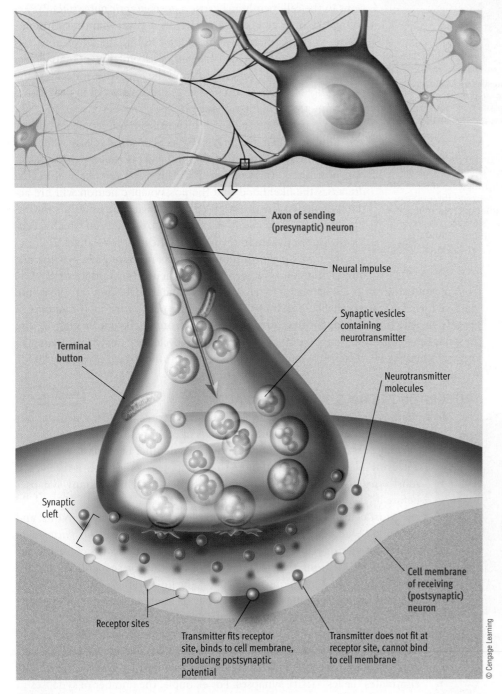

Axon of sending (presynaptic) neuron

Neural impulse

Synaptic vesicles containing neurotransmitter

Neurotransmitter molecules

Terminal button

Synaptic cleft

Cell membrane of receiving (postsynaptic) neuron

Receptor sites

Transmitter fits receptor site, binds to cell membrane, producing postsynaptic potential

Transmitter does not fit at receptor site, cannot bind to cell membrane

© Cengage Learning

FIGURE 3.3

The synapse. When a neural impulse reaches an axon's terminal buttons, it triggers the release of chemical messengers called neurotransmitters. The neurotransmitter molecules diffuse across the synaptic cleft and bind to receptor sites on the postsynaptic neuron. A specific neurotransmitter can bind only to receptor sites that its molecular structure will fit into, much like a key must fit a lock.

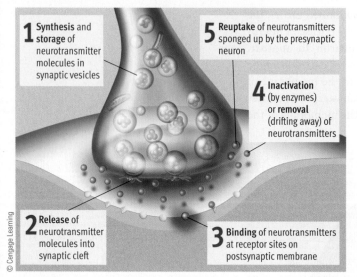

1 **Synthesis** and **storage** of neurotransmitter molecules in synaptic vesicles

5 **Reuptake** of neurotransmitters sponged up by the presynaptic neuron

4 **Inactivation** (by enzymes) or **removal** (drifting away) of neurotransmitters

2 **Release** of neurotransmitter molecules into synaptic cleft

3 **Binding** of neurotransmitters at receptor sites on postsynaptic membrane

© Cengage Learning

FIGURE 3.4

Overview of synaptic transmission. The main processes in synaptic transmission are summarized here. The five key processes involved in communication at synapses are (1) synthesis and storage, (2) release, (3) binding, (4) inactivation or removal, and (5) reuptake of neurotransmitters. As you'll see in this chapter and the remainder of the book, the effects of many phenomena—such as pain, drug use, and some diseases—can be explained in terms of how they alter one or more of these processes (usually at synapses releasing a specific neurotransmitter).

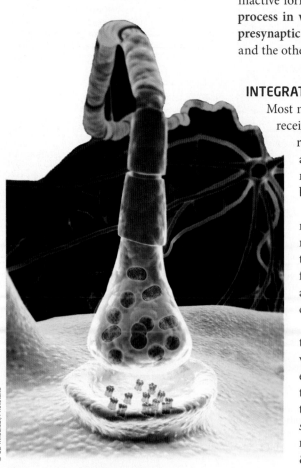

© 3D4Medical/Phototake

receiving cell. There they may bind with special molecules in the postsynaptic cell membrane at various *receptor sites.* These sites are specifically "tuned" to recognize and respond to some neurotransmitters but not to others.

RECEIVING SIGNALS: POSTSYNAPTIC POTENTIALS

PSYKTREK 2b

When a neurotransmitter and a receptor molecule combine, reactions in the cell membrane cause a *postsynaptic potential (PSP),* **a voltage change at a receptor site on a postsynaptic cell membrane.** Postsynaptic potentials do *not* follow the all-or-none law like action potentials do. Instead, postsynaptic potentials are *graded.* That is, they vary in size, and they increase or decrease the *probability* of a neural impulse in the receiving cell in proportion to the amount of voltage change.

Two types of messages can be sent from cell to cell: excitatory and inhibitory. An *excitatory PSP* is a positive voltage shift that *increases* the likelihood that the postsynaptic neuron will fire action potentials. An *inhibitory PSP* is a negative voltage shift that *decreases* the likelihood that the postsynaptic neuron will fire action potentials. The direction of the voltage shift, and thus the nature of the PSP (excitatory or inhibitory), depends on which receptor sites are activated in the postsynaptic neuron (Kandel, 2000).

The excitatory or inhibitory effects produced at a synapse last only a fraction of a second. Then neurotransmitters drift away from receptor sites or are inactivated by enzymes that metabolize (convert) them into inactive forms. Most are reabsorbed into the presynaptic neuron through *reuptake,* **a process in which neurotransmitters are sponged up from the synaptic cleft by the presynaptic membrane.** Reuptake allows synapses to recycle their materials. Reuptake and the other key processes in synaptic transmission are summarized in **Figure 3.4**.

INTEGRATING SIGNALS: A BALANCING ACT

PSYKTREK 2b

Most neurons are interlinked in complex, dense networks. In fact, a neuron may receive a symphony of signals from *thousands* of other neurons. That same neuron may pass its messages along to thousands of other neurons as well. Thus, a neuron must do a great deal more than simply relay messages it receives. It must *integrate* excitatory and inhibitory signals arriving at many synapses before it "decides" whether to fire a neural impulse.

Most neurons are interlinked in complex chains, pathways, circuits, and networks. Our perceptions, thoughts, and actions depend on *patterns* of neural activity in elaborate neural networks. These networks consist of interconnected neurons that frequently fire together or sequentially to perform certain functions (Song et al., 2005). The links in these neural networks are fluid, as new synaptic connections may be made while some old synaptic connections wither away (Hua & Smith, 2004).

Ironically, the *elimination of old synapses* appears to play a larger role in the sculpting of neural networks than the *creation of new synapses*. The nervous system normally forms more synapses than needed and then gradually eliminates the less-active synapses. For example, the number of synapses in the human visual cortex peaks at around age one and then declines (Huttenlocher, 1994). This elimination of old or less-active synapses is called *synaptic pruning.* It appears to be a key process in the formation of the neural networks that are crucial to communication in the nervous system (Tapia & Lichtman, 2008).

Neurotransmitters and Behavior

PsykTrek 2b, 4d

As we have seen, the nervous system relies on chemical couriers to communicate information between neurons. These neurotransmitters are fundamental to behavior, playing a key role in everything from muscle movements to moods and mental health.

Specific neurotransmitters function at specific kinds of synapses. You may recall that transmitters deliver their messages by binding to receptor sites on the postsynaptic membrane. However, a transmitter cannot bind to just any site. The binding process operates much like a lock and key, as was shown in **Figure 3.3**. Just as a key has to fit a lock to work, a transmitter has to fit into a receptor site for binding to occur. Hence, specific transmitters can deliver signals at only certain locations on cell membranes.

Why are there many different neurotransmitters, each of which works only at certain synapses? This variety and specificity reduces crosstalk between densely packed neurons, making the nervous system's communication more precise (Deutch & Roth, 2008). Let's look at some of the most interesting findings about how specific neurotransmitters regulate behavior, as summarized in **Table 3.1**.

ACETYLCHOLINE

PsykTrek 2b

The discovery that cells communicate by releasing chemicals was first made in connection with the transmitter *acetylcholine* (ACh). ACh has been found throughout the nervous system. It is the only transmitter between motor neurons and voluntary muscles. Every move you make—walking, talking, breathing—depends on ACh released to your muscles by motor neurons (Kandel & Siegelbaum, 2000). ACh also appears to contribute to attention, arousal, and memory. An inadequate supply of ACh in certain areas of the brain is associated with the memory losses seen in Alzheimer's disease (Bourgeois, Seaman, & Servis, 2003). Although ACh depletion does *not* appear to be the crucial causal factor underlying Alzheimer's disease, the drug treatments currently available, which can slow the progress of the disease (slightly), work by amplifying ACh activity (Neugroschl et al., 2005).

© Digital Vision/Getty Images

Cosmetic botox treatments temporarily reduce wrinkles by blocking ACh receptors at synapses between motor neurons and voluntary muscles (in the vicinity of the injection). This action basically paralyzes muscles to prevent wrinkles from forming. The cosmetic effects last only about three to five months, however, because the synapse adapts and new ACh receptors are gradually generated.

TABLE 3.1 **Common Neurotransmitters and Some of Their Relations to Behavior**

Neurotransmitter	Characteristics and Relations to Behavior	Disorders Associated with Dysregulation
Acetylcholine (ACh)	Released by motor neurons controlling skeletal muscles Contributes to the regulation of attention, arousal, and memory Some ACh receptors stimulated by nicotine	Alzheimer's disease
Dopamine (DA)	Contributes to control of voluntary movement Cocaine and amphetamines elevate activity at DA synapses Dopamine circuits in medial forebrain bundle characterized as "reward pathway"	Parkinsonism Schizophrenic disorders Addictive disorders
Norepinephrine (NE)	Contributes to modulation of mood and arousal Cocaine and amphetamines elevate activity at NE synapses	Depressive disorders
Serotonin	Involved in regulation of sleep and wakefulness, eating, aggression Prozac and similar antidepressant drugs affect serotonin circuits	Depressive disorders Obsessive-compulsive disorders Eating disorders
GABA	Serves as widely distributed inhibitory transmitter, contributing to regulation of anxiety and sleep/arousal Valium and similar antianxiety drugs work at GABA synapses	Anxiety disorders
Endorphins	Resemble opiate drugs in structure and effects Play role in pain relief and response to stress Contribute to regulation of eating behavior	

© Cengage Learning

Muhammed Ali is a well-known victim of Parkinson's disease. Roughly one million Americans suffer from this disease, which is caused by a decline in the synthesis of the neurotransmitter dopamine. The reduction in dopamine synthesis occurs because of the deterioration of a structure located in the midbrain.

MONOAMINES

PsykTrek 2b, 4d

The *monoamines* include three neurotransmitters: dopamine, norepinephrine, and serotonin. Neurons using these transmitters regulate many aspects of everyday behavior. Dopamine (DA), for example, is used by neurons that control voluntary movements. The degeneration of such neurons apparently causes *Parkinson's disease,* a neurological illness marked by tremors, muscular rigidity, and reduced control over voluntary movements (DeLong, 2000).

Serotonin-releasing neurons appear to play a prominent role in the regulation of sleep and wakefulness (Monti, Jantos, & Monti, 2008) and eating behavior (Klump & Culbert, 2007). Considerable evidence also suggests that neural circuits using serotonin regulate aggressive behavior in animals, and some preliminary evidence relates serotonin activity to aggression in humans (Carrillo et al., 2009; Wallner & Machatschke, 2009).

Abnormal levels of monoamines in the brain have been related to the development of certain psychological disorders. For example, people who suffer from depression appear to have lowered levels of activation at norepinephrine (NE) and serotonin synapses. Although numerous other biochemical changes may also contribute to depression, abnormalities at NE and serotonin synapses appear to play a central role, as most antidepressant drugs exert their main effects at these synapses (Thase, 2009). Abnormalities in serotonin circuits have also been implicated as a factor in eating disorders, such as anorexia and bulimia (Halmi, 2008), and in obsessive-compulsive disorders (Hollander & Simeon, 2008).

In a similar fashion, the dopamine hypothesis asserts that abnormalities in activity at dopamine synapses play an important role in the development of *schizophrenia.* This severe mental illness is marked by irrational thought, hallucinations, poor contact with reality, and deterioration of routine adaptive behavior. Afflicting roughly 1% of the population, schizophrenia requires hospitalization more often than any other psychological disorder (see Chapter 14). Studies suggest, albeit with many complications, that overactivity at DA synapses is the neurochemical basis for schizophrenia (Javitt & Laruelle, 2006). Why? Primarily because the therapeutic drugs that tame schizophrenic symptoms are known to block some DA receptor sites and thus reduce dopamine activity (Minzenberg, Yoon, & Carter, 2008).

Temporary alterations at monoamine synapses also appear to account for the powerful effects of some widely abused drugs, including amphetamines and cocaine. These stimulant drugs seem to exert most of their effects by creating a storm of increased activity at dopamine and norepinephrine synapses (King & Ellinwood, 2005; Repetto & Gold, 2005). Some theorists believe that the rewarding effects of most abused drugs depend on increased activity in a particular dopamine pathway (Koob, Everitt, & Robbins, 2008; see Chapter 5). Furthermore, dysregulation in this dopamine pathway appears to be the chief factor underlying drug craving and addiction (Nestler & Malenka, 2004).

GABA

PsykTrek 2b

Another group of transmitters consists of *amino acids.* One transmitter in this group, *gamma-aminobutyric acid* (GABA), is notable in that it seems to produce only *inhibitory* postsynaptic potentials. Some transmitters, such as ACh and NE, are versatile. They can produce either excitatory or inhibitory PSPs, depending on the synaptic receptors they bind to. However, GABA appears to have inhibitory effects at virtually all synapses where it is present. GABA receptors are widely distributed in the brain and may be present at 40% of all synapses. GABA appears to be responsible for much of the inhibition in the central nervous system. Studies suggest that GABA is involved in the regulation of anxiety in humans and that disturbances in GABA circuits may contribute to some types of anxiety disorders (Garakani et al., 2009). GABA circuits also play a central role in the expression of some types of seizures (Shank, Smith-Swintosky, & Twyman, 2000), and they contribute to the modulation of sleep (Siegel, 2004).

ENDORPHINS

In 1970, after a horseback-riding accident, Candace Pert, a graduate student working with scientist Solomon Snyder, lay in a hospital bed receiving frequent shots of *morphine,* a painkilling drug derived from the opium plant. This experience left her with a driving curiosity about how morphine works. A few years later, she and Snyder rocked the scientific world by showing that *morphine exerts its effects by binding to specialized receptors in the brain* (Pert & Snyder, 1973).

This discovery raised a perplexing question: Why would the brain be equipped with receptors for morphine, a powerful, addictive opiate drug not normally found in the body? It occurred to Pert and others that the nervous system must have its own, endogenous (internally produced) morphinelike substances. Investigators dubbed these as-yet undiscovered substances *endorphins*—**internally produced chemicals that resemble opiates in structure and effects.** A search for the body's natural opiate ensued. Soon, a number of endogenous opioids were identified (Hughes et al., 1975). Subsequent studies revealed that endorphins and their receptors are widely distributed in the human body and that they clearly contribute to the modulation of pain (Apkarian et al., 2005; Basbaum & Jessell, 2000), as we will discuss in Chapter 4. Subsequent research has suggested that the endogenous opioids also contribute to the regulation of eating behavior and the body's response to stress (Adam & Epel, 2007).

The discovery of endorphins has led to new theories and findings on the neurochemical bases of pain and pleasure. In addition to their painkilling effects, opiate drugs such as morphine and heroin produce highly pleasurable feelings of euphoria, which explains why heroin is so widely abused. Researchers suspect that the body's natural endorphins may also be capable of producing feelings of pleasure. This capacity might explain why joggers sometimes experience a "runner's high." The pain caused by a long run may trigger the release of endorphins, which neutralize some of the pain and create a feeling of exhilaration (Harte, Eifert, & Smith, 1995). The long-held suspicion that endorphins might underlie the "runner's high" experience was supported in a recent study that used brain-imaging technology to track endorphin release in the brain (Boecker et al., 2008). Ten joggers were administered brain scans just before and just after a 2-hour endurance run. As hypothesized, the post-run brain scans showed a surge in the production of endorphins in selected areas of the participants' brains.

In this section we have highlighted just a few of the more interesting connections between neurotransmitters and behavior. But biochemical processes in the nervous system are incredibly complex. Although scientists have learned a great deal about neurotransmitters and behavior, much still remains to be discovered.

© paul prescott/Shutterstock

Organization of the Nervous System

KEY LEARNING GOALS

3.4 Distinguish between the central nervous system and the peripheral nervous system.

Clearly, communication in the nervous system is fundamental to behavior. So far we have looked at how individual cells communicate with one another. In this section, we examine the organization of the nervous system as a whole.

Experts believe that there are roughly *100 billion* neurons in the human brain (Kandel, 2000). Obviously, this is only an *estimate*. If you counted them nonstop at the rate of one per second, you'd be counting for over 3000 years! And, remember, most neurons have synaptic connections to many other neurons, so there may be *100 trillion* synapses in a human brain!

The fact that neurons are so abundant as to be uncountable is probably why it is widely believed that "we only use 10% of our brains." This curious tidbit of folk wisdom is utter nonsense (McBurney, 1996). If 90% of the human brain consists of unused

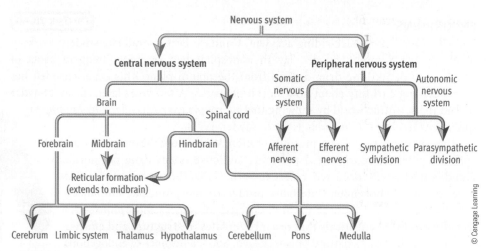

FIGURE 3.5

Organization of the human nervous system. This overview of the human nervous system shows the relationships of its various parts and systems. The brain is traditionally divided into three regions: the hindbrain, the midbrain, and the forebrain. The reticular formation runs through both the midbrain and the hindbrain on its way up and down the brainstem. These and other parts of the brain are discussed in detail later in the chapter. The peripheral nervous system is made up of the somatic nervous system, which controls voluntary muscles and sensory receptors, and the autonomic nervous system, which controls the involuntary activities of smooth muscles, blood vessels, and glands.

"excess baggage," localized brain damage would not be a problem much of the time. In reality, damage in even very tiny areas of brain usually has severe disruptive effects (Zillmer, Spiers, & Culbertson, 2008). Furthermore, brain-imaging research shows that even simple mental operations depend on activity spread across several or more areas in the brain. Even during sleep, the brain is highly active.

In any event, the multitudes of neurons in the nervous system have to work together to keep information flowing effectively. To see how the nervous system is organized to accomplish this task, we will divide it into parts. In many instances, the parts will be divided once again. **Figure 3.5** presents an organizational chart that shows the relationships among the major parts of the nervous system.

The Peripheral Nervous System

PSYKTREK 2a, 8c

The first and most important division separates the *central nervous system* (the brain and spinal cord) from the *peripheral nervous system*. The *peripheral nervous system* is made up of all those nerves that lie outside the brain and spinal cord. *Nerves* are

Concept Check 3.1

Linking Brain Chemistry to Behavior

Check your understanding of relations between brain chemistry and behavior by indicating which neurotransmitters or other biological chemicals have been linked to the phenomena listed below. Choose your answers from the following list: (a) acetylcholine, (b) norepinephrine, (c) dopamine, (d) serotonin, (e) endorphins. Indicate your choice (by letter) in the spaces on the left. You'll find the answers in Appendix A.

_____ 1. A transmitter involved in the regulation of sleep, eating, and aggression.

_____ 2. The two monoamines that have been linked to depression.

_____ 3. Chemicals that resemble opiate drugs in structure and that are involved in pain relief.

_____ 4. A neurotransmitter for which abnormal levels have been implicated in schizophrenia.

_____ 5. The only neurotransmitter between motor neurons and voluntary muscles.

bundles of neuron fibers (axons) that are routed together in the peripheral nervous system. This portion of the nervous system is just what it sounds like, the part that extends to the periphery (the outside) of the body. The peripheral nervous system can be subdivided into the somatic nervous system and the autonomic nervous system.

THE SOMATIC NERVOUS SYSTEM [PSYKTREK 2a]

The somatic nervous system lets you feel the world and move around in it. **The *somatic nervous system* is made up of nerves that connect to voluntary skeletal muscles and to sensory receptors.** These nerves are the cables that carry information from receptors in the skin, muscles, and joints to the central nervous system and that carry commands from the central nervous system to the muscles. These functions require two kinds of nerve fibers. *Afferent nerve fibers* **are axons that carry information inward to the central nervous system from the periphery of the body.** *Efferent nerve fibers* **are axons that carry information outward from the central nervous system to the periphery of the body.** Each body nerve contains many axons of each type. Thus, somatic nerves are "two-way streets" with incoming (afferent) and outgoing (efferent) lanes.

THE AUTONOMIC NERVOUS SYSTEM [PSYKTREK 2a, 8c]

The *autonomic nervous system (ANS)* **is made up of nerves that connect to the heart, blood vessels, smooth muscles, and glands.** As its name hints, the autonomic system is a separate (autonomous) system, although it is ultimately controlled by the central nervous system. The autonomic nervous system controls automatic, involuntary, visceral functions that people don't normally think about, such as heart rate, digestion, and perspiration (Powley, 2008).

The autonomic nervous system mediates much of the physiological arousal that occurs when people experience emotions. For example, imagine that you're arriving home alone one night when you notice that your front door is ajar and a window is broken. When you suspect that your home has been broken into, your heart rate and breathing speed up. As you cautiously make your way inside, your blood pressure may surge, you may get goosebumps, and your palms may begin to sweat. These difficult-to-control reactions are aspects of autonomic arousal. Walter Cannon (1932), one of the first psychologists to study this reaction, called it the *fight-or-flight response.* After Cannon carefully monitored this response in animals, he concluded that organisms generally respond to threat by preparing physically for attacking (fight) or fleeing (flight) the enemy.

The autonomic nervous system can be subdivided into two branches: the sympathetic division and the parasympathetic division (see **Figure 3.6**). **The *sympathetic division* is the branch of the autonomic nervous system that mobilizes the body's resources for emergencies.** It creates the fight-or-flight response. Activation of the sympathetic division slows digestive processes and drains blood from the periphery, lessening bleeding in the case of an injury. Key sympathetic nerves send signals to the adrenal glands, triggering the release of hormones that ready the body for

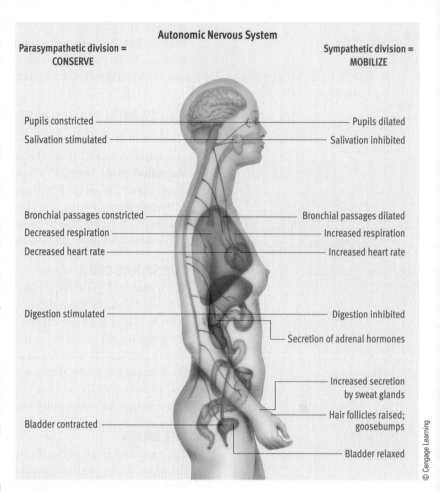

Autonomic Nervous System

Parasympathetic division = CONSERVE

Sympathetic division = MOBILIZE

Pupils constricted — Pupils dilated
Salivation stimulated — Salivation inhibited

Bronchial passages constricted — Bronchial passages dilated
Decreased respiration — Increased respiration
Decreased heart rate — Increased heart rate

Digestion stimulated — Digestion inhibited
— Secretion of adrenal hormones

— Increased secretion by sweat glands
— Hair follicles raised; goosebumps
Bladder contracted — Bladder relaxed

© Cengage Learning

FIGURE 3.6

The autonomic nervous system (ANS). The ANS is composed of the nerves that connect to the heart, blood vessels, smooth muscles, and glands. The ANS is divided into the sympathetic division, which mobilizes bodily resources in times of need, and the parasympathetic division, which conserves bodily resources. Some of the key functions controlled by each division of the ANS are summarized in the diagram.

© Werner Bollmann/Getty Images

exertion. In contrast, **the *parasympathetic division* is the branch of the autonomic nervous system that generally conserves bodily resources.** It activates processes that allow the body to save and store energy. For example, actions by parasympathetic nerves slow heart rate, reduce blood pressure, and promote digestion.

The Central Nervous System

PSYKTREK 2a

The central nervous system is the portion of the nervous system that lies within the skull and spinal column. Thus, **the *central nervous system (CNS)* consists of the brain and the spinal cord.** The CNS is bathed in its own special nutritive "soup," called *cerebrospinal fluid* (CSF). This fluid nourishes the brain and provides a protective cushion for it. Although derived from the blood, the CSF is carefully filtered. To enter the CSF, substances in the blood have to cross the *blood-brain barrier,* a semipermeable membrane that stops some chemicals, including drugs, from entering the CSF and affecting the brain.

THE SPINAL CORD

The *spinal cord* connects the brain to the rest of the body through the peripheral nervous system. Although the spinal cord looks like a cable from which the somatic nerves branch, it is part of the central nervous system. The spinal cord runs from the base of the brain to just below the level of the waist. It houses bundles of axons that carry the brain's commands to peripheral nerves and that relay sensations from the periphery of the body to the brain. Many forms of paralysis result from spinal cord damage, a fact that underscores the critical role it plays in transmitting signals from the brain to the neurons that move the body's muscles.

THE BRAIN

The crowning glory of the central nervous system is, of course, the *brain*. Anatomically, the *brain* is the part of the central nervous system that fills the upper portion of the skull. Although it weighs only about 3 pounds and could be held in one hand, the brain contains billions of interacting cells that integrate information from inside and outside the body, coordinate the body's actions, and enable people to talk, think, remember, plan, create, and dream. Because of its central importance for behavior, the brain is the subject of the next two sections of the chapter.

The Brain and Behavior

KEY LEARNING GOALS

3.5 Describe how lesioning, electrical stimulation, and various brain-imaging procedures are used to investigate brain function.

3.6 Know the principal functions of key structures in the brain.

3.7 Identify the four lobes in the cortex and their key functions, and summarize evidence on the brain's plasticity.

Scientists who want to find out how parts of the brain are related to behavior are faced with a formidable task, because mapping brain *function* requires a working brain. These scientists use a variety of specialized techniques to investigate brain-behavior relations. We will briefly discuss some of the innovative methods that permit scientists to look inside the brain and then outline the major findings of this research.

Looking Inside the Brain: Research Methods

PSYKTREK 2c

Researchers sometimes observe what happens when specific brain structures in animals are purposely disabled. *Lesioning* **involves destroying a piece of the brain.** It is typically done by inserting an electrode into a brain structure and passing a high-frequency electric current through it to burn the tissue and disable the structure. Another valuable technique is *electrical stimulation of the brain (ESB),* **which involves sending a weak electric current into a brain structure to stimulate (activate) it.** As with lesioning, the current is delivered through an implanted electrode, but the current is different. This sort of electrical stimulation does not exactly duplicate normal electrical signals in the brain. However, it is usually a close enough approximation to activate the brain struc-

(a) An X-ray beam and X-ray detector rotate around the patient's head, taking multiple X rays of a horizontal slice of the patient's brain.

X-ray source

Fan-shaped beam

X-ray detectors

© Cengage Learning

(b) A computer combines X rays to create an image of a horizontal slice of the brain. This scan shows a tumor (in red) on the right.

© Dan McCoy/Rainbow

FIGURE 3.7

CT technology. CT scans are used to examine aspects of brain structure. They provide computer-enhanced X rays of horizontal slices of the brain.

© SCOTT CAMAZINE/Getty Images

FIGURE 3.8

MRI scans. MRI scans can be used to produce remarkably high-resolution pictures of brain structure. A vertical view of a brain from the left side is shown here.

© NATIONAL CANCER INSTITUTE/SCIENCE PHOTO LIBRARY/Photo Researchers, Inc.

FIGURE 3.9

PET scans. PET scans are used to map brain activity rather than brain structure. They provide color-coded maps that show areas of high activity in the brain over time. The PET scan shown here pinpointed areas of high activity (indicated by the red and yellow colors) when a research participant was engaged in the production of speech.

tures in which the electrodes are lodged. Obviously, these invasive procedures are largely limited to animal research, although ESB is occasionally used on humans in the context of brain surgery required for medical purposes.

Fortunately, in recent decades, the invention of new brain-imaging devices has led to dramatic advances in scientists' ability to look inside the human brain (Raichle, 2006). The *CT (computerized tomography) scan* is a computer-enhanced X ray of brain structure. Multiple X rays are shot from many angles, and the computer combines the readings to create a vivid image of a horizontal slice of the brain (see **Figure 3.7**). The more recently developed *MRI (magnetic resonance imaging) scan* uses magnetic fields, radio waves, and computerized enhancement to map out brain structure. MRI scans provide much better images of brain structure than CT scans (Vythilingam et al., 2005), producing three-dimensional pictures of the brain that have remarkably high resolution (see **Figure 3.8**). Using CT and MRI scans, researchers have found abnormalities in brain structure among people suffering from specific types of mental illness, especially schizophrenia (Shenton & Kubicki, 2009; see Chapter 14).

In research on how brain and behavior are related, *PET (positron emission tomography) scans* have been especially valuable (Staley & Krystal, 2009). PET scans use radioactive markers to map chemical activity in the brain over time. Thus, a PET scan can provide a color-coded map indicating which areas of the brain become active when subjects clench their fist, sing, or contemplate the mysteries of the universe (see **Figure 3.9**). In efforts to pinpoint the brain areas that handle various types of mental tasks, neuroscientists are increasingly using *functional magnetic resonance imaging (fMRI),* which consists of several new variations on MRI technology that monitor blood flow and oxygen consumption in the brain to identify areas of high activity (Mason, Krystal, & Sanacora, 2009). This technology is exciting because, like PET scans, it can map actual *activity* in the brain over time, but with vastly greater precision. For example, using fMRI scans, researchers have identified patterns of brain activity associated with cocaine craving in cocaine addicts (Duncan et al., 2007), the contemplation of a loved one (Cheng et al., 2010), the visual recognition of shapes and textures (Stylianou-Korsnes et al., 2010), and the decision making required by risky gambles (Tom et al., 2007).

Now that we have discussed a few approaches to brain research, let's look at what scientists have discovered about the functions of various parts of the brain. The brain is divided into three major regions: the hindbrain, the midbrain, and the forebrain. The principal structures found in each of these regions are listed in the organizational chart of the nervous system in **Figure 3.5**. You can see where these regions are located in the brain by looking at **Figure 3.10** on the next page. They can be found easily in relation to the *brainstem*. The brainstem looks like its name—it appears to be a stem from which

FIGURE 3.10

Structures and areas in the human brain. (Top left) This photo of a human brain shows many of the structures discussed in this chapter. (Top right) The brain is divided into three major areas: the hindbrain, midbrain, and forebrain. These subdivisions actually make more sense for the brains of other animals than those of humans. In humans, the forebrain has become so large it makes the other two divisions look trivial. However, the hindbrain and midbrain aren't trivial; they control such vital functions as breathing, waking, and maintaining balance. (Bottom) This cross section of the brain highlights key structures and some of their principal functions. As you read about the functions of a brain structure, such as the corpus callosum, you may find visualizing it helpful.

PHOTO: Wadsworth collection

© Robert Kneschke/Shutterstock

Forebrain

Midbrain

Hindbrain

Cerebrum
Responsible for sensing, thinking, learning, emotion, consciousness, and voluntary movement

Corpus callosum
Bridge of fibers passing information between the two cerebral hemispheres

Amygdala
Part of limbic system involved in emotion and aggression

Thalamus
Relay center for cortex; handles incoming and outgoing signals

Hypothalamus
Responsible for regulating basic biological needs: hunger, thirst, temperature control

Cerebellum
Structure that coordinates fine muscle movement, balance

Pituitary gland
"Master" gland that regulates other endocrine glands

Pons
Involved in sleep and arousal

Reticular formation
Group of fibers that carry stimulation related to sleep and arousal through brainstem

Hippocampus
Part of limbic system involved in learning and memory

Medulla
Responsible for regulating largely unconscious functions such as breathing and circulation

Spinal cord
Responsible for transmitting information between brain and rest of body; handles simple reflexes

© Cengage Learning

the rest of the brain "flowers," like a head of cauliflower. At its lower end the stem is contiguous with the spinal cord. At its higher end it lies deep within the brain. We'll begin at the brain's lower end, where the spinal cord joins the brainstem. As we proceed upward, notice how the functions of brain structures go from the regulation of basic bodily processes to the control of "higher" mental processes.

The Hindbrain

PsykTrek 2d

The *hindbrain* **includes the cerebellum and two structures found in the lower part of the brainstem: the medulla and the pons.** The *medulla,* which attaches to the spinal cord, controls largely unconscious but essential functions, such as breathing, maintaining muscle tone, and regulating circulation. The *pons* (literally "bridge") includes a bridge of fibers that connects the brainstem with the cerebellum. The pons also contains several clusters of cell bodies involved with sleep and arousal.

The *cerebellum* **("little brain") is a relatively large and deeply folded structure adjacent to the back surface of the brainstem.** The cerebellum is involved in the coordination of movement and is critical to the sense of equilibrium, or physical balance (Mauk & Thach, 2008). Although the actual commands for muscular movements come from higher brain centers, the cerebellum plays a key role in the execution of these commands. It is your cerebellum that allows you to hold your hand out to the side and then smoothly bring your finger to a stop on your nose. This exercise is a useful roadside test for drunk driving because the cerebellum is one of the structures first depressed by alcohol. Damage to the cerebellum disrupts fine motor skills, such as those involved in writing, typing, or playing a musical instrument. Recent research has revealed that the cerebellum contributes to the control of other kinds of functions as well. Brain circuits running from the cerebellum to the prefrontal cortex appear to be involved in surprisingly higher-order functions, including attention, planning, and visual perception (Dum & Strick, 2009).

The Midbrain

PsykTrek 2d

The *midbrain* **is the segment of the brainstem that lies between the hindbrain and the forebrain.** The midbrain contains an area that is concerned with integrating sensory processes, such as vision and hearing (Stein, Wallace, & Stanford, 2000). An important system of dopamine-releasing neurons that projects into various higher brain centers originates in the midbrain. Among other things, this dopamine system is involved in the performance of voluntary movements. The decline in dopamine synthesis that causes Parkinson's disease is caused by degeneration of a structure located in the midbrain (DeLong, 2000).

Running through both the hindbrain and the midbrain is the *reticular formation.* Situated at the central core of the brainstem, the reticular formation contributes to the modulation of muscle reflexes, breathing, and pain perception (Saper, 2000). It is best known, however, for its role in the regulation of sleep and wakefulness. Activity in the ascending fibers of the reticular formation contributes to arousal (Coenen, 1998).

The Forebrain

PsykTrek 2e, 2f

The *forebrain* **is the largest and most complex region of the brain, encompassing a variety of structures, including the thalamus, hypothalamus, limbic system, and cerebrum.** This list is not exhaustive, and some of these structures have their own subdivisions, as you can see in the organizational chart of the nervous system (**Figure 3.5**). The thalamus, hypothalamus, and limbic system form the core of the forebrain. All three structures are located near the top of the brainstem. Above them is the *cerebrum*—the seat of complex thought. The wrinkled surface of the cerebrum is the *cerebral cortex*— the outer layer of the brain, the part that looks like a cauliflower.

THE THALAMUS: A RELAY STATION

PsykTrek 2e

The *thalamus* is a structure in the forebrain through which all sensory information (except smell) must pass to get to the cerebral cortex. This way station is made up of a number of clusters of cell bodies, or somas. Each cluster is concerned with relaying sensory information to a particular part of the cortex. However, it would be a mistake to characterize the thalamus as nothing more than a passive way station. The thalamus also appears to play an active role in integrating information from various senses.

THE HYPOTHALAMUS: A REGULATOR OF BIOLOGICAL NEEDS

PsykTrek 2e

The *hypothalamus* is a structure found near the base of the forebrain that is involved in the regulation of basic biological needs. It lies beneath the thalamus (*hypo* means "under," making the hypothalamus the area under the thalamus). Although no larger than a kidney bean, the hypothalamus contains various clusters of cells that have many key functions. One such function is to control the autonomic nervous system (Card, Swanson, & Moore, 2008). The hypothalamus also plays a major role in the regulation of basic biological drives related to survival, including the so-called "four F's": fighting, fleeing, feeding, and "mating."

THE LIMBIC SYSTEM: THE SEAT OF EMOTION

PsykTrek 2e

The *limbic system* is a loosely connected network of structures located roughly along the border between the cerebral cortex and deeper subcortical areas (hence the term *limbic,* which means "edge"). First described by Paul MacLean (1954), the limbic system is not a well-defined anatomical system with clear boundaries. Broadly speaking, it includes parts of the thalamus and hypothalamus, the *hippocampus,* the *amygdala,* and other nearby structures.

The *hippocampus* and adjacent structures clearly play a role in memory processes (Shrager & Squire, 2009). Some theorists believe that the hippocampal region is responsible for the *consolidation* of memories for factual information (Dudai, 2004). Consolidation involves the conversion of information into a durable memory code.

Similarly, there is ample evidence linking the limbic system to the experience of emotion, but the exact mechanisms of control are not yet well understood. Recent evidence suggests that the *amygdala* may play a central role in the learning of fear responses and the processing of other basic emotional responses (LeDoux, Schiller, & Cain, 2009; Phelps, 2006).

The limbic system also appears to contain emotion-tinged "pleasure centers." This intriguing possibility first surfaced, quite by chance, in brain stimulation research with rats. James Olds and Peter Milner (1954) accidentally discovered that a rat would press a lever repeatedly to send brief bursts of electrical stimulation to a specific spot in its brain where an electrode was implanted. Subsequent studies showed that rats and monkeys would press a lever *thousands of times* per hour to stimulate certain brain sites. Although the experimenters obviously couldn't ask the animals about it, they *inferred* that these self-stimulation sites produced some sort of pleasure.

Where are the pleasure centers located in the brain? Many of them have been found in the limbic system (Olds & Fobe, 1981). The heaviest concentration appears to be where the *medial forebrain bundle* (a bundle of axons) passes through the hypothalamus. The medial forebrain bundle is rich in dopamine-releasing neurons. The rewarding effects of ESB at self-stimulation sites may be largely mediated by the activation of these dopamine circuits (Koob et al., 2008). The pleasurable effects of opiates and stimulant drugs (cocaine and amphetamines) may also depend on excitation of this dopamine system (Wise, 1999, 2002). Recent evidence suggests that the so-called "pleasure centers" in the brain may not be anatomical centers so much as neural circuits releasing dopamine.

THE CEREBRUM: THE SEAT OF COMPLEX THOUGHT

PsykTrek 2f

The *cerebrum* is the largest and most complex part of the human brain. It includes the brain areas that are responsible for our most complex mental activities, including learning, remembering, thinking, and consciousness itself. **The *cerebral cortex* is the convoluted outer layer of the cerebrum.** The cortex is folded and bent, so that its large surface area—about 1.5 square feet—can be packed into the limited volume of the skull (Hubel & Wiesel, 1979).

The cerebrum is divided into two halves called hemispheres. Hence, **the *cerebral hemispheres* are the right and left halves of the cerebrum** (see **Figure 3.11**). The hemispheres are separated in the center of the brain by the longitudinal fissure (a split or crevice) that runs from the front to the back. This fissure descends to a thick band of fibers called the *corpus callosum* (also shown in **Figure 3.11**). **The *corpus callosum* is the major structure that connects the two cerebral hemispheres.** We'll discuss the functional specialization of the cerebral hemispheres in the next section of this chapter.

Each cerebral hemisphere is divided by deep fissures into four parts called *lobes.* To some extent, each of these lobes is dedicated to specific purposes. The location of these lobes can be seen in **Figure 3.12** on the next page.

The *occipital lobe,* at the back of the head, includes the cortical area where most visual signals are sent and visual processing is begun. This area is called the *primary visual cortex.* We will discuss how it is organized in Chapter 4.

The *parietal lobe* is forward of the occipital lobe. It includes the area that registers the sense of touch, called the *primary somatosensory cortex.* Various sections of this area receive signals from different regions of the body. When electrical stimulation is delivered in these parietal lobe areas, people report physical sensations—as if someone actually touched them on the arm or cheek, for example. The parietal lobe is also involved in integrating visual input and in monitoring the body's position in space.

The *temporal lobe* (meaning "near the temples") lies below the parietal lobe. Near its top, the temporal lobe contains an area devoted to auditory processing, the *primary auditory cortex.* As we will see momentarily, damage to an area in the temporal lobe on the left side of the brain can impair the ability to comprehend speech and language.

Continuing forward, we find the *frontal lobe,* the largest lobe in the human brain. It contains the principal areas that control the movement of muscles, the *primary motor cortex.* Electrical stimulation applied in these areas can cause actual muscle contractions. The amount of motor cortex allocated to the control of a body part depends not on the part's size but on the diversity and precision of its movements. Thus, more of the cortex is given to parts we have fine control over, such as the fingers, lips, and tongue. Less of the cortex is devoted to larger parts that make crude movements, such as the thighs and shoulders.

An area just forward of the primary motor cortex is where "mirror neurons" were first discovered accidentally in the mid-1990s. An Italian research team (Gallese et al., 1996)

Corpus callosum

© Cengage Learning

FIGURE 3.11

The cerebral hemispheres and the corpus callosum. In this drawing the cerebral hemispheres have been "pulled apart" to reveal the corpus callosum. This band of fibers is the communication bridge between the right and left halves of the human brain.

What areas of the brain are activated in these people?

© Apollofoto/Shutterstock

© photomak/Shutterstock

© Jason Stitt/Shutterstock

was recording activity in individual neurons as monkeys reached for various objects. A member of the team happened to reach out and pick up one of the designated objects, and much to his amazement the monkey's neuron fired just as it had when the monkey picked up the object itself. The researchers went on to find many such neurons in the frontal lobe, which they christened *mirror neurons*—**neurons that are activated by performing an action or by seeing another monkey or person perform the same action.** Research soon showed that humans also have mirror neuron circuits (Iacoboni & Dapretto, 2006; Rizzolatti & Craighero, 2004). Mirror neurons appear to provide a new model for understanding complex social cognition at a neural level. Recent research has suggested that mirror neurons may play a fundamental role in the acquisition of new motor skills (Buccino & Riggio, 2006); the imitation of others, which is crucial to much of human development (Rizzolatti, 2005); and the understanding of others' intentions and the ability to feel empathy for others (Kaplan & Iacoboni, 2006). Thus, the accidental discovery of mirror neurons may have a dramatic impact on brain-behavior research in the years to come.

The portion of the frontal lobe to the front of the motor cortex, called the *prefrontal cortex* (see the inset in **Figure 3.12**), is something of a mystery. This area is disproportionately large in humans, accounting for about one-third of the cerebral cortex (Huey, Krueger, & Grafman, 2006). Its apparent contribution to certain types of decision making (Summerfield & Koechlin, 2009) has led some theorists to suggest that the prefrontal cortex houses some sort of "executive control system," which is thought to monitor, organize, and direct thought processes (Beer, Shimamura, & Knight, 2004; Kane & Engle, 2002). Much remains to be learned, however, as the prefrontal cortex constitutes a huge

FIGURE 3.12

The cerebral cortex in humans. The cerebral cortex consists of right and left halves, called cerebral hemispheres. This diagram provides a view of the right hemisphere. Each cerebral hemisphere is divided into four lobes (which are highlighted in the bottom inset): the occipital lobe, the parietal lobe, the temporal lobe, and the frontal lobe. Each lobe has areas that handle particular functions, such as visual processing. The functions of the prefrontal cortex (see the inset) are something of a mystery, but they may include an executive control system that organizes and directs thought processes.

Primary somatosensory cortex

Primary motor cortex

Parietal lobe

Frontal lobe

Occipital lobe

Temporal lobe

Primary visual cortex

Primary auditory cortex

© Rob Wilkinson/Alamy

Prefrontal cortex

Parietal lobe

Frontal lobe

Occipital lobe

Temporal lobe

© Cengage Learning

chunk of the brain with many subareas whose specific functions are still being worked out (Miller & Wallis, 2008).

The Plasticity of the Brain

It was once believed that significant changes in the anatomy and organization of the brain were limited to early periods of development in both humans and animals. However, research has gradually demonstrated that the anatomical structure and functional organization of the brain are more flexible or "plastic" than widely assumed (Pascual-Leone, 2009). This conclusion is based on several lines of research.

First, studies have shown that aspects of experience can sculpt features of brain structure. For example, neuroimaging studies have shown that subjects given three months to practice and master a juggling routine show structural changes in brain areas known to handle the processing of visual and motor tasks (Draganski et al., 2004). *Second, research has shown that damage to incoming sensory pathways or the destruction of brain tissue can lead to neural reorganization.* For example, when scientists amputated the third finger in an owl monkey, the part of its cortex that formerly responded to the third finger gradually became responsive to the second and fourth fingers (Kaas, 2000). And in some blind people, areas in the occipital lobe that are normally dedicated to visual processing are "recruited" to help with verbal processing (Amedi et al., 2004).

Third, studies now indicate that the adult brain can generate new neurons (Gage, 2002). Until relatively recently it was believed that *neurogenesis—the formation of new neurons*—did not occur in adult humans. It was thought that the brain formed all its neurons by infancy at the latest (Gross, 2000). However, new evidence suggests that adult humans and monkeys can form new neurons in the olfactory bulb and the hippocampus (DiCicco-Bloom & Falluel-Morel, 2009). Furthermore, Elizabeth Gould (2004) and her colleagues have found that adult monkeys form *thousands* of new brain cells each day in an area of the hippocampus called the dentate gyrus. These new neurons then migrate to areas in the cortex where they sprout axons and form new synapses with existing neurons, becoming fully integrated into the brain's communication networks. Neuroscientists are now scrambling to figure out the functional significance of neurogenesis. Some theorists believe that it might contribute to the natural repair processes that occur after brain damage (Kozorovitskiy & Gould, 2007). Neurogenesis may also play an important role in learning and memory (Leuner, Gould, & Shors, 2006; see Chapter 7).

In sum, research suggests that the brain is not "hard wired" the way a computer is. It appears that the neural wiring of the brain is flexible and constantly evolving. That said, this plasticity is not unlimited. Rehabilitation efforts with people who have suffered brain damage clearly demonstrate that there are limits on the extent to which the brain can rewire itself (Zillmer et al., 2008). And the evidence suggests that the brain's plasticity declines with increasing age (Rains, 2002). Younger brains are more flexible than older brains. Still, the neural circuits of the brain show substantial plasticity, which certainly helps organisms to adapt to their environments.

Right Brain/Left Brain: Cerebral Specialization

As noted in the previous section. the cerebrum—the seat of complex thought—is divided into two separate hemispheres (see **Figure 3.11**). Recent decades have seen an exciting flurry of research on the specialized abilities of the right and left cerebral hemispheres. Some theorists have gone so far as to suggest that people really have two brains in one!

Broca's area
Wernicke's area

© Siri Stafford/Getty Images

FIGURE 3.13

Language processing in the brain. This view of the left hemisphere highlights the location of two centers for language processing in the brain: Broca's area, which is involved in speech production, and Wernicke's area, which is involved in language comprehension.

Courtesy of the Archives, California Institute of Technology

Roger Sperry

"Both the left and right hemispheres of the brain have been found to have their own specialized forms of intellect."

Hints of this hemispheric specialization have been available for many years, from cases in which one side of a person's brain has been damaged. The left hemisphere was implicated in the control of language as early as 1861, by Paul Broca, a French surgeon. Broca was treating a patient who had been unable to speak for 30 years. After the patient died, Broca showed that the probable cause of his speech deficit was a small lesion on the left side of the frontal lobe. Since then, many similar cases have shown that this area of the brain—known as *Broca's area*—plays an important role in the production of speech (see **Figure 3.13**). Another major language center—*Wernicke's area*—was identified in the temporal lobe of the left hemisphere in 1874. Damage in Wernicke's area (also shown in **Figure 3.13**) usually leads to problems with the *comprehension* of language.

Evidence that the left hemisphere usually processes language led scientists to characterize it as the "dominant" hemisphere. Because thoughts are usually coded in terms of language, the left hemisphere was given the lion's share of credit for handling the "higher" mental processes, such as reasoning, remembering, planning, and problem solving. Meanwhile, the right hemisphere came to be viewed as the "nondominant," or "dumb," hemisphere, lacking any special functions or abilities.

This characterization of the left and right hemispheres as major and minor partners in the brain's work began to change in the 1960s. It all started with landmark research by Roger Sperry, Michael Gazzaniga, and their colleagues who studied "split-brain" patients: individuals whose cerebral hemispheres had been surgically disconnected (Gazzaniga, 1970; Gazzaniga, Bogen, & Sperry, 1965; Levy, Trevarthen, & Sperry, 1972; Sperry, 1982). In 1981 Sperry received a Nobel prize in physiology/medicine for this work.

Bisecting the Brain: Split-Brain Research

PsykTrek SIM2, 2f

In *split-brain surgery* the bundle of fibers that connects the cerebral hemispheres (the **corpus callosum) is cut to reduce the severity of epileptic seizures.** It is a radical procedure that is chosen only in exceptional cases that have not responded to other forms of treatment (Wolford, Miller, & Gazzaniga, 2004). But the surgery provides scientists with an unusual opportunity to study people who have had their brain literally split in two.

To appreciate the logic of split-brain research, you need to understand how sensory and motor information is routed to and from the two hemispheres. *Each hemisphere's primary connections are to the opposite side of the body.* Thus, the left hemisphere controls, and communicates with, the right hand, right arm, right leg, right eyebrow, and so on. In contrast, the right hemisphere controls, and communicates with, the left side of the body.

Vision and hearing are more complex. Both eyes deliver information to both hemispheres, but input is still separated. Stimuli in the right half of the visual field are registered by receptors on the left side of each eye, which send signals to the left hemisphere. Stimuli in the left half of the visual field are transmitted by both eyes to the right hemisphere (see **Figure 3.14**). Auditory inputs to each ear also go to both hemispheres. However, connections to the opposite hemisphere are stronger or more immediate. That is, sounds presented to the right ear are registered in the left hemisphere first, while sounds presented to the left ear are registered more quickly in the right hemisphere.

For the most part, people don't notice this asymmetric, "crisscrossed" organization because the two hemispheres are in close communication with each other. Information received by one hemisphere is readily shared with the other via the corpus callosum. However, when the two hemispheres are surgically disconnected, the functional specialization of the brain becomes apparent.

In their classic study of split-brain patients, Gazzaniga, Bogen, and Sperry (1965) presented visual stimuli such as pictures, symbols, and words in a single visual field (the left or the right), so that the stimuli would be sent to only one hemisphere. The stimuli were projected onto a screen in front of the subjects, who stared at a fixation point (a spot) in the center of the screen. The images were flashed to the right or the left of the fixation point for only a split second. Thus, the subjects did not have a chance to move their eyes, and the stimuli were glimpsed in only one visual field.

When pictures were flashed in the right visual field and thus sent to the left hemisphere, the split-brain subjects were able to name and describe the objects depicted (such as a cup or spoon). However, the subjects were *not* able to name and describe the same objects when they were flashed in the left visual field and sent to the right hemisphere. These findings supported the notion that language is housed in the left hemisphere.

Although the split-brain subjects' right hemisphere was not able to speak up for itself, further tests revealed that it was processing the information presented. If subjects were given an opportunity to *point out a picture* of an object that had been flashed to the left visual field, they were able to do so. Furthermore, the right hemisphere (left hand) turned out to be *superior* to the left hemisphere (right hand) in assembling little puzzles and copying drawings, even though the subjects were right-handed. These findings provided the first compelling demonstration that the right hemisphere has its own special talents. Subsequent studies of additional split-brain patients showed the right hemisphere to be better than the left on a variety of visual-spatial tasks, including discriminating colors, arranging blocks, and recognizing faces.

Hemispheric Specialization in the Intact Brain   PsykTrek sim2, 2f

The problem with the split-brain operation, of course, is that it creates a highly abnormal situation. Moreover, the surgery is done only with people who suffer from prolonged, severe cases of epilepsy. These people may have had somewhat atypical brain organization even before the operation. Moreover, the number of split-brain patients has been quite small; only ten split-brain patients have been studied intensively (Gazzaniga, 2008). Thus, theorists couldn't help wondering whether it was safe to generalize broadly from the split-brain studies. For this reason, researchers developed methods that allowed them to study cerebral specialization in the intact brain.

One method involves looking at left-right imbalances in visual or auditory processing, called *perceptual asymmetries*. As we have seen, it is possible to present visual stimuli to just one visual field at a time. In normal individuals, the input sent to one hemisphere is quickly shared with the other. However, subtle differences in the "abilities" of the two hemispheres can be detected by precisely measuring how long it takes subjects to recognize different types of stimuli. For instance, when verbal stimuli are presented to the right visual field (and thus sent to the *left hemisphere* first), they are identified more quickly and more accurately than when they are presented to the left visual field (and sent to the right hemisphere first). The faster reactions in the left

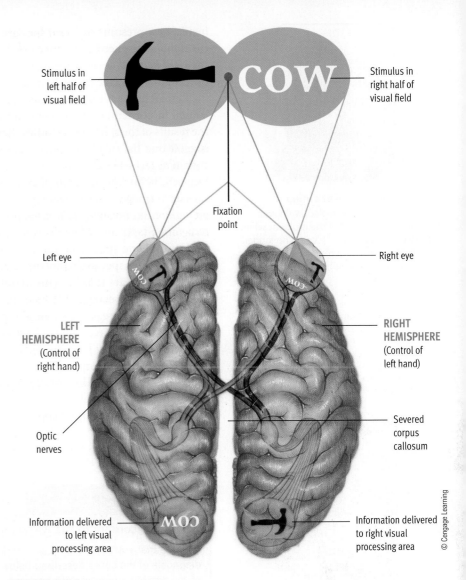

FIGURE 3.14

Visual input in the split brain. If a participant stares at a fixation point, the point divides the subject's visual field into right and left halves. Input from the right visual field (the word *cow* in this example) strikes the left side of each eye and is transmitted to the left hemisphere. Input from the left visual field (a picture of a hammer in this example) strikes the right side of each eye and is transmitted to the right hemisphere. Normally, the hemispheres share the information from the two halves of the visual field, but in split-brain patients, the corpus callosum is severed, and the two hemispheres cannot communicate. Hence, the experimenter can present a visual stimulus to just one hemisphere at a time.

Michael Gazzaniga

"Nothing can possibly replace a singular memory of mine: that of the moment when I discovered that case W. J. could no longer verbally describe (from his left hemisphere) stimuli presented to his freshly disconnected right hemisphere."

Courtesy of Michael S. Gazzaniga

hemisphere presumably occur because it can recognize verbal stimuli on its own, while the right hemisphere has to take extra time to "consult" the left hemisphere. In contrast, the *right hemisphere* is faster than the left on *visual-spatial* tasks, such as locating a dot or recognizing a face (Bradshaw, 1989; Bryden, 1982).

Researchers have used a variety of other approaches to explore hemispheric specialization in normal people. For the most part, their findings have converged nicely with the results of the split-brain studies (Reuter-Lorenz & Miller, 1998). Overall, the findings suggest that the two hemispheres are specialized, with each handling certain types of cognitive tasks better than the other (Corballis, 2003; Gazzaniga, 2005; Springer & Deutsch, 1998). *The left hemisphere is usually better on tasks involving verbal processing, such as language, speech, reading, and writing. The right hemisphere exhibits superiority on many tasks involving nonverbal processing, such as most spatial, musical, and visual recognition tasks, including the perception of emotions.*

Hemispheric specialization is not unique to humans, as it has been observed in a variety of other species (Vallortigara & Rogers, 2005). Although comparisons are complicated, it appears that humans manifest more cerebral specialization than other animals. Theorists speculate that hemispheric specialization is adaptive in an evolutionary sense in that it increases the neural capacity of the brain (Hopkins & Cantalupo, 2008). Interestingly, when researchers have studied variations in the strength of hemispheric specialization among humans, they have found links between weak lateralization and certain negative outcomes. For instance, weak lateralization has been associated with lower IQ scores (Corballis, Hattie, & Fletcher, 2008) and with elevated vulnerability to schizophrenia (Spironelli, Angrilli, & Stegagno, 2008). However, much remains to be learned about these intriguing correlations.

Concept Check 3.2

Relating Disorders to the Nervous System

Imagine that you are working as a neuropsychologist at a clinic. You are involved in the diagnosis of the cases described below. You are asked to identify the probable cause(s) of the disorders in terms of nervous system malfunctions. Based on the information in this chapter, indicate the probable location of any brain damage or the probable disturbance of neurotransmitter activity. The answers can be found in the back of the book in Appendix A.

Case 1. Miriam is exhibiting language deficits. In particular, she does not seem to comprehend the meaning of words. _____
_____
_____

Case 2. Camille displays tremors and muscular rigidity and is diagnosed as having Parkinson's disease. _____
_____
_____

Case 3. Ricardo, a 28-year-old computer executive, has gradually seen his strength and motor coordination deteriorate badly. He is diagnosed as having multiple sclerosis.
_____
_____

Case 4. Wendy is highly irrational, has poor contact with reality, and reports hallucinations. She is given a diagnosis of schizophrenic disorder. _____
_____
_____

© michaeljung/Shutterstock

The specialization of the right and left halves of the brain is a burgeoning area of research that has broad implications, which we will discuss further in the Personal Application. For now, however, let's leave the brain and turn our attention to the endocrine system.

The Endocrine System: Another Way to Communicate

KEY LEARNING GOALS

3.10 Identify the key elements of the endocrine system, and describe ways in which hormones regulate behavior.

The major way the brain communicates with the rest of the body is through the nervous system. However, the body has a second communication system that is also important to behavior. **The *endocrine system* consists of glands that secrete chemicals into the bloodstream that help control bodily functioning.** The messengers in this communication network are called hormones. *Hormones* **are the chemical substances released by the endocrine glands.** In a way, hormones are much like neurotransmitters in the nervous system, but they can't match the high speed of neural transmission and they tend to be less specific, as they often act on many target cells throughout the body. The major endocrine glands and their functions are shown in **Figure 3.15**. Hormone release tends to be *pulsatile*. That is, hormones tend to be released several times per day in brief bursts that last only a few minutes.

Much of the endocrine system is controlled by the nervous system through the *hypothalamus*. This structure at the base of the forebrain has intimate connections with the pea-sized *pituitary gland,* to which it is adjacent. **The *pituitary gland* releases a great variety of hormones that fan out within the body, stimulating actions in the other endocrine glands.** In this sense, the pituitary is the "master gland" of the endocrine system, although the hypothalamus is the real power behind the throne.

The intermeshing of the nervous system and the endocrine system can be seen in the fight-or-flight response described earlier. In times of stress, the hypothalamus sends signals along two pathways—through the autonomic nervous system and through the pituitary gland—to the adrenal glands (Clow, 2001). In response, the adrenal glands secrete hormones that radiate throughout the body, preparing it to cope with an emergency.

A topic of current research interest centers on the effects of *oxytocin*—**a hormone released by the pituitary gland, which regulates reproductive behaviors.** Oxytocin has long been known to trigger contractions when a woman gives birth and to stimulate the mammary glands to release milk for breastfeeding (Donaldson & Young, 2008). However, newer research suggests that this hormone has far-reaching effects on complex social behavior. For example, an extensive body of research indicates that oxytocin fosters adult-adult pair bonding in many mammals (Lim & Young, 2006), and preliminary research suggests that similar effects may be found in humans (Bartz & Hollander, 2006; Donaldson & Young, 2008). In one study male participants worked on a task in which they tried to infer

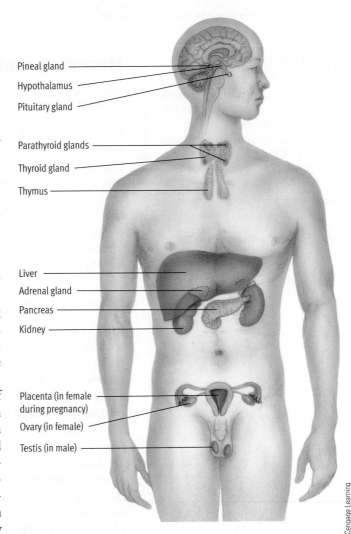

Pineal gland
Hypothalamus
Pituitary gland
Parathyroid glands
Thyroid gland
Thymus
Liver
Adrenal gland
Pancreas
Kidney
Placenta (in female during pregnancy)
Ovary (in female)
Testis (in male)

© Cengage Learning

FIGURE 3.15

The endocrine system. This graphic depicts most of the major endocrine glands. The endocrine glands secrete hormones into the bloodstream. These hormones regulate a variety of physical functions and affect many aspects of behavior.

people's mental states from subtle social cues, thus measuring their empathy. Performance was enhanced when subjects inhaled an oxytocin spray prior to working on this "mind-reading" task (Domes et al., 2007). Another study found that oxytocin increased males' empathy levels in response to photos of emotional situations (Hurlemann et al., 2010).

Recent research also suggests that oxytocin may foster trust in humans. In one fascinating study, male students participated in an investment-bargaining simulation in which the "investors" could send a portion of their financial stake to a "trustee," which tripled the money, but then they had to *hope* that the trustee would send a decent portion of the investment back to them (Kosfeld et al., 2005). Investors who inhaled an oxytocin spray before the simulation were far more trusting and sent more money to the trustees than control subjects. Other studies have also found a link between oxytocin and trusting behavior (Morhenn et al., 2008; Zak, Kurzban, & Matzner, 2005).

Research suggests that oxytocin, a hormone released by the pituitary gland, may help to foster empathy and trust in humans.

KEY LEARNING GOALS

3.11 Describe basic structures involved in genetic transmission, and discuss the nature of polygenic traits.

3.12 Compare the special methods used to investigate the influence of heredity, and discuss how heredity and environment interact.

Heredity and Behavior: Is It All in the Genes?

Most people realize that physical characteristics such as height, hair color, blood type, and eye color are largely shaped by heredity. But what about psychological characteristics, such as intelligence, moodiness, impulsiveness, and shyness? To what extent are people's behavioral qualities molded by their genes? As we saw in Chapter 1, questions about the relative importance of heredity versus environment are very old ones in psychology. The nature versus nurture debate will continue to surface in many of the upcoming chapters. To help you appreciate the complexities of this debate, we will outline some basic principles of genetics and describe the methods that investigators use to assess the effects of heredity.

Basic Principles of Genetics

Every cell in your body contains enduring messages from your mother and father. These messages are found on the *chromosomes* that lie within the nucleus of each cell. *Chromosomes* **are threadlike strands of DNA (deoxyribonucleic acid) molecules that carry genetic information.** With the exception of sex cells (sperm and eggs), every cell in humans contains 46 chromosomes. These chromosomes operate in 23 pairs, with one chromosome of each pair coming from each parent. Each chromosome, in turn, contains thousands of biochemical messengers called genes. *Genes* **are DNA segments that serve as the key functional units in hereditary transmission.**

If all offspring are formed by a union of the parents' sex cells, why aren't family members identical clones? The reason is that a single pair of parents can produce an extraordinary variety of combinations of chromosomes. Each parent's 23 chromosome pairs can be scrambled in over 8 million (2^{23}) different ways, yielding roughly 70 trillion possible configurations when sperm and egg unite. Thus, genetic transmission is a complicated process, and everything is a matter of probability. Except for identical twins, each person ends up with a unique genetic blueprint.

Although different combinations of genes explain why family members aren't all alike, the overlap among these combinations explains why family members do tend to resemble one another. Members of a family share more of the same genes than nonmembers (see **Figure 3.16**). The genetic overlap for identical twins is 100%. Parents and their children, and full siblings including fraternal twins, share 50% of their genes. More-distant relatives share smaller proportions of genes. For example, the genetic overlap between people and their grandparents, uncles, and aunts is 25%. First cousins' genetic overlap is 12.5%.

Like chromosomes, genes operate in pairs, with one gene of each pair coming from each parent. In the simplest scenario, a single pair of genes determines a trait. However, most human characteristics appear to be *polygenic traits,* **or characteristics that are influenced by more than one pair of genes.** For example, three to five gene pairs are thought to interactively determine skin color. Complex physical abilities, such as motor coordination, may be influenced by tangled interactions among a great many pairs of genes. Most psychological characteristics that appear to be affected by heredity seem to involve complex polygenic inheritance (Plomin et al., 2001).

Detecting Hereditary Influence: Research Methods PsykTrek 7d

How do scientists disentangle the effects of genetics and experience to determine how heredity affects human behavior? Researchers have designed special types of studies to assess the impact of heredity. The three most important methods are family studies, twin studies, and adoption studies.

FAMILY STUDIES PsykTrek 7d

In *family studies* researchers assess hereditary influence by examining blood relatives to see how much they resemble one another on a specific trait. If heredity affects the trait under scrutiny, researchers should find trait similarity among relatives. Furthermore, they should find more similarity among relatives who share more genes. For instance, siblings should exhibit more similarity than cousins.

Illustrative of this method are the numerous family studies conducted to assess the contribution of heredity to the development of schizophrenic disorders. These disorders strike approximately 1% of the population, yet 9% of the siblings of schizophrenic patients exhibit schizophrenia themselves (Gottesman, 1991). Thus, these first-degree relatives of schizophrenic patients show a risk for the disorder that is nine times higher than normal. This risk is greater than that observed for second-degree relatives, such as nieces and nephews (4%), which is greater than that found for third-degree relatives, such as first cousins (2%), and so on. This pattern of results supports the hypothesis that genetic inheritance influences the development of schizophrenic disorders (Kirov & Owen, 2009).

Family studies can indicate whether a trait runs in families. However, this correlation does not provide conclusive evidence that the trait is influenced by heredity. Why not? Because family members generally share not only genes but also similar environments. Furthermore, closer relatives are more likely to live together than distant relatives. Thus, genetic similarity and environmental similarity both tend to be greater for closer relatives. Either of these confounded variables could be responsible when greater

Relationship	Degree of relatedness	Genetic overlap
Identical twins		100%
Fraternal twins Brother or sister Parent or child	First-degree relatives	50%
Grandparent or grandchild Uncle, aunt, nephew, or niece Half-bother or half-sister	Second-degree relatives	25%
First cousin	Third-degree relatives	12.5%
Second cousin	Fourth-degree relatives	6.25%
Unrelated		0%

© Cengage Learning

FIGURE 3.16

Genetic relatedness. Research on the genetic bases of behavior takes advantage of the different degrees of genetic relatedness between various types of relatives. If heredity influences a trait, relatives who share more genes should be more similar with regard to that trait than are more distant relatives, who share fewer genes. Comparisons involving various degrees of biological relationships will come up frequently in later chapters.

trait similarity is found in closer relatives. Family studies can offer useful insights about the possible impact of heredity, but they cannot provide definitive evidence.

TWIN STUDIES

PsykTrek 7d

Twin studies can yield better evidence about the possible role of genetic factors. In *twin studies* researchers assess hereditary influence by comparing the resemblance of identical twins and fraternal twins with respect to a trait. *Identical (monozygotic) twins* emerge when a single fertilized egg splits for unknown reasons. Thus, they have exactly the same genetic blueprint; their genetic overlap is 100%. *Fraternal (dizygotic) twins* result when two separate eggs are fertilized simultaneously. Fraternal twins are no more alike in genetic makeup than any two siblings born to a pair of parents at different times. Their genetic overlap averages 50%.

Fraternal twins provide a useful comparison to identical twins because in both cases the twins usually grow up in the same home, at the same time, exposed to the same configuration of relatives, neighbors, peers, teachers, events, and so forth. Thus, both kinds of twins normally develop under equally similar environmental conditions. However, identical twins share more genetic kinship than fraternal twins. Consequently, if sets of identical twins tend to exhibit more similarity on a trait than sets of fraternal twins do, it is reasonable to infer that this greater similarity is probably due to heredity.

Twin studies have been conducted to assess the impact of heredity on a variety of traits. For example, researchers have found that identical twins tend to be more similar to each other than fraternal twins on measures of general intelligence and measures of specific personality traits, such as extraversion (see **Figure 3.17**; Plomin et al., 2008). These results support the notion that these traits are influenced to some degree by genetic makeup.

ADOPTION STUDIES

PsykTrek 7d

Adoption studies assess hereditary influence by examining the resemblance between adopted children and both their biological and their adoptive parents. If adopted children resemble their biological parents on a trait, even though they were not raised by them, genetic factors probably influence that trait. In contrast, if adopted children resemble their adoptive parents, even though they inherited no genes from them, environmental factors probably influence the trait.

In recent years, adoption studies have contributed to science's understanding of how genetics and the environment influence intelligence. The research shows modest similarity between adopted children and their biological parents, as indicated by an average

FIGURE 3.17

Twin studies of intelligence and personality. Identical twins trend to be more similar than fraternal twins (as reflected in higher correlations) with regard to intelligence and specific personality traits, such as extraversion. These findings suggest that intelligence and personality are influenced by heredity. (Data from Plomin et al., 2001)

correlation of .24 (McGue et al., 1993). Interestingly, adopted children resemble their adoptive parents just as much (also an average correlation of .24). These findings suggest that both heredity and environment have an influence on intelligence.

The Interplay of Heredity and Environment

We began this section by asking, is it all in the genes? When it comes to behavioral traits, the answer clearly is no. According to Robert Plomin (1993, 2004), perhaps the leading behavioral genetics researcher in the last decade, what scientists find again and again is that heredity and experience *jointly* influence most aspects of behavior. Moreover, their effects are interactive—they play off each other (Gottesman & Hanson, 2005; Rutter, 2006, 2007).

For example, consider what researchers have learned about the development of schizophrenic disorders. Although the evidence indicates that genetic factors influence the development of schizophrenia, it does not appear that anyone directly inherits the disorder itself. Rather, what people seem to inherit is a certain degree of *vulnerability* to the disorder (McDonald & Murphy, 2003). Whether this vulnerability is ever converted into an actual disorder depends on each person's experiences in life. Thus, as Danielle Dick and Richard Rose (2002) put it in a review of behavioral genetics research, "Genes confer dispositions, not destinies" (p. 73).

In recent years, research in the emerging field of *epigenetics* has only served to further demonstrate that genetic and environmental factors are inextricably intertwined. *Epigenetics* **is the study of heritable changes in gene expression that do not involve modifications to the DNA sequence.** It turns out that specific genes' effects can be dampened or silenced by chemical events at the cellular level, leading to alterations in traits, health, and behavior (Tsankova et al., 2007). Moreover, these chemical events can be stimulated by environmental events, such as poor nurturance when offspring are young, exposure to stress, or peculiarities in diet (McGowan, Meaney, & Szyf, 2008). What has surprised scientists is that these *epigenetic marks* that influence gene expression can be passed on to successive generations (Masterpasqua, 2009). Theorists suspect that epigenetic changes may contribute to a variety of psychological disorders, including schizophrenia (Zhang & Meaney, 2010). The finding that genes themselves are not exempt from environmental influence has a number of far-reaching implications. Among other things, it means that efforts to quantify the influence of heredity versus environment, informative though they may be, are ultimately artificial (Lickliter, 2009).

The Evolutionary Bases of Behavior

KEY LEARNING GOALS

3.13 Understand the key insights that represent the essence of Darwin's theory of evolution.

3.14 Describe subsequent refinements to evolutionary theory, and give some examples of animal behavior that represent adaptations.

To round out our look at the biological bases of behavior, we need to discuss how evolutionary forces have shaped many aspects of human and animal behavior. As you may recall from Chapter 1, *evolutionary psychology* is a relatively new theoretical perspective in the field that analyzes behavioral processes in terms of their adaptive significance. In this section, we will outline some basic principles of evolutionary theory and relate them to animal behavior. These ideas will create a foundation for forthcoming chapters, where we'll see how these principles can enhance our understanding of many aspects of human behavior.

Darwin's Insights

Charles Darwin, the legendary British naturalist, was *not* the first person to describe the process of evolution. Well before Darwin's time, other biologists who had studied the earth's fossil record noted that various species appeared to have undergone gradual

Michael Woodruff/Shutterstock

changes over the course of a great many generations. What Darwin contributed in his landmark book, *The Origin of Species* (1859), was a creative, new explanation for *how and why* evolutionary changes unfold over time. He identified *natural selection* as the engine that fuels the process of evolution (Dewsbury, 2009).

The mystery that Darwin set out to solve was complicated. He wanted to explain how the characteristics of a species might change over generations and why these changes tended to be surprisingly adaptive. In other words, he wanted to shed light on why organisms tend to have characteristics that serve them well in the context of their environments. How did giraffes acquire their long necks that allow them to reach high into acacia trees to secure their main source of food? How did woodpeckers develop their sharp, chisel-shaped beaks that permit them to probe trees for insects so effectively? Darwin's explanation for the seemingly purposive nature of evolution centered on four main insights.

First, he noted that organisms vary in endless ways, such as size, speed, strength, aspects of appearance, visual abilities, hearing capacities, digestive processes, cell structure, and so forth. Second, he noted that some of these characteristics are heritable—that is, they are passed down from one generation to the next. Although genes and chromosomes had not yet been discovered, the concept of heredity was well established. Third, borrowing from the work of Thomas Malthus, he noted that organisms tend to produce offspring at a pace that outstrips the local availability of food supplies, living space, and other important resources. As a population increases and resources dwindle, the competition for precious resources intensifies. Thus, it occurred to Darwin—and this was his grand insight—that variations in hereditary traits might affect organisms' ability to obtain the resources necessary for survival and reproduction. Fourth, building on this insight, Darwin argued that if a specific heritable trait contributes to an organism's survival or reproductive success, organisms with that trait should produce more offspring than those without the trait (or those with less of the trait), and the prevalence of that trait should gradually increase over generations—resulting in evolutionary change.

Although evolution is widely characterized as a matter of "survival of the fittest," Darwin recognized from the beginning that survival is important only insofar as it relates to reproductive success. Indeed, in evolutionary theory, *fitness* **refers to the reproductive success (number of descendants) of an individual organism relative to the average reproductive success in the population.** *Variations in reproductive success are what really fuels evolutionary change.* But survival is crucial because organisms typically need to mature and thrive before they can reproduce. So, Darwin theorized

© Bettmann/Corbis

Charles Darwin

"Can we doubt (remembering that many more individuals are born than can possibly survive) that individuals having any advantage, however slight, over others, would have the best chance of surviving and procreating their kind? . . . This preservation of favourable variations and the rejection of injurious variations, I call Natural Selection."

© Ienetstan/Shutterstock

Concept Check 3.3

Recognizing Hereditary Influence

Check your understanding of the methods scientists use to explore hereditary influences on specific behavioral traits by filling in the blanks in the descriptive statements below. The answers can be found in the back of the book in Appendix A.

1. The findings from family studies indicate that heredity may influence a trait if _____ show more trait similarity than _____.

2. The findings from twin studies suggest that heredity influences a trait if _____ show more trait similarity than _____.

3. The findings from adoption studies suggest that heredity influences a trait if children adopted at a young age share more trait similarity with their _____ than their _____.

4. The findings from family studies, twin studies, and adoption studies suggest that heredity does not influence a trait when _____ is not related to _____.

that there ought to be two ways in which traits might contribute to evolution: by providing either a survival advantage or a reproductive advantage. For example, a turtle's shell has great protective value that provides a survival advantage. In contrast, a firefly's emission of light is a courtship overture that provides a reproductive advantage.

To summarize, the principle of *natural selection* posits that heritable characteristics that provide a survival or reproductive advantage are more likely than alternative characteristics to be passed on to subsequent generations and thus they come to be "selected" over time. Please note, the process of natural selection works on *populations* rather than *individual organisms.* Evolution occurs when the gene pool in a population changes gradually as a result of selection pressures. Although there are occasional exceptions (Gould & Eldredge, 1977), this process tends to be extremely gradual—it generally takes thousands to millions of generations for one trait to be selected over another.

Darwin's theory had at least two important, far-reaching implications (Buss, 2009). First, it suggested that the awe-inspiring diversity of life is the result of an unplanned, natural process rather than divine creation. Second, it implied that humans are not unique and that they share a common ancestry with other species. Although these implications would prove highly controversial, Darwin's theory eventually gained considerable acceptance because it provided a compelling explanation for how the characteristics of various species gradually changed over many generations and for the functional, adaptive direction of these changes.

© Albie Venter/Shutterstock

Later Refinements to Evolutionary Theory

Although Darwin's evolutionary theory quickly gained many supporters, it also remained controversial for decades. Eventually, advances in the understanding of heredity were sufficient to permit Theodore Dobzhansky (1937) to write a fairly comprehensive account of the evolutionary process in genetic terms. Dobzhansky's synthesis of Darwin's ideas and modern genetics was enormously influential. By the 1950s the core tenets of evolutionary theory enjoyed widespread acceptance among scientists.

Contemporary models of evolution recognize that natural selection operates on the gene pool of a population. *Adaptations* are the key product of this process. An *adaptation* is an inherited characteristic that increased in a population (through natural selection) because it helped solve a problem of survival or reproduction during the time it emerged. Because of the slow, gradual nature of evolution, adaptations sometimes linger in a population even though they no longer provide a survival or reproductive advantage. For example, humans show a taste preference for fatty substances that was adaptive in an era of hunting and gathering, when dietary fat was a scarce source of important calories. However, in our modern world, where dietary fat is typically available in abundance, this taste preference leads many people to consume too much fat, resulting in obesity, heart disease, and other health problems. Thus, the preference for fatty foods has become a liability for human survival (although its impact on reproductive success is more difficult to gauge). As you will see, evolutionary psychologists have found that many aspects of human nature reflect the adaptive demands faced by our ancient ancestors rather than contemporary demands. Of course, as natural selection continues to work, these formerly adaptive traits should gradually be eliminated, but the process is extremely slow.

The behavior that helps this grasshopper hide from predators is a product of evolution, just like the physical characteristics that help it blend in with its surroundings.

Behaviors as Adaptive Traits

Scholarly analyses of evolution have focused primarily on the evolution of *physical characteristics* in the animal kingdom, but from the very beginning, Darwin recognized that natural selection was applicable to *behavioral traits* as well. Modern evolutionary psychology is based on the well-documented assumption that a species' typical patterns of behavior often reflect evolutionary solutions to adaptive problems.

Consider, for instance, the eating behavior of rats, which show remarkable caution when they encounter new foods. Rats are versatile animals that are found in an enormous range of habitats and can live off quite a variety of foods, but this diet variety can present risks, as they need to be wary of consuming toxic substances. When rats encounter unfamiliar foods, they consume only small amounts and won't eat two new foods together. If the consumption of a new food is followed by illness, they avoid that food in the future (Logue, 1991). These precautions allow rats to learn what makes them sick while reducing the likelihood of consuming a lethal amount of something poisonous. These patterns of eating behavior are highly adaptive solutions to the food selection problems faced by rats.

Let's look at some additional examples of how evolution has shaped organisms' behavior. Avoiding predators is a nearly universal problem for organisms. Because of natural selection, many species, such as the grasshopper shown in the photo on this page, have developed physical characteristics that allow them to blend in with their environments, making detection by predators more difficult. Many organisms also engage in elaborate *behavioral maneuvers* to hide themselves. For example, the pictured grasshopper has dug itself a small trench in which to hide and has used its midlegs to pull pebbles over its back (Alcock, 1998). This clever hiding behavior is just as much a product of evolution as the grasshopper's remarkable camouflage.

Many behavioral adaptations are designed to improve organisms' chances of reproductive success. Consider, for instance, the wide variety of species in which females choose which male to mate with. In many such species, females demand material goods and services from males in return for copulation opportunities. For example, in one type of moth, males have to spend hours extracting sodium from mud puddles, which they then transfer to prospective mates, who use it to supply their larvae with an important nutritional element (Smedley & Eisner, 1996). In the black-tipped hangingfly, females insist on a gift of food before they mate. They reject suitors bringing unpalatable food and tie the length of subsequent copulation to the size of the gift (Thornhill, 1976).

Reflecting on the Chapter's Themes

Three of our seven themes stood out in this chapter: (1) heredity and environment jointly influence behavior, (2) behavior is determined by multiple causes, and (3) psychology is empirical. Let's look at each of these points.

In Chapter 1, when it was first emphasized that heredity and environment jointly shape behavior, you may have been a little perplexed about how your genes could be responsible for your sarcastic wit or your interest in art. In fact, there are no genes for behavior per se. Experts do not expect to find genes for sarcasm or artistic interest, for example. Insofar as your hereditary endowment plays a role in your behavior, it does so *indirectly,* by molding the physiological machine that you work with. Thus, your genes influence your physiological makeup, which in turn influences your personality, temperament, intelligence, interests, and other traits. Bear in mind, however, that genetic factors do not operate in a vacuum. Genes exert their effects in an environmental context. The impact of genetic makeup depends on environment, and the impact of environment depends on genetic makeup.

It was evident throughout the chapter that behavior is determined by multiple causes, but this theme was particularly apparent in the discussions of schizophrenia. At different points in the chapter we saw that schizophrenia may be a function of (1) abnormalities in neurotransmitter activity (especially dopamine), (2) structural abnormalities in the brain identified with CT and MRI scans, and (3) genetic vulnerability to the illness. These findings do not contradict one another. Rather, they demonstrate that a complex array of biological factors are involved in the development of schizophrenia. In Chapter 14, we'll see that a host of environmental factors also play a role in the multifactorial causation of schizophrenia.

The empirical nature of psychology was apparent in the numerous discussions of the specialized research methods used to study the physiological bases of behavior. As you know, the empirical approach depends on precise observation. Throughout this chapter, you've seen how investigators have come up with innovative methods to observe and measure elusive phenomena such as neural impulses, brain function, cerebral specialization, and the impact of heredity on behavior. The point is that empirical methods are the lifeblood of the scientific enterprise. When researchers figure out how to better observe something, their findings usually facilitate major advances in our scientific knowledge. That is why the new brain-imaging techniques hold exciting promise for neuroscientists.

The importance of empiricism will also be apparent in the upcoming Personal Application and in the Critical Thinking Application that follows. In both applications you'll see the importance of learning to distinguish between scientific findings and conjecture based on those findings.

Personal
APPLICATION

Evaluating the Concept of "Two Minds in One"

KEY LEARNING GOALS

3.16 Describe and evaluate three popular beliefs regarding the specialization of the cerebral hemispheres.

Answer the following "true" or "false."

____ 1 Each half of the brain has its own special mode of thinking.

____ 2 Some people are left-brained while others are right-brained.

____ 3 The two hemispheres of the brain are specialized to handle different cognitive functions.

Do we have two minds in one that think differently? Do some of us depend on one side of the brain more than the other? Is the right side of the brain neglected? These questions are too complex to resolve with a simple "true" or "false," but in this Application we'll take a closer look at the issues involved in these generalizations about cerebral specialization. You'll learn that some of these ideas are plausible, but in many cases the hype has outstripped the evidence.

Cerebral Specialization and Cognitive Processes

PSYKTREK SIM2, 2f

Using a variety of methods, scientists have compiled mountains of data on the specialized abilities of the right and left hemispheres. These findings have led to extensive theorizing about how the right and left brains might be related to cognitive processes. Some of the more intriguing ideas include the following:

1. *The two hemispheres are specialized to process different types of cognitive tasks* (Corballis, 1991; Ornstein, 1977). Research findings have been widely interpreted as showing that the left hemisphere handles verbal tasks, including language, speech, writing, math, and logic, while the right hemisphere handles nonverbal tasks, including spatial problems, music, art, fantasy, and creativity. These conclusions have attracted a great deal of public interest and media attention. For example, **Figure 3.18** on the next page shows a *Newsweek* artist's depiction of how the brain supposedly divides its work.

2. *The two hemispheres have different modes of thinking* (Banich & Heller, 1998, Davis & Dean, 2005). According to this notion, the documented differences between the hemispheres in dealing with verbal and nonverbal materials are due to more basic differences in how the hemispheres process information. This theory holds that the reason the left hemisphere handles verbal material well is that it is analytic, abstract, rational, logical, and linear. In contrast, the right hemisphere is thought to be better equipped to handle spatial and musical material because it is synthetic, concrete, nonrational, intuitive, and holistic.

HOW THE BRAIN DIVIDES ITS WORK

FIGURE 3.18

Popular conceptions of hemispheric specialization. As this *Newsweek* diagram illustrates, depictions of hemispheric specialization in the popular press have often been oversimplified.

SOURCE: Cartoon courtesy of Roy Doty.

3. *People vary in their reliance on one hemisphere as opposed to the other* (Pink, 2005; Zenhausen, 1978). Allegedly, some people are "left-brained." Their greater dependence on their left hemisphere supposedly makes them analytic, rational, and logical. Other people are "right-brained." Their greater use of their right hemisphere supposedly makes them intuitive, holistic, and irrational. Being right-brained or left-brained is thought to explain many personal characteristics, such as whether an individual likes to read, is good with maps, or enjoys music. This notion of "brainedness" has even been used to explain occupational choice. Supposedly, right-brained people are more likely to become artists or musicians, while left-brained people are more likely to become writers or scientists.

Complexities and Qualifications

The ideas just outlined are intriguing and have clearly captured the imagination of the general public. However, the research on cerebral specialization is complex, and these ideas have to be qualified carefully

(Efron, 1990; Springer & Deutsch, 1998). Let's examine each point.

1. There *is* ample evidence that the right and left hemispheres are specialized to handle different types of cognitive tasks, *but only to a degree* (Brown & Kosslyn, 1993; Corballis, 2003). Doreen Kimura

(1973) compared the abilities of the right and left hemispheres to quickly recognize letters, words, faces, and melodies in a series of perceptual asymmetry studies. She found that the superiority of one hemisphere over the other on specific types of tasks was usually quite modest (see **Figure 3.19**). Most tasks probably engage both hemispheres, albeit to different degrees (Beeman & Chiarello, 1998).

Furthermore, people differ in their patterns of cerebral specialization (Springer & Deutsch, 1998). Some people display little specialization—that is, their hemispheres seem to have equal abilities on various types of tasks. Others even reverse the usual specialization, so that verbal processing might be housed in the right hemisphere. These unusual patterns are especially common among left-handed people (Josse & Tzourio-Mazoyer, 2004). Accomplished musicians may be another exception to the rule. Two recent studies found that experienced musicians exhibit more bilateral cerebral organization than comparable nonmusicians (Gibson, Folley, & Park, 2009; Patston et al., 2007). This bilaterality may develop because musicians often have to use both hands independently to play their instruments. If this explanation is accurate, it would provide another example of how

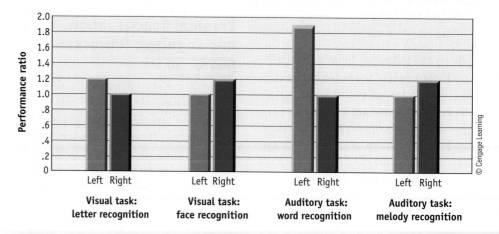

FIGURE 3.19

Relative superiority of one brain hemisphere over the other in studies of perceptual asymmetry. These performance ratios from a study by Doreen Kimura (1973) show the degree to which one hemisphere was "superior" to the other on each type of task in one study of normal participants. For example, the right hemisphere was 20% better than the left hemisphere in quickly recognizing melodic patterns (ratio 1.2 to 1). Most differences in the performance of the two hemispheres are quite small.

experience can shape brain organization. In any event, it is clear that the functional specialization of the cerebral hemispheres is not set in concrete.

2. Little direct evidence has been found to support the notion that each hemisphere has its own mode of thinking, or cognitive style (Bradshaw, 1989; Corballis, 2007). This notion is plausible, and there *is* some supportive evidence, but that evidence is inconsistent and more research is needed (Gordon, 1990; Reuter-Lorenz & Miller, 1998). One key problem with this idea is that aspects of cognitive style have proven difficult to define and measure (Brownell & Gardner, 1981). For instance, there is debate about the meaning of analytic versus synthetic thinking, or linear versus holistic thinking.

3. The evidence on the assertion that some people are left-brained while others are right-brained is inconclusive at best (Hellige, 1990). This idea has some credibility—if it means only that some people consistently display more activation of one hemisphere than the other. However, the practical significance of any such "preferences" remains to be determined. At present, researchers do not have convincing data linking brainedness to musical ability, occupational choice, or the like (Knecht et al., 2001; Springer & Deutsch, 1998).

In summary, the theories linking cerebral specialization to cognitive processes are highly speculative. There's nothing wrong with theoretical speculation. Unfortunately, the tentative, conjectural nature of these ideas about hemispheric spe-

Does artistic ability depend on being "right-brained"? The popular press has certainly suggested that this is the case, but as your text explains, there is no solid empirical evience to support this assertion.

cialization has gotten lost in the popular magazine descriptions of research on right and left brains (Coren, 1992). Commenting on this popularization, Hooper and Teresi (1986) note: "A widespread cult of the right brain ensued, and the duplex house that Sperry built grew into the Kmart of brain science. Today our hairdresser lectures us about the Two Hemispheres of the Brain" (p. 223). Cerebral specialization is an important and intriguing area of research. However, it is unrealistic to expect that the hemispheric divisions in the brain will provide a biological explanation for every dichotomy or polarity in modes of thinking.

Reality Check

Misconception

People are either left-brained or right-brained, and this disparity can predict their abilities and interests.

Reality

Pop psychology books with no scientific basis routinely discuss how being right-brained or left-brained ought to relate to personal talents and occupational choice. There is just one small problem. If you search the research literature there are no studies that have addressed these issues.

Building Better Brains: The Perils of Extrapolation

KEY LEARNING GOALS

3.17 Explain how neuroscience research has been overextrapolated to educational issues.

Summarizing the implications of certain widely discussed findings in brain research, science writer Ronald Kotulak (1996) concluded, "The first three years of a child's life are critically important to brain development" (pp. ix–x). Echoing this sentiment, the president of a U.S. educational commission asserted that "research in brain development suggests it is time to rethink many educational policies" (Bruer, 1999, p. 16). Based on research in the neurosciences (the various scientific disciplines that study the brain and the nervous system), many states in the 1990s launched elaborate and expensive programs intended to foster better neural development in infants. For example, the governor of Georgia at the time, Zell Miller, sought state funding to distribute classical music tapes to the state's infants, saying, "No one doubts that listening to music, especially at a very early age, affects the spatial-temporal reasoning that underlies math, engineering, and chess" (Bruer, 1999, p. 62). Well-intended educational groups have argued for the creation of schools for infants on the grounds that the first three years of life are especially critical to brain development.

What are these practical, new discoveries about the brain that will permit parents and educators to optimize infants' brain development? Well, we will discuss the pertinent research momentarily, but it is not as new or as practical as suggested in many quarters. Unfortunately, as we saw in our discussion of research on hemispheric specialization of the brain, the hype in the media has greatly outstripped the realities of what scientists have learned in the laboratory (Chance, 2001), providing an enlightening case study in the perils of overextrapolation.

The Key Findings on Neural Development

The education and childcare reformers who have used brain science as the basis for their campaigns have primarily cited two key findings: the discovery of critical periods in neural development and the demonstration that rats raised in "enriched environments" have more synapses than rats raised in "impoverished environments." Let's look at each of these findings.

A *critical period* is a limited time span in the development of an organism when it is optimal for certain capacities to emerge because the organism is especially responsive to certain experiences. The groundbreaking research on critical periods in neural development was conducted by David Hubel and Torsten Wiesel (1963) in the 1960s. They showed that if an eye of a newborn kitten is sewn shut early in its development (typically the first 4 to 6 weeks), the kitten will become permanently blind in that eye, but if the eye is covered for the same amount of time at later ages (after 4 months) blindness does not result. Such studies show that certain types of visual input are necessary during a critical period of development or neural pathways between the eye and brain will not form properly. Basically, what happens is that the inactive synapses from the closed eye are displaced by the active synapses from the open eye. Critical periods have been found for other aspects of neural development and in other species, but a great deal remains to be learned. Based on this type of research, some educational and childcare reformers have argued that the first three years of life are a critical period for human neural development.

The pioneering work on environment and brain development was begun in the 1960s by Mark Rosenzweig and his colleagues (1961, 1962). They raised some rats in an impoverished environment, (housed individually in small, barren cages) and other rats in an enriched environment (housed in groups in larger cages, with a variety of objects available for exploration), as shown in **Figure 3.20**. They found that the rats raised in the enriched environment performed better on problem-solving tasks than the impoverished rats and had slightly heavier brains and a thicker cerebral cortex in some areas. Subsequent research by William Greenough demonstrated that enriched environments resulted in heavier and thicker cortical areas by virtue of producing denser dendritic branching, more synapses, and richer neural networks (Greenough, 1975; Greenough & Volkmar, 1973). More recently, scientists have learned that enriched environments also promote the newly discovered process of *neurogenesis* in the brain (Nithiananthharajah & Hannan, 2006). Based on this type of research, some childcare reformers have argued that human infants need to be brought up in enriched environments during the critical period before age 3, to promote synapse formation and to enhance the development of their emerging neural circuits.

The findings on critical periods and enriched environments were genuine breakthroughs, but they certainly aren't *new* findings. Moreover, one can raise many doubts about whether this research can serve as a meaningful guide for decisions about day-care programs, educational policies, and welfare reform (Goswami, 2006; Thompson & Nelson, 2001).

The Tendency to Overextrapolate

Extrapolation occurs when an effect is estimated by extending beyond some known values or conditions. Extrapolation is a normal process, but some extrapolations are conservative, plausible projections drawn from directly relevant data, whereas others are wild leaps of speculation based on loosely related data. The extrapolations made regarding the educational implications of critical periods and environmental effects on synapse formation are highly conjectural *overextrapolations*. The studies that highlighted the possible importance of early experience in animals have all used extreme conditions to make their compari-

FIGURE 3.20

Enriched environments in the study of rats' neural development. In the studies by Rosenzweig and colleagues (1961, 1962), rats raised in an impoverished environment were housed alone in small cages, whereas rats raised in enriched environments were housed in groups and were given playthings that were changed daily. Although the enriched conditions provided more stimulating environments than what laboratory rats normally experience, they may not be any more stimulating than rats' natural habitats. Thus, the "enriched" condition may reveal more about the importance of normal stimulation than about the benefits of extra stimulation (Gopnik, Meltzoff, & Kuhl, 1999).

sons, such as depriving an animal of all visual input or raising it in stark isolation. The so-called "enriched" environments probably resemble normal conditions in the real world, whereas the standard laboratory environment may reflect extreme environmental deprivation (Gould, 2004). In light of the findings, it seems plausible to speculate that children probably need normal stimulation to experience normal brain development. However, great difficulty arises when these findings are extended to conclude that adding *more* stimulation to a normal environment will be beneficial to brain development (Shatz, 1992).

The ease with which people fall into the trap of overextrapolating has been particularly apparent in recent recommendations that infants listen to classical music to enhance their brain development. These recommendations have been derived from two studies that showed that college students'

performance on spatial reasoning tasks was enhanced slightly for about 10–15 minutes after listening to a brief Mozart recording (Rauscher, Shaw, & Ky, 1993, 1995). This finding, dubbed the "Mozart effect," has proven difficult to replicate (Gray & Della Sala, 2007; Steele, 2003), but the pertinent point here is that there was no research on how classical music affects *infants,* no research relating classical music to *brain development,* and no research on anyone showing *lasting effects.* Nonetheless, many people (including the governor of Georgia) were quick to extrapolate the shaky findings on the Mozart effect to infants' brain development.

Ironically, there is much better evidence linking *musical training* to enhanced cognitive performance. Studies have found an association between intelligence and the extent of individuals' exposure to music lessons (Schellenberg, 2004, 2005, 2006). Of course, if you think critically about this correlation, it might only mean that brighter youngsters are more likely to take music lessons (researchers are still working to sort it all out).

As discussed in Chapter 1, thinking critically about issues often involves asking questions such as: What is missing from this debate? Is there any contradictory evidence? In this case, there is some contradictory evidence. The basis for advocating infant educational programs is the belief that brain development is more rapid and malleable during the hypothesized critical period of birth to age 3 than

at later ages. However, Greenough's work on synaptic formation and other lines of research suggest that the brain remains malleable throughout life (Thompson & Nelson, 2001). Thus, advocates for the aged could just as readily argue for new educational initiatives for the elderly to help them maximize their intellectual potential. Another problem is the implicit assumption that greater synaptic density is associated with greater intelligence. There is quite a bit of evidence that infant animals and humans begin life with an overabundance of synaptic connections and that learning involves selective *pruning* of inactive synapses, which gradually give way to heavily used neural pathways (Huttenlocher, 2002; Rakic, Bourgeois, & Goldman-Rakic, 1994). Thus, in the realm of synapses, more may *not* be better.

In conclusion, there may be many valid reasons for increasing educational programs for infants, but research in neuroscience does not appear to provide a clear rationale for much in the way of specific infant care policies (Bruer, 2002). One problem in evaluating these proposals is that few people want to argue against high-quality child care or education. But modern societies need to allocate their limited resources to the programs that appear most likely to have beneficial effects, so even intuitively appealing ideas need to be subjected to critical scrutiny.

TABLE 3.2 Critical Thinking Skills Discussed in This Application

Skill	Description
Understanding the limits of extrapolation	The critical thinker appreciates that extrapolations are based on certain assumptions, vary in plausibility, and ultimately involve speculation.
Looking for contradictory evidence	In evaluating the evidence presented on an issue, the critical thinker attempts to look for contradictory evidence that may have been left out of the debate.

Review of Key Learning Goals

Communication in the Nervous System

3.1 Identify the various parts of the neuron and the main functions of glial cells.

Neurons receive, integrate, and transmit signals. Information is received at the dendrites, is passed through the soma and along the axon, and is transmitted to the dendrites of other cells at meeting points called synapses, where neurotransmitters are released from terminal buttons. Glial cells provide various types of support for neurons (nourishment, insulation, waste removal) and may contribute to signal transmission in the nervous system.

3.2 Describe the neural impulse, and explain how neurons communicate at chemical synapses.

The neural impulse is a brief change in a neuron's electrical charge that moves along an axon. An action potential is an all-or-none event. Neurons convey information about the strength of a stimulus by variations in their rate of firing. Action potentials trigger the release of chemicals called neurotransmitters that diffuse across a synapse to communicate with other neurons. Transmitters bind with receptors in the postsynaptic cell membrane, causing excitatory or inhibitory PSPs. Whether the postsynaptic neuron fires a neural impulse depends on the balance of excitatory and inhibitory PSPs.

1 **Synthesis** and **storage** of neurotransmitter molecules in synaptic vesicles

5 **Reuptake** of neurotransmitters sponged up by the presynaptic neuron

4 **Inactivation** (by enzymes) or **removal** (drifting away) of neurotransmitters

2 **Release** of neurotransmitter molecules into synaptic cleft

3 **Binding** of neurotransmitters at receptor sites on postsynaptic membrane

© Cengage Learning

3.3 Discuss some of the functions of acetylcholine, the monoamine neurotransmitters, GABA, and endorphins.

The transmitter ACh plays a key role in muscular movement. Serotonin circuits may contribute to the regulation of sleep and play a role in aggression and depression. Schizophrenia has been linked to overactivity at dopamine synapses. Cocaine and amphetamines appear to exert their main effects by altering activity at DA and NE synapses. GABA is a transmitter whose inhibitory effects appear to regulate anxiety and sleep. Endorphins, which resemble opiate drugs such as morphine, contribute to pain relief and may underlie the experience of the "runner's high."

Organization of the Nervous System

3.4 Distinguish between the central nervous system and the peripheral nervous system.

The peripheral nervous system consists of the nerves that lie outside the brain and spinal cord. It can be subdivided into the somatic nervous system, which connects to muscles and sensory receptors, and the autonomic nervous system, which connects to blood vessels, smooth muscles, and glands. The autonomic nervous system controls the largely automatic arousal that accompanies emotion and is divided into the sympathetic and the parasympathetic divisions. The central nervous system consists of the brain and spinal cord. The CNS is bathed in cerebrospinal fluid, which provides a protective cushion. The spinal cord connects the brain to the rest of the body through the peripheral nervous system.

The Brain and Behavior

3.5 Describe how lesioning, electrical stimulation, and various brain-imaging procedures are used to investigate brain function.

Neuroscientists use a variety of methods to investigate brain-behavior relations. Lesioning involves destroying a piece of the brain to see the effect on behavior. Another technique is electrical stimulation of areas in the brain in order to activate them. CT scans and MRI scans provide images of brain structure. PET scans and fMRI scans can track brain activity.

3.6 Know the principal functions of key structures in the brain.

In the hindbrain, the medulla regulates functions such as breathing and circulation, the cerebellum is involved in movement and balance, and the pons contributes to sleep and arousal. The midbrain plays a role in the coordination of sensory processes. In the forebrain, the thalamus is a relay station through which all sensory information (except smell) must pass to get to the cortex. The hypothalamus is involved in the regulation of basic biological drives such as hunger and sex. The limbic system is a network of loosely connected structures located along the border between the cortex and deeper subcortical areas. It includes the hippocampus, which appears to play a role in memory; the amygdala, which is involved in the regulation of emotion; and areas rich in self-stimulation sites.

Cerebrum
Responsible for sensing, thinking, learning, emotion, consciousness, and voluntary movement

Corpus callosum
Bridge of fibers passing information between the two cerebral hemispheres

Amygdala
Part of limbic system involved in emotion and aggression

Thalamus
Relay center for cortex; handles incoming and outgoing signals

Hypothalamus
Responsible for regulating basic biological needs: hunger, thirst, temperature control

Cerebellum
Structure that coordinates fine muscle movement, balance

Pituitary gland
"Master" gland that regulates other endocrine glands

Reticular formation
Group of fibers that carry stimulation related to sleep and arousal through brainstem

Hippocampus
Part of limbic system involved in learning and memory

Pons
Involved in sleep and arousal

Medulla
Responsible for regulating largely unconscious functions such as breathing and circulation

© Cengage Learning

3.7 Identify the four lobes in the cortex and their key functions, and summarize evidence on the brain's plasticity.

The cortex is the cerebrum's convoluted outer layer, which is subdivided into four lobes. These lobes and their primary known functions are the occipital lobe (vision), the parietal lobe (touch), the temporal lobe (hearing), and the frontal lobe (movement of the body). Mirror neurons are neurons that are activated by performing an action or by seeing another monkey or person perform the same action. Studies show that experience can affect brain structure, that brain damage can lead to neural reorganization, and that neurogenesis (formation of new neurons) can occur in some areas of the adult brain. Hence, the structure and function of the brain appear to be more plastic than widely appreciated.

Primary somatosensory cortex
Primary motor cortex
Parietal lobe
Frontal lobe
Occipital lobe
Temporal lobe
Primary visual cortex
Primary auditory cortex

© Rob Wilkinson/Alamy
© Cengage Learning

Right Brain/Left Brain: Cerebral Specialization

3.8 Explain how split-brain research changed our understanding of the brain's hemispheric organization.

The cerebrum is divided into right and left hemispheres connected by the corpus callosum. Evidence that the left cerebral hemisphere usually processes language led scientists to view it as the dominant hemisphere. However, studies of split-brain patients revealed that the right and left halves of the brain each have unique talents, with the right hemisphere being specialized to handle visual-spatial functions.

3.9 Describe research on cerebral specialization in normal subjects and what this research has revealed.

Studies of perceptual asymmetries in normal subjects have shown that the left hemisphere is better equipped to handle verbal processing, whereas the right hemisphere is more adept at nonverbal processing, including visual-spatial tasks, musical tasks, and the perception of emotion. Hemispheric specialization may be adaptive by virtue of increasing the brain's neural capacity. Weak lateralization is associated with certain negative outcomes.

The Endocrine System: Another Way to Communicate

3.10 Identify the key elements of the endocrine system, and describe ways in which hormones regulate behavior.

The endocrine system consists of glands that secrete hormones, which are chemicals involved in the regulation of basic bodily processes. Hormone release tends to be pulsatile. The control centers for the endocrine system are the hypothalamus and the pituitary gland. Hormones regulate the fight-or-flight response, which occurs in response to stress. Research suggests that the hormone oxytocin fosters bonding, empathy, and trust.

Heredity and Behavior: Is It All in the Genes?

3.11 Describe basic structures involved in genetic transmission, and discuss the nature of polygenic traits.

The basic units of genetic transmission are pairs of genes housed on chromosomes, which can be scrambled in an endless variety of ways. The key to the concept of genetic relatedness is that closer relatives share a larger proportion of genes than more-distant relatives. Most behavioral qualities appear to involve polygenic inheritance, which means that many pairs of genes play a role in influencing the traits.

3.12 Compare the special methods used to investigate the influence of heredity, and discuss how heredity and environment interact.

Family studies evaluate hereditary influence by examining blood relatives to see how much they resemble one another on a specific trait. Twin studies estimate hereditary influence by comparing the resemblance of identical twins and fraternal twins with respect to a trait. Adoption studies assess hereditary influence by examining the resemblance between adopted children and both their biological and their adoptive parents. Twin studies generally can provide the strongest evidence. Research indicates that most behavioral qualities are influenced jointly by heredity and environment, which play off of each other in complex interactions. New work in epigenetics has further demonstrated that genetic and environmental factors are deeply intertwined.

The Evolutionary Bases of Behavior

3.13 Understand the key insights that represent the essence of Darwin's theory of evolution.

Darwin argued that if a heritable trait contributes to an organism's survival or reproductive success, organisms with that trait should produce more offspring than those without the trait and that the prevalence of that trait should gradually increase over generations—thanks to natural selection. Fitness refers to organisms' reproductive success.

3.14 Describe subsequent refinements to evolutionary theory, and give some examples of animal behavior that represent adaptations.

Dobzhansky wrote a comprehensive account of the evolutionary process in genetic terms that was enormously influential. Because of the incremental nature of evolution, adaptations sometimes linger in a population even though they no longer provide a survival or reproductive advantage. Examples of behaviors sculpted by evolution include eating behavior, the avoidance of predators, and mating strategies.

Reflecting on the Chapter's Themes

3.15 Identify the three unifying themes that were highlighted in this chapter.

The interactive influence of heredity and environment was highlighted in this chapter, as was the multifactorial causation of behavior. The special research techniques used to study the biological bases of behavior show that empirical methods are the lifeblood of the scientific enterprise.

PERSONAL APPLICATION
Evaluating The Concept of "Two Minds In One"

3.16 Describe and evaluate three popular beliefs regarding the specialization of the cerebral hemispheres.

It is widely believed that the cerebral hemispheres are specialized to handle specific cognitive tasks, that each hemisphere has its own mode of thinking, and that people vary in their reliance on the right and left halves of the brain. The cerebral hemispheres *are* specialized for handling different cognitive tasks, but only to a degree, as most tasks engage both hemispheres. Moreover, people vary in their patterns of hemispheric specialization. Evidence on whether people vary in braineraness and whether the two hemispheres vary in cognitive style is inconclusive.

CRITICAL THINKING APPLICATION
Building Better Brains: The Perils of Extrapolation

3.17 Explain how neuroscience research has been overextrapolated to educational issues.

Some education and childcare reformers have used research in neuroscience as the basis for their campaigns. However, research has not demonstrated that birth to 3 is a critical period for human neural development or that specific enrichment programs can enhance brain development. These assertions are highly conjectural overextrapolations from existing data.

4

Sensation and Perception

PARADOX

We think we see the world as it is, but perception is inherently subjective and always a matter of interpretation.

Take a look at the photo below. What do you see? You probably answered, "a rose" or "a flower." But is that what you really see? No, this isn't a trick question. Let's examine the odd case of "Dr. P." It shows that there's more to seeing than meets the eye.

Dr. P was an intelligent and distinguished music professor who began to exhibit some worrisome behaviors that seemed to be related to his vision. Sometimes he failed to recognize familiar students by sight, though he knew them instantly by the sound of their voices. Sometimes he acted as if he saw faces in inanimate objects, cordially greeting fire hydrants and parking meters as if they were children. On one occasion, reaching for what he thought was his hat, he took hold of his wife's head and tried to put it on! Except for these kinds of visual mistakes, Dr. P was a normal, talented man.

Ultimately Dr. P was referred to Oliver Sacks, a neurologist, for an examination. During one visit, Sacks handed Dr. P a fresh red rose to see whether he would recognize it. Dr. P took the rose as if he were being given a model of a geometric solid rather than a flower. "About six inches in length," Dr. P observed, "a convoluted red form with a linear green attachment."

"Yes," Sacks persisted, "and what do you think it is, Dr. P?"

"Not easy to say," the patient replied. "It lacks the simple symmetry of the Platonic solids . . ."

"Smell it," the neurologist suggested. Dr. P looked perplexed, as if being asked to smell symmetry, but he complied and brought the flower to his nose. Suddenly, his confusion cleared up. "Beautiful. An early rose. What a heavenly smell" (Sacks, 1987, pp. 13−14).

What accounted for Dr. P's strange inability to recognize faces and familiar objects by sight? There was nothing wrong with his eyes. He could readily spot a pin on the floor. If you're thinking that he *must* have had something wrong with his vision, look again at the photo of the rose. What you see *is* "a convoluted red form with a linear green attachment." It doesn't occur to you to describe it that way only because, without thinking about it, you instantly perceive that combination of form and color as a flower. This is precisely what Dr. P was unable to do. He

could see perfectly well, but he was losing the ability to assemble what he saw into a meaningful picture of the world. Technically, he suffered from a condition called *visual agnosia,* an inability to recognize objects through sight. As Sacks (1987) put it, "Visually, he was lost in a world of lifeless abstractions" (p. 15).

As Dr. P's case illustrates, without effective processing of sensory input, our familiar world can become a chaos of confusing sensations. To acknowledge the needs to both take in and process sensory information, psychologists distinguish between sensation and perception. *Sensation* **is the stimulation of sense organs.** *Perception* **is the selection, organization, and interpretation of sensory input.** Sensation involves the absorption of energy, such as light or sound waves, by sensory organs, such as the eyes and ears. Perception involves organizing and translating sensory input into something meaningful. For example, when you look at the photo of the rose, your eyes are sensing the light reflected from the page, including areas of low reflection where ink has been deposited in an irregular shape. What you *perceive,* however, is a picture of a rose.

The distinction between sensation and perception stands out in Dr. P's case of visual agnosia. His eyes were doing their job of registering sensory input and transmitting signals to the brain. However, damage in his brain interfered with his ability to put these signals together into organized wholes. Thus, Dr. P's process of visual *sensation* was intact, but his process of visual *perception* was severely impaired.

Dr. P's case is unusual, of course. Normally, the processes of sensation and perception are difficult to separate because people automatically start organizing incoming sensory stimulation the moment it arrives. The distinction between sensation and perception has been useful in organizing theory and research, but in actual operation the two processes merge.

We'll begin our discussion of sensation and perception with a long look at vision, then take a briefer look at the other senses. As we examine each of the sensory systems, we'll see repeatedly that people's experience of the world depends on both the physical stimuli they encounter (sensation) and their active processing of stimulus inputs (perception). The chapter's Personal Application explores how principles of visual perception come into play in art and illusion. The Critical Thinking Application discusses how perceptual contrasts can be manipulated in persuasive efforts.

The Visual System: Essentials of Sight

"Seeing is believing." Good students are "bright," and a good explanation is "illuminating." This section is an "overview." Do you see the point? As these common expressions show, humans are visual animals. People rely heavily on their sense of sight, and they virtually equate it with what is trustworthy (seeing is believing). Although it is taken for granted, you'll see (there it is again) that the human visual system is amazingly complex. Furthermore, as in all sensory domains, what people "sense" and what they "perceive" may be quite different.

KEY LEARNING GOALS

4.1 Identify the three properties of light, and describe the role of key eye structures in vision.

4.2 Trace the routing of signals from the eye to the brain, and explain the brain's role in visual information processing.

4.3 Distinguish two types of color mixing, compare the trichromatic and opponent process theories of color vision, and describe research on how color can influence behavior.

The Stimulus: Light

PsykTrek 3a

For people to see, there must be light. *Light* is a form of electromagnetic radiation that travels as a wave, moving, naturally enough, at the speed of light. As **Figure 4.1(a)** shows, light waves vary in *amplitude* (height) and in *wavelength* (the distance between peaks). Amplitude affects mainly the perception of brightness, while wavelength affects mainly the perception of color. The lights humans normally see are mixtures of different wavelengths. Hence, light can also vary in its *purity* (how varied the mix is). Purity influences perception of the *saturation,* or richness, of colors. Saturation refers to the relative amount of whiteness in a color. As whiteness declines, saturation increases. Of course, most objects do not emit light, they reflect it (the sun, lamps, and fireflies being some exceptions).

What most people call light includes only the wavelengths that humans can see. But as **Figure 4.1(c)** shows, the visible spectrum is only a slim portion of the total range of wavelengths. Vision is a filter that permits people to sense only a fraction of the real world. Other animals have different capabilities and so live in a quite different visual world. For example, many insects can see shorter wavelengths than humans can see, in the *ultraviolet* spectrum, whereas many fish and reptiles can see longer wavelengths, in the *infrared* spectrum.

Although the sense of sight depends on light waves, in order for people to see, incoming visual input must be converted into neural impulses that are sent to the brain. Let's investigate how this transformation is accomplished.

The Eye: A Living Optical Instrument

PsykTrek 3a

The eyes serve two main purposes: They channel light to the neural tissue that receives it, called the *retina,* and they house that tissue. The structure of the eye is shown in **Figure 4.2**. Each eye is a living optical instrument that creates an image of the visual world on the light-sensitive retina that lines its inside back surface.

FIGURE 4.1

Light, the physical stimulus for vision. (a) Light waves vary in amplitude and wavelength. **(b)** Within the spectrum of visible light, amplitude (corresponding to physical intensity) affects mainly the experience of brightness. Wavelength affects mainly the experience of color, and purity is the key determinant of saturation. **(c)** If white light (such as sunlight) passes through a prism, the prism separates the light into its component wavelengths, creating a rainbow of colors. However, visible light is only the narrow band of wavelengths to which human eyes happen to be sensitive.

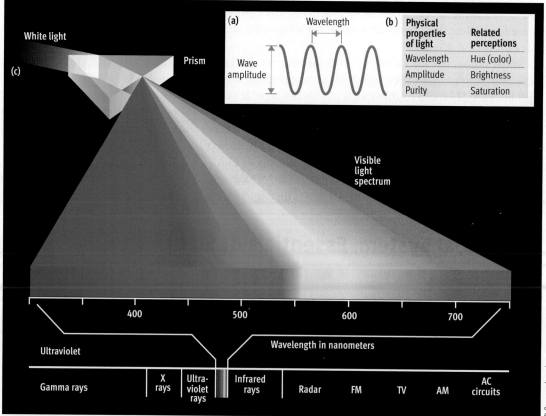

Physical properties of light	Related perceptions
Wavelength	Hue (color)
Amplitude	Brightness
Purity	Saturation

© Cengage Learning

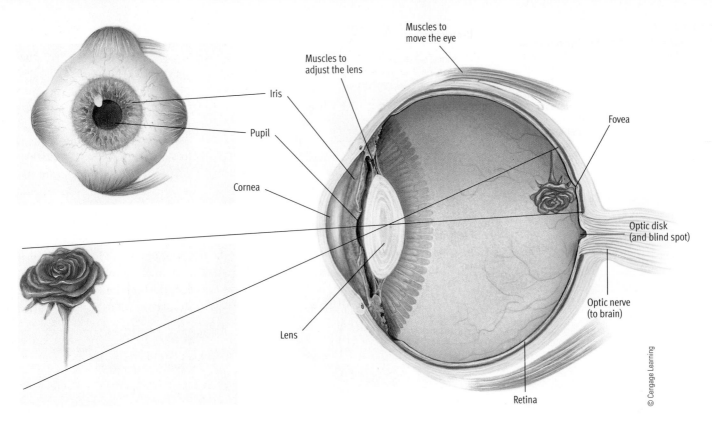

FIGURE 4.2

The human eye. Light passes through the cornea, pupil, and lens and falls on the light-sensitive surface of the retina, where images of objects are reflected upside down. The lens adjusts its curvature to focus the images falling on the retina. The pupil regulates the amount of light passing into the rear chamber of the eye.

Light enters the eye through a transparent "window" at the front, the *cornea*. The cornea and the crystalline *lens,* located behind it, form an upside down image of objects on the retina and adjust the focus of the image. It might seem disturbing that the image is upside down, but the arrangement works. It doesn't matter how the image sits on the retina, as long as the brain knows the rule for relating positions on the retina to the corresponding positions in the world. **The** *lens* **is a transparent eye structure that focuses the light rays falling on the retina.** The lens is made up of relatively soft tissue, capable of adjustments that facilitate a process called accommodation. *Accommodation* occurs when the curvature of the lens adjusts to alter visual focus. When you focus on a close object, the lens of your eye gets fatter (rounder) in order to give you a clear image. When you focus on distant objects, the lens flattens out to give you a better image.

A number of common visual problems are caused by focusing problems or defects in the lens (Guyton, 1991). For example, **in** *nearsightedness,* **close objects are seen clearly but distant objects appear blurry** because the focus of light from distant objects falls a little short of the retina (see **Figure 4.3** on the next page). This focusing problem occurs when the cornea or lens bends light too much or when the eyeball is too long. **In** *farsightedness,* **distant objects are seen clearly but close objects appear blurry** because the focus of light from close objects falls behind the retina (again, see **Figure 4.3**). This focusing problem typically occurs when the eyeball is too short. A *cataract* is a lens that is clouded. This defect occurs mainly in older persons, affecting three out of four people over the age of 65.

The eye also makes adjustments to alter the amount of light reaching the retina. The *iris* is the colored ring of muscle surrounding the *pupil,* or black center of the eye. **The** *pupil* **is the opening in the center of the iris that helps regulate the amount of light passing into the rear chamber of the eye.** When the pupil constricts, it lets less light into the eye, but it sharpens the image falling on the retina. When the pupil dilates

FIGURE 4.3

Nearsightedness and farsightedness. The pictures on the right simulate how a scene might look to nearsighted and far-sighted people. Nearsightedness occurs because light from distant objects focuses in front of the retina. Farsightedness results from the opposite situation—light from close objects focuses behind the retina.

Nearsightedness

Normal eye shape
Retina

Focus point falls in front of retina

Farsightedness

Normal eye shape
Retina

Focus point falls behind retina

© Cengage Learning; photos Craig McClain

(opens), it lets more light in, but the image is less sharp. In bright light, the pupils constrict to take advantage of the sharpened image. But in dim light, the pupils dilate. Image sharpness is sacrificed to allow more light to fall on the retina so that more remains visible.

The Retina: The Brain's Envoy in the Eye

PsykTrek 3b

The *retina* is the neural tissue lining the inside back surface of the eye; it absorbs light, processes images, and sends visual information to the brain. Much as the spinal cord is a complicated extension of the brain, the retina is the brain's envoy in the eye. About half as thick as a credit card, this thin sheet of neural tissue contains a complex network of specialized cells arranged in layers (Rodieck, 1998), as shown in **Figure 4.4**.

The axons that run from the retina to the brain converge at a single spot where they exit the eye. At that point, all the fibers dive through a hole in the retina called the *optic disk*. Since the optic disk is a *hole* in the retina, you cannot see the part of an image that falls on it. It is therefore known as the *blind spot*. Most people are not aware that they have a blind spot in each eye. Why? Because each eye compensates for the blind spot of the other and because the brain somehow "fills in" the missing part of the image (Churchland & Ramachandran, 1996).

VISUAL RECEPTORS: RODS AND CONES

PsykTrek 3b

The retina contains millions of receptor cells that are sensitive to light. Surprisingly, these receptors are located in the innermost layer of the retina (see **Figure 4.4**). Hence, light must pass through several layers of cells before it gets to the receptors that actually detect it. The retina contains two types of receptors, *rods* and *cones*. Their names are based on their shapes, as rods are elongated and cones are stubbier. Rods outnumber cones by a huge margin, as humans have 100−125 million rods, but only 5 million to 6.4 million cones (Frishman, 2001).

Receptor cells
(rods and
cones)

Bipolar cell

Amacrine cell

Light

Optic disk
(and blind spot)

Optic
nerve
fibers

Ganglion cell

Rod

Cone

Horizontal cell

© Cengage Learning

FIGURE 4.4

The retina. The close-up shows the several layers of cells in the retina. The cells closest to the back of the eye (the rods and cones) are the receptor cells that actually detect light. The intervening layers of cells receive signals from the rods and cones and form circuits that begin the process of analyzing incoming information before it is sent to the brain. These cells feed into many optic fibers, all of which head toward the "hole" in the retina where the optic nerve leaves the eye—the point known as the optic disk (which corresponds to the blind spot).

Cones are specialized visual receptors that play a key role in daylight vision and color vision. The cones handle most of people's daytime vision, because bright lights dazzle the rods. The special sensitivities of cones also allow them to play a major role in the perception of color. However, cones do not respond well to dim light, which is why you don't see color very well in low illumination. Nonetheless, cones provide better *visual acuity*—that is, sharpness and precise detail—than rods. Cones are concentrated most heavily in the center of the retina and quickly fall off in density toward its sides. The *fovea* is a tiny spot in the center of the retina that contains only cones; visual acuity is greatest at this spot (consult **Figure 4.2** again). When you want to see something in sharp focus, you usually move your eyes to center the object in the fovea.

Rods are specialized visual receptors that play a key role in night vision and peripheral vision. Rods handle night vision because they are up to 100 times more sensitive than cones to dim light (Kefalov, 2010). They handle the lion's share of peripheral vision because they greatly outnumber cones in the periphery (outer areas) of the retina. The density of the rods is greatest just outside the fovea and gradually decreases toward the periphery of the retina.

DARK AND LIGHT ADAPTATION

PSYKTREK 3b

You've probably noticed that when you enter a dark theater on a bright day, you stumble about almost blindly. But within minutes you can make your way about quite well in the dim light. This adjustment is called *dark adaptation*—the process in which the eyes become more sensitive to light in low illumination. **Figure 4.5** maps out the course of this process. It shows how, as time passes, you require less and less light to see. Dark adaptation is virtually complete in about 30 minutes, with considerable progress occurring in the first 10 minutes. The curve in **Figure 4.5** that charts this progress consists of two segments because cones adapt more rapidly than rods (Reeves, 2010).

When you emerge from a dark theater on a sunny day, you need to squint to ward off the overwhelming brightness, and the reverse of dark adaptation occurs. *Light adaptation* is the process in which the eyes become less sensitive to light in high illumination. As with dark adaptation, light adaptation improves your visual acuity under the prevailing circumstances.

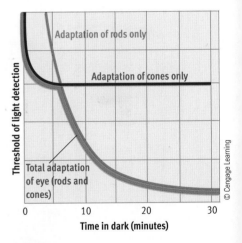

Adaptation of rods only

Adaptation of cones only

Threshold of light detection

Total adaptation of eye (rods and cones)

0   10   20   30

Time in dark (minutes)

© Cengage Learning

FIGURE 4.5

The process of dark adaptation. The declining thresholds over time indicate that your visual sensitivity is improving, as less and less light is required to see. Visual sensitivity improves markedly during the first 5 to 10 minutes after entering a dark room, as the eye's bright-light receptors (the cones) rapidly adapt to low light levels. However, the cones' adaptation, which is plotted in purple, soon reaches its limit, and further improvement comes from the rods' adaptation, which is plotted in red. The rods adapt more slowly than the cones, but they are capable of far greater visual sensitivity in low levels of light.

INFORMATION PROCESSING IN THE RETINA

In processing visual input, the retina transforms a pattern of light falling onto it into a very different representation of the visual scene. Light striking the retina's receptors (rods and cones) triggers the firing of neural signals that pass into the intricate network of cells in the retina. Thus, signals move from receptors to bipolar cells to ganglion cells, which in turn send impulses along the *optic nerve*—a collection of axons that connect the eye with the brain (refer back to **Figure 4.4**). These axons, which depart the eye through the optic disk, carry visual information, encoded as a stream of neural impulses, to the brain.

A great deal of complex information processing goes on in the retina itself before visual signals are sent to the brain. Ultimately, the information from as many as 130 million rods and cones converges to travel along "only" 1 million axons in the optic nerve (Slaughter, 1990). This means that the bipolar and ganglion cells in the intermediate layers of the retina integrate and compress signals from many receptors. The collection of rod and cone receptors that funnel signals to a particular visual cell in the retina (or ultimately in the brain) make up that cell's *receptive field*. Thus, **the *receptive field of a visual cell* is the retinal area that, when stimulated, affects the firing of that cell.**

Receptive fields in the retina come in a variety of shapes and sizes. Particularly common are circular fields with a center-surround arrangement (Levitt, 2010). In these receptive fields, light falling in the center has the opposite effect of light falling in the surrounding area. For example, the rate of firing of a visual cell might be *increased* by light in the center of its receptive field and *decreased* by light in the surrounding area. Other visual cells may work in just the opposite way. Either way, when receptive fields are stimulated, retinal cells send signals toward the brain.

Vision and the Brain

Light falls on the eye, but you see with your brain. Although the retina does a lot of information processing for a sensory organ, visual input is meaningless until it is processed in the brain.

Concept Check 4.1

Understanding Sensory Processes in the Retina

The receptors for vision are rods and cones in the retina. These two types of receptors have many important differences, which are compared systematically in the chart below. Fill in the missing information to finish the chart. Consult Appendix A for the answers.

Dimension	Rods	Cones
1. Physical shape	Elongated	
2. Number in the retina		5–6.4 million
3. Area of the retina in which they are dominant receptor	Periphery	
4. Critical to color vision		
5. Critical to peripheral vision		No
6. Sensitivity to dim light	Strong	
7. Speed of dark adaptation		Rapid

© Supri Suharjoto/Shutterstock

VISUAL PATHWAYS TO THE BRAIN

How does visual information get to the brain? Axons leaving the back of each eye form the optic nerves, which travel to the *optic chiasm,* **the point at which the axons from the inside half of each eye cross over and then project to the opposite half of the brain** (as we first discussed in Chapter 3—refer to **Figure 3.14**). This arrangement ensures that signals from both eyes go to both hemispheres of the brain. Thus, as **Figure 4.6** shows, axons from the left half of each retina carry signals to the left side of the brain, and axons from the right half of each retina carry information to the right side of the brain.

After reaching the optic chiasm, the optic nerve fibers split along two pathways. The main pathway projects into the thalamus, the brain's major relay station. Here, about 90% of the axons from the retinas synapse in the *lateral geniculate nucleus* (LGN) (Pasternak, Bisley, & Calkins, 2003). Visual signals are processed in the LGN and then distributed to areas in the occipital lobe that make up the *primary visual cortex.* After the initial cortical processing of visual input takes place here, signals are typically sent to the temporal and parietal lobes for additional processing. The second visual pathway leaving the optic chiasm branches off to an area in the midbrain (the *superior colliculus*)

FIGURE 4.6

Visual pathways through the brain. (a) Input from the right half of the visual field strikes the left side of each retina and is transmitted to the left hemisphere (shown in blue). Input from the left half of the visual field strikes the right side of each retina and is transmitted to the right hemisphere (shown in red). The nerve fibers from each eye meet at the optic chiasm, where fibers from the inside half of each retina cross over to the opposite side of the brain. After reaching the optic chiasm, the major visual pathway projects through the lateral geniculate nucleus (LGN) in the thalamus and onto the primary visual cortex (shown with solid lines). A second pathway detours through the superior colliculus and then projects through the thalamus and onto the primary visual cortex (shown with dashed lines). **(b)** This inset shows a side view of how the optic pathways project through the thalamus and onto the visual cortex in the back of the brain (the two pathways mapped out in diagram **(a)** are virtually indistinguishable from this angle).

before traveling through the thalamus to the occipital lobe. However, the second pathway projects into different areas of the thalamus and the occipital lobe than the main visual pathway does. The principal function of the second pathway appears to be the coordination of visual input with other sensory input (Casanova et al., 2001; Stein & Meredith, 1993).

INFORMATION PROCESSING IN THE VISUAL CORTEX PSYKTREK 3C

Visual input ultimately arrives in the primary visual cortex located in the occipital lobe. Research that won a Nobel prize for David Hubel and Torsten Wiesel (1962, 1963) demonstrated that cells in the visual cortex respond to very specific types of stimuli. Some are sensitive to lines, some respond to edges, and some only react to more complicated stimuli. Some respond best to a line of the correct width, oriented at the correct angle, and located in the correct position in its receptive field (see **Figure 4.7**).

The key point of all this is that the cells in the visual cortex seem to be highly specialized. They have been characterized as *feature detectors,* **neurons that respond selectively to very specific features of more complex stimuli.** Ultimately, most visual stimuli could be represented by combinations of lines such as those registered by these feature detectors. Some theorists believe that feature detectors are registering the basic building blocks of visual perception and that the brain somehow assembles the blocks into a coherent picture of complex stimuli (Maguire, Weisstein, & Klymenko, 1990).

After visual input is processed in the primary visual cortex, it is often routed to other cortical areas for additional processing. These signals travel through two streams that have sometimes been characterized as the *what* and *where pathways* (see **Figure 4.8**). The *ventral stream* processes the details of *what* objects are out there (the perception of form and color), while the *dorsal stream* processes *where* the objects are (the perception of motion and depth) (Connor et al., 2009).

As signals move farther along in the visual processing system, neurons become even more specialized or fussy about what turns them on, and the stimuli that activate them become more and more complex. For example, researchers have identified cells in the temporal lobe (along the *what pathway*) of monkeys and humans that are especially sensitive to pictures of faces (Kanwisher & Yovel, 2009). These neurons respond even to pictures that merely *suggest* the form of a face (Cox, Meyers, & Sinha, 2004).

The discovery of neurons that respond to facial stimuli raises an obvious question: Why does the cortex have face detectors? Theorists are far from sure, but one line of thinking is that the ability to quickly recognize faces—such as those of friends or foes—

David Hubel
"One can now begin to grasp the significance of the great number of cells in the visual cortex. Each cell seems to have its own specific duties."

Courtesy of David Hubel

FIGURE 4.7
Hubel and Wiesel's procedure for studying the activity of neurons in the visual cortex. As the cat is shown various stimuli, a microelectrode records the firing of a neuron in the cat's visual cortex. The figure shows the electrical responses of a visual cell apparently "programmed" to respond to lines oriented vertically.

probably has had adaptive significance over the course of evolution (Sugita, 2009). Thus, natural selection *may* have wired the brains of some species to quickly respond to faces. Consistent with this hypothesis, recent research has demonstrated that basic aspects of face perception are apparent in infants (McKone, Crookes, & Kanwisher, 2009).

Viewing the World in Color

PsykTrek 3d

So far, we've considered only how the visual system deals with light and dark. Let's journey now into the world of color. Of course, you can see perfectly well without seeing in color. Many animals get by with little or no color vision, and no one seemed to suffer back when photographs, movies, or TV shows were all in black and white. However, color adds not only spectacle but information to perceptions of the world. The ability to identify objects against a complex background is enhanced by the addition of color (Tanaka, Weiskopf, & Williams, 2001). Thus, some theorists have suggested that color vision evolved in humans and monkeys because it improved their abilities to find food through foraging, to spot prey, and to quickly recognize predators (Spence et al., 2006). Although the purpose of color vision remains elusive, scientists have learned a great deal about the mechanisms underlying the perception of color.

THE STIMULUS FOR COLOR

PsykTrek 3d

As noted earlier, the lights people see are mixtures of different wavelengths. Perceived color is primarily a function of the dominant wavelength in these mixtures. Although wavelength wields the greatest influence, the perception of color depends on complex blends of all three properties of light.

People can perceive many different colors. Indeed, experts estimate that humans can discriminate among millions of colors (Webster, 2010). Most of these diverse variations are the result of mixing a few basic colors. There are two kinds of color mixture: subtractive and additive. *Subtractive color mixing* **works by removing some wavelengths of light, leaving less light than was originally there.** You probably became familiar with subtractive mixing as a child when you mixed yellow and blue paints to make green. Paints yield subtractive mixing because pigments *absorb* most wavelengths, selectively reflecting back specific wavelengths that give rise to particular colors. Subtractive color mixing can also be demonstrated by stacking color filters. If you look through a sandwich of yellow and blue cellophane filters, they will block out certain wavelengths. The middle wavelengths that are left will look green.

Additive color mixing **works by superimposing lights, putting more light in the mixture than exists in any one light by itself.** If you shine red, green, and blue spotlights on a white surface, you'll have an additive mixture. As **Figure 4.9** on the next page shows, additive and subtractive mixtures of the same colors produce different results. Human processes of color perception parallel additive mixing much more closely than subtractive mixing, as you'll see in the following discussion of theories of color vision.

Can you imagine a world without color?

TRICHROMATIC THEORY OF COLOR VISION

PsykTrek 3d

The trichromatic theory of color vision (*tri* for "three," *chroma* for "color") was first stated by Thomas Young and modified later by Hermann von Helmholtz (1852). **The *trichromatic theory* holds that the human eye has three types of receptors with differing sensitivities to different light wavelengths.** Helmholtz believed that the eye contains specialized receptors sensitive to the wavelengths associated with red, green, or

FIGURE 4.8

The *what* and *where pathways* from the primary visual cortex. Cortical processing of visual input is begun in the primary visual cortex. From there, signals are shuttled onward to a variety of other areas in the cortex along a number of pathways. Two prominent pathways are highlighted here. The dorsal stream, or *where pathway*, which processes information about motion and depth, moves on to areas of the parietal lobe. The ventral stream, or *what pathway*, which processes information about color and form, moves on to areas of the temporal lobe.

FIGURE 4.9

Additive versus subtractive color mixing. Lights mix additively because all the wavelengths contained in each light reach the eye. If red, blue, and green lights are projected onto a white screen, they produce the colors shown on the left, with white at the intersection of all three lights. If paints of the same three colors were combined in the same way, the subtractive mixture would produce the colors shown on the right, with black at the intersection of all three colors.

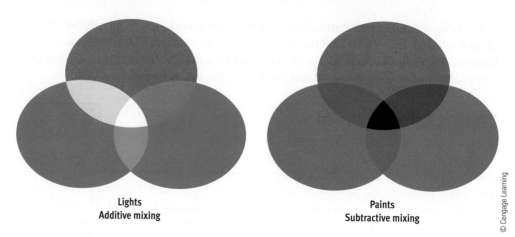

Lights
Additive mixing

Paints
Subtractive mixing

© Cengage Learning

Reality Check

Misconception

People who are color blind see the world in black and white.

Reality

The term color *blindness* is somewhat misleading, since only a tiny minority of those who are characterized as color blind are monochromats who see the world in black and white. The vast majority of color-blind people are dichromats who cannot see certain colors. Panel (a) below shows what the most common type of dichromat would see if presented with the batch of paper flowers shown in Panel (b).

(a)

(b)

SOURCE: From Goldstein, E. B. (2007). *Sensation and perception* (7 ed.). Belmont, CA: Wadsworth. Wadsworth is part of Cengage Learning, Inc. Reproduced by permission of Bruce Goldstein.

blue. According to this model, people can see all the colors of the rainbow because the eye does its own "color mixing" by varying the ratio of neural activity among these three types of receptors.

The impetus for the trichromatic theory was the demonstration that a light of any color can be matched by the additive mixture of three *primary colors.* (Any three colors that are appropriately spaced out in the visible spectrum can serve as primary colors, although red, green, and blue are usually used.) Does it sound implausible that three colors should be adequate for creating all other colors? If so, consider that this phenomenon is exactly what happens on your color TV screen or computer monitor (Stockman, 2010). Additive mixtures of red, green, and blue fool you into seeing all the colors of a natural scene.

Most of the known facts about color blindness also meshed well with trichromatic theory. *Color blindness* encompasses a variety of deficiencies in the ability to distinguish among colors. Color blindness occurs much more frequently in males than in females (Tait & Carroll, 2010). Most people who are color blind are *dichromats;* that is, they make do with only two types of color receptors. There are three types of dichromats, and each type is insensitive to one of the primary colors: red, green, or blue, although the latter is rare (Reid & Usrey, 2008). The three deficiencies, then, support the notion that there are three sets of receptors for color vision, as proposed by trichromatic theory.

OPPONENT PROCESS THEORY OF COLOR VISION

PSYKTREK 3d

Although trichromatic theory explained some facets of color vision well, it ran aground in other areas. Consider complementary afterimages, for instance. *Complementary colors* are pairs of colors that produce gray tones when mixed together. The various pairs of complementary colors can be arranged in a *color circle,* such as the one in **Figure 4.10**. If you stare at a strong color and then look at a white background, you'll see *an afterimage*—a visual image that persists after a stimulus is removed. The color of the afterimage will be the *complement* of the color you originally stared at. Trichromatic theory cannot account for the appearance of complementary afterimages.

Here's another peculiarity to consider. If you ask people to describe colors but restrict them to using three names, they run into difficulty. For example, using only red, green, and blue, they simply don't feel comfortable describing yellow as "reddish green." However, if you let them have just one more name, they usually choose yellow. Then they can describe any color quite well (Gordon & Abramov, 2001). If colors are reduced to three channels, why are four color names required to describe the full range of possible colors?

In an effort to answer questions such as these, Ewald Hering proposed the *opponent process theory* of color vision in 1878. The *opponent process theory* holds that color perception depends on receptors that make antagonistic responses to three pairs of colors. The three pairs of opponent colors he hypothesized were red versus green, yellow versus blue, and black versus white. The antagonistic processes in this theory provide plausible explanations for complementary afterimages and the need for four names (red, green, blue, and yellow) to describe colors. Opponent process theory also explains some aspects of color blindness. For instance, it can explain why dichromats typically find it hard to distinguish either green from red or yellow from blue.

RECONCILING THEORIES OF COLOR VISION

PsykTrek 3d

Advocates of trichromatic theory and opponent process theory argued about the relative merits of the two models for almost a century. Most researchers assumed that one theory must be wrong and the other must be right. In recent decades, however, it has become clear that *it takes both theories to explain color vision*. Eventually a physiological basis for both theories was found. Research that earned George Wald a Nobel prize demonstrated that *the eye has three types of cones*, with each type being most sensitive to a different band of wavelengths, as shown in **Figure 4.11** (Gegenfurtner, 2010; Wald, 1964). The three types of cones represent the three different color receptors predicted by trichromatic theory.

Researchers also discovered a biological basis for opponent processes. They found cells in the retina, the thalamus, and the visual cortex *that respond in opposite ways to red versus green and blue versus yellow* (Purves, 2009; Zrenner et al., 1990). For example, some ganglion cells in the retina are excited by green and inhibited by red. Other ganglion cells in the retina work in just the opposite way, as predicted by opponent process theory.

In summary, the perception of color appears to involve stages of information processing (Gegenfurtner, 2010; Hurvich, 1981). The receptors that do the first stage of processing (the cones) seem to follow the principles outlined in trichromatic theory. In later stages of processing, cells in the retina and the brain seem to follow the principles outlined in opponent process theory. As you can see, vigorous theoretical debate about color vision produced a solution that went beyond the contributions of either theory alone.

Effects of Color on Behavior

A newly emerging area of research concerns the effects that specific colors have on psychological functioning. Although there has long been an extensive popular literature on how colors affect behavior, it has mostly been based on speculation rather than empirical research. Recently, however, Andrew Elliot and his colleagues (Elliot & Maier, 2007; Moller, Elliot, & Maier, 2009) have formulated a theory of how color might influence behavior and have begun a series of experiments to test specific hypotheses. According

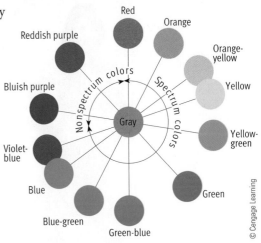

FIGURE 4.10

The color circle and complementary colors. Colors opposite each other on this color circle are complements, or "opposites." Additively mixing complementary colors produces gray. Opponent process principles help explain this effect as well as the other peculiarities of complementary colors.

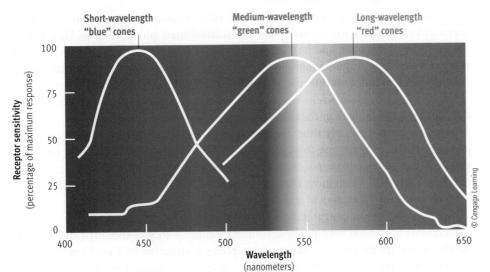

FIGURE 4.11

Three types of cones. Research has identified three types of cones that show varied sensitivity to different wavelengths of light. As the graph shows, these three types of cones correspond only roughly to the red, green, and blue receptors predicted by trichromatic theory, so it is more accurate to refer to them as cones sensitive to short, medium, and long wavelengths.

SOURCE: Based on Wald, G., & Brown, P. K. (1965). Human color vision and color blindness. *Cold Spring Harbor Laboratory Symposium of Quantitative Biology, 30,* 345–359 (p. 351). Copyright © 1965. Reprinted by permission of the author.

© Valentin Mosichev/Shutterstock

to Elliot et al. (2007), colors can have automatic, unconscious effects on behavior. They assert that these effects are probably rooted in the evolutionary significance of certain colors and learned associations.

In their first study of the behavioral effects of color, Elliot et al. (2007) theorized that red is associated with the danger of failure in achievement settings. Hence, they tested the hypothesis that exposure to the color red has a negative impact on performance in achievement situations. In one study, participants taking a subtest of an IQ test were exposed to a white, red, or green test booklet cover prior to taking the subtest. As hypothesized, subjects exposed to the red cover scored significantly lower on the test than those exposed to the green or white covers. Subsequent studies showed that the color red undermines performance in achievement contexts by evoking avoidance tendencies that disrupt attention (Elliot et al., 2009; Maier, Elliot, & Lichtenfeld, 2008).

Although red has negative effects in achievement contexts, Elliot et al. (2007) assert that it may have positive effects in sexual contexts. They review a number of ways in which the color red is associated with romance (red hearts on Valentine's day), lust (red light districts), and sexual liasons (the redness of aroused sexual organs). In a series of experiments, Elliot and Niesta (2008) found that that the color red inspires lust in men. For example, males evaluating a woman's attractiveness rated her as more sexually desirable when she wore red, as opposed to blue, green, or white. The influence of color on psychological functioning should be a fertile area of research in the future.

The Visual System: Perceptual Processes

KEY LEARNING GOALS

4.4 Discuss the subjectivity of form perception, inattentional blindness, and the concept of feature analysis.

4.5 Understand Gestalt principles of visual perception and the role of perceptual hypotheses in form perception.

4.6 Identify the monocular and binocular cues used in depth perception, and discuss cultural variations in depth perception.

4.7 Describe perceptual constancies, and discuss what visual illusions reveal about perception.

We have seen how sensory receptors in the eye transform light into neural impulses that are sent to the brain. We focus next on how the brain makes sense of it all—how does it convert streams of neural impulses into perceptions of chairs, doors, friends, automobiles, and buildings? In this section we explore *perceptual processes* in vision, such as the perception of forms, objects, depth, and so forth.

Perceiving Forms, Patterns, and Objects

PsykTrek 3c, 3e

The drawing in **Figure 4.12** is a poster for a circus act involving a trained seal. What do you see?

No doubt you see a seal balancing a ball on its nose and a trainer holding a fish and a whip. But suppose you had been told that the drawing is actually a poster for a costume ball. Would you have perceived it differently?

If you focus on the idea of a costume ball (stay with it a minute if you still see the seal and trainer), you will probably see a costumed man and woman in **Figure 4.12**. She's handing him a hat, and he has a sword in his right hand. This tricky little sketch was made ambiguous quite intentionally. It's a *reversible figure,* **a drawing that is compatible with two different interpretations that can shift back and forth.** Another classic reversible figure is shown in **Figure 4.13**. What do you see? A rabbit or a duck? It all depends on how you look at the drawing.

The key point is simply this: *The same visual input can result in radically different perceptions.* There is no one-to-one correspondence between sensory input and what you perceive. *This is a principal reason that people's experience of the world is subjective.* Perception involves much more than passively receiving signals from the outside world. It involves the *interpretation* of sensory input.

In this case, your interpretations result in two different "realities" because your *expectations* have been manipulated. Information given to you about the drawing has created a *perceptual set*—**a readiness to perceive a stimulus in a particular way.** A perceptual set creates a certain slant in how you interpret sensory input.

Form perception also depends on the *selection* of sensory input—that is, what people focus their attention on (Chun & Wolfe, 2001). A visual scene may include many objects and forms. Some of these may capture viewers' attention, while others may not. This fact has been demonstrated in dramatic fashion in studies of *inattentional blindness,* **which involves the failure to see fully visible objects or events in a visual display because one's attention is focused elsewhere.** In one such study (Simons & Chabris, 1999), participants watched a video of a group of people in white shirts passing a basketball laid over another video of people in black shirts passing a basketball (the two videos were partially transparent). The observers were instructed to focus on one of the two teams and press a key whenever that team passed the ball. Thirty seconds into the task, a woman carrying an umbrella clearly walked through the scene for four seconds. You might guess that this bizarre development would be noticed by virtually all the observers, but 44% of the participants failed to see the woman. Moreover, when someone in a gorilla suit strolled through the same scene, even more subjects (73%) missed the unexpected event!

Additional studies using other types of stimulus materials have demonstrated that people routinely overlook obvious forms that are unexpected (Most et al., 2005). Inattentional blindness has been attributed to subjects having a perceptual set that leads them to focus most of their attention on a specific feature in a scene (such as the basketball passes) while neglecting other facets of the scene (Most et al., 2001). Inattentional blindness may account for many automobile accidents, as accident reports often include the statement "I looked right there, but never saw them" (Shermer, 2004). The idea that we see much less of the world than we think we do surprises many people, but there is an auditory parallel that people take for granted (Mack, 2003). Think of how often you have had someone clearly say something to you, but you did not hear a word of what was said because you were "not listening." Inattentional blindness is essentially the same thing in the visual domain.

An understanding of how people perceive forms, patterns, and objects also requires knowledge of how people *organize and interpret* visual input. Several influential approaches to this question emphasize *feature analysis.*

FEATURE ANALYSIS: ASSEMBLING FORMS

PSYKTREK 3c

The information received by your eyes would do you little good if you couldn't recognize objects and forms—ranging from words on a page to the microwave in your kitchen and friends in the distance. According to some theories, perceptions of form and pattern entail *feature analysis* (Lindsay & Norman, 1977; Maguire et al., 1990). *Feature analysis* **is the process of detecting specific elements in visual input and assembling them into a more complex form.** In other words, you start with the components of a form, such as lines, edges, and corners, and build them into perceptions of squares, triangles, stop signs, bicycles, ice cream cones, and telephones. An application of this model of form perception is diagrammed in **Figure 4.14** on the next page.

Feature analysis assumes that form perception involves *bottom-up processing,* **a progression from individual elements to the whole** (see **Figure 4.15** on the next page). The plausibility of this model was bolstered greatly when Hubel and Wiesel showed that cells in the visual cortex operate as highly specialized feature detectors. Indeed, their findings strongly suggested that at least some aspects of form perception involve feature analysis.

Can feature analysis provide a complete account of how people perceive forms? Clearly not. A crucial problem for the theory is that form perception often does not involve bottom-up processing. In fact, there is ample evidence that perceptions of form frequently involve *top-down processing,* **a progression from the whole to the elements** (see **Figure 4.15**). For example, there is evidence that people can perceive a word before its individual letters, a phenomenon that has to reflect top-down processing (Johnston & McClelland, 1974). If readers depended exclusively on bottom-up processing, they would have to analyze the features of letters in words to recognize them and then assemble the letters into words. This task would be time-consuming and would slow down reading speed to a snail's pace.

© Cengage Learning

FIGURE 4.12
A poster for a trained seal act. Or is it? The picture is an ambiguous figure, which can be interpreted as either of two scenes, as explained in the text.

FIGURE 4.13
Another ambiguous figure. What animal do you see here? As the text explains, two very different perceptions are possible. This ambiguous figure was devised around 1900 by Joseph Jastrow, a prominent psychologist at the turn of the 20th century (Block & Yuker, 1992).

FIGURE 4.14

Feature analysis in form perception. One vigorously debated theory of form perception is that the brain has cells that respond to specific aspects or features of stimuli, such as lines and angles. Neurons functioning as higher-level analyzers then respond to input from these "feature detectors." The more input each analyzer receives, the more active it becomes. Finally, other neurons weigh signals from these analyzers and make a "decision" about the stimulus. In this way perception of a form is arrived at by assembling elements from the bottom up.

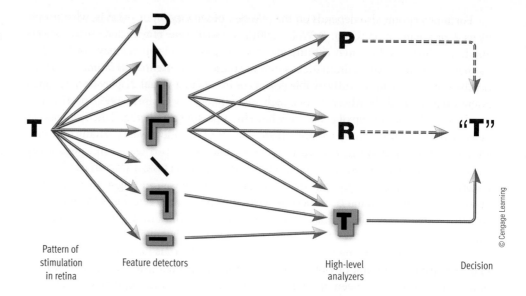

Pattern of stimulation in retina   Feature detectors   High-level analyzers   Decision

© Cengage Learning

FIGURE 4.15

Bottom-up versus top-down processing. As explained in these diagrams, bottom-up processing progresses from individual elements to whole elements, whereas top-down processing progresses from the whole to the individual elements.

© Cengage Learning

Archives of the History of American Psychology, University of Akron, Akron, Ohio

Max Wertheimer

"The fundamental 'formula' of Gestalt theory might be expressed in this way: There are wholes, the behaviour of which is not determined by that of their individual elements."

LOOKING AT THE WHOLE PICTURE: GESTALT PRINCIPLES

Sometimes a whole, as we perceive it, may have qualities that don't exist in any of the parts. This insight—*that the whole can be greater than the sum of its parts*—became the basic assumption of *Gestalt psychology,* an influential school of thought that emerged out of Germany during the first half of the 20th century (*Gestalt* is a German word for "form" or "shape").

A simple example of this principle, which you have experienced countless times, is the *phi phenomenon,* first described by Max Wertheimer in 1912. **The *phi phenomenon* is the illusion of movement created by presenting visual stimuli in rapid succession.** You encounter examples of the phi phenomenon nearly every day. For example, movies and TV consist of separate still pictures projected rapidly one after the other. You *see* smooth motion, but in reality the "moving" objects merely take slightly different positions in successive frames. Viewed as a whole, a movie has a property (motion) that isn't evident in any of its parts (the individual frames).

The Gestalt psychologists formulated a series of principles that describe how the visual system organizes a scene into discrete forms (Schirillo, 2010). Let's explore some of these principles.

Figure and Ground   Take a look at **Figure 4.16**. Do you see the figure as two silhouetted faces against a white background, or as a white vase against a black background?

This reversible figure illustrates the Gestalt principle of *figure and ground*. Dividing visual displays into figure and ground is a fundamental way in which people organize visual perceptions (Baylis & Driver, 1995). The figure is the thing being looked at, and the ground is the background against which it stands. Other things being equal, an object is more likely to be viewed as a figure when it is smaller in size, higher in contrast, or greater in symmetry (Palmer, 2003), and especially when it is lower in one's frame of view (Vecera & Palmer, 2006). More often than not, your visual field may contain many figures sharing a background. The following Gestalt principles relate to how these elements are grouped into higher-order figures (Palmer, 2003).

Proximity   Things that are near one another seem to belong together. The black dots in **Figure 4.17(a)** could be grouped into vertical columns or horizontal rows. However, people tend to perceive rows because of the effect of proximity (the dots are closer together horizontally).

Closure   People often group elements to create a sense of *closure*, or completeness. Thus, you may "complete" figures that actually have gaps in them. This principle is demonstrated in **Figure 4.17(b)**.

Similarity   People also tend to group stimuli that are similar. This principle is apparent in **Figure 4.17(c)**, where elements of similar darkness are grouped into the number 2.

FIGURE 4.16
The principle of figure and ground. Whether you see two faces or a vase depends on which part of this drawing you see as figure and which as background. Although this reversible drawing allows you to switch back and forth between two ways of organizing your perception, you can't perceive the drawing both ways at once.

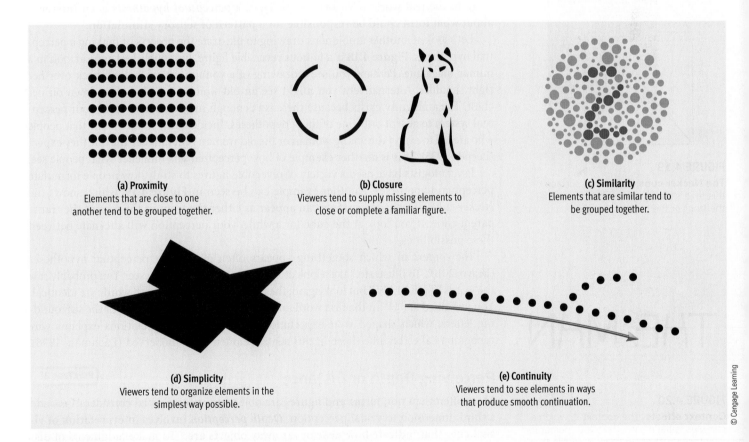

(a) Proximity
Elements that are close to one another tend to be grouped together.

(b) Closure
Viewers tend to supply missing elements to close or complete a familiar figure.

(c) Similarity
Elements that are similar tend to be grouped together.

(d) Simplicity
Viewers tend to organize elements in the simplest way possible.

(e) Continuity
Viewers tend to see elements in ways that produce smooth continuation.

FIGURE 4.17
Gestalt principles of perceptual organization. Gestalt principles help explain some of the factors that influence form perception. **(a) Proximity:** These dots might well be organized in vertical columns rather than horizontal rows, but because of proximity (the dots are closer together horizontally), they tend to be perceived in rows. **(b) Closure:** Even though the figures are incomplete, you fill in the blanks and see a circle and a dog. **(c) Similarity:** Because of similarity of color, you see dots organized into the number 2 instead of a random array. If you did not group similar elements, you wouldn't see the number 2 here. **(d) Simplicity:** You could view this as a complicated 11-sided figure, but given the preference for simplicity, you are more likely to see it as an overlapping rectangle and triangle. **(e) Continuity:** You tend to group these dots in a way that produces a smooth path rather than an abrupt shift in direction.

FIGURE 4.18
A famous reversible figure. What do you see? Consult the text to learn the two possible interpretations of this figure.

FIGURE 4.19
The Necker cube. The tinted surface of this reversible figure can become either the front or the back of the cube.

FIGURE 4.20
Context effects. The context in which a stimulus is seen can affect your perceptual hypotheses. The middle character in the word on the left is assumed to be an "H," whereas in the word on the right the same character is assumed to be an "A." In addition to showing the potential influence of context, this example shows the power of expectations and top-down processing.

Simplicity The Gestaltists' most general principle was the law of *Pragnanz*, which translates from German as "good form." The idea is that people tend to group elements that combine to form a good figure. This principle is somewhat vague in that it's often difficult to spell out what makes a figure "good" (Biederman, Hilton, & Hummel, 1991). Some theorists maintain that goodness is largely a matter of simplicity, asserting that people tend to organize forms in the simplest way possible (see **Figure 4.17(d)**).

Continuity The principle of continuity reflects people's tendency to follow in whatever direction they've been led. Thus, people tend to connect points that result in straight or gently curved lines that create "smooth" paths, as shown in **Figure 4.17(e)**.

Although Gestalt psychology is no longer an active theoretical orientation in modern psychology, its influence is still felt in the study of perception (Banks & Krajicek, 1991). The Gestalt psychologists raised many important questions that still occupy researchers, and they left a legacy of many useful insights about form perception that have stood the test of time (Sharps & Wertheimer, 2000).

FORMULATING PERCEPTUAL HYPOTHESES

In visual perception, the images projected on the retina are distorted, two-dimensional versions of their actual, three-dimensional counterparts. If the sensory input that people have to work with is so distorted, how do they get an accurate view of the world? One explanation is that people are constantly making and testing *hypotheses* about what's out there in the real world (Gregory, 1973). Thus, **a *perceptual hypothesis* is an inference about what form could be responsible for a pattern of sensory stimulation.**

Let's look at another ambiguous drawing to illustrate the process of making a perceptual hypothesis. **Figure 4.18** is a famous reversible figure, first published as a cartoon in a humor magazine. Perhaps you see a drawing of a young woman looking back over her right shoulder. Alternatively, you might see an old woman with her chin down on her chest. The ambiguity exists because there isn't enough information to force your perceptual system to accept only one of these hypotheses. Incidentally, studies show that people who are led to *expect* the young woman or the old woman generally see the one they expect (Leeper, 1935). This is another example of how perceptual sets influence what people see.

Psychologists have used a variety of reversible figures to study how people formulate perceptual hypotheses. Another example can be seen in **Figure 4.19**, which shows the *Necker cube*. The shaded surface can appear as either the front or the rear of the transparent cube. If you look at the cube for a while, your perception will alternate between these possibilities.

The *context* in which something appears often guides our perceptual hypotheses (Bravo, 2010). To illustrate, take a look at **Figure 4.20**. What do you see? You probably saw the words "THE MAN." But look again; the middle characters in both words are identical. You identified an "H" in the first word and an "A" in the second because of the surrounding letters, which shaped your expectations. The power of expectations explains why typographical errors like those in this sentence often pass unobered (Lachman, 1996).

Perceiving Depth or Distance

PSYKTREK 3f

More often than not, forms and figures are objects in space. Spatial considerations add a third dimension to visual perception. *Depth perception* **involves interpretation of visual cues that indicate how near or far away objects are.** To make judgments of distance, people rely on quite a variety of clues, which can be classified into two types: binocular cues and monocular cues (Hochberg, 1988; Proffitt & Caudek, 2003).

BINOCULAR CUES

PSYKTREK 3f

Because they are set apart, the eyes each have a slightly different view of the world. *Binocular depth cues* **are clues about distance based on the differing views of the two eyes.** The new 3D movies take advantage of this fact. Two cameras are used to record slightly different images of the same scene. The special polarized glasses that viewers wear separate the images for each eye. The brain then supplies the "depth," and you perceive a three-dimensional scene.

The principal binocular depth cue is *retinal disparity,* **which refers to the fact that objects within 25 feet project images to slightly different locations on the right and left retinas, so the right and left eyes see slightly different views of the object.** The closer an object gets, the greater the disparity between the images seen by each eye. Thus, retinal disparity increases as objects come closer, providing information about distance.

MONOCULAR CUES

PSYKTREK 3f

Monocular depth cues **are clues about distance based on the image in either eye alone.** There are two kinds of monocular cues to depth. One kind is the result of active use of the eye in viewing the world. For example, as an object comes closer, you may sense the accommodation (the change in the curvature of the lens) that must occur for the eye to adjust its focus.

The other kind of monocular cues are *pictorial depth cues*—**cues about distance that can be given in a flat picture.** There are many pictorial cues to depth, which is why paintings and photographs can seem so realistic that you feel you can climb right into them. Six prominent pictorial depth cues are described and illustrated in **Figure 4.21.**

© ImageSource/Getty Images

Linear perspective Parallel lines that run away from the viewer seem to get closer together.

Texture gradient As distance increases, a texture gradually becomes denser and less distinct.

Interposition The shapes of near objects overlap or mask those of more distant ones.

Relative size If separate objects are expected to be of the same size, the larger ones are seen as closer.

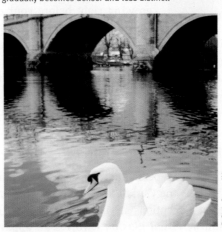

Height in plane Near objects are low in the visual field; more distant ones are higher up.

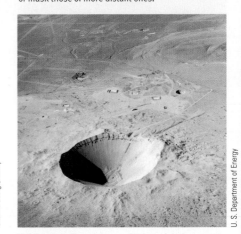

Light and shadow Patterns of light and dark suggest shadows that can create an impression of three-dimensional forms.

FIGURE 4.21

Pictorial cues to depth. Six pictorial depth cues are explained and illustrated here. Although one cue stands out in each photo, in most visual scenes several pictorial cues are present. Try looking at the light-and-shadow picture upside down. The change in shadowing reverses what you see.

BIZARRO

The first of these, *linear perspective,* is a depth cue reflecting the fact that lines converge in the distance. Because details are too small to see when they are far away, *texture gradients* can also provide information about depth. If an object comes between you and another object, it must be closer to you, a cue called *interposition. Relative size* is a cue because closer objects appear larger. *Height in plane* reflects the fact that distant objects appear higher in a picture. Finally, the familiar effects of shadowing make *light* and *shadow* useful in judging distance.

Some cultural differences appear to exist in the ability to take advantage of pictorial depth cues in two-dimensional drawings. These differences were first investigated by Hudson (1960, 1967), who presented pictures like the one in **Figure 4.22** to various cultural groups in South Africa. Hudson's approach was based on the assumption that subjects who indicate that the hunter is trying to spear the elephant instead of the antelope don't understand the depth cues (interposition, relative size, height in plane) in the picture, which place the elephant in the distance. Hudson found that subjects from a rural South African tribe (the Bantu), who had little exposure at that time to pictures and photos, frequently misinterpreted the depth cues in his pictures. Similar difficulties with depth cues in pictures have been documented for other cultural groups who have little experience with two-dimensional representations of three-dimensional space (Berry et al., 1992). Thus, the application of pictorial depth cues to pictures varies to some degree across cultures.

Recent research has shown that estimates of distance can be skewed by people's motivational states. Studies suggest that people see desirable objects as being closer to them than less desirable objects. For example, Balcetis and Dunning (2010) found that distance estimates of a bottle of water across a room were closer for participants who were very thirsty than for participants who were not thirsty. Thus, like other perceptual experiences, judgments of distance can be highly subjective.

FIGURE 4.22

Testing understanding of pictorial depth cues. In his cross-cultural research, Hudson (1960) asked subjects to indicate whether the hunter is trying to spear the antelope or the elephant. He found cultural disparities in subjects' ability to make effective use of the pictorial depth cues, which place the elephant in the distance and make it an unlikely target.

SOURCE: Adapted by permission from an illustration by Ilil Arbel in Deregowski, J. B. (1972, November). Pictorial perception and culture. *Scientific American, 227* (5), p. 83. Copyright © 1972 by Scientific American, Inc. All rights reserved.

Perceptual Constancies in Vision

When a person approaches you from the distance, his or her image on your retinas gradually changes in size. Do you perceive that person as growing right before your eyes? Of course not. Your perceptual system constantly makes allowances for this variation in visual input. In doing so, it relies in part on perceptual constancies. **A *perceptual constancy* is a tendency to experience a stable perception in the face of continually changing sensory input.** Among other things, people tend to view objects as having a stable size, shape, brightness, hue (color), and location in space (Goldstein, 2010). Perceptual constancies such as these help impose some order on the surrounding world.

The Power of Misleading Cues: Visual Illusions   (PsykTrek SIM3, 3g)

In general, perceptual constancies, depth cues, and principles of visual organization (such as the Gestalt laws) help people perceive the world accurately. Sometimes, however, perceptions are based on inappropriate assumptions, and *visual illusions* can result. **A *visual illusion* involves an apparently inexplicable discrepancy between the appearance of a visual stimulus and its physical reality.**

One famous visual illusion is the *Müller-Lyer illusion,* shown in **Figure 4.23**. The two vertical lines in this figure are equally long, but they certainly don't look that way. Why not? Several mechanisms probably play a role (Day, 1965; Gregory, 1978). The figure on the left looks like the outside of a building, thrust toward the viewer, while the one on the right looks like an inside corner, thrust away (see **Figure 4.24**). The vertical line in the left figure therefore seems closer. If two lines cast equally long retinal images but one seems closer, the closer one is assumed to be shorter. Thus, the Müller-Lyer illusion may be due largely to a combination of size constancy processes and misperception of depth.

The *Ponzo illusion,* shown in **Figure 4.25**, appears to result from the same factors (Coren & Girgus, 1978). The upper and lower horizontal lines are the same length, but the upper one appears longer. This illusion probably occurs because the converging lines convey linear perspective, a key depth cue suggesting that the upper line lies farther in the distance. **Figure 4.26** is a drawing by Stanford University psychologist Roger Shepard (1990) that creates a similar illusion. The second monster appears much larger than the first, even though they are really identical in size. This variation on the Ponzo

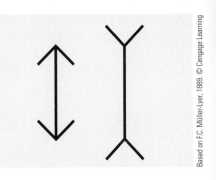

Based on F.C. Müller-Lyer, 1889. © Cengage Learning

FIGURE 4.23

The Müller-Lyer illusion. Go ahead, measure them: The two vertical lines are of equal length.

© Cengage Learning

FIGURE 4.24

Explaining the Müller-Lyer illusion. The figure on the left seems to be closer, since it looks like an outside corner, thrust toward you, whereas the figure on the right looks like an inside corner thrust away from you. Given retinal images of the same length, you assume that the "closer" line is shorter.

illusion and the other geometric illusions shown in **Figure 4.25** demonstrate that visual stimuli can be highly deceptive.

Yet another well-known visual illusion is the *moon illusion.* The full moon appears to be as much as 50% smaller when overhead than when looming on the horizon (Ross & Plug, 2002). As with many of the other illusions we have discussed, the moon illusion seems to result mainly from size constancy effects coupled with the misperception of distance (Coren & Aks, 1990; Kaufman et al., 2007).

Cross-cultural studies have uncovered some interesting differences among cultural groups in their tendency to see

© Philipe Ancheta/Shutterstock.com

A puzzling perceptual illusion common in everyday life is the moon illusion: the moon looks larger when at the horizon than when overhead.

Ponzo

Poggendorff

Upside-down T

Zollner

Ponzo (1913); Poggendorff (1860); Zollner (1860); © Cengage Learning

FIGURE 4.25

Four geometric illusions. Ponzo: The horizontal lines are the same length. **Poggendorff:** The two diagonal segments lie on the same straight line. **Upside-down T:** The vertical and horizontal lines are the same length. **Zollner:** The long diagonals are all parallel (try covering up some of the short lines if you don't believe it).

FIGURE 4.26

A monster of an illusion. The principles underlying the Ponzo illusion also explain the striking illusion seen here, in which two identical monsters appear to be quite different in size.

SOURCE: Shepard, R. N. (1990). *Mind sights.* New York: W. H. Freeman. Copyright © 1990 by Roger N. Shepard. Used by permission of Henry Holt & Co., LLC.

Unlike people in Western nations, the Zulus live in a culture where straight lines and right angles are scarce. Thus, they are not affected by such phenomena as the Müller-Lyer illusion nearly as much as people raised in environments that abound with rectangular structures.

certain illusions (Masuda, 2010). For example, Segall, Campbell, and Herskovits (1966) found that people from Western cultures are more susceptible to the Müller-Lyer illusion than people from some non-Western cultures. The most plausible explanation is that in the West, we live in a "carpentered world" dominated by straight lines, right angles, and rectangular rooms, buildings, and furniture. Thus, our experience prepares us to readily view the Müller-Lyer figures as inside and outside corners of buildings, inferences that help foster the illusion (Segall et al., 1990).

Like ambiguous figures, visual illusions demonstrate that human perceptions are not simple reflections of objective reality. Once again, we see that perception of the world is subjective. We will encounter this insight again as we examine other sensory systems, such as hearing, which we turn to next.

Concept Check 4.2

Recognizing Pictorial Depth Cues

Painters routinely attempt to create the perception of depth on a flat canvas by using pictorial depth cues. **Figure 4.21** describes and illustrates six pictorial depth cues, most of which are apparent in Vincent van Gogh's colorful piece titled *Corridor in the Asylum* (1889). Check your understanding of depth perception by trying to spot the depth cues in the painting.

In the list below, check off the depth cues used by van Gogh. The answers can be found in Appendix A. You can learn more about how artists use the principles of visual perception in the Personal Application at the end of this chapter.

_____ 1. Interposition

_____ 2. Height in plane

_____ 3. Texture gradient

_____ 4. Relative size

_____ 5. Light and shadow

_____ 6. Linear perspective

van Gogh, Vincent, *Corridor in the Asylum* (1889), gouache and watercolor, 24 3/8 x 18 1/2 inches (61.5 x 47 cm). Metropolitan Museum of Art. Bequest of Abby Aldrich Rockefeller, 1948. (48.190.2) Image © The Metropolitan Museum of Art. Image source: Art Resource, NY.

The Auditory System: Hearing

4.8 Identify the three properties of sound, and summarize information on human hearing capacities.

4.9 Describe how sensory processing occurs in the ear, and compare the place and frequency theories of pitch perception.

Like vision, the auditory (hearing) system provides input about the world "out there," but not until incoming information is processed by the brain. An auditory stimulus—a screech of tires, someone laughing, the hum of the refrigerator—produces sensory input in the form of sound waves reaching the ears. The perceptual system must somehow transform this stimulation into the psychological experience of hearing. We'll begin our discussion of hearing by looking at the stimulus for auditory experience: sound.

The Stimulus: Sound

PSYKTREK 3h

Sound waves are vibrations of molecules, which means that they must travel through some physical medium, such as air. They move at a fraction of the speed of light. Sound waves are usually generated by vibrating objects, such as a guitar string, a loudspeaker cone, or your vocal cords. However, they can also be generated by forcing air past a chamber (as in a pipe organ), or by suddenly releasing a burst of air (as when you clap).

Like light waves, sound waves are characterized by their *wavelength (frequency)*, their *amplitude*, and their *purity* (see **Figure 4.27**). These physical properties affect mainly the perceived (psychological) qualities of *pitch, loudness,* and *timbre,* respectively. However, they interact in complex ways to produce perceptions of these sound qualities (Hirsh & Watson, 1996).

Human Hearing Capacities

PSYKTREK 3h

Wavelengths of sound are described in terms of their *frequency,* which is measured in cycles per second, or *hertz* (Hz). For the most part, higher frequencies are perceived as having higher pitch. That is, if you strike the key for high C on a piano, it will produce higher-frequency sound waves than the key for low C. Although the perception of pitch depends mainly on frequency, the amplitude of the sound waves also influences it.

Just as the visible spectrum is only a portion of the total spectrum of light, so, too, what people can hear is only a portion of the available range of sounds. Humans can hear sounds ranging in frequency from a low of 20 Hz up to a high of about 20,000 Hz. Sounds at either end of this range are harder to hear, and sensitivity to high-frequency tones declines as adults grow older (Dubno, 2010). Other organisms have different capabilities. Low-frequency sounds under 10 Hz are audible to homing pigeons, for example. At the other extreme, bats and porpoises can hear frequencies well above 20,000 Hz.

In general, the greater the amplitude of sound waves, the louder the sound perceived. Whereas frequency is measured in hertz, amplitude is measured in *decibels* (dB). The relationship between decibels (which measure a physical property of sound) and loudness (a psychological quality) is complex. A rough rule of thumb is that perceived loudness doubles about every 6–10 decibels (Florentine & Heinz, 2010). As shown in **Figure 4.28** on the next page, the weakest sound a person can hear depends on its frequency. The human ear is most sensitive to sounds at frequencies near 2000 Hz. Thus, loudness ultimately depends on an interaction between amplitude and frequency.

Very loud sounds can have negative effects on the quality of your hearing. Even brief exposure to sounds over 120 decibels can be painful and may cause damage to your auditory system (Daniel, 2007). In recent years there has been great concern about hearing loss in young people using personal listening devices who play their music too loudly (Morata, 2007). Portable music players can easily deliver over 100 decibels through headphones. One study found significant hearing impairment in 14% of the young people sampled (Peng, Tao, Huang, 2009). Unfortunately, adolescents tend to not worry much about the risk of hearing loss (Vogel et al., 2008). However, it is a serious problem

(a) Wavelength — Air pressure — Amplitude

(b)

Physical properties of sound	Related perceptions
Wavelength/Frequency	Pitch
Amplitude	Loudness
Purity	Timbre

© Cengage Learning

FIGURE 4.27

Sound, the physical stimulus for hearing. (a) Like light, sound travels in waves—in this case, waves of air pressure. A smooth curve would represent a pure tone, such as that produced by a tuning fork. Most sounds, however, are complex. For example, the wave shown here is for middle C played on a piano. The sound wave for the same note played on a violin would have the same wavelength (or frequency) as this one, but the "wrinkles" in the wave would be different, corresponding to the differences in timbre between the two sounds. **(b)** The table shows the main relations between objective aspects of sound and subjective perceptions.

FIGURE 4.28

Sound pressure and auditory experience. The threshold for human hearing (graphed in green) is a function of both sound pressure (decibel level) and frequency. Human hearing is keenest for sounds at frequencies around 2000 Hz; at other frequencies, higher decibel levels are needed to produce sounds people can detect. On the other hand, the human threshold for pain (graphed in red) is almost purely a function of decibel level.

SOURCE: Decibel level examples from Atkinson, R. L., Atkinson R. C., Smith, E. F., & Hilgard, E. R., *Introduction to Psychology*, Ninth Edition, San Diego: Harcourt, copyright © 1987. Reprinted by permission of Cengage Learning. www.cengage.com/permissions.

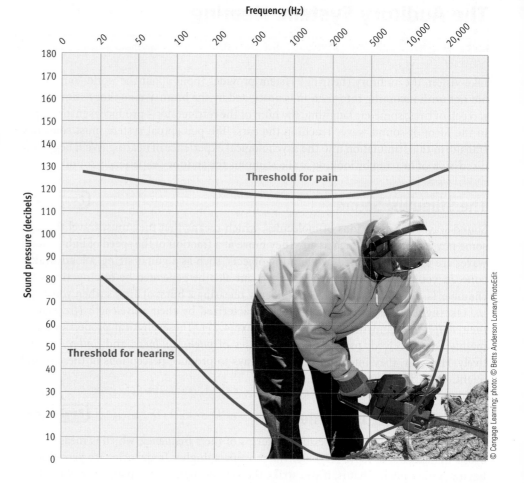

that is likely to lead to a great deal of preventable hearing loss given the increased popularity of portable music players (Daniel, 2007; Vogel et al., 2007).

People are also sensitive to variations in the purity of sounds. The purest sound is one that has only a single frequency of vibration, such as that produced by a tuning fork. Most everyday sounds are complex mixtures of many frequencies. The purity or complexity of a sound influences how *timbre* is perceived. To understand timbre, think of a note with precisely the same loudness and pitch played on a piano and then on a violin. The difference you perceive in the sounds is a difference in timbre.

Sensory Processing in the Ear (PSYKTREK 3h)

Like your eyes, your ears channel energy to the neural tissue that receives it. **Figure 4.29** shows that the human ear can be divided into three sections: the external ear, the middle ear, and the inner ear. Sound is conducted differently in each section. The external ear depends on the *vibration of air molecules*. The middle ear depends on the *vibration of movable bones*. And the inner ear depends on *waves in a fluid*, which are finally converted into a stream of neural signals sent to the brain (Moore, 2001).

The *external ear* consists mainly of the *pinna*, a sound-collecting cone. When you cup your hand behind your ear to try to hear better, you are augmenting that cone. Sound waves collected by the pinna are funneled along the auditory canal toward the *eardrum*, a taut membrane that vibrates in response.

In the *middle ear,* the vibrations of the eardrum are transmitted inward by a mechanical chain made up of the three tiniest bones in your body (the hammer, anvil, and stirrup), known collectively as the *ossicles.* The ossicles form a three-stage lever system that converts relatively large movements with little force into smaller motions with greater force. The ossicles serve to amplify tiny changes in air pressure.

The *inner ear* consists largely of **the *cochlea,* a fluid-filled, coiled tunnel that contains the receptors for hearing.** The term *cochlea* comes from the Greek word for a spiral-shelled snail, which this chamber resembles (see **Figure 4.29**). Sound enters the cochlea through the *oval window,* which is vibrated by the ossicles. The ear's neural tissue, which is functionally similar to the retina in the eye, lies within the cochlea. This tissue sits on the basilar membrane that divides the cochlea into upper and lower chambers. **The *basilar membrane,* which runs the length of the spiraled cochlea, holds the auditory receptors, called hair cells.** Waves in the fluid of the inner ear stimulate the hair cells. Like the rods and cones in the eye, the hair cells convert this physical stimulation into neural impulses that are sent to the brain (Hudspeth, 2000). These signals are routed through the thalamus to the auditory cortex, which is located mostly in the temporal lobes of the brain.

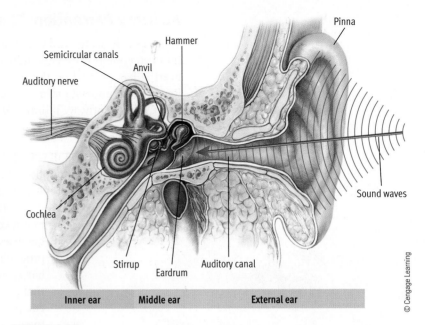

FIGURE 4.29

The human ear. Converting sound pressure to information processed by the nervous system involves a complex relay of stimuli. Waves of air pressure create vibrations in the eardrum, which in turn cause oscillations in the tiny bones in the inner ear (the hammer, anvil, and stirrup). As they are relayed from one bone to the next, the oscillations are magnified and then transformed into pressure waves moving through a liquid medium in the cochlea. These waves cause the basilar membrane to oscillate, stimulating the hair cells that are the actual auditory receptors (see **Figure 4.30**).

Concept Check 4.3

Comparing Vision and Hearing

Check your understanding of both vision and hearing by comparing key aspects of sensation and perception in these senses. The dimensions of comparison are listed in the first column below. The second column lists the answers for the sense of vision. Fill in the answers for the sense of hearing in the third column. The answers can be found in Appendix A in the back of the book.

Dimension	Vision	Hearing
1. Stimulus	Light waves	
2. Elements of stimulus and related perceptions	Wavelength/hue	
	Amplitude/brightness	
	Purity/saturation	
3. Receptors	Rods and cones	
4. Location of receptors	Retina	
5. Main location of processing in brain	Occipital lobe, Visual cortex	

Auditory Perception: Theories of Hearing

Theories of hearing need to account for how sound waves are physiologically translated into perceptions of pitch, loudness, and timbre. To date, most of the theorizing about hearing has focused on the perception of pitch, which is reasonably well understood. Researchers' understanding of loudness and timbre perception is primitive by comparison. Consequently, we'll limit our coverage to theories of pitch perception.

PLACE THEORY

There have been two influential theories of pitch perception: *place theory* and *frequency theory.* You'll be able to follow the development of these theories more easily if you can imagine the spiraled cochlea unraveled, so that the basilar membrane becomes a long, thin sheet, lined with about 25,000 individual hair cells (see **Figure 4.30**). Long ago, Hermann von Helmholtz (1863) proposed that specific sound frequencies vibrate specific portions of the basilar membrane, producing distinct pitches, just as plucking specific strings on a harp produces sounds of varied pitch. Thus, *place theory* holds **that perception of pitch corresponds to the vibration of different portions, or places, along the basilar membrane.** Place theory assumes that hair cells at various locations respond independently and that different sets of hair cells are vibrated by different sound frequencies. The brain then detects the frequency of a tone according to which area along the basilar membrane is most active.

FIGURE 4.30

The basilar membrane. This graphic shows how the cochlea might look if it were unwound and cut open to reveal the basilar membrane, which is covered with thousands of hair cells (the auditory receptors). Pressure waves in the fluid filling the cochlea cause oscillations to travel in waves down the basilar membrane, stimulating the hair cells to fire. Although the entire membrane vibrates, as predicted by frequency theory, the point along the membrane where the wave peaks depends on the frequency of the sound stimulus, as suggested by place theory.

FREQUENCY THEORY

Other theorists in the 19th century proposed an alternative theory of pitch perception, called frequency theory (Rutherford, 1886). *Frequency theory* **holds that perception of pitch corresponds to the rate, or frequency, at which the entire basilar membrane vibrates.** This theory views the basilar membrane as more like a drumhead than a harp. According to frequency theory, the whole membrane vibrates in response to sounds. However, a particular sound frequency, say 3000 Hz, causes the basilar membrane to vibrate at a corresponding rate of 3000 times per second. The brain detects the frequency of a tone by the rate at which the auditory nerve fibers fire.

RECONCILING PLACE AND FREQUENCY THEORIES

The competition between these two theories is similar to the dispute between the trichromatic and opponent process theories of color vision. Like that argument, the debate between place and frequency theories generated roughly a century of research. Although both theories proved to have some flaws, *both turned out to be valid in part.*

Helmholtz's place theory was basically on the mark except for one detail. The hair cells along the basilar membrane are not independent. They vibrate together, as suggested by frequency theory. The actual pattern of vibration, described in Nobel prize–winning research by Georg von Békésy (1947), is a traveling wave that moves along the basilar membrane. Place theory is correct, however, in that the wave peaks at a particular place, depending on the frequency of the sound wave.

The current thinking is that pitch perception depends on both place and frequency coding of vibrations along the basilar membrane (Moore, 2010; Yost, 2010). Low-frequency pure tones appear to be translated into pitch through frequency coding. High-frequency pure tones appear to rely on place coding. And complex tones seem to depend on complex combinations of frequency and place coding. Although much remains to be learned, once again we find that theories that were pitted against each other for decades are complementary rather than contradictory.

The Other Senses: Taste, Smell, and Touch

KEY LEARNING GOALS

4.10 Describe the stimulus and receptors for taste, and review research on individual differences in taste sensitivity.

4.11 Describe the stimulus and receptors for smell, and evaluate humans' olfactory capabilities.

4.12 Describe the stimulus and receptors for touch, and explain what is known about pain perception.

Psychologists have devoted most of their attention to the visual and auditory systems. Although less is known about the senses of taste, smell, and touch, they also play a critical role in people's experience of the world. Let's start by taking a brief look at what psychologists have learned about **the *gustatory system*—the sensory system for taste.**

Taste: The Gustatory System

True wine lovers go through an elaborate series of steps when they are served a good bottle of wine. Typically, they begin by drinking a little water to cleanse their palate. Then they sniff the cork from the wine bottle, swirl a small amount of the wine around in a glass, and sniff the odor emerging from the glass. Finally, they take a sip of the wine, rolling it around in their mouth for a short time before swallowing it. At last they are ready to indicate their approval or disapproval. Is all this activity really a meaningful way to put the wine to a sensitive test? Or is it just a harmless ritual passed on through tradition? You'll find out in this section.

The physical stimuli for the sense of taste are chemical substances that are soluble (dissolvable in water). The gustatory receptors are clusters of taste cells found in the *taste buds* that line the trenches around tiny bumps on the tongue. When these cells absorb chemicals dissolved in saliva, neural impulses are triggered that are routed through the thalamus to the cortex. Interestingly, taste cells have a short life. They last only about 10 days, and they are constantly being replaced (Cowart, 2005). New cells are born at the edge of the taste bud and migrate inward to die at the center.

It's generally agreed that there are four *primary tastes:* sweet, sour, bitter, and salty (Buck, 2000). However, scientists are increasingly recognizing a fifth primary taste called *umami,* a Japanese word for the *savory* taste of glutamate found in foods like meats and cheeses (DuBois, 2010). The case for umami as a fifth basic taste has been strengthened by recent evidence that umami substances activate specific receptors on the tongue (Di Lorenzo & Rosen, 2010). Sensitivity to the primary tastes is distributed somewhat unevenly across the tongue. However, Linda Bartoshuk (1993b), a leading authority on taste research, emphasizes that these variations in sensitivity are small and very complicated (see **Figure 4.31**). Taste signals are routed through the thalamus and sent on to the *insular cortex* in the frontal lobe, where the initial cortical processing takes place.

Research reveals that people vary considerably in their sensitivity to certain tastes. Bartoshuk (1993a) noted that these differences depend in part on the density of taste buds on the tongue, which appears to be a matter of genetic inheritance. People characterized as *nontasters*—as determined by their insensitivity to PTC (phenythiocarbamide), or its close relative, PROP (propylthiouracil)—tend to have about one-fourth as many taste buds per square centimeter as people at the other end of the spectrum, who are called *supertasters* (Miller & Reedy, 1990). Supertasters also have specialized taste receptors that are not found in

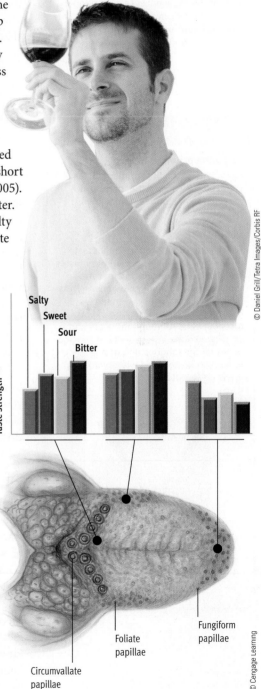

FIGURE 4.31

The tongue and taste. Taste buds are clustered around tiny bumps on the tongue called papillae. There are three types of papillae, which are distributed as shown here. The taste buds found in each type of papilla show slightly different sensitivities to the four basic tastes, as mapped out in the graph at the top. Thus, sensitivity to the primary tastes varies across the tongue, but these variations are small and all four primary tastes can be detected wherever there are taste receptors. (Data adapted from Bartoshuk, 1993a)

SOURCE: Adapted from Bartoshuk, L. M. (1993). Genetic and pathological taste variation: What can we learn from animal models and human disease? In D. Chadwick, J. Marsh, & J. Goode (Eds.), *The molecular basis of smell and taste transduction* (pp. 251–267). New York: Wiley.

Linda Bartoshuk

"Good and bad are so intimately associated with taste and smell that we have special words for the experiences (e.g., repugnant, foul). The immediacy of the pleasure makes it seem absolute and thus inborn. This turns out to be true for taste but not for smell."

Reality Check

Misconception

Sensitivity to the four primary tastes varies greatly across the tongue, as depicted in the tongue map shown below.

Reality

For decades it was reported that taste buds sensitive to the four primary tastes are distributed unevenly across the tongue in the manner shown here. However, these classic tongue maps were based on a misinterpretation of early research data. Although there are some small variations in sensitivity to specific tastes on the tongue, all four primary tastes can be detected wherever there are taste receptors.

nontasters (Bufe et al., 2005). In the United States, roughly 25% of people are nontasters, another 25% are supertasters, and the remaining 50% fall between these extremes and are characterized as *medium tasters* (Di Lorenzo & Youngentob, 2003).

Supertasters and nontasters respond similarly to many foods, but supertasters are much more sensitive to certain sweet and bitter substances (Prescott, 2010). These differences in taste sensitivity influence people's eating habits in ways that can have important repercussions for their physical health. For example, supertasters are less likely to be fond of sweets (Yeomans et al., 2007) and tend to consume fewer high-fat foods, both of which are likely to reduce their risk for cardiovascular disease (Duffy, Lucchina, & Bartoshuk, 2004). Supertasters also tend to react more negatively to alcohol and smoking, thereby reducing their likelihood of developing drinking problems or nicotine addiction (Duffy, Peterson, & Bartoshuk, 2004; Snedecor et al., 2006). The only health disadvantage identified for supertasters thus far is that they respond more negatively to many vegetables, which seems to hold down their vegetable intake (Basson et al., 2005; Dinehart et al, 2006). Overall, however, supertasters tend to have better health habits than nontasters, thanks to their strong reactions to certain tastes (Duffy, 2004).

Women are more likely to be supertasters than men (Bartoshuk, Duffy, & Miller, 1994). Some psychologists speculate that the gender gap in this trait may have evolutionary significance. Over the course of evolution, women have generally been more involved than men in feeding children. Increased reactivity to sweet and bitter tastes would have been adaptive in that it would have made women more sensitive to the relatively scarce high-caloric foods (which often taste sweet) needed for survival and to the toxic substances (which often taste bitter) that hunters and gatherers needed to avoid.

When you eat, you are constantly mixing food and saliva and moving it about in your mouth, so the stimulus is constantly changing. However, if you place a flavored substance in a single spot on your tongue, the taste will fade until it vanishes (Krakauer & Dallenbach, 1937). This fading effect is an example of *sensory adaptation—a gradual decline in sensitivity to prolonged stimulation.* Sensory adaptation is not unique to taste. This phenomenon occurs in other senses as well. In the taste system, sensory adaptation can leave aftereffects (Bartoshuk, 1988). For example, adaptation to a sour solution makes water taste sweet, whereas adaptation to a sweet solution makes water taste bitter.

Now that we've explored the dynamics of taste, we can return to our question about the value of the wine-tasting ritual. This elaborate ritual is indeed an authentic way to put wine to a sensitive test. The aftereffects associated with sensory adaptation make it wise to cleanse one's palate before tasting the wine. Sniffing the cork, and the wine in the glass, is important because odor is a major determinant of flavor. Swirling the wine in the glass helps release the wine's odor inside the glass. Rolling the wine around in your mouth is especially critical because it distributes the wine over the full range of taste cells. It also forces the wine's odor up into the nasal passages. Thus, each action in this age-old ritual makes a meaningful contribution to the tasting.

Smell: The Olfactory System

Humans are usually characterized as being relatively insensitive to smell. In this regard they are often compared unfavorably to dogs, which are renowned for their ability to track a faint odor over long distances. Are humans really inferior in the sensory domain of smell? Let's examine the facts.

The *olfactory system,* **the sensory system for smell,** resembles the sense of taste in many ways. The physical stimuli are chemical substances—volatile ones that can evaporate and be carried in the air. These chemical stimuli are dissolved in fluid—specifically, the mucus in the nose. The receptors for smell are *olfactory cilia,* hairlike structures located in the upper portion of the nasal passages (Getchell & Getchell, 1991) (see **Figure 4.32**). They resemble taste cells in that they have a short life and are constantly being replaced (Buck, 2000). Olfactory receptors have axons that synapse with cells in the *olfactory bulb* and then are routed directly to the olfactory cortex in the temporal lobe and other areas in the cortex (Scott, 2008). This arrangement is unique. *Smell is the only sensory system that is not routed through the thalamus before it projects onto the cortex.*

Odors cannot be classified as neatly as tastes, since efforts to identify primary odors have proven unsatisfactory (Doty, 1991). Humans have about 350 different types of olfactory receptors (Buck, 2004), most of which respond to a wide range of odors (Doty, 2001). Specific odors trigger responses in different *combinations* of receptors (Doty, 2010). Like the other senses, the sense of smell shows sensory adaptation. The perceived strength of an odor usually fades to less than half its original strength within about 4 minutes (Cain, 1988). Let's say you walk into your kitchen and find that the garbage has started to smell. If you stay in the kitchen without removing the garbage, the stench will soon start to fade.

How do human olfactory capacities compare to those of other species? We do have notably fewer olfactory receptors than many other animals (Wolfe et al., 2006). Our relative paucity of receptors probably reflects evolutionary trends that gradually allocated more and more of the brain to color vision (Gilad et al., 2004). However, recent studies have found that humans and monkeys, when compared to other mammals, have a better sense of smell than previously thought (Laska, Seibt, & Weber, 2000; Shepherd, 2004). For example, one innovative study (Porter et al., 2007) asked humans to get on their hands and knees to track the scent of chocolate oil that had been dribbled through a field. It found that the subjects performed quite well and that their patterns of tracking mimicked those of dogs. Gordon Shepherd (2004) offers several possible explanations for our surprising olfactory capabilities, including the fact that "humans smell with bigger and better brains" (p. 0574).

Touch: Sensory Systems in the Skin

The physical stimuli for touch consist of mechanical, thermal, and chemical energy that comes into contact with the skin. These stimuli can produce perceptions of tactile stimulation (the pressure of touch against the skin), warmth, cold, and pain. The human skin is saturated with at least six types of sensory receptors. To some degree, these different types of receptors are specialized for different functions, such as the registration of pressure, heat, cold, and so forth. However, these distinctions are not as clear as researchers had originally thought (Sinclair, 1981).

If you've been to a mosquito-infested picnic lately, you'll appreciate the need to quickly know where tactile stimulation is coming from. The sense of touch is set up to meet this need for tactile localization with admirable efficiency. Cells in the nervous system that respond to touch are sensitive to specific patches of skin. These skin patches, which vary considerably in size, are the functional equivalents of *receptive fields* in vision.

The nerve fibers that carry incoming information about tactile stimulation are routed through the thalamus and onward to the *somatosensory cortex* in the brain's parietal lobes. The entire body is sensitive to touch. However, in humans the bulk of the somatosensory cortex is devoted to processing signals coming from the fingers, lips, and tongue.

The receptors for pain are mostly free nerve endings in the skin. Pain messages are transmitted to the brain via two pathways that pass through different areas in the thalamus (Cholewiak & Cholewiak, 2010) (see **Figure 4.33** on the next page). One is a *fast pathway* that registers localized pain and relays it to the cortex in a fraction of a second. This is the system that hits you with sharp pain when you first cut your finger. The second system uses a *slow pathway*, routed through the limbic system, that lags a second or two behind the fast system. This pathway (which also carries information

FIGURE 4.32

The olfactory system. Odor molecules travel through the nasal passages and stimulate olfactory cilia. An enlargement of these hairlike olfactory receptors is shown in the inset. The olfactory axons transmit neural impulses through the olfactory bulb to the brain.

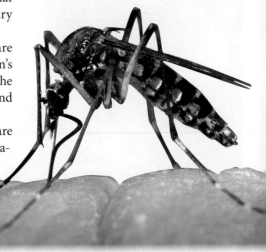

CDC/James Gathany

FIGURE 4.33

Pathways for pain signals. Pain signals are sent inward from receptors to the brain along the two ascending pathways. The fast pathway, shown in red, and the slow pathway, shown in black, depend on different types of nerve fibers and are routed through different parts of the thalamus. The gate-control mechanism hypothesized by Melzack and Wall (1965) apparently depends on signals in a descending pathway (shown in green) that originates in an area of the midbrain.

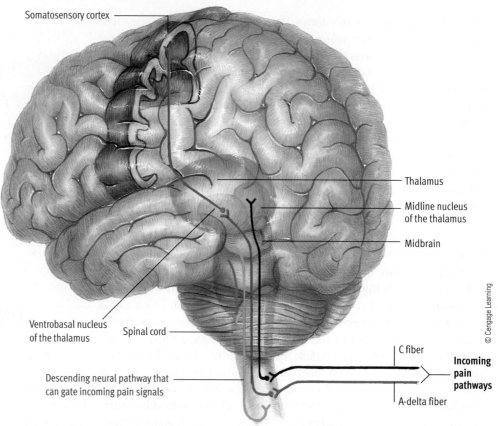

Somatosensory cortex

Thalamus

Midline nucleus of the thalamus

Midbrain

Ventrobasal nucleus of the thalamus

Spinal cord

C fiber

Incoming pain pathways

Descending neural pathway that can gate incoming pain signals

A-delta fiber

© Cengage Learning

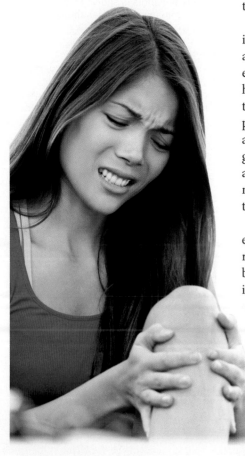

© Maridav/Shutterstock

about temperature) conveys the less localized, longer-lasting aching or burning pain that comes after the initial injury.

Pain perception is inherently subjective (Rollman, 2010). Some people with severe injuries report little pain, whereas other people with much more modest injuries report agonizing pain (Coderre, Mogil, & Bushnell, 2003). The perception of pain can be influenced greatly by beliefs, expectations, personality, mood, and other factors involving higher mental processes (Turk & Okifuji, 2003). The subjective nature of pain is illustrated by placebo effects. As we saw in Chapter 2, many people suffering from pain report relief when given a placebo—such as an inert "sugar pill" that is presented to them as if it were a painkilling drug (Benedetti, 2008; Stewart-Williams, 2004). Evidence regarding the subjective quality of pain has also come from studies that have found ethnic and cultural differences in pain tolerance (Ondeck, 2003). It appears that culture does not affect the process of pain perception so much as the willingness to tolerate certain types of pain (Zatzick & Dimsdale, 1990).

Several recent studies have also highlighted how contextual factors influence the experience of pain. For example, one recent study found that the experience of pain was reduced when female participants looked at a picture of their boyfriend or held their boyfriend's hand (Master et al., 2009). In a similar vein, another study found that looking at pleasant pictures reduced subjects' pain responses, while looking at unpleasant pictures led to stronger pain reactions (Roy et al., 2009). And a study by Gray and Wegner (2008) demonstrated that pain responses increase when participants believe that the pain was inflicted on them intentionally, rather than accidentally.

As you can see, then, tissue damage that sends pain impulses on their way to the brain doesn't necessarily result in the experience of pain. Cognitive and emotional processes that unfold in higher brain centers can sometimes block pain signals coming from peripheral receptors.

How are incoming pain signals blocked? In an influential effort to answer this question, Ronald Melzack and Patrick Wall (1965) devised the gate-control theory of pain. *Gate-control theory holds that incoming pain sensations must pass through a "gate" in the spinal cord that can be closed, thus blocking ascending pain signals.* The gate in this model is not an anatomical structure but a pattern of neural activity that inhibits incoming pain signals. Melzack and Wall suggested that this imaginary gate can be closed by signals from peripheral receptors or by signals from the brain. They theorized that the latter mechanism can help explain how factors such as attention and expectations can shut off pain signals. As a whole, research suggests that the concept of a gating mechanism for pain has merit (Craig & Rollman, 1999; Sufka & Price, 2002). However, relatively little support has been found for the neural circuitry originally hypothesized by Melzack and Wall. Other neural mechanisms, discovered after gate-control theory was proposed, appear to be responsible for blocking the perception of pain.

One of these discoveries was the identification of endorphins. As discussed in Chapter 3, *endorphins* are the body's own natural morphinelike painkillers, which are widely distributed in the central nervous system (Pert, 2002). For example, placebo effects in the treatment of pain often (but not always) depend on the action of endorphins (Eippert et al., 2009; Price, Finniss, & Benedetti, 2008). The other discovery involved the identification of a descending neural pathway that mediates the suppression of pain (Basbaum & Jessell, 2000). This pathway appears to originate in an area of the midbrain (see **Figure 4.33**). Neural activity in this pathway is probably initiated by endorphins. The circuits in this pathway inhibit the activity of neurons that would normally transmit incoming pain impulses to the brain.

Research also suggests that certain types of *glial cells* may contribute to the regulation of pain (Watkins, 2007). At least two types of glia in the spinal cord appear to play an important role in the experience of *chronic pain* (Milligan & Watkins, 2009). The discovery that glia play a role in the human pain system may eventually open up new avenues for treating chronic pain.

Reflecting on the Chapter's Themes

In this chapter, three of our unifying themes were highlighted: (1) psychology is theoretically diverse, (2) people's experience of the world is highly subjective, and (3) our behavior is shaped by our cultural heritage. Let's discuss the value of theoretical diversity first.

Contradictory theories about behavior can be disconcerting and frustrating for theorists, researchers, teachers, and students alike. Yet this chapter provided two dramatic demonstrations of how theoretical diversity can lead to progress in the long run. For decades, the trichromatic and opponent process theories of color vision and the place and frequency theories of pitch perception were viewed as fundamentally incompatible. These competing theories generated and guided the research that now provides a fairly solid understanding of how people perceive color and pitch. As you know, in each case the evidence eventually revealed that the opposing theories were not really incompatible. Both were needed to fully explain the sensory processes that each sought to explain individually. If it hadn't been for these theoretical debates, our current understanding of color vision and pitch perception might be far more primitive.

This chapter should have also enhanced your appreciation of why human experience of the world is highly subjective. As ambiguous figures and visual illusions clearly show, there is no one-to-one correspondence between sensory input and perceived experience of the world. Perception is an active process in which people organize and interpret the information received by the senses. Thus, individuals' experience of the world is subjective because the process of perception is inherently subjective.

Theoretical Diversity

Subjectivity of Experience

Cultural Heritage

The Five Major Senses

SENSE	STIMULUS	ELEMENTS OF THE STIMULUS

The Visual System: SIGHT

Light is electromagnetic radiation that travels in waves. Humans can register only a slim portion of the total range of wavelengths, from 400 to 700 nanometers.

© John White Photos/Alamy

Light waves vary in *amplitude, wavelength,* and *purity,* which influence perceptions as shown below.

Physical properties	Related perceptions
Wavelength	Hue (color)
Amplitude	Brightness
Purity	Saturation

The Auditory System: HEARING

Sound waves are vibrations of molecules, which means that they must travel through some physical medium, such as air. Humans can hear wavelengths between 20 and 20,000 Hz.

© Photodisc/Getty Images

Sound waves vary in *amplitude, wavelength,* and *purity,* which influence perceptions, as shown below.

Physical properties	Related perceptions
Wavelength	Pitch
Amplitude	Loudness
Purity	Timbre

The Gustatory System: TASTE

The stimuli for taste generally are chemical substances that are soluble (dissolvable in water). These stimuli are dissolved in the mouth's saliva.

© Lisa Woollett/Photofusion Picture Library/Alamy

It is generally, but not universally, agreed that there are four primary tastes: *sweet, sour, bitter,* and *salty.*

The Olfactory System: SMELL

© JGI/Blend Images/Getty Images

The stimuli are volatile chemical substances that can evaporate and be carried in the air. These chemical stimuli are dissolved in the mucus of the nose.

Efforts to identify primary odors have proven unsatisfactory. If primary odors exist, there must be a great many of them.

The Tactile System: TOUCH

The stimuli are mechanical, thermal, and chemical energy that impinge on the skin.

© IS713/Image Source Pink/Alamy

Receptors in the skin can register *pressure, warmth, cold,* and *pain.*

NATURE AND LOCATION OF RECEPTORS

The *retina*, which is neural tissue lining the inside back surface of the eye, contains millions of receptor cells called *rods* and *cones*. Rods play a key role in night and peripheral vision; cones play a key role in daylight and color vision.

Neural impulses are routed through the *LGN* in the *thalamus* and then distributed to the *primary visual cortex* at the back of the *occipital lobe*.

The receptors for hearing are tiny *hair cells* that line the *basilar membrane* that runs the length of the *cochlea*, a fluid-filled, coiled tunnel in the inner ear.

Neural impulses are routed through the *thalamus* and then sent to the *primary auditory cortex*, which is mostly located in the *temporal lobe*.

The gustatory receptors are clusters of *taste cells* found in the *taste buds* that line the trenches around tiny bumps in the tongue. Taste cells have a short life span (about 10 days) and are constantly being replaced.

Neural impulses are routed through the *thalamus* and on to the *insular cortex* in the frontal lobe.

The receptors for smell are *olfactory cilia*, hairlike structures in the upper portion of the nasal passages. Like taste cells, they have a short lifespan (about 30–60 days) and are constantly being replaced.

Neural impulses are routed through the *olfactory bulb* and then sent directly to the *olfactory cortex* in the *temporal lobe* and other cortical areas. Smell is the only sensory input not routed through the thalamus.

The human skin is saturated with at least six types of sensory receptors. The four types shown here respond to pressure, whereas *free nerve endings* in the skin respond to pain, warmth, and cold.

Neural impulses are routed through the *brainstem* and *thalamus* and on to the *somatosensory cortex* in the *parietal lobe*.

Finally, this chapter provided numerous examples of how cultural factors can shape behavior—in an area of research where one might expect to find little cultural influence. Most people are not surprised to learn that there are cultural differences in attitudes, values, social behavior, and development. But perception is widely viewed as a basic, universal process that should be invariant across cultures. In most respects it is, as the similarities among cultural groups in perception far outweigh the differences. Nonetheless, we saw cultural variations in depth perception, susceptibility to illusions, and pain tolerance. Thus, even a fundamental, heavily physiological process such as perception can be modified to some degree by one's cultural background.

The following Personal Application highlights the subjectivity of perception once again. It focuses on how painters have learned to use the principles of visual perception to achieve a variety of artistic goals.

Appreciating Art and Illusion

KEY LEARNING GOALS

4.14 Discuss how artists have used various principles of visual perception.

Answer the following multiple-choice question.
Artistic works such as paintings:
___ **a** render an accurate picture of reality.
___ **b** create an illusion of reality.
___ **c** provide an interpretation of reality.
___ **d** make us think about the nature of reality.
___ **e** do all of the above.

The answer to this question is (e), "all of the above." Historically, artists have had many and varied purposes, including each of those listed in the question (Goldstein, 2001). To realize their goals, artists have had to use a number of principles of perception—sometimes quite deliberately, and sometimes not. Here we'll use the example of painting to explore the role of perceptual principles in art and illusion.

The goal of most early painters was to produce a believable picture of reality. This goal immediately created a problem familiar to most of us who have attempted to draw realistic pictures: The real world is three-dimensional, but a canvas or a sheet of paper is flat. Paradoxically, then, painters who set out to recreate reality had to do

so by creating an *illusion* of three-dimensional reality.

Prior to the Renaissance, these efforts to create a convincing illusion of reality were awkward by modern standards. Why? Because artists did not understand how to use depth cues. This fact is apparent in **Figure 4.34**, a religious scene painted around 1300. The painting clearly lacks a sense of depth. The people seem paper-thin. They have no real position in space.

Although earlier artists made *some* use of depth cues, Renaissance artists manipulated the full range of pictorial depth cues and really harnessed the crucial cue of linear perspective (Solso, 1994). **Figure 4.35** dramatizes the resulting transition in art. This scene, painted by Italian Renaissance artists Gentile and Giovanni Bellini,

FIGURE 4.34

***Master of the Arrest of Christ* (detail, central part) by S. Francesco, Assisi, Italy (circa 1300).** Notice how the absence of depth cues makes the painting seem flat and unrealistic.

Maestro della catura di Cristo, Cattura de Christo, parte centrale, Assisi, S. Francisco. Scala/Art Resource, New York

seems much more realistic and lifelike than the painting in **Figure 4.34** because it uses a number of pictorial depth cues. Notice how the buildings on the sides converge to make use of linear perspective. Additionally, distant objects are smaller than nearby ones, an application of relative size. This painting also uses

height in plane, as well as interposition. By taking advantage of pictorial depth cues, an artist can enhance a painting's illusion of reality.

In the centuries since the Renaissance, painters have adopted a number of viewpoints about the portrayal of reality. For instance, the French Impressionists

FIGURE 4.35
A painting by the Italian Renaissance artists Gentile and Giovanni Bellini (circa 1480). In this painting a number of depth cues—including linear perspective, relative size, height in plane, and interposition—enhance the illusion of three-dimensional reality.

of the 19th century did not want to re-create the photographic "reality" of a scene. They set out to interpret a viewer's fleeting perception or impression of reality. To accomplish this end, they worked with color in unprecedented ways.

Consider, for instance, the work of Georges Seurat, a French artist who used a technique called pointillism. Seurat carefully studied what scientists knew about the composition of color in the 1880s, then applied this knowledge in a calculated, laboratory-like manner. Indeed, critics in his era dubbed him the "little chemist." Seurat constructed his paintings out of tiny dots of pure, intense colors (see **Figure 4.36**). He used additive color mixing, a departure from the norm in paint-

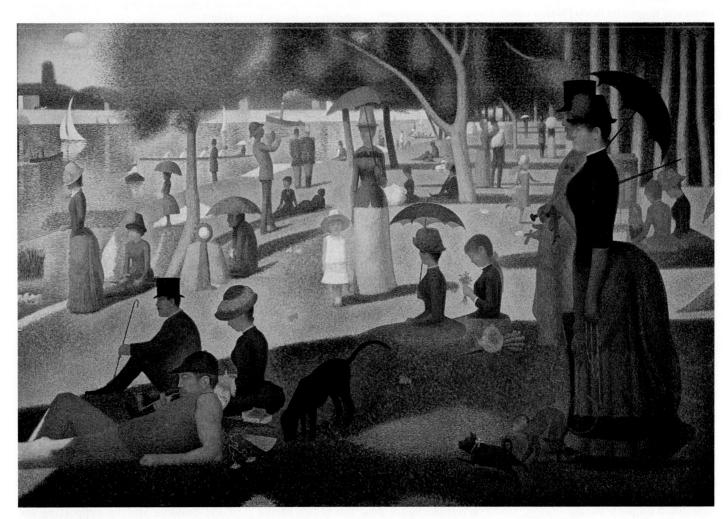

FIGURE 4.36
Georges Seurat's *Sunday Afternoon on the Island of La Grande Jatte* (without artist's border) (1884–1886). Seurat used thousands of tiny dots of color and the principles of color mixing; the eye and brain combine the points into the colors the viewer actually sees.

FIGURE 4.37

Violin and Grapes by Pablo Picasso (1912). This painting makes use of Gestalt principles of perceptual organization.

Pablo Picasso, _Violin and Grapes, Céret and Sorgues_ (spring–summer 1912), oil on canvas, 20 × 24 inches (50.6 × 61 cm). Collection, The Museum of Modern Art, New York, Mrs. David M. Levy Bequest (32.1960). Digital image © The Museum of Modern Art/ Licensed by SCALA/Art Resource, New York. © 2012 Estate of Pablo Picasso/Artists Rights Society (ARS), New York. Reproduction, including downloading is prohibited by copyright laws and international conventions without the express written permission of Artists Rights Society (ARS), New York.

FIGURE 4.38

Salvador Dali's _Slave Market with the Disappearing Bust of Voltaire_ (1940). This painting playfully includes a reversible figure (two nuns form the bust of Voltaire, a philosopher known for his stringent criticisms of the Catholic church).

Salvador Dali, _The Slave Market with the Disappearing Bust of Voltaire_, 1940, oil on canvas, 18-1/4 x 25-3/8 inches. Collection of The Salvador Dali Museum, St. Petersburg, FL. Copyright © 2006 The Salvador Dali Museum, Inc. © 2012 Salvador Dali, Gala-Salvador Dali Foundation/Artists Rights Society (ARS), New York.

ing, which usually depends on subtractive mixing of pigments. A famous result of Seurat's "scientific" approach to painting was _Sunday Afternoon on the Island of La Grande Jatte_ (see **Figure 4.36**). As the work of Seurat illustrates, modernist painters were moving away from attempts to re-create the world as it is literally seen.

If 19th-century painters liberated color, their successors at the turn of the 20th century liberated form. This was particularly true of the Cubists. Cubism was begun in 1909 by Pablo Picasso, a Spanish artist who went on to experiment with other styles in his prolific career. The Cubists didn't try to portray reality so much as to reassemble it. They attempted to reduce everything to combinations of geometric forms (lines, circles, triangles, rectangles, and such) laid out in a flat space, lacking depth. In a sense, they applied the theory of feature analysis to canvas, as they built their figures out of simple features.

The resulting paintings were decidedly unrealistic, but the painters would leave realistic fragments that provided clues about the subject. Picasso liked to challenge his viewers to decipher the subject of

his paintings. Take a look at the painting in **Figure 4.37** and see whether you can figure out what Picasso was portraying.

The work in **Figure 4.37** is titled _Violin and Grapes_. Note how Gestalt principles of perceptual organization are at work to create these forms. Proximity and similarity serve to bring the grapes together in the bottom right corner. Closure accounts for your being able to see the essence of the violin.

The Surrealists toyed with reality in a different way. Influenced by Sigmund Freud's writings on the unconscious, the Surrealists explored the world of dreams and fantasy. Specific elements in their paintings are often depicted realistically, but the strange combination of elements yields a disconcerting irrationality reminiscent of dreams. A prominent example of this style is Salvador Dali's _Slave Market with the Disappearing Bust of Voltaire_, shown in **Figure 4.38**. Notice the reversible figure near the center of the painting. The "bust of Voltaire" is made up of human figures in the distance, standing in front of an arch. Dali often used reversible figures to enhance the ambiguity of his bizarre visions.

Perhaps no one has been more creative in manipulating perceptual ambiguity than M. C. Escher, a modern Dutch artist. Escher closely followed the work of the Gestalt psychologists, and he readily acknowledged his debt to psychology as a source of inspiration (Teuber, 1974). _Waterfall_, a 1961 lithograph by Escher, is a perplexing drawing that appears to defy the law of gravity (see **Figure 4.39**). The puzzling problem here is that a level channel of water terminates in a waterfall that "falls" into the same channel two levels "below."

The Necker cube, a reversible figure mentioned earlier, was the inspiration for Escher's 1958 lithograph _Belvedere_, shown in **Figure 4.40**. You have to look carefully to realize that this is another impossible figure. Note that the top story runs at a right angle from the first story. Note also how the pillars are twisted around. The pillars that start on one side of the building end up supporting the second story on the other side! Escher's debt to the Necker cube is manifested in several places—for example, the drawing of a Necker cube on the floor next to the seated boy (on the lower left).

FIGURE 4.39
Escher's lithograph *Waterfall* (1961). Escher's clever manipulation of depth cues deceives the brain into seeing water flow uphill.

FIGURE 4.40
Escher's *Belvedere* (1958). This lithograph depicts an impossible figure inspired by the Necker cube. The cube appears in the architecture of the building, in the model held by the boy on the bench, and in the drawing lying at his feet.

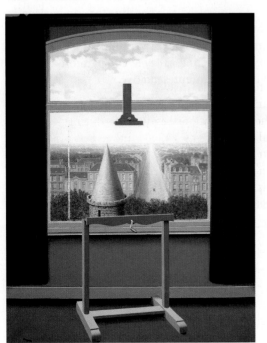

FIGURE 4.41
René Magritte's *Les Promenades d'Euclide* (1955). Notice how the pair of nearly identical triangles look quite different in different contexts.

While Escher challenged viewers to think about perception, Belgian artist René Magritte challenged people to think about the conventions of painting. Many of his works depict paintings on an easel, with the "real" scene continuing unbroken at the edges. The painting in **Figure 4.41** is such a picture within a picture. Ultimately, Magritte's painting blurs the line between the real world and the illusory world created by the artist, suggesting that there is no line—that everything is an illusion. In this way, Magritte "framed" the ageless, unanswerable question: What is reality?

Recognizing Contrast Effects: It's All Relative

4.15 Understand how contrast effects can be manipulated to influence or distort judgments.

You're sitting at home one night, when the phone rings. It's Simone, an acquaintance from school who needs help with a recreational program for youngsters that she runs for the local park district. She tries to persuade you to volunteer 4 hours of your time every Friday night throughout the school year to supervise the volleyball program. The thought of giving up your Friday nights and adding this sizable obligation to your already busy schedule makes you cringe with horror. You politely explain to Simone that you can't possibly afford to give up that much time and you won't be able to help her. She accepts your rebuff graciously, but the next night she calls again. This time she wants to know whether you would be willing to supervise volleyball every third Friday. You still feel like it's a big obligation that you really don't want to take on, but the new request seems much more reasonable than the original one. So, with a sigh of resignation, you agree to Simone's request.

What's wrong with this picture? Well, there's nothing wrong with volunteering your time for a good cause, but you just succumbed to a social influence strategy called the *door-in-the face technique*. The *door-in-the-face technique* involves making a large request that is likely to be turned down as a way to increase the chances that people will agree to a smaller request later (see **Figure 4.42**). The name for this strategy is derived from the expectation that the initial request will be quickly rejected (hence, the door is slammed in the salesperson's face). Although they may not be familiar with the strategy's name, many people use this manipulative tactic. For example, a husband who wants to coax his frugal wife into agreeing to buy a $30,000 sports car might begin by proposing that they purchase a $50,000 sports car. By the time the wife talks her husband out of the $50,000 car, the $30,000 price tag may look quite reasonable to her—which is what the husband wanted all along.

Research has demonstrated that the door-in-the-face technique is a highly effective persuasive strategy (Cialdini, 2007). One of the reasons it works so well is that it depends on a simple and pervasive perceptual principle: When it comes to perceptual experience, *everything is relative*. This relativity means that people are easily swayed by *contrast effects*. For example, lighting a match or a small candle in a dark room will produce a burst of light that seems quite bright, but if you light the same match or candle in a well-lit room, you may not even detect the additional illumination. The relativity of perception is apparent in the painting by Josef Albers shown in **Figure 4.43**. The two X's are exactly the same color, but the X in the top half looks yellow, whereas the X in the bottom half looks brown. These varied perceptions occur because of contrast effects—the two X's are contrasted against different background colors. Another example of how contrast effects can influence perception can be seen in **Figure 4.44**. The middle disk in each panel is exactly the same size, but the one in the top panel looks larger because it is surrounded by much smaller disks.

The same principles of relativity and contrast that operate when people make judgments about the intensity or color of visual stimuli also affect the way they make judgments in a wide variety of areas. For example, a 6' 3" basketball player, who is really quite tall, can look downright small when surrounded by teammates who are all over 6' 8". And a salary of $42,000 per year for your first full-time job may seem like a princely sum, until a close friend gets an offer of $75,000 a year. The assertion that everything is relative raises the issue of *relative to what? Comparators* are people, objects, events, and other standards that are used as a baseline for comparison in making judgments. It is fairly easy to manipulate many types of judgments by selecting *extreme* comparators that may be unrepresentative.

FIGURE 4.42

The door-in-the-face technique. The door-in-the-face technique is a frequently used compliance strategy in which you begin with a large request and work down to the smaller request you are really after. It depends in part on contrast effects.

FIGURE 4.43

Contrast effects in visual perception. This composition by Joseph Albers shows how one color can be perceived differently when contrasted against different backgrounds. The top X looks yellow and the bottom X looks brown, but they're really the same color.

SOURCE: Albers, Joseph. *Interaction of Color*. Copyright © 1963 and reprinted by permission of the publisher, Yale University Press.

FIGURE 4.44

Contrast effects in size perception. The middle disk in the top panel looks larger than the middle disk in the bottom panel, but they really are exactly the same size. This illusion occurs because of contrast effects created by the surrounding disks.

The influence of extreme comparators was demonstrated in some interesting studies of judgments of physical attractiveness. In one study, undergraduate males were asked to rate the attractiveness of an average-looking female (who was described as a potential date for another male in the dorm) presented in a photo either just before or just after the participants watched a TV show dominated by strikingly beautiful women (Kenrick & Gutierres, 1980). The female was viewed as less attractive when the ratings were obtained just after the men had seen gorgeous women on TV as opposed to when they hadn't. In other studies, both male and female participants have rated *themselves* as less attractive after being exposed to many pictures of extremely attractive

models (Little & Mannion, 2006; Thornton & Moore, 1993; Thornton & Maurice, 1999). Thus, contrast effects can influence important social judgments that are likely to affect how people feel about themselves and others.

Anyone who understands how easily judgments can be manipulated by a careful choice of comparators could influence your thinking. For example, a politician who is caught in some illegal or immoral act could sway public opinion by bringing to mind (perhaps subtly) the fact that many other politicians have committed acts that were much worse. When considered against a backdrop of more extreme comparators, the politician's transgression will probably seem less offensive. A defense attorney could use a similar strat-

egy in an attempt to obtain a lighter sentence for a client by comparing the client's offense to much more serious crimes. And a realtor who wants to sell you an expensive house that will require huge mortgage payments will be quick to mention other homeowners who have taken on even larger mortgages.

In summary, critical thinking is facilitated by conscious awareness of the way comparators can influence and perhaps distort a wide range of judgments. In particular, it pays to be vigilant about the possibility that others may manipulate contrast effects in their persuasive efforts. One way to reduce the influence of contrast effects is to consciously consider comparators that are both worse and better than the event you are judging, as a way of balancing the effects of the two extremes.

TABLE 4.1   Critical Thinking Skills Discussed in This Application

Skill	Description
Understanding how contrast effects can influence judgments and decisions	The critical thinker appreciates how striking contrasts can be manipulated to influence many types of judgments.
Recognizing when extreme comparators are being used	The critical thinker is on the lookout for extreme comparators that distort judgments.

© Cengage Learning

The Visual System: Essentials of Sight

4.1 Identify the three properties of light, and describe the role of key eye structures in vision.

Light varies in terms of wavelength, amplitude, and purity. Perceptions of color (hue) are primarily a function of light wavelength, while amplitude mainly affects brightness and purity mainly affects saturation. Light enters the eye through the cornea and pupil and is focused upside down on the retina by the lens. Distant objects appear blurry to nearsighted people and close objects appear blurry to farsighted people. The retina is the neural tissue in the eye that absorbs light, processes images, and sends visual signals to the brain. Cones, which are concentrated in the fovea, play a key role in daylight vision and color perception. Rods, which have their greatest density just outside the fovea, are critical to night vision and peripheral vision. Dark adaptation and light adaptation both involve changes in the retina's sensitivity to light. Receptive fields are areas in the retina that affect the firing of visual cells.

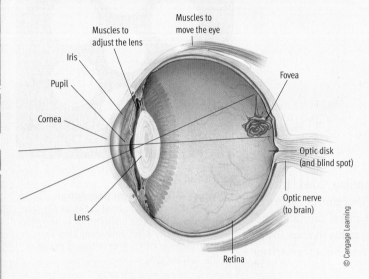

4.2 Trace the routing of signals from the eye to the brain, and explain the brain's role in visual information processing.

The optic nerves from the inside half of each eye cross at the optic chiasm and then project to the opposite half of the brain. Two visual pathways send signals to different areas of the primary visual cortex in the occipital lobe. The main pathway is routed through the LGN in the thalamus. After processing in the primary visual cortex, visual information is shuttled along the *what* and *where pathways* to other cortical areas. Research suggests that the visual cortex contains cells that function as feature detectors. The *what pathway* has neurons inside it that are especially sensitive to faces.

4.3 Distinguish two types of color mixing, compare the trichromatic and opponent process theories of color vision, and describe research on how color can influence behavior.

There are two types of color mixing: additive and subtractive. Human color perception depends on processes that resemble additive color mixing. The trichromatic theory holds that people have three types of receptors that are sensitive to wavelengths associated with red, green, and blue. The opponent process theory holds that color perception depends on receptors that make antagonistic responses to red versus green, blue

versus yellow, and black versus white. The evidence now suggests that both theories are necessary to account for color vision. A new line of research is exploring how various colors influence behavior. Evidence suggests that red undermines achievement strivings but enhances sexual attraction.

The Visual System: Perceptual Processes

4.4 Discuss the subjectivity of form perception, inattentional blindness, and the concept of feature analysis.

Reversible figures and perceptual sets demonstrate that the same visual input can result in very different perceptions. Form perception depends on both the selection and interpretation of sensory inputs. Inattentional blindness involves the failure to see readily visible objects. According to feature analysis theories, people detect specific elements in stimuli and build them into recognizable forms through bottom-up processing, but form perception also involves top-down processing.

4.5 Understand Gestalt principles of visual perception and the role of perceptual hypotheses in form perception.

Gestalt psychology emphasized that the whole may be greater than the sum of its parts (features), as illustrated by the phi phenomenon. Objects are more likely to be viewed as figure rather than ground when they are smaller, higher in contrast or symmetry, and lower in one's frame of view. The Gestalt principles of proximity, similarity, continuity, closure, and simplicity explain how we group elements into higher-order forms. Other approaches to form perception emphasize that people develop perceptual hypotheses about the external stimuli that could be responsible for various patterns of sensory stimulation.

4.6 Identify the monocular and binocular cues used in depth perception, and discuss cultural variations in depth perception.

Binocular cues such as retinal disparity can contribute to depth perception. But depth perception depends primarily on monocular cues. These include texture gradient, linear perspective, light and shadow, interposition, relative size, and height in plane. People from pictureless societies have some difficulty in applying pictorial depth cues to two-dimensional pictures.

4.7 Describe perceptual constancies and discuss what visual illusions reveal about perception.

A perceptual constancy is a tendency to experience a stable perception in the face of continually changing sensory input. People tend to view objects as having a stable size, shape, brightness, color, and location in space. Visual illusions demonstrate that perceptual hypotheses can be inaccurate and that perceptions are not simple reflections of objective reality. Researchers have found some cultural differences in susceptibility to certain illusions.

The Auditory System: Hearing

4.8 Identify the three properties of sound, and summarize information on human hearing capacities.

Sound varies in terms of wavelength (frequency), amplitude, and purity. Wavelength mainly affects perceptions of pitch, amplitude mainly influences perceptions of loudness, and purity is the key determinant of timbre. The human ear can detect sounds between 20 and 20,000 Hz, but it is most sensitive to sounds around 2000 Hz. Even brief exposure to sounds over 120 decibels can be painful and damaging.

4.9 Describe how sensory processing occurs in the ear, and compare the place and frequency theories of pitch perception.

Sound is transmitted through the external ear via air conduction to the middle ear, where sound waves are translated into the vibration of tiny bones called ossicles. In the inner ear, fluid conduction vibrates hair cells along the basilar membrane in the cochlea. These hair cells are the receptors for hearing. Place theory proposed that pitch perception depends on where vibrations occur along the basilar membrane. Frequency theory countered with the idea that pitch perception depends on the rate at which the basilar membrane vibrates. Modern evidence suggests that these theories are complementary rather than incompatible.

Pinna

Hammer

Semicircular canals

Anvil

Auditory nerve

Cochlea

Stirrup

Eardrum

Auditory canal

© Cengage Learning

The Other Senses: Taste, Smell, and Touch

4.10 Describe the stimulus and receptors for taste, and review research on individual differences in taste sensitivity.

The taste buds are sensitive to four basic tastes: sweet, sour, bitter, and salty. Umami may qualify as a fifth basic taste. Sensitivity to these tastes is distributed unevenly across the tongue, but the variations are small. Taste signals are routed through the thalamus and sent on to the insular cortex in the frontal lobe. Supertasters are much more sensitive to some tastes than nontasters, with medium tasters falling in between. Nontasters tend to be more susceptible to the lure of sweets, high-fat foods,

alcohol, and smoking, which means their consumption habits tend to be less healthy than those of supertasters. Women are more likely to be supertasters than men are.

4.11 Describe the stimulus and receptors for smell, and evaluate humans' olfactory capabilities.

Like taste, smell is a chemical sense. Chemical stimuli activate receptors, called olfactory cilia, that line the nasal passages. Most of these receptors respond to more than one odor. Smell is the only sense that is not routed through the thalamus. Sensory adaptation occurs in smell. When compared to other mammals, humans may have a better sense of smell than previously thought.

4.12 Describe the stimulus and receptors for touch, and explain what is known about pain perception.

The skin houses many types of sensory receptors. They respond to pressure, temperature, and pain. Tactile localization depends on receptive fields similar to those seen for vision. Pain signals are sent to the brain along two pathways that are characterized as fast and slow. The perception of pain is highly subjective and may be influenced by culture, mood, and contextual factors. Gate-control theory holds that incoming pain signals can be blocked in the spinal cord. Endorphins and a descending neural pathway appear responsible for this suppression of pain. Glial cells contribute to the modulation of chronic pain.

© Maridav/Shutterstock

Reflecting on the Chapter's Themes

4.13 Identify the three unifying themes that were highlighted in this chapter.

This chapter provided two dramatic demonstrations of the value of theoretical diversity. It also provided numerous examples of how and why people's experience of the world is highly subjective. Finally, it highlighted the importance of cultural background.

PERSONAL APPLICATION
Appreciating Art and Illusion

4.14 Discuss how artists have used various principles of visual perception.

After the Renaissance, painters began to routinely use pictorial depth cues to make their scenes more lifelike. Nineteenth-century painters, such as the Impressionists, manipulated color mixing in creative, new ways. The Cubists were innovative in manipulating form, as they applied the theory of feature analysis to canvas. The Surrealists toyed with reality, exploring the world of fantasy and dreams. Inspired by Gestalt psychology, Escher tried to stimulate viewers to think about the process of perception. Magritte challenged people to think about the conventions of painting and their relation to reality.

CRITICAL THINKING APPLICATION
Recognizing Contrast Effects: It's All Relative

4.15 Understand how contrast effects can be manipulated to influence or distort judgments.

The study of perception often highlights the relativity of experience. This relativity can be manipulated by arranging for contrast effects. For example, the door-in-the-face strategy depends on contrast effects. Critical thinking is enhanced by an awareness of how extreme comparators can distort many judgments.

5 Variations in Consciousness

PARADOX

Sleep seems like a single, uniform state of mental inactivity, but in reality sleep consists of a cyclical series of highly varied states characterized by a surprising amount of mental activity.

© Bloomimage/Corbis

Nathaniel Kleitman and Eugene Aserinsky couldn't believe their eyes—or their subject's eyes, either. It was the spring of 1952, and Kleitman, a prominent sleep researcher, was investigating the slow, rolling eye movements displayed by subjects at the onset of sleep. Kleitman had begun to wonder whether these eye movements might show up during later phases of sleep. The trouble was that watching a participant's closed eyelids all night long was a surefire way to put the *researcher* to sleep. Cleverly, Kleitman and Aserinsky, a graduate student, came up with a better way to document eye movements. They hooked subjects up to an apparatus that was connected to electrodes pasted near the eyes. The electrodes picked up the small electrical signals generated by moving eyeballs. These signals moved a pen on a chart recorder, much like an electroencephalograph (EEG) traces brain waves. The result was an objective record of sleepers' eye movements that could be studied at any time (Dement, 1992).

One night, while one of their subjects was asleep, the researchers were surprised to see a tracing in the recording that suggested a different, much more rapid, eye movement. This result was so unexpected that they at first thought the recording device was on the blink. Only when they decided to walk in and personally observe sleeping subjects were they convinced that the eye movements were real. The subjects were deeply asleep, yet the bulges in their closed eyelids showed that their eyeballs were moving laterally back and forth in sharp jerks. The researchers wondered: what in the world was going on?

In retrospect, it's amazing that no one had discovered these rapid eye movements before. It turns out that periods of rapid eye movement are a routine part of sleep in humans and many animals. In fact, you can observe them for yourself in your pet dog or cat. The phenomenon had been there for everyone to see for eons, but anyone who noticed must not have attached any significance to it.

Kleitman and Aserinsky's discovery might have remained something of an oddity, but then they had a brainstorm. Could the rapid eye movements perhaps be related to dreaming? With the help of William Dement, a graduate student who was interested in dreams, they soon found the answer. When Dement woke up subjects during periods of rapid eye movement, about 80% reported that they had just been having a vivid dream. By contrast, only a small minority of participants awakened from other phases of sleep reported that they had been dreaming. Subsequently, EEG recordings showed that periods of rapid eye movement were also associated with marked changes in brain-wave patterns. What Kleitman and his graduate students had stumbled on was considerably more than an oddity. It was a window into the most private aspect of consciousness imaginable—the experience of dreaming (Gottesmann, 2009). As you will learn in this chapter, the discovery of rapid eye movement (REM) sleep blossomed into a number of fascinating insights about what goes on during sleep. This is just one example of how modern psychologists have tried to come to grips with the slippery topic of consciousness.

We'll begin our tour of variations in consciousness with a few general points about the nature of consciousness. After that, much of the chapter will be a "bedtime story," as we take a long look at sleep and dreaming. We'll continue our discussion of consciousness by examining hypnosis, meditation, and the effects of mind-altering drugs. The Personal Application addresses a number of practical questions about sleep and dreams. Finally, the Critical Thinking Application returns to the topic of drugs and looks at the concept of alcoholism to highlight the power of definitions.

On the Nature of Consciousness

What is consciousness? *Consciousness* **is the awareness of internal and external stimuli.** Your consciousness includes (1) your awareness of external events ("The professor just asked me a hard question about medieval history"), (2) your awareness of your internal sensations ("My heart is racing and I'm starting to sweat"), (3) your awareness of your *self* as the unique being having these experiences ("Why me?"), and (4) your awareness of your thoughts about these experiences ("I'm going to make a fool of myself!"). In short, consciousness is personal awareness.

The contents of your consciousness are continually changing. Rarely does consciousness come to a standstill. It moves, it flows, it fluctuates, it wanders (Wegner, 1997). For example, in one study college students were prompted eight times a day to record whether their thoughts were wandering from what they were doing (Kane et al., 2007). On average, the participants reported that their mind was wandering from the task at hand about one-third of the time. Mind wandering was more likely when subjects were bored, anxious, tired, or stressed. Recognizing that consciousness fluctuates continuously, William James (1902) long ago named this flow the *stream of consciousness.* If you could tape-record your thoughts, you would find an endless flow of ideas that zigzag in all directions. As you will soon learn, even when you sleep your consciousness moves through a series of transitions. Constant shifting and changing seem to be part of the essential nature of consciousness.

Variations in Levels of Awareness

While William James emphasized the stream of consciousness, Sigmund Freud (1900) wanted to examine what goes on beneath the surface of this stream. As explained in Chapter 1, Freud argued that people's feelings and behavior are influenced by *unconscious* needs, wishes, and conflicts that lie below the surface of conscious awareness. According to Freud, the stream of consciousness has depth. Conscious and unconscious processes are different *levels of awareness.* Thus, Freud was one of the first theorists to recognize that consciousness is not an all-or-none phenomenon.

Since Freud's time, research has shown that people continue to maintain some awareness during sleep and even when they are put under anesthesia for surgery. How do we know? Because some stimuli can still penetrate awareness. For example, people under surgical anesthesia occasionally hear comments made during their surgery, which they later repeat to their surprised surgeons (Kihlstrom & Cork, 2007; Merikle, 2007). Research also indicates that while asleep some people remain aware of external events to some degree (K. B. Campbell, 2000; Dang-Vu et al., 2009). A good example is the new parent who can sleep through a loud thunderstorm or a buzzing alarm clock but who immediately hears the muffled sound of the baby crying down the hall. The parent's selective sensitivity to sounds means that some mental processing must be going on even during sleep.

Consciousness and Brain Activity

Consciousness does not arise from any distinct structure in the brain but rather is the result of activity in distributed networks of neural pathways (Kinsbourne, 1997; Singer, 2007). Scientists are increasingly using brain-imaging methods to explore the link between brain activity and consciousness (Wager, Hernandez, & Lindquist, 2009). But historically, the most commonly used indicator of variations in consciousness has been the EEG, which records activity from broad swaths of the cortex. **The *electroencephalograph (EEG)* is a device that monitors the electrical activity of the brain over time by means of recording electrodes attached to the surface of the scalp.** Ultimately, the EEG summarizes the rhythm of cortical activity in the brain in terms of line tracings called *brain waves.* These tracings vary in *amplitude* (height) and *frequency* (cycles per second, abbreviated *cps*). You can see what brain waves look like if you glance ahead to **Figure 5.2**. Human brain-wave activity is usually divided into four principal bands based on the frequency of the brain waves. These bands, named after letters in the Greek alphabet, are *beta* (13–24 cps), *alpha* (8–12 cps), theta (4–7 cps), and *delta* (under 4 cps).

Different patterns of EEG activity are associated with different states of consciousness, as is summarized in **Table 5.1**. For instance, when you are alertly engaged in problem solving, beta waves tend to dominate. When you are relaxed and resting, alpha waves increase. When you slip into deep, dreamless sleep, delta waves become more prevalent. Although these correlations are far from perfect, changes in brain activity are closely related to variations in consciousness (Wallace & Fisher, 1999).

TABLE 5.1   **EEG Patterns Associated with States of Consciousness**

EEG pattern	Frequency (cps)	Typical States of Consciousness
Beta (β)	13–24	Normal waking thought, alert problem solving
Alpha (α)	8–12	Deep relaxation, blank mind, meditation
Theta (θ)	4–7	Light sleep
Delta (Δ)	less than 4	Deep sleep

© Cengage Learning

Biological Rhythms and Sleep

KEY LEARNING GOALS

5.2 Summarize what is known about human biological clocks and their relationship to sleep.

5.3 Explain how getting out of sync with one's circadian rhythms can have effects on sleep.

Variations in consciousness are shaped in part by biological rhythms. Rhythms pervade the world around us. The daily alternation of light and darkness, the annual pattern of the seasons, and the phases of the moon all reflect this rhythmic quality of repeating cycles. Humans and many other animals display biological rhythms that are tied to these planetary rhythms (Foster, 2004; Kriegsfeld & Nelson, 2009). ***Biological rhythms are periodic fluctuations in physiological functioning.*** The existence of these rhythms means that organisms have internal "biological clocks" that somehow monitor the passage of time.

The Role of Circadian Rhythms

PSYKTREK 4a

Circadian rhythms **are the 24-hour biological cycles found in humans and many other species.** In humans, circadian rhythms are particularly influential in the regulation of sleep (Moore, 2006). However, daily cycles also produce rhythmic variations in blood pressure, urine production, hormonal secretions, and other physical functions (see **Figure 5.1**). These cycles also affect alertness, short-term memory, and other aspects of cognitive performance (Refinetti, 2006; Van Dongen & Dinges, 2005).

Research indicates that people generally fall asleep as their body temperature begins to drop and they awaken as it begins to ascend once again (Szymusiak, 2009). Investigators have concluded that circadian rhythms can leave individuals physiologically primed to fall asleep most easily at a particular time of day (Richardson, 1993). This optimal time varies from person to person, depending on their schedules, but each individual may have an "ideal" time for going to bed. Retiring at this ideal bedtime may also promote better-quality sleep during the night (Akerstedt et al., 1997). People often characterize themselves as a "night person" or a "morning person." These preferences reflect individual variations in circadian rhythms (Minkel & Dinges, 2009).

© Alex Staroseltsev/Shutterstock

FIGURE 5.1

Examples of circadian rhythms. These graphs show how alertness, core body temperature, and the secretion of growth hormone typically fluctuate in a 24-hour rhythm. Circadian rhythms are also seen for many other physiological functions.

SOURCE: Adapted from Coleman, R. (1986). *Wide awake at 3:00 A.M.* New York: W. H. Freeman. Copyright © 1986 by Richard M. Coleman. Reprinted by permission of Henry Holt & Co., LLC.

Researchers have a pretty good idea of how the day-night cycle resets human biological clocks. When exposed to light, some receptors in the retina send direct inputs to a small structure in the hypothalamus called the *suprachiasmatic nucleus* (SCN) (Weaver & Reppert, 2008). The SCN sends signals to the nearby *pineal gland,* whose secretion of the hormone *melatonin* plays a key role in adjusting biological clocks (Norman, 2009).

Ignoring Circadian Rhythms

PSYKTREK 4a

What happens when you ignore your biological clock and go to sleep at an unusual time? Typically, the quality of your sleep suffers. Getting out of sync with your circadian rhythms also causes *jet lag.* When you fly across several time zones, your biological clock keeps time as usual, even though official clock time changes. You then go to sleep at the "wrong" time and are likely to experience difficulty falling asleep and poor-quality sleep. This inferior sleep, which can continue to occur for several days, can make you feel fatigued, sluggish, and irritable during the daytime (Arendt, Stone, & Skene, 2005).

People differ in how quickly they can reset their biological clocks to compensate for jet lag, and the speed of readjustment depends on the direction traveled. Generally, it's easier to fly westward and lengthen your day than it is to fly eastward and shorten it (Arendt et al., 2005). This east-west disparity in jet lag is sizable enough to have an impact on the performance of sports teams. Studies have found that teams flying westward perform significantly better than teams flying eastward in professional baseball (Recht, Lew, & Schwartz, 1995) and college football (Worthen & Wade, 1999). A rough rule of thumb for jet lag is that the readjustment process takes about a day for each time zone crossed when flying eastward and about two-thirds of a day per time zone when flying westward (Monk, 2006).

© Steve Jacobs/iStockphoto

The rotating and late-night work shifts endured by many nurses, firefighters, and industrial workers also play havoc with biological rhythms. Shift rotation tends to have far more detrimental effects than jet lag (Monk, 2000). People suffering from jet lag get their circadian rhythms realigned within a matter of days, but workers on night or rotating shifts are constantly at odds with local time cues and normal rhythms. Studies show that such workers get less total sleep and poorer-quality sleep. These work schedules can also have a negative impact on employees' productivity and accident proneness at work, the quality of their social relations at home, and their mental health (Cruz, della Rocco, & Hackworth, 2000; Waage et al., 2009). Studies have also linked rotating shifts to a higher incidence of many physical diseases, including cancer, diabetes, ulcers, high blood pressure, and heart disease (Kriegsfeld & Nelson, 2009).

Realigning Circadian Rhythms

As scientists have come to appreciate the importance of circadian rhythms, they have begun to look for new ways to help people realign their daily rhythms. One promising line of research has focused on giving people small doses of the hormone melatonin, which appears to regulate the human biological clock. The evidence from a number of studies suggests that melatonin *can* reduce the effects of jet lag by helping travelers resynchronize their biological clocks, but the results are inconsistent (Arendt & Skeen, 2005; Monk, 2006). One reason for the inconsistent findings is that when melatonin is used to combat jet lag, the timing of the dose is crucial. But, because calculating the optimal timing is rather complicated, it is easy to get it wrong (Arendt, 2009).

A strategy that can help shift workers involves carefully planning their rotation schedules to reduce the severity of their circadian disruption (Smith, Fogg, & Eastman, 2009). The negative effects of shift rotation can be reduced if workers move through progressively later starting times (instead of progressively earlier starting times) and if they have longer periods between shift changes. Although enlightened scheduling practices can help, the unfortunate reality is that most people find rotating shift work very difficult (Arendt, 2010).

REM sleep is not unique to humans. Nearly all mammals and birds exhibit REM sleep. The only known exceptions among warm-blooded vertebrates are dolphins and some whales (Morrison, 2003). Dolphins are particularly interesting, as they sleep while swimming, resting one hemisphere of the brain while the other hemisphere remains alert.

foremost sleep researchers. The REM stage tends to be a "deep" stage of sleep in the conventional sense that it is relatively hard to awaken a person from it (although arousal thresholds vary during REM). The REM stage is also marked by irregular breathing and pulse rate. Muscle tone is extremely relaxed—so much so that bodily movements are minimal and the sleeper is virtually paralyzed. Although REM is a relatively deep sleep stage, EEG activity is dominated by high-frequency beta waves that resemble those observed when people are alert and awake (see **Figure 5.2** again).

This paradox is probably related to the association between REM sleep and dreaming. When researchers systematically awaken subjects from various stages of sleep to ask them whether they were dreaming, most dream reports come from awakenings during the REM stage (Dement, 1978; McCarley, 1994). Although decades of research have revealed that some dreaming occurs in the non-REM stages, dreaming is most frequent, vivid, and memorable during REM sleep (Pace-Schott, 2005).

To summarize, *REM sleep* **is a deep stage of sleep marked by rapid eye movements, high-frequency brain waves, and dreaming.** It is such a special stage of sleep that the other four stages are often characterized simply as "non-REM sleep." *Non-REM sleep* **consists of sleep stages 1 through 4, which are marked by an absence of rapid eye movements, relatively little dreaming, and varied EEG activity.**

REPEATING THE CYCLE

PsykTrek 4b

During the course of a night, people usually repeat the sleep cycle about four times. As the night wears on, the cycle changes gradually. The first REM period is relatively short, lasting only a few minutes. Subsequent REM periods get progressively longer, peaking at around 40–60 minutes. Additionally, non-REM intervals tend to get shorter, and descents into non-REM stages usually become more shallow. These trends can be seen in **Figure 5.3** on pages 148–149 which provides an overview of a typical night's sleep cycle. These trends mean that most slow-wave sleep occurs early in the sleep cycle and that REM sleep tends to pile up in the second half of the sleep cycle. Summing across the entire cycle, young adults typically spend about 15%–20% of their sleep time in slow-wave sleep and another 20%–25% in REM sleep (Rama et al., 2006).

What we have described thus far is the big picture—the typical structure of sleep averaged over many people. However, research by Tucker, Dinges, and Van Dongen (2007) has

FIGURE 5.3

An overview of the cycle of sleep. The white line charts how a typical, healthy young adult moves through the various stages of sleep during the course of a night. This diagram also shows how dreams and rapid eye movements tend to coincide with REM sleep, whereas posture changes occur in between REM periods (because the body is nearly paralyzed during REM sleep). Notice how the person cycles into REM four times, as descents into non-REM sleep get shallower and REM periods get longer. Thus, slow-wave sleep is prominent early in the night, while REM sleep dominates the second half of a night's sleep. Although these patterns are typical, keep in mind that sleep patterns vary from one person to another and that they change with age.

shown that the "architecture" of sleep—how quickly one falls asleep, how long one sleeps, how one cycles through the various stages—varies from one person to the next more than sleep researchers initially realized. And these personal variations are pretty stable from one night to the next, meaning that each of us has a signature sleep pattern.

Age, Culture, and Sleep

PSYKTREK 4b

Now that we have described the basic architecture of sleep, let's take a look at a couple of factors that contribute to variations in patterns of sleeping: age and culture.

AGE TRENDS

PSYKTREK 4b

Age alters the sleep cycle. What we have described so far is the typical pattern for young to middle-aged adults. Children, however, display different patterns (Bootzin et al., 2001; Roffwarg, Muzio, & Dement, 1966). Newborns will sleep six to eight times in a 24-hour period, often exceeding a total of 16 hours of sleep (see **Figure 5.4** on page 150). Fortunately for parents, during the first several months much of this sleep begins to get unified into one particularly long nighttime sleep period (Huber & Tononi, 2009). Interestingly, infants spend much more of their sleep time than adults do in the REM stage. In the first few months, REM accounts for about 50% of babies' sleep, as compared to 20% of adults' sleep. During the remainder of the first year, the REM portion of infants' sleep declines to roughly 30% (Ohayon et al., 2004). The REM portion of sleep continues to decrease gradually until it levels off at about 20% during adolescence (see **Figure 5.4**).

During adulthood, gradual, age-related changes in sleep continue. Although the proportion of REM sleep remains fairly stable (Floyd et al., 2007), the percentage of slow-wave sleep declines and the percentage of time spent in stage 1 increases slightly (Rissling & Ancoli-Israel, 2009). These shifts toward lighter sleep *may* contribute to the increased frequency of nighttime awakenings seen among the elderly (Klerman et al.,

REM

REM

The last REM period of the night has the fastest eye movements and may be the period from which dreams are best remembered.

© Cengage Learning

2004). As **Figure 5.4** shows, the average amount of total sleep time also declines with advancing age.

Until recently it was assumed that this decline in sleep time was due to older people having more difficulty initiating sleep or remaining asleep. In other words, it was

© michaeljung/Shutterstock

Concept Check 5.1

Comparing REM and non-REM Sleep

A table here could have provided you with a systematic comparison of REM sleep and non-REM sleep, but that would have deprived you of the opportunity to check your understanding of these sleep phases by creating your own table. Try to fill in each of the blanks below with a word or phrase highlighting the differences between REM and non-REM sleep with regard to the various characteristics specified. As usual, you can find the answers at the back of the book in Appendix A.

Characteristic	REM sleep	Non-REM sleep
1. Type of EEG activity		
2. Eye movements		
3. Dreaming		
4. Depth (difficulty in awakening)		
5. Percentage of total sleep (in adults)		
6. Increases or decreases (as percentage of sleep) during childhood		
7. Timing in sleep cycle (dominates early or late)		

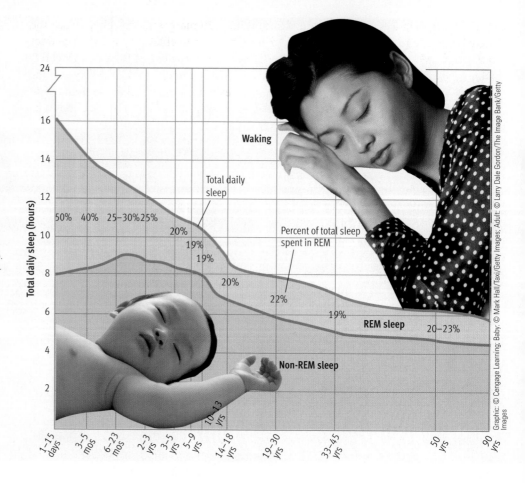

FIGURE 5.4

Changes in sleep patterns over the life span. Both the total amount of sleep per night and the portion of sleep that is REM sleep change with age. Sleep patterns change most dramatically during infancy, with total sleep time and amount of REM sleep declining sharply in the first two years of life. After a noticeable drop in the average amount of sleep in adolescence, sleep patterns remain relatively stable, although total sleep and slow-wave sleep continue to decline gradually with age.

SOURCE: Adapted from an updated revision of a figure in Roffwarg, H. P., Muzio, J. N., & Dement, W. C. (1966). Ontogenetic development of human sleep-dream cycle. *Science, 152,* 604–609. Copyright © 1966 by the American Association for the Advancement of Science. Adapted and revised by permission of the authors.

attributed to a decrease in their ability to sleep effectively. However, a recent, carefully controlled laboratory study that allowed for extended sleep opportunities found that older adults (ages 60–80) showed significantly less sleepiness during the day than younger adults (ages 18–30), even though the older group chose to sleep an average of 1.5 hours less per day (Klerman & Dijk, 2008). The authors conclude that the elderly may simply need less sleep than younger adults. Consistent with this line of thinking, another recent study yielded the surprising finding that older adults tolerate sleep deprivation with less impairment than younger adults (Duffy et al., 2009). Older people do have more difficulty adapting to circadian phase shifts, such as those produced by jet lag or rotating workshifts (Monk, 2005), but excessive daytime sleepiness does not increase with age (Young, 2004). The bottom line is that growing older, by itself, does not appear to lead to poor sleep if elderly people remain healthy (Vitiello, 2009).

CULTURAL VARIATIONS

Although age clearly affects the nature and structure of sleep itself, the psychological and physiological experience of sleep does not appear to vary much across cultures. For example, a cross-cultural survey of ten divergent countries (Soldatos et al., 2005) found relatively modest differences in the average amount of time that people sleep, or the time that it takes for them to fall asleep. That said, a recent poll of people in the United States found some ethnic disparities in subjective estimates of individuals' sleep quality (National Sleep Foundation, 2010). In this poll, whites (20%) and African Americans (18%) were more likely to report that they "rarely" or "never" enjoyed a good night's sleep than either Hispanics (14%) or Asians (9%). Another recent study also found that Asians reported fewer sleep complaints than other ethnic groups (Grandner, Patel et al., 2010b). The same study also looked at the influence of social class on sleep and concluded that lower income and education was associated with more sleep complaints.

Napping practices also vary along cultural lines. In many societies, shops close and activities are curtailed in the afternoon to permit people to enjoy a 1- to 2-hour midday nap. These "siesta cultures" are found mostly in tropical regions of the world (Webb & Dinges, 1989). There, this practice is adaptive in that it allows people to avoid working during the hottest part of the day. As a rule, the siesta tradition is not found in industrialized societies, where it conflicts with the emphasis on productivity and the philosophy that "time is money."

Doing Without: Sleep Deprivation

Scientific research on sleep deprivation presents something of a paradox. On the one hand, some studies suggest that sleep deprivation is not as detrimental as most people subjectively feel it to be. On the other hand, evidence suggests that sleep deprivation may be a major social problem, undermining efficiency at work and contributing to countless accidents.

Research has mostly focused on *partial sleep deprivation,* or *sleep restriction,* which occurs when people make do with substantially less sleep than normal over a period of time. Many sleep experts believe that much of American society suffers from chronic sleep deprivation (Walsh, Dement, & Dinges, 2005). It appears that more and more people are trying to squeeze additional waking hours out of their days as they attempt to juggle conflicting work, family, household, and school responsibilities, leading William Dement to comment that "Most Americans no longer know what it feels like to be fully alert" (Toufexis, 1990, p. 79).

How serious are the effects of partial sleep deprivation? The emerging consensus is that sleep restriction has far more negative effects than most people assume. Studies indicate that sleep restriction can impair individuals' attention, reaction time, motor coordination, and decision making and may also have negative effects on endocrine and immune system functioning (Dinges, Rogers, & Baynard, 2005). Sleep deprivation has also been blamed for a large proportion of transportation accidents and mishaps in the workplace (Walsh et al., 2005). For example, sleep restriction appears to be a contributing factor in many motor vehicle accidents (Abe et al., 2010). Unfortunately, research shows that sleep-deprived individuals are not particularly good at predicting if and when they will fall asleep (Kaplan, Itoi, & Dement, 2007). Thus, tired drivers often fail to pull off the road when they should.

William Dement

"Sleep deprivation is a major epidemic in our society. . . . Americans spend so much time and energy chasing the American dream, that they don't have much time left for actual dreaming."

Many traffic accidents occur because drivers get drowsy or fall asleep at the wheel. Although the effects of sleep deprivation seem innocuous, sleep loss can be deadly.

The unique quality of REM sleep led researchers to look into the effects of a special type of partial sleep deprivation—*selective deprivation*. In a number of laboratory studies, participants were awakened over a period of nights whenever they began to go into the REM stage. These subjects usually got a decent amount of sleep in non-REM stages, but they were selectively deprived of REM sleep.

What are the effects of REM deprivation? The evidence indicates that it has little impact on daytime functioning and task performance, but it *does* have some interesting effects on subjects' patterns of sleeping (Bonnet, 2005). As the nights go by in REM deprivation studies, it becomes necessary to awaken the participants more and more often to deprive them of their REM sleep, because they spontaneously shift into REM more and more frequently. Whereas most subjects normally go into REM about four times a night, REM-deprived participants start slipping into REM every time the researchers turn around. Furthermore, when a REM-deprivation experiment comes to an end and participants are allowed to sleep without interruption, they experience a "rebound effect." That is, they spend extra time in REM periods for one to three nights to make up for their REM deprivation (Bonnet, 2005).

Similar results have been observed when subjects have been selectively deprived of slow-wave sleep (Borbely & Achermann, 2005). What do theorists make of these spontaneous pursuits of REM and slow-wave sleep? They conclude that people must have specific *needs* for REM and slow-wave sleep—and rather strong needs, at that.

Why do we need REM and slow-wave sleep? Some influential studies suggest that REM and slow-wave sleep contribute to firming up learning that takes place during the day—a process called *memory consolidation* (Gais & Born, 2004; Stickgold, 2001). Efforts to explore this hypothesis have led to some interesting findings in recent years. For example, in one study participants were given training on a perceptual-motor task and then retested 12 hours later. Those who slept during the 12-hour interval showed substantial *improvement* in performance that was not apparent in participants who did not sleep (Walker et al., 2002). A number of similar studies have shown that sleep seems to enhance subjects' memory of specific learning activities that occurred during the day (Walker, 2009; Walker & Stickgold, 2004). These studies also find that the length of time spent in REM and SWS correlates with subjects' learning and memory performance (Walker & Stickgold, 2006). The theoretical meaning of these findings is still being debated, but the most widely accepted explanations center on how time spent in specific stages of sleep may stabilize or solidify memories formed during the day (Rasch & Born, 2008; Stickgold, 2005).

In related research, investigators have found that REM sleep appears to foster the recently discovered process of *neurogenesis* (Guzman-Marin et al., 2008; Meerlo et al., 2009). As noted in Chapter 3, **neurogenesis refers to the formation of new neurons.** This finding meshes with the data linking REM sleep to memory consolidation because other, independent lines of research suggest that neurogenesis contributes to learning (Leuner, Gould, & Shors, 2006; see Chapter 7).

Further underscoring the importance of REM sleep, some studies even suggest that REM may promote creative insights related to previous learning (Stickgold & Walker, 2004). In one study, participants worked on a challenging task requiring creativity before and after an opportunity to take a nap or enjoy quiet rest (Cai et al., 2009). The naps were monitored physiologically and subjects were divided into those who experienced REM during their nap and those who did not. The REM sleep group showed dramatic increases in creative performance after the nap that were not seen in the group without REM or the group that engaged in quiet rest (see **Figure 5.5**).

Sleep Loss and Health

In recent years, researchers have begun to investigate the notion that sleep deprivation might have serious health consequences. Accumulating evidence suggests that sleep loss can affect physiological processes in ways that may undermine physical health. For

FIGURE 5.5

Enhanced creativity after a nap with REM sleep. Participants in the Cai et al. (2009) study worked on a difficult measure of creativity and then were instructed to take a nap or engage in quiet rest. Napping subjects were divided into those who went into REM during their nap and those who did not. After their naps or quiet rest, participants worked on the creativity test again. Although the REM nappers only logged an average of 14 minutes in REM, their performance on the creativity test improved by almost 40%, whereas the other groups showed no improvement.

SOURCE: Adapted from Cai, D. J., Mednick, S. A., Harrison, E. M., Kanady, J. C., & Mednick, S. C. (2009). REM, not incubation, improves creativity by priming associative networks. *Proceedings of the National Academy of Sciences, 106*, 10130–10134.

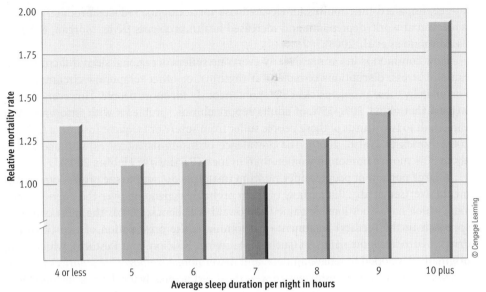

FIGURE 5.6

Mortality rates as a function of typical sleep duration. In a study of over 100,000 subjects followed for 10 years, Tamakoshi et al. (2004) estimated mortality rates in relation to typical sleep duration. The lowest mortality rate was found among those who slept 7 hours, so that figure was arbitrarily set to 1.00 and the mortality rates for other sleep lengths were calculated relative to that baseline. The rates shown here are averaged for males and females. As you can see, higher mortality rates are associated with both shorter sleep durations and longer sleep durations. Mortality rates were especially elevated among those who reported that they slept 10 or more hours per night.

example, sleep restriction appears to trigger hormonal changes that increase hunger (Grandner, Patel et al., 2010a). Consistent with this finding, studies have found a link between short sleep duration and increased obesity, which is a risk factor for a variety of health problems (Watanabe et al., 2010). Researchers have also found that sleep loss leads to impaired immune system functioning (Motivala & Irwin, 2007) and increased inflammatory responses (Patel et al., 2009), which are likely to heighten vulnerability to a variety of diseases. Thus, it is not surprising that studies have uncovered links between short sleep duration and an increased risk for diabetes (Knutson & Van Cauter, 2008), hypertension (Gangwisch et al., 2006), and coronary disease (Sabanayagam & Shankar, 2010).

These findings have motivated researchers to explore the correlation between habitual sleep time and overall mortality. The results of this research have provided a bit of a surprise. As expected, people who consistently sleep less than 7 hours exhibit an elevated mortality risk, but so do those who routinely sleep *more* than 8 hours. In fact, mortality rates are especially high among those who sleep over 10 hours (see **Figure 5.6**) (Chien et al., 2010; Grander, Hale et al., 2010). Researchers are now scrambling to figure out why long sleep duration is correlated with elevated mortality. It could be that prolonged sleep is a "marker" for other problems, such as depression or a sedentary lifestyle, that have negative effects on health (Patel et al., 2006). Bear in mind, also, that the studies linking typical sleep duration to mortality have depended on participants' *self-report estimates* of how long they normally sleep, which could be inaccurate. In any event, the relationship between sleep and health is an emerging area of research that will probably yield some interesting findings in the years to come.

Problems in the Night: Sleep Disorders

Not everyone is able to consistently enjoy the luxury of a good night's sleep. In this section we will briefly discuss what is known about a variety of sleep disorders.

INSOMNIA

Insomnia is the most common sleep disorder. *Insomnia* **refers to chronic problems in getting adequate sleep.** It occurs in three basic patterns: (1) difficulty in falling asleep initially, (2) difficulty in remaining asleep, and (3) persistent early-morning awakening. Insomnia may sound like a minor problem to those who haven't struggled with it, but it can be a very unpleasant ailment. Moreover, insomnia is associated with daytime

Reality Check

Misconception

The effects of partial sleep deprivation are generally modest and insignificant.

Reality

The basis for this belief is that the most obvious effect of sleep deprivation is increased sleepiness, which sounds pretty harmless. However, sleep deprivation impairs attention, motor coordination, decision making, and memory, and it increases the likelihood of many kinds of accidents. Moreover, sleep loss is associated with increased vulnerability to a variety of serious diseases and elevated mortality.

fatigue, impaired functioning, an elevated risk for accidents, reduced productivity, absenteeism at work, depression, and increased health problems (Kyle, Morgan, & Espie, 2010; Vgontzas et al., 2008).

How common is insomnia? Nearly everyone suffers occasional sleep difficulties because of stress, disruptions of biological rhythms, or other temporary circumstances. Fortunately, these problems clear up spontaneously for most people. However, studies suggest that about 30%–35% of adults report chronic problems with insomnia, and about half to two-thirds of these people suffer from severe or frequent insomnia (Brown, 2006; Zorick & Walsh, 2000). The prevalence of insomnia increases with age and is about 50% more common in women than in men (Partinen & Hublin, 2005).

A large portion of people suffering from insomnia do not pursue professional treatment (Sivertsen et al., 2006). Many of them probably depend on over-the-counter sleep aids, which have questionable value (Mahowald & Schenck, 2005). The most common approach in the medical treatment of insomnia is the prescription of two classes of drugs: *benzodiazepine sedatives* (such as Dalmane, Halcion, and Restoril), which were originally developed to relieve anxiety, and newer *nonbenzodiazepine sedatives* (such as Ambien, Sonata, and Lunesta), which were designed primarily for sleep problems (Mendelson, 2005). Both types of sedative medications are fairly effective in helping people fall asleep more quickly, and they reduce nighttime awakenings and increase total sleep (Lee-Chiong & Sateia, 2006; Mendelson, 2005).

Nonetheless, sedatives are a poor long-range solution for insomnia, for a number of reasons (Roehrs & Roth, 2000; Wesson et al., 2005). It is possible to overdose on sleeping pills, and some people become dependent on sedatives to fall asleep. Sedatives also have carryover effects that can make people drowsy and sluggish the next day and impair their functioning (Vermeeren, 2004). Moreover, with continued use sedatives gradually become less effective, so people need to increase their dose to more dangerous levels, creating a vicious circle of escalating dependency (Lader, 2002). Another problem is that when people abruptly discontinue their sleep medication, they can experience unpleasant withdrawal symptoms and increased insomnia (Lee-Chiong & Sateia, 2006). Fortunately, the newer nonbenzodiazepine sedatives have reduced (but not eliminated) many of the problems associated with previous generations of sleeping pills (Sanger, 2004).

OTHER SLEEP PROBLEMS

Although insomnia is the most common difficulty associated with sleep, people are plagued by many other types of sleep problems as well. Let's briefly look at the symptoms, causes, and prevalence of three additional sleep problems, as described by Kryger, Roth, and Dement (2005) and Hirshkowitz, Seplowitz-Hafkin, & Sharafkhaneh (2009).

Narcolepsy **is a disease marked by sudden and irresistible onsets of sleep during normal waking periods.** A person suffering from narcolepsy goes directly from wakefulness into REM sleep, usually for a short period (10–20 minutes). This is a potentially dangerous condition, as some victims fall asleep instantly, even while walking across a room or driving a car (Pelayo & Lopes, 2006). Narcolepsy is relatively uncommon, as it is seen in only about 0.05% of the population (Partinen & Hublin, 2005). Its causes are not well understood. Some individuals appear to be genetically predisposed to the disease (Mignot, 2005). Stimulant drugs have been used to treat this condition with modest success (Guilleminault & Fromherz, 2005). But as you will see in our upcoming discussion of drugs, stimulants carry many problems of their own.

Sleep apnea **involves frequent, reflexive gasping for air that awakens a person and disrupts sleep.** Some victims are awakened from their sleep hundreds of times a night. Apnea occurs when a person literally stops breathing for a minimum of 10 seconds. This disorder, which is usually accompanied by loud snoring, is seen in about 2% of women and about 4% of men, with a higher incidence among older adults, postmenopausal women, and obese people (Sanders & Givelber, 2006). As you might expect, sleep

"Wait! Don't! It can be dangerous to wake them!"

apnea can have a disruptive effect on sleep, leading to excessive daytime sleepiness. Sleep apnea is a more serious disorder than widely appreciated because it increases vulnerability to hypertension, coronary disease, and stroke (Hahn, Olson, & Somers, 2006). Apnea may be treated via lifestyle modifications (weight loss, reduced alcohol intake, improved sleep hygiene), drug therapy, special masks and oral devices that improve airflow, and upper airway and craniofacial surgery (Phillips & Kryger, 2005; Veasey, 2009).

Somnambulism, or sleepwalking, occurs when a person arises and wanders about while remaining asleep. About 15% of children and 3% of adults exhibit repetitive sleepwalking (Cartwright, 2006). Sleepwalking tends to occur during the first 3 hours of sleep, when individuals are in slow-wave sleep (Aldrich, 2000). Sleepwalkers may awaken during their journey, or they may return to bed without any recollection of their excursion. The causes of this unusual disorder are unknown, although it appears to have a genetic predisposition (Keefauver & Guilleminault, 1994). Also, episodes may be more likely in people who use nonbenzodiazepine sedatives, especially Ambien (Gunn & Gunn, 2006). Sleepwalking does not appear to be a manifestation of underlying emotional or psychological problems (Mahowald, 1993). However, while sleepwalking, some people have engaged in inappropriate aggressive or sexual behavior (Cartwright, 2006). Sleepwalkers are prone to accidents, including life-threatening incidents (Gunn & Gunn, 2006).

The World of Dreams

KEY LEARNING GOALS

5.7 Discuss the importance of dreams and findings on dream content.

5.8 Describe cultural variations in beliefs about dreams, and explain three theories of dreaming.

For the most part, dreams are not taken very seriously in Western societies. Paradoxically, though, Robert Van de Castle (1994) points out that dreams have sometimes changed the world. For example, Van de Castle describes how René Descartes's philosophy of dualism, Frederick Banting's discovery of insulin, Elias Howe's refinement of the sewing machine, and Mohandas Gandhi's strategy of nonviolent protest were all inspired by dreams. He also explains how Mary Shelley's *Frankenstein* and Robert Louis Stevenson's *The Strange Case of Dr. Jekyll and Mr. Hyde* emerged out of their dream experiences. In his wide-ranging discussion, Van de Castle also relates how the Surrealist painter Salvador Dali characterized his work as "dream photographs" and how legendary filmmakers Ingmar Bergman, Orson Welles, and Federico Fellini all drew on their dreams in making their films. Thus, Van de Castle concludes that "dreams have had a dramatic influence on almost every important aspect of our culture and history" (p. 10).

The Contents of Dreams

What do people dream about? Overall, dreams are not as exciting as advertised. Perhaps dreams are seen as exotic because people are more likely to remember their more bizarre nighttime dramas (De Koninck, 2000). After analyzing the contents of more than 10,000 dreams, Calvin Hall (1966) concluded that most dreams are relatively mundane. They tend to unfold in familiar settings with a cast of characters dominated by family, friends, and colleagues. People *are* more tolerant of logical discrepancies and implausible scenarios in their dreams than in their waking thought (Kahn, 2007), although they generally move through coherent virtual worlds in their dreams (Nielsen & Stenstrom, 2005). The one nearly universal element of dreams is a stable, coherent sense of self—people almost always experience dreams from a first-person perspective (Valli & Revonsuo, 2009).

Certain themes tend to be more common than others. **Figure 5.7** on the next page lists the most common dream themes reported by 1181 college students in one study of typical dream content (Nielsen et al., 2003). If you glance through this list, you will notice that people dream quite a bit about sex, aggression, and misfortune. As you can see, people often dream about negative and potentially traumatic events, including being killed. However, the notion that a traumatic dream could be fatal is nonsense. Hall

Rank	Dream content	Total prevalence
1	Chased or pursued, not physically injured	81.5%
2	Sexual experiences	76.5
3	Falling	73.8
4	School, teachers, studying	67.1
5	Arriving too late, e.g., missing a train	59.5
6	Being on the verge of falling	57.7
7	A person now alive as dead	54.1
8	Trying again and again to do something	53.5
9	Flying or soaring through the air	48.3
10	Vividly sensing . . . a presence in the room	48.3
11	Failing an examination	45.0
12	Physically attacked (beaten, stabbed, raped)	42.4
13	Being frozen with fright	40.7
14	A person now dead as alive	38.4
15	Being a child again	36.7
16	Being killed	34.5
17	Swimming	34.3
18	Insects or spiders	33.8
19	Being nude	32.6
20	Being inappropriately dressed	32.5
21	Discovering a new room at home	32.3
22	Losing control of a vehicle	32.0
23	Eating delicious foods	30.7
24	Being half awake and paralyzed in bed	27.2
25	Finding money	25.7

FIGURE 5.7

Common themes in dreams. Studies of dream content find that certain themes are particularly common. The data shown here are from a study of 1181 college students in Canada (Nielsen et al., 2003). This list shows the 25 dreams most frequently reported by the students. Total prevalence refers to the percentage of students reporting each dream.

SOURCE: Nielsen, T. A., Zadra, A. L., Simard, V., Saucier, S., Stenstrom, P, Smith, C., & Kuiken, D. (2003). The typical dreams of Canadian university students. *Dreaming, 13,* 211–235 [from Table 1, p. 217]. Copyright © 2003 Association for the Study of Dreams, American Psychological Association. Reprinted by permission.

was struck by how little people dream about public affairs and current events. Typically, dreams are self-centered; people dream mostly about themselves.

Though dreams seem to belong in a world of their own, what people dream about is affected by what is going on in their lives (Wamsley & Stickgold, 2009). If you're struggling with financial problems, worried about an upcoming exam, or sexually attracted to a classmate, these themes may very well show up in your dreams. Freud noticed long ago that the contents of waking life tend to spill into dreams. He labeled this spillover the *day residue.*

On occasion, the contents of dreams can also be affected by external stimuli experienced while one is dreaming (De Koninck, 2000). For example, William Dement sprayed water on one hand of sleeping subjects while they were in the REM stage (Dement & Wolpert, 1958). Subjects who weren't awakened by the water were roused by the experimenter a short time later and asked what they had been dreaming about. Dement found that 42% of the participants had incorporated the

SLEEP DISORDER RESEARCH

water into their dreams. They said that they had dreamt that they were in rainfalls, floods, baths, swimming pools, and the like. Some people report that they occasionally experience the same phenomenon at home when the sound of their alarm clock fails to awaken them. The alarm is incorporated into their dream as a loud engine or a siren, for instance.

Culture and Dreams

Striking cross-cultural variations occur in beliefs about the nature of dreams and the importance attributed to them (Lohmann, 2007). In modern Western society, we typically make a distinction between the "real" world we experience while awake and the "imaginary" world we experience while dreaming. Some people realize that events in the real world can affect their dreams, but few believe that events in their dreams hold any significance for their waking life. Although a small minority of individuals take their dreams seriously, in Western cultures dreams are largely written off as insignificant and meaningless (Tart, 1988).

In many non-Western cultures, however, dreams are viewed as important sources of information about oneself, about the future, or about the spiritual world (Kracke, 1991). Although no culture confuses dreams with waking reality, many view events in dreams as another type of reality that may be just as important as, or perhaps even more important than, events experienced while awake. In some instances, people are even held responsible for their dream actions. Among the New Guinea Arapesh, for example, an erotic dream about someone may be viewed as the equivalent of an adulterous act. In many cultures, dreams are seen as a window into the spiritual world, permitting communication with ancestors or supernatural beings (Bourguignon, 1972). People in some cultures believe that dreams provide information about the future—good or bad omens about upcoming battles, hunts, births, and so forth (Tedlock, 1992).

In regard to dream content, both similarities and differences occur across cultures in the types of dreams that people report (Domhoff, 2005b; Hunt, 1989). Some basic dream themes appear to be nearly universal (falling, being pursued, having sex). However, the contents of dreams vary some from one culture to another because people in different societies deal with different worlds while awake.

Theories of Dreaming

Many theories have been proposed to explain the purposes of dreaming (see **Figure 5.8** on the next page). Sigmund Freud (1900), who analyzed clients' dreams in therapy, believed that the principal purpose of dreams is *wish fulfillment*. He thought that people fulfill unmet needs from waking hours through wishful thinking in dreams. For example, if you were feeling unconscious guilt about being rude to a friend, you might dream about the incident in a way that renders you blameless. Freud asserted that the wish-fulfilling quality of many dreams may not be obvious because the unconscious attempts to censor and disguise the true meaning of dreams. Freud's influential theory sounded plausible when it was proposed over 100 years ago, but research has not provided much support for Freud's conception of dreaming (Fisher & Greenberg, 1996). Nonetheless, Freud's view remains popular among people. A recent study found that a substantial majority of people from three very different cultures endorsed the Freudian notion that dreams contain hidden truths (Morewedge & Norton, 2009).

Other theorists, such as Rosalind Cartwright, have proposed that dreams provide an opportunity to work through everyday problems (Cartwright, 1977; Cartwright & Lamberg, 1992). According to her cognitive, *problem-solving view,* there is considerable continuity between waking and sleeping thought. Proponents of this view believe that dreams allow people to engage in creative thinking about problems because dreams are not restrained by logic or realism. Research showing that REM sleep can enhance learning (Walker & Stickgold, 2004) has added new credibility to the problem-solving view of dreams (Cartwright, 2004).

Sigmund Freud
"[Dreams are] the royal road to the unconscious."

© National Library of Medicine

FIGURE 5.8
Three theories of dreaming. Dreams can be explained in a variety of ways. Freud stressed the wish-fulfilling function of dreams. Cartwright emphasizes the problem-solving function of dreams. Hobson asserts that dreams are merely a by-product of periodic neural activation. All three theories are speculative and have their critics.

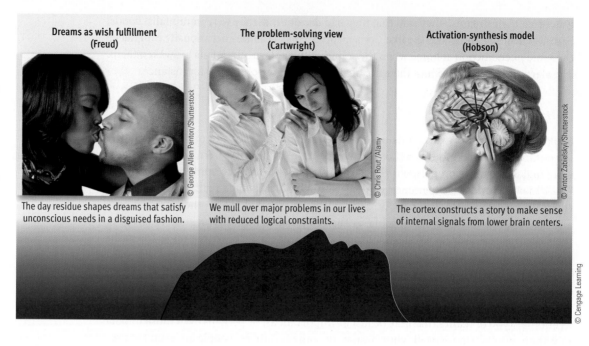

Dreams as wish fulfillment (Freud)	The problem-solving view (Cartwright)	Activation-synthesis model (Hobson)
The day residue shapes dreams that satisfy unconscious needs in a disguised fashion.	We mull over major problems in our lives with reduced logical constraints.	The cortex constructs a story to make sense of internal signals from lower brain centers.

J. Allan Hobson

"Activation-synthesis ascribes dreaming to brain activation in sleep. The principal engine of this activation is the reticular formation of the brainstem."

J. Allan Hobson and colleagues argue that dreams are simply the by-product of bursts of activity emanating from subcortical areas in the brain. Their *activation-synthesis model* (Hobson & McCarley, 1977; McCarley, 1994) and its more recent revisions (Hobson, 2007; Hobson, Pace-Schott, & Stickgold, 2000) propose that dreams are *side effects* of the neural activation that produces the beta brain waves during REM sleep that are associated with wakefulness. According to this model, neurons firing periodically in lower brain centers (especially the pons) send random signals to the cortex (the seat of complex thought). The cortex supposedly synthesizes (constructs) a dream to make sense out of these signals. In contrast to the theories of Freud and Cartwright, this theory obviously downplays the role of emotional factors as determinants of dreams. Like other theories of dreams, the activation-synthesis model has its share of critics. They point out that the model has a hard time explaining the fact that dreaming occurs outside of REM sleep, that damage to the pons does not eliminate dreaming, and that the contents of dreams are considerably more meaningful than the model would predict (Domhoff, 2005a; Foulkes, 1996; Solms, 2000a).

Hypnosis: Altered Consciousness or Role Playing?

KEY LEARNING GOALS

5.9 Discuss hypnotic susceptibility, and list some prominent effects of hypnosis.

5.10 Compare the role-playing and altered-state theories of hypnosis.

Hypnosis has a long and checkered history. It all began with a flamboyant 18th-century Austrian by the name of Franz Anton Mesmer (Pintar, 2010). Working in Paris, Mesmer claimed to cure people of illnesses through an elaborate routine involving a "laying on of hands." Mesmer had some complicated theories about how he had harnessed "animal magnetism." However, we know today that he had simply stumbled onto the power of suggestion. Eventually he was dismissed as a charlatan and run out of town by the local authorities. Although officially discredited, Mesmer inspired followers—practitioners of "mesmerism"—who continued to ply their trade. To this day, our language preserves the memory of Franz Mesmer: When we are under the spell of an event or a story, we are "mesmerized."

Eventually, a Scottish physician, James Braid, became interested in the trancelike state that could be induced by the mesmerists. It was Braid who popularized the term *hypnotism* in 1843, borrowing it from the Greek word for sleep (Pintar, 2010). Braid thought that hypnotism could be used to produce anesthesia for surgeries. However, just as hypnosis was catching on as a general anesthetic, more powerful and reliable chemical anesthetics were discovered. Interest in hypnotism then dwindled.

Since then, hypnotism has led a curious dual existence. On the one hand, it has been the subject of numerous scientific studies. Furthermore, it has enjoyed considerable use as a clinical tool by physicians, dentists, and psychologists for over a century and has empirically supported value in the treatment of a variety of psychological and physical ailments (Covino & Pinnell, 2010; Nash et al., 2009). On the other hand, an assortment of entertainers and quacks have continued in the less respectable tradition of mesmerism, using hypnotism for parlor tricks and chicanery.

Hypnotic Induction and Phenomena

Hypnosis **is a systematic procedure that typically produces a heightened state of suggestibility.** It may also lead to passive relaxation, narrowed attention, and enhanced fantasy. If only in popular films, virtually everyone has seen a *hypnotic induction* enacted with a swinging pendulum. Actually, many techniques can be used (Gibbons & Lynn, 2010). Usually, the hypnotist will suggest to the subject that he or she is relaxing. Repetitively, softly, subjects are told that they are getting tired, drowsy, or sleepy. Often, the hypnotist vividly describes bodily sensations that should be occurring. Subjects are told that their arms are going limp, that their feet are getting warm, that their eyelids are getting heavy. Gradually, most subjects succumb and become hypnotized.

People differ in how well they respond to hypnotic induction. About 10%–20% of people don't respond well at all. At the other end of the continuum, about 10%–15% of people are exceptionally good hypnotic subjects (Hilgard, 1965). Among people who are susceptible to hypnosis, many interesting effects can be produced. Some of the more prominent hypnotic phenomena include:

1. *Anesthesia.* Drugs are more reliable, but hypnosis can be surprisingly effective in the treatment of both acute and chronic pain (Boly et al., 2007; Jensen & Patterson, 2008). Although the practice is not widespread, some physicians and dentists use hypnosis as a substitute for anesthetic drugs.

2. *Sensory distortions and hallucinations.* Hypnotized subjects may be led to experience auditory or visual hallucinations (Spiegel, 2003b). They may hear sounds or see things that are not there, or fail to hear or see stimuli that are present (Spiegel et al., 1985). Subjects may also have their sensations distorted so that something sweet tastes sour or an unpleasant odor smells fragrant.

3. *Disinhibition.* Hypnosis can sometimes reduce inhibitions that would normally prevent subjects from acting in ways that they would see as immoral or unacceptable. In experiments, hypnotized subjects have been induced to throw what they believed to be nitric acid into the face of a research assistant. Similarly, stage hypnotists are sometimes successful in getting people to disrobe in public. This disinhibition effect may occur simply because hypnotized people feel that they cannot be held responsible for actions taken while hypnotized.

4. *Posthypnotic suggestions and amnesia.* Suggestions made during hypnosis may influence a participant's later behavior (Cox & Bryant, 2008). The most common posthypnotic suggestion is the creation of posthypnotic amnesia. That is, subjects who are told that they will remember nothing that happened while they were hypnotized do indeed usually remember nothing.

Theories of Hypnosis

Although a number of theories have been developed to explain hypnosis, it is still not well understood. One popular view is that hypnotic effects occur because participants

© AP Images/BOOKSTAVER

© Chuck Painter/Stanford News Service

Ernest Hilgard

"Many psychologists argue that the hypnotic trance is a mirage. It would be unfortunate if this skeptical view were to gain such popularity that the benefits of hypnosis are denied to the numbers of those who could be helped."

are put into a special, altered state of consciousness, called a *hypnotic trance* (Christensen, 2005). Although hypnotized subjects may feel as though they are in an altered state, they do not seem to show reliable alterations in brain activity that are unique to hypnosis (Burgess, 2007; Lynn et al., 2007). The failure to find special changes in brain activity that are consistently associated with hypnosis has led some theorists to conclude that hypnosis is a normal state of consciousness that is characterized by dramatic role playing.

HYPNOSIS AS ROLE PLAYING

The role-playing view asserts that hypnosis produces a normal mental state in which suggestible people act out the role of a hypnotic subject and behave as they think hypnotized people are supposed to (Barber, 1979; Kirsch, 2000; Spanos, 1991). According to this notion, it is subjects' *role expectations* that produce hypnotic effects, rather than a special trancelike state of consciousness.

Two lines of evidence support the role-playing view. First, many of the seemingly amazing effects of hypnosis have been duplicated by nonhypnotized subjects or have been shown to be exaggerated (Kirsch, 1997; Kirsch, Mazzoni, & Montgomery, 2007). This finding suggests that no special state of consciousness is required to explain hypnotic feats.

The second line of evidence involves demonstrations that hypnotized participants are often acting out a role. For example, Martin Orne (1951) regressed hypnotized subjects back to their sixth birthday and asked them to describe it. They responded with detailed descriptions that appeared to represent great feats of hypnosis-enhanced memory. However, instead of accepting this information at face value, Orne compared it with information that he had obtained from the participants' parents. It turned out that many of the subjects' memories were inaccurate and invented! Many other studies have also found that age-regressed subjects' recall of the distant past tends to be more fanciful than factual (Green, 1999). Thus, the role-playing explanation of hypnosis suggests that situational factors lead suggestible subjects to act out a certain role in a highly cooperative manner (Lynn, Kirsch, & Hallquist, 2008; Wagstaff et al., 2010).

HYPNOSIS AS AN ALTERED STATE OF CONSCIOUSNESS

Despite the doubts raised by role-playing explanations, many prominent theorists still maintain that hypnotic effects are attributable to a special, altered state of consciousness (Hilgard, 1986; Naish, 2006; Spiegel, 2003a; Woody & Sadler, 2008). These theorists argue that it is doubtful that role playing can explain all hypnotic phenomena. For instance, they assert that even the most cooperative subjects are unlikely to endure surgery without a drug anesthetic just to please their physician and live up to their expected role. They also cite studies in which hypnotized participants have continued to display hypnotic responses when they thought they were alone and not being observed (Perugini et al., 1998). If hypnotized participants were merely acting, they would drop the act when alone.

The most influential explanation of hypnosis as an altered state of awareness has been offered by Ernest Hilgard (1986, 1992). According to Hilgard, hypnosis creates a *dissociation* in consciousness. **Dissociation is a splitting off of mental processes into two separate, simultaneous streams of awareness.** In other words, Hilgard theorizes that hypnosis splits consciousness into two streams. One stream is in communication with the hypnotist and the external world, while the other is a difficult-to-detect "hidden observer." Hilgard believes that many hypnotic effects are a product of this divided consciousness. For instance, he suggests that a hypnotized subject might appear unresponsive to pain because the pain isn't registered in the portion of consciousness that communicates with other people.

One appealing aspect of Hilgard's theory is that *divided consciousness* is a common, normal experience. For example, people will often drive a car a great distance, responding to traffic signals and other cars, with no recollection of having consciously done so. In such cases, consciousness is clearly divided between driving and the person's thoughts about other matters. Interestingly, this common experience has long been known as *highway hypnosis*. In summary, Hilgard presents hypnosis as a plausible variation in consciousness that has continuity with everyday experience.

Meditation: Seeking Higher Consciousness

KEY LEARNING GOALS

5.11 Explain the nature of meditation, and describe its physiological correlates.

5.12 Assess the evidence on the long-term benefits of meditation.

Recent years have seen growing interest in the ancient discipline of meditation. *Meditation* **refers to a family of practices that train attention to heighten awareness and bring mental processes under greater voluntary control.** In North America, the most widely practiced approaches to meditation are those associated with yoga, Zen, and transcendental meditation (TM). All three are rooted in Eastern religions (Hinduism, Buddhism, and Taoism). However, meditation has been practiced throughout history as an element of all religious and spiritual traditions, including Judaism and Christianity (Walsh & Shapiro, 2006). Moreover, the practice of meditation can be largely divorced from religious beliefs. In fact, most Americans who meditate have only vague ideas regarding its religious significance. Of interest to psychology is the fact that meditation involves a deliberate effort to alter consciousness.

Approaches to meditation can be classified into two main styles that reflect how attention is directed: *focused attention* and *open monitoring* (Cahn & Polich, 2006; Manna et al., 2010). In focused attention approaches, attention is concentrated on a specific object, image, sound, or bodily sensation (such as breathing). The intent in narrowing attention is to clear the mind of its clutter. In open monitoring approaches, attention is directed to the contents of one's moment-to-moment experience in a nonjudgmental and nonreactive way. The intent in expanding attention is to become a detached observer of the flow of one's own sensations, thoughts, and feelings. Both approaches seek to achieve a "higher" form of consciousness than what people normally experience. The meditative disciplines that have received the most research attention are Transcendental Meditation (TM) and mindfulness meditation. Mindfulness meditation is an open monitoring approach with roots in Zen Buddhism, whereas TM is primarily a focused attention approach with roots in Hinduism.

What happens when an experienced meditator goes into the meditative state? One intriguing finding is that alpha and theta waves become more prominent in EEG recordings (Cahn & Polich, 2006; Lagopoulos et al., 2009). Many studies also find that subjects' heart rate, skin conductance, respiration rate, oxygen consumption, and carbon dioxide elimination decline (see **Figure 5.9**; Dillbeck & Orme-Johnson, 1987; Fenwick, 1987; Travis, 2001). Taken together, these changes suggest that meditation leads to a potentially beneficial physiological state characterized by suppression of bodily arousal. However, some researchers have argued that a variety of systematic relaxation training procedures can produce similar results (Holmes, 1987; Shapiro, 1984). Mere relaxation hardly seems like an adequate explanation for the transcendent experiences reported by many meditators. Thus, debate continues about whether there are physiological changes associated with meditation that are unique to a special state of consciousness (Shear & Jevning, 1999; Travis & Pearson, 2000).

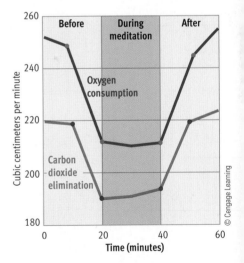

FIGURE 5.9

The suppression of physiological arousal during transcendental meditation. The physiological changes shown in the graph are evidence of physical relaxation during the meditative state. However, critics argue that similar changes may also be produced by systematic relaxation procedures.

SOURCE: Adapted from Wallace, R. K., & Benson, H. (1972, February). The physiology of meditation. *Scientific American, 226*, 85–90. Graphic redrawn from illustration on p. 86 by Lorelle A. Raboni. Copyright © 1972 by Scientific American, Inc.

What about the long-term benefits that have been claimed for meditation? Research suggests that meditation may have some value in reducing the effects of stress (Grossman et al., 2004). In particular, regular meditation is associated with lower levels of some "stress hormones" (Infante et al., 2001) and enhanced immune response (Davidson et al., 2003a). Studies also report that meditation may have beneficial effects on self-esteem (Emavardhana & Tori, 1997), mood and one's sense of control (Easterlin & Cardena, 1999), depression (Kabat-Zinn, 2003), and eating disorders (Kristeller, Baer, & Quillian-Wolever, 2006). In the physiological domain, research has suggested that meditation may help to control blood pressure (Barnes, Treiber, & Davis, 2001) and enhance patterns of sleep (Pattanashetty et al., 2010). Finally, although more difficult to measure, some theorists assert that meditation can enhance human potential by improving concentration, heightening awareness, and building emotional resilience (Walsh & Shapiro, 2006). At first glance these results are impressive, but they need to be viewed with some caution. Some of these effects may also be attainable through systematic relaxation or other mental focusing procedures (Shapiro, 1984; Smith, 1975). Critics also wonder whether placebo effects, sampling bias, and other methodological problems may have exaggerated some of the reported benefits of meditation (Bishop, 2002; Canter, 2003; Caspi & Burleson, 2005).

That said, the quality of meditation research appears to be improving, and recent years have brought some eye-opening findings. For example, a number of recent experiments have demonstrated that meditation can increase the tolerance of pain, which could have important implications for the management of a variety of health problems (Grant & Rainville, 2009; Grant et al., 2010; Zeidan et al., 2010). Grant and Rainville (2009) compared the pain sensitivity of thirteen experienced Zen meditators and thirteen comparable nonmeditators. Carefully controlled pain was administered by applying a heating plate to participants' calves. The meditators were able to handle considerably more pain than the non-meditators. Moreover, a follow-up study suggested that the meditators' greater pain tolerance was associated with increased thickness in brain regions that register pain (Grant et al., 2010). In other words, it appeared that meditation experience had produced enduring alterations in brain structure that were responsible for meditators' increased pain tolerance. Clearly, a great deal of additional research is needed, but these thought-provoking findings would seem to undermine the idea that meditation is nothing more than relaxation.

Concept Check 5.2

Relating EEG Activity to Variations in Consciousness

Early in the chapter we emphasized the intimate relationship between brain activity and variations in consciousness. Check your understanding of this relationship by indicating the kind of EEG activity (alpha, beta, theta, or delta) that would probably be dominant in each of the following situations. The answers are in Appendix A.

_____ 1. You are playing a video game.

_____ 2. You are deep in meditation.

_____ 3. You have just fallen asleep.

_____ 4. You are in the midst of a pleasant dream.

_____ 5. You are a novice typist, practicing your typing.

© lenetstan/Shutterstock

Altering Consciousness with Drugs

KEY LEARNING GOALS

5.13 Identify the major types of abused drugs and their main effects.

5.14 Understand why drug effects vary, how drugs affect the brain, and drug dependence.

5.15 Summarize evidence on the major health risks associated with drug abuse.

Like hypnosis and meditation, drugs are commonly used in deliberate efforts to alter consciousness. In this section, we focus on the use of drugs for nonmedical purposes, commonly referred to as "recreational drug use." Such drug use involves personal, moral, political, and legal issues that are not matters for science to resolve. However, the more knowledgeable you are about drugs, the more informed your decisions and opinions about them will be. Accordingly, this section describes the types of drugs that are most commonly used for recreational purposes and summarizes their effects on consciousness, behavior, and health.

Principal Abused Drugs and Their Effects

PsykTrek 4c

The drugs that people use recreationally are termed *psychoactive*. *Psychoactive drugs* **are chemical substances that modify mental, emotional, or behavioral functioning.** Not all psychoactive drugs produce effects that lead to recreational use. Generally, users prefer drugs that elevate their mood or produce other pleasurable alterations in consciousness. The principal types of recreational drugs are described in **Table 5.2** on the next page. The table lists representative drugs in each of six categories. It also summarizes how the drugs are taken, their medical uses, their effects on consciousness, and their common side effects (based on Julien, Advokat, & Comaty, 2008; Levinthal, 2008; Lowinson et al., 2005). The six categories of psychoactive drugs that we will focus on are narcotics, sedatives, stimulants, hallucinogens, cannabis, and alcohol.

Narcotics, or *opiates,* **are drugs derived from opium that are capable of relieving pain.** The main drugs in this category are heroin and morphine, although less potent opiates such as codeine, Demerol, and methadone are also abused. The emerging problem in this category is a relatively new drug called oxycodone (trade name: OxyContin). It's time-release format was supposed to make it an effective analgesic with less potential for abuse than the other opiates (Cicero, Inciardi, & Munoz, 2005). But people quickly learned that they could grind it up and gain a powerful high. This trend has led to a new epidemic of serious drug abuse, especially in rural areas of the United States (Tunnell, 2005). In sufficient dosages these drugs can produce an overwhelming sense of euphoria or well-being. This euphoric effect has a relaxing, "Who cares?" quality that makes the high an attractive escape from reality.

Sedatives **are sleep-inducing drugs that tend to decrease central nervous system activation and behavioral activity.** Historically, the most widely abused sedatives have been the *barbiturates*. But in recent decades stricter controls have reduced their availability and people have turned to the *benzodiazepine* sedatives, which, fortunately, have notably less appeal as a drug of abuse. People abusing sedatives, or "downers," generally consume larger doses than are prescribed for medical purposes. The desired effect is a euphoria similar to that produced by drinking large amounts of alcohol. Feelings of tension or dejection are replaced by a relaxed, pleasant state of intoxication, accompanied by loosened inhibitions.

Stimulants **are drugs that tend to increase central nervous system activation and behavioral activity.** Stimulants range from mild, widely available drugs, such as caffeine and nicotine, to stronger, carefully regulated ones, such as cocaine. We will focus on cocaine and amphetamines. Cocaine is a natural substance that comes from the coca shrub. In contrast, amphetamines ("speed") are synthesized in a pharmaceutical laboratory. Cocaine and amphetamines have fairly similar effects, except that cocaine produces a briefer high. Stimulants produce a euphoria very different from that created

"JUST TELL ME WHERE YOU KIDS GET THE IDEA TO TAKE SO MANY DRUGS."

© 2004 by Sidney Harris. ScienceCartoonPlus.com

by narcotics or sedatives. They produce a buoyant, elated, energetic, "I can conquer the world!" feeling accompanied by increased alertness. In recent years, cocaine and amphetamines have become available in much more potent (and dangerous) forms than before. "Crack" consists of relatively pure chips of cocaine that are usually smoked. Amphetamines are increasingly sold as a crystalline powder, called "crank," or "crystal meth" (short for methamphetamine), that may be snorted or injected intravenously.

Hallucinogens **are a diverse group of drugs that have powerful effects on mental and emotional functioning, marked most notably by distortions in sensory and perceptual experience.** The principal hallucinogens are LSD, mescaline, and psilocybin. These drugs have similar effects, although they vary in potency. Hallucinogens produce euphoria, increased sensory awareness, and a distorted sense of time. In some users, they lead to profound, dreamlike, "mystical" feelings that are difficult to describe. The latter effect is why they have been used in religious ceremonies for centuries in some cultures. Unfortunately, at the other end of the emotional spectrum hallucinogens can also produce nightmarish feelings of anxiety and paranoia, commonly called a "bad trip."

© Yuri Arcurs/Shutterstock

Cannabis **is the hemp plant from which marijuana, hashish, and THC are derived.** Marijuana is a mixture of dried leaves, flowers, stems, and seeds taken from the plant, while hashish comes from the plant's resin. Smoking is the usual route of ingestion for both marijuana and hashish. THC, the active chemical ingredient in cannabis, can be synthesized for research purposes (for example, to give to animals, which can't very well smoke marijuana). When smoked, cannabis has an immediate impact that may last several hours. The desired effects of the drug are a mild, relaxed euphoria and enhanced sensory awareness.

TABLE 5.2 Psychoactive Drugs: Methods of Ingestion, Medical Uses, and Effects

Drugs	Methods of Ingestion	Principal Medical Uses	Desired Effects	Potential Short-Term Side Effects
Narcotics (opiates) Morphine Heroin	Injected, smoked, oral	Pain relief	Euphoria, relaxation, anxiety reduction, pain relief	Lethargy, drowsiness, nausea, impaired coordination, impaired mental functioning, constipation
Sedatives Barbiturates Benzodiazepines	Oral, injected	Sleeping pill, anticonvulsant	Euphoria, relaxation, anxiety reduction, reduced inhibitions	Lethargy, drowsiness, severely impaired coordination, impaired mental functioning, emotional swings, dejection
Stimulants Amphetamines Cocaine	Oral, sniffed, injected, freebased, smoked	Treatment of hyperactivity and narcolepsy, local anesthetic (cocaine only)	Elation, excitement, increased alertness, increased energy, reduced fatigue	Increased blood pressure and heart rate, increased talkativeness, restlessness, irritability, insomnia, reduced appetite, increased sweating and urination, anxiety, paranoia, increased aggressiveness, panic
Hallucinogens LSD Mescaline Psilocybin	Oral	None	Increased sensory awareness, euphoria, altered perceptions, hallucinations, insightful experiences	Dilated pupils, nausea, emotional swings, paranoia, jumbled thought processes, impaired judgment, anxiety, panic reaction
Cannabis Marijuana Hashish THC	Smoked, oral	Treatment of glaucoma and chemotherapy-induced nausea and vomiting; other uses under study	Mild euphoria, relaxation, altered perceptions, enhanced awareness	Elevated heart rate, bloodshot eyes, dry mouth, reduced short-term memory, sluggish motor coordination, sluggish mental functioning, anxiety
Alcohol	Drinking	None	Mild euphoria, relaxation, anxiety reduction, reduced inhibitions	Severely impaired coordination, impaired mental functioning, increased urination, emotional swings, depression, quarrelsomeness, hangover

© Cengage Learning

Alcohol encompasses a variety of beverages containing ethyl alcohol, such as beers, wines, and distilled spirits. The concentration of ethyl alcohol varies from about 4% in most beers to 40% in 80-proof liquor—and occasionally more in higher-proof liquors. When people drink heavily, the central effect is a relaxed euphoria that temporarily boosts self-esteem, as problems seem to melt away and inhibitions diminish. Common side effects include impairments in mental and motor functioning, mood swings, and quarrelsomeness. Alcohol is the most widely used recreational drug in our society. Because alcohol is legal, many people use it casually without even thinking of it as a drug.

Factors Influencing Drug Effects

The drug effects summarized in **Table 5.2** are the *typical* ones. Drug effects can vary from person to person and even for the same person in different situations. The impact of any drug depends in part on the user's age, mood, motivation, personality, previous experience with the drug, body weight, and physiology. The dose and potency of a drug, the method of intake, and the setting in which a drug is taken are also likely to influence its effects (Leavitt, 1995). Our theme of *multifactorial causation* clearly applies to the effects of drugs.

So, too, does our theme emphasizing the *subjectivity of experience*. Expectations are potentially powerful factors that can influence the user's perceptions of a drug's effects. You may recall from the discussion of placebo effects in Chapter 2 that some people who are misled to *think* that they are drinking alcohol show signs of intoxication (Assefi & Garry, 2003). If people expect a drug to make them feel giddy, serene, or profound, their expectation may contribute to the feelings they experience.

A drug's effects can also change as the person's body develops a *tolerance* to the chemical. **Tolerance refers to a progressive decrease in a person's responsiveness to a drug as a result of continued use.** Tolerance usually leads people to consume larger and larger doses of a drug to attain the effects they desire. Most drugs produce tolerance, but some do so more rapidly than others. For example, tolerance to alcohol usually builds slowly, while tolerance to heroin increases much more quickly. **Table 5.3** indicates whether various categories of drugs tend to produce tolerance rapidly or gradually.

Mechanisms of Drug Action

PSYKTREK 4d

Most drugs have effects that reverberate throughout the body. However, psychoactive drugs work mainly by altering neurotransmitter activity in the brain. As we discussed in Chapter 3, *neurotransmitters* are chemicals that transmit signals between neurons at junctions called synapses.

TABLE 5.3 **Psychoactive Drugs: Tolerance, Dependence, Potential for Fatal Overdose, and Health Risks**

Drugs	Tolerance	Risk of Physical Dependence	Risk of Psychological Dependence	Fatal Overdose Potential	Health Risks
Narcotics (opiates)	Rapid	High	High	High	Infectious diseases, accidents, immune suppression
Sedatives	Rapid	High	High	High	Accidents
Stimulants	Rapid	Moderate	High	Moderate to high	Sleep problems, malnutrition, nasal damage, hypertension, respiratory disease, stroke, liver disease, heart attack
Hallucinogens	Gradual	None	Very low	Very low	Accidents, acute panic
Cannabis	Gradual	None	Low to moderate	Very low	Accidents, lung cancer, respiratory disease, pulmonary disease, increased vulnerability to psychosis
Alcohol	Gradual	Moderate	Moderate	Low to high	Accidents, liver disease, malnutrition, brain damage, neurological disorders, heart disease, stroke, hypertension, ulcers, cancer, birth defects

© Cengage Learning

The actions of amphetamines illustrate how drugs have selective, multiple effects on neurotransmitter activity. Amphetamines exert their main effects on two neurotransmitter systems: norepinephrine (NE) and dopamine (DA). Amphetamines appear to have two key effects at DA and NE synapses (Koob & Le Moal, 2006). First, they increase the release of dopamine and norepinephrine by presynaptic neurons. Second, they interfere with the reuptake of DA and NE from synaptic clefts. These actions serve to increase the levels of dopamine and norepinephrine at the affected synapses. Cocaine shares some of these actions, which is why cocaine and amphetamines produce similar stimulant effects.

Although specific drugs exert their initial effects in the brain on a wide variety of neurotransmitter systems, many theorists believe that virtually all abused drugs eventually increase activity in a particular neural pathway, called the *mesolimbic dopamine pathway* (Nestler & Malenka, 2004). This neural circuit—which runs from an area in the midbrain, through the *nucleus accumbens,* and on to the prefrontal cortex (see **Figure 5.10**)—has been described as a "reward pathway" (Pierce & Kumaresan, 2006). Large and rapid increases in the release of dopamine along this pathway are thought to be the neural basis of the reinforcing effects of most abused drugs (Knapp & Kornetsky, 2009; Volkow, Fowler, & Wang, 2004).

Drug Dependence

PsykTrek 4c

People can become either physically or psychologically dependent on a drug. Physical dependence is a common problem with narcotics, sedatives, and alcohol and is an occasional problem with stimulants. *Physical dependence* **exists when a person must continue to take a drug to avoid withdrawal illness.** The symptoms of withdrawal illness depend on the specific drug. Withdrawal from heroin, barbiturates, and alcohol can produce fever, chills, tremors, convulsions, vomiting, cramps, diarrhea, and severe aches and pains. Withdrawal from stimulants leads to a more subtle syndrome, marked by fatigue, apathy, irritability, depression, and disorientation.

Psychological dependence **exists when a person must continue to take a drug to satisfy intense mental and emotional craving.** Psychological dependence is more subtle than physical dependence, but the need it creates can be powerful. Cocaine, for instance, can produce an overwhelming psychological need for continued use. Psychological dependence is possible with all recreational drugs, although it seems rare for hallucinogens.

Both types of dependence are established gradually with repeated use of a drug. Drugs vary in their potential for creating either physical or psychological dependence. **Table 5.3** provides estimates of the risk of each kind of dependence for the six categories of recreational drugs covered in our discussion.

FIGURE 5.10

The "reward pathway" in the brain. The neural circuits shown here in blue make up the *mesolimbic dopamine pathway*. Axons in this pathway run from an area in the midbrain through the medial forebrain bundle to the *nucleus accumbens* and on to the prefrontal cortex. Recreational drugs affect a variety of neurotransmitter systems, but theorists believe that heightened dopamine activity in this pathway—especially the portion running from the midbrain to the nucleus accumbens—is responsible for the reinforcing effects of most abused drugs.

Labels on figure:
Area in midbrain
Dopamine projections to prefrontal cortex
Nucleus accumbens
Medial forebrain bundle (a path of axons that release dopamine)

Drugs and Health

PsykTrek 4c

Recreational drug use can affect physical health in a variety of ways. The three principal risks are overdose, tissue damage (direct effects), and health-impairing behavior that results from drug abuse (indirect effects).

OVERDOSE

PsykTrek 4c

Any drug can be fatal if a person takes enough of it, but some drugs are much more dangerous than others. **Table 5.3** shows estimates of the risk of accidentally consuming a *lethal* overdose of each listed drug. Drugs that are CNS depressants—sedatives, narcotics, and alcohol—carry the greatest risk of overdose. It's important to remember that these drugs are synergistic with each other, so many overdoses involve lethal *combinations* of CNS depressants. What happens when a person overdoses on these drugs? The respiratory system usually grinds to a halt, producing coma, brain damage, and death within a brief period. Fatal overdoses with CNS stimulants usually involve a heart attack, stroke, or cortical seizure. Years ago, deaths attributable to overdoses of stimulant drugs were relatively infrequent. However, cocaine overdoses have increased sharply as more people have experimented with smoking crack and using other more dangerous modes of ingestion (Repetto & Gold, 2005).

DIRECT EFFECTS

PsykTrek 4c

In some cases, drugs cause tissue damage directly. For example, chronic snorting of cocaine can damage nasal membranes. Cocaine use can also foster cardiovascular disease, and crack smoking is associated with a number of respiratory problems (Gold & Jacobs, 2005; Gourevitch & Arnsten, 2005). Long-term, excessive alcohol consumption is associated with an elevated risk for a wide range of serious health problems, including liver damage, ulcers, hypertension, stroke, heart disease, neurological disorders, and some types of cancer (Johnson & Ait-Daoud, 2005; Mack, Franklin, & Frances, 2003).

The health risks of marijuana have generated considerable debate in recent years. The available evidence suggests that chronic marijuana use increases the risk for respiratory and pulmonary disease (Aldington et al., 2007; Tashkin et al., 2002). Some studies have also found a link between long-term marijuana use and the risk for lung cancer, although the data are surprisingly inconsistent (Aldington et al., 2008; Mehra et al., 2006). Finally, there have been a rash of recent studies that report an unexpected link between cannabis use and severe, psychotic disorders, including schizophrenia (Degenhardt & Hall, 2006; DiForti et al., 2007). Obviously, the vast majority of marijuana users do not develop psychoses, but it appears that cannabis may trigger psychotic illness in individuals who have a genetic vulnerability to such disorders (D'Souza, 2007; Murray et al., 2007). Although these dangers are real, some other widely publicized dangers have been exaggerated by the popular press. For instance, contrary to popular reports, it appears that cannabis does *not* produce meaningful reductions in immune system response (Bredt et al., 2002; Klein, Friedman, & Specter, 1998) or any significant effects on male smokers' fertility or sexual functioning (Grinspoon, Bakalar, & Russo, 2005).

© Yellowj/Shtterstock

In 2011, after years of struggling with substance abuse, singer Amy Winehouse died from an accidental overdose of alcohol. Her tragic death illustrates the seductive risks of psychoactive drugs and that alcohol by itself can be quite dangerous.

© Featureflash/Shutterstock

INDIRECT EFFECTS

PsykTrek 4c

The negative effects of drugs on physical health are often indirect results of the drugs' impact on behavior. For instance, people using stimulants often do not eat or sleep properly. Sedatives increase the risk of accidental injuries because they severely impair motor coordination. People who abuse downers often trip down stairs, fall off stools, and suffer other mishaps. Many drugs, such as marijuana, impair driving ability, increasing the risk of automobile accidents (Ramaekers et al., 2004). Alcohol, for instance, may contribute to roughly 40% of all automobile deaths (Hingson & Sleet, 2006). Intravenous drug users risk contracting infectious diseases that can be spread by unsterilized needles. In recent years, acquired immune deficiency syndrome (AIDS) has been transmitted at an alarming rate through the population of intravenous drug users (Des Jarlais, Hagan, & Friedman, 2005).

The major health risks (other than overdose) of various recreational drugs are listed in the sixth column of **Table 5.3**. As you can see, alcohol appears to have the most diverse negative effects on physical health. The irony, of course, is that alcohol is the only recreational drug listed that is legal.

Reflecting on the Chapter's Themes

KEY LEARNING GOALS

5.16 Identify the five unifying themes highlighted in this chapter.

 Sociohistorical Context

 Subjectivity of Experience

 Cultural Heritage

 Multifactorial Causation

 Theoretical Diversity

This chapter highlighted five of our unifying themes. First, we saw how psychology evolves in a sociohistorical context. Research on consciousness dwindled to almost nothing after John B. Watson (1913, 1919) and others redefined psychology as the science of behavior. However, in the 1960s, people began to turn inward, showing a new interest in altering consciousness through drug use, meditation, hypnosis, and biofeedback. Psychologists responded to these social trends by beginning to study variations in consciousness in earnest. This shift shows how social forces can have an impact on psychology's evolution.

A second theme that surfaced in this chapter is the idea that people's experience of the world is highly subjective. We encountered this theme toward the end of the chapter when we discussed the subjective nature of drug effects, noting that the changes of consciousness produced by drugs depend significantly on personal expectations.

Third, we saw once again how culture molds some aspects of behavior. Although the basic physiological process of sleep appears largely the same from one society to another, culture influences certain aspects of sleep habits. And culture has a dramatic impact on whether people remember their dreams and how they interpret and feel about their dreams. If not for space constraints, we might also have discussed cross-cultural differences in patterns of recreational drug use, which vary considerably from one society to the next.

Fourth, we learned once again that behavior is governed by multifactorial causation. For example, we discussed how the effects

Concept Check 5.3

Recognizing the Unique Characteristics of Commonly Abused Drugs

From our discussion of the principal psychoactive drugs, it is clear that considerable overlap exists among the categories of drugs in terms of their methods of ingestion, medical uses, desired effects, and short-term side effects. Each type of drug, however, has at least one or two characteristics that make it different from the other types. Check your understanding of the unique characteristics of each type of drug by indicating which of them has the characteristics listed below. Choose from the following: (a) narcotics, (b) sedatives, (c) stimulants, (d) hallucinogens, (e) cannabis, and (f) alcohol. You'll find the answers in Appendix A.

_____ 1. Increases alertness and energy, reduces fatigue.

_____ 2. No recognized medical use. May lead to insightful or "mystical" experiences.

_____ 3. Used as a "sleeping pill" because it reduces CNS activity.

_____ 4. Increases one's risk for a number of diseases, including liver disease and neurological disorders.

_____ 5. Derived from opium; used for pain relief.

_____ 6. One likely health risk is respiratory and pulmonary disease.

of jet lag, sleep deprivation, and psychoactive drugs depend on a number of interacting factors.

Finally, the chapter illustrated psychology's theoretical diversity. We discussed conflicting theories about dreams, hypnosis, and meditation. For the most part, we did not see any of the opposing theories converging toward reconciliation, as we did in the previous chapter. However, it's important to emphasize that rival theories do not always merge neatly into tidy models of behavior. While it's always nice to resolve a theoretical debate, the debate itself can advance knowledge by stimulating and guiding empirical research.

Indeed, our upcoming Personal Application demonstrates that theoretical debates need not be resolved in order to advance knowledge. Many theoretical controversies and enduring mysteries remain in the study of sleep and dreams. Nonetheless, researchers have accumulated a great deal of practical information on these topics, which we'll discuss next.

Personal APPLICATION

Addressing Practical Questions About Sleep and Dreams

KEY LEARNING GOALS

5.17 Summarize the evidence on various practical questions about sleep and dreams.

Indicate whether the following statements are "true" or "false."
____ 1 Naps rarely have a refreshing effect.
____ 2 Some people never dream.
____ 3 When people cannot recall their dreams, it's because they are trying to repress them.

These assertions were drawn from the Sleep and Dreams Information Questionnaire (Palladino & Carducci, 1984), which measures practical knowledge about sleep and dreams. Are they true or false? You'll see in this Application.

Common Questions About Sleep

How much sleep do people need? The average amount of daily sleep for young adults is 7.5 hours. However, people differ considerably in how much they sleep, which suggests that sleep needs vary. As noted earlier, sleep experts believe that most people would function more effectively if they increased their amount of sleep (Banks & Dinges, 2007; Maas, 1998). Bear in mind, too, that research suggests that people who sleep 7–8 hours per night have the lowest mortality rates (Patel et al., 2004; Tamakoshi et al., 2004).

Can short naps be refreshing? Some naps are beneficial and some are not. The effectiveness of napping varies from person to person. Also, the benefits of any specific nap depend on the time of day and the amount of sleep one has had recently (Dinges, 1993). Naps tend to be more beneficial when they are rich in slow-wave sleep or REM sleep (Mednick & Drummond, 2009). Unfortunately, you're often just getting into these deeper stages of sleep when your nap time is up. Nonetheless, naps can enhance subsequent alertness and task performance and reduce sleepiness (Ficca et al., 2010). Evidence also suggests that naps can improve learning and memory—even more so than loading up on caffeine (Mednick et al., 2008). In conclusion, naps can be refreshing for many people, so the first statement opening this Application is false.

What is the significance of snoring? Snoring is a common phenomenon that is seen in roughly 30%–40% of adults (Hoffstein, 2005). Snoring increases after age 35, occurs in men more than women, and is more common among people who are overweight (Kryger, 1993; Stoohs et al., 1998). Many factors, including obesity, colds, allergies, smoking, and some drugs, can contribute to snoring, mainly by forcing people to breathe through their mouths while sleeping. Some people who snore loudly disrupt their own sleep as well as that of their bed partners. It can be difficult to prevent snoring in some people, whereas other people can reduce their snoring by losing weight or sleeping on their side instead of their back (Lugaresi et al., 1994). Snoring may seem like a trivial problem, but it is associated with sleep apnea and cardiovascular disease, and it may have more medical significance than most people realize (Dement & Vaughn, 1999; Olson & Park, 2006).

What can be done to avoid sleep problems? There are many ways to improve your chances of getting satisfactory sleep. Most of them involve developing sensible daytime habits that won't interfere with sleep (see Foldvary-Schaefer, 2006; Maas, 1998; Stepanski & Wyatt, 2003). For example, if you've been having trouble sleeping at night, it's a good idea to avoid daytime naps, so that you'll be tired when bedtime arrives. Some people find that daytime exercise helps them fall asleep more readily at bedtime (King et al., 1997).

People typically get very upset when they have difficulty falling asleep. Unfortunately, this emotional distress tends to make it even harder for people to get to sleep.

Baby. Many involve "boring yourself to sleep" by playing alphabet games, reciting poems, or listening to your clock. Another recommended strategy is to engage in some not-so-engaging activity. For instance, you might try reading your dullest textbook. It could turn out to be a superb sedative.

It's often a good idea to simply launch yourself into a pleasant daydream. This normal presleep process can take your mind off your difficulties. Whatever you think about, try to avoid ruminating about the current stresses and problems in your life. Research has shown that the tendency to ruminate is one of the key factors contributing to insomnia (Kales et al., 1984). Anything that relaxes you—whether it's music, meditation, prayer, a warm bath, or a systematic relaxation procedure—can aid you in falling asleep.

It's wise to minimize consumption of stimulants such as caffeine and nicotine. Because coffee and cigarettes aren't prescription drugs, people don't appreciate how much the stimulants they contain can heighten physical arousal. Many foods (such as chocolate) and beverages (such as cola drinks) contain more caffeine than people realize. Also, bear in mind that ill-advised eating habits can interfere with sleep. Try to avoid going to bed hungry, uncomfortably stuffed, or soon after eating foods that disagree with you. It's also a good idea to try to establish a reasonably regular bedtime. This habit will allow you to take advantage of your circadian rhythm, so you'll be trying to fall asleep when your body is primed to cooperate.

What can be done about insomnia? First, don't panic if you run into a little trouble sleeping. An overreaction to sleep difficulties can begin a vicious circle of escalating problems. If you jump to the conclusion that you are becoming an insomniac, you may approach sleep with anxiety that will aggravate the problem.

The harder you work at falling asleep, the less success you're likely to have. As noted earlier, temporary sleep problems are common and generally clear up on their own.

One sleep expert, Dianne Hales (1987), lists 101 suggestions for combating insomnia in her book *How to Sleep Like a*

Common Questions About Dreams

Does everyone dream? Yes. Some people just don't *remember* their dreams. However, when these people are brought into a sleep lab and awakened from REM sleep, they report having been dreaming—much to their surprise (statement 2 at the start of this Application is false).

© Elena Elisseeva/Shutterstock

Scientists have studied a small number of people who have sustained brain damage in the area of the *pons* that has wiped out their REM sleep, but even these people report dreams (Klosch & Kraft, 2005).

Why don't some people remember their dreams? The evaporation of dreams appears to be quite normal. Most dreams are lost forever unless unless people wake up during or just after a dream. Even then, dream recall fades quickly (Nir & Tononi, 2009). Most of the time, people who recall dreams are remembering their *last* dream from their final REM period. Hobson's (1989) educated guess is that people probably forget 95%–99% of their dreams. This forgetting is natural and is not due to repression (statement 3 is also false). People who never remember their dreams probably have a sleep pattern that puts too much time between their last REM/dream period and awakening, so even their last dream is forgotten.

Do dreams require interpretation? Yes, but interpretation may not be as difficult as generally assumed. People have long believed that dreams are symbolic and that it is necessary to interpret the symbols to understand the meaning of dreams. Freud, for instance, made a distinction between the *manifest content* and the *latent content* of a dream. The **manifest content consists of the plot of a dream at a surface level. The *latent content* refers to the hidden or disguised meaning of the events in the plot.** Thus, a Freudian therapist might equate such dream events as walking into a tunnel, mounting a horse, or riding a roller coaster with sexual intercourse. Freudian theorists assert that dream interpretation is a complicated task requiring considerable knowledge of symbolism.

However, many dream theorists argue that symbolism in dreams is less deceptive and mysterious than Freud thought (Faraday, 1974; Foulkes, 1985; Hall, 1979). Calvin Hall makes the point that dreams require some interpretation simply because they are more visual than verbal. That is, pictures need to be translated into ideas. According to Hall, dream symbolism is highly personal and the dreamer may be the person best equipped to decipher a dream. Unfortunately, you'll never know whether you're "correct," because there is no definitive way to judge the validity of different dream interpretations.

Is Alcoholism a Disease? The Power of Definitions

Alcoholism is a major problem in most—perhaps all—societies. It destroys countless lives, tears families apart, and is associated with an elevated risk for a variety of physical ailments (Johnson & Ait-Daoud, 2005). With roughly 15 million problem drinkers in the United States (Mack et al., 2003), it seems likely that alcoholism has touched the lives of a majority of Americans.

In almost every discussion about alcoholism someone will ask, "Is alcoholism a disease?" If alcoholism is a disease, it is a strange one, because the alcoholic is the most direct cause of his or her own sickness. If alcoholism is *not* a disease, what else might it be? Over the course of history, alcoholism has been categorized under many labels, from a personal weakness to a crime, a sin, a mental disorder, and a physical illness (Meyer, 1996). Each of these definitions carries important personal, social, political, and economic implications.

Consider, for instance, the consequences of characterizing alcoholism as a disease. If that is the case, alcoholics should be treated like diabetics, heart patients, or victims of other physical illnesses. That is, they should be viewed with sympathy and should be given appropriate medical and therapeutic interventions to foster recovery from their illness. These treatments should be covered by medical insurance and delivered by health care professionals. Just as important, if alcoholism is defined as a disease, it should lose much of its stigma. After all, we don't blame people with diabetes or heart disease for their illnesses. Yes, alcoholics admittedly contribute to their own disease (by drinking too much), but so do many victims of diabetes and heart disease who eat all the wrong foods, fail to control their weight, and so forth (McLellan et al., 2000). And, as is the case

with many physical illnesses, one can inherit a genetic vulnerability to alcoholism (Lin & Anthenelli, 2005), so it is difficult to argue that alcoholism is caused solely by one's behavior.

Alternatively, if alcoholism is defined as a personal failure or a moral weakness, alcoholics are less likely to be viewed with sympathy and compassion. They might be admonished to quit drinking, put in prison, or punished in some other way. These responses to their alcoholism would be administered primarily by the legal system rather than the health care system, as medical interventions are not designed to remedy moral failings. Obviously, the interventions that would be available would not be covered by health insurance, which would have enormous financial repercussions (for both health care providers and alcoholics).

The key point here is that definitions lie at the center of many complex debates. People tend to think of definitions as insignificant, arbitrary sets of words found buried in the obscurity of thick dictionaries compiled by ivory tower intellectuals. Much of this characterization may be accurate, but definitions are not insignificant. They are vested with enormous power to shape how people think about important issues. And an endless array of issues boil down to matters of definition. For example, the next time you hear people arguing over whether a particular movie is pornographic, whether the death penalty is cruel and unusual punishment, or whether spanking is child abuse, you'll find it helps to focus the debate on clarifying the definitions of the crucial concepts.

The Power to Make Definitions

So, how can we resolve the debate about whether alcoholism is a disease? Scientists generally try to resolve their debates by conducting research to achieve a better understanding of the phenomena under study. You may have noticed al-

ready that "we need more research on this issue" is a frequent refrain in this text. Is more research the answer in this case? For once, the answer is "no." There is no conclusive way to determine whether alcoholism is a disease. It is not as though there is a "right" answer to this question that we can discover through more and better research.

The question of whether alcoholism is a disease is a *matter of definition:* Does alcoholism fit the currently accepted definition of what constitutes a disease? If you consult medical texts or dictionaries, you will find that disease is typically defined as *an impairment in the normal functioning of an organism that alters its vital functions.* Given that alcoholism clearly impairs people's normal functioning and disrupts a variety of vital functions (see **Figure 5.11**), it seems reasonable to characterize it as a disease. This has been the dominant view in the United States since the middle of the 20th century (Maltzman, 1994; Meyer, 1996). This view has only been strengthened by recent evidence that addiction to alcohol (and other drugs) is the result of dysregulation in key neural circuits in the brain (Cami & Farre, 2003). Still, many critics express vigorous doubts about the wisdom of defining alcoholism as a disease (Peele, 1989, 2000). They often raise a question that comes up frequently in arguments about definitions: Who should have the power to make the definition? In this case, the power lies in the hands of the medical community, which seems sensible, given that disease is a medical concept. But some critics argue that the medical community has a strong bias in favor of defining conditions as diseases because doing so creates new markets and fuels economic growth for the health industry (Nikelly, 1994). Thus, debate about whether alcoholism is a disease seems likely to continue for the indefinite future.

To summarize, definitions generally do not emerge out of research. They are typically crafted by experts or authorities in a specific field who try to reach a con-

Brain Wernicke's syndrome, an acute condition characterized by mental confusion and ocular abnormalities; Korsakoff's syndrome, a psychotic condition characterized by impairment of memory and learning, apathy, and degeneration of the white brain matter

Eyes Tobacco-alcohol blindness; Wernicke's ophthalmoplegia, a reversible paralysis of the muscles of the eye

Pharynx Cancer of the pharynx

Esophagus Esophageal varices, an irreversible condition in which the person can die by drowning in his own blood when the varices open

Lungs Lowered resistance thought to lead to greater incidence of tuberculosis, pneumonia, and emphysema

Spleen Hypersplenism

Heart Alcoholic cardiomyopathy, a heart condition

Liver Acute enlargement of liver, which is reversible, as well as irreversible alcoholic's liver (cirrhosis)

Stomach Gastritis and ulcers

Pancreas Acute and chronic pancreatitis

Rectum Hemorrhoids

Testes Atrophy of the testes

Nerves Polyneuritis, a condition characterized by loss of sensation

Muscles Alcoholic myopathy, a condition resulting in painful muscle contractions

Blood and bone marrow Coagulation defects and anemia

© Cengage Learning

FIGURE 5.11

Physiological malfunctions associated with alcoholism. This chart amply demonstrates that alcoholism is associated with a diverse array of physiological maladies. In and of itself, however, this information does not settle the argument about whether alcoholism should be regarded as a disease. It all depends on one's definition of what constitutes a disease.

SOURCE: Edlin, G., & Golanty, E. (1992). *Health and wellness: A holistic approach.* Boston: Jones & Bartlett. Copyright © 1992 by Jones & Bartlett Publishers, Inc. www.jbpub.com. Reprinted by permission.

sensus about how to best define a particular concept. Thus, in analyzing the validity of a definition, you need to look not only at the definition itself but at where it came from. Who decided what the defi-nition should be? Does the source of the definition seem legitimate and appropriate? Did the authorities who formulated the definition have any biases that should be considered?

Definitions, Labels, and Circular Reasoning

One additional point about definitions is worth discussing. Perhaps because definitions are imbued with so much power, people have an interesting tendency to incorrectly use them as *explanations* for the phenomena they describe. This logical error, which equates *naming* something with *explaining* it, is sometimes called the *nominal fallacy*. Names and labels that are used as explanations often sound quite reasonable at first. *But definitions do not really have any explanatory value; they simply specify what certain terms mean.* Consider an example. Let's say your friend, Frank, has a severe drinking problem. You are sitting around with some other friends discussing why Frank drinks so much. Rest assured, at least one of these friends will assert that "Frank drinks too much because he is an alcoholic." This is *circular reasoning*, which is just as useless as explaining that Frank is an alcoholic because he drinks too much. It tells us nothing about *why* Frank has a drinking problem.

The diagnostic labels that are used in the classification of mental disorders—labels such as schizophrenia, depression, autism, and obsessive-compulsive disorder (see Chapter 14)—also seem to invite this type of circular reasoning. For example, people often say things like "That person is delusional because she is schizophrenic," or "He is afraid of small, enclosed places because he is claustrophobic." These statements may sound plausible, but they are no more logical or insightful than saying "She is a redhead because she has red hair." The logical fallacy of mistaking a label for an explanation will get us as far in our understanding as a dog gets in chasing its own tail.

TABLE 5.4 **Critical Thinking Skills Discussed in This Application**

Skill	Description
Understanding the way definitions shape how people think about issues	The critical thinker appreciates the enormous power of definitions and the need to clarify definitions in efforts to resolve disagreements.
Identifying the source of definitions	The critical thinker recognizes the need to determine who has the power to make specific definitions and to evaluate their credibility.
Avoiding the nominal fallacy in working with definitions and labels	The critical thinker understands that labels do not have explanatory value.

© Cengage Learning

On the Nature of Consciousness

5.1 Discuss the nature of consciousness and the relationship between consciousness and brain activity.

William James emphasized that consciousness is a continually changing stream of mental activity. Consciousness varies along a continuum of levels of awareness. People maintain some degree of awareness during sleep and sometimes while under anesthesia. Brain waves vary in amplitude and frequency (cps) and are divided into four bands: beta, alpha, theta, and delta. Beta waves are seen when people are alert, alpha waves are associated with relaxation, theta waves appear in light sleep, and delta wave dominate deep sleep.

Biological Rhythms and Sleep

5.2 Summarize what is known about human biological clocks and their relationship to sleep.

Biological rhythms are periodic fluctuations in physiological functioning, indicating that most organisms have internal biological clocks. The cycle of sleep and wakefulness is influenced considerably by circadian rhythms, which prime people to fall asleep most easily around specific times. Exposure to light resets biological clocks by affecting the activity of the suprachiasmatic nucleus and the pineal gland, which secretes the hormone melatonin.

5.3 Explain how getting out of sync with one's circadian rhythms can have effects on sleep.

Ignoring your biological clock by going to sleep at an unusual time may have a negative effect on your sleep. The unpleasant nature of jet lag and rotating shift work is due to sleep disruption attributable to being out of sync with one's circadian rhythms. Melatonin may have value in efforts to alleviate the effects of jet lag. Circadian-friendly rotation schedules can sometimes reduce the negative effects of rotating shift work.

The Sleep and Waking Cycle

5.4 Describe the nightly sleep cycle, and explain how age and culture influence sleep.

When people fall asleep, they pass through a series of stages in cycles of approximately 90 minutes. Slow-wave sleep consists of stages 3 and 4, during which delta waves are prominent. During the REM stage, sleepers experience rapid eye movements, brain waves that are characteristic of

waking thought, and vivid dreaming. The sleep cycle tends to be repeated about four times a night, as REM sleep gradually becomes more predominant and non-REM sleep dwindles. The REM portion of sleep declines during childhood, leveling off at around 20%. During adulthood, slow-wave sleep tends to decline. The elderly may need less sleep than younger adults. Culture appears to have little impact on the physiological experience of sleep. However, ethnicity is related to the prevalence of sleep complaints and culture influences napping patterns.

5.5 Describe evidence on the effects of sleep deprivation and the health ramifications of sleep loss.

Partial sleep deprivation tends to impair attention, motor coordination, and decision making. Increased sleepiness can be a significant problem that appears to contribute to many transportation accidents and mishaps at work. Research on selective sleep deprivation suggests that people need REM sleep and slow-wave sleep. REM sleep may contribute to memory consolidation, creativity, and neurogenesis. Short sleep duration is associated with a variety of health problems, including obesity, impaired immune function, and increased inflammation. People who sleep 7-8 hours per day have lower mortality rates than individuals who are long or short sleepers.

5.6 Identify the symptoms of insomnia, narcolepsy, sleep apnea, and somnambulism.

Insomnia consists of chronic problems getting adequate sleep. Sedative drugs can increase sleep time, but sleeping pills generally are a poor solution for insomnia. Narcolepsy is an infrequent but dangerous disease marked by sudden, irresistible onsets of sleep during normal waking periods. Sleep apnea involves frequent gasping for air, which occurs when people stop breathing during sleep. Somnambulism (sleepwalking) typically occurs during slow-wave sleep. Sleepwalkers are prone to accidents and should be awakened.

The World of Dreams

5.7 Discuss the importance of dreams and findings on dream content.

Dreams are not taken very seriously in Western cultures, but Van de Castle argues persuasively that dreams have influenced many important events. Dreams are not as bizarre as widely assumed, although people are more tolerant of logical discrepancies and implausible scenarios. People dream mostly about themselves. The content of one's dreams may be affected by what is going on in one's life and by external stimuli that are experienced during the dream.

5.8 Describe cultural variations in beliefs about dreams, and explain three theories of dreaming.

Cultures vary in beliefs about the importance of dreams. Some dream themes seem to be universal, but the contents of people's dreams vary across cultures because people in different societies deal with different worlds while awake. Freud argued that the principal purpose of dreams is wish fulfillment. Cartwright has articulated a problem-solving view, which

(a)	Ordinary Wakefulness — Fast, low-amplitude beta waves
(b)	Relaxed Wakefulness — Rhythmic alpha waves
(c)	Stage 1 Sleep — Small, irregular brain waves
(d)	Stage 2 Sleep — Appearance of spindle-shaped waves called sleep spindles
(e)	Stage 3/Stage 4 Sleep — Appearance of large, slow delta waves
(f)	REM Sleep — Similar to ordinary wakefulness

© Cengage Learning

Dreams as wish fulfillment (Freud)

The day residue shapes dreams that satisfy unconscious needs in a disguised fashion.

© George Allen Penton/Shutterstock

The problem-solving view (Cartwright)

We mull over major problems in our lives with reduced logical constraints.

© Chris Rout/Alamy

Activation-synthesis model (Hobson)

The cortex constructs a story to make sense of internal signals from lower brain centers.

© Anton Zabielskyi/Shutterstock

Graphic: © Cengage Learning

asserts that dreams allow people to engage in creative thinking. Hobson and colleagues assert that dreams are simple side effects of the neural activation seen during REM sleep that have relatively little meaning.

Hypnosis: Altered Consciousness or Role Playing?

5.9 Discuss hypnotic susceptibility, and list some prominent effects of hypnosis.

Hypnosis is a systematic procedure that typically produces a heightened state of suggestibility. People vary in their susceptibility to hypnosis. About 10%–15% of people are exceptionally good hypnotic subjects, whereas another 10%–20% of the population do not respond well. Hypnosis can produce anesthesia, sensory distortions, disinhibition, and posthypnotic amnesia.

5.10 Compare the role-playing and altered-state theories of hypnosis.

One approach to hypnosis is to view it as a normal state of consciousness in which subjects play the role of being hypnotized. Another approach asserts that hypnosis leads to an altered state in which consciousness is split into two dissociated streams of awareness.

Meditation: Seeking Higher Consciousness

5.11 Explain the nature of meditation, and describe its physiological correlates.

Meditation refers to a family of practices that train attention to heighten awareness and bring mental processes under greater voluntary control. Approaches to meditation can be classified into two main styles that reflect how attention is directed: focused attention and open monitoring. Studies suggest that meditation leads to a potentially beneficial physiological state characterized by increased alpha in EEG recordings and suppression of bodily arousal.

5.12 Assess the evidence on the long-term benefits of meditation.

Evidence suggests that meditation may reduce stress hormones, enhance self-esteem and mood, and reduce vulnerability to a variety of physical and psychological disorders. Some critics suggest that these benefits are not unique to meditation and that placebo effects may exaggerate the impact of meditation. Recent evidence suggests that meditation can increase pain tolerance and that it may be capable of producing alterations in brain structure.

Altering Consciousness with Drugs

5.13 Identify the major types of abused drugs and their main effects.

The principal categories of abused drugs are narcotics, sedatives, stimulants, hallucinogens, cannabis, and alcohol. Narcotics are opium derivatives that are capable of relieving pain. Sedatives decrease CNS activity, whereas stimulants increase activation in the central nervous system. Hallucinogens produce emotional changes and distortions in sensory experience. Cannabis use is associated with relaxed euphoria and enhanced sensory awareness. Alcohol produces a mild euphoria accompanied by reduced inhibitions.

5.14 Understand why drug effects vary, how drugs affect the brain, and drug dependence.

The effects of drugs depend on a host of factors, including the dose, the method of ingestion, subjective expectations, and tolerance to the drug. Psychoactive drugs exert their main effects in the brain, where they selectively alter neurotransmitter activity at synaptic sites in a variety of ways. For example, amphetamines increase activity at DA and NE synapses. The mesolimbic dopamine pathway may mediate the reinforcing effects of most abused drugs. Physical dependence exists when people must continue drug use to avoid withdrawal. Psychological dependence involves intense mental and emotional craving for a drug.

Area in midbrain

Dopamine projections to prefrontal cortex

Nucleus accumbens

Medial forebrain bundle (a path of axons that release dopamine)

Graphic: © Cengage Learning. © Anton Zabielskyi/Shutterstock

5.15 Summarize evidence on the major health risks associated with drug abuse.

Recreational drug use can prove harmful to health by producing an overdose, by causing tissue damage, or by increasing health-impairing behavior. The chances of accidentally consuming a lethal overdose are greatest for the CNS depressants and cocaine. Direct tissue damage occurs most frequently with alcohol and cocaine. Cannabis may increase risk for respiratory disease, lung cancer, and psychotic disorders, but some other concerns appear to be exaggerated.

Reflecting on the Chapter's Themes

5.16 Identify the five unifying themes highlighted in this chapter.

Five of our unifying themes were highlighted in this chapter. We saw that psychology evolves in a sociohistorical context, that experience is highly subjective, that culture influences many aspects of behavior, that behavior is determined by multiple causes, and that psychology is characterized by theoretical diversity.

PERSONAL APPLICATION
Addressing Practical Questions About Sleep and Dreams

5.17 Summarize the evidence on various practical questions about sleep and dreams.

Naps can prove helpful, but their effects vary. Snoring is fairly common but may have more medical significance than most people realize. Individuals troubled by transient insomnia should avoid panic, pursue effective relaxation, and try distracting themselves so they don't work too hard at falling asleep. Everyone dreams, but some people don't remember their dreams. Freud distinguished between the manifest and latent content of dreams. Freud asserted that dreams require interpretation, but modern theorists assert that this process may not be as complicated as Freud assumed.

CRITICAL THINKING APPLICATION
Is Alcoholism a Disease? The Power of Definitions

5.18 Recognize the influence of definitions, and understand the nominal fallacy.

Definitions lie at the center of many complex debates. Like many questions, the issue of whether alcoholism should be regarded as a disease is a matter of definition. In evaluating the validity of a definition, one should look not only at the definition but also at where it came from. People have a tendency to use definitions as explanations for the phenomena they describe. However, this nominal fallacy involves circular reasoning.

6 Learning

PARADOX

*The more parents try to suppress aggressive
behavior with physical punishment, the more
aggressive their children tend to be.*

© AKIRA/amanaimages/Corbis

Let's see if you can guess the answer to a riddle. What do the following scenarios have in common?

- In 1953 a Japanese researcher observed a young macaque (a type of monkey) on the island of Koshima washing a sweet potato in a stream before eating it. No one had ever seen a macaque do this before. Soon other members of the monkey's troop were showing the same behavior. Several generations later, macaques on Koshima still wash their potatoes before eating them (De Waal, 2001).

- In 2005 Wade Boggs was elected to baseball's Hall of Fame. Boggs was as renowned for his superstitions as he was for his great hitting. For 20 years Boggs ate chicken every day of the year. Before games he followed a strict set of rituals that included stepping on the bases in reverse order, running wind sprints at precisely 17 minutes past the hour, and tossing exactly three pebbles off the field. Every time he stepped up to hit during a game, he drew the Hebrew letter *chai* in the dirt with his bat. For Boggs, the slightest change in this routine was very upsetting (Gaddis, 1999; Vyse, 2000).

- Barn swallows in Minnesota have built nests inside a Home Depot warehouse store, safe from the weather and from predators. So how do they get in and out to bring food to their babies when the doors are closed? They flutter around the motion sensors that operate the doors until they open!

What common thread runs through these diverse situations? What connects a superstitious ballplayer to potato-washing monkeys and door-opening swallows?

The answer is *learning*. This may surprise you. When most people think of learning, they picture students reading textbooks or novices gaining proficiency in a skill, such as skiing or playing the guitar. To a psychologist, however, **learning is any relatively durable change in behavior or knowledge that is due to experience.** Macaques aren't born with the habit of washing their sweet potatoes, nor do swallows begin life knowing how to operate motion sensors. These behaviors are the product of experience—that is, they represent learning.

Learning is one of the most fundamental concepts in all of psychology. Learning shapes personal habits, such as nailbiting; personality traits, such as shyness; personal preferences, such as a distaste for formal clothes; and emotional responses, such as reactions to favorite songs. If all your learned responses could somehow be stripped away, little of your behavior would be left. You would not be able to talk, read a book, or cook yourself a hamburger. You would be about as complex and interesting as a turnip.

As the examples at the start of this chapter show, learning is not an exclusively human process. It is pervasive in the animal world as well, a fact that won't amaze anyone who has ever owned a dog or seen a trained seal in action. Indeed, many of the most fascinating discoveries in the study of learning originated in studies of animals.

In this chapter, you will see how fruitful the research into learning has been and how wide ranging its applications are. We will focus most of our attention on a specific kind of learning: conditioning. *Conditioning* **involves learning associations between events that occur in an organism's environment.** In investigating conditioning, psychologists study learning at a fundamental level. This strategy has paid off with insights that have laid the foundation for the study of more complex forms of learning. In the Personal Application, you'll see how you can harness the principles of conditioning to improve your self-control. The Critical Thinking Application shows how conditioning procedures can be used to manipulate emotions.

Classical Conditioning

Do you go weak in the knees at the thought of standing on the roof of a tall building? Does your heart race when you imagine encountering a harmless garter snake? If so, you can understand, at least to some degree, what it's like to have a phobia. *Phobias* are irrational fears of specific objects or situations. Mild phobias are common. Over the years, students in my classes have described their phobic responses to a diverse array of stimuli, including bridges, elevators, tunnels, heights, dogs, cats, bugs, snakes, professors, doctors, strangers, thunderstorms, and germs. If you have a phobia, you may have wondered how you managed to acquire such a foolish fear. Chances are, it was through

6.1 Describe Pavlov's demonstration of classical conditioning and the key elements in this form of learning.

6.2 Clarify how classical conditioning may shape emotions, physiological responses, and attitudes.

6.3 Describe acquisition, extinction, and spontaneous recovery in classical conditioning.

6.4 Explain what happens in generalization, discrimination, and higher-order conditioning.

classical conditioning (Antony & McCabe, 2003). *Classical conditioning* is a type of learning in which a stimulus acquires the capacity to evoke a response that was originally evoked by another stimulus. The process was first described in 1903 by Ivan Pavlov, and it was originally called *Pavlovian conditioning* in tribute to him. This learning process was characterized as "classical" conditioning decades later (starting in the 1940s) to distinguish it from other types of conditioning that attracted research interest around that time (Clark, 2004).

Pavlov's Demonstration: "Psychic Reflexes"

PsykTrek 5a

Pavlov was a prominent Russian physiologist who did Nobel prize–winning research on digestion. He was studying the role of saliva in the digestive processes of dogs when he stumbled onto what he called "psychic reflexes" (Pavlov, 1906). Like many great discoveries, Pavlov's was partly accidental, although he had the insight to recognize its significance. His subjects were dogs restrained in harnesses in an experimental chamber (see **Figure 6.1**). Their saliva was collected by means of a surgically implanted tube in the salivary gland. Pavlov would present meat powder to a dog and then collect the resulting saliva. As his research progressed, he noticed that dogs accustomed to the procedure would start salivating *before* the meat powder was presented. For instance, they would salivate in response to a clicking sound made by the device that was used to present the meat powder.

Intrigued by this unexpected finding, Pavlov decided to investigate further. He paired the presentation of the meat powder with various stimuli that would stand out in the laboratory situation. For instance, he used a simple auditory stimulus: the presentation of a tone. After the tone and the meat powder had been presented together a number of times, the tone was presented alone. What happened? The dogs responded by salivating to the sound of the tone alone.

What was so significant about a dog salivating when a tone was sounded? The key is that the tone had started out as a *neutral* stimulus. That is, it did not originally produce

Ivan Pavlov

"We have provisionally called the new reflexes 'conditioned reflexes.'"

FIGURE 6.1

Classical conditioning apparatus. An experimental arrangement similar to the one depicted here (taken from Yerkes & Morgulis, 1909) has typically been used in demonstrations of classical conditioning, although Pavlov's original setup (see inset) was quite a bit simpler. The dog is restrained in a harness. A tone is used as the conditioned stimulus (CS), and the presentation of meat powder is used as the unconditioned stimulus (US). The tube inserted into the dog's salivary gland allows precise measurement of its salivation response. The pen and rotating drum of paper on the left are used to maintain a continuous record of salivary flow. **(Inset)** The less elaborate setup that Pavlov originally used to collect saliva on each trial is shown here (Goodwin, 1991).

the response of salivation. However, Pavlov managed to change that by pairing the tone with a stimulus (meat powder) that *did* produce the salivation response. Through this process, the tone acquired the capacity to trigger the response of salivation. What Pavlov had demonstrated was how stimulus-response associations—the basic building blocks of learning—are formed by events in an organism's environment. Based on this insight, he built a broad theory of learning that attempted to explain aspects of emotion, temperament, neuroses, and language (Windholz, 1997).

Terminology and Procedures

PSYKTREK 5a

There is a special vocabulary associated with classical conditioning. It often looks intimidating, but it's really not all that mysterious. The bond Pavlov noted between the meat powder and salivation was a natural, unlearned association. It did not have to be created through conditioning. It is therefore called an *unconditioned* association. In unconditioned bonds, **the *unconditioned stimulus (US)* is a stimulus that evokes an unconditioned response without previous conditioning. The *unconditioned response (UR)* is an unlearned reaction to an unconditioned stimulus that occurs without previous conditioning.**

In contrast, the link between the tone and salivation was established through conditioning. It is therefore called a *conditioned* association. In conditioned bonds, **the *conditioned stimulus (CS)* is a previously neutral stimulus that has, through conditioning, acquired the capacity to evoke a conditioned response. The *conditioned response (CR)* is a learned reaction to a conditioned stimulus that occurs because of previous conditioning.**

In Pavlov's initial demonstration, the UR and CR were both salivation. When evoked by the US (meat powder), salivation was an unconditioned response. When evoked by the CS (the tone), salivation was a conditioned response. Although the unconditioned response and conditioned response sometimes consist of the same behavior, subtle differences usually exist between them, as conditioned responses often are weaker or less intense. And in some cases the UR and CR may be quite different, albeit intimately related. For example, if an animal is given a brief shock as a US, the unconditioned response is *pain*, whereas the conditioned response is *fear* of imminent pain. In any event, the procedures involved in classical conditioning are outlined in **Figure 6.2** on the next page. Pavlov's "psychic reflex" came to be called the *conditioned reflex*. Classically conditioned responses have traditionally been characterized as reflexes and are said to be *elicited* (**drawn forth**) because most of them are relatively automatic or involuntary. However, research in recent decades has demonstrated that classical conditioning is involved in a wider range of human and animal behavior than previously appreciated, including some types of nonreflexive responding (Allan, 1998; Turkkan, 1989). Finally, **a *trial* in classical conditioning consists of any presentation of a stimulus or pair of stimuli.** Psychologists are interested in how many trials are required to establish a particular conditioned bond. The number needed to form an association varies considerably. Although classical conditioning generally proceeds gradually, it can occur quite rapidly, sometimes in just one pairing of the conditioned stimulus and unconditioned stimulus.

Classical Conditioning in Everyday Life

PSYKTREK 5a

In laboratory experiments on classical conditioning, researchers have generally worked with extremely simple responses. Besides salivation, commonly studied favorites include eyelid closure, knee jerks, and the flexing of various limbs. The study of such simple responses has proven both practical and productive. However, these responses do not even begin to convey the rich diversity of everyday behavior that is regulated by

Reality Check

Misconception
In Pavlov's demonstration of the conditioned reflex, the conditioned stimulus was the ringing of a bell.

Reality
The details of Pavlov's studies have been distorted over the years as the cartoon below demonstrates. Pavlov did try using a bell as a CS, but in his classic 1906 article he reported that a bell was not a very effective stimulus because it tended to startle the dogs and disrupt their behavior (Goodwin, 1991). Pavlov used a variety of conditioned stimuli, but the sound of a tone was the preferred auditory stimulus.

Drawing by John Chase, www.chasetoons.com

FIGURE 6.2

The sequence of events in classical conditioning. (a) Moving downward, this series of three panels outlines the sequence of events in classical conditioning, using Pavlov's original demonstration as an example. **(b)** As we encounter other examples of classical conditioning throughout the book, you will see many diagrams like the one in this panel, which will provide snapshots of specific instances of classical conditioning.

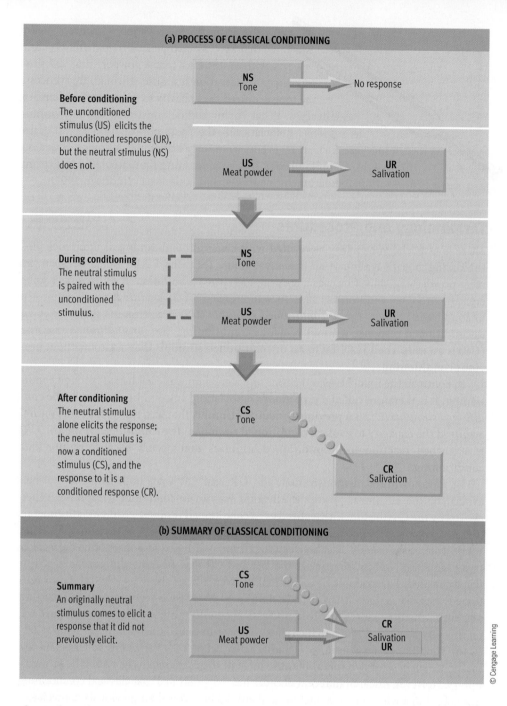

(a) PROCESS OF CLASSICAL CONDITIONING

Before conditioning
The unconditioned stimulus (US) elicits the unconditioned response (UR), but the neutral stimulus (NS) does not.

NS Tone → No response

US Meat powder → UR Salivation

During conditioning
The neutral stimulus is paired with the unconditioned stimulus.

NS Tone

US Meat powder → UR Salivation

After conditioning
The neutral stimulus alone elicits the response; the neutral stimulus is now a conditioned stimulus (CS), and the response to it is a conditioned response (CR).

CS Tone → CR Salivation

(b) SUMMARY OF CLASSICAL CONDITIONING

Summary
An originally neutral stimulus comes to elicit a response that it did not previously elicit.

CS Tone

US Meat powder → CR Salivation / UR

© Cengage Learning

classical conditioning. Let's look at some examples of classical conditioning drawn from everyday life.

CONDITIONED FEAR AND ANXIETY

PsykTrek 5a

Classical conditioning often plays a key role in shaping emotional responses such as fear and anxiety. Phobias are a good example of such responses. Case studies of patients suffering from phobias suggest that many irrational fears can be traced back to experiences that involve classical conditioning (Antony & McCabe, 2003; Muris & Mercklebach, 2001). It is easy to imagine how such conditioning can occur outside of the laboratory. For example, a student of mine was troubled by a bridge phobia so severe that she couldn't drive on interstate highways because of all the bridges that had to be crossed. She was able to pinpoint the source of her phobia as something that had happened during her childhood. Whenever her family drove to visit her grandmother, they had to cross a rickety, old bridge out in the countryside. Her father, in a misguided attempt at humor, made a major production out of these crossings. He would stop short of the bridge and carry on about the great danger. Obviously, he thought the bridge was safe or he wouldn't have driven across it. However, the naive young girl was terrified by her father's scare tactics. Thus, the bridge became a conditioned stimulus eliciting great fear (see **Figure 6.3**). Unfortunately, the fear spilled over to all bridges, and 40 years later she was still carrying the burden of this phobia.

Everyday anxiety responses that are less severe than phobias may also be products of classical conditioning. For instance, if you cringe when you hear the sound of a dentist's drill, this response is the result of classical conditioning. In this case, the pain you have experienced from dental drilling is the US. This pain has been paired with the sound of the drill, which became a CS eliciting your cringing behavior.

That is *not* to say that traumatic experiences associated with stimuli *automatically* lead to conditioned fears or phobias. Whether fear conditioning takes place depends on a constellation of factors. Conditioned fears are less likely to develop when events seem escapable and controllable and when people have a history of nontraumatic encounters in similar situations (for example, with dentists) (Mineka & Zinbarg, 2006).

© Dmitriy Shironosov/Shutterstock

FIGURE 6.3

Classical conditioning of a fear response. Many emotional responses that would otherwise be puzzling can be explained by classical conditioning. In the case of one woman's bridge phobia, the fear originally elicited by her father's scare tactics became a conditioned response to the stimulus of bridges.

OTHER CONDITIONED RESPONSES

PsykTrek 5a

Classical conditioning affects not only overt behaviors but *physiological processes* as well. For example, studies have demonstrated that the functioning of the immune system can be influenced by conditioning (Ader, 2001, 2003). Robert Ader and Nicholas Cohen (1984, 1993) have shown that classical conditioning procedures can lead to *immune suppression*—a decrease in the production of antibodies. In a typical study, animals are injected with a drug (the US) that *chemically* causes immune suppression while they are simultaneously given an unusual-tasting liquid to drink (the CS). Days later, after the chemically induced immune suppression has ended, some of the animals are reexposed to the CS by giving them the unusual-tasting solution. Measurements of antibody production indicate that animals exposed to the CS show a reduced immune response (see **Figure 6.4**).

Studies have also demonstrated that classical conditioning can influence *sexual arousal* (Pfaus, Kippin, & Centeno, 2001). For example, research has shown that quail can be conditioned to become sexually aroused by a neutral, nonsexual stimulus—such as a red light—that has been paired with opportunities to copulate (Domjan, 1992, 1994). Researchers have also conditioned quail to develop sexual fetishes for inanimate objects (Cetinkaya & Domjan, 2006; Koksal et al., 2004). Classical conditioning may also underlie the development of sexual fetishes in humans. It seems likely that humans may be conditioned to be aroused by objects—such as shoes, boots, leather, and undergarments—that have been paired with sexual encounters.

FIGURE 6.4

Classical conditioning of immune suppression. When a neutral stimulus is paired with a drug that chemically causes suppression of the immune response, it can become a CS that elicits immune suppression on its own. Thus, even the immune response can be influenced by classical conditioning.

EVALUATIVE CONDITIONING OF ATTITUDES

Pavlovian conditioning can also influence people's attitudes. In recent decades, researchers have shown great interest in a subtype of classical conditioning called *evaluative conditioning*. **Evaluative conditioning refers to changes in the liking of a stimulus that result from pairing that stimulus with other positive or negative stimuli.** In other words, evaluative conditioning involves the acquisition of likes and dislikes, or preferences, through classical conditioning. Typically, a neutral stimulus is paired with unconditioned stimuli that trigger positive reactions so that the neutral stimulus becomes a conditioned stimulus that elicits similar positive reactions. For example, in one recent study pleasant music paired with two unknown brands of root beer had significant effects on participants' liking for the root beers (Redker & Gibson, 2009). Another study showed that pairing an attractive face gazing directly at the viewer with various

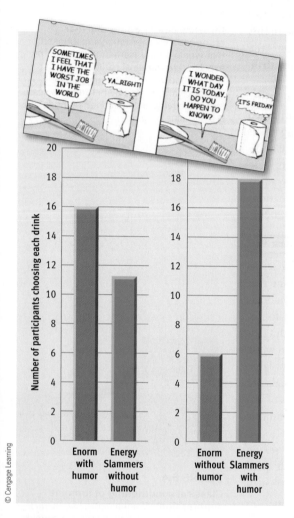

FIGURE 6.5

Evaluative conditioning with humor. In a study of evaluative conditioning, Strick et al. (2009) paired ten humorous or nonhumorous cartoons with two energy drinks. The nonhumorous control cartoons were created by taking an amusing cartoon and changing the text so it was no longer funny (see example at top). Pairing the energy drinks with humor had a positive effect on participants' attitudes about the drinks. Moreover, these positive attitudes influenced subjects' actual behavior when they later had a chance to consume one of the drinks. When the drink *Enorm* had been paired with humor, participants tended to prefer it, and when the drink *Energy Slammers* had been paired with humor, it was chosen far more often.

SOURCE: Adapted from Strick, M., van Baaren, R. B., Holland, R. W., & van Knippenberg, A. (2009). Humor in advertisements enhances product liking by mere association. *Journal of Experimental Psychology: Applied, 15*, 35-45. Figures 1 and 4. Copyright © 2009 American Psychological Association.

peppermint brands swayed subjects' brand preferences (Strick, Holland, & van Knippenberg, 2008). In another investigation, funny cartoons paired with two types of energy drinks increased participants' liking of the drinks (Strick et al., 2009; see **Figure 6.5**). Obviously, advertising campaigns routinely try to take advantage of evaluative conditioning (see the Personal Application for this chapter).

Basic Processes in Classical Conditioning   PsykTrek 5b

Classical conditioning is often portrayed as a mechanical process that inevitably leads to a certain result. This view reflects the fact that most conditioned responses are reflexive and difficult to control. Pavlov's dogs would have been hard pressed to withhold their salivation. However, this vision of classical conditioning as an "irresistible force" is misleading, because it fails to consider the many factors involved in classical conditioning (Kehoe & Macrae, 1998). In this section, we'll look at basic processes in classical conditioning to expand on the rich complexity of this form of learning.

ACQUISITION: FORMING NEW RESPONSES   PsykTrek 5b

We have already discussed *acquisition* without attaching a formal name to the process. **Acquisition refers to the initial stage of learning a new response tendency.** Pavlov theorized that the acquisition of a conditioned response depends on *stimulus contiguity*. Stimuli are contiguous if they occur together in time and space.

Stimulus contiguity is important, but learning theorists now realize that contiguity alone doesn't automatically produce conditioning (Miller & Grace, 2003). People are bombarded daily by countless stimuli that could be perceived as being paired, yet only some of these pairings produce classical conditioning. If conditioning does not occur with all the stimuli present in a situation, what determines its occurrence? Evidence suggests that stimuli that are novel, unusual, or especially intense have more potential to become CSs than routine stimuli, probably because they are more likely to stand out among other stimuli (Hearst, 1988).

EXTINCTION: WEAKENING CONDITIONED RESPONSES   PsykTrek 5b

Fortunately, a newly formed stimulus-response bond does not necessarily last indefinitely. If it did, learning would be inflexible, and organisms would have difficulty adapting to new situations. Instead, the right circumstances produce *extinction*, **the gradual weakening and disappearance of a conditioned response tendency.**

What leads to extinction in classical conditioning? The consistent presentation of the conditioned stimulus *alone*, without the unconditioned stimulus. For example, when Pavlov consistently presented only the tone to a previously conditioned dog, the tone gradually lost its capacity to elicit the response of salivation. Such a sequence of events is depicted in the left portion of **Figure 6.6**, which graphs the amount of salivation by a dog over a series of conditioning trials. Note how the salivation response declines during extinction.

For an example of extinction from outside the laboratory, let's assume that you cringe at the sound of a dentist's drill, which has been paired with pain in the past. You take a job as a dental assistant and you start hearing the drill (the CS) day in and day out without experiencing any pain (the US). Your cringing response will gradually diminish and extinguish altogether.

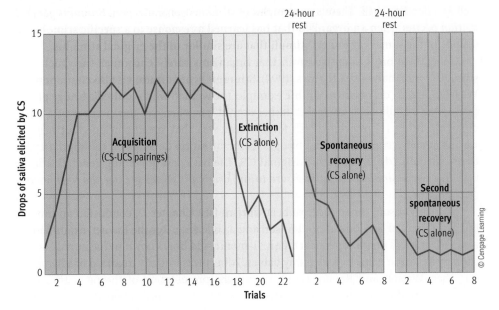

FIGURE 6.6

Acquisition, extinction, and spontaneous recovery. During acquisition, the strength of the dog's conditioned response (measured by the amount of salivation) increases rapidly and then levels off near its maximum. During extinction, the CR declines erratically until it's extinguished. After a "rest" period in which the dog is not exposed to the CS, a spontaneous recovery occurs, and the CS once again elicits a (weakened) CR. Repeated presentations of the CS alone reextinguish the CR, but after another "rest" interval, a weaker spontaneous recovery occurs.

SPONTANEOUS RECOVERY: RESURRECTING RESPONSES   PsykTrek 5b

Some conditioned responses can "reappear from the dead" after having been extinguished. Learning theorists use the term *spontaneous recovery* to describe such a resurrection from the graveyard of conditioned associations. **Spontaneous recovery is the reappearance of an extinguished response after a period of nonexposure to the conditioned stimulus.**

Pavlov (1927) observed this phenomenon in some of his early studies. He fully extinguished a dog's CR of salivation to a tone and then returned the dog to its home cage for a "rest interval" (a period of nonexposure to the CS). On a subsequent day, when the dog was brought back to the experimental chamber for retesting, the tone was sounded and the salivation response reappeared. However, the recovered response was weak: There was less salivation than when the response had been at its peak strength. If Pavlov consistently presented the CS by itself again, the response reextinguished quickly. Interestingly, in some of the dogs the response made still another spontaneous recovery (typically even weaker than the first) after they had spent another period in their cages (consult **Figure 6.6** once again).

Recent studies have uncovered a related phenomenon called the *renewal effect—if a response is extinguished in a different environment than it was acquired, the extinguished response will reappear if the animal is returned to the original environment where acquisition took place.* This phenomenon, along with the evidence on spontaneous recovery, suggests that extinction somehow *suppresses* a conditioned response rather than *erasing* a learned association. In other words, *extinction does not appear to lead to unlearning* (Bouton & Woods, 2009). The theoretical meaning of spontaneous recovery and the renewal effect is complex and the subject of some debate. However, their practical significance is quite simple: Even if you manage to rid yourself of an unwanted conditioned response (such as cringing when you hear a dental drill), there is an excellent chance that it may make a surprise reappearance later.

STIMULUS GENERALIZATION AND THE CASE OF LITTLE ALBERT   PsykTrek 5b

After conditioning has occurred, organisms often show a tendency to respond not only to the exact CS used but also to other, similar stimuli. For example, Pavlov's dogs might have salivated in response to a different tone, or you might cringe at the sound of a jeweler's as

John B. Watson

"Surely this proof of the conditioned origin of a fear response puts us on natural science grounds in our study of emotional behavior."

well as a dentist's drill. These are examples of stimulus generalization. *Stimulus generalization* occurs when an organism that has learned a response to a specific stimulus responds in the same way to new stimuli that are similar to the original stimulus.

Generalization is adaptive given that organisms rarely encounter the exact same stimulus more than once (Thomas, 1992). Stimulus generalization is also commonplace. We have already discussed a real-life example: the woman who acquired a bridge phobia during her childhood because her father scared her whenever they went over a particular old bridge. The original CS for her fear was that specific bridge, but her fear was ultimately *generalized* to all bridges. Generalization depends on the similarity between the new stimulus and the original CS. The basic law governing generalization is this: *The more similar new stimuli are to the original CS, the greater the likelihood of generalization.*

John B. Watson, the founder of behaviorism (see Chapter 1), conducted an influential early study of generalization. Watson and a colleague, Rosalie Rayner, examined the generalization of conditioned fear in an 11-month-old boy, known in the annals of psychology as "Little Albert." Like many babies, Albert was initially unafraid of a live white rat. Then Watson and Rayner (1920) paired the presentation of the rat with a loud, startling sound (made by striking a steel bar with a hammer). Albert *did* show fear in response to the loud noise. After seven pairings of the rat and the gong, the rat was established as a CS eliciting a fear response (see **Figure 6.7**). Five days later, Watson and Rayner exposed the youngster to other stimuli that resembled the rat in being white and furry. They found that Albert's fear re-

Concept Check **6.1**

Identifying Elements in Classical Conditioning

Check your understanding of classical conditioning by trying to identify the unconditioned stimulus (US), unconditioned response (UR), conditioned stimulus (CS), and conditioned response (CR) in each of the examples below. Fill in the diagram accompanying each example. You'll find the answers in Appendix A.

1. Sam is 3 years old. One night his parents build a roaring fire in the family room fireplace. The fire spits out a large ember that hits Sam in the arm, giving him a nasty burn that hurts a great deal for several hours. A week later, when Sam's parents light another fire in the fireplace, Sam becomes upset and fearful, crying and running from the room.

CS	
US	CR UR

2. Melanie is driving to work on a rainy highway when she notices that the brake lights of all the cars just ahead of her have come on. She hits her brakes but watches in horror as her car glides into a four-car pileup. She's badly shaken up in the accident. A month later she's driving in the rain again and notices that she tenses up every time she sees brake lights come on ahead of her.

CS	
US	CR UR

3. At the age of 24, Tyrone has recently developed an allergy to cats. When he's in the same room with a cat for more than 30 minutes, he starts wheezing. After a few such allergic reactions, he starts wheezing as soon as he sees a cat in a room.

CS	
US	CR UR

The conditioning of Little Albert. The diagram shows how Little Albert's fear response to a white rat was established. Albert's fear response to other white, furry objects illustrates generalization. In the photo, made from a 1919 film, John B. Watson and his collaborator, Rosalie Rayner, are shown with Little Albert before he was conditioned to fear the rat.

sponse generalized to a variety of stimuli, including a rabbit, a dog, a fur coat, a Santa Claus mask, and Watson's hair.

What happened to Little Albert? Did he grow up with a phobia of Santa Claus? There was endless speculation for decades because no one had any idea who Albert was or what had happened to him. He was taken from the hospital where Watson and Rayner conducted their study before they got around to extinguishing the conditioned fears they had created, and he was never heard of again. Recently, after 90 years of mystery, a team of history sleuths managed to track down Little Albert's identity and explain why he had vanished into thin air (Beck, Levinson, & Irons, 2009). It appears that his real name was Douglas Merritte, the son of a wet nurse who worked near Watson's lab. Sadly, Albert had a very brief life, perishing at the age of 6 from acquired hydrocephalus. Little information is available on his short life, so we will never know whether he experienced any ill effects from his participation in one of psychology's most legendary studies.

STIMULUS DISCRIMINATION

PsykTrek 5b

Stimulus discrimination is just the opposite of stimulus generalization. *Stimulus discrimination occurs when an organism that has learned a response to a specific stimulus does not respond in the same way to new stimuli that are similar to the original stimulus.* Like generalization, discrimination is adaptive in that an animal's survival may hinge on its being able to distinguish friend from foe, or edible from poisonous food (Thomas, 1992). Organisms can gradually learn to discriminate between the original CS and similar stimuli if they have adequate experience with both. For instance, let's say your dog runs around, excitedly wagging his tail, whenever he hears your car pull up in the driveway. Initially it will probably respond to *all* cars that pull into the driveway (stimulus generalization). However, if there is anything distinctive about the sound of your car, your dog may gradually respond with excitement only to your car and not to other cars (stimulus discrimination).

The development of stimulus discrimination usually requires that the original CS (your car) continues to be paired with the US (your arrival), while similar stimuli (the other cars) are not paired with the US. As with generalization, a basic law governs discrimination: *The less similar new stimuli are to the original CS, the greater the likelihood (and ease) of discrimination.* Conversely, if a new stimulus is quite similar to the original CS, discrimination will be relatively hard to learn.

HIGHER-ORDER CONDITIONING

PsykTrek 5b

Imagine that you were to conduct the following experiment. First, you condition a dog to salivate in response to the sound of a tone by pairing the tone with meat powder. Once

FIGURE 6.8

Higher-order conditioning. Higher-order conditioning involves a two-phase process. In the first phase, a neutral stimulus (such as a tone) is paired with an unconditioned stimulus (such as meat powder) until it becomes a conditioned stimulus that elicits the response originally evoked by the US (such as salivation). In the second phase, another neutral stimulus (such as a red light) is paired with the previously established CS (the tone), so that it also acquires the capacity to elicit the response originally evoked by the US.

the tone is firmly established as a CS, you pair the tone with a new stimulus, let's say a red light, for 15 trials. You then present the red light alone, without the tone. Will the dog salivate in response to the red light?

The answer is "yes." Even though the red light has never been paired with the meat powder, it will acquire the capacity to elicit salivation by virtue of being paired with the tone (see **Figure 6.8**). This is a demonstration of *higher-order conditioning,* **in which a conditioned stimulus functions as if it were an unconditioned stimulus.** Higher-order conditioning shows that classical conditioning does not depend on the presence of a genuine, natural US. An already established CS will do just fine. In higher-order conditioning, new conditioned responses are built on the foundation of already established conditioned responses. Many human conditioned responses are the product of higher-order conditioning. This process greatly extends the reach of classical conditioning.

Operant Conditioning

KEY LEARNING GOALS

6.5 Explain Skinner's principle of reinforcement, and describe the terminology and procedures in operant research.

6.6 Describe shaping, extinction, generalization, and discrimination in operant conditioning.

6.7 Identify various types of schedules of reinforcement, and discuss their typical effects.

6.8 Distinguish between positive and negative reinforcement and between escape learning and avoidance learning.

6.9 Describe punishment, and assess issues related to punishment as a disciplinary procedure.

Even Pavlov recognized that classical conditioning is not the only form of conditioning. Classical conditioning best explains reflexive responding that is largely controlled by stimuli that *precede* the response. However, humans and other animals make a great many responses that don't fit this description. Consider the response that you are engaging in right now: studying. It is definitely not a reflex (life might be easier if it were). The stimuli that govern it (exams and grades) do not precede it. Instead, your studying is mainly influenced by stimulus events that *follow* the response—specifically, its *consequences.*

In the 1930s, this kind of learning was named *operant conditioning* by B. F. Skinner (1938, 1953, 1969). The term was derived from his belief that in this type of responding, an organism "operates" on the environment instead of simply reacting to stimuli. Learning occurs because responses come to be influenced by the consequences that follow them. Thus, **operant conditioning is a form of learning in which voluntary responses come to be controlled by their consequences.** Learning theorists originally distinguished between classical and operant conditioning on the grounds that the former regulated reflexive, involuntary responses, whereas the latter governed voluntary responses. This distinction holds up much of the time, but it is not absolute. Research in recent decades has shown that classical conditioning sometimes contributes to the regulation of voluntary behavior; that operant conditioning can influence involuntary, visceral responses; and that the two types of conditioning jointly and interactively govern some aspects of behavior (Allan, 1998; Turkkan, 1989).

Skinner's Demonstration: It's All a Matter of Consequences

PSYKTREK 5c

B. F. Skinner had great admiration for Pavlov's work (Catania & Laties, 1999) and used it as the foundation for his own theory, even borrowing some of Pavlov's terminology (Dinsmoor, 2004). And, like Pavlov, Skinner (1953, 1969, 1984) conducted some deceptively simple research that became enormously influential. The fundamental principle of operant conditioning is uncommonly simple: *Skinner demonstrated that organisms tend to repeat those responses that are followed by favorable consequences.* This fundamental principle is embodied in Skinner's concept of reinforcement. **Reinforcement occurs when an event following a response increases an organism's tendency to make that response.** In other words, a response is strengthened because it leads to rewarding consequences.

The principle of reinforcement may be simple, but it is immensely powerful. Skinner and his followers have shown that much of people's everyday behavior is regulated by reinforcement. For example, you study hard because good grades are likely to follow as a result. You go to work because this behavior leads to receiving paychecks. Perhaps you work extra hard because promotions and raises tend to follow such behavior. You tell jokes, and your friends laugh—so you tell some more. The principle of reinforcement clearly governs complex aspects of human behavior. Paradoxically, though, this principle emerged out of Skinner's research on the behavior of rats and pigeons in exceptionally simple situations. Let's look at that research.

B. F. Skinner
"Operant conditioning shapes behavior as a sculptor shapes a lump of clay."

Terminology and Procedures

PSYKTREK 5c

Like Pavlov, Skinner created a prototype experimental procedure that has been repeated (with variations) thousands of times. In this procedure, an animal, typically a rat or a pigeon, is placed in an *operant chamber* that has come to be better known as a "Skinner box." **A *Skinner box* is a small enclosure in which an animal can make a specific response that is systematically recorded while the consequences of the response are controlled.** In the boxes designed for rats, the main response made available is pressing a small lever mounted on one side wall (see **Figure 6.9** on the next page). In the boxes made for pigeons, the designated response is pecking a small disk mounted on a side wall.

Operant responses such as lever pressing and disk pecking are said to be *emitted* rather than *elicited*. **To *emit* means to send forth.** This word was chosen because, as already noted, operant conditioning mainly governs *voluntary* responses instead of reflex responses.

The Skinner box permits the experimenter to control the reinforcement contingencies that are in effect for the animal. **Reinforcement contingencies are the circumstances or rules that determine whether responses lead to the presentation of reinforcers.** Typically, the experimenter manipulates whether positive consequences occur when the animal makes the designated response. The main positive consequence is usually delivery of a small bit of food into a cup mounted in the chamber. Because the animals are deprived of food for a while prior to the experimental session, their hunger virtually ensures that the food serves as a reinforcer.

© Vasiliy Koval/Shutterstock

The key dependent variable in most research on operant conditioning is the subjects' *response rate* over time. An animal's rate of lever pressing or disk pecking in the Skinner box is monitored continuously by a device known as a cumulative recorder (see **Figure 6.9**). **The *cumulative recorder* creates a graphic record of responding and reinforcement in a Skinner box as a function of time.** The recorder works by means of a roll of paper that moves at a steady rate underneath a movable pen. When there is no responding, the pen stays still and draws a straight horizontal line, reflecting the passage of time. Whenever the designated response occurs, however, the pen moves up a notch. The pen's movements produce a graphic summary of the animal's responding over time. The pen also makes slash marks to record the delivery of each reinforcer. The results of

FIGURE 6.9

Skinner box and cumulative recorder. (a) This diagram highlights some of the key features of an operant chamber, or Skinner box. In this apparatus designed for rats, the response under study is lever pressing. Food pellets, which may serve as reinforcers, are delivered into the food cup on the right. The speaker and light permit manipulations of visual and auditory stimuli, and the electric grid gives the experimenter control over aversive consequences (shock) in the box. **(b)** A cumulative recorder connected to the box keeps a continuous record of responses and reinforcements. A small segment of a cumulative record is shown here. The entire process is automatic as the paper moves with the passage of time; each lever press moves the pen up a step, and each reinforcement is marked with a slash. **(c)** This photo shows the real thing—a rat being conditioned in a Skinner box.

(b) Cumulative recorder

(a)
Skinner box

(c)

operant conditioning studies are usually portrayed in graphs. In these graphs, the horizontal axis is used to mark the passage of time, while the vertical axis is used to plot the accumulation of responses (consult the four graphs in **Figure 6.11** on page 193 for examples). In interpreting these graphs, the key consideration is the *slope* of the line that represents the record of responding. *A rapid response rate produces a steep slope, whereas a slow response rate produces a shallow slope.*

Basic Processes in Operant Conditioning

PsykTrek SIM4, 5c

Although the principle of reinforcement is strikingly simple, many other processes involved in operant conditioning make this form of learning just as complex as classical conditioning. In fact, some of the same processes are involved in both types of conditioning. In this section, we'll discuss how the processes of acquisition, extinction, generalization, and discrimination occur in operant conditioning.

ACQUISITION AND SHAPING

PsykTrek SIM4, 5c

As in classical conditioning, *acquisition* in operant conditioning is the formation of a new response tendency. However, the procedures used to establish a tendency to emit a voluntary operant response are different from those used to create a reflexive conditioned response. Operant responses are typically established through a gradual process called *shaping:* the reinforcement of closer and closer approximations of a desired response.

Shaping is necessary when an organism does not, on its own, emit the desired response. For example, when a rat is first placed in a Skinner box, it may not press the lever at all. In this case an experimenter begins shaping by releasing food pellets whenever the rat moves toward the lever. As this response becomes more frequent, the experimenter starts requiring a closer approximation of the desired response, possibly releasing food only when the rat actually touches the lever. As reinforcement increases the rat's tendency to touch the lever, the rat will spontaneously press the lever on occasion, finally providing the experimenter with an opportunity to reinforce the designated response. These reinforcements will gradually increase the rate of lever pressing.

Shaping molds many aspects of both human and animal behavior. For instance, it is the key to training animals to perform impressive tricks. When you go to a zoo, circus, or marine park and see bears riding bicycles, monkeys playing the piano, and whales leaping through hoops, you are witnessing the results of shaping. To demonstrate the power of shaping techniques, Skinner once trained some pigeons so that they appeared to play a crude version of Ping-Pong. They would run about at opposite ends of a tiny Ping-Pong table and peck the ball back and forth. Keller and Marian Breland, a couple of psychologists influenced by Skinner, applied shaping in their business of training animals for advertising and entertainment purposes. One of their better-known feats was shaping "Priscilla, the Fastidious Pig," to turn on a radio, eat at a kitchen table, put dirty clothes in a hamper, run a vacuum, and then "go shopping" with a shopping cart (see photo). Of course, Priscilla picked the sponsor's product off the shelf in her shopping expedition (Breland & Breland, 1961).

EXTINCTION

PsykTrek SIM4, 5c

In operant conditioning, *extinction* refers to the gradual weakening and disappearance of a response tendency because the response is no longer followed by reinforcement. Extinction begins in operant conditioning whenever previously available reinforcement is stopped. In laboratory studies with rats, this situation usually occurs when the experimenter stops delivering food as reinforcement for lever pressing. When the extinction process is begun, a brief surge often occurs in the rat's responding, followed by a gradual decline in response rate until it approaches zero. The same effects are generally seen in the extinction of human behavior.

Shaping—an operant technique in which an organism is rewarded for closer and closer approximations of the desired response—is used in teaching both animals and humans. It is the main means of training animals to perform unnatural tricks. Breland and Breland's (1961) famous subject, "Priscilla, the Fastidious Pig," is shown in the middle photo.

A key issue in operant conditioning is how much *resistance to extinction* an organism will display when reinforcement is halted. **Resistance to extinction occurs when an organism continues to make a response after delivery of the reinforcer for it has been terminated.** The greater the resistance to extinction, the longer the responding will continue. Thus, if a researcher stops giving reinforcement for lever pressing and the response tapers off slowly, the response shows high resistance to extinction. However, if the response tapers off quickly, it shows relatively little resistance to extinction.

Resistance to extinction may sound like a matter of purely theoretical interest, but actually it's quite practical. People often want to strengthen a response in such a way that it will be relatively resistant to extinction. For instance, most parents want to see their child's studying response survive even if the child hits a rocky stretch when studying doesn't lead to reinforcement (good grades). In a similar fashion, a casino wants to see patrons continue to gamble even if they encounter a lengthy losing streak.

STIMULUS CONTROL: GENERALIZATION AND DISCRIMINATION

Operant responding is ultimately controlled by its consequences, as organisms learn response-outcome (R-O) associations (Colwill, 1993). However, stimuli that *precede* a response can also influence operant behavior. When a response is consistently followed by a reinforcer in the presence of a particular stimulus, that stimulus comes to serve as a "signal" indicating that the response is likely to lead to a reinforcer. Once an organism learns the signal, it tends to respond accordingly (Honig & Alsop, 1992). For example, a pigeon's disk pecking may be reinforced only when a small light behind the disk is lit. When the light is out, pecking does not lead to the reward. Pigeons quickly learn to peck the disk only when it is lit. The light that signals the availability of reinforcement is called a discriminative stimulus. **Discriminative stimuli are cues that influence operant behavior by indicating the probable consequences (reinforcement or nonreinforcement) of a response.**

Discriminative stimuli play a key role in the regulation of operant behavior. For example, birds learn that hunting for worms is likely to be reinforced after a rain. Children learn to ask for sweets when their parents are in a good mood. Drivers learn to slow down when the highway is wet.

Reactions to a discriminative stimulus are governed by the processes of *stimulus generalization* and *stimulus discrimination,* just like reactions to a CS in classical conditioning. For instance, envision a cat that gets excited whenever it hears the sound of a can opener because that sound has become a discriminative stimulus signaling a good chance of its getting fed. If the cat also responded to the sound of a new kitchen appliance (say a blender), this response would represent *generalization*—responding to a new stimulus as if it were the original. *Discrimination* would occur if the cat learned to respond only to the can opener and not to the blender.

As you have learned in this section, the processes of acquisition, extinction, generalization, and discrimination in operant conditioning parallel these same processes in classical conditioning. **Table 6.1** compares these processes in the two kinds of conditioning.

Reinforcement: Consequences That Strengthen Responses

PsykTrek 5e

Although it is convenient to equate reinforcement with reward and the experience of pleasure, strict behaviorists object to this practice. Why? Because the experience of pleasure is an unobservable event that takes place within an organism. As explained in Chapter 1, most behaviorists believe that scientific assertions must be limited to what can be observed.

TABLE 6.1 Comparison of Basic Processes in Classical and Operant Conditioning

Process and Definition	Description in Classical Conditioning	Description in Operant Conditioning
Acquisition: The initial stage of learning	CS and US are paired, gradually resulting in CR.	Responding gradually increases because of reinforcement, possibly through shaping.
Extinction: The gradual weakening and disappearance of a conditioned response tendency	CS is presented alone until it no longer elicits CR.	Responding gradually slows and stops after reinforcement is terminated.
Stimulus generalization: An organism's responding to stimuli other than the original stimulus used in conditioning	CR is elicited by new stimulus that resembles original CS.	Responding increases in the presence of new stimulus that resembles original discriminative stimulus.
Stimulus discrimination: An organism's lack of response to stimuli that are similar to the original stimulus used in conditioning	CR is not elicited by new stimulus that resembles original CS	Responding does not increase in the presence of new stimulus that resembles original discriminative stimulus.

© Cengage Learning

In keeping with this orientation, Skinner said that reinforcement occurs whenever an outcome strengthens a response, as measured by an increase in the rate of responding. This definition avoids the issue of what the organism is feeling and focuses on observable events. Thus, the central process in reinforcement is the *strengthening of a response tendency.*

Reinforcement is therefore defined *after the fact,* in terms of its *effect* on behavior. Something that is clearly reinforcing for an organism at one time may not function as a reinforcer later (Catania, 1992). Food will reinforce lever pressing by a rat only if the rat is hungry. Similarly, something that serves as a reinforcer for one person may not function as a reinforcer for another person. For example, parental approval is a potent reinforcer for most children, but not all.

Operant theorists make a distinction between unlearned, or primary, reinforcers and conditioned, or secondary, reinforcers. *Primary reinforcers* **are events that are inherently reinforcing because they satisfy biological needs.** A given species has a limited number of primary reinforcers because these reinforcers are closely tied to physiological needs. In humans, primary reinforcers include food, water, warmth, sex, and perhaps affection expressed through hugging and close bodily contact. *Secondary,* **or** *conditioned, reinforcers* **are events that acquire reinforcing qualities by being associated with primary reinforcers.** The events that function as secondary reinforcers vary among members of a species because they depend on learning. Examples of common secondary reinforcers in humans include money, good grades, attention, flattery, praise, and applause. Most of the material things that people work hard to earn are secondary reinforcers. For example, people learn to find stylish clothes, sports cars, fine jewelry, elegant china, and state-of-the-art TVs reinforcing.

Patterns of Reinforcement

PSYKTREK 5d

In operant conditioning, a favorable outcome is much more likely to strengthen a response if the outcome follows *immediately.* If a delay occurs between a response and the positive outcome, the response may not be strengthened. Furthermore, studies show that the longer the delay between the designated response and the delivery of the reinforcer, the more slowly conditioning proceeds (Mazur, 1993; McDevitt & Williams, 2001).

Obviously, organisms make innumerable responses that do *not* lead to favorable consequences. It would be nice if people were reinforced every time they took an exam, watched a movie, hit a golf shot, asked for a date, or made a sales call. However, in the real world most responses are reinforced only some of the time. How does this situation affect the potency of reinforcers? To find out, operant psychologists have devoted an enormous amount of attention to how *schedules of reinforcement* influence operant behavior (Ferster & Skinner, 1957; Skinner, 1938, 1953).

A *schedule of reinforcement* is a specific pattern of presentation of reinforcers over time. The simplest pattern is continuous reinforcement. *Continuous reinforcement occurs when every instance of a designated response is reinforced.* In the laboratory, experimenters often use continuous reinforcement to shape and establish a new response before moving on to more realistic schedules involving intermittent, or partial, reinforcement. *Intermittent reinforcement occurs when a designated response is reinforced only some of the time.*

Which do you suppose leads to longer-lasting effects—being reinforced every time you emit a response, or being reinforced only some of the time? Studies show that, given an equal number of reinforcements, *intermittent* reinforcement makes a response more resistant to extinction than continuous reinforcement does (Falls, 1998; Schwartz & Robbins, 1995). This reality explains why behaviors that are reinforced only occasionally—such as temper tantrums in children—can be very durable and difficult to eliminate.

Reinforcement schedules come in many varieties, but four particular types of intermittent schedules have attracted the most interest. These schedules are described here along with examples drawn from the laboratory and everyday life (see **Figure 6.10** for additional examples).

Ratio schedules require the organism to make the designated response a certain number of times to gain each reinforcer. In a *fixed-ratio (FR) schedule,* **the reinforcer is given after a fixed number of nonreinforced responses.** *Examples:* (1) A rat is reinforced for every tenth lever press. (2) A salesperson receives a bonus for every fourth gym membership sold. In a *variable-ratio (VR) schedule,* **the reinforcer is given after a variable number of nonreinforced responses.** The number of nonreinforced responses varies around a predetermined average. *Examples:* (1) A rat is reinforced for every tenth lever press on the average. The exact number of responses required for reinforcement varies from one time to the next. (2) A slot machine in a casino pays off once every six tries on the average. The number of nonwinning responses between payoffs varies greatly from one time to the next.

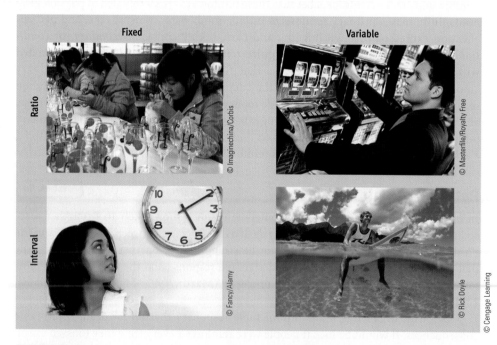

FIGURE 6.10

Reinforcement schedules in everyday life. Complex human behaviors are regulated by schedules of reinforcement. Piecework is reinforced on a fixed-ratio schedule. Playing slot machines is based on variable-ratio reinforcement. Watching the clock at work is rewarded on a fixed-interval basis (the arrival of quitting time is the reinforcer). Surfers waiting for a big wave are rewarded on a variable-interval basis.

Interval schedules require a time period to pass between the presentation of reinforcers. **In a *fixed-interval (FI) schedule*, the reinforcer is given for the first response that occurs after a fixed time interval has elapsed.** *Examples:* (1) A rat is reinforced for the first lever press after a 2-minute interval has elapsed and then must wait 2 minutes before being able to earn the next reinforcement. (2) Students can earn grades (let's assume the grades are reinforcing) by taking exams every three weeks. **In a *variable-interval (VI) schedule*, the reinforcer is given for the first response after a variable time interval has elapsed.** The interval length varies around a predetermined average. *Examples:* (1) A rat is reinforced for the first lever press after a 1-minute interval has elapsed, but the following intervals are 3 minutes, 2 minutes, 4 minutes, and so on—with an average length of 2 minutes. (2) A person repeatedly dials a busy phone number (getting through is the reinforcer).

More than 40 years of research has yielded an enormous volume of data on how these schedules of reinforcement are related to patterns of responding (Williams, 1988; Zeiler, 1977). Some of the more prominent findings are summarized in **Figure 6.11**, which depicts typical response patterns generated by each schedule. For example, with fixed-interval schedules, a pause in responding usually occurs after each reinforcer is delivered, and then responding gradually increases to a rapid rate at the end of the interval. This pattern of behavior yields a "scalloped" response curve. In general, *ratio schedules tend to produce more rapid responding than interval schedules.* Why? Because faster responding leads to quicker reinforcement when a ratio schedule is in effect. *Variable schedules tend to generate steadier response rates and greater resistance to extinction than their fixed counterparts.*

Most of the research on reinforcement schedules was conducted on rats and pigeons in Skinner boxes. However, psychologists have found that humans react to schedules of reinforcement in much the same way as lower animals (de Villiers, 1977; Perone, Galizio, & Baron, 1988). For example, when animals are placed on ratio schedules, shifting to a higher ratio (that is, requiring more responses per reinforcement) tends to generate faster responding. Managers who run factories that pay on a piecework basis (a fixed-ratio schedule) have seen the same reaction in humans. In a similar vein, most gambling is reinforced according to variable-ratio schedules, which tend to produce rapid, steady responding and great resistance to extinction—exactly what casino operators want.

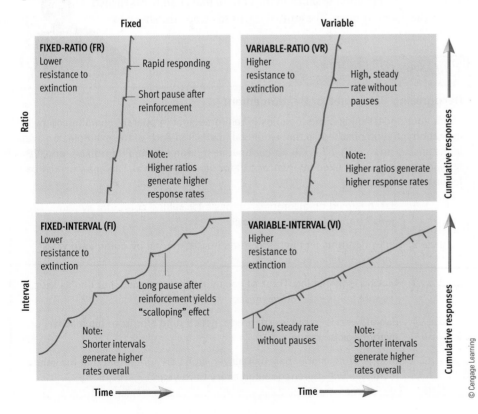

FIGURE 6.11

Schedules of reinforcement and patterns of response. In graphs of operant responding such as these, a steeper slope indicates a faster rate of response and the slash marks reflect the delivery of reinforcers. Each type of reinforcement schedule tends to generate a characteristic pattern of responding. In general, ratio schedules tend to produce more rapid responding than interval schedules (note the steep slopes of the FR and VR curves). In comparison to fixed schedules, variable schedules tend to yield steadier responding (note the smoother lines for the VR and VI schedules on the right).

Positive Reinforcement Versus Negative Reinforcement

PSYKTREK 5e, 5f

According to Skinner, reinforcement can take two forms, which he called *positive reinforcement* and *negative reinforcement* (see **Figure 6.12**). *Positive reinforcement* occurs **when a response is strengthened because it is followed by the presentation of a rewarding stimulus.** Thus far, for purposes of simplicity, our examples have involved positive reinforcement. Good grades, tasty meals, paychecks, scholarships, promotions, nice clothes, nifty cars, attention, and flattery are all positive reinforcers.

In contrast, *negative reinforcement* **occurs when a response is strengthened because it is followed by the removal of an aversive (unpleasant) stimulus.** Don't let the word "negative" confuse you. Negative reinforcement is reinforcement. Like all reinforcement, it involves a favorable outcome that strengthens a response tendency. However, this strengthening takes place because a response leads to the removal of an aversive stimulus rather than the arrival of a pleasant stimulus (see **Figure 6.12**).

In laboratory studies, negative reinforcement is usually accomplished as follows: While a rat is in a Skinner box, a moderate electric shock is delivered to the animal through the floor of the box. When the rat presses the lever, the shock is turned off for a period of time. Thus, lever pressing leads to removal of an aversive stimulus (shock). Although this sequence of events is different from those for positive reinforcement, it reliably strengthens the rat's lever pressing response.

Everyday human behavior is regulated extensively by negative reinforcement. Consider a handful of examples. You rush home in the winter to get out of the cold. You clean house to get rid of a mess. You give in to your child's begging to halt the whining. You give in to a roommate or spouse to bring an unpleasant argument to an end.

Negative reinforcement plays a key role in both escape learning and avoidance learning. **In *escape learning*, an organism acquires a response that decreases or ends some aversive stimulation.** Psychologists often study escape learning in the laboratory with dogs or rats that are conditioned in a *shuttle box*. The shuttle box has two compartments connected by a doorway, which can be opened and closed by the experimenter, as depicted in **Figure 6.13a**. In a typical study, an animal is placed in one compartment and the shock in the floor of that chamber is turned on, with the doorway open. The animal learns to escape the shock by

---

Concept Check 6.2

Recognizing Schedules of Reinforcement

Check your understanding of schedules of reinforcement in operant conditioning by indicating the type of schedule that would be in effect in each of the examples below. In the spaces on the left, fill in CR for continuous reinforcement, FR for fixed-ratio, VR for variable-ratio, FI for fixed-interval, and VI for variable-interval. The answers can be found in Appendix A.

_____ 1. Sarah is paid on a commission basis for selling computer systems. She gets a bonus for every third sale.

_____ 2. Juan's parents let him earn some pocket money by doing yard work *approximately* once a week.

_____ 3. Martha is fly-fishing. Think of each time that she casts her line as the response that may be rewarded.

_____ 4. Jamal, who is in the fourth grade, gets a gold star from his teacher for every book he reads.

_____ 5. Skip, a professional baseball player, signs an agreement that his salary increases will be renegotiated every third year.

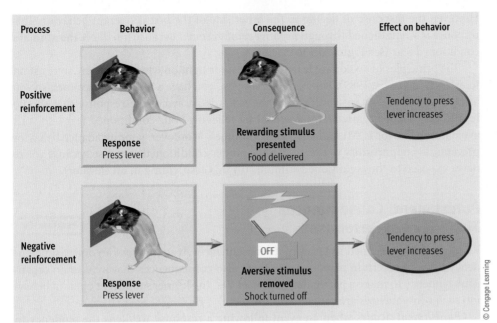

Process	Behavior	Consequence	Effect on behavior

Positive reinforcement

Response
Press lever

Rewarding stimulus presented
Food delivered

Tendency to press lever increases

Negative reinforcement

Response
Press lever

OFF

Aversive stimulus removed
Shock turned off

Tendency to press lever increases

© Cengage Learning

FIGURE 6.12

Positive reinforcement versus negative reinforcement. In positive reinforcement, a response leads to the presentation of a rewarding stimulus. In negative reinforcement, a response leads to the removal of an aversive stimulus. Both types of reinforcement involve favorable consequences and both have the same effect on behavior: The organism's tendency to emit the reinforced response is strengthened.

running to the other compartment. This escape response leads to the removal of an aversive stimulus (shock), so it is strengthened through negative reinforcement. If you were to leave a party where you were getting picked on by peers, you would be engaging in an escape response.

Escape learning often leads to avoidance learning. In *avoidance learning* an organism acquires a response that prevents some aversive stimulation from occurring. In shuttle box studies of avoidance learning, the experimenter simply gives the animal a signal that shock is forthcoming. The typical signal is a light that goes on a few seconds prior to the shock. At first the dog or rat runs only when shocked (escape learning). Gradually, however, the animal learns to run to the safe compartment as soon as the light comes on, showing avoidance learning. Similarly, if you were to quit going to parties because of your concern about being picked on by peers, you would be demonstrating avoidance learning.

Avoidance learning presents an interesting example of how classical conditioning and operant conditioning can work together to regulate behavior (Levis, 1989; Mowrer, 1947). In avoidance learning, the warning light that goes on before the shock becomes a CS (through classical conditioning) eliciting reflexive, conditioned fear in the animal.

(a)

Light

© Cengage Learning

(b)

1. Classical conditioning

CS
Light

US
Shock

CR
Fear
UR

2. Operant conditioning

Response

Run away

(negative reinforcement)

Aversive stimulus removed
Conditioned fear reduced

FIGURE 6.13

Escape and avoidance learning. (a) Escape and avoidance learning are often studied with a shuttle box like that shown here. Warning signals, shock, and the animal's ability to flee from one compartment to another can be controlled by the experimenter. **(b)** Avoidance begins because classical conditioning creates a conditioned fear that is elicited by the warning signal (panel 1). Avoidance continues because it is maintained by operant conditioning (panel 2). Specifically, the avoidance response is strengthened through negative reinforcement, since it leads to removal of the conditioned fear.

However, the response of fleeing to the other side of the box is operant behavior. This response is strengthened through *negative reinforcement* because it reduces the animal's conditioned fear (see **Figure 6.13b**).

The principles of avoidance learning shed some light on why phobias are so resistant to extinction (Levis, 1989). For example, suppose you have a phobia of elevators, so you always take the stairs instead. Taking the stairs is an avoidance response that should lead to consistent negative reinforcement by relieving your conditioned fear—so your avoidance behavior is strengthened and continues. Moreover, your avoidance behavior prevents any opportunity to extinguish the phobic conditioned response because you're never exposed to the conditioned stimulus (in this case, riding in an elevator).

Punishment: Consequences That Weaken Responses

PsykTrek 5e

Reinforcement is defined in terms of its consequences. It *strengthens* an organism's tendency to make a certain response. Are there also consequences that *weaken* an organism's tendency to make a particular response? Yes. In Skinner's model of operant behavior, such consequences are called *punishment.*

Punishment occurs when an event following a response weakens the tendency to make that response. In a Skinner box, the use of punishment is very simple. When a rat presses the lever or a pigeon pecks the disk, it receives a brief shock. This procedure usually leads to a rapid decline in the animal's response rate (Dinsmoor, 1998). Punishment typically involves presentation of an aversive stimulus (for instance, spanking a child). However, punishment may also involve the removal of a rewarding stimulus (for instance, taking away a child's TV-watching privileges).

The concept of punishment in operant conditioning is confusing to many students on two counts. First, they often confuse it with negative reinforcement, which is entirely different. Negative reinforcement involves the *removal* of an aversive stimulus, thereby *strengthening* a response. Punishment, on the other hand, involves the *presentation* of an aversive stimulus, thereby *weakening* a response. Thus, punishment and negative reinforcement are *opposite procedures* that *yield opposite effects* on behavior (see **Figure 6.14**).

FIGURE 6.14

Comparison of negative reinforcement and punishment. Although punishment can occur when a response leads to the removal of a rewarding stimulus, it more typically involves the presentation of an aversive stimulus. Students often confuse punishment with negative reinforcement because they associate both with aversive stimuli. However, as this diagram shows, punishment and negative reinforcement represent opposite procedures that have opposite effects on behavior.

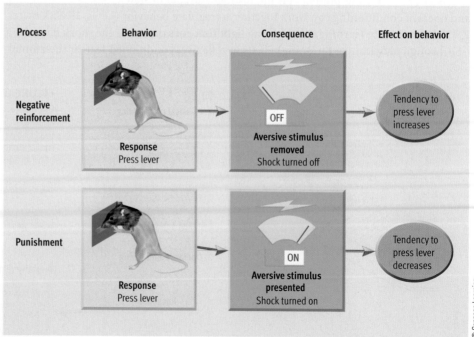

The second source of confusion involves the tendency to equate punishment with *disciplinary procedures* used by parents, teachers, and other authority figures. In the operant model, punishment occurs any time undesirable consequences weaken a response tendency. Defined in this way, the concept of punishment goes far beyond things like parents spanking children and teachers handing out detentions. For example, if you wear a new outfit and your schoolmates make fun of it, your behavior will have been punished and your tendency to emit this response (wear the same clothing) will probably decline. Similarly, if you go to a restaurant and have a horrible meal, your response will have been punished, and your tendency to go to that restaurant will probably decline.

Although punishment in operant conditioning encompasses far more than disciplinary acts, it *is* used frequently for disciplinary purposes. In light of this situation, it is worth looking at the research on punishment as a disciplinary measure. Controversy exists about the wisdom of using physical punishment. The main concern is that punishment may produce many undesirable side effects (McCord, 2005; Straus, 2000). Consistent with this analysis, a review of 88 studies (Gershoff, 2002) concluded that physical punishment is associated with poor-quality parent-child relations and with elevated aggression, delinquency, and behavioral problems in youngsters. Some critics have pointed out that the evidence linking spanking to negative effects is correlational, and correlation is no assurance of causation (Kazdin & Benjet, 2003). Perhaps spanking causes children to be more aggressive, but it's also plausible that aggressive children cause their parents to rely more on physical punishment.

© Di Carlo Darsa S/ Age fotostock

Although this critique has merit, evidence on the negative effects of corporal punishment has continued to pile up (Lynch et al., 2006; Mulvaney & Mebert, 2007). Many of the newer studies have statistically controlled for children's initial level of aggression and other confounding variables, which strengthens the case for a causal link between spanking and negative outcomes. For example, Straus and Paschall (2009) assessed how often children were spanked and their cognitive ability. They retested the children's cognitive ability four years later and found that those who were spanked showed a disadvantage in IQ scores. Another

Concept Check 6.3

Recognizing Outcomes in Operant Conditioning

Check your understanding of the various types of consequences that can occur in operant conditioning by indicating whether the examples below involve positive reinforcement (PR), negative reinforcement (NR), punishment (P), or extinction (E). The answers can be found in Appendix A.

_____ 1. Antonio gets a speeding ticket.

_____ 2. Diane's supervisor compliments her on her hard work.

_____ 3. Leon goes to the health club for a rare workout and pushes himself so hard that his entire body aches and he throws up.

_____ 4. Audrey lets her dog out so she won't have to listen to its whimpering.

_____ 5. Richard shoots up heroin to ward off tremors and chills associated with heroin withdrawal.

_____ 6. Sharma constantly complains about minor aches and pains to obtain sympathy from colleagues at work. Three co-workers who share an office with her decide to ignore her complaints instead of responding with sympathy.

© michaeljung/Shutterstock

carefully controlled study found that heavy use of physical punishment when children were age 3 was associated with higher levels of aggression at age 5 (Taylor et al., 2010). In light of findings such as these, an American Psychological Association task force concluded that parents should not use corporal punishment (Graham-Bermann, 2009).

Changing Directions in the Study of Conditioning

As you learned in Chapter 1, science is constantly evolving and changing in response to new research and new thinking. Such change certainly has occurred in the study of conditioning (Domjan, 1998). In this section, we will examine two major changes in thinking about conditioning that have emerged in recent decades. First, we'll consider the growing recognition that an organism's biological heritage can limit or channel conditioning. Second, we'll discuss the increased appreciation of the role of cognitive processes in conditioning.

Recognizing Biological Constraints on Conditioning

Learning theorists have traditionally assumed that the fundamental laws of conditioning have great generality—that they apply to a wide range of species. Although no one ever suggested that hamsters could learn physics, until the 1960s most psychologists assumed that associations could be conditioned between any stimulus an organism could register and any response it could make. However, findings in recent decades

Concept Check 6.4

Distinguishing Between Classical Conditioning and Operant Conditioning

Check your understanding of the usual differences between classical conditioning and operant conditioning by indicating the type of conditioning process involved in each of the following examples. In the space on the left, place a C if the example involves classical conditioning, an O if it involves operant conditioning, or a B if it involves both. The answers can be found in Appendix A.

_____ 1. Whenever Midori takes her dog out for a walk, she wears the same old blue windbreaker. Eventually, she notices that her dog becomes excited whenever she puts on this windbreaker.

_____ 2. The Wailing Creatures are a successful rock band with three hit albums to their credit. They begin their U.S. tour featuring many new, unreleased songs, all of which draw silence from their concert fans. The same fans cheer wildly when the Wailing Creatures play any of their old hits. Gradually, the band reduces the number of new songs it plays and starts playing more of the old standbys.

_____ 3. When Cindy and Mel first fell in love, they listened constantly to the Wailing Creatures' hit song "Transatlantic Obsession." Although several years have passed, whenever they hear this song, they experience a warm, romantic feeling.

_____ 4. For nearly 20 years Ralph has worked as a machinist in the same factory. His new foreman is never satisfied with his work and criticizes him constantly. After a few weeks of heavy criticism, Ralph experiences anxiety whenever he arrives at work. He starts calling in sick more and more frequently to evade this anxiety.

© lenetstan/Shutterstock

have demonstrated that there are limits to the generality of conditioning principles—limits imposed by an organism's biological heritage.

CONDITIONED TASTE AVERSION

A number of years ago, a prominent psychologist, Martin Seligman, dined out with his wife and enjoyed a steak with sauce béarnaise. About 6 hours afterward, he developed a wicked case of stomach flu and endured severe nausea. Subsequently, when he ordered sauce béarnaise, he was chagrined to discover that its aroma alone nearly made him throw up. Seligman's experience was not unique. Many people develop aversions to food that has been followed by nausea from illness, alcohol intoxication, or food poisoning (Rosenblum, 2009). However, Seligman was puzzled by what he called his "sauce béarnaise syndrome" (Seligman & Hager, 1972). On the one hand, it appeared to be the straightforward result of classical conditioning. A neutral stimulus (the sauce) had been paired with an unconditioned stimulus (the flu), which caused an unconditioned response (the nausea). Thus, the béarnaise sauce became a conditioned stimulus eliciting nausea (see **Figure 6.15**).

© Robyn Mackenzie/Shutterstock

On the other hand, Seligman recognized that his aversion to béarnaise sauce seemed to violate certain basic principles of conditioning. First, the lengthy delay of 6 hours between the CS (the sauce) and the US (the flu) should have prevented conditioning from occurring. In laboratory studies, a delay of more than *30 seconds* between the CS and US makes it difficult to establish a conditioned response, yet this conditioning occurred in just one pairing. Second, why was it that *only* the béarnaise sauce became a CS eliciting nausea? Why not other stimuli that were present in the restaurant? Shouldn't plates, knives, tablecloths, or his wife, for example, also trigger Seligman's nausea?

The riddle of Seligman's sauce béarnaise syndrome was solved by John Garcia (1989) and his colleagues. They conducted a series of studies on *conditioned taste aversion* (Garcia, Clarke, & Hankins, 1973; Garcia & Koelling, 1966; Garcia & Rusiniak, 1980). In these studies, they manipulated the kinds of stimuli preceding the onset of nausea and other noxious experiences in rats, using radiation to artificially induce the nausea. They found that when taste cues were followed by nausea, rats quickly acquired conditioned taste aversions. However, when taste cues were followed by other types of noxious stimuli (such as shock), rats did *not* develop conditioned taste aversions. Furthermore, visual and auditory stimuli followed by nausea also failed to produce conditioned aversions. In short, Garcia and his co-workers found that it was almost impossible to create certain associations, whereas taste-nausea associations (and odor-nausea associations) were almost impossible to prevent.

What is the theoretical significance of this unique readiness to make connections between taste and nausea? Garcia argues that it is a by-product of the evolutionary history of mammals. Animals that consume poisonous foods and survive must learn not to repeat their mistakes. Natural selection will favor organisms that quickly learn what *not* to eat. Thus, evolution may have biologically programmed some organisms to learn certain types of associations more easily than others.

PREPAREDNESS AND PHOBIAS

According to Martin Seligman (1971) and other theorists (Öhman, 1979; Öhman, Dimberg, & Öst, 1985), evolution has also programmed organisms to acquire certain fears more readily than others, because of a phenomenon called *preparedness*. **Preparedness involves species-specific predispositions to be conditioned in certain ways and not others.** Seligman believes that preparedness can explain why certain phobias are vastly more common than others. People tend to develop phobias to snakes, spiders, heights, and darkness relatively easily. However, even after having painful experiences with hammers, knives, hot stoves, and electrical outlets, people's phobic fears of these objects are rare. What characteristics do common phobic objects share? Most were once genuine threats to our ancient ancestors. Consequently, a fear response to such objects may

FIGURE 6.15

Conditioned taste aversion. Taste aversions can be established through classical conditioning, as in the "sauce béarnaise syndrome." However, as the text explains, taste aversions can be acquired in ways that *seem* to violate basic principles of classical conditioning.

© Cengage Learning

have survival value for our species. According to Seligman, evolutionary forces gradually wired the human brain to acquire conditioned fears of these stimuli easily and rapidly. Laboratory simulations of phobic conditioning have provided considerable support for the concept of preparedness (Mineka & Öhman, 2002).

People tend to develop phobias to snakes very easily but to hot stoves rarely, even though the latter can be just as painful. Preparedness theory can explain this paradox.

Recognizing Cognitive Processes in Conditioning

Pavlov, Skinner, and their followers traditionally viewed conditioning as a mechanical process in which stimulus-response associations are "stamped in" by experience. Learning theorists asserted that if creatures such as snails can be conditioned, conditioning can't depend on higher mental processes. This viewpoint did not go entirely unchallenged, but mainstream theories of conditioning did not allocate any role to cognitive processes. In recent decades, however, research findings have led theorists to shift toward more cognitive explanations of conditioning. Let's review some of this research.

SIGNAL RELATIONS

One theorist who was especially influential in demonstrating the importance of cognitive factors in classical conditioning was Robert Rescorla (1978, 1980; Rescorla & Wagner, 1972). Rescorla asserts that environmental stimuli serve as signals and that some stimuli are better, or more dependable, signals than others. A "good" signal is one that allows accurate prediction of the US. Hence, he has manipulated the *predictive value* of a conditioned stimulus by varying the proportion of trials in which the CS and US are paired. For example, in one study a CS (tone) and US (shock) were paired 100% of the time for one group of rats and only 50% of the time for another group.

What did Rescorla find when he tested the two groups of rats for conditioned fear? He found that the CS elicited a much stronger fear response in the group that had been exposed to the more dependable signal. Many other studies of signal relations have also shown that the predictive value of a CS is an influential factor governing classical conditioning (Rescorla, 1978). These studies suggest that classical conditioning may involve information processing rather than reflexive responding.

RESPONSE-OUTCOME RELATIONS AND REINFORCEMENT

Studies of response-outcome relations and reinforcement also highlight the role of cognitive processes in conditioning. Imagine that on the night before an important exam you study hard while repeatedly playing a Coldplay song. The next morning you earn an A on your exam. Does this result strengthen your tendency to play Coldplay's music before exams? Probably not. Chances are, you will recognize the logical relation between the response of studying hard and the reinforcement of a good grade, and only the response of studying will be strengthened (Killeen, 1981).

However, it's not out of the realm of possibility that you might develop a habit of playing Coldplay before big exams. Many years ago, B. F. Skinner argued that "superstitious behavior" could be established through *noncontingent reinforcement,* which occurs when a response is accidentally strengthened by a reinforcer that follows it, even though delivery of the reinforcer was not a result of the response. In a classic study, Skinner (1948) put eight pigeons in operant chambers that were set up to deliver reinforcement every 15 seconds, regardless of what responses the pigeons were making. In Skinner's judgment, six of the eight pigeons started displaying quirky, superstitious responses, such as head-bobbing or turning counter-clockwise. Skinner's theory that noncontingent reinforcement is the basis for superstitious behavior held sway for many years, but researchers eventually failed to replicate his findings (Staddon & Simmelhag, 1971).

That said, superstitious behavior is extremely common, and accidental reinforcements *may* sometimes contribute to these superstitions, along with various types of erroneous reasoning (Ono, 1987; Vyse, 1997). There are extensive anecdotal reports of athletes like Wade Boggs exhibiting superstitious responses such as wearing a special pair of socks, eating the same lunch, going through special rituals, and so on to enhance their chances of success (Bleak & Frederick, 1998; Ciborowski, 1997; Gmelch, 1978). And these quirks are certainly not limited to athletes (Wargo, 2008). For example, most people compulsively need to "knock on wood" after mentioning their good fortune in some area. One recent study (Risen & Gilovich, 2008) showed that many people subscribe to the belief that it is bad luck to "tempt fate." In one part of the study participants read about a student named Jon who had applied to prestigious Stanford University for graduate school and whose mother had sent him a Stanford T-shirt before he learned whether he had been accepted. The subjects believed that Jon's prospects of acceptance would be higher if he did not tempt fate by wearing the T-shirt before getting the results.

Contemporary research on superstitious behavior tends to ascribe it to normal cognitive biases and errors that promote irrational reasoning (discussed in Chapter 8) rather than to the unpredictable vagaries of operant conditioning (Pronin et al., 2006; Wegner & Wheatley, 1999). Interestingly, a recent study found that superstitious beliefs can actually enhance performance (Damisch, Stoberock, & Mussweiler, 2010). Participant golfers who were given a "lucky ball" sank more putts on a putting green than control subjects. And subjects who were allowed to hang onto a lucky charm performed better on memory and reasoning tasks than those who had to surrender their lucky charm. So, silly though they may seem, superstitions may actually influence people's outcomes.

In any case, it is clear that reinforcement is *not* automatic when favorable consequences follow a response. People actively reason out the relations between responses and the outcomes that follow. When a response is followed by a desirable outcome, the response is more likely to be strengthened if the person thinks that the response *caused* the outcome. In sum, modern, reformulated models of conditioning view it as a matter of detecting the *contingencies* among environmental events (Beckers et al., 2006; Penn & Povinelli, 2007).

Observational Learning

Can classical and operant conditioning account for all human learning? Absolutely not. Consider how people learn a fairly basic skill such as driving a car. They do not hop naively into an automobile and start emitting random responses until one leads to favorable consequences. On the contrary, most people learning to drive know exactly where to place the key and how to get started. How are these responses acquired? Through *observation*. Most new drivers have years of experience observing others drive, and they put those observations to work. Learning through observation accounts for a great deal of learning in both animals and humans.

Observational learning **occurs when an organism's responding is influenced by the observation of others, who are called models.** This process has been investigated extensively by Albert Bandura (1977, 1986). He does not see observational learning as entirely separate from classical and operant conditioning. Instead, he asserts that it greatly extends the reach of these conditioning processes. Whereas previous conditioning theorists emphasized the organism's direct experience, Bandura has demonstrated that both classical and operant conditioning can take place vicariously through observational learning.

Albert Bandura
"Most human behavior is learned by observation through modeling."

FIGURE 6.16

Observational learning. In observational learning, an observer attends to and stores a mental representation of a model's behavior (example: assertive bargaining) and its consequences (example: a good buy on a car). If the observer sees the modeled response lead to a favorable outcome, the observer's tendency to emit the modeled response will be strengthened.

Basic Processes

Essentially, observational learning involves being conditioned indirectly by virtue of observing another's conditioning (see **Figure 6.16**). To illustrate, suppose you observe a friend behaving assertively with a car salesperson. You see your friend's assertive behavior reinforced by the exceptionally good buy he gets on the car. Your own tendency to behave assertively with salespeople might well be strengthened as a result. Notice that the reinforcement is experienced by your friend, not you. The good buy should strengthen your friend's tendency to bargain assertively, but your tendency to do so may also be strengthened indirectly.

Bandura has identified four key processes that are crucial in observational learning. The first two—attention and retention—highlight the importance of cognition in this type of learning:

- *Attention.* To learn through observation, you must pay attention to another person's behavior and its consequences.

- *Retention.* You may not have occasion to use an observed response for weeks, months, or even years. Thus, you must store a mental representation of what you have witnessed in your memory.

- *Reproduction.* Enacting a modeled response depends on your ability to reproduce the response by converting your stored mental images into overt behavior.

Observational learning occurs in both humans and animals. For example, no one trained this dog to "pray" with its owner; the chihuahua just picked up the response through observation. In a similar vein, children acquire a diverse array of responses from role models through observational learning.

- *Motivation.* Finally, you are unlikely to reproduce an observed response unless you are motivated to do so. Your motivation depends on whether you encounter a situation in which you believe that the response is likely to pay off for you.

Observational Learning and the Media Violence Controversy

The power of observational learning has been at the center of a long-running controversy about the effects of media violence. Ever since television became popular in the 1950s, social critics have expressed concern about the amount of violence on TV. In the 1960s, Bandura and his colleagues conducted landmark research on the issue that remains widely cited and influential.

In one classic study, Bandura, Ross, and Ross (1963a) showed how the observation of filmed models can influence the learning of aggressive behavior in children. They manipulated whether or not nursery-school children saw an aggressive model on film and whether the aggressive model experienced positive or negative consequences. Soon after the manipulations, the children were taken to a room where their play was observed through a one-way mirror. Among the toys available in the room were two "Bobo dolls" that served as convenient targets for kicks, punches, and other aggressive responses. Children who had seen the aggressive model rewarded engaged in more aggression toward the toys than children in the other conditions did. This study was one of the earliest experimental demonstrations of a cause-and-effect relationship between exposure to TV depictions of aggression and increased aggressive behavior.

Decades of research since Bandura's pioneering work have indicated that media violence fosters increased aggression (Bushman & Huesmann, 2001). The short-term effects of media violence have been investigated in hundreds of experimental studies, which consistently demonstrate that exposure to TV and movie violence increases the likelihood of physical aggression, verbal aggression, aggressive thoughts, and aggressive emotions in both children and adults (Anderson et al., 2003).

A particular source of concern in recent research has been the finding that exposure to media violence appears to desensitize people to the effects of aggression in the real world. Desensitization means that people show muted reactions to real violence. For example, in one study participants were randomly assigned to play violent or nonviolent video games for 20 minutes. Their physiological reactions to video recordings of real-life aggression (prison fights, police confrontations, and such) were then monitored. The subjects who had played violent video games for a mere 20 minutes showed smaller physiological reactions to the aggression than those who played nonviolent games (Carnagey, Anderson, & Bushman, 2007).

A follow-up study suggested that the "numbing" effect of media violence makes people less sensitive to the suffering of others and less likely to help others in need

CALVIN AND HOBBES

Three Types of Learning

TYPE OF LEARNING	PROCEDURE	DIAGRAM	RESULT

CLASSICAL CONDITIONING

Ivan Pavlov

A neutral stimulus (for example, a tone) is paired with an unconditioned stimulus (such as food) that elicits an unconditioned response (salivation).

CS
Tone

US
Meat powder

CR
Salivation
UR

The neutral stimulus becomes a conditioned stimulus that elicits the conditioned response (for example, a tone triggers salivation).

OPERANT CONDITIONING

B. F. Skinner

In a stimulus situation, a response is followed by favorable consequences (reinforcement) or unfavorable consequences (punishment).

Response
Press lever

Rewarding or aversive stimulus presented or removed
Food delivery or shock

If reinforced, the response is strengthened (emitted more frequently); if punished, the response is weakened (emitted less frequently).

OBSERVATIONAL LEARNING

Albert Bandura

An observer attends to a model's behavior (for example, aggressive bargaining) and its consequences (for example, a good buy on a car).

Response
Bargain assertively

Rewarding stimulus presented
Good buy on car

The observer stores a mental representation of the modeled response; the observer's tendency to emit the response may be strengthened or weakened, depending on the consequences observed.

© Yuri Arcurs/Shutterstock

© Minerva Studio/Shutterstock

© Oleksiy Maksymenko Photography/Alamy

TYPICAL KINDS OF RESPONSES	EXAMPLES IN ANIMALS	EXAMPLES IN HUMANS
Mostly (but not always) involuntary reflexes and visceral responses	Dogs learn to salivate to the sound of a tone that has been paired with meat powder.	Little Albert learns to fear a white rat and other white, furry objects through classical conditioning.
Mostly (but not always) voluntary, spontaneous responses	Trained animals perform remarkable feats because they have been reinforced for gradually learning closer and closer approximations of responses they do not normally emit.	Casino patrons tend to exhibit high, steady rates of gambling, as most games of chance involve complex variable-ratio schedules of reinforcement.
Mostly voluntary responses, often consisting of novel and complex sequences	A dog spontaneously learns to mimic a human ritual.	A young boy performs a response that he has acquired through observation.

© Bettmann/Corbis

Archives of the History of American Psychology, University of Akron. From original footage, 1919–1920.

Courtesy of Animal Behavior Enterprises, Inc.

© Masterfile/ Royalty Free

© AP Images/Itsuo Inouye

© Mike Kemp/Age fotostock

FIGURE 6.17

The correlation between exposure to media violence and aggression. The more violence children watch on TV, the more aggressive they tend to be, but this correlation could reflect a variety of underlying causal relationships. Although watching violent shows probably causes increased aggressiveness, it is also possible that aggressive children are drawn to violent shows. Or perhaps a third variable (such as a genetic predisposition to aggressiveness) leads to both a preference for violent shows and high aggressiveness.

(Bushman & Anderson, 2009). In this study, participants who had just played a violent or nonviolent video game overheard a staged fight (just outside the door of the lab) in which one person was injured. The aggressive actor clearly had left the scene, so there was no perceived danger to the participants. Researchers monitored how long it took subjects to come out into the hall to offer help to the groaning victim. Participants who had just played a violent video game took much longer to help (average 73 seconds) than those who had just played a non-violent game (16 seconds). Thus, it appears that media violence can desensitize individuals to acts of aggression.

The real-world and long-term effects of media violence have been investigated through correlational research. The findings of these studies show that the more violence children watch on TV, the more aggressive they tend to be at home and at school (Huesmann & Miller, 1994). Of course, critics point out that this correlation could reflect a variety of causal relationships (see **Figure 6.17**). Perhaps high aggressiveness in children causes an increased interest in violent television shows. However, a handful of long-term studies that have followed the same subjects since the 1960s and 1970s have clarified the causal relations underlying the link between media violence and elevated aggression. These studies show that the extent of youngsters' exposure to media violence in childhood predicts their aggressiveness in adolescence and early adulthood, but not vice versa (Huesmann, 1986; Huesmann et al., 2003). In other words, high exposure to media violence precedes, and presumably contributes to the causation of, high aggressiveness.

The heated debate about media violence shows that observational learning plays an important role in regulating behavior. It represents a third major type of learning that builds on the first two types—classical conditioning and operant conditioning. These three basic types of learning are summarized and compared in the Illustrated Overview on pages 204–205.

KEY LEARNING GOALS

6.14 Identify the two unifying themes highlighted in this chapter.

Heredity and Environment

Sociohistorical Context

Reflecting on the Chapter's Themes

Two of our unifying themes stand out in this chapter: (1) nature and nurture interactively govern behavior, and (2) dense interconnections exist between psychology and events in the world at large. Let's examine each of these points in more detail.

In regard to nature versus nurture, research on learning has clearly and repeatedly demonstrated the enormous power of the environment and experience in shaping behavior. Indeed, many learning theorists once believed that *all* aspects of behavior could be explained in terms of environmental determinants. In recent decades, however, evidence on conditioned taste aversion and preparedness has shown that there are biological constraints on conditioning. Thus, even in explanations of learning—an area once dominated by nurture theories—we see again that heredity and environment jointly influence behavior.

The history of research on conditioning also shows how progress in psychology can seep into every corner of society. For example, Skinner's ideas on the power of positive reinforcement have influenced patterns of discipline in American society. Research on operant conditioning has also affected management styles in the business world, leading to an increased emphasis on positive reinforcement. The fact that the principles of conditioning are routinely applied in homes, businesses, child-care facilities, schools, and factories clearly shows that psychology is not an ivory tower endeavor.

In the upcoming Personal Application, you will see how you can apply the principles of conditioning to improve your self-control, as we discuss the technology of behavior modification.

Achieving Self-Control Through Behavior Modification

Answer the following "yes" or "no."

___ 1 Do you have a hard time passing up food, even when you're not hungry?

___ 2 Do you wish you studied more often?

___ 3 Would you like to cut down on your smoking or drinking?

___ 4 Do you experience difficulty in getting yourself to exercise regularly?

If you answered "yes" to any of these questions, you have struggled with the challenge of self-control. This Application discusses how you can use the principles and techniques of behavior modification to improve your self-control. *Behavior modification is a systematic approach to changing behavior through the application of the principles of conditioning.* Advocates of behavior modification assume that behavior is mainly a product of learning, conditioning, and environmental control. They further assume that *what is learned can be unlearned.* Thus, they set out to "recondition" people to produce more desirable and effective patterns of behavior.

The technology of behavior modification has been applied with great success in schools, businesses, hospitals, factories, childcare facilities, prisons, and mental health centers (Kazdin, 2001; O'Donohue, 1998; Rachman, 1992). Moreover, behavior modification techniques have proven particularly valuable in efforts to improve self-control. Our discussion will borrow liberally from an excellent book on self-modification by David Watson and Roland Tharp (2007). We will discuss four steps in the process

of self-modification, which are outlined in **Figure 6.18**.

Specifying Your Target Behavior

The first step in a self-modification program is to specify the target behavior(s) that you want to change. Behavior modification can only be applied to a clearly defined, overt response, yet many people have difficulty pinpointing the behavior they hope to alter. They tend to describe their problems in terms of unobservable personality *traits* rather than overt *behaviors*. For example, asked what behavior he would like to change, a man might say, "I'm too irritable." That statement may be true, but it is of little help in designing a self-modification program. To use a behavioral approach, vague statements about traits need to be translated into precise descriptions of specific target behaviors.

To identify target responses, you need to ponder past behavior or closely observe future behavior and list specific *examples* of responses that lead to the trait description. For instance, the man who regards himself as "too irritable" might identify two overly frequent responses, such as arguing with his wife and snapping at his children. These are specific behaviors for which he could design a self-modification program.

Gathering Baseline Data

The second step in behavior modification is to gather baseline data. You need to systematically observe your target behavior for a period of time (usually a week or two) before you work out the details of your program. In gathering your baseline data, you need to monitor three things.

First, you need to determine the initial response level of your target behavior. After all, you can't tell whether your program is working effectively unless you have a baseline for comparison. In most

cases, you would simply keep track of how often the target response occurs in a certain time interval. Thus, you might count the daily frequency of snapping at your children, smoking cigarettes, or biting your fingernails. *It is crucial to gather accurate data.* You should keep permanent written records, and it is usually best to portray these records graphically (see **Figure 6.19** on the next page).

Second, you need to monitor the *antecedents* of your target behavior. Anteced-

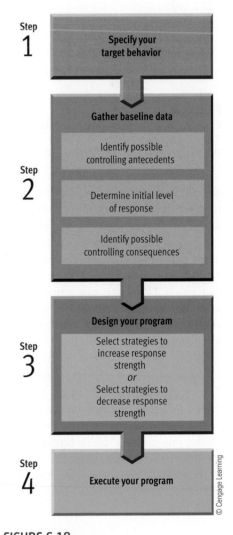

FIGURE 6.18

Steps in a self-modification program. This flowchart provides an overview of the four steps necessary to execute a self-modification program.

FIGURE 6.19

Example of recordkeeping in a self-modification program. Graphic records are ideal for tracking progress in behavior modification efforts. The records shown here illustrate what someone would be likely to track in a behavior modification program for weight loss.

ents are events that typically precede the target response. Often these events play a major role in evoking this behavior. For example, if your target is overeating, you might discover that the bulk of your over-eating occurs late in the evening while you watch TV. If you can pinpoint this kind of antecedent-response connection, you may be able to design your program to circumvent or break the link.

Third, you need to monitor the typical consequences of your target behavior. Try to identify the reinforcers that are maintaining an undesirable target behavior or the unfavorable outcomes that are suppressing a desirable target behavior. Bear in mind that a response may not be reinforced every time, as most behavior is maintained by intermittent reinforcement.

Designing Your Program

Once you have selected a target behavior and gathered adequate baseline data, it is time to plan your intervention program.

Generally speaking, your program will be designed to either increase or decrease the frequency of a target response.

INCREASING RESPONSE STRENGTH

Efforts to increase the frequency of a target response depend largely on the use of positive reinforcement. In other words, you reward yourself for behaving properly. Although the basic strategy is quite simple, doing it skillfully involves a number of considerations, including selecting the right reinforcer and arranging contingencies.

Selecting a Reinforcer To use positive reinforcement, you need to find a reward that will be effective for you. Reinforcement is subjective. What is reinforcing for one person may not be reinforcing for another. To determine your personal reinforcers you need to ask yourself questions such as: What do I like to do for fun? What makes me feel good? What would be a nice present? What would I hate to lose? (See **Figure 6.20.**)

You don't have to come up with spectacular new reinforcers that you've never experienced before. *You can use reinforcers that you are already getting.* However, you have to restructure the contingencies so that you get them only if you behave appropriately. For example, if you normally buy two DVDs per week, you might make these purchases contingent on studying a certain number of hours during the week.

Arranging the Contingencies Once you have chosen your reinforcer, you have to set up reinforcement contingencies. These contingencies will describe the exact behavioral goals that must be met and the reinforcement that may then be awarded. For example, in a program to increase exercise, you might make spending $50 on clothes (the reinforcer) contingent on having jogged 15 miles during the week (the target behavior).

Try to set behavioral goals that are both challenging and realistic. You want your goals to be challenging so that they lead to improvement in your behavior. However, setting unrealistically high goals—a common mistake in self-modification—often leads to unnecessary discouragement.

DECREASING RESPONSE STRENGTH

Let's turn now to the challenge of reducing the frequency of an undesirable response. You can go about this task in a number of ways. Your principal options include reinforcement, control of antecedents, and punishment.

Reinforcement Reinforcers can be used in an indirect way to decrease the frequency of a response. This may sound paradoxical, since you have learned that reinforcement strengthens a response. The trick lies in how you define the target behavior. For example, in the case of overeating you might define your target behavior as eating more than 1600 calories a day (an excess response that you want to decrease) or eating less than 1600 calories a day (a deficit response that you want to increase). You can choose the latter definition and reinforce yourself whenever you eat less than 1600 calories

Selecting a Reinforcer
1. What will be the rewards of achieving your goal?
2. What kind of praise do you like to receive, from yourself and others?
3. What kinds of things do you like to have?
4. What are your major interests?
5. What are your hobbies?
6. What people do you like to be with?
7. What do you like to do with those people?
8. What do you do for fun?
9. What do you do to relax?
10. What do you do to get away from it all?
11. What makes you feel good?
12. What would be a nice present to receive?
13. What kinds of things are important to you?
14. What would you buy if you had an extra $20? $50? $100?
15. On what do you spend your money each week?
16. What behaviors do you perform every day? (Don't overlook the obvious or commonplace.)
17. Are there any behaviors you usually perform instead of the target behavior?
18. What would you hate to lose?
19. Of the things you do every day, which would you hate to give up?
20. What are your favorite daydreams and fantasies?
21. What are the most relaxing scenes you can imagine?

FIGURE 6.20

Choosing a a self-modification program reinforcer. Finding a good reinforcer to use in a behavior modification program can require a lot of thought. The questions listed here can help people identify their personal reinforcers.

SOURCE: Adapted from Watson, D. L., & Tharp, R. G. (1997). *Self-directed behavior: Self-modification for personal adjustment.* Belmont, CA: Wadsworth. Wadsworth is a part of Cengage Learning, Inc. Reproduced by permission. www.cengage.com/permissions

in a day. Thus, you can reinforce yourself for not emitting a response, or for emitting it less, and thereby decrease a response through reinforcement.

Control of Antecedents A worthwhile strategy for decreasing the occurrence of an undesirable response may be to identify its antecedents and avoid exposure to them. This strategy is especially useful when you are trying to decrease the frequency of a consummatory response, such as smoking or eating. In the case of overeating, for instance, the easiest way to resist temptation is to avoid having to face it. Thus, you might stay away from favorite restaurants, minimize time spent in your kitchen, shop for groceries just after eating (when willpower is higher), and avoid purchasing favorite foods.

Punishment The strategy of decreasing unwanted behavior by punishing yourself for that behavior is an obvious option that people tend to overuse. The biggest problem with punishment in a self-modification effort is that it is difficult to follow through and punish yourself. Nonetheless, there may be situations in which your manipulations of reinforcers need to be bolstered by the threat of punishment. If you're going to use punishment, keep two guidelines in mind. First, do not use punishment alone. Use it in conjunction with positive reinforcement. If you set up a program in which you can earn only negative consequences, you probably won't stick to it. Second, use a relatively mild punishment so that you will actually be able to administer it to yourself.

Executing Your Program

Once you have designed your program, the next step is to put it to work by enforcing the contingencies that you have carefully planned. During this period, you need to continue to accurately record the frequency of your target behavior so you can evaluate your progress. The success of your program depends on your not "cheating." The most common form of cheating is to reward yourself when you have not actually earned it. You can reduce the likelihood of cheating by having someone other than yourself dole out the reinforcers and punishments.

Generally, when you design your program you should spell out the conditions under which you will bring it to an end. Doing so involves setting terminal goals such as reaching a certain weight, studying with a certain regularity, or going without cigarettes for a certain length of time. Often, it is a good idea to phase out your program by planning a gradual reduction in the frequency or potency of your reinforcement for appropriate behavior.

Manipulating Emotions: Pavlov and Persuasion

With all due respect to the great Ivan Pavlov, when we focus on his demonstration that dogs can be trained to slobber in response to a tone, it is easy to lose sight of the importance of classical conditioning. At first glance, most people do not see a relationship between Pavlov's slobbering dogs and anything that they are even remotely interested in. However, in the main body of the chapter, we saw that classical conditioning actually contributes to the regulation of many important aspects of behavior, including fears, phobias, and other emotional reactions; immune function; and even sexual arousal. In this Application you will learn that classical conditioning is routinely used to manipulate emotions in persuasive efforts. If you watch TV, you have been subjected to Pavlovian techniques. An understanding of these techniques can help you recognize when your emotions are being manipulated by advertisers, politicians, and the media.

Manipulation efforts using Pavlovian conditioning generally involve *evaluative conditioning*. As noted earlier in the chapter, evaluative conditioning consists of efforts to transfer the liking attached to a US to a new CS. The key to this process is simply to manipulate the automatic, subconscious associations that people make in response to various stimuli. Let's look at how this manipulation is done in advertising, business negotiations, and the world of politics.

Classical Conditioning in Advertising

The art of manipulating people's associations has been perfected by the advertising industry, leading Till and Priluck (2000) to comment, "Conditioning of attitudes towards products and brands has become generally accepted and has developed into a unique research stream" (p.

57). Advertisers consistently endeavor to pair the products they are peddling with stimuli that seem likely to elicit positive emotional responses (see **Figure 6.21**). An extensive variety of stimuli are used for this purpose. Products are paired with well-liked celebrity spokespersons; depictions of warm, loving families; beautiful pastoral scenery; cute, cuddly pets; enchanting, rosy-cheeked children; upbeat, pleasant music; and opulent surroundings that reek of wealth. Advertisers also like to pair their products with exciting events, such as the NBA Finals, and cherished symbols, such as flags and the Olympic rings insignia. But, above all else, advertisers like to link their products with sexual imagery and extremely attractive models—especially, glamorous, alluring women (Reichert, 2003; Reichert & Lambiase, 2003).

Advertisers mostly seek to associate their products with stimuli that evoke pleasurable feelings of a general sort, but in some cases they try to create more specific associations. For example, cigarette brands sold mainly to men are frequently paired with tough-looking men in rugged settings to create an association between the cigarettes and masculinity. In contrast, cigarette brands that are mainly marketed to women are paired with images that evoke feelings of femininity. In a similar vein, manufacturers of designer jeans typically seek to forge associations between their products and things that are young, urban, and hip. Advertisers marketing expensive automobiles or platinum credit cards pair their products with symbols of affluence, luxury, and privilege, such as mansions, butlers, and dazzling jewelry.

FIGURE 6.21

Classical conditioning in advertising. Many advertisers attempt to make their products conditioned stimuli that elicit pleasant emotional responses by pairing their products with attractive or popular people or sexual imagery.

© Cengage Learning

© Richard H. Cohen/Corbis

Classical Conditioning in Business Negotiations

In the world of business interactions, two standard practices are designed to get a company's customers to make an association between the company and pleasurable feelings. The first is to take customers out to dinner at fine restaurants. The provision of delicious food and fine wine in a luxurious environment is a powerful unconditioned stimulus that reliably elicits pleasant feelings that are likely to be associated with the host. The second practice is the strategy of entertaining customers at major events, such as concerts and football games. Over the last couple of decades, America's sports arenas have largely been rebuilt with vastly more "luxury skyboxes" to accommodate this business tactic. It reaches its zenith every year at the Super Bowl, where most of the seats go to the guests of Fortune 500 corporations. This practice pairs the host with both pleasant feelings and the excitement of a big event.

It is worth noting that these strategies take advantage of other processes besides classical conditioning. They also make use of the *reciprocity norm*—the social rule that one should pay back in kind what one receives from others (Cialdini, 2007). Thus, wining and dining clients creates a sense of obligation that they should reciprocate their hosts' generosity—presumably in their business dealings.

Classical Conditioning in the World of Politics

Like advertisers, candidates running for election need to influence the attitudes of many people quickly, subtly, and effectively—and they depend on evaluative conditioning to help them do so. For example, have you noticed how politicians show up at an endless variety of pleasant public events (such as the opening of a new mall) that often have nothing to do with their public service? When a sports team wins some sort of championship, local politicians are drawn like flies to the subsequent celebrations. They want to pair themselves with these positive events, so that they are associated with pleasant emotions.

Election campaign ads use the same techniques as commercial ads (except they don't rely much on sexual appeals). Candidates are paired with popular celebrities, wholesome families, pleasant music, and symbols of patriotism. Cognizant of the power of classical conditioning, politicians also exercise great care to ensure that they are not paired with people or events that might trigger negative feelings. For example, in the 2008 presidential election, it was reported that Republican candidate John McCain tried to minimize his public appearances with incumbent President George W. Bush because Bush's popularity ratings were extremely low.

The ultimate political perversion of the principles of classical conditioning probably occurred in Nazi Germany. The Nazis used many propaganda techniques to create prejudice toward Jews and members of other targeted groups (such as Gypsies). One such strategy was the repeated pairing of disgusting, repulsive images with stereotypical pictures of Jews. For example, the Nazis would show alternating pictures of rats or roaches crawling over filthy garbage and stereotypical Jewish faces, so that the two images would become associated in the minds of the viewers. Thus, the German population was conditioned to have negative emotional reactions to Jews and to associate them with vermin subject to extermination. The Nazis reasoned that if people would not hesitate to exterminate rats and roaches, then why not human beings associated with these vermin?

How effective are the efforts to manipulate people's emotions through classical conditioning? It's hard to say. In the real world, these strategies are always used in combination with other persuasive tactics, which creates multiple confounds that make it difficult to assess the impact of the Pavlovian techniques (Walther, Nagengast, & Trasselli, 2005). Laboratory research can eliminate these confounds, but surprisingly little research on these strategies has been published, and virtually all of it has dealt with advertising. The advertising studies suggest that classical conditioning can be effective and leave enduring imprints on consumers' attitudes (Grossman & Till, 1998; Shimp, Stuart, & Engle, 1991; Walther & Grigoriadis, 2003). And research indicates that sexual appeals in advertising are attention getting, likable, and persuasive (Reichert, Heckler, & Jackson, 2001). But a great deal of additional research is needed. Given the monumental sums that advertisers spend using these techniques, it seems reasonable to speculate that individual companies have data on their specific practices to demonstrate their efficacy, but these data are not made available to the public.

What can you do to reduce the extent to which your emotions are manipulated through Pavlovian procedures? Well, you could turn off your radio and TV, close up your magazines, stop your newspaper, disconnect your modem, and withdraw into a media-shielded shell, but that hardly seems realistic for most people. Realistically, the best defense is to make a conscious effort to become more aware of the pervasive attempts to condition your emotions and attitudes. Some research on persuasion suggests that *to be forewarned is to be forearmed* (Pfau et al., 1990). In other words, if you know how media sources try to manipulate you, you should be more resistant to their strategies.

TABLE 6.2 Critical Thinking Skills Discussed in This Application

Skill	Description
Understanding how Pavlovian conditioning can be used to manipulate emotions	The critical thinker understands how stimuli can be paired together to create automatic associations that people may not be aware of.
Developing the ability to detect conditioning procedures used in the media	The critical thinker can recognize Pavlovian conditioning tactics in commercial and political advertisements.

© Cengage Learning

Classical Conditioning

6.1 Describe Pavlov's demonstration of classical conditioning and the key elements in this form of learning.

Classical conditioning explains how a neutral stimulus can acquire the capacity to elicit a response originally elicited by another stimulus. This kind of conditioning was originally described by Ivan Pavlov, who conditioned dogs to salivate in response to the sound of a tone. The key elements in classical conditioning are the unconditioned stimulus (US), the unconditioned response (UR), the conditioned stimulus (CS), and the conditioned response (CR). Classically conditioned responses are said to be elicited.

CLASSICAL CONDITIONING

Summary
An originally neutral stimulus comes to elicit a response that it did not previously elicit.

CS
Tone

US
Meat powder

CR
Salivation
UR

© Cengage Learning

6.2 Clarify how classical conditioning may shape emotions, physiological responses, and attitudes.

Many kinds of everyday responses are regulated through classical conditioning, including emotions. For example, phobias and milder anxiety responses can be acquired when stimuli are paired with traumatic experiences. Even subtle physiological responses such as immune system functioning and sexual arousal respond to classical conditioning. Evaluative conditioning is a special form of classical conditioning that can shape attitudes when neutral stimuli are paired with unconditioned stimuli that elicit positive or negative reactions.

6.3 Describe acquisition, extinction, and spontaneous recovery in classical conditioning.

Acquisition refers to the initial stage of learning a new response tendency. Stimulus contiguity plays a key role in acquisition, but it does not produce conditioning automatically. Extinction is the gradual weakening and disappearance of a conditioned response, which happens when a CS is no longer paired with the US. Spontaneous recovery is the reappearance of an extinguished response after a period of nonexposure to the conditioned stimulus.

6.4 Explain what happens in generalization, discrimination, and higher-order conditioning.

Stimulus generalization occurs when an organism that has learned a response to a specific stimulus responds in the same way to new stimuli that are similar to the original stimulus. Watson and Rayner conducted an influential early study of generalization with a subject known as Little Albert, whose fear response to a rat generalized to a variety of other white, furry objects. The opposite of generalization is discrimination, which involves not responding to stimuli that resemble the original CS. Classical conditioning does not require a genuine unconditioned stimulus, as an already established CS can serve the same role. Higher-order conditioning occurs when a CS functions as if it were a US.

Operant Conditioning

6.5 Explain Skinner's principle of reinforcement, and describe the terminology and procedures in operant research.

Skinner pioneered the study of operant conditioning, working mainly with rats and pigeons in Skinner boxes. Reinforcement occurs when an event following a response increases an organism's tendency to emit that response. The key dependent variable in operant conditioning is the rate of response over time, which is tracked by a cumulative recorder. The results of operant conditioning studies are usually portrayed in graphs. In these graphs, a rapid response rate produces a steep slope, whereas a slow response rate produces a shallow slope.

Speaker
Signal lights
Lever
To food dispenser
Skinner box
Food pellet
Electric grid
To shock generator

© Cengage Learning

6.6 Describe shaping, extinction, generalization, and discrimination in operant conditioning.

Acquisition in operant conditioning often depends on shaping, which involves gradually reinforcing closer and closer approximations of the desired response. Shaping is the key to training animals to perform impressive tricks. In operant conditioning, extinction occurs when reinforcement for a response is terminated and the rate of that response declines. There are variations in resistance to extinction. Operant responses are regulated by discriminative stimuli that are cues for the likelihood of obtaining reinforcers. These stimuli are subject to the same processes of generalization and discrimination that occur in classical conditioning.

6.7 Identify various types of schedules of reinforcement, and discuss their typical effects.

Primary reinforcers are unlearned; secondary reinforcers acquire their reinforcing quality through conditioning. Delayed reinforcement undermines learning. Schedules of reinforcement influence patterns of operant responding. Intermittent schedules of reinforcement include fixed-ratio, variable-ratio, fixed-interval, and variable-interval schedules. Intermittent schedules produce greater resistance to extinction than continuous reinforcement. Ratio schedules tend to yield higher rates of response than interval schedules. Shorter intervals and higher ratios are associated with faster responding.

6.8 Distinguish between positive and negative reinforcement and between escape learning and avoidance learning.

Positive reinforcement occurs when a response is strengthened because it is followed by the presentation of a rewarding stimulus. Negative reinforcement occurs when a response is strengthened because it is followed by the removal of an aversive stimulus. Negative reinforcement plays a key role in both escape learning and avoidance learning. In escape learning, an organism acquires a response that decreases or ends aversive stimulation. In avoidance learning, an organism acquires a response that prevents aversive stimulation by learning a signal that serves as a warning of impending noxious stimulation. The process of avoidance learning may shed light on why phobias are so difficult to eliminate.

6.9 Describe punishment, and assess issues related to punishment as a disciplinary procedure.

Punishment involves aversive consequences that lead to a decline in response strength. Punishment and negative reinforcement are opposite procedures that yield opposite effects on behavior. When used as a disciplinary procedure, physical punishment is associated with poor quality parent-child relations, elevated aggression, delinquency, and behavioral problems. Recent research also suggests that corporal punishment may inhibit cognitive development in children.

Changing Directions in the Study of Conditioning

6.10 Articulate the theoretical significance of conditioned taste aversion and preparedness.

Conditioned taste aversions can be readily acquired even when a lengthy delay occurs between the CS and US. Preparedness appears to explain why people acquire phobias of ancient sources of threat much more readily than modern sources of threat. The findings on conditioned taste aversion and preparedness led to the conclusion that there are biological constraints on conditioning.

6.11 Understand the theoretical implications of research on signal relations and response-outcome relations.

Rescorla's work on signal relations showed that the predictive value of a CS is an influential factor governing classical conditioning. When a response is followed by a desirable outcome, the response is more likely to be strengthened if it appears to have caused the outcome. Noncontingent reinforcement, cognitive biases, and irrational reasoning appear to contribute to superstitious behavior. Studies of signal relations and response-outcome relations suggest that cognitive processes play a larger role in conditioning than originally believed.

Observational Learning

6.12 Explain the nature, importance, and basic processes of observational learning.

In observational learning, an organism is conditioned vicariously by watching a model's conditioning. Both classical and operant conditioning can occur through observational learning. Observational learning is important because it extends the reach of classical and operant conditioning. Observational learning depends on the processes of attention, retention, reproduction, and motivation. The roles of attention and retention illustrate the cognitive nature of observational learning.

Response
Bargain assertively

Rewarding stimulus presented
Good buy on car

© Yuri Arcurs/Shutterstock
© Minerva Studio/Shutterstock
© Oleksiy Maksymenko Photography/Alamy
© Cengage Learning

6.13 Discuss Bandura's research on TV models and aggression and modern research on the effects of media violence.

In a landmark study, Bandura and colleagues demonstrated that exposure to aggressive TV models led to increased aggression in children, especially when the TV models were reinforced for their aggression. In modern research on the effects of media violence, both experimental and correlational studies suggest that violent TV shows, movies, and video games contribute to increased aggression among children and adults. Exposure to media violence also appears to desensitize people to the effects of aggression in the real world.

Reflecting on the Chapter's Themes

6.14 Identify the two unifying themes highlighted in this chapter.

Two of our key themes were especially apparent in our coverage of learning and conditioning. One theme involves the interaction of biology and experience in learning. The other involves the way progress in psychology affects society at large.

PERSONAL APPLICATION
Achieving Self-Control Through Behavior Modification

6.15 Describe how to specify your target behavior and gather baseline data for a self-modification program.

Behavior modification techniques can be used to increase one's self-control. The first step in self-modification is to explicitly specify the overt, measurable target behavior to be increased or decreased. The second step is to gather data about the initial rate of the target response and to identify any typical antecedents or consequences associated with the behavior.

6.16 Discuss how to design, execute, and end a self-modification program.

In designing a program, if you are trying to increase the strength of a response, you'll depend on positive reinforcement contingencies that should be spelled out exactly. A number of strategies can be used to decrease the strength of a response, including reinforcement, control of antecedents, and punishment. In executing your program you should monitor your behavior carefully, resist the temptation to cheat, and decide how and when you will phase out your program.

CRITICAL THINKING APPLICATION
Manipulating Emotions: Pavlov and Persuasion

6.17 Recognize how classical conditioning is used to manipulate emotions.

Evaluative conditioning can be used to manipulate people's emotional responses. Advertisers routinely pair their products with stimuli that seem likely to elicit positive emotions or other specific feelings. The business practice of taking customers out to dinner or to major events also takes advantage of Pavlovian conditioning. Politicians also work to pair themselves with positive events. The best defense against these tactics is to become more aware of efforts to manipulate your emotions.

CS
Products (e.g., jeans)

US
Sexual imagery

CR
Pleasant emotional response
UR

© Cengage Learning

7 Human Memory

PARADOX

Forgetting (of information that is no longer relevant) can enhance memory (for more important information).

If you live in the United States, you've undoubtedly handled thousands of American pennies. Surely, then, you remember what a penny looks like—or do you? Take a look at **Figure 7.1**. Which drawing corresponds to a real penny?

Did you have a hard time selecting the real one? If so, you're not alone. Nickerson and Adams (1979) found that most people can't recognize the real penny in this collection of drawings. And their surprising finding was not a fluke. Undergraduates in England showed even worse memory for British coins (Jones, 1990). How can that be? Why do most of us have so poor a memory for an object we see every day?

Let's try another exercise. A definition of a word follows. It's not a particularly common word, but there's a good chance that you're familiar with it. Try to think of the word.

Definition: Favoritism shown or patronage granted by persons in high office to relatives or close friends.

If you can't think of the word, perhaps you can remember what letter of the alphabet it begins with, or what it sounds like. If so, you're experiencing the *tip-of-the-tongue phenomenon,* in which forgotten information feels like it's just out of reach. In this case, the word you may be reaching for is *nepotism.* You've probably endured the tip-of-the-tongue phenomenon while taking exams. You blank out on a term that you're sure you know. You may feel as if you're on the verge of remembering the term, but you can't quite come up with it. Later, perhaps while you're driving home, the term suddenly comes to you. "Of course," you may say to yourself, "how could I forget that?" That's an interesting question. Clearly, the term was stored in your memory.

As these examples suggest, memory involves more than taking in information and storing it in some mental compartment. In fact, psychologists probing the workings of memory have had to grapple with three enduring questions: (1) How does information get *into* memory? (2) How is information *maintained* in memory? (3) How is information *pulled back out* of memory? These three questions correspond to the three key

FIGURE 7.1

A simple memory test. Nickerson and Adams (1979) presented these fifteen versions of an object most people have seen hundreds or thousands of times and asked, "Which one is correct?" Can you identify the real penny?

SOURCE: Nickerson, R. S., & Adams, M. J. (1979). Long-term memory for a common object. *Cognitive Psychology, 11,* 287–307. Copyright © 1979 by Elsevier Science USA. Reproduced with permission from the publisher.

processes involved in memory (see **Figure 7.2**): *encoding* (getting information in), *storage* (maintaining it), and *retrieval* (getting it out).

Encoding **involves forming a memory code.** For example, when you form a memory code for a word, you might emphasize how it looks, how it sounds, or what it means. Encoding usually requires attention, which is why you may not be able to recall exactly what a penny looks like—most people don't pay much attention to the appearance of a penny. As you'll see throughout this chapter, memory is largely an active process. For the most part, you're unlikely to remember something unless you make a conscious effort to do so. *Storage* **involves maintaining encoded information in memory over time.** Psychologists have focused much of their memory research on trying to identify just what factors help or hinder memory storage. But, as the tip-of-the-tongue phenomenon shows, information storage isn't

PROCESS	ENCODING	STORAGE	RETRIEVAL
Definition	Involves forming a memory code	Involves maintaining encoded information in memory over time	Involves recovering information from memory stores
Analogy to information processing by a computer	Entering data through keyboard	Saving data in file on hard disk	Calling up file and displaying data on monitor

FIGURE 7.2

Three key processes in memory. Memory depends on three sequential processes: encoding, storage, and retrieval. Some theorists have drawn an analogy between these processes and elements of information processing by computers, as depicted here. The analogies for encoding and retrieval work pretty well, but the storage analogy is somewhat misleading. When information is stored on a hard drive, it remains unchanged indefinitely, and you can retrieve an exact copy. As you will learn in this chapter, memory storage is a much more dynamic process. Memories change over time and are rough reconstructions rather than exact copies of past events.

enough to guarantee that you'll remember something. You need to be able to get information out of storage. *Retrieval* **involves recovering information from memory stores.** Research issues concerned with retrieval include the study of how people search memory and why some retrieval strategies are more effective than others.

Most of this chapter is devoted to an examination of memory encoding, storage, and retrieval. These basic processes help explain the ultimate puzzle in the study of memory: why people forget. After our discussion of forgetting, we will take a brief look at the physiological bases of memory. Finally, we will discuss the controversy about whether there are separate memory systems for different types of information. The chapter's Personal Application provides some practical advice on how to improve your memory. The Critical Thinking Application discusses some reasons why memory is less reliable than people assume it to be.

Encoding: Getting Information into Memory

Have you ever been embarrassed because you couldn't remember someone's name? Perhaps you realized only 30 seconds after meeting someone that you had already "forgotten" his or her name. This familiar kind of forgetting frequently results from a failure to form a memory code for the name. When you're introduced to people, you're often busy sizing them up and thinking about what you're going to say. With your attention diverted, names go in one ear and out the other. You don't remember them because they are never encoded for storage.

This problem illustrates that encoding is an important process in memory. In this section, we discuss the role of attention in encoding, types of encoding, and ways to enrich the encoding process.

The Role of Attention

You generally need to pay attention to information if you intend to remember it (Lachter, Forster, & Ruthruff, 2004; Mulligan, 1998). For example, if you sit through a class lecture but pay little attention to it, you're unlikely to remember much of what the professor had to say. *Attention* **involves focusing awareness on a narrowed range of stimuli or events.** Psychologists routinely refer to "selective attention," but the words are really redundant. Attention *is* selection of input. Selective attention is critical to everyday functioning. If your attention were distributed equally among all stimulus inputs, life would be utter chaos. If you weren't able to filter out most of the potential stimulation around you, you wouldn't be able to read a book, converse with a friend, or even carry on a coherent train of thought.

The importance of attention to memory is apparent when participants are asked to focus their attention on two or more inputs simultaneously. Studies indicate that when participants are forced to divide their attention between memory encoding and some other task, large reductions in memory performance are seen (Craik, 2001; Craik & Kester, 2000). Actually, the negative effects of divided attention are not limited to memory. Divided attention can have a negative impact on the performance of quite a variety of tasks, especially when the tasks are complex or unfamiliar (Pashler, Johnston, & Ruthruff, 2001).

Although people tend to think that they can multitask with no deterioration in performance, research suggests that the human brain can effectively handle only one attention-consuming task at a time (Lien, Ruthruff, & Johnston, 2006). When people multitask, they are really switching their attention back and forth among tasks, rather than processing them simultaneously. That may be fine in many circumstances, but the cost of divided attention does have profound implications for the advisability of driving while conversing on a cell phone. Carefully controlled research clearly demonstrates that cell phone conversations undermine people's driving performance, even when hands-free phones are used (Horrey & Wickens, 2006; Kass, Cole, & Stanny, 2007; Strayer, Drews, & Crouch, 2006).

A recent study shed some light on why cell phone conversations are more distracting to drivers than conversations with passengers. The research showed that passengers adapt their conversation to the demands of the traffic and provide assistance to the driver (Drews, Pasupathi, & Strayer, 2008). In other words, when passengers see that traffic is heavy or that the driving task has become complicated, they reduce the rate and complexity of their communication and try to help the driver navigate through the situation. As distracting as cell phone conversations are, recent research indicates that texting while driving is substantially more dangerous (Drews et al., 2009).

© Elena Elisseeva/Shutterstock

Levels of Processing

PSYKTREK SIM5, 6a

Attention is critical to the encoding of memories. But not all attention is created equal. You can attend to things in different ways, focusing on different aspects of the stimulus input. According to some theorists, these qualitative differences in *how* people attend to information are the main factors influencing how much they remember. For example, Fergus Craik and Robert Lockhart (1972) argue that different rates of forgetting occur because some methods of encoding create more durable memory codes than others.

Craik and Lockhart propose that incoming information can be processed at different levels. For instance, they maintain that in dealing with verbal information, people engage in three progressively deeper levels of processing: structural, phonemic, and semantic encoding (see **Figure 7.3**). *Structural encoding* is relatively shallow processing that emphasizes the physical structure of the stimulus. For example, if words are flashed on a screen, structural encoding registers such things as how the words are printed (capital, lowercase, and so on) or their length (how many letters). Further analysis may result in *phonemic encoding,* which emphasizes what a word sounds like. Phonemic encoding involves naming or saying (perhaps silently) the words. Finally, *semantic encoding* emphasizes the *meaning* of verbal input; it involves thinking about the objects and actions the words represent. **Levels-of-processing theory** proposes that deeper levels of processing result in longer-lasting memory codes.

In one experimental test of levels-of-processing theory, Craik and Tulving (1975) compared the durability of structural, phonemic, and semantic encoding. They directed

Level of processing	Type of encoding	Example of questions used to elicit appropriate encoding
Shallow processing	*Structural encoding:* emphasizes the physical structure of the stimulus	Is the word written in capital letters?
Intermediate processing	*Phonemic encoding:* emphasizes what a word sounds like	Does the word rhyme with weight?
Deep processing	*Semantic encoding:* emphasizes the meaning of verbal input	Would the word fit in the sentence: "He met a _____ on the street"?

Depth of processing

© Cengage Learning

FIGURE 7.3

Levels-of-processing theory. According to Craik and Lockhart (1972), structural, phonemic, and semantic encoding—which can be elicited by questions such as those shown on the right in the figure—involve progressively deeper levels of processing.

subjects' attention to particular aspects of briefly presented stimulus words by asking them questions about various characteristics of the words (examples are in **Figure 7.3**). The questions were designed to engage the participants in different levels of processing. After responding to 60 words, the participants received an unexpected test of their memory for the words. As predicted, the subjects' recall was low after structural encoding, notably better after phonemic encoding, and highest after semantic encoding. The hypothesis that deeper processing leads to enhanced memory has been replicated in many studies (Craik, 2002; Lockhart & Craik, 1990). Levels-of-processing theory has been enormously influential; it has shown that memory involves more than just storage and has inspired a great deal of research on how processing considerations affect memory (Roediger, Gallo, & Geraci, 2002).

Enriching Encoding

PsykTrek 6a

Structural, phonemic, and semantic encoding are not the only processes involved in forming memory codes. Other dimensions that can enrich the encoding process and thereby improve memory include elaboration, visual imagery, and motivation to remember.

ELABORATION

Semantic encoding can often be enhanced through a process called elaboration. *Elaboration* is linking a stimulus to other information at the time of encoding. For example, let's say you read that phobias are often caused by classical conditioning, and you apply this idea to your own fear of spiders. In doing so, you are engaging in elaboration. The additional connections created by elaboration usually help people remember information. Differences in elaboration can help explain why different approaches to semantic processing result in varied amounts of retention (Toyota & Kikuchi, 2004, 2005; Willoughby, Motz, & Wood, 1997).

VISUAL IMAGERY

PsykTrek 6a

Imagery—the creation of visual images to represent the words to be remembered—can also be used to enrich encoding. Of course, some words are easier to create images for than others. If you were asked to remember the word *juggler,* you could readily form an image of someone juggling balls. However, if you were asked to remember the word *truth,* you would probably have more difficulty forming a suitable image. The difference is that *juggler* refers to a concrete object whereas *truth* refers to an abstract concept. Allan Paivio (1969) points out that it is easier to form images of concrete objects than of abstract concepts. He believes that this ease of image formation affects memory. For example, in one study he found that subjects given pairs of words to remember showed better recall for high-imagery than low-imagery pairings (see **Figure 7.4**), demonstrating that visual imagery enriches encoding (Paivio, Smythe, & Yuille, 1968). Similar results were observed in a more recent study that controlled for additional confounding factors (Paivio, Khan, & Begg, 2000).

According to Paivio (1986, 2007), imagery facilitates memory because it provides a second kind of memory code, and two codes are better than one. His *dual-coding theory* **holds that memory is enhanced by forming both semantic and visual codes, since either can lead to recall.** Although some aspects of his theory have been questioned, it's clear that the use of mental imagery can enhance memory in many situations (McCauley, Eskes, & Moscovitch, 1996). The value of visual imagery demonstrates once again that encoding plays a critical role in memory.

MOTIVATION TO REMEMBER

Another factor that appears to influence encoding effectiveness is one's motivation to remember (MTR) at the time of encoding. When MTR is high at the time of encoding—typically because the information is perceived to be important—people are more likely to exert extra effort to attend to and organize information in ways that facilitate future recall. In a recent investigation, participants were asked to memorize facts about six

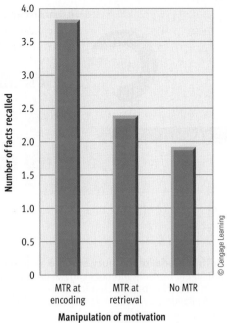

FIGURE 7.4

The effect of visual imagery on retention.
Paivio, Smythe, and Yuille (1968) asked
subjects to learn a list of sixteen pairs of
words. They manipulated whether the words
were concrete, high-imagery words or abstract, low-imagery words. In terms of imagery potential, the list contained four types of
pairings: high-high (*juggler-dress*), high-low
(*letter-effort*), low-high (*duty-hotel*), and
low-low (*quality-necessity*). The impact of
imagery was quite evident. The best recall
was of high-high pairings, and the worst
recall was of low-low pairings.

FIGURE 7.5

**The effect of motivation to remember
(MTR) on subsequent recall.** Participants'
motivation to remember was increased at
the time of encoding, at the time of retrieval, or not at all in a control condition.
Raising MTR at the time of encoding increased recall, but raising MTR at the time
of retrieval did not.

SOURCE: Adapted from Kassam, K. S., Gilbert,
D. T., Swencionis, J. K., & Wilson, T. D. (2009).
Misconceptions of memory: The Scooter Libby
effect. *Psychological Science, 20*(5), 551–552.
Copyright © 2009 Sage Publications. Reprinted by
permission of SAGE Publications.

people presented in photos (Kassam et al., 2009). Motivation to remember was manipulated, either at the time of encoding or at the time of retrieval, by offering participants a
financial bonus for every fact they recalled about a specific target person. The results
showed that increasing MTR at the time of encoding led to greater recall, whereas increasing MTR at the time of retrieval had little effect (see **Figure 7.5**). Thus, encoding
processes can be enhanced by strong motivation. But encoding is only one of the three
key processes in memory. We turn next to the process of storage, which for many people
is virtually synonymous with memory.

Storage: Maintaining Information in Memory

In their efforts to understand memory storage, theorists have historically related it to the
technologies of their age (Roediger, 1980). One of the earliest models used to explain
memory storage was the wax tablet. Both Aristotle and Plato compared memory to a
block of wax that differed in size and hardness for various individuals. Remembering,
according to this analogy, was like stamping an impression into the wax. As long as the
image remained in the wax, the memory would remain intact.

Modern theories reflect the technological advances of the 20th century. For example,
many theories formulated at the dawn of the computer age drew an analogy between
information storage by computers and information storage in human memory (Atkin-

Sensory memory · Short-term memory · Long-term memory

Rehearsal

Storage

Sensory input · Attention

Retrieval

© Cengage Learning

FIGURE 7.6

The Atkinson and Shiffrin model of memory storage. Atkinson and Shiffrin (1971) proposed that memory is made up of three information stores. *Sensory memory* can hold a large amount of information just long enough (a fraction of a second) for a small portion of it to be selected for longer storage. *Short-term memory* has a limited capacity, and unless aided by rehearsal, its storage duration is brief. *Long-term memory* can store an apparently unlimited amount of information for indeterminate periods.

son & Shiffrin, 1968, 1971; Broadbent, 1958; Waugh & Norman, 1965). The main contribution of these *information-processing theories* was to subdivide memory into three separate memory stores (Estes, 1999). According to the most influential model (Atkinson & Shiffrin, 1968, 1971), incoming information passes through two temporary storage buffers—the sensory store and short-term store—before it is transferred into a long-term store (see **Figure 7.6**). Like the wax tablet before it, the information-processing model of memory is a metaphor; the three memory stores are not viewed as anatomical structures in the brain but rather as functionally distinct types of memory.

Sensory Memory

PsykTrek 6b

Sensory memory **preserves information in its original sensory form for a brief time, usually only a fraction of a second.** Sensory memory allows the sensation of a visual pattern, sound, or touch to linger for a brief moment after the sensory stimulation is over. In the case of vision, people really perceive an *afterimage* rather than the actual stimulus. You can demonstrate the existence of afterimages for yourself by rapidly moving a light in circles in the dark. If you move the light fast enough, you should see a complete circle even though the light source is only a single point (see the adjacent photo). The sensory memory preserves the sensory image long enough for you to perceive a continuous circle rather than separate points of light.

The brief preservation of sensations in sensory memory gives you additional time to try to recognize stimuli. However, you'd better take advantage of sensory storage immediately, because it doesn't last long. In a classic experiment, George Sperling (1960) demonstrated that the memory trace in the visual sensory store decays in about one-quarter of a second. There is some debate about whether stimulus persistence really involves *memory storage* (Nairne, 2003). Some theorists view it as an artifact of the perceptual processing of incoming stimuli that is attributable to excitatory feedback in specific neural circuits (Francis, 1999). In other words, stimulus persistence may be more like an echo than a memory.

Because the image of the sparkler persists briefly in sensory memory, when the sparkler is moved fast enough, the blending of afterimages causes people to see a continuous stream of light instead of a succession of individual points.

Short-Term Memory

PsykTrek 6b

Short-term memory (STM) **is a limited-capacity store that can maintain unrehearsed information for up to about 20 seconds.** In contrast, information stored in long-term memory may last weeks, months, or years. Actually, you can maintain information in your short-term store for longer than 20 seconds. How? Primarily, by engaging in *rehearsal*—**the process of repetitively verbalizing or thinking about information.** You surely have used the rehearsal process on many occasions. For instance, when you get a phone number from an information operator, you probably recite it over and over until you can dial the number. Rehearsal keeps recycling the information through your short-term memory. In theory, this recycling could go on indefinitely, but in reality something eventually distracts you and breaks the rehearsal loop.

DURABILITY OF STORAGE

PsykTrek 6b

Without rehearsal, information in short-term memory is lost in 10 to 20 seconds (Nairne, 2003). This rapid loss was demonstrated in a study by Peterson and Peterson (1959). They measured how long undergraduates could remember three consonants if they couldn't rehearse them. To prevent rehearsal, the Petersons required the students to count backward by threes from the time the consonants were presented until they saw a light that signaled the recall test. Participants' recall accuracy was pretty dismal after only 15 seconds. Other approaches to the issue have suggested that the typical duration of STM storage may even be shorter (Baddely, 1986). Theorists originally believed that the loss of information from short-term memory was attributable purely to time-related *decay* of memory traces, but follow-up research showed that *interference* from competing material also contributes (Lewandowsky, Duncan, & Brown, 2004; Nairne, 2002).

CAPACITY OF STORAGE

PsykTrek 6b

Short-term memory is also limited in the number of items it can hold. The small capacity of STM was pointed out by George Miller (1956) in a famous paper called "The Magical Number Seven, Plus or Minus Two: Some Limits on Our Capacity for Processing Information." Miller noticed that people could recall only about seven items in tasks that required the use of STM. When short-term memory is filled to capacity, the insertion of new information "bumps out" some of the information currently in STM. The limited capacity of STM constrains people's ability to perform tasks in which they need to mentally juggle various pieces of information (Baddeley & Hitch, 1974).

The capacity of short-term memory may even be less than widely assumed. Nelson Cowan (2005, 2010) cites evidence indicating that the capacity of STM is *four* plus or minus *one*. The consensus on the capacity of STM seems to be moving toward this smaller estimate (Lustig et al., 2009). According to Cowan, the capacity of STM has historically been overestimated because researchers have often failed to take steps to prevent covert rehearsal or *chunking* by participants.

It has long been known that people can increase the capacity of their short-term memory by combining stimuli into larger, possibly higher-order units, called *chunks* (Simon, 1974). **A *chunk* is a group of familiar stimuli stored as a single unit.** You can demonstrate the effect of chunking by asking someone to recall a sequence of 12 letters grouped in the following way:

FB - INB - CC - IAIB - M

As you read the letters aloud, pause at the hyphens. Your subject will probably attempt to remember each letter separately because there are no obvious groups or chunks. But a string of 12 letters is too long for STM, so errors are likely. Now present the same string of letters to another person, but place the pauses in the following locations:

FBI - NBC - CIA - IBM

The letters now form four familiar chunks that should occupy only four slots in short-term memory, resulting in successful recall (Bower & Springston, 1970).

Reality Check

Misconception

The capacity of short-term memory (STM) is seven plus or minus two.

Reality

Calling this assertion a misconception is a little harsh, as this has been the conventional wisdom since the 1950s and there is room for argument on the matter. However, in the last decade or so researchers using more sophisticated methods have been chipping away at this maxim. The consensus among memory experts has shifted toward the belief that the capacity of STM is four plus or minus one.

To successfully chunk the letters I B M, a subject must first recognize these letters as a familiar unit. This familiarity has to be stored somewhere in long-term memory. Thus, in this case information was transferred from long-term into short-term memory. This type of transfer is not unusual. People routinely draw information out of their long-term memory banks to evaluate and understand information that they are working with in short-term memory.

SHORT-TERM MEMORY AS "WORKING MEMORY"

PsykTrek 6b

Research eventually suggested that short-term memory involves more than a simple rehearsal buffer, as originally believed. The findings prompted Alan Baddeley (1989, 1992, 2001, 2007) to propose a more complex model of short-term memory that characterizes it as *working memory*—**a modular system for temporary storage and manipulation of information.** Baddeley's model of working memory consists of four components (see **Figure 7.7**). The first component is the *phonological loop* that represented all of STM in earlier models. This component is at work when you use recitation to temporarily hold onto a phone number. Baddeley (2003) believes that the phonological loop evolved to foster the acquisition of language. The second component in working memory is a *visuospatial sketchpad* that permits people to temporarily hold and manipulate visual images. This component is at work when you try to mentally rearrange the furniture in your bedroom. The third component is the *central executive* system. It controls the deployment of attention, switching the focus of attention and dividing attention as needed. The fourth component is the *episodic buffer,* a temporary, limited capacity store that allows the various components of working memory to integrate information and serves as an interface between working memory and long-term memory.

The two key characteristics that originally defined short-term memory—small capacity and short storage duration—are still present in the concept of working memory. However, Baddeley's model accounts for evidence that STM handles a greater variety of functions and depends on more complicated processes than previously thought.

Baddeley's model of working memory has generated an enormous volume of research. For example, research has shown that people vary in how well they can juggle information in their working memory while fending off distractions (Engle, 2001). *Working memory capacity (WMC)* **refers to one's ability to hold and manipulate information in conscious attention.** WMC is a stable personal trait (Unsworth et al., 2005) that appears to be influenced to a considerable degree by heredity (Kremen et al., 2007). That said, WMC can be temporarily reduced by situational factors such as pressure to perform or excessive worry (Gimmig et al., 2006; Hayes, Hirsch, & Matthews, 2008).

Variations in working memory capacity correlate positively with measures of high-level cognitive abilities, such as reading comprehension, complex reasoning, and even intelligence (Conway, Kane, & Engle, 2003; Shelton et al., 2009, 2010). This finding has led some theorists to conclude that working memory capacity is critical to complex cognition and intelligence (Lepine, Barrouillet, & Camos, 2005). Variations in WMC also appear to influence musical ability, as reading music while playing an instrument taxes working memory capacity (Meinz & Hambrick, 2010). Some theorists argue that increases in WMC tens of thousands of years ago were crucial to the evolution of complex cognitive processes and creativity in humans (Coolidge & Wynn, 2009). Their analyses are highly speculative, but they highlight the profound importance of working memory capacity (Balter, 2010).

Long-Term Memory

PsykTrek 6b

Long-term memory (LTM) **is an unlimited capacity store that can hold information over lengthy periods of time.** Unlike sensory and short-term memory,

Alan Baddeley

"The concept of working memory proposes that a dedicated system maintains and stores information in the short term, and that this system underlies human thought processes."

FIGURE 7.7

Short-term memory as working memory. This diagram depicts the revised model of the short-term store proposed by Alan Baddeley. According to Baddeley (2001), working memory includes four components: a phonological loop, a visuospatial sketchpad, a central executive system, and an episodic buffer.

which decay rapidly, LTM can store information indefinitely. Long-term memories are durable. Some information may remain in LTM across an entire lifetime.

One point of view is that all information stored in long-term memory is stored there *permanently*. According to this view, forgetting occurs only because people sometimes cannot retrieve needed information from LTM. To draw an analogy, imagine that memories are stored in LTM like marbles in a barrel. According to this view, none of the marbles ever leak out. When you forget, you just aren't able to dig out the right marble, but it's there—somewhere. An alternative point of view assumes that some memories stored in LTM do vanish forever. According to this view, the barrel is leaky and some of the marbles roll out, never to return.

"The matters about which I'm being questioned, Your Honor, are all things I should have included in my long-term memory but which I mistakenly inserted in my short-term memory."

The existence of *flashbulb memories* is one piece of evidence that has been cited to support the notion that LTM storage may be permanent. At first glance, *flashbulb memories*, **which are unusually vivid and detailed recollections of momentous events,** provide striking examples of seemingly permanent storage (Brown & Kulik, 1977). Many American adults, for instance, can remember exactly where they were, what they were doing, and how they felt in 1963 when they learned that President John F. Kennedy had been shot. You may have a similar recollection related to the 1997 death of Princess Diana or the terrorist attacks that took place in New York and Washington, DC on September 11, 2001.

Does the evidence on flashbulb memories provide adequate support for the idea that LTM storage is permanent? No. research eventually showed that flashbulb memories are neither as accurate nor as special as once believed (Hirst et al., 2009; Schmolck, Buffalo, & Squire, 2000). Like other memories, they become less detailed and complete with time and are often inaccurate (Cubelli & Della Sala, 2008; Talarico & Rubin, 2009). Recent research suggests that it is not extraordinary accuracy or longevity that distinguish flashbulb memories. Rather, what makes them special is that people subjectively feel that these memories are exceptionally vivid, that they have exceptional confidence (albeit misplaced) in their memories' accuracy, and that more emotional intensity is attached to these recollections (Talarico & Rubin, 2003, 2007). So, perhaps flashbulb memories are "special," but not in the way originally envisioned.

Returning to the question at hand, the research findings on flashbulb memories clearly conflict with the hypothesis that memory storage is permanent. Although the possibility cannot be ruled out completely, there is no convincing evidence that memories are stored away permanently and that forgetting is all a matter of retrieval failure (Payne & Blackwell, 1998; Schacter, 1996).

Flashbulb memories are vivid and detailed recollections of momentous events. For example, many people will long remember exactly where they were and how they felt when they learned about the terrorist attacks on the World Trade Center.

Retrieval: Getting Information out of Memory

KEY LEARNING GOALS

7.6 Explain the tip-of-the-tongue phenomenon, and understand how context cues and schemas can influence retrieval.

7.7 Summarize research on the reconstructive nature of memory, and apply the concept of source monitoring to everyday memory errors.

Entering information into long-term memory is a worthy goal, but it is an insufficient one if you can't get the information back out again when you need it. Fortunately, recall often occurs without much effort. But occasionally a planned search of LTM is necessary. For instance, imagine that you were asked to recall the names of all 50 states in the United States. You would probably conduct your memory search systematically, recalling states in alphabetical order or by geographical location. Although this example is rather simple, retrieval is a complex process, as you'll see in this section.

Using Cues to Aid Retrieval

At the beginning of this chapter we discussed the *tip-of-the-tongue phenomenon*—the temporary inability to remember something you know, accompanied by a feeling that it's just out of reach. The tip-of-the-tongue phenomenon is a common experience that happens about once a week, although its occurrence increases with age (A. Brown, 1991; Burke & Shafto, 2004). It clearly represents a failure in retrieval. However, the exact mechanisms underlying this failure are the subject of debate. A number of explanations have been proposed for this phenomenon (Schwartz, 1999, 2002).

Fortunately, memories can often be jogged with *retrieval cues*—stimuli that help gain access to memories—such as hints, related information, or partial recollections. This was apparent when Roger Brown and David McNeill (1966) studied the tip-of-the-tongue phenomenon. They gave participants definitions of obscure words and asked them to think of the words. Our example at the beginning of the chapter (the definition for *nepotism*) was taken from their study. Brown and McNeill found that subjects groping for obscure words were correct in guessing the first letter of the missing word 57% of the time. This figure far exceeds chance and shows that partial recollections are often headed in the right direction.

Reinstating the Context of an Event

Let's test your memory: What did you have for breakfast two days ago? If you can't immediately answer, you might begin by imagining yourself sitting at the breakfast table (or wherever you usually have breakfast). Trying to recall an event by putting yourself back in the context in which it occurred involves working with *context cues* to aid retrieval.

Context cues often facilitate the retrieval of information (Smith, 1988). Most people have experienced the effects of context cues on many occasions. For instance, when people return after a number of years to a place where they used to live, they are typically flooded with long-forgotten memories. Or consider how often you have gone from one room to another to get something (scissors, perhaps), only to discover that you can't remember what you were after. However, when you return to the first room (the original context), you suddenly recall what it was ("Of course, the scissors!"). These examples illustrate the potentially powerful effects of context cues on memory.

The value of reinstating the context of an event may account for how hypnosis *occasionally* stimulates eyewitness recall in legal investigations (Meyer, 1992). The hypnotist usually attempts to reinstate the context of the event by telling the witness to imagine being at the scene of the crime once again. Although it is widely believed by

---

Concept Check 7.1

Comparing the Memory Stores

Check your understanding of the three memory stores by filling in the blanks in the table below. The column on the left lists three features of the memory stores that can be compared. The answers can be found in the back of the book in Appendix A.

Feature	Sensory memory	Short-term memory	Long-term memory
Main encoding format	*copy of input*		*largely semantic*
Storage capacity	*limited*		
Storage duration		*10–20 seconds*	

the general public that hypnosis can help people remember things that they would not normally recall (Green, 2003), extensive research has failed to demonstrate that hypnosis can reliably enhance retrieval (Mazzoni, Heap, & Scoboria, 2010). In fact, the notion that hypnotists can use age regression to recover long-lost memories by instructing subjects to go back in time and relive past events has been discredited (Mazzoni, Heap, & Scoboria, 2010). Quite to the contrary, research suggests that hypnosis often increases individuals' tendency to report *incorrect* information (Lynn, Neuschatz, & Fite, 2002; Mazzoni & Lynn, 2007). Moreover, popular beliefs about the supposed beneficial effects of hypnosis on memory often lead hypnotized subjects to feel overconfident about the accuracy of their recall (Scoboria et al., 2002).

Relying on Schemas

PsykTrek 6b

Imagine that you've just visited Professor Smith's office, which is shown in the adjacent photo. Take a brief look at the photo and then cover it up. Now pretend that you want to describe Professor Smith's office to a friend. Write down what you saw in the office (the picture).

After you finish, compare your description with the picture. Chances are, your description will include elements—filing cabinets, for instance—that were *not* in the office. This common phenomenon demonstrates how people rely on *schemas* in trying to retrieve memories.

A *schema* is an organized cluster of knowledge about a particular object or event abstracted from previous experience with the object or event. For example, college students have schemas for what professors' offices are like. When Brewer and Treyens (1981) tested the recall of thirty subjects who had briefly visited the office shown in the photo, most subjects recalled the desks and chairs. Few, though, recalled the wine bottle or the picnic basket, which aren't part of a typical office schema. Moreover, nine subjects in the Brewer and Treyens study falsely recalled that the office contained books. Perhaps you made the same mistake.

These results and other studies (Tuckey & Brewer, 2003) suggest that *people are more likely to remember things that are consistent with their schemas than things that are not.* Although this principle seems applicable much of the time, the inverse is also true: *People sometimes exhibit better recall of things that violate their schema-based expectations* (Koriat, Goldsmith, & Pansky, 2000; Neuschatz et al., 2002). If information really clashes with a schema, it may attract extra attention and deeper processing and thus become more memorable. For example, if you saw a slot machine in a professor's office, you would probably remember it. In short, the impact of schemas on memory can be difficult to predict, but it is apparent that schemas help to shape recall of events (Brewer, 2000).

Professor Smith's office is shown in this photo. Follow the instructions in the text to learn how Brewer and Treyens (1981) used it in a study of memory.

© Courtesy of W. F. Brewer

Reality Check

Misconception
Hypnosis can be used to retrieve memories of forgotten events.

Reality
For over a century, advocates of hypnosis have claimed that it can enhance recall but the empirical evidence is quite clear. Hypnosis does not improve memory retrieval. Quite to the contrary, hypnotized subjects are more likely than others to get things wrong—and to feel overconfident about their memories.

Reconstructing Memories

When you retrieve information from long-term memory, you're not able to pull up a "mental videotape" that provides an exact replay of the past. To some extent, your memories are sketchy *reconstructions* of the past that may be distorted and may include details that did not actually occur (Roediger, Wheeler, & Rajaram, 1993).

Elizabeth Loftus

"One reason most of us, as jurors, place so much faith in eyewitness testimony is that we are unaware of how many factors influence its accuracy."

Research by Elizabeth Loftus (1979, 1992, 2005) and others on the *misinformation effect* has shown that reconstructive distortions show up frequently in eyewitness testimony. **The *misinformation effect* occurs when participants' recall of an event they witnessed is altered by introducing misleading postevent information.** For example, in one study Loftus and Palmer (1974) showed participants a videotape of an automobile accident. Participants were then "grilled" as if they were providing eyewitness testimony, and biasing information was introduced. Some subjects were asked, "How fast were the cars going when they *hit* each other?" Other subjects were asked, "How fast were the cars going when they *smashed into* each other?" A week later, participants' recall of the accident was tested. They were asked whether they remembered seeing any broken glass in the accident (there was none). Subjects who had earlier been asked about the cars *smashing into* each other were more likely to "recall" broken glass. Why would they add this detail to their reconstructions of the accident? Probably because broken glass is consistent with their schema for cars *smashing* together (see **Figure 7.8**).

The misinformation effect, which has been replicated in "countless studies," is a remarkably reliable phenomenon that "challenged prevailing views about the validity of memory" (Zaragoza, Belli, & Payment, 2007, p. 37). Indeed, the effect is so difficult to escape, even subjects who have been forewarned can be swayed by postevent misinformation (Loftus, 2005). Consider, for instance, a recent study by Chan, Thomas, and Bulevich (2009). The investigators noted that in real-life situations, eyewitnesses are often immediately asked to systematically recall an event before there is much opportunity to introduce misinformation. In contrast, the typical misinformation experiment does not include a recall effort prior to the exposure to misinformation. Chan and colleagues reasoned that immediate recall should render an eyewitness less susceptible to misinformation. Surprisingly, however, immediate recall not only failed to reduce the misinformation effect, it actually increased the impact of misinformation!

Other research on the reconstructive nature of memory has demonstrated that the simple act of retelling a story can introduce inaccuracies into memory (Marsh, 2007). When people retell a story, they may streamline it, embellish the facts, exaggerate their role, and so forth. In such retellings, people may be aware that they are being a little loose with the facts (Marsh & Tversky, 2004). However, what is interesting is that their intentional distortions can reshape their subsequent recollections of the same events. Somehow, the "real" story and the storyteller's "spin" on it probably begin to blend imperceptibly. So, even routine retellings of events can contribute to the malleability of memory.

Source Monitoring

The misinformation effect appears to be due, *in part,* to the unreliability of source monitoring (Mitchell & Johnson, 2000). **Source monitoring is the process of making inferences about the origins of memories.** Marcia Johnson and her colleagues maintain that

FIGURE 7.8

The misinformation effect. In an experiment by Loftus and Palmer (1974), participants who were asked leading questions in which cars were described as *hitting* or *smashing* each other were prone to recall the same accident differently one week later, demonstrating the reconstructive nature of memory.

Leading question asked during witness testimony	Possible schemas activated	Response of subjects asked one week later, "Did you see any broken glass?" (There was none.)
"About how fast were the cars going when they hit each other?"		"Yes"—14%
"About how fast were the cars going when they smashed into each other?"		"Yes"—32%

© Cengage Learning

source monitoring is a crucial facet of memory retrieval that contributes to many of the mistakes that people make in reconstructing their experiences (Johnson, 1996, 2006; Johnson, Hashtroudi, & Lindsay, 1993). According to Johnson, memories are not tagged with labels that specify their sources. Thus, when people pull up specific memory records, they have to make decisions *at the time of retrieval* about where the memories came from (example: "Did I read that in the *New York Times* or *Rolling Stone*?"). Much of the time, these decisions are so easy and automatic, people make them without being consciously aware of the source-monitoring process. In other instances, however, they may consciously struggle to pinpoint the source of a memory. **A *source-monitoring error* occurs when a memory derived from one source is misattributed to another source.** For example, you might attribute something that your roommate said to your psychology professor, or something you heard on *Dr. Phil* to your psychology textbook. Inaccurate memories that reflect source-monitoring errors may seem quite compelling. People often feel quite confident about the authenticity of their assertions even though the recollections really are inaccurate (Lampinen, Neuschatz, & Payne, 1999).

Source-monitoring errors appear to be commonplace and may shed light on many interesting memory phenomena. For instance, in studies of eyewitness suggestibility, some subjects have gone so far as to insist that they "remember" seeing something that was only verbally suggested to them. Most theories have a hard time explaining how people can have memories of events that they never actually saw or experienced. But this paradox doesn't seem all that perplexing when it is explained as a source-monitoring error (Lindsay et al., 2004).

Reality Check

Misconception
Memory is like a mental videotape that can provide faithful reproductions of past events.

Reality
Countless studies in recent decades have demonstrated that memories are incomplete, distorted, fuzzy reconstructions of past events. The adjectives that best describe memory are not *exact* or *accurate*, but *fragile, fallible,* and *malleable.*

Forgetting: When Memory Lapses

KEY LEARNING GOALS

7.8 Describe Ebbinghaus's forgetting curve and three measures of retention.

7.9 Understand the potential causes of forgetting.

7.10 Summarize evidence on the controversy regarding recovered memories of childhood sexual abuse.

Forgetting gets a "bad press" that it may not deserve. People tend to view forgetting as a failure, weakness, or deficiency in cognitive processing. Although forgetting important information *can* be frustrating, some memory theorists argue that forgetting is actually adaptive. How so? Imagine how cluttered your memory would be if you never forgot anything. According to Daniel Schacter (1999), people need to forget information that is no longer relevant, such as out-of-date phone numbers, discarded passwords, and lines that were memorized for a tenth-grade play. Forgetting can reduce competition among memories that can cause confusion.

Although forgetting may be adaptive in the long run, the fundamental question of memory research remains: Why do people forget information that they would like to remember? There isn't one simple answer to this question. Research has shown that forgetting can be caused by defects in encoding, storage, retrieval, or some combination of these processes.

How Quickly We Forget: Ebbinghaus's Forgetting Curve

PsykTrek 6d

The first person to conduct scientific studies of forgetting was Hermann Ebbinghaus. He published a series of insightful memory studies way back in 1885. Ebbinghaus studied only one subject—himself. To give himself lots of new material to memorize, he invented *nonsense syllables*—consonant-vowel-consonant arrangements that do not correspond to words (such as BAF, XOF, VIR, and MEQ). He wanted to work with meaningless materials that would be uncontaminated by his previous learning.

Ebbinghaus was a remarkably dedicated researcher. For instance, in one study he went through over 14,000 practice repetitions, as he tirelessly memorized 420 lists of nonsense syllables (Slamecka, 1985). He tested his memory of these lists after various time intervals. **Figure 7.9** on the next page shows what he found. This diagram, called a

Hermann Ebbinghaus
"Left to itself every mental content gradually loses its capacity for being revived. . . . Facts crammed at examination time soon vanish."

FIGURE 7.9

Ebbinghaus's forgetting curve for nonsense syllables. From his experiments on himself, Ebbinghaus (1885) concluded that forgetting is extremely rapid immediately after the original learning and then levels off. Although this generalization remains true, subsequent research has shown that forgetting curves for nonsense syllables are unusually steep.

forgetting curve, **graphs retention and forgetting over time.** Ebbinghaus's forgetting curve shows a sharp drop in retention during the first few hours after the nonsense syllables were memorized. He forgot more than 60% of the syllables in less than 9 hours! Thus, he concluded that most forgetting occurs very rapidly after learning something.

That's a depressing conclusion. What is the point of memorizing information if you're going to forget it all right away? Fortunately, subsequent research showed that Ebbinghaus's forgetting curve was unusually steep (Postman, 1985). Forgetting isn't usually as swift or as extensive as Ebbinghaus thought. One problem was that he was working with such meaningless material. When participants memorize more meaningful material, such as prose or poetry, forgetting curves aren't nearly as steep. Studies of how well people recall their high school classmates suggest that forgetting curves for autobiographical information are much shallower (Bahrick, 2000). Also, different methods of measuring forgetting yield varied estimates of how quickly people forget. This variation underscores the importance of the methods used to measure forgetting, the matter we turn to next.

Measures of Forgetting

PSYKTREK SIM5, SIM6, 6d

To study forgetting empirically, psychologists need to be able to measure it precisely. Measures of forgetting inevitably measure retention as well. *Retention* **refers to the proportion of material retained (remembered).** In studies of forgetting, the results may be reported in terms of the amount forgotten or the amount retained. In these studies, the *retention interval* is the length of time between the presentation of materials to be remembered and the measurement of forgetting. Psychologists use three methods to measure forgetting/retention: recall, recognition, and relearning (Lockhart, 1992).

Who is the current U.S. secretary of state? What movie won the Academy Award for best picture last year? These questions involve recall measures of retention. **A** *recall measure* **requires participants to reproduce information on their own without any cues.** If you were to take a recall test on a list of 25 words you had memorized, you would simply be told to write down on a blank sheet of paper as many of the words as you could remember.

In contrast, in a recognition test you might be shown a list of 100 words and asked to choose the 25 words that you had memorized. **A** *recognition measure* **of retention requires participants to select previously learned information from an array of options.**

Subjects not only have cues to work with, they have the answers right in front of them. In educational testing, multiple-choice, true-false, and matching questions are recognition measures; essay questions and fill-in-the-blanks questions are recall measures.

If you're like most students, you probably prefer multiple-choice tests over essay tests. This preference is understandable, because evidence shows that recognition measures tend to yield higher scores than recall measures of memory for the same information (Lockhart, 2000). This tendency was demonstrated many years ago in a study by Luh (1922), who measured subjects' retention of nonsense syllables with both a recognition test and a recall test. He found that participants' performance on the recognition measure was far superior to their performance on the recall measure. There are two ways of looking at this disparity between recall and recognition tests. One view is that recognition tests are especially *sensitive* measures of retention. The other view is that recognition tests are excessively easy measures of retention.

The third method of measuring forgetting is relearning. **A *relearning measure* of retention requires a participant to memorize information a second time to determine how much time or effort is saved by having learned it before.** To use this method, a researcher measures how much time (or how many practice trials) a person needs in order to memorize something. At a later time, the participant is asked to relearn the information. The researcher measures how much more quickly the material is memorized the second time. Participants' *savings scores* provide an estimate of their retention. For example, if it takes you 20 minutes to memorize a list the first time and only 5 minutes to memorize it a week later, you've saved 15 minutes. Your savings score of 75% (15/20 = 3/4 = 75%) suggests that you have retained 75% and forgotten the remaining 25% of the information. Relearning measures can detect retention that is overlooked by recognition tests (Crowder & Greene, 2000).

Why We Forget

PSYKTREK 6d

Measuring forgetting is only the first step in the long journey toward explaining why forgetting occurs. In this section, we explore the possible causes of forgetting, looking at factors that may affect encoding, storage, and retrieval processes.

INEFFECTIVE ENCODING

PSYKTREK 6d

A great deal of forgetting may only *appear* to be forgetting. The information in question may never have been inserted into memory in the first place. Since you can't really forget something you never learned, this phenomenon is sometimes called *pseudoforgetting*. We opened the chapter with an example of pseudoforgetting. People usually assume that they know what a penny looks like. However, most people have actually failed to encode this information. Pseudoforgetting is usually attributable to *lack of attention*.

Even when memory codes are formed for new information, subsequent forgetting may be the result of ineffective or inappropriate encoding (Brown & Craik, 2000). The research on levels of processing shows that some approaches to encoding lead to more forgetting than others (Craik & Tulving, 1975). For example, if you're distracted while you read your textbooks, you may be doing little more than saying the words to yourself. This is an example of *phonemic encoding*, which is inferior to *semantic encoding* for retention of verbal material.

© rsooll/ Shutterstock

DECAY

PSYKTREK 6d

Instead of focusing on encoding, decay theory attributes forgetting to the impermanence of memory storage. **Decay theory proposes that forgetting occurs because memory traces fade with time.** The implicit assumption is that decay occurs in the physiological mechanisms responsible for memories. According to decay theory, the mere passage of time produces forgetting. This notion meshes nicely with commonsense views of forgetting.

As we saw earlier, decay *does* appear to contribute to the loss of information from the sensory and short-term memory stores. However, the critical task for theories of forgetting is to explain the loss of information from long-term memory. Researchers have *not* been able to demonstrate that decay causes LTM forgetting (Slamecka, 1992).

If decay theory is correct, the principal cause of forgetting should be the passage of time. In studies of long-term memory, however, researchers have repeatedly found that time passage is not as influential as what happens during the time interval. Research has shown that forgetting depends not on the amount of time that has passed since learning but on the amount, complexity, and type of information that subjects have had to absorb *during* the retention interval. The negative impact of competing information on retention is called *interference*.

INTERFERENCE

PsykTrek 6d

Interference theory proposes that people forget information because of competition from other material. Although demonstrations of decay in long-term memory have remained elusive, hundreds of studies have shown that interference influences forgetting (Anderson & Neely, 1996; Bjork, 1992). In many of these studies, researchers have controlled interference by varying the similarity between the original material given to subjects (the test material) and the material studied in the intervening period. Interference is assumed to be greatest when intervening material is most similar to the test material. Decreasing the similarity should reduce interference and cause less forgetting. This is exactly what McGeoch and McDonald (1931) found in an influential study. They had participants memorize test material that consisted of a list of two-syllable adjectives. They varied the similarity of intervening learning by having subjects then memorize one of five lists. In order of decreasing similarity to the test material, they were synonyms of the test words, antonyms of the test words, unrelated adjectives, nonsense syllables, and numbers. Later, subjects' recall of the test material was measured. The results showed that as the similarity of the intervening material decreased, the amount of forgetting also decreased—because of reduced interference.

There are two kinds of interference: *retroactive* and *proactive* (Jacoby, Hessels, & Bopp, 2001). *Retroactive interference* occurs when new information impairs the retention of previously learned information. Retroactive interference occurs between the original learning and the retest on that learning (see **Figure 7.10**). For example, the interference manipulated by McGeoch and McDonald (1931) was retroactive interference.

FIGURE 7.10

Retroactive and proactive interference. Retroactive interference occurs when learning produces a "backward" effect, reducing recall of previously learned material. Proactive interference occurs when learning produces a "forward" effect, reducing recall of subsequently learned material. For example, if you were to prepare for an economics test and then study psychology, the interference from the psychology study would be *retroactive* interference. However, if you studied psychology first and then economics, the interference from the psychology study would be *proactive* interference.

© Cengage Learning

In contrast, *proactive interference* occurs when previously learned information interferes with the retention of new information. Proactive interference is rooted in learning that comes before exposure to the test material. For example, when you get a new phone number, your old number (previous learning) may create proactive interference that hampers your recall of your new number. The evidence indicates that both types of interference can have powerful effects on how much you forget.

RETRIEVAL FAILURE

PSYKTREK 6d

People often remember things that they were unable to recall at an earlier time. This phenomenon may be obvious only during struggles with the tip-of-the-tongue phenomenon, but it happens frequently. In fact, a great deal of forgetting may be due to breakdowns in the process of retrieval.

Why does an effort to retrieve something fail on one occasion and succeed on another? That's a tough question. One theory is that retrieval failures may be more likely when a mismatch exists between retrieval cues and the encoding of the information you're searching for. According to Tulving and Thomson (1973), a good retrieval cue is consistent with the original encoding of the information to be recalled. If the sound of a word—its phonemic quality—was emphasized during encoding, an effective retrieval cue should emphasize the sound of the word. If the meaning of the word was emphasized during encoding, semantic cues should be best. A general statement of the principle at work here was formulated by Tulving and Thomson (1973). The *encoding specificity principle* states that the value of a retrieval cue depends on how well it corresponds to the memory code. This principle provides one explanation for the inconsistent success of retrieval efforts.

MOTIVATED FORGETTING

PSYKTREK 6d

Over a century ago, Sigmund Freud (1901) came up with an entirely different explanation for retrieval failures. As we noted in Chapter 1, Freud asserted that people often keep embarrassing, unpleasant, or painful memories buried in their unconscious. For example, a person who was deeply wounded by perceived slights at a childhood birthday party might suppress all recollection of that party. In his therapeutic work with patients, Freud recovered many such buried memories. He theorized that the memories were there all along, but their retrieval was blocked by unconscious avoidance tendencies.

The tendency to forget things one doesn't want to think about is called *motivated forgetting,* or to use Freud's terminology, *repression.* In Freudian theory, *repression* refers to keeping distressing thoughts and feelings buried in the unconscious (see Chapter 11). A number of experiments suggest that people don't remember anxiety-laden material as readily as emotionally neutral material, just as Freud proposed (Guenther, 1988; Reisner, 1998). Thus, when you forget unpleasant things such as a dental appointment, a promise to help a friend move, or a term paper deadline, motivated forgetting may be at work.

The Repressed Memories Controversy

PSYKTREK SIM6

Although the concept of repression has been around for a century, interest in this phenomenon has surged in recent years, thanks to a spate of prominent reports involving the return of long-lost memories of sexual abuse and other traumas during childhood. The media have been flooded with reports of adults accusing their parents, teachers, and neighbors of horrible child abuse decades earlier, based on previously repressed memories of these travesties. These parents, teachers, and neighbors have mostly denied the allegations. In an effort to make sense of the charges, some accused parents have argued that their children's recollections are false memories created inadvertently by well-intentioned therapists through the power of suggestion. What do psychologists and psychiatrists have to say about the recovery of repressed memories? They are sharply divided on the issue.

SUPPORT FOR RECOVERED MEMORIES

Many psychologists and psychiatrists, especially clinicians involved in the treatment of psychological disorders, accept recovered memories of abuse at face value (Banyard & Williams, 1999; Briere & Conte, 1993; Legault & Laurence, 2007; Skinner, 2001; Terr, 1994; Whitfield, 1995). They assert that sexual abuse in childhood is far more widespread than most people realize. For example, one large-scale survey (MacMillan et al., 1997), using a random sample of 9953 residents of Ontario, Canada, found that 12.8% of the females and 4.3% of the males reported that they had been victims of sexual abuse during childhood. Supporters further assert that there is ample evidence that it is common for people to bury traumatic incidents in their unconscious (Del Monte, 2000; Wilsnack et al., 2002). For instance, in a study of psychiatric patients hospitalized for posttraumatic or dissociative disorders (see Chapter 14), one-third of those who reported childhood sexual abuse said that they had experienced complete amnesia for the abuse at some point in their lives (Chu et al., 1999).

SKEPTICISM OF RECOVERED MEMORIES

In contrast, many other psychologists, especially memory researchers, have expressed skepticism about the recent upsurge of recovered memories of abuse (Kihlstrom, 2004; Loftus, 1998, 2003; McNally, 2003, 2007; Takarangi et al., 2008). The skeptics do *not* argue that people are lying about their previously repressed memories. Rather, they maintain that some suggestible people wrestling with emotional problems have been convinced by persuasive therapists that their emotional problems must be the result of abuse that occurred years before. Critics blame a small minority of therapists who presumably have good intentions but who operate under the questionable assumption that most or even all psychological problems are attributable to childhood sexual abuse (Lindsay & Read, 1994; Loftus & Davis, 2006; Spanos, 1994). Using hypnosis, dream interpretation, and leading questions, they supposedly prod and probe patients until they inadvertently create the memories of abuse that they are searching for (Lynn et al., 2003; Thayer & Lynn, 2006).

Psychologists who doubt the authenticity of repressed memories support their analysis by pointing to discredited cases of recovered memories (Brown, Goldstein, & Bjorklund, 2000). For example, with the help of a church counselor, one woman recovered memories of how her minister father had repeatedly raped her, got her pregnant, and then aborted the pregnancy with a coat-hanger, but subse-

Concept Check 7.2

Figuring Out Forgetting

Check your understanding of why people forget by identifying the probable causes of forgetting in each of the following scenarios. Choose from (a) motivated forgetting (repression), (b) decay, (c) ineffective encoding, (d) proactive interference, (e) retroactive interference, or (f) retrieval failure. You will find the answers in Appendix A.

_____ 1. Ellen can't recall the reasons for the Webster-Ashburton Treaty because she was daydreaming when it was discussed in history class.

_____ 2. Rufus hates his job at Taco Heaven and is always forgetting when he is scheduled to work.

_____ 3. Ray's new assistant in the shipping department is named Jason Timberlake. Ray keeps calling him Justin, mixing him up with the singer/actor Justin Timberlake.

_____ 4. Tania studied history on Sunday morning and sociology on Sunday evening. It's Monday, and she's struggling with her history test because she keeps mixing up prominent historians with influential sociologists.

quent evidence revealed that the woman was still a virgin and that her father had had a vasectomy years before (Brainerd & Reyna, 2005). The skeptics also point to published case histories that clearly involved suggestive questioning and to cases in which patients have recanted recovered memories of sexual abuse after realizing that these memories were implanted by their therapists (Loftus, 1994; Shobe & Schooler, 2001). Another problem for memory researchers is that some recovered memories have described incidents of abuse that occurred before the victim reached age 3. However, when adults are asked to recall their earliest memories, their oldest recollections typically don't go back that far (Bruce, Dolan, & Phillips-Grant, 2000; Hayne, 2007).

Those who question the accuracy of repressed memories also point to findings on the misinformation effect, research on source-monitoring errors, and other demonstrations of the relative ease of creating "memories" for events that never happened (Lindsay et al., 2004; Loftus & Cahill, 2007; Strange, Clifasefi, & Garry, 2007). For example, working with college students, Ira Hyman and his colleagues have managed to implant recollections of fairly substantial events (such as spilling a punch bowl at a wedding, being in a grocery store when the fire sprinkler system went off, being hospitalized for an earache) in about 25% of their subjects, just by asking them to elaborate on events supposedly reported by their parents (Hyman, Husband, & Billings, 1995; Hyman & Kleinknecht, 1999). Other studies have succeeded in implanting false memories of nearly drowning (Heaps & Nash, 2001), of being attacked by a vicious animal (Porter, Yuille, & Lehman, 1999), and of becoming ill after eating a certain food (Bernstein & Loftus, 2009). Moreover, subjects in these studies often feel very confident about their false memories, which frequently generate strong emotional reactions and richly detailed "recollections" (Loftus & Bernstein, 2005).

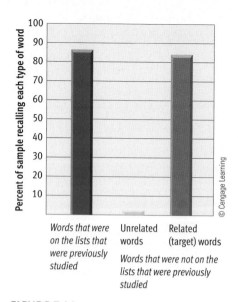

FIGURE 7.11

The prevalence of false memories observed by Roediger and McDermott (1995). The graph shown here summarizes the recognition test results in Study 1 conducted by Roediger and McDermott (1995). Participants correctly identified words that had been on the lists they had studied 86% of the time and only misidentified unrelated words that had not been on the lists 2% of the time, indicating that they were paying careful attention to the task. Nonetheless, they mistakenly reported that they "remembered" related target words that were not on the lists 84% of the time—a remarkably high prevalence of false memories.

Chart labels:
- Y-axis: Percent of sample recalling each type of word
- Words that were on the lists that were previously studied
- Unrelated words — Words that were not on the lists that were previously studied
- Related (target) words

In a similar vein, building on much earlier work by James Deese (1959), Henry Roediger and Kathleen McDermott (1995, 2000) have devised a simple laboratory paradigm that is remarkably reliable in producing memory illusions. In this procedure, now known as the *Deese-Roediger-McDermott (DRM) paradigm,* a series of lists of fifteen words are presented to participants, who are asked to recall the words immediately after each list is presented and are given a recognition measure of their retention at the end of the session. The trick is that each list consists of a set of words (such as *bed, rest, awake, tired*) that are strongly associated with another target word that is not on the list (in this case, *sleep*). When subjects *recall* the words on each list, they remember the nonpresented target word over 50% of the time, and when they are given the final *recognition* test, they typically indicate that about 80% of the nonstudied target words were presented in the lists (see **Figure 7.11**).

The memory illusions created in this experiment may seem trivial in comparison to the vivid, detailed recollections of previously forgotten sexual abuse that have generated the repressed memories controversy. But these false memories can be reliably created in normal, healthy participants in a matter of minutes, with little effort and no pressure or misleading information. Thus, this line of research provides a dramatic demonstration of how easy it is to get people to remember that they saw something they really didn't see (McDermott, 2007; Neuschatz et al., 2007).

CONCLUSIONS

So, what can we conclude about the recovered memories controversy? It seems pretty clear that therapists can unknowingly create false memories in their patients and that a significant portion of recovered memories of abuse are the product of suggestion (Follette & Davis, 2009; Ost, 2009). But it also seems likely that some cases of recovered memories are authentic (Brewin, 2007; Smith & Gleaves, 2007). It is difficult to estimate what proportion of recovered memories of abuse fall in each category. That said, recent evidence suggests that memories of abuse recovered through therapy are more likely to be false memories than those that are recovered spontaneously (McNally & Geraerts, 2009). People who report recovered memories of abuse seem to fall into two very different groups (Geraerts, Raymaekers, & Merckelbach, 2008). Some gradually recover memories of abuse with the assistance of suggestive therapeutic techniques, whereas others suddenly and unexpectedly recover memories of abuse when they encounter a relevant retrieval cue (such as returning to the scene of the abuse). A study that sought to corroborate reports of abuse from both groups found a much higher corroboration rate among those who recovered their memories spontaneously (37%) as opposed to those who recovered their memories in therapy (0%) (Geraerts et al., 2007).

The recovered memories controversy has inspired a great deal of research that has increased our understanding of just how fragile, fallible, malleable, and subjective human memory can be. Indeed, the implicit dichotomy underlying the repressed memories debate—that some memories are true, whereas others are false—is misleading and oversimplified. Research demonstrates that all human memories are imperfect reconstructions of the past that are subject to many types of distortion.

In Search of the Memory Trace: The Physiology of Memory

For decades, neuroscientists have ventured forth in search of the anatomical and neural bases of memory. A great deal of progress has been made, but much remains to be learned. In this section we'll look at some of the more influential research.

The Anatomy of Memory

Cases of amnesia (extensive memory loss) resulting from head injury are a useful source of clues about the anatomical bases of memory. There are two basic types of amnesia: retrograde and anterograde (see **Figure 7.12**). **In *retrograde amnesia* a person loses memories for events that occurred prior to the injury.** For example, a 25-year-old gymnast who sustains a head trauma might find 3 years, 7 years, or perhaps her entire lifetime erased. **In *anterograde amnesia* a person loses memories for events that occur after the injury.** For instance, after her accident, the injured gymnast might suffer impaired ability to remember people she meets, where she has parked her car, and so on.

Because victims' current memory functioning is impaired, cases of anterograde amnesia have been especially rich sources of information about the brain and memory. One well-known case, that of a man referred to as H.M., was followed from 1953 until his death in 2008 (Corkin, 1984, 2002; Scoville & Milner, 1957). H.M. had surgery to relieve debilitating epileptic seizures that occurred up to ten times a day. The surgery greatly reduced his seizures. Unfortunately, however, the surgery inadvertently wiped out most of his ability to form long-term memories. H.M.'s short-term memory remained fine, but he had no recollection of anything that had happened since 1953 (other than about the most recent 20 seconds of his life). He did not recognize the doctors treating him, he couldn't remember routes to and from places, and he didn't know his own age. H.M. was unable to remember what he ate a few minutes ago, let alone what he had done in the years since his surgery. At age 66, after he had gray hair for years, he could not remember whether he had gray hair when asked, even though he looked in the mirror every day. Although he could not form new long-term memories, H.M.'s intelligence remained intact. He could care for himself (around his own home), carry on complicated conversations, and solve crossword puzzles. This man's misfortune provided a golden opportunity for memory researchers.

In the decades after his surgery, over 100 researchers studied various aspects of H.M.'s memory performance, leading to several major discoveries about the nature of memory (Maugh, 2008). As one scientist put it in commenting on the case, "More was learned about memory by research with just one patient than was learned in the previous 100 years of research on memory" (Miller, 2009). More than 15 years prior to his

FIGURE 7.12
Retrograde versus anterograde amnesia. In retrograde amnesia, memory for events that occurred prior to the onset of amnesia is lost. In anterograde amnesia, memory for events that occur subsequent to the onset of amnesia suffers.

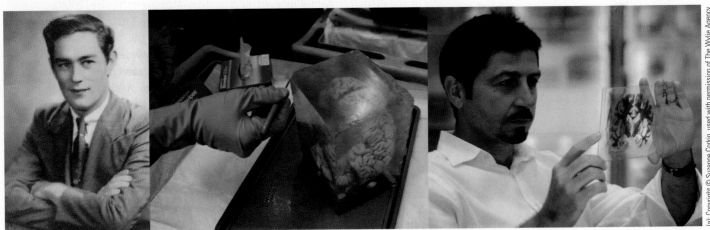

To protect his privacy, H.M. was identified only by his initials for over 50 years. After his death it was revealed that his name was Henry Molaison. He is shown as a young man in (a). His death triggered a complex, multifaceted team effort, orchestrated by Suzanne Corkin of MIT, to preserve, image, and dissect the brain of the most important research subject in the history of neuroscience. His brain is shown in a mold of gelatin in (b). The challenge of slicing Molaison's brain into razor-thin sections for preservation and digital imaging was allocated to Jacob Annese of UCSD, who spent years preparing for the delicate task. Annese is shown looking at a mounted slide of a brain slice in (c). The digital atlas of Molaison's brain will reveal the exact boundaries of his surgical lesions. This information will permit scientists to analyze the precise relations between his brain damage and 50 years of data on his memory performance.

FIGURE 7.13

The hippocampus and memory. The hippocampus and adjacent areas in the brain are thought to play an especially central role in memory. The hippocampus appears to be responsible for the initial consolidation of memories, which are then stored in diverse and widely distributed areas of the cortex.

Prefrontal cortex

Cerebral cortex

Hippocampus

© Cengage Learning

death, Suzanne Corkin arranged for H.M.'s brain to be donated to Massachusetts General Hospital, where it was immediately subjected to extensive brain imaging after he passed away in 2008. His brain was subsequently moved to a lab at the University of California, San Diego, where one year after H.M.'s death, it was cut into 2401 extremely thin slices for further study by scientists all over the world (Becker, 2009; Carey, 2009). The painstaking, methodical 53-hour dissection was broadcast live over the Internet, where portions of the process were watched by over 400,000 people.

H.M.'s memory losses were originally attributed to the removal of his *hippocampus* (see **Figure 7.13**), although theorists now understand that other nearby structures that were removed also contributed to H.M.'s dramatic memory deficits (Delis & Lucas, 1996). Based on decades of additional research, scientists now believe that the entire *hippocampal region* and adjacent areas in the cortex are critical for many types of long-term memory (Zola & Squire, 2000). Many scientists now refer to this broader memory complex as the *medial temporal lobe memory system* (Shrager & Squire, 2009).

Do these findings mean that memories are stored in the hippocampal region and adjacent areas? Probably not. Most theorists believe that the medial temporal lobe memory system plays a key role in the *consolidation* of memories (Dudai, 2004). **Consolidation is a hypothetical process involving the gradual conversion of information into durable memory codes stored in long-term memory.** According to this view, memories are consolidated in the hippocampal region and then stored in diverse and widely distributed areas of the cortex (Eichenbaum, 2004; Markowitsch, 2000). This setup allows new memories to become independent of the hippocampal region and to gradually be integrated with other memories already stored in various areas of the cortex (Frankland & Bontempi, 2005). Interestingly, recent research suggests that much of the consolidation process may unfold while people sleep (Stickgold & Walker, 2005).

The Neural Circuitry of Memory

PSYKTREK 6c

Richard Thompson (1989, 1992, 2005) and his colleagues have shown that specific memories may depend on *localized neural circuits* in the brain. In other words, memories may create unique, reusable pathways in the brain along which signals flow. Thompson has traced the pathway that accounts for a rabbit's memory of a conditioned eyeblink response. Thompson theorizes that other memories probably create entirely different pathways in other areas of the brain.

Another line of research suggests that memory formation results in *alterations in synaptic transmission* at specific sites. Eric Kandel (2001) and his colleagues have studied conditioned reflexes in a simple organism—a sea slug. In research that earned a Nobel prize for Kandel, they showed that reflex learning in the sea slug produces changes in the strength of specific synaptic connections by enhancing the availability and release of neurotransmitters at these synapses (Bailey & Kandel, 2009; Kennedy, Hawkins, & Kandel, 1992). Kandel believes that durable changes in synaptic transmission may be the neural building blocks of more complex memories as well.

Recent research suggests that the process of *neurogenesis*—the formation of new neurons—may contribute to the sculpting of neural circuits that underlie memory. As we noted in Chapter 3, scientists have recently discovered that new brain cells are formed constantly in the *dentate gyrus* of the *hippocampus* (Gould, 2004; Leuner & Gould, 2010). Animal studies show that manipulations that suppress neurogenesis lead to memory impairments on many types of learning tasks and that conditions that increase neurogenesis are associated with enhanced learning on many tasks (Leuner, Gould, & Shors, 2006). Neurogenesis may provide the brain with a supply of neurons that vary in age, and these variations may somehow allow the brain to "timestamp" some memories. The theorizing about how neurogenesis contributes to memory encoding is highly speculative (Jessberger, Aimone, & Gage, 2009). Nonetheless, research on neurogenesis is an exciting new line of investigation.

In summary, a number of anatomical structures and neural circuits appear to play a role in memory. Does all this sound confusing? It should, because it is. The bottom line is that neuroscientists are still assembling the pieces of the puzzle that will explain the physiological basis of memory. Although they have identified many of the puzzle pieces, they're not sure how the pieces fit together. Their difficulty is probably due to the complex, multifaceted nature of memory. Looking for the physiological basis for memory is only slightly less daunting than looking for the physiological basis for thought itself.

Eric Kandel
"Learning results from changes in the strength of the synaptic connections between precisely interconnected cells."

Systems and Types of Memory

KEY LEARNING GOALS

7.13 Compare and contrast declarative and nondeclarative memory.

7.14 Distinguish between episodic versus semantic memory and retrospective versus prospective memory.

Some theorists believe that evidence on the physiology of memory is confusing because investigators are unwittingly probing into several distinct memory systems that may have different physiological bases. The various memory systems are distinguished primarily by the types of information they handle.

Declarative Versus Procedural Memory

PSYKTREK 6c

The most basic division of memory into distinct systems contrasts *declarative memory* with *nondeclarative, or procedural, memory* (Squire, 2004, 2009; see **Figure 7.14** on the next page). The *declarative memory system* **handles factual information.** It contains recollections of words, definitions, names, dates, faces, events, concepts, and ideas. The *nondeclarative memory system* **houses memory for actions, skills, conditioned responses, and emotional memories.** It contains procedural memories of how to execute such actions as riding a bike, typing, and tying one's shoes. To illustrate the distinction, if you know the rules of tennis (the number of games in a set, scoring, and such), this factual information is stored in declarative memory. If you remember how to hit a serve and swing through a backhand, these perceptual-motor skills are stored in nondeclarative memory.

Support for the distinction between declarative and nondeclarative memory comes from evidence that the two systems seem to operate somewhat differently (Squire, Knowlton, & Musen, 1993). For example, the recall of factual information generally depends on conscious, effortful processes, whereas memory for conditioned reflexes is largely automatic and memories for skills often require little effort and attention (Johnson, 2003). People execute perceptual-motor tasks such as playing the piano or typing with little conscious awareness of what they're doing. In fact,

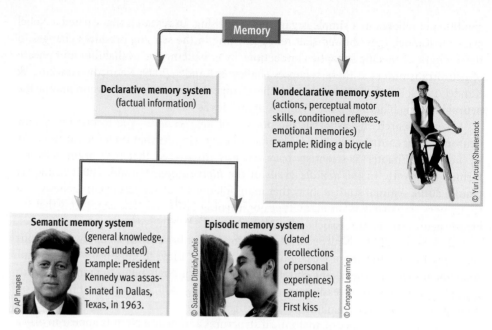

FIGURE 7.14

Theories of independent memory systems. Theorists have distinguished between declarative memory, which handles facts and information, and nondeclarative memory, which handles motor skills, conditioned responses, and emotional memories. Declarative memory is further subdivided into semantic memory (general knowledge) and episodic memory (dated recollections of personal experiences). The extent to which nondeclarative memory can be usefully subdivided remains the subject of debate.

performance on such tasks sometimes deteriorates if people think too much about what they're doing. Another disparity is that the memory for skills (such as typing and bike riding) doesn't decline much over long retention intervals, whereas declarative memory is more vulnerable to forgetting.

The notion that declarative and procedural memories are separate is supported by certain patterns of memory loss seen in amnesiacs. In many cases, declarative memory is severely impaired while procedural memory is left largely intact (Squire & Schrager, 2009). For example, H.M., the victim of amnesia discussed earlier, was able to learn and remember new motor skills, even though he couldn't remember what he looked like as he aged. The sparing of procedural memory in H.M. provided crucial evidence for the distinction between declarative and nondeclarative memory.

Semantic Versus Episodic Memory

Endel Tulving (1986, 1993, 2002) has further subdivided declarative memory into semantic and episodic memory (see **Figure 7.14**). Both contain factual information. However, episodic memory contains *personal facts* and semantic memory contains *general facts*. The **episodic memory system is made up of chronological, or temporally dated, recollections of personal experiences.** Episodic memory is a record of things you've done, seen, and heard. It includes information about *when* you did these things, saw them, or heard them. It contains recollections about being in a ninth-grade play, visiting the Grand Canyon, attending a Linkin Park concert, or going to a movie last weekend. Tulving (2001) emphasizes that the function of episodic memory is "time travel"—that is, to allow one to reexperience the past. He also speculates that episodic memory may be unique to humans.

The *semantic memory system* **contains general knowledge that is not tied to the time when the information was learned.** Semantic memory contains information such as Christmas is December 25th, dogs have four legs, the U.S. Supreme Court has nine justices, and Phoenix is located in Arizona. You probably don't remember when you learned these facts. Information like this is usually stored undated. The distinction between episodic and semantic memory can be better appreciated by drawing an analogy to books: Episodic memory is like an autobiography, while semantic memory is like an encyclopedia. The memory deficits seen in some cases of amnesia suggest that episodic and semantic memory are separate systems. For instance, some amnesiacs forget most

FIGURE 7.15

Retrospective versus prospective memory. Most memory research has explored the dynamics of *retrospective memory*, which focuses on recollections from the past. However, *prospective memory*, which requires people to remember to perform actions in the future, also plays an important role in everyday life.

Figure labels:
- Retrospective memory
- Prospective memory
- Remembering events from the past; previously learned information
- Remembering to perform actions in the future
- © Form Advertising/Alamy
- Past
- Future
- The present

personal facts, while their recall of general facts is largely unaffected (Szpunar & Mc-Dermott, 2009). However, debate continues about whether episodic and semantic memory have distinct neural bases.

Prospective Versus Retrospective Memory

A 1984 paper with a clever title, "Remembering to Do Things: A Forgotten Topic" (Harris, 1984), introduced yet another distinction between types of memory: *prospective memory* versus *retrospective memory* (see **Figure 7.15**). This distinction does not refer to independent *memory systems* but rather to fundamentally different types of *memory tasks*. **Retrospective memory involves remembering events from the past or previously learned information.** Retrospective memory is at work when you try to remember who won the Super Bowl last year or when you reminisce about your high school days. **Prospective memory involves remembering to perform actions in the future.** Examples of prospective memory tasks include remembering to bring your umbrella, to walk the dog, to call someone, or to grab the tickets for the big game. Experiments demonstrate that it is easy to forget such intentions, especially when you are confronted by interruptions and distractions (Einstein et al., 2003). People vary considerably in their ability to successfully carry out prospective memory tasks (Searleman, 1996). Individuals who appear deficient in prospective memory are often characterized as "absent-minded." Research suggests, with some caveats, that older adults are somewhat more vulnerable to problems with prospective memory than younger people are (McDaniel et al., 2003).

Concept Check 7.3

Recognizing Various Types of Memory

Check your understanding of the various types of memory discussed in this chapter by matching the definitions below with the following: (a) sensory memory, (b) short-term memory, (c) long-term memory, (d) declarative memory, (e) nondeclarative memory, (f) episodic memory, (g) semantic memory, (h) retrospective memory, and (i) prospective memory. The answers can be found in Appendix A.

_____ 1. Memory for factual information.

_____ 2. An unlimited capacity store that can hold information over lengthy periods of time.

_____ 3. The preservation of information in its original sensory form for a brief time, usually only a fraction of a second.

_____ 4. Chronological, or temporally dated, recollections of personal experiences.

_____ 5. The repository of memories for actions, skills, operations, and conditioned responses.

_____ 6. General knowledge that is not tied to the time when the information was learned.

_____ 7. Remembering to perform future actions.

_____ 8. A limited-capacity store that can maintain unrehearsed information for about 20 seconds.

Reflecting on the Chapter's Themes

 Subjectivity of Experience

 Theoretical Diversity

 Multifactorial Causation

One of our integrative themes—the idea that people's experience of the world is subjective—stood head and shoulders above the rest in this chapter. Let's briefly review how the study of memory has illuminated this idea.

First, our discussion of attention as inherently selective should have shed light on why people's experience of the world is subjective. To a great degree, what you see in the world around you depends on where you focus your attention. This is one of the main reasons why two people can be exposed to the "same" events and walk away with entirely different perceptions. Second, the reconstructive nature of memory should further explain people's tendency to view the world with a subjective slant. When you observe an event, you don't store an exact copy of the event in your memory. Instead, you store a rough, "bare bones" approximation of the event that may be reshaped as time goes by.

A second theme that was apparent in our discussion of memory was psychology's theoretical diversity. We saw illuminating theoretical debates about the nature of memory storage, the causes of forgetting, and the existence of multiple memory systems. Finally, the multifaceted nature of memory demonstrated once again that behavior is governed by multiple causes. For instance, your memory of a specific event may be influenced by your attention to it, your level of processing, your elaboration, how you search your memory store, how you reconstruct the event, and so forth. Given the multifaceted nature of memory, it should come as no surprise that there are many ways to improve memory. We discuss a variety of strategies in the Personal Application section.

Personal APPLICATION

Improving Everyday Memory

KEY LEARNING GOALS

7.16 Discuss the importance of rehearsal, distributed practice, and interference in efforts to improve everyday memory.

7.17 Discuss the value of deep processing, good organization, and mnemonic devices in efforts to improve everyday memory.

Answer the following "true" or "false."

_____ 1 Memory strategies were recently invented by psychologists.

_____ 2 Overlearning of information leads to poor retention.

_____ 3 Outlining what you read is not likely to affect retention.

_____ 4 Massing practice in one long study session is better than distributing practice across several shorter sessions.

Mnemonic devices are strategies for enhancing memory. They have a long and honorable history. In fact, one of the mnemonic devices covered in this Application— the method of loci—was described in Greece as early as 86–82 B.C. (Yates, 1966). Actually, mnemonic devices were even more crucial in ancient times than they are today. In ancient Greece and Rome, for instance, paper and pencils were not readily available for people to jot down things they needed to remember, so they had to depend heavily on mnemonic devices.

Are mnemonic devices the key to improving one's everyday memory? No. They clearly can be helpful in some situations (Wilding & Valentine, 1996), but they are not a cure-all. They can be hard to use and hard to apply to many everyday situations. Most books and training programs designed to improve memory probably overemphasize mnemonic techniques (Searleman & Herrmann, 1994). Although less exotic strategies such as increasing rehearsal, engaging in deeper processing, and organizing material are more crucial to everyday memory, we will discuss some popular mnemonics as we proceed through this Application. Along the way, you'll learn that all of our opening true-false statements are false.

Engage in Adequate Rehearsal `PsykTrek SIM5`

Practice makes perfect, or so you've heard. In reality, practice is not likely to guarantee perfection. However, it usually leads to improved retention. Studies show that retention improves with increased rehearsal (Greene, 1992). This improvement presumably occurs because rehearsal helps transfer information into long-term memory. Although the benefits of practice are well known, people have a curious tendency to overestimate their knowledge of a topic and how well they will perform on a subsequent memory test of this knowledge (Koriat & Bjork, 2005). That's one reason why it's a good idea to informally test yourself on information that you think you have mastered before confronting a real test.

In addition to checking your mastery, research suggests that testing actually enhances retention, a phenomenon dubbed the *testing effect* (Karpicke & Roediger, 2008; Roediger & Karpicke, 2006a). Studies have shown that taking a test on material increases performance on a subsequent test even more than studying for an equal amount of time. Interestingly, the testing effect is observed on both closed-book and open-book exams (Agarwal et al., 2008). And the favorable effects of testing are enhanced if participants are provided feedback on their test performance (Butler & Roediger, 2008). Moreover, recent studies have demonstrated that the laboratory findings on the testing effect replicate in real-world educational settings (Larsen, Butler, & Roediger, 2009). Unfortunately, given the recent nature of this discovery, relatively few students are aware of the value of testing in retention (Karpicke, Butler, & Roediger, 2009).

Why is testing so beneficial? The key appears to be that testing forces students to engage in effortful retrieval of information, which promotes future retention (Roediger et al., 2010). Indeed, even *unsuccessful* retrieval efforts can enhance retention (Kornell, Hays, & Bjork, 2009). In any event, self-testing appears to be an excellent memory tool. This suggests that it would be prudent to take the Practice Tests in this text (see Appendix A) or additional tests available on the website for the book.

One other point related to rehearsal is also worth mentioning. If you are memorizing some type of list, be aware of the serial-position effect, which is often observed when subjects are tested on their

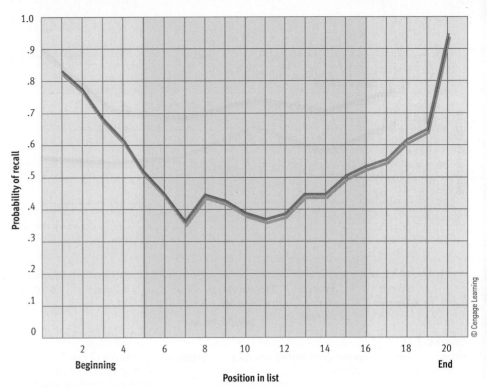

FIGURE 7.16

The serial-position effect. After learning a list of items to remember, people tend to recall more of the items from the beginning and the end of the list than from the middle, producing the characteristic U-shaped curve shown here. This phenomenon is called the serial-position effect.

SOURCE: Adapted from Rundus, D. (1971). Analysis of rehearsal processes in free recall. *Journal of Experimental Psychology, 89*, 63–77. Copyright © 1971 by the American Psychological Association.

memory of lists (Murdock, 2001). The *serial-position effect* occurs when subjects show better recall for items at the beginning and end of a list than for items in the middle (see **Figure 7.16**). The reasons for the serial-position effect are complex and need not concern us. However, its pragmatic implications are clear: If you need to memorize a list of, say, cranial nerves or past presidents, devote extra practice trials to items in the middle of the list and check your memorization of those items very carefully.

Schedule Distributed Practice and Minimize Interference

Let's assume that you need to study 9 hours for an exam. Should you "cram" all your studying into one 9-hour period (massed practice)? Or is it better to distribute your study among, say, three 3-hour periods on successive days (distributed practice)? The evidence indicates

that retention tends to be greater after distributed practice than after massed practice (Kornell et al., 2010; Rohrer & Taylor, 2006). Moreover, a review of over 300 experiments (Cepeda et al., 2006) showed that the longer the retention interval between studying and testing, the bigger the advantage for distributed practice, as shown in **Figure 7.17** on the next page. The same review concluded that the longer the retention interval, the longer the optimal "break" between practice trials. When an upcoming test is more than two days away, the optimal interval between practice periods appears to be around 24 hours. The superiority of distributed practice over massed practice suggests that cramming is an ill-advised approach to studying for exams (Dempster, 1996).

Because interference is a major cause of forgetting, you'll probably want to think about how you can minimize it. This issue is especially important for students, because memorizing information

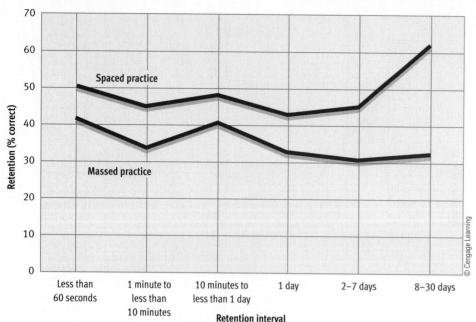

FIGURE 7.17

Effects of massed versus distributed practice on retention. In a review of over 300 experiments on massed versus distributed practice, Cepeda et al. (2006) examined the importance of the retention interval. As you can see, spaced practice was superior to massed practice at all retention intervals, but the gap widened at longer intervals. These findings suggest that distributed practice is especially advantageous when you need or want to remember material over the long haul.

for one course can interfere with the retention of information for another course. Thus, the day before an exam in a course, you should study for that course only—if possible. If demands in other courses make that plan impossible, you should study the test material last.

Engage in Deep Processing and Organize Information

Research on levels of processing suggests that how *often* you go over material is less critical than the *depth* of processing that you engage in (Craik & Tulving, 1975). If you expect to remember what you read, you have to fully comprehend its meaning (Einstein & McDaniel, 2004). Many students could probably benefit if they spent less time on rote memorization and more on paying attention to and analyzing the meaning of their reading assignments. In particular, it is useful to make material *personally* meaningful. When you read your textbooks, try to relate information to your own life and experi-

ence. For example, when you read about classical conditioning, try to think of your own responses that are attributable to classical conditioning.

It is also important to understand that retention tends to be greater when information is well organized (Einstein & McDaniel, 2004) Gordon Bower (1970) has shown that hierarchical organization is particularly helpful when it is applicable. Thus, it may be a good idea to *outline* reading assignments for school, since outlining forces you to organize material hierarchically. Consistent with this reasoning, there is some empirical evidence that outlining material from textbooks can enhance retention of that material (McDaniel, Waddill, & Shakesby, 1996).

Enrich Encoding with Mnemonic Devices [PsykTrek 6a]

Although it's often helpful to make information personally meaningful, it's not always easy to do so. For instance, when you study chemistry you may have a hard

time relating to polymers at a personal level. Thus, many mnemonic devices—such as acrostics, acronyms, and narrative methods—are designed to make abstract material more meaningful. Other mnemonic devices depend on visual imagery. As you may recall, Allan Paivio (1986, 2007) believes that visual images create a second memory code and that two codes are better than one.

ACROSTICS AND ACRONYMS

Acrostics are phrases (or poems) in which the first letter of each word (or line) functions as a cue to help you recall information to be remembered. For instance, you may remember the order of musical notes with the saying "Every Good Boy Does Fine." A slight variation on acrostics is the *acronym*—a word formed out of the first letters of a series of words. Students memorizing the order of colors in the light spectrum often store the name "Roy G. Biv" to remember red, orange, yellow, green, blue, indigo, and violet. Notice that this acronym takes advantage of the principle of chunking. Acrostics and acronyms that individuals create for themselves can be effective memory tools (Hermann, Raybeck, & Gruneberg, 2002).

RHYMES

Another verbal mnemonic that people often rely on is rhyming. You've probably repeated, "I before E except after C . . ." thousands of times. Perhaps you also remember the number of days in each month with the old standby, "Thirty days hath September . . ." Rhyming something to remember it is an old and useful trick.

LINK METHOD [PsykTrek 6a]

The *link method* involves forming a mental image of items to be remembered in a way that links them together. For instance, suppose that you need to remember some items to pick up at the drugstore: a news magazine, shaving cream, film, and pens. To remember these items, you might visualize a public figure on the magazine cover shaving with a pen while being photographed.

FIGURE 7.18

The method of loci. In this example from Bower (1970), a person about to go shopping pairs items to remember with familiar places (loci) arranged in a natural sequence: (1) hot dogs/driveway; (2) cat food/ garage interior; (3) tomatoes/front door; (4) bananas/coat closet shelf; (5) whiskey/kitchen sink. The shopper then uses imagery to associate the items on the shopping list with the loci, as shown in the drawing: (1) giant hot dog rolls down a driveway; (2) a cat noisily devours cat food in the garage; (3) ripe tomatoes are splattered on the front door; (4) bunches of bananas are hung from the closet shelf; (5) the contents of a bottle of whiskey gurgle down the kitchen sink. As the last panel shows, the shopper recalls the items by mentally touring the loci associated with them.

SOURCE: From Bower, G. H. (1970). Analysis of a mnemonic device. *American Scientist, 58,* 496–499. Copyright © 1970 by Scientific Research Society. Reprinted by permission.

The more bizarre you make your image, the more helpful it is likely to be (McDaniel & Einstein, 1986).

METHOD OF LOCI   PsykTrek 6a

The *method of loci* involves taking an imaginary walk along a familiar path where images of items to be remembered are associated with certain locations. The first step is to commit to memory a series of loci, or places along a path. Usu-ally these loci are specific locations in your home or neighborhood. Then envision each thing you want to remember in one of these locations. Try to form distinctive, vivid images. When you need to remember the items, imagine yourself walking along the path. The various loci on your path should serve as cues for the retrieval of the images that you formed (see **Figure 7.18**). Evidence suggests that the method of loci can be effective in in-creasing retention (Massen & Vterrodt-Plunnecke, 2006; Moe & De Beni, 2004). Moreover, this method ensures that items are remembered in their *correct order* because the order is determined by the sequence of locations along the pathway. A recent study found that using loci along a pathway from home to work was more effective than a pathway through one's home (Massen et al., 2009).

Understanding the Fallibility of Eyewitness Accounts

A number of years ago, the Wilmington, Delaware, area was plagued by a series of armed robberies committed by a perpetrator who was dubbed the "gentleman bandit" by the press because he was an unusually polite and well-groomed thief. The local media published a sketch of the gentleman bandit and eventually an alert resident turned in a suspect who resembled the sketch. Much to everyone's surprise, the accused thief was a Catholic priest named Father Bernard Pagano—who vigorously denied the charges. Unfortunately for Father Pagano, his denials and alibis were unconvincing and he was charged with the crimes. At the trial, *seven* eyewitnesses confidently identified Father Pagano as the gentleman bandit. The prosecution was well on its way to a conviction when there was a stunning turn of events—another man, Ronald Clouser, confessed to the police that he was the robber. The authorities dropped the charges against Father Pagano, and the relieved priest was able to return to his normal life (Rodgers, 1982).

This bizarre tale of mistaken identity—which sounds like it was lifted from a movie script—raises some interesting questions about memory. How could seven people "remember" seeing Father Pagnano commit armed robberies that he had nothing to do with? How could they mistake him for Ronald Clouser, when the two really didn't look very similar (see the adjacent photos)? How could the witnesses be so confident when they were so wrong? Perhaps you're thinking that this is just one case and it must be unrepresentative (which would be sound critical thinking). Well, yes, it is a rather extreme example of eyewitness fallibility, but researchers have compiled mountains of evidence that eyewitness testimony is not nearly as reliable or as accurate as widely assumed (Kassin et al., 2001; Wells, Memon, & Penrod, 2006). This finding is ironic in that people are most confident about their assertions when they can say "I saw it with my own eyes." Television news shows like to use the title "Eyewitness News" to create the impression that they chronicle events with great clarity and accuracy. And our legal system accords special status to eyewitness testimony because it is considered much more dependable than hearsay or circumstantial evidence.

So, why are eyewitness accounts surprisingly inaccurate? Well, a variety of factors and processes contribute. Let's briefly review some of the relevant processes that were introduced in the main body of the chapter; then we'll focus on two common errors in thinking that also play a role.

Can you think of any memory phenomena described in the chapter that seem likely to undermine eyewitness accuracy? You could point to the fact that *memory is a reconstructive process,* and eyewitness recall is likely to be *distorted by schemas* that people have for various events. Another consideration is that *witnesses sometimes make source-monitoring errors* and get confused about where they saw a face. For example, one rape victim mixed up her assailant with a guest on a TV show that she was watching when she was attacked. Fortunately, the falsely accused suspect had an airtight alibi, as he could demonstrate that he was on live television when the rape occurred (Schacter, 1996). Perhaps the most pervasive factor is the misinformation effect (Davis & Loftus, 2007). *Witnesses' recall of events is routinely distorted by information introduced after the event* by police officers, attorneys, news reports, and so forth. In addition to these factors, eyewitness inaccuracy is fueled by *hindsight bias* and *overconfidence effects.*

The Contribution of Hindsight Bias

Hindsight bias is the tendency to mold one's interpretation of the past to fit how events actually turned out. When you know the outcome of an event, this knowledge slants your recall of how the event unfolded and what your thinking was at the time. With the luxury of hindsight, people have a curious tendency to say, "I knew it all along" when explaining events that objectively would have been difficult to foresee. The tendency to exhibit the hindsight bias is normal, pervasive, and surprisingly strong (Guilbault et al., 2004). With regard to eyewitnesses, their recollections may often be distorted by knowing that a particular person has been arrested and accused of the crime in question. For example, Wells and Brad-

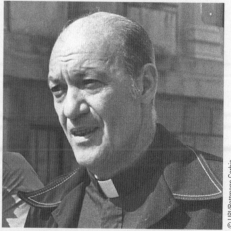

Although he doesn't look that much like the real "gentleman bandit," who is shown on the left, seven eyewitnesses identified Father Pagano (right) as the gentleman bandit, showing just how unreliable eyewitness accounts can be.

Although courts give special credence to eyewitness testimony, scientific evidence indicates that eyewitness accounts are less reliable than widely assumed.

field (1998) had simulated eyewitnesses select a perpetrator from a photo lineup. The participants' confidence in their identifications tended to be quite modest, which made sense given that the actual perpetrator was not even in the lineup. But when some subjects were told, "Good, you identified the actual suspect," they became highly confident about their identifications, which obviously were incorrect. In another study, participants read identical scenarios about a couple's first date that either had no ending or ended in a rape (described in one additional sentence). The subjects who received the rape ending reconstructed the story to be more consistent with their stereotypes of how rapes occur (Carli, 1999).

The Contribution of Overconfidence

Another flaw in thinking that contributes to inaccuracy in eyewitness accounts is people's tendency to be overconfident about the reliability of their memories. When tested for their memory of general information, people tend to overestimate their accuracy (Koriat & Bjork, 2005; Lichtenstein, Fischhoff, & Phillips, 1982). In studies of eyewitness recall, participants also tend to be overconfident about their recollections. Although jurors tend to be more convinced by eyewitnesses who appear confident, the evidence indicates that there is only a modest correlation between eyewitness confidence and eyewitness accuracy (Shaw, McClure, & Dykstra, 2007). Hence, many convictions of innocent people have been attributed to the impact of testimony from highly confident but mistaken eyewitnesses (Wells, Olson, & Charman, 2002).

Can you learn to make better judgments of the accuracy of your recall of everyday events? Yes, with effort you can get better at making accurate estimates of how likely you are to be correct in the recall of some fact or event. One reason that people tend to be overconfident is that if they can't think of any reasons they might be wrong, they assume they must be right. Thus, overconfidence is fueled by yet another common error in thinking—*the failure to seek disconfirming evidence.* Even veteran scientists fall prey to this weakness, as most people don't seriously consider why they might be wrong about something (Mynatt, Doherty, & Tweney, 1978).

Thus, to make more accurate assessments of what you know and don't know, it helps to engage in a deliberate process of considering why you might be wrong. Here is an example. Based on your reading of Chapter 1, write down the schools of thought associated with the following major theorists: William James, John B. Watson, and Carl Rogers. After you provide your answers, rate your confidence that the information you just provided is correct. Now, write three reasons that your answers might be wrong and three reasons that they might be correct. Most people will balk at this exercise, arguing that they cannot think of any reasons they might be wrong, but after some resistance, they can come up with several. Such reasons might include "I was half asleep when I read that part of the chapter" or "I might be confusing Watson and James." Reasons for thinking you're right could include "I distinctly recall discussing this with my friend" or "I really worked on those names in Chapter 1." After listing reasons that you might be right and might be wrong, rate your confidence in your accuracy once again. Guess what? Most people are less confident after going through such an exercise than they were before (depending, of course, on the nature of the topic).

The new confidence ratings tend to be more realistic than the original ratings (Koriat, Lichtenstein, & Fischhoff, 1980). Why? Because this exercise forces you to think more deeply about your answers and to search your memory for related information. Most people stop searching their memory as soon as they generate an answer they believe to be correct. Thus, the process of considering reasons you might be wrong about something—a process that people rarely engage in—is a useful critical thinking skill that can reduce overconfidence effects. Better assessment of what you know and don't know can be an important determinant of the quality of the decisions you make and the way you solve problems and reason from evidence.

TABLE 7.1 Critical Thinking Skills Discussed in This Application

Skill	Description
Understanding the limitations and fallibility of human memory	The critical thinker appreciates that memory is reconstructive and that even eyewitness accounts may be distorted or inaccurate.
Recognizing the bias in hindsight analysis	The critical thinker understands that knowing the outcome of events biases our recall and interpretation of the events.
Recognizing overconfidence in human cognition	The critical thinker understands that people are frequently overconfident about the accuracy of their projections for the future and their recollections of the past.
Understanding the need to seek disconfirming evidence	The critical thinker understands the value of thinking about how or why one might be wrong about something.

© Cengage Learning

Encoding: Getting Information into Memory

7.1 Clarify the role of attention and depth of processing in memory.

Attention, which facilitates encoding, is inherently selective and has been compared to a filter. Divided attention interferes with encoding and undermines memory, as well as performance on other tasks. Although people think that they can multitask, they are really switching their attention back and forth between tasks. Research clearly shows that cell phone conversations impair people's driving performance. According to Craik and Lockhart, structural, phonemic, and semantic encoding represent progressively deeper levels of processing. Levels-of-processing theory proposes that deeper processing generally results in better recall of information.

7.2 Explain how elaboration, visual imagery, and motivation to remember can enrich encoding.

Elaboration enriches encoding by linking a stimulus to other information. The creation of visual images to represent words can enrich encoding. According to dual-coding theory, visual imagery may facilitate memory by providing two memory codes rather than just one. Increasing the motivation to remember at the time of encoding can enhance memory.

Storage: Maintaining Information in Memory

7.3 Describe the sensory store in memory, and discuss the durability and capacity of short-term memory.

The sensory store preserves information in its original form, probably for only a fraction of a second. Some theorists view stimulus persistence as more like an echo than a memory. Short-term memory can maintain unrehearsed information for about 10-20 seconds. Short-term memory has a limited capacity that has long been believed to be about seven chunks of information. However, a more recent estimate suggesting that the capacity of STM is four items plus or minus one is becoming increasingly influential.

7.4 Describe Baddeley's model of working memory, and discuss research on working memory capacity.

Short-term memory appears to involve more than a simple rehearsal loop and has been reconceptualized by Baddeley as working memory. Working memory includes the phonological loop, the visuospatial sketchpad, a central executive system, and an episodic buffer. Individual differences in working memory capacity correlate with measures of many cognitive abilities.

7.5 Clarify the nature of long-term memory, and evaluate the notion that all memories are stored permanently.

Long-term memory is an unlimited capacity store that may hold information indefinitely. The existence of flashbulb memories suggests that LTM storage may be permanent, but the evidence is not convincing. Research has shown that that flashbulb memories are not as durable or accurate as claimed.

Retrieval: Getting Information out of Memory

7.6 Explain the tip-of-the-tongue phenomenon, and understand how context cues and schemas can influence retrieval.

The tip-of-the-tongue phenomenon is the temporary inability to remember something you know, which feels just out of reach. It clearly represents a failure in retrieval. Memories can be jogged by retrieval cues. Reinstating the context of an event can also facilitate recall. This factor may account for cases in which hypnosis appears to aid recall of previously forgotten information. However, hypnosis does not reliably enhance recall. A schema is an organized cluster of knowledge about a particular object or event. Schemas can influence the retrieval of events. Generally, people are more likely to remember things that are consistent with their schemas.

7.7 Summarize research on the reconstructive nature of memory, and apply the concept of source monitoring to everyday memory errors.

Memories are not exact replicas of past experiences, as memory is partially reconstructive. Research by Elizabeth Loftus on the misinformation effect shows that information learned after an event can alter one's memory of the event. Even the simple act of retelling a story can introduce inaccuracies into memory. Source monitoring is the process of making attributions about the origins of memories. According to Johnson, source-monitoring errors appear to be common and may explain why people sometimes "recall" something that was only verbally suggested to them or why they confuse their sources of information.

Forgetting: When Memory Lapses

7.8 Describe Ebbinghaus's forgetting curve and three measures of retention.

Ebbinghaus's early studies of nonsense syllables suggested that people forget very rapidly. Subsequent research showed that Ebbinghaus's forgetting curve was exceptionally steep. Forgetting can be measured by asking people to recall, recognize, or relearn information. Different methods of measuring retention often produce different estimates of forgetting. Recognition measures tend to yield higher estimates of retention than recall measures.

7.9 Understand the potential causes of forgetting.

Some forgetting, including pseudoforgetting, is caused by ineffective encoding of information, which is usually due to lack of attention. Decay theory proposes that forgetting occurs spontaneously with the passage of time. It has proven difficult to show that decay occurs in long-term memory. Interference theory proposes that people forget information because of competition from other material. Proactive interference occurs when old learning interferes with new information. Retroactive interference occurs when new learning interferes with old information. Forgetting may also be a matter of retrieval failure.

7.10 Summarize evidence on the controversy regarding recovered memories of childhood sexual abuse.

Recent years have seen a controversial surge of reports of recovered memories of sexual abuse in childhood. Those who tend to accept the validity of such recovered memories note that child abuse is quite common and argue that repression is a normal response to it. Memory researchers who tend to be skeptical about recovered memories argue that a minority of therapists prod their patients until they inadvertently create the memories of abuse that they are searching for. They point out that countless studies have demonstrated that it is not all that difficult to create false memories and that memory is more malleable and less reliable than assumed. Memories recovered spontaneously appear more likely to be authentic than memories recovered in therapy.

In Search of the Memory Trace: The Physiology of Memory

7.11 Distinguish between two types of amnesia, and identify the anatomical structures implicated in memory.

In retrograde amnesia, a person loses memory for events prior to the amnesia. In anterograde amnesia, a person shows memory deficits for events subsequent to the onset of the amnesia. Scientists learned a great deal from research on H.M.'s famous case of anterograde amnesia. Research suggests that the hippocampus and the broader medial temporal lobe system play a major role in memory. These areas may be crucial to the consolidation of memories.

7.12 Describe evidence on neural circuits and memory, and evidence on neurogenesis and memory.

Richard Thompson's research suggests that memory traces may consist of localized neural circuits. According to Eric Kandel, memory traces reflect alterations in neurotransmitter release at specific synapses. Neurogenesis may contribute to the sculpting of neural circuits for memories and provide a mechanism for time-stamping memories.

Systems and Types of Memory

7.13 Compare and contrast declarative and nondeclarative memory.

Declarative memory is memory for facts, whereas nondeclarative memory is memory for actions, skills, and conditioned responses. Declarative memory depends more on conscious attention, while nondeclarative memory is more automatic. Declarative memory is more vulnerable to forgetting. In contrast, memory for skills doesn't decline much over long retention intervals.

7.14 Distinguish between episodic versus semantic memory and retrospective versus prospective memory.

Endel Tulving subdivided declarative memory into episodic and semantic memory. Episodic memory is made up of temporally dated recollections of personal experiences, much like an autobiography. Semantic memory contains general facts, much like an encyclopedia. Prospective memory involves remembering to perform actions in the future. In contrast, retrospective memory involves remembering events from the past or previously learned information. Prospective memory tasks are more common in everyday life than is widely recognized.

Reflecting on the Chapter's Themes

7.15 Identify the three unifying themes highlighted in this chapter.

Our discussion of attention and memory enhances understanding of why people's experience of the world is highly subjective. Work on memory also highlights the field's theoretical diversity and shows that behavior is governed by multiple causes.

PERSONAL APPLICATION
Improving Everyday Memory

7.16 Discuss the importance of rehearsal, distributed practice, and interference in efforts to improve everyday memory.

Increased rehearsal facilitates memory. Testing yourself on material also enhances retention. It appears that testing forces students to engage in effortful retrieval of information, which promotes future retention. In memorizing lists, one should be wary of the serial-position effect. Distributed practice tends to be more efficient than massed practice. Study sessions should be scheduled in ways that minimize interference.

7.17 Discuss the value of deep processing, good organization, and mnemonic devices in efforts to improve everyday memory.

Deeper processing of material tends to result in greater retention. Evidence also suggests that organization enhances retention, so outlining texts may be valuable. Meaningfulness can be enhanced through the use of mnemonic devices such as acrostics, acronyms, and rhymes. The link method and the method of loci are mnemonic devices that depend on the value of visual imagery.

CRITICAL THINKING APPLICATION
Understanding the Fallibility of Eyewitness Accounts

7.18 Understand how hindsight bias and overconfidence contribute to the frequent inaccuracy of eyewitness memory.

Research indicates that eyewitness memory is not nearly as reliable or as accurate as widely believed. The hindsight bias, which is the tendency to reshape one's interpretation of the past to fit with known outcomes, often distorts eyewitness memory. People tend to be overconfident about their eyewitness recollections.

8

Cognition and Intelligence

PARADOX

There are widespread concerns about declining performance in schools, but research shows that average performance on IQ tests has increased steadily in recent decades.

© Science Source/Photo Researchers, Inc.

"Mr. Watson—Mr. Sherlock Holmes," said Stamford, introducing us. "How are you?" he said, cordially, gripping my hand with a strength for which I should hardly have given him credit. "You have been in Afghanistan, I perceive."

"How on earth did you know that?" I asked, in astonishment. (From A Study in Scarlet by Arthur Conan Doyle)

If you've ever read any Sherlock Holmes stories, you know that the great detective constantly astonished his loyal companion, Dr. Watson, with his extraordinary deductions. Obviously, Holmes could not arrive at his conclusions without a chain of reasoning. Yet to him even an elaborate reasoning process was a simple, everyday act. Consider his feat of knowing at once, upon first meeting Watson, that the doctor had been in Afghanistan. When asked, Holmes explained his reasoning as follows:

"I knew you came from Afghanistan. From long habit the train of thought ran so swiftly through my mind that I arrived at the conclusion without being conscious of the intermediate steps. There were such steps, however. The train of reasoning ran: 'Here is a gentleman of a medical type, but with the air of a military man. Clearly an army doctor, then. He has just come from the tropics, for his face is dark, and that is not the natural tint of his skin, for his wrists are fair. He has undergone hardship and sickness, as his haggard face says clearly. His left arm has been injured. He holds it in a stiff and unnatural manner. Where in the tropics could an English army doctor have seen much hardship and got his arm wounded? Clearly in Afghanistan.' The whole train of thought did not occupy a second."

Admittedly, Sherlock Holmes's deductive feats are fictional. But even to read about them—let alone imagine them, as Sir Arthur Conan Doyle did—is a remarkably complex mental act. Our everyday thought processes seem ordinary to us only because we take them for granted, just as Holmes saw nothing extraordinary in what to him was a simple deduction.

In reality, everyone is a Sherlock Holmes, continually performing magical feats of thought. Even elementary perception—for instance, watching a football game or a ballet—involves elaborate cognitive processes. People must sort through distorted, constantly shifting perceptual inputs and deduce what it is they are seeing out there in the real world. Imagine, then, the complexity of thought required to read a book, fix an automobile, or balance a checkbook. Of course, all this is not to say that human thought processes are flawless or unequaled. You probably own a $10 calculator that can run circles around you when it comes to computing square roots. As we'll see, some of the most interesting research in this chapter focuses on ways in which people's thinking can be limited, simplistic, or outright illogical.

Our topics in this chapter center on *thinking*. In the first half of the chapter, we will summarize research on cognition, or *how people think,* as we look at the subjects of problem solving and decision making. In the second half of the chapter, we will focus on *how well people think,* as measured by tests of intelligence. Thus, the first half of the chapter examines the intricacies of thinking *processes* (cognition), whereas the second half focuses on variations among people in thinking *ability* (intelligence).

The topics of cognition and intelligence have very different histories. As we will discuss later, the first useful tests of general mental ability were created between 1904 and 1916, and intelligence testing flourished throughout the 20th century. In contrast, during the first half of the 20th century, the study of cognition was actively discouraged by the theoretical dominance of behaviorism. Herbert Simon, a pioneer of cognitive psychology, recalls that "you couldn't use a word like *mind* in a psychology journal—you'd get your mouth washed out with soap" (Holden, 1986). Although it wasn't recognized until later, the 1950s brought a "cognitive revolution" in psychology (Baars, 1986). Renegade theorists, such as Simon, began to argue that behaviorists' exclusive focus on overt responses was doomed to yield an incomplete understanding of human functioning. More important, creative new approaches to research on problem solving, decision making, and reasoning led to exciting progress. Thus, it was only in the second half of the 20th century that the study of cognition grew into a robust, influential area of research. We will begin our discussion of cognitive processes by examining the topic of problem solving.

Herbert Simon
"You couldn't use a word like *mind* in a psychology journal—you'd get your mouth washed out with soap."

KEY LEARNING GOALS

8.1 List the three types of problems proposed by Greeno, and identify four common barriers to effective problem solving.

8.2 Review general problem-solving strategies and heuristics, and discuss cultural variations in cognitive style.

Problem Solving: In Search of Solutions

Look at the two problems below. Can you solve them?

In the Thompson family there are five brothers, and each brother has one sister. If you count Mrs. Thompson, how many females are there in the Thompson family?

Fifteen percent of the people in Topeka have unlisted telephone numbers. You select 200 names at random from the Topeka phone book. How many of these people can be expected to have unlisted phone numbers?

These problems, borrowed from Sternberg (1986, p. 214), are exceptionally simple, but many people fail to solve them. The answer to the first problem is two. The only females in the family are Mrs. Thompson and her one daughter, who is a sister to each of her brothers. The answer to the second problem is none. You won't find any people with unlisted phone numbers in the phone book.

Why do many people fail to solve these simple problems? You'll learn why in a moment, when we discuss barriers to effective problem solving. But first, let's examine a scheme for classifying problems into a few basic types.

Types of Problems

PSYKTREK SIM7, 7e

Problem solving **refers to active efforts to discover what must be done to achieve a goal that is not readily attainable.** Obviously, if a goal is readily attainable, there isn't a problem. But in problem-solving situations, one must go beyond the given information to overcome obstacles and reach a goal. Jim Greeno (1978) has proposed that problems can be categorized into three basic classes:

1. *Problems of inducing structure.* The person must discover the relations among the parts of the problem. The *series completion problems* and the *analogy problems* in **Figure 8.1** are examples of problems of inducing structure.

2. *Problems of arrangement.* The person must arrange the parts in a way that satisfies some criterion. The parts can usually be arranged in many ways. However, only one or a few of the arrangements form a solution. The *string problem* and the *anagrams* in **Figure 8.1** fit in this category.

3. *Problems of transformation.* The person must carry out a sequence of transformations in order to reach a specific goal. The *hobbits and orcs problem* and the *water jar problem* in **Figure 8.1** are examples of transformation problems. Transformation problems can be challenging. Even though you know exactly what the goal is, it's often not obvious how the goal can be achieved.

Greeno's list is not an exhaustive scheme for classifying problems, but it provides a useful system for understanding some of the variety seen in everyday problems.

Barriers to Effective Problem Solving

PSYKTREK 7e

On the basis of their studies of problem solving, psychologists have identified a number of barriers that frequently impede people's efforts to arrive at solutions. Common obstacles to effective problem solving include a focus on irrelevant information, functional fixedness, mental set, and imposition of unnecessary constraints.

IRRELEVANT INFORMATION

PSYKTREK 7e

We began our discussion of problem solving with two simple problems that people routinely fail to solve. The catch is that these problems contain *irrelevant information* that leads people astray. In the first problem, the number of brothers is irrelevant in deter-

A. Analogy

What word completes the analogy?

Merchant : Sell : : Customer : _____

Lawyer : Client : : Doctor : _____

B. String problem

Two strings hang from the ceiling but are too far apart to allow a person to hold one and walk to the other. On the table are a book of matches, a screwdriver, and a few pieces of cotton. How could the strings be tied together?

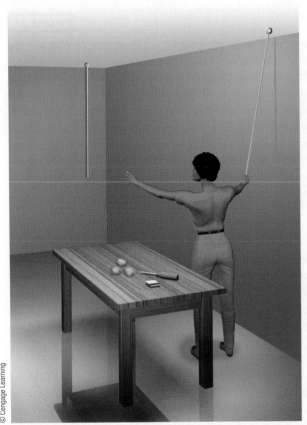

© Cengage Learning

C. Hobbits and orcs problem

Three hobbits and three orcs arrive at a river bank, and they all wish to cross onto the other side. Fortunately, there is a boat, but unfortunately, the boat can hold only two creatures at one time. Also, there is another problem. Orcs are vicious creatures, and whenever there are more orcs than hobbits on one side of the river, the orcs will immediately attack the hobbits and eat them up. Consequently, you should be certain that you never leave more orcs than hobbits on either river bank. How should the problem be solved? It must be added that the orcs, though vicious, can be trusted to bring the boat back! (From Matlin, 1989, p. 319)

D. Water jar problem

Suppose that you have a 21-cup jar, a 127-cup jar, and a 3-cup jar. Drawing and discarding as much water as you like, you need to measure out exactly 100 cups of water. How can this be done?

E. Anagram

Rearrange the letters in each row to make an English word.

RWAET

KEROJ

F. Series completion

What number or letter completes each series?

1 2 8 3 4 6 5 6 ____

A B M C D M ____

FIGURE 8.1

Six standard problems used in studies of problem solving. Try solving the problems and identifying which class each belongs to before reading further. The problems can be classified as follows. The *analogy problems* and *series completion problems* are problems of inducing structure. The solutions for the analogy problems are *Buy* and *Patient*. The solutions for the series completion problems are *4* and *E*. The *string problem* and the *anagram problems* are problems of arrangement. To solve the string problem, attach the screwdriver to one string and set it swinging as a pendulum. Hold the other string and catch the swinging screwdriver. Then you need only untie the screwdriver and tie the strings together. The solutions for the anagram problems are *WATER* and *JOKER*. The *hobbits and orcs problem* and the *water jar problem* are problems of transformation. The solutions for these two problems are outlined in **Figures 8.2** and **8.3** on the next page.

mining the number of females in the Thompson family. In the second problem, participants tend to focus on the figures of 15% and 200 names. But this numerical information is irrelevant, since all the names came out of the phone book.

Sternberg (1986) points out that people often incorrectly assume that all the numerical information in a problem is necessary to solve it. They therefore try to figure out how to use this information before they even consider whether it's relevant. Focusing on irrelevant information can have adverse effects on reasoning and problem solving (Gaeth & Shanteau, 2000). Thus, effective problem solving requires that you attempt to figure out what information is relevant and what is irrelevant before proceeding.

FIGURE 8.2

Solution to the hobbits and orcs problem. This problem is difficult because it is necessary to temporarily work "away" from the goal.

FIGURE 8.3

The method for solving the water jar problem. As explained in the text, the correct formula is B − A − 2C.

FUNCTIONAL FIXEDNESS `PSYKTREK 7e`

Another common barrier to successful problem solving is *functional fixedness*—the **tendency to perceive an item only in terms of its most common use.** Functional fixedness has been seen in the difficulties that people have with the string problem in **Figure 8.1** (Maier, 1931). Solving this problem requires finding a novel use for one of the objects: the screwdriver. Participants tend to think of the screwdriver in terms of its usual functions—turning screws and perhaps prying things open. They have a hard time viewing the screwdriver as a weight. Their rigid way of thinking about the screwdriver illustrates functional fixedness (Dominowski & Bourne, 1994). Ironically, young children appear to be less vulnerable to functional fixedness than older children or adults because they have less knowledge about the conventional uses of various objects (Defeyter & German, 2003).

MENTAL SET `PSYKTREK 7e`

Rigid thinking is also at work when a mental set interferes with effective problem solving. A *mental set* **exists when people persist in using problem-solving strategies that have worked in the past.** The effects of mental set were seen in a classic study by Abraham Luchins (1942). He asked subjects to work a series of water jar problems, like the one introduced earlier. Six such problems are outlined in **Figure 8.4**, which shows the capacities of the three jars and the amounts of water to be measured out. Try solving these problems.

Were you able to develop a formula for solving these problems? The first four all require the same strategy, which is described in **Figure 8.3**. You have to fill jar B, draw off the amount that jar A holds once, and draw off the amount that jar C holds twice. Thus, the formula for your solution is B − A − 2C. Although the fifth problem has an obvious and much simpler solution (A − C) (see **Figure 8.8** on page 254), Luchins found that most participants stuck with the more cumbersome strategy that they had used in problems 1–4. Moreover, most subjects couldn't solve the sixth problem in the allotted time, because they kept trying to use their proven strategy, which does not work for this problem. The participants' reliance on their "tried and true" strategy is an illustration of mental set in problem solving. Mental set may explain why having expertise in an area sometimes backfires and hampers problem-solving efforts (Leighton & Sternberg, 2003).

UNNECESSARY CONSTRAINTS `PSYKTREK 7e`

Effective problem solving requires specifying all the constraints governing a problem *without assuming any constraints that don't exist.* An example of a problem in which people place an unnecessary constraint on the solution is shown in **Figure 8.5** (Adams, 1980). Without lifting your pencil from the paper, try to draw four straight lines that will cross through all nine dots. If you struggle with this one, don't feel bad. When a time limit of a few minutes is imposed on this problem, the typical solution rate is 0% (MacGregor et al., 2001). The key factor that makes this a difficult problem is that most people will not draw lines outside the imaginary boundary that surrounds the dots. Notice that this constraint is not part of the problem statement. It's imposed only by the problem solver. Correct solutions, two of which are shown in **Figure 8.9** on page 254, extend outside the imaginary boundary. To solve this problem you need to literally "think outside the box." This popular slogan, spawned by the nine-dot problem, reflects the fact that people often make assumptions that impose unnecessary constraints on problem-solving efforts.

Approaches to Problem Solving

People use a variety of strategies in attempting to solve problems. In this section, we'll examine some general strategies.

TRIAL AND ERROR AND HEURISTICS

Trial and error is a common, albeit primitive, approach to solving problems. *Trial and error* **involves trying possible solutions sequentially and discarding those that are in error until one works.** Trial and error can be effective when there are relatively few possible solutions to be tried out. However, this method becomes impractical when the number of possible maneuvers is large. Consider, for instance, the problem shown in **Figure 8.6**. The challenge is to move just two matches to create a pattern containing four equal squares. Sure, you could use a trial-and-error approach in moving pairs of matches. But you'd better allocate plenty of time to this effort, as there are over 60,000 possible rearrangements to check out (see **Figure 8.10** on the next page for the solution).

Because trial and error is inefficient, people often use shortcuts called *heuristics* in problem solving. **A *heuristic* is a guiding principle or "rule of thumb" used in solving problems or making decisions.** Heuristics are often useful, but they don't guarantee success. Helpful heuristics in problem solving include forming subgoals, searching for analogies, changing the representation of the problem, and taking a break.

FORMING SUBGOALS

It is often useful to tackle problems by formulating *subgoals,* intermediate steps toward a solution (Catrambone, 1998). When you reach a subgoal, you've solved part of the problem. Some problems have fairly obvious subgoals, and research has shown that people take advantage of them. For instance, in analogy problems, the first subgoal usually is to figure out the possible relations between the first two parts of the analogy.

The wisdom of formulating subgoals can be seen in the *tower of Hanoi problem,* depicted in **Figure 8.7** on the next page. The terminal goal for this problem is to move all three rings on peg A to peg C while abiding by two restrictions: Only the top ring on a peg can be moved, and a ring must never be placed above a smaller ring. See whether you can solve the problem before continuing.

Dividing this problem into subgoals facilitates a solution (Kotovsky, Hayes, & Simon, 1985). If you think in terms of subgoals, your first task is to get ring 3 to the bottom of peg C. Breaking this task into sub-subgoals, subjects can figure out that they should move ring 1 to peg C, ring 2 to peg B, and ring 1 from peg C to peg B. These maneuvers allow you to place ring 3 at the bottom of peg C, thus meeting your first subgoal. Your next subgoal—getting ring 2 over to peg C—can be accomplished in just two steps: move ring 1 to peg A and ring 2 to peg C. It should then be obvious how to achieve your final subgoal—getting ring 1 over to peg C.

	Capacity of empty jars			Desired amount of water
Problem	A	B	C	
1	14	163	25	99
2	18	43	10	5
3	9	42	6	21
4	20	59	4	31
5	23	49	3	20
6	28	76	3	25

© Cengage Learning

FIGURE 8.4

Additional water jar problems. Using jars A, B, and C, with the capacities indicated in each row, figure out how to measure out the desired amount of water specified on the far right. The solutions are shown in **Figure 8.8**. (Based on Luchins, 1942)

SOURCE: *Cyclopedia of Puzzles,* Sam Lloyds, 1914.

FIGURE 8.5

The nine-dot problem. Without lifting your pencil from the paper, draw no more than four lines that will cross through all nine dots. For possible solutions, see **Figure 8.9**.

SOURCE: Adams, J. L. (1980). *Conceptual blockbusting: A guide to better ideas.* New York: W. H. Freeman. Copyright © 1980 by James L. Adams. Reprinted by permission of W. H. Freeman & Co.

FIGURE 8.6

The matchstick problem. Move two matches to form four equal squares. You can find the solution in **Figure 8.10**.

SOURCE: Kendler, H. H. (1974). *Basic psychology* (3rd ed., pp. 403, 404). Menlo Park, CA: Benjamin-Cummings. Copyright © 1974 The Benjamin-Cummings Publishing Co.

© Cengage Learning

CALVIN & HOBBES

PROBLEMS OFTEN LOOK OVERWHELMING AT FIRST.

THE SECRET IS TO BREAK PROBLEMS INTO SMALL, MANAGEABLE CHUNKS. IF YOU DEAL WITH *THOSE*, YOU'RE DONE BEFORE YOU KNOW IT.

FOR EXAMPLE, I'M SUPPOSED TO READ THIS ENTIRE HISTORY CHAPTER. IT LOOKS IMPOSSIBLE, SO I BREAK THE PROBLEM DOWN.

YOU FOCUS ON READING THE FIRST SECTION?

I ASK MYSELF, "DO I EVEN CARE?"

FIGURE 8.7

The tower of Hanoi problem. Your mission is to move the rings from peg A to peg C. You can move only the top ring on a peg and can't place a larger ring above a smaller one. The solution is explained in the text.

SEARCHING FOR ANALOGIES

Searching for analogies is another of the major heuristics for solving problems (Holyoak, 2005). We reason by analogy constantly (Sternberg, 2009), and these efforts to identify analogies can facilitate innovative thinking (Gassmann & Zeschky, 2008). If you can spot an analogy between problems, you may be able to use the solution to a previous problem to solve a current one. Of course, using this strategy depends on recognizing the similarity between the two problems, which may itself be a challenging problem. Nonetheless, recent studies of real-world problem-solving efforts show that we depend on analogies far more than most people appreciate. For example, one study of biologists' problem solving recorded during their lab meetings found that they used 3–15 analogies per hour (Dunbar & Blanchette, 2001). Another study recorded design engineers during their product development meetings and found that they came up with an average of 11 analogies per hour of deliberation (Christensen & Schunn, 2007).

Unfortunately, people often are unable to recognize that two problems are similar and that an analogy might lead to a solution (Kurtz & Lowenstein, 2007). One reason is

FIGURE 8.8

Solutions to the additional water jar problems. The solution for problems 1–4 is the same as the solution shown in **Figure 8.3** (B − A − 2C). This method will work for problem 5, but there also is a simpler solution (A − C), which is the only solution for problem 6. Many subjects exhibit a mental set on these problems, as they fail to notice the simpler solution for problem 5.

FIGURE 8.9

Two solutions to the nine-dot problem. The key to solving the problem is to recognize that nothing in the problem statement forbids going outside the imaginary boundary surrounding the dots.

SOURCE: *Cyclopedia of Puzzles,* Sam Lloyds, 1914.

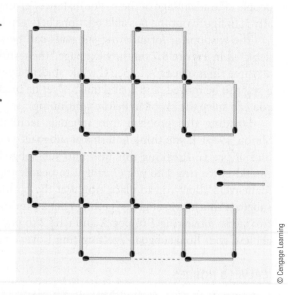

FIGURE 8.10

Solution to the matchstick problem. The key to solving this problem is to "open up" the figure, something many subjects are reluctant to do because they impose unnecessary constraints on the problem.

SOURCE: Kendler, H. H. (1974). *Basic psychology* (3rd ed., pp. 403, 404). Menlo Park, CA: Benjamin-Cummings. Copyright © 1974 The Benjamin-Cummings Publishing Co.

that they tend to focus on superficial, surface features of problems rather than their underlying structure (Bassok, 2003). Nonetheless, analogies can be a powerful tool in efforts to solve problems.

CHANGING THE REPRESENTATION OF THE PROBLEM

Whether you solve a problem often hinges on how you envision it—your *representation of the problem*. Many problems can be represented in a variety of ways, such as verbally, mathematically, or spatially. You might represent a problem with a list, a table, an equation, a graph, a matrix of facts or numbers, a hierarchical tree diagram, or a sequential flowchart (Halpern, 2003). When you fail to make progress with your initial representation of a problem, changing your representation is often a good strategy (Novick & Bassok, 2005). As an illustration, see whether you can solve the *Buddhist monk problem*:

At sunrise, a Buddhist monk sets out to climb a tall mountain. He follows a narrow path that winds around the mountain and up to a temple. He stops frequently to rest and climbs at varying speeds, arriving around sunset. After staying a few days, he begins his return journey. As before, he starts at sunrise, rests often, walks at varying speeds, and arrives around sunset. Prove that there must be a spot along the path that the monk will pass on both trips at precisely the same time of day.

Why should there be such a spot? The monk's walking speed varies. Shouldn't it all be a matter of coincidence if he reaches a spot at the same time each day? Moreover, if there is such a spot, how would you prove it? Participants who represent this problem in terms of verbal, mathematical, or spatial information struggle. Subjects who work with a graphic representation fare much better. The best way to represent the problem is to envision the monk (or two different monks) ascending and descending the mountain at the same time. The two monks must meet at some point. If you construct a graph (see **Figure 8.11**) you can vary the speed of the monks' descent in endless ways, but you can see that there's always a place where they meet.

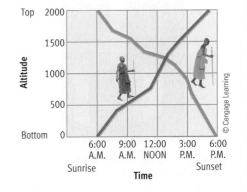

FIGURE 8.11
Solution to the Buddhist monk problem. If you represent this problem graphically and think in terms of two monks, it is readily apparent that the monk does pass a single spot at the same time each day.

Concept Check 8.1

Thinking About Problem Solving

Check your understanding of problem solving by answering some questions about the following problem. Begin by trying to solve the problem.

The candle problem.

Using the objects shown—candles, a box of matches, string, and some tacks—figure out how you could mount a candle on a wall so that it could be used as a light.

Work on the problem for a while, then turn to page 256 to see the solution. After you've seen the solution, respond to the following questions. The answers are in Appendix A.

1. If it didn't occur to you that the matchbox could be converted from a container to a platform, this illustrates _____ _____.

2. While working on the problem, if you thought to yourself, "How can I create a platform attached to the wall?" you used the heuristic of _____ _____.

3. If it occurred to you suddenly that the matchbox could be used as a platform, this realization would be an example of _____.

4. If you had a hunch that there might be some similarity between this problem and the string problem in **Figure 8.1** (the similarity is the novel use of an object), your hunch would illustrate the heuristic of _____ _____ _____.

5. In terms of Greeno's three types of problems, the candle problem is a(n) _____ problem.

The solution to the candle problem in Concept Check 8.1.

Craig McClain

TAKING A BREAK: INCUBATION

When a problem is resistant to solution, there is much to be said for taking a break and not thinking about it for a while. After the break, you may find that you see the problem in a different light, and new solutions may spring to mind. Obviously, there is no guarantee that a break will facilitate problem solving. But breaks pay off often enough that researchers have given the phenomenon a name: *incubation*. **An *incubation effect* occurs when new solutions surface for a previously unsolved problem after a period of not consciously thinking about the problem.** Depending on the nature of the problem, incubation periods may be measured in minutes, hours, or days. The likelihood of an incubation effect depends on a number of task-related factors, but on the whole, incubation does tend to enhance problem solving (Dodds, Ward, & Smith, 2011; Sio & Ormerod, 2009). Research suggests that incubation effects can even occur during sleep (Cai et al., 2009; Stickgold & Walker, 2004). Some theorists believe that incubation effects occur because people continue to work on problems at an unconscious level after conscious effort has been suspended (Ellwood et al., 2009). However, a host of alternative explanations for incubation effects have also been proposed (Helie & Sun, 2010).

Culture, Cognitive Style, and Problem Solving

Do the varied experiences of people from different cultures lead to cross-cultural variations in problem solving? Yes, at least to some degree. Researchers have found cultural differences in the cognitive style that people exhibit in solving problems.

Richard Nisbett and his colleagues (Nisbett et al., 2001; Nisbett & Miyamoto, 2005) have argued that people from Eastern Asian cultures (such as China, Japan, and Korea) display a *holistic cognitive style* that focuses on context and relationships among elements, whereas people from Western cultures (America and Europe) exhibit an *analytic cognitive style* that focuses on objects and their properties rather than context. To put it simply, *Easterners see wholes where Westerners see parts.*

In one test of this hypothesis, Masuda and Nisbett (2001) presented computer-animated scenes of fish and other underwater objects to Japanese and American participants and asked them to report what they had seen. The initial comments of American subjects typically referred to the focal fish, whereas the initial comments of Japanese

© vilainecrevette/Shutterstock.com

subjects usually referred to background elements. Furthermore, the Japanese participants made about 70% more statements about context or background and about twice as many statements about relationships between elements in the scenes. Based on these and many other findings, Nisbett et al. (2001) conclude that cultural differences in cognitive style are substantial and that "literally different cognitive processes are often invoked by East Asians and Westerners dealing with the same problem" (p. 305). These disparities in cognitive style seem to be rooted in variations in cultures' social orientation (Varnum et al., 2010). They appear to grow out of Western cultures' emphasis on the individual and independence as opposed to Eastern cultures' emphasis on the group and interdependence (see Chapters 11 and 12). Some theorists speculate that variations in cultural experiences may even lead to subtle cultural differences in neural structure, or how people's brains are "wired," but evidence on this hypothesis remains scant (Park & Huang, 2010).

Problems are not the only kind of cognitive challenge that people grapple with on a regular basis. Life also seems to constantly demand decisions. As you might expect, cognitive psychologists have shown great interest in the process of decision making, which is our next subject.

Decision Making: Choices and Chances

KEY LEARNING GOALS

8.3 Articulate Simon's theory of bounded rationality, and discuss research on decisions about preferences.

8.4 Understand the nature of risky decision making and the availability and representativeness heuristics.

8.5 Describe some common flaws in reasoning about decisions.

8.6 Describe the nature of fast and frugal heuristics, and discuss dual-process theories of decision making.

Decisions, decisions. Life is full of them. You decided to read this book today. Earlier today you decided when to get up, whether to eat breakfast, and if so, what to eat. Usually you make routine decisions like these with little effort. But on occasion you need to make important decisions that require more thought. Big decisions—such as selecting a car, a home, or a job—tend to be difficult. The alternatives usually have a number of facets that need to be weighed. For instance, in choosing among several cars, you may want to compare their costs, roominess, fuel economy, handling, acceleration, stylishness, reliability, safety features, and warranties.

Decision making involves evaluating alternatives and making choices among them. Most people try to be systematic and rational in their decision making. However, the work that earned Herbert Simon the 1978 Nobel prize in economics showed that people don't always live up to these goals. Before Simon's work, most traditional theories in economics assumed that people made rational choices to maximize their economic gains. Simon (1957) noted that people have a limited ability to process and evaluate information on numerous facets of possible alternatives. Thus, Simon's *theory of bounded rationality* asserts that people tend to use simple strategies in decision making that focus on only a few facets of available options and often result in "irrational" decisions that are less than optimal.

Spurred by Simon's analysis, psychologists have devoted several decades to the study of how cognitive biases distort people's decision making. Let's look at this research—and recent criticism that it has inspired.

Making Choices About Preferences

Many decisions involve choices about *preferences,* which can be made using a variety of strategies (Goldstein & Hogarth, 1997). Barry Schwartz (2004) has argued that people in modern societies are overwhelmed by an overabundance of such choices about preferences. For example, Schwartz describes how a simple visit to a local supermarket can require a consumer to choose from 285 varieties of cookies, 61 suntan lotions, 150 lipsticks, and 175 salad dressings. Increased choice is most tangible in the realm of consumer goods. But Schwartz argues that it also extends into more significant domains of life. Today, people tend to have unprecedented opportunities to make choices about how they will be educated, how and where they will work, how their intimate relationships will unfold, and even how they will look. Although enormous freedom of choice sounds attractive, Schwartz argues that the overabundance of choices in modern life has unexpected costs. He suggests that people routinely make errors even when choosing among a handful of alternatives and that errors become much more likely when decisions become more complex. And he explains how having more alternatives increases the potential for rumination and postdecision regret. Ultimately, he argues, the malaise associated with *choice overload* undermines individuals' happiness and contributes to depression.

Consistent with this analysis, recent research has suggested that when consumers have too many choices (for a specific product), they are more likely to leave a store empty-handed (Jessup et al., 2009). Why? Studies show that when there are many choices available, people are more likely to struggle deciding which is the best option and so defer their decision (White & Hoffrage, 2009). Researchers have also found that having to make a lot of decisions depletes mental resources and undermines subsequent self-control (Vohs et al., 2008). How many choices are too many? That depends on a host of factors, but it appears that people prefer more choices up to a point, and then further increases in options lead to decreased satisfaction with the situation (Reutskaja & Hogarth, 2009).

Reality Check

Misconception

In making choices, people like to have lots of options; the more options the better.

Reality

Having choices is a good thing, but having more choices is not necessarily better. People like to have a variety of options, but recent research on choice overload suggests only up to a point. An overabundance of options can make decisions difficult and unpleasant, foster decision paralysis (an inability to decide), and lead to postdecision regret.

© Yuri Arcurs/Shutterstock.com

Another line of research has looked at whether decisions about preferences work out better when people engage in conscious deliberation or go with intuitive, unconscious feelings based on minimal deliberation. Ap Dijksterhuis and colleagues (Dijksterhuis & Nordgren, 2006; Dijksterhuis & van Olden, 2006) have argued that, given the limited capacity of conscious thought, deliberate decisions should be superior to intuitive decisions when choices are simple, but intuitive, unconscious decisions should be superior when choices are complex. In a test of this hypothesis, they had a sample of people indicate how many facets they would evaluate in deciding to purchase 40 consumer products, such as shampoos, shoes, and cameras, yielding a *decision complexity* score for each product (Dijksterhuis et al., 2006). Subsequently, another group of participants picked a product from this list that they recently bought and they were asked how much conscious thought they put into the decision and how satisfied they were with their choice. **Figure 8.12** depicts participants' postchoice satisfaction for the six products that were chosen most frequently from the list. As predicted, conscious deliberation promoted greater satisfaction when decisions were simple. However, just the opposite occurred for complex decisions. Dijksterhuis calls this phenomenon the *deliberation-without-attention effect*—when people are faced with complex choices, they tend to make better decisions if they don't devote careful attention to the matter. Dijksterhuis believes that deliberations are taking place, but outside of conscious awareness. Along with other lines of research this effect suggests that intuition can sometimes be superior to logic and reflection (Gladwell, 2005; Myers, 2002).

Heuristics in Judging Probabilities

PSYKTREK 7f

- What are your chances of passing your next psychology test if you study only 3 hours?
- How likely is a major downturn in the stock market during the upcoming year?
- What are the odds of your getting into graduate school in the field of your choice?

FIGURE 8.12

Postchoice satisfaction as a function of decision complexity in the Dijksterhuis et al. (2006) study. Mean ratings of postchoice satisfaction for the six products chosen most often are shown here. The products are arranged, from left to right, in order of increasing decision complexity. For each product, participants' ratings of how much they deliberated about their purchase were split at the median, dividing them into conscious versus unconscious decision makers. When decision complexity was low, conscious deliberation was associated with greater satisfaction, but when decision complexity was high, conscious deliberation was associated with less satisfaction.

SOURCE: Dijksterhuis, A., Bos, M. W., Nordgren, L. F., & van Baaren, R. B. (2006). On making the right choice: The deliberation-without-attention effect. *Science,* *311*(5763), 1005–1007. Copyright © 2006 the American Association for the Advancement of Science. Reprinted by permission from the AAAS.

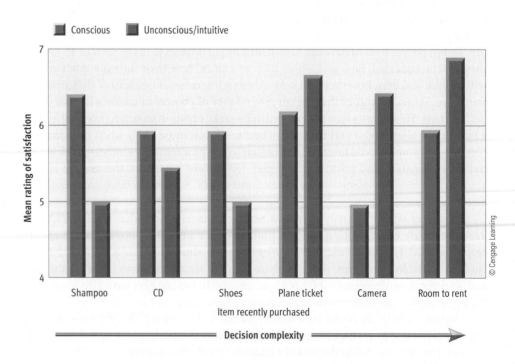

These questions ask you to make probability estimates. Such estimates are crucial in *risky decision making,* which involves making choices under conditions of uncertainty. Uncertainty exists when people don't know what will happen. Amos Tversky and Daniel Kahneman (1982; Kahneman & Tversky, 2000) have conducted extensive research on the *heuristics,* or mental shortcuts, that people use in grappling with probability estimates. This research earned Kahneman the Nobel prize in economics in 2002 (unfortunately, his collaborator, Amos Tversky, died in 1996).

Availability is one such heuristic. The *availability heuristic* involves basing the estimated probability of an event on the ease with which relevant instances come to mind. For example, you may estimate the divorce rate by recalling the number of divorces among your friends' parents. Recalling specific instances of an event is a reasonable strategy to use in estimating the event's probability. However, if instances occur frequently but you have difficulty retrieving them from memory, your estimate will be biased. For instance, it's easier to think of words that begin with a certain letter than words that contain that letter at some other position. Thus, people should tend to respond that there are more words starting with the letter *K* than words having a *K* in the third position. To test this hypothesis, Tversky and Kahneman (1973) selected five consonants (*K, L, N, R, V*) that occur more frequently in the third position of a word than in the first. Subjects were asked whether each of the letters appears more often in the first or third position. Most of the subjects erroneously believed that all five letters were much more frequent in the first than in the third position, confirming the hypothesis.

Representativeness is another guide in estimating probabilities identified by Kahneman and Tversky (1982). The *representativeness heuristic* involves basing the estimated probability of an event on how similar it is to the typical prototype of that event. To illustrate, imagine that you flip a coin six times and keep track of how often the result is heads (H) or tails (T). Which of the following sequences is more likely?

1. T T T T T T
2. H T T H T H

People generally believe that the second sequence is more likely. After all, coin tossing is a random affair, and the second sequence looks much more representative of a random process than the first. In reality, the probability of each exact sequence is precisely the same ($1/2 \times 1/2 \times 1/2 \times 1/2 \times 1/2 \times 1/2 = 1/64$). Overdependence on the representativeness heuristic has been used to explain quite a variety of decision-making tendencies (Teigen, 2004).

Common Flaws in Reasoning About Decisions

PsykTrek 7f

The pioneering work of Amos Tversky and Daniel Kahneman (1974, 1982) led to an explosion of research on risky decision making. In their efforts to identify the heuristics that people use in decision making, investigators stumbled onto quite a few misconceptions, oversights, and biases. It turns out that people deviate in predictable ways from optimal decision strategies—with surprising regularity (Dawes, 2001; Gilovich, Griffin, & Kahneman, 2002). Moreover, it appears that no one is immune to these errors in thinking. In recent research, Stanovich and West (2008) examined the relationship between intelligence (estimated by SAT scores) and the ability to avoid a variety of cognitive biases and flaws. For the most part, they found that cognitive ability did not correlate with the ability to avoid irrational errors in thinking. In other words, extremely bright people are just as vulnerable to irrational thinking as everyone else. Fortunately, however, some research suggests that increased awareness of common shortcomings in reasoning about decisions can lead to fewer errors in thinking and improved decision making (Lilienfeld, Ammirati, & Landfield, 2009; Milkman, Chugh, & Bazerman, 2009). With this goal in mind, let's look at some common pitfalls in decision making.

Daniel Kahneman
"The human mind suppresses uncertainty. We're not only convinced that we know more about our politics, our businesses, and our spouses than we really do, but also that what we don't know must be unimportant."

Amos Tversky
"People treat their own cases as if they were unique, rather than part of a huge lottery. You hear this silly argument that 'The odds don't apply to me.' Why should God, or whoever runs this lottery, give you special treatment?"

IGNORING BASE RATES

PsykTrek 7f

Steve is very shy and withdrawn, invariably helpful, but with little interest in people or in the world of reality. A meek and tidy soul, he has a need for order and structure and a passion for detail. Do you think Steve is a salesperson or a librarian? (Adapted from Tversky & Kahneman, 1974, p. 1124)

Using the *representativeness heuristic,* participants tend to guess that Steve is a librarian because he resembles their prototype of a librarian (Tversky & Kahneman, 1982). In reality, this is not a very wise guess, because *it ignores the base rates* of librarians and salespeople in the population. Virtually everyone knows that salespeople outnumber librarians by a wide margin (roughly 75 to 1 in the United States). This fact makes it much more likely that Steve is in sales. But in estimating probabilities, people often ignore information on base rates. People are particularly bad about applying base rates to themselves. For example, entrepreneurs starting new companies ignore the high failure rate for new businesses, and burglars underestimate the likelihood that they will end up in jail.

THE CONJUNCTION FALLACY

PsykTrek 7f

Let's look at another common mistake in decision-related reasoning. Imagine that you're going to meet a man who is an articulate, ambitious, power-hungry wheeler-dealer. Do you think it's more likely that he's a college teacher or a college teacher who's also a politician? People tend to guess that the man is a "college teacher who's a politician" because the description fits with the typical prototype of politicians. But stop and think for a moment. The broader category of college professors completely includes the smaller subcategory of college professors who are politicians (see **Figure 8.13**). The probability of being in the subcategory cannot be higher than the probability of being in the broader category. It's a logical impossibility! Tversky and Kahneman (1983) call this error the *conjunction fallacy.* **The *conjunction fallacy* occurs when people estimate that the odds of two uncertain events happening together are greater than the odds of either event happening alone.** It has generally been attributed to the powerful influence of the representativeness heuristic (Epstein, Donovan, & Denes-Raj, 1999).

THE GAMBLER'S FALLACY

PsykTrek 7f

Laura is in a casino watching people play roulette. The 38 slots in the roulette wheel include 18 black numbers, 18 red numbers, and 2 green numbers. Hence, on any one spin, the probability of red or black is slightly less than 50-50 (.474 to be exact). Although Laura hasn't been betting, she has been following the pattern of results in the game very carefully. The ball has landed in red seven times in a row. Laura concludes that black is long overdue and she jumps into the game, betting heavily on black.

Do you agree with Laura's reasoning? A great many people tend to believe that Laura has made a good bet (Stanovich, 2003). However, they're wrong. Laura's behavior illus-

© 2005 Steve Kelley. *The Times-Picayune.* Reprinted with permission of the creator.

College professors

College professors who are also politicians

FIGURE 8.13

The conjunction fallacy. People routinely fall victim to the conjunction fallacy, but as this diagram makes obvious, the probability of being in a subcategory (college professors who are politicians) cannot be higher than the probability of being in the broader category (college professors). As this case illustrates, it often helps to represent a problem in a diagram.

trates the *gambler's fallacy*—the belief that the odds of a chance event increase if the event hasn't occurred recently. People believe that the laws of probability should yield fair results and that a random process must be self-correcting (Burns & Corpus, 2004). These aren't bad assumptions in the long run. However, they don't apply to individual, independent events. The roulette wheel does not remember its recent results and make adjustments for them. Each spin of the wheel is an independent event. The probability of black on each spin remains at .474, even if red comes up 100 times in a row! The gambler's fallacy reflects the pervasive influence of the *representativeness heuristic*. In betting on black, Laura is predicting that future results will be more representative of a random process. This logic can be used to estimate the probability of black across a *string of spins*. But it doesn't apply to a *specific spin* of the roulette wheel.

OVERESTIMATING THE IMPROBABLE

PsykTrek 7f

Let's examine another issue that frequently crops up in working with probabilities. Various causes of death are paired up below. In each pairing, which is the more likely cause of death?

Asthma or tornadoes?
Accidental falls or firearms accidents?
Tuberculosis or floods?
Suicide or homicide?

Table 8.1 on the next page shows the actual mortality rates for each of the causes of death just listed. As you can see, the first choice in each pair is the more common cause of death. If you guessed wrong for several pairings, you may be a victim of the tendency to *overestimate the improbable*. People tend to greatly overestimate the likelihood of

TABLE 8.1   **Actual Mortality Rates for Selected Causes of Death**

Cause of Death	Rate	Cause of Death	Rate
Asthma	2,000	Tornadoes	25
Accidental falls	6,021	Firearms accidents	320
Tuberculosis	400	Floods	44
Suicide	11,300	Homicide	6,800

Note: Mortality rates are per 100 million people and are based on the *Statistical Abstract of the United States, 2001.*

dramatic, vivid—but infrequent—events that receive heavy media coverage. Thus, the number of fatalities resulting from tornadoes, floods, firearms accidents, and murders is usually overestimated (Slovic, Fischoff, & Lichtenstein, 1982). Fatalities due to asthma and other common diseases, which receive less media coverage, tend to be underestimated. This tendency to exaggerate the improbable has generally been attributed to the operation of the *availability heuristic* (Reber, 2004). Instances of floods, tornadoes, and such are readily available in memory because people are exposed to a great deal of publicity about such events.

LOSS AVERSION

In making decisions, people display a curious bias called *loss aversion*. That is, they tend to assume that losses will have more impact on them than gains of equal size (Kahneman & Tversky, 1979; Novemsky & Kahneman, 2005). Thus, most people expect that the negative impact of losing $1000 will be greater than the positive impact of wining $1000. Loss aversion can lead people to pass up excellent opportunities. For instance, subjects tend to decline a theoretical gamble in which they are given an 85% chance of doubling their life savings versus a 15% chance of losing their life savings, which mathematically is vastly more attractive than any bet one could place in a casino (Gilbert, 2006). The problem with loss aversion, as Daniel Gilbert and his colleagues have shown, is that people generally overestimate the intensity and duration of the negative emotions that they will experience after all sorts of losses, ranging from losing a job or romantic partner to botching an interview or watching one's team lose in a big game (Gilbert, Driver-Linn, & Wilson, 2002; Kermer et al., 2006).

The availability heuristic can be dramatized by juxtaposing the unrelated phenomena of tornadoes and asthma. People are routinely killed in tornadoes, but far more die annually from asthma (see **Table 8.1**). However, since the news media devote great attention to tornado fatalities, but rarely focus on deaths from asthma, people tend to assume that tornado-related deaths are much more common.

Evolutionary Analyses of Fast and Frugal Heuristics

A central conclusion of the last 30 years of research on decision making has been that human decision-making strategies are riddled with errors and biases that yield surprisingly irrational results (Goldstein & Hogarth, 1997; Risen & Gilovich, 2007; Shafir & LeBoeuf, 2002). However, some evolutionary psychologists have argued that humans only *seem* irrational because cognitive psychologists have been asking the wrong questions and formulating problems in the wrong ways—ways that have nothing to do with the adaptive problems that the human mind has evolved to solve (Cosmides & Tooby, 1996). Expanding on this view, Gerd Gigerenzer has asserted that humans' reasoning largely depends on "fast and frugal heuristics" that are quite a bit simpler than the complicated mental processes studied in traditional cognitive research (Gigerenzer, 2000, 2004, 2008; Goldstein & Gigerenzer, 1999; Todd & Gigerenzer, 2000, 2007). According to Gigerenzer, organisms from toads to stockbrokers have to make fast decisions under demanding circumstances with limited information. In most instances organisms (including humans) do not have the time, resources, or cognitive capacities to gather all the relevant information, consider all the possible options, calculate all the probabilities and risks, and then make the statistically optimal decision. Instead, they use quick and dirty heuristics that are less than perfect but that work well enough most of the time to be adaptive in the real world.

Gigerenzer and his colleagues have shown that fast and frugal heuristics can be surprisingly effective. One heuristic that is often used in selecting between alternatives based on some quantitative dimension is the *recognition heuristic,* which works as follows: If one of two alternatives is recognized and the other is not, assume that the recognized alternative has the higher value. Consider the following questions—Which city has more inhabitants: San Diego or San Antonio? Hamburg or Munich? In choosing between U.S. cities, American college students weighed a lifetime of facts useful for inferring population and made the correct choice 71% of the time. In choosing between German cities about which they knew very little, the same students depended on the recognition heuristic and chose correctly 73% of the time (Goldstein & Gigerenzer, 2002). Thus, the recognition heuristic allowed students to perform just as well with very limited knowledge as they did with extensive knowledge.

Concept Check 8.2

Recognizing Flaws in Decision Making

Check your understanding of common flaws in decision making by trying to identify the errors in reasoning apparent in the following examples. Write the letter for the relevant cognitive error in the space on the left choosing from the following: (a) neglect of base rates, (b) the conjunction fallacy, (c) the gambler's fallacy, (d) overestimation of the improbable, and (e) loss aversion. You can find the answers in Appendix A.

_____ 1. Alex is an outstanding linebacker for his high school football team. He is well aware that only a small minority of high school stars earn college scholarships and that an even tinier fraction of college athletes go on to play professional ball. Nonetheless, he is confident that he will be a star in the NFL someday.

_____ 2. Reggie is enjoying a delightful vacation at a plush beachfront hotel in Florida. But his friends cannot talk him into going into the ocean because he is extremely worried about the possibility of a shark attack.

_____ 3. Maurice and Whitney are the proud parents of four girls, but they still yearn for a baby boy. In contemplating whether to try to have another child in the hopes of adding a boy to the family, they figure "What the heck, the laws of probability are in our favor. Let's go for it."

Gigerenzer and his colleagues have studied a variety of other quick, one-reason decision-making strategies and shown that they can yield inferences that are just as accurate as much more elaborate strategies that carefully weigh many factors (Marewski, Gaissmaier, & Gigerenzer, 2010). And the researchers have demonstrated that people actually use these fast and frugal heuristics in a diverse array of situations (Gigerenzer & Todd, 1999; Rieskamp & Hoffrage, 1999). Thus, the study of fast and frugal heuristics promises to be an intriguing line of research in the study of human decision making.

How have traditional decision-making theorists responded to the challenge presented by Gigerenzer and other evolutionary theorists? They acknowledge that people often rely on fast and frugal heuristics, but they argue that this finding does not make decades of research on carefully reasoned approaches to decision making meaningless. Rather, they propose *dual-process theories* positing that people depend on two different modes or systems of thinking when making decisions (De Neys, 2006; Evans, 2007; Gilovich & Griffin, 2010; Kahneman, 2003). One system consists of quick, simple, effortless, automatic judgments, like Gigerenzer's fast and frugal heuristics, which traditional theorists prefer to characterize as "intuitive thinking." The second system consists of slower, more elaborate, effortful, controlled judgments, like those studied in traditional decision research. According to this view, the second system monitors and corrects the intuitive system as needed and takes over when complicated or important decisions loom. Thus, traditional theorists maintain that fast and frugal heuristics and reasoned, rule-governed decision strategies exist side by side and that both need to be studied to fully understand decision making.

Although sound decision making and effective problem solving obviously are key aspects of intelligence, there has been relatively little overlap between research on cognition and research on intelligence. As you have seen, cognitive research investigates how people use their intelligence; the focus is on *process*. In contrast, the study of intelligence has usually been approached from a testing perspective, which emphasizes measuring the *amount* of intelligence people have and figuring out why some have more than others. Let's look at how these measurements are made.

Measuring Intelligence

We'll begin our discussion with a brief overview of the history of intelligence testing, then we will address some practical questions about how intelligence tests work.

A Brief History

PsykTrek 7c

Intelligence tests were invented a little over a hundred years ago. The key breakthrough came in 1904, when a commission on education in France asked Alfred Binet to devise a test to identify mentally subnormal children. The commission wanted to single out youngsters in need of special training. It also wanted to avoid complete reliance on teachers' evaluations, which might often be subjective and biased. In response to this need, Binet and a colleague, Theodore Simon, created the first useful test of general mental ability in 1905. Their scale was a success because it was inexpensive, easy to administer, objective, and capable of predicting children's performance in school fairly well (Siegler, 1992). Thanks to these qualities, its use spread across Europe and America.

The Binet-Simon scale expressed a child's score in terms of "mental level" or "mental age." A child's *mental age* indicated that he or she displayed the mental ability typical of a child of that chronological (actual) age. Thus, a child with a mental age of 6 performed like the average 6-year-old on the test. Binet realized that his scale was a somewhat crude initial effort at measuring mental ability. He revised it in 1908 and again in 1911. Unfortunately, his revising came to an abrupt end with his death in 1911. However, other psychologists continued to build on Binet's work.

In America, Lewis Terman and his colleagues at Stanford University soon went to work on a major expansion and revision of Binet's test. Their work led to the 1916 publication of the Stanford-Binet Intelligence Scale (Terman, 1916). This revision was quite loyal to Binet's original conceptions. However, it incorporated a new scoring scheme based on William Stern's "intelligence quotient" (Minton, 2000). An *intelligence quotient (IQ)* is a child's mental age divided by chronological age, multiplied by 100. IQ scores originally involved actual quotients, calculated as follows:

$$IQ = \frac{\text{Mental age}}{\text{Chronological age}} \times 100$$

The IQ ratio placed all children (regardless of age) on the same scale, which was centered at 100 if their mental age corresponded to their chronological age (see **Table 8.2** for examples of IQ calculations).

Terman's technical and theoretical contributions to psychological testing were modest. Yet he made a strong case for the educational benefits of testing and became the key force behind American schools' widespread adoption of IQ tests (Chapman, 1988). As a result of his efforts, the Stanford-Binet quickly became the world's foremost intelligence test and the standard of comparison for virtually all intelligence tests that followed (White, 2000). Today, it remains one of the world's most widely used psychological tests.

Further advances in intelligence testing came from the work of David Wechsler (1939), who published the first high-quality IQ test designed specifically for *adults* in 1939. His test, the Wechsler Adult Intelligence Scale (WAIS), introduced two major innovations (Prifitera, 1994). First, Wechsler made his test less dependent on subjects' verbal ability than the Stanford-Binet. He included many items that required nonverbal reasoning. To highlight the distinction between verbal and nonverbal ability, he formalized the computation of separate scores for verbal IQ, performance (nonverbal) IQ, and full-scale (total) IQ. Second, Wechsler discarded the intelligence quotient in favor of a new scoring scheme based on the *normal distribution*. This scoring system has since been adopted by most other IQ tests, including the Stanford-Binet. Although the term *intelligence quotient* lingers on in our vocabulary, scores on intelligence tests are no longer based on an actual quotient, as you will see momentarily.

What Do Modern IQ Scores Mean?

PSYKTREK 7c

As we discussed, scores on intelligence tests once represented a ratio of mental age to chronological age. However, this system has given way to one based on the normal distribution and the *standard deviation,* a statistical index of variability in a data distribution, which is explained in Appendix B. The *normal distribution* is a symmetrical, bell-shaped curve that represents the pattern in which many characteristics are dispersed in the population. When a trait is normally distributed, most cases fall near the center of the distribution. The number of cases then gradually declines as one moves away from the center in either direction. The normal distribution provides a precise way to measure how people stack up in comparison to one another. The scores under the

Alfred Binet

"The intelligence of anyone is susceptible of development. With practice, enthusiasm, and especially with method one can succeed in increasing one's attention, memory, judgment, and in becoming literally more intelligent than one was before."

Lewis Terman

"It is the method of tests that has brought psychology down from the clouds and made it useful to men; that has transformed the 'science of trivialities' into the 'science of human engineering.'"

TABLE 8.2 **Calculating the Intelligence Quotient**

Measure	Child 1	Child 2	Child 3	Child 4
Mental age (MA)	6 years	6 years	9 years	12 years
Chronological age (CA)	6 years	9 years	12 years	9 years
$IQ = \dfrac{MA}{CA} \times 100$	$\dfrac{6}{6} \times 100 = 100$	$\dfrac{6}{9} \times 100 = 67$	$\dfrac{9}{12} \times 100 = 75$	$\dfrac{12}{9} \times 100 = 133$

normal curve are dispersed in a fixed pattern, with the standard deviation serving as the unit of measurement (see **Figure 8.14**). About 68% of the scores in the distribution fall within one standard deviation of the mean, whereas 95% of the scores fall within two standard deviations of the mean.

Psychologists eventually recognized that intelligence scores fall into a normal distribution. This insight permitted David Wechsler to devise a more sophisticated scoring system for his tests that has been adopted by virtually all subsequent IQ tests. In this system, raw scores are translated into *deviation IQ scores* **that locate respondents precisely within the normal distribution.** For most IQ tests, the mean of the distribution is set at 100 and the standard deviation (SD) is set at 15. These choices were made to provide continuity with the original IQ ratio (mental age to chronological age) that was centered at 100. In this system, which is shown in **Figure 8.14**, a score of 115 means that a person scored exactly one SD (15 points) above the mean. A score of 85 means that a person scored one SD below the mean. A score of 100 means that a person showed average performance. *The key point is that modern IQ scores indicate exactly where you fall in the normal distribution of intelligence.* Thus, a score of 120 does not indicate that you

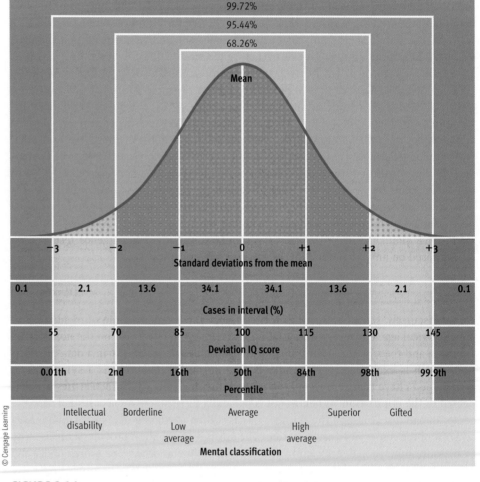

© Cengage Learning

FIGURE 8.14

The normal distribution. Many characteristics are distributed in a pattern represented by this bell-shaped curve. The horizontal axis shows how far above or below the mean a score is (measured in plus or minus standard deviations). The vertical axis is used to graph the number of cases obtaining each score. In a normal distribution, the cases are distributed in a fixed pattern. For instance, 68.26% of the cases fall between −1 and +1 standard deviation. Modern IQ scores indicate where a person's measured intelligence falls in the normal distribution. On most IQ tests, the mean is set at an IQ of 100 and the standard deviation at 15. Any deviation IQ score can be converted into a percentile score. The mental classifications at the bottom of the figure are descriptive labels that roughly correspond to ranges of IQ scores.

answered 120 questions correctly. Nor does it mean that you have 120 "units" of intelligence. A deviation IQ score places you at a specific point in the normal distribution of intelligence (based on the norms for your age group). Deviation IQ scores can be converted into *percentile scores,* as shown in **Figure 8.14.** A *percentile score* indicates the percentage of people who score at or below the score one has obtained.

Do Intelligence Tests Have Adequate Reliability? PSYKTREK SIM8, 7b

In the jargon of psychological testing, *reliability* **refers to the measurement consistency of a test.** A reliable test is one that yields similar results on repetition. Like other types of measuring devices, such as a stopwatch or a tire gauge, psychological tests need to be reasonably reliable. Estimates of reliability require the computation of correlation coefficients, which we introduced in Chapter 2. As you may recall, **a** *correlation coefficient* **is a numerical index of the degree of relationship between two variables** (see **Figure 8.15**). In gauging a test's reliability, the two variables that are correlated are typically two sets of scores from two administrations of the test. Do IQ tests produce consistent results when people are retested? Yes. Most IQ tests report commendable reliability estimates. The correlations generally range into the .90s (Kaufman, 2000), which is very high. In comparison to most other types of psychological tests, IQ tests are exceptionally reliable.

However, like other tests, they *sample* behavior, and a specific testing may yield an unrepresentative score. Variations in examinees' motivation to take an IQ test or in their anxiety about the test can sometimes produce misleading scores (Hopko et al., 2005; Zimmerman & Woo-Sam, 1984). The most common problem is that low motivation or high anxiety may drag a person's score down on a particular occasion. For instance, a fourth-grader who is made to feel that the test is extremely important may get jittery and be unable to concentrate. The same child might score much higher on a subsequent testing by another examiner who creates a more comfortable atmosphere. Although the reliability of IQ tests is excellent, caution is always in order in interpreting test scores.

Do Intelligence Tests Have Adequate Validity? PSYKTREK SIM8, 7b

Even if a test is quite reliable, we still need to be concerned about its validity. *Validity* **refers to the ability of a test to measure what it was designed to measure.** Validity can be estimated in several ways, depending on the nature of the test (Golden, Sawicki, &

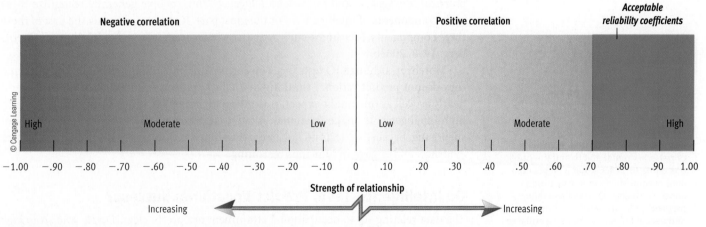

FIGURE 8.15
Correlation and reliability. As explained in Chapter 2, a positive correlation means that two variables co-vary in the *same* direction; a negative correlation means that two variables co-vary in the *opposite* direction. The closer the correlation coefficient gets to either −1.00 or +1.00, the stronger the relationship. At a minimum, reliability estimates for psychological tests must be moderately high positive correlations. Most reliability coefficients fall between .70 and .95.

© YanLev/Shutterstock

Franzen, 1990). In measuring an abstract personal quality such as intelligence, one needs to be concerned about the test's *construct validity*. Do intelligence tests measure what they're supposed to measure? Yes, but this answer has to be qualified very carefully. IQ tests are valid measures of the kind of intelligence that's necessary to do well in academic work. But if the purpose is to assess intelligence in a broader sense, the validity of IQ tests is questionable.

As you may recall, intelligence tests were originally designed with a relatively limited purpose in mind: to predict school performance. This has continued to be the principal purpose of IQ testing. Efforts to document the validity of IQ tests have usually concentrated on their relationship to grades in school. Typically, positive correlations in the .40s and .50s are found between IQ scores and school grades (Kline, 1991; Mackintosh, 1998). Moreover, a recent, huge study of over 70,000 children in England found an even stronger relationship between intelligence and educational achievement. When Deary and colleagues (2007) used a composite measure of intelligence (based on several tests) to predict a composite estimate of educational progress (based on 25 achievement tests) five years later, they found correlations in the vicinity of .70.

These correlations are about as high as one could expect, given that many factors besides a person's intelligence are likely to affect grades and school progress. For example, school grades may be influenced by a student's motivation or personality, not to mention teachers' subjective biases. Indeed, one study reported that measures of students' *self-discipline* are surprisingly strong predictors of students' performance (Duckworth & Seligman, 2005). Other studies suggest that students' subjective perceptions of their abilities influence their academic performance, even after controlling for actual IQ (Greven et al., 2009; Spinath et al., 2006). In other words, holding actual IQ constant, students who *think* they are talented tend to perform somewhat better than those with more negative views of their ability. Thus, given all the other factors likely to influence performance in school, IQ tests appear to be reasonably valid indexes of school-related intellectual ability, or academic intelligence.

But the abilities assessed by IQ tests are not as broad or general as widely assumed. When Robert Sternberg and his colleagues (1981) asked people to list examples of intelligence, they found that the examples fell into three categories: (1) *verbal intelligence*, (2) *practical intelligence*, and (3) *social intelligence*. Thus, people generally recognize three basic components of intelligence. For the most part, IQ tests assess only the first of these three components, focusing somewhat narrowly on academic/verbal intelligence (Sternberg, 1998, 2003b).

Moreover, although IQ tests focus on *cognitive* abilities, Stanovich (2009) argues that they do not predict rational thinking and effective decision making in the real world nearly as well as one might expect. According to Stanovich, it is routine for people with high intelligence to make irrational, ill-advised decisions. He explains that this is not surprising, because IQ tests do not assess the ability to think critically, weigh conflicting evidence, and engage in judicious reasoning.

Do Intelligence Tests Predict Vocational Success?

The data relating IQ to occupational attainment are pretty clear. *People who score high on IQ tests are more likely than those who score low to end up in high-status jobs* (Gottfredson, 2003b; Herrnstein & Murray, 1994; Schmidt & Hunter, 2004). Because IQ tests measure school ability fairly well and school performance is important in attaining certain occupations, this link between IQ scores and job status makes sense. Of course,

Reality Check

Misconception

IQ tests measure mental ability in a truly general sense.

Reality

IQ tests are characterized as measures of *general* mental ability and the public has come to believe that IQ tests measure mental ability in a truly broad sense. In reality, IQ tests have always focused only on the abstract reasoning and verbal fluency that are essential to academic success. The tests do not tap social competence, practical problem solving, creativity, mechanical ingenuity, or artistic talent.

the correlation between IQ and occupational attainment is moderate. For example, in a meta-analysis of many studies of the issue, Strenze (2007) found a correlation of .37 between IQ and occupational status. That figure means that there are plenty of exceptions to the general trend. Some people probably outperform brighter colleagues through bulldog determination and hard work. The relationship between IQ and income appears to be somewhat weaker. The meta-analysis by Strenze (2007) reported a correlation of .21 between IQ and income based on 31 studies. These findings suggest that intelligence fosters vocational success. However, the strength of the relationship is modest.

There is far more debate about whether IQ scores are effective predictors of performance *within* a particular occupation. On the one hand, research suggests that (a) there is a substantial correlation (about .50) between IQ scores and job performance, and (b) this correlation varies somewhat depending on the complexity of a job's requirements but does not disappear even for low-level jobs (Gottfredson, 2002; Ones, Viswesvaran, Dilchert, 2005; Schmidt, 2002). On the other hand, critics argue that the reported correlations have usually been corrected for statistical artifacts and that the raw, uncorrected correlations are lower (.30s) (Outtz, 2002). They also note that even a correlation of .50 would provide only modest accuracy in prediction (accounting for about 25% of the variation in job performance) (Goldstein, Zedeck, & Goldstein, 2002; Sternberg & Hedlund, 2002). Concerns have also been raised that when IQ tests are used for job selection they can have an adverse impact on employment opportunities for those in many minority groups that tend to score somewhat lower (on average) on such tests (Murphy, 2002; Outtz, 2002). In the final analysis, there is no question that intelligence is associated with vocational success. There is, however, room for argument about whether this association is strong enough to justify reliance on IQ testing in hiring employees.

Are IQ Tests Widely Used in Other Cultures?

In other Western cultures with European roots the answer is yes. In most non-Western cultures, the answer is only very little. IQ testing has a long history and continues to be a major enterprise in many Western countries, such as Britain, France, Norway, Canada, and Australia (Irvine & Berry, 1988). However, efforts to export IQ tests to non-Western societies have met with mixed results. The tests have been well received in some non-Western cultures, such as Japan, where the Binet-Simon scales were introduced as early as 1908 (Iwawaki & Vernon, 1988). But they have been met with indifference or resistance in other cultures, such as China and India (Chan & Vernon, 1988; Sinha, 1983). One reason is that some cultures have different conceptions of what intelligence is and value different mental skills (Baral & Das, 2004; Sternberg, 2007). Thus, the bottom line is that Western IQ tests do not translate well into the language and cognitive frameworks of many non-Western cultures (Berry, 1994; Sternberg, 2004).

"You can't build a hut, you don't know how to find edible roots and you know nothing about predicting the weather. In other words, you do terribly on our I.Q. test."

© 2004 by Sidney Harris/Science Cartoons Plus.com

Heredity and Environment as Determinants of Intelligence

KEY LEARNING GOALS

8.10 Summarize evidence that heredity affects intelligence, and discuss the concept of heritability.

8.11 Describe various lines of research that indicate that environment affects intelligence.

8.12 Evaluate heredity and socioeconomic disadvantage as explanations for cultural differences in IQ.

Most early pioneers of intelligence testing maintained that intelligence is inherited (Cravens, 1992). Small wonder, then, that this view lingers in our society. Gradually, however, it has become clear that both heredity and environment influence intelligence (Bartels et al., 2002; Davis, Arden, & Plomin, 2008; Plomin, 2003). Does this mean that the nature versus nurture debate has been settled with respect to intelligence? Absolutely not. Theorists and researchers continue to argue vigorously about which is more important, in part because the issue has such far-reaching social and political implications.

Theorists who believe that intelligence is largely inherited downplay the value of special educational programs for underprivileged groups (Herrnstein & Murray, 1994; Kanazawa, 2006; Rushton & Jensen, 2005). They assert that a child's intelligence cannot be increased noticeably, because genetic destiny cannot be altered. Other theorists take issue with this argument, pointing out that traits with a strong genetic component are not necessarily unchangeable (Flynn, 2007; Sternberg, Grigorenko, & Kidd, 2005). The people in this camp maintain that even more funds should be devoted to remedial education programs, improved schooling in lower-class neighborhoods, and college financial aid for the underprivileged. Because the debate over the role of heredity in intelligence has direct relevance to important social issues and political decisions, we'll take a detailed look at this complex controversy.

Evidence for Hereditary Influence

PsykTrek 7d

Researchers have long been aware that intelligence runs in families. However, *family studies* can determine only whether genetic influence on a trait is *plausible*, not whether it is certain. Family members share not just genes, but similar environments. If high intelligence (or low intelligence) appears in a family over several generations, this consistency could reflect the influence of either shared genes or shared environment. Because of this problem, researchers must turn to *twin studies* and *adoption studies* to obtain more definitive evidence on whether heredity affects intelligence.

TWIN STUDIES

PsykTrek 7d

The best evidence regarding the role of genetic factors in intelligence comes from studies that compare identical and fraternal twins. The rationale for twin studies is that both identical and fraternal twins normally develop under similar environmental conditions. However, identical twins share more genetic kinship than fraternal twins. Thus, if pairs of identical twins are more similar in intelligence than pairs of fraternal twins, it's presumably because of their greater genetic similarity. (See Chapter 3 for a more detailed explanation of the logic underlying twin studies.)

What are the findings of twin studies regarding intelligence? McGue and colleagues (1993) reviewed the results of over 100 studies of intellectual similarity for various kinds of kinship relations and childrearing arrangements. The key findings from their review are highlighted in **Figure 8.16**. This figure plots the average correlation observed for various types of relationships. As you can see, the average reported for identical twins (.86) is very high. This indicates that identical twins tend to be quite similar in intelligence. The average for fraternal twins (.60) is significantly lower. This correlation indicates that fraternal twins also tend to be similar in intelligence, but noticeably less similar than identical twins. These results support the notion that intelligence is inherited to a considerable degree (Bouchard, 1998; Plomin & Spinath, 2004).

Of course, critics have tried to poke holes in this line of reasoning. They argue that identical twins are more alike in IQ because parents and others treat them more similarly than they treat fraternal twins. This environmental explanation of the findings has some merit. After all, identical twins are always the same sex, and gender influences how a child is raised. However, this explanation seems unlikely in light of the evidence on identical twins reared apart as a result of family breakups or adoption (Bouchard, 1997; Bouchard et al., 1990). *Although reared in different environments,* these identical twins still display greater similarity in IQ (average correlation: .72) than fraternal twins reared together (average correlation: .60).

ADOPTION STUDIES

PsykTrek 7d

Research comparing adopted children to their biological parents also provides evidence about the effects of heredity (and of environment, as we shall see). If adopted children resemble their biological parents in intelligence even though they were not reared by

© Tom Wang/Shutterstock

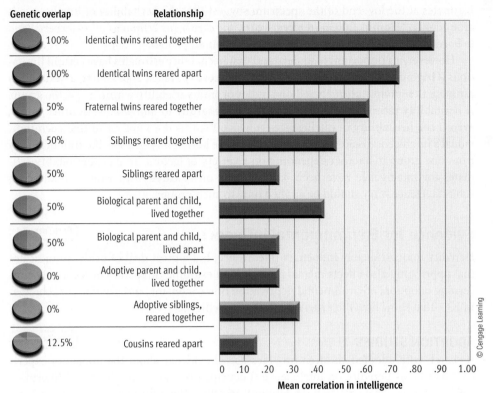

FIGURE 8.16

Studies of IQ similarity. The graph shows the mean correlations of IQ scores for people of various types of relationships, as obtained in studies of IQ similarity. Higher correlations indicate greater similarity. The results show that greater genetic similarity is associated with greater similarity in IQ, suggesting that intelligence is partly inherited (compare, for example, the correlations for identical and fraternal twins). However, the results also show that living together is associated with greater IQ similarity, suggesting that intelligence is partly governed by environment (compare, for example, the scores of siblings reared together and reared apart). (Data from McGue et al., 1993)

these parents, this finding supports the genetic hypothesis. The relevant studies indicate that there is indeed some measurable similarity between adopted children and their biological parents (Plomin et al., 2008) (refer again to **Figure 8.16**).

HERITABILITY ESTIMATES

PsykTrek 7d

Various experts have sifted through mountains of correlational evidence to estimate the *heritability* of intelligence. **A *heritability ratio* is an estimate of the proportion of trait variability in a population that is determined by variations in genetic inheritance.** Heritability can be estimated for any trait. For example, the heritability of height is estimated to be around 90% (Plomin, 1994). Heritability estimates for intelligence vary (see **Figure 8.17**). At the high end, some theorists estimate that the heritability of IQ ranges as high as 80% (Bouchard, 2004; Jensen, 1980, 1998). That is, they believe that only about 20% of the variation in intelligence is attributable to environmental factors.

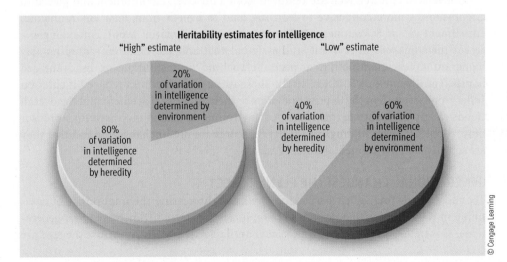

FIGURE 8.17

The concept of heritability. A heritability ratio is an estimate of the portion of variation in a trait determined by heredity—with the remainder presumably determined by environment—as these pie charts illustrate. Heritability estimates for intelligence range between a high of 80% and a low of 40%. The consensus estimate tends to hover around 50%. Bear in mind that heritability ratios are *estimates* and have certain limitations that are discussed in the text.

"I don't know anything about the bell curve, but I say heredity is everything."

Estimates at the low end of the spectrum suggest that the heritability of intelligence is around 40% (Plomin, 2003). *In recent years, the consensus estimates of the experts tend to hover around 50% (Petrill, 2005; Plomin & Spinath, 2004).*

However, it's important to understand that heritability estimates have certain limitations (Grigorenko, 2000; Johnson et al., 2009; Reeve & Hakel, 2002). First, a heritability estimate is a *group statistic* based on studies of trait variability within a specific group. A heritability estimate cannot be applied meaningfully to *individuals*. In other words, even if the heritability of intelligence truly is 60%, this does not mean that each individual's intelligence is 60% inherited. Second, the heritability of a specific trait may vary from one group to another depending on a variety of factors. To date, heritability estimates for intelligence have been based largely on research with white, middle-class subjects. Hence, they should be applied only to such groups.

Evidence for Environmental Influence

PsykTrek 7d

Heredity unquestionably influences intelligence, but a great deal of evidence indicates that upbringing also affects mental ability. We'll examine three lines of research—concerning adoption, environmental deprivation or enrichment, and generational changes in IQ—that show how life experiences shape intelligence.

ADOPTION STUDIES

PsykTrek 7d

Research with adopted children provides useful evidence about the impact of experience as well as heredity on intelligence (Locurto, 1990; Loehlin, Horn, & Willerman, 1997). Many of the correlations in **Figure 8.16** reflect the influence of the environment. For example, adopted children show some resemblance to their foster parents in IQ. This similarity is usually attributed to the fact that their foster parents shape their environment. Adoption studies also indicate that siblings reared together are more similar in IQ than siblings reared apart. This is true even for identical twins. Moreover, entirely unrelated children who are raised in the same home also show a significant resemblance in IQ. All of these findings indicate that environment influences intelligence.

ENVIRONMENTAL DEPRIVATION AND ENRICHMENT

If environment affects intelligence, then children who are raised in substandard circumstances should experience a gradual decrease in IQ as they grow older (since other children will be progressing more rapidly). This *cumulative deprivation hypothesis* was tested decades ago. Researchers studied children consigned to understaffed orphanages and children raised in the poverty and isolation of the back hills of Appalachia (Sherman & Key, 1932; Stoddard, 1943). Generally, investigators *did* find that environmental deprivation led to the predicted decline in IQ scores.

Conversely, children who are removed from a deprived environment and placed in circumstances more conducive to learning tend to benefit from their environmental enrichment (Scarr & Weinberg, 1977, 1983; Schiff & Lewontin, 1986). For example, a recent meta-analysis of relevant studies found that adopted children scored notably higher on IQ tests than siblings or peers "left behind" in institutions or disadvantaged homes (van IJzendoorn & Juffer, 2005). These gains are sometimes reduced if children suffer from severe, lengthy deprivation prior to their adoptive placement. But the overall trends clearly demonstrate that improved environments lead to increased IQ scores for most adoptees. These findings show that IQ scores are not unchangeable and that they are sensitive to environmental influences.

GENERATIONAL CHANGES: THE FLYNN EFFECT

The most interesting, albeit perplexing, evidence showcasing the importance of environment is the finding that performance on IQ tests has steadily increased over generations. This trend was not widely appreciated until relatively recently because the tests are revised periodically with new samples and scoring adjustments so that the mean IQ always remains at 100. However, in a study of the IQ tests used by the U.S. military, James Flynn noticed that the level of performance required to earn a score of 100 jumped upward every time the scoring was adjusted. Curious about this unexpected finding, he eventually gathered extensive data from 20 nations and demonstrated that IQ performance has been rising steadily all over the industrialized world since the 1930s (Flynn, 1987, 1999, 2003, 2007). Researchers who study intelligence are now scrambling to explain this trend, which has been dubbed the "Flynn effect." About the only thing they mostly agree on is that the Flynn effect has to be attributed to environmental factors, as the modern world's gene pool could not have changed overnight (in evolutionary terms, 70 years is like a fraction of a second) (Dickens & Flynn, 2001; Neisser, 1998; Sternberg et al., 2005).

At this point, the proposed explanations for the Flynn effect are conjectural, but it is worth reviewing some of them, as they highlight the diversity of environmental factors that may shape IQ performance. Some theorists attribute generational gains in IQ test performance to reductions in the prevalence of severe malnutrition among children (Colom, Lluis-Font, & Andres-Pueyo, 2005; Sigman & Whaley, 1998). Others attribute the Flynn effect to increased access to schooling and more demanding curricula in schools over the course of the last century (Blair et al., 2005). Patricia Greenfield (1998) argues that advances in technology, including much maligned media such as television and video games, have enhanced visuospatial skills and other specific cognitive skills that contribute to performance on IQ tests. Wendy Williams (1998) discusses the importance of a constellation of factors, including improved schools, smaller families, better-educated parents, and higher-quality parenting. All of these speculations have some plau-

Concept Check 8.3

Understanding Correlational Evidence on the Heredity-Environment Question

Check your understanding of how correlational findings relate to the nature versus nurture issue by indicating how you would interpret the meaning of each "piece" of evidence described below. The figures inside the parentheses are the median IQ correlations observed for the relationships described (based on McGue et al., 1993), which are shown in **Figure 8.16** on page 271.

In the spaces on the left, enter the letter H if the findings suggest that intelligence is shaped by heredity, enter the letter E if the findings suggest that intelligence is shaped by the environment, and enter the letter B if the findings suggest that intelligence is shaped by both (or either) heredity and environment. The answers can be found in Appendix A.

_____ 1. Identical twins reared apart are more similar (.72) than fraternal twins reared together (.60).

_____ 2. Identical twins reared together are more similar (.86) than identical twins reared apart (.72).

_____ 3. Siblings reared together are more similar (.47) than siblings reared apart (.24).

_____ 4. Biological parents and the children they rear are more similar (.42) than unrelated persons who are reared apart (no correlation if sampled randomly).

_____ 5. Adopted children show similarity to their biological parents (.24) and to their adoptive parents (.24).

sibility and are not mutually exclusive. Thus, the causes of the Flynn effect remain under investigation.

The Interaction of Heredity and Environment

PsykTrek 7d

Clearly, heredity and environment both influence intelligence to a significant degree (Dickens & Flynn, 2001; Petrill, 2005). And their effects involve intricate, dynamic, reciprocal interactions (Grigerenko, 2000; Johnson, 2010). Thus, many theorists now assert that the question of which is more important ought to take a backseat to the question of *how they interact* to govern IQ.

One line of thinking is that heredity may set certain limits on intelligence and that environmental factors determine where individuals fall within these limits (Bouchard, 1997; Weinberg, 1989). According to Sandra Scarr, a prominent advocate of this position, genetic makeup places an upper limit on a person's IQ that can't be exceeded even when environment is ideal. Heredity is also thought to place a lower limit on an individual's IQ, although extreme circumstances (for example, being locked in an attic for years) could drag a person's IQ beneath this boundary. Theorists use the term *reaction range* to refer to these genetically determined limits on IQ (or other traits).

According to the reaction-range model, children reared in high-quality environments that promote the development of intelligence should score near the top of their potential IQ range. Children reared under less ideal circumstances should score lower in their reaction range. The reaction range for most people is *estimated* to be around 20–25 points on the IQ scale (Weinberg, 1989). The concept of a reaction range can explain why high-IQ children sometimes come from poor environments. It can also explain why low-IQ children sometimes come from very good environments (see **Figure 8.18**). Moreover, it can explain these apparent paradoxes without discounting the importance of the environment.

Cultural Differences in IQ Scores

Although the full range of IQ scores is seen in all ethnic groups, the average IQ for many of the larger minority groups in the United States (such as blacks, Native Americans, and Hispanics) is somewhat lower than the average for whites. The typical disparity is around 10–15 points, depending on the group tested and the IQ scale used (Hunt & Carlson, 2007; Loehlin, 2000; Nisbett, 2005). However, data from the standardization samples for the Stanford-Binet and Wechsler scales suggest that the gap between blacks and whites has shrunk by about 4–7 points since the 1970s (Dickens & Flynn, 2006). There is relatively little argument about the existence of these group differences, variously referred to as racial, ethnic, or cultural differences in intelligence. The controversy concerns *why* the differences are found. A vigorous debate continues as to whether cultural differences in intelligence are due to the influence of heredity or of environment.

HERITABILITY AS AN EXPLANATION

In 1969 Arthur Jensen sparked a heated war of words by arguing that racial differences in average IQ are largely due to heredity. The cornerstone for Jensen's argument was his analysis suggesting that the heritability of intelligence is about 80%. Essentially, he asserted that (1) intelligence is largely genetic in origin, and (2) therefore, genetic factors are "strongly implicated" as the cause of ethnic differences in intelligence. Jensen's article triggered outrage and bitter criticism in many quarters, as well as a great deal of additional research on the determinants of intelligence. Twenty-five years later, Richard Herrnstein and Charles Murray (1994) reignited the same controversy with the publication of their widely discussed book *The Bell Curve*. They argued that ethnic differences in average intelligence are substantial, not easily reduced, and at least partly genetic in origin. The implicit message throughout *The Bell Curve* was that disadvantaged groups

Inherited reaction range · **Measured IQ, as shaped by interaction of heredity and environment**

Quality of environment (for realizing intellectual potential)

Enriched — Tom 84 · Kimberly 117 · Jerome 127

Average — Susan 84 · Chris 103 · Lee 122

Deprived — Jack 66 · Jill 97 · Alice 125

IQ scores: 55 · 70 · 85 · 100 · 115 · 130 · 145

Top row (left to right): © Rui Vale de Sousa/Shutterstock; © WoodyStock/Alamy; © R. Gino Santa Maria/Shutterstock. Middle row: © Luba V Nel/Shutterstock; © Corbis Cusp/Alamy; © Image Source/Alamy. Bottom row: © photobank.ch/ Shutterstock; © olly/Shutterstock; © swissmacky/Shutterstock.

© Cengage Learning

FIGURE 8.18

Reaction range. The concept of reaction range posits that heredity sets limits on one's intellectual potential (represented by the horizontal bars), while the quality of one's environment influences where one scores within this range (represented by the dots on the bars). People raised in enriched environments should score near the top of their reaction range, whereas people raised in poor-quality environments should score near the bottom of their range. Genetic limits on IQ can be inferred only indirectly, so theorists aren't sure whether reaction ranges are narrow (like Jerome's) or wide (like Kimberly's). The concept of reaction range can explain how two people with similar genetic potential can be quite different in intelligence (compare Tom and Jack) and how two people reared in environments of similar quality can score quite differently (compare Alice and Jack).

cannot avoid their fate because it is their genetic destiny. And as recently as 2010, based on an extensive review of statistical evidence, J. Phillipe Rushton and Arthur Jensen (2010) argued that genetic factors account for the bulk of the gap between races in average IQ.

As you might guess, these analyses and conclusions have elicited many lengthy and elaborate rebuttals. Critics argue that heritability explanations for ethnic differences in IQ have a variety of flaws and weaknesses (Brody, 2003; Devlin et al., 2002; Horn, 2002; Nisbett, 2005, 2009; Sternberg, 2003b, 2005a). For example, research suggests that the heritability of intelligence may be notably lower in samples drawn from the lower socioeconomic classes as opposed to higher socioeconomic classes (Turkheimer et al., 2003). However, heritability estimates for intelligence have largely been based on samples drawn from white, middle-class, North American and European populations (Grigerenko, 2000). Hence, there is doubt about the validity of applying these heritability estimates to other cultural groups.

Moreover, even if one accepts the assumption that the heritability of IQ is very high, it does not follow logically that differences in group averages must be due largely to heredity. Leon Kamin has presented a compelling analogy that highlights the logical fallacy in this reasoning (see **Figure 8.19** on the next page):

We fill a white sack and a black sack with a mixture of different genetic varieties of corn seed. We make certain that the proportions of each variety of seed are identical in each

Individual variation in corn plant heights within each group (cause: genetic variation in the seeds)

Field A: More fertile soil

Field B: Less fertile soil

Differences in average corn plant height between groups
(cause: the soils in which the plants were grown)

FIGURE 8.19

Genetics and between-group differences on a trait. Leon Kamin's analogy (see text) shows
how between-group differences on a trait (the average height of corn plants) could be due to
environment, even if the trait is largely inherited. The same reasoning presumably applies to
ethnic group differences in average intelligence.

*sack. We then plant the seed from the white sack in fertile Field A, while that from the
black sack is planted in barren Field B. We will observe that within Field A, as within
Field B, there is considerable variation in the height of individual corn plants. This variation will be due largely to genetic factors (seed differences). We will also observe, however,
that the average height of plants in Field A is greater than that in Field B. That difference
will be entirely due to environmental factors (the soil). The same is true of IQs: differences
in the average IQ of various human populations could be entirely due to environmental
differences, even if within each population all variation were due to genetic differences!
(Eysenck & Kamin, 1981, p. 97)*

Kamin's analogy shows that even if the heritability of intelligence is high, group differences in average IQ *could* still be caused entirely (or in part) by environmental factors
(Block, 2002). For decades, critics of Jensen's thesis have relied on this analogy rather
than actual data to make the point that between-groups differences in IQ do not necessarily reflect genetic differences. They depended on the analogy because no relevant data
were available. However, the discovery of the Flynn effect has provided compelling new
data that are directly relevant (Dickens & Flynn, 2001; Flynn, 2003). Generational gains
in IQ scores show that a between-groups disparity in average IQ (in this case the gap is
between generations rather than ethnic groups) can be environmental in origin, even
though intelligence is highly heritable.

SOCIOECONOMIC DISADVANTAGE AS AN EXPLANATION

Many social scientists argue that minority students' IQ scores are depressed because
these children tend to grow up in deprived environments that create a disadvantage—

both in school and on IQ tests. There is no question that, on the average, whites and minorities tend to be raised in very different circumstances. Most minority groups have endured a long history of economic discrimination and are greatly overrepresented in the lower social classes. A lower-class upbringing tends to carry a number of disadvantages that work against the development of a youngster's full intellectual potential (Bigelow, 2006; Evans, 2004; Lott, 2002; McLoyd, 1998; Noble, McCandliss, & Farah, 2007). In comparison to children from the middle and upper classes, lower-class children tend to be exposed to fewer books, to have fewer learning supplies, to have less privacy for concentrated study, and to get less parental assistance in learning. Typically, they also have poorer role models for language development, experience less pressure to work hard on intellectual pursuits, and attend poorer-quality schools.

In light of these disadvantages, it's not surprising that average IQ scores among children from lower social classes tend to run about 15 points below the average scores obtained by children from middle- and upper-class homes (Seifer, 2001; Williams & Ceci, 1997). This is the case even if race is factored out of the picture by studying whites exclusively. Admittedly, there is room for argument about the direction of the causal relationships underlying this association between social class and intelligence. Nonetheless, given the overrepresentation of minorities in the lower classes, many researchers argue that ethnic differences in intelligence are really social class differences in disguise.

New Directions in the Study of Intelligence

KEY LEARNING GOALS

8.13 Understand evidence on the brain correlates of intelligence and the link between IQ and mortality.

8.14 Explain Sternberg's cognitive analysis of intelligence and Gardner's theory of multiple intelligences.

Intelligence testing has been through a period of turmoil, and changes are on the horizon. In fact, many changes have occurred already. Let's look at some of the major new trends and projections for the future.

Exploring Biological Correlates of Intelligence

Researchers have begun to explore the relations between variations in intelligence and variations in specific characteristics of the brain. The early studies in this area used various measures of head size as an indicator of brain size. These studies generally found positive, but very small correlations (average = .15) between head size and IQ (Vernon et al., 2000). This result led researchers to speculate that head size is probably a very crude index of brain size. This line of research might have languished, but the invention of sophisticated brain-imaging technologies revived it. Since the 1990s, quite a few studies have examined the correlation between IQ scores and measures of overall brain volume based on MRI scans (see Chapter 3), yielding an average correlation of about .35 (Anderson, 2003; McDaniel, 2005; Rushton & Ankney, 2007). Thus, it appears that larger brains are predictive of greater intelligence.

© YAKOBCHUK VASYL/ Shutterstock

Many investigators suspect that the association between brain size and intelligence may reflect the enlargement of particular areas in the brain, or growth in certain types of brain tissue, rather than a global increase in brain size. Hence, these researchers are exploring whether IQ correlates with the size of specific regions in the brain. Based on their review of 37 brain imaging studies, Jung and Haier (2007) theorize that intelligence depends on interactions among a constellation of key areas in the brain, including the prefrontal cortex, Broca's and Wernicke's areas, the somatosensory association cortex, the visual association cortex, and the anterior cingulate. The evidence is complex and more data are needed, but researchers have found some intriguing correlations between the volume of these specific areas in the brain and measures of intelligence (Colom et al., 2009; Haier, 2009).

Other researchers have approached this question by analyzing the relations between intelligence and measures of the amount of gray matter or white matter in individuals' brains. According to Luders et al. (2009), the amount of gray matter should reflect the density of neurons and their dendrites, which may be predictive of information-processing capacity. In contrast, the amount of white matter should reflect the quantity of axons in the brain and their degree of myelinization, which may be predictive of the efficiency of neuronal communication. The findings thus far suggest that higher intelligence scores are correlated with increased volume of *both* gray matter and white matter, with the association being a little stronger for gray matter (Luders et al., 2009; Narr et al., 2007).

One obvious implication of these findings, eagerly embraced by those who tout the influence of heredity on intelligence, is that genetic inheritance gives some people larger brains than others and that larger brain size promotes greater intelligence (Rushton, 2003). However, as always, we must be cautious about interpreting correlational data. As discussed in Chapter 3, research has demonstrated that an enriched environment can produce denser neural networks and heavier brains in laboratory rats (Rosenzweig & Bennett, 1996). Thus, it is also possible that causation runs in the opposite direction—that developing greater intelligence promotes larger brain size, much like weightlifting can promote larger muscles.

Research on the biological correlates of intelligence has turned up another interesting finding. IQ scores measured in childhood correlate with longevity decades later (Deary, Whalley, & Starr, 2009; Deary et al., 2004). Quite a number of studies have arrived at the conclusion that *smarter people live longer* (Batty, Deary, & Gottfredson, 2007; Pearce et al., 2006) (see **Figure 8.20**). Why is higher IQ linked to increased longevity? Researchers have offered a variety of explanations (Arden, Gottfredson, & Miller, 2009; Batterham, Christensen, & Mackinnon, 2009; Gottfredson & Deary, 2004). One

FIGURE 8.20

The relationship between childhood IQ and mortality. Leon et al. (2009) examined the association between IQ measured at age 7 and mortality through the age of 57 in a sample of over 11,000 people in the UK. The data in the graph are age-adjusted *relative* morality rates in comparison to the reference group of people scoring near average (90–109) in intelligence. Thus, in comparison to the reference group, people who scored 70–79 were 22% more likely to die by age 57, and people who scored over 130 were less than half as likely to die by age 57. As you can see, there is a clear trend. As IQ scores go up, mortality rates decline.

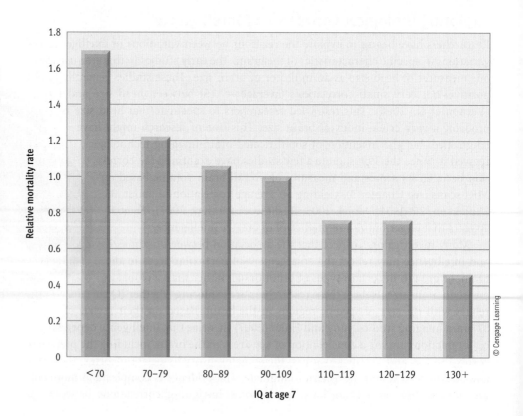

possibility is that good genes could foster both higher intelligence and resilient health. A second possibility is that health self-care is a complicated lifelong mission, for which brighter people are better prepared. In other words, smarter people may be more likely to avoid health-impairing habits (such as smoking and overeating), to be proactive about health (such as exercising and taking vitamins), and to use medical care more effectively (such as knowing when to seek treatment). A third possibility is that intelligence fosters career success and higher social class decreases mortality. People in higher socioeconomic classes tend to have less-stressful jobs with lower accident risks, reduced exposure to toxins and pathogens, better health insurance, and greater access to medical care. Thus, affluence could be the key factor linking intelligence to longevity. These explanations are not mutually exclusive. They might all contribute to the association between IQ and longevity.

Investigating Cognitive Processes in Intelligent Behavior

Investigators interested in intelligence and scholars who have studied cognition have traditionally pursued separate lines of research that only rarely have intersected. However, since the mid-1980s Robert Sternberg (1985, 1988b, 1991) has spearheaded an effort to apply a cognitive perspective to the study of intelligence. His cognitive approach emphasizes the need to understand how people use their intelligence.

In recent versions of his theory, Sternberg (1999, 2000b, 2003a, 2005b) has asserted that there are three aspects or facets of intelligence: analytical intelligence, creative intelligence, and practical intelligence (see **Figure 8.21**). *Analytical intelligence* involves abstract reasoning, evaluation, and judgment. It is the type of intelligence that is crucial to most schoolwork and that is assessed by conventional IQ tests. *Creative intelligence* involves the ability to generate new ideas and to be inventive in dealing with novel problems. *Practical intelligence* involves the ability to deal effectively with the kinds of problems that people encounter in everyday life, such as on the job or at home. A big part of practical intelligence involves acquiring *tacit knowledge*—what one needs to know in a particular environment in order to work efficiently that is not explicitly taught and that often is not even verbalized.

In a series of studies, Sternberg and his colleagues have gathered data suggesting that (1) all three facets of intelligence can be measured reliably, (2) the three facets of intelligence are relatively independent (uncorrelated), and (3) the assessment of all three aspects of intelligence can improve the prediction of intelligent behavior in the real world (Grigorenko & Sternberg, 2001; Henry, Sternberg, & Grigorenko, 2005). Some critics doubt that Sternberg's measures will facilitate better prediction of meaningful outcomes than traditional IQ tests (Gottfredson, 2003a), but that is an empirical question that should be resolved by future research. In any event, Sternberg certainly has been an articulate voice arguing for a broader, expanded concept of intelligence, which is a theme that has been echoed by others.

Expanding the Concept of Intelligence

In recent years, many theorists have concluded that traditional IQ tests are too narrow in focus. This view has been articulated particularly well by Howard Gardner (1983, 1993, 1999, 2004, 2006). According to Gardner, IQ tests have generally emphasized verbal and mathematical skills, to the exclusion of other important skills. He suggests the existence of a number of relatively independent *human intelligences,* which are listed in **Figure 8.22** on the next page. To build his list of separate intelligences, Gardner reviewed the evidence on cognitive capacities in normal individuals, people suffering from brain damage, and special populations, such as prodigies and idiot savants. He concluded that humans exhibit eight largely independent intelligences: logical-mathematical, linguistic, musical, spatial, bodily-kinesthetic, interpersonal, intrapersonal, and naturalist. These

Robert Sternberg
"To understand intelligent behavior, we need to move beyond the fairly restrictive tasks that have been used both in experimental laboratories and in psychometric tests of intelligence."

FIGURE 8.21
Sternberg's theory of intelligence. Sternberg's (2003a, 2005b) model of intelligence proposes that there are three aspects or types of intelligence: analytical intelligence, practical intelligence, and creative intelligence. According to Sternberg, traditional IQ tests focus almost exclusively on analytical intelligence. He believes that the prediction of real-world outcomes could be improved by broadening intelligence assessments to tap practical and creative intelligence.

TYPE OF INTELLIGENCE							
Logical-mathematical	Linguistic	Musical	Spatial	Bodily-kinesthetic	Interpersonal	Intrapersonal	Naturalist

CORE COMPONENTS

Sensitivity to, and capacity to discern, logical or numerical patterns; ability to handle long chains of reasoning	Sensitivity to the sounds, rhythms, and meanings of words; sensitivity to the different functions of language	Abilities to produce and appreciate rhythm, pitch, and timbre; appreciation of the forms of musical expressiveness	Capacities to perceive the visual-spatial world accurately and to perform transformations on one's initial perceptions	Abilities to control one's body movements and to handle objects skillfully	Capacities to discern and respond appropriately to the moods, temperaments, motivations, and desires of other people	Access to one's own feelings and the ability to discriminate among them and draw upon them to guide behavior; knowledge of one's own strengths, weaknesses, desires, and intelligences	Abilities to recognize and categorize objects and processes in nature

FIGURE 8.22

Gardner's eight intelligences. Howard Gardner has argued for an expanded view of intelligence. He asserts that humans display eight very different forms of intelligence, which he maintains are largely independent of each other.

Howard Gardner

"It is high time that the view of intelligence be widened to incorporate a range of human computational capacities. . . . But where is it written that intelligence needs to be determined on the basis of tests?"

intelligences obviously include a variety of talents that are not assessed by conventional IQ tests. Gardner is investigating the extent to which these intelligences are largely independent, as his theory asserts. For the most part, he has found that people tend to display a mixture of strong, intermediate, and weak abilities, which is consistent with the idea that the various types of intelligence are independent.

Gardner's books have been very popular and his theory clearly resonates with many people (Shearer, 2004). His ideas have had an enormous impact on educators' attitudes and beliefs around the world (Cuban, 2004; Kornhaber, 2004). He has raised thought-provoking questions about what abilities should be included under the rubric of intelligence (Eisner, 2004). However, he has his critics (Hunt, 2001; Klein, 1997; Morgan, 1996; Waterhouse, 2006). Some argue that his use of the term *intelligence* is so broad, encompassing virtually any valued human ability, it makes the term almost meaningless. These critics wonder whether there is any advantage to relabeling talents such as musical ability and motor coordination as forms of intelligence. Critics also note that Gardner's theory has not generated much research on the predictive value of measuring individual differences in the eight intelligences he has described. This research would require the development of tests to measure the eight intelligences, but Gardner is not particularly interested in the matter of assessment, and he loathes conventional testing. This situation makes it difficult to predict where his theory will lead, as research is crucial to the evolution of a theory.

Reflecting on the Chapter's Themes

KEY LEARNING GOALS

8.15 Identify the five unifying themes highlighted in this chapter.

Five of our unifying themes surfaced in this chapter. The first is the empirical nature of psychology. For many decades, psychologists paid little attention to cognitive processes, because most of them assumed that thinking is too private to be studied scientifically. During the 1950s and 1960s, however, psychologists began to devise creative new ways to measure mental processes. These innovations, which fueled the cognitive revolution, show that empirical methods are the lifeblood of the scientific enterprise.

Second, our review of cognition and intelligence demonstrated the importance of cultural factors. For example, we learned that there are striking cultural variations in cognitive style. We also saw that intelligence testing is largely a Western phenomenon and that ethnic differences in average intelligence may be largely cultural in origin. Thus, we see once again that if we hope to achieve a sound understanding of behavior, we need to appreciate the cultural contexts in which behavior unfolds.

Third, our coverage showed that intelligence is shaped by a complex interaction of hereditary and environmental factors. We've drawn a similar conclusion before in other chapters where we examined other topics. However, this chapter should have enhanced your appreciation of this idea by illustrating in detail how scientists arrive at this conclusion.

Fourth, we saw more evidence that psychology evolves in a sociohistorical context. Prevailing social attitudes have always exerted some influence on testing practices and the interpretation of test results. In the first half of the 20th century, a strong current of racial and class prejudice was apparent in the United States and Britain. This prejudice supported the idea that IQ tests measured innate ability and that "undesirable" groups scored poorly because of their genetic inferiority. Although these beliefs did not go unchallenged within psychology, their widespread acceptance in the field reflected the social values of the time. Today, the continuing, ferocious debate about the roots of cultural differences in intelligence shows that issues in psychology often have far-reaching social and political implications.

The final theme apparent in this chapter was the subjective nature of human experience, which was prominent in our discussion of peculiarities in human decision making.

 Empiricism

 Cultural Heritage

 Heredity and Environment

 Sociohistorical Context

 Subjectivity of Experience

Concept Check 8.4

Recognizing Conceptions of Intelligence

Check your understanding of various theories on the nature of intelligence by matching the names of their originators with the brief descriptions of the theories' main themes that appear below. Choose from the following theorists: (a) Alfred Binet, (b) Howard Gardner, (c) Arthur Jensen, (d) Sandra Scarr, (e) Robert Sternberg, and (f) David Wechsler. The answers are in Appendix A.

_____ 1. This theorist posited eight human intelligences: logical-mathematical, linguistic, musical, spatial, bodily-kinesthetic, interpersonal, intrapersonal, and naturalist.

_____ 2. This person distinguished between verbal and nonverbal ability and discarded the intelligence quotient in favor of a scoring scheme based on the normal distribution.

_____ 3. This theorist stated that the heritability of intelligence is very high and that IQ differences between ethnic groups are mainly due to genetics.

_____ 4. This theorist stated that heredity sets certain limits on intelligence and that environmental factors determine where one falls within those limits.

_____ 5. This person's theory posits that there are three facets of intelligence: analytical, practical, and creative intelligence.

Measuring and Understanding Creativity

Answer the following "true" or "false":

___ 1 Creative ideas often come out of nowhere.

___ 2 Creativity usually occurs in a burst of insight.

___ 3 Creativity and intelligence are unrelated.

Intelligence is not the only type of mental ability that psychologists have studied. They have devised tests to explore a variety of mental abilities. Among these, creativity is certainly one of the most interesting. People tend to view creativity as an essential trait for artists, musicians, and writers. However, it is important in *many* walks of life. In this Application, we'll discuss psychologists' efforts to measure and understand creativity. As we progress, you'll learn that all the statements above are false.

The Nature of Creativity

What makes thought creative? *Creativity* **involves the generation of ideas that are original, novel, and useful.** Creative thinking is fresh, innovative, and inventive. But novelty by itself is not enough. In addition to being unusual, creative thinking must be adaptive. It must be appropriate to the situation and problem.

DOES CREATIVITY OCCUR IN A BURST OF INSIGHT?

It is widely believed that creativity usually involves sudden flashes of insight and great leaps of imagination. Robert Weisberg (1986) calls this belief the "Aha! myth." Undeniably, creative bursts of in-

sight do occur (Feldman, 1988). However, the evidence suggests that major creative achievements generally are logical extensions of existing ideas, involving long, hard work and many small, faltering steps forward (Weisberg, 1993). Creative ideas do not come out of nowhere. They come from a deep well of experience and training in a specific area, whether it's music, painting, business, or science (Weisberg, 1999, 2006). As Snow (1986) puts it, "Creativity is not a light bulb in the mind, as most cartoons depict it. It is an accomplishment born of intensive study, long reflection, persistence, and interest" (p. 1033).

DOES CREATIVITY DEPEND ON DIVERGENT THINKING?

According to many theorists, the key to creativity lies in *divergent thinking*—thinking "that goes off in different directions," as J. P. Guilford (1959) put it. Guilford distinguished between convergent thinking and divergent thinking. **In convergent thinking one tries to narrow down a list of alternatives to converge on a single correct answer.** For example, when you take a multiple-choice exam, you try to eliminate incorrect options until you hit on the correct response. Most training in school encourages convergent thinking. **In *divergent thinking* one tries to expand the range of alternatives by generating many possible solutions.** Imagine that you work for an advertising agency. To come up with as many slogans as possible for a client's product, you must use divergent thinking. Some of your slogans may be clear losers, and eventually you will have to engage in convergent thinking to pick the best. But coming up with the range of new possibilities depends on divergent thinking.

Thirty years of research on divergent thinking has yielded mixed results. As a whole, the evidence suggests that divergent thinking contributes to creativity. However, it clearly does not represent the

essence of creativity, as originally proposed (Brown, 1989; Plucker & Renzulli, 1999; Weisberg, 2006). In retrospect, it was unrealistic to expect creativity to depend on a single cognitive skill.

Measuring Creativity   `PSYKTREK SIM8`

Although its nature may be elusive, creativity clearly is important in today's world. Creative masterpieces in the arts and literature enrich human existence. Creative inventions fuel technological progress. Thus, it is understandable that psychologists have been interested in measuring creativity with psychological tests.

HOW DO PSYCHOLOGICAL TESTS ASSESS CREATIVITY?   `PSYKTREK SIM8`

A diverse array of psychological tests have been devised to measure individuals' creativity (Plucker & Makel, 2010). Usually, the items on creativity tests give respondents a specific starting point and then require them to generate as many possibilities as they can in a short period of time. Typical items on a creativity test might include the following: (1) List as many uses as you can for a newspaper. (2) Think of as many fluids that burn as you can. (3) Imagine that people no longer need sleep and think of as many consequences as you can. Participants' scores on these tests depend on the *number* of alternatives they generate and on the *originality* and *usefulness* of the alternatives.

HOW WELL DO TESTS PREDICT CREATIVE PRODUCTIVITY?

In general, studies indicate that creativity tests are mediocre predictors of creative achievement in the real world (Hocevar & Bachelor, 1989; Plucker & Renzulli, 1999). Why? One reason is that these tests measure creativity in the abstract, as a *general trait*. However, the accumulation of evidence suggests that *creativity is specific to particular domains* (Amabile, 1996; Feist, 2004; Kaufman & Baer, 2002, 2004). Despite some rare exceptions, creative people usually excel in a single field, in which they typically have considerable training and expertise (Policastro & Gardner, 1999). An innovative physicist might have no potential to be a creative poet. Measuring this person's creativity outside of physics may be meaningless.

Correlates of Creativity

What are creative people like? Are they brighter or less well adjusted than average? A great deal of research has been conducted on the correlates of creativity.

IS THERE A CREATIVE PERSONALITY?

There is no single personality profile that accounts for creativity (Weisberg, 2006). However, investigators have found modest correlations between certain personality characteristics and creativity. Research suggests that highly creative people tend to be more independent, nonconforming, introverted, open to new experiences, self-confident, persistent, ambitious, dominant, and impulsive (Feist, 1998, 2010). At the core of this set of personality characteristics are the related traits of nonconformity and openness to new experiences. Creative people tend to think for themselves and are less easily influenced by the opinions of others than the average person is. The importance of openness to new experiences can be seen in a new line of research suggesting that living abroad enhances creativity.

Although living abroad has long been viewed as a rite of passage for creative artists and writers, no one thought to take an empirical look at its impact until recently. In a series of studies, Maddux and Galinsky (2009) found that the amount of time spent living abroad correlated positively with measures of creativity. Interestingly, time spent in tourist travel did *not* predict creativity. The contrasting effects of living and traveling abroad seems to depend on acculturation. Maddux and Galinsky found that the degree to which people adapted to foreign cultures was responsible for the association between living abroad and creativity. A subsequent study found that multicultural learning experiences appear to foster flexibility in thinking, which could enhance creativity (Maddux, Adam, & Galinsky, 2010).

ARE CREATIVITY AND INTELLIGENCE RELATED?

Are creative people exceptionally smart? Conceptually, creativity and intelligence represent different types of mental ability. Thus, it's not surprising that correlations between measures of creativity and measures of intelligence are generally weak (Sternberg & O'Hara, 1999). For example, a meta-analysis of many studies reported a correlation of only .17 (Kim, 2005).

IS THERE A CONNECTION BETWEEN CREATIVITY AND MENTAL ILLNESS?

There may be a connection between truly exceptional creativity and mental illness—in particular, mood disorders such as depression. When Nancy Andreasen studied 30 accomplished writers who had been invited as visiting faculty to the prestigious Iowa Writers Workshop, she found that 80% of her sample had suffered a mood disorder at some point in their lives (Andreasen, 1987, 2005). In a similar study of 59 female writers from another writers' conference, Ludwig (1994) found that 56% had experienced depression. These figures are far above the base rate (roughly 15%) for mood disorders in the general population. Other studies have also found an association between creativity and the prevalence of psychological disorders (Jamison, 1988; Ludwig, 1998; Post, 1996; Silvia & Kaufman, 2010). Perhaps the most ambitious examination of the issue has been Arnold Ludwig's (1995) analyses of the biographies of 1,004 people who achieved eminence in eighteen fields. He found greatly elevated rates of depression and other disorders among eminent writers, artists, and composers (see **Figure 8.23**). Thus, accumulating empirical data tentatively suggest that there may be a correlation between major creative achievement and vulnerability to mental disorders.

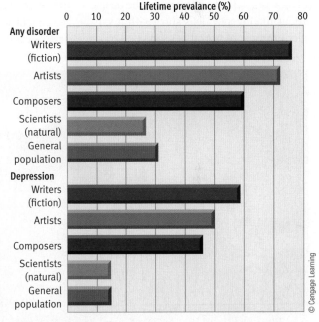

FIGURE 8.23

Estimated prevalence of psychological disorders among people who achieved creative eminence. Ludwig (1995) studied biographies of 1,004 people who had clearly achieved eminence in one of eighteen fields and tried to determine whether each person suffered from any specific mental disorders in his or her lifetime. The data summarized here show the prevalence rates for depression and for a mental disorder of any kind for four fields where creativity is often the key to achieving eminence. As you can see, the estimated prevalence of mental illness was extremely elevated among eminent writers, artists, and composers (but not natural scientists) in comparison to the general population, with depression accounting for much of this elevation.

The Intelligence Debate, Appeals to Ignorance, and Reification

A *fallacy* is a mistake or error in the process of reasoning. Cognitive scientists who study thinking processes have long lists of common errors that people make in their reasoning. One of these fallacies has a curious name, which is the *appeal to ignorance*. It involves misusing the general lack of knowledge or information on an issue (a lack of knowledge is a kind of ignorance) to support an argument. Before we tackle the more difficult issue of how this fallacy shows up in the debate about intelligence, let's start with a simpler example of how it is used.

Do ghosts exist? This is probably not the kind of question you expected to find in your psychology textbook, but it can clarify the appeal to ignorance. Those who assert that ghosts *do* exist will often support their conclusion by arguing that no one can prove that ghosts do *not* exist; therefore, ghosts must exist. The lack of evidence or inability to show that ghosts do not exist is used to conclude the opposite. Conversely, those who assert that ghosts *do not* exist often rely on the same logic. They argue that no one can prove that ghosts exist; therefore, they must not exist. Can you see what is wrong with these appeals to ignorance? The lack of information on an issue cannot be used to support any conclusion—other than the conclusion that we are too ignorant to draw a conclusion.

One interesting aspect of the appeal to ignorance is that the same appeal can be used to support two conclusions that are diametrically opposed to each other. This paradox is a telltale clue that appeals to ignorance involve flawed reasoning. It is easy to see what is wrong with appeals to ignorance when the opposite arguments (ghosts exist—ghosts do not exist) are presented together and the lack of evidence on the issue under discussion is obvious. However, when the same fallacy surfaces in more complex debates and the appeal to ignorance is not as blatant, the strategy can be more difficult to recognize. Let's look at how the appeal to ignorance has been used in the debate about intelligence.

As you saw in the main body of the chapter, the dispute about the relative contributions of nature and nurture to intelligence is one of psychology's longest-running controversies. This complex controversy is exceptionally bitter because it has far-reaching social and political repercussions. In this debate, one argument that has frequently been made is that we have little or no evidence that intelligence can be increased by environmental (educational) interventions; therefore, intelligence must be mostly inherited. In other words, the argument runs: No one has demonstrated that intelligence is largely shaped by environment, so it must be largely inherited. This argument was part of Jensen's (1969) landmark treatise that greatly intensified the debate about intelligence, and it was one of the arguments made by Herrnstein and Murray (1994) in their controversial book *The Bell Curve.* What the argument refers to is the evidence that educational enrichment programs such as Head Start, which have been designed to enhance the intellectual development of underprivileged children, generally have not produced substantial, long-term gains in IQ (Neisser et al., 1996). The programs produce other benefits, including enduring improvements in school achievement, but

Do ghosts exist? Littledean Hall, shown here, is said to be the home of 11 ghosts and is reputed to be the most haunted house in Great Britain. Those who believe in ghosts often support their view by arguing that no one can prove that ghosts do not exist. But as the text explains, this appeal to ignorance is logically flawed. This fallacy has also surfaced in some of the debates about the nature of intelligence.

© Simon Marsden, marsdenarchive.com

short-term gains in IQ scores typically have faded by the middle grades (Barnett, 2004). These findings may have some important implications for government policy in the educational arena, but the way in which they have been applied to the nature-nurture debate regarding intelligence has resulted in an appeal to ignorance. In its simplest form, the absence of evidence showing that environmental changes can increase intelligence is used to support the conclusion that intelligence is mostly determined by genetic inheritance. But the absence of evidence (ignorance) cannot be used to argue for or against a position.

By the way, if you have assimilated some of the critical thinking skills discussed in earlier chapters you may be thinking, "Wait a minute. Aren't there alternative explanations for the failure of educational enrichment programs to increase IQ scores?" Yes, one could argue that the programs failed to yield the expected increments in IQ scores because they were poorly planned, poorly executed, too brief, or underfunded (Ramey, 1999; Sigel, 2004). The inability of the enrichment programs to produce enduring increases in IQ does not necessarily imply that intelligence is unchangeable because it is largely a product of heredity. You may also be wondering, "Aren't there contradictory data?" Once again, the answer is yes. Some lesser-known educational enrichment programs attempted with smaller groups of children *have* yielded durable gains in IQ scores or other measures of academic achievement (Ramey & Ramey, 2004; Reynolds et al., 2001; Woodhead, 2004).

The dialogue on intelligence has also been marred by the tendency to engage in reification. ***Reification* occurs when a hypothetical, abstract concept is given a name and then treated as though it were a concrete, tangible object.** Some hypothetical constructs just become so familiar and so taken for granted that we begin to think about them as if they were real. People often fall into this trap with the Freudian personality concepts of id, ego, and superego (see Chapter 11). They begin to think of the *ego,* for instance, as a genuine entity that can be strengthened or controlled, when the ego is really nothing more than a hypothetical abstraction. The concept of intelligence has also been reified in many quarters. Like the ego, intelligence is nothing more than a useful abstraction—a hypothetical construct that is estimated, rather arbitrarily, by a collection of paper-and-pencil measures called IQ tests. Yet people routinely act as if intelligence is a tangible commodity, fighting vitriolic battles over whether it can be measured precisely, whether it can be changed, and whether it can ensure job success. This reification clearly contributes to the tendency for people to attribute excessive importance to the concept of intelligence. It would be wise to remember that intelligence is no more real than the concept of "environment" or "cyberspace" or "the American dream."

Reification has also occurred in the debate about the degree to which intelligence is inherited. Arguments about the heritability coefficient for intelligence often imply that there is a single, true number lurking somewhere "out there"

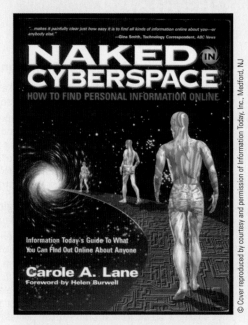

Reification occurs when we think of hypothetical constructs as if they were real. Like intelligence, the concept of cyberspace has been subject to reification. The fact that cyberspace is merely an abstraction becomes readily apparent when artists are asked to "draw" cyberspace for conference posters or book covers.

waiting to be discovered. In reality, heritability is a hypothetical construct that can be legitimately estimated in several ways that can lead to somewhat different results. Moreover, heritability ratios will vary from one population to the next, depending on the amount of genetic variability and the extent of environmental variability in the populations. No exactly accurate number that corresponds to "true heritability" awaits discovery (Hunt & Carlson, 2007; Sternberg, Grigorenko, & Kidd, 2005). Thus, it is important to understand that hypothetical constructs have great heuristic value in the study of complex phenomena such as human thought and behavior, but they do not actually exist in the world—at least not in the same way that a table or a person exists.

TABLE 8.3 **Critical Thinking Skills Discussed in This Application**

Skill	Description
Recognizing and avoiding appeals to ignorance	The critical thinker understands that the lack of information on an issue cannot be used to support an argument.
Recognizing and avoiding reification	The critical thinker is vigilant about the tendency to treat hypothetical constructs as if they were concrete things.
Looking for alternative explanations for findings and events	In evaluating explanations, the critical thinker explores whether there are other explanations that could also account for the findings or events under scrutiny.
Looking for contradictory evidence	In evaluating the evidence presented on an issue, the critical thinker attempts to look for contradictory evidence that may have been left out of the debate.

Problem Solving: In Search of Solutions

8.1 List the three types of problems proposed by Greeno, and identify four common barriers to effective problem solving.

James Greeno distinguished among three broad types of problems: problems of inducing structure, transformation problems, and arrangement problems. Common barriers to problem solving include being distracted by irrelevant information, succumbing to functional fixedness (only seeing an item's most common use), relying on mental set (persisting with strategies that have worked in the past), and placing unnecessary constraints on one's solutions.

8.2 Review general problem-solving strategies and heuristics, and discuss cultural variations in cognitive style.

Trial and error involves trying and discarding potential solutions to a problem until one works, whereas a heuristic is a rule of thumb used in searching for solutions to a problem. When people form subgoals, they break a problem into several parts. Other useful heuristics include searching for analogies between new problems and old problems, and changing the representation of problems. Research on incubation effects suggests that taking a break from a problem can sometimes enhance problem-solving efforts. Additional research suggests that there are cultural disparities in typical problem-solving strategies. Eastern cultures exhibit a more holistic cognitive style, whereas Western cultures display a more analytic cognitive style.

Decision Making: Choices and Chances

8.3 Articulate Simon's theory of bounded rationality and discuss research on decisions about preferences.

Herbert Simon's theory of bounded rationality suggests that human decision strategies are simplistic and often yield irrational results. Barry Schwartz argues that in modern societies people suffer from choice overload, which leads to rumination, regret, and diminished well-being. Recent research suggests that people prefer more choices up to a point, after which further increases in options lead to decreased satisfaction. Research on the deliberation-without-awareness effect suggests that intuitive, unconscious decisions may be more satisfying than those based on conscious deliberation, especially when choices are complex.

© Yuri Arcurs/Shutterstock.com

8.4 Understand the nature of risky decision making and the availability and representativeness heuristics.

Risky decision making involves making choices under conditions of uncertainty. The availability heuristic involves basing probability estimates on the ease with which relevant examples come to mind. The representativeness heuristic involves basing the estimated probability of an event on how similar it is to the prototype of that event.

8.5 Describe some common flaws in reasoning about decisions.

In estimating probabilities, people often ignore information on base rates because of the influence of the representativeness heuristic. The conjunction fallacy occurs when people estimate that the odds of two uncertain events happening together are greater than the odds of either event happening alone. The gambler's fallacy is the belief that the odds of a chance event increase if the event hasn't occurred recently. People tend to inflate estimates of improbable events that garner heavy coverage in the media, because of the availability heuristic. Research shows that people overestimate the impact of losses.

8.6 Describe the nature of fast and frugal heuristics, and discuss dual-process theories of decision making.

Evolutionary psychologists maintain that human decision making only *seems* irrational because cognitive psychologists have been asking the wrong questions and formulating problems in the wrong ways. Fast and frugal heuristics are extremely simple decision strategies that are surprisingly adaptive in the real world. Dual-process theories propose that people depend on two different modes of thinking in making decisions: fast and frugal heuristics and effortful, controlled deliberation.

Measuring Intelligence

8.7 Summarize the contributions of Binet, Terman, and Wechsler to the evolution of intelligence testing.

Modern intelligence testing began with the work of Alfred Binet, a French psychologist who published the first useful intelligence test in 1905. Binet's scale measured a child's mental age. Lewis Terman revised the original Binet scale to produce the Stanford-Binet in 1916. It introduced the intelligence quotient and became the standard of comparison for subsequent intelligence tests. David Wechsler devised an improved measure of intelligence for adults. He also introduced a new scoring system based on the normal distribution.

8.8 Explain the meaning of deviation IQ scores, and summarize evidence on the reliability and validity of IQ scores.

In the modern scoring system, deviation IQ scores indicate where people fall in the normal distribution of intelligence for their age group. On most tests, the mean is set at 100 and the standard deviation is set at 15. IQ tests are exceptionally reliable, with reliability coefficients typically ranging into the .90s. IQ tests are reasonably valid measures of academic intelligence in that they predict school performance fairly well. However, they do not measure intelligence in a truly general sense, as they do not tap social or practical intelligence and they do not predict rational thinking very well.

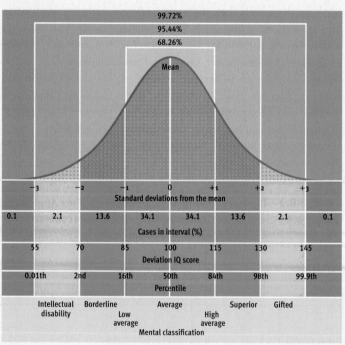

© Cengage Learning

8.9 Discuss how well IQ scores predict vocational success, and discuss the use of IQ tests in non-Western cultures.

IQ scores are associated with occupational attainment and income, but the correlations are modest. There is active debate about whether IQ scores predict performance within an occupation well enough to be used in hiring decisions. Intelligence testing is largely a Western enterprise, and IQ tests are not widely used in most non-Western cultures.

Heredity and Environment as Determinants of Intelligence

8.10 Summarize evidence that heredity affects intelligence, and discuss the concept of heritability.

Twin studies show that identical twins, even when raised apart, are more similar in IQ than fraternal twins, suggesting that intelligence is inherited. Adoption studies reveal that people resemble their parents in intelligence even when not raised by them. Estimates of the heritability of intelligence range from 40% to 80%, with the consensus estimate hovering around 50%; however, heritability ratios have certain limitations.

Heritability estimates for intelligence

"High" estimate

20% of variation in intelligence determined by environment

80% of variation in intelligence determined by heredity

"Low" estimate

40% of variation in intelligence determined by heredity

60% of variation in intelligence determined by environment

© Cengage Learning

8.11 Describe various lines of research that indicate that environment affects intelligence.

Studies show that adopted children resemble their parents and adoptive siblings in intelligence. The effects of environmental deprivation and enrichment also indicate that IQ is shaped by experience. And generational changes in IQ (the Flynn effect) can only be due to environmental factors. The concept of reaction range posits that heredity places limits on one's intellectual potential while the environment determines where one falls within these limits.

8.12 Evaluate heredity and socioeconomic disadvantage as explanations for cultural differences in IQ.

Arthur Jensen and the authors of *The Bell Curve* sparked controversy by arguing that cultural differences in average IQ are partly due to heredity. Even if the heritability of IQ is great, group differences in average intelligence could be entirely environmental in origin. Many theorists note that ethnicity co-varies with social class, so socioeconomic disadvantage may contribute to low IQ scores among minority students.

New Directions in the Study of Intelligence

8.13 Understand evidence on the brain correlates of intelligence and the link between IQ and mortality.

Recent research has uncovered a moderate positive correlation between IQ and overall brain volume estimated from MRI scans. Studies also suggest that IQ correlates with the size of specific areas in the brain and with the volume of gray and white matter. Researchers have also found that IQ measured in childhood correlates with longevity decades later. A variety of mechanisms may contribute to this surprising relationship.

8.14 Explain Sternberg's cognitive analysis of intelligence and Gardner's theory of multiple intelligences.

Robert Sternberg's theory uses a cognitive perspective, which emphasizes the need to understand how people use their intelligence. According to Sternberg, the three facets of successful intelligence are analytical, creative, and practical intelligence. Howard Gardner argues that the concept of intelligence should be expanded to encompass a diverse set of eight types of abilities. He believes that these eight intelligences are largely independent of one another.

Practical intelligence

Three facets of intelligence

Analytical intelligence

Creative intelligence

© Cengage Learning

Reflecting on the Chapter's Themes

8.15 Identify the five unifying themes highlighted in this chapter.

Five of our unifying themes surfaced in the chapter: the empirical nature of psychology, the importance of cultural factors, the interaction of heredity and environment, the way psychology evolves in a sociohistorical context, and the subjectivity of human experience.

PERSONAL APPLICATION
Measuring and Understanding Creativity

8.16 Evaluate the role of insight and divergent thinking in creativity, and discuss creativity tests.

Creativity involves the generation of original, novel, and useful ideas. Creativity does not usually involve sudden insight. Divergent thinking contributes to creativity but does not represent its essence. Creativity tests typically assess divergent thinking. Such tests are mediocre predictors of creative productivity in the real world. One problem is that creativity is specific to particular domains of expertise.

8.17 Clarify the associations between creativity and personality, intelligence, and mental illness.

Creative people are more likely than others to exhibit certain personality traits, but the correlations between creativity and personality are weak. Recent research suggests that living abroad may foster flexibility in thinking and enhance creativity The association between creativity and intelligence is also weak. Evidence suggests that creative geniuses may exhibit heightened vulnerability to mood disorders.

CRITICAL THINKING APPLICATION
The Intelligence Debate, Appeals to Ignorance, and Reification

8.18 Understand how appeals to ignorance and reification have cropped up in debates about intelligence.

The appeal to ignorance involves misusing the general lack of knowledge or information on an issue to support an argument. This fallacy has surfaced in the debate about intelligence, wherein it has been argued that because we have little or no evidence that intelligence can be increased by environmental interventions, intelligence must be mostly inherited. Reification occurs when a hypothetical construct, such as intelligence, is treated as though it were a tangible object.

9 Motivation and Emotion

PARADOX

Modern society seems obsessed with dieting, exercise, and weight loss, but the prevalence of obesity has risen in recent decades.

© Darryl Leniuk/Getty Images

It was a bright afternoon in May 1996, and 41-year-old Jon Krakauer was on top of the world—literally. Krakauer had just fulfilled a boyhood dream by climbing Mount Everest, the tallest peak on Earth. Clearing the ice from his oxygen mask, he looked down on a sweeping vista of ice, snow, and majestic mountains. His triumph should have brought him intense joy. Yet, he felt strangely detached. "I'd been fantasizing about this moment, and the release of emotion that would accompany it, for many years," he wrote later. "But now that I was finally here, standing on the summit of Mount Everest, I just couldn't summon the energy to care" (Krakauer, 1998, p. 6).

Why were Krakauer's emotions so subdued? A major reason was that he was physically exhausted. Climbing Mount Everest is an incredibly grueling experience. At just over 29,000 feet, the mountain's peak is at the altitude flown by jumbo jets. Because such high altitudes wreak havoc on the human body, Krakauer and his fellow climbers couldn't even approach the summit until they had spent six weeks acclimating at Base Camp, 17,600 feet above sea level. At Base Camp, Krakauer found that ordinary bodily functions became painfully difficult. On most nights, he awoke three or four times, gasping for breath and feeling like he was suffocating. His appetite vanished. "My body began consuming itself for sustenance. My arms and legs gradually began to wither to sticklike proportions" (Krakauer, 1998, p. 87).

At this point, you may be wondering why anyone would willingly undergo such extreme discomfort, but Base Camp was just the beginning. From Base Camp, it's another 2 vertical miles through the aptly named Death Zone to the summit. The final leg of the ascent is excruciating. By the time Krakauer reached the summit, every step was labored, every gasping breath hurt. He hadn't slept in 57 hours. He was bitterly cold. He was utterly exhausted. Instead of elation, he felt only apprehension. His oxygen-starved brain was barely functioning. But he understood that getting down from the summit would be just as dangerous as getting up.

The ensuing events proved just how dangerous an assault on Everest can be. During Krakauer's descent, a sudden, howling storm hit the mountain. Winds exceeding 100 miles per hour whipped the snow into a blinding white blur. Krakauer barely escaped with his life. Twelve men and women were not as fortunate. They died on the mountain, including several in Krakauer's own party. Some of them perished needlessly because they had fallen victim to "summit fever." Once they got close to the top, they refused to turn back despite extreme exhaustion and the obvious threat posed by the storm.

The saga of Jon Krakauer and the other climbers is packed with motivation riddles. Why would people push on toward a goal even at the risk of their lives? Why endure such a punishing and hazardous ordeal? In the case of Mount Everest, perhaps the most obvious motive is simply the satisfaction of conquering the world's tallest peak. When British climber George Leigh Mallory was asked why he wanted to climb Everest in the 1920s, his famous reply was, "Because it is there."

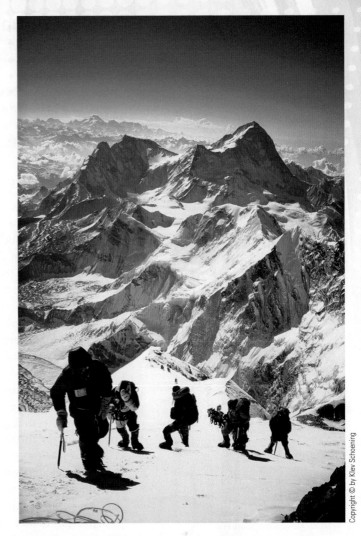

Jon Krakauer (the third person) and other climbers are seen here during their ascent of Mount Everest at an elevation of about 28,200 feet.

Some people seem to have an intense desire to take on the toughest challenges imaginable, to achieve something incredibly difficult. Yet—as is usually the case with human behavior—things are not quite so simple. Krakauer observed that a wide variety of motives drove the climbers he met on Everest. Such motives included desires for "minor celebrity, career advancement, ego massage, ordinary bragging rights, filthy lucre," and even a quest for "a state of grace" (Krakauer, 1998, p. 177).

Krakauer's story is also filled with strong emotions. He anticipated that he would experience a transcendent emotional high when he reached the summit of Mount Everest. As it turned out, his triumph was accompanied more by anxiety than by ecstasy. The harrowing events that followed left him emotionally numb at first. However, he was soon flooded with intense feelings of despair, grief, and guilt over the deaths of his companions. His tale illustrates the intimate connection between motivation and emotion—the topics we'll examine in this chapter.

KEY LEARNING GOALS

9.1 Compare drive, incentive, and evolutionary approaches to understanding motivation.

Motivational Theories and Concepts

Motives are the needs, wants, interests, and desires that propel people in certain directions. In short, *motivation* involves goal-directed behavior. Psychologists have devised a number of theoretical approaches to motivation. Let's look at some of these theories and related concepts.

Drive Theories

Many theories view motivational forces in terms of *drives.* The drive concept appears in a diverse array of theories that otherwise have little in common, such as psychoanalytic and behaviorist theories. The concept of drive was derived from Walter Cannon's (1932) observation that organisms seek to maintain *homeostasis,* a state of physiological equilibrium or stability. The body maintains homeostasis in various ways. For example, human body temperature normally fluctuates around 98.6 degrees Fahrenheit (see **Figure 9.1**). If your body temperature rises or drops noticeably, automatic responses occur: If your temperature goes up, you'll perspire. If your temperature goes down, you'll shiver. These reactions are designed to move your temperature back toward 98.6 degrees. Thus, your body reacts to many disturbances in physiological stability by trying to restore equilibrium.

Drive theories apply the concept of homeostasis to behavior. A *drive* **is a hypothetical, internal state of tension that motivates an organism to engage in activities that should reduce this tension.** These unpleasant states of tension are viewed as disruptions of the preferred equilibrium. According to drive theories, when individuals experience a drive, they're motivated to pursue actions that will lead to *drive reduction.* For example, the hunger motive has usually been viewed as a drive system. If you go without food for a while, you begin to experience some discomfort. This internal tension (the drive) motivates you to obtain food. Eating reduces the drive and restores physiological equilibrium.

Drive theories have been very influential, and the drive concept continues to be widely used in modern psychology. *However, drive theories cannot explain all motivation* (Berridge, 2004). Homeostasis appears irrelevant to some human motives, such as a "thirst for knowledge." And think of all the times that you've eaten when you weren't the least bit hungry. Drive theories can't explain this behavior very well. Incentive theories, which represent a different approach to motivation, can account for this behavior more readily.

Incentive Theories

Incentive theories propose that external stimuli regulate motivational states (Bolles, 1975; McClelland, 1975; Skinner, 1953). **An *incentive* is an external goal that has the capacity to motivate behavior.** Ice cream, a juicy steak, a monetary prize, approval from friends, an A on an exam, and a promotion at work are all incentives. Some of these incentives may reduce drives, but others may not.

Drive and incentive models of motivation are often contrasted as *push versus pull* theories. Drive theories emphasize how *internal* states of tension *push* people in certain directions. Incentive theories emphasize how *external* stimuli *pull* people in certain directions. According to drive theories, the source of motivation lies *within* the organism. According to incentive theories, the source of motivation lies *outside* the organism, in the environment. Thus, incentive models don't operate according to the principle of homeo-

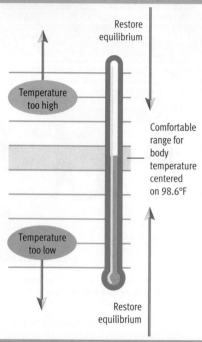

FIGURE 9.1

Temperature regulation as an example of homeostasis. The regulation of body temperature provides a simple example of how organisms often seek to maintain homeostasis, or a state of physiological equilibrium. When your temperature moves out of an acceptable range, automatic bodily reactions (such as sweating or shivering) occur that help restore equilibrium. Of course, these automatic reactions may not be sufficient by themselves, so you may have to take other actions (such as turning a furnace up or down) to bring your body temperature back into its comfort zone.

stasis, which hinges on internal changes in the organism. Rather, incentive theories emphasize environmental factors and downplay the biological bases of human motivation.

Evolutionary Theories

Psychologists who take an evolutionary perspective assert that the motives of humans and of other species are the products of evolution, just as anatomical characteristics are. They argue that natural selection favors behaviors that maximize reproductive success—that is, passing on genes to the next generation. Thus, they explain motives such as affiliation, achievement, dominance, aggression, and sex drive in terms of their adaptive value. If dominance is a crucial motive for a species, they say, it's because dominance provides a reproductive or survival advantage.

Evolutionary analyses of motivation are based on the premise that motives can best be understood in terms of the adaptive problems they have solved over the course of human history. For example, the need for dominance is thought to be greater in men than in women because it could facilitate males' reproductive success in a variety of ways. For instance, females may prefer mating with dominant males, dominant males may poach females from subordinate males, dominant males may intimidate male rivals in competition for sexual access, and dominant males may acquire more material resources that may increase mating opportunities (Buss, 1999). Consider, also, the *affiliation motive,* or need for belongingness. The adaptive benefits of affiliation for our ancestors probably included help with offspring, collaboration in hunting and gathering, mutual defense, opportunities for sexual interaction, and so forth (Baumeister & Leary, 1995). David Buss (1995) points out that it is not by accident that achievement, power (dominance), and intimacy are among the most heavily studied motives, as the satisfaction of each of these motives is likely to affect one's reproductive success.

Motivational theorists of all persuasions agree on one point: Humans display an enormous diversity of motives. These include a host of *biological motives,* such as hunger, thirst, and sex, and a variety of *social motives,* such as the needs for achievement, affiliation, autonomy, dominance, and order. Given the range and diversity of human motives, we can only examine a handful in depth. To a large degree, our choices reflect the motives psychologists have studied the most: hunger, sex, and achievement. After our discussion of these motivational systems, we will explore the elements of emotional experience and discuss various theories of emotion.

The Motivation of Hunger and Eating

KEY LEARNING GOALS

9.2 Summarize evidence on the physiological factors implicated in the regulation of hunger.

9.3 Explain how food availability, culture, and learning influence hunger.

Why do people eat? Because they're hungry. What makes them hungry? A lack of food. Any grade-school child can explain these basic facts. So hunger is a simple motivational system, right? Wrong! Hunger is deceptive. It only looks simple. Actually, it's a puzzling and complex motivational system. Despite extensive studies, scientists are still struggling to understand the factors that regulate eating behavior. Let's examine a few of these factors.

Biological Factors in the Regulation of Hunger

PsykTrek 2e, 8a

You have probably had embarrassing occasions when your stomach growled loudly at an untimely moment. Someone may have commented, "You must be starving!" Most people equate a rumbling stomach with hunger, and in fact, the first scientific theories of hunger were based on this simple equation. In a 1912 study, Walter Cannon and A. L. Washburn verified what most people have noticed based on casual observation: There is an association between stomach contractions and the experience of hunger.

Based on this correlation, Cannon theorized that stomach contractions *cause* hunger. However, as we've seen before, correlation is no assurance of causation. His theory was eventually discredited. Stomach contractions often accompany hunger, but they don't cause it. How do we know? Because later research showed that people continue to experience hunger even after their stomachs have been removed out of medical necessity (Wangensteen & Carlson, 1931). If hunger can occur without a stomach, then stomach contractions can't be the cause of hunger. This realization led to more elaborate theories of hunger that focus on (1) the role of the brain, (2) blood sugar level and digestive factors, and (3) hormones.

BRAIN REGULATION

Research with lab animals eventually suggested that the experience of hunger is controlled in the brain—specifically, in the hypothalamus. As we have noted in Chapter 3, the *hypothalamus* is a tiny structure involved in the regulation of a variety of biological needs related to survival (see **Figure 9.2**). In the 1940s and 1950s, researchers found that when they surgically destroyed animals' *lateral hypothalamus* (*LH*), the animals showed little or no interest in eating, as if their hunger center had been wiped out (Anand & Brobeck, 1951). In contrast, when researchers destroyed animals' *ventromedial nucleus of the hypothalamus* (*VMH*), the animals ate excessively and gained weight rapidly, as if their ability to recognize satiety (fullness) had been neutralized (Brobeck, Tepperman, & Long, 1943). These results led to the conclusion that the *lateral hypothalamus (LH)* and the *ventromedial nucleus of the hypothalamus (VMH)*, were the brain's on-off switches for the control of hunger (Stellar, 1954).

However, over the course of several decades, a variety of empirical findings undermined the dual-centers model of hunger (Valenstein, 1973; Winn, 1995). The current thinking is that the lateral and ventromedial areas of the hypothalamus are elements in the neural circuitry that regulates hunger. However, they are not the key elements, nor simple on-off centers (King, 2006; Meister, 2007). Today, scientists believe that two other areas of the hypothalamus—the *arcuate nucleus* and the *paraventricular nucleus*—play a larger role in the modulation of hunger (Scott, McDade, & Luckman, 2007) (see **Figure 9.2**). In recent years, the arcuate nucleus has been singled out as especially important (Becskei, Lutz, & Riediger, 2008). This area in the hypothalamus appears to contain a group of neurons that are sensitive to incoming hunger signals and another group of neurons that respond to satiety signals.

Contemporary theories of hunger focus more on *neural circuits* that pass through areas of the hypothalamus rather than on *anatomical centers* in the brain. These circuits depend on a large variety of neurotransmitters and they appear to be much more complicated than anticipated. Evidence suggests that the neural circuits regulating hunger are massively and reciprocally interconnected with extensive parallel processing (Powley, 2009). This complex neural circuitry is sensitive to a diverse range of physiological processes.

The rat on the left has had its ventromedial hypothalamus lesioned, resulting in a dramatic increase in weight.

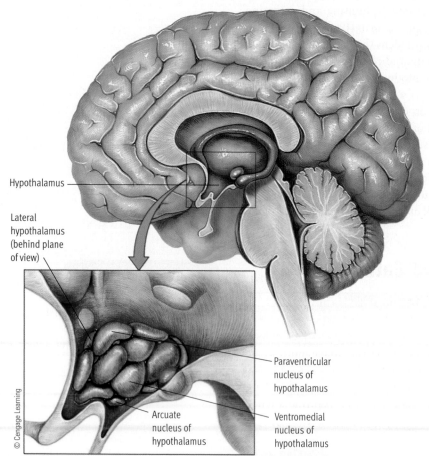

FIGURE 9.2

The hypothalamus. This small structure at the base of the forebrain plays a role in regulating a variety of human biological needs, including hunger. The detailed blow-up shows that the hypothalamus is made up of a variety of discrete areas. Scientists used to believe that the lateral and ventromedial areas were the brain's on-off centers for eating. However, more recent research suggests that the arcuate and paraventricular areas may be more crucial to the regulation of hunger and that thinking in terms of neural circuits rather than anatomical centers makes more sense.

DIGESTIVE AND HORMONAL REGULATION

PsykTrek 8a

The digestive system includes a variety of mechanisms that influence hunger (Ritter, 2004). It turns out that Walter Cannon was not entirely wrong in hypothesizing that the stomach regulates hunger. After you have consumed food, the stomach can send two types of signals to the brain that inhibit further eating (Woods & Stricker, 2008). The vagus nerve carries information about the stretching of the stomach walls that indicates when the stomach is full. Other nerves carry satiety messages that depend on how rich in nutrients the contents of the stomach are. Fluctuations in blood glucose levels also appear to influence hunger (Smith & Campfield, 1993).

A variety of hormones circulating in the bloodstream appear to contribute to the regulation of hunger. *Insulin,* a hormone secreted by the pancreas, must be present for cells to extract glucose from the blood. An inadequate supply of insulin causes diabetes, whereas higher insulin levels are associated with increased hunger. Moreover, insulin levels appear to be sensitive to fluctuations in the body's fat stores (Schwartz et al., 2000). These findings suggest that insulin secretions play a role in the determination of hunger.

At least two other hormones contribute to the short-term regulation of hunger. After the body goes without food for a while, the stomach secretes *ghrelin*, which causes stomach contractions and promotes hunger (Cummings, 2006). In contrast, after food is consumed, the upper intestine releases a hormone called *CCK* that delivers satiety signals to the brain, thus reducing hunger (Moran, 2004; Schwartz & Azzara, 2004)

Finally, evidence indicates that a hormone called *leptin* contributes to the long-term regulation of hunger, as well as the regulation of numerous other bodily functions (Ahima & Osei, 2004). Leptin is produced by fat cells throughout the body and released into the bloodstream. Leptin circulates through the bloodstream and ultimately provides the hypothalamus with information about the body's fat stores (Campfield, 2002). When leptin levels are high, the propensity to feel hungry diminishes. The hormonal signals that influence hunger (the fluctuations of insulin, ghrelin, CCK, and leptin) all seem to converge in the hypothalamus, especially the arcuate and paraventricular nuclei (Kuo et al., 2007; Näslund & Hellström, 2007).

Environmental Factors in the Regulation of Hunger

PsykTrek 8a

Hunger clearly is a biological need. But eating is not regulated by biological factors alone. Studies show that social and environmental factors govern eating to a considerable extent. Key environmental factors include the availability and palatability of food and learned preferences and habits.

FOOD AVAILABILITY AND RELATED CUES

PsykTrek 8a

Most of the research on the physiological regulation of hunger has been based on the assumption that hunger operates as a drive system in which homeostatic mechanisms are at work. However, some theorists emphasize the incentive value of food. They argue that humans and other animals are often motivated to eat not by the need to compensate for energy deficits but by the anticipated pleasure of eating (Hetherington & Rolls, 1996; Ramsay et al., 1996). This perspective has been bolstered by evidence that four variables exert significant influence over food consumption:

- *Palatability.* As you might expect, the better food tastes, the more of it people consume (de Castro, 2010). This principle is not limited to humans. The eating behavior of rats and other animals is also influenced by palatability.

- *Quantity available.* A powerful determinant of the amount eaten is the amount available. People tend to consume what is put in front of them. The more food people are served, the more they eat (Mrdjenovic & Levitsky, 2005; Rozin et al., 2003). For example, one study found that people consumed 45% more popcorn when it was served in larger containers (Wansink & Kim, 2005). Another study, in which participants unknowingly ate from soup bowls that imperceptibly refilled themselves, found that consumption

Reality Check

Misconception
Eating at night will lead to extra weight gain.

Reality
Changes in weight depend on one's caloric intake in relation to one's energy expenditure from physical activities and metabolic processes. *When* you consume your calories is irrelevant. It is the overall amount of caloric intake that is crucial.

soared 73% (Wansink, Painter, & North, 2005). Unfortunately, in recent decades, the size of grocery story packages, restaurant portions, and even dinnerware has increased steadily (Wansink, 2010). These bloated cues about what represents "normal" food consumption clearly fuel increased eating.

• *Variety.* Humans and animals increase their consumption when a greater variety of foods are available (Raynor & Epstein, 2001; Temple et al., 2008). As you eat a specific food, its incentive value declines. This phenomenon is called *sensory-specific satiety* (Havermans, Siep, & Jansen, 2010). If only a few foods are available, the appeal of all of them can decline quickly. But if many foods are available, people can keep shifting to new foods and end up eating more overall. This principle explains why people are especially likely to overeat at buffets, where many foods are available.

• *Presence of others.* On average, individuals eat 44% more when they eat with other people as opposed to eating alone. The more people present, the more food people tend to eat (de Castro, 2010). When two people eat together, they tend to use each other as guides and eat similar amounts (Salvy et al., 2007). When asked afterward, people seem oblivious to the fact that their eating is influenced by the presence of others (Vartanian, Herman, & Wansink, 2008).

Eating can also be triggered by exposure to environmental cues that have been associated with food. You have no doubt had your hunger aroused by television commercials for delicious-looking meals or by seductive odors coming from the kitchen. Consistent with this observation, studies have shown that exposure to soda and food advertisements incite hunger and lead to increased food intake (Harris, Bargh, & Brownell, 2009; Koordeman et al., 2010). Moreover, the foods consumed are not limited to those seen in the ads. And people tend to be unaware of how the ads influence their eating behavior. Thus, it's clear that hunger and eating are governed in part by the incentive qualities of food.

According to incentive models of hunger, the availability and palatability of food are key factors regulating hunger. An abundance of diverse foods tends to lead to increased eating.

LEARNED PREFERENCES AND HABITS

PSYKTREK 8a

Are you fond of eating calves' brains? How about eel or snake? Could I interest you in a grasshopper or some dog meat? Probably not. Yet these are delicacies in some regions of the world. Arctic Eskimos like to eat maggots! You probably prefer chicken, apples, eggs, lettuce, potato chips, pizza, cornflakes, or ice cream. These preferences are acquired through learning. People from different cultures display very different patterns of food consumption (Rozin, 2007). If you doubt this fact, just visit an ethnic grocery store.

Taste preferences are partly a function of learned associations formed through *classical conditioning* (Appleton, Gentry, & Shepherd, 2006). For instance, youngsters can be conditioned to prefer flavors paired with pleasant events. Of course, as we learned in Chapter 6, taste aversions can also be acquired through conditioning when foods are followed by nausea (Schafe & Bernstein, 1996). Eating habits are also shaped by *observational learning* (see Chapter 6). To a large degree, food preferences are a matter of exposure (Cooke, 2007). People generally prefer familiar foods. Geographical, cultural, religious, and ethnic factors limit people's access to certain foods, but repeated exposures to a new food usually lead to increased liking. However, as many parents have learned the hard way, forcing a child to eat a specific food can backfire and have a negative effect on the youngster's preference for the required food (Benton, 2004).

Food preferences are influenced greatly by culture. For example, the fried grasshoppers shown here would not be a treat for most Americans, but they are a delicacy in some cultures.

Sexual Motivation and Behavior

KEY LEARNING GOALS

9.4 Outline the four phases of the human sexual response.

9.5 Describe parental investment theory and gender differences in sexual activity and mating preferences.

9.6 Discuss the prevalence of homosexuality, and compare environmental and biological theories of sexual orientation.

How does sex resemble food? Sometimes it seems that people are obsessed with both. People joke and gossip about sex constantly. Magazines, novels, movies, and television shows are saturated with sexual activity and innuendo. The advertising industry uses sex to sell everything from mouthwash to designer jeans to automobiles. This intense interest in sex reflects the importance of sexual motivation. In this section, we will examine the physiology of the human sexual response, review evolutionary analyses of human sexual motivation, and discuss the roots of sexual orientation.

The Human Sexual Response

Assuming people are motivated to engage in sexual activity, exactly what happens to them physically? This may sound like a simple question, but scientists really knew very little about the physiology of the human sexual response before William Masters and Virginia Johnson did groundbreaking research in the 1960s. Masters and Johnson used physiological recording devices to monitor the bodily changes of volunteers engaging in sexual activities. Their observations and interviews with their subjects yielded a detailed description of the human sexual response and won them widespread acclaim. Masters and Johnson (1966, 1970) divided the sexual response cycle into four stages: excitement, plateau, orgasm, and resolution. **Figure 9.3** on the next page shows how the intensity of sexual arousal changes as women and men progress through these stages.

During the *excitement phase,* the level of physical arousal usually escalates rapidly. In both sexes, muscle tension, respiration rate, heart rate, and blood pressure increase quickly. *Vasocongestion*—engorgement of blood vessels—produces penile erection and swollen testes in males. In females, vasocongestion leads to a swelling and hardening of the clitoris, expansion of the vaginal lips, and vaginal lubrication. During the *plateau phase,* physiological arousal usually continues to build, but at a much slower pace. When foreplay is lengthy, arousal tends to fluctuate in both sexes.

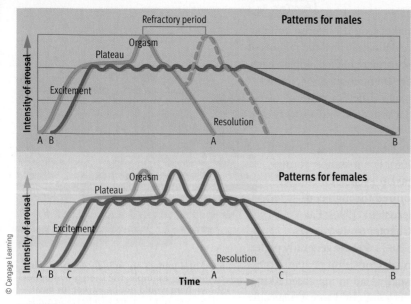

FIGURE 9.3

The human sexual response cycle. There are similarities and differences between men and women in patterns of sexual arousal. Pattern A, which culminates in orgasm and resolution, is the modal sequence for both sexes, but not something one can count on. Pattern B, which involves sexual arousal without orgasm followed by a slow resolution, is seen in both sexes but is more common among women. Pattern C, which involves multiple orgasms, is seen almost exclusively in women, as men go through a refractory period before they are capable of another orgasm.

SOURCE: Based on Masters, W. H., & Johnson, V. E. (1966). *Human sexual response.* Boston: Little, Brown. Copyright © 1966 Little, Brown and Company.

Orgasm occurs when sexual arousal reaches its peak intensity and is discharged in a series of muscular contractions that pulsate through the pelvic area. The subjective experience of orgasm is very similar for men and women, but women are more likely than men to experience more than one orgasm in a brief time period (pattern C in **Figure 9.3**). That said, women are also more likely than men to engage in intercourse without experiencing an orgasm. When respondents are asked whether they *always* have an orgasm with their partner, the gender gap in orgasmic consistency looks rather large. For example, among respondents ages 35–39, Laumann et al. (1994) found that 78% of men but only 28% of women reported always having an orgasm. However, a recent, major survey of sexual behavior approached the issue in a different way and found a smaller gender gap. Herbenick et al. (2010) asked respondents about many of the details of their *most recent sexual interaction* (what they did, how pleasurable it was, whether they had an orgasm, and so forth). As you can see in **Figure 9.4**, men were more likely to report having an orgasm, but the disparity was not as huge as when respondents were asked about *always* having an orgasm.

Whether this gender gap reflects attitudes and sexual practices versus physiological processes is open to debate. On the one hand, it's easy to argue that males' greater orgasmic consistency must be a product of evolution, as it would have obvious adaptive significance for promoting men's reproductive fitness. On the other hand, gender differences in the socialization of

Concept Check | 9.1

Understanding Factors in the Regulation of Hunger

Check your understanding of the effects of the various factors that influence hunger by indicating whether hunger and eating would tend to increase or decrease in each of the situations described below. Indicate your choice by marking an I (increase), a D (decrease), or a ? (can't be determined without more information) next to each situation. You'll find the answers in Appendix A at the back of the book.

_____ 1. Jameer's stomach has just secreted the hormone, ghrelin.

_____ 2. The leptin levels in Marlene's bloodstream have increased in recent weeks.

_____ 3. Norman wasn't hungry, but his roommate just brought home a delicious-looking pizza that smells great.

_____ 4. You're offered an exotic, strange-looking food from another culture and told that everyone in that culture loves it.

_____ 5. Darius is eating at a huge buffet where an enormous variety of foods are available.

_____ 6. You have just been served your meal at a new restaurant. You are astonished by the enormous size of the meal.

guilt feelings about sex, as well as sexual scripts and practices that are less than optimal for women, could play a part (Lott, 1987).

During the *resolution phase,* the physiological changes produced by sexual arousal gradually subside. If orgasm has not occurred, the reduction in sexual tension may be relatively slow. After orgasm, men experience a *refractory period,* a time following orgasm during which they are largely unresponsive to further stimulation. The length of the refractory period varies from a few minutes to a few hours and increases with age.

Evolutionary Analyses of Human Sexual Motivation

The task of explaining sexual behavior is obviously crucial to evolutionary psychologists, given their fundamental thesis that natural selection is fueled by variations in reproductive success. The thinking in this area has been guided by Robert Trivers's (1972) *parental investment theory.* **Parental investment refers to what each sex has to invest—in terms of time, energy, survival risk, and forgone opportunities (to pursue other goals)—to produce and nurture offspring.** For example, the efforts required to guard eggs, build nests, and nourish offspring represent parental investments. In most species, striking disparities exist between males and females in their parental investment, and these discrepancies shape mating strategies. So how does this theory apply to humans?

As with many mammalian species, human males are *required* to invest little in the production of offspring beyond the act of copulation. Hence, their reproductive potential is maximized by mating with as many females as possible. The situation for females is quite different. Females have to invest nine months in pregnancy, and our female ancestors typically had to devote at least several additional years to nourishing offspring through breastfeeding. These realities place a ceiling on the number of offspring women can produce, regardless of how many males they mate with. Hence, females have little or no incentive for mating with many males. Instead, females can optimize their reproductive potential by being selective in mating. Thus, in humans, males are thought to compete with other males for the relatively scarce and valuable "commodity" of reproductive opportunities.

Parental investment theory predicts that in comparison to women, men will show more interest in sexual activity, more desire for variety in sexual partners, and more willingness to engage in uncommitted sex (see **Figure 9.5**). In contrast, females are thought to be the conservative, discriminating sex that is highly selective in choosing partners. This selectivity supposedly involves seeking partners who have the greatest ability to contribute toward feeding and caring for offspring. Why? Because in the world of our ancient ancestors, males' greater strength and agility would have been crucial assets in the never-ending struggle to find food and shelter and defend territory. A female who chose a mate who was lazy or unreliable or who had no hunting, fighting, building, farming, or other useful economic skills would have suffered a substantial disadvantage in her efforts to raise her children and pass on her genes.

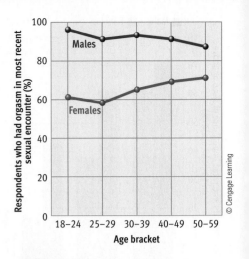

FIGURE 9.4

The gender gap in orgasm consistency. In their sexual interactions, men reach orgasm more reliably than women. When respondents are asked whether they *always* have an orgasm, the gender gap is huge. But the new data shown here, which indiciate whether people had an orgasm in their most recent sexual encounter, suggest that the gender gap is quite a bit smaller, although not insignificant. The new data also indicate that the gender gap diminishes in older age groups. (Data from Herbenick et al., 2010)

FIGURE 9.5

Parental investment theory and mating preferences. Parental investment theory suggests that basic differences between males and females in parental investment have great adaptive significance and lead to gender differences in mating tendencies and preferences, as outlined here.

Males ▉ Females ▉

(y-axis) Respondents who rated importance of sex 6 or above on 10-point scale (%)

80
70
60
50
40
30
20
10
0

25–54   55–64   65–74

Age bracket

© Cengage Learning

FIGURE 9.6

The gender gap in interest in sex.
Lindau and Gavrilova (2010) summarized data from a nationally representative sample of over 3000 participants. In the survey, respondents were asked to rate how much thought and effort they put into the sexual aspect of their lives. The rating scale ranged from 0 (none) to 10 (very much). The graph shows the percentage of respondents who gave a rating of 6 or greater. As you can see, males generally expressed a greater interest in sex than females. The gender gap was modest in the 25–54 age range, but widened considerably in older age groups.

GENDER DIFFERENCES IN PATTERNS OF SEXUAL ACTIVITY

Consistent with evolutionary theory, males generally show a greater interest in sex than females do (Peplau, 2003). Men think about sex more often than women. They also initiate sex more often (Morokoff et al., 1997). Males have more frequent and varied sexual fantasies (Okami & Shackelford, 2001), and their subjective ratings of their sex drive tend to be higher than those of females (Ostovich & Sabini, 2004). When heterosexual couples are asked about their sex lives, male partners are more likely than their female counterparts to report that they would like to have sex more often. The findings of a recent study suggest that this disparity in sexual motivation only widens when people reach middle age (Lindau & Gavrilova, 2010). As you can see in **Figure 9.6**, in the 55–64 age bracket, 62% of men but only 38% of women report that they are still very interested in sex.

Men are also more motivated than women to pursue sex with a greater variety of partners (McBurney, Zapp, & Streeter, 2005). For example, Buss and Schmitt (1993) found that college men indicated that they would ideally like to have eighteen sex partners across their lives. College women, on the other hand, reported that they would prefer only five partners. Similar findings were observed in a follow-up study that examined desire for sexual variety in over 16,000 subjects from ten major regions of the world (Schmitt et al., 2003). Males expressed a desire for more partners than females in all ten world regions. In most cases the differences were substantial.

© Dmitry Melnikov/Shutterstock

Clear gender disparities are also seen in regard to people's willingness to engage in casual or uncommitted sex. For example, in a compelling field study, Clark and Hatfield (1989) had average-looking men approach female (college-age) strangers and ask if they would go back to the man's apartment to have sex with him. None of the women agreed to this proposition. But when Clark and Hatfield had average-looking women approach males with the same proposition 75% of the men eagerly agreed!

GENDER DIFFERENCES IN MATE PREFERENCES

Parental investment theory suggests some glaring disparities should exist between men and women in what they look for in a long-term mate (see **Figure 9.5** again). The theory predicts that men should place more emphasis than women on such partner characteristics as youthfulness (which allows for more reproductive years) and attractiveness (which is assumed to be correlated with health and fertility). In contrast, parental investment theory predicts that women should place more emphasis than men on partner characteristics such as intelligence, ambition, education, income, and social status (which are associated with the ability to provide more material resources). If these evolutionary analyses of sexual motivation are on the mark, gender differences in mating preferences should be virtually universal and thus transcend culture.

© Dmitry Shironosov/Shutterstock

To test this hypothesis, David Buss (1989) and fifty scientists from around the world surveyed more than 10,000 people from thirty-seven cultures about what they looked for in a mate. As predicted by parental investment theory, they found that women placed a higher value than men on potential partners' status, ambition, and financial prospects. These priorities were not limited to industrialized or capitalist countries. They were apparent in third-world cultures, socialist countries, and all varieties of economic systems. In contrast, men around the world consistently showed more interest than women in potential partners' youthfulness and physical attractiveness. A number of studies, using diverse samples and a variety of research methods, have replicated the disparities between males and females in mating priorities and preferences (Neuberg, Kenrick, & Schaller, 2010; Shackelford, Schmitt, & Buss, 2005).

David Buss

"Evolutionary psychologists develop hypotheses about the psychological mechanisms that have evolved in humans to solve particular adaptive problems that humans have faced under ancestral conditions."

CRITICISM AND ALTERNATIVE EXPLANATIONS

So, the findings on gender differences in sexual behavior and mating priorities mesh nicely with predictions derived from evolutionary theory. But evolutionary theory has its share of critics. Some skeptics argue that there are alternative explanations for the findings. For example, women's emphasis on males' material resources could be a by-product of cultural and economic forces rather than the result of biological imperatives (Eagly & Wood, 1999). Women may have learned to value males' economic clout because their own economic potential has historically been limited in virtually all cultures (Hrdy, 1997; Kasser & Sharma, 1999). In a similar vein, Roy Baumeister has argued that the gender disparity in sexual motivation may be largely attributable to extensive cultural processes that serve to suppress female sexuality (Baumeister & Twenge, 2002). Evolutionary theorists counter these arguments by pointing out that the cultural and economic processes at work may themselves be products of evolution.

Evolutionary theory posits that men can maximize their reproductive fitness by seeking youthful partners, whereas women can maximize their reproductive success by searching for mates that are rich in material resources that can be invested in children. Obviously, this theory can explain why attractive young women often become romantically involved with much older men who happen to be wealthy.

BIZARRO

The Mystery of Sexual Orientation

Sex must be a contentious topic, as the controversy swirling around evolutionary explanations of gender differences in sexuality is easily equaled by the controversy surrounding the determinants of *sexual orientation*. *Sexual orientation* refers to a person's preference for emotional and sexual relationships with individuals of the same sex, the other sex, or either sex. *Heterosexuals* seek emotional-sexual relationships with members of the other sex, *bisexuals* with members of either sex, and *homosexuals* with members of the same sex. The terms *gay* and *straight* have become widely used to refer to homosexuals and heterosexuals, respectively. Although *gay* can refer to homosexuals of either sex, most homosexual women prefer to call themselves *lesbians*.

People tend to view heterosexuality and homosexuality as an all-or-none distinction. However, in a large-scale survey of sexual behavior, Alfred Kinsey and his colleagues (1948, 1953) discovered that many people who define themselves as heterosexuals have had homosexual experiences—and vice versa. Thus, Kinsey and others have concluded that it is more accurate to view heterosexuality and homosexuality as end points on a continuum (Haslam, 1997). Indeed, Kinsey devised a seven-point scale, shown in **Figure 9.7** on the next page, that can be used to characterize individuals' sexual orientation.

FIGURE 9.7

Homosexuality and hetero-sexuality as end points on a continuum. Sex researchers view heterosexuality and homosexuality as falling on a continuum rather than make an all-or-none distinction. Kinsey and his associates (1948, 1953) created this 7-point scale (from 0 to 6) to describe people's sexual orientation.

0	1	2	3	4	5	6
Exclusively heterosexual	Predominantly heterosexual, only incidentally homosexual	Predominantly heterosexual, more than incidentally homosexual	Equally heterosexual and homosexual	Predominantly homosexual, more than incidentally heterosexual	Predominantly homosexual, only incidentally heterosexual	Exclusively homosexual

© Cengage Learning

How common is homosexuality? No one knows for sure. Part of the problem is that this question is vastly more complex than it appears at first glance (LeVay, 1996; Savin-Williams, 2006). Given that sexual orientation is best represented as a continuum, where do you draw the lines between heterosexuality, bisexuality, and homosexuality? And how do you handle the distinction between overt behavior and latent desire? Where, for instance, do you put a person who is married and has never engaged in homosexual behavior but who reports homosexual fantasies and acknowledges being strongly drawn to members of the same sex? The other part of the problem is that many people have extremely prejudicial attitudes about homosexuality, which makes gays reluctant to give candid information about their sexuality (Herek, 2000, 2009). Small wonder then that estimates of the portion of the population that is homosexual vary widely. A frequently cited estimate of the number of people who are gay is 10%, but surveys suggest that this percentage may be an overestimate. Michaels (1996) combined data from two of the better large-scale surveys to arrive at the estimates shown in **Figure 9.8**. As you can see, the numbers are open to varying interpretations, but as a whole they suggest that about 5%–8% of the population could reasonably be characterized as homosexual.

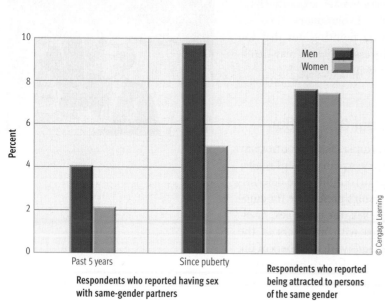

© Nicholas Piccillo/Shutterstock

© Cengage Learning

FIGURE 9.8

How common is homosexuality? The answer to this question is both complex and controversial. Michaels (1996) brought together data from two large-scale surveys to arrive at the estimates shown here. If you look at how many people have actually had a same-sex partner in the last five years, the figures are relatively low, but if you count those who have had a same-sex partner since puberty the figures more than double. Still another way to look at the situation is to ask people whether they are attracted to others of the same sex (regardless of their actual behavior). This approach suggests that about 8% of the population could be characterized as homosexual.

ENVIRONMENTAL THEORIES OF HOMOSEXUALITY

Over the years many environmental theories have been floated to explain the origins of homosexuality. However, when tested empirically, these theories have received remarkably little support. For example, psychoanalytic and behavioral theorists, who usually agree on very little, both proposed environmental explanations for the development of homosexuality. The Freudian theorists argued that a male is likely to become gay when raised by a weak, detached, ineffectual father who is a poor heterosexual role model and by an overprotective, overly attached mother, with whom the boy identifies. Behavioral theorists argued that homosexuality is a learned preference acquired when same-sex stimuli have been paired with sexual arousal, perhaps through chance seductions by adult homosexuals. Extensive research on homosexuals' upbringing and childhood experiences have failed to support either of these theories (Bell, Weinberg, & Hammersmith, 1981). Similarly, there is no evidence that parents' sexual orientation is linked to that of their children (Patterson, 2003). That is, homosexual parents are no more likely to produce homosexual offspring than heterosexual parents are.

However, efforts to research homosexuals' personal histories have yielded a number of interesting insights. Extremely feminine behavior in young boys or masculine behavior in young girls does predict the subsequent development of homosexuality (Bailey & Zucker, 1995). For example, Rieger and colleagues (2008) asked homosexual and heterosexual adults to supply childhood home videos. Independent judges were asked to rate how gender nonconforming the young children were in the videos. Rieger and colleagues found that children who would eventually identify as homosexual in adulthood were more gender nonconforming than those who identified as heterosexual. This finding held for both males and females. Consistent with this finding, most gay men and women report that they can trace their homosexual leanings back to their early childhood, even before they understood what sex was really about (Bailey, 2003). Most also report that because of negative parental and societal attitudes about homosexuality, they initially struggled to deny their sexual orientation. Thus, they felt that their homosexuality was not a matter of choice and not something that they could readily change (Breedlove, 1994). Although people's subjective recollections of the past need to be interpreted with caution, these findings suggest that the roots of homosexuality are more biological than environmental.

BIOLOGICAL THEORIES OF HOMOSEXUALITY

Like environmental theorists, biological theorists were frustrated for quite a while in their efforts to explain the roots of homosexuality. However, that picture changed dramatically in the 1990s (Gladue, 1994). In one landmark investigation, Bailey and Pillard (1991) studied gay men who had either a twin brother or an adopted brother. They found that 52% of the participants' identical twins were gay, that 22% of their fraternal twins were gay, and that 11% of their adoptive brothers were gay. A companion study (Bailey et al., 1993) of lesbians yielded a similar pattern of results (see **Figure 9.9**). Given that identical twins share more genetic overlap than fraternal twins, who share more genes than unrelated adoptive siblings, these results suggest that there is a genetic predisposition to homosexuality (Hyde, 2005b) (see Chapter 3 for an explanation of the logic underlying twin and adoption studies).

Many theorists suspect that the roots of homosexuality may lie in the organizing effects of prenatal hormones on neurological development (James, 2005). Several lines of research suggest that hormonal secretions during critical periods of prenatal development may shape sexual development, organize the brain in a lasting manner, and influence subsequent sexual orientation (Berenbaum & Snyder, 1995). For example, researchers have found elevated rates of homosexuality among women exposed to abnormally high androgen levels during prenatal development (because their mothers had an adrenal disorder or were given a synthetic hormone to reduce the risk of miscarriage) (Breedlove, 1994; Meyer-Bahlburg et al., 1995). Several other independent lines of research suggest that abnormalities in prenatal hormonal secretions may foster a predisposition to homosexuality (Mustanski, Chivers, & Bailey, 2002).

Despite the recent breakthroughs, much remains to be learned about the determinants of sexual orientation. One complication that has emerged relatively recently is that the pathways to homosexuality may be somewhat different for males as opposed to females. Females' sexuality appears to be characterized by more *plasticity* than males' sexuality (Baumeister, 2000, 2004). In other words, women's sexual behavior may be more easily shaped and modified by sociocultural factors. For example, although sexual orientation is assumed to be a stable characteristic, research shows that lesbian and bisexual women often change their sexual orientation over the course of their adult years (Diamond, 2003, 2007, 2008). And, in comparison to gay males, lesbians are less likely

Percentage of relatives with gay sexual orientation

© Cengage Learning

FIGURE 9.9

Genetics and sexual orientation. If relatives who share more genetic relatedness show greater similarity on a trait than relatives who share less genetic overlap, this evidence suggests a genetic predisposition to the characteristic. Studies of both gay men and lesbian women have found a higher prevalence of homosexuality among their identical twins than their fraternal twins, who, in turn, are more likely to be homosexual than their adoptive siblings. These findings suggest that genetic factors influence sexual orientation. (Data from Bailey & Pillard, 1991; Bailey et. al., 1993)

© AP Images/Peter Kramer

Some people were baffled when actress Lindsay Lohan became involved with DJ Samantha Ronson after a history of heterosexual relationships. Although shifts in sexual orientation like this are uncommon among males, research has shown that females' sexual orientation tends to be characterized by more plasticity than that of males.

to trace their homosexuality back to their childhood and are more likely to indicate that their attraction to the same sex emerged during adulthood (Tolman & Diamond, 2001). These findings suggest that sexual orientation may be more fluid and malleable in women than in men. The debate about the roots of sexual orientation shows once again that the nature versus nurture issue can have far-reaching social and political implications.

Achievement: In Search of Excellence

KEY LEARNING GOALS

9.7 Describe the need for achievement and how it has been measured.

9.8 Explain how the need for achievement and situational factors influence achievement strivings.

At the beginning of this chapter, we discussed Jon Krakauer's laborious, grueling effort to reach the summit of Mount Everest. He and the other climbers confronted incredible perils and endured extraordinary hardships to achieve their goal. What motivates people to push themselves so hard? In all likelihood, it's a strong need for achievement. The *achievement motive* **is the need to master difficult challenges, to outperform others, and to meet high standards of excellence.** Above all else, the need for achievement involves the desire to excel, especially in competition with others.

Research on achievement motivation was pioneered by David McClelland and his colleagues (McClelland, 1985; McClelland et al., 1953). McClelland argued that achievement motivation is of the utmost importance—that it is the spark that ignites economic growth, scientific progress, inspirational leadership, and masterpieces in the creative arts.

Individual Differences in the Need for Achievement `PSYKTREK 8b`

The need for achievement is a fairly stable aspect of personality. Thus, research in this area has focused mostly on individual differences in achievement motivation. In this research, investigators usually measure participants' need for achievement with some variant of the Thematic Apperception Test (TAT) (Smith, 1992; Spangler, 1992). The TAT is a *projective* test, one that requires subjects to respond to vague, ambiguous stimuli in ways that may reveal personal motives and traits (see Chapter 11). The stimulus materials for the TAT are pictures of people in ambiguous scenes open to interpretation. Examples include a man working at a desk and a woman seated in a chair staring off into space. Participants are asked to write or tell stories about what's happening in the scenes and what the characters are feeling. The themes of these stories are then scored to measure the strength of various needs. **Figure 9.10** shows examples of stories dominated by themes of achievement and, as another example, affiliation needs.

The research on individual differences in achievement motivation has yielded interesting findings on the characteristics of people who score high in the need for achievement. For instance, they tend to work harder and more persistently on tasks than people low in

David McClelland

"People with a high need for achievement are not gamblers; they are challenged to win by personal effort, not by luck."

FIGURE 9.10

Measuring motives with the Thematic Apperception Test (TAT). Subjects taking the TAT tell or write stories about what is happening in a scene, such as this one showing a man at work. The two stories shown here illustrate strong affiliation motivation and strong achievement motivation. The italicized parts of the stories are thematic ideas that would be identified by a TAT scorer.

SOURCE: Stories reprinted by permission of Dr. David McClelland.

Affiliation arousal
George is an engineer who is working late. He is *worried that his wife will be annoyed* with him for neglecting her. She has been *objecting* that he cares more about his work than his wife and family. He seems *unable to satisfy* both his boss and his wife, but he *loves her* very much and will do his best to *finish up* fast and get home to her.

Achievement arousal
George is an engineer who *wants to win* a competition in which the man with the *most practicable drawing* will be awarded the contract to build a bridge. He is taking a moment to think *how happy he will be* if he wins. He has been *baffled by how to make such a long span strong*, but he remembers to *specify a new steel alloy* of great strength, submits his entry, but does not win, and is *very unhappy*.

the need for achievement (Brown, 1974), and they handle negative feedback about task performance more effectively than others (Fodor & Carver, 2000). They are also more likely than others to delay gratification in order to pursue long-term goals (Mischel, 1961; Raynor & Entin, 1982). As you might guess, given these characteristics, researchers often find a positive correlation between high need for achievement and educational attainment (Hustinx et al., 2009). In terms of careers, those with a high achievement need typically go into competitive occupations that provide them with an opportunity to excel (Collins, Hanges, & Locke, 2004; Stewart & Roth, 2007). Apparently, their persistence and hard work often pay off. High achievement motivation correlates positively with measures of career success in business (Amyx & Alford, 2005; Winter, 2010).

Do people high in achievement need always tackle the biggest challenges available? Not necessarily. A curious finding has emerged in laboratory studies in which subjects have been asked to choose the difficulty level of a task to work on. Participants high in the need for achievement tend to select tasks of intermediate difficulty (McClelland & Koestner, 1992). For instance, in a study in which subjects playing a ring-tossing game were allowed to stand as close to or as far away from the target peg as they wanted, high achievers tended to prefer a moderate degree of challenge (Atkinson & Litwin, 1960). Research on the situational determinants of achievement behavior has suggested a reason.

Situational Determinants of Achievement Behavior [PsykTrek 8b]

Your achievement drive is not the only determinant of how hard you work. Situational factors can also influence achievement strivings. John Atkinson (1974, 1981, 1992) has elaborated extensively on McClelland's original theory of achievement motivation and has identified some important situational determinants of achievement behavior. Atkinson theorizes that the tendency to pursue achievement in a particular situation depends on:

- The strength of one's *motivation* to *achieve* success, which is viewed as a stable aspect of personality.
- One's estimate of the *probability of success* for the task at hand; such estimates vary from task to task.
- The *incentive value* of success, which depends on the tangible and intangible rewards for success on the specific task.

The last two variables are situational determinants of achievement behavior. That is, they vary from one situation to another. According to Atkinson, the pursuit of achievement increases as the probability of success and incentive value of success go up. Let's apply Atkinson's model to a simple example. Given a certain motivation to achieve success, you will pursue a good grade in calculus less vigorously if your professor gives impossible exams (thus lowering your expectancy of success) or if a good grade in calculus is not required for your major (lowering the incentive value of success).

The joint influence of these situational factors may explain why high achievers prefer tasks of intermediate difficulty. Atkinson notes that the probability of success and the incentive value of success on tasks are interdependent to some degree. As tasks get easier, success becomes less satisfying. As tasks get harder, success becomes more satisfying but becomes less likely. When the probability and incentive value of success are weighed together, moderately challenging tasks seem to offer the best overall value.

We turn next to the study of emotion. Motivation and emotion are often intertwined (Zurbriggen & Sturman, 2002). On the one hand, *emotion can cause motivation*. For example, *anger* about your work schedule may motivate you to look for a new job. *Jealousy* of an ex-girlfriend may motivate you to ask out her roommate. On the other hand, *motivation can cause emotion*. For example, your motivation to win a photography contest may lead to great *anxiety* during the judging and either *elation* if you win or *gloom* if you don't. Although motivation and emotion are closely related, they're *not* the same thing. We'll analyze the nature of emotion in the next section.

Reality Check

Misconception

People with high achievement motivation are risk takers who prefer very challenging tasks.

Reality

People who score high in achievement motivation seem to *need* to experience success; many of them fear failure. Hence, they tend to select tasks that are moderately challenging and pursue goals that are reasonably realistic. They are not necessarily the most daring risk takers.

The Elements of Emotional Experience

9.9 Describe the cognitive and physiological components of emotion.

9.10 Explain how emotions are reflected in facial expressions, and describe the facial feedback hypothesis.

9.11 Review cross-cultural similarities and variations in emotional experience.

The most profound and important experiences in life are saturated with emotion. Think of the *joy* that people feel at weddings, the *grief* they feel at funerals, the *ecstasy* they feel when they fall in love. Emotions also color everyday experiences. For instance, you might experience *anger* when a professor treats you rudely, *dismay* when you learn that your car needs expensive repairs, and *happiness* when you see that you aced your economics exam. Clearly, emotions play an important role in people's lives.

Exactly what is an emotion? Everyone has plenty of personal experience with emotion, but it's an elusive concept to define (LeDoux, 1995). Emotion includes cognitive, physiological, and behavioral components, which are summarized in the following definition: *Emotion* involves (1) **a subjective conscious experience (the cognitive component)** accompanied by (2) **bodily arousal (the physiological component)** and (3) **characteristic overt expressions (the behavioral component).** That's a pretty complex definition. Let's take a closer look at each of these three components.

The Cognitive Component

PSYKTREK 8c

In studying the cognitive component of emotions, psychologists generally rely on individuals' highly subjective verbal reports of what they're experiencing. These reports indicate that emotions are potentially intense internal feelings that sometimes seem to have a life of their own. People can't switch their emotions on and off like a bedroom light. If it were that simple, you could choose to be happy whenever you wanted. As Joseph LeDoux puts it, "Emotions are things that happen to us rather than things we will to occur" (1996, p. 19).

People's cognitive appraisals of events in their lives are key determinants of the emotions they experience (Clore & Ortony, 2008; Ellsworth & Scherer, 2003). A specific event, such as giving a speech, may be a highly threatening and thus anxiety-arousing occasion for one person but a routine matter for another. The conscious experience of emotion includes an *evaluative* aspect. People characterize their emotions as pleasant or unpleasant (Barrett

Emotions involve automatic reactions that can be difficult to control.

Concept Check 9.2

Understanding the Determinants of Achievement Behavior

According to John Atkinson, one's pursuit of achievement in a particular situation depends on several factors. Check your understanding of these factors by identifying each of the following vignettes as an example of one of the following three determinants of achievement behavior: (a) need for achievement, (b) perceived probability of success, and (c) incentive value of success. The answers can be found in Appendix A.

_____ 1. Belinda is nervously awaiting the start of the finals of the 200-meter dash in the last meet of her high school career. "I've gotta win this race! This is the most important race of my life!"

_____ 2. Corey grins as he considers the easy time he's going to have this semester. "This class is supposed to be a snap. I hear the professor gives A's and B's to nearly everyone."

_____ 3. Diana's just as hard-charging as ever. She's gotten the highest grade on every test throughout the semester, yet she's still up all night studying for the final. "I know I've got an A in the bag, but I want to be the best student Dr. McClelland's ever had!"

et al., 2007; Nesse & Ellsworth, 2009). These evaluative reactions can be automatic and subconscious (Ferguson & Bargh, 2004).

In recent years a curious finding has emerged regarding people's cognitive assessments of their emotions—they are not very good at anticipating their emotional responses to future events. Research on *affective forecasting*—**efforts to predict one's emotional reactions to future events**—demonstrates that people reliably mispredict their future feelings in response to good and bad events, such as getting a promotion at work, taking a long-awaited vacation, or getting a poor grade in an important class (Wilson & Gilbert, 2003, 2005). People tend to be reasonably accurate in anticipating whether events will generate positive or negative emotions, but they often are way off in predicting the intensity and duration of their emotional reactions.

For example, Dunn, Wilson, and Gilbert (2003) asked college students to predict what their overall level of happiness would be if a campus housing lottery assigned them to a desirable or an undesirable dormitory. The students expected that their dormitory assignments would have a pretty dramatic effect on their well-being. But when their happiness was assessed a year after actually being assigned to the good or bad dorms, it was clear that their happiness was not affected by their dorm assignments. In a similar vein, research shows that young professors overestimate the unhappiness they will feel five years after being turned down for tenure, college students overestimate how despondent they will be after the breakup of a romantic relationship, and applicants overestimate how distressed they will feel after being rejected for a job (Gilbert et al., 1998).

Why are our predictions of our emotional reactions surprisingly inaccurate? Many factors can contribute (Hoerger et al., 2009; Wilson & Gilbert, 2003). One consideration is that most of us do not fully appreciate how effective people tend to be in rationalizing, discounting, and overlooking failures and mistakes. People exhibit a host of cognitive biases that help them insulate themselves from the emotional fallout of life's difficulties. As you can see, emotions are not only hard to regulate, they are also hard to predict.

The Physiological Component

PsykTrek 8c

Emotional processes are closely tied to physiological processes, but the interconnections are enormously complex. The biological bases of emotions are diffuse and multifaceted, involving many areas in the brain, as well as the autonomic nervous system and the endocrine system.

AUTONOMIC AROUSAL

PsykTrek 8c

Imagine your reaction as your car spins out of control on an icy highway. Your fear is accompanied by a variety of physiological changes. Your heart rate and breathing accelerate. Your blood pressure surges, and your pupils dilate. The hairs on your skin stand erect, giving you "goose bumps," and you start to perspire. Although your reactions may not always be as obvious as in this scenario, *emotions are accompanied by physical arousal* (Larsen et al., 2008). Surely you've experienced a "knot in your stomach" or a "lump in your throat" thanks to anxiety.

Much of the physiological arousal associated with emotion occurs through the actions of the *autonomic nervous system* (Janig, 2003). This system regulates the activity of glands, smooth muscles, and blood vessels (see **Figure 9.11** on the next page). As you may recall from Chapter 3, the autonomic nervous system is responsible for the highly emotional *fight-or-flight response,* which is largely controlled by the release of adrenal *hormones* that radiate throughout the body. Hormonal changes clearly play a crucial role in emotional responses to stress and may contribute to many other emotions as well (Baum, Grunberg, & Singer, 1992).

The connection between emotion and autonomic arousal provides the basis for the *polygraph,* or lie detector, **a device that records autonomic fluctuations while a subject is questioned.** The polygraph was invented in 1915 by psychologist William Marston— who also dreamed up the comic book superhero Wonder Woman (Knight, 2004). A

FIGURE 9.11

Emotion and autonomic arousal.
The autonomic nervous system (ANS) is composed of the nerves that connect to the heart, blood vessels, smooth muscles, and glands (consult Chapter 3 for more information). The ANS is divided into the *sympathetic division,* which mobilizes bodily resources in response to stress, and the *parasympathetic division,* which conserves bodily resources. Emotions are frequently accompanied by sympathetic ANS activation, which leads to goose bumps, sweaty palms, and the other physical responses listed on the left side of the diagram.

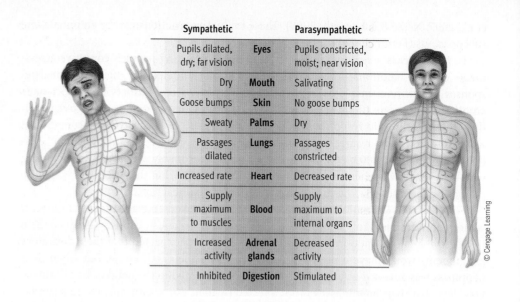

Sympathetic		Parasympathetic
Pupils dilated, dry; far vision	**Eyes**	Pupils constricted, moist; near vision
Dry	**Mouth**	Salivating
Goose bumps	**Skin**	No goose bumps
Sweaty	**Palms**	Dry
Passages dilated	**Lungs**	Passages constricted
Increased rate	**Heart**	Decreased rate
Supply maximum to muscles	**Blood**	Supply maximum to internal organs
Increased activity	**Adrenal glands**	Decreased activity
Inhibited	**Digestion**	Stimulated

© Cengage Learning

polygraph can't actually detect lies. It's really an emotion detector. It monitors key indicators of autonomic arousal, typically heart rate, blood pressure, respiration rate, and *galvanic skin response (GSR),* **which is an increase in the electrical conductivity of the skin that occurs when sweat glands increase their activity.** The assumption is that when people lie, they experience emotion (presumably anxiety) that produces noticeable changes in these physiological indicators (see **Figure 9.12**). The polygraph examiner asks a subject a number of nonthreatening questions to establish the person's baseline on these indicators. Then the examiner asks the critical questions (for example, "Were you at home on the night of the burglary?") and observes whether the subject's autonomic arousal changes.

Paper direction

Respiration

Galvanic skin response (GSR)

Blood pressure

© RIA Novosti/The Image Works

© Cengage Learning

| What department do you work in? | Who is your supervisor? | Have you ever taken money from the bank? | Have you ever falsified bank records? |

FIGURE 9.12

Emotion and the polygraph. A lie detector measures the autonomic arousal that most people experience when they tell a lie. After using nonthreatening questions to establish a baseline, a polygraph examiner looks for signs of arousal (such as the sharp change in GSR shown here) on incriminating questions. Unfortunately, as your text explains, the polygraph is not a very dependable index of whether people are lying.

The polygraph has been controversial since its invention (Grubin & Madsen, 2005). Polygraph advocates claim that lie detector tests are about 85%–90% accurate and that the validity of polygraph testing has been demonstrated in empirical studies. However, these claims clearly are not supported by the evidence (Iacono & Lykken, 1997; Iacono & Patrick, 1999). Methodologically sound research on the validity of polygraph testing is surprisingly sparse (largely because it is difficult research to do), and the limited evidence is not very impressive (Branaman & Gallagher, 2005; Lykken, 1998; Saxe & Ben-Shakhar, 1999). Part of the problem is that people who are telling the truth may experience emotional arousal when they respond to incriminating questions. Another problem is that some people can lie without experiencing anxiety or autonomic arousal. The polygraph *is* a potentially useful tool that can help police check out leads and alibis. However, polygraph results are not reliable enough to be submitted as evidence in most types of courtrooms.

NEURAL CIRCUITS

PSYKTREK 8c

The autonomic responses that accompany emotions are ultimately controlled in the brain. The hypothalamus, amygdala, and adjacent structures in the *limbic system* have long been viewed as the seat of emotions in the brain (Izard & Saxton, 1988; MacLean, 1993).

Recent evidence suggests that the *amygdala* plays a particularly central role in the acquisition of conditioned fears (LeDoux & Phelps, 2008). According to Joseph LeDoux (1996, 2000), sensory inputs capable of eliciting emotions arrive in the thalamus, which simultaneously routes the information along two separate pathways: to the nearby amygdala and to areas in the cortex (see **Figure 9.13**). The amygdala processes the information very quickly. If it detects a threat, it almost instantly triggers activity in the

FIGURE 9.13

The amygdala and fear. Emotions are controlled by a constellation of interacting brain systems, but the amygdala appears to play a particularly crucial role. According to LeDoux (1996), sensory inputs that can trigger fear (such as seeing a snake while out walking) arrive in the thalamus and then are routed along a fast pathway (shown in red) directly to the amygdala, and along a slow pathway (shown in blue) which allows the cortex time to think about the situation. Activity in the fast pathway also elicits the autonomic arousal and hormonal responses that are part of the physiological component of emotion. (Adapted from LeDoux, 1994) hypothalamus that leads to the autonomic arousal and hormonal responses. The processing in this pathway is extremely fast, so that emotions may be triggered even before the cortex has had a chance to really "think" about the input. LeDoux believes that this rapid-response pathway evolved because it is a highly adaptive warning system that can "be the difference between life and death." Consistent with LeDoux's theory, evidence indicates that the amygdala can process emotion independent of cognitive awareness (Phelps, 2005). Research linking the amygdala to emotion has focused mainly on fear. However, some evidence suggests that the amygdala may play a role in positive emotions as well (Murray, 2007).

The Behavioral Component

At the behavioral level, people reveal their emotions through characteristic overt expressions such as smiles, frowns, furrowed brows, clenched fists, and slumped shoulders. In other words, *emotions are expressed in "body language," or nonverbal behavior.*

Facial expressions reveal a variety of basic emotions. In an extensive research project, Paul Ekman and Wallace Friesen have asked participants to identify what emotion a person was experiencing on the basis of facial cues in photographs. They have found that subjects are generally successful in identifying six fundamental emotions: happiness, sadness, anger, fear, surprise, and disgust (Ekman & Friesen, 1975, 1984). Furthermore, the identification of emotions from facial expressions tends to occur quickly and automatically (Tracy & Robins, 2008).

Some theorists believe that muscular feedback from one's own facial expressions contributes to one's conscious experience of emotions (Izard, 1990; Tomkins, 1991). Proponents of the *facial-feedback hypothesis* assert that facial muscles send signals to the brain and that these signals help the brain recognize the emotion that one is experiencing. According to this view, smiles, frowns, and furrowed brows help create the experience of various emotions. Consistent with this idea, studies show that if subjects are instructed to contract their facial muscles to mimic facial expressions associated with certain emotions, they tend to report that they actually experience these emotions to some degree (Kleinke, Peterson, & Rutledge, 1998; Levenson, 1992).

The facial expressions that go with various emotions may be largely innate (Eibl-Ebesfeldt, 1975; Izard, 1994). For the most part, people who have been blind since birth smile and frown much like everyone else, even though they've never seen a smile or frown (Galati, Scherer, & Ricci-Bitti, 1997). In an influential, recent study, David Matsumoto and Bob Willingham (2009) carefully photographed the facial expressions of congenitally blind judo athletes in the Paralympic Games and sighted judo athletes in the Olympic Games. The photos for comparison were taken just after the athletes had won or lost their crucial final matches (for gold, silver, or bronze medals). The analysis of thousands of photos of numerous athletes yielded clear results. The facial expressions of sighted and blind athletes were indistinguishable. These findings strongly support the hypothesis that the facial expressions that go with emotions are wired into the human brain.

In a creative application of naturalistic observation, Matsumoto and Willingham (2009) shot photos of the award ceremonies for congenitally blind and sighted athletes to gain insight into whether facial expressions of emotion are innate.

Culture and the Elements of Emotion

Are emotions innate reactions that are universal across cultures? Or are they socially learned reactions that are culturally variable? The research on this lingering question has not yielded a simple answer. Investigators have found both strong similarities and sharp differences among cultures in the experience of emotion.

CROSS-CULTURAL SIMILARITIES IN EMOTIONAL EXPERIENCE

After demonstrating that Western subjects could discern specific emotions from facial expressions, Ekman and Friesen (1975) took their facial-cue photographs on the road to other societies to see whether nonverbal expressions of emotion transcend cultural boundaries. For example, they tested participants in Argentina, Spain, Japan, and other countries. They found considerable cross-cultural agreement in the identification of happiness, sadness, anger, fear, surprise, and disgust based on facial expressions (see **Figure 9.14**). Still, Ekman and Friesen wondered whether this agreement might be the result of learning rather than biology. They were concerned that people in different cultures often share considerable exposure to Western mass media (magazines, newspapers, television, and so forth), which provide many visual depictions of people's emotional reactions. To rule out this explanation, they took their photos to a remote area in New Guinea and showed them to a group of natives (the Fore) who had had virtually no contact with Western culture. Even the people from this preliterate culture did a fair job of identifying the emotions portrayed in the pictures (see **Figure 9.14**). Cross-cultural similarities have also been found in the cognitive appraisals that lead to certain emotions (Matsumoto, Nezlek, & Koopmann, 2007). Likewise, researchers have found little cultural variance in the physiological arousal that accompanies emotional experience (Breugelmans et al., 2005).

© urosr/ Shutterstock

CROSS-CULTURAL DIFFERENCES IN EMOTIONAL EXPERIENCE

The cross-cultural similarities in emotional experience are impressive. Yet, researchers have also found many cultural disparities in how people think about and express their emotions (Mesquita, 2003; Mesquita & Leu, 2007). For example, fascinating variations have been observed in how cultures categorize emotions. Some basic categories of emotion that are universally understood in Western cultures appear to go unrecognized— or at least unnamed—in some non-Western cultures. James Russell (1991) has compiled numerous examples of English words for emotions that have no equivalent in other languages. For example, Tahitians have no word that corresponds to *sadness*. Many

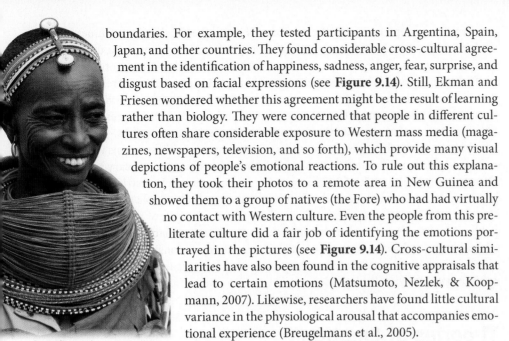

Country	Agreement in judging photos (%)			
	Fear	Disgust	Happiness	Anger
United States	85	92	97	67
Brazil	67	97	95	90
Chile	68	92	95	94
Argentina	54	92	98	90
Japan	66	90	100	90
New Guinea	54	44	82	50

© Cengage Learning

FIGURE 9.14

Cross-cultural comparisons of people's ability to recognize emotions from facial expressions. Ekman and Friesen (1975) found that people in highly disparate cultures showed fair agreement on the emotions portrayed in these photos. This consensus across cultures suggests that facial expressions of emotions may be universal and that they have a strong biological basis.

SOURCE: Data from Ekman, P., & Friesen, W. V. (1975). *Unmasking the Face.* Englewood Cliffs, NJ: Prentice-Hall. © 1975 by Paul Ekman, photographs courtesy of Paul Ekman.

non-Western groups, including the Yoruba of Nigeria, the Kaluli of New Guinea, and the Chinese, lack a word for *depression*. The concept of *anxiety* seems to go unrecognized among Eskimos and the Yoruba, and the Quichua of Ecuador lack a word for *remorse*.

Cultural disparities have also been found in regard to nonverbal expressions of emotion. Although the natural facial expressions associated with basic emotions appear to be universal, people can and do learn to control and modify these expressions. ***Display rules* are norms that regulate the appropriate expression of emotions.** They prescribe when, how, and to whom people can show various emotions. These norms vary from one culture to another (Ekman, 1992). Attitudes about specific emotions vary as well (Eid & Diener, 2001). The Ifaluk of Micronesia, for instance, severely restrict expressions of happiness because they believe that this emotion often leads people to neglect their duties (Lutz, 1987). Japanese culture emphasizes the suppression of negative emotions in public. More so than in other cultures, the Japanese are socialized to mask emotions such as anger, sadness, and disgust with stoic facial expressions or polite smiling. Thus, nonverbal expressions of emotions vary somewhat across cultures because of culture-specific attitudes and display rules.

Theories of Emotion

KEY LEARNING GOALS

9.12 Compare the James-Lange and Cannon-Bard theories of emotion.

9.13 Explain the two-factor theory of emotion and evolutionary theories of emotion.

How do psychologists explain the experience of emotion? A variety of theories and conflicting models exist. Some have been vigorously debated for over a century. As we describe these theories, you'll recognize a familiar bone of contention. Like theories of motivation, theories of emotion differ in their emphasis on the innate biological basis of emotion versus the social, environmental basis.

James-Lange Theory

`PSYKTREK 8d`

As we noted in Chapter 1, William James was an early theorist who urged psychologists to explore the functions of consciousness. James (1884) developed a theory of emotion over 100 years ago that remains influential today. At about the same time, he and Carl Lange (1885) independently proposed that the *conscious experience of emotion results from one's perception of autonomic arousal*. Their theory stood common sense on its head. Everyday logic suggests that when you stumble onto a rattlesnake in the woods, the conscious experience of fear leads to autonomic arousal (the fight-or-flight response). The James-Lange theory of emotion asserts the opposite. It posits that the perception of autonomic arousal leads to the conscious experience of fear (see **Figure 9.15**). In other words, while you might assume that your pulse is racing because you're fearful, James and Lange argue that you're fearful because your pulse is racing.

The James-Lange theory emphasizes the physiological determinants of emotion. According to this view, *different patterns of autonomic activation lead to the experience of different emotions*. Hence, people supposedly distinguish emotions such as fear, joy, and anger on the basis of the exact configuration of physical reactions they experience. Decades of research have supported the concept of *autonomic specificity*—that different emotions are accompanied by different patterns of autonomic activation (Janig, 2003; Levenson, 2003). However, the question of whether people identify their emotions from these varied patterns of autonomic activation remains unresolved.

Cannon-Bard Theory

`PSYKTREK 8d`

Walter Cannon (1927) found the James-Lange theory unconvincing. Cannon pointed out that physiological arousal may occur without the experience of emotion (if one

FIGURE 9.15

Theories of emotion. Three influential theories of emotion are contrasted with one another and with the commonsense view. The James-Lange theory was the first to suggest that feelings of arousal cause emotion, rather than vice versa. Schachter built on this idea by adding a second factor—interpretation (appraisal and labeling) of arousal.

exercises vigorously, for instance). He also argued that visceral changes are too slow to precede the conscious experience of emotion. Finally, he argued that people experiencing very different emotions, such as fear, joy, and anger, exhibit almost identical patterns of autonomic arousal.

Thus, Cannon espoused a different explanation of emotion. Later, Philip Bard (1934) elaborated on it. The resulting Cannon-Bard theory argues that emotion occurs when the *thalamus* sends signals *simultaneously* to the cortex (creating the conscious experience of emotion) and to the autonomic nervous system (creating visceral arousal). The Cannon-Bard model is compared to the James-Lange model in **Figure 9.15**. Cannon and Bard were off the mark a bit in pinpointing the thalamus as the neural center for emotion. However, many modern theorists agree with the Cannon-Bard view that emotions originate in subcortical brain structures (LeDoux, 1996; Panksepp, 1991; Rolls, 1990). Likewise, most modern theorists accept the notion that people do *not* infer their emotions from different patterns of autonomic activation (Frijda, 1999; Wagner, 1989).

Schachter's Two-Factor Theory

PSYKTREK 8d

In another influential analysis, Stanley Schachter asserted that people look at situational cues to differentiate between alternative emotions. According to Schachter (1964; Schachter & Singer, 1962, 1979), the experience of emotion depends on two factors: (1) autonomic arousal and (2) cognitive interpretation of that arousal. Schachter

Stanley Schachter
"Cognitive factors play a major role in determining how a subject interprets his bodily feelings."

proposed that when you experience physiological arousal, you search your environment for an explanation (see **Figure 9.15** again). If you're stuck in a traffic jam, you'll probably label your arousal as anger. If you're taking an important exam, you'll probably label it as anxiety. If you're celebrating your birthday, you'll probably label it as happiness.

Schachter agrees with the James-Lange view that emotion is inferred from arousal. However, he also agrees with the Cannon-Bard position that different emotions yield indistinguishable patterns of arousal. He reconciles these views by arguing that people look to external rather than internal cues to differentiate and label their specific emotions. In essence, Schachter suggests that people think along the following lines: "If I'm aroused and you're obnoxious, I must be angry."

In a classic test of the two-factor theory, Dutton and Aron (1974) arranged for young men crossing a footbridge in a park to encounter a young woman who asked them to stop briefly to fill out a questionnaire. The woman offered to explain the research at some future time and gave the men her phone number. Autonomic arousal was manipulated by enacting this scenario on two very different bridges. One was a long suspension bridge that swayed precariously 230 feet above a river (see below). The other bridge was a solid, safe structure above a small stream. The experimenters reasoned that the men crossing the frightening bridge would be experiencing emotional arousal and that some of them might attribute that arousal to the woman rather than to the bridge. If so, they might mislabel their emotion as lust rather than fear and infer that they were attracted to the woman. The dependent variable was how many of the men later called the woman to pursue a date. As predicted, more of the men who met the woman on the precarious bridge called her for a date. Thus, the findings supported the theory that people often infer emotion from their physiological arousal and label that emotion in accordance with their cognitive explanation for it.

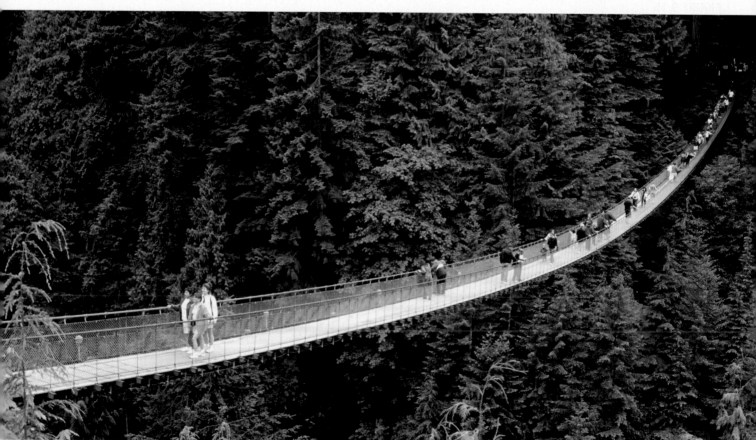

© SuperStock/ Age fotostock

Evolutionary Theories of Emotion

In recent years, some theorists interested in emotion have returned to ideas espoused by Charles Darwin over a century ago. Darwin (1872) believed that emotions developed because of their adaptive value. Fear, for instance, would help an organism avoid danger and thus would aid in survival. Thus, Darwin viewed human emotions as a product of evolution. This premise serves as the foundation for several modern theories of emotion developed independently by S. S. Tomkins (1980, 1991), Carroll Izard (1984, 1991), and Robert Plutchik (1984, 1993).

These *evolutionary theories* consider emotions to be largely innate reactions to certain stimuli. As such, emotions should be immediately recognizable under most conditions without much thought. After all, primitive animals that are incapable of complex thought seem to have little difficulty in recognizing their emotions. Evolutionary theorists believe that emotion evolved before thought. They assert that thought plays a relatively small role in emotion, although they admit that learning and cognition may have some influence on human emotions. Evolutionary theories generally assume that emotions originate in subcortical brain structures (such as the hypothalamus and most of the limbic system) that evolved before the higher brain areas (in the cortex) associated with complex thought.

Evolutionary theories also assume that evolution has equipped humans with a small number of innate emotions with proven adaptive value. Thus, the principal question that evolutionary theories of emotion wrestle with is, *What are the fundamental emotions?* Evolutionary theorists attempt to identify these primary emotions by searching for universals—emotions that are expressed and recognized in the same way in widely disparate cultures. **Figure 9.16** summarizes the conclusions of the leading theorists in this area. As you can see, Tomkins, Izard, and Plutchik have not come up with identical lists. However, there is considerable agreement. All three conclude that people exhibit eight to ten primary emotions. Moreover, six of these emotions appear on all three lists: fear, anger, joy, disgust, interest, and surprise.

Silvan Tomkins	Carroll Izard	Robert Plutchik
Fear	Fear	Fear
Anger	Anger	Anger
Enjoyment	Joy	Joy
Disgust	Disgust	Disgust
Interest	Interest	Anticipation
Surprise	Surprise	Surprise
Contempt	Contempt	
Shame	Shame	
	Sadness	Sadness
Distress		
	Guilt	
		Acceptance

© Cengage Learning

FIGURE 9.16

Primary emotions. Evolutionary theories of emotion attempt to identify primary emotions. Three leading theorists—Silvan Tomkins, Carroll Izard, and Robert Plutchik—have compiled different lists of primary emotions, but this chart shows great overlap among the basic emotions identified by these theorists. (Based on Mandler, 1984)

Concept Check 9.3

Understanding Theories of Emotion

Check your understanding of theories of emotion by matching the theories we discussed with the statements below. Let's borrow William James's classic example: Assume that you just stumbled onto a bear in the woods. The first statement expresses the commonsense explanation of your fear. Each of the remaining statements expresses the essence of a different theory; indicate which theory in the spaces provided. The answers are provided in Appendix A.

1. You tremble because you're afraid.

   Common sense

2. You're afraid because you're trembling.

3. You're afraid because situational cues (the bear) suggest that's why you're trembling.

4. You're afraid because the bear has elicited an innate primary emotion.

© Ienetstan/Shutterstock

KEY LEARNING GOALS

9.14 Identify the five unifying themes highlighted in this chapter.

Reflecting on the Chapter's Themes

Cultural Heritage

Sociohistorical Context

Theoretical Diversity

Heredity and Environment

Multifactorial Causation

Five of our organizing themes were particularly prominent in this chapter: the influence of cultural contexts, the dense connections between psychology and society at large, psychology's theoretical diversity, the interplay of heredity and environment, and the multiple causes of behavior.

Our discussion of motivation and emotion demonstrated once again that there are both similarities and differences across cultures in behavior. The neural, biochemical, genetic, and hormonal processes underlying hunger and eating, for instance, are universal. However, cultural factors influence what people prefer to eat and how much they eat. In a similar vein, researchers have found a great deal of cross-cultural similarity in the cognitive, physiological, and expressive elements of emotional experience, but they have also found cultural variations in how people think about and express their emotions. Thus, as we have seen in previous chapters, psychological processes are characterized by both cultural variance and invariance.

Our discussion of the controversies surrounding evolutionary theory and the determinants of sexual orientation show once again that psychology is not an ivory tower enterprise. It evolves in a sociohistorical context that helps shape the debates in the field, and these debates often have far-reaching social and political ramifications for society at large. We ended the chapter with a discussion of various theories of emotion, which showed once again that psychology is characterized by great theoretical diversity.

Finally, we repeatedly saw that biological and environmental factors jointly govern behavior. For example, we learned that eating behavior, sexual desire, and the experience of emotion all depend on complicated interactions between biological and environmental determinants. Indeed, complicated interactions permeated the entire chapter. Thus, if we want to fully understand behavior, we have to take multiple causes into account.

PERSONAL APPLICATION

Exploring the Ingredients of Happiness

KEY LEARNING GOALS

9.15 Identify the factors that do and do not correlate with happiness, and articulate three conclusions about the dynamics of happiness.

Answer the following "true" or "false."

___ 1 The empirical evidence indicates that most people are relatively unhappy.

___ 2 Although wealth doesn't *guarantee* happiness, wealthy people are much more likely to be happy than the rest of the population.

___ 3 People who have children are happier than people without children.

___ 4 Good health is an essential requirement for happiness.

The answer to all these questions is "false." These assertions are all reasonable and widely believed hypotheses about the prevalence and correlates of happiness. Yet, they have *not* been supported by empirical research. Due in part to a new emphasis on positive psychology, recent years have brought a surge of interest in the correlates of *subjective well-being—individuals' personal perceptions of their overall happiness and life satisfaction.* The findings of this research are quite interesting. As you have already seen from our true-false questions, many commonsense notions about happiness appear to be inaccurate.

How Happy Are People?

One of these inaccuracies is the apparently widespread assumption that most people are relatively unhappy. Writers, social scientists, and the general public seem to believe that people around the world are predominantly dissatisfied and unhappy. However, empirical surveys consistently find that the vast majority of respondents—even those who are poor or disabled—characterize themselves as fairly happy (Diener & Diener, 1996; Myers & Diener, 1995). When people are asked to rate their happiness, only a small minority place themselves below the neutral point on the various scales used (see **Figure 9.17**). When the average subjective well-being of entire nations is computed, based on almost 1000 surveys, the means cluster toward the positive end of the scale (Tov & Diener, 2007). That's not to say that everyone is equally happy. Researchers find substantial and thought-

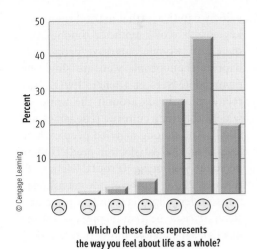

FIGURE 9.17

Measuring happiness with a nonverbal scale. Researchers have used a variety of methods to estimate the distribution of happiness. For example, in one study in the United States, respondents were asked to examine the seven facial expressions shown and select the one that "comes closest to expressing how you feel about your life as a whole." As you can see, the vast majority of participants chose happy faces. (Data adapted from Myers, 1992)

provoking disparities among people in subjective well-being, which we will analyze momentarily. The overall picture, though, seems rosier than anticipated.

Factors That Do Not Predict Happiness

Let's begin our discussion of individual differences in happiness by highlighting those things that turn out to be relatively unimportant determinants of subjective well-being. Quite a number of factors that you might expect to be influential appear to bear little or no relationship to general happiness.

Money There *is* a positive correlation between income and subjective feelings of happiness. The association is surprisingly weak, however. Within specific nations, the correlation between income and happiness tends to fall somewhere between .12 and .20 (Diener & Biswas-Diener, 2002; Johnson & Krueger, 2006). Obviously, being poor can contribute to unhappiness. Yet it seems once people ascend above a certain level of income, additional wealth does not appear to fos-

ter greater happiness. One recent study in the United States estimated that once people exceed an income of around $75,000, little relation is seen between wealth and subjective well-being (Kahneman & Deaton, 2010).

Why isn't money a better predictor of happiness? One reason is that there seems to be a disconnect between actual income and how people feel about their financial situation. Research (Johnson & Krueger, 2006) suggests that the correlation between actual wealth and people's subjective perceptions of whether they have enough money to meet their needs is surprisingly modest (around .30). Another problem with money is that pervasive advertising and rising income fuel escalating material desires (Frey & Stutzer, 2002; Kasser et al., 2004). When these growing material desires outstrip what people can afford, dissatisfaction is likely (Solberg et al., 2002). Thus, complaints about not having enough money are routine even among people who are very affluent by objective standards. Interestingly, there is some evidence that people who place an especially strong emphasis on the pursuit of wealth and materialistic goals tend to be somewhat

less happy than others (Kasser, 2002; Van Boven, 2005). Research has also suggested that wealthy people become jaded in a way that undermines their ability to savor positive experiences (Quoidbach et al., 2010).

Age Age and happiness are consistently found to be unrelated. Age accounts for less than 1% of the variation in people's happiness (Inglehart, 1990; Myers & Diener, 1997). The key factors influencing subjective well-being may shift some as people grow older—work becomes less important, health more so. But people's average level of happiness tends to remain remarkably stable over the life span.

Parenthood Children can be a tremendous source of joy and fulfillment. However, they can also be a tremendous source of headaches and hassles. Compared to childless couples, parents worry more and experience more marital problems (Argyle, 1987). Apparently, the good and bad aspects of parenthood balance each other out, because the evidence indicates that people who have children are neither more nor less happy than people without children (Argyle, 2001).

"Who can say? I suppose I'm as happy as my portfolio will allow me to be."

Intelligence and attractiveness Intelligence and physical attractiveness are highly valued traits in modern society. But researchers have *not* found an association between either characteristic and happiness (Diener, Wolsic, & Fujita, 1995; Diener, Kesebir & Tov, 2009).

Moderately Good Predictors of Happiness

Research has identified two facets of life that appear to have a *moderate* association with subjective well-being: health and social activity.

Health Good physical health would seem to be an essential requirement for happiness, but people adapt to health problems. Research reveals that individuals who develop serious, disabling health conditions aren't as unhappy as one might guess (Myers, 1992; Riis et al., 2005). Furthermore, Freedman (1978) argues that good health does not, by itself, produce happiness, because people tend to take good health for granted. Considerations such as these may help to explain why researchers find only a moderate positive correlation (average = .32) between health status and subjective well-being (Argyle, 1999). While health may promote happiness to a moderate degree, happiness may also foster better health, as recent research has found a positive correlation between happiness and longevity (Veenhoven, 2008).

Social Activity Humans are social animals, and interpersonal relations do appear to contribute to people's happiness. Those who are satisfied with their social support and friendship networks and those who are socially active report above-average levels of happiness (Diener & Seligman, 2004; Myers, 1999). One recent study that periodically recorded participants' daily conversations found that people who had more deep, substantive conversations were happier than those who mostly engaged in small talk (Mehl et al., 2010). This finding is not all that surprising, in that one would expect that people with richer social networks would have more deep conversations.

Strong Predictors of Happiness

The list of factors that turn out to have fairly strong associations with happiness is surprisingly short. The key ingredients of happiness appear to involve love, work, and personality.

Love and Marriage. Romantic relationships can be stressful, but people consistently rate being in love as one of the critical ingredients of happiness (Myers, 1999). Furthermore, although people complain a lot about their marriages, the evidence indicates that marital status is a key correlate of happiness. Among both men and women, married people are happier than people who are single or divorced (Myers & Diener, 1995). This relationship holds around the world in widely different cultures (Diener et al., 2000). And among married people, their level of marital satisfaction predicts their personal well-being (Proulx, Helms, & Buehler, 2007). However, the causal relations underlying this correlation are unclear. It may be that happiness causes marital satisfaction more than marital satisfaction promotes happiness.

Work People often complain about their jobs. Hence, one might not expect work to be a key source of happiness, but it is. Although less critical than love and marriage, job satisfaction has a substantial association with general happiness (Judge & Klinger, 2008; Warr, 1999). Studies also show that unemployment has strong negative effects on subjective well-being (Lucas et al., 2004). It is difficult to sort out whether job satisfaction causes happiness or vice versa, but evidence suggests that causation flows both ways (Argyle, 2001).

Genetics and Personality The best predictor of individuals' future happiness is their past happiness (Lucas & Diener, 2008). Some people seem destined to be happy and others unhappy, regardless of their triumphs or setbacks. Evidence suggests that happiness does not depend on external circumstances—buying a nice house, getting promoted—as much as internal factors, such as one's outlook on life (Lyubomirsky, Sheldon, & Schkade, 2005). With this reality in mind, researchers have investigated whether there might be a hereditary basis for variations in happiness. These studies suggest that people's genetic predispositions account for a substantial portion of the variance in happiness, perhaps as much as

© INSADCO Photography/Alamy

Research shows that happiness does not depend on people's positive and negative experiences as much as one would expect. Some people, presumably because of their personality, seem destined to be happy in spite of major setbacks, and others seem destined to cling to unhappiness even though their lives seem reasonably pleasant.

50% (Lyubomirsky et al., 2005; Stubbe et al., 2005). How can one's genes influence one's happiness? Presumably, by shaping one's temperament and personality, which are known to be heritable (Weiss, Bates, & Luciano, 2008). As a result, researchers have begun to look for links between personality and subjective well-being, and they have found some interesting correlations. For example, *extraversion* is one of the better predictors of happiness. People who are outgoing, upbeat, and sociable tend to be happier than others (Fleeson, Malanos, & Achille, 2002). Additional personality correlates of happiness include conscientiousness, agreeableness, self-esteem, and optimism (Lucas, 2008; Lyubomirsky, Tkach, & DiMatteo, 2006).

Conclusions About Subjective Well-Being

We must be cautious in drawing inferences about the *causes* of happiness, because the available data are correlational (see **Figure 9.18**). Nonetheless, the empirical findings suggest a number of worthwhile insights about the roots of happiness.

First, research on happiness shows that the determinants of subjective well-being are precisely that: subjective. *Objective realities are not as important as subjective feelings*. In other words, your health, your wealth, your job, and your age are not as influential as how you *feel* about your health, wealth, job, and age (Schwarz & Strack, 1999). Second, *when it comes to happiness, everything is relative* (Argyle, 1999; Hagerty, 2000). In other words, you evaluate what you have relative to what the people around you have and relative to what you expected to have. Generally, we compare ourselves with others who are similar to us. Thus, people who are wealthy assess what they have by comparing themselves with their wealthy friends and neighbors, and their *relative* standing is crucial (Boyce, Brown, & Moore, 2010). This is yet another reason underlying the low correlation between wealth and happiness.

Third, *research on subjective well-being indicates that people often adapt to their circumstances*. This adaptation effect is one reason that increases in income don't necessarily bring increases in happiness. **Hedonic adaptation occurs when the mental scale that people use to judge the pleasantness-unpleasantness of their experiences shifts so that their neutral point, or baseline for comparison, changes.** Unfortunately, when people's experiences improve, hedonic adaptation may *sometimes* put them on a *hedonic treadmill*. Their neutral point moves upward, so that the improvements yield no real benefits (Kahneman, 1999). However, when people have to grapple with major setbacks, hedonic adaptation probably helps protect their mental and

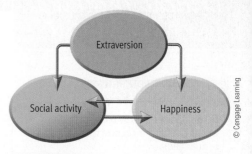

FIGURE 9.18

Possible causal relations among the correlates of happiness. Although we have considerable data on the correlates of happiness, it is difficult to untangle the possible causal relationships. For example, we know that there is a moderate positive correlation between social activity and happiness, but we can't say for sure whether high social activity causes happiness or whether happiness causes people to be more socially active. Moreover, in light of the research showing that a third variable—extraversion—correlates with both variables, we have to consider the possibility that extraversion causes both greater social activity and greater happiness.

physical health. For example, people who are sent to prison and people who develop debilitating diseases are not as unhappy as one might assume, because they adapt to their changed situations and evaluate events from a new perspective (Frederick & Loewenstein, 1999). That's not to say that hedonic adaptation in the face of life's difficulties is inevitable or complete, but people adapt to setbacks much better than widely assumed (Lucas, 2007).

Analyzing Arguments: Making Sense out of Controversy

Consider the following argument: "Dieting is harmful to your health because the tendency to be obese is largely inherited." What is your reaction to this reasoning? Do you find it convincing? We hope not, as this argument is seriously flawed. Can you see what's wrong? There is no relationship between the conclusion that "dieting is harmful to your health" and the reason given that "the tendency to be obese is largely inherited." The argument is initially seductive because most people know that obesity *is* largely inherited. So, the reason provided represents a true statement. But the reason is unrelated to the conclusion advocated. This scenario may strike you as odd. But if you start listening carefully to discussions about controversial issues, you will probably notice that people often cite irrelevant considerations in support of their favored conclusions.

This chapter was loaded with controversial issues that sincere, well-meaning people could argue about for weeks. Are gender differences in mating preferences a product of evolution or of modern economic realities? Is there a biological basis for homosexuality? Unfortunately, arguments about issues such as these are typically unproductive in terms of moving toward resolution or agreement because most people know little about the rules of argumentation. In this application, we will explore what makes arguments sound or unsound in the hope of improving your ability to analyze and think critically about arguments.

The Anatomy of an Argument

In everyday usage, the word *argument* is used to refer to a dispute or disagreement between two or more people. However, in the technical language of rhetoric, an *argument* consists of one or more premises that are used to provide support for a conclusion. *Premises* are the reasons that are presented to persuade someone that a conclusion is true or probably true. *Assumptions* are premises for which no proof or evidence is offered. Assumptions are often left unstated. For example, suppose that your doctor tells you that you should exercise regularly because regular exercise is good for your heart. In this simple argument, the conclusion is "You should exercise regularly." The premise that leads to this conclusion is the idea that "exercise is good for your heart." An unstated assumption is that everyone wants a healthy heart.

In the language of argument analysis, premises are said to support (or not support) conclusions. A conclusion may be supported by one reason or by many reasons. One way to visualize these possibilities is to draw an analogy between the reasons that support a conclusion and the legs that support a table (Halpern, 2003). A table top (conclusion) could be supported by one strong leg (a single strong reason) or many thin legs (lots of weaker reasons). Of course, the reasons provided for a conclusion may fail to support the conclusion. Returning to our table analogy, the table top might not be supported because the legs are too thin (very weak reasons) or because the legs are not attached (irrelevant reasons).

Arguments can get pretty complicated, as they usually have more parts than just premises and conclusions. In addition, there often are *counterarguments,* which are reasons that take support away from a conclusion. And sometimes the most important part of an argument is something that is not there—reasons that have been omitted, either deliberately or not, that would lead to a different conclusion if they were supplied. Given

© Mlenny Photography/iStockphoto

all the complex variations that can occur in arguments, it is impossible to give you simple rules for judging arguments, but we can highlight some common fallacies and then provide some criteria you can apply in thinking critically about arguments.

Common Fallacies

As noted in previous chapters, cognitive scientists have compiled lengthy lists of fallacies that people frequently display in their arguments. This section describes five common fallacies. To illustrate each one, we will assume the role of someone arguing that pornographic material on the Internet (cyberporn) should be banned or heavily regulated.

Irrelevant Reasons Reasons cannot provide support for an argument unless they are relevant to the conclusion. Arguments that depend on irrelevant reasons—either intentionally or inadvertently—are quite common. You already saw one example at the beginning of this application. The Latin term for this fallacy is *non sequitur,* which literally translates to "it doesn't follow." In other words, the conclusion does not follow from the premise. For example, in the debate about Internet pornography, you might hear the following *non sequitur:* "We need to regulate cyberporn because research has shown that most date rapes go unreported."

Circular Reasoning In *circular reasoning* the premise and conclusion are simply restatements of each other. People vary their wording a little so it isn't obvious, but when you look closely, the conclusion is the premise. For example, in arguments about Internet pornography you might hear someone assert, "We need to control cyberporn because it is currently unregulated."

Slippery Slope The concept of *slippery slope* argumentation takes its name from the notion that if you are on a slippery slope and you don't dig your heels in, you will slide and slide until you reach bottom. A slippery slope argument typically asserts that if you allow X to happen, things will spin out of control and far worse events will follow. The trick is that no inherent connection exists between X and the events that are predicted to follow. For example, in the debate about medical marijuana, opponents have argued, "If you legalize medical marijuana, the next thing you know cocaine and heroin will be legal." In the debate about cyberporn, a slippery slope argument might go, "If we don't ban cyberporn, the next thing you know, grade school children will be watching smut in their school libraries."

Weak Analogies An *analogy* asserts that two concepts or events are similar in some way. Hence, you can draw conclusions about event B because of its similarity to event A. Analogies can be very useful in thinking about complex issues. However, some analogies are weak or inappropriate because the similarity between A and B is superficial, minimal, or irrelevant to the issue at hand. For example, in the debate about Internet erotica, someone might argue, "Cyberporn is morally offensive, just like child molestation. We wouldn't tolerate child molestation, so we shouldn't permit cyberporn."

False Dichotomy A *false dichotomy* creates an either-or choice between two outcomes: the outcome advocated and some obviously horrible outcome that any sensible person would want to avoid. These outcomes are presented as the only possible ones, when in reality many other outcomes are possible, including some that lie between the extremes depicted in the false dichotomy. In the debate about Internet pornography, someone might argue, "We can ban cyberporn, or we can hasten the moral decay of modern society."

Evaluating the Strength of Arguments

In everyday life, you frequently need to assess the strength of arguments made by friends, family, co-workers, politicians, media pundits, and so forth. You may also want to evaluate your own arguments when you write papers or speeches for school or prepare presentations for your work. The following questions can help you to make systematic evaluations of arguments (adapted from Halpern, 2003):

- What is the conclusion?
- What are the premises provided to support the conclusion? Are the premises valid?
- Does the conclusion follow from the premises? Are there any fallacies in the chain of reasoning?
- What assumptions have been made? Are they valid assumptions? Should they be stated explicitly?
- What are the counterarguments? Do they weaken the argument?
- Is there anything that has been omitted from the argument?

TABLE 9.1 Critical Thinking Skills Discussed in This Application

Skill	Description
Understanding the elements of an argument	The critical thinker understands that an argument consists of premises and assumptions that are used to support a conclusion.
Recognizing and avoiding common fallacies, such as irrelevant reasons, circular reasoning, slippery slope reasoning, weak analogies, and false dichotomies	The critical thinker is vigilant about conclusions based on unrelated premises, conclusions that are rewordings of premises, unwarranted predictions that things will spin out of control, superficial analogies, and contrived dichotomies.
Evaluating arguments systematically	The critical thinker carefully assesses the validity of the premises, assumptions, and conclusions in an argument, and considers counterarguments and missing elements.

© Cengage Learning

Chapter 9 — Review of Key Learning Goals

Motivational Theories and Concepts

9.1 Compare drive, incentive, and evolutionary approaches to understanding motivation.

Drive theories apply a homeostatic model to motivation. They assume that organisms seek to reduce unpleasant states of tension called drives. In contrast, incentive theories emphasize how external goals energize behavior. Evolutionary theorists explain motives in terms of their adaptive value. Humans display an enormous diversity of biological and social motives.

The Motivation of Hunger and Eating

9.2 Summarize evidence on the physiological factors implicated in the regulation of hunger.

In the brain, the lateral and ventromedial areas of the hypothalamus were once viewed as on-off centers for the control of hunger. However, that model proved to be an oversimplification, as the arcuate and paraventricular areas of the hypothalamus may be more important. Contemporary theories of hunger focus more on neural circuits than on anatomical centers in the brain. The stomach can send two types of signals to the brain that can inhibit eating. Hormonal regulation of hunger depends primarily on insulin, ghrelin, CCK, and leptin.

9.3 Explain how food availability, culture, and learning influence hunger.

Organisms consume more food when it is palatable, when more is available, and when there is greater variety. The presence of others and environmental cues, such as advertisements for food, can also promote eating. Cultural traditions also shape food preferences. Learning processes, such as classical conditioning and observational learning, exert a great deal of influence over what people eat.

Sexual Motivation and Behavior

9.4 Outline the four phases of the human sexual response.

The human sexual response cycle can be divided into four stages: excitement, plateau, orgasm, and resolution. The subjective experience of orgasm is fairly similar for both sexes. Intercourse leads to orgasm in women less consistently than in men, but women are much more likely to be multiorgasmic.

9.5 Describe parental investment theory and gender differences in sexual activity and mating preferences.

Parental investment theory asserts that gender differences in parental investment shape differences between males and females in mating pref-erences and sexual behavior. Consistent with this theory, males tend to think about and initiate sex more than females do, and they have more sexual partners and more interest in casual sex than females. Gender differences in mating preferences appear to largely transcend cultural boundaries. Males emphasize potential partners' youthfulness and attractiveness, whereas females emphasize potential partners' status, ambition, and financial prospects.

	Males	Females
Biological reality	Reproduction involves minimal investment of time, energy, and risk	Reproduction involves substantial investment of time, energy, and risk
Evolutionary significance	Maximize reproductive success by seeking more sexual partners with high reproductive potential	Maximize reproductive success by seeking partners willing to invest material resources in your offspring
Behavioral outcomes	More interest in uncommitted sex; greater number of sex partners over lifetime; look for youth and attractiveness in partners	Less interest in uncommitted sex; smaller number of sex partners over lifetime; look for income, status, and ambition in partners

© Cengage Learning

9.6 Discuss the prevalence of homosexuality, and compare environmental and biological theories of sexual orientation.

Alfred Kinsey viewed heterosexuality and homosexuality not as an all-or-none distinction but as end points on a continuum. Data on the prevalence of homosexuality suggest that 5%–8% of the population may be gay. Although most gays can trace their homosexual leanings back to early childhood, research has not supported Freudian or behavioral theories of sexual orientation. Recent studies suggest that there is a genetic predisposition to homosexuality. Idiosyncrasies in prenatal hormonal secretions may also contribute to the development of homosexuality. The pathways into homosexuality may be somewhat different for males and females, with females displaying greater plasticity in sexual orientation.

Achievement: In Search of Excellence

9.7 Describe the need for achievement and how it has been measured.

Achievement, which was first investigated by David McClelland, involves the need to master difficult challenges and to excel, especially in competition with others. The need for achievement is usually measured with a projective test called the TAT, which asks people to respond to vague, ambiguous stimuli in ways that may reveal personal motives.

9.8 Explain how the need for achievement and situational factors influence achievement strivings.

People who are relatively high in the need for achievement work harder and more persistently than others. They delay gratification well and pursue competitive careers. However, in choosing challenges they often select tasks of intermediate difficulty. Situational factors also influence achievement behavior. The pursuit of achievement tends to increase when the probability and incentive value of success are high. The joint influence of these factors may explain why people high in achievement need tend to prefer challenges of intermediate difficulty.

The Elements of Emotional Experience

9.9 Describe the cognitive and physiological components of emotion.

The cognitive component of emotion involves subjective feelings that have an evaluative aspect. Emotions can be automatic and intense, and they are not easy to control. People's cognitive appraisals of events in their lives determine the emotions they experience. Research on affective forecasting shows that people are surprisingly bad at predicting the intensity and duration of their emotional reactions to events. The most readily apparent aspect of the physiological component of emotion is autonomic arousal. This arousal is the basis for the lie detector, which is really an emotion detector. Polygraphs are not all that accurate in assessing individuals' veracity. The amygdala appears to be the hub of an emotion-processing system in the brain that modulates conditioned fears.

9.10 Explain how emotions are reflected in facial expressions, and describe the facial feedback hypothesis.

At the behavioral level, emotions are expressed through body language, with facial expressions being particularly prominent. People can identify six fundamental emotions from facial expressions. Ekman and Friesen have found considerable cross-cultural agreement in the identification of emotions based on facial expressions. Advocates of the facial-feedback hypothesis maintain that facial muscles send signals that help the brain recognize the emotion one is experiencing. The facial expressions that go with various emotions may be largely innate.

9.11 Review cross-cultural similarities and variations in emotional experience.

Cross-cultural similarities have been found in the facial expressions associated with specific emotions, the cognitive appraisals that provoke emotions, and the physiological underpinnings of emotion. However, there are some striking cultural variations in how people categorize their emotions. Some basic categories of emotion that are universally understood in Western cultures appear to go unrecognized in some non-Western cultures. Display rules, which are norms that govern how much people show their emotions, vary across cultures.

Theories of Emotion

9.12 Compare the James-Lange and Cannon-Bard theories of emotion.

Common sense suggests that emotions cause autonomic arousal, but the James-Lange theory asserted that emotion results from one's perception of autonomic arousal. The James-Lange theory also asserted that different patterns of autonomic activation lead to the experience of different emotions. The Cannon-Bard theory asserted that people do *not* infer their emotions from patterns of autonomic activation and that emotions originate in subcortical areas of the brain.

9.13 Explain the two-factor theory of emotion and evolutionary theories of emotion.

According to Schachter's two-factor theory, people infer emotion from arousal and then label the emotion in accordance with their cognitive explanation for the arousal. Evolutionary theories of emotion maintain that emotions are innate reactions that require little cognitive interpretation. Evolutionary theorists seek to identify a small number of innate, fundamental emotions.

Reflecting on the Chapter's Themes

9.14 Identify the five unifying themes highlighted in this chapter.

Our look at motivation and emotion showed once again that psychology is characterized by theoretical diversity, that biology and environment shape behavior interactively, that behavior is governed by multiple causes, that psychological processes are characterized by both cultural variance and invariance, and that psychology evolves in a sociohistorical context.

PERSONAL APPLICATION
Exploring the Ingredients of Happiness

9.15 Identify the factors that do and do not correlate with happiness, and articulate three conclusions about the dynamics of happiness.

Research suggests that many notions about happiness appear to be incorrect, including the notion that most people are unhappy. Factors such as income, age, parenthood, intelligence, and attractiveness are largely uncorrelated with subjective well-being. Physical health and good social relationships appear to have a modest association with feelings of happiness. The only factors that are good predictors of happiness are love and marriage, work satisfaction, and personality and genetics. Research on happiness indicates that objective realities are not as important as subjective feelings. Studies also demonstrate that subjective well-being is a relative concept. The evidence also indicates that people adapt to their circumstances, although such hedonic adaptation is not necessarily complete.

CRITICAL THINKING APPLICATION
Analyzing Arguments: Making Sense out of Controversy

9.16 Identify the key elements in arguments, and recognize common fallacies in arguments.

An argument consists of one or more premises used to provide support for a conclusion. Assumptions are premises for which no proof is offered. A conclusion may be supported by one or by many reasons. Arguments are often marred by fallacies in reasoning, such as irrelevant reasons, weak analogies, or circular reasoning, in which the premise and conclusion are simply restatements of each other. In a slippery slope scenario, people assert that if you allow X to happen, far worse events will follow. False dichotomies create either-or choices when in reality there could be other outcomes.

10 Human Development Across the Life Span

PARADOX

Some diseases that typically emerge in middle or late adulthood may be traceable to events that occurred before birth.

© Getty Images

In high school, kids called her "catfish" because of her outsized lips. Her attempts at modeling brought more than 100 rejections—she was too short, too skinny, too scarred. Today, she's been named "Most Beautiful Woman in the World" by *People* magazine, is one of the highest-paid actors in the world, and is known for her humanitarian work for the United Nations. Let's take a closer look at the life of Angelina Jolie.

Angelina was born to two actors, but she didn't have a fairy-tale life. Her father had an affair with one of his theater students when Angelina was six months old, and the family broke apart. Her mother was so traumatized by the split, she couldn't bear to be with Angelina because she reminded her too much of her former husband. As a result, Angelina was mostly raised by nannies and babysitters in her early years.

The story of Angelina Jolie's metamorphosis from an awkward, insecure "wild child," into an elegant, self-assured public figure provides a dramatic demonstration of how human development is marked by both continuity and transition.

Angelina's childhood was marked by frequent moves to rented and ever-smaller houses as her mother struggled to make ends meet. Attending Beverly Hills High School, Angelina felt out of place among the well-scrubbed rich kids in preppy clothes. Angelina wore all-black, often second-hand clothes and punk get-ups. "I didn't feel clean and, like, pretty," she said (Morton, 2010, p. 75). Taken on modeling calls by her mother, Angelina was self-conscious and nervous. Although her father, Jon Voigt, was a famous Oscar-winning actor, she didn't want to be an actress. She wanted to be a funeral director. Her first tattoo was the Japanese character for "death." She hung out at the arcade with the outcasts, experimenting with drugs. At 14, she dyed her hair purple and went slam-dancing with her live-in punk boyfriend. She continued to rebel against convention when, at her wedding to actor Jonny Lee Miller, she wore black rubber pants and a white shirt with the groom's name written in her blood across the back. The media couldn't write enough about the "wild child."

But in her mid-20s, Angelina underwent a transformation. Preparing for her role as a humanitarian aid worker in *Beyond Borders*, and filming *Lara Croft: Tomb Raider* in Cambodia, she saw conditions that would change her forever. The plight of displaced people in Cambodia and the news of refugees fleeing massacres in the Darfur region of Northern Africa affected her deeply. She contacted the United Nations to learn more and asked to help. The U.N. sent her to paparazzi-free zones: trouble spots in Sierra Leone and Tanzania. In 2001, the U.N. High Commissioner for Refugees made Angelina an official Goodwill Ambassador. Since then, Angelina has been on twenty daunting U.N. field missions to places such as Thailand, Sudan, and Ecuador, where she often has had to endure extremely primitive living conditions.

Angelina's transition from an insecure teenager to a self-assured adult and from a wild child to humanitarian were startling. Yet there was also a strong element of continuity in her life. Consider, for instance, her rebelliousness. When Angelina was a child, her mother dressed her in frilly white dresses. Angelina rebeled and wore all black. When her mother dragged her to acting auditions, Angelina refused to read the lines. As she has matured, Angelina has remained a rebel, vigorously fighting for more-humane treatment of oppressed refugee populations. In a sense, she rechanneled her defiance. "In my early 20s I was fighting with myself," Jolie says. "Now I take that punk in me to Washington, and I fight for something important" (Swibel, 2006).

Another personality trait that has remained constant throughout her life is empathy. Perhaps because of her own uprooted childhood, Angelina was always maternal to younger children. Photos from when she was 5 show her with her arm protectively around Sean Stogel, then 3, whom she taught how to blow bubbles. From the age of 12, Angelina knew that she wanted to adopt underprivileged children. As an adult, she has followed through on this desire, adopting three orphans from far-flung corners of the globe (Cambodia, Ethiopia, and Vietnam). And, of course, her continued empathy for the plight of the world's downtrodden is manifested in her remarkably unselfish commitment to humanitarian missions.

What does Angelina Jolie have to do with developmental psychology? Although her story is obviously unique in many ways, it provides an interesting illustration of the two themes that permeate the study of human development: *transition* and *continuity*. In investigating human development, psychologists study how people evolve through transitions over time. In looking at these transitions, developmental psychologists inevitably find continuity with the past. This continuity may be the most fascinating element in Angelina's story. The metamorphosis of the insecure, wild teenager into an influential, self-assured public figure was a more radical transformation than most people go through. Nonetheless, the threads of continuity connecting Angelina's childhood to the development of her adult personality were quite obvious.

Development is the sequence of age-related changes that occur as a person progresses from conception to death. It is a reasonably orderly, cumulative process that includes both the biological and behavioral changes that take place as people grow older. An infant's newfound ability to grasp objects, a child's gradual mastery of grammar, an adolescent's spurt in physical growth, a young adult's increasing commitment to a vocation, and an older adult's transition into the role of grandparent all represent development. These transitions are predictable changes that are related to age.

Traditionally, psychologists have been most interested in development during childhood. Our coverage reflects this emphasis. However, decades of research have clearly shown that development is a lifelong process. In this chapter, we divide the life span into four broad periods: the prenatal period, between conception and birth, childhood, adolescence, and adulthood. We examine aspects of development that are especially dynamic during each period. Let's begin by looking at events that occur before birth, during prenatal development.

KEY LEARNING GOALS

10.1 Outline the major events of the three stages of prenatal development.

10.2 Summarize the impact of environmental factors on prenatal development.

Progress Before Birth: Prenatal Development

Development begins with conception. Conception occurs when fertilization creates **a zygote, a one-celled organism formed by the union of a sperm and an egg.** All the other cells in your body developed from this single cell. Each of your cells contains enduring messages from your parents carried on the *chromosomes* that lie within its nucleus. Each chromosome houses many *genes,* the functional units in hereditary transmission. Genes carry the details of your hereditary blueprints, which are revealed gradually throughout life (see Chapter 3 for more information on genetic transmission).

The *prenatal period* **extends from conception to birth, usually encompassing nine months of pregnancy.** Significant development occurs before birth. In fact, development during the prenatal period is remarkably rapid. If you were an average-sized newborn and your physical growth had continued during the first year of your life at a prenatal pace, by your first birthday you would have weighed 200 pounds! Fortunately, you didn't grow at that rate, because in the final weeks before birth the frenzied pace of prenatal development tapers off dramatically.

In this section, we'll examine the usual course of prenatal development and discuss how environmental events can leave their mark on development even before birth exposes the newborn to the outside world.

The Course of Prenatal Development

PsykTrek 9a

The prenatal period is divided into three phases: (1) the germinal stage (the first 2 weeks), (2) the embryonic stage (2 weeks to 2 months), and (3) the fetal stage (two months to birth). Some key developments in these phases are outlined here.

GERMINAL STAGE

PsykTrek 9a

The *germinal stage* **is the first phase of prenatal development, encompassing the first 2 weeks after conception.** This brief stage begins when a zygote is created through fertilization. Within 36 hours, rapid cell division begins. The zygote becomes a microscopic mass of multiplying cells. This mass slowly migrates along the mother's fallopian tube to the uterine cavity. On about the seventh day, the cell mass begins to implant itself in the uterine wall. This process takes about a week and is far from automatic. Many zygotes are rejected at this point. As many as one in five pregnancies end with the woman never being aware that conception has occurred (Simpson & Juaniaux, 2007).

During the implantation process, the placenta begins to form (Buster & Carson, 2002). **The *placenta* is a structure that allows oxygen and nutrients to pass into the fetus from the mother's bloodstream and bodily wastes to pass out to the mother.** This critical exchange takes place across thin membranes that block the passage of blood cells, keeping the fetal and maternal bloodstreams separate.

EMBRYONIC STAGE

PsykTrek 9a

The *embryonic stage* **is the second stage of prenatal development, lasting from 2 weeks until the end of the second month.** During this stage, most of the vital organs and

Prenatal development is remarkably rapid. Top left: This 30-day-old embryo is just 6 millimeters in length. Bottom left: At 14 weeks, the fetus is approximately 2 inches long. Note the well-developed fingers. The fetus can already move its legs, feet, hands, and head and displays a variety of basic reflexes. Right: After 4 months of prenatal development, facial features are beginning to emerge.

bodily systems begin to form in the developing organism, which is now called an *embryo*. Structures such as the heart, spine, and brain emerge gradually as cell division becomes more specialized. Although the embryo is typically only about an inch long at the end of this stage, it's already beginning to look human. Arms, legs, hands, feet, fingers, toes, eyes, and ears are already discernible.

The embryonic stage is a period of great vulnerability because virtually all the basic physiological structures are being formed. If anything interferes with normal development during the embryonic phase, the effects can be devastating. Most miscarriages occur during this period (Simpson & Juaniaux, 2007). Most major structural birth defects also result from problems that occur during the embryonic stage (Niebyl & Simpson, 2007).

FETAL STAGE

PsykTrek 9a

The *fetal stage* is the third stage of prenatal development, lasting from 2 months through birth. The first 2 months of the fetal stage bring rapid bodily growth, as muscles and bones begin to form (Moore & Persaud, 2008). The developing organism, now called a *fetus*, becomes capable of physical movements as skeletal structures harden. Organs formed in the embryonic stage continue to grow and gradually begin to function. The sense of hearing, for example, is functional by around 20–24 weeks (Hepper, 2003).

During the final 3 months of the prenatal period, brain cells multiply at a brisk pace. A layer of fat is deposited under the skin to provide insulation, and the respiratory and digestive systems mature (Adolph & Berger, 2011). All of these changes ready the fetus for life outside the cozy, supportive environment of its mother's womb. Sometime between 23 weeks and 26 weeks the fetus reaches the *threshold of viability*—the age at which a baby can survive in the event of a premature birth (Moore & Persaud, 2008). At 23 weeks the probability of survival is still slim (about 10%–20%), but it climbs rapidly over the next month, to around a 75% survival rate at 26 weeks (Iams & Romero, 2007). Unfortunately, a great many of the premature infants born near the threshold of viability go on to experience a wide range of developmental problems (Cunningham et al., 2010; Eichenwald & Stark, 2008).

Environmental Factors and Prenatal Development

Although the fetus develops within the protective buffer of the womb, events in the external environment can affect it indirectly through the mother, as the developing organism and its mother are linked via the placenta.

© LWA/Larry Williams/Getty Images

Nutrition Maternal nutrition is very important, as the developing fetus needs a variety of essential nutrients. Severe maternal malnutrition increases the risk of birth complications and neurological deficits for the newborn (Coutts, 2000; Fifer, Monk, & Grose-Fifer, 2001). The impact of moderate malnutrition is more difficult to gauge because it is often confounded with other risk factors associated with poverty, such as drug abuse and limited access to health care (Guerrini, Thomson, & Gurling, 2007). Still, even when pregnant women have ample access to food, it is important for them to consume a balanced diet that includes essential vitamins and minerals. For example, a diet rich in folic acid can reduce the likelihood of a variety of birth defects (Reynolds, 2002).

Stress and Emotion Recent studies suggest that maternal emotions can have an impact on prenatal development. For example, anxiety and depression in pregnant women are associated with an increased prevalence of various behavioral problems in their offspring (Bergner, Monk, & Werner, 2008). Moreover, research suggests that prospective mothers' emotional reactions to stressful events can disrupt the delicate hormonal balance that fosters healthy prenatal development (Douglas, 2010).

Drug Use Another major source of concern is the mother's consumption of drugs. Unfortunately, most drugs consumed by a pregnant woman can slip through the membranes of the placenta. Virtually all "recreational" drugs can be harmful, with sedatives, narcotics, cocaine, and methamphetamine being particularly dangerous (Finnegan & Kandall, 2005; Singer et al., 2002). Problems can even be caused by drugs prescribed for legitimate medical reasons and by some over-the-counter drugs (Niebyl & Simpson, 2007). Tobacco use during pregnancy is also problematic. Smoking appears to increase a mother's risk for miscarriage, stillbirth, and prematurity, and newborns' risk for sudden infant death syndrome (Shea & Steiner, 2008), as well as attention deficits, hyperactivity, and conduct problems (Button, Maughan, & McGuffin, 2007).

Alcohol Consumption Alcohol consumption during pregnancy also carries serious risks. It has long been clear that *heavy* drinking by a mother can be hazardous to a fetus. *Fetal alcohol syndrome* is a collection of congenital (inborn) problems associated with excessive alcohol use during

Concept Check 10.1

Understanding the Stages of Prenatal Development

Check your understanding of the stages of prenatal development by filling in the blanks in the chart below. The first column contains descriptions of a main event from each of the three stages. In the second column, write the name of the stage; in the third column, write the term used to refer to the developing organism during that stage; and in the fourth column, write the time span (in terms of weeks or months) covered by the stage. The answers are in Appendix A at the back of the book.

Event	Stage	Term for organism	Time span
1. Uterine implantation	_____	_____	_____
2. Muscle and bone begin to form	_____	_____	_____
3. Vital organs and body systems begin to form	_____	_____	_____

© Supri Suharjoto/Shutterstock

pregnancy. Typical problems manifested in childhood include microcephaly (a small head), heart defects, irritability, hyperactivity, and delayed motor development (Hannigan & Armant, 2000; Pellegrino & Pellegrino, 2008). Fetal alcohol syndrome is the most common known cause of mental retardation (Niccols, 2007). Furthermore, many children fall short of the criteria for fetal alcohol syndrome but still show serious impairments attributable to their mothers' drinking during pregnancy (Willford, Leech, & Day, 2006). A long-running study of pregnant women's drinking found that higher alcohol intake was associated with an elevated risk for deficits in IQ, motor skills, and attention span, and with increased impulsive, antisocial, and delinquent behavior (Streissguth, 2007). Clearly, even moderate drinking during pregnancy can have enduring and substantial negative effects.

Maternal Illness The placenta screens out quite a number of infectious agents, but not all. Thus, many maternal illnesses can interfere with prenatal development. Diseases such as measles, rubella (German measles), syphilis, and chickenpox can be hazardous to the fetus (Bernstein, 2007); the nature of any damage depends, in part, on when the mother contracts the illness. The HIV virus that causes AIDS can also be transmitted by pregnant women to their offspring. The transmission of AIDS may occur prenatally through the placenta, during delivery, or through breastfeeding. Up through the mid-1990s, about 20%–30% of HIV-positive pregnant women passed the virus on to their babies, but improved antiretroviral drugs (given to the mother) and more cautious obstetrical care have reduced this figure to about 2% in the United States (Cotter & Potter, 2006).

Environmental Toxins Research also suggests that babies in the womb are exposed to a surprising variety of *environmental toxins* that can affect them (Houlihan et al., 2005). For example, prenatal exposure to air pollution has been linked to impairments in cognitive development at age 5 (Edwards et al., 2010). In a similar vein, exposure to the chemicals used in flame-retardant materials correlates with slower mental and physical development up through age 6 (Herbstman et al., 2010).

Fetal Origins of Adult Disease Research on prenatal development has generally focused on its connection to the risk for birth defects and adverse outcomes that are apparent during early childhood. Recently, however, researchers have begun to explore the links between prenatal factors and *adults'* physical and mental health. Recent evidence suggests that events during prenatal development can "program" the fetal brain in ways that influence the person's vulnerability to various types of illness decades later. For example, prenatal malnutrition has been linked to vulnerability to schizophrenia, which usually emerges in late adolescence or early adulthood (Brown & Susser, 2008). Low birth weight, which is a marker for a variety of prenatal disruptions, has been found to be associated with an increased risk of heart disease many decades later in adulthood (Roseboom, de Rooij, & Painter, 2006). Studies have also linked aspects of prenatal development to adults' risk for depression and other mood disorders (Bale et al., 2010), obesity (Huang, Lee, & Lu, 2007), diabetes (Whincup et al., 2008), and some types of cancer (Ahlgren et al., 2007). These findings on the fetal origins of disease are provoking a dramatic reassessment of the factors that influence health and illness.

The Wondrous Years of Early Childhood

A certain magic is associated with childhood. Young children have an extraordinary ability to captivate adults' attention. Legions of parents gush to friends and strangers alike about the cute things their kids do. Most wondrous of all are the rapid and momentous developmental changes of the childhood years. Helpless infants become curious toddlers almost overnight. In this section you'll see what psychologists have learned about motor development, the development of attachment relationships, and language development.

KEY LEARNING GOALS

10.3 Understand the role of maturation and cultural variations in motor development.

10.4 Describe Harlow's and Bowlby's views on attachment, and discuss research on patterns of attachment.

10.5 Trace the development of human language during childhood.

Exploring the World: Motor Development

Motor development **refers to the progression of muscular coordination required for physical activities.** Basic motor skills include grasping and reaching for objects, manipulating objects, sitting up, crawling, walking, and running.

Early progress in motor skills has traditionally been attributed almost entirely to the process of maturation (Adolph & Berger, 2011). *Maturation* **is development that reflects the gradual unfolding of one's genetic blueprint.** It is a product of genetically programmed physical changes that come with age—as opposed to experience and learning. However, research that has taken a closer look at the *process* of motor development suggests that infants are active agents rather than passive organisms waiting for their brain and limbs to mature (Adolph & Berger, 2011; Thelen, 1995). According to this view, the driving force behind motor development is infants' ongoing exploration of their world and their need to master specific tasks (such as grasping a larger toy or looking out a window). Progress in motor development is attributed to infants' experimentation and their learning and remembering the consequences of their activities. Although modern researchers acknowledge that maturation facilitates motor development, they assert that its contribution has been overestimated (Bertenthal & Clifton, 1998).

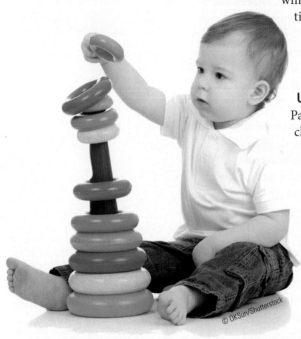

© OKSun/Shutterstock

UNDERSTANDING DEVELOPMENTAL NORMS

Parents often pay close attention to early motor development, comparing their child's progress with developmental norms. *Developmental norms* **indicate the typical (median) age at which individuals display various behaviors and abilities.** Developmental norms are useful benchmarks as long as parents don't expect their children to progress exactly at the pace specified in the norms. Some parents get unnecessarily alarmed when their children fall behind developmental norms. What these parents overlook is that developmental norms are group *averages*. Variations from the average are entirely normal. This normal variation stands out in **Figure 10.1**, which indicates the age at which 25%, 50%, and 90% of youngsters can demonstrate various motor skills. As **Figure 10.1** shows, a substantial portion of children don't achieve a particular milestone until long after the average time cited in norms.

CULTURAL VARIATIONS AND THEIR SIGNIFICANCE

Cross-cultural research has highlighted the dynamic interplay between experience and maturation in motor development. Relatively rapid motor development has been observed in some cultures that provide special practice in basic motor skills (Adolph, Karasik, & Tamis-Lemonda, 2010). For example, the Kipsigis people of Kenya begin active efforts to train their infants to sit up, stand, and walk soon after birth. Thanks to this training, Kipsigis children achieve these developmental milestones (but not others) about a month earlier than babies in the United States (Super, 1976). In contrast, relatively slow motor development has been found in some cultures that discourage motor exploration (Adolph, Karasik, & Tamis-Lemonda, 2010). Cultural variations in the emergence of basic motor skills show that environmental factors can accelerate or slow early motor development.

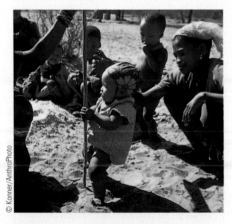

© Konner/AnthroPhoto

Tribes across the world use a variety of methods to foster rapid development of motor abilities in their children. The Kung San of the Kalahari, Botswana, teach their young to dance quite early, using poles to develop the kinesthetic sense of balance.

Early Emotional Development: Attachment

[PSYKTREK 9e]

Attachment **refers to the close emotional bonds of affection that develop between infants and their caregivers.** Researchers have shown a keen interest in how infant-mother attachments are formed early in life. Children eventually form attachments to many people, including their fathers, siblings, grandparents, and others (Cassidy, 2008). However, a child's first important attachment usually occurs with his or her mother because she is typically the main caregiver in the early months of life (Lamb & Lewis, 2011).

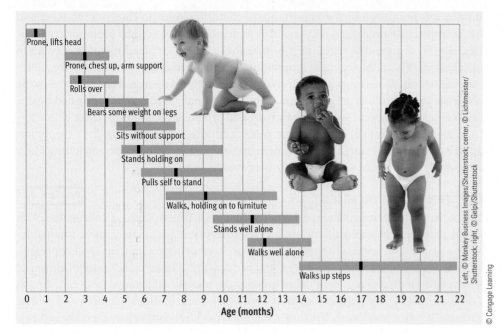

FIGURE 10.1
Milestones in motor development. The left edge, interior mark, and right edge of each bar indicate the age at which 25%, 50%, and 90% of infants have mastered each motor skill shown. Developmental norms typically report only the median age of mastery (the interior mark), which can be misleading in light of the variability in age of mastery apparent in this chart.

Prone, lifts head
Prone, chest up, arm support
Rolls over
Bears some weight on legs
Sits without support
Stands holding on
Pulls self to stand
Walks, holding on to furniture
Stands well alone
Walks well alone
Walks up steps

Age (months)

Left, © Monkey Business Images/Shutterstock; center, © Lichtmeister/Shutterstock; right, © Gelpi/Shutterstock
© Cengage Learning

Contrary to popular belief, infants' attachment to their mothers is *not* instantaneous. Initially, babies show relatively little in the way of a special preference for their mother. At 2–3 months of age, infants may smile and laugh more when they interact with their mother, but they can be handed over to strangers such as babysitters with relatively little difficulty. This situation gradually changes. By about 6–8 months of age, infants begin to show a pronounced preference for their mother's company and often protest when separated from her (Lamb, Ketterlinus, & Fracasso, 1992). This is the first manifestation of *separation anxiety*—emotional distress seen in many infants when they are separated from people with whom they have formed an attachment. Separation anxiety may occur with other familiar caregivers as well as the mother. It typically peaks at around 14–18 months and then begins to decline.

THEORIES OF ATTACHMENT

PsykTrek 9e

Why do children gradually develop a special attachment to their mothers? This question sounds simple enough. However, it has been the subject of a lively theoretical dialogue. Behaviorists have argued that the infant-mother attachment develops because mothers are associated with the powerful, reinforcing event of being fed. Thus, the mother becomes a conditioned reinforcer. However, this reinforcement theory of attachment came into question as a result of Harry Harlow's famous studies of attachment in infant rhesus monkeys (Harlow, 1958, 1959).

Harlow removed monkeys from their mothers at birth and raised them in the laboratory with two types of artificial "substitute mothers." One type of artificial mother was made of terry cloth and could provide "contact comfort" (see the adjacent photo). The other type was made of wire. Half of the monkeys were fed from a bottle attached to a wire mother and the other half were fed by a cloth mother. The young monkeys' attachment to their substitute mothers was tested by introducing a frightening stimulus, such as a strange toy. If reinforcement through feeding were the key to attachment, the frightened monkeys should have scampered off to the mother that had fed them. This was not the case. The young monkeys scrambled for their cloth mothers, even if they were *not* fed by them.

Harlow's work made a simple reinforcement explanation of attachment unrealistic for animals, let alone for more complex human beings. Attention then turned to an alternative explanation of attachment proposed by John Bowlby (1969, 1973, 1980).

© Nina Leen/Time Life Pictures/Getty Images

Even if fed by a wire surrogate mother, Harlow's infant monkeys cuddled up with a terry cloth surrogate that provided contact comfort. When threatened by a frightening toy, the monkeys sought security from their terry cloth mothers.

Harry Harlow
"The little we know about love does not transcend simple observation, and the little we write about it has been written better by poets and novelists."

Reality Check

Misconception
A strong attachment relationship depends on infant-mother bonding during the first few hours after birth.

Reality
Bonding immediately after birth can be a magic moment for mothers and probably should be encouraged for their sake. But there is no empirical evidence that this practice leads to healthier attachment relationships in the long run.

Bowlby was impressed by the importance of contact comfort to Harlow's monkeys and by the apparently unlearned nature of this preference. Influenced by evolutionary theories, Bowlby argued that there must be a biological basis for attachment. According to his view, infants are biologically programmed to emit behavior (smiling, cooing, clinging, and so on) that triggers an affectionate, protective response from adults. Bowlby also asserted that adults are programmed by evolutionary forces to be captivated by this behavior and to respond with warmth, love, and protection. Obviously, these characteristics would be adaptive in terms of promoting children's survival. Bowlby's theory has guided most of the research on attachment over the last several decades, including Mary Ainsworth's influential work on patterns of attachment.

PATTERNS OF ATTACHMENT

PSYKTREK 9e

Infant-mother attachments vary in quality. Mary Ainsworth and her colleagues (1978) found that these attachments fall into three categories. Fortunately, most infants develop a *secure attachment*. They play and explore comfortably with their mother present, become visibly upset when she leaves, and are quickly calmed by her return. However, some children display a pattern called *anxious-ambivalent attachment* (also called *resistant attachment*). They appear anxious even when their mothers are near and protest excessively when she leaves, but they are not particularly comforted when she returns. Children in the third category seek little contact with their mothers and often are not distressed when she leaves. This condition is labeled *avoidant attachment*.

Maternal behaviors appear to have considerable influence over the type of attachment that emerges between an infant and mother (Ainsworth et al., 1978; Posada et al., 2007). Mothers who are sensitive and responsive to their children's needs are more likely to promote secure attachments than mothers who are relatively insensitive or inconsistent in their responding (Nievar & Becker, 2008; van den Boom, 2001). However, infants are not passive bystanders as this process unfolds. They are active participants who influence the process with their crying, smiling, fussing, and babbling. Difficult infants who spit up most of their food, make bathing a major battle, and rarely smile may sometimes slow the process of attachment (van IJzendoorn & Bakermans-Kranenburg, 2004). Thus, the type of attachment that emerges between an infant and mother may depend on the nature of the infant's temperament as well as the mother's sensitivity (Kagan & Fox, 2006).

Evidence suggests that the quality of the attachment relationship can have important consequences for children's subsequent development. Based on their attachment experiences, children develop *internal working models* of the dynamics of close relationships that influence their future interactions with a wide range of people (Bretherton & Munholland, 2008; Johnson, Dweck, & Chen, 2007). Infants with a relatively secure attachment *tend* to become resilient, sociable, competent toddlers with high self-esteem (Ranson & Urichuk, 2006; Thompson, 2008). In their preschool years, such children display more persistence, curiosity, self-reliance, and leadership and have better peer relations (Weinfield et al., 2008). In middle childhood, they exhibit more positive moods, healthier strategies for coping with stress, and fewer problems with hostility and aggression (Fearon et al., 2010; Kerns et al., 2007). Studies have also found a relationship between secure attachment and more advanced cognitive development during childhood and adolescence (Ranson & Urichuk, 2006).

CULTURE AND ATTACHMENT

PSYKTREK 9e

Separation anxiety emerges in children at about 6–8 months and peaks at about 14–18 months in cultures around the world (Grossmann & Grossmann, 1990). These findings, which have been replicated in quite a variety of non-Western cultures, suggest that attachment is a universal feature of human development. However, studies have found some modest cultural variations in the proportion of infants who fall into the three attachment categories described by Ainsworth. Working mostly with white, middle-class subjects in the United States, researchers have found that 67% of infants display a secure attachment, 21% an avoidant attachment, and 12% an anxious-ambivalent attachment (van IJzendoorn & Sagi-Schwartz, 2008). Interestingly, studies in Japan and Germany have yielded somewhat different estimates of the prevalence of various types of attachment, as shown in **Figure 10.2**. That said, the differences are small, and secure attachment appears to be the predominant type of attachment around the world.

Learning to Communicate: Language Development

The early course of language development is similar across very different cultures (Gleitman & Newport, 1996; Slobin, 1992), and language development tends to unfold at roughly the same pace for most children, even though children obviously are reared in diverse home environments. These findings suggest that language development is determined by biological maturation more than personal experience.

MOVING TOWARD PRODUCING WORDS

Long before infants utter their first words, they are making progress in learning the sound structure of their native language. By 7.5 months, infants begin to recognize common word forms (Houston, Santelmann, & Jusczyk, 2004), and by 8 months many infants show the first signs of understanding the meanings of familiar words (Swingley, 2008). During the first 6 months of life, a baby's vocalizations are dominated by crying, cooing, and laughter, which have limited value as a means of communication. Soon, infants are *babbling*. Their babbling gradually becomes more complex and increasingly resembles the language spoken by parents and others in the child's environment (Hoff, 2005).

At around 10 to 13 months of age, most children begin to utter sounds that correspond to words. Most infants' first words are similar in phonetic form and meaning—even in different languages (Waxman, 2002). The initial words resemble the syllables that infants most often babble spontaneously. For example, words such as *dada, mama,* and *papa* are names for parents in many languages because they consist of sounds that are easy to produce.

USING WORDS

After children utter their first words, their vocabulary grows slowly for the next few months (Dapretto & Bjork, 2000). Toddlers typically can say between 3 and 50 words by 18 months. However, their *receptive vocabulary* is larger than their *productive vocabulary*. That is, they can comprehend more words spoken by others than they can actually produce to express themselves (Pan & Uccelli, 2009). Thus, toddlers can *understand* 50 words months before they can *say* 50 words. Children generally acquire nouns before verbs because the meanings of nouns, which often refer to distinct, concrete objects, tend to be easier to encode than the meanings of verbs, which often refer to more abstract relationships (Poulin-Dubois & Graham, 2007).

Youngsters' vocabularies soon begin to grow at a dizzying pace, as a *vocabulary spurt* often begins at around 18 months when toddlers realize that everything has a name (Camaioni, 2001; see **Figure 10.3** on the next page). By the first grade, the average child has a vocabulary of approximately 10,000 words, which builds to an astonishing 40,000 words by the fifth grade (Anglin, 1993). In building these impressive vocabularies, some 2-year-olds learn as many as 20 new words every week. *Fast mapping* appears to be one factor underlying this rapid growth of vocabulary (Carey, 2010; Gershkoff-Stowe & Hahn, 2007). *Fast mapping* **is the process by which children map a word onto an underlying concept after only one exposure.** Thus, children often add words like *tank, board,* and *tape* to their vocabularies after their first encounter with objects that illustrate these concepts.

Of course, these efforts to learn new words are not flawless. Toddlers often make errors, such as overextensions and underextensions (Harley, 2008). **An** *overextension*

FIGURE 10.2

Cultural variations in attachment patterns. This graph shows the prevalence of secure, avoidant, and anxious-ambivalent attachment patterns found in specific studies in Germany, Japan, and the United States. As you can see, secure attachment is the most common pattern in all three societies, as it is around the world. However, there are some modest cultural differences in the prevalence of each pattern of attachment, which are probably attributable to cultural variations in childrearing practices. (Data from van IJzendoorn & Kroonenberg, 1988)

FIGURE 10.3

The vocabulary spurt. Children typically acquire their first 10–15 words very slowly, but they soon go through a *vocabulary spurt*—a period during which they rapidly acquire many new words. The vocabulary spurt usually begins at around 18 months, but children vary, as these graphs of three toddlers' vocabulary growth show.

SOURCE: Adapted from Goldfield, B. A., & Resnick, J. S. (1990). Early lexical acquisition: Rate, content, and the vocabulary spurt. *Journal of Child Language, 17,* 171–183. Copyright © 1990 by Cambridge University Press. Adapted by permission. Photo: Courtesy of Wayne Weiten.

occurs when a child incorrectly uses a word to describe a wider set of objects or actions than it is meant to. For example, a child might use the word *ball* for anything round—oranges, apples, even the moon. Overextensions usually appear in children's speech between ages 1 and 2-1/2. Specific overextensions typically last up to several months. Toddlers also tend to be guilty of *underextensions,* which occur when a child incorrectly uses a word to describe a narrower set of objects or actions than it is meant to. For example, a child might use the word *doll* to refer only to a single, favorite doll. Overextensions and underextensions show that toddlers are actively trying to learn the rules of language— albeit with mixed success.

COMBINING WORDS

Children typically begin to combine words into sentences near the end of their second year. Early sentences are characterized as "telegraphic" because they resemble old-fashioned telegrams, which omitted nonessential words because senders were charged by the word (Bochner & Jones, 2003). *Telegraphic speech* consists mainly of content words; articles, prepositions, and other less critical words are omitted. Thus, a child might say, "Give doll" rather than "Please give me the doll." Although not unique to the English language, telegraphic speech is not cross-culturally universal, as was once thought (de Villiers & de Villiers, 1999).

By the end of their third year, most children can express complex ideas such as the plural or the past tense. However, their efforts to learn the rules of language continue to generate revealing mistakes. *Overregularizations* occur when grammatical rules are incorrectly generalized to irregular cases where they do not apply. For example, children will say things like "The girl goed home" or "I hitted the ball." Cross-cultural research suggests that these overregularizations occur in all languages (Slobin, 1985). Most theorists believe that overregularizations demonstrate that children are working actively to master the *rules* of language (Marcus, 1996). Children don't learn the fine points of grammar and usage in a single leap but gradually acquire them in small steps. Youngsters make their largest strides in language development in their first 4 to 5 years. However, they continue to refine their language skills during their school-age years.

Personality and Cognitive Development in Childhood

KEY LEARNING GOALS

10.6 Describe the basic tenets of Erikson's theory and his stages of childhood personality development.

10.7 Outline Piaget's stages of cognitive development, and evaluate the notion that some cognitive abilities may be innate.

10.8 Discuss Kohlberg's stages of moral development and criticism of his theory.

Many other aspects of development are especially dynamic during childhood. In this section we'll examine personality development, cognitive development, and the development of moral reasoning, which is closely tied to cognitive development. We will begin with a look at the work of Erik Erikson and introduce the concept of developmental stages.

Becoming Unique: Personality Development

PsykTrek 9b

How do individuals develop their unique sets of personality traits over time? Many theories have addressed this question. The first major theory of personality development was put together by Sigmund Freud back around the turn of the 20th century. As we'll discuss in Chapter 11, he claimed that the basic foundation of an individual's personal-

Infancy

Adulthood

Infancy

(a) Continuous development

(b) Discontinuous development (stages)

© Cengage Learning

FIGURE 10.4

Stage theories of development. Some theories view development as a relatively continuous process, albeit not as smooth and perfectly linear as shown on the left **(a)**. In contrast, stage theories assume that development is marked by major discontinuities, as shown on the right **(b)**, that bring fundamental, qualitative changes in capabilities or characteristic behavior.

ity is firmly laid down by age 5. Half a century later, Erik Erikson (1963) proposed a sweeping revision of Freud's theory that has proven influential. Like Freud, Erikson concluded that events in early childhood leave a permanent stamp on adult personality. However, unlike Freud, Erikson theorized that personality continues to evolve over the entire life span.

Building on Freud's earlier work, Erikson devised a stage theory of personality development. As you'll see in this chapter, many theories describe development in terms of stages. A *stage* is a developmental period during which characteristic patterns of behavior are exhibited and certain capacities become established. Stage theories assume that (1) individuals must progress through specified stages in a particular order because each stage builds on the previous stage, (2) progress through these stages is strongly related to age, and (3) development is marked by major discontinuities that usher in dramatic transitions in behavior (see **Figure 10.4**).

ERIKSON'S STAGE THEORY

PsykTrek 9b

Erikson divided the life span into eight stages. Each stage brings a *psychosocial crisis* involving transitions in important social relationships. According to Erikson, personality is shaped by how individuals deal with these psychosocial crises. Each crisis is a potential turning point that can yield different outcomes. Erikson described the stages in terms of these alternative outcomes, which represent personality traits that people display over the remainder of their lives. All eight stages in Erikson's theory are charted in **Figure 10.5**. We describe the first four childhood stages here and discuss the remaining stages in the upcoming sections on adolescence and adulthood.

Erik Erikson

"Human personality in principle develops according to steps predetermined in the growing person's readiness to be driven toward, to be aware of, and to interact with a widening social radius."

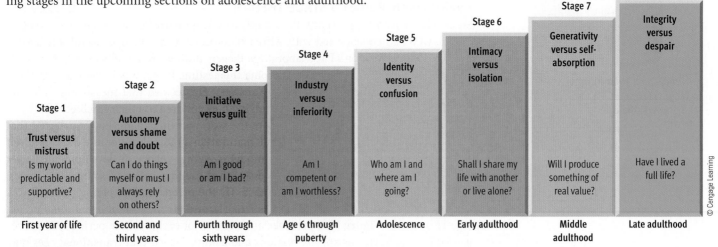

Stage 1	Stage 2	Stage 3	Stage 4	Stage 5	Stage 6	Stage 7	Stage 8
Trust versus mistrust Is my world predictable and supportive?	**Autonomy versus shame and doubt** Can I do things myself or must I always rely on others?	**Initiative versus guilt** Am I good or am I bad?	**Industry versus inferiority** Am I competent or am I worthless?	**Identity versus confusion** Who am I and where am I going?	**Intimacy versus isolation** Shall I share my life with another or live alone?	**Generativity versus self-absorption** Will I produce something of real value?	**Integrity versus despair** Have I lived a full life?
First year of life	Second and third years	Fourth through sixth years	Age 6 through puberty	Adolescence	Early adulthood	Middle adulthood	Late adulthood

© Cengage Learning

FIGURE 10.5

Erikson's stage theory. Erikson's theory of personality development asserts that people evolve through eight stages over the life span. Each stage is marked by a *psychosocial crisis* that involves confronting a fundamental question, such as "Who am I and where am I going?" The stages are described in terms of alternative traits that are potential outcomes from the crises. Development is enhanced when a crisis is resolved in favor of the healthier alternative (which is listed first for each stage).

Trust Versus Mistrust Erikson's first stage encompasses the first year of life. During this time an infant has to depend completely on adults to take care of its basic needs for such necessities as food, a warm blanket, and changed diapers. If an infant's basic biological needs are adequately met by its caregivers and sound attachments are formed, the child should develop an optimistic, trusting attitude toward the world. However, if the infant's basic needs are taken care of poorly, a more distrusting, insecure personality may result.

Autonomy Versus Shame and Doubt Erikson's second stage unfolds during the second and third years of life. During this time parents begin toilet training and other efforts to regulate the child. The child must begin to take some personal responsibility for feeding, dressing, and bathing. If all goes well, he or she acquires a sense of self-sufficiency. But if parents are never satisfied with the child's efforts and if parent-child conflicts are constant, the child may develop a sense of personal shame and self-doubt.

Initiative Versus Guilt In Erikson's third stage, roughly from ages 3 to 6, the challenge facing children is to function socially within their families. If children think only of their own needs and desires, family members may begin to instill feelings of guilt, and self-esteem may suffer. But if children learn to get along well with siblings and parents, a sense of self-confidence should begin to grow.

Industry Versus Inferiority In the fourth stage (age 6 through puberty), the challenge of learning to function socially is extended beyond the family to the broader social realm of the neighborhood and school. Children who are able to function effectively in this less nurturant social sphere where productivity is highly valued should develop a sense of competence.

The Growth of Thought: Cognitive Development ⬢ PSYKTREK 9c

Cognitive development refers to transitions in youngsters' patterns of thinking, including reasoning, remembering, and problem solving. The investigation of cognitive development has been dominated by the theory of Jean Piaget (Kessen, 1996). Much of our discussion of cognitive development is devoted to Piaget's theory and the research it generated, although we'll also delve into other approaches to cognitive development.

OVERVIEW OF PIAGET'S STAGE THEORY ⬢ PSYKTREK 9c

Swiss scholar Jean Piaget (1929, 1952, 1983) was in his early 20s when he met Theodore Simon, who had collaborated with Alfred Binet in devising the first useful intelligence tests. Working in Simon's Paris laboratory, Piaget administered intelligence tests to children to develop better test norms. In doing this testing, Piaget was intrigued by the reasoning underlying the children's *wrong* answers. He decided that measuring children's intelligence was less interesting than studying how children *use* their intelligence.

Noting that children actively explore the world around them, Piaget asserted that interaction with the environment and maturation gradually alter the way children think. Like Erikson's theory, Piaget's model is a *stage theory* of development. Piaget proposed that children's thought processes go through a series of four major stages: (1) the *sensorimotor period* (birth to age 2), (2) the *preoperational period* (ages 2 to 7), (3) the *concrete operational period* (ages 7 to 11), and (4) the *formal operational period* (age 11 onward). **Figure 10.6** provides an overview of each of these periods. Piaget regarded his age norms as approximations and acknowledged that transitional ages may vary from one child to another.

Sensorimotor Period The first stage in Piaget's theory is the *sensorimotor period,* lasting from birth to about age 2. Piaget called this stage *sensorimotor* because infants are developing the ability to coordinate their sensory input with their motor actions. The

Jean Piaget
"It is virtually impossible to draw a clear line between innate and acquired behavior patterns."

Stage 1	Stage 2	Stage 3	Stage 4

Stage 1

Sensorimotor period

Coordination of sensory input and motor responses; development of object permanence

Stage 2

Preoperational period

Development of symbolic thought marked by irreversibility, centration, and egocentrism

Stage 3

Concrete operational period

Mental operations applied to concrete events; mastery of conservation, hierarchical classification

Stage 4

Formal operational period

Mental operations, applied to abstract ideas; logical, systematic thinking

Birth to 2 years	2 to 7 years	7 to 11 years	Age 11 through adulthood

FIGURE 10.6

Piaget's stage theory. Piaget's theory of cognitive development identifies four stages marked by fundamentally different modes of thinking through which youngsters evolve. The approximate age norms and some key characteristics of thought at each stage are summarized here.

major development during the sensorimotor stage is the gradual appearance of symbolic thought. At the beginning of this stage, a child's behavior is dominated by innate reflexes; infants aren't "thinking" as much as they are simply responding to stimuli. But by the end of the stage, the child can use mental symbols to represent objects (for example, a mental image of a favorite toy). The key to this transition is the acquisition of the concept of object permanence.

Object permanence develops when a child recognizes that objects continue to exist even when they are no longer visible. Although you surely take the permanence of objects for granted, infants aren't aware of this permanence at first. If you show a 3-month-old child an eye-catching toy and then cover the toy with a pillow, the child will not attempt to search for the toy. Piaget inferred from this observation that the child does not understand that the toy continues to exist under the pillow. The notion of object permanence does not dawn on children overnight. The first signs of this insight usually appear between 4 and 8 months of age. Progress is gradual, and Piaget believed that children typically don't master the concept of object permanence until they're about 18 months old.

Preoperational Period The *preoperational period* extends roughly from age 2 to age 7. During this stage children gradually improve in their use of mental images. Although progress in symbolic thought continues, Piaget emphasized the *shortcomings* in preoperational thought.

Consider a simple problem that Piaget presented to youngsters. He would take two identical beakers and fill each with the same amount of water. After a child had agreed that the two beakers contained the same amount of water, he would pour the water from one of the beakers into a much taller and thinner beaker (see **Figure 10.7** on the next page). He would then ask the child whether the two differently shaped beakers still contained the same amount of water. Confronted with a problem like this, children in the preoperational period generally said "no." They typically focused on the higher water line in the taller beaker and insisted that there was more water in it. They had not yet mastered the principle of conservation. *Conservation* **is Piaget's term for the awareness that physical quantities remain constant in spite of changes in their shape or appearance.**

Step 1
The child agrees that beakers A and B contain the same amount of water.

Step 2
The child observes as the water from beaker B is poured into beaker C, which is shaped differently.

Step 3
The child is asked: "Do beakers A and C contain the same amount of water?"

© Cengage Learning

FIGURE 10.7

Piaget's conservation task. After watching the transformation shown, a preoperational child will usually answer that the taller beaker contains more water. In contrast, the child in the concrete operations period tends to respond correctly, recognizing that the amount of water in beaker C remains the same as the amount in beaker A.

Why are preoperational children unable to solve conservation problems? According to Piaget, their inability to understand conservation is the result of some basic flaws in preoperational thinking. These flaws include centration, irreversibility, and egocentrism.

Centration **is the tendency to focus on just one feature of a problem, neglecting other important aspects.** When working on the conservation problem with water, preoperational children tend to concentrate on the height of the water while ignoring the width. They have difficulty focusing on several aspects of a problem at once.

Irreversibility **is the inability to envision reversing an action.** Preoperational children can't mentally "undo" something. For instance, in grappling with the conservation of water, they don't think about what would happen if the water were poured back from the tall beaker into the original beaker.

Egocentrism **in thinking is characterized by a limited ability to share another person's viewpoint.** Indeed, Piaget felt that preoperational children fail to appreciate that there are points of view other than their own. For instance, if you ask a preoperational girl whether her sister has a sister, she'll probably say "no" if they are the only two girls in the family. She's unable to view sisterhood from her sister's perspective (this example also shows irreversibility).

A notable feature of egocentrism is *animism—***the belief that all things are living,** just like oneself. Thus, youngsters attribute lifelike, human qualities to inanimate objects, asking questions such as, "When does the ocean stop to rest?" or "Why does the wind get so mad?"

Concrete Operational Period The development of mental operations marks the beginning of the *concrete operational period,* which usually lasts from about age 7 to age 11. Piaget called this stage *concrete* operations because children can perform operations only on images of tangible objects and actual events. Among the operations that children master during this stage are reversibility and decentration. *Reversibility* permits a child to mentally undo an action. *Decentration* allows the child to focus on more than one feature of a problem simultaneously. The newfound ability to coordinate several aspects of a problem helps the child appreciate that there are several ways to look at things. This ability in turn leads to a *decline in egocentrism and gradual mastery of conservation* as it applies to liquid, mass, number, volume, area, and length.

As children master concrete operations, they develop a variety of new problem-solving capacities. Let's examine another problem studied by Piaget. Give a preoperational child seven carnations and three daisies. Tell the child the names for the two types of flowers. Then ask the child to sort them into carnations and daisies. That should be no problem. Now ask the child whether there are more carnations or more daisies. Most children will correctly respond that there are more carnations. Now ask the child whether there are more carnations or more flowers. At this point, most preoperational children will stumble and respond incorrectly that there are more carnations than flowers. Generally, preoperational children can't handle *hierarchical classification* problems that require them to focus simultaneously on two levels of classification. However, the child who has advanced to the concrete

© michaeljung/Shutterstock

operational stage is not as limited by centration and can work successfully with hierarchical classification problems.

Formal Operational Period The final stage in Piaget's theory is the *formal operational period*. It typically begins at around 11 years of age. In this stage, children begin to apply their operations to *abstract* concepts in addition to concrete objects. Indeed, during this stage, youngsters come to *enjoy* the contemplation of abstract concepts. Many adolescents spend hours mulling over hypothetical possibilities related to abstractions such as justice, love, and free will. Thought processes in the formal operational period can be characterized as relatively systematic, logical, and reflective.

According to Piaget, youngsters graduate to relatively adult modes of thinking in the formal operations stage. He did *not* mean to suggest that no further cognitive development occurs once children reach this stage. However, he believed that after children achieve formal operations, further developments in thinking are changes in *degree* rather than fundamental changes in the *nature* of thinking.

EVALUATING PIAGET'S THEORY

Jean Piaget made a landmark contribution to psychology's understanding of children in general and their cognitive development in particular (Beilin, 1992). He founded the field of cognitive development and fostered a new view of children that saw them as active agents constructing their own worlds (Fischer & Hencke, 1996). Piaget's theory guided an enormous volume of productive research that continues through today (Brainerd, 1996; Feldman, 2003). This research has supported many of Piaget's central ideas (Flavell, 1996). In such a far-reaching theory, however, there are bound to be some weak spots. Here are some criticisms of Piaget's theory:

1. In many aspects, Piaget appears to have underestimated young children's cognitive development (Birney et al., 2005). For example, researchers have found evidence that children understand object permanence much earlier than Piaget thought (Birney & Sternberg, 2011).

2. Another problem is that children often simultaneously display patterns of thinking that are characteristic of several stages. This "mixing" of stages and the fact that the transitions between stages are gradual rather than abrupt call into question the value of organizing cognitive development in terms of stages (Bjorklund, 2005; Krojgaard, 2005).

Concept Check 10.2

Recognizing Piaget's Stages

Check your understanding of Piaget's theory by indicating the stage of cognitive development illustrated by each of the examples below. For each scenario, fill in the letter for the appropriate stage in the space on the left. The answers are in Appendix A.

a. Sensorimotor period   c. Concrete operational period

b. Preoperational period   d. Formal operational period

_____ 1.   Upon seeing a glass lying on its side, Sammy says, "Look, the glass is tired. It's taking a nap."

_____ 2.   Maria is told that a farmer has nine cows and six horses. The teacher asks, "Does the farmer have more cows or more animals?" Maria answers, "More animals."

_____ 3.   Alice is playing in the living room with a small red ball. The ball rolls under the sofa. She stares for a moment at the place where the ball vanished and then turns her attention to a toy truck sitting in front of her.

3. Piaget believed that his theory described universal processes that should lead children everywhere to progress through uniform stages of thinking at roughly the same ages. Subsequent research has shown that the *sequence* of stages is largely invariant, but the *timetable* that children follow in passing through these stages varies considerably across cultures (Dasen, 1994; Rogoff, 2003). Thus, Piaget underestimated the influence of cultural factors on cognitive development. Indeed, it seems fair to say that Piaget underestimated the importance of environmental factors in general while focusing too heavily on the role of maturation (Birney et al., 2005; Maratsos, 2007).

ARE SOME COGNITIVE ABILITIES INNATE?

The frequent finding that Piaget underestimated infants' cognitive abilities has led to a rash of studies suggesting that infants have a surprising grasp of many complex concepts. Studies have shown that infants understand basic properties of objects and some of the rules that govern them (Baillargeon, 2002, 2004). At 3 to 4 months of age, infants understand that objects are distinct entities with boundaries, that objects move in continuous paths, that one solid object cannot pass through another, that an object cannot pass through an opening that is smaller than the object, and that objects on slopes roll down rather than up (Baillargeon, 2008; Spelke & Newport, 1998). Infants also understand that liquids are different from objects. For example, 5-month-old infants expect that liquids will change shape as they move and that they can be penetrated by solid objects (Hespos, Ferry, & Rips, 2009).

In this line of research, perhaps the most stunning discovery has been the finding that *infants seem to exhibit surprisingly sophisticated numerical abilities* (Lipton & Spelke, 2004; Wood & Spelke, 2005). If 5-month-old infants are shown a sequence of events in which one object is added to another behind a screen, they expect to see two objects when the screen is removed, and they exhibit surprise when their expectation is violated. This expectation suggests that they understand that $1 + 1 = 2$ (Wynn, 1992, 1996). Similar manipulations suggest that infants also understand that $2 - 1 = 1$, that $2 + 1 = 3$, that $3 - 1 = 2$, and other, more complicated calculations (Hauser & Carey, 1998; McCrink & Wynn, 2004; Wynn, 1998).

Again and again in recent years, research has shown that infants appear to understand surprisingly complex concepts that they have had virtually no opportunity to learn about. These findings have led some theorists to conclude that certain basic cognitive abilities are biologically prewired into humans' neural architecture (Spelke & Kinzler, 2007). As you might anticipate, evolutionary theorists maintain that this prewiring is a product of natural selection, and they strive to understand its adaptive significance for our ancient ancestors (Hauser & Carey, 1998; Wynn, 1998).

The Development of Moral Reasoning

PsykTrek 9d

In Europe, a woman was near death from cancer. One drug might save her, a form of radium that a druggist in the same town had recently discovered. The druggist was charging $2,000, ten times what the drug cost him to make. The sick woman's husband, Heinz, went to everyone he knew to borrow the money, but he could only get together about half of what it cost. He told the druggist that his wife was dying and asked him to sell it cheaper or let him pay later. But the druggist said, "No." The husband got desperate and broke into the man's store to steal the drug for his wife. Should the husband have done that? Why? (Kohlberg, 1969, p. 379)

What's your answer to Heinz's dilemma? Would you have answered the same way 5 years ago? Can you guess what you might have said at age 6? By presenting similar dilemmas to participants and studying their responses, Lawrence Kohlberg (1976, 1984; Colby & Kohlberg, 1987) developed a model of *moral development*. What is morality? That's a complicated question that philosophers have debated for centuries. For our purposes, it will suffice to say that *morality* involves the ability to distinguish right from wrong and to behave accordingly.

KOHLBERG'S STAGE THEORY

PSYKTREK 9d

Kohlberg's model is the most influential of a number of competing theories that attempt to explain how youngsters develop a sense of right and wrong. His work was derived from much earlier work by Piaget (1932). Piaget theorized that moral development is determined by cognitive development. By this he meant that the way individuals think out moral issues depends on their level of cognitive development. This assumption provided the springboard for Kohlberg's research.

Kohlberg's theory focuses on moral *reasoning* rather than overt *behavior*. This point is best illustrated by describing Kohlberg's method of investigation. He presented his participants with thorny moral questions such as Heinz's dilemma. He then asked them what the actor in the dilemma should do, and more important, why. It was the *why* that interested Kohlberg. He examined the nature and progression of subjects' moral reasoning.

The result of this work is the stage theory of moral reasoning outlined in **Figure 10.8**. Kohlberg found that individuals progress through a series of three levels of moral development. Each of these levels can be broken into two sublevels, yielding a total of six stages. Each stage represents a different approach to thinking about right and wrong.

Younger children at the *preconventional level* think in terms of external authority. Acts are wrong because they are punished, or right because they lead to positive consequences. Older children who have reached the *conventional level* of moral reasoning see rules as necessary for maintaining social order. They therefore accept these rules as their own. They "internalize" these rules not to avoid punishment but to be virtuous and win approval from others. Moral thinking at this stage is relatively inflexible. Rules are viewed as absolute guidelines that should be enforced rigidly.

During adolescence, some youngsters move on to the *postconventional level*. This level involves working out a personal code of ethics. Acceptance of rules is less rigid, and moral thinking shows some flexibility. Subjects at the postconventional level allow for the possibility that someone might not comply with some of society's rules if they conflict with personal ethics. For example, participants at this level might applaud a newspaper reporter who goes to jail rather than reveal a source of information who was promised anonymity.

© Bob Daemmrich/PhotoEdit

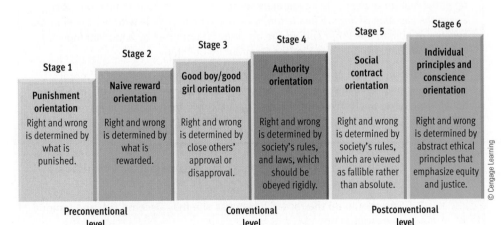

Stage 1	Stage 2	Stage 3	Stage 4	Stage 5	Stage 6
Punishment orientation	**Naive reward orientation**	**Good boy/good girl orientation**	**Authority orientation**	**Social contract orientation**	**Individual principles and conscience orientation**
Right and wrong is determined by what is punished.	Right and wrong is determined by what is rewarded.	Right and wrong is determined by close others' approval or disapproval.	Right and wrong is determined by society's rules, and laws, which should be obeyed rigidly.	Right and wrong is determined by society's rules, which are viewed as fallible rather than absolute.	Right and wrong is determined by abstract ethical principles that emphasize equity and justice.
Preconventional level		**Conventional level**		**Postconventional level**	

© Cengage Learning

FIGURE 10.8

Kohlberg's stage theory. Kohlberg's model describes three levels of moral reasoning, each of which can be divided into two stages. This chart summarizes some of the key facets in how individuals think about right and wrong at each stage.

EVALUATING KOHLBERG'S THEORY

How has Kohlberg's theory fared in research? The central ideas have received reasonable support. Progress in moral reasoning is indeed closely tied to cognitive development (Walker, 1988). Studies also show that youngsters generally do move through Kohlberg's stages of moral reasoning in the order that he proposed (Walker, 1989). Furthermore, relations between age and level of moral reasoning are in the predicted directions (Rest, 1986). Although these findings support Kohlberg's model, like all influential theorists, he has his critics. They have raised the following issues:

1. It's not unusual to find that a person shows signs of several adjacent levels of moral reasoning at a particular point in development (Walker & Taylor, 1991). As we noted in the critique of Piaget, this mixing of stages is a problem for virtually all stage theories.

2. Evidence is mounting that Kohlberg's dilemmas may not be valid indicators of moral development in some cultures (Nucci, 2002). Some critics believe that the value judgments built into Kohlberg's theory reflect a liberal, individualistic ideology characteristic of modern Western nations that is much more culture-specific than Kohlberg appreciated (Miller, 2006).

3. A consensus is building that Kohlberg's theory led to a constricted focus on reasoning about interpersonal conflicts while ignoring many other important aspects of moral development (Walker, 2007). Thus, contemporary researchers are increasingly turning their attention to other dimensions of moral development, including the development of empathy (Eisenberg, Spinrad, & Sadovsky, 2006), the emergence of conscience (Grusec, 2006), and the development of prosocial (helping, sharing) behavior (Carlo, 2006).

Concept Check 10.3

Analyzing Moral Reasoning

Check your understanding of Kohlberg's theory of moral development by analyzing hypothetical responses to the following moral dilemma.

A midwest biologist has conducted numerous studies demonstrating that simple organisms such as worms and paramecia can learn through conditioning. It occurs to her that perhaps she could condition fertilized human ova, to provide a dramatic demonstration that abortions destroy adaptable, living human organisms. This possibility appeals to her, as she is ardently opposed to abortion. However, there is no way to conduct the necessary research on human ova without sacrificing the lives of potential human beings. She desperately wants to conduct the research, but obviously, the sacrifice of human ova is fundamentally incompatible with her belief in the sanctity of human life. What should she do? Why? [Submitted by a student (age 13) to Professor Barbara Banas at Monroe Community College]

In the spaces on the left of each numbered response, indicate the level of moral reasoning shown, choosing from the following: (a) preconventional level, (b) conventional level, or (c) postconventional level. The answers are in Appendix A.

_____ 1. She should do the research. Although it's wrong to kill, there's a greater good that can be realized through the research.

_____ 2. She shouldn't do the research because people will think that she's a hypocrite and condemn her.

_____ 3. She should do the research because she may become rich and famous as a result.

The Transition of Adolescence

KEY LEARNING GOALS

10.9 Review the physiological changes of puberty, and summarize research on neural development in adolescence.

10.10 Discuss identity formation in adolescence and the stage of emerging adulthood.

Adolescence is a bridge between childhood and adulthood. During this time, individuals continue to experience significant changes in cognitive, moral, and social development. However, the most dynamic areas of development during adolescence are physical changes and related transitions in emotional and personality development.

Physiological Changes

Recall for a moment your junior high school days. Didn't it seem that your body grew so fast that your clothes just couldn't "keep up"? This phase of rapid growth in height and weight is called the *adolescent growth spurt*. Brought on by hormonal changes, it typically starts at about age 10 in girls and at about 12 in boys (Archibald, Graber, & Brooks-Dunn, 2003).

In addition to growing taller and heavier, children begin to develop the physical features that characterize adults of their respective sexes. These features are termed *secondary sex characteristics*—**physical features that distinguish one sex from the other but that are not essential for reproduction.** For example, males go through a voice change, develop facial hair, and experience greater skeletal and muscle growth in the upper torso, leading to broader shoulders (see **Figure 10.9**). Females experience breast growth and a widening of the pelvic bones plus increased fat deposits in this area, resulting in wider hips (Susman & Rogol, 2004).

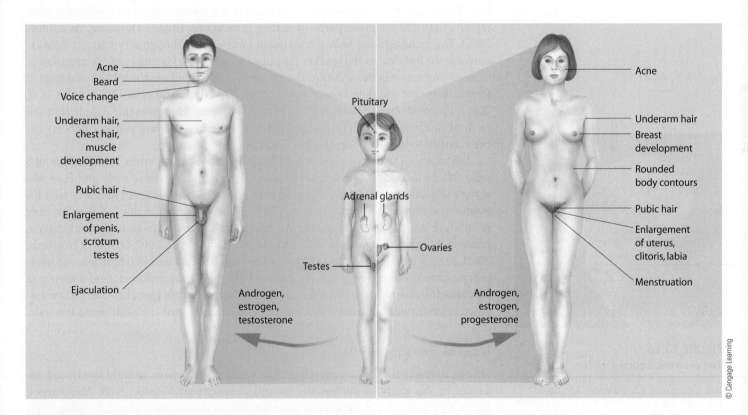

© Cengage Learning

FIGURE 10.9

Physical development at puberty. Hormonal changes during puberty lead not only to a growth spurt but also to the development of secondary sex characteristics. The pituitary gland sends signals to the adrenal glands and gonads (ovaries and testes), which secrete hormones responsible for various physical changes that differentiate males and females.

Soon, youngsters reach *puberty*—**the stage during which sexual functions reach maturity, which marks the beginning of adolescence.** It is during puberty that the *primary sex characteristics*—**the structures necessary for reproduction**—develop fully. In the male, these include the testes, penis, and related internal structures. Primary sex characteristics in the female include the ovaries, vagina, uterus, and other internal structures.

In females, puberty is typically signaled by *menarche*—**the first occurrence of menstruation,** which reflects the culmination of a series of hormonal changes (Pinyerd & Zipf, 2005). American girls typically reach menarche at ages 12–13, with further sexual maturation continuing until approximately age 16 (Susman, Dorn, & Schiefelbein, 2003). American boys typically experience *spermarche*—**the first occurrence of ejaculation**—at ages 13–14, with further sexual maturation continuing until approximately age 18 (Archibald et al., 2003).

Interestingly, *generational* changes have occurred in the timing of puberty over the last 150 years. Today's adolescents begin puberty at a younger age, and complete it more rapidly, than their counterparts in earlier generations (Bellis, Downing, & Ashton, 2006). This trend appears to be occurring in both sexes, although more precise data are available for females, as the marker for puberty (menarche) is more readily apparent in females (Herman-Giddens, 2006). The reasons for this trend are the subject of debate. It seems likely that multiple factors have contributed (Archibald et al., 2003; Bellis et al. 2006). The most obvious potential causes are widespread improvements in nutrition and medical care, which would probably explain why the trend toward younger puberty has been limited to modern, "developed" countries.

The timing of puberty varies from one adolescent to the next over a range of about 5 years (10–15 for girls, 11–16 for boys). Generally, *girls who mature early and boys who mature late seem to experience more subjective distress and emotional difficulty with the transition to adolescence* (Susman et al., 2003). However, in both males and females, early maturation is associated with greater use of alcohol and drugs, more high-risk behavior, greater aggression, and more trouble with the law (Lynne et al., 2007; Steinberg & Morris, 2001). Among females, early maturation is also correlated with earlier experience of intercourse, more unwanted pregnancies, a greater risk for eating problems, and a variety of psychological disorders (Archibald et al., 2003). Thus, we might speculate that early maturation often thrusts both sexes (but especially females) toward the adult world too soon.

FIGURE 10.10

The prefrontal cortex. Recent research suggests that neural development continues throughout adolescence. Moreover, the chief site for much of this development is the prefrontal cortex, which appears to be the last area of the brain to mature fully. This discovery may have fascinating implications for understanding the adolescent brain, as the prefrontal cortex appears to play a key role in emotional regulation and self-control.

Prefrontal cortex

Neural Development

Thanks to modern brain-imaging technology, recent years have brought significant advances in the study of adolescents' neural development (Giedd, 2008; McAnarney, 2008). This research has uncovered some interesting developmental trends during adolescence. For example, the volume of white matter in the brain grows throughout adolescence (Blakemore, 2008). This means that *neurons are becoming more myelinated* (see Chapter 3), which presumably leads to enhanced conductivity and connectivity in the brain. In contrast, gray matter decreases in volume (Toga, Thompson, & Sowell, 2006). This finding is thought to reflect the process of *synaptic pruning*—the elimination of less-active synapses—that plays a key role in the formation of neural networks (see Chapter 3).

Perhaps the most interesting discovery about the adolescent brain has been that increased myelinization and synaptic pruning are most pronounced in the *prefrontal cortex* (Blakemore, 2008; see **Figure 10.10**). Thus, *the prefrontal cortex appears to be the last area of the brain to fully mature.* This maturation may not be complete until one's mid-20s (Gogtay et al., 2004). Much has been made of this finding because the prefrontal cortex has been characterized as an "executive control center." It appears to be crucial to high-level cognitive functions, such as planning, organizing, emotional regulation, and response inhibition (Casey et al., 2005). Theorists have suggested that the immaturity of the prefrontal cortex may explain why risky behavior (such as reckless driving, experimentation with drugs, dangerous stunts, unprotected sex, and so forth) peaks during adolescence and then declines in adulthood (Compas, 2004; Steinberg, 2008).

That said, Kuhn (2006) notes that media pundits have gotten carried away, blaming the immaturity of the adolescent prefrontal cortex for "just about everything about teens that adults have found perplexing" (p. 59). Other factors also contribute to risky behavior during adolescence. One of these factors is susceptibility to peer influence (Steinberg, 2007). Adolescents spend a great deal of time with their peers. One elegant lab study found that the presence of peers more than doubled the number of risks taken by teenagers in a video game involving in-the-moment decisions about crash risks (Gardner & Steinberg, 2005). In contrast, older adults' risk taking was not elevated by the presence of peers (see **Figure 10.11**).

The Search for Identity

PsykTrek 9b

Erik Erikson was especially interested in personality development during adolescence, which is the fifth of the eight major life stages he described. The psychosocial crisis during this stage pits *identity* against *confusion* as potential outcomes. According to Erikson (1968), the main challenge of adolescence is the struggle to form a clear sense of identity. This struggle involves working out a stable concept of oneself as a unique individual and embracing an ideology or system of values that provides a sense of direction. In Erikson's view, adolescents grapple with questions such as "Who am I?" and "Where am I going in life?"

Adolescents deal with identity formation in a variety of ways. According to James Marcia (1966, 1980, 1994), the presence or absence of a sense of commitment (to life goals and values) and a sense of crisis (active questioning and exploration) can combine to produce four different *identity statuses.* In order of increasing maturity, Marcia's four identity statuses begin with *identity diffusion,* a state of rudderless apathy, with no commitment to an ideology. *Identity foreclosure* is a premature commitment to visions, values, and roles—typically those prescribed by one's parents. Foreclosure is associated

FIGURE 10.11

Peer influence on risk taking. Gardner and Steinberg (2005) had adolescents, young adults, and adults play a video game involving simulated driving in which participants had to make quick decisions about crash risks. The dependent variable, which indexed subjects' risk taking, was the number of crashes experienced. Some participants played the video game alone, whereas others played in the presence of peers. The data showed that the presence of peers increased risk taking by young adults moderately and by adolescents considerably, but adults' risk taking was unaffected. These findings suggest that susceptibility to peer influence may increase risky behavior among adolescents and young adults.

SOURCE: Adapted from Steinberg, L. (2007). Risk taking in adolescence: New perspectives from brain and behavioral science. *Current Directions in Psychological Science, 16,* 55–59. Copyright © 2007 Blackwell Publishing.

with conformity and not being very open to new experiences (Kroger, 2003). An *identity moratorium* involves delaying commitment for a while to experiment with alternative ideologies and careers. *Identity achievement* involves arriving at a sense of self and direction after some consideration of alternative possibilities. Identity achievement is associated with higher self-esteem, conscientiousness, security, achievement motivation, and capacity for intimacy (Kroger, 2003). However, recent research suggests that people tend to reach identity achievement at later ages than originally envisioned by Marcia. In one recent, large-scale study (Meeus et al., 2010), by late adolescence only 22%–26% of the sample had reached identity achievement. Thus, the struggle for a sense of identity routinely extends into young adulthood.

Emerging Adulthood as a New Developmental Stage

The finding that the search for identity routinely extends into adulthood is one of many considerations that have led Jeffrey Arnett to make the radical claim that we ought to recognize the existence of a new developmental stage in modern societies. He calls this stage *emerging adulthood*. According to Arnett (2000, 2004, 2006), the years between ages 18 and 25 (roughly) have become a distinct, new transitional stage of life. He attributes the rise of this new developmental period to a variety of demographic trends. For example, more people are delaying marriage and parenthood until their late 20s or early 30s. More people stay in school for lengthier periods, and young people face more barriers to financial independence.

Arnett (2000, 2006) maintains that emerging adulthood is marked by a number of distinct features. A central feature is the subjective feeling that one is in between adolescence and adulthood. When 18- to 25-year-olds are asked, "Do you feel like you have reached adulthood?" the modal response is "Yes and no." They don't feel like adolescents, but most don't see themselves as adults either. Another feature of emerging adulthood is that it is an age of possibilities. It tends to be a time of great optimism about one's personal future. A third aspect of emerging adulthood is that it is a self-focused time of life. People in this period tend to be unfettered by duties, commitments, and social obligations, giving them unusual autonomy and freedom to explore new options. Finally, Arnett has found that emerging adulthood is a period of continued struggles with identity issues. Arnett's provocative theory has already inspired a good deal of research on the dynamics and developmental significance of emerging adulthood (Aquilino, 2006; Côté, 2006; Labouvie-Vief, 2006; Tanner, 2006).

The Expanse of Adulthood

KEY LEARNING GOALS

10.11 Discuss personality development in adulthood and trace typical transitions in family relations during the adult years.

10.12 Describe the physical changes associated with aging, and summarize information on Alzheimer's disease.

10.13 Understand how intelligence, memory, and mental speed change in later adulthood.

The concept of development was once associated almost exclusively with childhood and adolescence. Today, however, development is widely recognized as a lifelong journey. Interestingly, patterns of development during the adult years are becoming increasingly diverse. The boundaries between young, middle, and late adulthood are becoming blurred as more and more people have children later than one is "supposed" to, retire earlier than one is "supposed" to, and so forth. In the upcoming pages we will look at some of the major developmental transitions in adult life. As we do, you should bear in mind that in adulthood (even more so than childhood or adolescence) there are many divergent pathways and timetables.

Personality Development

PsykTrek 9b

Research on adult personality development has been dominated by one key question: How stable is personality over the life span? We'll look at this issue and Erikson's view of adulthood in our discussion of personality development in the adult years.

THE QUESTION OF STABILITY

How common are significant personality changes in adulthood? Is a grouchy 20-year-old going to be a grouchy 40-year-old and a grouchy 65-year-old? After tracking subjects through adulthood, many researchers have been impressed by the amount of change observed (Helson, Jones, & Kwan, 2002; Whitbourne et al., 1992). In contrast, many other researchers have concluded that personality tends to be quite stable over periods of 20 to 40 years (Caspi & Herbener, 1990; Costa & McCrae, 1994, 1997). A review of 150 relevant studies, involving almost 50,000 participants, concluded that personality in early adulthood is a good predictor of personality in late adulthood (Roberts & DelVecchio, 2000).

Clearly, researchers assessing the stability of personality in adulthood have reached very different conclusions. How can these contradictory conclusions be reconciled? It appears that *both* are accurate—they just reflect different ways of looking at the data (Bertrand & Lachman, 2003). As noted in Chapter 8, psychological test scores are *relative* measures. They show how one scores *relative to other people*. Raw scores are converted into *percentile scores* that indicate the precise degree to which one is above or below average on a particular trait. The data indicate that these percentile scores tend to be remarkably stable over lengthy spans of time—people's relative standing on personality traits doesn't tend to change much (Kandler et al., 2010; Roberts, Wood, & Caspi, 2008).

However, if we examine participants' raw scores on a test of the Big Five traits (see Chapter 11), we can see meaningful developmental trends. For example, adults' mean raw scores on extraversion, neuroticism, and openness to experience tend to decline moderately with increasing age, while measures of agreeableness and conscientiousness tend to increase (Bertrand & Lachman, 2003; Caspi, Roberts, & Shiner, 2005; see **Figure 10.12**). Recent research with a nationally representative sample found that self-esteem tends to increase slowly from early adulthood through middle-age, peaking at about age 60 (Orth, Trzesniewski, & Robins, 2010). After age 60, self-esteem tends to gradually decline. Women and men tend to show similar trajectories, although women score slightly lower in self-esteem across most of the life span. In sum, it appears that personality in adulthood is characterized by *both* stability and change.

ERIKSON'S VIEW OF ADULTHOOD

Insofar as personality changes during the adult years, Erik Erikson's (1963) theory offers some clues about the kinds of changes people can expect. In his eight-stage model of development over the life span, Erikson divided adulthood into three stages (see again **Figure 10.5**):

Intimacy Versus Isolation In early adulthood, the key concern is whether one can develop the capacity to share intimacy with others. Successful resolution of the challenges in this stage should promote empathy and openness, rather than shrewdness and manipulativeness.

Generativity Versus Self-Absorption In middle adulthood, the key challenge is to acquire a genuine concern for the welfare of future generations, which results in providing unselfish guidance to younger people. Self-absorption is characterized by self-indulgent concerns with meeting one's own needs and desires.

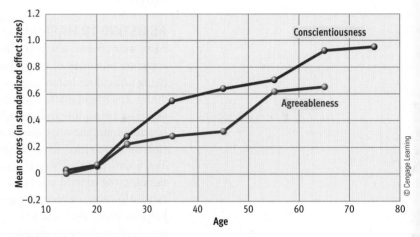

FIGURE 10.12

Examples of personality trends in the adult years. According to Brent Roberts and Daniel Mroczek (2008), when researchers examine participants' mean raw scores on personality measures, they find meaningful trends over the decades of adulthood. The trends for two specific traits—agreeableness and conscientiousness—are shown here as examples. Using subjects' test scores in adolescence as a baseline, you can see how measures of agreeableness and conscientiousness increase substantially over the decades.

SOURCE: Roberts, B. W., & Mroczek, D. (2008). Personality trait change in adulthood. *Current Directions in Psychological Science, 17*, 31–35. Copyright © 2008 Blackwell Publishing.

PsykTrek 9b

Integrity Versus Despair During the retirement years, the challenge is to avoid the tendency to dwell on the mistakes of the past and on one's imminent death. People need to find meaning and satisfaction in their lives, rather than wallow in bitterness and resentment.

Transitions in Family Life

Many of the important transitions in adulthood involve changes in family responsibilities and relationships. Everyone emerges from a family, and most people go on to form their own families. However, the transitional period during which young adults are "between families" until they form a new family is being prolonged by more and more people. The percentage of young adults who are postponing marriage until their late twenties or early thirties has risen steadily (see **Figure 10.13**). This trend is probably the result of a number of factors. Chief among them are the availability of new career options for women, increased educational requirements in the world of work, and increased emphasis on personal autonomy. Nonetheless, over 90% of adults eventually marry.

ADJUSTING TO MARRIAGE

Most new couples are pretty happy, but 8%–14% of newlyweds score in the distressed range on measures of marital satisfaction, with the most commonly reported problems being difficulties balancing work and marriage and financial concerns (Schramm et al., 2005). You might guess that partners who cohabit prior to getting married ought to have an easier transition and greater marital success. However, until recently research demonstrated just the opposite. Studies found an association between premarital cohabitation and increased divorce rates (Bumpass & Lu, 2000; Cohan & Kleinbaum, 2002; Teachman, 2003). Theorists speculated that people inclined to cohabit were less traditional, more individualistic, and had a weaker commitment to the institution of marriage. However, in recent years the findings on the effects of cohabitation have become less consistent (de Vaus, Qu, & Weston, 2005; Liefbroer & Dourleijn, 2006). One reason may be that cohabitation prior to marriage has gradually become the norm rather than the exception. In the 1970s only about 10% of couples lived together before marriage, but

FIGURE 10.13

Median age at first marriage. The median age at which people in the United States marry for the first time has been creeping up for both males and females since the mid-1960s. This trend indicates that more people are postponing marriage. (Data from the U. S. Bureau of the Census)

by the 1990s that figure had risen to 60% (Tach & Halpern-Meekin, 2009). The findings of a recent, large-scale study in Australia that looked at trends over decades (from 1945 to 2000) suggest that the impact of cohabitation may be changing (Hewitt & de Vaus, 2009). Cohabitants had higher rates of marital dissolution up through 1988, but then the trend started to gradually reverse itself, with cohabitants showing lower rates of divorce. More data are needed, but changes in the composition of the population of people who cohabit may be altering the effect of cohabitation on marital stability.

One major source of conflict in many new marriages is the negotiation of marital roles in relation to career commitments. More and more women are aspiring to demanding careers. However, research shows that husbands' careers continue to take priority over their wives' career ambitions (Cha, 2010; Haas, 1999). Moreover, many husbands maintain traditional role expectations about housework, child care, and decision making. Men's contribution to housework has increased noticeably since the 1960s. But studies indicate that wives are still doing the bulk of the household chores in the United States and all over the world, even when they work outside the home (Greenstein, 2009; Sayer, 2005). Nonetheless, most wives do not view their division of labor as unfair (Braun et al., 2008) because most women don't expect a 50-50 split (Coltrane, 2001).

ADJUSTING TO PARENTHOOD

Although an increasing number of people are choosing to remain childless, the vast majority of married couples continue to have children. Most couples are happy with their decision to have children. However, the arrival of the first child represents a major transition, and the disruption of routines can be emotionally draining (Bost et al., 2002). The transition to parenthood tends to have more impact on mothers than fathers (Nomaguchi & Milkie, 2003). The transition is more difficult when a wife's expectations regarding how much the father will be involved in child care are not met (Fox, Bruce, & Combs-Orme, 2000). A review of decades of research on parenthood and marital satisfaction, found that (1) parents exhibit lower marital satisfaction than comparable nonparents, (2) mothers of infants report the steepest decline in marital satisfaction, and (3) the more children couples have, the lower their marital satisfaction tends to be (Twenge, Campbell, & Foster, 2003). Although these findings are distressing, crisis during the transition to first parenthood is far from universal.

As children grow up, parental influence over them tends to decline. As this happens, the early years of parenting—that once seemed so difficult—are often recalled with fondness. When youngsters reach adolescence and seek to establish their own identities, gradual realignments occur in parent-child relationships. On the one hand, these relations generally are not as bitter or contentious as widely assumed (Laursen, Coy, & Collins, 1998). On the other hand, adolescents do spend less time in family activities, and their closeness to their parents declines while conflicts become more frequent (Smetana, Campione-Barr, & Metzger, 2006). The conflicts tend to involve everyday matters (chores and appearance) more than substantive issues (sex and drugs) (Collins & Laursen, 2006).

SALLY FORTH

SALLY FORTH © King Features Syndicate

Reality Check

Misconception
Children are a key ingredient of marital bliss.

Reality
Children can be a source of great joy, but they also are a source of considerable stress. Although other factors are also at work, studies show that marital satisfaction generally declines after the arrival of children and often increases after grown children leave home.

Aging and Physiological Changes

People obviously experience many physical changes as they progress through adulthood. In both sexes, hair tends to thin out and become gray. Many males confront receding hairlines and baldness. To the dismay of many, the proportion of body fat tends to increase with age. Overall, weight tends to increase in most adults through the mid-50s, when a gradual decline may begin. These changes have little functional significance. In our youth-oriented society, however, they often lead people to view themselves as unattractive (Aldwin & Gilmer, 2004).

Curiously though, when elderly people are asked how old they feel, they mostly report feeling quite a bit younger than they actually are. For instance, in a study of people over the age of 70, on average the subjects reported that they felt 13 years younger than their chronological age (Kleinspehn-Ammerlahn, Kotter-Grühn, & Smith, 2008). Obviously, there is some wishful thinking at work here, but it appears to be beneficial. Evidence suggests that feeling younger than one's real age is associated with better health and cognitive functioning and reduced mortality risk (Kotter-Grühn et al., 2009).

In the sensory domain, the key developmental changes occur in vision and hearing. The proportion of people with 20/20 visual acuity declines with age. Farsightedness and difficulty seeing in low illumination become more common (Schieber, 2006). Hearing sensitivity begins declining gradually in early adulthood but usually isn't noticeable until after age 50. Hearing loss tends to be greater in men than in women and for high-frequency sounds more than low-frequency sounds (Yost, 2000). Even mild hearing loss can undermine speech perception and put an added burden on cognitive processing (Wingfield, Tun, & McCoy, 2005). These sensory losses would be more problematic, but in modern society they can usually be partially compensated for with eyeglasses, contacts, and hearing aids.

Age-related changes also occur in hormonal functioning during adulthood. Among women, these changes lead to *menopause*. This ending of menstrual periods, accompanied by a loss of fertility, typically occurs at around age 50 (Grady, 2006). Most women experience at least some unpleasant symptoms, such as hot flashes, headaches, night sweats, mood changes, sleep difficulties, and reduced sex drive, but the degree of discomfort varies considerably (Grady, 2006; Williams et al., 2007). Not long ago, menopause was thought to be almost universally accompanied by severe emotional strain. However, it is now clear that most women experience relatively modest psychological distress (George, 2002; Walter, 2000).

Aging and Neural Changes

The amount of brain tissue and the brain's weight decline gradually in late adulthood, mostly after age 60 (Victoroff, 2005). These trends appear to reflect both a decrease in the number of active neurons in some areas of the brain and shrinkage of still-active neurons, with neuron loss perhaps being less important than once believed (Albert & Killiany, 2001). Although this gradual loss of brain tissue sounds alarming, it is a normal part of the aging process. Its functional significance is the subject of some debate, but it doesn't appear to be a key factor in any of the age-related dementias. **A *dementia* is an abnormal condition marked by multiple cognitive deficits that include memory impairment.** Dementia can be caused by quite a variety of diseases, such as Alzheimer's disease, Parkinson's disease, Huntington's disease, and AIDS, to name just a few (Caine & Lyness, 2000). The prevalence of many of these diseases increases with age. Thus, dementia is seen in about 5%–8% of people ages 65–70, and 15%–20% of those ages 75–80 (Richards & Sweet, 2009). However, it is important to emphasize that dementia and "senility" are not part of the normal aging process.

Alzheimer's disease accounts for roughly 70% of all cases of dementia (Albert, 2008). The disease is accompanied by major structural deterioration in the brain. Alzheimer's patients exhibit profound and widespread loss of neurons and brain tissue and the accumulation of characteristic neural abnormalities known as neuritic plaques and neurofibrillary tangles (Haroutunian & Davis, 2003). The hallmark early symptom is the forgetting of newly learned information after surprisingly brief periods of time (Albert & Killiany, 2001). Impairments of working memory, attention, and executive function (planning, staying on task) are also quite common (Storandt, 2008). The course of the disease is one of progressive deterioration, typically over a period of 8 to 10 years, ending in death (Albert, 2008).

The causes that launch this debilitating neural meltdown are not well understood. Genetic factors clearly contribute (Mc-Queen & Blacker, 2008). Their exact role, though, remains unclear (Bertram & Tanzi, 2008). Recent evidence also implicates chronic inflammation as a contributing factor (Heneka et al., 2010). Some "protective" factors that diminish vulnerability to Alzheimer's disease have been identified (Hertzog et al., 2009). For example, risk is reduced among those who engage in regular exercise (Radak et al., 2010) and those with lower cardiovascular risk factors, such as absence of high blood pressure and high cholesterol (Qui, De Ronchi, & Fratiglioni, 2010). Decreased vulnerability to Alzheimer's is also associated with frequent participation in stimulating cognitive activities (Karp et al., 2009) and maintenance of active social engagement with friends and family (Krueger et al., 2009).

Aging and Cognitive Changes

Numerous studies report decreases in older adults' memory capabilities (Hoyer & Verhaeghen, 2006). Many researchers maintain that the memory losses associated with normal aging tend to be moderate and are *not* experienced by everyone (Dixon & Cohen, 2003; Shimamura et al., 1995). However, Salthouse (2003, 2004) takes a much more pessimistic view, arguing that age-related decreases in memory are substantial in magnitude, that they begin in early adulthood, and that they affect everyone. One reason for these varied conclusions may be that a variety of memory types can be assessed (see Chapter 7 for a review of various systems of memory).

In the cognitive domain, aging seems to take its toll on *speed* first. Many studies indicate that speed in learning, solving problems, and processing information tends to decline with age (Salthouse, 1996). The evidence suggests that the erosion of processing speed may be a gradual, lengthy trend beginning in middle adulthood (see **Figure 10.14**). The general nature of this trend (across differing tasks) suggests that it may be the result of age-related changes in neurological functioning (Salthouse, 2000), but doubts have been raised about this conclusion (Hartley, 2006). Although mental speed declines with age, problem-solving ability remains largely unimpaired if older people are given adequate time to compensate for their reduced speed.

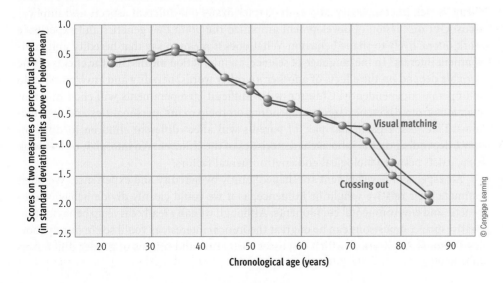

FIGURE 10.14

Age and mental speed. Many studies have found that mental speed decreases with age. The data shown here, from Salthouse (2000), are based on two perceptual speed tasks. The data points are means for large groups of subjects expressed in terms of how many standard deviations (see Appendix B) they are above or below the mean for all ages (which is set at 0). Similar age-related declines are seen on many tasks that depend on mental speed.

SOURCE: Adapted from Salthouse, T. A. (2000). Aging and measures of processing speed. *Biological Psychology, 54,* 35–54. Reproduced by permission of Elsevier Science.

A hot issue in recent years has been whether high levels of mental activity in late adulthood can delay the typical age-related declines in cognitive functioning. This possibility is sometimes referred to as the "use it or lose it" hypothesis. Several lines of evidence seem to provide support for this notion. For example, people who continue to work further into old age, especially people who remain in mentally demanding jobs, tend to show smaller decrements in cognitive abilities than their age-mates (Bosma et al., 2002; Schooler, 2007). Other studies suggest that continuing to engage in intellectually challenging activities in late adulthood serves to buffer against cognitive declines (Kliegel, Zimprich, & Rott, 2004; Yaffe et al., 2009). For example, one recent study of 488 people between the ages of 75 and 85 found that participation in leisure activities (such as reading, writing, working crossword puzzles, and playing board games) was associated with a reduced decline in memory functioning (Hall et al., 2009).

With findings such as these in mind, some scientists have developed elaborate and challenging cognitive training programs for elderly people that are intended to slow their cognitive decline. Studies of these interventions have yielded promising results (Ball, Edwards, & Ross, 2007; Mahncke et al., 2006; Willis et al., 2006). For example, one recent study had subjects over the age of 65 spend one hour a day, five days a week, for 8 weeks on a computerized training program (Smith et al., 2009). Subsequent tests showed that the training enhanced many aspects of memory performance. That said, the improvement was not dramatic, just 4%. These findings are intriguing, but the evidence on memory training in the elderly is a mixed bag and there are skeptics (Papp, Walsh, & Snyder, 2009; Salthouse, 2006). It remains to be seen whether modest training effects can prevent or delay the onset of Alzheimer's disease.

KEY LEARNING GOALS

10.14 Identify the five unifying themes highlighted in this chapter.

Theoretical
Diversity

Sociohistorical
Context

Multifactorial
Causation

Cultural Heritage

Heredity and
Environment

Reflecting on the Chapter's Themes

Five of our seven integrative themes surfaced to some degree in our coverage of human development. We saw theoretical diversity in our discussions of cognitive development and personality development. We saw that psychology evolves in a sociohistorical context, investigating complex, real-world issues—such as the effects of cohabitation—that emerge as our society changes. We encountered multifactorial causation of behavior in the development of attachment, among other things. We saw cultural invariance and cultural diversity in our examination of attachment, motor development, cognitive development, and moral development.

But above all else, we saw how heredity and environment jointly mold behavior. We've encountered the dual influence of heredity and environment before, but this theme is rich in complexity, and each chapter draws out different aspects and implications. Our discussion of development amplified the point that genetics and experience work *interactively* to shape behavior. What does it mean to say that heredity and environment interact? In the language of science, an interaction means that the effects of one variable depend on the effects of another. In other words, heredity and environment do not operate independently. Children with "difficult" temperaments will elicit different reactions from different parents, depending on the parents' personalities and expectations. Likewise, a particular pair of parents will affect different children in different ways, depending on the inborn characteristics of the children. An interplay, or feedback loop, exists between biological and environmental factors.

All aspects of development are shaped jointly by heredity and experience. We often estimate their relative weight or influence, as if we could cleanly divide behavior into genetic and environmental components. Although we can't really carve up behavior that neatly, such comparisons can be of great theoretical interest, as you'll see in our upcoming Personal Application, which discusses the nature and origins of gender differences in behavior.

Understanding Gender Differences

10.15 Summarize evidence on gender differences in behavior, and assess the significance of these differences.

10.16 Explain how biological and environmental factors are thought to contribute to gender differences.

Answer the following "true" or "false."

____ **1** Females are more socially oriented than males.

____ **2** Males outperform females on most spatial tasks.

____ **3** Females are more irrational than males.

____ **4** Males are less sensitive to nonverbal cues than females.

____ **5** Females are more emotional than males.

Are there genuine behavioral differences between the sexes similar to those mentioned above? If so, why do these differences exist? How do they develop? These are the complex and controversial questions that we'll explore in this Personal Application.

Before proceeding further, we need to clarify how some key terms are used, as terminology in this area of research has been evolving and remains a source of confusion (Deaux, 1993; Unger & Crawford, 1993). *Sex* **refers to the biologically based categories of female and male.** In contrast, *gender* **refers to culturally constructed distinctions between femininity and masculinity.** Individuals are born female or male. However, they become feminine or masculine through complex developmental processes that take years to unfold.

The statements at the beginning of this Application reflect popular gender stereotypes in our society. *Gender stereotypes* **are widely held beliefs about females' and males' abilities, personality traits, and social behavior.** Table 10.1 lists some characteristics that are part of the masculine and feminine stereotypes in North American society. The table

shows something you may have already noticed on your own. The male stereotype is much more flattering, suggesting that men have virtually cornered the market on competence and rationality. After all, everyone knows that females are more dependent, emotional, irrational, submissive, and talkative than males. Right? Or is that not the case? Let's look at the research.

How Do the Sexes Differ in Behavior?

Gender differences **are actual disparities between the sexes in typical behavior or average ability.** Mountains of research, literally thousands of studies, exist on gender differences. What does this research show? Are the stereotypes of males and females accurate? Well, the findings are a mixed bag. The research indicates that genuine behavioral differences *do* exist between the sexes and that people's stereotypes are not entirely inaccurate (Eagly, 1995; Swim, 1994). But the differ-

TABLE 10.1   Elements of Traditional Gender Stereotypes

Masculine	Feminine
Active	Aware of others' feelings
Adventurous	Considerate
Aggressive	Creative
Ambitious	Cries easily
Competitive	Devotes self to others
Dominant	Emotional
Independent	Enjoys art and music
Leadership qualities	Excitable in a crisis
Likes math and science	Expresses tender feelings
Makes decisions easily	Feelings hurt easily
Mechanical aptitude	Gentle
Not easily influenced	Home oriented
Outspoken	Kind
Persistent	Likes children
Self-confident	Neat
Skilled in business	Needs approval
Stands up under pressure	Tactful
Takes a stand	Understanding

SOURCE: Adapted from Ruble, T. L. (1983). Sex stereotypes: Issues of change in the 70s. *Sex Roles, 9,* 397–402. Copyright © 1983 Plenum Publishing Group. Adapted with kind permission of Springer Science and Business Media.

© Cengage Learning

ences are fewer in number, smaller in size, and far more complex than stereotypes suggest. As you'll see, only two of the differences mentioned in our opening true-false questions (the even-numbered items) have been largely supported by the research.

COGNITIVE ABILITIES

In the cognitive domain, it appears that there are three genuine—albeit very small—gender differences. First, on the average, females tend to exhibit slightly better *verbal skills* than males (Halpern et al., 2007). In particular, females seem stronger on tasks that require rapid access to semantic and other information in long-term memory (Halpern, 1997, 2004). Second, starting during high school, males show a slight advantage on tests of *mathematical ability*. When all students are compared, males' advantage is quite small. Indeed, in a recent review of research, Hyde and Mertz (2009) conclude that the gender gap in math has disappeared in the general population in the United States. Around the world, though, small to modest gender disparities are still seen in some countries, especially those that do not endorse equal opportunities for men and women (Else-Quest, Hyde, & Linn, 2010). Also, at the high end of the ability distribution, a gender gap is still found in the United States. About three to four times as many males as females manifest exceptional math skills (Wai et al., 2010). Third, starting in the grade-school years, males tend to score higher than females on most measures of *visual-spatial ability* (Halpern et al., 2007). The size of these gender differences varies from moderate to small depending on the exact nature of the spatial task. Males appear to be strongest on tasks that require visual transformations in working memory (Halpern, 2004).

SOCIAL BEHAVIOR

In regard to social behavior, research findings support the existence of some additional gender differences. First, studies indicate that males tend to be much more *physically aggressive* than females (Archer, 2005). This disparity shows up early in childhood. Its continuation into adulthood is supported by the fact that men account for a grossly disproportionate number of the violent crimes in our society (Kenrick, Trost, & Sundie, 2004). The findings on *verbal aggression* are more complex, as females appear to exhibit more relational aggression (snide remarks and so forth) (Archer, 2005). Second, there are gender differences in *nonverbal communication*. The evidence indicates that females are more sensitive than males to subtle nonverbal cues (Hall, Carter, & Horgan, 2000; Hampson, van Anders, & Mullin, 2006) and that they pay more attention to interpersonal information (Hall & Mast, 2008). Third, males are more *sexually active* than females in a variety of ways. For example, males have more permissive attitudes about casual, premarital, and extramarital sex (Baumeister, Catanese, & Vohs, 2001; Hyde, 2005a; see Chapter 9).

SOME QUALIFICATIONS

Although research has identified some genuine gender differences in behavior, bear in mind that these are group differences that indicate nothing about individuals. Essentially, research results compare the "average man" with the "average woman." However, you are—and every individual is—unique. The average female and male are ultimately figments of our imagination. Furthermore, the genuine group differences noted are relatively small (Hyde, 2005a, 2007). **Figure 10.15** shows how scores on a trait, perhaps verbal ability, might be distributed for men and women. Although the group averages are detectably different, you can see the great variability within each group (sex) and the huge overlap between the two group distributions.

Biological Origins of Gender Differences

What accounts for the development of gender differences? To what degree are

they the product of learning or of biology? This question is yet another manifestation of the *nature versus nurture* issue. Investigations of the biological origins of gender differences have centered on the evolutionary bases of behavior, hormones, and brain organization.

EVOLUTIONARY EXPLANATIONS

Evolutionary psychologists argue that gender differences in behavior reflect different natural selection pressures operating on males and females over the course of human history (Archer, 1996; Geary, 2007). For example, as we discussed in Chapter 9, males supposedly are more sexually active and permissive because they invest less than females in the process of procreation and can maximize their reproductive success by seeking many sexual partners (Schmitt, 2005; Webster, 2009). The gender gap in aggression is also explained in terms of reproductive fitness. Because females are more selective about mating than males, males have to engage in more competition for sexual partners than females do. Greater aggressiveness is thought to be adaptive for males in this competition for sexual access because it should foster social dominance over other males. It should also facilitate the acquisition of the material resources emphasized by females when evaluating potential partners (Campbell, 2005; Cummins, 2005). Evolutionary theorists assert that gender differences in spatial ability reflect

the division of labor in ancestral hunting-and-gathering societies in which males typically handled the hunting and females the gathering. Males' superiority on most spatial tasks has been attributed to the adaptive demands of hunting (Newcombe, 2007; Silverman & Choi, 2005; see Chapter 1).

Evolutionary analyses of gender differences are interesting, but controversial. On the one hand, it seems quite plausible that evolutionary forces could have led to some divergence between males and females in typical behavior. On the other hand, evolutionary hypotheses are highly speculative and difficult to test empirically (Eagly & Wood, 1999; Halpern, 1997). The crucial problem for some critics is that evolutionary analyses are so "flexible" they can be used to explain almost anything. For example, if the situation regarding spatial ability were reversed—if females scored higher than males—evolutionary theorists might attribute females' superiority to the adaptive demands of gathering food, weaving baskets, and making clothes—and it would be difficult to prove otherwise (Cornell, 1997).

THE ROLE OF HORMONES

Hormones play a key role in sexual differentiation during prenatal development. The high level of androgens (the principal class of male hormones) in males and the low level of androgens in

FIGURE 10.15

The nature of gender differences. Gender differences are group differences that indicate little about individuals because of the great overlap between the groups. For a given trait, one gender may score higher on the average, but far more variation occurs within each gender than between the genders.

females lead to the differentiation of male and female genital organs. The critical role of prenatal hormones becomes apparent when something interferes with normal prenatal hormonal secretions. About a half-dozen endocrine disorders can cause overproduction or underproduction of specific gonadal hormones during prenatal development. Scientists have also studied children born to mothers who were given an androgenlike drug to prevent miscarriage. The general trend in this research is that females exposed prenatally to abnormally high levels of androgens exhibit more male-typical behavior than other females do. Likewise, males exposed prenatally to abnormally low levels of androgens exhibit more female-typical behavior than other males (Hines, 2004).

These findings suggest that prenatal hormones contribute to the shaping of gender differences in humans. But there are some problems with this evidence (Basow, 1992; Fausto-Sterling, 1992; Jordan-Young, 2010). First, the evidence is much stronger for females than for males. Second, it's always dangerous to draw conclusions about the general population based on small samples of people who have abnormal conditions. However, a recent study that approached the issue in a new way circumvented both of these problems. In this study, the level of testosterone (a critical androgen) in

mothers' amniotic fluid was assessed and correlated with a later measure of their children's gender-typical play. Fetal testosterone levels were positively correlated with male-typical play in both boys and girls (Auyeung et al., 2009). These findings are important in that they are based on "normal" subjects from the general population and because they show similar trends for both males and females. Looking at the evidence as a whole, it does seem likely that prenatal hormones contribute to gender differences in behavior. However, a great deal remains to be learned.

DIFFERENCES IN BRAIN ORGANIZATION

Interpretive problems have also cropped up in efforts to link gender differences to specialization of the cerebral hemispheres in the brain (see **Figure 10.16**). As you may recall from Chapter 3, in most people the left hemisphere is more actively involved in verbal processing, whereas the right hemisphere is more active in visual-spatial processing (Gazzaniga, Ivry, & Mangum, 2009). After these findings surfaced, theorists began to wonder whether this division of labor in the brain might be related to gender differences in verbal and spatial skills. Consequently, they began looking for sex-related disparities in brain organization.

Some thought-provoking findings *have* been reported. For instance, some studies have found that *males tend to exhibit more cerebral specialization than females* (Boles, 2005; Voyer, 1996). In other words, there's a trend for males to depend more heavily than females do on the left hemisphere in verbal processing and more heavily on the right in spatial processing. Differences between males and females have also been found in the size of the corpus callosum, the band of fibers that connects the two hemispheres of the brain. Some studies suggest that *females tend to have a larger corpus callosum* (Gur & Gur, 2007;

FIGURE 10.16

The cerebral hemispheres and the corpus callosum. In this drawing the cerebral hemispheres have been "pulled apart" to reveal the corpus callosum, the band of fibers that connects the right and left halves of the brain. Research has shown that the right and left hemispheres are specialized to handle different types of cognitive tasks (see Chapter 3), leading some theorists to speculate that patterns of hemispheric specialization might contribute to gender differences in verbal and spatial abilities.

Corpus callosum

© Cengage Learning

Resnick, 2006). This might allow for better interhemispheric transfer of information, which, in turn, might underlie the less lateralized organization of females' brains (Innocenti, 1994). Thus, some theorists have concluded that differences between the sexes in brain organization are responsible for gender differences in verbal and spatial ability (Clements et al., 2006).

This idea is intriguing, but psychologists have a long way to go before they can explain gender differences in terms of right brain/left brain specialization. Studies have not been consistent in finding that males have more specialized brain organization than females (Kaiser et al., 2009). In fact, a recent meta-analysis of twenty-six neuroimaging studies concluded that there was no gender disparity in language lateralization (Sommer et al., 2008). Also, serious doubts have been raised about the finding that females have a larger corpus callosum (Fine, 2010;

© Aliaksei Lasevich/Shutterstock

Halpern et al., 2007). Moreover, even if these findings were replicated consistently, no one is really sure just how these findings would account for the observed gender differences in cognitive abilities (Fine, 2010).

In summary, researchers have made some intriguing progress in their efforts to document the biological roots of gender differences in behavior. However, the idea that "anatomy is destiny" has proven difficult to demonstrate. Many theorists remain convinced that gender differences are largely shaped by experience. Let's examine their evidence.

Environmental Origins of Gender Differences

All societies make efforts to train children about gender roles. *Gender roles* **are expectations about what is appropriate behavior for each sex.** Although gender roles are in a period of transition in modern Western society, there are still many disparities in how males and females are brought up. Investigators have identified three key processes involved in the development of gender roles: operant conditioning, observational learning, and self-socialization. First we'll examine these processes. Then we'll look at the principal sources of gender-role socialization: families, schools, and the media.

OPERANT CONDITIONING

In part, gender roles are shaped by the power of reward and punishment—the key processes in *operant conditioning* (see Chapter 6). Parents, teachers, peers, and others often reinforce (usually with tacit approval) "gender-appropriate" behavior and respond negatively to "gender-inappropriate" behavior (Bussey & Bandura, 1999; Matlin, 2008). If you're a man, you might recall getting hurt as a young boy and being told that "big boys don't cry." If you succeeded in inhibiting your crying, you may have earned an approving smile or even something tangible like an ice cream cone. The reinforcement probably strengthened your tendency to "act like a man" and suppress emotional displays. If

you're a woman, chances are your crying wasn't discouraged as gender-inappropriate. Studies suggest that fathers encourage and reward gender-appropriate behavior in their youngsters more than mothers do and that boys experience more pressure to behave in gender-appropriate ways than girls do (Levy, Taylor, & Gelman, 1995).

OBSERVATIONAL LEARNING

Observational learning (see Chapter 6) by children can lead to the imitation of adults' gender-appropriate behavior. Children imitate both males and females, but most children tend to imitate same-sex role models more than opposite-sex role models (Bussey & Bandura, 1984; Frey & Ruble, 1992). Thus, imitation often leads young girls to play with dolls, dollhouses, and toy stoves, while young boys are more likely to tinker with toy trucks, miniature gas stations, or tool kits.

SELF-SOCIALIZATION

Children themselves are active agents in their own gender-role socialization. Several *cognitive theories* of gender-role development emphasize self-socialization (Bem, 1985; Cross & Markus, 1993; Martin & Ruble, 2004). Self-socialization entails three steps. First, children learn to classify themselves as male or female and to recognize their sex as a permanent quality. Second, this self-categorization motivates them to value those characteristics and behaviors associated with their sex. Third, they strive to bring their behavior in line with what is considered gender-appropriate in their culture. In other words, children get involved in their own socialization. They work diligently to discover the rules that are supposed to govern their behavior.

© Jaimie Duplass/Shutterstock

SOURCES OF GENDER-ROLE SOCIALIZATION

There are three main sources of influence in gender-role socialization: families, schools, and the media. Of course, we are now in an era of transition in gender roles. Thus, the generalizations that follow may say more about how you were socialized than about how children will be socialized in the future.

Families A great deal of gender-role socialization takes place in the home (Berenbaum, Martin, & Ruble, 2008; Pomerantz, Ng, & Wang, 2004). For example, fathers engage in more "roughhousing" play with their sons than with their daughters, even in infancy (McBride-Chang & Jacklin, 1993). As children grow, boys and girls are encouraged to play with different types of toys (Freeman, 2007; Wood, Desmarais, & Gugula,

© Here's Looking at You/Brand X/
Jupiter Images

on gender (Cunningham, 2001). For example, girls wash dishes and boys mow the lawn.

Schools Schools and teachers clearly contribute to the socialization of gender roles (Berenbaum, Martin, & Ruble, 2008). The books that children use in learning to read can influence their ideas about what is suitable behavior for males and females (Diekman & Murnen, 2004). Traditionally, males have been more likely to be portrayed as clever, heroic, and adventurous in these books, while females have been more likely to be shown doing domestic chores. Preschool and grade-school teachers frequently reward gender-appropriate behavior in their pupils (Fagot et al., 1985; Ruble & Martin, 1998). Interestingly, teachers tend to pay greater attention to males, helping them, praising them, and scolding them more than females (Sadker & Sadker, 1994). Schools may play a key role in the gender gap in outstanding math performance, as Hyde and Mertz (2009) note that girls traditionally have been much less likely than boys to be encouraged to enroll in advanced math, chemistry, and physics courses.

2002). Generally, boys have less leeway to play with "feminine" toys than girls do with "masculine" toys. When children are old enough to help with household chores, the assignments tend to depend

Media Television and other mass media are another source of gender-role socialization (Bussey & Bandura, 2004). Although some improvement has occurred in recent years, television shows have traditionally depicted men and women in stereotypical ways (Galambos, 2004; Signorielli, 2001). Women are often portrayed as submissive, passive, and emotional. Men are more likely to be portrayed as independent, assertive, and competent. Even commercials contribute to the socialization of gender roles (Lippa, 2005; Signorielli, McLeod, & Healy, 1994). Recent research found an association between children's exposure to gender stereotyping in the media and their beliefs about gender roles (Oppliger, 2007).

Conclusion

As you can see, the findings on gender and behavior are complex and confusing. Nonetheless, the evidence does permit one very general conclusion—a conclusion that you have seen before and will see again. Taken as a whole, the research in this area suggests that biological factors and environmental factors both contribute to gender differences in behavior—as they do to all other aspects of development.

Are Fathers Essential to Children's Well-Being?

Are fathers essential for children to experience normal, healthy development? This question is currently the subject of heated debate. A number of social scientists have mounted a thought-provoking argument that father absence is the chief factor underlying a variety of modern social ills. For example, David Blankenhorn (1995) argues that "fatherlessness is the most harmful demographic trend of this generation. It is the leading cause of declining child well-being in our society" (p. 1). Expressing a similar view, David Popenoe (2009) maintains that "today's fatherlessness has led to social turmoil—damaged children, unhappy children, aimless children, children who strike back with pathological behavior and violence" (p. 192). The belief that fathers are crucial to healthy development has become widely accepted. This conventional wisdom has been strongly endorsed by both President George W. Bush and President Barack Obama, and it has guided government policy in a variety of areas.

The Basic Argument

What is the evidence for the proposition that fathers are essential to healthy development? Over the last 40 years, the proportion of children growing up without a father in the home has more than doubled. During the same time, we have seen dramatic increases in teenage pregnancy, juvenile delinquency, violent crime, drug abuse, eating disorders, teen suicide, and family dysfunction. Moreover, mountains of studies have demonstrated an association between father absence and an elevated risk for these problems. Summarizing this evidence, Popenoe (2009) asserts that "fatherless children have a risk factor two to three times that of fathered children for a wide range of negative out-

comes, including dropping out of high school, giving birth as a teenager, and becoming a juvenile delinquent" (p. 192). This leads him to infer that "fathers have a unique and irreplaceable role to play in child development" (p. 197). Working from this premise, Popenoe concludes, "If present trends continue, our society could be on the verge of committing social suicide" (p. 192). Echoing this dire conclusion, Blankenhorn (1995) comments that "to tolerate the trend of fatherlessness is to accept the inevitability of continued societal recession" (p. 222).

You might be thinking, "What's all the fuss about?" Surely, proclaiming the importance of fatherhood ought to be no more controversial than advocacy for motherhood or apple pie. But the assertion that a father is *essential* to a child's well-being has some interesting political implications. It suggests that heterosexual marriage is the only appropriate context in which to raise children and that other family configurations are fundamentally deficient. Based on this line of reasoning, some people have argued for new laws that would make it more difficult to obtain a divorce and have advocated other policies and programs that would favor traditional families over families headed by single mothers, cohabiting parents, and gay and lesbian parents (Silverstein & Auerbach, 1999). Not surprisingly, the belief that children need both a mother and a father has surfaced repeatedly in the legal wrangling over same-sex marriage. Thus, the question about the importance of fathers is creating a great deal of controversy because it is really a question about alternatives to traditional family structure.

Evaluating the Argument

In light of the far-reaching implications of the view that fathers are essential to normal development, it makes sense to subject this view to critical scrutiny. How could you use critical thinking skills to evaluate this argument? At least three previously discussed ideas seem pertinent.

First, it is important to recognize that the position that fathers are essential for healthy development rests on a foundation of correlational evidence. As we have seen repeatedly, *correlation is no assurance of causation*. Yes, there has been an increase in fatherlessness that has been paralleled by increases in teenage pregnancy, drug abuse, eating disorders, and other disturbing social problems. But think of all the other changes that have occurred in American culture over the last 40 years, such as the decline of organized religion, the growth of mass media, dramatic shifts in sexual mores, and so forth. Increased fatherlessness has co-varied with a host of other cultural trends. Thus, it is highly speculative to infer that father absence is the chief cause of most modern social problems.

Second, it always pays to think about whether there are *alternative explanations* for findings that you might have doubts about. What other factors might

Are fathers crucial to children's well-being? This seemingly simple question has sparked heated debate.

© Andresr/Shutterstock

account for the association between father absence and children's maladjustment? Think for a moment: What is the most frequent cause of father absence? Obviously, it is divorce. Divorces tend to be highly stressful events that disrupt children's entire lives. Although the evidence suggests that a majority of children seem to survive divorce without lasting detrimental effects, it is clear that divorce elevates youngsters' risk for a wide range of negative developmental outcomes (Amato, 2006; Amato & Dorius, 2010; Hetherington, 1999, 2003). Given that father absence and divorce are often intertwined, it is possible that the negative effects of divorce account for much of the association between father absence and social problems.

Are there any other alternative explanations for the correlation between fatherlessness and social maladies? Yes, critics point out that the prevalence of father absence co-varies with socioeconomic status: Father absence is much more common in low-income families (Anderson, Kohler, & Letiecq, 2002). Thus, the effects of father absence are entangled to some extent with the many powerful, malignant effects of poverty, which might account for much of the correlation between fatherlessness and negative outcomes (McLoyd, 1998).

A third possible strategy in thinking critically about the effects of father absence would be to ask *if there is contradictory evidence*. Once again, the answer is yes. Biblarz and Stacey (2010) reviewed studies comparing pairs of heterosexual parents against pairs of lesbian parents. If fathers are essential, the adjustment of children raised by heterosexual parents should be superior to that of children raised by lesbian parents. But the studies found negligible differences between these parental configurations.

A fourth possible strategy in thinking critically about the effects of father absence would be to look for some of the *fallacies in reasoning* introduced in Chapter 9 (irrelevant reasons, circular reasoning, slippery slope, weak analogies, and false dichotomy). A couple of the quotes from Popenoe and Blankenhorn were chosen to give you an opportunity to detect two of these fallacies in a new context. Take a look at the quotes once again and see whether you can spot the fallacies.

Popenoe's assertion that "if present trends continue, our society could be on the verge of social suicide" is an example of *slippery slope argumentation*, which involves predictions that if one allows X to happen, things will spin out of control and catastrophic events will follow. "Social suicide" is a little vague, but it sounds as if Popenoe is predicting that father absence will lead to the destruction of modern American culture. The other fallacy that you might have spotted was the *false dichotomy* apparent in Blankenhorn's assertion that "to tolerate the trend of fatherlessness is to accept the inevitability of continued societal recession." A false dichotomy creates an either-or choice between the position one wants to advocate (in this case, new social policies to reduce father absence) and some obviously horrible outcome that any sensible person would want to avoid (social decay), while ignoring other possible outcomes that might lie between these extremes.

In summary, we can find a number of flaws and weaknesses in the argument that fathers are *essential* to normal development. However, our critical evaluation of this argument *does not mean that fathers are unimportant*. Many types of evidence suggest that fathers generally make significant contributions to their children's development (Anderson et al., 2002; Phares, 1996; Rohner & Veneziano, 2001). We could argue with merit that fathers typically provide a substantial advantage for children that fatherless children do not have. But there is a crucial distinction between arguing that fathers *promote* normal, healthy development and arguing that fathers are *necessary* for normal, healthy development. If fathers are *necessary*, children who grow up without them could not achieve the same level of well-being as those who have fathers. It is clear, however, that a great many children from single-parent homes turn out just fine.

Fathers surely are important, and it seems likely that father absence *contributes* to a variety of problems in modern society. So, why do Blankenhorn (1995) and Popenoe (2009) argue for the much stronger conclusion—that fathers are *essential*? They appear to prefer the stronger conclusion because it raises much more serious questions about the viability of nontraditional family forms. Thus, they seem to want to advance a *political agenda* that champions traditional family values. They are certainly entitled to do so, but when research findings are used to advance a political agenda—whether conservative or liberal—a special caution alert should go off in your head. When a political agenda is at stake, it pays to scrutinize arguments with extra care, because research findings are more likely to be presented in a slanted fashion. The field of psychology deals with a host of complex questions that have profound implications for a wide range of social issues. The skills and habits of critical thinking can help you find your way through the maze of reasons and evidence that hold up the many sides of these complicated issues.

TABLE 10.2   Critical Thinking Skills Discussed in This Application

Skill	Description
Understanding the limitations of correlational evidence	The critical thinker understands that a correlation between two variables does not demonstrate that there is a causal link between the variables.
Looking for alternative explanations for findings and events	In evaluating explanations, the critical thinker explores whether there are other explanations that could also account for the findings or events under scrutiny.
Recognizing and avoiding common fallacies, such as irrelevant reasons, circular reasoning, slippery slope reasoning, weak analogies, and false dichotomies	The critical thinker is vigilant about conclusions based on unrelated premises, conclusions that are rewordings of premises, unwarranted predictions that things will spin out of control, superficial analogies, and contrived dichotomies.

© Cengage Learning

Progress Before Birth: Prenatal Development

10.1 Outline the major events of the three stages of prenatal development.

Prenatal development proceeds through the germinal (first 2 weeks), embryonic (2 weeks to 2 months), and fetal stages (2 months to birth) as the zygote becomes differentiated into a human organism. The embryonic stage is a period of great vulnerability, as most physiological structures are being formed. The fetal stage brings rapid growth as physiological systems mature. The fetus reaches the threshold of viability at around 23-26 weeks.

© Petit Format/Science Source/Photo Researchers, Inc.

10.2 Summarize the impact of environmental factors on prenatal development.

Maternal malnutrition during the prenatal period has been linked to birth complications and other subsequent problems. Maternal emotions can have an impact on prenatal development. Maternal use of illicit drugs can be dangerous to the unborn child. Even normal social drinking and routine tobacco use can be hazardous during prenatal development. A variety of maternal illnesses can interfere with prenatal development. Environmental toxins are also a source of concern. Recent evidence suggests that prenatal development can "program" the fetal brain in ways that influence vulnerability to various types of illness decades later.

The Wondrous Years of Early Childhood

10.3 Understand the role of maturation and cultural variations in motor development.

Early motor development is thought to depend primarily on maturation. However, infants' exploration and learning may play a larger role than previously realized. Developmental norms for motor skills and other types of development are only group averages. Cultural variations in the pacing of motor development demonstrate the potential importance of environment and learning.

10.4 Describe Harlow's and Bowlby's views on attachment, and discuss research on patterns of attachment.

Infants begin to show attachments around 6-8 months of age, when separation anxiety surfaces. Harry Harlow's work with monkeys undermined the reinforcement explanation of attachment. John Bowlby proposed an influential evolutionary theory that attachment relationships have survival value. Infant-mother attachments fall into three categories: secure, anxious-ambivalent, and avoidant. Research shows that attachment emerges out of an interplay between infant and mother. Cultural

© Nina Leen/Time Life Pictures/Getty Images

variations in childrearing can affect the patterns of attachment seen in a society, but secure attachment is predominant around the world.

10.5 Trace the development of human language during childhood.

The initial vocalizations by infants are similar across languages, but their babbling gradually begins to resemble the sounds from their surrounding language. Children typically utter their first words around their first birthday. A vocabulary spurt often begins at around 18 months. Most children begin to combine words by the end of their second year. Their early sentences are telegraphic. Over the next several years, children gradually learn the complexities of grammar.

Personality and Cognitive Development in Childhood

10.6 Describe the basic tenets of Erikson's theory and his stages of childhood personality development.

Like other stage theories, Erik Erikson's theory assumes that individuals must progress through a series of specified stages in a particular order and that development is marked by major discontinuities. Erikson's theory of personality development proposes that individuals evolve through eight stages over the life span. In each stage the person wrestles with two opposing tendencies evoked by that stage's psychosocial crisis. Erikson's four stages during childhood are thought to determine the degree to which children exhibit trust, autonomy, initiative, and industriousness.

10.7 Outline Piaget's stages of cognitive development, and evaluate the notion that some cognitive abilities may be innate.

The key advance during the sensorimotor period is the child's gradual recognition of the permanence of objects. The preoperational period is marked by certain deficiencies in thinking—notably, centration, irreversibility, and egocentrism. During the concrete operations period, children develop the ability to perform operations on mental representations. The stage of formal operations ushers in more abstract, systematic, and logical thought. Piaget may have underestimated some aspects of children's cognitive development, as well as the impact of culture and environment. Recent research has shown that infants appear to understand surprisingly complex concepts that they have had virtually no opportunity to learn about.

Stage 1 Sensorimotor period: Coordination of sensory input and motor responses; development of object permanence — Birth to 2 years

Stage 2 Preoperational period: Development of symbolic thought marked by irreversibility, centration, and egocentrism — 2 to 7 years

Stage 3 Concrete operational period: Mental operations applied to concrete events; mastery of conservation, hierarchical classification — 7 to 11 years

Stage 4 Formal operational period: Mental operations, applied to abstract ideas; logical, systematic thinking — Age 11 through adulthood

© Cengage Learning

10.8 Discuss Kohlberg's stages of moral development and criticism of his theory.

According to Kohlberg, moral reasoning progresses through six stages that are related to age and determined by cognitive development. Preconventional thinking emphasizes external authority. Conventional moral reasoning focuses on adherence to social order. Postconventional reasoning involves working out a personal code of ethics. Age-related progress in moral reasoning has been found in research, although a great deal of overlap occurs between adjacent stages, and Kohlberg's theory is more culture-specific than he realized.

The Transition of Adolescence

10.9 Review the physiological changes of puberty, and summarize research on neural development in adolescence.

The growth spurt at puberty is a prominent event involving the development of reproductive maturity and secondary sex characteristics. Generational changes have been seen in the timing of puberty. Girls who mature early and boys who mature late experience more subjective distress with the transition to adolescence. However, in both sexes, early sexual maturation is associated with a greater variety of behavioral problems. During adolescence neurons are becoming more myelinated, while synaptic pruning continues to sculpt neural networks. The prefrontal cortex, which has been characterized as an executive control center, appears to be the last area of the brain to mature fully. This reality may contribute to adolescent risk taking.

Prefrontal cortex

© RimDream/Shutterstock

© Cengage Learning

10.10 Discuss identity formation in adolescence and the stage of emerging adulthood.

According to Erik Erikson, the key challenge of adolescence is to make some progress toward a sense of identity. James Marcia identified four patterns of identity formation: foreclosure, moratorium, identity diffusion, and identity achievement. Jeffrey Arnett argues that we ought to recognize the existence of a new developmental stage in modern societies, which he has christened emerging adulthood. Central features of this stage include feeling in between adolescence and adulthood and experiencing continued identity formation.

The Expanse of Adulthood

10.11 Discuss personality development in adulthood, and trace typical transitions in family relations during the adult years.

During adulthood, personality is marked by both stability and change, as percentile scores remain stable, but mean raw scores change in predictable ways. Agreeableness and conscientiousness tend to increase in the adult years, while extraversion and openness to experience tend to decline. Those who move successfully through the three stages of adulthood posited by Erik Erikson should develop intimacy, generativity, and integrity. Premarital cohabitation used to be predictive of an increased likelihood of marital dissolution later, but the situation seems to be changing. Difficulty adjusting to marriage is more likely when spouses have different role expectations, especially about housework. The transition to parenthood can be stressful, but realistic expectations can help.

10.12 Describe the physical changes associated with aging, and summarize information on Alzheimer's disease.

During adulthood, age-related physiological transitions include changes in appearance, sensory losses (especially in vision and hearing), and hormonal changes. Drastic mental decline is not a part of the normal aging

process, but dementia is seen in about 5%-8% of people ages 65-70 and 15%-20% of those aged 75-80. Alzheimer's disease has a subtle onset marked by chronic forgetting of newly learned information, followed by a progressive deterioration over 8-10 years. The causes of this debilitating disease are not well understood, although genetic factors and chronic inflammation appear to contribute.

10.13 Understand how intelligence, memory, and mental speed change in later adulthood.

Many studies have found decreases in older adults' memory capabilities. Mental speed declines in late adulthood, but many people remain productive well into old age. Some studies suggest that high levels of mental activity in late adulthood can delay the typical age-related declines in cognitive functioning.

Reflecting on the Chapter's Themes

10.14 Identify the five unifying themes highlighted in this chapter.

This chapter showed that psychology is theoretically diverse, that psychology evolves in a sociohistorical context, that multifactorial causation is the norm, and that culture affects many aspects of behavior, but above all else, it demonstrated that heredity and environment jointly mold behavior.

PERSONAL APPLICATION
Understanding Gender Differences

10.15 Summarize evidence on gender differences in behavior, and assess the significance of these differences.

Gender differences in behavior are fewer in number than gender stereotypes suggest. In the cognitive domain, research reviews suggest that there are genuine gender differences in verbal ability, mathematical ability, and spatial ability. In regard to social behavior, differences have been found in aggression, nonverbal communication, and sexual behavior. But most gender differences in behavior are very small in magnitude.

10.16 Explain how biological and environmental factors are thought to contribute to gender differences.

Evolutionary theorists maintain that gender differences exist because males and females have confronted different adaptive demands over the course of human history. Extensive evidence suggests that prenatal hormones contribute to human gender differences. Research linking gender differences to cerebral specialization is intriguing, but highly speculative. A vast research literature shows that gender differences are shaped by socialization processes. Operant conditioning, observational learning, and self-socialization contribute to the development of gender differences. Families, schools, and the media are among the main sources of gender-role socialization.

CRITICAL THINKING APPLICATION
Are Fathers Essential to Children's Well-being?

10.17 Clarify and critique the argument that fathers are essential for healthy development.

Some social scientists have argued that father absence is the chief cause of a number of social problems and that fathers are essential for normal, healthy development. Critics note that all the relevant data are correlational, making causal inferences speculative. They also argue that there are contradictory data and alternative explanations for the association between father absence and negative developmental outcomes.

11 Personality

PARADOX

Personality tests have a number of shortcomings and weaknesses, but they remain invaluable measurement instruments for both research and clinical work.

Richard Branson was sure that he was about to die. He was high above the Atlantic Ocean, alone in a capsule attached to the biggest balloon in the world. Per Lindstrand, the balloon's pilot, was somewhere in the icy waves far below. He and Branson had just become the first people ever to cross the Atlantic in a hot-air balloon. But when an emergency landing at sea failed, Lindstrand had leaped into the water. Before Branson could follow, the balloon had shot back up into the sky. Now Branson—who had never flown in a balloon before his all-too-brief training for the trip—was stranded in midair with no clear idea how to save himself.

Hastily Branson scribbled a note to his family: "I love you." Then he began trying to vent the huge balloon in a desperate attempt to guide it safely earthward. Much to his own surprise, he was able to get close enough to the sea to jump for it. A rescue helicopter plucked him out of the waves. (Lindstrand was saved by a passing fisherman.)

After this frightening brush with death, Branson swore that he would never risk his life so foolishly again. Yet three years later, he and Lindstrand were at it again. This time they attempted to become the first people to cross the Pacific in a hot-air balloon. The trip turned into another terrifying ordeal. At one point the balloon caught fire when they were thousands of feet above empty ocean—and once again they were nearly killed. But that didn't stop them from planning their next exploit—trying to become the first hot-air balloonists to fly completely around the world (Branson, 2005; Brown, 1998).

When people describe Richard Branson, they are apt to use words such as *adventurous, brave, daring, impulsive,* and *reckless.* These are the kinds of words used to characterize what we call "personality." And Branson—a self-made billionaire and one of the richest people in the world—may be as famous for his exuberant personality as he is for his immense wealth.

A high school dropout, Branson is the founder of the Virgin group of companies, including the Virgin Atlantic airline and Virgin Galactic, which aims to become the first company to fly tourists into space. Branson is a brash, shrewd, and relentless entrepreneur who loves cutting a deal. But he also loves parties, practical jokes, and flamboyant publicity stunts. Most of all, he relishes finding new fields to conquer.

Most people would agree that Richard Branson has an unusual personality. But what exactly *is* personality? And why are personalities so different? Why is one person daring, while another is timid? Why is one person high-spirited and outgoing, while another is quiet and shy? Was Richard Branson born with the self-confidence and daring he is renowned for, or were

Richard Branson, the founder of the Virgin group of companies, clearly manifests a powerful and unusual personality. But everyone has his or her own unique personality, which makes the study of personality a fascinating area of inquiry in psychology.

environment and learning critical in shaping his personality? Consider that Branson's parents stressed the importance of being strong and independent, starting at an early age. But perhaps the roots of Branson's personality lie in biological inheritance. Branson (2005) describes his mother as a woman of dazzling energy and fierce determination who also has a taste for adventure. During World War II, she talked her way into pilot training on the condition that she disguise herself as a boy. Maybe Branson's genetic makeup is responsible for his being an "adrenaline junkie."

Psychologists have approached questions like these from a variety of perspectives. Traditionally, the study of personality has been dominated by "grand theories" that attempt to explain a great many facets of behavior. Our discussion will reflect this emphasis, as we'll devote most of our time to the sweeping theories of Freud, Skinner, Rogers, and several others. In recent decades, however, the study of personality has shifted toward narrower research programs that examine specific issues related to personality. This trend is reflected in our review of biological, cultural, and other contemporary approaches to personality in the last several sections of the chapter. In the Personal Application, we'll examine how psychological tests are used to measure aspects of personality. The Critical Thinking Application will explore how hindsight bias can taint people's analyses of personality.

The Nature of Personality

KEY LEARNING GOALS

11.1 Clarify the meaning of personality and personality traits.

11.2 Describe the five-factor model of personality and the relationship between the Big Five traits and life outcomes.

Personality is a complex hypothetical construct that has been defined in a variety of ways. Let's take a closer look at the concepts of personality and personality traits.

Defining Personality: Consistency and Distinctiveness

What does it mean to say that someone has an optimistic personality? This assertion indicates that the person has a fairly *consistent tendency* to behave in a cheerful, hopeful, enthusiastic way, looking at the bright side of things across a wide variety of situations. Although no one is entirely consistent in behavior, this quality of *consistency across situations* lies at the core of the concept of personality.

Distinctiveness is also central to the concept of personality. Personality is used to explain why everyone does not act the same way in similar situations. If you were stuck in an elevator with three people, each might react differently. One might crack jokes to relieve tension. Another might make ominous predictions that "we'll never get out of here." The third person might calmly think about how to escape. These varied reactions to the same situation occur because each person has a different personality. Each person has traits that are seen in other people, but each individual has his or her own distinctive *set* of personality traits.

In summary, the concept of personality is used to explain (1) the stability in a person's behavior over time and across situations (consistency) and (2) the behavioral differences among people reacting to the same situation (distinctiveness). We can combine these ideas into the following definition: **Personality refers to an individual's unique set of consistent behavioral traits.** Let's explore the concept of *traits* in more detail.

© iodrakon/Shutterstock

Personality Traits: Dispositions and Dimensions

Everyone makes remarks like "Jan is very *conscientious*." Or you might assert that "Jamaal is too *timid* to succeed in that job." These descriptive statements refer to personality traits. **A *personality trait* is a durable disposition to behave in a particular way in a variety of situations.** Adjectives such as *honest, dependable, moody, impulsive, suspicious, anxious, excitable, domineering,* and *friendly* describe dispositions that represent personality traits. People use an enormous number of these trait terms to describe one another's personality. One prominent personality theorist, Gordon Allport (1937, 1961), went through an unabridged dictionary and identified over 4500 personality traits!

Most approaches to personality assume that some traits are more basic than others. According to this notion, a small number of fundamental traits determine other, more superficial traits. For example, a person's tendency to be impulsive, restless, irritable, boisterous, and impatient might all be derived from a more basic tendency to be excitable. A number of theorists have taken on the challenge of identifying the basic traits that form the core of personality. In recent decades, the most influential model has been the *five-factor model of personality,* which we turn to next.

The Five-Factor Model of Personality Traits

Robert McCrae and Paul Costa (1987, 1997, 2003, 2008) have used elaborate statistical methods to identify the crucial dimensions that underlie the diverse personality traits that people exhibit. McCrae and Costa maintain that most personality traits are derived from just five higher-order traits that have come to be known as the "Big Five" (see **Figure 11.1**):

- *Extraversion.* People who score high in extraversion are characterized as outgoing, sociable, upbeat, friendly, assertive, and gregarious. They also have a more positive outlook on life and are motivated to pursue social contact, intimacy, and interdependence (Wilt & Revelle, 2009).

- *Neuroticism.* People who score high in neuroticism tend to be anxious, hostile, self-conscious, insecure, and vulnerable. They also tend to exhibit more impulsiveness and emotional instability than others (Widiger, 2009).

- *Openness to experience.* Openness is associated with curiosity, flexibility, vivid fantasy, imaginativeness, artistic sensitivity, and unconventional attitudes. People who are high in openness also tend to be tolerant of ambiguity and have less need for closure on issues than others (McCrae & Sutin, 2009).

- *Agreeableness.* Those who score high in agreeableness tend to be sympathetic, trusting, cooperative, modest, and straightforward. Agreeableness is also correlated with empathy and helping behavior (Graziano & Tobin, 2009).

- *Conscientiousness.* Conscientious people tend to be diligent, disciplined, well-organized, punctual, and dependable. Conscientiousness is associated with strong self-discipline and the ability to regulate oneself effectively (Roberts et al., 2009).

FIGURE 11.1
The five-factor model of personality.
Trait models attempt to break personality down into its basic dimensions. McCrae and Costa (1985, 1987, 1997) maintain that personality can be described adequately with the five higher-order traits identified here, which are widely referred to as the "Big Five."

Correlations have been found between the Big Five traits and quite a variety of important life outcomes (Ozer & Benet-Martinez, 2006). For instance, higher grades (GPA) in both high school and college are associated with higher conscientiousness, primarily because conscientious students work harder (Noftle & Robins, 2007). Several of the Big Five traits are associated with occupational attainment (career success). Extraversion and conscientiousness are positive predictors of occupational attainment, whereas neuroticism is a negative predictor (Roberts, Caspi, & Moffitt, 2003). The likelihood of divorce can also be predicted by personality traits, as neuroticism elevates the probability of divorce, whereas agreeableness and conscientiousness reduce it (Roberts et al., 2007). Finally, and perhaps most important, two of the Big Five traits are related to health and mortality over the course of the life span. Neuroticism is associated with an elevated prevalence of physical and mental disorders (Lahey, 2009; Widiger, 2009), whereas conscientiousness is correlated with the experience of less illness and with reduced mortality (Kern & Friedman, 2008). In other words, conscientious people live longer than others!

McCrae and Costa maintain that personality can be described adequately by measuring the basic traits that they've identified. Their bold claim has been supported in many studies by other researchers, and the Big Five model has become the dominant conception of personality structure in contemporary psychology (John, Naumann, & Soto, 2008; McCrae, 2005). However, some theorists have argued that more than five traits are necessary to account for most of the variation seen in human personality (Boyle, 2008; Lee & Ashton, 2008).

The debate about how many dimensions are necessary to describe personality is likely to continue. As you'll see throughout the chapter, the study of personality is an area in psychology that has a long history of "dueling theories." We'll divide these diverse personality theories into four broad groups that share certain assumptions, emphases, and interests: (1) psychodynamic perspectives, (2) behavioral perspectives, (3) humanistic perspectives, and (4) biological perspectives. We'll begin our discussion of personality theories by examining the ideas of Sigmund Freud.

Psychodynamic Perspectives

Psychodynamic theories include all the diverse theories descended from the work of Sigmund Freud that focus on unconscious mental forces. Freud inspired many scholars who followed in his intellectual footsteps. Some of these followers simply refined and updated Freud's theory. Others veered off in new directions and established independent, albeit related, schools of thought. Today, the psychodynamic umbrella covers a large collection of loosely related theories that we can only sample in this text. In this section, we'll examine the ideas of Sigmund Freud in some detail. Then we'll take a briefer look at the psychodynamic theories of Carl Jung and Alfred Adler.

Freud's Psychoanalytic Theory

[PSYKTREK 10a]

Born in 1856, Sigmund Freud grew up in a middle-class Jewish home in Vienna, Austria. Freud lived in the Victorian era, which was marked by sexual repression. His outlook was also affected by World War I, which devastated Europe. Freud was a physician specializing in neurology when he began his medical practice in Vienna toward the end of the 19th century. Like other neurologists in his era, he often treated people troubled by nervous problems such as irrational fears, obsessions, and anxieties. Eventually he devoted himself to the treatment of mental disorders using an innovative procedure he had developed, which he called *psychoanalysis*. It required lengthy verbal interactions with patients during which Freud probed deeply into their lives (as we'll learn more about in Chapter 15).

Freud's (1901, 1924, 1940) *psychoanalytic theory* grew out of his decades of interactions with his clients in psychoanalysis. Psychoanalytic theory attempts to explain personality, motivation, and psychological disorders by focusing on the influence of early childhood experiences, on unconscious motives and conflicts, and on the methods people use to cope with their sexual and aggressive urges.

Most of Freud's contemporaries were uncomfortable with his theory, for at least three reasons. First, in arguing that people's behavior is governed by unconscious factors of which they are unaware, Freud made the disconcerting suggestion that individuals are not masters of their own minds. Second, in claiming that adult personalities are shaped by childhood experiences and other factors beyond one's control, he suggested that people are not masters of their own destinies. Third, by emphasizing the importance of how people cope with their sexual urges, he offended those who held the conservative, Victorian values of his time. Thus, Freud endured a great deal of criticism, condemnation, and outright ridicule, even after his work began to attract favorable attention. Let's examine the ideas that generated so much controversy.

Sigmund Freud

© National Library of Medicine

"No one who, like me, conjures up the most evil of those half-tamed demons that inhabit the human beast, and seeks to wrestle with them, can expect to come through the struggle unscathed."

STRUCTURE OF PERSONALITY

[PSYKTREK 10a]

Freud divided personality structure into three components: the id, the ego, and the superego. He saw a person's behavior as the outcome of interactions among these three components.

The *id* **is the primitive, instinctive component of personality that operates according to the pleasure principle.** Freud referred to the id as the reservoir of psychic energy. By this he meant that the id houses the raw biological urges (to eat, sleep, defecate, copulate, and so on) that energize human behavior. The id operates according to **the *pleasure principle,* which demands immediate gratification of its urges.** The id engages in *primary-process thinking,* which is primitive, illogical, irrational, and fantasy oriented.

The *ego* **is the decision-making component of personality that operates according to the reality principle.** The ego mediates between the id, with its forceful desires for immediate satisfaction, and the external social world, with its expectations and norms regarding suitable behavior. The ego considers social realities—society's norms, etiquette, rules, and customs—in deciding how to behave. The ego is guided by **the *reality* *principle,* which seeks to delay gratification of the id's urges until appropriate outlets and situations can be found.** In short, to stay out of trouble, the ego often works to tame the unbridled desires of the id.

In the long run, the ego wants to maximize gratification, just as the id does. However, the ego engages in *secondary-process thinking,* which is relatively rational, realistic, and oriented toward problem solving. Thus, the ego strives to avoid negative consequences from society and its representatives (for example, punishment by parents or teachers) by behaving "properly." It also attempts to achieve long-range goals that sometimes require putting off gratification.

While the ego concerns itself with practical realities, **the *superego* is the moral component of personality that incorporates social standards about what represents right and wrong.** Throughout their lives, but especially during childhood, people receive training about what constitutes good and bad behavior, and many social norms regarding morality are eventually internalized. The superego emerges out of the ego at around 3 to 5 years of age. In some people, the superego can become irrationally demanding in its striving for moral perfection, and they become plagued by excessive feelings of guilt.

According to Freud, the id, ego, and superego are distributed differently across three levels of awareness, which we'll describe next.

LEVELS OF AWARENESS

PsykTrek 10a

Perhaps Freud's most enduring insight was his recognition of how unconscious forces can influence behavior. He inferred the existence of the unconscious from a variety of observations that he made with his patients. For example, he noticed that "slips of the tongue" often revealed a person's true feelings (hence the expression "Freudian slip"). He also realized that his patients' dreams often expressed hidden desires. Most important, through psychoanalysis he often helped patients discover feelings and conflicts they had previously been unaware of.

Freud contrasted the unconscious with the conscious and preconscious, creating three levels of awareness. **The *conscious* consists of whatever one is aware of at a particular point in time.** For example, at this moment your conscious may include the train of thought in this text and a dim awareness in the back of your mind that your eyes are getting tired and you're beginning to get hungry. **The *preconscious* contains material just beneath the surface of awareness that can easily be retrieved.** Examples might include your middle name, what you had for supper last night, or an argument you had with a friend yesterday. **The *unconscious* contains thoughts, memories, and desires that are well below the surface of conscious awareness but that nonetheless exert great influence on behavior.** Examples of material that might be found in your unconscious include a forgotten trauma from childhood, hidden feelings of hostility toward a parent, and repressed sexual desires.

Freud's conception of the mind is often compared to an iceberg that has most of its mass hidden beneath the water's surface (see **Figure 11.2** on the next page). He believed that the unconscious (the mass below the surface) is much larger than the conscious or preconscious. As you can see in **Figure 11.2**, he proposed that the ego and superego operate at all three levels of awareness. In contrast, the id is entirely unconscious, expressing its urges at a conscious level through the ego. Of course, the id's desires for immediate satisfaction often trigger internal conflicts with the ego and superego. These conflicts play a key role in Freud's theory.

CONFLICT AND THE TYRANNY OF SEX AND AGGRESSION

PsykTrek 10a

Freud assumed that behavior is the outcome of an ongoing series of internal conflicts. He saw internal battles between the id, ego, and superego as routine. Why? Because the id wants to gratify its urges immediately, but the norms of civilized society frequently

Freud's psychoanalytic theory was based on decades of clinical work. He treated a great many patients in the consulting room pictured here. The room contains numerous artifacts from other cultures—and the original psychoanalytic couch.

Reality Check

Misconception
People are generally aware of the factors that influence their behavior.

Reality
Freud's insight from over a century ago, that people are often unaware of the unconscious factors that shape their behavior, has proven prophetic. Decades of research on perception, cognition, and social behavior have repeatedly demonstrated that unconscious goals, attitudes, and thoughts exert enormous influence over human behavior (Bargh, Gollwitzer, & Oettingen, 2010; Dijksterhuis, 2010).

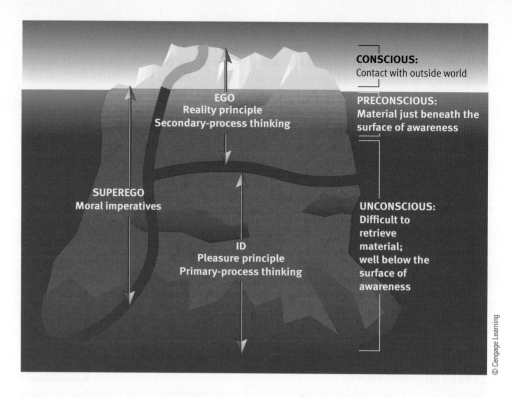

FIGURE 11.2

Freud's model of personality structure.
Freud theorized that people have three levels of awareness: the conscious, the preconscious, and the unconscious. The enormous size of the unconscious is often dramatized by comparing it to the portion of an iceberg that lies beneath the water's surface. Freud also divided personality structure into three components—id, ego, and superego—which operate according to different principles and exhibit different modes of thinking. In Freud's model, the id is entirely unconscious, but the ego and superego operate at all three levels of awareness.

"ALL I WANT FROM THEM IS A SIMPLE MAJORITY ON THINGS."

dictate otherwise. For example, your id might feel an urge to clobber a co-worker who constantly irritates you. However, society frowns on such behavior, so your ego would try to hold this urge in check. Hence, you would find yourself in conflict. You may be experiencing conflict at this very moment; in Freudian terms, your id may be secretly urging you to abandon reading this chapter so that you can fix a snack and watch some television. Your ego may be weighing this appealing option against your society-induced need to excel in school.

Freud believed that internal conflicts are a routine part of people's lives. He asserted that conflicts centering on sexual and aggressive impulses are especially likely to have far-reaching consequences. Why did he emphasize sex and aggression? Two reasons were prominent in his thinking. First, he thought that sex and aggression are subject to more complex and ambiguous social controls than other basic motives. Thus, people often get inconsistent messages about what's appropriate. Second, he noted that the aggressive and sexual drives are thwarted more regularly than other basic, biological urges. Think about it: If you get hungry or thirsty, you can simply head for a nearby vending machine or a drinking fountain. But when you see an attractive person who inspires lustful urges, you don't normally walk over and propose hooking up in a nearby broom closet. Freud ascribed great importance to these needs because social norms dictate that they're routinely frustrated.

ANXIETY AND DEFENSE MECHANISMS

PSYKTREK 10a

Most internal conflicts are trivial and are quickly resolved. Occasionally, however, a conflict will linger for days, months, or even years, creating internal tension. More often than not, such prolonged and troublesome conflicts involve sexual and aggressive impulses that society wants to tame. These conflicts are often played out entirely in the unconscious. Although you may not be aware of these unconscious battles, they can produce *anxiety* that slips to the surface of conscious awareness.

The arousal of anxiety is a crucial event in Freud's theory of personality functioning. Anxiety is distressing, so people try to rid themselves of this unpleasant emotion any way they can. This effort to ward off anxiety often involves the use of defense mechanisms. **Defense mechanisms are largely unconscious reactions that protect a person from unpleasant emotions such as anxiety and guilt.** Typically, they're mental maneuvers that work through self-deception (see **Table 11.1**). Consider *rationalization,* **which is creating false but plausible excuses to justify unacceptable behavior.** For example, after cheating someone in a business transaction, you might reduce your guilt by rationalizing that "everyone does it."

According to Freud, the most basic and widely used defense mechanism is repression. *Repression* **is keeping distressing thoughts and feelings buried in the unconscious.** People tend to repress desires that make them feel guilty, conflicts that make them anxious, and memories that are painful. As pointed out in Chapter 7, repression has been called "motivated forgetting." If you forget a dental appointment or the name of someone you don't like, repression may be at work.

Self-deception can also be seen in projection and displacement. *Projection* **is attributing one's own thoughts, feelings, or motives to another.** Usually, the thoughts one projects onto others are those that would make one feel guilty. For example, if lusting for a co-worker makes you feel guilty, you might attribute any latent sexual tension between the two of you to the *other person's* desire to seduce you. *Displacement* **is diverting emotional feelings (usually anger) from their original source to a substitute target.** If your boss gives you a hard time at work and you come home and slam the door, kick the dog, and scream at your spouse, you're displacing your anger onto irrelevant targets. Unfortunately, social constraints often force people to hold back their anger, and they end up lashing out at the people they love the most.

Other prominent defense mechanisms include reaction formation, regression, and identification. *Reaction formation* **is behaving in a way that's exactly the opposite of one's true feelings.** Guilt about sexual desires often leads to reaction formation. Freud theorized that many homophobic males who ridicule homosexuals are defending against their own latent homosexual impulses. The telltale sign of reaction formation is the exaggerated quality of the opposite behavior. *Regression* **is a reversion to immature patterns of behavior.** When anxious about their self-worth, some adults respond with childish boasting and bragging (as opposed to subtle efforts to impress others). For example, a fired executive having difficulty finding a new job might start making

TABLE 11.1 Defense Mechanisms, with Examples

Defense Mechanism	Definition	Example
Repression	Keeping distressing thoughts and feelings buried in the unconscious	A traumatized soldier has no recollection of the details of a close brush with death.
Projection	Attributing one's own thoughts, feelings, or motives to another	A woman who dislikes her boss thinks she likes her boss but feels that the boss doesn't like her.
Displacement	Diverting emotional feelings (usually anger) from their original source to a substitute target	After a parental scolding, a young girl takes her anger out on her little brother.
Reaction formation	Behaving in a way that is exactly the opposite of one's true feelings	A parent who unconsciously resents a child spoils the child with outlandish gifts.
Regression	A reversion to immature patterns of behavior	An adult has a temper tantrum when he doesn't get his way.
Rationalization	Creating false but plausible excuses to justify unacceptable behavior	A student watches TV instead of studying, saying that "additional study wouldn't do any good anyway."
Identification	Bolstering self-esteem by forming an imaginary or real alliance with some person or group	An insecure young man joins a fraternity to boost his self-esteem.
Sublimation	Channeling unconscious, unacceptable impulses into socially acceptable or admirable activities	A person obsessed with sex becomes a sex therapist and helps others with their sexual problems

© Cengage Learning

ridiculous statements about his incomparable talents and achievements. Such bragging is regressive when it's marked by massive exaggerations that virtually anyone can see through. *Identification* **is bolstering self-esteem by forming an imaginary or real alliance with some person or group.** Young people often shore up fragile feelings of self-worth by identifying with rock stars, movie stars, or famous athletes. Adults may join exclusive country clubs or civic organizations as a means of boosting their self-esteem via identification.

Finally, Freud described the defense of *sublimation,* **which occurs when unconscious, unacceptable impulses are channeled into socially acceptable, perhaps even admirable, behaviors.** For example, intense aggressive impulses might be rechanneled by taking up boxing or football. Freud believed that many creative endeavors, such as painting, poetry, and sculpture, are sublimations of sexual urges. For instance, he argued that Leonardo da Vinci's painting of Madonna figures was a sublimation of his longing for intimacy with his mother (Freud, 1910). By definition, sublimation is regarded as a relatively healthy defense mechanism.

DEVELOPMENT: PSYCHOSEXUAL STAGES

PSYKTREK 10a

Freud made the rather startling claim that the basic foundation of an individual's personality has been laid down by the tender age of 5. To shed light on these crucial early years, Freud formulated a stage theory of development. He emphasized how young children deal with their immature but powerful sexual urges (he used the term *sexual* in a general way to refer to many urges for physical pleasure). According to Freud, these urges shift in focus as children progress from one stage of development to another. Indeed, the names for the stages (oral, anal, genital, and so on) are based on where children are focusing their erotic energy during that period. Thus, *psychosexual stages* **are developmental periods with a characteristic sexual focus that leave their mark on adult personality.**

Freud theorized that each psychosexual stage has its own unique developmental challenges or tasks (see **Table 11.2**). The way these challenges are handled supposedly shapes personality. The notion of

---

Concept Check 11.1

Identifying Defense Mechanisms

Check your understanding of defense mechanisms by identifying specific defenses in the story below. Each example of a defense mechanism is underlined, with a number beneath it. Write in the defense at work in each case in the numbered spaces after the story. The answers are in Appendix A.

My boyfriend recently broke up with me after we had dated seriously for several years. At first, I cried a great deal and <u>locked myself in my room, where I pouted endlessly.</u> *I was sure that my former boyfriend felt as miserable as I did.* <u>I told several friends that he was probably lonely and depressed.</u> *Later, I decided that I hated him.* <u>I was happy about the breakup and talked about how much I was going to enjoy my newfound freedom.</u> *I went to parties and socialized a great deal and just forgot about him.* <u>It's funny—at one point I couldn't even remember his phone number!</u> *Then I started pining for him again. But eventually I began to look at the situation more objectively. I realized that he had many faults and that* <u>we were bound to break up sooner or later, so I was better off without him.</u>

1. _____   4. _____

2. _____   5. _____

3. _____

fixation plays an important role in this process. *Fixation* **involves a failure to move forward from one stage to another as expected.** Essentially, the child's development stalls for a while. Fixation can be caused by excessive *gratification* of needs at a particular stage or by excessive *frustration* of those needs. Either way, fixations left over from childhood affect adult personality. Generally, fixation leads to an overemphasis on the psychosexual needs prominent during the fixated stage. Freud described a series of five psychosexual stages. Let's examine some of the highlights in this sequence and how fixation might occur.

Oral Stage The oral stage encompasses the first year of life. During this period, the main source of erotic stimulation is the mouth (in biting, sucking, chewing, and so on). In Freud's view, the way the child's feeding experience is handled is crucial to subsequent development. He attributed considerable importance to the manner in which the child is weaned from the breast or the bottle. According to Freud, fixation at the oral stage could form the basis for obsessive eating or smoking (among many other things) later in life.

Anal Stage In their second year, children get their erotic pleasure from their bowel movements, through either the expulsion or retention of feces. The significant event at this time is toilet training, which represents society's first systematic effort to regulate the child's biological urges. Severely punitive toilet training leads to a variety of possible outcomes. For example, excessive punishment might produce a latent feeling of hostility toward the "trainer," usually the mother. This hostility might generalize to women as a class. Another possibility is that heavy reliance on punitive measures could lead to an association between genital concerns and the anxiety that the punishment arouses. This genital anxiety derived from severe toilet training could evolve into anxiety about sexual activities later in life.

© Finnbarr Webster/Alamy

Phallic Stage In the third through fifth years, the genitals become the focus for the child's erotic energy, largely through self-stimulation. During this pivotal stage, the *Oedipal complex* emerges. That is, little boys develop an erotically tinged preference for their mother. They also feel hostility toward their father, whom they view as a competitor for mom's affection. Similarly, little girls develop a special attachment to their father. Around the same time, they learn that little boys have different genitals and supposedly develop *penis envy*. According to Freud, young girls feel hostile toward their mother because they blame her for their anatomical "deficiency." To summarize, in the *Oedipal complex* **children manifest erotically tinged desires for their opposite-sex parent, accompanied by feelings of hostility toward their same-sex parent.** The name for this syndrome was taken from the Greek myth in which Oedipus, not knowing the identity of his real parents, inadvertently killed his father and married his mother.

TABLE 11.2 Freud's Stages of Psychosexual Development

Stage	Approximate Ages	Erotic Focus	Key Tasks and Experiences
Oral	0–1	Mouth (sucking, biting)	Weaning (from breast or bottle)
Anal	2–3	Anus (expelling or retaining feces)	Toilet training
Phallic	4–5	Genitals (masturbating)	Identifying with adult role models; coping with Oedipal crisis
Latency	6–12	None (sexually repressed)	Expanding social contacts
Genital	Puberty onward	Genitals (being sexually intimate)	Establishing intimate relationships; contributing to society through working

© Cengage Learning

According to Freud, the way parents and children deal with the sexual and aggressive conflicts inherent in the Oedipal complex is of paramount importance. The child has to resolve the Oedipal dilemma by purging the sexual longings for the opposite-sex parent and by crushing the hostility felt toward the same-sex parent. In Freud's view, healthy psychosexual development hinges on the resolution of the Oedipal conflict. Why? Because continued hostility toward the same-sex parent may prevent the child from identifying adequately with that parent. Freudian theory predicts that without such identification, many aspects of the child's development won't progress as they should.

Latency and Genital Stages From around age 5 through puberty, the child's sexuality is largely suppressed—it becomes *latent*. Important events during this *latency stage* center on expanding social contacts beyond the immediate family. With the advent of puberty, the child progresses into the *genital stage.* Sexual urges reappear and focus on the genitals once again. At this point, sexual energy is normally channeled toward peers of the other sex, rather than toward oneself as in the phallic stage.

In arguing that the early years shape personality, Freud did not mean that personality development comes to an abrupt halt in middle childhood. However, he did believe that the foundation for adult personality is solidly entrenched by this time. He maintained that future developments are rooted in early, formative experiences and that significant conflicts in later years are replays of crises from childhood.

In fact, Freud believed that unconscious sexual conflicts rooted in childhood experiences cause most personality disturbances. His steadfast belief in the psychosexual origins of psychological disorders eventually led to bitter theoretical disputes with two of his most brilliant colleagues: Carl Jung and Alfred Adler. Jung and Adler both argued that Freud overemphasized sexuality. Freud summarily rejected their ideas. Hence, Jung and Adler felt compelled to go their own way, with each developing his own psychodynamic theory of personality.

Jung's Analytical Psychology

Carl Jung was an established young psychiatrist in Switzerland when he began to write to Freud in 1906. When the two men had their first meeting, they were so taken by each other's insights, they talked nonstop for 13 hours! They exchanged 359 letters before their friendship and theoretical alliance were torn apart in 1913.

Jung called his new approach *analytical psychology* to differentiate it from Freud's psychoanalytic theory. Like Freud, Jung (1921, 1933) emphasized the unconscious determinants of personality. However, he proposed that the unconscious consists of two layers. The first layer, called the *personal unconscious,* is essentially the same as Freud's version of the unconscious. The personal unconscious houses material that is not within one's conscious awareness, because it has been repressed or forgotten. In addition, Jung theorized the existence of a deeper layer that he called the collective unconscious. **The *collective unconscious* is a storehouse of latent memory traces inherited from people's ancestral past.** According to Jung, each person shares the collective unconscious with the entire human race. It contains the "whole spiritual heritage of mankind's evolution, born anew in the brain structure of every individual" (Jung, quoted in Campbell, 1971, p. 45).

Jung called these ancestral memories *archetypes.* They are not memories of actual, personal experiences. Instead, **archetypes are emotionally charged images and thought forms that have universal meaning.** These archetypal images and ideas show up frequently in dreams and are often manifested in a culture's use of symbols in art, literature, and religion. According to Jung, symbols from very different cultures often show striking similarities because they emerge from archetypes that are shared by the entire human race. For instance, Jung found numerous cultures in which the *mandala,* or "magic circle," has served as a symbol of the unified wholeness of the self. Jung felt that an understanding of archetypal symbols helped him make sense of his patients' dreams. He thought that dreams contain important messages from the unconscious, and like Freud, depended extensively on dream analysis in his treatment of patients.

Adler's Individual Psychology

Growing up in Vienna, Alfred Adler was a sickly child who was overshadowed by an exceptionally successful older brother. Nonetheless, he went on to earn his medical degree and gradually became interested in psychiatry. He was a charter member of Freud's inner circle—the Vienna Psychoanalytic Society. However, he soon began to develop his own approach to personality, which he called *individual psychology.*

Like Jung, Adler (1917, 1927) argued that Freud had gone overboard in centering his theory on sexual conflicts. According to Adler, the foremost source of human motivation is a striving for superiority. In his view, this striving does not necessarily translate into the pursuit of dominance or high status. Adler saw *striving for superiority* as a universal drive to adapt, improve oneself, and master life's challenges. He noted that young children understandably feel weak and helpless in comparison with more competent older children and adults. These early inferiority feelings supposedly motivate them to acquire new skills and develop new talents.

Adler asserted that everyone has to work to overcome some feelings of inferiority. He called this process compensation. *Compensation* involves efforts to overcome imagined or real inferiorities by developing one's abilities. Adler believed that compensation is entirely normal. However, in some people inferiority feelings can become excessive, which can result in what is widely known today as an *inferiority complex*—exaggerated feelings of weakness and inadequacy. Adler thought that either parental pampering or parental neglect could cause an inferiority complex. Thus, he agreed with Freud on the importance of early childhood experiences. However, he focused on different aspects of parent-child relations.

Evaluating Psychodynamic Perspectives

The psychodynamic approach has provided a number of far-reaching, truly "grand" theories of personality. These theories yielded some bold new insights when they were first presented. Although one might argue about exact details of interpretation, psychodynamic theory and research have demonstrated that (1) unconscious forces can influence behavior, (2) internal conflict often plays a key role in generating psychological distress, (3) early childhood experiences can influence adult personality, and (4) people use defense mechanisms to reduce their experience of unpleasant emotions (Bornstein, 2003; Porcerelli et al., 2010; Solms, 2004; Westen, Gabbard, & Ortigo, 2008).

In addition to being praised, psychodynamic formulations have also been criticized on several grounds, including the following (Crews, 2006; Eysenck, 1990b; Kramer, 2006; Torrey, 1992):

1. *Poor testability.* Scientific investigations require testable hypotheses. Psychodynamic ideas have often been too vague and conjectural to permit a clear scientific test. For instance, how would you prove or disprove the assertion that the id is entirely unconscious?

2. *Unrepresentative samples.* Freud's theories were based on an exceptionally narrow sample of upper-class, neurotic, sexually repressed Viennese women. They were not even remotely representative of Western European culture, let alone other cultures.

3. *Inadequate evidence.* The empirical evidence on psychodynamic theories has often been characterized as "inadequate." Psychodynamic theories depend too heavily on clinical case studies in which it's much too easy for clinicians to see what they expect to see. Reexaminations of Freud's own clinical work suggest that he frequently distorted his patients' case histories to make them mesh with his theory (Esterson, 2001;

© SuperStock/SuperStock

Adler's theory has been used to analyze the tragic life of the legendary actress Marilyn Monroe (Ansbacher, 1970). During her childhood, Monroe suffered from parental neglect that left her with acute feelings of inferiority. Her inferiority feelings led her to overcompensate by flaunting her beauty, marrying celebrities (Joe DiMaggio and Arthur Miller), keeping film crews waiting for hours, and seeking the adoration of her fans.

Powell & Boer, 1995) and that there was a substantial disparity between Freud's writings and his actual therapeutic methods (Lynn & Vaillant, 1998). Insofar as researchers have accumulated evidence on psychodynamic theories, the evidence has provided only modest support for many of the central hypotheses (Westen, Gabbard, & Ortigo, 2008; Wolitzky, 2006).

4. *Sexism.* Many critics have argued that psychodynamic theories are characterized by a sexist bias against women. Freud believed that females' penis envy made them feel inferior to men. He also thought that females tended to develop weaker superegos and to be more prone to psychological distress than men. The sex bias in modern psychodynamic theories has been reduced considerably. Nonetheless, the psychodynamic approach has generally provided a rather male-centered point of view (Lerman, 1986; Person, 1990).

It's easy to ridicule Freud for concepts such as penis envy, and it's easy to point to Freudian ideas that have turned out to be wrong. However, Freud and his colleagues deserve great credit for breaking new ground with their speculations about personality dynamics. Psychodynamic theories have had extraordinary impact on modern intellectual thought. In psychology as a whole, no other school of thought has been so influential—with the exception of behaviorism, to which we turn next.

KEY LEARNING GOALS

11.7 Understand Skinner's and Bandura's contributions to behavioral views of personality.

11.8 Identify Mischel's principal thesis, and evaluate the behavioral approach to personality.

Behavioral Perspectives

Behaviorism is a theoretical orientation based on the premise that scientific psychology should study only observable behavior. As we saw in Chapter 1, behaviorism has been a major school of thought in psychology since 1913, when John B. Watson argued that psychology should abandon its earlier focus on the mind and mental processes and focus exclusively on overt behavior. In this section, we'll examine three behavioral views of personality: those of B. F. Skinner, Albert Bandura, and Walter Mischel. For the most part, you'll see that behaviorists explain personality the same way they explain everything else—in terms of learning.

Skinner's Ideas Applied to Personality

PSYKTREK 10b

As we noted in Chapters 1 and 6, modern behaviorism's most prominent theorist has been B. F. Skinner, an American psychologist who lived from 1904 to 1990. Working at Harvard University, Skinner achieved renown for his research on learning in lower organisms, mostly rats and pigeons. Skinner's (1953, 1957) principles of *operant conditioning* were never meant to be a theory of personality. However, his ideas have affected thinking in all areas of psychology and have been applied to the explanation of personality. Here we'll examine Skinner's views as they relate to personality structure and development.

PERSONALITY STRUCTURE: A VIEW FROM THE OUTSIDE

PSYKTREK 10b

Skinner made no provision for internal personality structures similar to Freud's id, ego, and superego because such structures can't be observed. Following in the tradition of Watson, Skinner showed little interest in what goes on "inside" people. Instead, he focused on how the external environment molds overt behavior. Indeed, he argued for a strong brand of *determinism,* asserting that behavior is fully determined by environmental stimuli.

How can Skinner's theory explain the consistency that can be seen in individuals' behavior? According to his view, people show some consistent patterns of behavior because they have some stable *response tendencies* that they have acquired through experience. These response tendencies may change in the future, as a result of new experience.

B. F. Skinner
"The objection to inner states is not that they do not exist, but that they are not relevant."

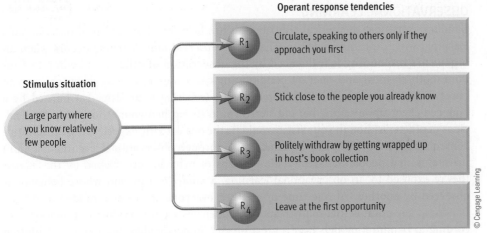

Operant response tendencies

Stimulus situation

Large party where you know relatively few people

R₁ → Circulate, speaking to others only if they approach you first

R₂ → Stick close to the people you already know

R₃ → Politely withdraw by getting wrapped up in host's book collection

R₄ → Leave at the first opportunity

© Cengage Learning

FIGURE 11.3

A behavioral view of personality.
Staunch behaviorists devote little attention to the structure of personality because it is unobservable, but they implicitly view personality as an individual's collection of response tendencies. A possible hierarchy of response tendencies for a particular person in specific stimulus situation (a large party) is shown here.

But they're enduring enough to create a certain degree of consistency in a person's behavior. Implicitly, then, Skinner viewed an individual's personality as a *collection of response tendencies that are tied to various stimulus situations*. A specific situation may be associated with a number of response tendencies that vary in strength, depending on past conditioning (see **Figure 11.3**).

PERSONALITY DEVELOPMENT AS A PRODUCT OF CONDITIONING PSYKTREK 10b

Skinner's theory accounts for personality development by explaining how various response tendencies are acquired through learning (Bolling, Terry, & Kohlenberg, 2006). He believed that most human responses are shaped by the type of conditioning that he described: operant conditioning. As we discussed in Chapter 6, Skinner maintained that environmental consequences—reinforcement, punishment, and extinction—determine people's patterns of responding. On the one hand, when responses are followed by favorable consequences (reinforcement), they are strengthened. For example, if your joking at a party pays off with favorable attention, your tendency to joke at parties will increase. On the other hand, when responses lead to negative consequences (punishment), they are weakened. Thus, if your impulsive decisions always backfire, your tendency to be impulsive will decline.

Response tendencies are constantly being strengthened or weakened by new experiences. Because of this, Skinner's theory views personality development as a continuous, lifelong journey. Unlike Freud and many other theorists, Skinner saw no reason to break the developmental process into stages. Nor did he attribute special importance to early childhood experiences.

© Jose Luis Pelaez Inc/Age fotostock RF

Bandura's Social Cognitive Theory PSYKTREK 10b

Albert Bandura is one of several behaviorists who have added a cognitive flavor to behaviorism since the 1960s. These theorists take issue with Skinner's "pure" behaviorism. They point out that humans obviously are conscious, thinking, feeling beings. Moreover, they argue that in neglecting cognitive processes, Skinner ignored the most distinctive and important feature of human behavior. Bandura and like-minded theorists originally called their modified brand of behaviorism *social learning theory*. Today, Bandura refers to his model as *social cognitive theory*.

Bandura (1986, 1999a, 2006) agrees with the fundamental thrust of behaviorism in that he believes that personality is largely shaped through learning. However, he contends that conditioning is not a mechanical process in which people are passive participants. Instead, he maintains that people actively seek out and process information about their environment to maximize favorable outcomes. In focusing on information processing, he brings unobservable cognitive events into the picture.

Photo by Keeble, courtesy of Albert Bandura

Albert Bandura
"Most human behavior is learned by observation through modeling."

© Vanessa Nel/Shutterstock

OBSERVATIONAL LEARNING

PsykTrek 10b

Bandura's foremost theoretical contribution has been his description of observational learning, which we introduced in Chapter 6. *Observational learning* **occurs when an organism's responding is influenced by the observation of others.** According to Bandura, both classical and operant conditioning can occur indirectly when one person observes another's conditioning. For example, watching your sister get burned by a bounced check upon selling her old stereo could strengthen your tendency to be suspicious of others. Although your sister would be the one actually experiencing the negative consequences, they might also influence you—through observational learning. Bandura maintains that people's characteristic patterns of behavior are shaped by the *models* they're exposed to. In observational learning, **a *model* is a person whose behavior is observed by another.** At one time or another, everyone serves as a model for others. Bandura's key point is that many response tendencies are the product of imitation. According to Bandura, models have a great impact on personality development. Children learn to be assertive, conscientious, self-sufficient, dependable, easygoing, and so forth by observing parents, teachers, relatives, siblings, and peers behaving in these ways.

SELF-EFFICACY

PsykTrek 10b

Bandura discusses how a variety of personal factors (aspects of personality) govern behavior. In recent years, the factor he has emphasized the most is self-efficacy (Bandura, 1990, 1993, 1995). *Self-efficacy* **refers to one's belief about one's ability to perform behaviors that should lead to expected outcomes.** When self-efficacy is high, individuals feel confident that they can execute the responses necessary to earn reinforcers. When self-efficacy is low, individuals worry that the necessary responses may be beyond their abilities. Perceptions of self-efficacy are subjective and specific to certain kinds of tasks. For instance, you might feel extremely confident about your ability to handle difficult social situations. On the other hand, you might be doubtful about your ability to handle academic challenges.

© Brand X Pictures/Getty Images

Perceptions of self-efficacy can influence which challenges people tackle and how well they perform. Studies have found that feelings of greater self-efficacy are associated with reduced procrastination (Steel, 2007), greater success in giving up smoking (Schnoll et al., 2010), greater adherence to an exercise regimen (Ayotte, Margrett, & Hicks-Patrick, 2010), more effective weight-loss efforts (Linde et al., 2006), reduced disability from problems with chronic pain (Hadjistavropoulos et al., 2007), better study habits (Prat-Sala & Redford, 2010), higher levels of academic performance (Weiser & Riggio, 2010), reduced vulnerability to anxiety and depression in childhood (Muris, 2002), less jealousy in romantic relationships (Hu, Zhang, & Li, 2005), enhanced performance in athletic competition (Kane et al., 1996), greater success in searching for a new job (Saks, 2006), higher work-related performance (Stajkovic & Luthans, 1998), and reduced strain from occupational stress (Grau, Salanova, & Peiro, 2001), among many other things.

Mischel and the Person-Situation Controversy

Walter Mischel is another prominent social learning theorist. Mischel's (1973, 1984) chief contribution to personality theory has been to focus attention on the extent to which situational factors govern behavior. According to Mischel, people make responses that they think will lead to reinforcement in the situation at hand. For example, if you believe that hard work in your job will pay off by leading to raises and promotions, you'll probably be diligent and industrious. But if you think that hard work in your job is unlikely to be rewarded, you may behave in a lazy and irresponsible manner. Thus, Mischel's version of social learning theory predicts that people will often behave differently in different situations. Mischel (1968, 1973) reviewed decades of research and concluded that, indeed, people exhibit far less consistency across situations than had been widely assumed. For example, a person who is shy in one context might be quite outgoing in another. Other models of personality largely ignore this inconsistency. Mischel's provocative theories sparked a robust debate about the relative importance of the *person* as opposed to the *situation* in determining behavior. The ensuing research led to a growing recognition that *both* the person and the situation are important determinants of behavior (Fleeson, 2004; Roberts & Pomerantz, 2004).

Evaluating Behavioral Perspectives

Behavioral theories are firmly rooted in extensive empirical research. Skinner's ideas have shed light on how environmental consequences and conditioning mold people's characteristic behavior. Bandura's social learning theory has expanded the horizons of behaviorism and increased its relevance to the study of personality. Mischel deserves credit for increasing psychology's awareness of how situational factors shape behavior.

Of course, each theoretical approach has its shortcomings, and the behavioral approach is no exception. The behaviorists used to be criticized because they neglected cognitive processes, which clearly are important factors in human behavior. The rise of social cognitive theory blunted this criticism. However, social cognitive theory undermines the foundation on which behaviorism was built—the idea that psychologists should study only observable behavior. Thus, some critics complain that behavioral theories aren't very behavioral anymore. Other critics argue that behaviorists have indiscriminately generalized from animal behavior to human behavior (Liebert & Liebert, 1998; Maddi, 1989). Humanistic theorists, whom we shall cover next, have been particularly vocal in criticizing behavioral views.

Humanistic Perspectives

Humanistic theory emerged in the 1950s as something of a backlash against the behavioral and psychodynamic theories that we have just discussed (Cassel, 2000). The principal charge hurled at these two models was that they are dehumanizing (DeCarvalho, 1991). Freudian theory was criticized for its belief that behavior is dominated by primitive, animalistic drives. Behaviorism was criticized for its preoccupation with animal research. Critics argued that both schools of thought are too deterministic—that they fail to recognize that humans are free to chart their own courses of action—and that they fail to appreciate the unique qualities of human behavior.

Many of these critics blended into a loose alliance that came to be known as humanism, because of its exclusive focus on human behavior. *Humanism* is a theoretical orientation that emphasizes the unique qualities of humans, especially their freedom and their potential for personal growth. In contrast to most psychodynamic and behavioral theorists, humanistic theorists, such as Carl Rogers and Abraham Maslow, take an optimistic view of human nature. They assume (1) that people can rise above their primitive animal heritage, (2) that people are largely conscious and rational beings who are not dominated by unconscious, irrational conflicts, and (3) that people are not helpless pawns of deterministic forces. Humanistic theorists also maintain that a person's subjective view of the world is more important than objective reality (Wong, 2006). According to this notion, if you think that you're homely or bright or sociable, then this belief will influence your behavior more than the realities of how homely, bright, or sociable you actually are.

Misconception
People's behavior is largely determined by their personality and character.

Reality
Mischel's argument that situational forces shape much of our behavior has proven compelling. That is not to say that personality is irrelevant. But research has shown again and again that situational factors are more powerful determinants of behavior than laypersons or scientists would have guessed (Benjamin & Simpson, 2009; Ross & Nisbett, 1991; Zimbardo, 2004).

KEY LEARNING GOALS

11.9 Explain the impetus for humanism, and articulate Rogers's views on the self-concept.

11.10 Describe Maslow's key insights, and evaluate the humanistic approach to personality.

Carl Rogers

"I have little sympathy with the rather prevalent concept that man is basically irrational, and that his impulses, if not controlled, will lead to destruction of others and self. Man's behavior is exquisitely rational, moving with subtle and ordered complexity toward the goals his organism is endeavoring to achieve."

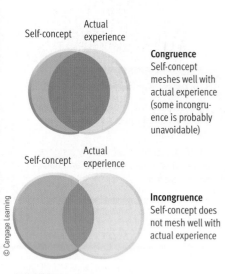

Self-concept   Actual
               experience

Congruence
Self-concept meshes well with actual experience (some incongruence is probably unavoidable)

Self-concept   Actual
               experience

Incongruence
Self-concept does not mesh well with actual experience

FIGURE 11.4

Rogers's view of personality structure.
In Rogers's model, the self-concept is the only important structural construct. However, Rogers acknowledged that one's self-concept may not be consistent with the realities of one's actual experience—a condition called incongruence.

Rogers's Person-Centered Theory

PSYKTREK 10c

Carl Rogers (1951, 1961, 1980) was one of the fathers of the human potential movement. This movement emphasizes self-realization through sensitivity training, encounter groups, and other exercises intended to foster personal growth. Like Freud, Rogers based his personality theory on his extensive therapeutic interactions with many clients. Because of its emphasis on a person's subjective point of view, Rogers called his approach a *person-centered theory.*

THE SELF

PSYKTREK 10c

Rogers viewed personality structure in terms of just one construct. He called this construct the *self,* although it's more widely known today as the *self-concept.* A *self-concept* **is a collection of beliefs about one's own nature, unique qualities, and typical behavior.** Your self-concept is your own mental picture of yourself. It's a collection of self-perceptions. For example, a self-concept might include beliefs such as "I'm easygoing" or "I'm sly and crafty" or "I'm pretty" or "I'm hardworking."

Rogers stressed the subjective nature of the self-concept. Your self-concept may not be entirely consistent with your experiences. Most people tend to distort their experiences to some extent to promote a relatively favorable self-concept. For example, you may believe that you're quite bright, but your grade transcript might suggest otherwise. Rogers called the gap between self-concept and reality "incongruence." *Incongruence* **is the degree of disparity between one's self-concept and one's actual experience.** In contrast, if a person's self-concept is reasonably accurate, it's said to be *congruent* with reality (see **Figure 11.4**). Everyone experiences a certain amount of incongruence. The crucial issue is how much. As we'll see, Rogers held that too much incongruence undermines one's psychological well-being.

DEVELOPMENT OF THE SELF

PSYKTREK 10c

In terms of personality development, Rogers was concerned with how childhood experiences promote congruence or incongruence between one's self-concept and one's experience. According to Rogers, people have a strong need for affection, love, and acceptance from others. Early in life, parents provide most of this affection. Rogers maintained that some parents make their affection *conditional.* That is, it depends on the child's behaving well and living up to expectations. When parental love seems conditional, children often block out of their self-concept those experiences that make them feel unworthy of love. They do so because they're worried about parental acceptance, which appears precarious. At the other end of the spectrum, some parents make their affection *unconditional.* Their children have less need to block out unworthy experiences because they've been assured that they're worthy of affection, no matter what they do.

Rogers believed that unconditional love from parents fosters congruence and that conditional love fosters incongruence. He further theorized that if individuals grow up believing that affection from others is highly conditional, they will go on to distort more and more of their experiences in order to feel worthy of acceptance from a wider and wider array of people.

© MBI/Alamy

ANXIETY AND DEFENSE

PSYKTREK 10c

According to Rogers, experiences that threaten people's personal views of themselves are the principal cause of troublesome anxiety. The more inaccurate your self-concept is, the more likely you are to have experiences that clash with your self-perceptions.

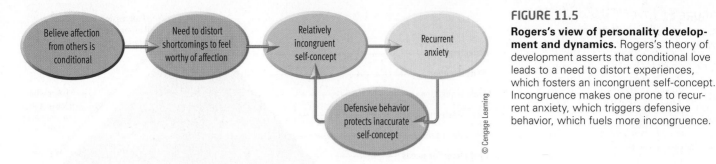

FIGURE 11.5

Rogers's view of personality development and dynamics. Rogers's theory of development asserts that conditional love leads to a need to distort experiences, which fosters an incongruent self-concept. Incongruence makes one prone to recurrent anxiety, which triggers defensive behavior, which fuels more incongruence.

Thus, people with highly incongruent self-concepts are especially likely to be plagued by recurrent anxiety (see **Figure 11.5**). To ward off this anxiety, individuals often behave defensively in an effort to reinterpret their experience so that it appears consistent with their self-concept. Thus, they ignore, deny, and twist reality to protect and perpetuate their self-concept. For example, a young lady who is selfish but unable to face that reality might attribute friends' comments about her selfishness to their jealousy of her good looks.

Maslow's Theory of Self-Actualization   PSYKTREK 10c

Abraham Maslow (1970) was a prominent humanistic theorist who argued that psychology should take a greater interest in the nature of the healthy personality, instead of dwelling on the causes of disorders. "To oversimplify the matter somewhat," he said, "it is as if Freud supplied to us the sick half of psychology and we must now fill it out with the healthy half" (Maslow, 1968, p. 5). Maslow's key contributions were his analysis of how motives are organized hierarchically and his description of the healthy personality.

HIERARCHY OF NEEDS   PSYKTREK 10c

Maslow proposed that human motives are organized into a *hierarchy of needs*—a systematic arrangement of needs, according to priority, in which basic needs must be met before less basic needs are aroused. This hierarchical arrangement is usually portrayed as a pyramid (see **Figure 11.6**). The needs toward the bottom of the pyramid, such as physiological or security needs, are the most basic. Higher levels in the pyramid consist of progressively less basic needs. When a person manages to satisfy a level of needs reasonably well (complete satisfaction is not necessary), *this satisfaction activates needs at the next level.*

Like Rogers, Maslow argued that humans have an innate drive toward personal growth—that is, evolution toward a higher state of being. Thus, he described the needs in the uppermost reaches of his hierarchy as *growth needs*. These include the needs for

Abraham Maslow

"It is as if Freud supplied to us the sick half of psychology and we must now fill it out with the healthy half."

Need for self-actualization: Realization of potential

Aesthetic needs: Order and beauty

Cognitive needs: Knowledge and understanding

Esteem needs: Achievement and gaining of recognition

Belongingness and love needs: Affiliation and acceptance

Safety and security needs: Long-term survival and stability

Physiological needs: Hunger, thirst, and so forth

Progression if lower needs are satisfied

Regression if lower needs are not being satisfied

FIGURE 11.6

Maslow's hierarchy of needs. According to Maslow, human needs are arranged in a hierarchy, and people must satisfy their basic needs before they can satisfy higher needs. In the diagram, higher levels in the pyramid represent progressively less basic needs. Individuals progress upward in the hierarchy when lower needs are satisfied reasonably well, but they may regress back to lower levels if basic needs are no longer satisfied.

FIGURE 11.7

Proposed revision of Maslow's pyramid. According to Kenrick and colleagues (2010), the lower levels of needs in Maslow's hierarchy have been supported by research, but the needs in the upper portion of his pyramid should be replaced. Working from an evolutionary perspective, Kenrick et al. argue that humans' highest needs involve motives related to reproductive fitness, as shown here.

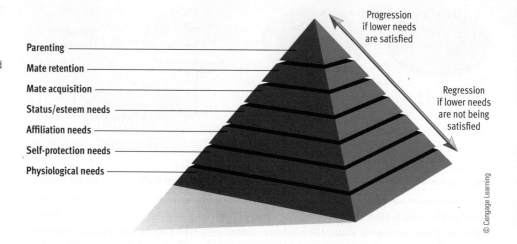

Parenting

Mate retention

Mate acquisition

Status/esteem needs

Affiliation needs

Self-protection needs

Physiological needs

Progression if lower needs are satisfied

Regression if lower needs are not being satisfied

© Cengage Learning

knowledge, understanding, order, and aesthetic beauty. Foremost among them is the ***need for self-actualization,* which is the need to fulfill one's potential.** It is the highest need in Maslow's motivational hierarchy. Maslow summarized this concept with a simple statement: "What a man *can* be, he *must* be." According to Maslow, individuals will be frustrated if they are unable to fully utilize their talents or pursue their true interests. For example, if you have great musical talent but must work as an accountant, your need for self-actualization will be thwarted.

Maslow's pyramid has penetrated popular culture to a remarkable degree (Peterson and Park, 2010). But recently, almost 70 years after Maslow first proposed his influential pyramid of needs, theorists have proposed a major renovation. Working from an evolutionary perspective, Kenrick and colleagues (2010) argue for a reworking of the upper levels of Maslow's hierarchy. They acknowledge that decades of research and theory provide support for the priority of the first four levels of needs. But they contend that the higher needs in the pyramid are not that fundamental and that they are really pursued in service of esteem needs—that people seek knowledge, beauty, and self-actualization to impress others. After grouping Maslow's higher needs with the esteem needs, Kenrick et al. (2010) fill in the upper levels of their revised hierarchy with needs related to reproductive fitness—that is, passing on one's genes. Specifically, they propose that the top three needs in the pyramid should be the need to find a mate, the need to retain a mate, and the need to successfully parent offspring (see **Figure 11.7**).

It hard to say whether this sweeping revision of Maslow's pyramid will gain traction. Most commentaries thus far acknowledge that Kenrick and his colleagues have compiled some compelling arguments in favor of their renovated pyramid. However, such a radical transformation of an iconic theoretical model is bound to invite second-guessing. For example, critics have argued that the revised hierarchy is no longer uniquely human (Kesebir, Graham, & Oishi, 2010) and that it is premature to dismiss the need for self-actualization (Peterson & Park, 2010).

THE HEALTHY PERSONALITY

PSYKTREK 10c

Because of his interest in self-actualization, Maslow conducted research to analyze the nature of the healthy personality. He called people with exceptionally healthy personalities *self-actualizing persons* because of their commitment to continued personal growth. Maslow identified various traits characteristic of self-actualizing people. Many of these traits are listed in **Figure 11.8**. In brief, Maslow found that self-actualizers are accurately tuned in to reality and that they're at peace with themselves. He found that they're open and spontaneous and that they retain a fresh appreciation of the world around them. Socially, they're sensitive to others' needs and enjoy rewarding interpersonal relations. However, they're not dependent on others for approval or uncomfortable with solitude. They thrive on their work, and they enjoy their sense of humor. Maslow also noted that they have "peak experiences" (profound emotional highs) more often than others. Finally, he found that they strike a nice balance between many polarities in personality. For instance, they can be both childlike and mature, both rational and intuitive, both conforming and rebellious.

Evaluating Humanistic Perspectives

The humanists added a refreshing new perspective to the study of personality. Their argument that a person's subjective views may be more important than objective reality has proven compelling. The humanistic approach also deserves credit for making the self-concept an important construct in psychology. Finally, one could argue that the humanists' optimistic, growth- and health-oriented approach laid the foundation for the emergence of the positive psychology movement that is increasingly influential in contemporary psychology (Sheldon & Kasser, 2001; Taylor, 2001).

Of course, the balance sheet has a negative side as well (Burger, 2008; Wong, 2006). Critics argue that (1) many aspects of humanistic theory are difficult to put to a scientific test, (2) humanists have been unrealistically optimistic in their assumptions about human nature and their descriptions of the healthy personality, and (3) more experimental research is needed to catch up with the theorizing in the humanistic camp.

Biological Perspectives

Could personality be a matter of genetic inheritance? This possibility was largely ignored for many decades of personality research until Hans Eysenck made a case for genetic influence in the 1960s. In this section, we'll discuss Eysenck's theory and look at more recent behavioral genetics research on the heritability of personality. We'll also examine evolutionary perspectives on personality.

Eysenck's Theory

PSYKTREK 10d

Hans Eysenck was born in Germany but fled to London during the era of Nazi rule. He went on to become one of Britain's most prominent psychologists. Eysenck (1967, 1982, 1990a) views personality structure as a hierarchy of traits, in which many superficial traits are derived from a smaller number of more basic traits, which are derived from a handful of fundamental higher-order traits, as shown in **Figure 11.9** on the next page.

According to Eysenck, "Personality is determined to a large extent by a person's genes" (1967, p. 20). How is heredity linked to personality in Eysenck's model? In part, through conditioning concepts borrowed from behavioral theory (consult Chapter 6 for an overview of classical conditioning). Eysenck theorizes that some people can be conditioned more readily than others because of differences in their physiological functioning. These variations in "conditionability" are assumed to influence the personality traits that people acquire through conditioning processes.

Characteristics of self-actualizing people

- Clear, efficient perception of reality and comfortable relations with it
- Spontaneity, simplicity, and naturalness
- Problem centering (having something outside themselves they "must" do as a mission)
- Detachment and need for privacy
- Autonomy, independence of culture and environment
- Continued freshness of appreciation
- Mystical and peak experiences
- Feelings of kinship and identification with the human race
- Strong friendships, but limited in number
- Democratic character structure
- Ethical discrimination between good and evil
- Philosophical, unhostile sense of humor
- Balance between polarities in personality

© Cengage Learning

FIGURE 11.8

Maslow's view of the healthy personality. Humanistic theorists emphasize psychological health instead of maladjustment. Maslow's description of characteristics of self-actualizing people evokes a picture of the healthy personality.

SOURCE: Adapted from Potkay, C. R., & Allen, B. P. (1986). *Personality: Theory, research and application.* Pacific Grove, CA: Brooks/Cole. Copyright © 1986 by C. R. Potkay & B. P. Allen. Adapted by permission of the author.

KEY LEARNING GOALS

11.11 Outline Eysenck's view of personality, and summarize behavioral genetics research on personality.

11.12 Articulate evolutionary explanations for why the Big Five traits are important, and evaluate the biological approach to personality.

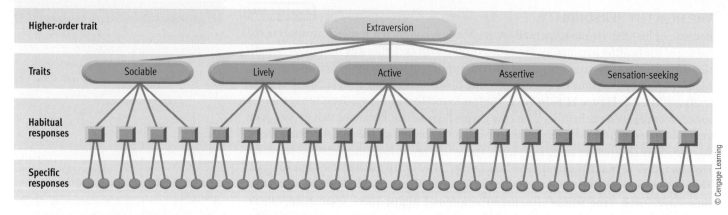

Higher-order trait			Extraversion		
Traits	Sociable	Lively	Active	Assertive	Sensation-seeking
Habitual responses					
Specific responses					

© Cengage Learning

FIGURE 11.9

Eysenck's model of personality structure. Eysenck described personality structure as a hierarchy of traits. In this scheme, a few higher-order traits, such as extraversion, determine a host of lower-order traits, which determine a person's habitual responses.

SOURCE: Eysenck, H. J. (1976). *The biological basis of personality.* Springfield, IL: Charles C. Thomas. Reprinted by permission of the publisher.

Eysenck has shown a special interest in explaining variations in *extraversion-introversion*. He has proposed that introverts tend to have high levels of physiological arousal, which make them more easily conditioned than extraverts. According to Eysenck, such people acquire more conditioned inhibitions than others. These inhibitions make them more bashful, tentative, and uneasy in social situations, leading them to turn inward. As a result, they become introverted.

Concept Check   11.2

Recognizing Key Concepts in Personality Theories

Check your understanding of psychodynamic, behavioral, and humanistic personality theories by identifying key concepts from these theories in the scenarios below. The answers can be found in Appendix A.

1. Thirteen-year-old Sarah watches a TV show in which the leading female character manipulates her boyfriend by acting helpless and purposely losing a tennis match against him. The female lead repeatedly expresses her slogan, "Never let them [men] know you can take care of yourself." Sarah becomes more passive and less competitive around boys her own age.

   Concept: _____

2. Yolanda has a secure, enjoyable, reasonably well-paid job as a tenured English professor at a state university. Her friends are dumbfounded when she announces that she's going to resign and give it all up to try writing a novel. She tries to explain, "I need a new challenge, a new mountain to climb. I've had this lid on my writing talents for years, and I've got to break free. It's something I have to try. I won't be happy until I do."

   Concept: _____

3. Vladimir, who is 4, seems to be emotionally distant from and inattentive to his father. He complains whenever he's left with his dad. In contrast, he cuddles up in bed with his mother frequently and tries very hard to please her by behaving properly.

   Concept: _____

© Ienetstan/Shutterstock

Behavioral Genetics and Personality

PsykTrek 10d

Recent research in behavioral genetics has provided impressive support for the idea that personality is largely inherited (Livesley, Jang, & Vernon, 2003; Rowe & van den Oord, 2005). For instance, in twin studies of the Big Five personality traits, identical twins have been found to be much more similar than fraternal twins on all five traits (Loehlin, 1992). These findings strongly suggest that genetic factors exert considerable influence over personality.

© Image Source/Alamy

Some skeptics wonder whether identical twins might exhibit more trait similarity than fraternal twins because they're treated more alike. In other words, they wonder whether environmental factors (rather than heredity) could be responsible for identical twins' greater personality resemblance. This nagging question can be answered only by studying identical twins reared apart. Fortunately, an influential twin study at the University of Minnesota provided the necessary data (Tellegen et al., 1988). This study was the first to administer the same personality test to identical and fraternal twins reared apart, as well as together. Most of the twins reared apart were separated quite early in life (median age of 2.5 months) and remained separated for a long time (median period of almost 34 years). The results revealed that identical twins reared apart were substantially more similar in personality than fraternal twins reared together. The *heritability estimates* (see Chapter 8) for the traits examined ranged from 40% to 58%. Overall, five decades of research on the determinants of the Big Five traits suggests that the heritability of each trait is in the vicinity of 50% (Krueger & Johnson, 2008). Thus, behavioral genetics research supports the notion that genetic blueprints shape the contours of individuals' personality.

Research on the heritability of personality has inadvertently turned up a surprising finding: *shared family environment* appears to have remarkably little impact on personality. This unexpected finding has been observed quite consistently in behavioral genetics research (Beer, Arnold, & Loehlin, 1998; Rowe & van den Oord, 2005). It is surprising in that social scientists have long assumed that the family environment shared by children growing up together led to some personality resemblance among them. This finding has led researchers to explore how children's subjective environments vary *within* families. But scientists continue to be perlexed by the minimal impact of shared family environment.

The Evolutionary Approach to Personality

In the realm of biological perspectives on personality, the most recent development has been the emergence of evolutionary theory. Evolutionary theorists assert that personality has a biological basis because natural selection has favored certain traits over the course of human history (Figueredo et al., 2005, 2009). Thus, evolutionary analyses focus on how various personality traits—and the ability to recognize these traits in others—may have contributed to reproductive fitness in ancestral human populations.

For example, David Buss (1991, 1995, 1997) has argued that the Big Five personality traits stand out as important dimensions of personality across a variety of cultures because those traits have had significant adaptive implications. Buss points out that humans historically have depended heavily on groups, which afford protection from predators or enemies, opportunities for sharing food, and a diverse array of other benefits. In the context of these group interactions, people have had to make difficult but crucial judgments about the characteristics of others, asking such questions as: Who will make a good member of my group? Who can I depend on when in need? Who will share their resources? According to Buss, the Big Five emerge as fundamental dimensions of personality because humans have evolved special sensitivity to variations in the ability to bond with others (extraversion), the willingness to cooperate and collaborate (agreeableness), the tendency to be reliable and ethical (conscientiousness), the capacity

Reality Check

Misconception
Parents exert a great deal of influence over the personality of their offspring.

Reality
This seems like a logical supposition, but when behavioral genetics researchers have attempted to quantify the impact of shared family environment on personality, they have been stunned by its lack of influence. Other types of research in developmental psychology have suggested that parents have some influence over their children's personality (Maccoby, 2000), but this influence appears to be much more modest than widely assumed (Cohen, 1999; Harris, 1998).

to be an innovative problem solver (openness to experience), and the ability to handle stress (low neuroticism). In a nutshell, Buss argues that the Big Five reflect the most salient features of others' adaptive behavior over the course of evolutionary history.

Daniel Nettle (2006) takes this line of thinking one step further. He asserts that the traits themselves (as opposed to the ability to recognize them in others) are products of evolution that were adaptive in ancestral environments. For example, he discusses how extraversion could have promoted mating success, how agreeableness could have fostered the effective building of coalitions, and so forth.

Evaluating Biological Perspectives

Researchers have compiled convincing evidence that biological factors help shape personality, and findings on the meager effects of shared family environment have launched intriguing new approaches to the investigation of personality development. Nonetheless, we must take note of some weaknesses in biological approaches to personality. Critics assert that too much emphasis has been placed on heritability estimates that vary depending on sampling and statistical procedures (Funder, 2001). Critics also argue that efforts to carve behavior into genetic and environmental components are ultimately artificial. The effects of nature and nurture are twisted together in complicated interactions that can't be separated cleanly (Plomin, 2004; Rutter, 2007). For example, a genetically influenced trait, such as a young child's surly, sour temperament, might evoke a particular style of parenting. In essence then, the child's genes have molded his or her environment. Thus, genetic and environmental influences on personality are not entirely independent.

Concept Check   11.3

Understanding the Implications of Major Theories: Who Said This?

Check your understanding of the implications of the personality theories we've discussed by indicating which theorist is likely to have made the statements below. The answers are in Appendix A.

Choose from the following theorists: (a) Alfred Adler, (b) Albert Bandura, (c) Hans Eysenck, (d) Sigmund Freud, (e) Abraham Maslow, (f) Walter Mischel.

_____ 1. "If you deliberately plan to be less than you are capable of being, then I warn you that you'll be deeply unhappy for the rest of your life."

_____ 2. "I feel that the major, most fundamental dimensions of personality are likely to be those on which [there is] strong genetic determination of individual differences."

_____ 3. "People are in general not candid over sexual matters . . . they wear a heavy overcoat woven of a tissue of lies, as though the weather were bad in the world of sexuality."

Contemporary Empirical Approaches to Personality

KEY LEARNING GOALS

11.13 Understand the nature, correlates, and social consequences of narcissism.

11.14 Describe the chief concepts of terror management theory.

So far, our coverage has been devoted to grand, panoramic theories of personality. In this section we'll examine some contemporary empirical approaches that are narrower in scope. In modern personality research programs, investigators typically attempt to describe and measure an important personality trait and ascertain its relationship to other traits and specific behaviors. To get a sense of this kind of research, we'll take a look at research on a trait called *narcissism*. We'll also look at an influential new approach called *terror management theory* that focuses on personality dynamics rather than personality traits.

Narcissism

Narcissism **is a personality trait marked by an inflated sense of importance, a need for attention and admiration, a sense of entitlement, and a tendency to exploit others.** The term is drawn from the Greek myth of Narcissus, who was an attractive young man in search of love. In the mythical tale he eventually saw his reflection in water, fell in love with his own image, and gazed at it until he died, thus illustrating the perils of excessive self-love. The concept of narcissism was originally popularized over a century ago by pioneering sex researcher Havelock Ellis (1898) and Sigmund Freud (1914).

Narcissism was not widely discussed outside of psychoanalytic circles until the 1980s, when some researchers developed scales intended to assess narcissism as a normal personality trait (as opposed to a pathological syndrome). Of these scales, the Narcissistic Personality Inventory (NPI) (Raskin & Hall, 1979, 1981; Raskin & Terry, 1988), has become the most widely used measure of narcissism.

Studies have painted an interesting portrait of those who score high in narcissism (Rhodewalt & Peterson, 2009). Narcissists have highly positive, but easily-threatened self-concepts. Above all else, their behavior is driven by a need to maintain their fragile self-esteem. They are far more interested in making themselves look powerful and successful than they are in forging lasting bonds with others (Campbell & Foster, 2007). They display a craving for approval and admiration that resembles an addiction (Baumeister & Vohs, 2001). Hence, they proactively work overtime to impress people with self-aggrandizing descriptions of their accomplishments. As you might guess, in this era of social networking via the Internet, those who are high in narcissism tend to post relatively blatant self-promotional content on Facebook and similar websites (Buffardi & Campbell, 2008; Mehdizadeh, 2010).

The social consequences of narcissism are interesting (Back, Schmukle, & Egloff, 2010; Paulhus, 1998). When they first meet people, narcissists are often perceived as charming, self-assured, humorous, and perhaps even charismatic. Thus, initially, they tend to be well-liked. With repeated exposure, however, their constant need for attention, brazen boasting, and sense of entitlement tend to wear thin. Eventually, they tend to be viewed as arrogant, self-centered, and unlikable.

Based on a variety of social trends, Jean Twenge and colleagues (2008) suspected that narcissism might be increasing in recent generations. To test this hypothesis, they gathered data from 85 studies dating back to the 1980s in which American college students had been given the NPI. Their analysis revealed that NPI scores have been rising, going from a mean of about 15.5 in the 1980s to almost 17.5 in 2005–2006. This finding was replicated in a recent study that extended the trend through 2009 (Twenge & Foster, 2010). In a discussion of the possible ramifications of this trend, Twenge and Campbell (2009) have argued that rising narcissism has fueled an obsessive concern about being physically attractive in young people, leading to unhealthy diet-

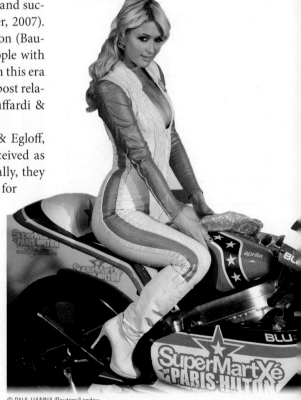

© PAUL HANNA/Reuters/Landou

Major Theories of Personality

THEORIST AND ORIENTATION	SOURCE OF DATA AND OBSERVATIONS	KEY ASSUMPTIONS
A PSYCHODYNAMIC VIEW Sigmund Freud	Case studies from clinical practice of psychoanalysis	Past events in childhood determine our adult personality. Our behavior is dominated by unconscious, irrational wishes, needs, and conflicts. Personality development progresses through stages.
A BEHAVIORAL VIEW B. F. Skinner	Laboratory experiments, primarily with animals 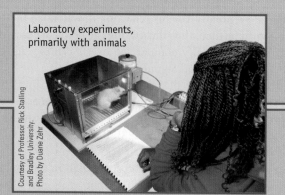	Behavior is determined by the environment, although this view was softened by Bandura's social cognitive theory. Nurture (learning and experience) is more influential than nature (heredity and biological factors). Situational factors exert great influence over behavior.
A HUMANISTIC VIEW Carl Rogers	Case studies from clinical practice of client-centered therapy	People are free to chart their own courses of action; they are not hapless victims governed by the environment. People are largely conscious, rational beings who are not driven by unconscious needs. A person's subjective view of the world is more important than objective reality.
A BIOLOGICAL VIEW Hans Eysenck	Twin, family, and adoption studies of heritability; factor analysis studies of personality structure	Behavior is largely determined by evolutionary adaptations, the wiring of the brain, and heredity. Nature (heredity and biological factors) is more influential than nurture (learning and experience).

Illustrations of Freud, Skinner, Rogers, and Eysenck © Cengage Learning

MODEL OF PERSONALITY STRUCTURE

Three interacting components (id, ego, superego) operating at three levels of consciousness

Collections of response tendencies tied to specific stimulus situations

Self-concept, which may or may not mesh well with actual experience

Hierarchy of traits, with specific traits derived from more fundamental, general traits

VIEW OF PERSONALITY DEVELOPMENT

Emphasis on fixation or progress through psychosexual stages; experiences in early childhood (such as toilet training) can leave lasting mark on adult personality

© Finnbarr Webster/Alamy

© Jose Luis Pelaez Inc./ Age fotostock RF

Personality evolves gradually over the life span (not in stages); responses (such as extraverted joking) followed by reinforcement (such as appreciative laughter) become more frequent

Children who receive unconditional love have less need to be defensive; they develop more accurate, congruent self-concept; conditional love fosters incongruence

© MBI/Alamy

Emphasis on unfolding of genetic blueprint with maturation; inherited predispositions interact with learning experiences

ROOTS OF DISORDERS

Unconscious fixations and unresolved conflicts from childhood, usually centering on sex and aggression

Maladaptive behavior due to faulty learning; the "symptom" is the problem, not a sign of under-lying disease

Incongruence between self and actual experience (inaccurate self-concept); over-dependence on others for approval and sense of worth

Genetic vulnera-bility activated in part by environ-mental factors ing, overuse of cosmetic surgery, and steroid-fueled body building. They also assert that narcissists' "me-first" attitude has led to increased materialism and overconsumption of the earth's resources, which have contributed to the current environmental crisis and economic meltdown.

Terror Management Theory

Terror management theory emerged as an influential perspective in the 1990s. Although the theory borrows from Freudian and evolutionary formulations, it provides its own unique analysis of the human condition. Developed by Sheldon Solomon, Jeff Greenberg, and Tom Pyszczynski (1991, 2004b), this fresh perspective is currently generating a huge volume of research.

One of the chief goals of terror management theory is to explain why people need self-esteem. Unlike other animals, humans have evolved complex cognitive abilities that permit self-awareness and contemplation of the future. These cognitive capacities make humans keenly aware that life can be snuffed out at any time. The collision between humans' self-preservation instinct and their awareness of the inevitability of death creates the potential for experiencing anxiety, alarm, and terror when people think about their mortality (see **Figure 11.10**).

How do humans deal with this potential for terror? According to terror management theory, "What saves us is culture. Cultures provide ways to view the world—worldviews—that 'solve' the existential crisis engendered by the awareness of death" (Pyszczynski, Solomon, & Greenberg, 2003, p. 16). Cultural worldviews diminish anxiety by providing answers to universal questions such as: Why am I here? What is the meaning of life? Cultures create stories, traditions, and institutions that give their members a sense of being part of an enduring legacy and thus soothe their fear of death.

Where does self-esteem fit into the picture? Self-esteem is viewed as a sense of personal worth that depends on one's confidence in the validity of one's cultural worldview and the belief that one is living up to the standards prescribed by that worldview. Hence, self-esteem buffers people from the profound anxiety associated with the awareness that they are transient animals destined to die. In other words, self-esteem serves a *terror management* function (refer to **Figure 11.10**).

The notion that self-esteem functions as an *anxiety buffer* has been supported by numerous studies (Pyszczynski et al., 2004; Schmeichel et al., 2009). In many of these experiments, researchers have manipulated what they call **mortality salience—the degree to which subjects' mortality is prominent in their minds**. Typically, mortality

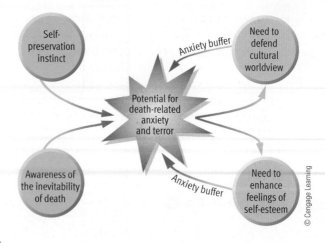

FIGURE 11.10

Overview of terror management theory. This graphic maps out the relations among the key concepts proposed by terror management theory. The theory asserts that humans' unique awareness of the inevitability of death fosters a need to defend one's cultural worldview and one's self-esteem, which serve to protect one from mortality-related anxiety.

salience is temporarily increased by asking participants to briefly think about their own future death. Consistent with the anxiety buffer hypothesis, reminding people of their mortality leads subjects to engage in a variety of behaviors that are likely to bolster their self-esteem, thus reducing anxiety.

Increasing mortality salience also leads people to work harder at defending their cultural worldview (Arndt & Vess, 2008; Burke, Martens, & Faucher, 2010). For instance, after briefly pondering their mortality, research participants (1) hand out harsher penalties to moral transgressors, (2) respond more negatively to people who criticize their country, and (3) show more respect for cultural icons, such as a flag. This need to defend one's cultural worldview may even fuel prejudice and aggression (Greenberg et al., 2009). Reminding subjects of their mortality leads to (1) more negative evaluations of people from different religious or ethnic backgrounds, (2) more stereotypic thinking about minorities, and (3) more aggressive behavior toward people with opposing political views. Terror management theory has yielded novel hypotheses regarding many phenomena, and these predictions have been supported in hundreds of experiments (Burke, Martens, & Faucher, 2010).

Culture and Personality

KEY LEARNING GOALS

11.15 Clarify how researchers have found both cross-cultural similarities and disparities in personality.

Are there connections between culture and personality? In recent years psychology's new interest in cultural factors has led to a renaissance of culture-personality research (Church, 2010). This research has sought to determine whether Western personality constructs are relevant to other cultures and whether cultural differences can be seen in the prevalence of specific personality traits. As with cross-cultural research in other areas of psychology, these studies have found evidence of both continuity and variability across cultures.

For the most part, continuity has been apparent in cross-cultural comparisons of the *trait structure* of personality. When English language personality scales have been translated and administered in other cultures, the predicted dimensions of personality have emerged from the factor analyses (Chiu, Kim, & Wan, 2008). For example, when scales that tap the Big Five personality traits have been administered and subjected to factor analysis in other cultures, the usual five traits have typically surfaced (Katigbak et al., 2002; McCrae & Costa, 2008). Thus, research tentatively suggests that the basic dimensions of personality trait structure may be universal.

On the other hand, some cross-cultural variability is seen when researchers compare the average trait scores of samples from various cultural groups. For example, in a study comparing 51 cultures, McCrae et al. (2005a) found that Brazilians scored relatively high in neuroticism, Australians in extraversion, Germans in openness to experience, Czechs in agreeableness, and Malaysians in conscientiousness, to give but a handful of examples. These findings should be viewed as preliminary, since more data are needed from larger and more carefully selected samples. Nonetheless, the findings suggest that there may be genuine cultural differences on some personality traits. That said, the cultural disparities in average trait scores that were observed were modest in size.

The availability of the data from the McCrae et al. (2005a) study allowed Terracciano et al. (2005) to evaluate the concept of *national character*—the idea that various cultures have widely recognized prototype personalities. Terracciano and his colleagues asked subjects from many cultures to describe the *typical* member of *their* culture on rating forms guided by the five-factor model. Generally, subjects displayed substantial agreement on these ratings of what was typical for their culture. The averaged ratings, which served as the measures of each culture's national character, were then correlated with the actual mean trait scores for various cultures compiled in the McCrae et al. (2005a) study. The results were definitive—the vast majority of the correlations were extremely low and

FIGURE 11.11

An example of inaccurate perceptions of national character. Terracciano et al. (2005) found that perceptions of national character (the prototype or typical personality for a particular culture) are largely inaccurate. The data shown here for one culture—Canadians—illustrates this inaccuracy. Mean scores on the Big Five traits for a sample of real individuals from Canada are graphed in red. Averaged perceptions of national character for Canadians are graphed in blue. The discrepancy between perception and reality is obvious. Terracciano et al. found similar disparities between views of national character and actual trait scores for a majority of the cultues they studied. (Adapted from McCrae & Terracciano, 2006)

often even negative. In other words, there was little or no relationship between perceptions of national character and actual trait scores for various cultures (see **Figure 11.11**). People's beliefs about national character, which often fuel cultural prejudices, turned out to be profoundly inaccurate stereotypes (McCrae & Terracciano, 2006).

Perhaps the most interesting and influential work on culture and personality has been that of Hazel Markus and Shinobu Kitayama (1991, 1994, 2003). Their research has compared American and Asian conceptions of the self. According to Markus and Kitayama, American parents teach their children to be self-reliant, to feel good about themselves, and to view themselves as special individuals. Children are encouraged to excel in competitive endeavors and to strive to stand out from the crowd. They are told that "the squeaky wheel gets the grease" and that "you have to stand up for yourself." Thus, Markus and Kitayama argue that *American culture fosters an independent view of the self.* American youngsters learn to define themselves in terms of their personal attributes, abilities, accomplishments, and possessions. Their unique strengths and achievements become the basis for their sense of self-worth. Thus, they are prone to emphasize their uniqueness.

Most of us take this individualistic mentality for granted. However, Markus and Kitayama marshal convincing evidence that this view is *not* universal. They argue that in Asian cultures such as Japan and China, socialization practices foster a more *interdependent view of the self,* which emphasizes the fundamental connectedness of people to each other (see **Figure 11.12**). In these cultures, parents teach their children that they can rely on family and friends, that they should be modest about their personal accomplishments so they don't diminish others' achievements, and that they should view themselves as part of a larger social matrix. Children are encouraged to fit in with others and to avoid standing out from the crowd. A popular adage in Japan reminds children that "the nail that stands out gets pounded down." Hence, Markus and Kitayama assert that Asian youngsters typically learn to define themselves in terms of the groups they belong to. Their harmonious relations with others and their pride in group achievements become the basis for their sense of self-worth. Thus, Asian and American conceptions of self appear to be noticeably different.

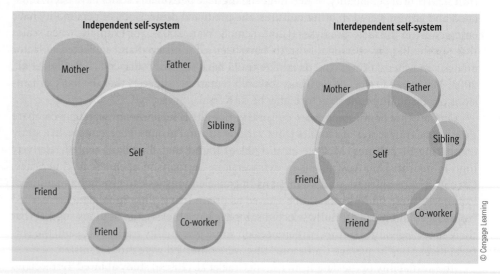

FIGURE 11.12

Culture and conceptions of self. According to Markus and Kitayama (1991), Western cultures foster an independent view of the self as a unique individual who is separate from others, as diagrammed on the left. In contrast, Asian cultures encourage an interdependent view of the self as part of an interconnected social matrix, as diagrammed on the right. The interdependent view leads people to define themselves in terms of their social relationships (for instance, as someone's daughter, employee, colleague, or neighbor).

SOURCE: Adapted from Markus, H. R., & Kitayama, S. (1991). Culture and the self: Implications for cognition, emotion, and motivation. *Psychological Review, 98,* 224–253. Copyright © 1991 by the American Psychological Association. Adapted by permission of the author.

Reflecting on the Chapter's Themes

KEY LEARNING GOALS

11.16 Identify the three unifying themes highlighted in this chapter.

The preceding discussion of culture and personality obviously highlighted the text's theme that people's behavior is influenced by their cultural heritage. This chapter has also been ideally suited for embellishing on two other unifying themes: psychology's theoretical diversity and the idea that psychology evolves in a sociohistorical context.

No other area of psychology is characterized by as much theoretical diversity as the study of personality, where there are literally dozens of insightful theories. Some of this diversity exists because different theories attempt to explain different facets of behavior. Of course, much of this diversity reflects genuine disagreements on basic questions about personality. These disagreements should be apparent on pages 384–385, where you'll find an Illustrated Overview of the ideas of Freud, Skinner, Rogers, and Eysenck, as representatives of the psychodynamic, behavioral, humanistic, and biological approaches to personality.

The study of personality also highlights the sociohistorical context in which psychology evolves. Personality theories have left many marks on modern culture. The theories of Freud, Adler, and Skinner have had an enormous impact on childrearing practices. The ideas of Freud and Jung have found their way into literature (influencing the portrayal of fictional characters) and the visual arts. For example, Freud's theory helped inspire surrealism's interest in the world of dreams, while Maslow's hierarchy of needs and Skinner's affirmation of the value of positive reinforcement have given rise to new approaches to management in the world of business and industry.

Sociohistorical forces also leave their imprint on psychology. This chapter provided many examples of how personal experiences, prevailing attitudes, and historical events have contributed to the evolution of ideas in psychology. For example, Freud's pessimistic view of human nature and his emphasis on the dark forces of aggression were shaped to some extent by his exposure to the hostilities of World War I. Freud's emphasis on sexuality was surely influenced by the Victorian climate of sexual repression that existed in his youth. Adler's views also reflected the social context in which he grew up. His interest in inferiority feelings and compensation appears to have sprung from his own sickly childhood and the difficulties he had to overcome.

Progress in the study of personality has also been influenced by developments in other areas of psychology. For instance, the enterprise of psychological testing originally emerged out of efforts to measure general intelligence. Eventually, however, the principles of psychological testing were applied to the challenge of measuring personality. In the upcoming Personal Application we discuss the logic and limitations of personality tests.

Cultural Heritage

Theoretical Diversity

Sociohistorical Context

Personal APPLICATION

Understanding Personality Assessment

KEY LEARNING GOALS

11.17 Explain how personality inventories and projective tests work, and evaluate their strengths and weaknesses.

Answer the following "true" or "false."

___ 1 Responses to personality tests are subject to unconscious distortion.

___ 2 The results of personality tests are often misunderstood.

___ 3 Personality test scores should be interpreted with caution.

___ 4 Personality tests serve many important functions.

If you answered "true" to all four questions, you earned a perfect score. Yes, personality tests are subject to distortion. Admittedly, test results are often misunderstood, and they should be interpreted cautiously. In spite of these problems, however, psychological tests can be quite useful.

Personality tests can be helpful in (1) making clinical diagnoses of psychological disorders, (2) vocational counseling, (3) personnel selection in business and industry, and (4) measuring specific personality traits for research purposes. Personality tests can be divided into two broad categories: *self-report inventories* and *projective tests*. In this Personal Application, we'll discuss some representative tests from both categories. We'll also discuss their strengths and weaknesses.

Self-Report Inventories

PSYKTREK 7a

Self-report inventories are personality tests that ask individuals to answer a series of questions about their characteristic behavior. The logic underlying this approach is very simple. Who knows you better? Who has known you longer? Who has more access to your private feelings? We'll look at two examples of self-report scales, the MMPI and the NEO Personality Inventory.

THE MMPI

The most widely used self-report inventory is the Minnesota Multiphasic Personality Inventory (MMPI) (Butcher, 2005, 2006). The MMPI was originally designed to aid clinicians in the diagnosis of psychological disorders. It measures ten personality traits that, when mani-

fested to an extreme degree, are thought to be symptoms of disorders. Examples include traits such as paranoia, depression, and hysteria.

Are the MMPI clinical scales valid? That is, do they measure what they were designed to measure? Originally, it was assumed that the ten clinical subscales would provide direct indexes of specific types of disorders. In other words, a high score on the depression scale would be indicative of depression, a high score on the paranoia scale would be indicative of a paranoid disorder, and so forth. However, research revealed that the relations between MMPI scores and various types of mental illness are much more complex than originally anticipated. People with most types of disorders show elevated scores on *several* MMPI subscales. This means that certain score *profiles* are indicative of specific disorders (see **Figure 11.13**). Thus, the interpretation of the MMPI is quite complicated—perhaps overly complicated, according to some critics (Helmes, 2008). Still, the MMPI can be a helpful diagnostic tool for the clinician. The fact that the inventory has been translated into more than 115 languages is a testimonial to its usefulness (Butcher, 1990).

THE NEO PERSONALITY INVENTORY

As we noted in the main body of the chapter, many theorists believe that only

five trait dimensions are required to provide a full description of personality. This view led to the creation of the NEO Personality Inventory. Developed by Paul Costa and Robert McCrae (1985, 1992), the NEO Inventory is designed to measure the Big Five traits: neuroticism, extraversion, openness to experience, agreeableness, and conscientiousness. In spite of its relatively short life span, the NEO inventory is widely used in research and clinical work, and updated revisions of the scale have been released (Costa & McCrae, 2008; McCrae & Costa, 2007). An example of a NEO personality profile (averaged from many respondents) was shown in our discussion of culture and personality (see **Figure 11.12**).

STRENGTHS AND WEAKNESSES OF SELF-REPORT INVENTORIES

To appreciate the strengths of self-report inventories, consider how else you might inquire about an individual's personality. For instance, if you want to know how assertive someone is, why not just ask the person? Why administer an elaborate 50–item personality inventory that measures assertiveness? The advantage of the personality inventory is that it can provide a more objective and more precise estimate of the person's assertiveness.

Of course, self-report inventories are only as accurate as the information that respondents provide. They are susceptible

FIGURE 11.13

MMPI profiles. Scores on the ten clinical scales of the MMPI are often plotted as shown here to create a profile for a client. The normal range for scores on each subscale is 50 to 65. People with disorders frequently exhibit elevated scores on several clinical scales rather than just one.

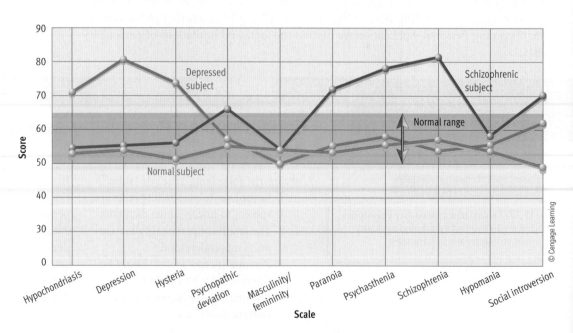

© Cengage Learning

to several sources of error (Ben-Porath, 2003; Kline, 1995; Paulhus, 1991), including the following:

1. *Deliberate deception.* Some self-report inventories include many questions whose purpose is easy to figure out. This problem makes it possible for some respondents to intentionally fake particular personality traits (Rees & Metcalfe, 2003). Some studies suggest that deliberate faking is a serious problem when personality scales are used to evaluate job applicants (Birkeland et al., 2006). Other studies, however, suggest that the problem is not all that significant (Hogan, Barrett, & Hogan, 2007).

2. *Social desirability bias.* Without realizing it, some people consistently respond to questions in ways that make them look good. The social desirability bias isn't a matter of deception so much as wishful thinking.

3. *Response sets.* A response set is a systematic tendency to respond to test items in a particular way that is unrelated to the content of the items. For instance, some people, called "yea-sayers," tend to agree with virtually every statement on a test. Other people, called "nay-sayers," tend to disagree with nearly every statement.

Test developers have devised a number of strategies to reduce the impact of deliberate deception, social desirability bias, and response sets (Berry, Wetter, & Baer, 1995; Lanyon & Goodstein, 1997). For instance, it's possible to insert a "lie scale" into a test to assess the likelihood that a respondent is engaging in deception. The best way to reduce the impact of social desirability bias is to identify items that are sensitive to this bias and drop them from the test. Problems with response sets can be reduced by systematically varying the way in which test items are worded.

Projective Tests PsykTrek 7a

Projective tests, which take a rather indirect approach to the assessment of personality, are used extensively in clinical work. *Projective tests ask participants to respond to vague, ambiguous stimuli in ways that may reveal the subjects' needs, feelings, and personality traits.* The Rorschach test, for instance, consists of a series of ten inkblots. Respondents are asked to describe what they see in the blots. In the Thematic Apperception Test (TAT), a series of pictures of simple scenes is presented to individuals who are asked to tell stories about what is happening in the scenes and what the characters are feeling. For instance, one TAT card shows a young boy contemplating a violin resting on a table in front of him.

THE PROJECTIVE HYPOTHESIS PsykTrek 7a

The "projective hypothesis" is that ambiguous materials can serve as a blank screen onto which people project their characteristic concerns, conflicts, and desires (Frank, 1939). Thus, a competitive person who is shown the TAT card of the boy at the table with the violin might concoct a story about how the boy is contemplating an upcoming musical competition at which he hopes to excel. The same card shown to a person high in impulsiveness might elicit a story about how the boy is planning to sneak out the door to go dirt-bike riding with friends.

The scoring and interpretation of projective tests is very complicated. Rorschach responses may be analyzed in terms of content, originality, the feature of the inkblot that determined the response, and the amount of the inkblot used, among other criteria. In fact, six different systems exist for scoring the Rorschach (Adams & Culbertson, 2005).

TAT stories are examined in terms of heroes, needs, themes, and outcomes.

STRENGTHS AND WEAKNESSES OF PROJECTIVE TESTS

Proponents of projective tests assert that the tests have two unique strengths. First, they are not transparent to respondents. That is, the subject doesn't know how the test provides information to the tester. Hence, it may be difficult for people to engage in intentional deception (Groth-Marnat, 1997). Second, the indirect approach used in these tests may make them especially sensitive to unconscious, latent features of personality.

Unfortunately, the scientific evidence on projective measures is unimpressive (Garb, Florio, & Grove, 1998; Hunsley, Lee, & Wood, 2003; Lanyon & Goodstein, 1997). In a thorough review of the relevant research, Lillienfeld, Wood, and Garb (2000) conclude that projective tests tend to be plagued by inconsistent scoring, low reliability, inadequate test norms, cultural bias, and poor validity estimates. They also assert that, contrary to advocates' claims, projective tests are susceptible to some types of intentional deception (primarily, faking poor mental health). Based on their analysis, Lillienfeld and his colleagues argue that projective tests should be referred to as projective "techniques" or "instruments" rather than tests because "most of these techniques as used in daily clinical practice do not fulfill the traditional criteria for psychological tests" (p. 29). In spite of these problems, projective tests continue to be used by many clinicians. Although the questionable scientific status of these techniques is a very real problem, their continued popularity suggests that they yield subjective information that many clinicians find useful (Viglione & Rivera, 2003).

Hindsight in Everyday Analyses of Personality

KEY LEARNING GOALS

11.18 Understand how hindsight bias affects everyday analyses and theoretical analyses of personality.

Consider the case of two close sisters who grew up together: Lorena and Christina. Lorena grew into a frugal adult who is careful about spending her money, only shops when there are sales, and saves every penny she can. In contrast, Christina became an extravagant spender who lives to shop and never saves any money. How do the sisters explain their striking personality differences? Lorena attributes her thrifty habits to the fact that her family was so poor when she was a child that she learned the value of being careful with money. Christina attributes her extravagant spending to the fact that her family was so poor that she learned to really enjoy any money that she might have. Now, it *is* possible that two sisters could react to essentially the same circumstances quite differently. But the more likely explanation is that both sisters have been influenced by *hindsight bias*—the tendency to mold one's interpretation of the past to fit how events actually turned out. We saw how hindsight can distort memory in Chapter 7. Here, we will see how hindsight tends to make people feel as if they are personality experts and how it creates interpretive problems even for scientific theories of personality.

The Prevalence of Hindsight Bias

Hindsight bias is *ubiquitous,* which means that it occurs in many settings, with all sorts of people (Blank, Musch, & Pohl, 2007; Sanna & Schwarz, 2006). Most of the time, people are not aware of the way their explanations are skewed by the fact that the outcome is already known. The experimental literature on hindsight bias offers a rich array of findings on how the knowledge of an out-

come biases the way people think about its causes (Fischhoff, 2007; Guilbault et al., 2004). For example, when college students were told the results of a hypothetical experiment, each group of students could "explain" why the studies turned out the way they did, even though different groups were given opposite results to explain (Slovic & Fischhoff, 1977). The students believed that the results of the studies were obvious when they were told what the experimenter found. Yet, when they were given only the information that was available before the outcome was known, it was not obvious at all. This bias is also called the "I knew it all along" effect because that is the typical refrain of people when they have the luxury of hindsight.

Indeed, afterward, people often act as if events that would have been difficult to predict had in fact been virtually *inevitable.* Looking back at the 2008 crash of the U.S. mortgage system and ensuing financial meltdown, for instance, many people today act as though these events were bound to happen. In reality, though, these landmark events were predicted by almost no one. It appears that outcome knowledge warps judgments in two ways (Erdfelder, Brandt, & Bröder, 2007). First, knowing the outcome of an event impairs one's recall of earlier expectations about the event. Second, outcome knowledge shapes how people reconstruct their thinking about the event.

Hindsight bias shows up in many contexts. For example, when a couple announces that they are splitting up, many people in their social circle will typically claim they "saw it coming." When a football team loses in a huge upset, you will hear many fans claim, "I knew they were overrated and vulnerable." When public authorities make a difficult decision that leads to a disastrous outcome—such as officials' decision not to evacuate New Orleans in preparation for Hurricane Katrina until relatively late—many of the pundits in the press are quick to criticize, often asserting that only incompetent

fools could have failed to foresee the catastrophe. Interestingly, people are not much kinder to themselves when they make ill-fated decisions. When individuals make tough calls that lead to negative results—such as buying a car that turns out to be a lemon, or investing in a stock that plummets—they often say things like, "Why did I ignore the obvious warning signs?" or "How could I have been such an idiot?"

Hindsight and Personality

Hindsight bias appears to be pervasive in everyday analyses of personality. Think about it: If you attempt to explain why you are so suspicious, why your mother is so domineering, or why your best friend is so insecure, the starting point in each case will be the personality outcome. It would probably be impossible to reconstruct the past without being swayed by your knowledge of these outcomes. Thus, hindsight makes everybody an expert on personality, as we can all come up with plausible explanations for the personality traits of people we know well. Perhaps

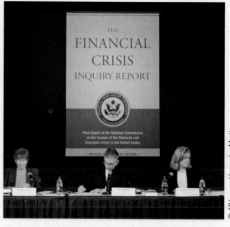

When public officials make complicated decisions that backfire, critics are often quick to argue that the officials should have shown greater foresight. This type of hindsight bias has been apparent in casual discussions and formal analyses of the 2008 economic meltdown in the United States. With the luxury of hindsight it is easy to second-guess bank and stock market regulators who failed to foresee the financial crisis that triggered a worldwide recession.

this is why Judith Harris (1998) ignited a firestorm of protest when she wrote a book arguing that parents have relatively little effect on their children's personalities beyond the genetic material that they supply.

In her book *The Nurture Assumption,* Harris summarizes behavioral genetics research (which we discussed in the main body of the chapter; see p. 381) and other evidence suggesting that family environment has surprisingly little impact on children's personality. There is room for debate on this complex issue (Kagan, 1998; Tavris, 1998). Our chief interest here, though, is that Harris made a cogent, compelling argument that attracted extensive coverage in the press, which generated an avalanche of commentary from angry parents who argued that *parents do matter.* For example, *Newsweek* magazine received 350 letters, mostly from parents who provided examples of how they thought they had influenced their children's personalities. However, parents' retrospective analyses of their children's personality development have to be treated with great skepticism. These analyses are likely to be distorted by hindsight bias (not to mention the selective recall commonly seen in anecdotal reports).

Unfortunately, hindsight bias is so prevalent, it also presents a problem for scientific theories of personality. For example, the issue of hindsight bias has been raised in many critiques of psychoanalytic theory (Torrey, 1992). Freudian theory was originally built mainly on a foundation of case studies of patients in therapy. Obviously, Freudian therapists who knew what their patients' adult personalities were like probably went looking for the types of childhood experiences hypothesized by Freud (oral fixations, punitive toilet training, Oedipal conflicts, and so forth) in their efforts to explain their patients' personalities.

Another problem with hindsight bias is that once researchers know an outcome, more often than not they can fashion some plausible explanation for it. For instance, Torrey (1992) describes a study inspired by Freudian theory that examined breast-size preferences among men. The original hypothesis was that men who scored higher in dependence— thought to be a sign of oral fixation— would manifest a stronger preference for women with large breasts. When the actual results of the study showed just the opposite—that dependence was associated with a preference for smaller breasts—the finding was attributed to reaction formation (the defense mechanism that involves behaving in a way opposite of one's true feelings). Instead of failing to support Freudian theory, the unexpected findings were simply reinterpreted in a way that was consistent with Freudian theory.

Hindsight bias also presents thorny problems for evolutionary theorists, who generally work backward from known outcomes to reason out how adaptive pressures in humans' ancestral past may have led to those outcomes (Cornell, 1997). Consider, for instance, evolutionary theorists' assertion that the Big Five traits are found to be fundamental dimensions of personality around the world because those specific traits have had major adaptive implications over the course of human history (Buss, 1995; Nettle, 2006). Their explanation makes sense, but what would have happened if some *other traits* had shown up in the Big Five? Would the evolutionary view have been weakened if dominance or paranoia had turned up in the Big Five? Probably not. With the luxury of hindsight, evolutionary theorists surely could have constructed plausible explanations for how these traits promoted reproductive success in the distant past. Thus, hindsight bias is a fundamental feature of human

cognition and the scientific enterprise is not immune to this problem.

Other Implications of "20-20 Hindsight"

Our discussion of hindsight has focused on its implications for thinking about personality, but there is ample evidence that hindsight can bias thinking in all sorts of domains. For example, consider the practice of obtaining second opinions on medical diagnoses. The doctor providing the second opinion usually is aware of the first physician's diagnosis, which creates a hindsight bias (Arkes et al., 1981). Second opinions would probably be more valuable if the doctors rendering them were not aware of previous diagnoses. Hindsight also has the potential to distort legal decisions in many types of cases where jurors evaluate defendants' responsibility for known outcomes, such as a failed surgery (Harley, 2007). For example, in trials involving allegations of negligence, jurors' natural tendency to think "how could they have failed to foresee this problem?" may exaggerate the appearance of negligence (LaBine & LaBine, 1996).

Hindsight bias is powerful. The next time you hear of an unfortunate outcome to a decision made by a public official, carefully examine the way news reporters describe the decision. You will probably find that they believe that the disastrous outcome should have been obvious, because they can clearly see what went wrong after the fact. Similarly, if you find yourself thinking, "Only a fool would have failed to anticipate this disaster" or "I would have forseen this problem," take a deep breath and try to review the decision *using only information that was known at the time the decision was being made.* Sometimes good decisions based on the best available information can have terrible outcomes. Unfortunately, the clarity of "20-20 hindsight" makes it difficult for people to learn from their own and others' mistakes.

TABLE 11.3 Critical Thinking Skill Discussed in This Application

Skill	Description
Recognizing the bias in hindsight analysis	The critical thinker understands that knowing the outcome of events biases one's recall and interpretation of the events.

© Cengage Learning

Review of Key Learning Goals

The Nature of Personality

11.1 Clarify the meaning of personality and personality traits.

The concept of personality focuses on consistency in people's behavior over time and across situations and on what traits make people distinctive from one another. Thus, personality refers to an individual's unique constellation of consistent behavioral traits. A personality trait is a durable disposition to behave in a particular way.

11.2 Describe the five-factor model of personality and the relationship between the Big Five traits and life outcomes.

The five-factor model has become the dominant conception of personality structure. The Big Five personality traits are extraversion, neuroticism, openness to experience, agreeableness, and conscientiousness. The Big Five traits are predictive of important life outcomes. For example, occupational attainment is predicted by extraversion, conscientiousness, and neuroticism. Health and mortality are related to neuroticism and conscientiousness.

© Iodrakon/Shutterstock

Psychodynamic Perspectives

11.3 Explain Freud's view of personality structure and the role of conflict and anxiety.

Freud described personality structure in terms of three components—the id, ego, and superego—which are routinely involved in an ongoing series of internal conflicts. Freud described three levels of awareness: the conscious, the preconscious, and the unconscious. His theory emphasized the importance of unconscious processes. Freud theorized that conflicts centering on sex and aggression are especially likely to lead to significant anxiety.

CONSCIOUS:
Contact with outside world

EGO
Reality principle
Secondary-process thinking

PRECONSCIOUS:
Material just beneath the surface of awareness

SUPEREGO
Moral imperatives

UNCONSCIOUS:
Difficult to retrieve material; well below the surface of awareness

ID
Pleasure principle
Primary-process thinking

© Cengage Learning

11.4 Identify key defense mechanisms, and outline Freud's view of development.

According to Freud, anxiety and other unpleasant emotions are often warded off with defense mechanisms. Key defense mechanisms include rationalization, repression, projection, displacement, reaction formation, regression, identification, and sublimation. Freud believed that the first 5 years of life are extremely influential in shaping adult personality. He described a series of five psychosexual stages of development: oral, anal, phallic, latency, and genital. Certain experiences during these stages can

have lasting effects on adult personality. Resolution of the Oedipal complex is thought to be particularly critical to healthy development.

11.5 Summarize the psychodynamic theories proposed by Jung and Adler.

The most innovative concept in Jung's analytical psychology was the collective unconscious, a storehouse of latent memory traces inherited from people's ancestral past. Archetypes are emotionally charged images that have universal meaning. Adler's individual psychology emphasizes how people strive for superiority to compensate for their feelings of inferiority. He explained personality disturbances in terms of inferiority complexes.

11.6 Evaluate the strengths and weaknesses of the psychodynamic approach to personality.

Overall, psychodynamic theories have produced many groundbreaking insights about the unconscious, the role of internal conflict, and the importance of early childhood experiences in personality development. However, psychodynamic theories have been criticized for their poor testability, reliance on unrepresentative samples, inadequate base of empirical evidence, and male-centered views.

Behavioral Perspectives

11.7 Understand Skinner's and Bandura's contributions to behavioral views of personality.

Skinner's followers view personality as a collection of response tendencies tied to specific stimulus situations. They assume that personality development is a lifelong process in which response tendencies are shaped and reshaped by learning, especially operant conditioning. Bandura's social cognitive theory focuses on how observational learning can contribute to individuals' characteristic patterns of behavior. High self-efficacy has been related to successful health regimens, academic success, high athletic performance, and reduced vulnerability to anxiety, depression, and jealousy, among many other things.

11.8 Identify Mischel's principal thesis, and evaluate the behavioral approach to personality.

Mischel has questioned the degree to which people display consistency in behavior across situations. Mischel's arguments have increased awareness of the situational determinants of behavior. Behavioral approaches to personality are based on rigorous research and have provided ample insights into how environmental factors mold personalities. The approach has been criticized in that behavioral theories are not very behavioral anymore. Critics also complain that behaviorists are too quick to generalize from animal research to human behavior.

Humanistic Perspectives

11.9 Explain the impetus for humanism, and articulate Rogers's views on the self-concept.

Humanism emerged as a backlash against psychodynamic and behavioral theories, which were viewed as overly deterministic and dehumanizing. Humanistic theories take an optimistic view of people's conscious, rational ability to chart their own courses of action. Rogers focused on the self-concept as the critical aspect of personality. Incongruence is the degree of disparity between one's self-concept and actual experience. Rogers maintained that unconditional love fosters congruence, whereas conditional love fosters incongruence. Incongruence makes one vulnerable to recurrent anxiety and defensive behavior.

11.10 Describe Maslow's key insights, and evaluate the humanistic approach to personality.

Maslow theorized that needs are organized hierarchically and that psychological health depends on fulfilling one's need for self-actualization, which is the need to realize one's human potential. His work led to the description of self-actualizing persons as idealized examples of psychological health. Recently, theorists have proposed a major revision of Maslow's pyramid of needs in which the higher, growth needs are replaced by motives related to reproductive fitness. Humanistic theories deserve credit for highlighting the importance of subjective views of oneself and psychological health. Humanistic theories lack a firm base of research, are difficult to put to an empirical test, and may be overly optimistic about human nature.

treatment for moral transgressions, elevated respect for cultural icons, and increased prejudice.

Biological Perspectives

11.11 Outline Eysenck's view of personality, and summarize behavioral genetics research on personality.

Eysenck views personality structure as a hierarchy of traits. He believes that heredity influences individual differences in physiological functioning that affect how easily people acquire conditioned inhibitions. Twin studies of the Big Five personality traits find that identical twins are more similar in personality than fraternal twins, thus suggesting that personality is partly inherited. Estimates for the heritability of personality hover in the vicinity of 50%. Recent research in behavioral genetics has suggested that shared family environment has surprisingly little impact on personality.

11.12 Articulate evolutionary explanations for why the Big Five traits are important, and evaluate the biological approach to personality.

According to Buss, the ability to recognize and judge others' status on the Big Five traits may have contributed to reproductive fitness. Nettle argues that the Big Five traits themselves (rather than the ability to recognize them) are products of evolution that were adaptive in ancestral times. Researchers have compiled convincing evidence that genetic factors exert considerable influence over personality. However, the biological approach has been criticized because efforts to carve personality into genetic and environmental components are ultimately artificial.

Contemporary Empirical Approaches to Personality

11.13 Understand the nature, correlates, and social consequences of narcissism.

Narcissism is a trait marked by an inflated sense of self, a need for attention, and a sense of entitlement. People who score high in narcissism work overtime trying to impress others with self-aggrandizing tales of their accomplishments, all to protect their fragile self-esteem. They often are well-liked at first but are eventually seen as arrogant and self-centered. Research suggests that levels of narcissism have been increasing in recent generations.

11.14 Describe the chief concepts of terror management theory.

Terror management theory proposes that self-esteem and faith in a cultural worldview shield people from the profound anxiety associated with their mortality. Consistent with this analysis, increasing mortality salience leads people to make efforts to bolster their self-esteem and defend their worldviews. Manipulations of mortality salience lead to harsh

Culture and Personality

11.15 Clarify how researchers have found both cross-cultural similarities and disparities in personality.

The basic trait structure of personality may be much the same across cultures, as the Big Five traits usually emerge in cross-cultural studies. However, some cultural variability has been seen when researchers compare average trait scores for various cultural groups. Perceptions of national character tend to be inaccurate stereotypes. Markus and Kitayama assert that American culture fosters an independent conception of self as a unique individual who is separate from others. In contrast, Asian cultures foster an interdependent view of the self, as part of an interconnected social matrix.

Reflecting on the Chapter's Themes

11.16 Identify the three unifying themes highlighted in this chapter.

The study of personality illustrates how psychology is characterized by great theoretical diversity. It also demonstrates how ideas in psychology are shaped by sociohistorical forces and how cultural factors influence psychological processes.

PERSONAL APPLICATION
Understanding Personality Assessment

11.17 Explain how personality inventories and projective tests work, and evaluate their strengths and weaknesses.

Self-report inventories ask subjects to describe themselves. The MMPI is a widely used inventory that measures pathological aspects of personality. The NEO personality inventory measures the Big Five personality traits. Self-report inventories are vulnerable to certain sources of error, including deception, the social desirability bias, and response sets. Projective tests, such as the Rorschach and the TAT, assume that subjects' responses to ambiguous stimuli reveal something about their personality. While the projective hypothesis seems plausible, projective tests' reliability and validity are disturbingly low.

CRITICAL THINKING APPLICATION
Hindsight in Everyday Analyses of Personality

11.18 Understand how hindsight bias affects everyday analyses and theoretical analyses of personality.

Hindsight bias often leads people to assert that "I knew it all along" in discussing outcomes that they did not actually predict. Thanks to hindsight, people can almost always come up with plausible-sounding explanations for known personality traits. Psychoanalytic and evolutionary theories of personality have also been accused of falling victim to hindsight bias.

12 Social Behavior

PARADOX

In an emergency, the greater the number of bystanders, the less likely they are to provide help.

Audrey, a 16-year-old junior in high school, takes her cell phone with her everywhere, yet she is loathe to actually talk on her phone. She will do anything to avoid phone conversations. The immediacy of real-time conversation intimidates her. It's not that her phone goes unused. She uses it constantly for texting, which she prefers because she has more control over the communication. She can take time to think and edit her thoughts. She also uses her phone's camera all day long. She snaps away

and posts many pictures to Facebook. "I like to feel that my life is up there," she says. But the life depicted on her Facebook profile is a carefully crafted one. She agonizes over which photos to post. Which ones will portray her in the best light? Which ones will project an appealing "bad" girl image without going too far?

The comments Audrey gets about what she posts shape what she does next. Say Audrey experiments with a flirty style on Facebook. If she gets a good response from her Facebook friends, she'll escalate the flirty tone. One day, she tries out "an ironic, witty" tone in her wall posts. The response is not particularly enthusiastic, so she backs off. Friends who know Audrey in real life give her some leeway as she bends reality a bit. She reciprocates by not challenging their self-presentations.

But sometimes a little spat online can spin out of control. Audrey clashed with a classmate, Logan, in a chat room one day. Feeling she'd been wrong, she apologized to him the next day at school. But Logan wasn't satisfied. He brought the quarrel back online, this time posting his side of the story on Audrey's Facebook page, where all her friends would see it. Audrey felt she had to fight back to counter his smoldering version of what had happened. Day after day, Audrey spent hours in angry online exchanges as friends from both sides joined in the fray. Even six months later, she and Logan, who had been "really good friends" avoided each other in the hall. Eventually, Logan apologized, but it was "an online apology. It's cheap. It's easy. All you have to do is type 'I'm sorry.' You don't have to have any emotion, any believability in your voice or anything," Audrey said. "With an online apology, there are still unanswered questions: 'Is he going to act weird to me now? Are we just going to be normal?' You don't know how the two worlds are going to cross."

Despite her own beliefs about doing certain things in person, Audrey acknowledges that she once broke up with a boyfriend online. She readily admits that she endorses the norm that one should not break off a relationship via text or other online communication, but she claims she just couldn't help herself. "I felt so bad, because I really did care for him, and I couldn't get my-

self to say it. . . . I wasn't trying to chicken out, I just couldn't form the words, so I had to do it online, and I wish I hadn't. He deserved to have me do it in person. . . . I'm very sorry for it. I just think it was a really cold move, and kind of lame."

Source: Turkle, S. (2011). *Alone together*. New York: Basic Books, pp. 189–197.

The preceding account is a real story, taken from Sherry Turkle's book *Alone Together* (2011), which provides a fascinating analysis of how modern technology is altering the fabric of our social relationships. Audrey's story illustrates something that you probably already know—social relationships assume enormous importance in our lives. Audrey, like most of us, is deeply concerned about how others perceive her. She agonizes over the demise of her friendship with Logan and her inability to break up with her boyfriend face-to-face. Audrey's story also illustrates how advances in technology are reshaping the nature of our social behavior. More and more of our social interactions are migrating onto the Internet. Intimate relationships are increasingly forged at online dating sites. Work groups are conducting more and more of their business from distant locations via the Internet. People routinely form their impressions of others from what is posted on social networking sites. Whether these shifts will prove to be fundamental or superficial alterations in our social landscape remains to be seen.

In any event, in this chapter we take a look at our social world. *Social psychology* **is the branch of psychology concerned with the way individuals' thoughts, feelings, and behaviors are influenced by others.** Social psychologists study how people are affected by the actual, imagined, or implied presence of others. Their interest is not limited to individuals' interactions with others, as people can engage in social behavior even when they're alone. For instance, if you were driving by yourself on a deserted highway and tossed your trash out your car window, your littering would be a social action. It would defy social norms, reflect your socialization and attitudes, and have repercussions (albeit, small) for other people in your society. Social psychologists often study individual behavior in a social context. This interest in understanding individual behavior should be readily apparent in our first section, on person perception.

© Stuwdamdorp/Alamy

Person Perception: Forming Impressions of Others

KEY LEARNING GOALS

12.1 Understand how physical appearance and stereotypes may influence impressions of others.

12.2 Discuss the subjectivity of social perception and evolutionary explanations for bias in person perception.

Can you remember the first meeting of your introductory psychology class? What kind of impression did your professor make on you that day? Did your instructor appear to be confident? Easygoing? Pompous? Open-minded? Cynical? Friendly? Were your first impressions supported or undermined by subsequent observations? When you interact with people, you're constantly engaged in *person perception,* **the process of forming impressions of others.** In this section we consider some of the factors that influence, and often distort, people's perceptions of others.

Effects of Physical Appearance

PsykTrek SIM10

"Don't judge a book by its cover." People know better than to let physical attractiveness determine their perceptions of others' personal qualities. Or do they? Recent studies have found that good-looking people command more of our attention than less-attractive individuals do (Lorenzo, Biesanz, & Human, 2010; Maner et al., 2007). And a number of studies have shown that judgments of others' personality are often swayed by their appearance, especially their physical attractiveness. People tend to ascribe desirable personality characteristics to those who are good-looking. Attractive people tend to be seen as more sociable, friendly, poised, warm, and well adjusted than those who are less attractive (Macrae & Quadflieg, 2010; van Leeuwen, Matthijs, & Macrae, 2004). In reality, research findings suggest that little correlation exists between attractiveness and personality traits (Feingold, 1992). Why do we inaccurately assume that a connection exists between good looks and personality? One reason is that extremely attractive people are vastly overrepresented in the entertainment media, where they are mostly portrayed in a highly favorable light (Smith, McIntosh, & Bazzini, 1999). Another reason is that our perceptions are swayed by our desire to bond with attractive people (Lemay, Clark, & Greenberg, 2010).

© R. Gino Santa Maria/Shutterstock

You might guess that physical attractiveness would influence perceptions of competence less than perceptions of personality, but the data suggest otherwise. A review of the relevant research found that people have a surprisingly strong tendency to view good-looking individuals as more competent than less-attractive individuals (Langlois et al., 2000). This bias pays off for good-looking people, as they tend to secure better jobs and earn higher salaries than less-attractive individuals (Collins & Zebrowitz, 1995; Senior et al., 2007). For example, research on attorneys whose law school class photos were evaluated by independent raters found that physical attractiveness boosted income by 10%–12% (Engemann & Owyang, 2005). Another study (Judge, Hurst, & Simon, 2009) compared the impact of brains versus beauty on income. As one would expect (and hope), intelligence was more strongly related to earnings (correlation = .50) than good looks. But the correlation of .24 between attractiveness and income was not trivial.

Observers are also quick to draw inferences about people based on how they move, talk, and gesture—that is, their style of nonverbal expressiveness. Moreover, these inferences tend to be fairly accurate (Ambady & Rosenthal, 1993; Borkenau et al., 2004). For example, based on a mere 10 seconds of videotape, participants can guess strangers' sexual orientation (heterosexual-homosexual) with some accuracy (Ambady, Hallahan, & Conner, 1999). Based on similar "thin slices" of behavior, observers can make accurate judgments of individuals' racial prejudice, social status, and intelligence (Ambady & Weisbuch, 2010). Even static photographs can provide telling cues about personality. One recent study found that participants were able to make meaningful inferences about stimulus persons' extraversion, openness to experience, agreeableness, and self-esteem based on simple photographs (Naumann et al., 2009).

DILBERT

Stereotypes

Stereotypes can have a dramatic effect on the process of person perception. **Stereotypes are widely held beliefs that people have certain characteristics because of their membership in a particular group.** The most common stereotypes in our society are those based on gender, age, and membership in ethnic or occupational groups. People who subscribe to traditional *gender stereotypes* tend to assume that women are emotional, submissive, illogical, and passive, while men are unemotional, dominant, logical, and aggressive. Preconceived notions that Jews are mercenary, blacks have rhythm, Germans are methodical, and Italians are passionate are examples of common *ethnic stereotypes. Occupational stereotypes* suggest that lawyers are manipulative, computer programmers are nerdy, accountants are conforming, artists are moody, and so forth.

Stereotyping is a normal cognitive process that is often automatic and that saves on the time and effort required to get a handle on people individually (Fiske & Russell, 2010). Stereotypes save energy by simplifying our social world. However, this conservation of energy often comes at some cost in terms of accuracy (Stangor, 2009). Stereotypes tend to be broad overgeneralizations that ignore the diversity within social groups and foster inaccurate perceptions of people (Hilton & von Hippel, 1996). Obviously, not all males, Jews, and lawyers behave alike. Most people who subscribe to stereotypes realize that not all members of a group are identical. For instance, they may admit that some men aren't competitive, some Jews aren't mercenary, and some lawyers aren't manipulative. However, people may still tend to assume that males, Jews, and lawyers are *more likely* than others to have these characteristics. Even if stereotypes mean only that people think in terms of slanted *probabilities,* their expectations may lead them to misperceive individuals with whom they interact. As we've noted in previous chapters, perception is subjective. People often see what they expect to see.

Subjectivity in Person Perception

Stereotypes and other schemas create biases in person perception that often lead to confirmation of people's expectations about others. If any ambiguity exists in someone's behavior, people are likely to interpret what they see in a way that's consistent with their expectations (Olson, Roese, & Zanna, 1996). People not only see what they expect to see, they also tend to overestimate how often they see it (Johnson & Mullen, 1994; Shavitt et al., 1999). The *illusory correlation* occurs when people estimate that they have encountered more confirmations of an association between social traits than they have actually seen. People also tend to underestimate the number of disconfirmations they have encountered, as illustrated by statements like "I've never met an honest lawyer."

Memory processes can contribute to confirmatory biases in person perception in a variety of ways. Often, individuals selectively recall facts that fit with their schemas and stereotypes (Fiske, 1998; Quinn, Macrae, & Bodenhausen, 2003). Evidence for such a tendency was found in a study by Cohen (1981). In this experiment, subjects watched a videotape of a woman, described as either a waitress or a librarian, who engaged in a variety of activities, including listening to classical music, drinking beer, and watching TV. When asked to recall what the woman did during the filmed sequence, participants tended to remember activities consistent with their stereotypes of waitresses and librarians. For instance, participants who thought the woman was a waitress tended to recall her drinking beer, whereas subjects who thought she was a librarian tended to recall her listening to classical music.

An Evolutionary Perspective on Bias in Person Perception

Why is the process of person perception riddled with bias? Evolutionary psychologists argue that many of the biases seen in social perception were adaptive in humans' ancestral environment (Krebs & Denton, 1997). For example, they argue that person perception is swayed by physical attractiveness because attractiveness was associated with reproductive potential in women and with health, vigor, and the accumulation of material resources in men.

Evolutionary theorists attribute the human tendency to automatically categorize others to our distant ancestors' need to quickly separate friend from foe. They assert that humans are programmed by evolution to immediately classify people as members of an *ingroup—a group that one belongs to and identifies with,* or as members of an *outgroup—a group that one does not belong to or identify with.* This crucial categorization is thought to structure subsequent perceptions. As Krebs and Denton (1997) put it, "It is as though the act of classifying others as ingroup or outgroup members activates two quite different brain circuits" (p. 27). Ingroup members tend to be viewed in a favorable light, whereas outgroup members tend to be viewed in terms of various negative stereotypes. According to Krebs and Denton, these negative stereotypes ("They are inferior; they are all alike; they will exploit us") move outgroups out of our domain of empathy, so we feel justified in not liking them. Thus, evolutionary psychologists assert that much of the bias in person perception is due to cognitive mechanisms that have been wired into the human brain by natural selection.

Attribution Processes: Explaining Behavior

It's Friday evening and you're sitting around at home feeling bored. You call a few friends to see whether they'd like to go out. They all say that they'd love to go, but they have other commitments and they can't. Their commitments sound vague, and you feel that their reasons for not going out with you are rather flimsy. How do you explain these rejections? Do your friends really have commitments? Are they worn out by school and work? Are they just lazy and apathetic about going out? These questions illustrate a process that people engage in routinely: the explanation of behavior. *Attributions* play a key role in these explanatory efforts, and they have significant effects on social relations.

What are attributions? *Attributions* are inferences that people draw about the causes of events, others' behavior, and their own behavior. If you conclude that a friend turned down your invitation because she's overworked, you've made an attribution about the cause of her behavior (and, implicitly, rejected other possible explanations). If you conclude that you're stuck at home with nothing to do because you failed to plan ahead, you've made an attribution about the cause of an event (being stuck at home). If you conclude that you failed to plan ahead because you're a procrastinator, you've made an attribution about the cause of your own behavior. *Why do people make attributions?* Individuals make attributions because they have a strong need to understand their experiences. They want to make sense out of their own behavior, others' actions, and the events in their lives.

Internal Versus External Attributions

PSYKTREK 12a

Fritz Heider (1958) was the first to describe how people make attributions. He asserted that people tend to locate the cause of behavior either *within a person,* attributing it to personal factors, or *outside a person,* attributing it to environmental factors.

Elaborating on Heider's insight, various theorists have agreed that explanations of behavior and events can be categorized as internal or external attributions (Jones & Davis, 1965; Kelley, 1967; Weiner, 1974). **Internal attributions ascribe the causes of behavior to personal dispositions, traits, abilities, and feelings. External attributions ascribe the causes of behavior to situational demands and environmental constraints.** For example, if a friend's business fails, you might attribute it to your friend's lack of business knowledge (an internal, personal factor) or to negative trends in the nation's economic climate (an external, situational explanation). Parents who find out that their teenage son has just banged up the car may blame it on his carelessness (an internal attribution) or on slippery road conditions (an external attribution).

Internal and external attributions can have a tremendous impact on everyday interpersonal interactions. Blaming a friend's business failure on poor business smarts as opposed to a poor economy will have a great impact on how you view your friend—not to mention on whether you'll lend him or her money in the future. Likewise, if parents attribute their son's automobile accident to slippery road conditions, they're likely to deal with the event very differently than if they attribute it to his carelessness.

Attributions for Success and Failure

PSYKTREK 12a

Some psychologists have sought to discover additional dimensions of attributional thinking besides the internal-external dimension. After studying the attributions that people make in explaining success and failure, Bernard Weiner (1980, 1986, 1994) concluded that people often focus on the *stability* of the causes underlying behavior. According to Weiner, the stable-unstable dimension in attribution cuts across the internal-external dimension, creating four types of attributions for success and failure, as shown in **Figure 12.1**.

Let's apply Weiner's model to a concrete event. Imagine that you're contemplating why you failed to get a job that you wanted. You might attribute your setback to internal factors that are stable (lack of ability) or unstable (inadequate effort to put together an eye-catching résumé). Or you might attribute your setback to external factors that are stable (too much outstanding competition) or unstable (bad luck). If you got the job, the explanations you might offer for your success would fall into the same four categories: internal-stable (your

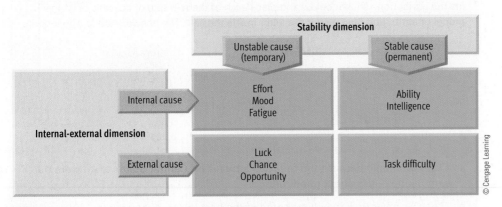

© Cengage Learning

FIGURE 12.1

Weiner's model of attributions for success and failure. Weiner's model assumes that people's explanations for success and failure emphasize internal versus external causes and stable versus unstable causes. Examples of causal factors that fit into each of the four cells in Weiner's model are shown in the diagram.

SOURCE: Weiner, B., Friese, I., Kukla, A., Reed, L., & Rosenbaum, R. M. (1972). Perceiving the causes of success and failure. In E. E. Jones, D. E. Kanouse, H. H. Kelley, R. E. Nisbett, S. Valins, & B. Weiner (Eds.) *Perceiving the causes of behavior.* Morristown, NJ: General Learning Press. Used by permission of Bernard Weiner.

excellent ability), internal-unstable (your hard work to assemble a superb résumé), external-stable (lack of top-flight competition), and external-unstable (good luck).

Bias in Attribution

PSYKTREK 12a

Attributions are only inferences. Your attributions may not be the correct explanations for events. Paradoxical as it may seem, people often arrive at inaccurate explanations even when they contemplate the causes of *their own behavior*. Attributions ultimately represent guesswork about the causes of events, and these guesses tend to be slanted in certain directions. Let's look at the principal biases seen in attribution.

ACTOR-OBSERVER BIAS

PSYKTREK 12a

Your view of your own behavior can be quite different from the view of someone else observing you. When an actor (the person exhibiting the behavior) and an observer draw inferences about the causes of the actor's behavior, they often make different attributions. The *fundamental attribution error* **refers to observers' bias in favor of internal attributions in explaining others' behavior.** Of course, in many instances, an internal attribution may not be an "error." However, observers have a curious tendency to overestimate the likelihood that an actor's behavior reflects personal qualities rather than situational factors (Krull, 2001). Why? Primarily because attributing others' behavior to their dispositions is a relatively effortless, almost automatic process. In contrast, explaining people's behavior in terms of situational factors requires more thought and effort (see **Figure 12.2**) (Krull & Erickson, 1995). Another factor favoring internal attributions is that many people feel that few situations are so coercive that they negate all freedom of choice (Forsyth, 2004).

To illustrate the gap that often exists between actors' and observers' attributions, imagine that you're visiting your bank and you fly into a rage over a mistake made on your account. Observers who witness your rage

Concept Check   12.1

Analyzing Attributions

Check your understanding of attribution processes by analyzing possible explanations for an athletic team's success. Imagine that the women's track team at your school has just won a regional championship that qualifies it for the national tournament. Around the campus, you hear people attribute the team's success to a variety of factors. Examine the attributions shown below and place each of them in one of the cells of Weiner's model of attribution (just record the letter inside the cell). The answers are in Appendix A.

	Unstable cause (temporary)	Stable cause (permanent)
Internal cause		
External cause		

a. "They won only because the best two athletes on Central State's team were out with injuries—talk about good fortune!"

b. "They won because they have some of the best talent in the country."

c. "Anybody could win this region; the competition is far below average in comparison to the rest of the country."

d. "They won because they put in a great deal of last-minute effort and practice, and they were incredibly fired up for the regional tourney after last year's near miss."

are likely to make an internal attribution and infer that you are surly, temperamental, and quarrelsome. They may be right, but if asked, you'd probably attribute your rage to the frustrating situation. Perhaps you're normally a calm, easygoing person, but today you've been in line for 20 minutes, you just straightened out a similar error by the same bank last week, and you're being treated rudely by the teller. Observers often are unaware of situational considerations such as these. Hence, they tend to make internal attributions for another's behavior (Gilbert, 1998).

In contrast, the circumstances that have influenced an actor's behavior tend to be more salient to the actor. Hence, actors are more likely than observers to locate the cause of their behavior in the situation. In general, then, *actors favor external attributions for their behavior, while observers are more likely to explain the same behavior with internal attributions* (Jones & Nisbett, 1971; Krueger, Ham, & Linford, 1996).

SELF-SERVING BIAS

PsykTrek 12a

The self-serving bias in attribution comes into play when people attempt to explain success and failure (Mezulis et al., 2004; Shepperd, Malone, & Sweeny, 2008). **The *self-serving bias* is the tendency to attribute one's successes to personal factors and one's failures to situational factors.** In explaining *failure,* the usual actor-observer biases are apparent. But in explaining *success,* the usual actor-observer differences are reversed to some degree: Actors prefer internal attributions so they can take credit for their triumphs. Interestingly, this bias grows stronger as time passes after an event, so that people tend to take progressively more credit for their successes and less blame for their failures (Burger, 1986).

Culture and Attributions

Do the patterns of attribution observed in subjects from Western societies transcend culture? More research is needed, but the preliminary evidence suggests not. Some interesting cultural disparities have emerged in research on attribution processes.

According to Harry Triandis (1989, 1994, 2001), cultural differences in *individualism* versus *collectivism* influence attributional tendencies as well as other aspects of social behavior. *Individualism* **involves putting personal goals ahead of group goals and defining one's identity in terms of personal attributes rather than group memberships.** In contrast, *collectivism* **involves putting group goals ahead of personal goals and defining one's identity in terms of the groups one belongs to** (such as one's family, tribe, work group, social class, caste, and so on). In comparison to individualistic cultures, collectivist cultures place a higher priority on shared values and resources, cooperation, mutual interdependence, and concern for how one's actions will affect other group members. Generally speaking, North American and Western European cultures tend to be individualistic, whereas Asian, African, and Latin American cultures tend to be collectivistic (Hofstede, 1980, 1983, 2001).

How does individualism versus collectivism relate to patterns of attribution? The evidence suggests that collectivist cultures may promote different attributional biases than individualistic cultures do. For example, people from collectivist societies appear to be less susceptible to the *fundamental attribution error* than those from individualistic societies (Choi, Nisbett, & Norenzayan, 1999; Triandis, 2001). And the *self-serving bias* may be particularly prevalent in individualistic, Western societies, where an emphasis on competition and high self-esteem motivates people to try to impress others, as well as themselves (Mezulis et al., 2004). In contrast, Japanese individuals exhibit a *self-effacing bias* in explaining success (Akimoto & Sanbonmatsu, 1999). That is, they tend to attribute their successes to help they receive from others or to the ease of the task, while downplaying the importance of their ability.

Traditional model of attribution

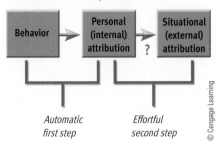

Alternative two-step model of attribution

Automatic first step *Effortful second step*

FIGURE 12.2

An alternative view of the fundamental attribution error. According to Gilbert (1989) and others, the nature of attribution processes favors the *fundamental attribution error.* Traditional models of attribution assume that internal and external attributions are an either-or proposition requiring equal amounts of effort. In contrast, the two-step model of attribution posits that people tend to automatically make internal attributions with little effort, then *may* expend additional effort to adjust for the influence of situational factors, which can lead to an external attribution. Thus, external attributions for others' behavior require more thought and effort, which makes them less common than personal attributions.

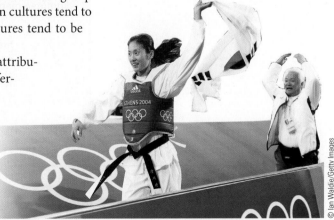

Triumphant athletes from cultures high in collectivism typically exhibit different attributional biases than winning athletes from Western societies that are high in individualism. Collectivist cultures tend to promote a self-effacing bias in explaining success, rather than a self-serving bias.

Interpersonal Attraction: Liking and Loving

KEY LEARNING GOALS

12.5 Understand the role of physical attractiveness, similarity, and reciprocity in attraction.

12.6 Discuss theoretical views of love and how culture and the Internet relate to romantic relationships.

12.7 Understand evolutionary analyses of mating preferences.

© Andres Rodriguez/Alamy

"I just don't know what she sees in him. She could do so much better for herself. I suppose he's a nice guy, but they're just not right for each other." Can't you imagine someone in your social circle making these comments in discussing a mutual friend's new boyfriend? You've probably heard similar remarks on many occasions. These comments illustrate people's interest in analyzing the dynamics of attraction. *Interpersonal attraction* **refers to positive feelings toward another person.** Social psychologists use this term broadly to encompass a variety of experiences, including liking, friendship, admiration, lust, and love.

Key Factors in Attraction

Many factors influence who is attracted to whom. Here we'll discuss factors that promote the development of liking, friendship, and love. Although these are different types of attraction, the interpersonal dynamics at work in each are surprisingly similar.

PHYSICAL ATTRACTIVENESS

It is often said that "beauty is only skin deep." But the empirical evidence suggests that most people don't really believe this saying (Fitness, Fletcher, & Overall, 2003). The importance of physical attractiveness was shown in a study of college students in which unacquainted men and women were sent off on a "get-acquainted" date (Sprecher & Duck, 1994). The researchers were mainly interested in how communication might affect the process of attraction.

Concept Check 12.2

Recognizing Bias in Social Cognition

Check your understanding of bias in social cognition by identifying various types of errors that are common in person perception and attribution. Imagine that you're a nonvoting student member of a college committee at Southwest State University that is hiring a new political science professor. As you listen to the committee's discussion, you hear examples of (a) the illusory correlation effect, (b) stereotyping, and (c) the fundamental attribution error. Indicate which of these is at work in the excerpts from committee members' deliberations below. The answers are in Appendix A.

_____ 1. "I absolutely won't consider the fellow who arrived 30 minutes late for his interview. Anybody who can't make a job interview on time is either irresponsible or hopelessly disorganized. I don't care what he says about the airline messing up his reservations."

_____ 2. "You know, I was very, very impressed with the young female applicant, and I would love to hire her, but every time we add a young woman to the faculty in liberal arts, she gets pregnant within the first year." The committee chairperson, who has heard this line from this professor before replies, "You always say that, so I finally did a systematic check of what's happened in the past. Of the last 14 women hired in liberal arts, only one has become pregnant within a year."

_____ 3. "The first one I want to rule out is the guy who's been practicing law for the last ten years. Although he has an excellent background in political science, I just don't trust lawyers. They're all ambitious, power hungry, manipulative cutthroats. He'll be a divisive force in the department."

© Christo/Shutterstock

However, to put this factor in context they also measured participants' perceptions of their date's physical attractiveness and similarity to themselves. They found that the quality of communication during the date did have some effect on females' interest in friendship, but the key determinant of romantic attraction for both sexes was the physical attractiveness of the other person. Consistent with this finding, research has shown, as one might expect, that attractive people of both sexes enjoy greater mating success than their less-attractive peers (Rhodes, Simmons, & Peters, 2005). Many other studies have demonstrated the singular prominence of physical attractiveness in the initial stage of dating and have shown that it continues to influence the course of commitment as relationships evolve (McNulty, Neff, & Karney, 2008; Patzer, 2006). In the realm of romance, being physically attractive appears to be more important for females' desirability (Gottschall, 2007; Regan, 2003). For example, in a study of college students (Speed & Gangestad, 1997), the correlation between romantic popularity (assessed by peer ratings) and physical attractiveness was higher for females (.76) than for males (.47).

Although people prefer physically attractive partners in romantic relationships, they may consider their own level of attractiveness in pursuing dates. What people want in a partner may be different from what they are willing to settle for (Regan, 1998). **The matching hypothesis proposes that males and females of approximately equal physical attractiveness are likely to select each other as partners.** The matching hypothesis is supported by evidence that dating and married couples tend to be similar in level of physical attractiveness (Regan, 1998, 2008). Not surprisingly, research suggests that attractive people expect to date more-attractive individuals and unattractive people expect to date less-attractive partners (Montoya, 2008). One recent study relevant to the matching hypothesis examined requests to get acquainted at the HOTorNOT.com website, where members routinely rate each others' level of physical attractiveness (Lee et al., 2008). As one would expect, more-attractive members were more selective in agreeing to get acquainted with others than less-attractive members were. The study also looked at whether less-attractive persons deluded themselves into thinking that their prospective partners were more attractive than others perceived them to be. The results did not support this "rationalization" hypothesis. Instead, the data suggested that less-attractive people place less weight on physical attractiveness than good-looking people do.

SIMILARITY EFFECTS

Is it true that "birds of a feather flock together," or do "opposites attract"? Research provides far more support for the former than the latter (Surra et al., 2006). Married and dating couples tend to be similar in age, race, religion, social class, education, intelligence, physical attractiveness, and attitudes (Kalmijn, 1998; Watson et al., 2004). The similarity principle operates in both friendships and romantic relationships regardless of sexual orientation (Fehr, 2008; Morry, 2007, 2009; Peplau & Fingerhut, 2007). In a longitudinal study of best friends, researchers found that similarity among friends in 1983 actually predicted their closeness in 2002—19 years later (Ledbetter, Griffin, & Sparks (2007). The most obvious explanation for these correlations is that similarity causes attraction (Byrne, 1997). However, research also suggests that attraction can foster similarity (Anderson, Keltner, & John, 2003) as people who are close gradually modify their attitudes in ways that make them more congruent, a phenomenon they called *attitude alignment*.

RECIPROCITY EFFECTS

In interpersonal attraction, *reciprocity* **involves liking those who show that they like you.** In general, research indicates that we tend to like those who show that they like us and that we tend to see others as liking us more if we like them. Thus, it appears that liking breeds liking and loving promotes loving (Sprecher, 1998). Reciprocating attraction generally entails providing friends and intimate partners with positive feedback that results in a *self-enhancement* effect—in other words, you help them feel good about themselves (Sedikides & Strube, 1997).

© Warren Goldswain/Shutterstock

According to the matching hypothesis, males and females who are similar in physical attractiveness are likely to be drawn together. This type of matching may also influence the formation of friendships.

Reality Check

Misconception

In the realm of romance, opposites attract.

Reality

There is absolutely no empirical evidence to support this folklore. Research consistently shows that couples tend to be similar in intelligence, education, social status, ethnicity, physical attractiveness, and attitudes. Dissimilarity does not foster attraction.

"It would never work out between us, Tom—We're from two totally different tiers of the upper middle class."

Adult attachment style

Secure
I find it relatively easy to get close to others and am comfortable depending on them and having them depend on me. I don't often worry about being abandoned or about someone getting too close to me.

Avoidant
I am somewhat uncomfortable being close to others; I find it difficult to trust them, difficult to allow myself to depend on them. I am nervous when anyone gets too close, and often love partners want me to be more intimate than I feel comfortable being.

Anxious/ambivalent
I find that others are reluctant to get as close as I would like. I often worry that my partner doesn't really love me or won't want to stay with me. I want to merge completely with another person, and this desire sometimes scares people away.

FIGURE 12.3

Attachment and romantic relationships. According to Hazan and Shaver (1987), people's romantic relationships in adulthood are similar in form to their attachment patterns in infancy, which fall into three categories. The three attachment styles seen in adult intimate relations are described here. (Based on Hazan and Shaver, 1986, 1987)

Perspectives on the Mystery of Love

PsykTrek 12b

Love has proven to be an elusive subject. It's difficult to define and study because there are many types of love (Berscheid, 2006). Nonetheless, psychologists have begun to make some progress in their study of love. Let's look at their theories and research.

PASSIONATE AND COMPANIONATE LOVE

PsykTrek 12b

In an influential analysis, some theorists have proposed that romantic relationships are characterized by two kinds of love: passionate love and companionate love (Berscheid, 1988; Hatfield & Rapson, 1993). *Passionate love* **is a complete absorption in another that includes tender sexual feelings and the agony and ecstasy of intense emotion.** Passionate love has its ups and downs. It's associated with large swings in positive and negative emotions (Reis & Aron, 2008). *Companionate love* **is warm, trusting, tolerant affection for another whose life is deeply intertwined with one's own.** Passionate and companionate love *may* coexist. They don't, however, necessarily go hand in hand. Research suggests that, as a general rule, companionate love is more strongly related to relationship satisfaction than passionate love is (Fehr, 2001).

Research suggests that passionate love is a powerful motivational force that produces profound changes in people's thinking, emotion, and behavior (Reis & Aron, 2008). Interestingly, brain-imaging research indicates that when people think about someone they are passionately in love with, these thoughts light up the dopamine circuits in the brain that are known to be activated by cocaine and other addictive drugs (Aron, Fisher, & Mashek, 2005). Perhaps that explains why passionate love sometimes resembles an addiction.

LOVE AS ATTACHMENT

PsykTrek 12b

In another groundbreaking analysis of love, Hazan and Shaver (1987) have looked at similarities between adult love and attachment relationships in infancy. We noted in Chapter 10 that infant-caretaker bonding, or *attachment,* emerges in the first year of life. Early attachments vary in quality, and infants tend to fall into three groups (Ainsworth et al., 1978). Most infants develop a *secure attachment.* However, some are very anxious when separated from their caretaker, a syndrome called *anxious-ambivalent attachment.* A third group of infants, characterized by *avoidant attachment,* never bond very well with their caretaker.

According to Hazan and Shaver, romantic love is an attachment process, and people's intimate relationships in adulthood follow the same form as their attachments in infancy. In their theory, a person who had an anxious-ambivalent attachment in infancy will tend to have romantic relations marked by anxiety and ambivalence in adulthood. In other words, people relive their early bonding experiences with their parents in their romantic relationships in adulthood.

Hazan and Shaver's (1987) initial survey study provided striking support for their theory. They found that adults' love relationships could be sorted into groups that paralleled the three patterns of attachment seen in infants (see **Figure 12.3**). *Secure adults* found it relatively easy to get close to others and described their love relations as trusting. *Anxious-ambivalent adults* reported a preoccupation with love accompanied by expectations of rejection, and they described their love relations as volatile and marked by jealousy. *Avoidant adults* found it difficult to get close to others and described their love relations as lacking intimacy and trust. Research eventually showed that attachment patterns are reasonably stable over time (Mikulincer & Shaver, 2007) and that people's working models of attachment are carried forward from one relationship to the next (Brumbaugh & Fraley, 2006). These findings supported the notion that individuals' infant attachment experiences shape their intimate relations in adulthood.

Research on the correlates of adult attachment styles has grown exponentially since the mid-1990s. Consistent with the original theory, research has shown that securely attached individuals have more committed, satisfying, interdependent, well-adjusted, and longer-lasting relationships compared to people with anxious-ambivalent or avoidant attachment styles (Feeney, 2008). Moreover, studies have shown that people with different attachment styles are predisposed to think, feel, and behave differently in their relationships (Mikulincer & Shaver, 2008). For example, anxious-ambivalent people tend to report more intense emotional highs and lows in their romantic relationships. They also report having more conflicts with their partners, that these conflicts are especially stressful, and that these conflicts often have a negative impact on how they feel about their relationship (Campbell et al., 2005). In a similar vein, attachment anxiety promotes *excessive reassurance seeking*—the tendency to persistently ask for assurances from partners that one is worthy of love (Shaver, Schachner, & Mikulincer, 2005).

Culture and Close Relationships

The limited evidence available suggests both similarities and differences among cultures in romantic relationships (Hendrick & Hendrick, 2000; Schmitt, 2005). For the most part, similarities have been seen when research has focused on what people look for in prospective mates—such as mutual attraction, kindness, and intelligence (Buss, 1989, 1994b). Cultures vary, however, in their emphasis on love—especially passionate love—as a prerequisite for marriage. Although romantic love appears to be found in all cultures (Buss, 2006), passionate love as the basis for marriage is an 18th-century invention of Western culture (Stone, 1977). As Hatfield and Rapson (1993) note, "Marriage-for-love represents an ultimate expression of individualism" (p. 2). In contrast, marriages arranged by families and other go-betweens remain common in cultures high in collectivism, including India, Japan, and China (Hatfield, Rapson, & Martel, 2007). This practice is declining in some societies as a result of Westernization. Nonetheless, in collectivist societies people contemplating marriage still tend to think in terms of "What will my parents and other people say?" rather than "What does my heart say?" (Triandis, 1994). Although romantic love is routinely seen in collectivist societies (Lieberman & Hatfield, 2006), subjects from societies high in individualism tend to report that romantic love is more important for marriage than subjects from collectivist cultures do (Dion & Dion, 2006; Levine et al., 1995).

© Jon Bower Japan/Alamy

The Internet and Close Relationships

In recent years the Internet has dramatically expanded opportunities for people to meet and develop close relationships through social networking sites (Google+, Facebook), online dating services, e-mail, and chat rooms. Some critics worry that this trend will undermine face-to-face interactions and that many people will be lured into dangerous liaisons by unscrupulous people. But research to date generally paints a positive picture of the Internet's impact on people's connections with one another (Whitty, 2008). For example, the Internet offers a wealth of opportunities to interact for those who suffer from physical infirmities or social anxieties (McKenna & Bargh, 2000). Also, Internet groups provide a safer venue than real life for individuals with stigmatized identities (for example, gay people) to interact and receive support.

Critics are concerned that Internet relationships tend to be superficial. Research, however, suggests that virtual relationships are just as intimate as face-to-face ones and are sometimes even closer (Bargh, McKenna, & Fitzsimons, 2002). Moreover, many virtual relationships evolve into face-to-face interactions (Boase & Wellman, 2006). Researchers find that romantic relationships that begin on the Internet seem to be just as stable over two years as traditional relationships (McKenna, Green, & Gleason, 2002). The relevance of the Internet to interpersonal attraction is not limited to dating. Many people join various types of social networking sites in the hopes of making new friends, and their hopes are often realized (Fehr, 2008; McKenna, 2008).

The power of similarity effects provides the foundation for some of the Internet's most successful online dating sites. Prior to 2000 web dating sites were basically just an electronic variation on the personal ads that had been around for decades—with the addition of sophisticated search capabilities. But in 2000 eHarmony.com launched the first matching website. This site claims to use a "scientific approach" to matching people based on compatibility. Members fill out lengthy questionnaires about their attitudes, values, interests, and so forth, and then matching algorithms are used to identify people who exhibit promising similarity. The commercial success of eHarmony.com has led many other online dating sites to add matching services. These sites have not published their matching formulas, so it is hard to say just how scientific they are, but many of the sites employ legitimate research experts as consultants (Sprecher et al., 2008). Hence, it seems likely that many of them use matching algorithms that are grounded in empirical research on interpersonal attraction. Of course, as you have already learned in this chapter, similarity is just one of many factors that plays a role in the dynamics of attraction. Still, it is interesting to note that the growth of the Internet has brought psychological science into play in the domain of close relationships.

An Evolutionary Perspective on Attraction

Evolutionary psychologists have a great deal to say about heterosexual attraction. For example, they assert that physical appearance is an influential determinant of attraction because certain aspects of good looks can be indicators of sound health, good genes, and high fertility, all of which can contribute to reproductive potential (Gallup & Frederick, 2010). Consistent with the evolutionary view, research has found that some standards of attractiveness are more consistent across cultures than previously believed (Sugiyama, 2005). For example, *facial symmetry* seems to be a key element of attractiveness in highly diverse cultures (Fink & Penton-Voak, 2002). Facial symmetry is thought to be valued because a variety of environmental insults and developmental abnormalities are associated with physical asymmetries, which may serve as markers of relatively poor genes or health (Fink et al., 2006).

The most thoroughly documented findings on the evolutionary bases of heterosexual attraction are those on gender differences in mating preferences, which appear to be consistent across highly varied cultures (Neuberg, Kenrick, & Schaller, 2010). In keeping with the notion that humans are programmed by evolution to behave in ways that enhance their reproductive fitness, evidence indicates that men generally are more interested than women in seeking youthfulness and physical attractiveness in their mates because these traits should be associated with greater reproductive potential (see Chapter 9). On the other hand, research shows that women place a greater premium on prospective mates' ambition, social status, and financial potential because these traits should be associated with the ability to invest material resources in children (Li et al., 2002; Shackelford et al., 2005). There are some qualifications to these trends, but even these caveats make evolutionary sense. For example, when women are asked what they prefer in a *short-term partner* (for casual sex) they value physical attractiveness just as much as men (Li & Kenrick, 2006). And very attractive women, aware of their own high mate value, want it all—they want prospective male partners to exhibit excellent economic potential *and* physical attractiveness (Buss & Shackelford, 2008).

Does the gender gap in mating priorities influence the tactics people actually use in pursuing romantic relationships? Yes, evidence indicates that during courtship men tend to emphasize their material resources, whereas women are more likely to work at enhancing their appearance (Buss, 1988). Interestingly, the tactics used by both sexes may include efforts at deception (Rowatt, Cunningham, & Druen, 1999). Consistent with evolutionary theory, women report that they are most upset when men exaggerate their social status, their financial resources, or the depth of their romantic commitment to the woman, whereas men are most upset when women conceal a history of "promiscuity" (Haselton et al., 2005).

Attitudes: Making Social Judgments

Social psychology's interest in attitudes has a much longer history than its interest in attraction. Indeed, in its early days social psychology was defined as the study of attitudes. In this section we'll discuss the nature of attitudes, efforts to change attitudes through persuasion, and theories of attitude change.

What are attitudes? *Attitudes* **are positive or negative evaluations of objects of thought.** "Objects of thought" may include social issues (capital punishment or gun control, for example), groups (liberals, farmers), institutions (the Lutheran church, the Supreme Court), consumer products (yogurt, computers), and people (the president, your next-door neighbor).

Components and Dimensions of Attitudes

Social psychologists have traditionally viewed attitudes as being made up of three components: a cognitive component, an affective component, and a behavioral component. However, in recent years it has become apparent that many attitudes do not include all three components (Fazio & Olson, 2003). Thus, it is more accurate to say that attitudes may include up to three components (Banaji & Heiphetz, 2010). The *cognitive component* of an attitude is made up of the beliefs that people hold about the object of an attitude. The *affective component* consists of the *emotional feelings* stimulated by an object of thought. The *behavioral component* consists of *predispositions to act* in certain ways toward an attitude object. **Figure 12.4** on the next page provides concrete examples of how someone's attitude about gun control might be divided into its components.

Attitudes also vary along several crucial dimensions. These include their *strength, accessibility,* and *ambivalence* (Olson & Maio, 2003). Definitions of *attitude strength* differ. However, strong attitudes are genereally viewed as ones that are firmly held (resistant to change), that are durable over time, and that have a powerful impact on behavior (Petty, Wheeler, & Tormala, 2003). The *accessibility* of an attitude refers to how often one thinks about it and how quickly it comes to mind. Highly accessible attitudes are quickly and readily available (Fabrigar, MacDonald, & Wegener, 2005). Attitude accessibility is correlated with attitude strength, as highly accessible attitudes *tend* to be strong. But the concepts are distinct and there is no one-to-one correspondence. *Ambivalent attitudes* are conflicted evaluations that include both positive and negative feelings about an object of thought (Fabrigar et al., 2005). When ambivalence is high, an attitude tends to be more pliable in the face of persuasion (Fabrigar & Wegener, 2010).

How well do attitudes predict actual behavior? Research on attitudes has yielded a surprising answer to this question. Studies have repeatedly shown that attitudes are mediocre predictors of people's behavior (Ajzen & Fishbein, 2005). When Wallace and colleagues (2005) reviewed 797 attitude-behavior studies, they found that the average

KEY LEARNING GOALS

12.8 Analyze the structure of attitudes and the link between attitudes and behavior.

12.9 Distinguish between explicit and implicit attitudes, and explain how implicit attitudes are measured.

12.10 Summarize how source, message, and receiver factors influence the process of persuasion.

12.11 Clarify various theories of attitude formation and change.

FIGURE 12.4
The possible components of attitudes.
Attitudes may include cognitive, affective, and behavioral components, as illustrated here for a hypothetical person's attitude about gun control.

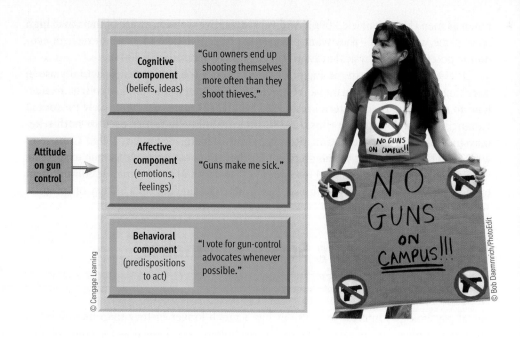

Cognitive component (beliefs, ideas) — "Gun owners end up shooting themselves more often than they shoot thieves."

Attitude on gun control

Affective component (emotions, feelings) — "Guns make me sick."

Behavioral component (predispositions to act) — "I vote for gun-control advocates whenever possible."

© Cengage Learning

© Bob Daemmrich/PhotoEdit

correlation between attitudes and behavior was .41. That correlation is high enough to conclude that attitudes are a meaningful predictor of actual behavior, but they do not predict behavior nearly as well as most people assume.

Why aren't attitude-behavior relations more consistent? One consideration is that people fail to factor in the influence of attitude strength (Fabrigar & Wegener, 2010). Although strong attitudes predict behavior reasonably well, many attitudes are not strongly held and are only weak predictors of behavior. Inconsistent relations between attitudes and behavior are also seen because behavior depends on situational constraints (Ajzen & Fishbein, 2000, 2005). Your subjective perceptions of how people expect you to behave are especially important. For instance, you may be strongly opposed to marijuana use. However, you may not say anything when friends start passing a joint around at a party because you don't want to turn the party into an argument. In another situation, though, governed by different norms, such as a class discussion, you may speak out forcefully against marijuana use.

Implicit Attitudes: Looking Beneath the Surface

In recent years, theorists have begun to make a distinction between explicit and implicit attitudes (Bohner & Dickel, 2011). *Explicit attitudes* **are attitudes that one holds consciously and can readily describe.** For the most part, these overt attitudes are what social psychologists have always studied until fairly recently. *Implicit attitudes* **are covert attitudes that are expressed in subtle automatic responses over which one has little conscious control.** It was only in the mid-1990s that social psychologists started digging beneath the surface to explore the meaning and importance of implicit attitudes. Implicit attitudes were discovered in research on prejudice, and their role in various types of prejudice continues to be the main focus of current inquiry.

Why are implicit attitudes a central issue in the study of prejudice? Because in modern societies most people have been taught that prejudicial attitudes are inappropriate and something to be ashamed of. At the same time, however, people grow up in a culture where negative stereotypes about certain groups are widely disseminated. Although most people want to be unbiased, research has shown that these negative ideas can seep into one's subconscious mind and contaminate one's reactions to others. Thus, many people express explicit attitudes that condemn prejudice but unknowingly harbor implicit attitudes that reflect subtle forms of prejudice (Devine & Sharp, 2009; Dovidio & Gaertner, 2008).

How are implicit attitudes measured? A number of techniques have been developed, but the most widely used is the Implicit Association Test (IAT) (Greenwald & Banaji, 1995; Greenwald, McGhee, & Schwartz, 1998). This computer-administered test measures how quickly people associate carefully chosen pairs of concepts. Let's consider how the IAT would be used to assess implicit prejudice against blacks. A series of words and pictures are presented onscreen and subjects are urged to respond to these stimuli as quickly and as accurately as possible. In the first series of trials respondents are instructed to press a specific key with their left hand if the stimulus is a black person or a positive word and to press another key with their right hand if the stimulus is a white person or a negative word (see **Figure 12.5**). In the second series of trials the instructions are changed and participants are told to press the left-hand key if the stimulus is a black person or a negative word and to press the right-hand key if the stimulus is a white person or positive word. The various types of stimuli are presented in quick succession and the computer records precise reaction times. Research shows that reaction times are quicker when liked faces are paired with positive words and disliked faces with negative words. So, if respondents have negative implicit attitudes about African Americans, the second series of trials will yield shorter average reaction times. And if this is so, the size of the difference between average reaction times in the two series provides an index of the strength of participants' implicit racism.

Since 1998, millions of people have responded to a web-based version of the IAT (Nosek, Banaji, & Greenwald, 2002; Nosek, Greenwald, & Banaji, 2007). Although surveys of people's explicit attitudes suggest that prejudice has declined considerably, the IAT results show that over 80% of respondents, both young and old, show negative implicit attitudes about the elderly. And about three-quarters of white respondents exhibit implicit prejudice against blacks. The findings also indicate that implicit prejudice against gays, the disabled, and the obese is common.

Do IAT scores based on tiny differences in reaction times predict prejudicial behavior in the real world? Yes, IAT scores are predictive of subtle, but potentially important differences in behavior (Greenwald et al., 2009). For instance, white participants' degree of implicit racial prejudice predicts how far they choose to sit from a black partner whom they expect to work with on a task (Amodio & Devine, 2006). Higher implicit racism scores in white subjects are also associated with decreased smiling, reduced eye contact, shorter speaking time, and more speech hesitations in interracial interactions (Devos, 2008).

Trying to Change Attitudes: Factors in Persuasion

Every day you're bombarded by efforts to alter your attitudes. In light of this reality, let's examine some of the factors that determine whether persuasion works. The process of persuasion includes four basic elements: the source, receiver, message, and channel (see

FIGURE 12.5

Measuring implicit attitudes. The IAT assesses implicit prejudice against blacks by tracking how quickly subjects respond to images of black and white people paired with positive or negative words. If participants are prejudiced against African Americans, they will react more quickly to the pairings in the condition on the right. The IAT has been used to measure implicit attitudes toward a variety of groups.

Graphic: © Cengage Learning;
Face photo: © Bill Aron/PhotoEdit

FIGURE 12.6

Overview of the persuasion process.
The process of persuasion essentially boils down to *who* (the source) communicates *what* (the message) *by what means* (the channel) *to whom* (the receiver). Thus, four sets of variables influence the process of persuasion: source, message, channel, and receiver factors. The diagram lists some of the more important factors in each category (including some that are not discussed in the text due to space limitations).

SOURCE: Based on Lippa, R. A. (1994). *Introduction to social psychology.* Belmont, CA: Brooks/Cole Publishing Company. Copyright © 1994 by Wadsworth. Reprinted by permission of the author.

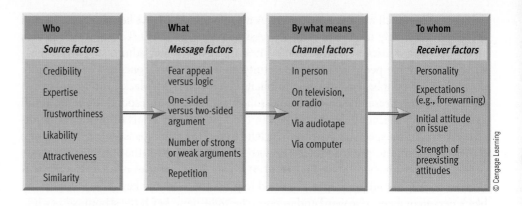

Who	What	By what means	To whom
Source factors	**Message factors**	**Channel factors**	**Receiver factors**
Credibility	Fear appeal versus logic	In person	Personality
Expertise	One-sided versus two-sided argument	On television, or radio	Expectations (e.g., forewarning)
Trustworthiness	Number of strong or weak arguments	Via audiotape	Initial attitude on issue
Likability	Repetition	Via computer	Strength of preexisting attitudes
Attractiveness			
Similarity			

© Cengage Learning

Figure 12.6). The *source* is the person who sends a communication, and the *receiver* is the person to whom the message is sent. Thus, if you watch a presidential news conference on TV, the president is the source, and you and millions of other viewers are the receivers. The *message* is the information transmitted by the source, and the *channel* is the medium through which the message is sent. Although the research on communication channels is interesting, we'll confine our discussion to source, message, and receiver variables.

SOURCE FACTORS

Occasional exceptions to the general rule are seen, but persuasion tends to be more successful when the source has high *credibility* (Albarracin & Vargas, 2010). What gives a person credibility? Either expertise or trustworthiness. *Expertise* tends to be more influential when an argument is ambiguous or when the receiver is not motivated to pay close attention to the argument (Chaiken & Maheswaran, 1994; Reimer, Mata, & Stoecklin, 2004). People try to convey their expertise by mentioning their degrees, their training, and their experience or by showing an impressive grasp of the issue at hand. Expertise is a plus, but *trustworthiness* can be even more important. Many people tend to accept messages from trustworthy sources with little scrutiny (Priester & Petty, 1995, 2003). Trustworthiness is undermined when a source appears to have something to gain. In contrast, trustworthiness is enhanced when people appear to argue against their own best interests (Hunt, Smith, & Kernan, 1985). *Likability* also increases the effectiveness of a persuasive source (Johnson, Maio, & Smith-McLallen, 2005). In addition, people respond better to sources who share *similarity* with them in ways that are relevant to the issue at hand (Hilmert, Kulik, & Christenfeld, 2006).

MESSAGE FACTORS

If you were going to give a speech to a local community group advocating a reduction in state taxes on corporations, you'd probably wrestle with a number of questions about how to structure your message. Should you look at both sides of the issue, or should you just present your side? Should you deliver a low-key, logical speech? Or should you try to strike fear into the hearts of your listeners? These questions are concerned with message factors in persuasion.

In general, two-sided arguments seem to be more effective than one-sided presentations (Petty & Wegener, 1998). Just mentioning that an issue has two sides can increase your credibility with an audience. Fear appeals appear to work—if they are successful in arousing fear. Research reveals that many messages intended to induce fear fail to do so. However, studies involving a wide range of issues (nuclear policy, auto safety, dental hygiene, and so on) have shown that messages that are effective in arousing fear tend to increase persuasion (Ruiter, Abraham, & Kok, 2001). Fear appeals are most likely to work when your listeners view the dire consequences that you describe as exceedingly unpleasant, are fairly probable if they don't take your advice, and are avoidable if they do (Das, de Wit, & Stroebe, 2003).

Frequent repetition of a message also seems to be an effective strategy (Dechêne et al., 2010), probably because of the mere exposure effect first described by Robert Zajonc. The *mere exposure effect* **is the finding that repeated exposures to a stimulus promotes greater liking of the stimulus.** In a groundbreaking study (Zajonc, 1968), participants were exposed to unfamiliar Turkish words 0, 1, 2, 5, 10, or 25 times. Subsequently, the subjects were asked to rate the degree to which they thought the words referred to something good or bad. The more subjects had been exposed to a specific word, the more favorably they rated it. Zajonc observed remarkably similar findings when participants rated the favorability of selected Chinese pictographs (the symbols used in Chinese writing) and when they rated the likability of people shown in yearbook photos (see **Figure 12.7**). The mere exposure effect has been replicated with many types of stimuli including sounds, nonsense syllables, meaningful words, line drawings, photographs, and various types of objects (Albarracin & Vargas, 2010; Bornstein, 1989).

RECEIVER FACTORS

What about the receiver of the persuasive message? Are some people easier to persuade than others? Undoubtedly, but transient factors such as the forewarning a receiver gets about a persuasive effort seem to be more influential than the receiver's personality. Consider, for instance, the old adage that "to be forewarned is to be forearmed." The value of *forewarning* does apply to targets of persuasive efforts (Janssen, Fennis, & Pruyn, 2010). When you shop for a new car, you *expect* salespeople to work at persuading you, and to some extent this forewarning reduces the impact of their arguments.

Furthermore, studies show that *stronger attitudes are more resistant to change* (Eagly & Chaiken, 1998; Miller & Peterson, 2004). Strong attitudes may be tougher to alter because they tend to be embedded in networks of beliefs that might also require change (Erber, Hodges, & Wilson, 1995). Finally, *resistance can promote resistance.* That is, when people successfully resist persuasive efforts to change specific attitudes, they often become more certain about those attitudes (Tormala & Petty, 2002, 2004).

Our review of source, message, and receiver variables has shown that attempting to change attitudes through persuasion involves a complex interplay of factors—and we haven't even looked beneath the surface yet. How do people acquire attitudes in the first place? What dynamic processes within people produce attitude change? We turn to these theoretical issues next.

Theories of Attitude Formation and Change

PSYKTREK 12c

Many theories have been proposed to explain the mechanisms at work in attitude change, whether or not it occurs in response to persuasion. We'll look at three theoretical perspectives: learning theory, dissonance theory, and the elaboration likelihood model.

LEARNING THEORY

PSYKTREK 12c

We've seen repeatedly that the concepts of *learning* and *conditioning* can help explain a wide range of phenomena, from conditioned fears to the acquisition of gender roles to the development of personality traits. Now we can add attitude formation and change to our list. Attitudes may be learned from parents, peers, the media, cultural traditions and other social influences (Banaji & Heiphetz, 2010).

The affective, or emotional, component in an attitude can be created through a special subtype of *classical conditioning*, called evaluative conditioning (Olson & Fazio, 2001, 2002; Walther & Langer, 2008). As we discussed in Chapter 6, *evaluative conditioning* consists of efforts to transfer the emotion attached to an unconditioned stimulus (US) to a new conditioned stimulus (CS) (Kruglanski & Stroebe, 2005; Schimmack & Crites, 2005). Advertisers routinely try to take advantage of evaluative conditioning by

FIGURE 12.7

The mere exposure effect. In seminal research on the mere exposure effect, Robert Zajonc (1968) manipulated how often participants were exposed to various unfamiliar, neutral stimuli. As the data show here, he found that increased exposures led to increased liking. The mere exposure effect may shed light on why repetition is an effective strategy in persuasion.

Reality Check

Misconception
Familiarity breeds contempt: The more we are exposed to something, the less we like it.

Reality
People often comment that they are sick of an incessant commercial or overexposed celebrity, but a large body of research shows that repeated exposures to something, even neutral as opposed to favorable exposures, generally lead to increased liking.

FIGURE 12.8

Classical conditioning of attitudes in advertising. Advertisers routinely pair their products with likable celebrities in the hope that their products will come to elicit pleasant emotional responses. As discussed in Chapter 6, this special type of classical conditioning is called *evaluative conditioning*. See the Critical Thinking Application in Chapter 6 for a more in-depth discussion of this practice.

pairing their products with stimuli that elicit pleasant emotional responses, such as extremely attractive models, highly likable spokespersons, and cherished events, such as the Olympics (Till & Priluck, 2000). This conditioning process is diagrammed in **Figure 12.8**. Evaluative conditioning can occur without awareness and seems to be exceptionally resistant to extinction (Albarracin & Vargas, 2010).

Operant conditioning may come into play when you openly express an attitude, such as "I believe that husbands should do more housework." Some people may endorse your view, while others may jump down your throat. Agreement from other people generally functions as a reinforcer. It strengthens your tendency to express a specific attitude (Bohner & Schwarz, 2001). Disagreement often functions as a form of punishment. Thus, it may gradually weaken your commitment to your viewpoint.

Another person's attitudes may rub off on you through *observational learning* (Banaji & Heiphetz, 2010). If you hear your uncle say, "Republicans are nothing but puppets of big business" and your mother heartily agrees, your exposure to your uncle's attitude and your mother's reinforcement of your uncle may influence your attitude toward the Republican party. Studies show that parents and their children tend to have similar political attitudes (Sears, 1975). Also, college students living in residence halls tend to show some convergence in attitudes (Cullum & Harton, 2007). Observational learning presumably accounts for much of this similarity. The opinions of teachers, coaches, co-workers, talk-show hosts, rock stars, and so forth are also likely to sway people's attitudes through observational learning.

Concept Check 12.3

Understanding Attitudes and Persuasion

Check your understanding of the components of attitudes and the elements of persuasion by analyzing hypothetical political strategies. Imagine you're working on a political campaign and you're invited to join the candidate's inner circle in strategy sessions, as staff members prepare the candidate for upcoming campaign stops. During the meetings, you hear various strategies discussed. For each strategy below, indicate which component of voters' attitudes (cognitive, affective, or behavioral) is being targeted for change, and indicate which element in persuasion (source, message, or receiver factors) is being manipulated. The answers are in Appendix A.

1. "You need to convince this crowd that your program for regulating nursing homes is sound. Whatever you do, don't acknowledge the two weaknesses in the program that we've been playing down. I don't care if you're asked point blank. Just slide by the question and keep harping on the program's advantages."

   _____

   _____

2. "You haven't been smiling enough lately, especially when the TV cameras are rolling. Remember, you can have the best ideas in the world, but if you don't seem likable, you're not gonna get elected. By the way, I think I've lined up some photo opportunities that should help us create an image of sincerity and compassion."

   _____

   _____

3. "This crowd is already behind you. You don't have to alter their opinions on any issue. Get right to work convincing them to contribute to the campaign. I want them lining up to donate money."

   _____

   _____

DISSONANCE THEORY

Leon Festinger

"Cognitive dissonance is a motivating state of affairs. Just as hunger impels a person to eat, so does dissonance impel a person to change his opinions or his behavior."

Leon Festinger's *dissonance theory* assumes that inconsistency among attitudes propels people in the direction of attitude change. Dissonance theory burst into prominence in 1959 when Festinger and J. Merrill Carlsmith published a landmark study. Let's look at their findings and at how dissonance theory explains them.

Festinger and Carlsmith (1959) had male college students come to a laboratory and work on excruciatingly dull tasks, such as turning pegs repeatedly. When a subject's hour was over, the experimenter confided that some participants' motivation was being manipulated by telling them that the task was interesting and enjoyable before they started it. Then, after a moment's hesitation, the experimenter asked if the subject could help him out of a jam. His usual helper was delayed and he needed someone to testify to the next "subject" (really an accomplice) that the experimental task was interesting. He offered to pay the subject if he would tell the person in the adjoining waiting room that the task was enjoyable and involving.

This entire scenario was enacted to coax participants into doing something that was inconsistent with their true feelings. Some subjects received a token payment of $1 for their effort, while others received a more substantial payment of $20 (an amount equivalent to about $120 today, in light of inflation). Later, a second experimenter inquired about the participants' true feelings regarding the dull experimental task. **Figure 12.9** summarizes the design of the Festinger and Carlsmith study.

Who do you think rated the task more favorably—the subjects who were paid $1 or those who were paid $20? Both common sense and learning theory would predict that the subjects who received the greater reward ($20) should come to like the task more. In reality, however, the participants who were paid $1 exhibited more favorable attitude change—just as Festinger and Carlsmith had predicted. Why? Dissonance theory provides an explanation.

According to Festinger (1957), **cognitive dissonance exists when related attitudes or beliefs are inconsistent— that is, when they contradict each other.** Festinger's model assumes that dissonance is possible only when cognitions are relevant to each other, since unrelated cognitions ("I am hardworking" and "Fire engines are red") can't contradict each other. However, when cognitions are related, they may be consonant ("I am hardworking" and "I'm staying overtime to get an important job done") or dissonant ("I am hardworking" and "I'm playing hooky from work"). When aroused, cognitive dissonance is supposed to create an unpleasant state of tension that motivates people to reduce their dissonance—usually by altering their cognitions.

In the study by Festinger and Carlsmith (1959), the subjects' contradictory cognitions were "The task is boring" and "I told someone the task was enjoyable." The participants who were paid $20 for lying had an obvious reason for behaving inconsistently with their true attitudes, so these subjects experienced little dissonance. In contrast, the participants paid $1 had no readily apparent justification for their lie and experienced high dissonance. To reduce it, they tended to persuade themselves that the task was more enjoyable than they had originally thought. *Thus, dissonance theory sheds light on why people sometimes come to believe their own lies.*

Cognitive dissonance is also at work when people turn attitude somersaults to justify efforts that haven't panned

FIGURE 12.9

Design of the Festinger and Carlsmith (1959) study. The manipulations of variables and the results of Festinger and Carlsmith's (1959) landmark study of attitude change are outlined here.

PsykTrek 12c

© Cengage Learning

Courtesy of Professor Jerry Suls

Hypothesis: High dissonance about counterattitudinal behavior will cause attitude change

Random assignment: Subjects randomly assigned to experimental and control groups

Manipulation of independent variable:
- *Experimental group:* Subjects paid $1 for saying task is fun (high dissonance)
- *Control group:* Subjects paid $20 for saying task is fun (low dissonance)

Measurement of dependent variable: Dull task is rated more enjoyable by the high-dissonance subjects

Conclusion: Dissonance about counterattitudinal behavior does cause attitude change out, a syndrome called *effort justification*. Aronson and Mills (1959) studied effort justification by putting college women through a "severe initiation" before they could qualify to participate in what promised to be an interesting discussion of sexuality. In the initiation, the women had to read obscene passages out loud to a male experimenter. After all that, the highly touted discussion of sexuality turned out to be a boring, taped lecture on reproduction in lower animals. Subjects in the severe initiation condition experienced highly dissonant cognitions ("I went through a lot to get here" and "This discussion is terrible"). How did they reduce their dissonance? Apparently by changing their attitude about the discussion, since they rated it more favorably than participants in two control conditions. Effort justification may be at work in many facets of everyday life. For example, music fans who pay hundreds of dollars for scalped concert tickets will tend to view the concert favorably, even if the artists show up in a stupor and play out of tune.

Dissonance theory has been tested in hundreds of studies with mixed, but largely favorable, results. The dynamics of dissonance appear to underlie many important types of attitude changes (Draycott & Dabbs, 1998; Keller & Block, 1999; Petty et al., 2003). And research has largely supported Festinger's claim that dissonance involves genuine psychological discomfort and even physiological arousal (Devine et al., 1999; Visser & Cooper, 2003).

ELABORATION LIKELIHOOD MODEL

PSYKTREK 12C

The *elaboration likelihood model* of attitude change, originally proposed by Richard Petty and John Cacioppo (1986), asserts that there are two basic "routes" to persuasion (Petty & Briñol, 2008; Petty & Wegener, 1999). The *central route* is taken when people carefully ponder the content and logic of persuasive messages. The *peripheral route* is taken when persuasion depends on nonmessage factors, such as the attractiveness and credibility of the source, or on conditioned emotional responses (see **Figure 12.10**). For example, a politician who campaigns by delivering carefully researched speeches that thoughtfully analyze complex issues is following the central route to persuasion. In contrast, a politician who depends on marching bands, flag waving, celebrity endorsements, and emotional slogans is following the peripheral route.

Both routes can lead to effective persuasion and attitude change. However, according to the elaboration likelihood model, the durability of attitude change depends on the extent to which people elaborate on (think about) the contents of persuasive communications. Studies suggest that the central route to persuasion leads to more enduring attitude change than the peripheral route (Petty & Wegener, 1998). Research also suggests that attitudes changed through central processes predict behavior better than attitudes changed through peripheral processes (Kruglanski & Stroebe, 2005; Petty & Briñol, 2010).

FIGURE 12.10

The elaboration likelihood model.
According to the elaboration likelihood model (Petty & Cacioppo, 1986), the central route to persuasion leads to more elaboration of message content and more enduring attitude change than the peripheral route to persuasion.

Central route: Persuasion based on content and logic of the message → High elaboration: Careful processing of the information → More durable attitude change

Peripheral route: Persuasion based on nonmessage factors such as attractiveness, credibility, emotion → Low elaboration: Minimal processing of the information → Less durable attitude change

© Cengage Learning

Conformity and Obedience: Yielding to Others

KEY LEARNING GOALS

12.12 Understand Asch's work on conformity and Milgram's research on obedience.

12.13 Discuss cultural variations in conformity and obedience, and describe the Stanford Prison Simulation.

Since the 1950s, social psychologists have shown an enduring fascination with the subject of social influence. Work in this area has yielded some of the most famous and influential studies in the history of psychology. Let's look at this research.

Conformity

PSYKTREK 12e

If you keep a well-manicured lawn and praise the music of Radiohead, are you exhibiting conformity? According to social psychologists, it depends on whether your behavior is the result of group pressure. **Conformity occurs when people yield to real or imagined social pressure.** For example, if you maintain a well-groomed lawn only to avoid complaints from your neighbors, you're yielding to social pressure. If you like Radiohead because you genuinely enjoy their music, that's *not* conformity. However, if you like Radiohead because doing so is "hip" and your friends would question your taste if you didn't, then you're conforming.

In the 1950s, Solomon Asch (1951, 1955, 1956) devised a clever procedure that minimized ambiguity about whether subjects were conforming, allowing him to investigate the variables that govern conformity. Let's re-create one of Asch's (1955) classic experiments. The participants are male undergraduates recruited for a study of visual perception. A group of seven subjects are shown a large card with a vertical line on it. They are then are asked to indicate which of three lines on a second card matches the original "standard line" in length (see **Figure 12.11**). All seven participants are given a turn at the task. They each announce their choice to the group. The subject in the sixth chair doesn't know it, but everyone else in the group is an accomplice of the experimenter. They're about to make him wonder whether he has taken leave of his senses.

The accomplices give accurate responses on the first two trials. On the third trial, line number 2 clearly is the correct response, but the first five "subjects" all say that line number 3 matches the standard line. The genuine subject is bewildered and can't believe his ears. Over the course of the next 15 trials, the accomplices all give the same incorrect response on 11 of them. How does the real subject respond? The line judgments are easy and unambiguous. So, if the participant consistently agrees with the accomplices, he isn't making honest mistakes—he's conforming.

Averaging across all 50 subjects, Asch (1955) found that the young men conformed on 37% of the trials. The participants varied considerably in their tendency to conform, however. Of the fifty subjects, thirteen never caved in to the group, while 14 conformed on more than half the trials. One could argue that the results show that people confronting a unanimous majority generally tend to *resist* the pressure to conform (Hodges & Geyer, 2006). However, given how clear and easy the line judgments were, most social scientists viewed the findings as a dramatic demonstration of humans' propensity to conform (Levine, 1999).

In subsequent studies, *group size* and *group unanimity* turned out to be key determinants of conformity (Asch, 1956). To examine the impact of group size, Asch repeated his procedure with groups that included from 1 to 15 accomplices. Little conformity was seen when a subject was pitted against just one person, but conformity increased rapidly as group size went from two to four, peaked at a group size of seven, and then leveled off. Thus, Asch reasoned that as groups grow larger, conformity increases—up to a point—a conclusion that has been echoed by other researchers (Cialdini & Trost, 1998).

Solomon Asch

"That we have found the tendency to conformity in our society so strong that reasonably intelligent and well-meaning young people are willing to call white black is a matter of concern."

FIGURE 12.11

Stimuli used in Asch's conformity studies. Subjects were asked to match a standard line (top) with one of three other lines displayed on another card (bottom). The task was easy—until experimental accomplices started responding with obviously incorrect answers, creating a situation in which Asch evaluated subjects' conformity.

SOURCE: Adapted from Asch, S. (1955). Opinion and social pressure. *Scientific American, 193* (5), 31–35. Based on illustrations by Sara Love. Copyright © 1955 by Scientific American, Inc. All rights reserved.

However, group size made little difference if just one accomplice "broke" with the others, wrecking their unanimous agreement. The presence of another dissenter lowered conformity to about one-quarter of its peak, even when the dissenter made *inaccurate* judgments that happened to conflict with the majority view. Apparently, the participants just needed to hear someone else question the accuracy of the group's perplexing responses. The importance of unanimity in fostering conformity has been replicated in subsequent research (Nemeth & Chiles, 1988).

Obedience

PsykTrek 12e

Obedience **is a form of compliance that occurs when people follow direct commands, usually from someone in a position of authority.** To a surprising extent, when an authority figure says, "Jump!" many people simply ask, "How high?"

MILGRAM'S STUDIES

PsykTrek 12e

Stanley Milgram wanted to study this tendency to obey authority figures. Like many other people after World War II, he was troubled by how readily the citizens of Germany followed the orders of dictator Adolf Hitler, even when the orders required shockingly immoral actions, such as the slaughter of millions of Jews. Milgram, who had worked with Solomon Asch, set out to design a standard laboratory procedure for the study of obedience, much like Asch's procedure for studying conformity. The clever experiment that Milgram devised became one of the most famous and controversial studies in the annals of psychology (Blass, 2009).

Milgram's (1963) participants were a diverse collection of forty men from the local community. They were told that they would be participating in a study concerned with the effects of punishment on learning. When they arrived at the lab, they drew slips of paper from a hat to get their assignments. The drawing was rigged so that the subject always became the "teacher" and an experimental accomplice (a likable 47-year-old accountant) became the "learner."

The learner was strapped into an electrified chair through which a shock could be delivered whenever he made a mistake on the task (see **Figure 12.12**). The subject was then taken to an adjoining room that housed the shock generator that he would control in his role as the teacher. Although the apparatus looked and sounded realistic, it was a fake and the learner was never shocked.

Stanley Milgram

"The essence of obedience is that a person comes to view himself as the instrument for carrying out another person's wishes, and he therefore no longer regards himself as responsible for his actions."

FIGURE 12.12

Milgram's experiment on obedience. The photo on the left shows the "learner" being connected to the shock generator during one of Milgram's experimental sessions. The photo on the right shows the fake shock generator used in the study. The surprising results of the Milgram (1963) study are summarized in the bar graph. Although subjects frequently protested, the vast majority (65%) delivered the entire series of shocks to the learner.

SOURCE: Photos Copyright © 1965 by Stanley Milgram. From the film *Obedience*, distributed by The Pennsylvania State University. Reprinted by permission of Alexandra Milgram.

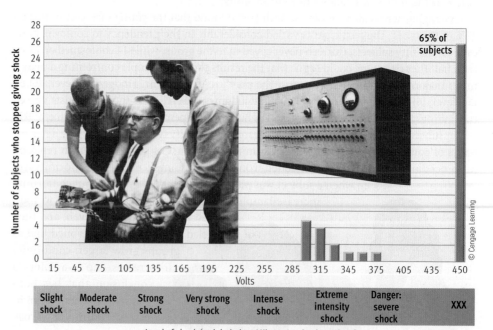

As the "learning experiment" proceeded, the accomplice made many mistakes that necessitated shocks. The teacher was instructed to increase the shock level after each wrong answer. At 300 volts, the learner began to pound on the wall between the two rooms in protest and soon stopped responding to the teacher's questions. From this point forward, participants frequently turned to the experimenter for guidance. Whenever they did so, the experimenter firmly indicated that the teacher should continue to give stronger and stronger shocks to the now-silent learner. The dependent variable was the maximum shock the participant was willing to administer before refusing to go on.

As **Figure 12.12** shows, twenty-six of the forty subjects (65%) administered all 30 levels of shock. Although they tended to obey the experimenter, many subjects voiced and displayed considerable distress about harming the learner. The horrified participants groaned, bit their lips, stuttered, trembled, and broke into a sweat, but continued administering the shocks. Based on these results, Milgram concluded that obedience to authority was even more common than he or others anticipated. Before the study was conducted, Milgram had described it to forty psychiatrists and had asked them to predict how much shock subjects would be willing to administer to their innocent victims. Most of the psychiatrists had predicted that fewer than 1% of the subjects would continue to the end of the series of shocks!

In interpreting his results, Milgram argued that strong pressure from an authority figure can make decent people do indecent things to others. Applying this insight to Nazi war crimes and other travesties, Milgram asserted that some sinister actions may not be due to actors' evil character so much as to situational pressures that can lead normal people to engage in acts of treachery and violence. Thus, he arrived at the disturbing conclusion that given the right circumstances, any of us might obey orders to inflict harm on innocent strangers.

THE ENSUING CONTROVERSY

PSYKTREK 12e

Milgram's study evoked a controversy that continues through today. Some critics argued that Milgram's results wouldn't generalize to the real world (Orne & Holland, 1968). For example, Baumrind (1964) asserted that subjects who agree to participate in a scientific study *expect to obey* orders from an experimenter. Milgram (1964, 1968) replied by pointing out that so do soldiers and bureaucrats in the real world who are accused of villainous acts performed in obedience to authority. "I reject Baumrind's argument that the observed obedience doesn't count because it occurred where it is appropriate," said Milgram (1964). "That is precisely why it *does* count." Overall, the weight of evidence supports the generalizability of Milgram's results. They were consistently replicated for many years, in diverse settings, with a variety of subjects and procedural variations (Blass, 1999, 2009; Miller, 1986).

Critics also questioned the ethics of Milgram's experimental procedures (Baumrind, 1964; Kelman, 1967). They noted that without prior consent, participants were exposed to extensive deception that could undermine their trust in people and severe stress that could leave emotional scars. Milgram's defenders argued that the brief distress experienced by his subjects was a small price to pay for the insights that emerged from his obedience studies. Looking back, however, many psychologists seem to share the critics' concerns about the ethical implications of Milgram's groundbreaking work. His procedure is questionable by contemporary standards of research ethics, and no replications of his obedience study were conducted in the United States from the mid-1970s until recently (Elms, 2009), when Jerry Burger (2009) crafted a very cautious, *partial* replication that incorporated a variety of additional safeguards to protect the welfare of the participants.

Burger (2009) wanted to see whether Milgram's findings would hold up 45 years later. After all, the world has changed in countless ways since Milgram's original research in the early 1960s. To accommodate modern ethical standards, Burger had to change some features of the Milgram procedure. Among other things, he screened participants with great care, excluding those who seemed likely to experience excessive stress; he emphasized repeatedly that participants could withdraw from the study without penalty at any time; and he provided instant debriefing after each participant completed the procedure. Most important, he enacted Milgram's scenario only up through the level of 150 volts. Burger chose 150 volts as the maximum because in Milgram's series of studies the vast majority of subjects who went past this point went on to administer all the levels of shock. Interestingly, in spite of the extra precautions, Burger's study yielded obedience rates that were only slightly lower than those observed by Milgram 45 years earlier. Given Burger's repeated assurances that participants could withdraw from the study (which one would expect to reduce obedience) it seems likely that people today are just as prone to obedience as they were 45 years ago.

Cultural Variations in Conformity and Obedience

Are conformity and obedience unique to American culture? By no means. The Asch and Milgram experiments have been repeated in many other societies, where they have yielded results roughly similar to those seen in the United States. Thus, the phenomena of conformity and obedience seem to transcend culture.

The replications of Milgram's obedience study have largely been limited to industrialized nations similar to the United States. Many of these studies have reported even *higher* obedience rates than those seen in Milgram's American samples (Smith & Bond, 1994). Thus, the surprisingly high level of obedience observed by Milgram does not appear to be peculiar to the United States. The Asch experiment has been repeated in a more diverse range of societies than the Milgram experiment. Various theorists have hypothesized that collectivistic cultures, which emphasize respect for group norms, cooperation, and harmony, encourage more conformity than individualistic cultures, with their emphasis on independence (Kim & Markus, 1999; Matsumoto, 1994). Consistent with this analysis, replications of the Asch experiment have tended to find somewhat higher levels of conformity in collectivistic cultures than in individualistic cultures (Bond & Smith, 1996; Smith, 2001).

The Power of the Situation: The Stanford Prison Simulation

The research of Asch and Milgram provided dramatic demonstrations of the potent influence that situational factors can have on social behavior. The power of the situation was underscored once again, about a decade after Milgram's obedience research, in another landmark study conducted by Philip Zimbardo, who, ironically, was a high school classmate of Milgram's. Zimbardo and his colleagues designed the Stanford Prison Simulation to investigate why prisons tend to become abusive, degrading violent environments (Haney, Banks, & Zimbardo, 1973; Zimbardo, Haney, & Banks, 1973). Like Milgram, Zimbardo wanted to see how much the power of the situation would shape the behavior of normal, average subjects.

The participants were college students recruited for a study of prison life through a newspaper ad. After seventy volunteers were given an extensive battery of tests and interviews, the researchers chose twenty-four students who appeared to be physically healthy and psychologically stable to be the subjects. A coin flip determined which of them would be "guards" and which would be the "prisoners" in a simulated prison set up at Stanford University. The prisoners were "arrested" at their homes, handcuffed, and transported to a mock prison on the Stanford campus. Upon arrival, they were ordered to strip, sprayed with a delousing agent, given prison uniforms (smocks), assigned numbers as their identities, and locked up in iron-barred cells. The subjects assigned to be guards were given khaki uniforms, billy clubs, whistles, and reflective sunglasses. They were told that they could run their prison in whatever way they wanted except that they were not allowed to use physical punishment.

What happened? In short order, confrontations occurred between the guards and prisoners, and the guards quickly devised a variety of sometimes cruel strategies to

Philip Zimbardo

"But in the end, I called off the experiment not because of the horror I saw out there in the prison yard, but because of the horror of realizing that I could have easily traded places with the most brutal guard or become the weakest prisoner full of hatred at being so powerless."

maintain total control over their prisoners. Meals, blankets, and bathroom privileges were selectively denied to some prisoners to achieve control. The prisoners were taunted, humiliated, called demeaning names. They were forced to beg for opportunities to go to the bathroom. Pointless, petty rules were strictly enforced. Difficult prisoners were punished with hard labor (doing pushups and jumping jacks, cleaning toilets with their bare hands). And the guards creatively turned a 2-foot by 2-foot closet into a "hole" for solitary confinement of rebellious prisoners. Although there was some variation among the guards, collectively they became mean, malicious, and abusive in fulfilling their responsibilities. How did the prisoners react? A few of them showed signs of emotional disturbance and had to be released early, but they mostly became listless, apathetic, and demoralized. The study was designed to run two weeks, but Zimbardo decided to end it prematurely after just 6 days because he was concerned about the rapidly escalating abuse and degradation of the prisoners. The subjects were debriefed, offered counseling, and sent home.

How did Zimbardo and his colleagues explain the stunning transformations of their subjects? First, they attributed the participants' behavior to the enormous influence of social roles. *Social roles* **are widely shared expectations about how people in certain positions are supposed to behave.** We have role expectations for salespeople, waiters, ministers, medical patients, students, bus drivers, tourists, flight attendants, and, of course, prison guards and prisoners. The participants had a rough idea of what it meant to act like a guard or a prisoner, and they were gradually consumed by their roles (Haney & Zimbardo, 1998). Second, the researchers attributed their subjects' behavior to the compelling power of situational factors. Before the study began, the tests and interviews showed no measurable differences in personality or character between those randomly assigned to be guards versus prisoners. The stark differences in their behavior had to be due to the radically different situations that they found themselves in. As Haney and Zimbardo (1998) put it, the study "demonstrated the power of situations to overwhelm people and elicit from them unexpectedly cruel, yet 'situationally appropriate' behavior" (p. 719). As a result, Zimbardo, like Milgram before him, concluded that situational pressures can lead normal, decent people to behave in sinister, repugnant ways.

Behavior in Groups: Joining with Others

KEY LEARNING GOALS

12.14 Discuss the nature of groups, the bystander effect, and social loafing.

12.15 Explain group polarization and groupthink.

Social psychologists study groups as well as individuals, but exactly what is a group? Are all the divorced fathers living in Baltimore a group? Are three strangers moving skyward in an elevator a group? What if the elevator gets stuck? How about four students from your psychology class who study together regularly? How about a jury working to render a verdict in a trial? The Boston Celtics? Some of these collections of people are groups and others aren't. Let's examine the concept of a group to find out which of these collections qualify.

In social psychologists' eyes, **a** *group* **consists of two or more individuals who interact and are interdependent.** The divorced fathers in Baltimore aren't likely to qualify on either count. Strangers sharing an elevator might interact briefly, but they're not interdependent. However, if the elevator gets stuck and they have to deal with an emergency together, they could suddenly become a group. Your psychology classmates who study together qualify as a group, since they interact and depend on each other to achieve shared goals. So do the members of a jury and a sports team such as the Celtics. Historically, most groups have interacted on a face-to-face basis, but advances in telecommunications are rapidly changing that situation. In the era of the Internet, people can interact, become interdependent, and develop a group identity without ever meeting in person (Bargh & McKenna, 2004; O'Leary & Cummings, 2007). Indeed, Hackman and

© Purestock RF/age fotostock

Katz (2010) assert that the nature of groups is evolving because of advances in technology. They note that traditionally groups tended to be intact and stable with clear boundaries, whereas membership in modern groups is often continuously changing. Traditional groups usually have a designated leader, whereas modern groups often are self-managing with shared leadership. Similarly, traditional groups tended to be created in a top-down fashion, whereas modern groups often coalesce on their own to explore shared interests. It will be interesting to see whether these shifts have an impact on how groups function.

Behavior Alone and in Groups: The Case of the Bystander Effect

Imagine that you have a precarious medical condition and that you must go through life worrying about whether someone will leap forward to provide help if the need ever arises. Wouldn't you feel more secure around larger groups? After all, there's "safety in numbers." Logically, as group size increases, the probability of having a good Samaritan on the scene increases. Or does it? We've seen before that human behavior isn't necessarily logical. When it comes to helping behavior, many studies have uncovered an apparent paradox called the *bystander effect:* **People are less likely to provide needed help when they are in groups than when they are alone.**

Evidence that your probability of getting help *declines* as group size increases was first described by John Darley and Bibb Latané (1968), who were conducting research on the determinants of helping behavior. In the Darley and Latané study, students in individual cubicles connected by an intercom participated in discussion groups of three sizes. Early in the discussion, a student who was an experimental accomplice hesitantly mentioned that he was prone to seizures. Later in the discussion, the same accomplice faked a severe seizure and cried out for help. Although a majority of participants sought assistance for the student, the tendency to seek help *declined* with increasing group size.

Similar trends have been seen in many other experiments, in which over 6000 subjects have had opportunities to respond to apparent emergencies, including fires, asthma attacks, faintings, crashes, and flat tires, as well as less pressing needs to answer a door or to pick up objects dropped by a stranger. Pooling the results of this research, Latané and Nida (1981) estimated that participants who were alone provided help 75% of the time, whereas participants in the presence of others provided help only 53% of the time.

What accounts for the bystander effect? A number of factors may be at work, but the most important appears to be the *diffusion of responsibility* that occurs in a group situation. If you're by yourself when you encounter someone in need of help, the responsibility to provide help rests squarely on your shoulders. However, if other people are present, the responsibility is divided among you, and you may all say to yourselves "Someone else will help." A reduced sense of responsibility may contribute to other aspects of behavior in groups, as we'll see in the next section.

Group Productivity and Social Loafing

Have you ever driven through a road construction project—at a snail's pace, of course—and become irritated because so many workers seem to be just standing around? Maybe the irony of the posted sign "Your tax dollars at work" made you imagine that they were all dawdling. And then again, perhaps not. Individuals' productivity often does decline in larger groups (Latané, Williams, & Harkins, 1979).

Two factors appear to contribute to reduced individual productivity in larger groups. One factor is *reduced efficiency* resulting from the *loss of coordination* among workers' efforts. As you put more people on a yearbook staff, for instance, you'll probably create more and more duplication of effort and increase how often group members end up working at cross purposes.

The second factor contributing to low productivity in groups involves *effort* rather than efficiency. *Social loafing* is a reduction in effort by individuals when they work in groups as compared to when they work by themselves. To investigate social loafing, Latané et al. (1979) measured the sound output produced by subjects who were asked to cheer or clap as loudly as they could. So they couldn't see or hear other group members, participants were told that the study concerned the importance of sensory feedback and were asked to don blindfolds and put on headphones through which loud noise was played. This maneuver permitted a simple deception: Subjects were led to *believe* that they were working alone or in a group of two or six, when in fact *individual* output was actually measured.

When subjects *thought* that they were working in larger groups, their individual output declined. Because lack of coordination could not affect individual output, the participants' decreased sound production had to be attributable to reduced effort. Latané and his colleagues also had the same subjects clap and shout in genuine groups of two and six and found an additional decrease in production that was attributed to loss of coordination. **Figure 12.13** shows how social loafing and loss of coordination combined to reduce productivity as group size increased.

Social loafing and the bystander effect appear to share a common cause: diffusion of responsibility in groups (Comer, 1995; Latané, 1981). As group size increases, the responsibility for getting a job done is divided among more people. Many group members then ease up because their individual contribution is less recognizable. Thus, social loafing occurs in situations where individuals can "hide in the crowd."

That said, social loafing is *not* inevitable. For example, social loafing is less likely when individuals' personal contributions to productivity are readily identifiable (Hoigaard & Ingvaldsen, 2006). And social loafing is reduced when people work in smaller and more cohesive groups (Shiue, Chiu, & Chang, 2010). Finally, cultural factors influence the likelihood of social loafing. Research suggests that social loafing is less prevalent in collectivistic cultures, which place a high priority on meeting group goals and contributing to one's ingroups (Karau & Williams, 1995; Smith, 2001).

FIGURE 12.13

The effect of loss of coordination and social loafing on group productivity. The amount of sound produced per person declined noticeably when subjects worked in actual groups of two or six (orange line). This decrease in productivity reflects both loss of coordination and social loafing. Sound per person also declined when subjects merely thought they were working in groups of two or six (purple line). This smaller decrease in productivity is attributed to social loafing.

SOURCE: Adapted from Latané, B., Williams, K., & Harkins, S. (1979). Many hands make light the work: The causes and consequences of social loafing. *Journal of Personality and Social Psychology, 37,* 822–832. Copyright © 1979 by the American Psychological Association. Adapted by permission of the author.

Concept Check   12.4

Scrutinizing Common Sense

Check your understanding of the implications of research in social psychology by indicating whether the common sense assertions listed below have been supported by empirical findings. Do the trends in research summarized in this chapter indicate that the following statements are true or false? The answers are in Appendix A.

_____ 1. Generally, in forming their impressions of others, people don't judge a book by its cover.

_____ 2. When it comes to attraction, birds of a feather flock together.

_____ 3. In the realm of love, opposites attract.

_____ 4. If you're the target of persuasion, to be forewarned is to be forearmed.

_____ 5. When you need help, there's safety in numbers.

Decision Making in Groups

Productivity is not the only issue that commonly concerns groups. When people join together in groups, they often have to make decisions about what the group will do and how it will use its resources. Whether it's your study group deciding what type of pizza to order, a jury deciding on a verdict, or Congress deciding whether to pass a bill, groups make decisions. Social psychologists have discovered some interesting tendencies in group decision making. We'll take a brief look at two of these, *group polarization* and *groupthink*.

GROUP POLARIZATION

Who leans toward more cautious decisions: individuals or groups? Common sense suggests that groups will work out compromises that cancel out members' extreme views. Hence, the collective wisdom of the group should yield relatively conservative choices. Is common sense correct? To investigate this question, Stoner (1961) asked individual participants to give their recommendations on tough decisions and then asked the same subjects to engage in group discussion to arrive at joint recommendations. When Stoner compared individuals' average recommendation against their group decision generated through discussion, he found that groups arrived at *riskier* decisions than individuals did. Stoner's finding was replicated in other studies (Pruitt, 1971), and the phenomenon acquired the name *risky shift*.

However, investigators eventually determined that groups can shift either way, toward risk or caution, depending on which way the group is leaning to begin with (Friedkin, 1999; Myers & Lamm, 1976). A shift toward a more extreme position, an effect called *polarization,* is often the result of group discussion (Van Swol, 2009). Thus, **group polarization occurs when group discussion strengthens a group's dominant point of view and produces a shift toward a more extreme decision in that direction** (see **Figure 12.14**). Group polarization does not involve widening the gap between factions in a group, as its name might suggest. In fact, group polarization can contribute to consensus in a group, as we'll see in our discussion of groupthink.

GROUPTHINK

In contrast to group polarization, which is a normal process in group dynamics, groupthink is more like a "disease" that can infect decision making in groups. **Groupthink occurs when members of a cohesive group emphasize concurrence at the expense of critical thinking in arriving at a decision.** As you might imagine, groupthink doesn't produce very effective decision making. Indeed, groupthink often leads to major blunders that may look incomprehensible after the fact. Irving Janis (1972) first described groupthink in his effort to explain how President John F. Kennedy and his advisers could have miscalculated so badly in deciding to invade Cuba at the Bay of Pigs in 1961. The attempted invasion failed miserably and, in retrospect, seemed remarkably ill-conceived. Applying his many years of research on group dynamics to the Bay of Pigs fiasco, Janis developed a model of groupthink.

When groups get caught up in groupthink, members suspend their critical judgment and the group starts censoring dissent as the pressure to conform increases. Soon, everyone begins to think alike. Moreover, "mind guards" try to shield the group from information that contradicts the group's view. If the group's view is challenged from outside, victims of groupthink tend to think in simplistic "us versus them" terms. Members begin to overestimate the ingroup's unanimity, and they

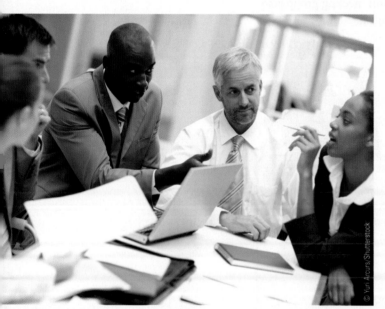

Many types of groups have to arrive at collective decisions. The social dynamics of group decisions are complicated, and a variety of factors can undermine effective decision making.

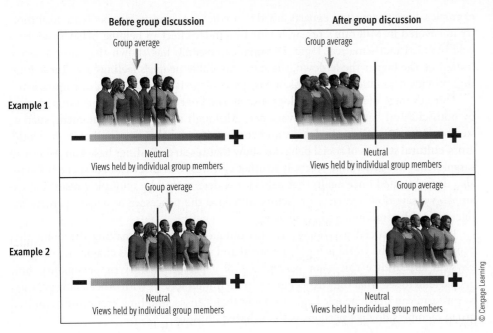

Before group discussion

Example 1

Group average

Neutral
Views held by individual group members

After group discussion

Group average

Neutral
Views held by individual group members

Example 2

Group average

Neutral
Views held by individual group members

Group average

Neutral
Views held by individual group members

© Cengage Learning

FIGURE 12.14

Group polarization. Two examples of group polarization are diagrammed here. In the first example (top) a group starts out mildly opposed to an idea, but after discussion sentiment against the idea is stronger. In the second example (bottom), a group starts out with a favorable disposition toward an idea, and this disposition is strengthened by group discussion.

begin to view the outgroup as the enemy. Groupthink also promotes incomplete gathering of information. Like individuals, groups often display a confirmation bias, as they tend to seek and focus on information that supports their initial views (Schulz-Hardt et al., 2000).

What causes groupthink? One key precondition is high group cohesiveness. *Group cohesiveness* **refers to the strength of the liking relationships linking group members to each other and to the group itself.** Members of cohesive groups are close-knit, are committed, have "team spirit," and are loyal to the group. Cohesiveness itself isn't bad. It can help groups achieve great things. But Janis maintains that the danger of groupthink is greater when groups are highly cohesive. Groupthink is also more likely when a group works in relative isolation, when its power structure is dominated by a strong, directive leader, and when it is under pressure to make a major decision quickly.

Reflecting on the Chapter's Themes

KEY LEARNING GOALS

12.16 Identify the four unifying themes highlighted in this chapter.

Our discussion of social psychology has provided a penetrating look at four of our seven unifying themes: psychology's commitment to empiricism, the importance of cultural factors, multifactorial causation, and the extent to which people's experience of the world is highly subjective. Let's consider the virtues of empiricism first.

It's easy to question the need to do scientific research on social behavior, because studies in social psychology often seem to verify common sense. While most people wouldn't presume to devise their own theory of color vision or question the significance of REM sleep, everyone has beliefs about the nature of love, how to persuade others, and the limits of obedience. Thus, when studies show that credibility enhances persuasion or that good looks facilitate attraction, it's tempting to conclude that social psychologists go to great lengths to document the obvious, and some critics say, "Why bother?"

You saw why in this chapter. Research in social psychology has repeatedly shown that the predictions of logic and common sense are often wrong. Consider just a few

 Empiricism

 Cultural Heritage

 Multifactorial Causation

 Subjectivity of Experience

examples. Even psychiatric experts failed to predict the remarkable obedience to authority uncovered in Milgram's research. The bystander effect in helping behavior violates cold-blooded mathematical logic. Dissonance research has shown that after a severe initiation, the bigger the letdown, the more favorable people's feelings are. These findings provide dramatic illustrations of why psychologists put their faith in empiricism.

Our coverage of social psychology also showed once again that behavior is marked by both cultural variance and invariance. Although basic social phenomena such as stereotyping, attraction, obedience, and conformity probably occur all over the world, cross-cultural studies of social behavior show that research findings based on American samples may not generalize precisely to other cultures. Our discussion of social behavior also demonstrated once again that behavior is determined by multiple causes. For example, we saw how a variety of factors influence the processes of person perception, interpersonal attraction, and persuasion.

Research in social psychology is also uniquely suited for making the point that people's view of the world is highly personal and subjective. In this chapter we saw how physical appearance can color perceptions of a person's ability or personality, how people tend to see what they expect to see in their interactions with others, how pressure to conform can make people begin to doubt their senses, and how groupthink can lead group members down a perilous path of shared illusions.

Personal APPLICATION

Understanding Prejudice

KEY LEARNING GOALS

12.17 Relate person perception processes and attributional bias to prejudice.

12.18 Relate attitude formation, intergroup competition, and ingroups versus outgroups to prejudice.

Answer the following "true" or "false."
___ 1 Prejudice and discrimination amount to the same thing.
___ 2 Stereotypes are always negative or unflattering.
___ 3 Ethnic and racial groups are the only widespread targets of prejudice in modern society.

Prejudice is a major social problem. It can harms victims' self-concepts, suppress their potential, create enormous stress in their lives, and promote tension and strife between groups (Inzlicht & Kang, 2010; Major & Townsend, 2010). The first step toward reducing prejudice is to understand its roots. Hence, in this Application we'll strive to achieve a better understanding of why prejudice is so common. Along the way, you'll learn the answers to the opening true-false questions.

Prejudice and discrimination are closely related concepts. In fact, the terms have become nearly interchangeable in popular use. Social scientists, however, prefer to define their terms precisely, so let's clarify which is which. *Prejudice* **is a negative attitude held toward members of a group.** Like other attitudes, prejudice can include three components (see **Figure 12.15**): beliefs ("Indians are mostly alcoholics"), emotions ("I despise Jews"), and behavioral dispositions ("I wouldn't hire a

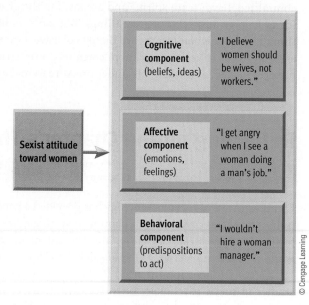

FIGURE 12.15

The three potential components of prejudice as an attitude. Attitudes can consist of up to three components. The tricomponent model of attitudes, applied to prejudice against women, would view sexism as negative beliefs about women (cognitive component) that lead to emotional reactions (affective component), and promote a readiness to discriminate against women (behavioral component).

Mexican"). Racial prejudice receives the lion's share of publicity, but prejudice is not limited to ethnic groups. Women, homosexuals, the aged, the disabled, and the mentally ill are also targets of widespread prejudice. Thus, many people hold prejudicial attitudes toward one group or another, and many have been victims of prejudice.

Prejudice may lead to *discrimination, which involves behaving differently, usually unfairly, toward the members of a group.* Prejudice and discrimination tend to go hand in hand, but attitudes and behavior do not necessarily correspond (see **Figure 12.16**). In our discussion, we'll concentrate primarily on the attitude of prejudice. Let's begin by looking at processes in person perception that promote prejudice.

Stereotyping [PSYKTREK 12d]

Perhaps no factor plays a larger role in prejudice than *stereotypes.* However, stereotypes are not inevitably negative. Although a massive overgeneralization, it's hardly insulting to assert that Americans are ambitious or that the Japanese are industrious. Unfortunately, many people

FIGURE 12.16

Relationship between prejudice and discrimination. As these examples show, prejudice can exist without discrimination and discrimination without prejudice. In the green cells, there is a disparity between attitude and behavior.

do subscribe to derogatory stereotypes of various ethnic groups. Studies suggest that negative racial stereotypes have diminished over the last 50 years, but they're not a thing of the past (Zarate, 2009). According to a variety of investigators, modern racism has merely become more subtle (Dovidio, Gaertner, & Kawakami, 2010).

Research indicates that prejudicial stereotypes are so pervasive and insidious they often operate automatically (Bodenhausen, Todd, & Richeson, 2009;

Devine & Sharp, 2009), even in people who truly renounce prejudice. Thus, a heterosexual man who rejects prejudice against homosexuals may still feel uncomfortable sitting next to a gay man on a bus, even though he regards his reaction as inappropriate.

Stereotypes also persist because the *subjectivity* of person perception makes it likely that people will see what they expect to see when they actually come into contact with members of groups that they view with prejudice (Fiske & Russell, 2010). For example, Duncan (1976) had white subjects watch and evaluate interaction on a TV monitor that was supposedly live (actually it was a videotape), and he varied the race of a person who gets into an argument and gives another person a slight shove. The shove was coded as "violent behavior" by 73% of the participants when the actor was black but by only 13% of the participants when the actor was white. As we've noted before, people's perceptions are highly subjective. Because of stereotypes, even "violence" may lie in the eye of the beholder.

Making Biased Attributions [PSYKTREK 12d]

Attribution processes can also help perpetuate stereotypes and prejudice. Research taking its cue from Weiner's (1980) model of attribution has shown that people often make *biased attributions for*

Members of many types of groups are victims of prejudice. Besides racial minorities, others that have been stereotyped and discriminated against include gays and lesbians, women, the homeless, and those who are overweight.

success and failure. For example, men and women don't get equal credit for their successes (Swim & Sanna, 1996). Observers often discount a woman's success by attributing it to good luck, sheer effort, or the ease of the task (except on traditional feminine tasks). In comparison, a man's success is more likely to be attributed to his outstanding ability (see **Figure 12.17**). For example, one study found that when a man and woman collaborate on a stereotypically "male" task, both male and female observers downplay the woman's contribution (Heilman & Haynes, 2005). These biased patterns of attribution help sustain the stereotype that men are more competent than women.

Recall that the *fundamental attribution error* is a tendency to explain events by pointing to the personal characteristics of the actors as causes (internal attributions). Research suggests that people are particularly likely to make this error when evaluating targets of prejudice (Hewstone, 1990). Thus, when people take note of ethnic neighborhoods dominated by crime and poverty, they blame the personal qualities of the residents for these problems, while downplaying or ignoring other explanations emphasizing situational factors (job discrimination, poor police service, and so on).

Forming and Preserving Prejudicial Attitudes ｟PSYKTREK 12d｠

If prejudice is an attitude, where does it come from? Many prejudices appear to be handed down as a legacy from parents (Killen, Richardson, & Kelly, 2010). Prejudicial attitudes can be found in children as young as ages 4 or 5 (Aboud & Amato, 2001). Research suggests that parents' racial attitudes often influence their children's racial attitudes (Sinclair, Dunn, & Lowery, 2004). This transmission of prejudice across generations presumably depends to some extent on *observational learning.* For example, if a young boy hears his father ridicule homosexuals, his exposure to his father's attitude is likely to affect his attitude about gays. If the boy

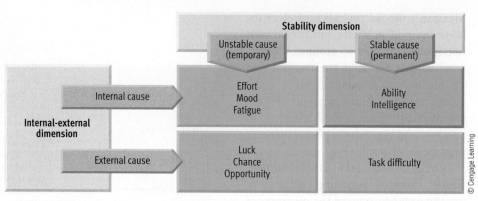

FIGURE 12.17
Bias in the attributions used to explain success and failure by men and women.
Attributions about the two sexes often differ. For example, men's successes tend to be attributed to their ability and intelligence (blue cell), whereas women's successes tend to be attributed to hard work, good luck, or low task difficulty (green cells). These attributional biases help to perpetuate the belief that men are more competent than women.

then goes to school and makes disparaging remarks about gays that are reinforced by approval from peers, his prejudice will be strengthened through *operant conditioning.* Consistent with this analysis, one study found that college students' opinions on racial issues were swayed by overhearing others voice racist or antiracist sentiments (Blanchard, Lilly, & Vaughn, 1991). Of course, prejudicial attitudes, are not acquired only through direct experience. Stereotypic portrayals of various groups in the media can also foster prejudicial attitudes (Mastro, Behm-Morawitz, Kopacz, 2008; Mutz & Goldman, 2010).

Competition Between Groups

One of the oldest and simplest explanations for prejudice is that competition between groups can fuel animosity. If two groups compete for scarce resources, such as good jobs and affordable housing, one group's gain is the other's loss. *Realistic group conflict theory* asserts that intergroup hostility and prejudice are a natural outgrowth of fierce competition between groups.

A classic study at Robbers' Cave State Park in Oklahoma provided support for this theory many years ago (Sherif et al., 1961). The subjects were 11-year-old

white boys attending a three-week summer camp at the park. They did not know that the camp counselors were actually researchers (their parents knew). The boys were randomly assigned to one of two groups. During the first week, the boys got to know the other members of their own group through typical camp activities. They gradually developed group identities, choosing to call themselves the Rattlers and the Eagles. In the second week, the Rattlers and Eagles were put into a series of competitive situations, such as a football game, a treasure hunt, and a tug of war, with trophies and other prizes at stake. As predicted by realistic group conflict theory, hostile feelings quickly erupted between the two groups. Food fights broke out in the mess hall, cabins were ransacked, and group flags were burned.

If competition between innocent groups of children pursuing trivial prizes can foster hostility, you can imagine what is likely to happen when adults from very different backgrounds battle for genuinely important resources. Research has repeatedly shown that conflict over scarce resources can fuel prejudice and discrimination (Esses, Jackson, & Bennett-AbuAyyash, 2010). In fact, even the mere *perception* of competition can breed prejudice.

Homeless people are often viewed with prejudice. Because of the fundamental attribution error, people tend to blame the homeless for their plight.

Dividing the World into Ingroups and Outgroups

PSYKTREK 12d

As noted in the main body of the chapter, when people join together in groups, they sometimes divide the social world into "us versus them," or *ingroups versus outgroups*. This distinction has a profound impact on how people perceive, evaluate, and remember others (Dovidio & Gaertner, 2010). People tend to think simplistically about outgroups. They tend to see diversity among the members of their own group but to overestimate the homogeneity of the outgroup (Boldry, Gaertner, & Quinn,

2007). At a simple, concrete level, the essence of this process is captured by the statement "They all look alike." The illusion of homogeneity in the outgroup makes it easier to sustain stereotypic beliefs about its members (Rothbart, 2001). Furthermore, as you might anticipate, people tend to evaluate outgroup members less favorably than ingroup members (Reynolds, Turner, & Haslam, 2000). People routinely engage in outgroup derogation—in other words, they "trash" outgroups so that they can feel superior to them.

Our discussion has shown that a plethora of processes conspire to create

and maintain personal prejudices against a diverse array of outgroups. Most of the factors at work reflect normal, routine processes in social behavior. Thus, it is understandable that most people—whether privileged or underprivileged, minority members or majority members—probably harbor some prejudicial attitudes. Our analysis of the causes of prejudice may have permitted you to identify prejudices of your own or their sources. Perhaps an enhanced awareness of your personal prejudices may help you become a little more tolerant of the endless diversity seen in human behavior.

Analyzing Credibility and Social Influence Tactics

You can run, but you cannot hide. This statement aptly sums up the situation that exists when it comes to persuasion and social influence. There is no way to evade the constant, never-ending efforts of others to shape your attitudes and behavior. In this Application we will discuss two topics that can enhance your resistance to manipulation. First, we will outline some ideas that can be useful in evaluating the credibility of a persuasive source. Second, we will describe some widely used social influence strategies that it pays to know about.

Evaluating Credibility

The salesperson at your local health food store swears that a specific herb combination improves memory and helps people stay healthy. A popular singer touts a psychic hotline, where the operators can "really help" with the important questions in life. Speakers at a "historical society" meeting claim that the Holocaust never happened. These are just a few real-life examples of the pervasive attempts to persuade the public to believe something. In these examples, the "something" people are expected to believe runs counter to the conventional or scientific view, but who is to say who is right? After all, people are entitled to their own opinions, aren't they?

Yes, people *are* entitled to their own opinions, but that does not mean that all opinions are equally valid. Some opinions are just plain wrong and others are highly questionable. People are not equally believable. In deciding what to believe, it is important to carefully examine the evidence presented and the logic of the argument that supports the conclusion (see the Critical Thinking Applica-

tion for Chapter 9). In deciding what to believe, you also need to decide *whom* to believe, a task that requires assessing the *credibility* of the source of the information. Let's look at some questions that can provide guidance in this process.

Does the source have a vested interest in the issue at hand? If the source is likely to benefit in some way from convincing you of something, you need to take a skeptical attitude. In the examples provided here, it is easy to see how the sales clerk and popular singer will benefit if you buy the products they are selling. But what about the so-called historical society? How would members benefit by convincing large numbers of people that the Holocaust never happened? Like the sales clerk and singer, they are also selling something, in this case a particular view of history that they hope will influence future events in certain ways. Of course, the fact that sources have a vested interest does not necessarily mean that their arguments are invalid. But a source's credibility needs to be evaluated with extra caution when the person or group has something to gain.

What are the source's credentials? Does the person have any special training, an advanced degree, or any other basis for claiming special knowledge about the topic? The usual training for a sales clerk or singer does not include how to assess research results in medical journals or to evaluate claims of psychic powers. The Holocaust deniers are more difficult to evaluate. Some of them have studied history and written books on the topic. However, the books are mostly self-published, and few of these "experts" hold positions at reputable universities where scholars are subject to peer evaluation. That's *not* to say that legitimate credentials ensure a source's credibility. A number of popular diets that are widely regarded by nutritional experts as worthless, if not hazardous (Drewnowski, 1995; Dwyer, 1995), were created and marketed by genuine physicians. Of course, these physicians have a *vested interest* in the

diets, as they have made millions of dollars from them.

Is the information grossly inconsistent with the conventional view on the issue? Just being different from the mainstream view certainly does *not* make a conclusion wrong. But claims that vary radically from most other information on a subject should raise a red flag that leads to careful scrutiny. Bear in mind that charlatans and hucksters are often successful because they typically try to persuade people to believe things that they want to believe. Wouldn't it be great if we could effortlessly enhance our memory, foretell the future, eat all we want and still lose weight, and earn hundreds of dollars per hour working at home? And wouldn't it be nice if the Holocaust never happened? It is prudent to be wary of wishful thinking.

Recognizing Social Influence Strategies

It pays to understand social influence strategies because advertisers, salespeople, and fundraisers—not to mention friends and neighbors—frequently rely on them to manipulate people's behavior. Let's look at four basic strategies: the foot-in-the-door technique, misuse of the reciprocity norm, the lowball technique, and feigned scarcity.

Door-to-door salespeople have long recognized the importance of gaining a *little* cooperation from sales targets (getting a "foot in the door") before hitting them with the real sales pitch. The *foot-in-the-door technique* involves getting people to agree to a small request to increase the chances that they will agree to a larger request later. This technique is widely used in all walks of life. For example, groups seeking donations often ask people to simply sign a petition first.

In an early study of the foot-in-the-door technique (Freedman & Fraser, 1966), the large request involved asking homemakers whether a team of six men doing consumer research could come into their home to classify *all* their household products. Only 22% of the control subjects agreed to this outlandish request. However, when the same request was made three days after a small request (to answer a few questions about soap preferences), 53% of the participants agreed to the larger request. Why does the foot-in-the-door technique work? According to Burger (1999), quite a variety of processes contribute to its effectiveness, including people's tendency to try to behave consistently (with their initial response) and their reluctance to renege on their sense of commitment to the person who made the initial request.

Most of us have been socialized to believe in the *reciprocity norm*—the rule that we should pay back in kind what we receive from others. Robert Cialdini (2008) has written extensively about how the reciprocity norm is used in social influence efforts. For example, groups seeking donations routinely send address labels, key rings, and other small gifts with their pleas. Salespeople using the reciprocity principle distribute free samples to prospective customers. When they return a few days later, most of the customers feel obligated to buy some of their products. The reciprocity rule is meant to promote fair exchanges in social interactions. However, when people manipulate the reciprocity norm, they usually give something of minimal value in the hopes of getting far more in return (Howard, 1995).

The lowball technique is even more deceptive. The name for this technique derives from a common practice in automobile sales, in which a customer is offered a terrific bargain on a car. The bargain price gets the customer to commit to

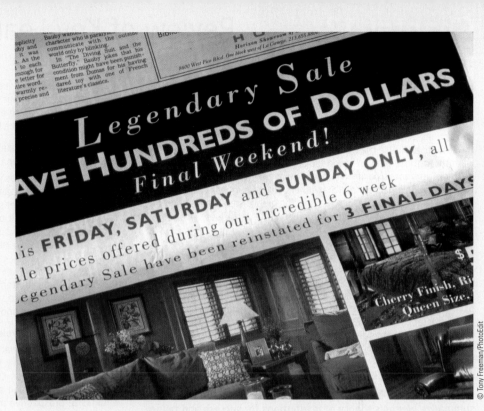

Advertisers often try to artificially create scarcity to make their products seem more desirable.

buying the car. Soon after this commitment is made, however, the dealer starts revealing some hidden costs. Typically, the customer learns that options assumed to be included in the original price are actually going to cost extra or that a promised low loan rate has "fallen through." Once they have committed to buying a car, most customers are unlikely to cancel the deal. Thus, **the lowball technique involves getting someone to commit to a seemingly attractive proposition before its hidden costs are revealed.** Car dealers aren't the only ones who use this technique, which is a surprisingly effective strategy (Cialdini & Griskevicius, 2010).

A number of years ago, Jack Brehm (1966) demonstrated that telling people they can't have something only makes them want it more. This phenomenon helps explain why companies often try to create the impression that their products are in scarce supply. Scarcity threatens your freedom to choose a product, thus creating an increased desire for the scarce commodity. Advertisers frequently feign scarcity to drive up the demand for products. Thus, we constantly see ads that scream "limited supply available," "for a limited time only," "while they last," and "time is running out." Like genuine scarcity, feigned scarcity can enhance the desirability of a commodity (Cialdini & Griskevicius, 2010).

TABLE 12.1 **Critical Thinking Skills Discussed in This Application**

Skill	Description
Judging the credibility of an information source	The critical thinker understands that credibility and bias are central to determining the quality of information and looks at factors such as vested interests, credentials, and appropriate expertise.
Recognizing social influence strategies	The critical thinker is aware of manipulative tactics such as the foot-in-the-door and lowball techniques, misuse of the reciprocity norm, and feigned scarcity.

Person Perception: Forming Impressions of Others

12.1 Understand how physical appearance and stereotypes may influence impressions of others.

Perceptions of others can be distorted by physical appearance. People tend to attribute desirable characteristics, such as intelligence, competence, and warmth, to those who are good-looking. Observers can draw surprisingly accurate inferences based on others' nonverbal expressiveness. Stereotypes are widely held beliefs that others will have certain characteristics because of their membership in a specific group. Stereotypes tend to be broad overgeneralizations that foster inaccurate perceptions of people.

12.2 Discuss the subjectivity of social perception and evolutionary explanations for bias in person perception.

In interacting with others, people tend to see what they expect to see. People also tend to overestimate how often their expectations are confirmed, a phenomenon called the illusory correlation effect. Evolutionary psychologists argue that many biases in person perception were adaptive in humans' ancestral past. The tendency to automatically categorize others into ingroups and outgroups may reflect the primitive need to quickly separate friend from foe.

Attribution Processes: Explaining Behavior

12.3 Distinguish between internal and external attributions, and summarize Weiner's theory of attributions for success and failure.

Internal attributions ascribe behavior to personal dispositions and traits, whereas external attributions locate the cause of behavior in the environment. Weiner's model proposes that attributions for success and failure should be analyzed in terms of the stability of causes, as well as along the internal-external dimension, yielding four possible types of attributions: internal-stable, internal-unstable, external-stable, and external-unstable.

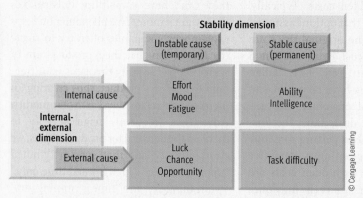

12.4 Identify some types of bias in patterns of attribution, including cultural variations.

Observers favor internal attributions to explain another's behavior, which is called the fundamental attribution error, while actors favor external attributions to explain their own behavior. The self-serving bias is the tendency to attribute one's good outcomes to personal factors and one's bad outcomes to situational factors. Cultures vary in their emphasis on individualism as opposed to collectivism, which can influence attributional tendencies. The fundamental attribution error and the self-serving bias in attribution may be more prevalent in Western cultures that are high in individualism.

Interpersonal Attraction: Liking and Loving

12.5 Understand the role of physical attractiveness, similarity, and reciprocity in attraction.

People tend to like and love others who are physically attractive. The matching hypothesis asserts that people who are similar in physical at-

tractiveness are more likely to be drawn together than those who are not. Research suggests that similarity causes attraction, although attitude alignment may also be at work. Reciprocity, which involves liking those who show that they like you, fosters attraction.

12.6 Discuss theoretical views of love and how culture and the Internet relate to romantic relationships.

Passionate love involves complete absorption in another along with sexual feelings, whereas companionate love involves a trusting, tolerant entwinement. Hazan and Shaver's theory suggests that love relationships in adulthood mimic attachment patterns in infancy. People tend to fall into three attachment subtypes: secure, avoidant, and anxious-ambivalent. Those who are secure tend to have more-committed, satisfying relationships. The characteristics people seek in prospective mates are much the same around the world. However, cultures vary in their emphasis on passionate love as a prerequisite for marriage. Although critics are concerned that Internet relationships are superficial, Internet-initiated relationships appear to be just as intimate and stable as relationships forged offline.

12.7 Understand evolutionary analyses of mating preferences.

According to evolutionary psychologists, certain aspects of good looks, such as facial symmetry, influence attraction because they are indicators of reproductive fitness. Consistent with evolutionary theory, men tend to seek youthfulness and attractiveness in their mates, whereas women emphasize prospective mates' social status and financial potential. The gender gap in mating priorities influences people's courtship tactics.

Attitudes: Making Social Judgments

12.8 Analyze the structure of attitudes and the link between attitudes and behavior.

Attitudes may be made up of cognitive, affective, and behavioral components. The cognitive component consists of beliefs, the affective component of emotional feelings, and the behavioral component of predispositions to act in certain ways. Attitudes also vary along three dimensions: strength, accessibility, and ambivalence. Attitudes and behavior aren't as consistent as one might assume, for a variety of reasons, including the need to consider situational pressures.

12.9 Distinguish between explicit and implicit attitudes, and explain how implicit attitudes are measured.

Explicit attitudes are attitudes that are held consciously and can readily be described. Implicit attitudes are covert attitudes that are expressed in subtle automatic responses. Implicit attitudes are measured by testing how quickly people associate carefully chosen pairs of concepts. Research with the IAT suggests that most people harbor covert prejudices, which do affect overt behavior.

12.10 Summarize how source, message, and receiver factors influence the process of persuasion.

A source of persuasion who is credible, expert, trustworthy, likable, and similar tends to be relatively effective in stimulating attitude change. Although there are some situational limitations, two-sided arguments and fear arousal are effective elements in persuasive messages. Repetition of a message is also helpful, perhaps because of the mere exposure effect. Persuasion is more difficult when a receiver is forewarned and when strong attitudes are targeted.

Who	What	By what means	To whom
Source factors	**Message factors**	**Channel factors**	**Receiver factors**
Credibility	Fear appeal versus logic	In person	Personality
Expertise	One-sided versus two-sided argument	On television, or radio	Expectations (e.g., forewarning)
Trustworthiness		Via audiotape	Initial attitude on issue
Likability	Number of strong or weak arguments	Via computer	
Attractiveness			Strength of preexisting attitudes
Similarity	Repetition		

SOURCE: Based on Lippa, R. A. (1994). *Introduction to social psychology*. Belmont, CA: Brooks/Cole Publishing Company. Copyright © 1994 by Wadsworth. Reprinted by permission of the author. Graphic: © Cengage Learning

12.11 Clarify various theories of attitude formation and change.

Attitudes may be shaped through classical conditioning, operant conditioning, and observational learning. Festinger's dissonance theory asserts that inconsistent attitudes cause tension and that people alter their attitudes to reduce cognitive dissonance. Dissonance theory has been used to explain attitude change following counterattitudinal behavior and efforts that haven't panned out. The elaboration likelihood model holds that the central route to persuasion, which depends on the logic of persuasive messages, tends to yield longer-lasting attitude change than the peripheral route, which depends on nonmessage factors.

Conformity and Obedience: Yielding to Others

12.12 Understand Asch's work on conformity and Milgram's research on obedience.

Asch found that subjects often conform to the group, even when the group reports inaccurate judgments on a simple line-judging task. Conformity becomes more likely as group size increases, up to a group size of seven, then levels off. If a small group isn't unanimous, conformity declines rapidly. In Milgram's landmark study of obedience to authority, participants showed a remarkable tendency, despite their misgivings, to follow orders to shock an innocent stranger. Milgram concluded that situational pressures can make decent people do indecent things. Critics asserted that Milgram's results were not generalizable to the real world and that his methods were unethical. The generalizability of Milgram's findings has stood the test of time, as Burger's recent replication verified. But Milgram's work did lead to stricter ethical standards for research.

12.13 Discuss cultural variations in conformity and obedience, and describe the Stanford Prison Simulation.

The Asch and Milgram experiments have been replicated in many cultures, showing that conformity and obedience are common around the world. Generally, slightly higher rates of conformity have been found in collectivist cultures. The Stanford Prison Simulation, in which normal, healthy students were randomly assigned to be prisoners or guards, demonstrated that social roles and situational pressures can exert great influence over behavior. Like Milgram, Zimbardo showed that situational forces can lead normal people to exhibit surprisingly callous, abusive behavior.

Behavior in Groups: Joining with Others

12.14 Discuss the nature of groups, the bystander effect, and social loafing.

A group consists of two or more people who interact and are interdependent. People are more likely to help someone in need when they are alone than when a group is present. This phenomenon, called the bystander effect, occurs primarily because a group creates diffusion of responsibility. Individuals' productivity often declines in larger groups because of loss of coordination and because of social loafing. Social loafing seems to be due mostly to diffusion of responsibility. It may be less prevalent in collectivist cultures.

12.15 Explain group polarization and groupthink.

Group polarization occurs when discussion leads a group to shift toward a more extreme decision in the direction the group was already leaning. In groupthink, a cohesive group suspends critical judgment in a misguided effort to promote agreement in decision making.

Reflecting on the Chapter's Themes

12.16 Identify the four unifying themes highlighted in this chapter.

Our study of social psychology highlighted four of the text's unifying themes: the value of empiricism, the cultural limits of research based on American samples, the subjectivity of perception, and the multifactorial causation of behavior.

PERSONAL APPLICATION
Understanding Prejudice

12.17 Relate person perception processes and attributional bias to prejudice.

Stereotyping is a key process contributing to prejudice. Although racial stereotypes have diminished, modern racism has merely become more subtle. Stereotypes are highly resistant to change because people tend to see what they expect to see. Attributional biases, such as the tendency to assume that others' behavior reflects their dispositions, can contribute to prejudice.

12.18 Relate attitude formation, intergroup competition, and ingroups versus outgroups to prejudice.

Negative attitudes about groups are often acquired through observational learning and strengthened through operant conditioning. Realistic group conflict theory posits that competition between groups for scarce resources fosters prejudice. The propensity to see outgroups as homogenous serves to strengthen prejudice and promote outgroup derogation.

CRITICAL THINKING APPLICATION
Analyzing Credibility and Social Influence Tactics

12.19 Identify useful criteria for evaluating credibility, and recognize standard social influence strategies.

Useful criteria in judging credibility include whether a source has vested interests or appropriate credentials. One should also consider why information might not coincide with conventional wisdom. To resist manipulative efforts, it helps to be aware of social influence tactics such as the foot-in-the-door technique, misuse of the reciprocity norm, the lowball technique, and feigned scarcity.

13

Stress, Coping, and Health

PARADOX

*Even when people are under severe stress, they
continue to experience positive emotions.*

© Angela Coppola/Corbis

You're in your car headed home from school with a classmate. Traffic is barely moving. A radio report indicates that the traffic jam is only going to get worse. You groan as you fiddle impatiently with the radio dial. Another motorist nearly takes your fender off trying to cut into your lane. Your pulse quickens as you shout insults at the unknown driver, who can't even hear you. You think about the term paper that you have to work on tonight. Your stomach knots up as you think about all the research you still have to do. If you don't finish that paper soon, you won't be able to find any time to study for your math test, not to mention your biology quiz. Suddenly, you remember that you promised the person you're dating that the two of you would get together tonight. There's no way. Another fight looms on the horizon. Your classmate asks how you feel about the tuition increase that the college announced yesterday. You've been trying not to think about it. You're already in debt up to your ears. Your parents are bugging you about changing schools, but you don't want to leave your friends. Your heartbeat quickens as you contemplate the debate you're sure to have with your parents. You feel wired with tension as you realize that the stress in your life never seems to let up.

In this chapter we'll discuss the nature of stress, how people cope with stress, and the potential effects of stress. Our examination of the relationship between stress and physical illness will lead us into a broader discussion of the psychology of health. The way people in health professions think about physical illness has changed considerably in the past 20 to 30 years. The traditional view of physical illness as a purely biological phenomenon has given way to a biopsychosocial model of illness (Friedman & Adler, 2007; Suls, Luger, & Martin, 2010). **The *biopsychosocial model* holds that physical illness is caused by a complex interaction of biological, psychological, and sociocultural factors.** This model does not suggest that biological factors are unimportant. It simply asserts that these factors operate in a psychological and social context that is also influential.

The Nature of Stress

KEY LEARNING GOALS

13.1 Evaluate the impact of minor stressors and people's appraisals of stress.

13.2 Identify four major types of stress.

The term *stress* has been used in different ways by different theorists. We'll define *stress* **as any circumstances that threaten or are perceived to threaten one's well-being and tax one's coping abilities.** The threat may be to immediate physical safety, long-range security, self-esteem, reputation, peace of mind, or many other things that one values. This is a complex concept, so let's explore it a little further.

Stress as an Everyday Event

The word *stress* tends to spark images of overwhelming, traumatic crises. People may think of terrorist attacks, hurricanes, military combat, and nuclear accidents. Undeniably, major disasters of this sort are extremely stressful (Kim et al., 2008; van Griensven et al., 2007). However, these unusual events are only a small part of what constitutes stress. Many everyday events such as waiting in line, having car trouble, shopping for Christmas presents, misplacing your checkbook, and staring at bills you can't pay are also stressful. Of course, major and minor stressors are not entirely independent. A major stressful event, such as going through a divorce, can trigger a cascade of minor stressors, such as looking for an attorney, taking on new household responsibilities, and so forth (Pillow, Zautra, & Sandler, 1996).

You might guess that minor stresses would produce minor effects, but that isn't necessarily true. Richard Lazarus and his colleagues have developed a scale to measure everyday hassles. They have shown that routine hassles may have significant harmful effects on mental and physical health (Delongis, Folkman, & Lazarus, 1988; Johnson & Sherman, 1997). Why would minor hassles be related to mental health? The answer isn't entirely clear yet. It may be because of the *cumulative* nature of stress (Seta, Seta, & McElroy, 2002). Stress adds up. Routine stresses at home, at school, and at work might be fairly benign individually, but collectively they could create great strain.

Appraisal: Stress Lies in the Eye of the Beholder

The experience of feeling stressed depends on what events one notices and how one appraises them (Monroe & Slavich, 2007). Events that are stressful for one person may be routine for another (Steptoe, 2007). For example, many people find flying in an airplane

Richard Lazarus
"We developed the Hassle Scale because we think scales that measure major events miss the point. The constant, minor irritants may be much more important than the large, landmark changes."

somewhat stressful, but frequent flyers may not be bothered at all. Some people enjoy the excitement of going out on a date with someone new; others find the uncertainty terrifying.

In discussing appraisals of stress, Lazarus and Folkman (1984) distinguish between primary and secondary appraisal (see **Figure 13.1**). *Primary appraisal* **is an initial evaluation of whether an event is (1) irrelevant to you, (2) relevant but not threatening or (3) stressful.** When you view an event as stressful, you are likely to make a *secondary appraisal,* **which is an evaluation of your coping resources and options for dealing with the stress.** Thus, your primary appraisal would determine whether you saw an upcoming job interview as stressful. Your secondary appraisal would determine how stressful the interview appeared, in light of your assessment of your ability to deal with the event.

Often, people aren't very objective in their appraisals of potentially stressful events. A study of hospitalized patients awaiting surgery showed only a slight correlation between the objective seriousness of a person's upcoming surgery and the amount of fear the patient experienced (Janis, 1958). Clearly, some people are more prone than others to feel threatened by life's difficulties. A number of studies have shown that anxious, neurotic people report more stress than others (Cooper & Bright, 2001; Espejo et al., 2011), as do people who are relatively unhappy (Cacioppo et al., 2008). Thus, stress lies in the eye (actually, the mind) of the beholder. People's appraisals of stressful events are highly subjective.

Major Types of Stress

An enormous variety of events can be stressful for one person or another. Although they're not entirely independent, the four principal types of stress are (1) frustration, (2) conflict, (3) change, and (4) pressure. As you read about each type, you'll surely recognize some familiar adversaries.

FRUSTRATION

PSYKTREK 11f

As psychologists use the term, *frustration* **is experienced whenever the pursuit of some goal is thwarted.** In essence, you experience frustration when you want something and you can't have it. Everyone has to deal with frustration virtually every day. Traffic jams, difficult commutes, and annoying drivers, for instance, are a routine source of frustration that can elicit anger and aggression (Evans & Wener, 2006; Schaefer, 2005). Fortunately, most frustrations are brief and insignificant. You may be quite upset when you go to a repair shop to pick up your ailing laptop and find that it hasn't been fixed as promised. However, a week later you'll probably have your computer back, and the frustration will be forgotten. Of course, some frustrations—such as failing to get a promotion at work or losing a boyfriend or girlfriend—can be sources of significant stress.

FIGURE 13.1

Primary and secondary appraisal of stress. *Primary appraisal* is an initial evaluation of whether an event is (1) irrelevant to you, (2) relevant, but not threatening, or (3) stressful. When you view an event as stressful, you are likely to make a *secondary appraisal,* which is an evaluation of your coping resources and options for dealing with the stress. (Based on Lazarus & Folkman, 1994)

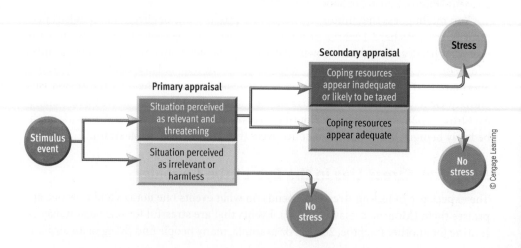

© Cengage Learning

CONFLICT

Like frustration, conflict is an unavoidable feature of everyday life. The perplexing question "Should I or shouldn't I?" comes up countless times in one's life. *Conflict* **occurs when two or more incompatible motivations or behavioral impulses compete for expression.** As we discussed in Chapter 11, Sigmund Freud proposed a century ago that internal conflicts generate considerable psychological distress.

Conflicts come in three types, which were originally described by Kurt Lewin (1935) and investigated extensively by Neal Miller (1944, 1959). These three basic types of conflict—approach-approach, avoidance-avoidance, and approach-avoidance—are diagrammed in **Figure 13.2.**

In an *approach-approach conflict* **a choice must be made between two attractive goals.** The problem, of course, is that you can choose just one of the two goals. For example: You have a free afternoon—should you play tennis or racquetball? You can't afford both the blue sweater and the gray jacket—which should you buy? Among the three kinds of conflict, the approach-approach type tends to be the least stressful. Nonetheless, approach-approach conflicts over important issues may sometimes be troublesome. If you're torn between two appealing college majors or two attractive boyfriends, for example, you may find the decision-making process quite stressful.

In an *avoidance-avoidance conflict* **a choice must be made between two unattractive goals.** Forced to choose between two repelling alternatives, you are, as they say, "caught between a rock and a hard place." For example, should you continue to collect unemployment checks, or should you take that boring job at the car wash? Or suppose you have painful backaches. Should you submit to surgery that you dread, or should you continue to live with the pain? Obviously, avoidance-avoidance conflicts are most unpleasant and highly stressful.

In an *approach-avoidance conflict* **a choice must be made about whether to pursue a single goal that has both attractive and unattractive aspects.** For instance, imagine that you're offered a promotion that will mean a large increase in pay, but you'll have to move to a city that you hate. Approach-avoidance conflicts are common and can be quite stressful. Any time you have to take a risk to pursue some desirable outcome, you're likely to find yourself in an approach-avoidance conflict. Should you risk rejection by approaching that attractive person in class? Should you risk your savings by investing in a new business that could fail? Approach-avoidance conflicts often produce *vacillation* (Miller, 1944). That is, you go back and forth, beset by indecision. You decide to go ahead, then you decide not to, and then you decide to go ahead again.

FIGURE 13.2

Types of conflict. Psychologists have identified three basic types of conflict. In approach-approach and avoidance-avoidance conflicts, a person is torn between two goals. In an approach-avoidance conflict, only one goal is under consideration, but it has both positive and negative aspects.

CHANGE

Thomas Holmes and Richard Rahe have led the way in exploring the idea that life changes—including positive events, such as getting married or getting promoted—represent a key type of stress. *Life changes* are **any noticeable alterations in one's living circumstances that require readjustment.** Based on their theory, Holmes and Rahe (1967) developed the Social Readjustment Rating Scale (SRRS) to measure life change as a form of stress. The scale assigns numerical values to forty-three major life events. These values are supposed to reflect the magnitude of the readjustment required by each change (see **Table 13.1**). In using the scale, respondents are asked to indicate how often they experienced any of these forty-three events during a certain time period (typically, the past year). The numbers associated with each checked event are then added. This total is an index of the amount of change-related stress the person has recently experienced.

The SRRS and similar scales based on it have been used in over 10,000 studies by researchers all over the world (Dohrenwend, 2006). Overall, these studies have shown that people with higher scores tend to be more vulnerable to many kinds of physical illness and to many types of psychological problems as well (Derogatis & Coons, 1993; Scully, Tosi, & Banning, 2000; Surtees & Wainwright, 2007). These results have attracted a great deal of attention. The SRRS has even been reprinted in many popular newspapers and magazines. The attendant publicity has led to the widespread conclusion that life change is inherently stressful.

However, experts have criticized this research, citing problems with the methods used and problems in interpreting the findings (Dohrenwend, 2006; Monroe, 2008; Wethington, 2007). At this point, it's a key interpretive issue that concerns us. A variety of critics have collected evidence showing that the SRRS does not measure *change* exclusively (McLean & Link, 1994; Turner & Wheaton, 1995). In reality, it assesses a wide range of kinds of stressful experiences. Thus, we have little reason to believe that change is *inherently* or *inevitably* stressful. Undoubtedly, some life changes may be quite challenging, but others may be quite benign.

PRESSURE

At one time or another, most people have remarked that they're "under pressure." What does this mean? *Pressure* involves **expectations or demands that one behave in a certain way.** You are under pressure to *perform* when you're expected to execute tasks and responsibilities quickly, effi-

---

Concept Check 13.1

Identifying Types of Conflict

Check your understanding of the three basic types of conflict by identifying the type experienced in each of the following examples. The answers are in Appendix A.

Examples

_____ 1. John can't decide whether to take a boring job in a car wash or to go on welfare.

_____ 2. Desiree wants to apply to a highly selective law school, but she hates to risk the possibility of rejection.

_____ 3. Vanessa has been shopping for a new car and is torn between a nifty little sports car and a classy sedan, both of which she really likes.

Types of conflict

a. approach-approach

b. avoidance-avoidance

c. approach-avoidance

© Supri Suharjoto/Shutterstock

TABLE 13.1 Social Readjustment Rating Scale

Life Event	Mean Value	Life Event	Mean Value
Death of a spouse	100	Son or daughter leaving home	29
Divorce	73	Trouble with in-laws	29
Marital separation	65	Outstanding personal achievement	28
Jail term	63	Spouse begins or stops work	26
Death of a close family member	63	Begin or end school	26
Personal injury or illness	53	Change in living conditions	25
Marriage	50	Revision of personal habits	24
Fired at work	47	Trouble with boss	23
Marital reconciliation	45	Change in work hours or conditions	20
Retirement	45	Change in residence	20
Change in health of family member	44	Change in school	20
Pregnancy	40	Change in recreation	19
Sex difficulties	39	Change in church activities	19
Gain of a new family member	39	Change in social activities	18
Business readjustment	39	Mortgage or loan for lesser purchase (car, TV, etc.)	17
Change in financial state	38	Change in sleeping habits	16
Death of a close friend	37	Change in number of family get-togethers	15
Change to a different line of work	36	Change in eating habits	15
Change in number of arguments with spouse	35	Vacation	13
Mortgage or loan for major purchase (home, etc.)	31	Christmas	12
Foreclosure of mortgage or loan	30	Minor violations of the law	11
Change in responsibilities at work	29		

© Cengage Learning

SOURCE: Adapted from Holmes, T. H., & Rahe, R. (1967). The Social Readjustment Rating Scale. *Journal of Psychosomatic Research, 11*, 213–218. Copyright © 1967 by Elsevier Science Publishing Co. Reprinted by permission.

ciently, and successfully. For example, salespeople are usually under pressure to move merchandise. Professors at research institutions are often under pressure to publish in respected journals. Stand-up comedians are under intense pressure to make people laugh. Pressures to *conform* to others' expectations are also common. Businessmen are expected to wear suits and ties. Suburban homeowners are expected to keep their yards well groomed. Teenagers are expected to respect their parents' values and rules.

Although widely discussed by the general public, the concept of pressure has received scant attention from researchers. However, Weiten (1988b, 1998) has devised a scale to measure pressure as a form of life stress. It assesses self-imposed pressure, pressure from work and school, and pressure from family relations, peer relations, and intimate relations. In research with this scale, a strong relationship has been found between

Pressure comes in two varieties: pressure to perform and pressure to conform. For example, standup comedians are under intense pressure to make audiences laugh (pressure to perform), whereas corporate employees are often expected to dress in certain ways (pressure to conform).

Left: Stockbyte/Getty Images; right:
© Craig Grant/iStockphoto

pressure and a variety of psychological symptoms and problems. In fact, pressure has turned out to be more strongly related to measures of mental health than the SRRS and other established measures of stress. Moreover, a recent 15-year study of over 12,000 nurses found that increased pressure at work was related to an increased risk for heart disease (Väänänen, 2010). Participants who reported that their pressure at work was much too high were almost 50% more likely to develop heart disease than subjects who experienced normal levels of pressure.

We tend to think of pressure as something imposed by outside forces. However, studies of high school and college students find that *pressure is often self-imposed* (Kouzma & Kennedy, 2004; Misra & Castillo, 2004). For example, you might sign up for extra classes to get through school quickly. Actually, self-imposed stress is not unique to pressure. Research suggests that other forms of stress can also be self-generated (Roberts & Ciesla, 2007). One implication of this finding is that people might have more control over a substantial portion of the stress in their lives than they realize.

Responding to Stress

The human response to stress is complex and multidimensional. Stress affects the individual at several levels. Consider again the chapter's opening scenario. You're driving home in heavy traffic and thinking about overdue papers, tuition increases, and parental pressures. Let's look at some of the reactions that were mentioned. When you groan in reaction to the traffic report, you're experiencing an *emotional response* to stress, in this case annoyance and anger. When your pulse quickens and your stomach knots up, you're exhibiting *physiological responses* to stress. When you shout insults at another driver, your verbal aggression is a *behavioral response* to the stress at hand. Thus, we can analyze a person's reactions to stress at three levels: (1) emotional responses, (2) physiological responses, and (3) behavioral responses. **Figure 13.3** provides an overview of the stress process.

Concept Check 13.2

Recognizing Sources of Stress

Check your understanding of the major sources of stress by indicating which type or types of stress are at work in each of the examples below. Bear in mind that the four basic types of stress are not mutually exclusive. There's some potential for overlap, so a specific experience might include both change and pressure, for instance. The answers are in Appendix A.

Examples

_____ 1. Marie is stuck in line at the bank.

_____ 2. Tamika decides that she won't be satisfied unless she gets straight A's this year.

_____ 3. Jose has just graduated from business school and has taken an exciting new job.

_____ 4. Morris has just been fired from his job and needs to find another.

Types of stress

a. frustration

b. conflict

c. change

d. pressure

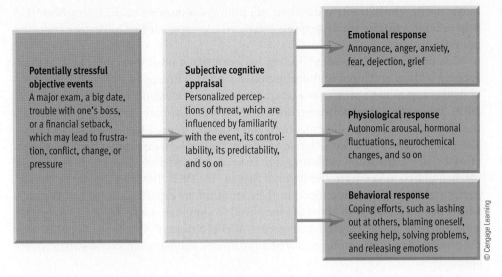

FIGURE 13.3

Overview of the stress process.
A potentially stressful event, such as a major exam, elicits a subjective appraisal of how threatening the event is. If the event is viewed with alarm, the stress may trigger emotional, physiological, and behavioral reactions, as people's response to stress is multidimensional.

© Cengage Learning

Emotional Responses

PsykTrek 11g

When people are under stress, they often react emotionally. Studies that have tracked stress and mood on a daily basis have found intimate relationships between the two (Affleck et al., 1994; van Eck, Nicolson, & Berkhof, 1998).

EMOTIONS COMMONLY ELICITED

PsykTrek 11g

No simple one-to-one connections have been found between certain types of stressful events and particular emotions. However, researchers *have* begun to uncover some strong links between *specific cognitive reactions to stress* (appraisals) and specific emotions (Smith & Lazarus, 1993). For example, self-blame tends to lead to guilt, helplessness to sadness, and so forth. Many emotions can be evoked by stressful events, but some are certainly more likely than others. Common emotional responses to stress include (a) annoyance, anger, and rage, (b) apprehension, anxiety, and fear, and (c) dejection, sadness, and grief (Lazarus, 1993; Woolfolk & Richardson, 1978).

Investigators have tended to focus heavily on the connection between stress and negative emotions. However, research shows that positive emotions also occur during periods of stress (Finan, Zautra, & Wershba, 2011; Folkman, 2008). Although this finding seems counterintuitive, researchers have found that people experience a diverse array of pleasant emotions even while enduring the most dire of circumstances (Folkman et al., 1997). Consider, for example, a study that examined subjects' emotional functioning early in 2001 and again in the weeks following the 9/11 terrorist attacks in the United States (Fredrickson et al., 2003). Like most U.S. citizens, these subjects reported many negative emotions in the aftermath of 9/11, including anger, sadness, and fear. However, within this "dense cloud of anguish" positive emotions also emerged. For example, people felt gratitude for the safety of their loved ones, many took stock and counted their blessings, and quite a few reported renewed love for their friends and family. Fredrickson et al. (2003) also found that the frequency of pleasant emotions correlated positively with a measure of subjects' resilience. Thus, contrary to common sense, positive emotions do *not* vanish during times of severe stress. Moreover, these positive emotions appear to play a key role in helping people bounce back from the difficulties associated with stress (Tugade & Fredrickson, 2004).

How do positive emotions promote resilience in the face of stress? Barbara Fredrickson's (2001, 2005, 2006) *broaden-and-build theory of positive emotions* can shed light on this question. First, positive emotions alter people's mindsets, broadening their scope of attention, and increasing their creativity and flexibility in problem solving. Second, positive emotions can undo the lingering effects of negative emotions and thus short-circuit the potentially damaging physiological responses to stress that we will discuss

FIGURE 13.4

Positive emotions and longevity. To look at the relation between positive emotions and longevity, Abel and Kruger (2010) used the intensity of baseball players' smiles in photographs as a rough indicator of the players' characteristic emotional tone. All the photos in the *Baseball Register* for 1952 were reviewed and classified as showing no smile, a partial smile, or a big smile. Then the age at death was determined for the players (except the 46 who were still alive in June 2009). As you can see, greater smile intensity was associated with living longer.

momentarily. Third, positive emotions can promote rewarding social interactions that help to build valuable social support, enhanced coping strategies, and other enduring personal resources.

One particularly interesting finding has been that a positive emotional style is associated with an enhanced immune response (Cohen & Pressman, 2006). Positive emotions also appear to be protective against heart disease (Davidson, Mostofsky, & Whang, 2010). These effects probably contribute to the recently discovered association between the tendency to report positive emotions and longevity (Ong, 2010; Xu & Roberts, 2010). Yes, people who experience a high level of positive emotions appear to live longer than others! One recent study exploring this association looked at photos of major league baseball players taken from the *Baseball Register* for 1952. The intensity of the players' smiles was used as a crude index of their tendency to experience positive emotions, which was then related to how long they lived. As you can see in **Figure 13.4**, greater smile intensity predicted greater longevity (Abel & Kruger, 2010). Thus, it appears that the benefits of positive emotions may be more diverse and more far reaching than widely appreciated.

EFFECTS OF EMOTIONAL AROUSAL

PSYKTREK 11g

Emotional responses are a natural and normal part of life. Even unpleasant emotions serve important purposes. Like physical pain, painful emotions can serve as warnings that one needs to take action. However, strong emotional arousal can also interfere with efforts to cope with stress. For example, there's evidence that high emotional arousal can interfere with attention and memory retrieval and can impair judgment and decision making (Lupien & Maheu, 2007; Mandler, 1993).

Although emotional arousal may hurt coping efforts, that isn't *necessarily* the case. The *inverted-U hypothesis* predicts that task performance should improve with increased emotional arousal—up to a point, after which further increases in arousal become disruptive and performance deteriorates (Anderson, 1990; Mandler, 1993). This idea is referred to as the inverted-U hypothesis because when performance is plotted as a function of arousal, the resulting graphs approximate an upside-down U (see **Figure 13.5**). In these graphs, the level of arousal at which performance peaks is characterized as the *optimal level of arousal* for a task.

This optimal level appears to depend in part on the complexity of the task at hand. The conventional wisdom is that *as a task becomes more complex, the optimal level of*

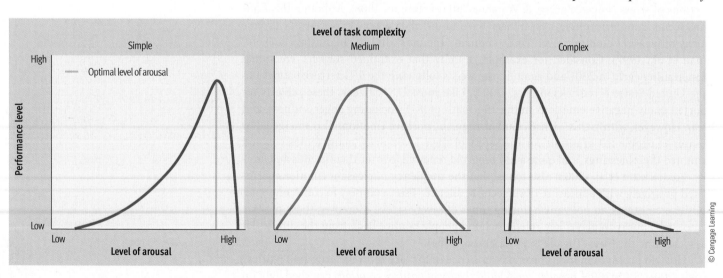

FIGURE 13.5

Arousal and performance. Graphs of the relationship between emotional arousal and task performance tend to resemble an inverted U, as increased arousal is associated with improved performance up to a point, after which higher arousal leads to poorer performance. The optimal level of arousal for a task depends on the complexity of the task. On complex tasks, a relatively low level of arousal tends to be optimal. On simple tasks, however, performance may peak at a much higher level of arousal.

arousal (for peak performance) tends to decrease. This relationship is depicted in **Figure 13.5**. As you can see, a fairly high level of arousal should be optimal on simple tasks (such as driving 8 hours to help a friend in a crisis). However, performance should peak at a lower level of arousal on complex tasks (such as making a major decision in which you have to weigh many factors). Thus, emotional arousal could have either beneficial or disruptive effects on coping, depending on the nature of the stressful demands one encounters.

Physiological Responses

PSYKTREK 11g

As we just discussed, stress frequently elicits strong emotional responses. Now we'll look at the important physiological changes that often accompany these emotions.

THE GENERAL ADAPTATION SYNDROME

PSYKTREK 11g

Concern about the physical effects of stress was first voiced by Hans Selye (1936, 1956), a Canadian scientist who coined the term *stress* while launching stress research many decades ago (Russell, 2007). Selye (1956, 1974, 1982) explained stress reactions in terms of what he called the general adaptation syndrome. The *general adaptation syndrome* is **a model of the body's stress response, consisting of three stages: alarm, resistance, and exhaustion** (see **Figure 13.6**). In the first stage, an *alarm reaction* occurs when an organism first recognizes the existence of a threat: Physiological arousal increases as the body musters its resources to combat the challenge. Selye's alarm reaction is essentially the fight-or-flight response described in Chapters 3 and 9.

However, Selye took his investigation of stress a few steps further by exposing laboratory animals to *prolonged stress,* similar to the chronic stress often endured by humans. As stress continues, the organism may progress to the second phase of the general adaptation syndrome, the *stage of resistance.* During this phase, physiological changes stabilize as coping efforts get under way. Typically, physiological arousal continues to be higher than normal, although it may level off somewhat as the organism becomes accustomed to the threat.

If the stress continues over a substantial period of time, the organism may enter the third stage, the *stage of exhaustion.* According to Selye, the body's resources for fighting stress are limited. If the stress can't be overcome, the body's resources may be depleted. Eventually, he thought, the organism would experience hormonal exhaustion, although we now know that the crux of the problem is that chronic overactivation of the stress response can have damaging physiological effects on a variety of organ systems (Sapolsky, 2007). These harmful physiological effects can lead to what Selye called "diseases of adaptation."

BRAIN-BODY PATHWAYS

PSYKTREK 11g

Even in cases of moderate stress, you may notice that your heart has started beating faster, you've begun to breathe harder, and you're perspiring more than usual. How does all this (and much more) happen? It appears that there are two major pathways along which the brain sends signals to the endocrine system (Dallman, Bhatnagar, & Viau,

Hans Selye

"There are two main types of human beings: 'racehorses,' who thrive on stress and are only happy with a vigorous, fast-paced lifestyle; and 'turtles,' who in order to be happy require peace, quiet, and a generally tranquil environment."

FIGURE 13.6

The general adaptation syndrome.
According to Selye, the physiological response to stress can be broken into three phases. During the first phase, the body mobilizes its resources for resistance after a brief initial shock. In the second phase, resistance levels off and eventually begins to decline. If the third phase of the general adaptation syndrome is reached, resistance is depleted, leading to health problems and exhaustion.

DILBERT

FIGURE 13.7

Brain-body pathways in stress. In times of stress, the brain sends signals along two pathways. The pathway through the autonomic nervous system controls the release of catecholamine hormones that help mobilize the body for action. The pathway through the pituitary gland and the endocrine system controls the release of corticosteroid hormones that increase energy and ward off tissue inflammation.

2007; Tsigos, Kyrou, & Chrousos, 2005). As we noted in Chapter 3, the *endocrine system* consists of glands located at various sites in the body that secrete chemicals called *hormones*. The hypothalamus is the gland in the brain that appears to initiate action along these two pathways.

The first pathway (see **Figure 13.7**) is routed through the autonomic nervous system (ANS). Your hypothalamus activates the sympathetic division of the ANS. A key part of this activation involves stimulating the central part of the adrenal glands (the adrenal medulla) to release large amounts of *catecholamines* into the bloodstream. These hormones radiate throughout your body, producing a number of physiological changes. The net result of catecholamine elevation is that your body is mobilized for action (Lundberg, 2007).

The second pathway involves more direct communication between the brain and the endocrine system (see **Figure 13.7**). The hypothalamus sends signals to the so-called master gland of the endocrine system, the pituitary gland. In turn, the pituitary secretes a hormone (ACTH) that stimulates the outer part of the adrenal glands (the adrenal cortex) to release another important set of hormones—*corticosteroids.* These hormones stimulate the release of chemicals that help increase your energy and help inhibit tissue inflammation in case of injury (Munck, 2007).

Recent research suggests that there may be sex differences in reactivity along both of these brain-body pathways. Evidence suggests that females' stress responses tend to be milder than males' stress reactions, at least from puberty through menopause (Kajantie & Phillips, 2006; Kudielka & Kirschbaum, 2005). The fact that this gender gap is found only between puberty and menopause suggests that females' higher levels of the hormone estrogen may play a key role in toning down women's physiological reactivity to stress. Some theorists speculate that this gender disparity in stress reactivity may contribute to the higher prevalence of cardiovascular disorders and certain other diseases in men (Kajantie, 2008).

An important new finding in research on stress and the brain is that stress can interfere with neurogenesis (McEwen, 2009; Mirescu & Gould, 2006). As you may recall from Chapter 3, scientists have recently discovered that the adult brain is capable of *neurogenesis*—the formation of new neurons, primarily in key areas in the hippocampus. In Chapter 14 we will discuss evidence that suppressed neurogenesis may be a key cause of depression (Dranovsky & Hen, 2006). Thus, the capacity of stress to hinder neurogenesis may have important ramifications. This is currently the subject of intense research.

Behavioral Responses

PSYKTREK 11g

People respond to stress at several levels. However, it's clear that behavior is the crucial dimension of their reactions. Most behavioral responses to stress involve coping. **Coping refers to efforts to master, reduce, or tolerate the demands created by stress.** Notice that this definition is neutral as to whether coping efforts are healthful or maladaptive. The popular use of the term often implies that coping is inherently healthful. When people say that someone "coped with her problems," the implication is that she handled them effectively.

In reality, however, coping responses may be adaptive or maladaptive (Folkman & Moskowitz, 2004; Kleinke, 2007). For example, if you were flunking a history course at midterm, you might cope with this stress by (1) increasing your study efforts, (2) seeking help from a tutor, (3) blaming your professor, or (4) giving up on the class without really trying. Clearly, the first two of these coping responses would be more adaptive than the last two. In this section we'll focus most of our attention on styles of coping that tend to be less than ideal. We'll discuss more healthful coping strategies in the Personal Application on stress management.

GIVING UP AND BLAMING ONESELF

PSYKTREK 11g

When confronted with stress, people sometimes simply give up and withdraw from the battle. Some people routinely respond to stress with fatalism and resignation. They passively accept setbacks that might be dealt with effectively. This syndrome is referred to as *learned helplessness* (Seligman, 1974, 1992). **Learned helplessness is passive behavior produced by exposure to unavoidable aversive events.** Learned helplessness seems to occur when individuals come to believe that events are beyond their control. As you might guess, giving up is not a highly regarded method of coping. Consistent with this view, many studies suggest that learned helplessness can contribute to depression (Isaacowitz & Seligman, 2007).

Although giving up is clearly less than optimal in many contexts, new research suggests that when people struggle to pursue goals that turn out to be unattainable, it sometimes makes sense for them to cut their losses and disengage from the goal (Wrosch & Scheier, 2003). Recent studies have shown that people who are better able to disengage from unattainable goals report better health and exhibit lower levels of a key stress hormone (Wrosch et al., 2007). Given the way people in our competitive culture tend to disparage the concept of "giving up," the authors note that it might be better to characterize this coping tactic as "goal adjustment."

Blaming oneself is another common response when people are confronted by stressful difficulties. The tendency to become highly self-critical in response to stress has been noted by a number of influential theorists. Albert Ellis (1973, 1987) calls this phenomenon "catastrophic thinking." According to Ellis, catastrophic thinking causes, aggravates, and perpetuates emotional reactions to stress that are often problematic (see the Personal Application for this chapter). Although there is something to be said for recognizing one's weaknesses and taking responsibility for one's failures, Ellis maintains that excessive self-blame can be very unhealthy.

Albert Ellis
"People largely disturb themselves by thinking in a self-defeating, illogical, and unrealistic manner."

Courtesy of Albert Ellis Institute

Concept Check 13.3

Tracing Brain-Body Pathways in Stress

Check your understanding of the two major pathways along which the brain sends signals to the endocrine system in the event of stress by separating the eight terms below into two sets of four and arranging each set in the appropriate sequence. You'll find the answers in Appendix A.

ACTH	corticosteriods
adrenal cortex	hypothalamus
adrenal medulla	pituitary
catecholamines	sympathetic division of the ANS

Pathway 1

_____

_____

_____

_____

Pathway 2

_____

_____

_____

_____

© Christo/Shutterstock

STRIKING OUT AT OTHERS

PsykTrek 11g

People often respond to stressful events by striking out at others with aggressive behavior. *Aggression* **is any behavior that is intended to hurt someone, either physically or verbally.** Many years ago, a team of psychologists (Dollard et al., 1939) proposed the *frustration-aggression hypothesis,* which held that aggression is always caused by frustration. Decades of research have supported this idea of a causal link between frustration and aggression (Berkowitz, 1989). However, this research has also shown that there isn't an inevitable, one-to-one correspondence between the two.

Sigmund Freud theorized that behaving aggressively could get pent-up emotion out of one's system and thus be adaptive. He coined the term *catharsis* **to refer to this release of emotional tension.** The Freudian notion that it is a good idea to vent anger has become widely disseminated and accepted in modern society. Books, magazines, and self-appointed experts routinely advise that it is healthy to "blow off steam" and thereby release and reduce anger. However, experimental research generally has *not* supported the catharsis hypothesis. Indeed, *most studies find just the opposite: Behaving in an aggressive manner tends to fuel more anger and aggression* (Bushman, 2002; Lohr et al., 2007). Other behaviors, such as talking or writing about one's problems, may have some value in releasing pent-up emotions (see the Personal Application), but aggressive behavior is not cathartic.

© Monkey Business Images/Shutterstock

INDULGING ONESELF

PsykTrek 11g

Stress sometimes leads to reduced impulse control, or *self-indulgence* (Tice, Bratslavsky, & Baumeister, 2001). When troubled by stress, many people engage in excessive or unwise patterns of eating, drinking, smoking, using drugs, spending money, and so forth. It makes sense that when things are going poorly in one area of their lives, people may try to compensate by pursuing substitute forms of satisfaction. Thus, it's not surprising that studies have linked stress to increases in eating (O'Connor & Conner, 2011), smoking (McClernon & Gilbert, 2007), gambling (Wood & Griffiths, 2007), and consumption of alcohol and drugs (Grunberg, Berger, & Hamilton, 2011). A new manifestation of this coping strategy that has attracted much attention recently is the tendency to immerse oneself in the online world of the Internet. Kimberly Young (1998, 2009) has called this syndrome *Internet addiction.* In some cases it can interfere with people's functioning at work, at school, or at home.

© Lucky Business/Shutterstock

DEFENSIVE COPING

PsykTrek 10a, 11g

Many people exhibit consistent styles of defensive coping in response to stress (Vaillant, 1994). We noted in Chapter 11 that Sigmund Freud originally developed the concept of the *defense mechanism.* Though rooted in the psychoanalytic tradition, this concept has gained widespread acceptance from psychologists of most persuasions (Cramer, 2000). Building on Freud's initial insights, modern psychologists have broadened the scope of the concept and added to Freud's list of defense mechanisms.

Defense mechanisms **are largely unconscious reactions that protect a person from unpleasant emotions such as anxiety and guilt.** Many specific defense mechanisms have been identified. For example, Laughlin (1979) lists forty-nine different defenses. We described eight common defense mechanisms in our discussion of Freud's theory in the previous chapter: repression, projection, displacement, reaction formation, regression, rationalization, identification, and sublimation (consult **Table 11.1**).

CATHY

The main purpose of defense mechanisms is to shield individuals from the emotional discomfort so often elicited by stress. They accomplish this purpose through *self-deception,* distorting reality so that it doesn't appear so threatening. Defense mechanisms operate at varying levels of awareness, although they're largely unconscious (Cramer, 2001; Erdelyi, 2001).

Generally, defensive coping is less than optimal because avoidance and wishful thinking rarely solve personal problems (Bolger, 1990; Holahan & Moos, 1990). That said, Shelley Taylor and Jonathon Brown (1988, 1994) have reviewed evidence suggesting that "positive illusions" may sometimes be adaptive for mental health. Some of the personal illusions that people create through defensive coping may help them deal with life's difficulties. Roy Baumeister (1989) theorizes that it's all a matter of degree and that there is an "optimal margin of illusion." According to Baumeister, extreme distortions of reality are maladaptive, but small illusions can be beneficial.

CONSTRUCTIVE COPING

PSYKTREK 11g

Our discussion thus far has focused on coping strategies that are less than ideal. Of course, people also exhibit many healthful strategies for dealing with stress. We'll use the term *constructive coping* to refer to relatively healthful efforts that people make to deal with stressful events. No strategy of coping can *guarantee* a successful outcome. Even the best coping responses may turn out to be ineffective in some circumstances. Thus, the concept of constructive coping is simply meant to convey a healthful, positive approach, without promising success.

What makes certain coping strategies constructive? Frankly, it's a gray area in which psychologists' opinions vary to some extent. Nonetheless, a consensus about the nature of constructive coping has emerged from the sizable literature on stress management. Key themes in this literature include the following:

1. Constructive coping involves confronting problems directly. It is task relevant and action oriented. It entails a conscious effort to rationally evaluate your options so that you can try to solve your problems.

2. Constructive coping is based on reasonably realistic appraisals of your stress and coping resources. A little self-deception may sometimes be adaptive. However, excessive self-deception and highly unrealistic negative thinking clearly are not.

3. Constructive coping involves learning to recognize, and in some cases inhibit, potentially disruptive emotional reactions to stress.

4. Constructive coping includes making efforts to ensure that your body is not especially vulnerable to the potentially damaging effects of stress.

The principles just described provide a rather general and abstract picture of constructive coping. We'll look at patterns of constructive coping in more detail in the Personal Application, which discusses various stress management strategies that people can use. We turn next to some of the possible outcomes of struggles with stress.

Shelley Taylor

"Rather than perceiving themselves, the world, and the future accurately, most people regard themselves, their circumstances, and the future as considerably more positive than is objectively likely. . . . These illusions are not merely characteristic of human thought; they appear actually to be adaptive, promoting rather than undermining good mental health."

Stress and Physical Health

KEY LEARNING GOALS

13.6 Review the evidence linking personality factors, emotional reactions, and depression to coronary heart disease.

13.7 Discuss how stress affects immune functioning, and assess the link between stress and illness.

13.8 Identify some factors that moderate the impact of stress, and explain how stress may have positive effects.

People struggle with many stresses every day. Most stresses come and go without leaving any enduring imprint. However, when stress is severe or when many stressful demands pile up, one's mental or physical health may be affected. In Chapter 14 you'll learn that chronic stress contributes to many types of psychological disorders, including depression, schizophrenia, and anxiety disorders. In this section, we'll discuss the link between stress and physical illness.

Prior to the 1970s, it was thought that stress contributed to the development of only a few physical diseases, such as high blood pressure, ulcers, and asthma, which were called *psychosomatic diseases.* However, in the 1970s, research began to uncover new links between stress and a great variety of diseases previously believed to be purely physiological in origin (Dimsdale et al., 2005; Dougall & Baum, 2001). Let's look at some of this research.

Personality, Hostility, and Heart Disease

Heart disease accounts for nearly 30% of the deaths in the United States every year. *Coronary heart disease* involves a reduction in blood flow in the coronary arteries, which supply the heart with blood. This type of heart disease accounts for about 90% of heart-related deaths. Established risk factors for coronary disease include smoking, lack of exercise, high cholesterol levels, and high blood pressure (Bekkouche et al., 2011). Recently, attention has shifted to the possibility that *inflammation* may contribute to elevated coronary risk (Miller & Blackwell, 2006). Evidence is mounting that inflammation plays a key role in the initiation and progression of coronary disease, as well as the acute complications that trigger heart attacks (Nabi et al., 2008).

Research on the relationship between *psychological* factors and heart attacks began in the 1960s and 1970s, when a pair of cardiologists, Meyer Friedman and Ray Rosenman (1974), discovered an apparent connection between coronary risk and a syndrome they called the *Type A personality,* which involves self-imposed stress and intense reactions to stress. The *Type A personality* **includes three elements: (1) a strong competitive orientation, (2) impatience and time urgency, and (3) anger and hostility.** Type A's are ambitious, hard-driving perfectionists who are exceedingly time-conscious. They routinely try to do several things at once. They fidget frantically over the briefest delays. Often they are highly competitive, achievement-oriented workaholics who drive themselves with many deadlines. They are easily irritated and are quick to anger. In contrast, **the *Type B personality* is marked by relatively relaxed, patient, easygoing, amicable behavior.** Type B's are less hurried, less competitive, and less easily angered than Type A's.

Decades of research uncovered a relatively modest correlation between Type A behavior and increased coronary risk. More often than not, studies found a correlation between Type A personality and an elevated incidence of heart disease, but the findings were not as strong nor as consistent as expected (Baker, Suchday, & Krantz, 2007; Myrtek, 2007). However, in recent decades, researchers have found a stronger link between personality and coronary risk by focusing on a specific component of the Type A personality: *anger and hostility* (Chida & Steptoe, 2009; Powell & Williams, 2007). For example, in one study of almost 13,000 men and women who had no prior history of heart disease, investigators found an elevated incidence of heart attacks among participants who exhibited an angry temperament (Williams et al., 2000). The participants, who were followed for a median period of 4.5 years, were classified as being low (37.1% of the subjects), moderate

© Alex James Bramwell/Shvutterstock

(55.2%), or high (7.7%) in the tendency to experience anger. Among participants with normal blood pressure, the high-anger subjects experienced almost three times as many coronary events as the low-anger subjects (see **Figure 13.8**). The results of this study and many others suggest that hostility may be the crucial toxic element in the Type A syndrome.

Emotional Reactions, Depression, and Heart Disease

Work on personality risk factors has dominated research on how psychological functioning contributes to heart disease. However, recent studies suggest that emotional reactions may also be critical. *One line of research has supported the hypothesis that transient mental stress and the resulting emotions that people experience can tax the heart* (Bekkouche et al., 2011; Dimsdale, 2008). Based on anecdotal evidence, cardiologists and laypersons have long voiced suspicions that strong emotional reactions might trigger heart attacks in individuals with coronary disease, but it has been difficult to document this connection. However, advances in cardiac monitoring have facilitated investigation of the issue.

As suspected, laboratory experiments with cardiology patients have shown that brief periods of mental stress can trigger sudden symptoms of heart disease (Baker, Suchday, & Krantz, 2007). Overall, the evidence suggests that mental stress can elicit cardiac symptoms in about 30%–70% of patients with stable coronary disease (Kop, Gottdiener, & Krantz, 2001). Outbursts of anger may be particularly dangerous (Lampert et al., 2009). Moreover, a recent study also demonstrated that mental stress can trigger temporary increases in the *inflammation* that is thought to contribute to cardiovascular risk (Kop et al., 2008).

Another line of research has implicated depression as a risk factor for heart disease (Goldston & Baillie, 2008). *Depressive disorders,* which are characterized by persistent feelings of sadness and despair, are a fairly common form of mental illness (see Chapter 14). In many studies, elevated rates of depression have been found among patients suffering from heart disease. However, experts have tended to explain this correlation by asserting that being diagnosed with heart disease makes people depressed. However, recent evidence suggests that the causal relations may be just the opposite—*that the emotional dysfunction of depression may cause heart disease* (Frasure-Smith & Lesperance, 2005). For example, a recent study of almost 20,000 people who were initially free of heart disease reported striking results: Participants who suffered from depression were 2.7 times more likely to die of heart disease during the follow-up period than people who were not depressed (Surtees et al., 2008). Because the participants' depressive disorders preceded their heart attacks, it can't be argued that their heart disease caused their depression. Overall, studies have found that depression roughly doubles one's chances of developing heart disease (Herbst et al., 2007; Lett et al., 2004).

Stress, Other Diseases, and Immune Functioning

The development of questionnaires to measure life stress has allowed researchers to look for correlations between stress and a variety of diseases. These researchers have uncovered many connections between stress and illness. For example, researchers have found an association between life stress and the course of rheumatoid arthritis (Davis et al., 2008). Other studies have connected stress to the development of diabetes (Landel-Graham, Yount, & Rudnicki, 2003), herpes (Padgett & Sheridan, 2000), fibromyalgia (Wood, 2007), and flare-ups of irritable bowel syndrome (Blanchard & Keefer, 2003). These are just a handful of representative examples of studies relating stress to a great variety of physical diseases. Why should stress increase the risk for so many kinds of illness? A partial answer may lie in the body's immune functioning.

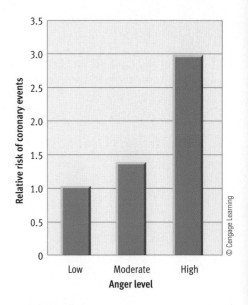

FIGURE 13.8

Anger and coronary risk. Working with a large sample of healthy men and women who were followed for a median of 4.5 years, Williams et al. (2000) found an association between participants' propensity to get angry and the likelihood of a coronary event. Among subjects who manifested normal blood pressure at the beginning of the study, a moderate anger level was associated with a 36% increase in coronary attacks, and a high level of anger nearly tripled participants' risk for coronary disease.

The *immune response* is the body's defensive reaction to invasion by bacteria, viral agents, or other foreign substances. The immune response works to protect organisms from many forms of disease. A wealth of studies indicate that experimentally induced stress can impair immune functioning *in animals* (Ader, 2001; Rose, 2007). That is, stressors such as crowding, shock, food restriction, and restraint reduce various aspects of immune reactivity in laboratory animals (Prolo & Chiappelli, 2007).

Some studies have also related stress to suppressed immune activity *in humans* (Kiecolt-Glaser & Glaser, 1995). In one study, medical students provided researchers with blood samples so that their immune response could be assessed (Kiecolt-Glaser et al., 1984). They provided a baseline sample a month before final exams. They then contributed a high-stress sample on the first day of their finals. The subjects also responded to the SRRS to measure recent stress. Reduced levels of immune activity were found during the extremely stressful finals week. Reduced immune activity was also correlated with higher scores on the SRRS. In another study, investigators exposed quarantined volunteers to respiratory viruses that cause the common cold and found that those under high stress were more likely to be infected by the viruses (Cohen, Tyrell, & Smith, 1993).

Research in this area has mainly focused on the link between stress and immune suppression. However, recent studies have revealed other important connections between stress, immune function, and vulnerability to illness. Recent findings suggest that exposure to long-term stress can sometimes promote chronic inflammation (Christian et al., 2009; Robles, Glaser, & Kiecolt-Glaser, 2005). Scientists have only begun to fully appreciate the potential ramifications of this chronic inflammation in recent years. As we noted earlier, inflammation has recently been recognized as a major factor in the development of heart disease. But that's not all. Research has also demonstrated that chronic inflammation contributes to a diverse array of diseases, including arthritis, osteoporosis, respiratory diseases, diabetes, Alzheimer's disease, and some types of cancer (Feuerstein et al., 2007). Thus, chronic inflammation resulting from immune system dysregulation may be another key mechanism underlying the association between stress and wide variety of diseases.

Sizing Up the Link Between Stress and Illness

A wealth of evidence shows that stress is related to physical health. Converging lines of evidence suggest that stress contributes to the *causation* of illness (Cohen, Janicki-Deverts, & Miller, 2007; Pedersen, Bobvjerg, & Zachariae, 2011). But we have to put this intriguing finding in perspective. Virtually all of the relevant research is correlational, so it can't demonstrate conclusively that stress *causes* illness (Smith & Gallo, 2001; see Chapter 2 for a discussion of correlation and causation). Subjects' elevated levels of stress and illness could both be due to a third variable, perhaps some aspect of personality (see **Figure 13.9**). For instance, some evidence suggests that neuroticism may make people overly prone to interpret events as stressful and overly prone to interpret unpleasant sensations as symptoms of illness. Such a trend would inflate the correlation between stress and illness (Espejo et al., 2011).

In spite of methodological problems favoring inflated correlations, the research in this area consistently indicates that the *strength* of the relationship between stress and health is *modest*. The correlations typically fall in the .20s and .30s (Cohen, Kessler, & Gordon, 1995). Clearly, stress is not an irresistible force that produces inevitable effects on health. Actually, this fact should come as no surprise, as stress is but one factor operating in a complex network of biopsychosocial determinants of health. Other key factors include one's genetic endowment, exposure to infectious agents and environmental toxins, nutrition, exercise, alcohol and drug use, smoking, use of medical care, and cooperation with medical advice. Furthermore, some people handle stress better than others, which is the matter we turn to next.

© Cengage Learning

FIGURE 13.9

The stress-illness correlation. One or more aspects of personality, physiology, or memory could play the role of a postulated third variable in the relationship between high stress and high incidence of illness. For example, neuroticism may lead some subjects to view more events as stressful and to remember more illness, thus inflating the apparent correlation between stress and illness.

Factors Moderating the Impact of Stress

Some people seem to be able to withstand the ravages of stress better than others (Holahan & Moos, 1994). Why? Because certain factors can lessen the impact of stress on physical and mental health. We'll look at two such factors—social support and personality—to shed light on individual differences in how well people tolerate stress.

SOCIAL SUPPORT

Friends may be good for your health! This startling conclusion emerges from studies on social support as a moderator of stress. *Social support* **refers to various types of aid and emotional sustenance provided by members of one's social networks.** Many studies have found positive correlations between high social support and greater immune functioning (Uchino, Uno, & Holt-Lunstad, 1999). In contrast, the opposite of social support—loneliness and social isolation—was found to predict reduced immune responding in one study of college students (Pressman et al., 2005). In recent decades, a vast number of studies have found evidence that social support is favorably related to physical health (Taylor, 2007; Uchino & Birmingham, 2011).

The favorable effects of social support are strong enough to have an impact on participants' mortality. A recent meta-analysis of 148 studies reported that solid social support increased people's odds of survival by roughly 50% (Holt-Lunstad, Smith, & Layton, 2010). The strength of social support's impact on mortality was surprising. To put this finding in perspective, the researchers compared the effect of low social support on mortality with that of other established risk factors. They found that the negative effect of inadequate social support is greater than the negative effects of being obese, not exercising, drinking excessively, and smoking (up to 15 cigarettes per day).

Recent research suggests that cultural disparities exist in the type of social support that people prefer. Studies have found that Asians and Asian Americans are reluctant to seek support from others and that they assert that social support is not all that helpful to them (Kim et al., 2006; Taylor et al., 2004). In an effort to shed light on this puzzling observation, Shelley Taylor and colleagues (2007) discovered that Asians can benefit from social support, but they prefer a different kind of support than Americans. Taylor et al. (2007) distinguish between *explicit social support* (overt emotional solace and instrumental aid from others) and *implicit social support* (the comfort that comes from knowing that one has access to close others who will be supportive). Research has shown that Americans generally prefer and pursue explicit social support. In contrast, Asians do not feel comfortable seeking explicit social support because they worry about the strain it will place on their friends and family (Kim, Sherman, & Taylor, 2008). But Asians do benefit from the implicit support that results when they spend time with close others (without discussing their problems) and when they remind themselves that they belong to valued social groups that would be supportive if needed.

© Piotr Marcinski/Shutterstock

OPTIMISM AND CONSCIENTIOUSNESS

Optimism **is as a general tendency to expect good outcomes.** A number of studies have found a correlation between optimism and relatively good physical health (Rasmussen, Scheier, & Greenhouse, 2009). Researchers have also found that optimism is associated with more-effective immune functioning (Segerstrom & Sephton, 2010). The potential importance of optimism is illustrated by research suggesting that optimism fosters reduced mortality and greater longevity (Peterson et al., 1998). Why is optimism beneficial to health? Research suggests that optimists cope with stress in more adaptive ways than pessimists (Carver, Scheier, & Segerstrom, 2010). Optimists are more likely to engage in action-oriented, problem-focused coping. They are more willing than pessimists to seek social support, and they are more likely to emphasize the positive in their appraisals of stressful events. In comparison, pessimists are more likely to deal with stress by giving up or engaging in denial.

Optimism is not the only personality trait that has been examined as a possible moderator of physical health. Howard Friedman and his colleagues have found evidence that *conscientiousness,* one of the Big Five personality traits discussed in Chapter 11, may have an impact on physical health (Kern & Friedman, 2008; Martin, Friedman, & Schwartz, 2007). They have related personality measures to longevity in sample of individuals who have been followed closely by researchers since 1921. Data were available on six personality traits, which were measured when the subjects were children. The one trait that predicted greater longevity was conscientiousness. Why does conscientiousness promote longevity? According to Friedman (2007), several considerations may contribute, but the key one appears to be that conscientiousness fosters better health habits. People who are high in conscientiousness are less likely than others to exhibit unhealthy habits, such as excessive drinking, drug abuse, dangerous driving, smoking, overeating, and risky sexual practices (Bogg & Roberts, 2004; Roberts, Walton, & Bogg, 2005).

Positive Effects of Stress

Our discussion of the link between stress and illness may have given you the impression that the effects of stress are entirely negative, but this most certainly is not the case. Recent years have brought increased interest in the positive aspects of the stress process, including favorable outcomes that follow in the wake of stress (Folkman & Moskowitz, 2000). To some extent, the new focus on the possible benefits of stress reflects a new emphasis on "positive psychology." As we noted in Chapter 1, the advocates of positive psychology argue for increased research on well-being, courage, perseverance, tolerance, and other human strengths and virtues (Seligman, 2003). One of these strengths is resilience in the face of stress (Seligman & Csikszentmihalyi, 2000), and in fact studies indicate that resilience is not as uncommon as widely assumed (Bonanno, 2005).

Research on resilience suggests that stress can promote personal growth or self-improvement (Calhoun & Tedeschi, 2006, 2008). For example, studies of people grappling with major health problems show that the majority of respondents report that they derived benefits from their adversity (Tennen & Affleck, 1999). Stressful events sometimes force people to develop new skills, reevaluate priorities, learn new insights, and acquire new strengths. In other words, the adaptation process initiated by stress may lead to personal changes that are changes for the better. Confronting a stressful challenge may lead to improvements in specific coping abilities and reduced reactivity to future stressful events (Bower, Moskowitz, & Epel, 2009). Thus, researchers have begun to explore the growth potential of stressful events (Helgeson, Reynolds, & Tomich, 2006).

KEY LEARNING GOALS

13.9 Evaluate the negative health impact of smoking, substance abuse, and lack of exercise.

13.10 Clarify the relationship between behavioral factors and AIDS.

Health-Impairing Behavior

Some people seem determined to dig an early grave for themselves. They do precisely those things that are bad for their health. For example, some people drink heavily even though they know that they're damaging their liver. Others eat all the wrong foods even though they know that they're increasing their risk of a second heart attack. Behavior that's downright *self-destructive* is surprisingly common. In this section we'll discuss how health is affected by smoking, alcohol and drug use, and lack of exercise, and we'll look at behavioral factors in AIDS.

Smoking

The smoking of tobacco is widespread in our culture. The percentage of people who smoke has declined noticeably since the mid-1960s (see **Figure 13.10**). Nonetheless, about 21% of adult men and 18% of adult women in the United States continue to smoke regularly. Smokers face a much greater risk of premature death than nonsmokers. For example, the average smoker has an estimated life expectancy *13 to 14 years shorter* than that of a similar nonsmoker (Schmitz & Delaune, 2005). The overall risk is positively correlated with the number of cigarettes smoked and their tar and nicotine content.

Why are mortality rates higher for smokers? Smoking increases the likelihood of developing a surprisingly large range of diseases (Thun, Apicella, & Henley, 2000). Lung cancer and heart disease kill the largest number of smokers. However, smokers also have an elevated risk for oral, bladder, and kidney cancer, as well as cancers of the larynx, esophagus, and pancreas; for arteriosclerosis, hypertension, stroke, and other cardiovascular diseases; and for bronchitis, emphysema, and other pulmonary diseases. Most smokers know about the risks associated with tobacco use. Interestingly, though, they tend to underestimate the risks as applied to themselves (Ayanian & Cleary, 1999).

Sadly, the dangers of smoking are not limited to smokers themselves. Family members and co-workers who spend a lot of time around smokers are exposed to *second-hand smoke* or *environmental tobacco smoke.* Second-hand smoke can increase their risk for a variety of illnesses, including lung cancer (Vineis, 2005) and heart disease (Venn & Britton, 2007). Young children may be particularly vulnerable to the effects of second-hand smoke (U.S. Department of Health and Human Services, 2006).

Studies show that if people can give up smoking, their health risks decline reasonably quickly (Kenfield et al., 2008; Williams et al., 2002). Evidence suggests that most smokers would like to quit but are reluctant to give up a major source of pleasure. They also worry about craving cigarettes, gaining weight, becoming anxious and irritable, and feeling less able to cope with stress (Grunberg, Faraday, & Rahman, 2001).

Unfortunately, it's difficult to give up cigarettes. People who enroll in formal smoking cessation programs are only slightly more successful than people who try to quit on their own (Swan, Hudman, & Khroyan, 2003). Long-term success rates peak in the vicinity of only 25%. Many studies report even lower figures. Nonetheless, the fact that there are nearly 40 million ex-smokers in the United States indicates that it is possible

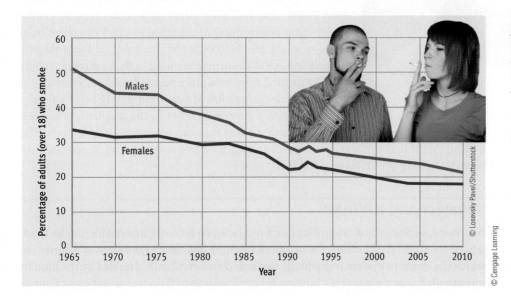

FIGURE 13.10

The prevalence of smoking in the United States. This graph shows how the percentage of U.S. adults who smoke has declined steadily since the mid-1960s. Although considerable progress has been made, smoking still accounts for a huge number of premature deaths in the United States each year. (Based on data from the Centers for Disease Control and Prevention)

Misconception

If you can't quit smoking the first time you try, you are unlikely to succeed in the future.

Reality

People attempting to give up smoking usually fail several or more times before eventually succeeding. Hence, if your first effort to quit smoking ends in failure, you should not give up hope—try again in a few weeks or a few months.

to quit smoking successfully. Interestingly, many people fail several times before they eventually succeed. Research suggests that the readiness to give up smoking builds gradually as people cycle through periods of abstinence and relapse (Prochaska, 1994; Prochaska et al., 2004).

Alcohol and Drug Use

PSYKTREK 4c

Although there is some thought-provoking evidence that *moderate* drinking may offer some protection against cardiovascular disease (Brien et al., 2011; Ronksley et al., 2011), heavy consumption of alcohol clearly increases one's risk for a host of diseases (Johnson & Ait-Daoud, 2005). Recreational drug use is another common health-impairing habit. Unlike smoking or inactivity, drugs can kill directly and immediately. And in the long run, alcohol and various recreational drugs can elevate one's risk for infectious diseases; respiratory, pulmonary, and cardiovascular diseases; liver disease; gastrointestinal problems; cancer; neurological disorders; and pregnancy complications (see Chapter 5).

Lack of Exercise

Considerable evidence links lack of exercise to poor health. Conversely, research indicates that regular exercise is associated with increased longevity (Kokkinos et al., 2008; Lee & Skerrett, 2001). A meta-analysis of 33 studies with over 100,000 male and female participants found substantial reductions in mortality among those who were high in fitness (Kodama et al., 2009). Unfortunately, physical fitness appears to be declining in the United States. Only about one-third of American adults get an adequate amount of regular exercise (Carlson et al., 2010).

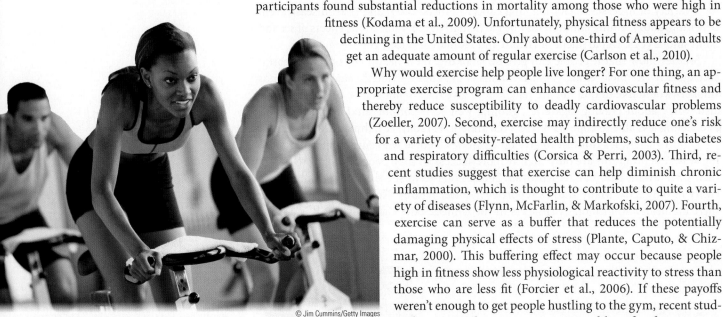

© Jim Cummins/Getty Images

Why would exercise help people live longer? For one thing, an appropriate exercise program can enhance cardiovascular fitness and thereby reduce susceptibility to deadly cardiovascular problems (Zoeller, 2007). Second, exercise may indirectly reduce one's risk for a variety of obesity-related health problems, such as diabetes and respiratory difficulties (Corsica & Perri, 2003). Third, recent studies suggest that exercise can help diminish chronic inflammation, which is thought to contribute to quite a variety of diseases (Flynn, McFarlin, & Markofski, 2007). Fourth, exercise can serve as a buffer that reduces the potentially damaging physical effects of stress (Plante, Caputo, & Chizmar, 2000). This buffering effect may occur because people high in fitness show less physiological reactivity to stress than those who are less fit (Forcier et al., 2006). If these payoffs weren't enough to get people hustling to the gym, recent studies have turned up a new, unexpected benefit of exercise—it can facilitate the generation of new brain cells (Cotman, Berchtold, & Christie, 2007; Pereira et al., 2007). As noted earlier in the chapter (see p. 444), *neurogenesis* appears to be an important process that can be suppressed by stress. The finding that this neurodevelopmental process can be promoted by simple exercise may turn out to have profound implications.

Behavior and HIV/AIDS

At present, some of the most problematic links between behavior and health may be those related to AIDS. AIDS stands for *acquired immune deficiency syndrome,* **a disorder in which the immune system is gradually weakened and eventually disabled by the human immunodeficiency virus (HIV).** Being infected with the HIV virus is *not* equivalent to having AIDS, which is in fact the final stage of the HIV infection process, typically manifested about 10 years after the original infection. With the onset of AIDS, one is left virtually defenseless against numerous infectious agents. AIDS inflicts its harm indirectly by opening the door to other diseases. The symptoms of AIDS vary widely depending on the specific constellation of diseases that one develops (Cunningham & Selwyn, 2005). Unfortunately, the worldwide prevalence of this deadly disease continues to increase at an alarming rate, especially in certain regions of Africa (UNAIDS, 2009).

Prior to 1996–1997, the average length of survival for people after the onset of the AIDS syndrome was about 18 to 24 months. Encouraging advances in the treatment of AIDS with drug regimens referred to as *highly active antiretroviral therapy (HAART)* hold out promise for substantially longer survival (Anthony & Bell, 2008; Bhaskaran et al., 2008). But these drugs have been rushed into service, and their long-term efficacy is yet to be determined. Medical experts are concerned that the general public has gotten the impression that these treatments have transformed AIDS from a fatal disease to a manageable one. This may be a premature conclusion, as HIV strains are evolving.

The HIV virus is transmitted through person-to-person contact involving the exchange of bodily fluids, primarily semen and blood. The two principal modes of transmission in the United States have been sexual contact and the sharing of needles by intravenous (IV) drug users. In the United States, sexual transmission has occurred primarily among gay and bisexual men, but heterosexual transmission has increased in recent years (Centers for Disease Control, 2011). In the world as a whole, infection through heterosexual relations has been much more common from the beginning. In heterosexual relations, male-to-female transmission is estimated to be about eight times more likely than female-to-male transmission (Ickovics, Thayaparan, & Ethier, 2001). The HIV virus can be found in the tears and saliva of infected individuals, but the concentrations are low and there is no evidence that the infection can be spread through casual contact. Even most forms of noncasual contact, including kissing, hugging, and sharing food with infected individuals, appear safe (Kalichman, 1995).

One problem related to transmission is that many young heterosexuals who are sexually active with a variety of partners foolishly downplay their risk for HIV. They greatly underestimate the probability that their sexual partners previously may have used IV drugs or had unprotected sex with an infected individual. Also, many young people inaccurately believe that prospective sexual partners who carry the HIV virus will exhibit telltale signs of illness. In reality, many HIV carriers do not know themselves that they are HIV-positive. In one study that screened over 5000 men for HIV, 77% of those who tested HIV-positive were previously unaware of their infection (MacKellar et al., 2005).

Reactions to Illness

KEY LEARNING GOALS

13.11 Discuss differences in the willingness to seek medical treatment and some barriers to effective patient-provider communication.

13.12 Review the extent to which people tend to adhere to medical advice.

Some people respond to physical symptoms and illnesses by ignoring warning signs of developing diseases. In contrast, others actively seek to conquer their diseases. Let's examine the decision to seek medical treatment, communication with health providers, and factors that affect adherence to medical advice.

Deciding to Seek Treatment

Have you ever experienced nausea, diarrhea, stiffness, headaches, cramps, chest pains, or sinus problems? Of course you have; everyone experiences some of these problems periodically. However, whether someone views these sensations as *symptoms* is a matter of individual interpretation. When two persons experience the same unpleasant sensations, one may shrug them off as a nuisance while the other may rush to a physician (Martin & Leventhal, 2004). Studies suggest that people who are relatively high in anxiety and neuroticism tend to report more symptoms of illness than others do (Petrie & Pennebaker, 2004). Those who are extremely attentive to bodily sensations and health concerns also report more symptoms than the average person (Barsky, 1988).

The biggest problem in regard to treatment seeking is the tendency of many people to delay the pursuit of needed professional consultation. Delays can be critical, because early diagnosis and quick intervention may facilitate more effective treatment of many health problems (Petrie & Pennebaker, 2004). Unfortunately, procrastination is the norm even when people are faced with a medical emergency, such as a heart attack (Martin & Leventhal, 2004). Why do people dawdle in the midst of a crisis? Robin Di-Matteo (1991), a leading expert on patient behavior, mentions a number of reasons, noting that people delay because they often (a) misinterpret and downplay the significance of their symptoms, (b) fret about looking silly if the problem turns out to be nothing, (c) worry about "bothering" their physician, (d) are reluctant to disrupt their plans (to go out to dinner, see a movie, and so forth), and (e) waste time on trivial matters (such as taking a shower, gathering personal items, or packing clothes) before going to a hospital emergency room.

Communicating with Health Providers

A large portion of medical patients leave their doctors' offices not understanding what they have been told and what they are supposed to do (Johnson & Carlson, 2004). This situation is most unfortunate because good communication is a crucial requirement for sound medical decisions, informed choices about treatment, and appropriate follow-through by patients (Buckman, 2002; Haskard et al., 2008).

There are many barriers to effective provider-patient communication (DiMatteo, 1997; Marteau & Weinman, 2004). Economic realities dictate that medical visits generally be quite brief, allowing little time for discussion. Many providers use too much medical jargon and overestimate their patients' understanding of technical terms. Patients who are upset and worried about their illness may simply forget to report some symptoms or to ask questions they meant to ask. Other patients are evasive about their real concerns because they fear a serious diagnosis. Many patients are reluctant to challenge doctors' authority and are too passive in their interactions with providers.

What can you do to improve your communication with health care providers? The key is to not be a passive consumer of medical services (Ferguson, 1993; Kane, 1991). Arrive at a medical visit on time, with your questions and concerns prepared in advance. Try to be accurate and candid in replying to your doctor's questions. If you don't understand something the doctor says, don't be embarrassed about asking for clarification. And if you have doubts about the suitability or feasibility of your doctor's recommendations, don't be afraid to voice them.

© iofoto/Shutterstock

Adhering to Medical Advice

Many patients fail to follow the instructions they receive from physicians and other health care professionals. The evidence suggests that *nonadherence* to medical advice may occur 30% of the time when short-term treatments are prescribed for acute conditions and 50% of the time when long-term treatments are needed for chronic illness (Johnson & Carlson, 2004). Nonadherence takes many forms. Patients may fail to begin a treatment regimen, may stop the regimen early, may reduce or increase the levels of treatment that were prescribed, or may be inconsistent and unreliable in following treatment procedures (Dunbar-Jacob & Schlenk, 2001). Nonadherence has been linked to increased sickness, treatment failures, and higher mortality (Christensen & Johnson, 2002; DiMatteo et al., 2002). Moreover, nonadherence wastes expensive medical visits and medications and increases hospital admissions, leading to enormous economic costs. DiMatteo (2004b) speculates that in the United States alone, nonadherence may be a $300 billion a year drain on the health care system.

Why don't people comply with the advice that they've sought out from highly regarded health care professionals? Physicians tend to attribute noncompliance to patients' personal characteristics, but research indicates that personality traits and demographic factors are surprisingly unrelated to adherence rates (DiMatteo, 2004b; Marteau & Weinman, 2004). One factor that *is* related to adherence is patients' *social support*. Adherence is improved when patients have family members, friends, or co-workers who remind them about, and help them comply with, treatment requirements (DiMatteo, 2004a). Other considerations that influence the likelihood of adherence include the following (Dunbar-Jacob & Schlenk, 2001; Johnson & Carlson, 2004):

1. Frequently, nonadherence occurs because the patient doesn't understand the instructions as given. Highly trained professionals often forget that what seems obvious and simple to them may be obscure and complicated to many of their patients.

2. Another key factor is how aversive or difficult the instructions are. If the prescribed regimen is unpleasant, adherence will tend to decrease. And the more that following instructions interferes with routine behavior, the less probable it is that the patient will cooperate successfully.

3. If a patient has a negative attitude toward a physician, the probability of noncompliance will increase. When patients are unhappy with their interactions with the doctor, they're more likely to ignore the medical advice provided, no matter how important it may be.

Reflecting on the Chapter's Themes

13.13 Identify the two unifying themes highlighted in this chapter.

Which of our themes were prominent in this chapter? As you probably noticed, our discussion of stress and health illustrated multifactorial causation and the subjectivity of experience.

Our discussion of the psychology of health provided a particularly complex illustration of multifactorial causation. As we noted in Chapter 1, people are likely to think simplistically, in terms of single causes. In recent years, the highly publicized research linking stress to health has led many people to point automatically to stress as an explanation for illness. In reality, stress has only a modest impact on physical health. Stress can increase the risk for illness, but health is governed by a dense network of factors. Important factors include inherited vulnerabilities, exposure to infectious agents, health-impairing habits, reactions to symptoms, treatment-seeking behavior, compliance with medical advice, optimism, and social support. In other words, stress is but one actor on a crowded stage. This should be apparent in **Figure 13.11** on the next page, which shows the multitude of biopsychosocial factors that jointly influence physical health. It illustrates multifactorial causation in all its complexity.

Multifactorial Causation

Subjectivity of Experience

Biological factors

Environmental toxins

Genetic predisposition

Physiological reactivity

Infectious agents

Immune response

Physical health and illness

Stress

Social support

Coping tactics

Health education

Personality

Pollution control

Psychological (behavioral) factors

Health-related habits

Reactions to illness

Medical care

Sanitation

Social (system) factors

© Steve Sant/Alamy

© Cengage Learning

FIGURE 13.11

Biopsychosocial factors in health. Physical health can be influenced by a remarkably diverse set of variables, including biological, psychological, and social factors. The variety of factors that affect health provide an excellent example of multifactorial causation.

The subjectivity of experience was demonstrated by the frequently repeated point that stress lies in the eye of the beholder. The same job promotion may be stressful for one person and invigorating for another. One person's pressure is another's challenge. When it comes to stress, objective reality is not nearly as important as subjective perceptions. More than anything else, the impact of stressful events seems to depend on how people view them. The critical importance of stress appraisals will continue to be apparent in our Personal Application on stress management. Many stress-management strategies depend on altering one's appraisals of events.

Personal
APPLICATION

Improving Coping and Stress Management

KEY LEARNING GOALS

13.14 Analyze the adaptive value of rational thinking, humor, and release of pent-up emotions.

13.15 Assess the adaptive value of forgiving others, relaxing, and increasing one's fitness.

Answer the following "true" or "false."

___ 1 The key to managing stress is to avoid or circumvent it.

___ 2 It's best to suppress emotional reactions to stress.

___ 3 Laughing at one's problems is immature.

___ 4 Exercise has little or no impact on stress resistance.

Courses and books on stress management have multiplied at a furious pace in recent decades. They summarize experts' advice on how to cope with stress more effectively. How do these experts feel about the four statements above? As you'll see in this Personal Application, most would agree that all four are false.

The key to managing stress does not lie in avoiding it. Stress is an inevitable element in the fabric of modern life. As Hans Selye (1973) noted, "Contrary to public opinion, we must not—and indeed can't—avoid stress" (p. 693). Thus, most stress-management programs train people to use more effective coping strategies. In this Application, we'll examine a variety of constructive coping tactics, beginning with Albert Ellis's ideas about changing one's appraisals of stressful events.

Reappraisal: Ellis's Rational Thinking

Albert Ellis is a prominent theorist who believes that people can short-circuit their emotional reactions to stress by altering their appraisals of stressful events. Ellis's insights about stress appraisal are the foundation for a widely used system of therapy called *rational-emotive behavior therapy* (Ellis, 1977, 1987), and several popular books on effective coping (Ellis, 1985, 1999, 2001).

Ellis maintains that *you feel the way you think*. He argues that problematic emotional reactions are caused by negative self-talk, which he calls catastrophic thinking. *Catastrophic thinking* involves **unrealistically pessimistic appraisals of stress that exaggerate the magnitude of one's problems.** According to Ellis, people unwittingly believe that stressful events cause their emotional turmoil, but he maintains that emotional reactions to personal setbacks are actually caused by overly negative appraisals of stressful events (see **Figure 13.12**).

Ellis theorizes that unrealistic appraisals of stress are derived from irrational assumptions that people hold. He maintains that if you scrutinize your catastrophic thinking, you'll find that your reasoning is based on a logically indefensible premise, such as "I must have approval from everyone" or "I must perform well in all endeavors." These

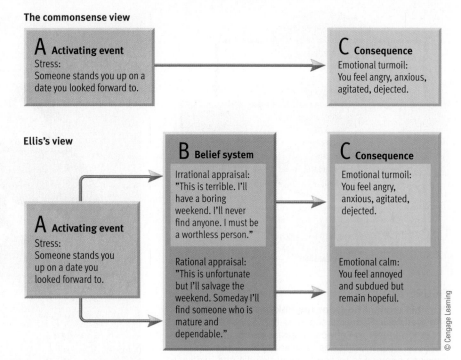

FIGURE 13.12

Albert Ellis's model of emotional reactions. Although most people attribute their negative emotional reactions directly to negative events that they experience, Ellis argues that events themselves do *not* cause emotional distress; rather, distress is caused by the way people *think* about negative events. According to Ellis, the key to managing stress is to change one's appraisal of stressful events.

faulty assumptions, which people often hold unconsciously, generate catastrophic thinking and emotional turmoil. How can you reduce your unrealistic appraisals of stress? Ellis asserts that you must learn (1) how to detect catastrophic thinking and (2) how to dispute the irrational assumptions that cause it.

Humor as a Stress Reducer

A number of years ago, the Chicago suburbs experienced their worst flooding in about a century. Thousands of people saw their homes wrecked when two rivers spilled over their banks. As the waters receded, the flood victims returning to their homes were subjected to the inevitable TV interviews. A remarkable number of victims, surrounded by the ruins of their homes, *joked* about their misfortune. When the going gets tough, it may pay to laugh about it. In a study of coping styles, McCrae (1984) found that 40% of his subjects used humor to deal with stress.

Empirical evidence showing that humor moderates the impact of stress has been accumulating over the last 25 years (Abel, 1998; Lefcourt, 2001, 2005). How does humor help to reduce the effects of stress and promote wellness? Several explanations have been proposed (see **Figure 13.13** on the next page). One possibility is that humor affects appraisals of stressful events (Abel, 2002). Jokes can help people to put a less threatening spin on their trials and tribulations. Another possibility is that humor increases the experience of positive emotions (Martin, 2002). These emotions may help people bounce back from stressful events (Tugade & Fredrickson, 2004). Another hypothesis is that a good sense of humor facilitates rewarding social interactions, which promote social support, a factor known to buffer the effects of stress (Martin, 2002). Finally, Lefcourt and colleagues (1995) argue that high-humor people may benefit from not taking themselves as seriously as low-humor people do. As they put it, "If per-

FIGURE 13.13

Possible explanations for the link between humor and wellness. Research suggests that a good sense of humor buffers the effects of stress and promotes wellness. Four hypothesized explanations for the link between humor and wellness are outlined in the middle column of this diagram. As you can see, humor may have a variety of beneficial effects.

In September 1994, Reg and Maggie Green were vacationing in Italy when their seven-year-old son Nicholas was shot and killed during a highway robbery. In an act of forgiveness that stunned Europe, the Greens chose to donate their son's organs, which went to seven Italians. The Greens, shown here five years after the incident, have weathered their horrific loss better than most, perhaps in part because of their willingness to forgive.

sons do not regard themselves too seriously and do not have an inflated sense of self-importance, then defeats, embarrassments, and even tragedies should have less pervasive emotional consequences for them" (p. 375).

Releasing Pent-up Emotions and Forgiving Others

Although there's no guarantee of it, you can sometimes reduce stress-induced physiological arousal by *expressing* your emotions. For instance, evidence is accumulating that writing or talking about life's difficulties can be valuable in dealing with stress (Lyubomirsky, Sousa, & Dickerhoof, 2006; Smyth & Pennebaker, 1999). In one study of college students, half of the subjects were asked to write three essays about their difficulties in adjusting to college, while the other half wrote three

essays about superficial topics. The subjects who wrote about their personal problems enjoyed better health in the following months than the other subjects did (Pennebaker, Colder, & Sharp, 1990). Subsequent studies have replicated this finding and shown that emotional disclosure is associated with better immune functioning (Slatcher & Pennebaker, 2005; Smyth & Pennebaker, 2001). So, if you can find a good listener, you may be able to discharge problematic emotions by letting your fears, misgivings, and frustrations spill out in a candid conversation.

People tend to experience hostility and other negative emotions when they feel "wronged"—that is, when they believe that the actions of another person were harmful, immoral, or unjust. People's natural inclination in such situations is either to seek revenge or to avoid further contact with the offender (McCullough, 2001).

Forgiving someone involves counteracting these natural tendencies and releasing the person from further liability for his or her transgression. Research suggests that forgiving is associated with better adjustment and well-being (McCullough & Witvliet, 2002; Worthington & Scherer, 2004). This includes enhanced mood and reduced physical symptoms (Bono, McCullough, & Root, 2008). For example, in one study of divorced or permanently separated women reported by McCullough (2001), the extent to which the women had forgiven their former husbands was positively related to several measures of well-being.

Relaxing and Minimizing Physiological Vulnerability

Relaxing is a valuable stress-management technique that can soothe emotional tur-

FIGURE 13.14

Physical fitness and mortality. Blair and colleagues (1989) studied death rates among men and women who exhibited low, medium, or high physical fitness. As you can see, fitness was associated with lower mortality rates in both sexes.

moil and suppress problematic physiological arousal (McGuigan & Lehrer, 2007; Smith, 2007). The value of relaxation became apparent to Herbert Benson (1975) as a result of his research on meditation. Benson, a Harvard Medical School cardiologist, believes that relaxation is the key to many of the beneficial effects of meditation. Anything that relaxes you—whether it's music, meditation, prayer, or a warm bath—can be helpful. Experts have also devised a variety of systematic relaxation procedures that can make relaxation efforts more effective. You may want to learn about techniques such as *progressive relaxation* (Jacobson, 1938), *autogenic training* (Schultz & Luthe, 1959), or the *relaxation response* (Benson & Klipper, 1988).

As this chapter has made clear, the wear and tear of stress can be injurious to one's physical health. To combat this potential problem, it helps to keep your body in relatively sound shape. The potential benefits of regular exercise are substantial, including increased longevity (Lee & Skerrett, 2001). Moreover, research has shown that you don't have to be a dedicated athlete to benefit from exercise (Blair et al., 1989); even a moderate amount of exercise reduces your risk of disease (Richardson et al., 2004; see **Figure 13.14**).

Embarking on an exercise program is difficult for many people. Exercise is time-consuming, and if you're out of shape, your initial attempts may be painful and discouraging. To avoid these problems, it's wise to (1) select an activity that you find enjoyable, (2) increase your participation gradually, (3) exercise regularly without overdoing it, and (4) rein-

force yourself for your efforts (Greenberg, 2002).

Good sleep habits can also help in the effort to minimize physiological vulnerability to stress. As we discussed in Chapter 5, sleep loss can undermine immune system responding (Motivala & Irwin, 2007) and fuel inflammatory responses (Patel et al., 2009). Evidence also suggests that poor sleep quality is associated with poor health (Benham, 2010) and that sleep loss can elevate mortality (Chien et al., 2010). Thus, sound sleep patterns can contribute to stress management. The results of a recent study suggest that people need to get a sufficient amount of sleep and that they should strive for consistency in their patterns of sleeping (Barber et al., 2010).

Critical Thinking
APPLICATION

Thinking Rationally About Health Statistics and Decisions

KEY LEARNING GOALS

13.16 Understand important considerations in evaluating health statistics and making health decisions.

With so many conflicting claims about the best ways to prevent or treat diseases, how can anyone ever decide what to do? It seems that every day a report in the media claims that yesterday's health news was wrong. The inconsistency of health news is only part of the problem. We are also overwhelmed by health-related statistics. As mathematics pundit John Allen Paulos (1995) puts it, "Health statistics may be bad for our mental health. Inundated by too many of them, we tend to ignore them completely, to accept them blithely, to disbelieve them closemindedly, or simply to misinterpret their significance" (p. 133).

Making personal decisions about health-related issues may not be easy. Even medical personnel often struggle to make sense out of health statistics (Gigerenzer at al., 2007). Yet it's particularly important to try to think rationally and systematically about such issues. In this Application, we'll discuss a few insights that can help you to think critically about statistics on health risks. Then we'll briefly outline a systematic approach to thinking through health decisions.

Evaluating Statistics on Health Risks

News reports seem to suggest that there are links between virtually everything people do, touch, and consume and some type of physical illness. For example, media have reported that coffee consumption is related to hypertension, that sleep loss is related to mortality, and that a high-fat diet is related to heart disease. Such reports are enough to send even the most subdued person into a panic. Fortu-

nately, your evaluation of data on health risks can become more sophisticated by considering the following factors.

Correlation Is No Assurance of Causation It is not easy to conduct experiments on health risks, so the vast majority of studies linking lifestyle and demographic factors to diseases are correlational studies. Hence, it pays to remember that no causal link may yexist between two variables that happen to be correlated. Thus, when you hear that a factor is related to some disease, try to dig a little deeper and find out *why* scientists think this factor is associated with the disease. The suspected causal factor may be something very different from what was measured.

Statistical Significance Is Not Equivalent to Practical Significance Reports on health statistics often emphasize that the investigators uncovered "statistically significant" findings. Statistically significant findings are results that are not likely to be due to chance fluctuations. Statistical significance is a useful concept, but it

can sometimes be misleading (Matthey, 1998). Medical studies are often based on rather large samples, because they tend to yield more reliable conclusions than small samples. However, when a large sample is used, weak relationships and small differences between groups can turn out to be statistically significant, and these small differences may not have much practical importance. For example, in one study of sodium (salt) intake and cardiovascular disease, which used a sample of over 14,000 participants, He et al. (1999) found a statistically significant link between high sodium intake and the prevalence of hypertension among normal-weight subjects. However, this statistically significant difference was not particularly large. The prevalence of hypertension among subjects with the lowest sodium intake was 19.1% compared to 21.8% for subjects with the highest sodium intake—not exactly a difference worthy of panic.

Base Rates Should Be Considered in Evaluating Probabilities In evaluating whether a possible risk factor is associ-

© by Jim Borgman/Cincinnati Enquirer. Used by permission of UNIVERSAL UCLICK. All rights reserved.

Image labels: Today's Random Medical News — from the New England Journal of Panic-Inducing Gobbledygook. JIM BORGMAN CINCINNATI ENQUIRER 1997. Wheel 1: SMOKING, EXERCISE, FATTY FOODS, STRESS, RED WINE, DAYCARE, COMPUTER TERMINALS, COFFEE. CAN CAUSE. Wheel 2: HEART DISEASE, BREAST CANCER, SPONTANEOUS REMISSION, GLAUCOMA, DEPRESSION, SEXUAL DYSFUNCTION, A FEELING OF WELL-BEING, HYPOTHERMIA. IN. Wheel 3: CHILDREN, TWINS, ARTHRITIS SUFFERERS, 7 OUT OF 10 WOMEN, RATS, OVERWEIGHT SMOKERS, MEN 25-40, TWO-INCOME FAMILIES. ACCORDING TO A REPORT RELEASED TODAY.... NEWS.

462 CHAPTER 13

ated with some disease, people often fail to consider the base rates of these events. If the base rate of a disease is relatively low, a small increase can sound quite large if it's reported as a percentage. For example, in the He et al. (1999) study, the prevalence of diabetes among subjects with the lowest sodium intake was 2.1% compared to 3.8% for subjects with the highest sodium intake. Based on this small but statistically significant difference, one could say (the investigators did not) that high sodium intake was associated with an 81% increase ([3.8 − 2.1] ÷ 2.1) in the prevalence of diabetes. This would be technically accurate, but an exaggerated way of portraying the results. Base rates should also be considered when evaluating claims made about the value of medications and other medical treatments. If the base rate of a disease is low, a very modest decrease reported as a percentage can foster exaggerated perceptions of treatment benefits. For instance, Gigerenzer at al. (2007) describe an advertisement for Lipitor (a drug intended to lower cholesterol levels) claiming that Lipitor reduced the risk of stroke by 48%. Although this was technically accurate, in absolute terms the protective benefits of Lipitor were actually rather modest. After four years, 1.5% of those taking Lipitor had a stroke versus 2.8% of those taking the placebo.

Thinking Systematically About Health Decisions

Health decisions are oriented toward the future, which means that there are always uncertainties. And they usually involve weighing potential risks and benefits. None of these variables is unique to health decisions—uncertainty, risks, and benefits play prominent roles in economic and political decisions as well as in personal decisions. To illustrate, let's apply some basic principles of quantitative reasoning to a treatment decision involving whether to prescribe Ritalin for a boy who has been diagnosed with attention deficit disorder (ADD). Keep in mind that the general principles applied in this example can be used for a wide variety of decisions.

Seek Information to Reduce Uncertainty Gather information and check it carefully for accuracy, completeness, and the presence or absence of conflicting information. For example, is the diagnosis of ADD correct? Look for conflicting information that does not fit with this diagnosis. If the child can sit and read for a long period of time, maybe the problem is an undetected hearing loss that makes him appear to be hyperactive in some situations. As you consider the additional information, begin quantifying the degree of uncertainty or its "flip side," your degree of confidence that the diagnosis is correct. If you decide that you are not confident about the diagnosis, you may be trying to solve the wrong problem.

Make Risk-Benefit Assessments What are the risks and benefits of Ritalin? How likely is this child to benefit from Ritalin, and just how much improvement can be expected? If the child is 8 years old and unable to read and is miserable in school and at home, any treatment that could reduce his problems deserves serious consideration. As in the first step, the quantification is at an approximate level.

List Alternative Courses of Action What are the alternatives to Ritalin? How well do they work? What are the risks associated with the alternatives, including the risk of falling further behind in school? Consider the pros and cons of each alternative. A special diet that sometimes works might be a good first step along with the decision to start drug therapy if the child does not show improvement over some time period. What are the relative success rates for different types of treatment for children like the one being considered? In order to answer these questions, you will need to use probability estimates in your decision making.

As you can see from this example, many parts of the problem have been quantified (confidence in the diagnosis, likelihood of improvement, probability of negative outcomes, and so forth). Precise probability values were not used because often the actual numbers are not known. Some of the quantified values reflect value judgments, others reflect likelihoods, and others assess the degree of uncertainty. If you are thinking that the quantification of many unknowns in decision making is a lot of work, you are right. But, it is work worth doing. Whenever there are important decisions to be made about health, the ability to think with numbers will help you reach a better decision. And yes, that assertion is a virtual certainty.

TABLE 13.2   Critical Thinking Skills Discussed in This Application

Skill	Description
Understanding the limitations of correlational evidence	The critical thinker understands that a correlation between two variables does not demonstrate that there is a causal link between the variables.
Understanding the limitations of statistical significance	The critical thinker understands that weak relationships can be statistically significant when large samples are used in research.
Utilizing base rates in making predictions and evaluating probabilities	The critical thinker appreciates that the initial proportion of some group or event needs to be considered in weighing probabilities.
Seeking information to reduce uncertainty	The critical thinker understands that gathering more information can often decrease uncertainty, and reduced uncertainty can facilitate better decisions.
Making risk-benefit assessments	The critical thinker is aware that most decisions have risks and benefits that need to be weighed carefully.
Generating and evaluating alternative courses of action	In problem solving and decision making, the critical thinker knows the value of generating as many alternatives as possible and assessing their advantages and disadvantages.

© Cengage Learning

The Nature of Stress

13.1 Evaluate the impact of minor stressors and people's appraisals of stress.

Stress involves circumstances and experiences that are perceived as threatening. Stress is a common, everyday event, and even seemingly minor stressors, such as daily hassles, can be problematic. To a large degree, stress is subjective and lies in the eye of the beholder. People's primary appraisals of events determine what they find stressful, and their secondary appraisals influence the degree of stress experienced.

13.2 Identify four major types of stress.

Four principal types of stress are frustration, conflict, change, and pressure. Frustration occurs when an obstacle prevents one from attaining some goal. The three principal types of conflict are approach-approach, avoidance-avoidance, and approach-avoidance. The third type is especially stressful. Vacillation is a common response to approach-avoidance conflict. A large number of studies with the SRRS suggest that life change is stressful. Although this may be true, it is now clear that the SRRS is a measure of general stress rather than just change-related stress. Two kinds of pressure (to perform and conform) also appear to be stressful.

Responding to Stress

13.3 Discuss the role of positive emotions in response to stress, and describe the effects of emotional arousal.

Stress often triggers emotional reactions, such as anger, fear, and sadness, but positive emotions are common as well. Fredrickson's broaden-and-build theory asserts that positive emotions broaden thinking and build coping resources. Evidence suggests that people who experience high levels of positive emotions live longer than others. Emotional arousal may interfere with coping. According to the inverted-U hypothesis, task performance improves with increased arousal up to a point and then declines. The optimal level of arousal on a task depends on the complexity of the task.

13.4 Describe Selye's general adaptation syndrome and other physiological responses to stress.

Selye's general adaptation syndrome describes three stages of physiological reactions to stress: alarm, resistance, and exhaustion. Diseases of adaptation may appear during the stage of exhaustion. There are two major pathways along which the brain sends signals to the endocrine system in response to stress, leading to the release of catecholamines and corticosteroids. Stress may suppress neurogenesis in the brain.

13.5 Evaluate the adaptive value of common coping strategies.

The behavioral response to stress takes the form of coping. Giving up is not a highly regarded approach to coping, but studies suggest that people who are able to disengage from unattainable goals exhibit better health. Aggression tends to fuel more anger and increase rather than decrease stress. Self-indulgence is another coping pattern that tends to be of limited value. Defensive coping is quite common. Defense mechanisms protect against emotional distress through self-deception. Some evidence suggests that small positive illusions about one's life may be healthful, but serious distortions are maladaptive. Relatively healthful coping tactics are termed constructive coping. Constructive coping is action-oriented and based on realistic appraisals of stress.

Stress and Physical Health

13.6 Review the evidence linking personality factors, emotional reactions, and depression to coronary heart disease.

The Type A personality has been implicated as a contributing cause of coronary heart disease, but the evidence has been equivocal. Recent research suggests that hostility may be the most toxic element of the Type A syndrome. Transient, stress-induced emotional reactions can elicit cardiac symptoms and may fuel inflammatory responses. Although depression can be a result of heart disease, research also suggests that depression can increase one's risk for cardiovascular disease.

13.7 Discuss how stress affects immune functioning, and assess the link between stress and illness.

Stress appears to play a role in a host of diseases, perhaps because it can temporarily suppress the effectiveness of the immune system. Exposure to long-term stress can also promote chronic inflammation, which can contribute to many diseases. Although there's little doubt that stress can contribute to the development of physical illness, the link between stress and illness is modest, and causality is ambiguous. Stress is only one factor in a complex network of biopsychosocial variables that shape health.

13.8 Identify some factors that moderate the impact of stress, and explain how stress may have positive effects.

Social support is a key moderator of the relationship between stress and both physical and mental health. Studies have even found that social support is related to mortality. Asians prefer implicit social support, whereas Americans prefer explicit social support. Optimism is associated with relatively good physical health. Optimism may lead to more effective coping with stress. Recent research suggests that conscientiousness is associated with better health

© Piotr Marcinski/Shutterstock

habits and greater longevity. Research on the effects of stress has concentrated on negative outcomes, but positive effects may also occur. Research on resilience suggests that stress can promote personal growth and improved coping. Resilience in the face of severe stress is not as uncommon as widely assumed.

Health-Impairing Behavior

13.9 Evaluate the negative health impact of smoking, substance abuse, and lack of exercise.

Smokers have much higher mortality rates than nonsmokers because they are more vulnerable to a host of diseases. Health risks decline reasonably quickly for people who give up smoking, but quitting is difficult and relapse rates are high. Alcohol and drug abuse can kill directly as well as elevate one's risk for many forms of illness. Lack of exercise can increase one's vulnerability to cardiovascular and obesity-related health problems. In contrast, regular exercise can diminish chronic inflammation, buffer the effects of stress, and facilitate neurogenesis.

13.10 Clarify the relationship between behavioral factors and AIDS.

Aspects of behavior influence one's risk of AIDS, which is transmitted through person-to-person contact involving the exchange of bodily fluids, primarily semen and blood. The two principal modes of transmission in the United States have been sexual contact and the sharing of needles by IV drug users. One problem related to transmission is that many young heterosexuals who are sexually active with a variety of partners foolishly downplay their risk for HIV.

Reactions to Illness

13.11 Discuss differences in the willingness to seek medical treatment and some barriers to effective patient-provider communication.

People high in anxiety or neuroticism report more symptoms of illness than others. The biggest problem in regard to treatment seeking is the tendency

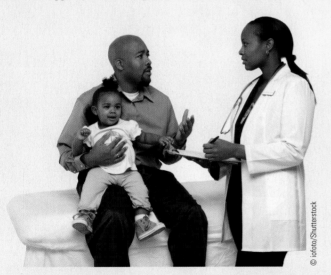
© iofoto/Shutterstock

of many people to delay the pursuit of needed treatment. There are many barriers to effective communication between patients and health care providers, such as brief visits, overdependence on medical jargon, and patients' evasiveness and forgetfulness. The key for patients in improving communication is to not be a passive consumer of medical services.

13.12 Review the extent to which people tend to adhere to medical advice.

Noncompliance with medical advice is a major problem, which may occur 30% of the time in the context of short-term treatments and 50% of the time in long-term treatments. The likelihood of nonadherence is greater

when instructions are difficult to understand, when recommendations are difficult to follow, and when patients are unhappy with their doctor.

Reflecting on the Chapter's Themes

13.13 Identify the two unifying themes highlighted in this chapter.

Two of our integrative themes were prominent in this chapter. First, we saw that behavior and health are influenced by multiple causes. Second, we saw that experience is highly subjective, as stress lies in the eye of the beholder.

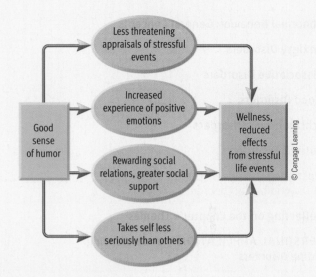
© Cengage Learning

PERSONAL APPLICATION
Improving Coping and Stress Management

13.14 Analyze the adaptive value of rational thinking, humor, and release of pent-up emotions.

According to Ellis, emotional distress is often attributable to catastrophic thinking and irrational assumptions that underlie it. Ellis emphasizes the importance of reappraising stressful events and thinking in more rational ways about life's difficulties. Humor may be useful in efforts to redefine stressful situations. Humor can also increase positive emotions and enhance social support. In some cases, releasing pent-up emotions may pay off. In particular, writing about one's difficulties can foster better health.

13.15 Assess the adaptive value of forgiving others, relaxing, and increasing one's fitness.

Stress can also be reduced by learning to be more forgiving toward those who may have wronged you. Relaxation techniques can dampen stress-induced arousal and reduce the wear and tear of stress. Physical vulnerability may also be reduced by striving to increase one's fitness through regular exercise. Even moderate levels of exercise can decrease disease risks. Good sleep habits can also help to minimize vulnerability to stress.

CRITICAL THINKING APPLICATION
Thinking Rationally About Health Statistics and Decisions

13.16 Understand important considerations in evaluating health statistics and making health decisions.

Evaluations of statistics on health risks can be enhanced by remembering that correlation is no assurance of causation, that statistical significance is not equivalent to practical significance, and that base rates need to be considered in assessing probabilities. In trying to think systematically about health decisions, one should seek information to reduce uncertainty, make risk-benefit assessments, and consider alternative courses of action.

14 Psychological Disorders

PARADOX

Antonyms such as mental health versus mental illness suggest a sharp distinction between those who are normal and those who are not, but it's often difficult to draw a line that clearly separates normality from abnormality.

Actress Jessica Alba used to unplug every single appliance in her house because she worried it would catch fire. She would also check and recheck her doors to ensure that they were locked.

Soccer star David Beckham acknowledges more elaborate concerns that involve symmetry and matching. He is not comfortable unless everything is arranged in straight lines or in pairs. For instance, if he has five cans of Pepsi in a refrigerator, he has to get rid of one to restore even pairs. When he enters a hotel room he immediately has to put away all the leaflets and books to restore order to the room.

For Alba and Beckham, these aren't just little eccentricities of being a celebrity. They're manifestations of obsessive-compulsive behavior. Comedian and talk show host Howie Mandel explains the disorder in his 2009 autobiography, *Here's the Deal: Don't Touch Me.* Mandel doesn't shake hands, because of his fear of germs, but "it's not just that I'm scared of germs," he says. There's nothing wrong with shaking hands with someone and then washing your hands. But "there *is* something wrong with being totally consumed that you didn't get everything off your hand, that there's things crawling, so you wash it again, and you're so consumed that you wash it

© AP Images/Charles Sykes

again, and you wash it again and you wash it again and you wash it again," Mandel says. "When you can't get past that, that's obsessive-compulsive disorder. It's not that you're afraid of germs, it's that you obsess about that thought and have to do things like handwashing to relieve the worry. I always have intrusive thoughts and rituals."

What causes such abnormal behavior? Does Mandel have a mental illness, or does he just behave strangely? What is the basis for judging behavior as normal versus abnormal? How common are such disorders? Can they be cured? These are just a few of the questions that we will address in this chapter as we discuss psychological disorders and their complex causes.

Abnormal Behavior: General Concepts

KEY LEARNING GOALS

14.1 Evaluate the medical model of psychological disorders, and identify the key criteria of abnormality.

14.2 Outline the structure of the DSM diagnostic system.

Misconceptions about abnormal behavior are common. Consequently, we need to clear up some preliminary issues before we describe the various types of disorders. In this section, we will discuss (1) the medical model of abnormal behavior, (2) the criteria of abnormal behavior, and (3) the classification of psychological disorders.

The Medical Model Applied to Abnormal Behavior

There's no question that Howie Mandel's extreme fear of germs is abnormal. But does it make sense to view his unusual and irrational behavior as an illness? This is a controversial question. The *medical model* **proposes that it is useful to think of abnormal behavior as a disease.** This point of view is the basis for many of the terms used to refer to abnormal behavior, including mental *illness,* psychological *disorder,* and *psychopathology* (*pathology* refers to manifestations of disease). The medical model gradually became the dominant way of thinking about abnormal behavior during the 18th and 19th centuries. Its influence remains strong today.

The medical model clearly represented progress over earlier models of abnormal behavior. Prior to the 18th century, most conceptions of abnormal behavior were based on superstition. People who behaved strangely were thought to be possessed by demons, to be witches in league with the devil, or to be victims of God's punishment. Their disorders were "treated" with chants, rituals, exorcisms, and such. If individuals' behavior was seen as threatening, they were candidates for chains, dungeons, torture, and death.

The rise of the medical model brought improvements in the treatment of those who exhibited abnormal behavior. As victims of an illness, they were viewed with more sympathy and less hatred and fear. Although living conditions in early asylums were often deplorable, gradual progress was made toward more humane care of the mentally ill. It took time, but ineffective approaches to treatment eventually gave way to scientific investigation of the causes and cures of psychological disorders.

Photograph by Jeffrey A. Schaler, permission granted, www.szasz.com

Thomas Szasz

"Minds can be 'sick' only in the sense that jokes are 'sick' or economies are 'sick.'"

However, in recent decades, some critics have suggested that the medical model may have outlived its usefulness (Boyle, 2007; Kiesler, 1999). Some critics are troubled because medical diagnoses of abnormal behavior pin potentially derogatory labels on people (Hinshaw, 2007; Overton & Medina, 2008). Being labeled as psychotic, schizophrenic, or mentally ill carries a social stigma that can be difficult to shake. Those characterized as mentally ill are viewed as erratic, dangerous, incompetent, and inferior (Corrigan & Larson, 2008). These stereotypes promote distancing, disdain, prejudice, and rejection. Unfortunately, the stigma associated with psychological disorders appears to be deep rooted and not easily reduced. In recent decades research has increasingly demonstrated that many psychological disorders are at least partly attributable to genetic and biological factors, making them appear more similar to physical illnesses, which carry far less stigma (Pescosolido, 2010; Schnittker, 2008). You would think that these trends would lead to a reduction in the stigma associated with mental illness, but research suggests that the stigmatization of mental disorders has remained stable or perhaps even increased (Hinshaw & Stier, 2008; Schnittker, 2008).

Another line of criticism has been voiced by Thomas Szasz (1974, 1990). He asserts that "strictly speaking, disease or illness can affect only the body; hence there can be no mental illness. . . . Minds can be 'sick' only in the sense that jokes are 'sick' or economies are 'sick'" (1974, p. 267). He further argues that abnormal behavior usually involves a deviation from social norms rather than an illness. He contends that such deviations are "problems in living" rather than medical problems. According to Szasz, the medical model's disease analogy converts moral and social questions about what is acceptable behavior into medical questions.

The criticism of the medical model has some merit, and it is important to recognize the social roots and ramifications of the medical model. However, the bottom line is that the medical model continues to dominate thinking about psychological disorders. Medical concepts such as *diagnosis, etiology,* and *prognosis* have proven valuable in the treatment and study of abnormality. ***Diagnosis* involves distinguishing one illness from another. *Etiology* refers to the apparent causation and developmental history of an illness. A *prognosis* is a forecast about the probable course of an illness.** These medically based concepts have widely shared meanings that permit clinicians, researchers, and the public to communicate more effectively in their discussions of abnormal behavior.

Criteria of Abnormal Behavior

If your next-door neighbor scrubs his front porch twice every day and spends virtually all his time cleaning and recleaning his house, is he normal? If your sister-in-law goes to one physician after another seeking treatment for ailments that appear imaginary, is she psychologically healthy? How are we to judge what's normal and what's abnormal? More important, who's to do the judging?

These are complex questions. In a sense, *all* people make judgments about normality in that they all express opinions about others' (and perhaps their own) mental health. Of course, formal diagnoses of psychological disorders are made by mental health professionals. In making these diagnoses, clinicians rely on a variety of criteria, the foremost of which are the following:

1. *Deviance.* As Szasz has pointed out, people are often said to have a disorder because their behavior deviates from what their society considers acceptable. What constitutes normality varies somewhat from one culture to another. However, all cultures have such norms. When people violate these standards and expectations, they may be labeled mentally ill. For example, *transvestic fetishism* is a sexual disorder in which a man achieves sexual arousal by dressing in women's clothing. This behavior is regarded as disordered because a man who wears a dress, brassiere, and nylons is deviating from our culture's norms. This example illustrates the arbitrary nature of cultural standards regarding normality, as the same overt behavior (cross-sex dressing) is acceptable for women but deviant for men.

This man's hoarding behavior clearly represents a certain type of deviance, but does that mean he has a psychological disorder? The criteria of mental illness are more subjective and complicated than most people realize. To some extent, judgments of mental health represent value judgments.

2. *Maladaptive behavior.* In many cases, people are judged to have a psychological disorder because their everyday adaptive behavior is impaired. This is the key criterion in the diagnosis of substance use (drug) disorders. In and of itself, alcohol and drug use is not terribly unusual or deviant. However, when the use of cocaine, for instance, begins to interfere with a person's social or occupational functioning, a substance use disorder exists. In such cases, it is the maladaptive quality of the behavior that makes it disordered.

3. *Personal distress.* Frequently, the diagnosis of a psychological disorder is based on an individual's report of great personal distress. This is usually the criterion met by people who are troubled by depression or anxiety disorders. Depressed people, for instance, may or may not exhibit deviant or maladaptive behavior. Such people are usually labeled as having a disorder when they describe their subjective pain and suffering to friends, relatives, and mental health professionals.

Although two or three criteria may apply in a particular case, people are often viewed as disordered when only one criterion is met. As you may have already noticed, diagnoses of psychological disorders involve *value judgments* about what represents normal or abnormal behavior (Sadler, 2005; Widiger & Sankis, 2000). The criteria of mental illness are not nearly as value-free as the criteria of physical illness. In evaluating physical diseases, people can usually agree that a malfunctioning heart or kidney is pathological, regardless of their personal values. However, judgments about mental illness reflect prevailing cultural values, social trends, and political forces, as well as scientific knowledge (Kutchins & Kirk, 1997, Mechanic, 1999).

Antonyms such as *normal* versus *abnormal* and *mental health* versus *mental illness* imply that people can be divided neatly into two distinct groups: those who are normal and those who are not. In reality, it is often difficult to draw a line that clearly separates normality from abnormality. On occasion, everybody acts in deviant ways, everyone displays some maladaptive behavior, and everyone experiences personal distress. People are judged to have psychological disorders only when their behavior becomes *extremely* deviant, maladaptive, or distressing. Thus, normality and abnormality exist on a continuum. It's a matter of degree, not an either-or proposition.

Reality Check

Misconception

People with psychological disorders typically exhibit highly bizarre behavior.

Reality

This is true only in a small minority of cases, usually involving relatively severe disorders. The vast majority of people with psychological disorders do not display strange behavior. On the surface most are indistinguishable from those without disorders.

FIGURE 14.1
Overview of the DSM-IV diagnostic system. The *Diagnostic and Statistical Manual of Mental Disorders* is the formal classification system used in the diagnosis of psychological disorders. DSM-IV is a *multiaxial* system, which means that information is recorded on the five axes described here. A new edition of the DSM system is tentatively scheduled for release in 2013. (Adapted for educational purposes from American Psychiatric Association, 1994, 2000)

Axis I
Clinical Syndromes

Axis I is used to record most types of disorders, including anxiety disorders, dissociative disorders, mood disorders, schizophrenic disorders, eating disorders, substance-related disorders, somatoform disorders, sexual and gender-identity disorders, organic mental disorders, and disorders usually first diagnosed in childhood.

Axis II
Personality Disorders or Mental Retardation

Personality disorders are longstanding patterns of extreme, inflexible personality traits that are deviant or maladaptive and lead to impaired functioning or subjective distress.

Mental retardation (intellectual disability) refers to subnormal general mental ability accompanied by deficiencies in adaptive skills, originating before age 18.

Axis III
General Medical Conditions

Physical disorders or conditions are recorded on this axis. Examples include diabetes, arthritis, and hemophilia.

Axis IV
Psychosocial and Environmental Problems

Axis IV is for reporting psychosocial and environmental problems that may affect the diagnosis, treatment, and prognosis of mental disorders (Axes I and II). A psychosocial or environmental problem may be a negative life event, an environmental difficulty or deficiency, a familial or other interpersonal stressor, an inadequacy of social support or personal resources, or another problem that describes the context in which a person's difficulties have developed.

Axis V
Global Assessment of Functioning (GAF) Scale

Axis V is used to make estimates of an individual's current level of adaptive functioning (in social and occupational behavior, viewed as a whole) and of the individual's highest level of functioning in the past year. A 100-point scale is used, with higher scores reflecting better functioning.

© Cengage Learning

Psychodiagnosis: The Classification of Disorders **PsykTrek SIM9**

Lumping all psychological disorders together would make it extremely difficult to understand them better. A sound taxonomy of mental disorders can facilitate empirical research and enhance communication among scientists and clinicians (First, 2008; Zimmerman & Spitzer, 2009). Thus, a great deal of effort has been invested in devising an elaborate system for classifying psychological disorders. This classification system, published by the American Psychiatric Association, is outlined in a book titled the *Diagnostic and Statistical Manual of Mental Disorders.* The current, fourth edition, referred to as DSM-IV, was released in 1994 and revised slightly in 2000.

DSM-IV employs a multiaxial system of classification. It asks for judgments about individuals on five separate "axes" (see **Figure 14.1**). The diagnoses of disorders are made on Axes I and II. Clinicians record most types of disorders on Axis I, while they use Axis II to list long-running personality disorders or mental retardation (intellectual disability). People may receive diagnoses on both Axes I and II. The remaining axes are used to record supplemental information. A patient's physical disorders are listed on Axis III (General Medical Conditions). On Axis IV (Psychosocial and Environmental Problems), the clinician makes notations regarding the types of stress experienced by the individual in the past year. On Axis V (Global Assessment of Functioning), estimates are made of the individual's current level of adaptive functioning (in social and occupational behavior, viewed as a whole) and of the individual's highest level of functioning in the past year.

Concept Check 14.1

Applying the Criteria of Abnormal Behavior

Check your understanding of the criteria of abnormal behavior by identifying the criteria met by each of the examples below and checking them off in the table provided. Remember, a specific behavior may meet more than one criterion. The answers are in Appendix A.

Behavioral Examples

1. Alan's performance at work has suffered because he has been drinking alcohol to excess. Several co-workers have suggested that he seek help for his problem, but he thinks that they're getting alarmed over nothing. "I just enjoy a good time once in a while," he says.

2. Monica has gone away to college and feels lonely, sad, and dejected. Her grades are fine, and she gets along okay with the other students in the dormitory, but inside she's choked with gloom, hopelessness, and despair.

3. Boris believes that he's Napoleon reborn. He believes that he is destined to lead the U.S. military forces into a great battle to recover California from space aliens.

4. Natasha panics with anxiety whenever she leaves her home. Her problem escalated gradually until she was absent from work so often that she was fired. She hasn't been out of her house in nine months and is deeply troubled by her problem.

Criteria Met by Each Example

	Maladaptive behavior	Deviance	Personal distress
1. Alan	_____	_____	_____
2. Monica	_____	_____	_____
3. Boris	_____	_____	_____
4. Natasha	_____	_____	_____

© michaeljung/Shutterstock

Work is currently underway to formulate the next edition of the diagnostic system (e.g., Andrews et al., 2009; Helzer et al., 2008b; Regier et al., 2009), which will be identified as DSM-5 (instead of DSM-V), to facilitate incremental updates (such as DSM-5.1). It is tentatively scheduled for publication in 2013. Clinical researchers have been collecting data, holding conferences, and formulating arguments about whether various syndromes should be added, eliminated, redefined, or renamed. One major change in the preliminary draft for DSM-5 is that the multiaxial system will be retired. The distinction between Axis I and Axis II disorders will be discarded. Clinicians will still be encouraged to make notations about patients' medical conditions, stressors, and global functioning, but there will be no formal axes for this supplemental information. Many of the proposed revisions for DSM-5 have been highly controversial. Some prominent critics have argued vigorously that implementation of DSM-5 should be delayed pending further research, but at this point it appears that the American Psychiatric Association will proceed with the publication of DSM-5 in 2013. Hence, we will mention some of the less contentious revisions that seem likely to make it into the final version.

One major issue in the development of DSM-5 has been whether to reduce the system's commitment to a categorical approach. In recent years many critics of the DSM system have questioned the fundamental axiom that the diagnostic system is built on—the assumption that people can reliably be placed in discontinuous (nonoverlapping) diagnostic categories (Helzer et al., 2008a; Widiger & Trull, 2007). These critics note that there is enormous overlap among various disorders in symptoms, making the boundaries between diagnoses much fuzzier than would be ideal. They also point out that people often qualify for more than one diagnosis. Because of problems such as these, some theorists have argued that the current *categorical approach* to diagnosis should be replaced by a *dimensional approach*. A dimensional approach would describe individuals' pathology in terms of how they score on a limited number of continuous dimensions, such as the degree to which they exhibit anxiety, depression, agitation, hypochondria, paranoia, and so forth (Kraemer, 2008; Widiger, Livesley, & Clark, 2009). The practical logistics of shifting to a dimensional approach to psychological disorders are formidable. Agreement would have to be reached about what dimensions to assess and how to measure them. At this juncture, it appears that DSM-5 will retain a categorical approach, but it looks like there will be significant movement toward supplementing it with a dimensional approach for at least some disorders (Regier et al., 2009).

We are now ready to start examining the specific types of psychological disorders. Obviously, in this chapter we cannot cover all 200 or so disorders listed in the DSM system. However, we will introduce most of the major categories of disorders to give you an overview of the many forms abnormal behavior takes. In discussing each set of disorders, we will begin with brief descriptions of the specific subtypes that fall in the category. If data are available, we will discuss the *prevalence* of the disorders in that category (how common they are in the population). Then we'll focus on the *etiology* of that set of disorders.

Anxiety Disorders

PSYKTREK SIM9

KEY LEARNING GOALS

14.3 Identify five anxiety disorders and the symptoms associated with each.

14.4 Discuss how biology, conditioning, cognition, and stress can contribute to the development of anxiety disorders.

Everyone experiences anxiety from time to time. It is a natural and common reaction to many of life's difficulties. For some people, however, anxiety becomes a chronic problem. These people experience high levels of anxiety with disturbing regularity. *Anxiety disorders* are a class of disorders marked by feelings of excessive apprehension and anxiety. There are five principal types of anxiety disorders: generalized anxiety disorder, phobic disorder, panic disorder, obsessive-compulsive disorder, and posttraumatic stress disorder. However, the current proposal for DSM-5 would remove obsessive-compulsive disorder from the anxiety disorders category and put it in its own special category. Studies suggest that anxiety disorders are quite common. Over the course of their lives, roughly 19% of people experience an anxiety disorder (Dew, Bromet, & Switzer, 2000; Regier & Burke, 2000).

Generalized Anxiety Disorder

PSYKTREK 11a

Generalized anxiety disorder is marked by a chronic, high level of anxiety that is not tied to any specific threat. People with this disorder worry constantly about yesterday's mistakes and tomorrow's problems. They worry about minor matters related to family, finances, work, and personal illness. They hope that their worrying will help to ward off negative events (Beidel & Stipelman, 2007). Nonetheless, they worry about how much they worry (Barlow et al., 2003). They often dread decisions and brood over them endlessly. Their anxiety is often accompanied by physical symptoms, such as trembling, muscle tension, diarrhea, dizziness, faintness, sweating, and heart palpitations. Generalized anxiety disorder tends to have a gradual onset, has a lifetime prevalence of about 5%–6%, and is seen more frequently in females than males (Rowa & Antony, 2008).

Phobic Disorder

PSYKTREK 11a

In a phobic disorder, an individual's troublesome anxiety has a specific focus. A *phobic disorder* is marked by a persistent and irrational fear of an object or situation that presents no realistic danger. The following case provides an example of a phobic disorder:

Hilda is 32 years of age and has a rather unusual fear. She is terrified of snow. She cannot go outside in the snow. She cannot even stand to see snow or hear about it on the weather report. Her phobia severely constricts her day-to-day behavior. Probing in therapy revealed that her phobia was caused by a traumatic experience at age 11. Playing at a ski lodge, she was buried briefly by a small avalanche of snow. She had no recollection of this experience until it was recovered in therapy. (Adapted from Laughlin, 1967, p. 227)

As Hilda's unusual snow phobia illustrates, people can develop phobic responses to virtually anything. Nonetheless, certain types of phobias are relatively common, including acrophobia (fear of heights), claustrophobia (fear of small, enclosed places), brontophobia (fear of storms), hydrophobia (fear of water), and various animal and insect phobias (McCabe & Antony, 2008; see **Figure 14.2**). Many people troubled by phobias realize that their fears are irrational but still are unable to calm themselves when confronted by a phobic object.

Panic Disorder and Agoraphobia

PSYKTREK 11a

A *panic disorder* is characterized by recurrent attacks of overwhelming anxiety that usually occur suddenly and unexpectedly. These paralyzing attacks are accompanied by physical symptoms of anxiety. After a number of anxiety attacks, victims often become apprehensive, wondering when their next panic attack will occur. Their concern about exhibiting panic in public may increase to the point where they are afraid to leave home. This fear creates a condition called *agoraphobia,* which is a common complication of panic disorders.

Agoraphobia is a fear of going out to public places (its literal meaning is "fear of the marketplace or open places"). Because of this fear, some people become prisoners confined to their homes, although many

FIGURE 14.2

Common phobic fears. This graph shows the lifetime prevalence of the most common types of phobic fears reported by participants in a study by Curtis et al. (1998). As you can see, a very substantial number of people struggle with a variety of specific phobias. Bear in mind that only a portion of these people qualify for a diagnosis of phobic disorder, which is merited only if individuals' phobias seriously impair their everyday functioning.

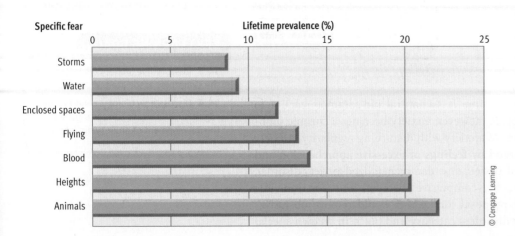

© Cengage Learning

will venture out if accompanied by a trusted companion (Hollander & Simeon, 2008). As its name suggests, agoraphobia was once viewed as a phobic disorder. However, in DSM-III and DSM-IV it was characterized as a common complication of panic disorder. In DSM-5 it appears that it will be listed as a separate anxiety disorder that may or may not co-exist with panic disorder. About two-thirds of people who are diagnosed with panic disorder are female (Taylor, Cox, & Asmundson, 2009). The onset of panic disorder typically occurs during late adolescence or early adulthood (McClure-Tone & Pine, 2009).

Obsessive-Compulsive Disorder

PSYKTREK 11a

Obsessions are *thoughts* that repeatedly intrude on one's consciousness in a distressing way. Compulsions are *actions* that one feels forced to carry out. Therefore, *obsessive-compulsive disorder (OCD)* **is marked by persistent, uncontrollable intrusions of unwanted thoughts (obsessions) and urges to engage in senseless rituals (compulsions).** To illustrate, let's examine the bizarre behavior of a man once reputed to be the wealthiest person in the world:

The famous industrialist Howard Hughes was obsessed with the possibility of being contaminated by germs. This led him to devise extraordinary rituals to minimize the possibility of such contamination. He would spend hours methodically cleaning a single telephone. He once wrote a three-page memo instructing assistants on exactly how to open cans of fruit for him. (Adapted from Barlett & Steele, 1979, pp. 227–237)

Obsessions often center on inflicting harm on others, personal failures, suicide, or sexual acts. People troubled by obsessions may feel that they have lost control of their mind. Compulsions usually involve stereotyped rituals that may temporarily relieve the anxiety produced by one's obsessions. As we saw at the beginning of the chapter, common examples include constant handwashing, repetitive cleaning and ordering of things, and endless rechecking of locks, faucets, and such (Pato et al., 2008). **Figure 14.3** on the next page shows the most common compulsions seen in OCD patients. Many of us can be compulsive at times. Indeed, a recent study found that 17% of a sample of people without a mental disorder reported a significant obsession or compulsion (Fullana et al., 2009). However, full-fledged obsessive-compulsive disorders occur in roughly 2%–3% of the population (Zohar, Fostick, & Juven-Wetzler, 2009). OCD can be a particularly severe disorder and is often associated with serious social and occupational impairments (Torres et al., 2006).

© Matthew Benoit/Shutterstock

As a young man (shown in the photo), Howard Hughes was a handsome, dashing daredevil pilot and movie producer who appeared to be reasonably well adjusted. However, as the years went by, his behavior gradually became more and more maladaptive, as obsessions and compulsions came to dominate his life. In his later years (shown in the drawing), he spent most of his time in darkened rooms, naked, unkempt, and dirty, following bizarre rituals to alleviate his anxieties. (The drawing was done by an NBC artist and was based on descriptions from men who had seen Hughes.)

FIGURE 14.3

Common compulsions in OCD patients.
The most common compulsions reported by a sample of 550 OCD patients are shown here. Nearly half of the OCD patients reported multiple compulsions.

SOURCE: Pato, M. T., Fanous, A., Eisen, J. L., & Phillips, K. A. (2008). Anxiety disorders: Obsessive-compulsive disorder. In A. Tasman, J. Kay, J. A. Lieberman, M. B. First, & M. Maj (Eds.), *Psychiatry* (3rd ed.), 1443–1471. Chichester, England: Wiley-Blackwell.

© Cengage Learning

Posttraumatic Stress Disorder

Posttraumatic stress disorder (PTSD) **involves enduring psychological disturbance attributed to the experience of a major traumatic event.** PTSD was first recognized as a disorder in the 1970s in the aftermath of the Vietnam war, when a great many veterans were traumatized by their combat experiences. Research eventually showed that PTSD can be caused by a variety of traumatic events besides harrowing war experiences. For example, PTSD is often seen after a rape or assault, a severe automobile accident, a natural disaster, or the witnessing of someone's death. Although people tend to assume that such events are relatively uncommon, research shows that a majority of adults have been exposed to one or more serious traumatic events (Norris & Slone, 2007). Common symptoms of PTSD include reexperiencing the event in the form of nightmares and flashbacks, emotional numbing, alienation, problems in social relations, an increased sense of vulnerability, and elevated arousal, anxiety, anger, and guilt (McClure-Tone & Pine, 2009).

Research suggests that about 7% of people have suffered from PTSD at some point in their lives (Resick, Monson, & Rizvi, 2008). Currently, there is great concern about the number of military returnees from the Afghanistan and Iraq wars who will develop PTSD (Ramchand et al., 2010; Sundin et al., 2010). Similar to what happened with Vietnam veterans, the preliminary data suggest that these troops are showing greatly elevated rates of PTSD.

A variety of factors are predictors of individuals' risk for PTSD (Keane, Marshall, & Taft, 2006; McNally, 2009). As you might expect, increased vulnerability is associated with greater personal injuries and losses, greater intensity of exposure to the traumatic event, and more exposure to the grotesque aftermath of the event. One key predictor of vulnerability is the *intensity of one's reaction at the time of the traumatic event* (Ozer et al., 2003). Individuals who have especially intense emotional reactions during or immediately after the traumatic event go on to show highly elevated vulnerability to PTSD.

Military and other personnel who have served in the wars in Iraq and Afghanistan will almost surely exhibit greatly elevated rates of posttraumatic stress disorder.

© Robert Nickelsberg/ Getty Images

Etiology of Anxiety Disorders

PSYKTREK 11a

Like most psychological disorders, anxiety disorders develop out of complicated interactions among a variety of biological and psychological factors.

BIOLOGICAL FACTORS

PsykTrek 11a

In studies that assess the impact of heredity on psychological disorders, investigators look at *concordance rates*. **A *concordance rate* indicates the percentage of twin pairs or other pairs of relatives that exhibit the same disorder.** If relatives who share more genetic similarity show higher concordance rates than relatives who share less genetic overlap, this finding supports the genetic hypothesis. The results of both *twin studies* (see **Figure 14.4**) and *family studies* (see Chapter 3 for discussions of both methods) suggest that there is a moderate genetic predisposition to anxiety disorders (Fyer, 2009).

Recent evidence suggests that a link may exist between anxiety disorders and neurochemical activity in the brain. As you learned in Chapter 3, *neurotransmitters* are chemicals that carry signals from one neuron to another. Therapeutic drugs (such as Valium or Xanax) that reduce excessive anxiety appear to alter neurotransmitter activity at synapses that release a neurotransmitter called GABA. This finding and other lines of evidence suggest that disturbances in the neural circuits using GABA may play a role in some types of anxiety disorders (Rowa & Antony, 2009). Abnormalities in neural circuits using serotonin have been implicated in obsessive-compulsive disorders (Pato et al., 2008). In short, scientists are beginning to unravel the neurochemical bases for anxiety disorders.

CONDITIONING AND LEARNING

PsykTrek 11a

Many anxiety responses may be *acquired through classical conditioning* and *maintained through operant conditioning* (see Chapter 6). According to Mowrer (1947), an originally neutral stimulus (the snow in Hilda's case, for instance) may be paired with a frightening event (the avalanche) so that it becomes a conditioned stimulus eliciting anxiety (see **Figure 14.5**). Once a fear is acquired through classical conditioning, the person may start avoiding the anxiety-producing stimulus. The avoidance response is negatively reinforced because it is followed by a reduction in anxiety. This process involves operant conditioning (see **Figure 14.5**). Thus, separate conditioning processes may create and then sustain specific anxiety responses (Levis, 1989). Consistent with this view, studies find that a substantial portion of people suffering from phobias can identify a traumatic conditioning experience that probably contributed to their anxiety disorder (McCabe & Antony, 2008; Mineka & Zinbarg, 2006).

The tendency to develop phobias of certain types of objects and situations may be explained by Martin Seligman's (1971) concept of *preparedness*. Like many theorists, Seligman believes that classical conditioning creates most phobic responses. *However, he suggests that people are biologically prepared by their evolutionary history to acquire some fears much more easily than others.* His theory would explain why people develop phobias of ancient sources of threat (such as snakes and spiders) much more readily than modern sources of threat (such as electrical outlets or hot irons). As we noted in Chapter 6, Arne Öhman and Susan Mineka (2001) have updated the notion of preparedness, which they call an *evolved module for fear learning*. They maintain that this evolved module is automatically activated by stimuli related to past survival threats in evolutionary history and that it is relatively resistant to intentional efforts to suppress the resulting fears. Consistent with this view, phobic stimuli associated with evolutionary threats tend to produce more rapid conditioning of fears and stronger fear responses (Mineka & Öhman, 2002).

COGNITIVE FACTORS

PsykTrek 11a

Cognitive theorists maintain that certain styles of thinking make some people particularly vulnerable to anxiety disorders (Craske & Waters, 2005). According to these theorists, some people are more likely to suffer from anxiety problems because they tend to (a) misinterpret harmless situations as threatening, (b) focus excessive attention on perceived threats, and (c) selectively recall information that seems threatening (Beck,

FIGURE 14.4

Twin studies of anxiety disorders.
The concordance rate for anxiety disorders in identical twins is higher than that for fraternal twins, who share less genetic overlap. These results suggest that there is a genetic predisposition to anxiety disorders. (Data based on Noyes et al., 1987; Slater & Shields, 1969; Torgersen, 1979, 1983)

(a) Classical conditioning: Acquisition of phobic fear

(b) Operant conditioning: Maintenance of phobic fear (negative reinforcement)

FIGURE 14.5

Conditioning as an explanation for phobias. (a) Many phobias appear to be acquired through classical conditioning when a neutral stimulus is paired with an anxiety-arousing stimulus. **(b)** Once acquired, a phobia may be maintained through operant conditioning. Avoidance of the phobic stimulus reduces anxiety, resulting in negative reinforcement.

FIGURE 14.6

Cognitive factors in anxiety disorders.
Eysenck and his colleagues (1991) compared how subjects with anxiety problems and nonanxious subjects tended to interpret sentences that could be viewed as threatening or nonthreatening. Consistent with cognitive models of anxiety disorders, anxious subjects were more likely to interpret the sentences in a threatening light.

1997; McNally, 1994, 1996). In one intriguing test of the cognitive view, anxious and nonanxious subjects were asked to read thirty-two sentences that could be interpreted in either a threatening or a nonthreatening manner (Eysenck et al., 1991). For instance, one such sentence was "The doctor examined little Emma's growth," which could mean that the doctor checked her height or the growth of a tumor. As **Figure 14.6** shows, the anxious participants interpreted the sentences in a threatening way more often than the nonanxious participants did. Thus, consistent with our theme that human experience is highly subjective, the cognitive view holds that some people are prone to anxiety disorders because they see threat in every corner of their lives (Aikens & Craske, 2001; Riskind, 2005).

STRESS

PSYKTREK 11a

Obviously, cases of posttraumatic stress disorder are attributed to individuals' exposure to extremely stressful incidents. Research has also demonstrated that other types of anxiety disorders can be stress related (Beidel & Stipelman, 2007; Sandin et al., 2004). For instance, Faravelli and Pallanti (1989) found that patients with panic disorder had experienced a dramatic increase in stress in the month prior to the onset of their disorder. In another study, Brown and colleagues (1998) found an association between stress and the development of social phobia. Thus, there is reason to believe that high stress often helps precipitate the onset of anxiety disorders.

Concept Check   14.2

Distinguishing Among Anxiety Disorders

Check your understanding of the nature of anxiety disorders by making preliminary diagnoses for the cases described below. Read each case summary and write your tentative diagnosis in the space provided. The answers are in Appendix A.

1. Malcolm religiously follows an exact schedule every day. His showering and grooming ritual takes two hours. He follows the same path in walking to his classes every day, and he always sits in the same seat in each class. He can't study until his apartment is arranged perfectly. Although he tries not to, he thinks constantly about flunking out of school. Both his grades and his social life are suffering from his rigid routines.

   Preliminary diagnosis:

   _____

2. Jane has an intense fear of thunderstorms. Lightning and thunder terrify her. If she is home when a thunderstorm hits, she drops everything she is doing and runs to her basement. If she is out and about when a thunderstorm hits, she goes into a panic. She carefully monitors weather predictions to avoid this calamity. Because of her fear of thunderstorms she often misses work and she is worried that she may be fired.

   Preliminary diagnosis:

   _____

3. Nathan recently returned from a six-month tour of military duty in Afghanistan where he saw a close friend die in combat. He keeps reliving the nightmare of seeing his friend die. He reports chronic feelings of anxiety, anger, and emotional numbing.

   Preliminary diagnosis:

   _____

Dissociative Disorders

KEY LEARNING GOALS

14.5 Distinguish among three dissociative disorders.

14.6 Discuss the etiology of dissociative identity disorder.

Dissociative disorders are probably the most controversial set of disorders in the diagnostic system, sparking heated debate among normally subdued researchers and clinicians (Simeon & Loewenstein, 2009). *Dissociative disorders* **are a class of disorders in which people lose contact with portions of their consciousness or memory, resulting in disruptions in their sense of identity.** We'll describe three dissociative syndromes—dissociative amnesia, dissociative fugue, and dissociative identity disorder. All of these disorders are relatively uncommon.

Dissociative Amnesia and Fugue

Dissociative amnesia and fugue are overlapping disorders characterized by serious memory deficits. *Dissociative amnesia* **is a sudden loss of memory for important personal information that is too extensive to be due to normal forgetting.** Memory losses may occur for a single traumatic event (such as an automobile accident or home fire) or for an extended period of time surrounding the event. Cases of amnesia have been observed after people have experienced disasters, accidents, combat stress, physical abuse, and rape or after they have witnessed the violent death of a parent, among other things (Arrigo & Pezdek, 1997; Cardeña & Gleaves, 2007). In *dissociative fugue,* **people lose their memory for their entire lives along with their sense of personal identity.** These people forget their name, their family, where they live, and where they work! In spite of this wholesale forgetting, they remember matters unrelated to their identity, such as how to drive a car and how to do math.

Dissociative Identity Disorder

Dissociative identity disorder (DID) **involves the coexistence in one person of two or more largely complete, and usually very different, personalities.** The name for this disorder used to be *multiple personality disorder,* which still enjoys informal usage. In dissociative identity disorder, the divergences in behavior go far beyond those that people normally display in adapting to different roles in life. People with "multiple personalities" feel that they have more than one identity. Each personality has his or her own name, memories, traits, and physical mannerisms. Although it is rare, this syndrome is frequently portrayed in novels, movies, and television shows, such as the satirical film *Me, Myself, and Irene,* a 2000 release starring Jim Carrey, and most recently the Showtime series the *United States of Tara.* In popular media portrayals, the syndrome is often mistakenly called *schizophrenia.* As you will see later, schizophrenic disorders are entirely different.

In dissociative identity disorder, the various personalities generally report that they are unaware of each other (Eich et al., 1997). The alternate personalities commonly display traits that are quite foreign to the original personality. For instance, a shy, inhibited person might develop a flamboyant, extraverted alternate personality. Transitions between identities often occur suddenly. The disparities between identities can be bizarre: Different personalities may assert that they are different in age, race, gender, and sexual orientation (Kluft, 1996). Dissociative identity disorder is seen more often in women than in men (Simeon & Loewenstein, 2009).

Starting in the 1970s, a dramatic increase was seen in the diagnosis of multiple-personality disorder (Kihlstrom, 2001). Only 79 well-documented cases had accumulated up through 1970, but by the late-1990s about 40,000 cases were estimated to have been reported (Lilienfeld & Lynn, 2003). Some theorists believe that the disorder used to be underdiagnosed—that is, it often went undetected (Maldonado & Spiegel, 2008).

However, other theorists argue that a handful of clinicians have begun overdiagnosing the condition and that some clinicians even contribute to the emergence of DID (McHugh, 1995; Powell & Gee, 1999). Consistent with this view, a survey of all the psychiatrists in Switzerland found that 90% of them had never seen a case of dissociative identity disorder, whereas three of the psychiatrists had each seen more than 20 patients with dissociative identity disorder (Modestin, 1992). The data from this study suggest that 6 psychiatrists (out of 655 surveyed) accounted for two-thirds of the dissociative identity disorder diagnoses in Switzerland.

Etiology of Dissociative Disorders

Dissociative amnesia and fugue are usually attributed to excessive stress. However, relatively little is known about why this extreme reaction to stress occurs in a tiny minority of people but not in the vast majority who are subjected to similar stress.

The causes of dissociative identity disorder are particularly obscure. Some skeptical theorists (Lilienfeld et al., 1999; Spanos, 1994, 1996) believe that people with multiple personalities are engaging in intentional role playing to use mental illness as a face-saving excuse for their personal failings. They argue that a small minority of therapists help create DID in their patients by subtly encouraging the emergence of alternate personalities. According to these skeptics, dissociative identity disorder is a creation of modern North American culture, much as demonic possession was a creation of early Christianity.

In spite of these concerns, many clinicians are convinced that dissociative identity disorder is an authentic disorder (Cardeña & Gleaves, 2007; van der Hart & Nijenhuis, 2009). They argue that there is no incentive for either patients or therapists to manufacture cases of multiple personalities, which are often greeted with skepticism and outright hostility. They maintain that most cases of dissociative identity disorder are rooted in severe emotional trauma that occurred during childhood (Maldonado & Spiegel, 2008). A substantial majority of people with dissociative identity disorder report a childhood history of rejection from parents and of physical and sexual abuse (Foote et al., 2006; van der Hart & Nijenhuis, 2009). However, this abuse typically has not been independently verified (Lilienfeld & Lynn, 2003). Moreover, this association would not be unique to DID, as a history of child abuse elevates the likelihood of *many* disorders, especially among females (MacMillan et al., 2001). In the final analysis, little is known about the causes of dissociative identity disorder, which remains a controversial diagnosis (Barry-Walsh, 2005).

Mood Disorders

PsykTrek SIM9

KEY LEARNING GOALS

14.7 Describe the two major mood disorders and their relation to suicide.

14.8 Understand how genetic, neural, cognitive, social, and stress factors are related to the development of mood disorders.

What did Abraham Lincoln, Marilyn Monroe, Kurt Cobain, Vincent van Gogh, Ernest Hemingway, Winston Churchill, Ted Turner, Sting, Billy Joel, Jim Carrey, and Ben Stiller have in common? Yes, they all achieved great prominence, albeit in different ways at different times. But, more pertinent to our interest, they all suffered from severe mood disorders. Although mood disorders can be crippling, people with mood disorders may still achieve greatness, because such disorders tend to be *episodic*. In other words, mood disturbances often come and go, interspersed among periods of normality. These episodes of disturbance can vary greatly in length, but they typically last 3 to 12 months (Akiskal, 2000).

Mood disorders **are a class of disorders marked by emotional disturbances of varied kinds that may spill over to disrupt physical, perceptual, social, and thought processes.** There are two basic types of mood disorders: bipolar and unipolar (see **Figure 14.7**). People with *bipolar disorder* experience emotional extremes at both ends

Mood disorders are common and have affected many successful, well-known people, such as Gwyneth Paltrow and Owen Wilson.

of the mood continuum, going through periods of both *depression and mania* (excitement and elation). The mood swings in bipolar disorder can be patterned in many ways. People with *unipolar disorder* experience emotional extremes at just one end of the mood continuum, as they are troubled only by periodic bouts of *depression* (for the most part, patients do not exhibit manic episodes only). In DSM-5 it appears that depressive disorders and bipolar disorders will be separated into two distinct categories.

Major Depressive Disorder

PSYKTREK 11b

Everyone gets depressed once in a while. Thus, the line between normal and abnormal depression can be difficult to draw (Akiskal, 2009). Ultimately, a subjective judgment is required. Crucial considerations in this judgment include the duration of the depression and its disruptive effects. When a depression significantly impairs everyday adaptive behavior for more than a few weeks, there is reason for concern.

FIGURE 14.7

Episodic patterns in mood disorders. Time-limited episodes of emotional disturbance come and go unpredictably in mood disorders. People with unipolar disorder suffer from bouts of depression only, whereas people with bipolar disorder experience both manic and depressive episodes. The time between episodes of disturbance and the length of the episodes varies greatly.

TABLE 14.1 Comparisons of Common Symptoms in Manic and Depressive Episodes

Characteristics	Manic Episode	Depressive Episode
Emotional	Elated, euphoric, very sociable, impatient at any hindrance	Gloomy, hopeless, socially withdrawn, irritable
Cognitive	Characterized by racing thoughts, flight of ideas, desire for action, and impulsive behavior; talkative, self-confident; experiencing delusions of grandeur	Characterized by slowness of thought processes, obsessive worrying, inability to make decisions, negative self-image, self-blame and delusions of guilt and disease
Motor	Hyperactive, tireless, requiring less sleep than usual, showing increased sex drive and fluctuating appetite	Less active, tired, experiencing difficulty in sleeping, showing decreased sex drive and decreased appetite

© Cengage Learning

SOURCE: Sarason, I. G., & Sarason, B. G. (1987). *Abnormal psychology: The problem of maladaptive behavior.* Upper Saddle River, NJ: Prentice-Hall. © 1987 Prentice-Hall, Inc. Reprinted by permission.

In *major depressive disorder* people show persistent feelings of sadness and despair and a loss of interest in previous sources of pleasure. Negative emotions form the heart of the depressive syndrome, but many other symptoms may also appear. The most common symptoms of depression are summarized and compared with the symptoms of mania in **Table 14.1**. A central feature of depression is *anhedonia*—a diminished ability to experience pleasure. Depressed people lack the energy or motivation to tackle the tasks of living, to the point where they often have trouble getting out of bed (Craighead et al., 2008). Hence, they often give up things that they used to enjoy, such as hobbies, favorite foods, or spending time with friends. Reduced appetite and insomnia are common. People with depression often lack energy. They tend to move sluggishly and talk slowly. Anxiety, irritability, and brooding are commonly observed. Self-esteem tends to sink as the depressed person begins to feel worthless. Depression plunges people into feelings of hopelessness, dejection, and boundless guilt. The severity of abnormal depression varies considerably.

The onset of depression can occur at any point in the life span. However, a substantial majority of cases emerge before age 40 (Hammen, 2003). The vast majority (75%–95%) of people who suffer from depression experience more than one episode over the course of their lifetime (Joska & Stein, 2008). The average number of depressive episodes is five to six. The average length of these episodes is about 6 months (Akiskal, 2009). Although depression tends to be episodic, some people suffer from chronic major depression that may persist for years (Klein, 2010). Such chronic depression is associated with a particularly severe impairment of functioning. People with chronic depression tend to have a relatively early onset and high rates of additional disorders.

© manzrussali/Shutterstock

How common are depressive disorders? Well, estimates of the prevalence of depression vary quite a bit from one study to another because of the previously mentioned difficulty in drawing a line between normal dejection and abnormal depression. That said, depression clearly is a common disorder. The pooled data from two influential, large-scale studies (see **Figure 14.16** on page 498) yielded a lifetime prevalence estimate of 13%–14%. A more recent study of a nationally representative sample of over 9000 adults estimated that the lifetime prevalence of depressive disorder was 16.2% (Kessler et al., 2003). That estimate suggests that over 30 million people in the United States have suffered or will suffer from depression!

Research indicates that the prevalence of depression is about twice as high in women as it is in men (Nolen-Hoeksema & Hilt, 2009). The many possible explanations for this gender gap are the subject of considerable debate. The gap does *not* appear to be attributable to differences in genetic makeup (Kessler et al., 2003). A small portion of the disparity may be the result of women's elevated vulnerability to depression at certain points in their reproductive life cycle (Nolen-Hoeksema & Hilt, 2009). Obviously, only women have to worry about postpartum and postmenopausal depression. Susan Nolen-

Hoeksema (2001) argues that women experience more depression than men because they are far more likely to be victims of sexual abuse and somewhat more likely to endure poverty, sexual harassment, and excessive pressure to be thin and attractive. In other words, she attributes the higher prevalence of depression among women to their experience of greater stress and adversity. Nolen-Hoeksema also believes that women have a greater tendency than men to *ruminate* about setbacks and problems. Evidence suggests that this tendency to dwell on one's difficulties elevates vulnerability to depression, as we will discuss momentarily.

Bipolar Disorder

(PSYKTREK 11b)

Bipolar disorder (formerly known as *manic-depressive disorder*) is marked by the experience of both depressed and manic periods. The symptoms seen in manic periods generally are the opposite of those seen in depression (see **Table 14.1** for a comparison). In a manic episode, a person's mood becomes elevated to the point of euphoria. Self-esteem skyrockets as the person bubbles over with optimism, energy, and extravagant plans. He or she becomes hyperactive and may go for days without sleep. The individual talks rapidly and shifts topics wildly, as his or her mind races at breakneck speed. Judgment is often impaired. Some people in manic periods gamble impulsively, spend money frantically, or become sexually reckless. Like depressive disorder, bipolar disorder varies considerably in severity.

You may be thinking that the euphoria in manic episodes sounds appealing. If so, you are not entirely wrong. In their milder forms, manic states can seem attractive. The increases in energy, self-esteem, and optimism can be deceptively seductive (Goodwin & Jamison, 2007). However, manic periods often carry a paradoxical negative undercurrent of uneasiness and irritability. Moreover, mild manic episodes usually escalate to higher levels that become scary and disturbing. Impaired judgment leads many victims to do things that they greatly regret later, as you'll see in the following case history:

Robert, a dentist, awoke one morning with the idea that he was the most gifted dental surgeon in his tri-state area. He decided that he should try to provide services to as many people as possible, so that more people could benefit from his talents. Thus, he decided to remodel his two-chair dental office so that he could simultaneously attend to 20 patients. That same day, impatient to get rolling on his remodeling, he rolled up his sleeves, got himself a sledgehammer, and began to knock down the walls in his office. Annoyed when that didn't go so well, he smashed his dental tools, washbasins and X-ray equipment. Later, Robert's wife became concerned about his behavior and summoned two of her adult daughters for assistance. The daughters responded quickly, arriving at the family home with their husbands. In the ensuing discussion, Robert made sexual advances toward his daughters. He had to be subdued by their husbands. (Adapted from Kleinmuntz, 1980, p. 309)

Although not rare, bipolar disorder is much less common than unipolar disorder. Bipolar disorder affects roughly about 1% of the population (Merikangas & Pato, 2009). Unlike depressive disorder, bipolar disorder is seen equally often in males and females (Rihmer & Angst, 2009). The onset of bipolar disorder is age related. The typical age of onset is in the late teens.

"Those? Oh, just a few souvenirs from my biopolar-disorder days."

Mood Disorders and Suicide

A tragic, heartbreaking problem associated with mood disorders is suicide. Suicide is the eleventh leading cause of death in the United States, accounting for about 30,000 deaths annually. Official statistics may underestimate the scope of the problem. Many suicides are disguised as accidents, either by the suicidal person or by the survivors who try to cover up afterward. Moreover, experts estimate that suicide attempts may outnumber completed suicides by a ratio of as much as ten to one (Sudak, 2009). Anyone can commit suicide, but some groups are at higher risk than others (Carroll-Ghosh, Victor, & Bourgeois, 2003). Evidence suggests that women *attempt* suicide three times more often than men. But men are more likely to actually kill themselves in an attempt, so they *complete* four times as many suicides as women.

With the luxury of hindsight, it is recognized that about 90% of the people who complete suicide suffer from some type of psychological disorder, although in some cases this disorder may not be readily apparent beforehand (Melvin et al., 2008). As you might expect, suicide rates are highest for people with mood disorders. They account for about 60% of completed suicides (Mann & Currier, 2006). Both bipolar disorder and depression are associated with dramatic elevations in suicide rates. Studies suggest that the lifetime risk of completed suicide is about 15%–20% for people with bipolar disorder and about 10% for those who have grappled with depression (Sudak, 2009).

Etiology of Mood Disorders

PsykTrek 11b

Quite a bit is known about the etiology of mood disorders, although the puzzle hasn't been assembled completely. There appear to be a number of routes into these disorders, involving intricate interactions among psychological and biological factors.

GENETIC VULNERABILITY

PsykTrek 11b

The evidence strongly suggests that genetic factors influence the likelihood of developing major depression or bipolar disorder (Kelsoe, 2009; Lohoff & Berrettini, 2009). *Twin studies* have found a huge disparity between identical and fraternal twins in concordance rates for mood disorders. The concordance rate for identical twins is much higher (see **Figure 14.8**). This evidence suggests that heredity can create a *predisposition* to mood disorders. Environmental factors probably determine whether this predisposition is converted into an actual disorder. The influence of genetic factors appears to be stronger for bipolar disorder than for unipolar disorder (Kieseppa et al., 2004; Merikangas & Risch, 2003).

NEUROCHEMICAL AND NEUROANATOMICAL FACTORS

PsykTrek 11b

Heredity may influence susceptibility to mood disorders by creating a predisposition toward certain types of neurochemical abnormalities in the brain. Correlations have been found between mood disorders and abnormal levels of two neurotransmitters in the brain: norepinephrine and serotonin (Duman, Polan, & Schatzberg, 2008), although other neurotransmitter disturbances may also contribute (Dunlop, Garlow, & Nemeroff, 2009). The details remain elusive, but low levels of serotonin appear to be a crucial factor underlying most forms of depression (Johnson et al., 2009).

Studies have also found some interesting correlations between mood disorders and a variety of structural abnormalities in the brain (Flores et al., 2004). Perhaps the best-documented correlation is the association between depression and *reduced hippocampal volume* (Davidson, Pizzagalli, & Nitschke, 2009; Videbech, 2006). The *hippocampus,* which is known to play a major role in memory consolidation (see Chapter 7), tends to be about 8%–10% smaller in depressed subjects than in normal subjects (Videbech & Ravnkilde, 2004). A relatively new theory of the biological bases of depression may be able to account for this finding. The springboard for this theory is the discovery that the human brain continues to generate new neurons (neurogenesis) in adulthood, especially in the hippocampal formation (Gage, 2002) (see Chapter 3). Recent evidence suggests that depression occurs when major life stress causes neurochemical reactions that suppress this neurogenesis, resulting in reduced hippocampal volume (Duman et al., 2008; Jacobs, 2004). According to this view, the suppression of neurogenesis is the central cause of depression, and antidepressant drugs are successful because they promote neurogenesis

FIGURE 14.8

Twin studies of mood disorders.
The concordance rate for mood disorders in identical twins is much higher than that for fraternal twins, who share less genetic overlap. These results suggest that there is a genetic predisposition to mood disorders. (Data from Berrettini 2006, © Cengage Learning 2014)

(Duman & Monteggia, 2006). A great deal of additional research will be required to fully test this innovative new model of the biological bases of depressive disorders.

COGNITIVE FACTORS

PSYKTREK 11b

A variety of theories emphasize how cognitive factors contribute to depressive disorders (Christensen, Carney, & Segal, 2006). We will discuss Aaron Beck's (1976, 1987, 2008) influential cognitive theory of depression in Chapter 15, where his approach to therapy is described. In this section, we'll examine Martin Seligman's *learned helplessness model* of depression. Based largely on animal research, Seligman (1974) proposed that depression is caused by *learned helplessness*—passive "giving up" behavior produced by exposure to unavoidable aversive events (such as uncontrollable shock in the lab). He originally considered learned helplessness to be a product of conditioning but eventually revised his theory, giving it a cognitive slant. The reformulated theory of learned helplessness asserts that the roots of depression lie in how people explain the setbacks and other negative events that they experience (Abramson, Seligman, & Teasdale, 1978). According to Seligman (1990), people who exhibit a *pessimistic explanatory style* are especially vulnerable to depression. These people tend to attribute their setbacks to their personal flaws instead of to situational factors. Moreover, they tend to draw global, far-reaching conclusions about their personal inadequacies based on these setbacks.

In accord with this line of thinking, Susan Nolen-Hoeksema (1991, 2000) has found that depressed people who *ruminate* about their depression remain depressed longer than those who try to distract themselves. People who respond to depression with rumination repetitively focus their attention on their feelings of depression. They think constantly about how sad, lethargic, and unmotivated they are. Excessive rumination tends to foster and amplify episodes of depression by increasing negative thinking, impairing problem solving, and undermining social support (Nolen-Hoeksema, Wisco, & Lyubomirsky, 2008). As we noted earlier, Nolen-Hoeksema believes that women have a greater tendency to ruminate than men and that this disparity may be a major reason why depression is more prevalent in women.

In sum, cognitive models of depression maintain that negative thinking is what leads to depression in many people. The principal problem with cognitive theories is their difficulty in separating cause from effect (Rehm, Wagner, & Ivens-Tyndal, 2001). Does negative thinking cause depression? Or does depression cause negative thinking (see **Figure 14.9**)? A *clear* demonstration of a causal link between negative thinking and depression is not possible, because it would require manipulating people's explanatory style (which is not easy to change) in sufficient degree to produce full-fledged depressive disorders (which would not be ethical). However, research has provided impressive evidence consistent with a causal link between negative thinking and vulnerability to depression. Lauren Alloy and her colleagues (1999) assessed the explanatory style of a sample of first-year college students who were not depressed at the outset of the study. The students were characterized as being at high risk or low risk for depression based on whether they exhibited a negative cognitive style. The follow-up data over the next 2.5 years on students who had no prior history of depression showed dramatic differences between the two groups in vulnerability to depression. During this relatively brief period, a major depressive disorder emerged in 17% of the high-risk students in comparison to only 1% of the low-risk students. The high-risk subjects also displayed a much greater incidence of minor depressive episodes (39% versus 6%). These findings and other data from the study suggest that negative thinking makes a causal contribution to the development of depressive disorders.

INTERPERSONAL ROOTS

PSYKTREK 11b

Behavioral approaches to understanding depression emphasize how inadequate social skills put people on the road to depressive disorders (see **Figure 14.10** on the next page; Ingram, Scott, & Hamill, 2009). According to this notion, depression-prone people lack

Susan Nolen-Hoeksema

"By adolescence, girls appear to be more likely than boys to respond to stress and distress with rumination—focusing inward on feelings of distress and personal concerns rather than taking action to relieve their distress."

FIGURE 14.9

Interpreting the correlation between negative thinking and depression. Cognitive theories of depression assume that consistent patterns of negative thinking cause depression. Although these theories are highly plausible, depression could cause negative thoughts, or both could be caused by a third factor, such as neurochemical changes in the brain.

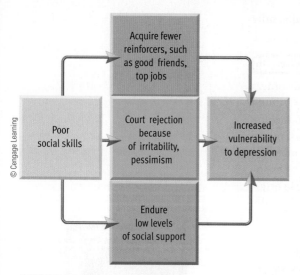

© Cengage Learning

FIGURE 14.10

Interpersonal factors in depression. Behavioral theories about the etiology of depression emphasize how inadequate social skills may contribute to the development of the disorder through several mechanisms, as diagrammed here.

the social finesse needed to acquire many important kinds of reinforcers, such as good friends, top jobs, and desirable spouses. This lack of reinforcers could understandably lead to negative emotions and depression. Consistent with this theory, researchers have found correlations between poor social skills and depression (Petty, Sachs-Ericsson, & Joiner, 2004). Evidence also suggests that depressed people unintentionally court rejection from others because they tend to be irritable, pessimistic, unpleasant companions (Joiner & Timmons, 2009). Another problem is that depressed people tend to have fewer sources of social support than nondepressed people. This situation is unfortunate in that low social support can increase vulnerability to depression (Lakey & Cronin, 2008). Research suggests that lack of social support may make a larger contribution to depression in women than in men (Kendler, Myers, & Prescott, 2005).

PRECIPITATING STRESS

PsykTrek 11b

Mood disorders sometimes appear mysteriously in people who are leading benign, nonstressful lives. For this reason, experts used to believe that stress has little influence on mood disorders. However, advances in the measurement of personal stress have altered this picture. The evidence available today suggests the existence of a moderately strong link between stress and the onset of mood disorders (Monroe, Slavich, & Georgiades, 2009). Stress also appears to affect how people with mood disorders respond to treatment and whether they experience a relapse of their disorder (Monroe & Hadjiyannakis, 2002).

Schizophrenic Disorders

PsykTrek SIM9

KEY LEARNING GOALS

14.9 Identify the general characteristics and subtypes of schizophrenia.

14.10 Explain how biological factors may contribute to the development of schizophrenia.

14.11 Summarize how family dynamics and stress may play a role in the etiology of schizophrenia.

Literally, *schizophrenia* means "split mind." However, when Eugen Bleuler coined the term in 1911 he was referring to the fragmentation of thought processes seen in the disorder—not to a "split personality." Unfortunately, writers in the popular media often assume that the split-mind notion, and thus schizophrenia, refers to the rare syndrome in which a person manifests two or more personalities. As you have already learned, this syndrome is actually called *multiple-personality disorder* or *dissociative identity disorder*. Schizophrenia is a much more common, and altogether different, type of disorder.

Schizophrenic disorders **encompass a class of disorders marked by delusions, hallucinations, disorganized speech, and deterioration of adaptive behavior.** Prevalence estimates suggest that about 1% of the population may suffer from schizophrenic disorders (Lauriello, Bustillo, & Keith, 2005). That may not sound like much, but it means that in the United States alone several million people may be troubled by schizophrenic disturbances. Moreover, schizophrenia is an extremely costly illness for society, because it is a severe, debilitating illness that tends to have an early onset and often requires lengthy hospital care (Samnaliev & Clark, 2008).

General Symptoms

PsykTrek 11c

There are a number of distinct schizophrenic syndromes. Yet, they share some general characteristics that we will examine before looking at the subtypes. Many of these characteristics are apparent in the following case history, adapted from Sheehan (1982).

Sylvia was first diagnosed as schizophrenic at age 15. She has been in and out of many types of psychiatric facilities since then. She has never been able to hold a job for any length of time. During severe flare-ups of her disorder, her personal hygiene deteriorates. She rarely washes, she wears clothes that neither fit nor match, she smears makeup on heavily but randomly, and she slops food all over herself. Sylvia occasionally hears voices talking to her. She tends to be argumentative, aggressive, and emotionally volatile. Over the years, she has been involved in innumerable fights with fellow patients, psychiatric staff members, and strangers. Her thoughts can be highly irrational, as is apparent from the following quote:

"Mick Jagger wants to marry me. If I have Mick Jagger, I don't have to covet Geraldo Rivera. Mick Jagger is St. Nicholas and the Maharishi is Santa Claus. I want to form a gospel rock group called the Thorn Oil, but Geraldo wants me to be the music critic on Eyewitness News, so what can I do? Got to listen to my boyfriend. Teddy Kennedy cured me of my ugliness. I'm pregnant with the son of God. They're eating the patients here. I'm Joan of Arc. I'm Florence Nightingale. The door between the ward and the porch is the dividing line between New York and California. Forget about Zip Codes. I need shock treatments. The body is run by electricity. My wiring is all faulty." (Adapted from Shee-han, 1982; quotation from pp. 104–105)

Sylvia's case clearly shows that schizophrenic thinking can be bizarre and that schizophrenia can be a severe and crippling disorder. Although no single symptom is inevitably present, the following symptoms are commonly seen in schizophrenia (Lewis, Escalona, & Keith, 2009; Liddle, 2009).

Delusions and Irrational Thought Cognitive deficits and disturbed thought processes are the central, defining feature of schizophrenic disorders (Barch, 2003; Heinrichs, 2005). Various kinds of delusions are common. *Delusions* **are false beliefs that are maintained even though they clearly are out of touch with reality.** For example, one patient's delusion that he was a tiger (with a deformed body) persisted for 15 years (Kulick, Pope, & Keck, 1990). More typically, affected persons believe that their private thoughts are being broadcast to other people, that thoughts are being injected into their mind against their will, or that their thoughts are being controlled by some external force (Maher, 2001). In *delusions of grandeur,* people maintain that they are famous or important. Sylvia expressed an endless array of grandiose delusions, such as thinking that Mick Jagger wanted to marry her, that she had dictated the hobbit stories to J. R. R. Tolkien, and that she was going to win the Nobel prize for medicine. In addition to delusions, the schizophrenic person's train of thought deteriorates. Thinking becomes chaotic rather than logical and linear. A "loosening of associations" occurs, as the person shifts topics in disjointed ways. The quotation from Sylvia illustrates this symptom dramatically. The entire quote involves a wild flight of ideas in which the thoughts mostly have no apparent connection to each other.

Deterioration of Adaptive Behavior Schizophrenia usually involves a noticeable deterioration in the quality of the person's routine functioning in work, social relations, and personal care. Friends will often make remarks such as "Hal just isn't himself anymore." This deterioration is readily apparent in Sylvia's inability to get along with others or to function in the work world. It's also apparent in her neglect of personal hygiene.

Distorted Perception A variety of perceptual distortions may occur with schizophrenia, the most common being auditory hallucinations, which are reported by about 75% of patients (Combs & Mueser, 2007). *Hallucinations* **are sensory perceptions that occur in the absence of a real, external stimulus or are gross distortions of perceptual input.** Schizophrenics commonly report that they hear voices of nonexistent or absent people talking to them. Sylvia, for instance, said she heard messages from former Beatle Paul McCartney. These voices often provide an insulting, running commentary on the person's behavior ("You're an idiot for shaking his hand"). They may be argumentative ("You don't need a bath"), and they may issue commands ("Prepare your home for visitors from outer space").

Reality Check

Misconception

Schizophrenia refers to the syndrome in which a person manifests two or more personalities.

Reality

Literally, *schizophrenia* means "split mind." However, when Eugen Bleuler coined the term in 1911, he was referring to the fragmentation of thought processes seen in the disorder—not to a "split personality." Unfortunately, writers in the popular media often erroneously equate the split-mind notion with split personality. As you have already learned, this syndrome is actually called *dissociative identity disorder* or *multiple-personality disorder.*

Disturbed Emotion Normal emotional tone can be disrupted in a variety of ways. Some victims show a flattening of emotions. In other words, they show little emotional responsiveness. Others show inappropriate emotional responses that don't jell with the situation or with what they are saying. People with schizophrenia may also become emotionally volatile. Because of this volatility, acts of aggression can be a problem with some schizophrenic patients (Serper, 2011; Wehring & Carpenter, 2011).

Subtypes and Course

PSYKTREK 11c

Four subtypes of schizophrenic disorders have traditionally been recognized. The major symptoms of each subtype are described below (Lewis et al., 2009; Minzenberg, Yoon, & Carter, 2008). However, it should be noted that one of the more radical proposals for DSM-5 is to discard these subtypes because two of them are rarely seen in clinical practice (catatonic and disorganized) and another (undifferentiated) isn't a subtype as much as a hodgepodge of "leftovers."

Paranoid Type As its name implies, *paranoid schizophrenia* **is dominated by delusions of persecution, along with delusions of grandeur.** In this common form of schizophrenia, people come to believe that they have many enemies who want to harass and oppress them. They may become suspicious of friends and relatives, or they may attribute the persecution to mysterious, unknown persons. They are convinced that they are being watched and manipulated. To make sense of this persecution, they often develop delusions of grandeur. They believe that they must be enormously important people, frequently seeing themselves as great inventors or as great religious or political leaders.

Catatonic Type *Catatonic schizophrenia* **is marked by striking motor disturbances, ranging from muscular rigidity to random motor activity.** Some patients go into an extreme form of withdrawal known as a catatonic stupor. They may remain virtually motionless and seem oblivious to the environment around them for long periods of time. Others go into a state of catatonic excitement. They become hyperactive and incoherent. Some alternate between these dramatic extremes. The catatonic subtype is not particularly common, and its prevalence seems to be declining.

Disorganized Type In *disorganized schizophrenia,* **a particularly severe deterioration of adaptive behavior is seen.** Prominent symptoms include emotional indifference, frequent incoherence, and virtually complete social withdrawal. Aimless babbling and giggling are common. Delusions often center on bodily functions ("My brain is melting out my ears").

Undifferentiated Type People who are clearly schizophrenic but who cannot be placed into any of the three previous categories are said to have *undifferentiated schizophrenia,* **which is marked by idiosyncratic mixtures of schizophrenic symptoms.** The undifferentiated subtype is fairly common.

Course and Outcome Schizophrenic disorders usually emerge during adolescence or early adulthood. About 75% of cases manifest by the age of 30 (Perkins, Miller-Anderson, & Lieberman, 2006). Those who develop schizophrenia usually have a long history of peculiar behavior and cognitive and social deficits, although most do not manifest a full-fledged psychological disorder during childhood (Walker et al., 2004). The emergence of schizophrenia may be sudden, but it is usually insidious and gradual. Once the disorder clearly emerges, its course is variable, but patients tend to fall into three broad groups. Some patients, presumably those with milder disorders, are treated successfully and enjoy a full recovery. Other patients experience a partial recovery and can return to independent living for a time. However, they experience regular relapses

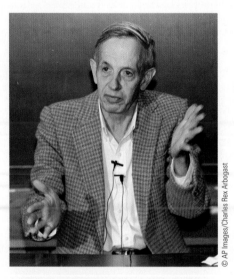

John Nash, the Nobel Prize–winning mathematician whose story was told in the film *A Beautiful Mind,* has struggled with paranoid schizophrenia since 1959.

© AP Images/Charles Rex Arbogast

over the remainder of their lives. Finally, a third group of patients endure chronic illness marked by relentless deterioration and extensive hospitalization. Estimates of the percentage of patients falling in each category vary. Overall, the preponderance of studies have suggested that only about 20% of schizophrenic patients enjoy a full recovery (Perkins et al., 2006; Robinson et al., 2004). However, to some extent, this low recovery rate may reflect the poor to mediocre quality of mental health care available for severe disorders in many countries. When comprehensive, well-coordinated, quality care is initiated promptly, recovery rates in the vicinity of 50% have been found (Hopper et al., 2007; Liberman & Kopelowicz, 2005). Although schizophrenia is often viewed as a disorder marked by relentless deterioration, it is clear that a good portion of patients experience a reasonable degree of recovery (Jablensky, 2009).

Etiology of Schizophrenia

You can probably identify, at least to some extent, with people who suffer from mood disorders and anxiety disorders. You can probably imagine events that could unfold that might leave you struggling with depression or grappling with anxiety. But what could possibly account for Sylvia's thinking that she was Joan of Arc or that she had dictated the hobbit novels to Tolkien? As mystifying as these delusions may seem, you'll see that the etiology of schizophrenic disorders is not all that different from the etiology of other psychological disorders. We'll begin our discussion by examining the matter of genetic vulnerability.

Concept Check **14.3**

Distinguishing Schizophrenic and Mood Disorders

Check your understanding of the nature of schizophrenic and mood disorders by making preliminary diagnoses for the cases described below. Read each case summary and write your tentative diagnosis in the space provided. The answers are in Appendix A.

1. Max hasn't slept in four days. He's determined to write the "great American novel" before his class reunion, which is a few months away. He expounds eloquently on his novel to anyone who will listen, talking at such a rapid pace that no one can get a word in edgewise. He feels like he's wired with energy and is supremely confident about the novel, even though he's only written 10 to 20 pages. Last week, he charged $5000 worth of new computer equipment, which is supposed to help him write his book.

   Preliminary diagnosis: _____

2. Eduardo maintains that he invented the atomic bomb, even though he was born after its invention. He says he invented it to punish homosexuals, Nazis, and short people. It's short people that he's really afraid of. He's sure that all the short people on TV are talking about him. He thinks that short people are conspiring to make him look like a Republican. Eduardo frequently gets in arguments with people and is emotionally volatile. His grooming is poor, but he says it's okay because he's the Secretary of State.

   Preliminary diagnosis: _____

3. Margaret has hardly gotten out of bed for weeks, although she's troubled by insomnia. She doesn't feel like eating and has absolutely no energy. She feels dejected, discouraged, spiritless, and apathetic. Friends stop by to try to cheer her up, but she tells them not to waste their time on "pond scum."

   Preliminary diagnosis: _____

© Supri Suharjoto/Shutterstock

Psychological Disorders **487**

GENETIC VULNERABILITY

PsykTrek 11c

Evidence is plentiful that hereditary factors play a role in the development of schizophrenic disorders (Glatt, 2008; Kirov & Owen, 2009). For instance, in twin studies, concordance rates average around 48% for identical twins, in comparison to about 17% for fraternal twins (Gottesman, 1991, 2001). Studies also indicate that a child born to two schizophrenic parents has about a 46% probability of developing a schizophrenic disorder (as compared to the probability in the general population of about 1%). These and other findings that show the genetic roots of schizophrenia are summarized in **Figure 14.11**. Overall, the picture is similar to that seen for mood disorders. Several converging lines of evidence indicate that some people inherit a *vulnerability* to schizophrenia (Cornblatt et al., 2009). Some theorists suspect that genetic factors may account for as much as 80% of the variability in susceptibility to schizophrenia (Pogue-Geile & Yokley, 2010).

NEUROCHEMICAL FACTORS

PsykTrek 11c

Like mood disorders, schizophrenic disorders appear to be accompanied by changes in the activity of one or more neurotransmitters in the brain (Patel, Pinals, & Breier, 2008). The *dopamine hypothesis* asserts that excess dopamine activity is the neurochemical basis for schizophrenia. This hypothesis makes sense because most of the drugs that are useful in the treatment of schizophrenia are known to dampen dopamine activity in the brain (Javitt & Laruelle, 2006). However, the evidence linking schizophrenia to high dopamine levels is riddled with inconsistencies, complexities, and interpretive problems (Bobo et al., 2008). In recent years, the dopamine hypothesis has become more nuanced and complex. Researchers believe that dysregulation occurs in dopamine circuits and that the nature of this dysregulation may vary in different regions of the brain (Howes & Kapur, 2009). Scientists are also investigating whether dysfunctions in neural circuits using glutamate play a role in schizophrenia (Downar & Kapur, 2008).

Recent research has suggested that marijuana use during adolescence may help precipitate schizophrenia in young people who have a genetic vulnerability to the disorder (Degenhardt & Hall, 2006; McGrath et al., 2010). This unexpected finding has generated considerable debate about whether and how cannabis might contribute to the emergence of schizophrenia (Castle, 2008; DeLisi, 2008). Some critics have suggested that it could be that schizophrenia leads to cannabis use rather than vice versa. In other words, emerging psychotic symptoms may prompt young people to turn to marijuana to self-medicate. However, a carefully controlled long-term study in Germany found no evidence in support of the self-medication explanation (Kuepper et al., 2011). After controlling for age, sex, social class, use of other drugs, occurrence of childhood trauma, and the presence of other disorders, the study found that marijuana use roughly doubled the risk of psychotic disturbance. The current thinking is that the key chemical ingredient in marijuana (THC)

FIGURE 14.11

Genetic vulnerability to schizophrenic disorders. Relatives of schizophrenic patients have an elevated risk for schizophrenia. This risk is greater among closer relatives. Although environment also plays a role in the etiology of schizophrenia, the concordance rates shown here suggest that there is a genetic vulnerability to the disorder. These concordance estimates are based on pooled data from forty studies conducted between 1920 and 1987. (Data adapted from Gottesman, 1991)

© Cengage Learning

may increase neurotransmitter activity in dopamine circuits in certain areas of the brain (Di Forti et al., 2007; Kuepper et al., 2010). The data on this issue are still preliminary. More research will be needed to fully understand the association between marijuana use and schizophrenia.

STRUCTURAL ABNORMALITIES IN THE BRAIN

PsykTrek 11c

For decades, studies have suggested that individuals with schizophrenia exhibit a variety of deficits in attention, perception, and information processing (Belger & Barch, 2009; Harvey, 2010). These cognitive deficits suggested that schizophrenic disorders may be caused by neurological defects (Perry & Braff, 1994). Until recent decades, this theory was based more on speculation than on actual research. However, advances in brain imaging technology have yielded mountains of intriguing data since the mid-1980s. The most reliable finding is that CT scans and MRI scans (see Chapter 3) suggest an association between enlarged brain ventricles (the hollow, fluid-filled cavities in the brain depicted in **Figure 14.12**) and schizophrenic disturbance (Shenton & Kubicki, 2009). Enlarged ventricles are assumed to reflect the degeneration of nearby brain tissue. The significance of enlarged ventricles is hotly debated, however. This structural deterioration could be a *consequence* of schizophrenia, or it could be a contributing *cause* of the illness.

Brain-imaging studies have also uncovered other structural abnormalities including reductions in both gray matter and white matter in specific brain regions (Bobo et al., 2008; Karlsgodt, Sun, & Cannon, 2010). These reductions seem to reflect losses of synaptic density and of myelinization (see Chapter 3). These findings suggest that schizophrenia is caused by disruptions in the brain's neural connectivity, which impairs the normal communication among neural circuits (Karlsgodt et al., 2010).

THE NEURODEVELOPMENTAL HYPOTHESIS

PsykTrek 11c

The *neurodevelopmental hypothesis* of schizophrenia asserts that schizophrenia is caused in part by various disruptions in the normal maturational processes of the brain before or at birth (Fatemi & Folsom, 2009). According to this hypothesis, insults to the brain during sensitive phases of prenatal development or during birth can cause subtle neurological damage that elevates individuals' vulnerability to schizophrenia years later in adolescence and early adulthood (see **Figure 14.13**). What are the sources of these early insults to the brain? Thus far, research has focused on viral infections or malnutrition during prenatal development and on obstetrical complications during the birth process.

The evidence on viral infections has been building since Sarnoff Mednick and his colleagues (1988) discovered an elevated incidence of schizophrenia among individuals

Right ventricle
Left ventricle
Third ventricle
Fourth ventricle

photo: © RimiDream/Shutterstock; art: © Cengage Learning

FIGURE 14.12

Schizophrenia and the ventricles of the brain. Cerebrospinal fluid (CSF) circulates around the brain and spinal cord. The hollow cavities in the brain filled with CSF are called ventricles. The four ventricles in the human brain are depicted here. Studies with CT scans and MRI scans suggest an association between enlarged ventricles in the brain and the occurrence of schizophrenic disturbance.

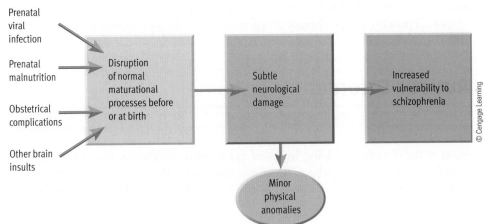

Prenatal viral infection
Prenatal malnutrition
Obstetrical complications
Other brain insults

Disruption of normal maturational processes before or at birth

Subtle neurological damage

Increased vulnerability to schizophrenia

Minor physical anomalies

© Cengage Learning

FIGURE 14.13

The neurodevelopmental hypothesis of schizophrenia. Recent findings have suggested that insults to the brain sustained during prenatal development or at birth may disrupt crucial maturational processes in the brain, resulting in subtle neurological damage that gradually becomes apparent as youngsters develop. This neurological damage is believed to increase both vulnerability to schizophrenia and the incidence of minor physical anomalies (slight anatomical defects of the head, face, hands, and feet).

who had been in their second trimester of prenatal development during a 1957 influenza epidemic in Finland. Quite a number of subsequent studies have found a link between exposure to influenza and other infections during prenatal development and increased prevalence of schizophrenia (Brown & Derkits, 2010). Another study, which investigated the possible impact of prenatal malnutrition, found an elevated incidence of schizophrenia in a group of people who were prenatally exposed to a severe famine in 1944–1945 resulting from a Nazi blockade of food deliveries in the Netherlands during World War II (Susser et al., 1996). Other research has shown that schizophrenic patients are more likely than control subjects to have experienced obstetrical complications when they were born (Kelly et al., 2004; Murray & Bramon, 2005). Finally, research suggests that minor physical anomalies (slight anatomical defects of the head, hands, feet, and face) that would be consistent with prenatal neurological damage are more common among people with schizophrenia than among others (McNeil, Canton-Graae, & Ismail, 2000; Schiffman et al., 2002).

Collectively, these diverse studies argue for a relationship between early neurological trauma and a predisposition to schizophrenia (King, St-Hilaire, & Heidkamp, 2010). Much remains to be learned about the neurodevelopmental bases of schizophrenia, but this relatively new line of inquiry should increase our understanding of the etiology of schizophrenic disorders.

EXPRESSED EMOTION

PsykTrek 11c

Research on expressed emotion has primarily focused on how this element of family dynamics influences the *course* of schizophrenic illness, after the onset of the disorder (Leff & Vaughn, 1985). *Expressed emotion* is the degree to which a relative of a schizophrenic patient displays highly critical or emotionally overinvolved attitudes toward the patient. Audiotaped interviews of relatives' communication are carefully evaluated for critical comments, resentment toward the patient, and excessive emotional involvement (overprotective, overconcerned attitudes) (Hooley, 2004).

Studies show that a family's expressed emotion is a good predictor of the course of a schizophrenic patient's illness (Hooley, 2007). After release from a hospital, schizophrenic patients who return to a family high in expressed emotion show relapse rates three times that of patients who return to a family low in expressed emotion (Hooley, 2009) (see **Figure 14.14**). Part of the problem for patients returning to homes high in expressed emotion is that their families probably are sources of stress rather than of social support (Cutting & Docherty, 2000).

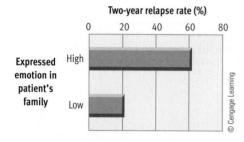

Two-year relapse rate (%)

Expressed emotion in patient's family — High / Low

© Cengage Learning

FIGURE 14.14

Expressed emotion and relapse rates in schizophrenia. Schizophrenic patients who return to a home that is high in expressed emotion have higher relapse rates than those who return to a home low in expressed emotion. Thus, unhealthy family dynamics can influence the course of schizophrenia. (Data adapted from Leff & Vaughn, 1981)

PRECIPITATING STRESS

PsykTrek 11c

Most theories of schizophrenia assume that stress plays a key role in triggering schizophrenic disorders (Walker & Tessner, 2008). According to this notion, various biological and psychological factors influence individuals' *vulnerability* to schizophrenia. High stress may then serve to precipitate a schizophrenic disorder in someone who is vulnerable (McGlashan & Hoffman, 2000). Research indicates that high stress can also trigger relapses in patients who have made progress toward recovery (Walker, Mittal, & Tessner, 2008).

KEY LEARNING GOALS

14.12 Describe the symptoms, prevalence, and etiology of autistic disorder.

Autistic Disorder

Many of the disorders we have discussed can be seen in children. For example, phobic disorders, obsessive-compulsive disorders, and depression are routinely seen among children, as well as adults. However, DSM-IV includes a special category for *disorders usually first diagnosed in infancy, childhood, or adolescence.* This category includes intellectual disability (mental retardation), learning disorders, attention-deficit disorders, and pervasive developmental disorders, such as autism. In this section we'll discuss autism, a diagnosis that has garnered increased attention in recent years. *Autistic disorder,* or *autism,* **is characterized by profound impairment of social interaction and communication and severely restricted interests and activities, apparent by the age of 3.** In DSM-5 it appears that autism will be lumped with *Asperger's disorder* and other milder forms of the disease into a single diagnostic category called *autism spectrum disorder.*

Symptoms and Prevalence

The central feature of autistic disorder is the child's lack of interest in other people. Children with autism act as though people in their environment are no different than nearby inanimate objects, such as toys, pillows, or chairs. They don't tend to make eye contact with others or need physical contact with their caretakers. They make no effort to connect with people and fail to bond with their parents or to develop normal peer relationships. Verbal communication can be greatly impaired, as about one-third of autistic children fail to develop speech (Wetherby & Prizant, 2005). Among those who do develop speech, their ability to initiate and sustain a conversation is limited, and their use of language tends to be marked by peculiarities, such as *echolalia,* which involves rote repetition of others' words. Autistic children's interests are restricted in that they tend to become preoccupied with objects or repetitive body movements (spinning, body rocking, playing with their hands, and so forth). They can also be extremely inflexible, in that minor changes in their environment can trigger rages and tantrums. Some autistic children exhibit self-injurious behavior, such as banging their heads, pulling their hair, or hitting themselves. About one-half of autistic children exhibit subnormal IQ scores (Volkmar et al., 2009).

Parents of autistic children typically become concerned about their child's development by about 15–18 months of age and usually seek professional consultation by about 24 months. The diagnosis of autism is almost always made before affected children reach age 3. More often than not, autism turns out to be a lifelong affliction requiring extensive family and institutional support throughout adulthood. However, with early and effective intervention, around 15%–20% of autistic individuals are able to live independently in adulthood, and another 20%–30% approach this level of functioning (Volkmar et al., 2009).

Until relatively recently, the prevalence of autism was thought to be well under 1% (Newsschaffer, 2007; Shattuck, 2006). Since the mid-1990s, however, there has been a dramatic (roughly fourfold) increase in the diagnosis of autism, with prevalence estimates approaching 1% (Brugha et al., 2011; Weintraub, 2011). Most experts believe that this surge in autism is largely due to greater awareness of the syndrome and the use of broader diagnostic criteria (Wing & Potter, 2009). Contemporary prevalence estimates usually include related syndromes, such as Asperger's disorder, that are milder forms of the disease that used to go uncounted. Although these explanations make sense, scientists have not ruled out the possibility that there has been a genuine increase in the prevalence of autism (Weintraub, 2011). Males account for about 80% of autism diagnoses,

Children with autism often fail to make eye contact with others and tend to find social attention unpleasant.

Three Categories of Psychological Disorders

AXIS I CATEGORY	SUBTYPES	PREVALENCE/ WELL-KNOWN VICTIM

ANXIETY DISORDERS

Edvard Munch's *The Scream* expresses overwhelming feelings of anxiety.

Generalized anxiety disorder: Chronic, high level of anxiety not tied to any specific threat

Phobic disorder: Persistent, irrational fear of object or situation that presents no real danger

Panic disorder: Recurrent attacks of overwhelming anxiety that occur suddenly and unexpectedly

Obsessive-compulsive disorder: Persistent, uncontrollable intrusions of unwanted thoughts and urges to engage in senseless rituals

Posttraumatic stress disorder: Enduring psychological disturbance attributable to the experience of a major traumatic event

0 2 4 6 8 10 12 14 16 18 20

19%

Prevalence

Comedian Howie Mandel suffers from obsessive-compulsive disorder.

MOOD DISORDERS

Major depressive disorder: Two or more major depressive episodes marked by feelings of sadness, worthlessness, despair

Bipolar disorder: One or more manic episodes marked by inflated self-esteem, grandiosity, and elevated mood and energy, usually accompanied by major depressive episodes

Vincent Van Gogh's *Portrait of Dr. Gachet* captures the profound dejection experienced in depressive disorders.

0 2 4 6 8 10 12 14 16 18 20

15%

Prevalence

Actress Gwyneth Paltrow has suffered from depression.

SCHIZOPHRENIC DISORDERS

The perceptual distortions seen in schizophrenia probably contributed to the bizarre imagery apparent in this portrait of a cat painted by Louis Wain.

Paranoid schizophrenia: Delusions of persecution and delusions of grandeur; frequent auditory hallucinations

Catatonic schizophrenia: Motor disturbances ranging from immobility to excessive, purposeless activity

Disorganized schizophrenia: Flat or inappropriate emotions; disorganized speech and adaptive behavior

Undifferentiated schizophrenia: Idiosyncratic mixtures of schizophrenic symptoms that cannot be placed into above three categories

0 2 4 6 8 10 12 14 16 18 20

1%

Prevalence

John Nash, the Nobel Prize-winning mathematician whose story was told in the film *A Beautiful Mind*, has struggled with schizophrenia.

ETIOLOGY: BIOLOGICAL FACTORS

Genetic vulnerability: Twin studies and other evidence suggest a mild genetic predisposition to anxiety disorders.

Concordance rate (%)
0 10 20 30 40 50 60 70

Identical twins
Fraternal twins

Neurochemical bases: Disturbances in neural circuits releasing GABA may contribute to some disorders; abnormalities at serotonin synapses have been implicated in obsessive-compulsive disorders.

Genetic vulnerability: Twin studies and other evidence suggest a genetic predisposition to mood disorders.

Concordance rate (%)
0 10 20 30 40 50 60 70

Identical twins
Fraternal twins

Suppressed neurogenesis: Disruption of neurogenesis may lead to reduced volume in the hippocampus and to depression.

Neurochemical bases: Disturbances in neural circuits releasing norepinephrine may contribute to some mood disorders; abnormalities at serotonin synapses have also been implicated as a factor in depression.

Genetic vulnerability: Twin studies and other evidence suggest a genetic predisposition to schizophrenic disorders.

Concordance rate (%)
0 10 20 30 40 50 60 70

Identical twins
Fraternal twins

Neurochemical bases: Overactivity in neural circuits releasing dopamine is associated with schizophrenia; but abnormalities in other neurotransmitter systems may also contribute.

Structural abnormalities in brain: Enlarged brain ventricles are associated with schizophrenia, but they may be an effect rather than a cause of the disorder.

Data from Berrettini 2006

ETIOLOGY: PSYCHOLOGICAL FACTORS

Learning: Many anxiety responses may be acquired through classical conditioning or observational learning; phobic responses may be maintained by operant reinforcement.

CS Snow

US Buried in avalanche

CR Fear UR

Stress: High stress may help to precipitate the onset of anxiety disorders.

Anxious subjects
Nonanxious subjects

30 35 40 45 50 55 60
Threatening interpretations endorsed (%)

Cognition: People who misinterpret harmless situations as threatening and who focus excessive attention on perceived threats are more vulnerable to anxiety disorders.

Interpersonal roots: Behavioral theories emphasize how inadequate social skills can result in a paucity of reinforcers and other effects that make people vulnerable to depression.

Acquire fewer reinforcers, such as good friends, top jobs

Poor social skills

Court rejection because of irritability, pessimism

Endure low levels of social support

Increased vulnerability to depression

Negative thinking → Depression

Stress: High stress can act as precipitating factor that triggers depression or bipolar disorder.

Cognition: Negative thinking can contribute to the development of depression; rumination may extend and amplify depression.

Expressed emotion: A family's expressed emotion is a good predictor of the course of a schizophrenic patient's illness.

Stress: High stress can precipitate schizophrenic disorder in people who are vulnerable to schizophrenia.

Two-year relapse rate (%)
20 40 60 80

Expressed emotion in patient's family
High
Low

Disruption of normal maturational processes before or at birth → Subtle neurological damage → Increased vulnerability to schizophrenia

The neurodevelopmental hypothesis: Insults to the brain sustained during prenatal development or at birth may disrupt maturational processes in the brain resulting in elevated vulnerability to schizophrenia.

although curiously, females tend to exhibit more severe impairments (Ursano et al., 2008).

Etiology of Autism

Autism was originally blamed on cold, aloof parenting (Bettelheim, 1967), but that view was eventually discredited by research (Bhasin & Schendel, 2007). Given its appearance so early in life, most theorists today view autism as a disorder that originates in biological dysfunctions. Consistent with that viewpoint, twin studies and family studies have demonstrated that genetic factors make a major contribution to autistic disorders (McPartland et al., 2008). Many theorists believe that autism must be attributable to some sort of brain abnormality, but there has been relatively little progress in pinpointing the nature of this abnormality. Some studies suggest that autism may be due to damage to the *amygdala*, a brain structure that is intimately involved in the processing of fear responses (see Chapters 3 and 9), but the evidence is mixed (Schumann & Amaral, 2006; Volkmar et al., 2009).

One hypothesis that has garnered a great deal of publicity is the idea that autism may be caused by the mercury that is used as a preservative in some childhood vaccines (Kirby, 2005). However, research has failed to find an association between vaccinations and the development of autism (Jick & Kaye, 2004; Madsen et al., 2002; Paul, 2009; Wing & Potter, 2009). Widespread belief in the apparently spurious relationship between autism and vaccinations may simply be due to the fact that children get scheduled vaccinations around the same age (12–15 months) that parents first start to realize that their children are not developing normally (Doja & Roberts, 2006). The popularity of the vaccination hypothesis may also be a result of the explanatory void that it fills, as science has yet to achieve a sound understanding of the causes of autism.

KEY LEARNING GOALS

14.13 Identify the four unifying themes highlighted in this chapter.

 Multifactorial Causation

 Heredity and Environment

 Sociohistorical Context

 Cultural Heritage

Reflecting on the Chapter's Themes

Our examination of abnormal behavior and its roots has highlighted four of our organizing themes: multifactorial causation, the interplay of heredity and environment, the sociohistorical context in which psychology evolves, and the influence of culture on psychological phenomena.

We can safely assert that every disorder described in this chapter has multiple causes. The development of mental disorders involves an interplay among a variety of psychological, biological, and social factors. We also saw that most psychological disorders depend on an interaction of genetics and experience. This interaction shows up most clearly in the *stress-vulnerability models* for mood disorders and schizophrenic disorders. *Vulnerability* to these disorders seems to depend primarily on heredity, whereas *stress* is largely a function of the environment. According to stress-vulnerability theories, disorders emerge when high vulnerability intersects with high stress. Thus, the impact of heredity depends on the environment, and the effect of environment depends on heredity.

This chapter also demonstrated that psychology evolves in a sociohistorical context. We saw that modern conceptions of normality and abnormality are largely shaped by empirical research, but social trends, prevailing values, and political realities also play a role. Finally, our discussion of psychological disorders showed once again that psychological phenomena are shaped to some degree by cultural parameters, as cultural norms influence what is regarded as abnormal. Indeed, the influence of culture will be apparent in our upcoming Personal Application on eating disorders. These disorders are largely a creation of modern, affluent, Western culture.

Understanding Eating Disorders

KEY LEARNING GOALS

14.14 Describe the subtypes, history, and prevalence of eating disorders.

14.15 Outline how genetic factors, personality, culture, family dynamics, and disturbed thinking contribute to eating disorders.

Answer the following "true" or "false."

____ **1** Although they have only attracted attention in recent years, eating disorders have a long history and have always been fairly common.

____ **2** People with anorexia nervosa are much more likely to recognize that their eating behavior is pathological than people suffering from bulimia nervosa.

____ **3** The prevalence of eating disorders is twice as high in women as it is in men.

____ **4** The binge-and-purge syndrome seen in bulimia nervosa is not common in anorexia nervosa.

All of the above statements are false, as you will see in this Application. The psychological disorders that we discussed in the main body of the chapter have largely been recognized for centuries and are generally found in one form or another in all cultures and societies. Eating disorders present a sharp contrast to this picture. They have only been recognized in recent decades and have largely been confined to affluent, Westernized cultures (Russell, 1995; Szmukler & Patton, 1995). In spite of these fascinating differences, eating disorders have much in common with traditional forms of pathology.

Description

Most people don't seem to take eating disorders as seriously as other types of psychological disorders. Yet, you will see that they are dangerous and debilitating (Thompson, Roehrig, & Kinder, 2007). No psychological disorder is associated with a greater elevation in mortality

(Striegel-Moore & Bulik, 2007). *Eating disorders are severe disturbances in eating behavior characterized by preoccupation with weight concerns and unhealthy efforts to control weight.* The majority of cases consist of two sometimes overlapping syndromes: *anorexia nervosa* and *bulimia nervosa. Anorexia nervosa involves intense fear of gaining weight, disturbed body image, refusal to maintain normal weight, and use of dangerous measures to lose weight.* Two subtypes have been observed (Herzog & Delinsky, 2001). In *restricting type anorexia nervosa,* people drastically reduce their intake of food, sometimes literally starving themselves. In *binge-eating/purging type anorexia nervosa,* individuals attempt to lose weight by forcing themselves to vomit after meals, by misusing laxatives and diuretics, and by engaging in excessive exercise.

Eating disorders have become distressingly common among young women in Western cultures. No matter how frail they become, people suffering from anorexia insist that they are too fat.

© Angela Hampton Picture Library/Alamy

Both types suffer from disturbed body image. No matter how frail they become, they insist that they are too fat. Their morbid fear of obesity means that they are never satisfied with their weight. If they gain a pound or two, they panic. The only thing that makes them happy is to lose more weight. The common result is a relentless decline in body weight. People entering treatment for anorexia nervosa are typically 25%–30% below their normal weight (Hsu, 1990). Because of their disturbed body image, individuals suffering from anorexia generally do *not* appreciate the maladaptive quality of their behavior. Hence, they rarely seek treatment on their own. They are typically coaxed or coerced into treatment by friends or family members who are alarmed by their appearance.

Anorexia nervosa eventually leads to a cascade of medical problems. These problems may include *amenorrhea* (a loss of menstrual cycles in women), gastrointestinal problems, low blood pressure, *osteoporosis* (a loss of bone density), and metabolic disturbances that can lead to cardiac arrest or circulatory collapse (Halmi, 2008; Russell, 2009). Anorexia is a serious illness that leads to death in 5%–10% of patients (Steinhausen, 2002).

Bulimia nervosa involves habitually engaging in out-of-control overeating followed by unhealthy compensatory efforts, such as self-induced vomiting, fasting, abuse of laxatives and diuretics, and excessive exercise. The eating binges are usually carried out in secret and are followed by intense guilt and concern about gaining weight. These feelings motivate ill-advised strategies to undo the effects of the overeating. However, vomiting prevents the absorption of only about half of recently consumed food, and laxatives and diuretics have negligible impact on caloric intake. So, individuals suffering from bulimia nervosa typically maintain a reasonably normal weight (Fairburn, Cooper, & Murphy, 2009). Medical problems associated with bulimia nervosa include cardiac arrythmias, dental problems, metabolic deficiencies, and gastrointestinal problems (Halmi, 2002, 2008).

Obviously, bulimia nervosa shares many features with anorexia nervosa, such as a morbid fear of becoming obese, preoccupation with food, and rigid, maladaptive approaches to controlling weight that are grounded in naive all-or-none thinking. However, the syndromes also differ in crucial ways. First and foremost, bulimia is a much less life-threatening condition. Second, although their appearance is usually more "normal" than that seen with anorexia, people with bulimia are much more likely to recognize that their eating behavior is pathological and are more likely to cooperate with treatment (Guarda et al., 2007). Nonetheless, like anorexia, bulimia is associated with elevated mortality rates (Crow et al., 2009).

History and Prevalence

Historians have been able to track down descriptions of anorexia nervosa that date back centuries. Thus, the disorder is *not* entirely new. However, anorexia nervosa did not become a common affliction until the middle of the 20th century (Vandereycken, 2002). Although binging and purging have a long history in some cultures, they were not part of pathological efforts to control weight. Bulimia nervosa appears to be an entirely new syndrome that emerged gradually in the middle of the 20th century and was first recognized in the 1970s (Steiger & Bruce, 2009).

Both disorders are a product of modern, affluent Western culture, in which food is generally plentiful and the desirability of being thin is widely endorsed. Until recently, these disorders were not seen outside of Western cultures (Hoek, 2002). However, advances in communication have exported Western culture to far-flung corners of the globe. Hence, eating disorders have started showing up in many non-Western societies, especially affluent Asian countries (Becker & Fay, 2006; Lee & Katzman, 2002).

There is a huge gender gap in the likelihood of developing eating disorders. About 90%–95% of individuals with anorexia nervosa and bulimia ner-

vosa are female (Thompson & Kinder, 2003). This staggering discrepancy appears to be a result of cultural pressures rather than biological factors (Smolak & Murnen, 2001). Western standards of attractiveness emphasize slenderness more for females than for males, and women generally experience greater pressure to be physically attractive than men do (Strahan et al., 2008). Eating disorders mostly afflict *young* women. The typical age of onset for anorexia is 14 to 18; for bulimia it is 15 to 21 (see **Figure 14.15**).

How common are eating disorders in Western societies? Studies of young women suggest that about 1% develop anorexia nervosa and about 2%–3% develop bulimia nervosa (Anderson & Yager, 2005). However, prevalence rates appear to be trending higher in more recent studies (Thompson et al., 2007). In some respects, these figures may only scratch the surface of the problem. Evidence suggests that as many as 20% of female college students are struggling with transient bulimic symptoms (Anderson & Yager, 2005). And community surveys suggest that there may be more undiagnosed eating disorders among men than generally appreciated (Hudson et al., 2007).

Etiology of Eating Disorders

Like other types of psychological disorders, eating disorders are caused by multiple determinants that work interactively. Let's take a brief look at some of the factors that contribute to the development of anorexia nervosa and bulimia nervosa.

GENETIC VULNERABILITY

The evidence is not nearly as strong or complete as it is for many other types of psychopathology (such as anxiety, mood, and schizophrenic disorders), but some people may inherit a genetic vulnerability to eating disorders (Thornton, Mazzeo, & Bulik, 2011). Studies show that relatives of patients with eating disorders have elevated rates of anorexia nervosa and bulimia nervosa (Bulik, 2004). And twin studies suggest that a genetic predisposition may be at work (Steiger, Bruce, & Israel, 2003).

PERSONALITY FACTORS

Certain personality traits may increase vulnerability to eating disorders. There are innumerable exceptions, but victims of anorexia nervosa tend to be obsessive, rigid, and emotionally restrained, where-

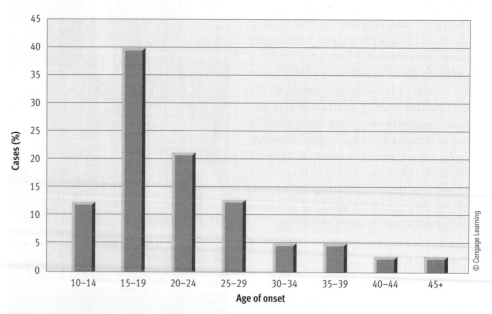

FIGURE 14.15

Age of onset for anorexia nervosa. Eating disorders mostly emerge during adolescence, as these data for anorexia nervosa show. This graph shows how age of onset was distributed in a sample of 166 female patients from Minnesota. As you can see, over half the patients experienced the onset of their illness before the age of 20, with vulnerability clearly peaking between the ages of 15 and 19. (Based on data from Lucas et al., 1991) as victims of bulimia nervosa tend to be impulsive, overly sensitive, and low in self-esteem (Anderluh, Tchauturia, & Rube-Hesketh, 2003; Wonderlich, 2002). Recent research also suggests that perfectionism is a risk factor for anorexia (Steiger & Bruce, 2009).

CULTURAL VALUES

The contribution of cultural values to the increased prevalence of eating disorders can hardly be overestimated (Anderson-Fye & Becker, 2004; Striegel-Moore & Bulik, 2007). In Western society, young women are socialized to believe that they must be attractive. To be attractive they think they must be as thin as the actresses and fashion models that dominate the media (Levine & Harrison, 2004). Thanks to this cultural milieu, many young women are dissatisfied with their weight because the societal ideals pro-moted by the media are unattainable for most of them (Thompson & Stice, 2001). Unfortunately, in a small portion of these women, the pressure to be thin, in combination with genetic vulnerability, family pathology, and other factors, leads to unhealthy efforts to control weight.

THE ROLE OF THE FAMILY

Quite a number of theorists stress how family dynamics can contribute to the development of anorexia and bulimia in young women (Haworth-Hoeppner, 2000). The principal issue appears to be that some mothers contribute to eating disorders simply by endorsing society's message that "you can never be too thin" and by modeling unhealthy dieting behaviors of their own (Francis & Birch, 2005). In conjunction with media pressures, this role-modeling leads many daughters to internalize the idea that the thinner you are, the more attractive you are.

COGNITIVE FACTORS

Many theorists emphasize the role of disturbed thinking in the etiology of eating disorders (Williamson et al., 2001). For example, anorexic patients' typical belief that they are fat when they are really wasting away is a dramatic illustration of how thinking goes awry. Patients with eating disorders display rigid, all-or-none thinking and many maladaptive beliefs. Such thoughts may include "I must be thin to be accepted," "If I am not in complete control, I will lose all control," "If I gain one pound, I'll go on to gain enormous weight." Additional research is needed to determine whether distorted thinking is a *cause* or merely a *symptom* of eating disorders.

Working with Probabilities in Thinking About Mental Illness

As you read about the various types of psychological disorders, did you think to yourself that you or someone you know was being described? On the one hand, there is no reason to be alarmed. The tendency to see yourself and your friends in descriptions of pathology is a common response. It is sometimes called the *medical students' syndrome* because beginning medical students often erroneously believe that they or their friends have whatever diseases they are currently learning about. On the other hand, realistically speaking, it *is* quite likely that you know *many* people with psychological disorders. Recent data on the prevalence of psychological disorders—which are summarized in **Figure 14.16**—suggest that the likelihood of anyone having at least one DSM disorder at some point during his or her life is about 44%.

This estimate strikes most people as surprisingly high. Why is this so? One reason is that when people think about psychological disorders they tend to think of severe disorders, such as bipolar disorder or schizophrenia, which are relatively infrequent, rather than "ordinary" disturbances, such as anxiety and depressive disorders, which are much more common. When it comes to mental illness, people tend to think of patients in straightjackets or of obviously psychotic homeless people who do not reflect the broad and diverse population of people who suffer from psychological disorders. In other words, their *prototypes* or "best examples" of mental illness consist of severe disorders that are infrequent. Hence, they underestimate the prevalence of mental disorders. This distortion illustrates the influence of the *representative-*

ness heuristic, which is basing the estimated probability of an event on how similar it is to the typical prototype of that event (see Chapter 8).

Do you still find it hard to believe that the overall prevalence of psychological disorders is about 44%? Another reason this number seems surprisingly high is that many people do not understand that the probability of having *at least one* disorder is much higher than the probability of having the most prevalent disorder by itself. For example, the probability of having a substance use disorder, the single most common type of disorder, is approximately 24%, but the probability of having a substance use disorder *or* an anxiety disorder *or* a mood disorder *or* a schizophrenic disorder jumps to 44%. These "or" relationships represent *cumulative probabilities.*

What about "and" relationships—that is, relationships in which we want to know the probability of someone having condition A *and* condition B? For exam-

ple, given the lifetime prevalence estimates (from **Figure 14.16**) for each category of disorder, which are shown in the parentheses, what is the probability of someone having a substance use disorder (24% prevalence) *and* an anxiety disorder (19%) *and* a mood disorder (15%) *and* a schizophrenic disorder (1%) during his or her lifetime? Such "and" relationships represent *conjunctive probabilities.* Stop and think: What must be true about the probability of having all four types of disorders? Will this probability be less than 24%, between 24% and 44%, or over 44%? You may be surprised to learn that this figure is under 1%. You can't have all four disorders unless you have the least frequent disorder (schizophrenia), which has a prevalence of 1%, so the answer *must* be 1% or less. Moreover, of all of the people with schizophrenia, only a tiny subset of them are likely to have all three of the other disorders, so the answer is surely well under 1% (see **Figure 14.17**). If this type of question strikes you as con-

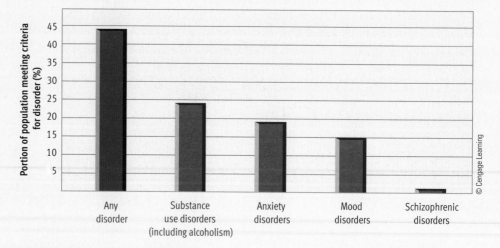

FIGURE 14.16

Lifetime prevalence of psychological disorders. The estimated percentages of people who have, at any time in their life, suffered from one of four types of psychological disorders or from a disorder of any kind (left blue bar) are shown here. Prevalence estimates vary somewhat from one study to the next, depending on the exact methods used in sampling and assessment. The estimates shown here are based on pooling data from Wave 1 and 2 of the Epidemiological Catchment Area studies and the National Comorbidity Study, as summarized by Regier and Burke (2000) and Dew, Bromet, and Switzer (2000). These studies collectively evaluated over 28,000 subjects.

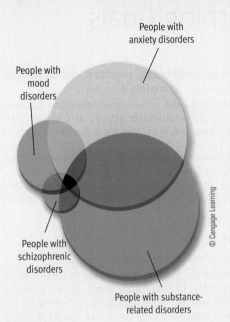

FIGURE 14.17
Conjunctive probabilities. The probability of someone having all four disorders depicted here cannot be greater than the probability of the least common condition by itself, which is 1% for schizophrenia. The intersection of all four disorders (shown in black) has to be a subset of schizophrenic disorders and has to be well under 1%. Efforts to think about probabilities can sometimes be facilitated by creating diagrams that show the relationships and overlap among various events.

People with anxiety disorders

People with mood disorders

People with schizophrenic disorders

People with substance-related disorders

trived, think again. Epidemiologists have devoted an enormous amount of research to the estimation of *comorbidity*—the coexistence of two or more disorders—because it can greatly complicate treatment issues.

These are two examples of using statistical probabilities as a critical thinking tool. Let's apply this type of thinking to another problem dealing with physical health. Here is a problem used in a study by Tversky and Kahneman (1983, p. 308) that many physicians got wrong:

A health survey was conducted in a sample of adult males in British Columbia, of all ages and occupations. Please give your best estimate of the following values:

What percentage of the men surveyed have had one or more heart attacks? _____

What percentage of the men surveyed both are over 55 years old and have had one or more heart attacks? _____

Fill in the blanks above with your best guesses. Of course, you probably have only a very general idea about the prevalence of heart attacks, but go ahead and fill in the blanks anyway.

The actual values are not as important in this example as the relative values are. Over 65% of the physicians who participated in the experiment by Tversky and Kahneman gave a higher percentage value for the second question than for the first. What is wrong with their answers? The second question is asking about the conjunctive probability of two events. Hopefully, you see why this figure *must* be less than the probability of either one of these events occurring alone. Of all of the men in the survey who had had a heart attack, only some of them are also over 55, so the second number must be smaller than the first. As we saw in Chapter 8, this common error in thinking is called the *conjunction fallacy*. The *conjunction fallacy* occurs when people estimate that the odds of two uncertain events happening together are greater than the odds of either event happening alone.

Why did so many physicians get this problem wrong? They were vulnerable to the conjunction fallacy because they were influenced by the *representativeness heuristic,* or the power of prototypes. When physicians think "heart attack," they tend to envision a man over the age of 55. Hence, the second scenario fit so well with their prototype of a heart attack victim that they carelessly overestimated its probability.

Let's consider some additional examples of erroneous reasoning about probabilities involving how people think about psychological disorders. Many people tend to stereotypically assume that mentally ill people are likely to be violent. People also tend to wildly overestimate (37-fold in one study) how often the insanity defense is used in criminal trials (Silver, Cirincione, & Steadman, 1994). These mistaken beliefs reflect the influence of **the *availability heuristic,* which is basing the estimated probability of an event on the ease with which relevant instances come to mind.** Because of the availability heuristic, people tend to overestimate the probability of dramatic events that receive heavy media coverage, even when these events are rare, because examples of the events are easy to retrieve from memory. Violent acts by former psychiatric patients tend to get lots of attention in the press. And because of the *hindsight bias,* journalists tend to question why authorities couldn't foresee and prevent the violence (see the Critical Thinking Application for Chapter 11), so the mental illness angle tends to be emphasized. In a similar vein, press coverage is usually intense when a defendant in a murder trial mounts an insanity defense.

In sum, the various types of statistics that come up in thinking about psychological disorders demonstrate that we are constantly working with probabilities, even though we may not realize it. Critical thinking requires a good understanding of the laws of probability because there are very few certainties in life.

TABLE 14.2   Critical Thinking Skills Discussed in this Application

Skill	Description
Understanding the limitations of the representativeness heuristic	The critical thinker understands that focusing on prototypes can lead to inaccurate probability estimates.
Understanding cumulative probabilities	The critical thinker understands that the probability of at least one of several events occurring is additive, and increases with time and the number of events.
Understanding conjunctive probabilities	The critical thinker appreciates that the probability of two uncertain events happening together is less than the probability of either event happening alone.
Understanding the limitations of the availability heuristic	The critical thinker understands that the ease with which examples come to mind may not be an accurate guide to the probability of an event.

© Cengage Learning

Abnormal Behavior: General Concepts

14.1 Evaluate the medical model of psychological disorders, and identify the key criteria of abnormality.

The medical model assumes that it is useful to view abnormal behavior as a disease. This view has been criticized on the grounds that it turns questions about deviance into medical questions. Mental illness carries a stigma that can be difficult to shake and creates additional difficulties for those who suffer from psychological disorders. Nonetheless, the medical model has been useful, as medical concepts such as diagnosis, etiology, and prognosis have proven valuable. Three criteria are used in deciding whether people suffer from psychological disorders: deviance, personal distress, and maladaptive behavior. Judgments about abnormality reflect cultural values. Often it is difficult to clearly draw a line between normality and abnormality.

14.2 Outline the structure of the DSM diagnostic system.

The DSM is the official psychodiagnostic classification system in the United States. This system asks for information about patients on five axes. Diagnoses of disorders are made on Axes I and II. Supplemental information about medical conditions, recent stress, and overall functioning are made on the other three axes. The current version is DSM-IV. Work is under way on DSM-5, which may supplement the current categorical approach with a dimensional approach, which would describe individuals' pathology in terms of how they score on a limited number of continuous dimensions.

Anxiety Disorders

14.3 Identify five anxiety disorders and the symptoms associated with each.

Generalized anxiety disorder is marked by chronic, high anxiety, whereas phobic disorder involves irrational fears of specific objects or situations. Panic disorder is demonstrated by recurrent panic attacks and agoraphobia, which is a fear of going out to public places. Obsessive-compulsive disorder is dominated by intrusions of unwanted thoughts (obsessions) and urges to engage in senseless rituals (compulsions). Posttraumatic stress disorder consists of enduring disturbance due to the experience of a major traumatic event. Common symptoms in PTSD include nightmares, flashbacks, alienation, problems in social relations, an increased sense of vulnerability, and elevated arousal.

14.4 Discuss how biology, conditioning, cognition, and stress can contribute to the development of anxiety disorders.

Studies suggest that there is a weak genetic predisposition to anxiety disorders. Abnormalities in neurotransmitter activity at GABA or serotonin synapses may also play a role. Many anxiety responses, especially phobias, may be caused by classical conditioning and maintained by operant conditioning, with preparedness influencing which phobias condition most readily. Cognitive theorists maintain that a tendency to overinterpret harmless situations as threatening makes some people more vulnerable to anxiety disorders. Stress may also predispose people to anxiety disorders.

Dissociative Disorders

14.5 Distinguish among three dissociative disorders.

Dissociative amnesia involves sudden memory loss that is too extensive to be due to normal forgetting. In dissociative fugue people also lose their sense of identity. Dissociative identity disorder is marked by the coexistence of two or more very different personalities. Since the 1970s a dramatic and controversial increase has occurred in the diagnosis of dissociative identity disorder.

14.6 Discuss the etiology of dissociative identity disorder.

Some theorists believe that people with dissociative identity disorder are engaging in intentional role playing to use an exotic mental illness as a face-saving excuse for their personal failings. Other theorists view dissociative identity disorder as an authentic disorder rooted in emotional trauma that occurred during childhood.

Mood Disorders

14.7 Describe the two major mood disorders and their relation to suicide.

Mood disorders tend to be episodic. Major depression is marked by profound sadness, slowed thought processes, and loss of interest in previous sources of pleasure. Bipolar disorder involves the experience of both manic episodes and periods of depression. Manic episodes are characterized by inflated self-esteem, high energy, grandiose plans, and racing thoughts. Depression is quite common, whereas the lifetime prevalence of bipolar disorder is about 1%. Depression is about twice as common in women as it is in men. Both types of mood disorders are associated with greatly elevated rates of suicide. They account for about 60% of completed suicides.

Compulsive symptoms at admission

SOURCE: Pato, M. T., Fanous, A., Eisen, J. L., & Phillips, K. A. (2008). Anxiety disorders: Obsessive-compulsive disorder. In A. Tasman, J. Kay, J. A. Lieberman, M. B. First, & M. Maj (Eds.), *Psychiatry* (3rd ed.), 1443–1471. Chichester, England: Wiley-Blackwell.

14.8 Understand how genetic, neural, cognitive, social, and stress factors are related to the development of mood disorders.

Evidence indicates that people vary in their genetic vulnerability to mood disorders. These disorders are accompanied by changes in neurochemical activity in the brain. Abnormalities at norepinephrine and serotonin synapses appear particularly critical. Reduced hippocampal volume and suppressed neurogenesis are also associated with depression. Cognitive models posit that negative thinking contributes to depression. A pessimistic explanatory style has been implicated, as has a tendency to ruminate about one's problems. Interpersonal inadequacies may contribute to depressive disorders. Poor social skills may lead to a paucity of life's reinforcers and frequent rejection. Mood disorders may also be precipitated by high stress.

Schizophrenic Disorders

14.9 Identify the general characteristics and subtypes of schizophrenia.

Disturbed, irrational thought processes, including delusions, are the defining feature of schizophrenic disorders. Schizophrenia is also characterized by deterioration of everyday adaptive behavior, auditory hallucinations, and disturbed emotion. Schizophrenic disorders are classified as paranoid, catatonic, disorganized, or undifferentiated. Schizophrenic disorders usually emerge during adolescence or young adulthood. The course of the disorder tends to involve chronic deterioration for many patients, but with prompt, effective care recovery is possible.

14.10 Explain how biological factors may contribute to the development of schizophrenia.

Twin studies and other research show that some people inherit a genetic vulnerability to schizophrenia. The dopamine hypothesis asserts that excess dopamine activity is the neurochemcial basis for schizophrenia. The dopamine hypothesis may explain why recent research has uncovered a link between marijuana use and vulnerability to schizophrenia. Structural abnormalities in the brain, such as enlarged ventricles, are associated with schizophrenia, but their causal significance is unclear. The neurodevelopmental hypothesis of schizophrenia asserts that schizophrenia is attributable to disruptions in the normal maturational processes of the brain before or at birth that are caused by prenatal viral infections, obstetrical complications, and other insults to the brain.

14.11 Summarize how family dynamics and stress may play a role in the etiology of schizophrenia.

Patients who come from homes high in expressed emotion have elevated relapse rates, suggesting that unhealthy family dynamics play a role in schizophrenia. High stress may also contribute to the onset of schizophrenia and to relapse after treatment.

Autistic Disorder

14.12 Describe the symptoms, prevalence, and etiology of autistic disorder.

Autism is characterized by profound impairment of social interaction and communication and by severely restricted interests and activities, which is apparent by the age of 3. Autism tends be a lifelong affliction requiring extensive family and institutional support throughout adulthood. Since the mid-1990s there has been a dramatic increase in the diagnosis of autism, with prevalence estimates approaching 1%. This increase is probably due to greater awareness of the syndrome and the use of broader diagnostic criteria. Genetic factors contribute to autistic disorders, but little else is known about the etiology of autism. Research has failed to find an association between vaccinations and the development of autism.

Reflecting on the Chapter's Themes

14.13 Identify the four unifying themes highlighted in this chapter.

This chapter highlighted four of our unifying themes, showing that behavior is governed by multiple causes, that heredity and environment jointly influence mental disorders, that psychology evolves in a sociohistorical context, and that psychological phenomena are shaped to some degree by cultural parameters.

PERSONAL APPLICATION
Understanding Eating Disorders

14.14 Describe the subtypes, history, and prevalence of eating disorders.

The principal eating disorders are anorexia nervosa and bulimia nervosa. Anorexia and bulimia both lead to a cascade of medical problems, but anorexia is more dangerous. Both disorders are largely a product of affluent, Westernized culture that weren't recognized until the 20th century. Females account for 90%-95% of eating disorders. Among young women, about 1% develop anorexia nervosa and about 2%-3% develop bulimia nervosa, typically between the ages of 15 to 20.

14.15 Outline how genetic factors, personality, culture, family dynamics, and disturbed thinking contribute to eating disorders.

There appears to be a genetic predisposition to eating disorders. Certain personality traits increase the vulnerability to eating disorders. Cultural pressures on young women to be thin clearly help to foster eating disorders. Families that endorse the idea that you can never be too thin can help to promote eating disorders. Rigid, disturbed thinking can also contribute to the development of these disorders.

Age of onset for anorexia nervosa

CRITICAL THINKING APPLICATION
Working with Probabilities in Thinking About Mental Illness

14.16 Understand how mental heuristics can distort estimates of cumulative and conjunctive probabilities.

Cumulative probabilities are additive, whereas conjunctive probabilities are always less than the likelihood of any one of the events happening alone. Probability estimates can be distorted by the representativeness heuristic. For example, people's "best examples" of mental disorders consist of severe disorders that are infrequent, leading them to underestimate the prevalence of mental disorders. Probability estimates can also be distorted by the availability heuristic, which leads people to overestimate the likelihood of events that receive heavy media coverage.

15

Treatment of Psychological Disorders

PARADOX

Psychotherapy is both an art and a science.

© Sigrid Olsson/PhotoAlto/Corbis

What do you picture when you hear the term *psychotherapy*? Unless you've had some personal exposure to therapy, your image of it has likely been shaped by portrayals you've seen on television or in the movies. A good example is the 1999 film *Analyze This,* a comedy starring Billy Crystal as psychiatrist Ben Sobol and Robert De Niro as Paul Vitti, a mob boss who is suffering from "panic attacks." Complications develop when Vitti—a man no one says "no" to—demands that Dr. Sobol cure him of his problem before his rivals in crime turn his "weakness" against him.

With his glasses and beard, Billy Crystal's Dr. Sobol resembles many people's picture of a therapist. Like many movie therapists, Dr. Sobol practices "talk therapy." He listens attentively as his patients talk about what is troubling them. Occasionally he offers comments that reflect their thoughts and feelings back to them or that offer some illuminating insight into their problems. We can get a feeling for his approach from a funny scene in which the uneducated Vitti turns Dr. Sobol's techniques on him:

VITTI: Hey, let's see how you like it. Let's talk about your father.

SOBOL: Let's not.

VITTI: What kind of work does your father do?

SOBOL: It's not important.

VITTI: You paused.

SOBOL: I did not.

VITTI: You just paused. That means you had a feeling, like a thought . . .

SOBOL: You know, we're running out of time. Let's not waste it talking about my problems.

VITTI: Your father's a problem?

SOBOL: No!

VITTI: That's what you just said.

SOBOL: I did not!

VITTI: Now you're upset.

SOBOL: (getting upset): I am not upset!

VITTI: Yes you are.

SOBOL: Will you stop it!

VITTI: You know what, I'm getting good at this.

As in this scene, the film derives much of its humor from popular conceptions—and misconceptions—about therapy. The technique that Vitti makes fun of does resemble one type of therapeutic process. Like Vitti, many people do associate needing therapy with having a shameful weakness. Further, therapy is often of considerable benefit in helping people make significant changes in their lives—even if those changes are not as dramatic as Vitti's giving up his life of crime at the end of the movie. On the other hand, the film's comic exaggerations

The popular film *Analyze This* derived much of its humor from common misconceptions about the process of psychotherapy.

also highlight some misconceptions about therapy, including the following:

• Vitti is driven to see a "shrink" because he feels like he's "falling apart." In fact, therapists help people with all kinds of problems. People need not have severe symptoms of mental illness to benefit from therapy.

• Dr. Sobol is a psychiatrist, but most therapists are not. And although Dr. Sobol quotes Freud and the film's plot turns on interpreting a dream (in this case, it's the psychiatrist's dream!), most therapists make little or no use of Freudian techniques.

• Dr. Sobol relies on "talk therapy" to produce insights that will help his patients overcome their troubles. In reality, this approach is only one of the many techniques used by therapists.

• Dr. Sobol "cures" Vitti by getting him to acknowledge a traumatic event in his childhood (the death of his father) that is at the root of his problems. But only rarely does therapy produce a single dramatic insight that results in wholesale change for the client.

In this chapter, we'll take a down-to-earth look at *psychotherapy,* using the term in its broadest sense, to refer to all the diverse approaches used in the treatment of mental disorders and psychological problems. We'll start by discussing some general questions about how treatment is provided. After considering these issues, we'll examine the goals, techniques, and effectiveness of some of the more widely used approaches to therapy and discuss recent trends and issues in treatment, including changes in institutional treatment. In the Personal Application, we'll look at practical questions related to finding and choosing a therapist. And in the Critical Thinking Application we'll address problems involved in determining whether therapy actually helps.

KEY LEARNING GOALS

15.1 Identify the three major categories of therapy, and discuss patterns of treatment seeking.

15.2 Identify the various types of mental health professionals involved in the provision of therapy.

Elements of the Treatment Process

Sigmund Freud is widely credited with launching modern psychotherapy. Ironically, the landmark case that inspired Freud was actually treated by one of his colleagues, Josef Breuer. Around 1880, Breuer began to treat a young woman known in the annals of psychiatry as Anna O (her real name, which came out years later, was Bertha Pappenheim). Anna exhibited a variety of physical maladies, including headaches, coughing, and a loss of feeling and movement in her right arm. Much to his surprise, Breuer discovered that Anna's physical symptoms cleared up when he encouraged her to talk about emotionally charged experiences from her past.

When Breuer and Freud discussed the case, they speculated that talking things through had enabled Anna to drain off bottled up emotions that had caused her symptoms. Breuer found the intense emotional exchange in this treatment not to his liking, so he didn't follow through on his discovery. However, Freud applied Breuer's insight to other patients. His successes led him to develop a systematic treatment procedure, which he called *psychoanalysis*. Anna O called her treatment "the talking cure." However, as you'll see, psychotherapy isn't always curative, and many modern therapies place little emphasis on talking.

Freud's breakthrough ushered in a century of progress for psychotherapy. Psychoanalysis spawned many offspring as Freud's followers developed their own systems of treatment. Since then, approaches to psychotherapy have steadily grown more numerous, more diverse, and more effective.

Treatments: How Many Types Are There?

In their efforts to help people, psychotherapists use many treatment methods. One expert (Kazdin, 1994) estimates that there may be over 400 different approaches to treatment! Fortunately, we can impose some order on this chaos. As varied as therapists' procedures are, approaches to treatment can be classified into three major categories:

1. *Insight therapies.* Insight therapy is "talk therapy" in the tradition of Freud's psychoanalysis. In insight therapies, clients engage in complex, often lengthy verbal interactions with their therapist. The goal in these discussions is to pursue increased insight regarding the nature of the client's difficulties and to sort through possible solutions.

2. *Behavior therapies.* Behavior therapies are based on the principles of learning, which were introduced in Chapter 6. Instead of emphasizing personal insights, behavior therapists make direct efforts to alter problematic responses (phobias, for instance) and maladaptive habits (drug use, for instance).

3. *Biomedical therapies.* Biomedical approaches to therapy involve interventions into a person's biological functioning. The most widely used procedures are drug therapy and electroconvulsive (shock) therapy. In recent decades, drug therapy has become the dominant mode of treatment for psychological disorders. As **Figure 15.1** shows, one large-scale study found that 57% of mental health patients were treated with medication only, up from 44% just nine years earlier (Olfson & Marcus, 2010). As the name bio*medical* therapies suggests, these treatments have traditionally been provided only by physicians with a medical degree (usually psychiatrists). This situation is changing, however, as psychologists have been campaigning for prescription privileges (Price, 2008). The chief rationale for this campaign is that many rural areas and underserved populations have inadequate access to psychiatrists (Ax et al., 2008). To date, psychologists have obtained prescription authority in two states (New Mexico and Louisiana), and they have made legislative progress toward this goal in many other states (Long, 2005; Munsey, 2008).

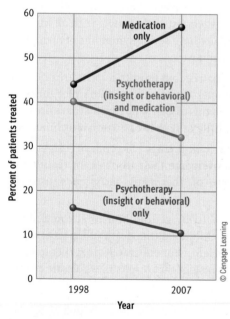

FIGURE 15.1

Escalating reliance on drug therapy.
Using data from an ongoing national survey focusing on patterns of health care, Olfson and Marcus (2010) found some interesting trends in outpatient treatment for psychological disorders. Comparing treatment procedures in 1998 and 2007, they found that the percentage of patients treated with medication exclusively increased from 44% to 57%. During the same time period, the percentage of patients treated with insight or behavioral therapy alone, or in combination with drug therapy, declined.

Clients: Who Seeks Therapy?

People seeking mental health treatment represent the full range of human problems: anxiety, depression, unsatisfactory interpersonal relations, troublesome habits, poor self-control, low self-esteem, marital conflicts, self-doubt, a sense of emptiness, and feelings of personal stagnation. Among adults, the two most common presenting problems are depression and anxiety disorders (Olfson & Marcus, 2010).

People vary considerably in their willingness to seek psychotherapy. People often delay for many years before finally seeking treatment for their psychological problems (Wang, Berglund et al., 2005). As you can see in **Figure 15.2**, women are more likely than men to receive therapy. In terms of ethnicity, whites are more likely to pursue treatment than blacks or Hispanics. Treatment is also more likely when people have medical insurance and when they have more education (Olfson & Marcus, 2010; Wang, Lane et al., 2005). *Unfortunately, it appears that many people who need therapy don't receive it.* Research suggests that only about one-third of the people who need treatment get it (Kessler et al., 2005). People who could benefit from therapy do not seek it for a variety of reasons. Lack of health insurance and cost concerns appear to be major barriers to obtaining needed care for many people. Perhaps the biggest roadblock is the stigma surrounding the receipt of mental health treatment. Unfortunately, many people equate seeking therapy with admitting personal weakness.

Therapists: Who Provides Professional Treatment?

Friends and relatives may provide you with excellent advice about your personal problems, but their assistance does not qualify as therapy. Psychotherapy refers to *professional* treatment by someone with special training. However, a common source of confusion about psychotherapy is the variety of "helping professions" involved (Murstein & Fontaine, 1993). Psychology and psychiatry are the principal professions involved in the

FIGURE 15.2

Therapy utilization rates. Olfson and Marcus (2010) analyzed data on the use of outpatient mental health services in the United States in relation to various demographic variables. In regard to marital status, utilization rates are particularly high among those who are divorced or not married. The use of therapy is also greater among those who have more education. Females are more likely to pursue therapy than males are, but utilization rates are relatively low among ethnic minorities and those who lack health insurance.

delivery of psychotherapy, providing the lion's share of mental health care. However, treatment is also provided by other types of therapists (**see Table 15.1**). Let's look at these mental health professions.

PSYCHOLOGISTS

Two types of psychologists may provide therapy, although the distinction between them is more theoretical than real. *Clinical psychologists* **and** *counseling psychologists* **specialize in the diagnosis and treatment of psychological disorders and everyday behavioral problems.** In theory, clinical psychologists' training emphasizes the treatment of full-fledged disorders. In contrast, counseling psychologists' training is supposed to be slanted toward the treatment of everyday adjustment problems in normal people. In practice, however, clinical and counseling psychologists overlap greatly in training, skills, and the clientele they serve (Morgan & Cohen, 2008). Both types of psychologists must earn a doctoral degree (Ph.D., Psy.D., or Ed.D.). In providing therapy, psychologists use either insight or behavioral approaches. Clinical and counseling psychologists do psychological testing as well as psychotherapy, and many also conduct research.

PSYCHIATRISTS

Psychiatrists **are physicians who specialize in the diagnosis and treatment of psychological disorders.** Many psychiatrists also treat everyday behavioral problems. However, in comparison to psychologists, psychiatrists devote more time to relatively severe disorders (schizophrenia, mood disorders) and less time to everyday marital, family, job, and school problems. Psychiatrists have an M.D. degree. Their graduate training requires four years of coursework in medical school and a four-year apprenticeship in a residency at a hospital. In comparison to psychologists, psychiatrists are more likely to use psychoanalysis and less likely to use group therapies or behavior therapies. That said, contemporary psychiatrists primarily depend on medication as their principal mode of treatment (Mojtabai & Olfson, 2008).

OTHER MENTAL HEALTH PROFESSIONALS

Several other mental health professions provide psychotherapy services. *Psychiatric social workers* and *psychiatric nurses* often work as part of a treatment team with a psychologist or psychiatrist. Social workers have traditionally worked in hospitals and

TABLE 15.1 **Types of Therapists**

Profession	Degree	Education beyond Bachelor's degree	Typical roles and activities
Clinical psychologist	PhD or PsyD	5–7 years	Psychological testing, diagnosis, treatment with insight or behavior therapy
Counseling psychologist	PhD, PsyD, or EdD	5–7 years	Similar to clinical psychologist, but more focus on work, career, and adjustment problems
Psychiatrist	MD	8 years	Diagnosis and treatment, primarily with biomedical therapies, but also insight therapies
Clinical social worker	MSW, DSW	2–5 years	Insight and behavior therapy, often help inpatients with their return to the community
Psychiatric nurse	RN, MA, or PhD	0–5 years	Inpatient care, insight and behavior therapy
Counselor	BA or MA	0–2 years	Vocational counseling, drug counseling, rehabilitation counseling
Marriage and family therapist	MA or PhD	2–5 years	Marital/couples therapy, family therapy

© Cengage Learning

social service agencies. However, many also provide a wide range of therapeutic services as independent practitioners. Many kinds of *counselors* also provide therapeutic services. They often specialize in particular types of problems, such as vocational counseling, marital counseling, rehabilitation counseling, and drug counseling.

Marriage and family therapists generally have a master's degree that prepares them to work with couples experiencing relationship problems or with dysfunctional families. They are licensed as independent practitioners in all but two states (Bowers, 2007). Marital and family therapy has experienced enormous growth since the 1980s (Lebow, 2008).

There are clear differences among the helping professions in their education, training, and approach to therapy. That said, their roles in the treatment process overlap considerably. In this chapter, we will refer to psychologists or psychiatrists as needed, but otherwise we'll use the terms *clinician, therapist,* and *mental health professional* to refer to psychotherapists of all kinds, regardless of their professional degree.

Now that we have discussed the basic elements in psychotherapy, we can examine specific approaches to treatment in terms of their goals, procedures, and effectiveness. We'll begin with some representative insight therapies.

Insight Therapies

KEY LEARNING GOALS

15.3 Explain the logic of psychoanalysis and the techniques by which analysts probe the unconscious.

15.4 Understand the role of therapeutic climate and therapeutic process in client-centered therapy.

15.5 Explain how group therapy, couples therapy, and family therapy are generally conducted.

15.6 Assess the efficacy of insight therapies.

Many schools of thought offer ideas about how to conduct insight therapy. Therapists with various theoretical orientations use different methods to pursue different kinds of insights. However, what these varied approaches have in common is that *insight therapies* **involve verbal interactions intended to enhance clients' self-knowledge and thus promote healthful changes in personality and behavior.** In this section, we'll delve into psychoanalysis, related psychodynamic approaches, and client-centered therapy. Then we'll discuss how insight therapy can be done with groups, couples, and families, as well as individuals.

Psychoanalysis

PSYKTREK 11d

After the case of Anna O, Sigmund Freud worked as a psychotherapist for almost 50 years in Vienna. Through a painstaking process of trial and error, he developed innovative techniques for the treatment of psychological disorders and distress. His system of *psychoanalysis* came to dominate psychiatry for many decades. Although this dominance has eroded in recent decades, a diverse collection of psychoanalytic approaches to therapy continue to evolve and to remain influential today (Gabbard, 2005; Luborsky, O'Reilly-Landry, & Arlow, 2011; Ursano, Sonnenberg, & Lazar, 2008).

Psychoanalysis **is an insight therapy that emphasizes the recovery of unconscious conflicts, motives, and defenses through techniques such as free association and transference.** To appreciate the logic of psychoanalysis, we have to look at Freud's thinking about the roots of mental disorders. Freud mostly treated anxiety-dominated disturbances, such as phobic, panic, obsessive-compulsive, and conversion disorders, which were then called *neuroses*.

Freud believed that neurotic problems are caused by unconscious conflicts left over from early childhood. As explained in Chapter 11, he thought that people depend on defense mechanisms to avoid confronting these conflicts, which remain hidden in the depths of the unconscious (see **Figure 15.3** on the next page). However, he noted that defensive maneuvers tend to be only partially successful in alleviating anxiety, guilt, and other distressing emotions. With this model in mind, let's take a look at the therapeutic procedures used in psychoanalysis.

Sigmund Freud
"The news that reaches your consciousness is incomplete and often not to be relied on."

FIGURE 15.3

Freud's view of the roots of disorders.
According to Freud, unconscious conflicts between the id, ego, and superego sometimes lead to anxiety. This discomfort may lead to pathological reliance on defensive behavior.

Intrapsychic conflict (between id, ego, and superego) → Anxiety → Reliance on defense mechanisms

© Cengage Learning

PROBING THE UNCONSCIOUS

PsykTrek 11d

Given Freud's assumptions, we can see that the logic of psychoanalysis is quite simple. The analyst attempts to probe the murky depths of the unconscious to discover the unresolved conflicts causing the client's neurotic behavior. In this effort to explore the unconscious, the therapist relies on two techniques: free association and dream analysis.

In *free association* clients spontaneously express their thoughts and feelings exactly as they occur, with as little censorship as possible. In free associating, clients talk about anything that comes to mind, no matter how trivial, silly, or embarrassing it might be. The analyst studies these free associations for clues about what is going on in the unconscious. In *dream analysis* the therapist interprets the symbolic meaning of the client's dreams. For Freud, dreams were the "royal road to the unconscious," the most direct means of access to patients' innermost conflicts, wishes, and impulses. Psychoanalytic clients are encouraged and trained to remember their dreams, which they then describe in therapy.

To better illustrate these matters, let's look at an actual case treated through psychoanalysis (adapted from Greenson, 1967, pp. 40–41). Mr. N was troubled by an unsatisfactory marriage. He claimed to love his wife, but he preferred sexual relations with prostitutes. Mr. N reported that his parents also endured lifelong marital difficulties. His childhood conflicts about their relationship appeared to be related to his problems. Both dream analysis and free association can be seen in the following description of a session in Mr. N's treatment:

Mr. N reported a fragment of a dream. All that he could remember is that he was waiting for a red traffic light to change when he felt that someone had bumped into him from behind. . . . The associations led to Mr. N's love of cars, especially sports cars. He loved the sensation, in particular, of whizzing by those fat, old expensive cars. . . . His father always hinted that he had been a great athlete, but he never substantiated it. . . . Mr. N doubted whether his father could really perform. His father would flirt with a waitress in a cafe or make sexual remarks about women passing by, but he seemed to be showing off. If he were really sexual, he wouldn't resort to that.

As is characteristic of free association, Mr. N's train of thought meandered about with little direction. Nonetheless, clues about his unconscious conflicts were apparent. What did Mr. N's therapist extract from this session? The therapist saw sexual overtones in the dream fragment, where Mr. N was bumped from behind. The therapist also inferred that Mr. N had a competitive orientation toward his father, based on the free association about whizzing by fat, old expensive cars. As you can see, analysts must *interpret* their clients' dreams and free associations. Contrary to popular belief, analysts generally don't try to dazzle clients with startling revelations. Instead, analysts move forward inch by inch, offering interpretations that should be just out of the client's own reach. Mr. N's therapist eventually offered the following interpretations to his client:

I said to Mr. N near the end of the hour that I felt he was struggling with his feelings about his father's sexual life. He seemed to be saying that his father was sexually not a very potent man. . . . He also recalls that he once found a packet of condoms under his father's pillow when he was an adolescent and he thought, "My father must be going to prosti-

tutes." I then intervened and pointed out that the condoms under his father's pillow seemed to indicate more obviously that his father used the condoms with his mother, who slept in the same bed. However, Mr. N wanted to believe his wish-fulfilling fantasy: mother doesn't want sex with father and father is not very potent. The patient was silent and the hour ended.

As you may have already guessed, the therapist concluded that Mr. N's difficulties were rooted in an *Oedipal complex* (see Chapter 11). The patient had unresolved sexual feelings toward his mother and hostile feelings about his father. These unconscious conflicts, rooted in Mr. N's childhood, were distorting his intimate relations as an adult.

RESISTANCE AND TRANSFERENCE

PSYKTREK 11d

How would you expect Mr. N to respond to the therapist's suggestion that he was in competition with his father for the sexual attention of his mother? Obviously, most clients would have great difficulty accepting such an interpretation. Freud fully expected clients to display some resistance to therapeutic efforts. *Resistance refers to largely unconscious defensive maneuvers intended to hinder the progress of therapy.* Resistance is assumed to be an inevitable part of the psychoanalytic process (Samberg & Marcus, 2005). Why would clients try to resist the helping process? Because they don't want to face up to the painful, disturbing conflicts that they have buried in their unconscious. Although they have sought help, they are reluctant to confront their real problems. Analysts use a variety of strategies to deal with clients' resistance. Often, a key consideration is the handling of transference.

Transference **occurs when clients start relating to their therapists in ways that mimic critical relationships in their lives.** Thus, a client might start relating to a therapist as if the therapist were an overprotective mother, a rejecting brother, or a passive spouse. In a sense, the client *transfers* conflicting feelings about important people onto the therapist. Psychoanalysts often encourage transference so that clients can reenact relations with crucial people in the context of therapy. These reenactments can help bring repressed feelings and conflicts to the surface, allowing the client to work through the conflicts.

Undergoing psychoanalysis is not easy. It can be a slow, painful process of self-examination that routinely requires three to five years of hard work. It tends to be a lengthy process because patients need time to gradually work through their problems and genuinely accept unnerving revelations (Williams, 2005). Ultimately, if resistance and transference can be handled effectively, the therapist's interpretations should lead the client to profound insights. For instance, Mr. N eventually admitted, "The old boy is probably right, it does tickle me to imagine that my mother preferred me and I could beat out my father. Later, I wondered whether this had something to do with my own screwed-up sex life with my wife." According to Freud, once clients recognize the unconscious sources of conflicts, they can resolve these conflicts and discard their neurotic defenses.

© Photos 12/Alamy

MODERN PSYCHODYNAMIC TREATMENTS

Though still available, classical psychoanalysis as done by Freud is not widely practiced anymore (Kay & Kay, 2008). Freud's psychoanalytic method was geared to a particular kind of clientele that he was seeing in Vienna a century ago. As his followers fanned out across Europe and America, many found it necessary to adapt psychoanalysis to different cultures, changing times, and new kinds of patients (Karasu, 2005). Thus, many variations on Freud's original approach to psychoanalysis have developed over the years. These descendants of psychoanalysis are collectively known as *psychodynamic approaches* to therapy.

Focus on emotional experience
Psychodynamic therapies encourage exploration of patients' emotional feelings.

Exploration of efforts to avoid distressing thoughts and feelings
Psychodynamic therapies probe patients' defense mechanisms and resistance.

Identification of recurring patterns in patients' lives
Psychodynamic therapies attempt to help patients recognize and understand recurring themes in their thoughts, feelings, and relationships.

Discussion of past experience
Psychodynamic therapies have a developmental slant, which emphasizes exploration of early childhood experiences and attachments.

Analysis of interpersonal relationships
Psychodynamic therapies focus heavily on patients' social relationships, especially with attachment figures.

Focus on the therapeutic relationship
Psychodynamic therapies pay careful attention to the relationship between the therapist and patient and the potential for transference.

Exploration of fantasy life
Psychodynamic therapies encourage exploration of patients' fantasies, dreams, and daydreams, which can offer useful clues about how they view their social worlds.

Distinctive features of psychodynamic therapies

© Cengage Learning

FIGURE 15.4

Core features of psychodynamic therapies. In an article on the efficacy of psychodynamic therapies, Jonathan Shedler (2010) outlined the distinctive aspects of modern psychodynamic techniques and processes. The seven features described here represent the core of contemporary psychodynamic treatment.

Courtesy of Carl Rogers Memorial Library

Carl Rogers
"To my mind, empathy is in itself a healing agent."

As a result, today we have a rich diversity of psychodynamic approaches (Magnavita, 2008). Recent reviews of these treatments suggest that interpretation, resistance, and transference continue to play key roles in therapeutic effects (Hoglend et al., 2008; Luborsky & Barrett, 2006). Other central features of modern psychodynamic therapies include (1) a focus on emotional experience, (2) exploration of efforts to avoid distressing thoughts and feelings, (3) identification of recurring patterns in patients' life experiences, (4) discussion of past experience, especially events in early childhood, (5) analysis of interpersonal relationships, (6) a focus on the therapeutic relationship itself, and (7) exploration of dreams and other aspects of fantasy life (Shedler, 2010; see **Figure 15.4**). Recent research suggests that psychodynamic approaches can be helpful in the treatment of a diverse array of disorders (Gibbons, Crits-Christoph, & Hearon, 2008; Leichsenring & Rabung, 2008; Shedler, 2010).

Client-Centered Therapy [PSYKTREK 11d]

You may have heard of people going into therapy to "find themselves" or to "get in touch with their real feelings." These now-popular phrases emerged out of the *human potential movement*. This movement was stimulated in part by the work of Carl Rogers (1951, 1986). Using a humanistic perspective, Rogers devised client-centered therapy (also known as person-centered therapy) in the 1940s and 1950s.

Client-centered therapy **is an insight therapy that emphasizes providing a supportive emotional climate for clients, who play a major role in determining the pace and direction of their therapy.** Rogers's theory about the principal causes of neurotic anxieties is quite different from the Freudian explanation. As discussed in Chapter 11, Rogers maintains that most personal distress is to the result of inconsistency, or "incongruence," between a person's self-concept and reality (see **Figure 15.5**). According to his theory, incongruence makes people feel threatened by realistic feedback about themselves from others. According to Rogers, anxiety about such feedback often leads to reliance on defense mechanisms, to distortions of reality, and to stifled personal growth. Excessive incongruence is thought to be rooted in clients' overdependence on others for approval and acceptance.

Given Rogers's theory, client-centered therapists stalk insights that are quite different from the repressed conflicts that psychoanalysts go after. Client-centered therapists

FIGURE 15.5

Rogers's view of the roots of disorders. Rogers's theory asserts that anxiety and self-defeating behavior are rooted in an incongruent self-concept that makes one prone to recurrent anxiety, which triggers defensive behavior, which fuels more incongruence.

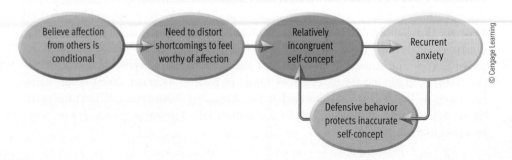

© Cengage Learning

help clients realize that they do not have to worry constantly about pleasing others and winning acceptance. These clinicians help people restructure their self-concept to correspond better to reality. Ultimately, they try to foster self-acceptance and personal growth.

THERAPEUTIC CLIMATE

PSYKTREK 11d

According to Rogers, the *process* of therapy is not as important as the emotional *climate* in which the therapy takes place. He believes that it is critical for the therapist to provide a warm, supportive climate that creates a safe environment in which clients can confront their shortcomings without feeling threatened. The lack of threat should reduce clients' defensive tendencies and thus help them open up. To create this supportive atmosphere, client-centered therapists must provide three conditions: (1) *genuineness* (honest communication), (2) *unconditional positive regard* (nonjudgmental acceptance of the client), and (3) *accurate empathy* (understanding of the client's point of view).

THERAPEUTIC PROCESS

PSYKTREK 11d

In client-centered therapy, the client and therapist work together as equals. The therapist provides relatively little guidance and keeps interpretation and advice to a minimum (Raskin, Rogers, & Witty, 2011). The therapist's key task is *clarification*. The client-centered therapist tries to function like a human mirror, reflecting statements back to the client, but with enhanced clarity. He or she helps clients become more aware of their true feelings by highlighting themes that may be obscure in the clients' rambling discourse.

By working with clients to clarify their feelings, client-centered therapists hope to gradually build toward more far-reaching insights. In particular, they try to help clients better understand their interpersonal relationships and become more comfortable with their genuine selves. Obviously, these are ambitious goals. Client-centered therapy resembles psychoanalysis in that both seek to achieve a major reconstruction of a client's personality.

Client-centered therapists emphasize the importance of a supportive emotional climate in therapy. They also work to clarify, rather than interpret, the feelings expressed by their patients.

Group Therapy

Many approaches to insight therapy, such as client-centered therapy, can be conducted on either an individual or group basis. *Group therapy* is the simultaneous treatment of several clients in a group. Because of economic pressures in mental health care, the use of group therapy appears likely to grow in future years (Burlingame & Baldwin, 2011). Although group therapy can be conducted in a variety of ways, we can provide a general overview of the process (see Cox, Vinogradov, & Yalom, 2008; Spitz, 2009; Stone, 2008).

A therapy group typically consists of four to twelve people, with six to eight participants regarded as ideal (Cox et al., 2008). The therapist usually screens the participants, excluding persons who seem likely to be disruptive. Some theorists maintain that judicious selection of participants is crucial to effective group treatment (Schlapobersky & Pines, 2009). In group therapy, participants essentially function as therapists for one another (Stone, 2008). Group members describe their problems, trade viewpoints, share experiences, and discuss coping strategies. Most important, they provide acceptance and emotional support for each other. In this atmosphere, group members work at peeling away the social masks that cover their insecurities. As members come to value each other's opinions, they work hard to display healthy changes. In group treatment, the therapist's responsibilities include selecting participants,

Group treatments have proven particularly helpful when members share similar problems, such as alcoholism, overeating, or having been sexually abused as a child. Many approaches to insight therapy that were originally designed for individuals—such as client-centered therapy—have been adapted for treatment of groups.

setting goals for the group, initiating and maintaining the therapeutic process, and preventing interactions among group members that might be psychologically harmful (Cox et al., 2008). The therapist often plays a relatively subtle role in group therapy, staying in the background and focusing mainly on promoting group cohesiveness.

Group therapies obviously save time and money, which can be critical in understaffed mental hospitals and other institutional settings (Cox et al., 2008). Therapists in private practice usually charge less for group than individual therapy, making therapy affordable for more people. However, group therapy is *not* just a less costly substitute for individual therapy (Knauss, 2005; Stone, 2008). Group therapy has unique strengths of its own, and certain kinds of problems are especially well suited to group treatment.

Couples and Family Therapy

Like group therapy, marital and family therapy rose to prominence after World War II. As their names suggest, these interventions are defined in terms of who is being treated. *Couples* or *marital therapy* **involves the treatment of both partners in a committed, intimate relationship, in which the main focus is on relationship issues.** Couples therapy is not limited to married couples. It is frequently provided to cohabiting couples, including gay couples. *Family therapy* **involves the treatment of a family unit as a whole, in which the main focus is on family dynamics and communication.** Family therapy often emerges out of efforts to treat children or adolescents with individual therapy. A child's therapist, for instance, might come to the realization that treatment is likely to fail because the child returns to a home environment that contributes to the child's problems, and so proposes a broader family intervention.

As with other forms of insight therapy, there are different schools of thought about how to conduct couples and family therapy (Goldenberg, Goldenberg, & Pelavin, 2011). Some of these diverse systems are extensions of influential approaches to individual therapy, including psychodynamic, humanistic, and behavioral treatments. Other approaches are based on innovative models of families as complex systems and explicit rejection of individual models of treatment. Although the various approaches to couples and family therapy differ in terminology and in their theoretical models of relationship and family dysfunction, they tend to share two common goals. First, they seek to understand the entrenched patterns of interaction that produce distress. In this endeavor they view individuals as parts of a family eco-

---

Concept Check 15.1

Understanding Therapists' Conceptions of Disorders

Check your understanding of various approaches to insight therapy covered in the text by matching each approach with the appropriate explanation of the typical origins of clients' psychological disorders. The answers are in Appendix A.

Theorized Causes of Disorders

_____ 1. Problems rooted in families' or couples' social ecosystem

_____ 2. Problems rooted in unconscious conflicts left over from childhood

_____ 3. Problems rooted in inaccurate self-concept and excessive concern about pleasing others

Therapy

a. Psychoanalysis

b. Client-centered therapy

c. Couples and family therapy

system, and they assume that people behave as they do because of their role in the system (Lebow, 2008). Second, they seek to help couples and families improve their communication and move toward healthier patterns of interaction.

How Effective Are Insight Therapies?

Evaluating the effectiveness of any approach to psychotherapy is a complex matter (Crits-Christoph & Gibbons, 2009; Hill & Lambert, 2004). For one thing, psychological disorders sometimes clear up on their own, a phenomenon called *spontaneous remission*. If a client experiences a recovery after treatment, we cannot automatically assume that the recovery was due to the treatment (see the Critical Thinking Application). Evaluations of insight therapies are especially complicated given that various schools of thought pursue entirely different goals. Judgments of therapeutic outcome in insight therapy tend to be subjective, with little consensus about the best way to assess therapeutic progress. Moreover, people enter therapy with diverse problems of varied severity, so the efficacy of treatment can be evaluated meaningfully only for specific clinical problems.

Despite these difficulties, thousands of outcome studies have been conducted to evaluate the effectiveness of insight therapy. These studies have examined a broad range of clinical problems and used a variety of methods to assess therapeutic outcomes, including looking at scores on psychological tests and ratings by family members, as well as therapists' and clients' ratings. These studies consistently indicate that insight therapy *is* superior to no treatment or to placebo treatment and that the effects of therapy are reasonably durable (Lambert, 2011; Lambert & Archer, 2006; Torres & Saunders, 2009). And when insight therapies are compared head-to-head against drug therapies, they usually show roughly equal efficacy (Arkowitz & Lilienfeld, 2007; Pinquart, Duberstein, & Lyness, 2006). Studies generally find the greatest improvement early in treatment (the first thirteen to eighteen weekly sessions), with further gains gradually diminishing over time (Lambert, Bergin, & Garfield, 2004). Overall, about 50% of patients show a clinically meaningful recovery within about twenty sessions, and another 25% of patients achieve this goal after about forty-five sessions (Lambert & Ogles, 2004). Of course, these broad generalizations mask considerable variability in outcome, but the general trends are encouraging.

Behavior Therapies

KEY LEARNING GOALS

15.7 Describe the procedures of systematic desensitization, aversion therapy, and social skills training.

15.8 Articulate the goals and techniques of cognitive therapy, and evaluate the efficacy of behavior therapies.

Behavior therapy is different from insight therapy in that behavior therapists make no attempt to help clients achieve grand insights about themselves. Why not? Because behavior therapists believe that such insights aren't necessary to produce constructive change. For example, consider a client troubled by compulsive gambling. The behavior therapist doesn't care whether this behavior is rooted in unconscious conflicts or parental rejection. What the client needs is to get rid of the maladaptive behavior. Consequently, the therapist simply designs a program to eliminate the compulsive gambling.

Behavior therapies involve the application of the principles of learning and conditioning to direct efforts to change clients' maladaptive behaviors. Behavior therapies are based on two main assumptions (Stanley & Beidel, 2009). *First, it is assumed that behavior is a product of learning.* No matter how self-defeating or pathological a client's behavior might be, the behaviorist believes that it is the result of past conditioning. *Second, it is assumed that what has been learned can be unlearned.* Thus, behavior therapists attempt to change clients' behavior by applying the principles of classical conditioning, operant conditioning, and observational learning (see Chapter 6). Behavior therapy involves designing specific procedures for specific types of problems, as you'll see in our discussion of systematic desensitization.

Systematic Desensitization

PsykTrek 11e

Devised by Joseph Wolpe (1958), systematic desensitization revolutionized psychotherapy by giving therapists their first useful alternative to traditional "talk therapy" (Fishman & Franks, 1992). *Systematic desensitization is a behavior therapy used to reduce clients' phobic responses.* The treatment assumes that most anxiety responses are acquired through classical conditioning (as discussed in Chapter 14). According to this model, a harmless stimulus (for instance, a bridge) may be paired with a fear-arousing event (lightning striking it), so that it becomes a conditioned stimulus eliciting anxiety. The goal of systematic desensitization is to weaken the association between the conditioned stimulus (the bridge) and the conditioned response of anxiety (see **Figure 15.6**).

Systematic desensitization involves three steps. *In the first step, the therapist helps the client build an anxiety hierarchy.* This is a list of anxiety-arousing stimuli related to the specific source of anxiety, such as flying, academic tests, or snakes. The client ranks the stimuli from the least anxiety arousing to the most anxiety arousing. *The second step involves training the client in deep muscle relaxation.* This second phase may begin during early sessions while the therapist and client are still constructing the anxiety hierarchy. *In the third step, the client tries to work through the hierarchy, learning to remain relaxed while imagining each stimulus.* Starting with the least anxiety-arousing stimulus, the client imagines the situation as vividly as possible while relaxing. If the client experiences strong anxiety, he or she drops the imaginary scene and concentrates on relaxation. The client keeps repeating this process until he or she can imagine a scene with little or no anxiety. Once a particular scene is conquered, the client moves on to the next stimulus situation in the anxiety hierarchy. Gradually, over a number of therapy sessions, the client progresses through the hierarchy, unlearning troublesome anxiety responses.

The effectiveness of systematic desensitization in reducing phobic responses is well documented (Spiegler & Guevremont, 2010). That said, interventions emphasizing direct exposures to anxiety-arousing situations have become behavior therapists' treatment of choice for phobic and other anxiety disorders (Rachman, 2009). In *exposure therapies* clients are confronted with situations that they fear so that they learn that these situations are really harmless. The exposures take place in a controlled setting and often involve a gradual progression from less-feared to more-feared stimuli. These real-life exposures to anxiety-arousing situations usually prove harmless and individuals' anxiety responses decline. In recent decades, some therapists have resorted to highly realistic virtual-reality presentations of feared situations via computer-generated imagery (Meyerbröker & Emmelkamp, 2010; Reger et al., 2011). Exposure therapies are versatile in that they can be used with the full range of anxiety disorders, including obsessive-compulsive disorder, posttraumatic stress disorder, and panic disorder.

Aversion Therapy

PsykTrek 11e

Aversion therapy uses classical conditioning to create a negative response to a stimulus that has elicited problematic behavior. For example, alcoholics may be given an *emetic drug* (one that causes nausea and vomiting) in conjunction with their favorite

Joseph Wolpe
"Neurotic anxiety is nothing but a conditioned response."

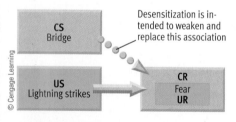

FIGURE 15.6

The logic underlying systematic desensitization. Behaviorists argue that many phobic responses are acquired through classical conditioning. For example, a person traumatized by a lightning strike while crossing a bridge might develop a phobia of bridges, as diagrammed here. Systematic desensitization targets the conditioned associations between phobic stimuli and fear responses.

drinks during therapy sessions (Landabaso et al., 1999). By pairing the drug with alcohol, the therapist hopes to create a conditioned aversion to alcohol. Aversion therapy takes advantage of the automatic, reflexive nature of responses produced through classical conditioning. Admittedly, alcoholics treated with aversion therapy know that they won't be given an emetic outside of their therapy sessions. However, their reflex response to the stimulus of alcohol may be changed so that they respond to it with nausea and distaste (see **Figure 15.7**). Obviously, this response should make it much easier to resist the urge to drink.

Aversion therapy is not a widely used technique, and it usually is only one element in a larger treatment program. Troublesome behaviors treated successfully with aversion therapy have included drug and alcohol abuse, sexual deviance, gambling, shoplifting, stuttering, cigarette smoking, and overeating (Bordnick et al., 2004; Emmelkamp, 1994; Grossman & Ruiz, 2004; Maletzky, 2002).

Social Skills Training

Many psychological problems grow out of interpersonal difficulties. Behavior therapists point out that people are not born with social finesse—they acquire social skills through learning. Unfortunately, some people have not learned how to be friendly, how to make conversation, how to express anger appropriately, and so forth. As a result, behavior therapists are increasingly using social skills training in efforts to improve clients' social abilities. This approach to therapy has yielded promising results in the treatment of social anxiety (Bögels & Voncken, 2008), autism (Cappadocia & Weiss, 2010), attention deficit disorder (Monastra, 2008) and schizophrenia (Kurtz & Mueser, 2008).

Social skills training **is a behavior therapy designed to improve interpersonal skills that emphasizes modeling, behavioral rehearsal, and shaping.** With *modeling,* clients are encouraged to watch socially skilled friends and colleagues so that they can acquire appropriate responses (eye contact, active listening, and so on) through observation. In *behavioral rehearsal,* the client tries to practice social techniques in structured role-playing exercises. The therapist provides corrective feedback and uses approval to reinforce progress. Eventually, of course, clients try their newly acquired skills in real-world interactions. Usually, they are given specific homework assignments. *Shaping* is used in that clients are gradually asked to handle more complicated and delicate social situations. For example, a nonassertive client may begin by working on making requests of friends. Only much later will he be asked to tackle standing up to his boss at work.

Cognitive-Behavioral Treatments

In Chapter 14, we learned that cognitive factors play a key role in the development of many anxiety and mood disorders. Citing the importance of such findings, behavior therapists started to focus more attention on their clients' cognitions in the 1970s (Hollon & DiGiuseppe, 2011). *Cognitive-behavioral treatments* **use combinations of verbal interventions and behavior modification techniques to help clients change maladaptive patterns of thinking.** Some of these treatments, such as Albert Ellis's (1973) *rational-emotive behavior therapy* and Aaron Beck's (1976) *cognitive therapy,* emerged out of an insight therapy tradition, whereas other treatments, such as the systems developed by Donald Meichenbaum (1977) and Michael Mahoney (1974), emerged from the behavioral tradition. We will focus on Beck's cognitive therapy (Newman & Beck, 2009) as an example of a cognitive-behavioral treatment (see Chapter 13 for a discussion of some of Ellis's ideas).

Cognitive therapy **uses specific strategies to correct habitual thinking errors that underlie various types of disorders.** Cognitive therapy was originally devised as a treatment for depression. However, in recent decades cognitive therapy has been applied fruitfully to a wide range of disorders (Beck & Weishaar, 2011; Hollon, Stewart, & Strunk, 2006). According to cognitive therapists, depression and other disorders are

Systematic desensitization is a behavioral treatment for phobias. Early studies of the procedure's efficacy often used people who had snake phobias as research subjects because people with snake phobias were relatively easy to find. This research showed that systematic desensitization is generally an effective treatment.

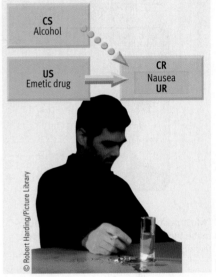

FIGURE 15.7

Aversion therapy. Aversion therapy uses classical conditioning to create an aversion to a stimulus that has elicited problematic behavior. For example, in the treatment of drinking problems, alcohol may be paired with a nausea-inducing drug to create an aversion to drinking.

Negative thinking

- Blame setbacks on personal inadequacies
- Focus selectively on negative events
- Make unduly pessimistic projections about future
- Draw negative conclusions about personal worth

→ Increased vulnerability to depression

© Cengage Learning

FIGURE 15.8

Beck's view of the roots of disorders. Beck's theory initially focused on the causes of depression, although it was gradually broadened to explain other disorders. According to Beck, depression is caused by the types of negative thinking shown here.

Courtesy of Aaron T. Beck

Aaron Beck

"Most people are barely aware of the automatic thoughts which precede unpleasant feelings or automatic inhibitions."

caused by "errors" in thinking (see **Figure 15.8**). For example, they assert that depression-prone people tend to (1) blame their setbacks on personal inadequacies without considering circumstantial explanations, (2) focus selectively on negative events while ignoring positive events, (3) make unduly pessimistic projections about the future, and (4) draw negative conclusions about their worth as a person based on insignificant events. For instance, imagine that you got a low grade on a minor quiz in a class. If you made the kinds of errors in thinking just described, you might blame the grade on your woeful stupidity, dismiss comments from a classmate that it was an unfair test, gloomily predict that you will surely flunk the course, and conclude that you are not genuine college material.

The goal of cognitive therapy is to change clients' negative thoughts and maladaptive beliefs (Kellogg & Young, 2008). To begin, clients are taught to detect their automatic negative thoughts—the self-defeating statements that people are prone to make when analyzing problems. Examples might include "I'm just not smart enough," "No one really likes me," or "It's all my fault." Clients are then trained to subject these automatic thoughts to reality testing. The therapist helps them to see how unrealistically negative the thoughts are.

Cognitive therapy uses a variety of behavioral techniques, such as modeling, systematic monitoring of one's behavior, and behavioral rehearsal (Beck & Weishaar, 2011). For example, cognitive therapists often give their clients "homework assignments" that focus on changing clients' overt behaviors. Clients may be instructed to engage in overt responses on their own, outside of the clinician's office.

How Effective Are Behavior Therapies?

Behavior therapists have historically placed more emphasis on the importance of measuring therapeutic outcomes than insight therapists have. Thus, there has been a good deal of research on the effectiveness of behavior therapy (Jacob & Pelham, 2005; Stanley & Beidel, 2009). Of course, behavior therapies are not well suited to the treatment of some types of problems (vague feelings of discontent, for instance). Furthermore, it's misleading to make global statements about the effectiveness of behavior therapies, because they include many types of procedures designed for very different purposes. For example, the value of systematic desensitization for phobias has no bearing on the value of aversion therapy for sexual deviance. For our purposes, it is sufficient to note that there is favorable evidence on the efficacy of most of the widely used behavioral interventions (Zinbarg & Griffith, 2008). Behavior therapies can make important contributions to the treatment of phobias, obsessive-compulsive disorders, sexual dysfunction, schizophrenia, drug-related problems, eating disorders, psychosomatic disorders, hyperactivity, autism, and mental retardation (Emmelkamp, 2004; Hollon & Dimidjian, 2009; Wilson, 2011).

Biomedical Therapies

KEY LEARNING GOALS

15.9 Summarize the therapeutic actions and side effects of four categories of psychiatric drugs.

15.10 Evaluate the overall efficacy of drug treatments, and discuss controversies surrounding pharmaceutical research.

15.11 Describe electroconvulsive therapy, and assess its therapeutic effects and risks.

Biomedical therapies are physiological interventions intended to reduce symptoms associated with psychological disorders. These therapies assume that psychological disorders are caused, at least in part, by biological malfunctions. As we discussed in the previous chapter, this assumption clearly has merit for many disorders, especially the more severe ones. We will discuss the two standard biomedical approaches to psychotherapy, drug therapy and electroconvulsive (shock) therapy.

Treatment with Drugs

PSYKTREK 11e

Since the 1950s drug therapy has become increasingly important in the treatment of psychological disorders. Therapeutic drugs fall into four major groups: antianxiety drugs, antipsychotic drugs, antidepressant drugs, and mood stabilizers.

ANTIANXIETY DRUGS

PSYKTREK 11e

Most of us know someone who pops pills to relieve anxiety. *Antianxiety drugs,* **which reduce tension, apprehension, and nervousness,** are the drugs used in this common coping strategy. The most popular of these drugs are Valium and Xanax (trade names for the generic drugs diazepam and alprazolam, respectively).

Valium, Xanax, and other similar drugs are often called *tranquilizers*. These drugs exert their effects almost immediately. They can be fairly effective in relieving feelings of anxiety (Dubovsky, 2009). However, their effects are measured in hours, so their impact is relatively short-lived. Antianxiety drugs are routinely prescribed for people with anxiety disorders, but they are also given to millions of people who simply suffer from chronic nervous tension.

All the drugs used to treat psychological disorders have potentially troublesome side effects that show up in some patients but not others. The most common side effects of Valium and Xanax are drowsiness, lightheadedness, cottonmouth, depression, nausea, and constipation. These drugs also have potential for abuse, drug dependence, and overdose, although these risks have probably been exaggerated in the press (Martinez, Marangell, & Martinez, 2008). Another drawback is that patients who have been on antianxiety drugs for a while often experience unpleasant withdrawal symptoms when their drug treatment is stopped (Edwards et al., 2008).

ANTIPSYCHOTIC DRUGS

PSYKTREK 11e

Antipsychotic drugs are used primarily in the treatment of schizophrenia. They are also given to people with severe mood disorders who become delusional. *Antipsychotic drugs* **are used to gradually reduce psychotic symptoms, including hyperactivity, mental confusion, hallucinations, and delusions.** The traditional antipsychotics appear to decrease activity at dopamine synapses. However, the exact relationship between their neurochemical effects and their clinical effects remains obscure (Miyamoto et al., 2008).

Concept Check 15.2

Understanding Therapists' Goals

Check your understanding of therapists' goals by matching various therapies with the appropriate description. The answers are in Appendix A.

Principal Therapeutic Goals

_____ 1. Elimination of maladaptive behaviors or symptoms

_____ 2. Acceptance of genuine self, personal growth

_____ 3. Recovery of unconscious conflicts, character reconstruction

_____ 4. Detection and reduction of negative thinking

Therapy

a. Psychoanalysis

b. Client-centered therapy

c. Cognitive therapy

d. Behavior therapy

© Christo/Shutterstock

FIGURE 15.9

The time course of antipsychotic drug effects. Antipsychotic drugs reduce psychotic symptoms gradually, over a span of weeks, as graphed here. In contrast, patients given placebo medication show little improvement.

SOURCE: Cole, J. O., Goldberg, S. C., & Davis, J. M. (1966). Drugs in the treatment of psychosis. In P. Solomon (Ed.), *Psychiatric drugs*. New York: Grune & Stratton. From data in the NIMH-PSC Collaborative Study I. Reprinted by permission of J. M. Davis.

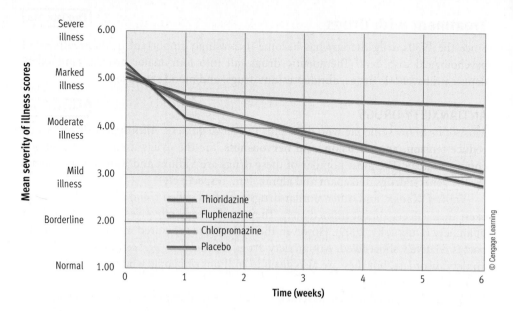

Studies suggest that antipsychotic drugs reduce psychotic symptoms in about 70% of patients, albeit in varied degrees (Kane, Stroup, & Marder, 2009). When antipsychotic drugs are effective, they work their magic gradually, as shown in **Figure 15.9**. Patients usually begin to respond within two days to a week. Further improvement may occur for several months. Many schizophrenic patients are placed on antipsychotics indefinitely because these drugs can reduce the likelihood of a relapse into an active schizophrenic episode (van Kammen, Hurford, & Marder, 2009).

Antipsychotic drugs undeniably make a major contribution to the treatment of severe mental disorders, but they are not without problems. They have many unpleasant side effects (Dolder, 2008; Muench & Hamer, 2010). Drowsiness, constipation, and cottonmouth are common. Tremors, muscular rigidity, and impaired coordination may also occur. After being released from a hospital, many patients who have been placed on antipsychotics stop their drug regimen because of the side effects. Unfortunately, after patients stop taking antipsychotic medication, about 70% relapse within a year (van Kammen et al., 2009). One recent study found that even brief periods of partial noncompliance with one's drug regimen increased the risk of relapse (Subotnik et al., 2011). In addition to their nuisance side effects, antipsychotics may cause a more severe and lasting problem called *tardive dyskinesia,* which is seen in about 20%–30% of patients who receive long-term treatment with traditional antipsychotics (Kane et al., 2009). ***Tardive dyskinesia* is a neurological disorder marked by involuntary writhing and ticlike movements of the mouth, tongue, face, hands, or feet.** Once this debilitating syndrome emerges, there is no cure, although spontaneous remission sometimes occurs after the discontinuation of antipsychotic medication (Pi & Simpson, 2000).

Psychiatrists currently rely primarily on a newer class of antipsychotic agents called *atypical* or *second-generation antipsychotic drugs* (Marder, Hurford, & van Kammen, 2009). These drugs appear to be roughly similar to the first-generation antipsychotics in therapeutic effectiveness, but they offer several advantages over the older drugs (Meltzer & Bobo, 2009). For instance, they can help some treatment-resistant patients who do not respond to traditional antipsychotics, and they produce fewer unpleasant side effects and carry less risk for tardive dyskinesia. Of course, like all powerful drugs, they carry some risks: Second-generation antipsychotics appear to increase patients' vulnerability to diabetes and cardiovascular problems.

ANTIDEPRESSANT DRUGS

PSYKTREK 11e

As their name suggests, *antidepressant drugs* gradually elevate mood and help bring people out of a depression. Reliance on antidepressants has increased dramatically in the last 10–15 years, as these drugs have become the most frequently prescribed class of medication in the United States (Olfson & Marcus, 2009). Today, the most widely prescribed antidepressants are the *selective serotonin reuptake inhibitors (SSRIs),* which slow the reuptake process at serotonin synapses. The drugs in this class, which include Prozac (fluoxetine), Paxil (paroxetine), and Zoloft (sertraline), seem to yield rapid therapeutic gains in the treatment of depression (Boland & Keller, 2008) while producing fewer unpleasant or dangerous side effects than previous generations of antidepressants (Sussman, 2009). However, there is some doubt about how effective the SSRIs (and other antidepressants) are in relieving episodes of depression among patients suffering from bipolar disorder (Berman et al., 2009). Bipolar patients do not seem to respond as well as those who suffer from depression only, and in some cases antidepressants appear to foster a switch back into a manic episode (Altshuler et al., 2006).

Like antipsychotic drugs, the various types of antidepressants exert their effects gradually over a period of weeks, but about 60% of patients' improvement tends to occur in the first two weeks (Gitlin, 2009). A recent analysis that looked carefully at the severity of patients' depression when medication was initiated found that people with serious depression benefit the most from antidepressants (Fournier et al, 2010). This analysis focused on six studies that measured patients' initial level of depression precisely and included patients with the full range of symptom severity (many drug trials exclude patients with mild illness). The most provocative aspect of the findings was that antidepressants provided a relatively modest benefit for patients with mild to moderate depression.

A major concern in recent years has been evidence from a number of studies that SSRIs may increase the risk for suicide (Healy & Whitaker, 2003; Holden, 2004). The challenge of collecting definitive data on this issue is much more daunting than one might guess. The crux of the problem is that suicide rates are already elevated among people who exhibit the disorders for which SSRIs are prescribed (Berman, 2009). Some researchers have collected data that suggest that suicide rates have *declined* slightly because of widespread prescription of SSRIs (Baldessarini et al., 2007; Isacsson et al., 2009). In contrast, others have found no association between SSRIs and suicide (Lapiere, 2003; Simon et al., 2006).

Overall, however, when antidepressants are compared to placebo treatment, the data suggest that antidepressants lead to a slight elevation in the risk of suicidal behavior, from roughly 2% to 4% (Bridge et al., 2007; Dubicka, Hadley, & Roberts, 2006; Hammad, Laughren, & Racoosin, 2006). The increased suicide risk appears to mainly be a problem among a small minority of children and adolescents in the first month after starting antidepressants, especially during the first nine days (Jick, Kaye, & Jick, 2004). Thus, patients starting on SSRIs should be carefully monitored by their physicians and families (Culpepper et al., 2004). Regulatory warnings from the U.S. Food and Drug Administration (FDA) have led to a decline in the prescription of SSRIs among adolescents (Nemeroff et al., 2007). This trend has prompted concern that increases in suicide may occur among untreated individuals (Dudley et al., 2008). This concern seems legitimate in that suicide risk clearly peaks in the month prior to people beginning treatment for depression, whether that treatment involves SSRIs or psychotherapy (Simon & Savarino, 2007). This pattern presumably occurs because the escalating agony of depression finally prompts people to seek treatment, but it also suggests that getting treatment with drugs or therapy reduces suicidal risk. In the final analysis, this is a complex issue, but the one thing experts seem to agree on is that adolescents starting on SSRIs should be monitored closely.

MOOD STABILIZERS

Mood stabilizers **are drugs used to control mood swings in patients with bipolar mood disorders.** The principal drugs in this category are *lithium* and *valproate*. Both have proven valuable in preventing *future* episodes of both mania and depression in patients with bipolar illness (Muzina, Kemp, Calabrese, 2008; Post & Altshuler, 2009). They can also be used in efforts to bring patients with bipolar illness out of *current* manic or depressive episodes. However, antipsychotics and antidepressants are more commonly used for these purposes. On the negative side of the ledger, lithium does have some dangerous side effects if its use isn't managed skillfully (Jefferson & Greist, 2009). Lithium levels in the patient's blood must be monitored carefully, because high concentrations can be toxic and even fatal. Kidney and thyroid gland complications are the other major problems associated with lithium therapy.

EVALUATING DRUG THERAPIES

Drug therapies can produce clear therapeutic gains for many kinds of patients. What's especially impressive is that they can be effective with severe disorders that otherwise defy therapeutic endeavors. Nonetheless, drug therapies are controversial. Critics have raised a number of issues (Bentall, 2009; Breggin, 2008; Healy, 2004; Kirsch, 2010; Whitaker, 2002). First, some critics argue that drug therapies are not as effective as advertised and that they often produce superficial, short-lived curative effects. For example, Valium does not really solve problems with anxiety; it merely provides temporary relief from an unpleasant symptom. Moreover, relapse rates are substantial when drug regimens are discontinued. Second, critics charge that many drugs are overprescribed and many patients overmedicated. According to these critics, a number of physicians routinely hand out prescriptions without giving adequate consideration to more complicated and difficult interventions. Consistent with this line of criticism, a recent study of office visits to psychiatrists found that they increasingly prescribe two and even three medications to patients, even though relatively little is known about the interactive effects of psychiatric drugs (Mojtabai & Olfson, 2010). Third, some critics charge that the damaging side effects of therapeutic drugs are underestimated by psychiatrists and that these side effects are often worse than the illnesses that the drugs are supposed to cure.

Critics maintain that the negative effects of psychiatric drugs are not fully appreciated because the pharmaceutical industry has managed to gain undue influence over the research enterprise as it relates to drug testing (Angell, 2004; Healy, 2004; Insel, 2010; L. J. Weber, 2006). Today, most researchers who investigate the benefits and risks of medications and write treatment guidelines have lucrative financial arrangements with the pharmaceutical industry (Bentall, 2009; Lurie et al., 2006; Pachter et al., 2007). Their studies are funded by drug companies, and they often receive substantial consulting fees. Unfortunately, these financial ties appear to undermine the objectivity required in scientific research, as studies funded by drug companies are far less likely to report unfavorable results than nonprofit-funded studies (Bekelman, Li, & Gross, 2003; Perlis et al., 2005). Industry-financed drug trials also tend to be much too brief to detect the long-term risks associated with new drugs (Vandenbroucke & Psaty, 2008). Additionally, when unfavorable results emerge, the data are often withheld from publication (Antonuccio, Danton, & McClanahan, 2003; Rising, Bacchetti, & Bero, 2008; Turner et al., 2008). Also, research designs are often slanted in a variety of ways so as to exaggerate the positive effects and minimize the negative effects of the drugs under scrutiny (Carpenter, 2002; Chopra, 2003; Moncrieff, 2001). The conflicts of interest that appear to be pervasive in contemporary drug research raise grave concerns that require attention from researchers, universities, and federal agencies.

© Frank Cotham/The New Yorker Collection/www.cartoonbank.com

"I medicate first and ask questions later."

Electroconvulsive Therapy (ECT)

In the 1930s, a Hungarian psychiatrist named Ladislas von Meduna speculated that epilepsy and schizophrenia could not coexist in the same body. On the basis of this observation, which turned out to be inaccurate, von Meduna theorized that it might be useful to induce epileptic-like seizures in schizophrenic patients. Initially, a drug was used to trigger these seizures. However, by 1938 a pair of Italian psychiatrists (Cerletti & Bini,

1938) demonstrated that it was safer to elicit the seizures with electric shock. Thus, modern electroconvulsive therapy was born.

Electroconvulsive therapy (ECT) **is a biomedical treatment in which electric shock is used to produce a cortical seizure accompanied by convulsions.** In ECT, electrodes are attached to the skull over the temporal lobes of the brain. A light anesthesia is administered, and the patient is given a variety of drugs to minimize the likelihood of complications, such as spinal fractures. An electric current is then applied for about a second. The current triggers a brief (5–20 seconds) convulsive seizure, during which the patient usually loses consciousness. The patient normally awakens in an hour or two. People typically receive three treatments a week over a period of two to seven weeks (Fink, 2009).

The clinical use of ECT peaked in the 1940s and 1950s, before effective drug therapies were widely available. ECT has long been controversial, and its use declined in the 1960s and 1970s. Nonetheless, the use of ECT has seen a resurgence in recent decades, and it is not a rare form of therapy. Although only about 8% of psychiatrists administer ECT (Hermann et al., 1998), it is estimated that about 100,000 people receive ECT treatments yearly in the United States (Hermann et al., 1995). Some critics argue that ECT is overused because it is a lucrative procedure that boosts psychiatrists' income while consuming relatively little of their time in comparison to insight therapy (Frank, 1990). Conversely, some ECT advocates argue that ECT is underutilized because the public harbors many misconceptions about its risks and side effects (McDonald et al., 2004).

EFFECTIVENESS OF ECT

The evidence on the therapeutic efficacy of ECT is open to varied interpretations. Proponents maintain that it is a remarkably effective treatment for major depression (Fink, 2009; Prudic, 2009). Moreover, they note that many patients who do not benefit from antidepressant medication improve in response to ECT (Nobler & Sackeim, 2006). However, opponents argue that the available studies are flawed and inconclusive and that ECT is probably no more effective than a placebo (Rose et al., 2003). Overall, there does seem to be enough favorable evidence to justify *conservative* use of ECT in treating severe mood disorders in patients who have not responded to medication (Carney & Geddes, 2003; Metzger, 1999). Unfortunately, relapse rates after ECT are distressingly high. For example in one well-controlled study, 64% of patients relapsed within 6 months and the median time to relapse was only 8.6 weeks (Prudic et al., 2004). These relapse rates, however, can be reduced by giving ECT patients antidepressant drugs (Sackeim et al., 2001, 2009).

Concept Check **15.3**

Understanding Biomedical Therapies

Check your understanding of biomedical therapies by matching each treatment with its chief use. The answers are in Appendix A.

Treatment	Chief Purpose
_____ 1. Antianxiety drugs	a. To reduce psychotic symptoms
_____ 2. Antipsychotic drugs	b. To bring a major depression to an end
_____ 3. Antidepressant drugs	c. To suppress tension, nervousness, and apprehension
_____ 4. Mood stabilizers	d. To prevent future episodes of mania or depression in bipolar disorders
_____ 5. Electroconvulsive therapy (ECT)	

Illustrated OVERVIEW

Five Major Approaches to Treatment

THERAPY/FOUNDER

ROOTS OF DISORDERS

PSYCHOANALYSIS

Developed by Sigmund Freud in Vienna, from the 1890s through the 1930s

Intrapsychic conflict (among id, ego, and superego) → Anxiety → Reliance on defense mechanisms

Unconscious conflict resulting from fixations in earlier development cause anxiety, which leads to defensive behavior. The repressed conflicts typically center on sex and aggression.

CLIENT-CENTERED THERAPY

Created by Carl Rogers at the University of Chicago during the 1940s and 1950s

Need to distort shortcomings to feel worthy of affection → Relatively incongruent self-concept → Recurrent anxiety

Defensive behavior protects inaccurate self-concept

Overdependence on acceptance from others fosters incongruence, which leads to anxiety and defensive behavior and thwarts personal growth.

BEHAVIOR THERAPY

Launched primarily by South African Joseph Wolpe's description of systematic desensitization in 1958

Maladaptive patterns of behavior are acquired through learning. For example, many phobias are thought to be created through classical conditioning and maintained by operant conditioning.

CS Bridge
US Lightning strikes
CR Fear UR

COGNITIVE–BEHAVIORAL TREATMENTS

One approach devised by Aaron Beck at the University of Pennsylvania in the 1960s and 1970s

Pervasive negative thinking about events related to self fosters anxiety and depression, and other forms of pathology.

Blame setbacks on personal inadequacies
Focus selectively on negative events
Make unduly pessimistic projections about future
Draw negative conclusions about personal worth
→ Increased vulnerability to depression

BIOMEDICAL THERAPY

Many researchers contributed; key breakthroughs in drug treatment made around 1950 by John Cade in Australia, Henri Laborit in France, and Jean Delay and Pierre Deniker, also in France

Most disorders are attributed to genetic predisposition and physiological malfunctions, such as abnormal neurotransmitter activity.

For example, schizophrenia appears to be associated with overactivity at dopamine synapses.

Unless otherwise stated, art on this page © Cengage Learning.

THERAPEUTIC GOALS

THERAPEUTIC TECHNIQUES

Insights regarding unconscious conflicts and motives; resolution of conflicts; personality reconstruction

Free association, dream analysis, interpretation, transference

Increased congruence between self-concept and experience; acceptance of genuine self; self-determination and personal growth

Genuineness, empathy, unconditional positive regard, clarification, reflecting back to client

Elimination of maladaptive symptoms; acquisition of more adaptive responses

Classical and operant conditioning, systematic desensitization, aversive conditioning, social skills training, reinforcement, shaping, punishment, extinction, biofeedback

Reduction of negative thinking; substitution of more realistic thinking

Thought stopping, recording of automatic thoughts, refuting of negative thinking, homework assignments

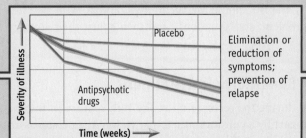

Elimination or reduction of symptoms; prevention of relapse

Antianxiety, antidepressant, antipsychotic, and mood-stabilizing drugs, electro-convulsive therapy

SOURCE: Cole, J. O., Goldberg, S. C., & Davis, J. M. (1966). Drugs in the treatment of psychosis. In P. Solomon (Ed.), *Psychiatric drugs*. New York: Grune & Stratton. From data in the NIMH-PSC Collaborative Study I. Reprinted by permission of J. M. Davis.

RISKS ASSOCIATED WITH ECT

Even ECT proponents acknowledge that memory losses, impaired attention, and other cognitive deficits are common short-term side effects of electroconvulsive therapy (Rowny & Lisanby, 2008; Sackeim et al., 2007). However, advocates assert that these deficits are mild and usually disappear within a month or two (Glass, 2001). An American Psychiatric Association task force (2001) concluded that there is no objective evidence that ECT causes structural damage in the brain or that it has any lasting negative effects on the ability to learn and remember information. In contrast, ECT critics maintain that ECT-induced cognitive deficits are often significant and sometimes permanent (Breggin, 1991; Rose et al., 2003), although their evidence seems to be largely anecdotal. Given the doubts that have been raised about the efficacy and risks of electroconvulsive therapy, it appears that this treatment will remain controversial for some time to come.

Current Trends and Issues in Treatment

As we saw in our discussion of insight, behavioral, and drug therapy, recent decades have brought many changes in the world of mental health care. In this section, we'll discuss two trends that are not tied to a specific mode of treatment. Specifically, we'll look at the trend toward blending various approaches to therapy and efforts to respond more effectively to increasing cultural diversity in Western societies.

Blending Approaches to Treatment

In this chapter, we have reviewed many approaches to treatment. However, there is no rule that a client must be treated with just one approach. Often, a clinician will use several techniques in working with a client. For example, a depressed person might receive cognitive therapy, social skills training, and antidepressant medication. Multiple approaches are particularly likely when a treatment team provides therapy. Studies suggest that combining approaches to treatment has merit (Glass, 2004; Szigethy & Friedman, 2009).

The value of multiple approaches to treatment may explain why a significant trend seems to have crept into the field of psychotherapy. There's now a movement *away* from strong loyalty to individual schools of thought and a corresponding move toward integrating various approaches to therapy (Castonguay et al., 2003; D. A. Smith, 1999). Most clinicians used to depend exclusively on one system of therapy while rejecting the utility of all others. This era of fragmentation may be drawing to a close. One survey of psychologists' theoretical orientations found that 36% of the respondents described themselves as *eclectic* in approach (Norcross, Hedges, & Castle, 2002). **Eclecticism in the practice of therapy involves drawing ideas from two or more systems of therapy instead of committing to just one system.** Advocates of eclecticism, such as Arnold Lazarus (1995, 2008), maintain that therapists should ask themselves, "What is the best approach for this specific client, problem, and situation?" and then adjust their strategy accordingly.

Increasing Multicultural Sensitivity in Treatment

Modern psychotherapy emerged during the second half of the 19th century in Europe and America. It was spawned in part by a cultural milieu that viewed the person as an independent, reflective, rational being, capable of self-improvement (Cushman, 1992). Psychological disorders were assumed to have natural causes, like physical diseases do, and to be susceptible to medical treatments derived from scientific research. But the individualized, medicalized institution of modern psychotherapy reflects Western cultural values that are far from universal (Sue & Sue, 1999). In many nonindustrialized societies, psychological disorders are attributed to supernatural forces (possession, witchcraft, angry gods, and so forth), and victims seek help from priests, shamans, and folk healers, rather than doctors (Wittkower & Warnes, 1984). Thus, efforts to export Western psychotherapies to non-Western cultures have met with mixed success. Indeed, the highly culture-bound origins of modern therapies have raised questions about their applicability to ethnic minorities *within* Western culture (Miranda et al., 2005).

Research on how cultural factors influence the process and outcome of psychotherapy has increased in recent years. Its growth has been motivated in part by the need to improve mental health services for ethnic minority groups in American society (Lee & Ramirez, 2000; Worthington, Soth-McNett, & Moreno, 2007). Studies suggest that American minority groups generally underutilize therapeutic services (Bender et al., 2007; Folsom et al., 2007; Sue et al., 2009). Why? A variety of barriers appear to contribute to this problem (Snowden & Yamada, 2005; U.S. Department of Health and Human Services, 1999; Zane et al., 2004). One major consideration is that many members of minority groups have a history of frustrating interactions with American bureaucracies. Hence, they tend to be distrusting of large, intimidating institutions, such as hospitals and community mental health centers. Another issue is that most hospitals and mental health agencies are not adequately staffed with therapists who speak the languages used by minority groups in their service areas. Yet another problem is that the vast majority of therapists have been trained almost exclusively in the treatment of white, middle-class Americans. As a result, they often are not familiar with the cultural backgrounds and unique characteristics of various ethnic groups. This culture gap often leads to misunderstandings, ill-advised treatment strategies, and reduced rapport. Consistent with this assertion, recent research found that psychiatrists spend less time with African American patients than white patients (Olfson, Cherry, & Lewis-Fernandez, 2009). Another study of over 3500 African American participants found that only 27% of their mental health visits resulted in "minimally adequate care" (Neighbors et al., 2007). And a recent study of over 15,000 people suffering from depression found that Mexican Americans and African Americans were notably less likely to receive treatment than whites, as can be seen in **Figure 15.10** (González et al., 2010).

What can be done to improve mental health services for American minority groups? Researchers in this area have offered a variety of suggestions (Hong, Garcia, & Soriano, 2000; Miranda et al., 2005; Pedersen, 1994; Yamamoto et al., 1993). Discussions of possible solutions usually begin with the need to recruit and train more ethnic minority therapists. Studies show that ethnic minorities are more likely to go to mental health facilities staffed by a higher proportion of people who share their ethnic background (Snowden & Hu, 1996; Sue, Zane, & Young, 1994). Individual therapists have been urged to work harder at building a vigorous *therapeutic alliance* (a strong supportive bond) with their ethnic clients. A strong therapeutic alliance is associated with better therapeutic outcomes regardless of ethnicity, but some studies suggest that it is especially crucial for minority clients (Bender et al., 2007; Comas-Diaz, 2006). Finally, most authorities urge further investigation of how traditional approaches to therapy can be modified and tailored to be more compatible with specific cultural groups' attitudes, values, norms, and traditions (Hwang, 2006). A recent review of seventy-six studies that examined the effects of culturally adapted interventions found clear evidence that this tailoring process tends to yield positive effects (Griner & Smith, 2006; Sue et al., 2009). The benefits are particularly notable when a treatment is tailored to a single, specific cultural group rather than a mixture of several or more cultural groups.

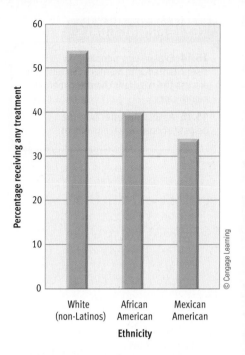

FIGURE 15.10

Ethnicity and treatment for depression. In a nationally representative sample of almost 16,000 subjects, Gonzales and colleagues (2010) identified participants suffering from depression and ascertained what types of treatment they had received. When they analyzed these data in relation to ethnicity, they found that members of minority groups were less likely than whites to get treatment. The data graphed here show the percentage of patients receiving treatment of any kind.

© Ali Haider/epa/Corbis

Institutional Treatment in Transition

KEY LEARNING GOALS

15.14 Explain why people grew disenchanted with mental hospitals, and discuss the resultant change in mental health care.

15.15 Assess the effects of the deinstitutionalization movement.

Traditionally, much of the treatment of mental illness has been carried out in institutional settings, primarily in mental hospitals. **A *mental hospital* is a medical institution specializing in providing inpatient care for psychological disorders.** In the United States, a national network of state-funded mental hospitals started to emerge in the 1840s through the efforts of Dorothea Dix and other reformers. Prior to these reforms, the mentally ill who were poor were housed in jails and poorhouses or were left to wander the countryside. Today, mental hospitals continue to play an important role in the delivery of mental health services. However, since World War II, institutional care for mental illness has undergone a series of major transitions—and the dust hasn't settled yet. Let's look at how institutional care has evolved in recent decades.

Disenchantment with Mental Hospitals

By the 1950s, it had become apparent that public mental hospitals were not fulfilling their goals very well (Mechanic, 1980; Menninger, 2005). Experts began to realize that hospitalization often *contributed* to the development of pathology instead of curing it.

What were the causes of these unexpected negative effects? Part of the problem was that the facilities were usually underfunded (Hogan & Morrison, 2008). The lack of adequate funding meant that the facilities were overcrowded and understaffed. Hospital personnel were undertrained and overworked, making them hard-pressed to deliver minimal custodial care. Despite gallant efforts at treatment, the demoralizing conditions made most public mental hospitals decidedly nontherapeutic (Scull, 1990). These problems were aggravated by the fact that state mental hospitals served large geographic regions but were rarely placed near major population centers. As a result, most patients were uprooted from their community and isolated from their social support networks.

Disenchantment with the public mental hospital system inspired the *community mental health movement* that emerged in the 1960s (Duckworth & Borus, 1999; Huey et al., 2009). The community mental health movement emphasizes (1) local, community-based care, (2) reduced dependence on hospitalization, and (3) the prevention of psychological disorders. Community mental health centers were intended to supplement mental hospitals with decentralized and more accessible services. However, they have had their own funding struggles (Dixon & Goldman, 2004).

Deinstitutionalization

Mental hospitals continue to care for many people troubled by chronic mental illness, but their role in patient care has diminished. Since the 1960s, a policy of deinstitutionalization has been followed in the United States, as well as most other Western countries (Fakhoury & Priebe, 2002). *Deinstitutionalization refers to transferring the treatment of mental illness from inpatient institutions to community-based facilities that emphasize outpatient care.* This shift in responsibility was made possible by two developments: (1) the emergence of effective drug therapies for severe disorders and (2) the deployment of community mental health centers to coordinate local care (Goff & Gudeman, 1999).

The exodus of patients from mental hospitals has been dramatic. The average inpatient population in state and county mental hospitals had dropped from a peak of nearly 550,000 in the mid-1950s to around 70,000 by 2000, as shown in **Figure 15.11**. This trend does not mean that hospitalization for mental illness has

FIGURE 15.11

Declining inpatient population at state and county mental hospitals. The inpatient population in public mental hospitals has declined dramatically since the late 1950s, as a result of deinstitutionalization and the development of effective antipsychotic medication. (Data from the National Institute of Mental Health) become a thing of the past. A great many people are still hospitalized, but the shift has been toward placing them in local general hospitals for brief periods instead of distant psychiatric hospitals for long periods (Hogan & Morrison, 2008). In keeping with the philosophy of deinstitutionalization, these local facilities try to get patients stabilized and back into the community as swiftly as possible.

How has deinstitutionalization worked out? It gets mixed reviews. On the positive side, many people have benefited by avoiding disruptive and unnecessary hospitalization. Ample evidence suggests that alternatives to hospitalization can be as effective as and less costly than inpatient care (McGrew et al., 1999; Reinharz, Lesage, & Contandriopoulos, 2000). Moreover, follow-up studies of discharged patients reveal that a substantial majority prefer the greater freedom provided by community-based treatment (Leff, 2006).

Nonetheless, some unanticipated problems have arisen (Elpers, 2001; Munk-Jorgensen, 1999; Talbott, 2004). Many patients suffering from chronic psychological disorders had nowhere to go when they were released. They had no families, friends, or homes to return to. Many had no work skills and were poorly prepared to live on their own. These people were supposed to be absorbed by "halfway houses," sheltered workshops, and other types of intermediate care facilities. Unfortunately, many communities were never able to fund and build the planned facilities (Hogan & Morrison, 2003; Lamb, 1998). Thus, deinstitutionalization left two major problems in its wake: a "revolving door" population of people who flow in and out of psychiatric facilities, and a sizable population of homeless mentally ill people.

Mental Illness, the Revolving Door, and Homelessness

Most of the people caught in the mental health system's revolving door suffer from chronic, severe disorders (usually schizophrenia) that often require hospitalization (Haywood et al., 1995). However, they respond to drug therapies in the hospital. Once they're stabilized through drug therapy, they no longer qualify for expensive hospital treatment according to the new standards created by deinstitutionalization and managed care. Thus, they're sent back out the door, into communities that often aren't prepared to provide adequate outpatient care. Because they lack appropriate care and support, their condition deteriorates, and they soon require readmission to a hospital, where the cycle begins once again. Over two-thirds of all psychiatric inpatient admissions involve rehospitalizing a former patient. Moreover, 40% to 50% of patients are readmitted within a year of their release (Bridge & Barbe, 2004).

DOONESBURY

Deinstitutionalization has also been blamed for the growing population of homeless people. Studies have consistently found elevated rates of mental illness among the homeless. Taken as a whole, the evidence suggests that roughly one-third of homeless people suffer from severe mental illness (schizophrenic and mood disorders), that another one-third or more are struggling with alcohol and drug problems, that many qualify for multiple diagnoses, and that the prevalence of mental illness among the homeless may be increasing (Bassuk et al., 1998; Folsom et al., 2005; Haugland et al., 1997; North et al., 2004; Vazquez, Munoz, & Sanz, 1997). In essence, homeless shelters have become a *de facto* element of America's mental health care system (Callicutt, 2006).

Ultimately, it's clear that our society is not providing adequate care for a sizable segment of the mentally ill population (Appelbaum, 2002; Elpers, 2000; Gittelman, 2005; Torrey, 1996). That's not a new development. Inadequate care for mental illness has always been the norm. Societies always struggle with the problem of what to do with the mentally ill and how to pay for their care (Duckworth & Borus, 1999). Ours is no different. Unfortunately, in recent years the situation has deteriorated rather than improved. Although overall health care spending has been increasing steadily in recent years, funding for mental health care has diminished dramatically (Geller, 2009). The number of beds in general hospitals dedicated to psychiatric care has declined precipitously since the late 1990s (Liptzin, Gottlieb, & Summergrad, 2007). Today, most states have a shortage of psychiatric beds, resulting in waiting lists for admission, overcrowding, and increasingly brief hospitalizations (Geller, 2009).

KEY LEARNING GOALS

15.16 Identify the two unifying themes highlighted in this chapter.

 Cultural Heritage

 Theoretical Diversity

Reflecting on the Chapter's Themes

In our discussion of psychotherapy, one of our unifying themes—the value of theoretical diversity—was particularly prominent, and one other theme—the importance of culture—surfaced briefly. Let's discuss the latter theme first. The approaches to psychotherapy described in this chapter are products of modern, white, middle-class, Western culture. Some of these therapies have proven useful in some other cultures, but many have turned out to be irrelevant or counterproductive when used with different cultural groups. Thus, we have seen once again that Western psychology cannot assume that its theories and practices have universal applicability.

As for theoretical diversity, its value can be illustrated with a rhetorical question: Can you imagine what the state of modern psychotherapy would be if everyone in psychology and psychiatry had simply accepted Freud's theories about the nature and treatment of psychological disorders? If not for theoretical diversity, mental health treatment might still be in the dark ages. Psychoanalysis can be a useful method of therapy, but we would have a tragic state of affairs if that were the *only* treatment available to people experiencing psychological distress. Multitudes of people have benefited from alternative approaches to treatment that emerged out of tension between psychoanalytic theory and various other theoretical perspectives.

Given that people have diverse problems, rooted in varied origins, it is fortunate that they can choose from a diverse array of approaches to treatment. The illustrated overview on pages 522–523 summarizes and compares the approaches that we've discussed in this chapter. This overview shows that the major approaches to therapy each have their own vision of the nature of human discontent and the ideal remedy.

Of course, diversity can be confusing. The range and variety of available treatments in modern psychotherapy leaves many people puzzled about their options. Thus, in our Personal Application we'll sort through the practical issues involved in selecting a therapist.

Looking for a Therapist

Answer the following "true" or "false."

___ **1** Psychotherapy is an art as well as a science.

___ **2** Psychotherapy can be harmful or damaging to a client.

___ **3** Mental health treatment does not have to be expensive.

___ **4** The type of professional degree that a therapist holds is relatively unimportant.

All of these statements are true. Do any of them surprise you? If so, you're in good company. Many people know relatively little about the practicalities of selecting a therapist.

The task of finding an appropriate therapist is no less complex than shopping for any other major service. Should you see a psychologist or a psychiatrist? Should you opt for individual therapy or group therapy? Should you see a client-centered therapist or a behavior therapist? The unfortunate part of this complexity is that people seeking psychotherapy often feel overwhelmed by personal difficulties. The last thing they need is to be confronted by yet another complex problem.

Nonetheless, the importance of finding a good therapist cannot be overestimated. Therapy can sometimes have harmful rather than helpful effects. We have already discussed how drug therapies and ECT can sometimes be damaging. But problems are not limited to biological interventions. Talking about your problems with a therapist may sound pretty harmless, but studies indicate that insight therapies can also backfire (Lambert & Ogles, 2004; Lillienfeld, 2007). Although a great many talented thera-

pists are available, psychotherapy, like any other profession, has incompetent practitioners as well. Therefore, you should shop for a skilled therapist, just as you would for a good attorney or a good mechanic.

In this Application, we'll go over some information that should be helpful if you ever have to look for a therapist for yourself or for a friend or family member (based on Beutler, Bongar, & Shurkin, 2001; Bruckner-Gordon, Gangi, & Wallman, 1988; Ehrenberg & Ehrenberg, 1994; Pittman, 1994).

Where Do You Find Therapeutic Services?

Psychotherapy can be found in a variety of settings. Contrary to general belief, most therapists are not in private practice. Many work in institutional settings such as community mental health centers, hospitals, and human service agencies. The principal sources of therapeutic services are described in **Table 15.2**. The exact collection of therapeutic services available will vary from one community to another. To find out what your com-

munity has to offer, it is a good idea to consult your friends, your local phone book, or your local community mental health center.

Is the Therapist's Profession or Sex Important?

Psychotherapists may be trained in psychology, psychiatry, social work, counseling, psychiatric nursing, or marriage and family therapy. Researchers have *not* found any reliable associations between therapists' professional background and therapeutic efficacy (Beutler et al., 2004). This is probably because many talented therapists can be found in all of these professions. Thus, the type of degree that a therapist holds doesn't need to be a crucial consideration in your selection process. It *is* true that currently only psychiatrists can prescribe drugs in most states. However, critics argue that many psychiatrists are too quick to use drugs to solve problems (Breggin, 1991). In any case, other types of therapists can refer you to a psychiatrist if they think that drug therapy would be helpful. If you have a health insurance policy that covers

TABLE 15.2 Principal Sources of Therapeutic Services

Source	Comments
Private practitioners	Self-employed therapists are listed in the Yellow Pages under their professional category, such as psychologists or psychiatrists. Private practitioners tend to be relatively expensive, but they also tend to be highly experienced therapists.
Community mental health centers	Community mental health centers have salaried psychologists, psychiatrists, and social workers on staff. The centers provide a variety of services and often have staff available on weekends and at night to deal with emergencies.
Hospitals	Several kinds of hospitals provide therapeutic services. There are both public and private mental hospitals that specialize in the care of people with psychological disorders. Many general hospitals have a psychiatric ward, and those that do not usually have psychiatrists and psychologists on staff and on call. Although hospitals tend to concentrate on in-patient treatment, many provide outpatient therapy as well.
Human service agencies	Various social service agencies employ therapists to provide short-term counseling. Depending on your community, you may find agencies that deal with family problems, juvenile problems, drug problems, and so forth.
Schools and workplaces	Most high schools and colleges have counseling centers where students can get help with personal problems. Similarly, some large businesses offer in-house counseling to their employees.

© Cengage Learning

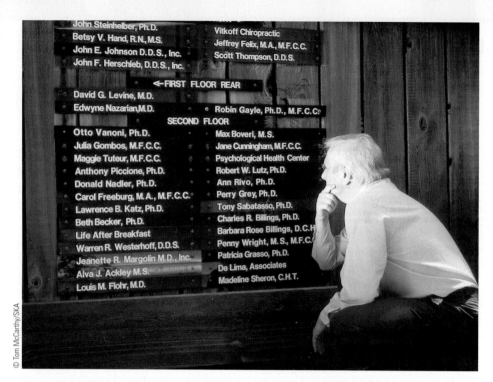

© Tom McCarthy/SKA

Finding the right therapist is no easy task. You need to take into account the therapist's training and orientation, fees charged, and personality. An initial visit should give you a good idea of what a particular therapist is like.

health insurance plans provide at least partial reimbursement for the cost of psychotherapy.

Is the Therapist's Theoretical Approach Important?

Logically, you might expect that the diverse approaches to therapy would vary in effectiveness. For the most part, that is *not* what researchers find, however. After reviewing many studies of therapeutic efficacy, Jerome Frank (1961) and Lester Luborsky and his colleagues (1975) both quote the dodo bird who has just judged a race in *Alice in Wonderland:* "Everybody has won, and *all* must have prizes." Improvement rates for various theoretical orientations usually come out pretty close in most studies (Lambert, Bergin, & Garfield, 2004; Luborsky et al., 2002; Wampold, 2001; see **Figure 15.12**).

However, these findings are a little misleading, as these estimates of overall effectiveness have been averaged across many types of patients and many types of problems. Most experts seem to think that *for certain types of problems, some approaches to therapy are more effective than others* (Beutler, 2002; Crits-Christoph,

psychotherapy, you may want to check to see whether it carries any restrictions about the therapist's profession.

Whether a therapist's gender is important depends on your attitude (Nadelson, Notman, & McCarthy, 2005). If *you* feel that the therapist's sex is important, then for you it is. The therapeutic relationship must be characterized by trust and rapport. Feeling uncomfortable with a therapist of one sex or the other could inhibit the therapeutic process. Thus, you should feel free to look for a male or female therapist if you prefer to do so.

Is Treatment Always Expensive?

Psychotherapy does not have to be prohibitively expensive. Private practitioners tend to be the most expensive, charging between $75 and $140 per (50-minute) hour. These fees may seem high, but they are in line with those of similar professionals, such as dentists and attorneys. Community mental health centers and social service agencies are usually supported by tax dollars. Consequently, they can charge lower fees than most therapists in private practice. Many of these

organizations use a sliding scale, so that clients are charged according to how much they can afford to pay. Thus, most communities have inexpensive opportunities for treatment. Moreover, many

FIGURE 15.12

Estimates of the effectiveness of various approaches to psychotherapy. Smith and Glass (1977) reviewed nearly 400 studies in which clients who were treated with a specific type of therapy were compared with a control group made up of individuals with similar problems who went untreated. The bars indicate the percentile rank (on outcome measures) attained by the average client treated with each type of therapy when compared to control subjects. The higher the percentile, the more effective the therapy was. As you can see, the various approaches were fairly similar in their overall effectiveness.

SOURCE: Adapted from Smith, M. L., & Glass, G. V. (1977). Meta-analysis of psychotherapy outcome series. *American Psychologist, 32,* 752–760. Copyright © 1977 by the American Psychological Association.

Therapy is both a science and an art. It is scientific in that practitioners are guided in their work by a huge body of empirical research. It is an art in that therapists often have to be creative in adapting their treatment procedures to individual patients and their idiosyncrasies.

1997; Norcross, 1995). For example, Martin Seligman (1995) asserts that panic disorders respond best to cognitive therapy, that specific phobias are most amenable to treatment with systematic desensitization, and that obsessive-compulsive disorders are best treated with behavior therapy or medication. Thus, for a specific type of problem, a therapist's theoretical approach may make a difference.

It is also important to point out that the finding that different approaches to therapy are roughly equal in overall efficacy does not mean that all *therapists* are created equal. Some therapists unquestionably are more effective than others. However, these variations in effectiveness appear to depend on individual therapists' personal skills rather than on their theoretical orientation (Beutler et al., 2004). Good, bad, and mediocre therapists are found within each school of thought. Indeed, the tremendous variation among individual therapists in skills may be one of the main reasons it is hard to find efficacy differences between theoretical approaches to therapy (Staines, 2008).

The key point is that effective therapy requires skill and creativity. Arnold Lazarus, who devised multimodal therapy, emphasizes that therapists "straddle the fence between science and art." Therapy is scientific in that interventions are based on extensive theory and empirical research (Forsyth & Strong, 1986). Ultimately, though, each client is a unique human being, and the therapist has to creatively fashion a treatment program that will help that individual (Goodheart, 2006).

What Is Therapy Like?

It is important to have realistic expectations about therapy. Otherwise, you may be unnecessarily disappointed. Some people expect miracles. They expect to turn their life around quickly with little effort. Others expect their therapist to run their lives for them. These are unrealistic expectations.

Therapy usually is a slow process. Your problems are not likely to melt away quickly. Moreover, therapy is hard work, and your therapist is only a facilitator. Ultimately, you have to confront the challenge of changing your behavior, your feelings, or your personality. This process may not be pleasant. You may have to face up to some painful truths about yourself. As Ehrenberg and Ehrenberg (1994) point out, "Psychotherapy takes time, effort, and courage."

From Crisis to Wellness—But Was It the Therapy?

KEY LEARNING GOALS

15.18 Understand how placebo effects and regression toward the mean can complicate the evaluation of therapy.

It often happens this way. Problems seem to go from bad to worse. The trigger could be severe pressures at work, an emotional fight with your spouse, or a child's unruly behavior spiraling out of control. At some point, you recognize that it might be wise to seek professional assistance from a therapist, but where do you turn? If you are like most people, you will probably hesitate before actively seeking professional help. People hesitate because therapy carries a stigma, because the task of finding a therapist is daunting, and because they hope that their psychological problems will clear up on their own—which *does* happen with some regularity. When people finally decide to pursue mental health care, it is often because they feel like they have reached rock bottom in terms of their functioning and have no choice. Motivated by their crisis, they enter into treatment, looking for a ray of hope. Will therapy help them feel better?

It may surprise you to learn that the answer *generally* would be "yes," even if professional treatment itself was utterly worthless. People entering therapy are likely to get better, regardless of whether their treatment is effective, for two major reasons: placebo effects and regression toward the mean. *Placebo effects* occur **when people's expectations lead them to experience some change even though they receive a fake treatment** (such as getting a sugar pill instead of a real drug). Clients generally enter therapy with expectations that it will have positive effects, and as we have emphasized throughout this text, *people have a remarkable tendency to see what they expect to see.* Because of this factor, studies of the efficacy of medical drugs always include a placebo condition in which subjects are given fake

medication (see Chapter 2). Researchers are often quite surprised by just how much the placebo subjects improve (Fisher & Greenberg, 1997; Walsh et al., 2002). Placebo effects can be powerful and should be taken into consideration whenever efforts are made to evaluate the efficacy of some approach to treatment.

The other factor at work is the main focus in this Application. It is an interesting statistical phenomenon that we have not discussed previously. *Regression toward the mean* occurs when people who score extremely high or low on some trait are measured a second time and their new scores fall closer to the mean (average). Regression effects work in both directions: On the second measurement high scorers tend to fall back toward the mean and low scorers tend to creep upward toward the mean. For example, let's say we wanted to evaluate the effectiveness of a one-day coaching program intended to improve performance on the SAT test. We reason that coaching is most likely to help students who have performed poorly on the test. So, we recruit a sample of high school students who have previously scored in the bottom 20% on the SAT. Thanks to regression toward the mean, most of these students will score higher if they take the SAT a second time, so our coaching program may *look* effective even if it has no value. By the way, if we set out to see whether our coaching program could increase the performance of high scorers, regression effects would be working *against* us. The processes underlying regression toward the mean are complex matters of probability, but they can be approximated by a simple principle: If you are near the bottom, you have almost

nowhere to go but up, and if you are near the top, you have almost nowhere to go but down.

What does all of this have to do with the effects of professional treatment for psychological problems and disorders? Well, recall that most people enter psychotherapy during a time of severe crisis, when they are at a really low point in their lives. If you measure the mental health of a group of people entering therapy, most will get relatively low scores. If you measure their mental health again a few months later, chances are that most of them will score higher—with or without therapy—because of regression toward the mean. This is not a matter of idle speculation. In studies of therapeutic efficacy, data on *untreated (control group) subjects* demonstrate that poor scores on measures of mental health regress toward the mean when participants are assessed a second time (Flett, Vredenburg, & Krames, 1995; Hsu, 1995).

Does the fact that most people will get better even without therapy mean that there is no sound evidence that psychotherapy works? No. Regression effects, along with placebo effects, do create major headaches for researchers evaluating the efficacy of various therapies, but these problems *can* be neutralized. Control groups, random assignment, placebo

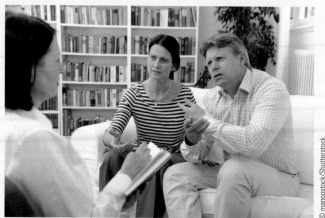

Placebo effects and regression toward the mean are two prominent factors that make it difficult to evaluate the efficacy of various approaches to therapy.

conditions, and statistical adjustments can be used to control for regression and placebo effects, as well as for other threats to validity. As discussed in the main body of the chapter, researchers have accumulated rigorous evidence that most approaches to therapy have demonstrated efficacy. However, our discussion of placebo and regression effects shows you some of the complexities that make this type of research far more complicated than might be anticipated.

Recognizing how regression toward the mean can occur in a variety of contexts is an important critical thinking skill, so let's look at some additional examples. Think about an outstanding young pro baseball player who has a fabulous first season and is named "Rookie of the Year." What sort of performance would you predict for this athlete the next year? Statistically speaking, our Rookie of the Year is likely to perform well above average the next year, but not as well as he did in his first year. If you are a sports fan, you may recognize this pattern as the "sophomore slump." Many sports columnists have written about the sophomore slump, which they typically blame on the athlete's personality or motivation ("He got lazy,'" "He got cocky," "The money and fame went to his head," and so forth). A simple appeal to regression toward the mean could explain this sort of outcome, with no need to criticize the personality or motivation of the athlete. Of course, sometimes the Rookie of the Year performs even better during his second year. Thus, our baseball example can be used to emphasize an important point. Regression toward the mean is not an inevitability. It is a statistical tendency

that predicts what will happen far more often than not, but it is merely a matter of probability—which means it is a much more reliable principle when applied to groups (say, the top ten rookies in a specific year) rather than to individuals.

People who do not understand regression toward the mean can make some interesting mistakes in their efforts to improve task performance. For instance, Kahneman and Tversky (1973) worked with Israeli flight instructors who, logically enough, would praise students when they handled a difficult maneuver exceptionally well and criticize students when they exhibited particularly poor performance. Because of regression toward the mean, the students' performance tended to decline after they earned praise for extremely good work and to improve after they earned criticism for extremely bad work. Taking note of this trend, the flight instructors erroneously concluded that praise led to poorer performance and criticism led to improved performance—until the concept of regression toward the mean was explained to them. Many parents and coaches working to train children have probably made the same mistake and naively inferred that praise has a negative effect on subsequent performance, when what they were really witnessing was regression toward the mean.

Let's return to the world of therapy for one last thought about the significance of both regression and placebo effects. Over the years, a host of quacks, charlatans, con artists, herbalists, and faith healers have marketed an endless array of worthless treatments for both psychological problems and physical

Placebo effects and regression toward the mean can help explain why phony, worthless treatments can have sincere supporters who really believe that the bogus interventions are effective.

maladies. In many instances, people who have been treated with these phony therapies have expressed satisfaction or even praise and gratitude. For instance, you may have heard someone sincerely rave about some herbal remedy or psychic advice that you were pretty sure was really worthless. If so, you were probably puzzled by their glowing testimonials. Well, you now have two explanations for why people can honestly believe that they have derived great benefit from harebrained, bogus treatments: placebo effects and regression effects. The people who provide testimonials for worthless treatments may have experienced *genuine* improvements in their conditions, but those improvements were probably the results of placebo effects and regression toward the mean. Placebo and regression effects add to the many reasons that you should always be skeptical about anecdotal evidence. And they help explain why charlatans can be so successful and why unsound, ineffective treatments can have sincere proponents.

TABLE 15.3   Critical Thinking Skills Discussed in This Application

Skill	Description
Recognizing situations in which placebo effects might occur	The critical thinker understands that if people have expectations that a treatment will produce a certain effect, they may experience that effect even if the treatment was fake or ineffectual.
Recognizing situations in which regression toward the mean may occur	The critical thinker understands that when people are selected for their extremely high or low scores on some trait, their subsequent scores will probably fall closer to the mean.
Recognizing the limitations of anecdotal evidence	The critical thinker is wary of anecdotal evidence, which consists of personal stories used to support one's assertions. Anecdotal evidence tends to be unrepresentative, inaccurate, and unreliable.

© Cengage Learning

© Tony Freeman/PhotoEdit

Elements of the Treatment Process

15.1 Identify the three major categories of therapy, and discuss patterns of treatment seeking.

Approaches to treatment are diverse, but they can be grouped into three categories: insight therapies, behavior therapies, and biomedical therapies. Clients bring a wide variety of problems to therapy. The most common problems are depression and anxiety. People vary in their willingness to seek treatment. Unfortunately, many people who need therapy do not receive it, in part because of the stigma attached to therapy.

15.2 Identify the various types of mental health professionals involved in the provision of therapy.

Therapists come from a variety of professional backgrounds. Clinical and counseling psychologists, psychiatrists, clinical social workers, psychiatric nurses, counselors, and marriage and family therapists are the principal providers of therapeutic services. Each of these professions show different preferences for approaches to treatment. Psychologists typically practice insight or behavior therapy. Psychiatrists rely more heavily on drug therapies.

Types of Therapists

Profession	Degree	Education beyond Bachelor's degree	Typical roles and activities
Clinical psychologist	PhD or PsyD	5–7 years	Psychological testing, diagnosis, treatment with insight or behavior therapy
Counseling psychologist	PhD, PsyD, or EdD	5–7 years	Similar to clinical psychologist, but more focus on work, career, and adjustment problems
Psychiatrist	MD	8 years	Diagnosis and treatment, primarily with biomedical therapies, but also insight therapies
Clinical social worker	MSW, DSW	2–5 years	Insight and behavior therapy, often help inpatients with their return to the community
Psychiatric nurse	RN, MA, or PhD	0–5 years	Inpatient care, insight and behavior therapy
Counselor	BA or MA	0–2 years	Vocational counseling, drug counseling, rehabilitation counseling
Marriage and family therapist	MA or PhD	2–5 years	Marital/couples therapy, family therapy

© Cengage Learning

Insight Therapies

15.3 Explain the logic of psychoanalysis and the techniques by which analysts probe the unconscious.

Freudian approaches to therapy assume that neuroses originate from unresolved conflicts lurking in the unconscious. Therefore, in psychoanalysis free association (discussing whatever comes to mind with no censorship) and dream analysis are used to explore the unconscious. When an analyst's probing hits sensitive areas, resistance, which involves unconscious defensive maneuvers to hinder progress, can be expected.

The transference relationship may be used to overcome this resistance so that the client can handle interpretations that lead to insight.

15.4 Understand the role of therapeutic climate and therapeutic process in client-centered therapy.

Rogers's client-centered therapy assumes that neurotic anxieties are derived from incongruence between a person's self-concept and reality. Accordingly, the client-centered therapist emphasizes trying to provide a supportive climate marked by genuineness, unconditional positive regard, and empathy. The process of client-centered therapy depends on clarification of the client's feelings to promote self-acceptance.

© Cengage Learning

15.5 Explain how group therapy, couples therapy, and family therapy are generally conducted.

Participants in group therapy essentially act as therapists for one another, exchanging insights and emotional support. The therapist sets goals for the group and works to maintain a supportive climate. Group therapy is less expensive and has some advantages in comparison to individual therapy. Couples therapy involves the treatment of both partners in a committed, intimate relationship. Family therapy involves the treatment of a family unit as a whole. Marital and family therapists seek to understand the entrenched patterns of interaction that produce distress for their clients and attempt to help couples and families improve their communication.

15.6 Assess the efficacy of insight therapies.

Evaluating the effectiveness of any approach to therapy is complex and difficult, as different therapies pursue different goals and clients vary in the severity of their problems. Nonetheless, the weight of empirical evidence suggests that insight therapies are superior to no treatment or to placebo treatment. Studies generally find the greatest improvement early in treatment.

Behavior Therapies

15.7 Describe the procedures of systematic desensitization, aversion therapy, and social skills training.

Behavior therapies use the principles of learning in direct efforts to change specific aspects of behavior. Wolpe's systematic desensitization is a treatment designed to relieve phobias. It involves the construction of an anxiety hierarchy, relaxation training, and step-by-step movement through the hierarchy, pairing relaxation with each phobic stimulus. In aversion therapy, a stimulus associated with an unwanted response is paired with an unpleasant stimulus in an effort to eliminate the maladaptive response. Social skills training can improve clients' interpersonal skills through shaping, modeling, and behavioral rehearsal.

15.8 Articulate the goals and techniques of cognitive therapy, and evaluate the efficacy of behavior therapies.

Cognitive-behavioral treatments concentrate on changing the way clients think about events in their lives. Cognitive therapists reeducate clients to detect and challenge automatic negative thoughts that cause depression and anxiety. Cognitive therapy also depends on modeling, behavioral rehearsal, and homework assignments. Behavior therapists have historically placed more emphasis on the importance of measuring therapeutic outcomes than insight therapists have. There is ample evidence that behavior therapies are effective in the treatment of a wide variety of disorders.

Biomedical Therapies

15.9 Summarize the therapeutic actions and side effects of four categories of psychiatric drugs.

Antianxiety drugs are fairly effective in reducing feelings of anxiety, but their impact is short-lived. They produce some nuisance side effects, and there can be complications involving abuse, dependence, and overdose. Antipsychotic drugs reduce psychotic symptoms in about 70% of patients. Traditional antipsychotics can have a variety of serious side effects, which have been reduced in the newer, atypical antipsychotics. Antidepressants are used to bring people out of episodes of depression. SSRIs are the dominant type used today. Side effects tend to be manageable, although there are concerns that antidepressants may increase suicide risk slightly. Mood stabilizers are used to prevent the recurrence of episodes of disturbance in people with bipolar mood disorders.

15.10 Evaluate the overall efficacy of drug treatments, and discuss controversies surrounding pharmaceutical research.

Drug therapies can be quite effective, but they have their drawbacks. All of the drugs produce side effects, some of which can be troublesome. Some critics maintain that drugs' curative effects are superficial and that some drugs are overprescribed. Disturbing questions have been raised about the scientific impartiality of contemporary research on therapeutic drugs.

15.11 Describe electroconvulsive therapy, and assess its therapeutic effects and risks.

Electroconvulsive therapy (ECT) is used to trigger a cortical seizure that is believed to have therapeutic value for mood disorders, especially depression. Evidence about the effectiveness of ECT is contradictory but seems sufficient to justify conservative use of the procedure. Cognitive deficits are the principal risk, with much debate about how severe and enduring these deficits tend to be.

Current Trends and Issues in Treatment

15.12 Discuss the merits of blending approaches to therapy.

Combinations of insight, behavioral, and biomedical therapies are often used fruitfully in the treatment of psychological disorders. Many modern therapists are eclectic, using specific ideas, techniques, and strategies gleaned from a number of theoretical approaches.

15.13 Analyze the barriers that lead to underutilization of mental health services by ethnic minorities, and describe possible solutions to the problem.

Because of cultural, language, and access barriers, therapeutic services are underutilized by most ethnic minorities in America. More culturally responsive approaches to treatment will require more minority therapists, more effort to build strong therapeutic alliances, and additional investigation of how traditional therapies can be tailored to be more compatible with specific ethnic groups' cultural heritage.

Institutional Treatment in Transition

15.14 Explain why people grew disenchanted with mental hospitals, and discuss the resultant change in mental health care.

Experts eventually realized that mental hospitals often contributed to the development of pathology instead of curing it, in part because they tended to be underfunded and understaffed, leading to demoralizing conditions. Disenchantment with the negative effects of mental hospitals led to the advent of more localized community mental health centers and a policy of deinstitutionalization.

15.15 Assess the effects of the deinstitutionalization movement.

As a result of deinstitutionalization, long-term hospitalization for mental disorders is largely a thing of the past. Deinstitutionalization has worked well for some patients, but it has spawned some unanticipated problems, including the revolving door problem and increased homelessness.

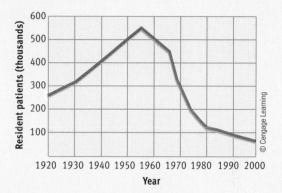

Reflecting on the Chapter's Themes

15.16 Identify the two unifying themes highlighted in this chapter.

Our discussion of psychotherapy highlighted the value of theoretical diversity. Conflicting theoretical orientations have generated varied approaches to treatment. Our coverage of therapy also showed once again that cultural factors shape psychological processes.

PERSONAL APPLICATION
Looking for a Therapist

15.17 Discuss some practical considerations in seeking therapy, including the importance of therapists' theoretical approach.

Therapeutic services are available in many settings, and such services need not be expensive. Both excellent and mediocre therapists can be found in all of the mental health professions. Thus, therapists' personal skills are more important than their professional degree. Whether a therapist's sex is important depends on the client's attitude. The various theoretical approaches appear to be fairly similar in overall effectiveness. However, for certain types of problems, some approaches are probably more effective than others, and all therapists are not created equal. It is important to have realistic expectations about therapy.

CRITICAL THINKING APPLICATION
From Crisis to Wellness—But Was It the Therapy?

15.18 Understand how placebo effects and regression toward the mean can complicate the evaluation of therapy.

People entering therapy are likely to get better even if their treatment is ineffective, because of placebo effects and regression toward the mean. Regression toward the mean occurs when people selected for their extremely high or low scores on some trait are measured a second time and their new scores fall closer to the mean. Regression and placebo effects may also help explain why people can often be deceived by phony, ineffectual treatments.

Practice Tests and Answers to the Concept Checks

PART 1: CHAPTER PRACTICE TESTS

Chapter 1 Practice Test

1. For which of the following is Wilhelm Wundt primarily known?
   A. The establishment of the first formal laboratory for research in psychology
   B. The distinction between mind and body as two separate entities
   C. The discovery of how signals are conducted along nerves in the body
   D. The development of the first formal program for training in psychotherapy

2. Which of the following approaches might William James criticize for examining a movie frame by frame instead of seeing the motion in the motion picture?
   A. Structuralism
   B. Functionalism
   C. Dualism
   D. Humanism

3. Fred, a tennis coach, insists that he can make any reasonably healthy individual into an internationally competitive tennis player. Fred is echoing the thoughts of:
   A. Sigmund Freud.
   B. John B. Watson.
   C. Abraham Maslow.
   D. William James.

4. Which of the following is a statement with which Skinner's followers would agree?
   A. The whole is greater than the sum of its parts.
   B. The goal of behavior is self-actualization.
   C. Nature is more influential than nurture.
   D. Free will is an illusion.

5. Which of the following approaches has the most optimistic view of human nature?
   A. Humanism
   B. Behaviorism
   C. Psychoanalysis
   D. Structuralism

6. Which of the following historical events created a demand for clinicians that was far greater than the supply?
   A. World War I
   B. The Depression
   C. World War II
   D. The Korean War

7. _____ psychology examines behavioral processes in terms of their adaptive value for a species over the course of many generations.
   A. Clinical   C. Evolutionary
   B. Cognitive   D. Physiological

8. The study of the endocrine system and genetic mechanisms would most likely be undertaken by a:
   A. clinical psychologist.
   B. physiological psychologist.
   C. social psychologist.
   D. educational psychologist.

9. A multifactorial causation approach to behavior suggests that:
   A. most behaviors can be explained best by single-cause explanations.
   B. most behavior is governed by a complex network of inter-related factors.
   C. data need to be analyzed by the statistical technique called factor analysis in order for the data to make sense.
   D. explanations of behavior tend to build up from the simple to the complex in a hierarchical manner.

10. Psychology's answer to the question of whether we are "born" or "made" tends to be that:
    A. we are "born."
    B. we are "made."
    C. we are both "born" and "made."
    D. neither is correct.

11. A good reason for taking notes in your own words, rather than verbatim, is that:
    A. most lecturers are quite wordy.
    B. "translating" on the spot is good mental exercise.
    C. it reduces the likelihood that you'll later engage in plagiarism.
    D. it forces you to assimilate the information in a way that makes sense to you.

12. Critical thinking skills:
    A. are abstract abilities that cannot be identified.
    B. usually develop spontaneously through normal content instruction.
    C. usually develop spontaneously without any instruction.
    D. need to be deliberately taught because they often do not develop by themselves with standard content instruction.

Answers

1. A p. 3	**7.** C p. 14
2. A p. 5	**8.** B p. 17
3. B p. 8	**9.** B pp. 20–21
4. D p. 9	**10.** C p. 22
5. A pp. 10–11	**11.** D p. 25
6. C p. 12	**12.** D p. 26

Chapter 2 Practice Test

1. Theories permit researchers to move from:
   A. understanding to application.
   B. concept to description.
   C. application to control.
   D. description to understanding.

2. Researchers must describe the actions that will be taken to measure or control each variable in their studies. In other words, they must:
   A. provide operational definitions of their variables.
   B. decide whether their studies will be experimental or correlational.
   C. use statistics to summarize their findings.
   D. decide how many subjects should participate in their studies.

3. A researcher found that clients who were randomly assigned to same-sex groups participated more in group therapy sessions than clients who were randomly assigned to coed groups. In this experiment, the independent variable was:
   A. the amount of participation in the group therapy sessions.
   B. whether or not the group was same-sex or coed.
   C. the clients' attitudes toward group therapy.
   D. how much the clients' mental health improved.

4. In a study of the effect of a new teaching technique on students' achievement test scores, an important extraneous variable would be the students':
   A. hair color.
   B. athletic skills.
   C. IQ scores.
   D. sociability.

5. Whenever you have a cold, you rest in bed, take aspirin, and drink plenty of fluids. You can't determine which remedy is most effective because of which of the following problems?
   A. Sampling bias
   B. Distorted self-report data
   C. Confounding of variables
   D. Experimenter bias

6. Which of the following correlation coefficients would indicate the strongest relationship between two variables?
   A. .58
   B. .19
   C. −.97
   D. −.05

7. A psychologist monitors a group of nursery school children during the school day, recording each instance of helping behavior as it occurs, without any intervention. The psychologist is using:
   A. the experimental method.
   B. naturalistic observation.
   C. case studies.
   D. the survey method.

8. Among the advantages of descriptive/correlational research is (are):
   A. it can often be used in circumstances in which an experiment would be unethical or impossible.
   B. it permits researchers to examine subjects' behavior in natural, real-world circumstances.
   C. it can demonstrate conclusively that two variables are causally related.
   D. both a and b.

9. Sampling bias exists when:
   A. the sample is representative of the population.
   B. the sample is not representative of the population.
   C. two variables are confounded.
   D. the effect of the independent variable can't be isolated.

10. Critics of deception in research have assumed that deceptive studies are harmful to subjects. The empirical data on this issue suggest that:
    A. many deceptive studies do have significant negative effects on subjects.
    B. most participants in deceptive studies report that they enjoyed the experience and didn't mind being misled.
    C. deceptive research seriously undermines subjects' trust in others.
    D. both a and c.

11. Which of the following would not be included in the results section of a journal article?
    A. Descriptive statistics summarizing the data
    B. Statistical analysis of the data
    C. Graphs and/or tables presenting the data pictorially
    D. Interpretation, evaluation, and implications of the data

12. Anecdotal evidence:
    A. is often concrete, vivid, and memorable.
    B. tends to influence people.
    C. is fundamentally flawed and unreliable.
    D. is all of the above.

Answers

1. D p. 32
2. A p. 33
3. B p. 37
4. C p. 38
5. C p. 39
6. C p. 42
7. B pp. 43–44
8. D p. 46
9. B p. 50
10. B p. 53
11. D p. 57
12. D pp. 58–59

Chapter 3 Practice Test

1. A neural impulse is initiated when a neuron's charge momentarily becomes less negative, or even positive. This event is called:
   A. an action potential.
   B. a resting potential.
   C. impulse facilitation.
   D. neuromodulation.

2. Neurons convey information about the strength of stimuli by varying:
   A. the size of their action potentials.
   B. the speed of their action potentials.
   C. the rate at which they fire action potentials.
   D. all of the above.

3. Alterations in activity at dopamine synapses have been implicated in the development of:
   A. anxiety.
   B. schizophrenia.
   C. Alzheimer's disease.
   D. nicotine addiction.

4. Jim has just barely avoided a head-on collision on a narrow road. With heart pounding, hands shaking, and body perspiring, Jim recognizes that these are signs of the body's fight-or-flight response, which is controlled by the:
   A. empathetic division of the peripheral nervous system.
   B. parasympathetic division of the autonomic nervous system.
   C. somatic division of the peripheral nervous system.
   D. sympathetic division of the autonomic nervous system.

5. The thalamus can be characterized as:
   A. a regulatory mechanism.
   B. the consciousness switch of the brain.
   C. a relay station.
   D. a bridge between the two cerebral hemispheres.

6. The _____ lobe is to hearing as the occipital lobe is to vision.
   A. frontal
   B. temporal
   C. parietal
   D. cerebellar

7. The scientist who won a Nobel prize for his work with split-brain patients is:
   A. Walter Cannon.
   B. Paul Broca.
   C. Roger Sperry.
   D. James Olds.

8. In people whose corpus callosums have not been severed, verbal stimuli are identified more quickly and more accurately:
   A. when sent to the right hemisphere first.
   B. when sent to the left hemisphere first.
   C. when presented to the left visual field.
   D. when presented auditorally rather than visually.

9. Hormones are to the endocrine system as _____ are to the nervous system.
   A. nerves
   B. synapses
   C. neurotransmitters
   D. action potentials

10. Adopted children's similarity to their biological parents is generally attributed to _____; adopted children's similarity to their adoptive parents is generally attributed to _____.
    A. heredity; the environment
    B. the environment; heredity
    C. the environment; the environment
    D. heredity; heredity

11. In evolutionary theory, *fitness* refers to:
    A. the ability to survive.
    B. the ability to adapt to environmental demands.
    C. reproductive success.
    D. the physical skills necessary for survival.

12. For which of the following assertions is the empirical evidence strongest?
    A. The two cerebral hemispheres are specialized to handle different types of cognitive tasks.
    B. Schools should be reformed to better educate the right hemisphere.
    C. Each hemisphere has its own cognitive style.
    D. Some people are right-brained, while others are left-brained.

Answers

1. A p. 66
2. C p. 66
3. B p. 70
4. D p. 73
5. C pp. 76, 78
6. B pp. 79–80
7. C p. 82
8. B pp. 83–84
9. C p. 85
10. A p. 88
11. C p. 90
12. A pp. 94–95

Chapter 4 Practice Test

1. The term used to refer to the stimulation of the sense organs is:
   A. sensation.
   B. perception.
   C. transduction.
   D. adaptation.

2. Perception of the brightness of a color is affected mainly by:
   A. the wavelength of light waves.
   B. the amplitude of light waves.
   C. the purity of light waves.
   D. the saturation of light waves.

3. In farsightedness:
   A. close objects are seen clearly but distant objects appear blurry.
   B. the focus of light from close objects falls behind the retina.
   C. the focus of light from distant objects falls a little short of the retina.
   D. both A and B occur.
   E. both A and C occur.

4. The collection of rod and cone receptors that funnel signals to a particular visual cell in the retina make up that cell's:
   A. blind spot.
   B. optic disk.
   C. opponent process field.
   D. receptive field.

5. The primary visual cortex is located in the:
   A. occipital lobe.
   B. temporal lobe.
   C. parietal lobe.
   D. frontal lobe.

6. Which theory would predict that the American flag would have a green, black, and yellow afterimage?
   A. Subtractive color mixing
   B. Opponent process theory
   C. Additive color mixing
   D. Trichromatic theory

7. A readiness to perceive a stimulus in a particular way is referred to as (a):
   A. Gestalt.
   B. feature analysis.
   C. perceptual set.
   D. congruence.

8. In a painting, train tracks may look as if they go off into the distance because the artist draws the tracks as converging lines, a monocular cue to depth known as:
   A. interposition.
   B. texture gradient.
   C. relative size.
   D. linear perspective.

9. Perception of pitch can best be explained by:
   A. place theory.
   B. frequency theory.
   C. both place theory and frequency theory.
   D. neither theory.

10. In what way(s) is the sense of taste like the sense of smell?
    A. There are four primary stimulus groups for both senses.
    B. Both systems are routed through the thalamus on the way to the cortex.
    C. The physical stimuli for both senses are chemical substances dissolved in fluid.
    D. All of the above.
    E. None of the above.

11. The fact that theories originally seen as being incompatible, such as the trichromatic and opponent process theories of color vision, are now seen as both being necessary to explain sensory processes illustrates:
    A. that psychology evolves in a sociohistorical context.
    B. the subjectivity of experience.
    C. the value of psychology's theoretical diversity.
    D. the nature-nurture controversy.

12. In the study by Kenrick and Gutierres (1980), exposing male subjects to a TV show dominated by extremely beautiful women:
    A. had no effect on their ratings of the attractiveness of a prospective date.
    B. increased their ratings of the attractiveness of a prospective date.
    C. decreased their ratings of the attractiveness of a prospective date.
    D. decreased their ratings of their own attractiveness.

Answers

1. A p. 101
2. B p. 102
3. B pp. 103–104
4. D p. 106
5. A p. 107
6. B p. 110
7. C p. 112
8. D pp. 117–118
9. C p. 124
10. C pp. 125–127
11. C p. 129
12. C p. 137

Chapter 5 Practice Test

1. An EEG would indicate primarily _____ activity while you take this test.
   A. alpha
   B. beta
   C. delta
   D. theta

2. Readjusting your biological clock would be most difficult under which of the following circumstances?
   A. Flying west from Los Angeles to Hawaii
   B. Flying north from Miami to New York
   C. Flying east from Hawaii to Los Angeles
   D. Flying south from New York to Miami

3. As the sleep cycle evolves through the night, people tend to:
   A. spend more time in REM sleep and less time in non-REM sleep.
   B. spend more time in non-REM sleep and less time in REM sleep.
   C. spend a more or less equal amount of time in REM sleep and non-REM sleep.
   D. spend more time in stage 4 sleep and less time in REM sleep.

4. Newborn infants spend about _____ % of their sleep time in REM, and adults spend about _____ % of their sleep time in REM.
   A. 20; 50
   B. 50; 20
   C. 20; 20
   D. 50; 50

5. After being selectively deprived of REM sleep, people typically experience:
   A. hypochondriasis.
   B. non-REM dysfunction.
   C. emotional breakdowns.
   D. a temporary increase in time spent in REM.

6. Which of the following is *not* true of sleeping pills?
   A. Sleeping pills are an excellent long-range solution for all types of insomnia.
   B. There is some danger of overdose.
   C. Sleeping pills can make people sluggish and drowsy the next day.
   D. Sleeping pills gradually become less effective with continued use.

7. The activation-synthesis theory of dreaming contends that:
   A. dreams are simply the by-product of bursts of activity in the brain.
   B. dreams provide an outlet for energy invested in socially undesirable impulses.
   C. dreams represent the brain's attempt to purge information taken in during waking hours.
   D. dreams are an attempt to restore a neurotransmitter balance within the brain.

8. A common driving experience is "highway hypnosis," in which one's consciousness seems to be divided between the driving itself and one's conscious train of thought. This phenomenon has been cited to support the idea that hypnosis is:
   A. an exercise in role playing.
   B. a dissociated state of consciousness.
   C. a goal-directed fantasy.
   D. not an altered state of consciousness.

9. Amphetamines work by increasing activity at _____ synapses in a variety of ways.
   A. GABA and glycine
   B. serotonin and dopamine
   C. acetylcholine
   D. norepinephrine and dopamine

10. Which of the following drugs would be most likely to result in a fatal overdose?
    A. LSD
    B. Mescaline
    C. Marijuana
    D. Narcotics

11. Which of the following is a true statement about naps?
    A. Daytime naps invariably lead to insomnia.
    B. Daytime naps are invariably refreshing and an efficient way to rest.
    C. Daytime naps are not very efficient ways to sleep, but their effects are variable and they can be beneficial.
    D. Taking many naps during the day can substitute for a full night's sleep.

12. Definitions:
    A. generally emerge out of research.
    B. often have great explanatory value.
    C. generally exert little influence over how people think.
    D. are usually constructed by experts or authorities in a specific field.

Answers

1. B p. 142
2. C p. 144
3. A pp. 147–149
4. B pp. 148, 150
5. D p. 152
6. A p. 154
7. A p. 158
8. B pp. 160–161
9. D p. 166
10. D pp. 165–167
11. C p. 169
12. D pp. 172–173

Chapter 6 Practice Test

1. After repeated pairings of a tone with meat powder, Pavlov found that a dog will salivate when the tone is presented. Salivation to the tone is a(n):
   A. unconditioned stimulus.
   B. unconditioned response.
   C. conditioned stimulus.
   D. conditioned response.

2. Sam's wife always wears the same black nightgown whenever she is "in the mood" for sexual relations. Sam becomes sexually aroused as soon as he sees his wife in the nightgown. For Sam, the nightgown is a(n):
   A. unconditioned stimulus.
   B. unconditioned response.
   C. conditioned stimulus.
   D. conditioned response.

3. Watson and Rayner (1920) conditioned "Little Albert" to fear white rats by banging a hammer on a steel bar as he played with a white rat. Later, it was discovered that Albert feared not only white rats but white stuffed toys and Santa's beard as well. Albert's fear of these other objects can be attributed to:
   A. shaping.
   B. stimulus generalization.
   C. stimulus discrimination.
   D. an overactive imagination.

4. The phenomenon of higher-order conditioning shows that:
   A. only a genuine, natural US can be used to establish a CR.
   B. auditory stimuli are easier to condition than visual stimuli.
   C. visual stimuli are easier to condition than auditory stimuli.
   D. an already established CS can be used in the place of a natural US.

5. In a Skinner box, the dependent variable is usually:
   A. the force with which the lever is pressed or the disk is pecked.
   B. the schedule of reinforcement used.
   C. the rate of responding.
   D. the speed of the cumulative recorder.

6. A primary reinforcer has _____ reinforcing properties; a secondary reinforcer has _____ reinforcing properties.
   A. biological; acquired
   B. conditioned; unconditioned
   C. weak; potent
   D. immediate; delayed

7. The steady, rapid responding of a person playing a slot machine is an example of the pattern of responding typically generated on a _____ schedule of reinforcement.
   A. fixed-ratio
   B. variable-ratio
   C. fixed-interval
   D. variable-interval

8. Positive reinforcement _____ the rate of responding; negative reinforcement _____ the rate of responding.
   A. increases; decreases
   B. decreases; increases
   C. increases; increases
   D. decreases; decreases

9. Research on avoidance learning suggests that conditioned fear acquired through _____ conditioning plays a key role.
   A. classical
   B. operant
   C. reinforcement
   D. intermittent

10. The studies by Garcia and his colleagues demonstrate that rats easily learn to associate a taste CS with a(n) _____ US.
    A. shock
    B. visual
    C. auditory
    D. nausea-inducing

11. Albert Bandura:
    A. was the first to describe species-specific learning tendencies.
    B. was the founder of behaviorism.
    C. pioneered the study of classical conditioning.
    D. pioneered the study of observational learning.

12. In designing a self-modification program, control of antecedents should be used:
    A. by people who are in poor physical condition.
    B. only when your usual reinforcers are unavailable.
    C. when you want to decrease the frequency of a response.
    D. when you are initially not capable of making the target response.

Answers

1. D pp. 179–180
2. C pp. 179–180
3. B pp. 184–185
4. D p. 186
5. C p. 187
6. A p. 191
7. B pp. 192–193
8. C pp. 194–195
9. A pp. 195–196
10. D p. 199
11. D p. 201
12. C p. 209

Chapter 7 Practice Test

1. Getting information into memory is called _____;
   getting information out of memory is called _____.
   A. storage; retrieval
   B. encoding; storage
   C. encoding; retrieval
   D. storage; encoding

2. The word *big* is flashed on a screen. A mental picture of the
   word *big* represents a _____ code; the definition "large
   in size" represents a _____ code; "sounds like pig"
   represents a _____ code.
   A. structural; phonemic; semantic
   B. phonemic; semantic; structural
   C. structural; semantic; phonemic
   D. phonemic; structural; semantic

3. The capacity of short-term memory is:
   A. about 50,000 words.
   B. unlimited.
   C. about 25 stimuli.
   D. thought to be 7 plus or minus 2 chunks of information,
      although some theorists suggest it may be 4 plus or minus 1
      chunks.

4. Which statement best represents current evidence on the dura-
   bility of long-term storage?
   A. All forgetting involves breakdowns in retrieval.
   B. LTM is like a barrel of marbles in which none of the marbles
      ever leak out.
   C. There is no convincing evidence that all one's memories are
      stored away permanently.
   D. All long-term memories gradually decay at a constant rate.

5. An organized cluster of knowledge about a particular object or
   sequence of events is called a:
   A. semantic network.
   B. conceptual hierarchy.
   C. schema.
   D. retrieval cue.

6. The tip-of-the-tongue phenomenon:
   A. is a temporary inability to remember something you know,
      accompanied by a feeling that it's just out of reach.
   B. is clearly due to a failure in retrieval.
   C. reflects a permanent loss of information from LTM.
   D. is both A and B.

7. Loftus's work on eyewitness testimony has demonstrated that:
   A. Memory errors are surprisingly infrequent.
   B. Memory errors are mainly due to repression.
   C. Information given after an event can alter a person's memory
      of the event.
   D. Information given after an event cannot alter a person's
      memory of the event.

8. If decay theory is correct:
   A. information can never be permanently lost from long-term
      memory.
   B. forgetting is simply a case of retrieval failure.
   C. the principal cause of forgetting should be the passage of
      time.
   D. all of the above.

9. Amnesia in which people lose memories for events that oc-
   curred prior to their injury is called _____ amnesia.
   A. anterograde
   B. retrospective
   C. retrograde
   D. episodic

10. Your knowledge that birds fly, that the sun rises in the east, and
    that 2 + 2 = 4 is contained in your _____ memory.
    A. episodic
    B. procedural
    C. implicit
    D. semantic

11. Dorothy memorized her shopping list. When she got to the
    store, however, she found she had forgotten many of the items
    from the middle of the list. This is an example of:
    A. inappropriate encoding.
    B. retrograde amnesia.
    C. proactive interference.
    D. the serial-position effect.

12. The tendency to mold one's interpretation of the past to fit how
    events actually turned out is called:
    A. the overconfidence effect.
    B. selective amnesia.
    C. retroactive interference.
    D. the hindsight bias.

Answers

1. C pp. 215–216
2. C p. 217
3. D p. 221
4. C p. 223
5. C p. 225
6. D p. 224
7. C p. 226
8. C pp. 229–230
9. C p. 235
10. D pp. 237–238
11. D p. 241
12. D p. 244

Chapter 8 Practice Test

1. Problems that require a common object to be used in an unusual way may be difficult to solve because of:
   A. mental set.
   B. irrelevant information.
   C. unnecessary constraints.
   D. functional fixedness.

2. The nine-dot problem:
   A. is the basis for the saying "think outside the box."
   B. is difficult because people assume constraints that are not part of the problem.
   C. is solved through forming subgoals.
   D. is both A and B.

3. A heuristic is:
   A. a flash of insight.
   B. a guiding principle or "rule of thumb" used in problem solving or decision making.
   C. a methodical procedure for trying all possible solutions to a problem.
   D. a way of making a compensatory decision.

4. According to Nisbett, Eastern cultures tend to favor a(n) _____ cognitive style, whereas Western cultures tend to display a(n) _____ cognitive style.
   A. analytic; holistic
   B. holistic; analytic
   C. logical; emotional
   D. emotional; logical

5. The work of Herbert Simon on decision making showed that:
   A. people generally make rational choices that maximize their gains.
   B. people can evaluate an unlimited number of alternatives effectively.
   C. people tend to focus on only a few aspects of their available options and often make "irrational" decisions as a result.
   D. the more options people consider, the better their decisions tend to be.

6. When you estimate the probability of an event by judging the ease with which relevant instances come to mind, you are relying on:
   A. an additive decision-making model.
   B. the representativeness heuristic.
   C. the availability heuristic.
   D. a noncompensatory model.

7. The belief that the probability of heads is higher after a long string of tails:
   A. is rational and accurate.
   B. is an example of the "gambler's fallacy."
   C. reflects the influence of the representativeness heuristic.
   D. is both B and C.

8. On most modern IQ tests, a score of 115 would be:
   A. about average.
   B. about 15% higher than the average of one's age mates.
   C. an indication of genius.
   D. one standard deviation above the mean.

9. IQ tests have proven to be good predictors of:
   A. social intelligence.
   B. practical problem-solving intelligence.
   C. school performance.
   D. all of the above.

10. Saying that the heritability of intelligence is 60% would mean that:
    A. 60% of a person's intelligence is due to heredity.
    B. 60% of the variability in intelligence scores in a group is estimated to be due to genetic variations.
    C. intelligence is 40% inherited.
    D. heredity affects intelligence in 60% of the members of the group.

11. Evidence indicating that upbringing affects one's mental ability is provided by which of the following findings?
    A. Identical twins are more similar in IQ than fraternal twins.
    B. There is more than a chance similarity between adopted children and their biological parents.
    C. Siblings reared together are more similar in IQ than siblings reared apart.
    D. Identical twins reared apart are more similar in IQ than siblings reared together.

12. According to theories that use the concept of reaction range, the upper limits of an individual's intellectual potential are:
    A. determined during the first year of life.
    B. largely set by heredity.
    C. determined by a person's unique experiences.
    D. determined by one's heritability quotient.

Answers

1. D p. 252
2. D pp. 252–253
3. B p. 253
4. B p. 256
5. C p. 257
6. C p. 259
7. D pp. 260–261
8. D pp. 266–267
9. C p. 268
10. B pp. 271–272
11. C pp. 270–273
12. B p. 274

Chapter 9 Practice Test

1. Although Jackson had a huge breakfast and felt stuffed, he ate three of the donuts that a colleague brought to a morning meeting. His behavior is consistent with:
   A. incentive theories of motivation.
   B. drive theories of motivation.
   C. evolutionary theories of motivation.
   D. the Cannon-Bard theory of motivation.

2. Results of the early studies of hypothalamic manipulations in animals implied that the lateral hypothalamus and the ventromedial nucleus of the hypothalamus may be on-off centers for the control of:
   A. emotion.
   B. hunger.
   C. thirst.
   D. sex drive.

3. Which of the following statements is false?
   A. Insulin is a hormone secreted by the pancreas.
   B. Insulin must be present for cells to utilize glucose.
   C. Leptin levels correlate with levels of the body's fat stores.
   D. Ghrelin secretions are associated with decreased hunger.

4. Which of the following has *not* been found in research on gender differences in sexual interest?
   A. Men think about sex more than women.
   B. Men initiate sex more frequently than women.
   C. Women are more interested in having many partners than men are.
   D. Men are more interested in uncommitted/casual sex than women.

5. Kinsey maintained that sexual orientation:
   A. depends on early classical conditioning experiences.
   B. should be viewed as a continuum.
   C. depends on normalities and abnormalities in the amygdala.
   D. should be viewed as an either-or distinction.

6. One's need for achievement is usually assessed using the:
   A. McClelland Achievement Inventory.
   B. MMPI.
   C. Thematic Apperception Test.
   D. Atkinson Manifest Needs Scale.

7. A polygraph (lie detector) works by:
   A. monitoring physiological indexes of autonomic arousal.
   B. directly assessing the truthfulness of a person's statements.
   C. monitoring the person's facial expressions.
   D. doing all of the above.

8. Which of the following statements about emotional experience is true?
   A. The facial expressions associated with various emotions vary widely across cultures.
   B. Some basic emotions go unnamed in some cultures.
   C. People can identify 11 fundamental emotions from others' facial expressions.
   D. Display rules do not vary across different cultures.

9. According to the James-Lange theory of emotion:
   A. the experience of emotion depends on autonomic arousal and on one's cognitive interpretation of that arousal.
   B. different patterns of autonomic activation lead to the experience of different emotions.
   C. emotion occurs when the thalamus sends signals simultaneously to the cortex and to the autonomic nervous system.
   D. emotions develop because of their adaptive value.

10. The fact that eating behavior, sexual behavior, and the experience of emotion all depend on interactions between biological and environmental determinants lends evidence to which of the text's organizing themes?
    A. Psychology's theoretical diversity
    B. Psychology's empiricism
    C. People's experience of the world is subjective
    D. The joint influence of heredity and environment

11. Which of the following statements is (are) true?
    A. For the most part, people are pretty happy.
    B. Age is largely unrelated to happiness.
    C. Income is largely unrelated to happiness.
    D. All of the above are true.

12. The sales pitch "We're the best dealership in town because the other dealerships just don't stack up against us" is an example of:
    A. a false dichotomy.
    B. semantic slanting.
    C. circular reasoning.
    D. a slippery slope.

Answers

1. A pp. 290–291
2. B p. 292
3. D p. 293
4. C p. 298
5. B pp. 299–300
6. C p. 302
7. A pp. 305–306
8. B pp. 308–310
9. B pp. 310–311
10. D p. 314
11. D pp. 314–315
12. C p. 319

Chapter 10 Practice Test

1. The stage of prenatal development during which the developing organism is most vulnerable to injury is the:
   A. zygotic stage.
   B. germinal stage.
   C. fetal stage.
   D. embryonic stage.

2. Developmental norms:
   A. can be used to make extremely precise predictions about the age at which an individual child will reach various developmental milestones.
   B. indicate the maximum age at which a child can reach a particular developmental milestone and still be considered "normal."
   C. indicate the average age at which individuals reach various developmental milestones.
   D. involve both A and B.

3. The behavioral, reinforcement explanation of the basis for infant-caregiver attachment was undermined by the research of:
   A. Erik Erikson.
   B. Harry Harlow.
   C. Lawrence Kohlberg.
   D. Lev Vygotsky.

4. The quality of infant-caregiver attachment depends:
   A. on the quality of bonding in the first few hours of life.
   B. exclusively on the infant's temperament.
   C. on the interaction between the infant's temperament and the caregiver's responsiveness.
   D. on how stranger anxiety is handled.

5. The 2-year-old child who refers to every four-legged animal as "doggie" is making which of the following errors?
   A. Underextension
   B. Overextension
   C. Overregularization
   D. Underregularization

6. During the second year of life, toddlers begin to take some personal responsibility for feeding, dressing, and bathing themselves in an attempt to establish what Erikson calls a sense of:
   A. superiority.
   B. industry.
   C. generativity.
   D. autonomy.

7. Five-year-old David watches as you pour water from a short, wide glass into a tall, narrow one. He says there is now more water than before. This response demonstrates that:
   A. David understands the concept of conservation.
   B. David does not understand the concept of conservation.
   C. David's cognitive development is "behind" for his age.
   D. both B and C are happening.

8. Which of the following is *not* one of the criticisms of Piaget's theory of cognitive development?
   A. Piaget may have underestimated the cognitive skills of children in some areas.
   B. Piaget may have underestimated the influence of cultural and environmental factors on cognitive development.
   C. The simultaneous mixing of stages raises questions about the value of analyzing development in terms of stages.
   D. Evidence for the theory is based on children's answers to questions.

9. If a child's primary reason for not drawing pictures on the living room wall with crayons is to avoid the punishment that would inevitably follow this behavior, she would be said to be at which level of moral development?
   A. Conventional
   B. Postconventional
   C. Preconventional
   D. Unconventional

10. Girls who mature _____ and boys who mature _____ feel more subjective distress about the transition of puberty.
   A. early; early
   B. early; late
   C. late; early
   D. late; late

11. One aspect of cognition that may decline in middle and late adulthood is:
   A. math ability.
   B. cognitive speed.
   C. abstract reasoning.
   D. none of the above.

12. Males have been found to differ slightly from females in three well-documented areas of mental abilities. Which of the following is *not* one of these?
   A. Verbal ability
   B. Mathematical ability
   C. Intelligence
   D. Visual-spatial abilities

Answers

1. D p. 325
2. C pp. 328–329
3. B p. 329
4. C p. 330
5. B pp. 331–332
6. D pp. 333–334
7. B pp. 335–336
8. D pp. 337–338
9. C p. 339
10. B p. 342
11. B p. 349
12. C p. 351

Chapter 11 Practice Test

1. Harvey Hedonist has devoted his life to the search for physical pleasure and immediate need gratification. Freud would say that Harvey is dominated by:
   A. his ego.
   B. his superego.
   C. his id.
   D. Bacchus.

2. Furious at her boss for what she considers to be unjust criticism, Clara turns around and takes out her anger on her subordinates. Clara may be using the defense mechanism of:
   A. displacement.
   B. reaction formation.
   C. identification.
   D. replacement.

3. Freud believed that most personality disturbances are due to:
   A. the failure of parents to reinforce healthy behavior.
   B. a poor self-concept resulting from excessive parental demands.
   C. unconscious and unresolved sexual conflicts rooted in child-hood experiences.
   D. the exposure of children to unhealthy role models.

4. According to Alfred Adler, the prime motivating force in a person's life is:
   A. physical gratification.
   B. existential anxiety.
   C. striving for superiority.
   D. the need for power.

5. Which of the following learning mechanisms does B. F. Skinner see as being the major means by which behavior is learned?
   A. Classical conditioning
   B. Operant conditioning
   C. Observational learning
   D. Insight learning

6. Always having been a good student, Irving is confident that he will do well in his psychology course. According to Bandura's social cognitive theory, Irving would be said to have:
   A. strong feelings of self-efficacy.
   B. a sense of superiority.
   C. strong feelings of narcissism.
   D. strong defense mechanisms.

7. Which of the following did Carl Rogers believe fosters a congruent self-concept?
   A. Conditional love
   B. Appropriate role models
   C. Immediate need gratification
   D. Unconditional love

8. What need was Abraham Maslow expressing when he said, "What a man can be, he must be"?
   A. The need for superiority
   B. The need for unconditional love
   C. The need for self-actualization
   D. The need to achieve

9. The most convincing evidence for the theory that personality is heavily influenced by genetics is provided by strong personality similarity between:
   A. identical twins reared together.
   B. identical twins reared apart.
   C. fraternal twins reared together.
   D. nontwins reared together.

10. In which of the following cultures is an independent view of the self most likely to be the norm?
    A. China
    B. Japan
    C. Korea
    D. United States

11. Which of the following is *not* a shortcoming of self-report personality inventories?
    A. The accuracy of the results is a function of the honesty of the respondent.
    B. Respondents may attempt to answer in a way that makes them look good.
    C. There is sometimes a problem with "yea-sayers" or "nay-sayers."
    D. They are objective measures.

12. In *The Nurture Assumption*, Judith Harris argues that the evidence indicates that family environment has _____ on children's personalities.
    A. largely positive effects
    B. largely negative effects
    C. surprisingly little effect
    D. a powerful effect

Answers
1. C pp. 364–365
2. A p. 367
3. C p. 370
4. C p. 371
5. B p. 373
6. A p. 374
7. D pp. 376–377
8. C p. 378
9. B p. 381
10. D p. 388
11. D pp. 390–391
12. C p. 393

Chapter 12 Practice Test

1. Stereotypes:
   A. reflect normal cognitive processes that frequently are automatic.
   B. are widely held beliefs that people have certain characteristics because of their membership in a particular group.
   C. tend to be broad overgeneralizations that ignore the diversity within social groups.
   D. are all of the above.

2. You believe that short men have a tendency to be insecure. The concept of illusory correlation implies that you will:
   A. overestimate how often you meet short men who are insecure.
   B. underestimate how often you meet short men who are insecure.
   C. overestimate the frequency of short men in the population.
   D. falsely assume that shortness in men causes insecurity.

3. A father suggests that his son's low marks in school are due to the child's laziness. The father has made _____ attribution.
   A. an external
   B. an internal
   C. a situational
   D. a high consensus

4. The fundamental attribution error refers to the tendency of:
   A. observers to favor external attributions in explaining the behavior of others.
   B. observers to favor internal attributions in explaining the behavior of others.
   C. actors to favor external attributions in explaining the behavior of others.
   D. actors to favor internal attributions in explaining their behavior.

5. Which of the following factors is *not* one that influences interpersonal attraction?
   A. Physical attractiveness
   B. Similarity
   C. Reciprocity
   D. Latitude of acceptance

6. According to Hazan and Shaver (1987):
   A. romantic relationships in adulthood follow the same form as attachment relationships in infancy.
   B. those who had ambivalent attachments in infancy are doomed never to fall in love as adults.
   C. those who had avoidant attachments in infancy often overcompensate by becoming excessively intimate in their adult love relationships.
   D. all of the above are the case.

7. Which of the following variables does *not* tend to facilitate persuasion?
   A. Source credibility
   B. Source trustworthiness
   C. Forewarning of the receiver
   D. A two-sided argument

8. Cognitive dissonance theory predicts that after people engage in behavior that contradicts their true feelings, they will:
   A. convince themselves they really didn't perform the behavior.
   B. change their attitude to make it more consistent with their behavior.
   C. change their attitude to make it less consistent with their behavior.
   D. do nothing.

9. The elaboration likelihood model of attitude change suggests that:
   A. the peripheral route results in more enduring attitude change.
   B. the central route results in more enduring attitude change.
   C. only the central route to persuasion can be effective.
   D. only the peripheral route to persuasion can be effective.

10. The results of Milgram's (1963) study imply that:
    A. in the real world, most people will refuse to follow orders to inflict harm on a stranger.
    B. many people will obey an authority figure even if innocent people get hurt.
    C. most people are willing to give obviously wrong answers when ordered to do so.
    D. most people stick to their own judgment, even when group members unanimously disagree.

11. It appears that social loafing is due to:
    A. social norms that stress the importance of positive interactions among group members.
    B. duplication of effort among group members.
    C. diffusion of responsibility in groups.
    D. a bias toward making internal attributions about the behavior of others.

12. Groupthink occurs when members of a cohesive group:
    A. are initially unanimous about an issue.
    B. stress the importance of caution in group decision making.
    C. emphasize concurrence at the expense of critical thinking in arriving at a decision.
    D. shift toward a less extreme position after group discussion.

Answers

1. D p. 399
2. A pp. 399–400
3. B p. 401
4. B p. 402
5. D pp. 404–405
6. A p. 406
7. C pp. 412–413
8. B p. 415
9. B p. 416
10. B pp. 418–419
11. C p. 423
12. C pp. 424–425

Chapter 13 Practice Test

1. The notion that health is governed by a complex interaction of biological, psychological, and sociocultural factors is referred to as the:
   A. medical model.
   B. multifactorial model.
   C. biopsychosocial model.
   D. interactive model.

2. The four principal types of stress are:
   A. frustration, conflict, pressure, and anxiety.
   B. frustration, anger, pressure, and change.
   C. anger, anxiety, depression, and annoyance.
   D. frustration, conflict, pressure, and change.

3. You want very badly to ask someone for a date, but you are afraid to risk rejection. You are experiencing:
   A. an approach-avoidance conflict.
   B. an avoidance-avoidance conflict.
   C. optimized arousal.
   D. conformity pressure.

4. Research suggests that a high level of arousal may be most optimal for the performance of a task when:
   A. the task is complex.
   B. the task is simple.
   C. the rewards are high.
   D. an audience is present.

5. The alarm stage of Hans Selye's general adaptation syndrome is essentially the same as:
   A. the fight-or-flight response.
   B. constructive coping.
   C. approach-avoidance conflict.
   D. secondary appraisal.

6. The brain structure responsible for initiating action along the two major pathways through which the brain sends signals to the endocrine system is the:
   A. hypothalamus.
   B. thalamus.
   C. corpus callosum.
   D. medulla.

7. Which of the following is accurate in regard to defense mechanisms?
   A. There are many different defense mechanisms.
   B. They are used to ward off unpleasant emotions.
   C. They work through self-deception.
   D. All of the above are accurate.

8. Which element of the Type A personality seems to be most strongly related to increased coronary risk?
   A. Time consciousness
   B. Perfectionism
   C. Ambitiousness
   D. Hostility

9. Research has found that optimists are more likely than pessimists to:
   A. take their time in confronting problems.
   B. identify the negatives before they identify the positives.
   C. engage in action-oriented, problem-focused coping.
   D. seek social support only after they have exhausted all individual efforts to deal with the problem.

10. Which of the following has *not* been found to be a mode of transmission for the HIV virus?
    A. Sexual contact among homosexual men
    B. The sharing of needles by intravenous drug users
    C. Heterosexual contact
    D. Sharing food

11. The fact that health is governed by a dense network of factors is an illustration of the theme of:
    A. psychology in a sociohistorical context.
    B. the phenomenology of experience.
    C. multifactorial causation.
    D. empiricism.

12. In evaluating health statistics, it is useful to:
    A. remember that statistical significance is equivalent to practical significance.
    B. remember that correlation is a reliable indicator of causation.
    C. consider base rates in thinking about probabilities.
    D. do all of the above.

Answers

1. C p. 435
2. D p. 436
3. A p. 437
4. B pp. 442–443
5. A p. 443
6. A p. 444
7. D pp. 446–447
8. D pp. 448–449
9. C pp. 451–452
10. D p. 455
11. C pp. 457–458
12. C pp. 462–463

Chapter 14 Practice Test

1. According to Thomas Szasz, abnormal behavior usually involves:
   A. behavior that is statistically unusual.
   B. behavior that deviates from social norms.
   C. a disease of the mind.
   D. biological imbalance.

2. Although Sue always feels a high level of dread, worry, and anxiety, she still manages to meet her daily responsibilities. Sue's behavior:
   A. should not be considered abnormal because her adaptive functioning is not impaired.
   B. should not be considered abnormal because everyone sometimes experiences worry and anxiety.
   C. can still be considered abnormal because she feels great personal distress.
   D. both a and b are true.

3. A concordance rate indicates:
   A. the percentage of relatives who exhibit the same disorder.
   B. the percentage of people with a given disorder who are currently receiving treatment.
   C. the prevalence of a given disorder in the general population.
   D. the rate of cure for a given disorder.

4. The observation that people acquire phobias of ancient sources of threat (such as snakes) much more readily than modern sources of threat (such as electrical outlets) can best be explained by:
   A. classical conditioning.
   B. operant conditioning.
   C. observational learning.
   D. preparedness/an evolved module for fear learning.

5. Which of the following statements about dissociative identity disorder is true?
   A. The original personality is always aware of the alternate personalities.
   B. Dissociative identity disorder is an alternate name for schizophrenia.
   C. The personalities are typically all quite similar to one another.
   D. Starting in the 1970s, there was a dramatic increase in the diagnosis of dissociative identity disorder.

6. People with unipolar disorder experience _____; people with bipolar disorder experience _____.
   A. alternating periods of depression and mania; mania only
   B. depression only; alternating periods of depression and mania
   C. mania only; alternating periods of depression and mania
   D. alternating periods of depression and mania; depression and mania simultaneously

7. People who consistently come up with _____ explanations for negative events are more prone to depression.
   A. overly optimistic
   B. pessimistic
   C. delusional
   D. dysthymic

8. Mary believes that while she sleeps at night, space creatures are attacking her and invading her uterus, where they will multiply until they are ready to take over the world. Mary was chosen for this task, she believes, because she is the only one with the power to help the space creatures succeed. Mary would most likely be diagnosed as _____ schizophrenic.
   A. paranoid
   B. catatonic
   C. disorganized
   D. undifferentiated

9. Most of the drugs that are useful in the treatment of schizophrenia are known to dampen _____ activity in the brain, suggesting that disruptions in the activity of this neurotransmitter may contribute to the development of the disorder.
   A. norepinephrine
   B. serotonin
   C. acetylcholine
   D. dopamine

10. Research suggests that there is an association between schizophrenia and:
    A. atrophied brain ventricles.
    B. enlarged brain ventricles.
    C. hippocampal degeneration.
    D. abnormalities in the cerebellum.

11. Victims of _____ are more likely to recognize that their eating behavior is pathological; the more life-threatening eating disorder is _____.
    A. anorexia nervosa; bulimia nervosa
    B. bulimia nervosa; anorexia nervosa
    C. anorexia nervosa; anorexia nervosa
    D. bulimia nervosa; bulimia nervosa

12. About _____ of patients with eating disorders are female.
    A. 40%
    B. 50%−60%
    C. 75%
    D. 90%−95%

Answers

1. B p. 468
2. C pp. 468−469
3. A p. 475
4. D p. 475
5. D p. 477
6. B pp. 478−479
7. B p. 483
8. A p. 486
9. D p. 488
10. B p. 489
11. B p. 496
12. D p. 496

Chapter 15 Practice Test

1. One key problem with the provision of psychotherapy is that:
   A. there are too many different approaches to treatment.
   B. there are too many different professions involved.
   C. there is a shortage of qualified therapists.
   D. there are many people who need therapy but do not receive treatment.

2. After undergoing psychoanalysis for several months, Karen has suddenly started "forgetting" to attend her therapy sessions. Karen's behavior is most likely a form of:
   A. resistance.
   B. transference.
   C. insight.
   D. catharsis.

3. The key task of the client-centered therapist is:
   A. interpretation of the client's thoughts, feelings, memories, and behaviors.
   B. clarification of the client's feelings.
   C. confrontation of the client's irrational thoughts.
   D. modification of the client's problematic behaviors.

4. Evaluating the effectiveness of psychotherapy is complicated and difficult because:
   A. disorders sometimes clear up on their own.
   B. different approaches to treatment pursue entirely different goals.
   C. clients' problems vary in severity.
   D. all of the above are involved.

5. Systematic desensitization is particularly effective for the treatment of _____ disorders.
   A. generalized anxiety
   B. panic
   C. obsessive-compulsive
   D. phobic

6. Linda's therapist has her practice active listening skills in structured role-playing exercises. Later, Linda is gradually asked to practice these skills with family members, friends, and finally, her boss. Linda is undergoing:
   A. systematic desensitization.
   B. cognitive restructuring.
   C. a token economy.
   D. social skills training.

7. After being released from a hospital, many schizophrenic patients stop taking their antipsychotic medication because:
   A. their mental impairment causes them to forget.
   B. of the unpleasant side effects.
   C. most schizophrenics don't believe they are ill.
   D. all of the above are involved.

8. Selective serotonin reuptake inhibitors (SSRIs) appear to have value for the treatment of _____ disorders.
   A. depressive
   B. schizophrenic
   C. dissociative
   D. alcoholic

9. Modern psychotherapy:
   A. was spawned by a cultural milieu that viewed the self as an independent, rational being.
   B. embraces universal cultural values.
   C. has been successfully exported to most non-Western cultures.
   D. both B and C.

10. Many people repeatedly go in and out of mental hospitals. Typically, such people are released because _____; they are eventually readmitted because _____.
    A. they have been stabilized through drug therapy; their condition deteriorates once again because of inadequate outpatient care
    B. they run out of funds to pay for hospitalization; they once again can afford it
    C. they have been cured of their disorder; they develop another disorder
    D. they no longer want to be hospitalized; they voluntarily recommit themselves

11. The type of professional training a therapist has:
    A. is the most important indicator of his or her competence.
    B. should be the major consideration in choosing a therapist.
    C. is not all that important because talented therapists can be found in all of the mental health professions.
    D. both A and B are true.

12. Which of the following could be explained by regression toward the mean?
    A. You get an average bowling score in one game and a superb score in the next game.
    B. You get an average bowling score in one game and a very low score in the next game.
    C. You get an average bowling score in one game and another average score in the next game.
    D. You get a terrible bowling score in one game and an average score in the next game.

Answers

1. D p. 505
2. A p. 509
3. B p. 511
4. D p. 513
5. D p. 514
6. D p. 515
7. B p. 518
8. A p. 519
9. A pp. 524–525
10. A p. 527
11. C p. 529
12. D p. 532

PART 2: ANSWERS TO THE CONCEPT CHECKS

Chapter 1

Concept Check 1.1

1. c. Sigmund Freud (1905, pp. 77–78) arguing that it is possible to probe into the unconscious depths of the mind.

2. a. Wilhelm Wundt (1904 revision of an earlier text, p. v) campaigning for a new, independent science of psychology.

3. b. William James (1890) commenting negatively on the structuralists' efforts to break consciousness into its elements and his view of consciousness as a continuously flowing stream.

Concept Check 1.2

1. b. B. F. Skinner (1971, p. 17) explaining why he believes that freedom is an illusion.

2. c. Carl Rogers (1961, p. 27) commenting on others' assertion that he had an overly optimistic (Pollyannaish) view of human potential and discussing humans' basic drive toward personal growth.

3. a. John B. Watson (1930, p. 103) dismissing the importance of genetic inheritance while arguing that traits are shaped entirely by experience.

Concept Check 1.3

1. c. Thomas and Chess's (1977) well-known New York Longitudinal Study is a landmark in developmental psychology.

2. a. Olds and Milner (1954) made this discovery by accident and thereby opened up a fascinating line of inquiry in physiological psychology.

3. e. Zuckerman (1971) pioneered the study of sensation seeking as a personality trait.

Chapter 2

Concept Check 2.1

1. IV: Film violence (present versus absent).
   DV: Heart rate and blood pressure (there are two DVs).

2. IV: Courtesy training (training versus no training).
   DV: Number of customer complaints.

3. IV: Stimulus complexity (high versus low) and stimulus contrast (high versus low) (there are two IVs).
   DV: Length of time spent staring at the stimuli.

4. IV: Group size (large versus small).
   DV: Conformity.

Concept Check 2.2

1. b and e. The other three conclusions all equate correlation with causation.

2. a. Negative. As age increases, more people tend to have visual problems and acuity tends to decrease.

   b. Positive. Studies show that highly educated people tend to earn higher incomes and that people with less education tend to earn lower incomes.

   c. Negative. As shyness increases, the size of one's friendship network should decrease. However, research suggests that this inverse association may be weaker than widely believed.

Concept Check 2.3

Methodological flaw	Study 1	Study 2
Sampling bias	✓	✓
Placebo effects	✓	
Confounding of variables	✓	
Distortions in self-report data		✓
Experimenter bias	✓	

Explanations for Study 1. Sensory deprivation is an unusual kind of experience that may intrigue certain potential subjects, who may be more adventurous or more willing to take risks than the population at large. Using the first 80 students who sign up for this study may not yield a sample that is representative of the population. Assigning the first 40 subjects who sign up to the experimental group may confound these extraneous variables with the treatment (students who sign up most quickly may be the most adventurous). In announcing that he will be examining the detrimental effects of sensory deprivation, the experimenter has created expectations in the subjects. These expectations could lead to placebo effects that have not been controlled for with a placebo group. The experimenter has also revealed that he has a bias about the outcome of the study. Because he supervises the treatments, he knows which subjects are in the experimental and control groups, thus aggravating potential problems with experimenter bias. For example, he might unintentionally give the control group subjects better instructions on how to do the pursuit-rotor task and thereby slant the study in favor of finding support for his hypothesis.

Explanations for Study 2. Sampling bias is a problem because the researcher has sampled only subjects from a low-income, inner-city neighborhood. A sample obtained in this way is not likely to be representative of the population at large. People are sensitive about the issue of racial prejudice, so distortions in self-report data are also likely. Many subjects may be swayed by social desirability bias and rate themselves as less prejudiced than they really are.

Chapter 3

Concept Check 3.1

1. d. Serotonin.

2. b and d. Norepinephrine and serotonin.

3. e. Endorphins.

4. c. Dopamine.

5. a. Acetylcholine.

Concept Check 3.2

1. Left hemisphere damage, probably to Wernicke's area.

2. Deficit in dopamine synthesis in an area of the midbrain.

3. Deterioration of myelin sheaths surrounding axons.

4. Disturbance in dopamine activity.

Please note that neuropsychological assessment is not as simple as this introductory exercise may suggest. There are many possible causes of most disorders, and we discussed only a handful of leading causes for each.

Concept Check 3.3

1. Closer relatives; more distant relatives.
2. Identical twins; fraternal twins.
3. Biological parents; adoptive parents.
4. Genetic overlap or closeness; trait similarity.

Chapter 4

Concept Check 4.1

Dimension	Rods	Cones
1. Physical shape	Elongated	Stubby
2. Number in the retina	125 million	5–6.4 million
3. Area of the retina in which they are dominant receptor	Periphery	Center/fovea
4. Critical to color vision	No	Yes
5. Critical to peripheral vision	Yes	No
6. Sensitivity to dim light	Strong	Weak
7. Speed of dark adaptation	Slow	Rapid

Concept Check 4.2

✓ 1. Interposition. The arches in front cut off part of the corridor behind them.

✓ 2. Height in plane. The back of the corridor is higher on the horizontal plane than the front of the corridor is.

✓ 3. Texture gradient. The more distant portions of the hallway are painted in less detail than the closer portions are.

✓ 4. Relative size. The arches in the distance are smaller than those in the foreground.

✓ 5. Light and shadow. Light shining in from the crossing corridor (it's coming from the left) contrasts with shadow elsewhere.

✓ 6. Linear perspective. The lines of the corridor converge in the distance.

Concept Check 4.3

Dimension	Vision	Hearing
1. Stimulus	Light waves	Sound waves
2. Elements of related perceptions	Wavelength/hue Amplitude/brightness Purity/saturation	Frequency/pitch Amplitude/loudness Purity/timbre
3. Receptors	Rods and cones	Hair cells
4. Location of receptors	Retina	Basilar membrane
5. Main location of processing in brain	Occipital lobe, visual cortex	Temporal lobe, auditory cortex

Chapter 5

Concept Check 5.1

Characteristic	REM sleep	Non-REM sleep
1. Type of EEG activity	"Wide awake" brain waves, mostly beta	Varied, lots of delta waves
2. Eye movements	Rapid, lateral	Slow or absent
3. Dreaming	Frequent, vivid	Less frequent
4. Depth (difficulty in awakening)	Difficult to awaken	Varied, generally easier to awaken
5. Percentage of total sleep (in adults)	About 20%	About 80%
6. Increases or decreases (as percentage of sleep) during childhood	Percent decreases	Percent increases
7. Timing in sleep (dominates early or late)	Dominates later in cycle	Dominates early in cycle

Concept Check 5.2

1. Beta. Video games require alert information processing, which is associated with beta waves.
2. Alpha. Meditation involves relaxation, which is associated with alpha waves, and studies show increased alpha in meditators.
3. Theta. In stage 1 sleep, theta waves tend to be prevalent.
4. Beta. Dreams are associated with REM sleep, which paradoxically produces "wide awake" beta waves.
5. Beta. If you're a beginner, typing will require alert, focused attention, which should generate beta waves.

Concept Check 5.3

1. c. Stimulants.
2. d. Hallucinogens.
3. b. Sedatives.
4. f. Alcohol.
5. a. Narcotics.
6. e. Cannabis.

Chapter 6

Concept Check 6.1

1. CS: Fire in fireplace
   US: Pain from burn   CR/UR: Fear
2. CS: Brake lights in rain
   US: Car accident   CR/UR: Tensing up
3. CS: Sight of cat
   US: Cat dander   CR/UR: Wheezing

Concept Check 6.2

1. FR. Each sale is a response and every third response earns reinforcement.
2. VI. A varied amount of time elapses before the response of doing yard work can earn reinforcement.
3. VR. Reinforcement occurs after a varied number of unreinforced casts (time is irrelevant; the more casts Martha makes, the more reinforcers she will receive).
4. CR. The designated response (reading a book) is reinforced (with a gold star) each and every time.
5. FI. A fixed time interval (3 years) has to elapse before Skip can earn a salary increase (the reinforcer).

Concept Check 6.3

1. Punishment.

2. Positive reinforcement.

3. Punishment.

4. Negative reinforcement (for Audrey); the dog is positively reinforced for its whining.

5. Negative reinforcement.

6. Extinction. When Sharma's co-workers start to ignore her complaints, they are trying to extinguish the behavior (which had been positively reinforced when it won sympathy).

Concept Check 6.4

1. Classical conditioning. Midori's blue windbreaker is a CS eliciting excitement in her dog.

2. Operant conditioning. Playing new songs leads to negative consequences (punishment), which weaken the tendency to play new songs. Playing old songs leads to positive reinforcement, which gradually strengthens the tendency to play old songs.

3. Classical conditioning. The song was paired with the passion of new love so that it became a CS eliciting emotional, romantic feelings.

4. Both. Ralph's workplace is paired with criticism so that his workplace becomes a CS eliciting anxiety. Calling in sick is operant behavior that is strengthened through negative reinforcement (because it reduces anxiety).

Chapter 7

Concept Check 7.1

Feature	Sensory memory	Short-term memory	Long-term memory
1. Main encoding format	Copy of input	Largely phonemic	Largely semantic
2. Storage	Limited capacity	Small	No known limit
3. Storage duration	About ¼ second	Up to 20 seconds	Minutes to years

Concept Check 7.2

1. Ineffective encoding due to lack of attention.

2. Retrieval failure due to motivated forgetting.

3. Proactive interference (previous learning of Justin Timberlake's name interferes with new learning).

4. Retroactive interference (new learning of sociology interferes with older learning of history).

Concept Check 7.3

1. d. Declarative memory.

2. c. Long-term memory.

3. a. Sensory memory.

4. f. Episodic memory.

5. e. Nondeclarative memory.

6. g. Semantic memory.

7. i. Prospective memory.

8. b. Short-term memory.

Chapter 8

Concept Check 8.1

1. Functional fixedness.

2. Forming subgoals.

3. Insight.

4. Searching for analogies.

5. Arrangement problem.

Concept Check 8.2

1. a. Neglect of base rates.

2. d. Overestimation of the improbable due to availability heuristic.

3. c. Gambler's fallacy.

Concept Check 8.3

1. H. Given that the identical twins were reared apart, their greater similarity in comparison to fraternals reared together can only be due to heredity. This comparison is probably the most important piece of evidence supporting the genetic determination of IQ.

2. E. We tend to associate identical twins with evidence supporting heredity, but in this comparison genetic similarity is held constant because both sets of twins are identical. The only logical explanation for the greater similarity in identicals reared together is the effect of their being reared together (environment).

3. E. This comparison is similar to the previous one. Genetic similarity is held constant and a shared environment produces greater similarity than being reared apart.

4. B. This is nothing more than a quantification of the observation that intelligence runs in families. Because families share both genes and environment, either or both could be responsible for the observed correlation.

5. B. The similarity of adopted children to their biological parents can only be due to shared genes, and the similarity of adopted children to their foster parents can only be due to shared environment, so these correlations show the influence of both heredity and environment.

Concept Check 8.4

1. b   2. f   3. c   4. d   5. e

Chapter 9

Concept Check 9.1

1. I. The secretion of ghrelin by the stomach tends to trigger stomach contractions and promote hunger.

2. I. Hunger increases when the amount of glucose in the blood decreases.

3. I or ?. Food cues generally trigger hunger and eating, but reactions vary among individuals.

4. D. Food preferences are mostly learned, and we tend to like what we are accustomed to eating. Most people will not be eager to eat a strange-looking food.

5. I. People tend to eat more when a variety of foods are available.

6. I. The more people are served, the more they tend to eat. Large portions tend to increase eating.

Concept Check 9.2

1. c. Incentive value of success.
2. b. Perceived probability of success.
3. a. Need for achievement.

Concept Check 9.3

2. James-Lange theory
3. Schachter's two-factor theory
4. Evolutionary theories

Chapter 10

Concept Check 10.1

	Event	Stage	Organism	Time span
1.	Uterine implantation	Germinal	Zygote	0–2 weeks
2.	Muscle and bone begin to form	Fetal	Fetus	2 months to birth
3.	Vital organs and body systems begin to form	Embryonic	Embryo	2 weeks to 2 months

Concept Check 10.2

1. b. Animism is characteristic of the preoperational period.
2. c. Mastery of hierarchical classification occurs during the concrete operational period.
3. a. Lack of object permanence is characteristic of the sensorimotor period.

Concept Check 10.3

1. c. Commitment to personal ethics is characteristic of postconventional reasoning.
2. b. Concern about approval of others is characteristic of conventional reasoning.
3. a. Emphasis on positive or negative consequences is characteristic of preconventional reasoning.

Chapter 11

Concept Check 11.1

1. Regression.
2. Projection.
3. Reaction formation.
4. Repression.
5. Rationalization.

Concept Check 11.2

1. Bandura's observational learning. Sarah imitates a role model from television.
2. Maslow's need for self-actualization. Yolanda is striving to realize her fullest potential.
3. Freud's Oedipal complex. Vladimir shows preference for his opposite-sex parent and emotional distance from his same-sex parent.

Concept Check 11.3

1. Maslow (1971, p. 36) commenting on the need for self-actualization.
2. Eysenck (1977, pp. 407–408) commenting on the biological roots of personality.
3. Freud (in Malcolm, 1980) commenting on the repression of sexuality.

Chapter 12

Concept Check 12.1

	Unstable	Stable
Internal	d	b
External	a	c

Concept Check 12.2

1. c. Fundamental attribution error (assuming that arriving late reflects personal qualities).
2. a. Illusory correlation effect (overestimating how often one has seen confirmations of the assertion that young, female professors get pregnant soon after being hired).
3. b. Stereotyping (assuming that all lawyers have certain traits).

Concept Check 12.3

1. *Target:* Cognitive component of attitudes (beliefs about program for regulating nursing homes).

   Persuasion: Message factor (advice to use one-sided instead of two-sided arguments).
2. *Target:* Affective component of attitudes (feelings about candidate).

   Persuasion: Source factor (advice on appearing likable, sincere, and compassionate).
3. *Target:* Behavioral component of attitudes (making contributions).

   Persuasion: Receiver factor (considering audience's initial position regarding the candidate).

Concept Check 12.4

1. False.
2. True.
3. False.
4. True.
5. False.

Chapter 13

Concept Check 13.1

1. b. A choice between two unattractive options.
2. c. Weighing the positive and negative aspects of a single goal.
3. a. A choice between two attractive options.

Concept Check 13.2

1. a. Frustration due to delay.

2. d. Pressure to perform.

3. c. Change associated with leaving school and taking a new job.

4. a. Frustration due to loss of job.

    c. Change in life circumstances.

    d. Pressure to perform (in quickly obtaining new job).

Concept Check 13.3

Pathway 1: hypothalamus, sympathetic division of the ANS, adrenal medulla, catecholamines.

Pathway 2: pituitary, ACTH, adrenal cortex, corticosteroids.

Chapter 14

Concept Check 14.1

	Deviance	Maladaptive behavior	Personal distress
1. Alan		✓	
2. Monica			✓
3. Boris	✓		
4. Natasha	✓	✓	✓

Concept Check 14.2

1. Obsessive-compulsive disorder (key symptoms: frequent rituals, obsession with ordering things).

2. Phobic disorder (key symptoms: persistent and irrational fear of thunderstorms, interference with work functioning).

3. Posttraumatic stress disorder (key symptoms: enduring disturbance due to exposure to traumatic event, nightmares, emotional numbing).

Concept Check 14.3

1. Bipolar disorder, manic episode (key symptoms: extravagant plans, hyperactivity, reckless spending).

2. Paranoid schizophrenia (key symptoms: delusions of persecution and grandeur, along with deterioration of adaptive behavior).

3. Major depression (key symptoms: feelings of despair, low self-esteem, lack of energy).

Chapter 15

Concept Check 15.1

1. c.

2. a.

3. b.

Concept Check 15.2

1. d.

2. b

3. a

4. c

Concept Check 15.3

1. c.

2. a.

3. b.

4. d.

5. b.

Statistical Methods

Empiricism depends on observation; precise observation depends on measurement; and measurement requires numbers. Thus, scientists routinely analyze numerical data to arrive at their conclusions. Over 3000 empirical studies are cited in this text, and all but a few of the simplest ones required a statistical analysis. *Statistics* **is the use of mathematics to organize, summarize, and interpret numerical data.** We discussed correlation briefly in Chapter 2, but in this appendix we look at a variety of statistics.

To illustrate statistics in action, let's assume that we want to test a hypothesis that has generated quite an argument in your psychology class. The hypothesis is that college students who watch a great deal of television aren't as bright as those who watch TV infrequently. For the fun of it, your class decides to conduct a correlational study of itself, collecting survey and psychological test data. Your classmates all agree to respond to a short survey on their TV viewing habits. Because everyone at your school has had to take the SAT, the class decides to use scores on the SAT verbal subtest as an index of how bright students are. All of them agree to allow the records office at the college to furnish their SAT scores to the professor, who replaces each student's name with a subject number (to protect students' right to privacy). Let's see how we could use statistics to analyze the data collected in our pilot study (a small, preliminary investigation).

Graphing Data

PSYKTREK 1c

After collecting our data, our next step is to organize the data to get a quick overview of our numerical results. Let's assume that there are 20 students in your class, and when they estimate how many hours they spend per day watching TV, the results are as follows:

3	2	0	3	1
3	4	0	5	1
2	3	4	5	2
4	5	3	4	6

One of the simpler things that we can do to organize data is to create a *frequency distribution*—**an orderly arrangement of scores indicating the frequency of each score or group of scores.** Figure B.1(a) shows a frequency distribution for our data on TV viewing. The column on the left lists the possible scores (estimated hours of TV viewing) in order, and the column on the right lists the number of subjects with each score. Graphs can provide an even better overview of the data. One approach is to portray the data in a *histogram,* **which is a bar graph that presents data from a frequency distribution.** Such a histogram, summarizing our TV viewing data, is presented in **Figure B.1(b).**

Another widely used method of portraying data graphically is the *frequency polygon*—**a line figure used to present data from a frequency distribution.** **Figures B.1(c)** and **B.1(d)** show how our TV viewing data can be converted from a histogram to a frequency polygon. In both the bar graph and the line figure, the horizontal axis lists the possible scores and the vertical axis is used to indicate the frequency of each score. This use of

Score	Tallies	Frequency
6	I	1
5	III	3
4	IIII	4
3	IIII I	5
2	III	3
1	II	2
0	II	2

(a) Frequency distribution

(b) Histogram

(c) Conversion of histogram into frequency polygon

(d) Frequency polygon

FIGURE B.1

Graphing data. (a) Our raw data are tallied into a frequency distribution. **(b)** The same data are portrayed in a bar graph called a histogram. **(c)** A frequency polygon is plotted over the histogram. **(d)** The resultant frequency polygon is shown by itself.

© Cengage Learning

```
0
0
1
1
2
2
2
2
3 ────── Mode
3          (most frequent score)
3 ────── Median
3          (middle of score distribution)
3
4
4
4
4
5
5
5
6
60 ÷ 20 = 3.00   Mean (arithmetic average
                       of summed scores)
```

FIGURE B.2

Measures of central tendency. The mean, median, and mode sometimes yield different results, but they usually converge, as in the case of our TV viewing data.

the axes is nearly universal for frequency polygons, although sometimes it is reversed in histograms (the vertical axis lists possible scores, so the bars become horizontal).

Our graphs improve on the jumbled collection of scores that we started with, but **descriptive statistics, which are used to organize and summarize data,** provide some additional advantages. Let's see what the three measures of central tendency tell us about our data.

Measuring Central Tendency

PSYKTREK 1c

In examining a set of data, it's routine to ask "What is a typical score in the distribution?" For instance, in this case we might compare the average amount of TV watching in our sample against national estimates to determine whether our subjects appear to be representative of the population. The three measures of central tendency, the median, the mean, and the mode, give us indications regarding the typical score in a data set. The **median is the score that falls in the center of a distribution, the mean is the arithmetic average of the scores,** and the **mode is the score that occurs most frequently.**

All three measures of central tendency are calculated for our TV viewing data in **Figure B.2.** As you can see, in this set of data, the mean, median, and mode all turn out to be the same score, which is 3. The correspondence among the three measures of central tendency seen in our TV viewing data is quite common, but there are situations in which the mean, median, and mode can yield very different estimates of central tendency. To illustrate, imagine that you're interviewing for a sales position at a company. Unbeknownst to you, the company's five salespeople earned the following incomes in the previous year: $20,000, $20,000, $25,000, $35,000, and $200,000. You ask how much the typical salesperson earns in a year. The sales director proudly announces that her five salespeople earned *a mean* income of $60,000 last year. However, before you order that expensive, new sports car, you had better inquire about the *median* and *modal* income for the sales staff. In this case, one extreme score ($200,000) has inflated the mean, making it unrepresentative of the sales staff's earnings. In this instance, the median ($25,000) and the mode ($20,000) both provide better estimates of what you are likely to earn.

In general, the mean is the most useful measure of central tendency because additional statistical manipulations can be performed on it that are not possible with the median or mode. However, the mean is sensitive to extreme scores in a distribution, which can sometimes make the mean misleading. Thus, lack of agreement among the three measures of central tendency usually occurs when a few extreme scores pull the mean away from the center of the distribution, as shown in **Figure B.3.** The curves

(a) Symmetrical distribution

(b) Negatively skewed distribution

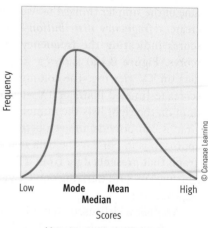

(c) Positively skewed distribution

FIGURE B.3

Measures of central tendency in skewed distributions. In a symmetrical distribution (**a**), the three measures of central tendency converge. However, in a negatively skewed distribution (**b**) or in a positively skewed distribution (**c**), the mean, median, and mode are pulled apart as shown here. Typically, in these situations the median provides the best index of central tendency.

plotted in **Figure B.3** are simply "smoothed out" frequency polygons based on data from many subjects. They show that when a distribution is symmetric, the measures of central tendency fall together, but this is not true in skewed or unbalanced distributions.

Figure B.3(b) shows a *negatively skewed distribution,* in which most scores pile up at the high end of the scale (the negative skew refers to the direction in which the curve's "tail" points). A *positively skewed distribution,* in which scores pile up at the low end of the scale, is shown in **Figure B.3(c).** In both types of skewed distributions, a few extreme scores at one end pull the mean, and to a lesser degree the median, away from the mode. In these situations, the mean may be misleading and the median usually provides the best index of central tendency.

In any case, the measures of central tendency for our TV viewing data are reassuring because they all agree and they fall reasonably close to national estimates regarding how much young adults watch TV. Given the small size of our group, this agreement with national norms doesn't *prove* that our sample is representative of the population, but at least there's no obvious reason to believe that they're unrepresentative.

Measuring Variability

PSYKTREK 1c

Of course, everyone in our sample did not report identical TV viewing habits. Virtually all data sets are characterized by some variability. *Variability* **refers to how much the scores tend to vary or depart from the mean score.** For example, the distribution of golf scores for a mediocre, erratic golfer would be characterized by high variability, while scores for an equally mediocre but more consistent golfer would show less variability.

The *standard deviation* **is an index of the amount of variability in a set of data.** It reflects the dispersion of scores in a distribution. This principle is portrayed graphically in **Figure B.4**, where the two distributions of golf scores have the same mean but the one on the left has less variability because the scores are bunched up in the center (for the consistent golfer). The distribution in **Figure B.4(b)** is characterized by more variability, as the erratic golfer's scores are more spread out. This distribution will yield a higher standard deviation than the distribution in **Figure B.4(a)**.

The formula for calculating the standard deviation is shown in **Figure B.5**, where d stands for each score's deviation from the mean and Σ stands for summation. A step-by-step application of this formula to our TV viewing data, shown in **Figure B.5**, reveals that the standard deviation for our TV viewing data is 1.64. The standard deviation has a variety of uses. One of these uses will surface in the next section, where we discuss the normal distribution.

TV viewing score (X)	Deviation from mean (d)	Deviation squared (d^2)
0	−3	9
0	−3	9
1	−2	4
1	−2	4
2	−1	1
2	−1	1
2	−1	1
3	0	0
3	0	0
3	0	0
3	0	0
3	0	0
4	+1	1
4	+1	1
4	+1	1
4	+1	1
5	+2	4
5	+2	4
5	+2	4
$N = 20$ 6	+3	9
$\Sigma X = 60$		$\Sigma d^2 = 54$

$$\text{Mean} = \frac{\Sigma X}{N} = \frac{60}{20} = 3.0$$

$$\text{Standard deviation} = \sqrt{\frac{\Sigma d^2}{N}} = \sqrt{\frac{54}{20}}$$

$$= \sqrt{2.70} = 1.64$$

© Cengage Learning

FIGURE B.5

Steps in calculating the standard deviation. (1) Add the scores (ΣX) and divide by the number of scores (N) to calculate the mean (which comes out to 3.0 in this case). (2) Calculate each score's deviation from the mean by subtracting the mean from each score (the results are shown in the second column). (3) Square these deviations from the mean and total the results to obtain (Σd^2) as shown in the third column. (4) Insert the numbers for N and Σd^2 into the formula for the standard deviation and compute the results.

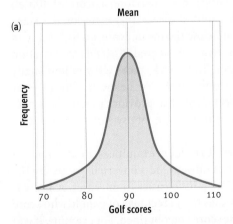

(a)

Mean

Frequency

Golf scores

© Cengage Learning

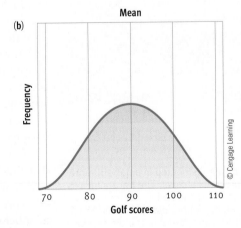

(b)

Mean

Frequency

Golf scores

FIGURE B.4

The standard deviation and dispersion of data. Although both these distributions of golf scores have the same mean, their standard deviations will be different. In (**a**) the scores are bunched together and there is less variability than in (**b**), yielding a lower standard deviation for the data in distribution (**a**).

The Normal Distribution

The hypothesis in our study is that brighter students watch less TV than relatively dull students. To test this hypothesis, we're going to correlate TV viewing with SAT scores. But to make effective use of the SAT data, we need to understand what SAT scores mean, which brings us to the normal distribution.

The *normal distribution* **is a symmetrical, bell-shaped curve that represents the pattern in which many human characteristics are dispersed in the population.** A great many physical qualities (for example, height, nose length, and running speed) and psychological traits (intelligence, spatial reasoning ability, introversion) are distributed in a manner that closely resembles this bell-shaped curve. When a trait is normally distributed, most scores fall near the center of the distribution (the mean) and the number of scores gradually declines as one moves away from the center in either direction (see **Figure B.6**). The normal distribution is *not* a law of nature. It's a mathematical function, or theoretical curve, that approximates the way nature seems to operate.

The normal distribution is the bedrock of the scoring system for most psychological tests, including the SAT. As we discuss in Chapter 8, psychological tests are *relative measures*; they assess how people score on a trait in comparison to other people. The normal distribution gives us a precise way to measure how people stack up in comparison to one another. The scores under the normal curve are dispersed in a fixed pattern, with the standard deviation serving as the unit of measurement, as shown in **Figure B.6**. About 68% of the scores in the distribution fall within plus or minus 1 standard deviation of the mean, while 95% of the scores fall within plus or minus 2 standard deviations of the mean. Given this fixed pattern, if you know the mean and standard deviation of a normally distributed trait, you can tell where any score falls in the distribution for the trait.

Although you may not have realized it, you probably have taken many tests in which the scoring system is based on the normal distribution. On the SAT, for instance, raw scores (the number of items correct on each subtest) are converted into standard scores that indicate where you fall in the normal distribution for the trait measured. In this conversion, the mean is set arbitrarily at 500 and the standard deviation at 100, as shown in **Figure B.7**. Therefore, a score of 400 on the SAT verbal subtest means that you scored 1 standard deviation below the mean, while an SAT score of 600 indicates that you scored 1 standard deviation above the mean. Thus, SAT scores tell you how many standard deviations above or below the mean your score was. This system also provides the metric for IQ scales and many other types of psychological tests (see Chapter 8).

Test scores that place examinees in the normal distribution can always be converted to percentile scores, which are a little easier to interpret. A *percentile score* **indicates the percentage of people who score at or below the score you obtained.** For example, if you score at the 60th percentile, 60% of the people who take the test score the same or below you, while the remaining 40% score above you. There are tables available that permit us to convert any standard deviation

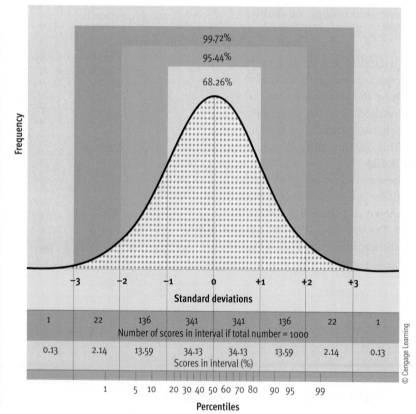

FIGURE B.6

The normal distribution. Many characteristics are distributed in a pattern represented by this bell-shaped curve (each dot represents a case). The horizontal axis shows how far above or below the mean a score is (measured in plus or minus standard deviations). The vertical axis shows the number of cases obtaining each score. In a normal distribution, most cases fall near the center of the distribution, so that 68.26% of the cases fall within plus or minus 1 standard deviation of the mean. The number of cases gradually declines as one moves away from the mean in either direction, so that only 13.59% of the cases fall between 1 and 2 standard deviations above or below the mean, and even fewer cases (2.14%) fall between 2 and 3 standard deviations above or below the mean.

placement in a normal distribution into a precise percentile score. **Figure B.6** gives some percentile conversions for the normal curve.

Of course, not all distributions are normal. As we saw in **Figure B.3**, some distributions are skewed in one direction or the other. As an example, consider what would happen if a classroom exam were much too easy or much too hard. If the test were too easy, scores would be bunched up at the high end of the scale, as in **Figure B.3(b)**. If the test were too hard, scores would be bunched up at the low end, as in **Figure B.3(c)**.

Measuring Correlation

PSYKTREK 1d

To determine whether TV viewing is related to SAT scores, we have to compute a *correlation coefficient*—a numerical index of the degree of relationship that exists between two variables. As discussed in Chapter 2, a *positive* correlation means that the two variables—say *X* and *Y*—covary together. This means that high scores on variable *X* are associated with high scores on variable *Y* and that low scores on *X* are associated with low scores on *Y*. A *negative* correlation indicates that there is an inverse relationship between two variables. This means that people who score high on variable *X* tend to score low on variable *Y*, whereas those who score low on *X* tend to score high on *Y*. In our study, we hypothesized that as TV viewing increases, SAT scores will decrease, so we should expect a negative correlation between TV viewing and SAT scores.

The *magnitude* of a correlation coefficient indicates the *strength* of the association between two variables. This coefficient can vary between 0 and ±1.00. The coefficient is usually represented by the letter *r* (for example, *r* = .45). A coefficient near 0 tells us that there is no relationship between two variables. A coefficient of +1.00 or −1.00 indicates that there is a perfect, one-to-one correspondence between two variables. A perfect correlation is found only rarely when working with real data. The closer the coefficient is to either −1.00 or +1.00, the stronger the relationship is.

The direction and strength of correlations can be illustrated graphically in scatter diagrams. A *scatter diagram* is a graph in which paired X and Y scores for each subject are plotted as single points. **Figure B.8** below shows scatter diagrams for positive correlations in the upper half and for negative correlations in the bottom half. A perfect positive correlation and a perfect negative correlation are shown on the far left. When a

FIGURE B.7

The normal distribution and SAT scores. The normal distribution is the basis for the scoring system on many standardized tests. For example, on the SAT, the mean is set at 500 and the standard deviation at 100. Hence, an SAT score tells you how many standard deviations above or below the mean you scored. For example, a score of 700 means you scored 2 standard deviations above the mean.

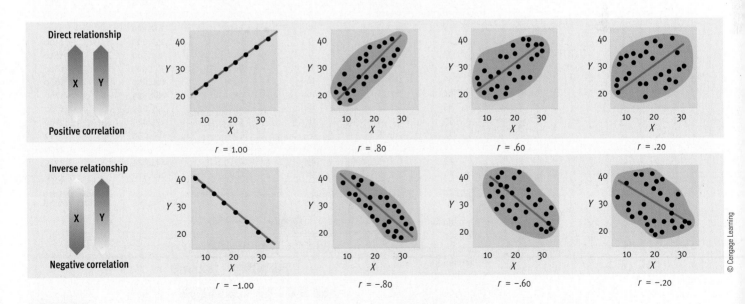

FIGURE B.8

Scatter diagrams of positive and negative correlations. Scatter diagrams plot paired *X* and *Y* scores as single points. Score plots slanted in the opposite direction result from positive (top row) as opposed to negative (bottom row) correlations. Moving across both rows (to the right), you can see that progressively weaker correlations result in more and more scattered plots of data points.

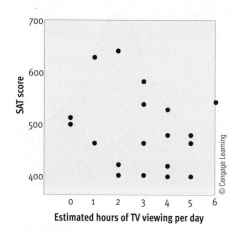

FIGURE B.9

Scatter diagram of the correlation between TV viewing and SAT scores.
Our hypothetical data relating TV viewing to SAT scores are plotted in this scatter diagram. Compare it to the scatter diagrams seen in **Figure B.8** and see whether you can estimate the correlation between TV viewing and SAT scores in our data (see the text for the answer).

FIGURE B.10

Computing a correlation coefficient.
The calculations required to compute the Pearson product-moment coefficient of correlation are shown here. The formula looks intimidating, but it's just a matter of filling in the figures taken from the sums of the columns shown above the formula.

© Cengage Learning

correlation is perfect, the data points in the scatter diagram fall exactly in a straight line. However, positive and negative correlations yield lines slanted in the opposite direction because the lines map out opposite types of associations. Moving to the right in **Figure B.8**, you can see what happens when the magnitude of a correlation decreases. The data points scatter farther and farther from the straight line that would represent a perfect relationship.

What about our data relating TV viewing to SAT scores? **Figure B.9** shows a scatter diagram of these data. Having just learned about scatter diagrams, perhaps you can estimate the magnitude of the correlation between TV viewing and SAT scores. The scatter diagram of our data looks a lot like the one seen in the bottom right corner of **Figure B.8**, suggesting that the correlation will be in the vicinity of $-.20$.

The formula for computing the most widely used measure of correlation—the Pearson product-moment correlation—is shown in **Figure B.10**, along with the calculations for our data on TV viewing and SAT scores. The data yield a correlation of $r = -.24$. This coefficient of correlation reveals that we have found a weak inverse association between TV viewing and performance on the SAT. Among our subjects, as TV viewing increases, SAT scores decrease, but the trend isn't very strong. We can get a better idea of how strong this correlation is by examining its predictive power.

Correlation and Prediction

PSYKTREK 1d

As the magnitude of a correlation increases (gets closer to either -1.00 or $+1.00$), our ability to predict one variable based on knowledge of the other variable steadily increases. This relationship between the magnitude of a correlation and predictability can

Subject number	TV viewing score (X)	X^2	SAT score (Y)	Y^2	XY
1	0	0	500	250,000	0
2	0	0	515	265,225	0
3	1	1	450	202,500	450
4	1	1	650	422,500	650
5	2	4	400	160,000	800
6	2	4	675	455,625	1350
7	2	4	425	180,625	850
8	3	9	400	160,000	1200
9	3	9	450	202,500	1350
10	3	9	500	250,000	1500
11	3	9	550	302,500	1650
12	3	9	600	360,000	1800
13	4	16	400	160,000	1600
14	4	16	425	180,625	1700
15	4	16	475	225,625	1900
16	4	16	525	275,625	2100
17	5	25	400	160,000	2000
18	5	25	450	202,500	2250
19	5	25	475	225,625	2375
20	6	36	550	302,500	3300
$N = 20$	$\Sigma X = 60$	$\Sigma X^2 = 234$	$\Sigma Y = 9815$	$\Sigma Y^2 = 4{,}943{,}975$	$\Sigma XY = 28{,}825$

Formula for Pearson product-moment correlation coefficient

$$r = \frac{(N)\,\Sigma XY - ((\Sigma X)\,\Sigma Y)}{\sqrt{[(N)\,\Sigma X^2 - (\Sigma X)^2]\,[(N)\,\Sigma Y^2 - (\Sigma Y)^2]}}$$

$$= \frac{(20)\,(28{,}825) - (60)\,(9815)}{\sqrt{[(20)\,(234) - (60)^2]\,[(20)\,(4{,}943{,}975) - (9815)^2]}}$$

$$= \frac{-12{,}400}{\sqrt{[1080]\,[2{,}545{,}275]}}$$

$$= -.237$$

© Cengage Learning

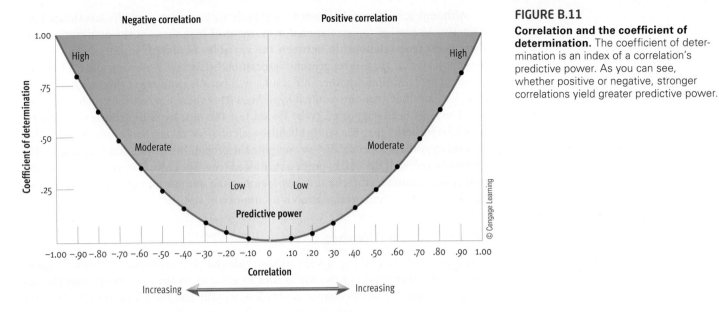

Correlation and the coefficient of determination. The coefficient of determination is an index of a correlation's predictive power. As you can see, whether positive or negative, stronger correlations yield greater predictive power.

be quantified precisely. All we have to do is square the correlation coefficient (multiply it by itself) and this gives us the *coefficient of determination,* **the percentage of variation in one variable that can be predicted based on the other variable.** Thus, a correlation of .70 yields a coefficient of determination of .49 (.70 × .70 = .49), indicating that variable *X* can account for 49% of the variation in variable *Y*. **Figure B.11** shows how the coefficient of determination goes up as the magnitude of a correlation increases.

Unfortunately, a correlation of −.24 doesn't give us much predictive power. We can account for only a little over 6% of the variation in variable *Y*. So, if we tried to predict individuals' SAT scores based on how much TV they watched, our predictions wouldn't be very accurate. Although a low correlation doesn't have much practical, predictive utility, it may still have theoretical value. Just knowing that there is a relationship between two variables can be theoretically interesting. However, we haven't yet addressed the question of whether our observed correlation is strong enough to support our hypothesis that there is a relationship between TV viewing and SAT scores. To make this judgment, we have to turn to inferential statistics and the process of hypothesis testing.

Hypothesis Testing

Inferential statistics go beyond the mere description of data. *Inferential statistics* **are used to interpret data and draw conclusions.** They permit researchers to decide whether their data support their hypotheses.

In our study of TV viewing we hypothesized that we would find an inverse relationship between amount of TV watched and SAT scores. Sure enough, that's what we found. However, we have to ask ourselves a critical question: Is this observed correlation large enough to support our hypothesis, or might a correlation of this size have occurred by chance?

We have to ask a similar question nearly every time we conduct a study. Why? Because we are working only with a sample. In research, we observe a limited *sample* (in this case, 20 subjects) to draw conclusions about a much larger *population* (college students in general). There's always a possibility that if we drew a different sample from the population, the results might be different. Perhaps our results are unique to our sample and not generalizable to the larger population. If we were able to collect data on the entire population, we would not have to wrestle with this problem, but our dependence on a sample necessitates the use of inferential statistics to precisely evaluate the likelihood that our results are due to chance factors in sampling. Thus, inferential statistics are the key to making the inferential leap from the sample to the population (see **Figure B.12**).

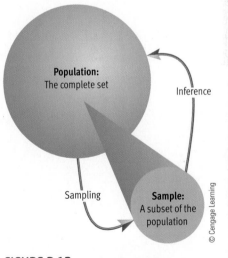

The relationship between the population and the sample. In research, we are usually interested in a broad population, but we can observe only a small sample from the population. After making observations of our sample, we draw inferences about the population, based on the sample. This inferential process works well as long as the sample is reasonably representative of the population.

Although it may seem backward, in hypothesis testing we formally test the *null* hypothesis. As applied to correlational data, the **null hypothesis is the assumption that there is no true relationship between the variables observed.** In our study, the null hypothesis is that there is no genuine association between TV viewing and SAT scores. We want to determine whether our results will permit us to *reject* the null hypothesis and thus conclude that our *research hypothesis* (that there is a relationship between the variables) has been supported. Why do we test the null hypothesis instead of the research hypothesis? Because our probability calculations depend on assumptions tied to the null hypothesis. Specifically, we compute the probability of obtaining the results that we have observed if the null hypothesis is indeed true. The calculation of this probability hinges on a number of factors. A key factor is the amount of variability in the data, which is why the standard deviation is an important statistic.

Statistical Significance

When we reject the null hypothesis, we conclude that we have found *statistically significant* results. **Statistical significance is said to exist when the probability that the observed findings are due to chance is very low, usually less than 5 chances in 100.** This means that if the null hypothesis is correct and we conduct our study 100 times, drawing a new sample from the population each time, we will get results such as those observed only 5 times out of 100. If our calculations allow us to reject the null hypothesis, we conclude that our results support our research hypothesis. Thus, statistically significant results typically are findings that *support* a research hypothesis.

The requirement that there be less than 5 chances in 100 that research results are due to chance is the *minimum* requirement for statistical significance. When this requirement is met, we say the results are significant at the .05 level. If researchers calculate that there is less than 1 chance in 100 that their results are due to chance factors in sampling, the results are significant at the .01 level. If there is less than a 1 in 1000 chance that findings are attributable to sampling error, the results are significant at the .001 level. Thus, there are several *levels* of significance that you may see cited in scientific articles.

Because we are only dealing in matters of probability, there is always the possibility that our decision to accept or reject the null hypothesis is wrong. The various significance levels indicate the probability of erroneously rejecting the null hypothesis (and inaccurately accepting the research hypothesis). At the .05 level of significance, there are 5 chances in 100 that we have made a mistake when we conclude that our results support our hypothesis, and at the .01 level of significance the chance of an erroneous conclusion is 1 in 100. Although researchers hold the probability of this type of error quite low, the probability is never zero. This is one of the reasons that competently executed studies of the same question can yield contradictory findings. The differences may be due to chance variations in sampling that can't be prevented.

What do we find when we evaluate our data linking TV viewing to students' SAT scores? The calculations indicate that, given our sample size and the variability in our data, the probability of obtaining a correlation of −.24 by chance is greater than 20%. That's not a high probability, but it's not low enough to reject the null hypothesis. Thus, our findings are not strong enough to allow us to conclude that we have supported our hypothesis.

Statistics and Empiricism

In summary, conclusions based on empirical research are a matter of probability, and there's always a possibility that the conclusions are wrong. However, two major strengths of the empirical approach are its precision and its intolerance of error. Scientists can give you precise estimates of the likelihood that their conclusions are wrong, and because they're intolerant of error, they hold this probability extremely low. It's their reliance on statistics that allows them to accomplish these goals.

The Psychology of Environmental Sustainability

by Britain A. Scott (University of St. Thomas) and Susan M. Koger (Willamette University)

What do pollution, deforestation, the extinction of species, and climate change have in common? You might instantly respond, "They're all environmental problems." But if you stop to think about it, is it really the *environment* that has the problems? What ties all these issues together is their cause: *maladaptive human behavior.* Particularly for the last 150 years, we humans have been behaving in ways that are *unsustainable.* We burn fossil fuels that pollute the air and change the climate, dump wastes into water and soil, overconsume resources, and invade the habitats of other species. Because the real problem is destructive human behaviors—and underlying thoughts, attitudes, feelings, values, and decisions—psychologists are increasingly applying their expertise to these issues (e.g., Clayton & Myers, 2009; Koger & Winter, 2010). As you will see, psychological insights are critical to the achievement of a *sustainable world*—**one in which human activities and needs are balanced with those of other species and future generations, taking into account ecological as well as social and economic factors** (Schmuck & Schultz, 2002).

The earliest psychological research on environmental issues emerged in the 1970s, against a backdrop of growing public concern about air and water pollution and nuclear waste. Most of this research was conducted by *environmental psychologists,* **researchers who study how individuals are affected by, and interact with, their physical environments.** Importantly, the term *environmental* in this context does not refer specifically to the natural environment. Only a minority of environmental psychologists study nature-related topics, such as how spending time in nature restores one's ability to pay attention and cope with stress (Kaplan, 1995). Most environmental psychologists study human-built environments, focusing on topics such as noise, crowding, and urban design.

In the 1990s, holistic thinkers calling themselves *ecopsychologists* began promoting the idea that modern living erodes people's sense of *connection to nature,* leaving them developmentally deprived and psychologically distressed (Roszak, 1992; Roszak, Gomes, & Kanner, 1995). Convinced by this notion, some clinicians have incorporated ecopsychological therapies into their practices. Their goal is to revive a connection to nonhuman nature that may help people feel better and guide them to behave in more environmentally friendly ways (e.g., Buzzell & Chalquist, 2009). Empirical research testing the validity of the ecopsychological premise has emerged over the past decade, and the first peer-reviewed research journal on the topic, *Ecopsychology,* made its debut in 2009. Specifically, several researchers have created measures to *operationally define* (see Chapter 2) the connection to nature (e.g., Mayer & Frantz, 2004; Nisbet, Zelenski, & Murphy, 2009; Schultz, 2000). If we can *measure* it, we can determine whether it is related to mental well-being and if it predicts pro-environmental attitudes and sustainable behavior, as ecopsychologists propose.

Over the past several years, another label has emerged to describe the work of researchers in traditional branches of psychology (primarily social, behavioral, and cognitive) who study how to promote pro-environmental behaviors (e.g., energy conservation) and decrease anti-environmental behavior (e.g., material consumption). *Conservation psychology* **is defined as the study of the interactive relationships between humans and the rest of nature, with a particular focus on applying psychological theory and research to enhance conservation of natural resources** (Saunders, 2003). Some, but not all, environmental psychologists and ecopsychologists see their work fitting this definition.

In the following section, we will review some facts regarding how humans are negatively affecting the larger systems upon which our lives depend. We then go on to illustrate how many subdisciplines of psychology can aid in understanding—and hopefully solving—the foundational problems in people's thinking and behavior. (Note: A more thorough discussion of these issues is available in Koger & Winter, 2010.)

The Escalating Environmental Crisis

Unless you've been living in a cave without media access, you are at least somewhat familiar with the environmental issues currently confronting humanity. In fact, you may even feel tired of hearing the "gloom and doom" reports concerning melting ice caps and rising sea levels, toxic chemicals in the air and water, overpopulation, dwindling forests, and species losses. It may all seem too depressing, overwhelming, and perhaps even terrifying. Or maybe it doesn't seem to have much to do with you personally, and you feel powerless to make any difference.

Such responses are understandable and consistent with an evolutionary perspective. Human cognitive and perceptual systems evolved in an environment where the primary threats to safety were sudden and dramatic. As a result, people have difficulty responding to slowly developing but potentially calamitous conditions, especially when the consequences seem far away in terms of time or place. People discount distant dangers and take them less seriously than "risks with negative outcomes that occur for sure, now, here, and to us" (Gattig & Hendrickx, 2007, p. 22). The tendency is to delay action until problems are large scale and readily apparent rather than working to prevent the problems. Unfortunately, by then it may be too late.

Let's take, for example, the problem of *global warming*. Gases such as carbon dioxide, methane, and nitrous oxide trap heat in the atmosphere. The naturally resulting *greenhouse effect* is necessary to maintain a climate suitable for life on this planet. Gas levels

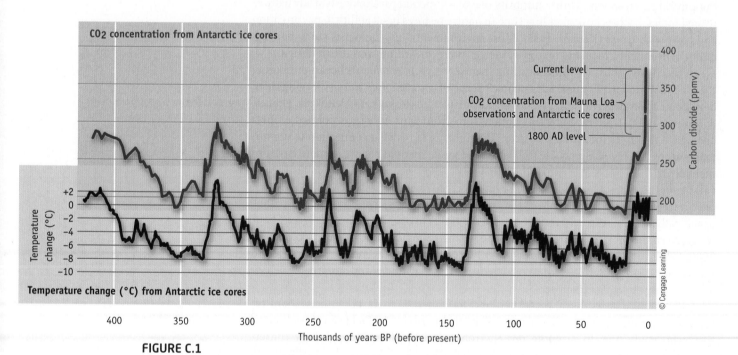

FIGURE C.1

Long-term trends in atmospheric carbon dioxide concentration and temperature. Scientists have sampled ice cores in Antarctica to study fluctuations in atmospheric concentrations of carbon dioxide (CO_2), the dominant greenhouse gas. Over the past 400,000 years, there has been a very strong correlation between temperature variations and CO_2 levels. With the beginning of the Industrial Revolution in the 1800s, CO_2 concentrations began a dramatic and unprecedented increase, rising rapidly from 280 ppmv (parts per million by volume) to current levels of 376 ppmv. Note that this represents an increase of 77 ppmv relative to the highest concentrations reached during the course of the preceding 400,000 years (Woods Hole Research Center, 2009). Thus, it is highly unlikely that these recent trends reflect "natural" variability.

vary naturally to some extent, but as you have probably heard, modern living has created an unprecedented increase in greenhouse gas concentrations (see **Figure C.1**). Simultaneously, our forests, which act as the lungs of the Earth by converting carbon dioxide to oxygen, have been rapidly shrinking because of logging and the clearing of forest land for other uses. As a result, carbon dioxide in the atmosphere is at the "highest level in 650,000 years" (Gardner & Prugh, 2008, p. 3) and is clearly correlated with planetary warming (see **Figure C.2**). Although it is not possible to establish causation from these correlational analyses, the "scientific consensus [is] that global warming is happening and that it is induced by human activity" (Associated Press, 2010).

The years between 2001 and 2011 were eleven of the twelve warmest since 1850, when recording of global temperatures began. January 2012 was the 323rd consecutive month with a global temperature higher than the 20th-century average (National Oceanic and Atmospheric Administration, 2012). The trends suggest that many warming greenhouse gases, including CO_2 and methane, will continue to rise if current industrial and social practices do not change dramatically and quickly. In its most recent report, the Intergovernmental Panel on Climate Change (2007) predicted that the planet could warm as much as 11 degrees Fahrenheit by 2100. That may not sound like much, but let's put that number in perspective: during the last ice age the world was only 9 degrees cooler than it is today. Thus, we are facing the real possibility of planetary temperature changes of ice age magnitudes within this century.

You may be wondering why the warming of the planet matters. It matters because of the associated global *climactic changes*. For example, we are already witnessing melting of the Earth's ice caps, and it's not just the polar bears that are in trouble. Melting ice is threatening people living on islands and near the ocean because it leads to rising sea levels, erosion, and flooding. A recent report states that the melting is happening so quickly that sea levels may rise 5 feet in this century (Ritter, 2011). This means that U.S. coastal cities such as Miami, New Orleans, Tampa, and Virginia Beach could lose more than 10% of their land by 2100 (Weiss, Overpeck, & Strauss, 2011).

Climate changes will mean flooding in some regions and drought in others. Tornados, typhoons, and hurricanes will likely become more intense. The U.S. Centers for Disease Control and Prevention (2009) are gearing up in anticipation of the possibility of millions of people suffering from malnutrition, disease, and injury as a result of extreme weather. These physical hardships will have significant mental health impacts. Loss, disruption, and displacement, as well as worry about future consequences, will create profound stress. There will likely be an increase in acute and posttraumatic stress disorders and related problems such as anxiety, substance abuse, grief, depression, and suicide (Fritze et al., 2008). And, of course climate change will affect everyone, not just people in flooded or drought-ridden areas. As many as 20%–30% of known plant and animal species are at an increased risk for extinction because of climate change. Species extinction means a

FIGURE C.2

Trends in global average temperature and carbon dioxide concentration since 1880. Evidence for a changing climate is also seen in average increases of global temperatures, which are correlated with escalating atmospheric CO_2 levels since the beginning of the Industrial Revolution in 1880. CO_2 measurements since 1958 are from the Mauna Loa Observatory in Hawaii; earlier data are from ice cores in Antarctica.

decrease in the *biodiversity* that is necessary to maintain healthy *ecosystems* (Lovejoy & Hannah, 2005)—ecosystems on which we all rely for basic life support.

Given the dire nature of these predicted outcomes, why aren't people responding collectively and as individuals to reduce use of fossil fuels and associated emissions? As Harvard Psychologist Daniel Gilbert (2006) put it, "Environmentalists despair that global warming is happening so fast. In fact, it isn't happening fast enough." Humans respond best to threats that are "PAINful: i.e., Personal, Abrubt, Immoral, and happening Now" (Gilbert, 2008; see also Frantz & Mayer, 2009). But, despite the "hard-wiring" of the human brain that makes it difficult for people to anticipate and plan for long-term problems on the scale of global climate change, our species is capable of dramatic and rapid behavioral change. Consider, for example, the pace of the technological revolution. As undergraduates, the two of us relied on typewriters for writing papers after engaging in library research with massive printed publication indexes and bound volumes of journals. (Can you imagine?) Now, the idea of using anything other than high-speed computers and the Internet to conduct research and write papers seems horribly inefficient and cumbersome. In theory, the human capacity for behavioral adaptation could help us reverse current ecological trends.

However, before someone changes his or her behaviors, that person must recognize which behaviors need changing, know how to change them, and feel that changing them is worthwhile. In fact, the majority of people will not even initiate change until they experience a personal crisis (Beddoe et al., 2009), commonly known as "hitting bottom," or until risks become salient and personally relevant. Breaking any *addiction*—whether to unsustainable consumption, to substances like alcohol, or to the Internet requires

FIGURE C.3

A graphic overview of the concept of the ecological footprint. The ecological footprint is a tool used to estimate an individual's, a group's, a nation's, or the world population's impact on the planet. (Based on Global Footprint Network, www.footprintnetwork.org/en/index.php/GFN/page/footprint_basics_overview/)

patience and perseverance because most people relapse (i.e., fall back on old habits). This perspective from the psychology of addiction helps us understand why many people don't feel galvanized to respond to issues like climate change: Such environmental risks probably don't seem personally relevant to most people. What does environmental destruction have to do with you as an individual? You yourself do not produce industrial wastes or log forests. What, then, is each person doing to deplete the capacity of the planet to sustain human life? The best way to address these questions is to consider individuals' extravagant use and misuse of the world's natural resources.

Human impacts on the planet can be estimated by using the *ecological footprint*—a measure of how fast a person (or population) consumes resources and generates waste in comparison to how rapidly nature can absorb the waste and replenish the resources (see **Figure C.3**). People who live in the United States have the largest footprints in the world, consuming considerably more resources and generating more waste than any other people on the planet. Unfortunately, the gap between this ecological footprint and the planet's *carrying capacity* is growing at an alarming pace (see **Figure C.4**). "If everyone in the world had an ecological footprint equivalent to that of the typical North American or Western European, global society would overshoot the planet's biocapacity three to five fold" (Kitzes et al., 2008, p. 468). In other words, if everyone lived like those in the United States do, more than three additional planets would be needed to support this lifestyle!

People living in the United States are by far the biggest users of the world's energy. Less than 5% of the global population lives in the United States, and the country holds only about 3% of the planet's oil (Kunstler, 2005), yet U.S. residents use a staggering *25%* of the total commercial supply: 18,771,000 barrels of oil *per day*—72% of which is used for transportation (U.S. Energy Information Administration, 2010). The next largest consumer is China, but consider this: China has *four times* the population of the United States and uses less than half of the amount of oil. Each person in the United States uses, on average, more than thirty times the amount of gasoline as the average person in a developing country (World Resources Institute, 2001). This "addiction to oil" is fostering a dangerously unstable international political climate. Middle Eastern countries rest on more than 60% of the planet's oil reserves, inspiring military-based foreign policies that emphasize control and access (e.g., Winter & Cava, 2006). Wars over access to resources including oil will likely become more common.

Amazingly, much of this huge expenditure of energy is wasted (Miller, 2007). People in North America waste over 43% of their energy by selecting energy-inefficient automobiles, appliances, and home heating systems when more efficient choices are available. Energy expert Amory Lovins puts it plainly, "If the United States wants to save a lot of oil and money and increase national security, there are two simple ways to do it: Stop driving Petropigs and stop living in energy sieves" (quoted in Miller, 2007, p. 385).

FIGURE C.4

Trends in the collective ecological footprint of the United States. This graph shows how the ecological footprint of the United States has increased dramatically since the 1960s in relation to the (decreasing) carrying capacity that our habitat can support. Carrying capacity, or "biocapacity," varies depending on ecosystem management, agricultural practices (such as fertilizer use and irrigation), ecosystem degradation, and weather. Overall, biocapacity is diminishing as population pressures, changing climates, and urbanization degrade land and other resources. As you can see, the trends are not encouraging.

SOURCE: www.footprintnetwork.org/en/index.php/GFN/page/trends/us/. Global Footprint Network 2008 National Footprint Accounts. Reprinted with permission.

Those living in the United States also overuse and abuse water. The toxic chemicals used in industrial production, as well as those used to kill pests like bugs and weeds, clean houses, and even groom and beautify people and pets, are polluting groundwater, lakes, rivers, and oceans. Demand for water from growing populations in arid locations is lowering reservoirs and aquifers. At least one-quarter of the groundwater that is currently withdrawn is not being replenished. For example, Las Vegas has doubled in population since 1990. The city gets 90% of its water from the Colorado River, which is experiencing the worst drought in its recorded history (Hutchinson, 2007). Already more than *1 billion* people on the planet do not have safe drinking water. In contrast, people in the developed world pollute and waste gallons of drinking-quality water every time they flush the toilet.

The wasteful use of energy and water are two of the primary contributors to the enormous ecological footprint of the U.S. population. Another major factor is diet. Livestock farming produces more greenhouse gases than transportation (Food and Agriculture Organization of the United Nations, 2006), and it has been estimated that it takes 600 gallons of water to produce just one hamburger (Kreith, 1991). Recently, Japanese researchers have estimated that the CO_2 emissions associated with the production of just 2.2 pounds of beef is equivalent to the amount emitted by an average European car every 155 miles (Bittman, 2008). Thus, if U.S. citizens merely decreased meat consumption by 20%, the energy savings and reduction in greenhouse gases would be equivalent to all of us trading in our average sedans for a Prius (Walsh, 2008). Yet, as a result of increasing affluence in other parts of the world and a rapidly expanding global population, worldwide meat consumption is projected to rise 53% by 2030 (World Resources Institute, 2010).

Most people in the United States regularly eat food that is out of season or does not grow in their region. This means that their food must travel long distances to get to them. It is typical in the United States for food to travel more than 1500 miles from its source to the dinner table (Pirog & Benjamin, 2003). Popular convenience foods are subject to energy-intensive processing and are packaged in containers and wrappers that cannot be reused or recycled. Further, 34 million tons of food is *wasted* every year in the United States (U.S. Environmental Protection Agency, 2011), about 39% of the edible food supply (Stokstad, 2009). Most of that food ends up in landfills, and as it rots it releases methane, a greenhouse gas that is twenty times more powerful than carbon dioxide at trapping heat in the atmosphere (U.S. EPA, 2011).

Energy, water, and food are not the only things consumed in unsustainable ways. In fact, *overconsumption of consumer goods constitutes the biggest drain on the Earth's carrying capacity*. Many people suffer from *affluenza*, an "unsustainable addiction to overconsumption and materialism" (Miller, 2007, p. 19). Those who are addicted to consumption use shopping as a coping strategy similar to overeating, using alcohol and drugs, or surfing the Internet. Each person in North America consumes, directly or indirectly, vastly more raw materials than those in developing countries and even more than people in other developed nations. And the things people buy—clothes, electronics, cars, furnishings—are produced from materials that leave a long trail of pollution elsewhere that is invisible to the U.S. consumer. A pair of pants made of polyester and sold in an American department store may be sewn in a sweatshop in Indonesia, from synthetic material manufactured in Singapore, which comes from oil refined in Mexico. U.S. consumer culture is spreading quickly, so that people in developing countries are aiming for "the good life," hurrying to develop the same extravagant lifestyles modeled in movies, television, advertising, and tourism.

Conspicuous consumption of convenience foods and consumer goods yields astonishing amounts of solid waste. Each person in North America generates more than 4.5 pounds of garbage per day (Miller, 2007). People throw away approximately 2.5 million nonreturnable plastic bottles *every hour* and toss about 25 billion Styrofoam coffee cups in the garbage each year. Electronic waste, or "e-waste," is growing exponentially. Every year, people living in the United States discard an estimated 130 million cell phones and 100 million computers, monitors, and television sets, only recycling about 10% (Miller, 2007). But even careful household recycling will not change the biggest solid waste problem. Commercial and industrial activities generate 98.5% of the waste. Average citizens sponsor this enormous waste production every time they buy a product that was inefficiently manufactured, is overpackaged, is not recyclable or biodegradable, or has traveled a long distance to get to them (which describes the vast majority of consumer products, including some that are misleadingly labeled "eco-friendly").

Ironically, there is evidence that overconsumption is not "delivering the goods." Rather, happiness is predicted by quality relationships, fulfilling work, and a positive outlook—not how much stuff we own (see Chapter 9). In fact, the race to pay for material possessions is likely to detract from these primary ingredients of happiness. Thus, attempting to meet psychological needs through overconsumption jeopardizes not only people's physical habitat but also their psychological well-being (Kasser & Kanner, 2004). You may have heard of the 3 Rs: Reduce, Reuse, Recycle. But effective solutions to environmental problems must start with *Refusing* to buy things that aren't really necessary and choosing sustainably produced options for the things that are (Miller, 2007).

As you were reading this section, did you feel despair? Anxiety? Irritation? Hopelessness? Did you scan the material, thinking to yourself that you already knew it? Did you find yourself growing overwhelmed, angry, or afraid? Did you feel guilty, defensive, or skeptical? Did you feel a sense of apathy? These *psychological* reactions are important because they determine how such problems are understood and what people are willing and able to do about them. In fact, the environmental crisis we face has been named the "pivotal psychological reality of our time" (Macy, 1995, p. 241). It would be naive to suggest that any one academic discipline will provide all the solutions to the environmental crisis; however, as we will show in the following sections, psychology has a lot to offer for understanding the roots of environmental destruction, the psychological forces maintaining it, and what it will take for people to change.

Insights from Social Psychology

As you may recall from Chapter 12, social psychology is primarily about the power of situational influences to shape behavior. Many environmentally damaging behaviors arise from *social norms*—informal, unwritten "rules" about what is appropriate or typical. Some researchers distinguish between *injunctive norms* (what is expected or approved of) and *descriptive norms* (what most people actually do) (Cialdini, Reno, & Kallgren, 1990). In the case of environmentally responsible behaviors, injunctive and descriptive norms often clash; that is, most people approve of environmentally responsible behaviors but don't actually engage in them. Cialdini (2003) argued that environmental campaigns that highlight people's environmentally irresponsible behavior may backfire because they inadvertently focus attention on descriptive norms for *anti*-environmental behavior!

To test the importance of these two types of norms, researchers conducted a series of field experiments on littering. Thanks in large part to an aggressive nationwide

Good intentions do not necessarily result in good behavior. Most people endorse environmentally responsible behaviors such as not littering, but depending on the situation, their actual behavior may be quite different. Social psychology can shed light on these disparities between attitudes and behavior.

© Dan Sullivan/Alamy

anti-littering campaign in the 1970s, the United States has a general injunctive norm against littering. Still, in some places the descriptive norm is to litter. Researchers tested how these norms interact to influence behavior. They found that in a littered setting, seeing a confederate litter made participants more likely to litter; however, in a *clean* setting, participants who saw a confederate litter were *less* likely to do so themselves, as compared to those who saw no littering behavior. Can you figure out why? It's because the stark contrast between the clean setting and the confederate's littering brought to mind the injunctive norm against littering (Cialdini et al., 1990).

Though social psychologists focus on the power of situational influence, they recognize that behavior is also shaped by internal factors such as attitudes and values. Individuals whose behavior is guided by *egocentric* and *materialistic* values that emphasize personal wealth and status tend to exhibit fewer environmentally friendly actions (Schultz et al., 2005). Still, *biocentric* values are no guarantee of environmentally friendly behavior. There is often a gap between people's attitudes and their behaviors. Even individuals with pro-environmental attitudes often find that situational constraints can make it difficult (or costly, inconvenient, or awkward) to act in an attitude-consistent manner (Kollmus & Agyeman, 2002).

Sometimes when individuals behave in an attitude-discrepant way, they experience *cognitive dissonance*, an uncomfortable state of arousal that motivates them to change their behaviors or their attitudes to bring them in sync with each other (Festinger, 1957; see also Chapter 12). In a few studies, researchers have successfully induced a state of cognitive dissonance that led to increased environmentally friendly behavior. For example, students on their way to the gym were intercepted and asked whether they ever wasted water (all did) and whether they would sign their name to a public message about the importance of water conservation (all did). Researchers lurking in the locker room found that these students took shorter showers after their workouts than students who hadn't been reminded of their own hypocritical behavior (Dickerson, et al., 1992). However, as long as individuals can justify their attitude-discrepant behavior to themselves, dissonance will not be aroused and their behavior is unlikely to change.

Many environmental problems result from people acting out of self-interest in the moment, ultimately harming the greater whole. *Social dilemmas* contribute to environmental degradation in several ways (e.g., Gardner & Stern, 2002; Osbaldiston & Sheldon, 2002; Vlek & Steg, 2007):

- First, in *commons dilemmas*, individuals take more than their fair share of a communal resource (such as oil or water).

- Second, in *public goods dilemmas*, individuals contribute less than their fair share to a communal resource (such as not wanting to pay higher taxes for bus services).

- Third, in *risk dilemmas*, an individual's behavior exposes the greater whole to hazards (e.g., a homeowner uses toxic herbicides because she wants a green lawn).

- Fourth, *ecological dilemmas* occur when acting from self-interest upsets larger systems (e.g., a landowner fills in a wetland on his property, thereby interfering with waterfowl migration).

In these examples, rewards to the individual are more immediate and compelling than the delayed costs to the population. People don't always act in self-interest, however. Individuals will sometimes forgo personal benefits in favor of a common goal (such as driving less to reduce global emissions) if they identify with the group and feel responsible toward it (Dawes, 1980; Van Vugt, 2002) and if they perceive the long-term benefits as personally relevant (Milinski et al., 2008).

The founder of experimental social psychology, Kurt Lewin, emphasized that behavior is a function of both the situation and *the person*. How people define their *self-concepts* and their *social identities* certainly has implications for environmentally relevant behaviors. For example, negative stereotypes about environmentalists discourage some individuals from behaving in overtly sustainable ways. (Do you know anyone who is afraid of being perceived as a "tree-hugger"?) Recently, some social psychologists have turned their attention to the notion of the *ecologically connected self*. Theoretically, the more one defines oneself as *part of nature*, the more empathy one should have for other living things (Bragg, 1996). Several studies support the idea that an ecologically connected self is positively correlated with environmentally friendly attitudes and behaviors (e.g., Clayton, 2003; Mayer & Frantz, 2004; Schultz, 2001). Yet, it is probably safe to say that the self-concepts of most people living in industrialized countries today lack a sense of ecological connection.

Insights from Theories of Personality

As you learned in Chapter 11, one of the earliest personality theorists was Sigmund Freud, who believed that personality is shaped by how one resolves unconscious conflicts in early childhood. Because most of Freud's ideas cannot be empirically tested, they have inspired vigorous criticism. Still, his suggestion that people use unconscious defenses to ward off emotional discomfort seems relevant for understanding environmental issues. Awareness of the probable collapse of the planet's ecosystems *should* trigger powerful and uncomfortable feelings, but people often fail to act on those feelings. If people do use ego-protective *defense mechanisms* as proposed by Freud and his daughter Anna (A. Freud, 1936), this may explain how people can "know" about environmental problems and yet not change their behaviors.

Four defense mechanisms seem particularly applicable to people's ecologically unfriendly behaviors. *Rationalization* is one of the most common. For instance, though people may feel guilty about driving alone, they convince themselves, "I have to drive because carpooling is too inconvenient. *Identification* leads people to purchase nonessential status symbols so they can feel good about themselves. *Denial* about environmental problems includes minimizing their severity, seeing them as irrelevant, and seeing oneself as not responsible (Opotow & Weiss, 2000). Finally, *projection* occurs when people perceive in others what they fail to perceive in themselves. One of us recalls vehemently grumbling about all the cars on the road during rush hour, only to be reminded by her 3-year-old in the backseat, "But Mommy, you're traffic, too!"

Contemporary personality theorists focus on traits, rather than unconscious motivations. Some personality traits are associated with caring for nonhuman nature. For example, Broida and colleagues (1993) found that college students classed as Intuitive and Feeling on the Myers-Briggs Type Inventory tended to be more ecologically concerned and more opposed to animal experimentation than other personality types.

Mathews and Herzog (1997) administered the Sixteen Personality Factor Inventory to college students and found that two personality factors—sensitivity and imaginativeness—were positively correlated with attitudes toward animals. Furnham, McManus, and Scott (2004) measured the Big Five personality traits and found that openness was positively related to liking of animals and believing that animals have feelings. More recently, researchers have found a positive relationship between openness and general environmental concern (Hirsh, 2010) and pro-environmental behaviors (Markowitz et al., 2012).

Insights from Behavioral Psychology

As you read in Chapter 6, one of the best-known behavioral psychologists, B. F. Skinner, argued that what people do depends on the consequences of their behavior: reinforcement encourages behavior, while punishment discourages it. Toward the end of his career, Skinner took a particular interest in environmental issues. In an address to the American Psychological Association, he criticized the efforts of environmental activists as inconsistent with operant learning principles. He said they should stop inspiring guilt, fear, and shame to motivate greener behaviors. Instead, they should help individuals see the potentially reinforcing consequences of sustainable lifestyles (Skinner, 1987). Yet, the benefits associated with environmentally *damaging* behaviors are often more obvious than the rewards of environmentally *sustainable* behaviors. For instance, can you think of any environmentally unfriendly behaviors that are rewarded by convenience or social status? Is it harder to think of environmentally friendly behaviors that are similarly reinforced?

One of the most common ways governments and companies reinforce pro-environmental behavior is through financial rewards. Although temporary incentives, such as tax rebates, can help motivate greener choices, their effectiveness may be limited. Often, when the incentive goes away, so does the behavior (Abrahamse, Alloy, & Metalsky, 2005; Lehman & Geller, 1994). More powerful and enduring than financial rewards may be *social* reinforcers. For example, imagine being rewarded for energy-efficient driving not only by earning virtual dollars to buy online merchandise but also by earning points that would show all of your Facebook friends how green you are—and how much greener you are than they (Pritchard, 2010). By creating social status competition, researchers have been able to motivate people to choose less desirable but greener products over more luxurious nongreen products, especially when the greener product was the more expensive option and their choices were made public (Griskevicius, Tybur, & Van den Bergh, 2010).

Besides the use of reinforcement, another behavior modification strategy involves altering *discriminative (antecedent) stimuli* (see Chapter 6). For example, prominently placed bins in areas where drinks are consumed serve as *prompts* to recycle cans and bottles (Lehman & Geller, 2004). Another example is placing signs over light switches reminding people to turn off the lights when they leave a room. Research suggests that the more specific the prompt, the greater its effectiveness. A sign saying "Faculty and students please turn off lights after 5 pm" is more effective than one reading "Conserve Electricity." Polite prompts are more effective than demanding ones (the word *please* can make a difference), and the closer the prompt is to the point of behavior, the better (a sign over a light switch is more effective than a sign across the room). Thus, polite, salient, and specific reminders can change behavior (Geller, Winett, & Everett, 1982; Lehman & Geller, 2004).

Although providing information is a technique widely used by environmental groups, there is little evidence that education alone changes what people actually do (see reviews by Abrahamse et al., 2005; Gardner & Stern, 2002; Lehman & Geller, 2004). *Modeling* environmentally friendly behavior can be more effective than simply describing it (see Bandura, 1977 and Chapter 6). For instance, in one classic study, participants were exposed to a video showing a person turning down a thermostat, wearing warmer clothes, and using heavy blankets. With this treatment, viewers reduced their energy use by 28% (Winett et al., 1982). A more recent study involved users of a Facebook application who had been posting and commenting on climate change news stories. These participants reported increases in both their knowledge about climate change science and their pro-environmental behavior. Importantly, they claimed that it wasn't the information that motivated their behavior change; it was the peer modeling they witnessed in the online community (Robelia, Greenhow, & Burton, 2011).

Insights from Cognitive Psychology

From the perspective of cognitive psychology, much environmentally destructive behavior is maintained by cognitive biases such as those described in Chapter 8. The tendency to depend on mental shortcuts called *heuristics* can lead to underestimation of the risks of environmental hazards. For example, the *availability heuristic* may explain why people downplay the significance of global warming. Most of us can't easily visualize melting ice caps and rising sea levels, so the perils of climate change don't easily come to mind. On the other hand, environmental hazards that have received dramatic media coverage, such as oil spills, feature prominently in our memories. Therefore, we may devote a lot of attention and resources to the vivid events, while neglecting the less vivid, but more insidious, hazards (Gardner & Stern, 2002).

Although the use of mental shortcuts is automatic, it is possible to temporarily override this tendency. When people are sufficiently motivated and not mentally overloaded, they are capable of careful, logical, effortful reasoning. The key may be for each person to increase his or her awareness of the potential for errors in thinking. In this way, individuals will become better environmental decision makers . . . or will they? The question is whether "coldly rational" judgments are always superior to emotionally driven ones when it comes to environmental issues (Slovic et al., 2004). For example, after reading a description of nuclear energy that emphasized the negatives ("Waste is highly radioactive and contaminated with plutonium, a deadly element"), participants not only raised their estimates of the risks of nuclear power (as would be logically expected) but also *lowered* their estimates of the benefits of nuclear power—even though the description had not said anything about benefits. The researchers explained this change in participants' benefit estimates as being due to an overall increase in negative feelings about nuclear power (Finucane et al., 2000). Participants had used the *affect* (emotion-based) *heuristic* in making their judgments. Clearly, heuristics may sometimes bias people in an anti-environmental direction and sometimes in a pro-environmental direction.

Many cognitive biases protect people from threats to their self-esteem and feelings of security. They help people feel good about themselves in spite of their behavior or circumstances. *Comparative optimism* leads individuals to believe they are less vulnerable than other people to all types of risks, including environmental threats, even though objectively there is no reason to think the risks are any different for one individual versus another (Pahl et al., 2005). *False consensus* helps people maintain positive self-esteem by convincing themselves that many others engage in the same undesirable behaviors as they do. For example, when a water shortage prompted a temporary shower ban at Princeton University in 1999, researchers conducted a 5-day field study during and after the ban (Benoît & Norton, 2003). They found that students who ignored the ban and showered as usual overestimated how many other people were similarly irresponsible. Finally, *false polarization* is the tendency to perceive the views of those on the opposing side of a debate as more extreme than they really are. In the shower ban study, participants believed that people who showered cared much less about the greater good than those who did not shower. However, self-report data suggested that the actual attitudinal positions of these two groups were quite close. Can you see how this cognitive bias might contribute to the current political divide between Democrats and Republicans in the United States when it comes to environmental issues?

Insights from Developmental Psychology

The discipline of psychology emerged in an urban-industrialized context during the last century. This is probably why developmental psychologists have largely overlooked the vital role that nature plays in humans' cognitive, emotional, and social development. Only since the 1990s have some developmentalists turned their attention toward topics such as children's relationship with animals, their understanding of life and ecological systems, their moral reasoning about environmental issues, and the implications of their experiences (or lack thereof) in natural settings.

Developmental psychologists have almost completely neglected the study of children's relationship with animals. This is surprising given that animals are a primary focus in children's lives: as companions (live, stuffed, or imaginary), as captive or wild specimens, as characters in books and film, and as creatures the children themselves pretend to be. Recently, however, a few developmental psychologists have proposed that in order to fully understand development, researchers must extend the list of important childhood influences to include animals—perhaps even putting them at the top of the list (Melson, 2001, 2003; Myers, 2007).

As you may know from personal experience, one thing children learn about through their experience with animals is death. But even without firsthand experience, young children intuitively perceive, categorize, and think about living things differently than nonliving things—and they see connections among plants, animals, and humans. This naive understanding of nature is called *folkbiology* (Inagaki & Hatano, 2002). Seeing the similarities between themselves and other species inspires children to see nature as "something worthy of moral consideration" (Gebhard, Nevers, & Billmann-Mahecha, 2003, p. 92). Indeed, research on children's moral reasoning suggests that children sometimes adopt a *biocentric* perspective, where they view plants and animals as having rights and as deserving respect, just as people do. In several cross-cultural studies, children showed strong moral prohibitions against pollution, damage to natural systems, and other species (reviewed in Kahn, 2003). Research on children's folkbiology and environmentally related moral reasoning will not only broaden our understanding of cognitive development in general but may also help psychologists to better understand why and how adults' unsustainable behaviors may be influenced by *anthropocentric* (human-centered) thinking and ignorance about ecology.

Increasingly, child development experts are becoming convinced that children need outdoor experiences to fully develop their emotional, physical, mental, and social capabilities (e.g., Kahn & Kellert, 2002), a theory that captured the attention of the general public with the publication of *Last Child in the Woods: Saving Our Children from Nature Deficit Disorder* (Louv, 2005). Children may need opportunities for spontaneous and independent play in natural areas to fully develop their perceptual systems, their love relationships and empathy, and their sense of self (e.g., Kellert, 2002). Experiences in nature may also be vital for children's mental health. Children living in rural communities with more "nearby nature" have less psychological distress, including anxiety and depression, and fewer conduct disorders, such as bullying,

Experience with animals during childhood can have an impact on people's attitudes about nature in general, not to mention their feelings about the importance of preserving endangered species.

than those living in urban areas (Wells & Evans, 2003). And recent studies suggest that symptoms of *attention deficit hyperactivity disorders* can be ameliorated by time spent in natural settings (Faber Taylor & Kuo, 2009; van den Berg & van den Berg, 2011).

Unfortunately, many children today spend very little time outside, and when they do go out they experience only degraded and polluted conditions, making identification with nature more difficult (Kahn, 2007). More time inside generally means more screen time—as much as 6 to 9 hours per day engaged with electronic media (Roberts, Foehr, & Rideout, 2005). Technology bombards children with images and advertisements that promote an environmentally destructive consumer culture (Kasser, 2002; Linn, 2008). Further, time spent inside stunts children's understanding of, and appreciation for, the natural world. Research on adults suggests that experiences in nature during childhood—and having family members who modeled appreciation for nature—are significant predictors of a pro-environmental orientation (e.g., Guiney & Oberhauser, 2009; Horwitz, 1996). In fact, some investigators have argued that love of nature and concern about its protection are developed *only* with consistent outdoor experiences (Chawla, 1988). This means that children who spend most of their time indoors may be ultimately less likely to engage in pro-environmental actions.

Insights from Health and Clinical Psychology

You read in Chapter 13 about the physiology of stress and its associated behavioral and health problems. It turns out that many aspects of contemporary environments that are ecologically unsound are also significant human stressors. Urban noise, traffic, crowding, pollution, and living near toxic industries or waste sites are all associated with increased stress and related symptoms such as anxiety, depression, anger, and aggression (Kuo & Sullivan, 2001; Lundberg, 1998). The effects of catastrophic environmental events can cause *posttraumatic stress disorder* (see Chapter 14). For example, mental health services were needed to treat depression, anxiety, and PTSD in approximately 250,000 survivors of Hurricane Katrina in 2005 (Siegel, 2007).

The manufacture, use, and disposal of tens of thousands of industrial and household chemicals are causing or contributing to increased rates of various forms of cancer, birth defects, reproductive abnormalities, immune system dysfunction, neurological impairments, and developmental disabilities, all significant stressors in their own right (e.g., Koger, Schettler, & Weiss, 2005; U.S. EPA., 2008). More than 85,000 chemicals are currently registered with the Environmental Protection Agency, including commonly used pesticides and household chemicals (e.g., paint thinners, cleaning agents, bleach). In addition, certain ingredients in plastics, electronics, and cosmetics are known to be toxic to humans and other animals. The net result is deteriorating health of human beings on physical, mental, emotional, and social levels, as well as degradation of the planet. The health of humans is directly related to the health of the planet Earth.

Perhaps not surprisingly, people strongly prefer healthy, natural settings that include bodies of water, plants, trees, and sunlight over urban environments filled with buildings and cars (Kaplan & Kaplan, 1989; van den Berg, Hartig, & Staats, 2007). Walking in natural settings, or simply having views of plants, can alleviate symptoms of stress (e.g., Kaplan & Kaplan, 1989) by activating the *parasympathetic nervous system* (see Chapters 3 and 13), providing recovery by reducing blood pressure and heart rate. Activities such as gardening, caring for indoor plants, and interacting with nonhuman animals such as pet dogs can all reduce stress (Frumkin, 2001). Spending time in nature can also provide recovery from prolonged work and concentration. You can probably relate to the worn-out feeling that accompanies intense studying during midterm and final exams. As little as 20 minutes spent in a natural setting has been shown to relieve this attentional fatigue (Berman, Jonides, & Kaplan, 2008).

Given their restorative benefits, natural environments have long been used in outpatient and nature-immersion therapies (Chalquist, 2009). For instance, Jordan and Marshall (2010) point out that Freud took his clients outside for analytic walks during

In recent years, psychologists have conducted some interesting research on the effects of exposure to natural settings (like the top two photos) versus human-created urban environments (like the bottom two photos). This research indicates that natural environments can decrease individuals' response to stress.

top left: © Martyn Osman/Alamy; top right: © Noam Armonn/Alamy; bottom left: © Optic Design/Alamy; bottom right: © EschCollection Royalty Free/Alamy

the therapy hour. *Wilderness therapy* programs take advantage of nature as a backdrop for traditional therapeutic techniques or integrate wilderness skills and interaction as a part of therapy itself. Most wilderness therapy programs are designed for adolescents struggling with behavioral and emotional problems, but other client populations have included attachment-challenged adults (Bettmann & Jasperson, 2008), families (Swank & Daire, 2010), and women who have suffered abuse (Cole, Erdman, & Rothblum, 1994; McBride & Korell, 2005). Because wilderness therapy programs have historically suffered from a lack of consistency in methods, quality, and practitioner credentials, as well as a lack of ethical oversight, some providers banded together in 1997 to form the Outdoor Behavioral Health Industry Council. Outcome research conducted by members of this organization and others is beginning to generate evidence for the effectiveness of nature-based therapy for improving self-perceptions, emotional well-being, resiliency, and social functioning (e.g., Chalquist, 2009; Russell, 2005).

Intact and healthy ecosystems are vital for human well-being, but valuing natural resources only for the ways in which they can benefit humankind is a limited and anthropocentric view. As Greenway (1995) put it, "Perhaps the clearest evidence of our recovery will be that we do not demand that wilderness heal us. We will have learned to let it be. For a wilderness that must heal us is surely a commodity, just as when we can only look at wilderness as a source of endless wealth" (pp. 134–135).

What You Can Personally Do

I am only one. But still I am one.
I cannot do everything, but still I can do something;
And because I cannot do everything,
I will not refuse to do the something that I can do.

—Quote from Edward Everett Hale (1822–1909),
    original source unknown

Many excellent guides are available (both online and in print) on how to become more environmentally responsible. You can start by taking the online quiz at http://www.myfootprint.org/ to determine your own ecological footprint and consider ways to alter your daily life based on your quiz results. You might also consider developing a *behavior modification* project (see the Personal Application in Chapter 6) addressing some of your environmentally relevant behaviors.

Six aspects of human lifestyles most significantly and adversely affect the environment (Gardner & Stern, 2008; Miller, 2007): agriculture, transportation, home energy use, water use, overall resource consumption and waste, and toxic chemical production, use, and disposal. We recommend that you think about these issues and take the following steps toward walking more lightly on the Earth. If you don't feel you can do all of them, select at least a few to get you started on a more sustainable lifestyle, and then add a new one each month.

AGRICULTURE

- Reduce your meat consumption by eating *no meat* one day per week, then increase to two days, and so forth.
- Buy locally grown food for at least one month a year, and then try to increase this.
- Buy organically produced food or grow some of your own.

TRANSPORTATION

- Walk, bike, carpool, or take mass transit as much as you can.
- If possible, work at home or live near your work or school.
- When you have to drive, note that fuel efficiency can be dramatically increased by
  - reducing your speed;
  - avoiding rapid acceleration and sudden stops;
  - shutting off the engine rather than idling;
  - keeping tires inflated;
  - getting regular tune-ups; and
  - turning off your air conditioner.
- Record the distance you drive for one week, and then try to reduce the amount by 10%. Once you accomplish that, try reducing by 15% or more.
- When you purchase a new car, buy a small, fuel-efficient (greater than 35 mpg) model.

HOME ENERGY USE

- Turn down the heat by at least a few degrees in winter, and avoid using air conditioning (or turn the thermostat up a few degrees) in the summer.
- Turn off computers, printers, and other appliances when not in use.
- Replace your light bulbs with compact fluorescent bulbs.

WATER USE

- Always turn off the water while brushing your teeth and shaving.
- Take showers instead of baths, and limit them to 5 minutes if you can.
- Turn off the water while soaping up and shampooing.
- Reuse cups and plates when possible, rather than washing after each use.
- Only run dishwashers and clothes-washers with full loads.
- Use the flushing rule: "If it's yellow, let it mellow, if it's brown, flush it down" (urine is sterile).

RESOURCE CONSUMPTION

- The two most important ways to reduce consumption and waste are *refusing* to buy things you don't really need, or that you could borrow or rent, and *reusing* as many items as possible (coffee cups, canvas or other bags for groceries, and your own *to-go* container for leftovers when you eat out). Refusing and reusing will save you money, as well as reduce your environmental impact. Recycling is important, but it still requires energy and encourages the production and use of more and more stuff. Keep a list of things you refused to buy or reused, and try to expand the list each month. (Refer to the "Unshopping Card" in **Figure C.5**.)
- Beware of "green-washing"—many products are misleadingly labeled "eco-friendly" or "all natural."
- Buy secondhand items of all kinds whenever possible.
- Give away, donate to charity, or sell items you no longer need or use, rather than throwing them away—especially during move-out time at the end of the school year!
- Junk mail generates an astonishing amount of waste, utilizes an incredible amount of natural resources, and contributes to climate change. Let organizations know that you don't want to receive their newsletters, catalogs, and solicitations, and be sure to recycle mailings you can't refuse.

TOXIC CHEMICALS

- Pesticides are designed to kill bugs (insecticides), weeds (herbicides), rodents, and so forth. They are directly toxic to humans as well, producing cancers and learning disabilities, among other disorders. Don't use any pesticides in your home, lawn, or garden, and educate others about their impacts on human health and neurological function, as well as detrimental effects on biodiversity.
- Avoid chemical cleansers. Baking soda and vinegar are excellent alternatives to many cleaning products; vinegar is also an effective herbicide.
- Many plastics, cosmetics, and personal care products contain chemicals that disrupt normal hormone functions (e.g., phthalates and bisphenol A or BPA). Don't buy bottled water, don't reheat or microwave foods in plastic containers, use fewer products with fewer ingredients, and don't trust claims like "dermatologist-tested," "natural," or "organic." Read the ingredient labels and avoid fragrances, dyes, parabens or -paraben, and things you can't pronounce.
- Reduce use of plastics by bringing your own refillable containers, buying in bulk, buying things with minimal packaging, and purchasing products in recyclable and recycled packaging.
- Dispose of household toxic products properly. Many items—paints, pesticides, batteries, and even energy-efficient compact fluorescent light bulbs—contain toxic ingredients. Drop these items off at a local household hazardous waste site.

Glossary

A

Absolute refractory period The minimum length of time after an action potential during which another action potential cannot begin.

Achievement motive The need to master difficult challenges, to outperform others, and to meet high standards of excellence.

Acquired immune deficiency syndrome (AIDS) A disorder in which the immune system is gradually weakened and eventually disabled by the human immunodeficiency virus (HIV).

Acquisition The formation of a new conditioned response tendency.

Action potential A brief change in a neuron's electrical charge.

Adaptation An inherited characteristic that increased in a population (through natural selection) because it helped solve a problem of survival or reproduction during the time it emerged. See also *Sensory adaptation*.

Additive color mixing Formation of colors by superimposing lights, putting more light in the mixture than exists in any one light by itself.

Adoption studies Research studies that assess hereditary influence by examining the resemblance between adopted children and both their biological and their adoptive parents.

Affective forecasting Efforts to predict one's emotional reactions to future events.

Afferent nerve fibers Axons that carry information inward to the central nervous system from the periphery of the body.

Afterimage A visual image that persists after a stimulus is removed.

Aggression Any behavior that is intended to hurt someone, either physically or verbally.

Agoraphobia A fear of going out to public places.

Alcohol A variety of beverages containing ethyl alcohol.

Amnesia See *Anterograde amnesia, Retrograde amnesia*.

Anecdotal evidence Personal stories about specific incidents and experiences.

Anhedonia A diminished ability to experience pleasure.

Animism The belief that all things are living.

Anorexia nervosa Eating disorder characterized by intense fear of gaining weight, disturbed body image, refusal to maintain normal weight, and dangerous measures to lose weight.

Anterograde amnesia Loss of memories for events that occur after a head injury.

Antianxiety drugs Medications that relieve tension, apprehension, and nervousness.

Antidepressant drugs Medications that gradually elevate mood and help bring people out of a depression.

Antipsychotic drugs Medications used to gradually reduce psychotic symptoms, including hyperactivity, mental confusion, hallucinations, and delusions.

Anxiety disorders A class of disorders marked by feelings of excessive apprehension and anxiety.

Approach-approach conflict A conflict situation in which a choice must be made between two attractive goals.

Approach-avoidance conflict A conflict situation in which a choice must be made about whether to pursue a single goal that has both attractive and unattractive aspects.

Archetypes According to Jung, emotionally charged images and thought forms that have universal meaning.

Argument One or more premises used to provide support for a conclusion.

Assumptions Premises for which no proof or evidence is offered.

Attachment A close, emotional bond of affection between infants and their caregivers.

Attention Focusing awareness on a narrowed range of stimuli or events.

Attitudes Orientations that locate objects of thought on dimensions of judgment.

Attributions Inferences that people draw about the causes of events, others' behavior, and their own behavior.

Autistic disorder Childhood psychological disorder characterized by profound impairment of social interaction and communication and severely restricted interests and activities, apparent by the age of 3.

Autonomic nervous system (ANS) The system of nerves that connect to the heart, blood vessels, smooth muscles, and glands.

Availability heuristic Basing the estimated probability of an event on the ease with which relevant instances come to mind.

Aversion therapy A behavior therapy in which an aversive stimulus is paired with a stimulus that elicits an undesirable response.

Avoidance-avoidance conflict A conflict situation in which a choice must be made between two unattractive goals.

Avoidance learning Learning that has occurred when an organism engages in a response that prevents aversive stimulation from occurring.

Axon A long, thin fiber that transmits signals away from the neuron cell body to other neurons, or to muscles or glands.

B

Basilar membrane A structure that runs the length of the cochlea in the inner ear and holds the auditory receptors, called hair cells.

Behavior Any overt (observable) response or activity by an organism.

Behavior modification A systematic approach to changing behavior through the application of the principles of conditioning.

Behavior therapies Application of the principles of learning to direct efforts to change clients' maladaptive behaviors.

Behaviorism A theoretical orientation based on the premise that scientific psychology should study only observable behavior.

Binocular depth cues Clues about distance based on the differing views of the two eyes.

Biological rhythms Periodic fluctuations in physiological functioning.

Biomedical therapies Physiological interventions intended to reduce symptoms associated with psychological disorders.

Biopsychosocial model A model of illness that holds that physical illness is caused by a complex interaction of biological, psychological, and sociocultural factors.

Bipolar disorder (formerly known as manic-depressive disorder) Mood disorder marked by the experience of both depressed and manic periods.

Bisexuals Persons who seek emotional-sexual relationships with members of either sex.

Bottom-up processing In form perception, progression from individual elements to the whole.

Bounded rationality. See *Theory of bounded rationality*.

Bulimia nervosa Eating disorder characterized by habitually engaging in out-of-control overeating followed by unhealthy compensatory efforts, such as self-induced vomiting, fasting, abuse of laxatives and diuretics, and excessive exercise.

Bystander effect A paradoxical social phenomenon in which people are less likely to provide needed help when they are in groups than when they are alone.

C

Cannabis The hemp plant from which marijuana, hashish, and THC are derived.

Case study An in-depth investigation of an individual subject.

Catastrophic thinking Unrealistically pessimistic appraisals of stress that exaggerate the magnitude of one's problems.

Catatonic schizophrenia A type of schizophrenia marked by striking motor disturbances, ranging from muscular rigidity to random motor activity.

Catharsis The release of emotional tension.

Central nervous system (CNS) The brain and the spinal cord.

Centration The tendency to focus on just one feature of a problem, neglecting other important aspects.

Cerebellum A relatively large and deeply folded structure located adjacent to the back surface of the brainstem.

Cerebral cortex The convoluted outer layer of the cerebrum.

Cerebral hemispheres The right and left halves of the cerebrum.

Channel The medium through which a message is sent.

Chromosomes Threadlike strands of DNA (deoxyribonucleic acid) molecules that carry genetic information.

Chunk A group of familiar stimuli stored as a single unit.

Circadian rhythms The 24-hour biological cycles found in humans and many other species.

Classical conditioning A type of learning in which a neutral stimulus acquires the ability to evoke a response that was originally evoked by another stimulus.

Client-centered therapy An insight therapy that emphasizes providing a supportive emotional climate for clients, who play a major role in determining the pace and direction of their therapy.

Clinical psychologists Psychologists who specialize in the diagnosis and treatment of psychological disorders and everyday behavioral problems.

Clinical psychology The branch of psychology concerned with the diagnosis and treatment of psychological problems and disorders.

Cochlea The fluid-filled, coiled tunnel in the inner ear that contains the receptors for hearing.

Coefficient of determination The percentage of variation in one variable that can be predicted based on the other variable.

Cognition The mental processes involved in acquiring knowledge.

Cognitive-behavioral treatments A varied combination of verbal interventions and behavioral modification techniques used to help clients change maladaptive patterns of thinking.

Cognitive development Transitions in youngsters' patterns of thinking, including reasoning, remembering, and problem solving.

Cognitive dissonance A psychological state that exists when related cognitions are inconsistent.

Cognitive therapy An insight therapy that emphasizes recognizing and changing negative thoughts and maladaptive beliefs.

Collective unconscious According to Jung, a storehouse of latent memory traces inherited from people's ancestral past.

Collectivism Putting group goals ahead of personal goals and defining one's identity in terms of the groups one belongs to.

Color blindness Deficiency in the ability to distinguish among colors.

Comorbidity The coexistence of two or more disorders.

Companionate love Warm, trusting, tolerant affection for another whose life is deeply intertwined with one's own.

Comparators People, objects, events, and other standards that are used as a baseline for comparisons in making judgments.

Compensation According to Adler, efforts to overcome imagined or real inferiorities by developing one's abilities.

Complementary colors Pairs of colors that produce gray tones when added together.

Concordance rate The percentage of twin pairs or other pairs of relatives that exhibit the same disorder.

Conditioned reinforcers See *Secondary reinforcers.*

Conditioned response (CR) A learned reaction to a conditioned stimulus that occurs because of previous conditioning.

Conditioned stimulus (CS) A previously neutral stimulus that has, through conditioning, acquired the capacity to evoke a conditioned response.

Conditioning Learning associations between events that occur in an organism's environment.

Cones Specialized visual receptors that play a key role in daylight vision and color vision.

Conflict A state that occurs when two or more incompatible motivations or behavioral impulses compete for expression.

Conformity The tendency for people to yield to real or imagined social pressure.

Confounding of variables A condition that exists whenever two variables are linked together in a way that makes it difficult to sort out their independent effects.

Conjunction fallacy An error that occurs when people estimate that the odds of two uncertain events happening together are greater than the odds of either event happening alone.

Connectionist models See *Parallel distributed processing (PDP) models.*

Conscious Whatever one is aware of at a particular point in time.

Consciousness One's awareness of internal and external stimuli.

Conservation Piaget's term for the awareness that physical quantities remain constant in spite of changes in their shape or appearance.

Conservation psychology The study of the interactive relationships between humans and the rest of nature, with a particular focus on how to enhance conservation of natural resources.

Consolidation A hypothetical process involving the gradual conversion of information into durable memory codes stored in long-term memory.

Constructive coping Relatively healthful efforts that people make to deal with stressful events.

Continuous reinforcement Reinforcing every instance of a designated response.

Control group Subjects in a study who do not receive the special treatment given to the experimental group.

Convergent thinking Narrowing down a list of alternatives to converge on a single correct answer.

Coping Active efforts to master, reduce, or tolerate the demands created by stress.

Corpus callosum The structure that connects the two cerebral hemispheres.

Correlation The extent to which two variables are related to each other.

Correlation coefficient A numerical index of the degree of relationship between two variables.

Counseling psychologists Psychologists who specialize in the treatment of everyday adjustment problems.

Couples therapy The treatment of both partners in a committed, intimate relationship, in which the main focus is on relationship issues.

Creativity The generation of ideas that are original, novel, and useful.

Critical period A limited time span in the development of an organism when it is optimal for certain capacities to emerge because the organism is especially responsive to certain experiences.

Critical thinking Purposeful, reasoned, goal-directed thinking that involves solving problems, formulating inferences, working with probabilities, and making carefully thought-out decisions.

Culture The widely shared customs, beliefs, values, norms, institutions, and other products of a community that are transmitted socially across generations.

Culture-bound disorders Abnormal syndromes found only in a few cultural groups.

Cumulative recorder A graphic record of reinforcement and responding in a Skinner box as a function of time.

D

Dark adaptation The process in which the eyes become more sensitive to light in low illumination.

Data collection techniques Procedures for making empirical observations and measurements.

Decay theory The idea that forgetting occurs because memory traces fade with time.

Decision making The process of evaluating alternatives and making choices among them.

Declarative memory system Memory for factual information.

Defense mechanisms Largely unconscious reactions that protect a person from unpleasant emotions such as anxiety and guilt.

Deinstitutionalization Transferring the treatment of mental illness from inpatient institutions to community-based facilities that emphasize outpatient care.

Delusions False beliefs that are maintained even though they are clearly out of touch with reality.

Dementia An abnormal condition marked by multiple cognitive defects that include memory impairment.

Dendrites Branchlike parts of a neuron that are specialized to receive information.

Dependent variable In an experiment, the variable that is thought to be affected by the manipulation of the independent variable.

Depth perception Interpretation of visual cues that indicate how near or far away objects are.

Descriptive statistics Statistics that are used to organize and summarize data.

Development The sequence of age-related changes that occur as a person progresses from conception to death.

Developmental norms The average age at which individuals display various behaviors and abilities.

Deviation IQ scores Scores that locate subjects precisely within the normal distribution, using the standard deviation as the unit of measurement.

Diagnosis Distinguishing one illness from another.

Discrimination Behaving differently, usually unfairly, toward the members of a group.

Discriminative stimuli Cues that influence operant behavior by indicating the probable consequences (reinforcement or nonreinforcement) of a response.

Disorganized schizophrenia A type of schizophrenia in which particularly severe deterioration of adaptive behavior is seen.

Displacement Diverting emotional feelings (usually anger) from their original source to a substitute target.

Display rules Cultural norms that regulate the appropriate expressions of emotions.

Dissociation A splitting off of mental processes into two separate, simultaneous streams of awareness.

Dissociative amnesia A sudden loss of memory for important personal information that is too extensive to be due to normal forgetting.

Dissociative disorders A class of disorders in which people lose contact with portions of their consciousness or memory, resulting in disruptions in their sense of identity.

Dissociative fugue A disorder in which people lose their memory for their entire lives along with their sense of personal identity.

Dissociative identity disorder A type of dissociative disorder characterized by the coexistence in one person of two or more largely complete, and usually very different, personalities. Also called multiple-personality disorder.

Divergent thinking Trying to expand the range of alternatives by generating many possible solutions.

Door-in-the-face technique Making a large request that is likely to be turned down as a way to increase the chances that people will agree to a smaller request later.

Double-blind procedure A research strategy in which neither subjects nor experimenters know which subjects are in the experimental or control groups.

Dream analysis A psychoanalytic technique in which the therapist interprets the symbolic meaning of the client's dreams.

Drive An internal state of tension that motivates an organism to engage in activities that should reduce the tension.

Dual-coding theory Paivio's theory that memory is enhanced by forming semantic and visual codes because either can lead to recall.

E

Eating disorders Severe disturbances in eating behavior characterized by preoccupation with weight concerns and unhealthy efforts to control weight.

Eclecticism In psychotherapy, drawing ideas from two or more systems of therapy instead of committing to just one system.

Efferent nerve fibers Axons that carry information outward from the central nervous system to the periphery of the body.

Ego According to Freud, the decision-making component of personality that operates according to the reality principle.

Egocentrism A limited ability to share another person's viewpoint.

Elaboration Linking a stimulus to other information at the time of encoding.

Electrical stimulation of the brain (ESB) Sending a weak electric current into a brain structure to stimulate (activate) it.

Electrocardiograph (EKG) A device that records the contractions of the heart.

Electroconvulsive therapy (ECT) A biomedical treatment in which electric shock is used to produce a cortical seizure accompanied by convulsions.

Electroencephalograph (EEG) A device that monitors the electrical activity of the brain over time by means of recording electrodes attached to the surface of the scalp.

Electromyograph (EMG) A device that records muscular activity and tension.

Electrooculograph (EOG) A device that records eye movements.

Elicit To draw out or bring forth.

Embryonic stage The second stage of prenatal development, lasting from two weeks until the end of the second month.

Emit To send forth.

Emotion A subjective conscious experience (the cognitive component) accommpanied by bodily arousal (the physiological component) and by characteristic overt expression (the behavioral component).

Empiricism The premise that knowledge should be acquired through observation.

Encoding Forming a memory code.

Encoding specificity principle The idea that the value of a retrieval cue depends on how well it corresponds to the memory code.

Endocrine system A group of glands that secrete chemicals into the bloodstream that help control bodily functioning.

Endorphins The entire family of internally produced chemicals that resemble opiates in structure and effects.

Environmental psychology The subdiscipline concerned with the study of how individuals are affected by, and interact with, their physical environments.

Epigenetics The study of heritable changes in gene expression that do not involve modifications to the DNA sequence.

Episodic memory system Chronological, or temporally dated, recollections of personal experiences.

Escape learning A type of learning in which an organism acquires a response that decreases or ends some aversive stimulation.

Etiology The apparent causation and developmental history of an illness.

Evaluative conditioning Efforts to transfer the emotion attached to a UCS to a new CS.

Evolutionary psychology Theoretical perspective that examines behavioral processes in terms of their adaptive value for a species over the course of many generations.

Experiment A research method in which the investigator manipulates a variable under carefully controlled conditions and observes whether any changes occur in a second variable as a result.

Experimental group The subjects in a study who receive some special treatment in regard to the independent variable.

Experimenter bias A phenomenon that occurs when a researcher's expectations or preferences about the outcome of a study influence the results obtained.

Explicit attitude Attitudes that people hold consciously and can readily describe.

Exposure therapies An approach to behavior therapy in which clients are confronted with situations they fear so they learn these situations are really harmless.

Expressed emotion The degree to which a relative of a schizophrenic patient displays highly critical or emotionally overinvolved attitudes toward the patient.

External attributions Ascribing the causes of behavior to situational demands and environmental constraints.

Extinction The gradual weakening and disappearance of a conditioned response tendency.

Extraneous variables Any variables other than the independent variable that seem likely to influence the dependent variable in a specific study.

F

Family studies Scientific studies in which researchers assess hereditary influence by examining blood relatives to see how much they resemble each other on a specific trait.

Family therapy The treatment of a family unit as a whole, in which the main focus is on family dynamics and communication.

Farsightedness A visual deficiency in which distant objects are seen clearly but close objects appear blurry.

Fast mapping The process by which children map a word onto an underlying concept after only one exposure.

Feature analysis The process of detecting specific elements in visual input and assembling them into a more complex form.

Feature detectors Neurons that respond selectively to very specific features of more complex stimuli.

Fetal alcohol syndrome A collection of congenital (inborn) problems associated with excessive alcohol use during pregnancy.

Fetal stage The third stage of prenatal development, lasting from two months through birth.

Fitness The reproductive success (number of descendants) of an individual organism relative to the average reproductive success of the population.

Fixation According to Freud, failure to move forward from one psychosexual stage to another as expected.

Fixed-interval (FI) schedule A reinforcement schedule in which the reinforcer is given for the first response that occurs after a fixed time interval has elapsed.

Fixed-ratio (FR) schedule A reinforcement schedule in which the reinforcer is given after a fixed number of nonreinforced responses.

Flashbulb memories Unusually vivid and detailed recollections of momentous events.

Foot-in-the-door technique Getting people to agree to a small request to increase the chances that they will agree to a larger request later.

Forebrain The largest and most complicated region of the brain, encompassing a variety of structures, including the thalamus, hypothalamus, limbic system, and cerebrum.

Forgetting curve A graph showing retention and forgetting over time.

Fovea A tiny spot in the center of the retina that contains only cones; visual acuity is greatest at this spot.

Free association A psychoanalytic technique in which clients spontaneously express their thoughts and feelings exactly as they occur, with as little censorship as possible.

Frequency distribution An orderly arrangement of scores indicating the frequency of each score or group of scores.

Frequency polygon A line figure used to present data from a frequency distribution.

Frequency theory Theory holding that perception of pitch corresponds to the rate, or frequency, at which the entire basilar membrane vibrates.

Frustration The feeling that people experience in any situation in which their pursuit of some goal is thwarted.

Functional fixedness The tendency to perceive an item only in terms of its most common use.

Functionalism A school of psychology based on the belief that psychology should investigate the function or purpose of consciousness, rather than its structure.

Fundamental attribution error Observers' bias in favor of internal attributions in explaining others' behavior.

G

Galvanic skin response (GSR) An increase in the electrical conductivity of the skin that occurs when sweat glands increase their activity.

Gambler's fallacy The belief that the odds of a chance event increase if the event hasn't occurred recently.

Gender Culturally constructed distinctions between masculinity and femininity.

Gender differences Actual disparities between the sexes in typical behavior or average ability.

Gender roles Expectations about what is appropriate behavior for each sex.

Gender stereotypes Widely held beliefs about males' and females' abilities, personality traits, and behavior.

General adaptation syndrome Selye's model of the body's stress response, consisting of three stages: alarm, resistance, and exhaustion.

Generalized anxiety disorder A psychological disorder marked by a chronic, high level of anxiety that is not tied to any specific threat.

Genes DNA segments that serve as the key functional units in hereditary transmission.

Germinal stage The first phase of prenatal development, encompassing the first two weeks after conception.

Glia Cells found throughout the nervous system that provide various types of support for neurons.

Group Two or more individuals who interact and are interdependent.

Group cohesiveness The strength of the liking relationships linking group members to each other and to the group itself.

Group polarization A phenomenon that occurs when group discussion strengthens a group's dominant point of view and produces a shift toward a more extreme decision in that direction.

Group therapy The simultaneous treatment of several clients in a group.

Groupthink A process in which members of a cohesive group emphasize concurrence at the expense of critical thinking in arriving at a decision.

Gustatory system The sensory system for taste.

H

Hallucinations Sensory perceptions that occur in the absence of a real, external stimulus, or gross distortions of perceptual input.

Hallucinogens A diverse group of drugs that have powerful effects on mental and emotional functioning, marked most prominently by distortions in sensory and perceptual experience.

Halo effect Phenomenon that occurs in self-reports when someone's overall evaluation of a person, object, or institution spills over to influence more specific ratings.

Health psychology The subfield of psychology concerned with how psychosocial factors relate to the promotion and maintenance of health and with the causation, prevention, and treatment of illness.

Hedonic adaptation An effect that occurs when the mental scale that people use to judge the pleasantness-unpleasantness of their experiences shifts so that their neutral point, or baseline for comparison, changes.

Heritability ratio An estimate of the proportion of trait variability in a population that is determined by variations in genetic inheritance.

Heterosexuals Persons who seek emotional-sexual relationships with members of the other sex.

Heuristic A strategy, guiding principle, or rule of thumb used in solving problems or making decisions.

Hierarchy of needs Maslow's systematic arrangement of needs according to priority, which assumes that basic needs must be met before less basic needs are aroused.

Higher-order conditioning A type of conditioning in which a conditioned stimulus functions as if it were an unconditioned stimulus.

Hindbrain The part of the brain that includes the cerebellum and two structures found in the lower part of the brainstem: the medulla and the pons.

Hindsight bias The tendency to mold one's interpretation of the past to fit how events actually turned out.

Histogram A bar graph that presents data from a frequency distribution.

Homeostasis A state of physiological equilibrium or stability.

Homosexuals Persons who seek emotional-sexual relationships with members of the same sex.

Hormones The chemical substances released by the endocrine glands.

Humanism A theoretical orientation that emphasizes the unique qualities of humans, especially their freedom and their potential for personal growth.

Hypnosis A systematic procedure that typically produces a heightened state of suggestibility.

Hypothalamus A structure found near the base of the forebrain that is involved in the regulation of basic biological needs.

Hypothesis A tentative statement about the relationship between two or more variables.

I

Id According to Freud, the primitive, instinctive component of personality that operates according to the pleasure principle.

Identification Bolstering self-esteem by forming an imaginary or real alliance with some person or group.

Illusory correlation A misperception that occurs when people estimate that they have encountered more confirmations of an association between social traits than they have actually seen.

Immune response The body's defensive reaction to invasion by bacteria, viral agents, or other foreign substances.

Implicit attitudes Covert attitudes that are expressed in subtle automatic responses that people have little conscious control over.

Inattentional blindness The failure to see fully visible objects or events in a visual display because one's attention is focused elsewhere.

Incentive An external goal that has the capacity to motivate behavior.

Incongruence The degree of disparity between one's self-concept and one's actual experience.

Incubation effect A phenomenon that occurs when new solutions surface for a previously unsolved problem after a period of not consciously thinking about the problem.

Independent variable In an experiment, a condition or event that an experimenter varies in order to see its impact on another variable.

Individualism Putting personal goals ahead of group goals and defining one's identity in terms of personal attributes rather than group memberships.

Inferential statistics Statistics that are used to interpret data and draw conclusions.

Ingroup The group that people belong to and identify with.

Insight therapies Psychotherapy methods characterized by verbal interactions intended to enhance clients' self-knowledge and thus promote healthful changes in personality and behavior.

Insomnia Chronic problems in getting adequate sleep.

Intelligence quotient (IQ) A child's mental age divided by chronological age, multiplied by 100.

Interference theory The idea that people forget information because of competition from other material.

Intermittent reinforcement A reinforcement schedule in which a designated response is reinforced only some of the time.

Internal attributions Ascribing the causes of behavior to personal dispositions, traits, abilities, and feelings.

Interpersonal attraction Positive feelings toward another.

Introspection Careful, systematic observation of one's own conscious experience.

Irreversibility The inability to envision reversing an action.

J

Journal A periodical that publishes technical and scholarly material, usually in a narrowly defined area of inquiry.

L

Latent content According to Freud, the hidden or disguised meaning of the events in a dream.

Learned helplessness Passive behavior produced by exposure to unavoidable aversive events.

Learning A relatively durable change in behavior or knowledge that is due to experience.

Lens The transparent eye structure that focuses the light rays falling on the retina.

Lesioning Destroying a piece of the brain.

Levels-of-processing theory The theory holding that deeper levels of mental processing result in longer-lasting memory codes.

Lie detector See *Polygraph*.

Life changes Any noticeable alterations in one's living circumstances that require readjustment.

Light adaptation The process whereby the eyes become less sensitive to light in high illumination.

Limbic system A densely connected network of structures roughly located along the border between the cerebral cortex and deeper subcortical areas.

Link method Forming a mental image of items to be remembered in a way that links them together.

Long-term memory (LTM) An unlimited capacity store that can hold information over lengthy periods of time.

Long-term potentiation (LTP) A long-lasting increase in neural excitability at synapses along a specific neural pathway.

Lowball technique Getting someone to commit to an attractive proposition before revealing the hidden costs.

M

Major depressive disorder Mood disorder characterized by persistent feelings of sadness and despair and a loss of interest in previous sources of pleasure.

Manic-depressive disorder See *Bipolar disorder*.

Manifest content According to Freud, the plot of a dream at a surface level.

Marital therapy. See *couples therapy*.

Matching hypothesis The idea that males and females of approximately equal physical attractiveness are likely to select each other as partners.

Maturation Development that reflects the gradual unfolding of one's genetic blueprint.

Mean The arithmetic average of the scores in a distribution.

Median The score that falls exactly in the center of a distribution of scores.

Medical model The view that it is useful to think of abnormal behavior as a disease.

Meditation A family of mental exercises in which a conscious attempt is made to focus attention in a nonanalytical way.

Menarche The first occurrence of menstruation.

Mental age In intelligence testing, a score that indicates that a child displays the mental ability typical of a child of that chronological (actual) age.

Mental hospital A medical institution specializing in providing inpatient care for psychological disorders.

Mental set Persisting in using problem-solving strategies that have worked in the past.

Mere exposure effect The finding that repeated exposures to a stimulus promotes greater liking of the stimulus.

Message The information transmitted by a source.

Meta-analysis A research technique that combines the statistical results of many studies of the same question, yielding an estimate of the size and consistency of a variable's effects.

Method of loci A mnemonic device that involves taking an imaginary walk along a familiar path where images of items to be remembered are associated with certain locations.

Midbrain The segment of the brain stem that lies between the hindbrain and the forebrain.

Mirror neurons Neurons that are activated by performing an action or by seeing another monkey or person perform the same action.

Misinformation effect Phenomenon that occurs when participants' recall of an event they witnessed is altered by introducing misleading postevent information.

Mnemonic devices Strategies for enhancing memory.

Mode The score that occurs most frequently in a distribution.

Model A person whose behavior is observed by another.

Monocular depth cues Clues about distance based on the image from either eye alone.

Mood disorders A class of disorders marked by emotional disturbances of varied kinds that may spill over to disrupt physical, perceptual, social, and thought processes.

Mood stabilizers Drugs used to control mood swings in patients with bipolar mood disorders.

Mortality salience The degree to which subjects' mortality is prominent in their minds.

Motivation Goal-directed behavior.

Motor development The progression of muscular coordination required for physical activities.

Multiple-personality disorder See *Dissociative identity disorder*.

Myelin sheath Insulating material, derived from glial cells, that encases some axons of neurons.

N

Narcissism A personality trait marked by an inflated sense of importance, a need for attention and admiration, a sense of entitlement, and a tendency to exploit others.

Narcolepsy A disease marked by sudden and irresistible onsets of sleep during normal waking periods.

Narcotics (opiates) Drugs derived from opium that are capable of relieving pain.

Natural selection Principle stating that inherited characteristics that provide a survival or reproductive advantage are more likely than alternative characteristics to be passed on to subsequent generations and thus come to be "selected" over time.

Naturalistic observation A descriptive research method in which the researcher engages in careful, usually prolonged, observation of behavior without intervening directly with the subjects.

Nearsightedness A visual deficiency in which close objects are seen clearly but distant objects appear blurry.

Need for self-actualization The need to fulfill one's potential.

Negative reinforcement The strengthening of a response because it is followed by the removal of an aversive (unpleasant) stimulus.

Negatively skewed distribution A distribution in which most scores pile up at the high end of the scale.

Neurogenesis The formation of new neurons.

Neurons Individual cells in the nervous system that receive, integrate, and transmit information.

Neurotransmitters Chemicals that transmit information from one neuron to another.

Nondeclarative memory system The repository for memories for actions, skills, conditioned responses, and emotional memories. Also called *procedural memory*.

Non-REM (NREM) sleep Sleep stages 1 through 4, which are marked by an absence of rapid eye movements, relatively little dreaming, and varied EEG activity.

Nonsense syllables Consonant-vowel-consonant arrangements that do not correspond to words.

Normal distribution A symmetric, bell-shaped curve that represents the pattern in which many characteristics are dispersed in the population.

Null hypothesis In inferential statistics, the assumption that there is no true relationship between the variables being observed.

O

Obedience A form of compliance that occurs when people follow direct commands, usually from someone in a position of authority.

Object permanence Recognizing that objects continue to exist even when they are no longer visible.

Observational learning A type of learning that occurs when an organism's responding is influenced by the observation of others, who are called models.

Obsessive-compulsive disorder (OCD) A type of anxiety disorder marked by persistent, uncontrollable intrusions of unwanted thoughts (obsessions) and urges to engage in senseless rituals (compulsions).

Oedipal complex According to Freud, children's manifestation of erotically tinged desires for their opposite-sex parent, accompanied by feelings of hostility toward their same-sex parent.

Olfactory system The sensory system for smell.

Operant conditioning A form of learning in which voluntary responses come to be controlled by their consequences.

Operational definition A definition that describes the actions or operations that will be used to measure or control a variable.

Opiates. See *Narcotics*.

Opponent process theory The idea that color perception depends on receptors that make antagonistic responses to three pairs of colors.

Optic chiasm The point at which the axons from the inside half of each eye cross over and then project to the opposite half of the brain.

Optimism A general tendency to expect good outcomes.

Outgroup People who are not part of the ingroup.

Overextension Mistake in language learning that occurs when a child incorrectly uses a word to describe a wider set of objects or actions than it is meant to.

Overregulation Mistake in language learning in which a child incorrectly generalizes grammatical rules to irregular cases where they do not apply.

Oxycontin A hormone released by the pituitary gland, which regulates reproductive behaviors.

P

Panic disorder A type of anxiety disorder characterized by recurrent attacks of overwhelming anxiety that usually occur suddenly and unexpectedly.

Parallel distributed processing (PDP) models Models of memory that assume cognitive processes depend on patterns of activation in highly interconnected computational networks that resemble neural networks. Also called connectionist models.

Paranoid schizophrenia A type of schizophrenia that is dominated by delusions of persecution along with delusions of grandeur.

Parasympathetic division The branch of the autonomic nervous system that generally conserves bodily resources.

Parental investment What each sex invests—in terms of time, energy, survival risk, and forgone opportunities—to produce and nurture offspring.

Participants The persons or animals whose behavior is systematically observed in a study.

Passionate love A complete absorption in another that includes tender sexual feelings and the agony and ecstasy of intense emotion.

Pavlovian conditioning See *Classical conditioning*.

Percentile score A figure that indicates the percentage of people who score below the score one has obtained.

Perception The selection, organization, and interpretation of sensory input.

Perceptual constancy A tendency to experience a stable perception in the face of continually changing sensory input.

Perceptual hypothesis An inference about what form could be responsible for a pattern of sensory stimulation.

Perceptual set A readiness to perceive a stimulus in a particular way.

Peripheral nervous system All those nerves that lie outside the brain and spinal cord.

Person perception The process of forming impressions of others.

Personality An individual's unique constellation of consistent behavioral traits.

Personality trait A durable disposition to behave in a particular way in a variety of situations.

Phi phenomenon The illusion of movement created by presenting visual stimuli in rapid succession.

Phobic disorder A type of anxiety disorder marked by a persistent and irrational fear of an object or situation that presents no realistic danger.

Physical dependence The condition that exists when a person must continue to take a drug to avoid withdrawal illness.

Pictorial depth cues Clues about distance that can be given in a flat picture.

Pituitary gland The "master gland" of the endocrine system; it releases a great variety of hormones that fan out through the body, stimulating actions in the other endocrine glands.

Place theory The idea that perception of pitch corresponds to the vibration of different portions, or places, along the basilar membrane.

Placebo effects The fact that subjects' expectations can lead them to experience some change even though they receive an empty, fake, or ineffectual treatment.

Placenta A structure that allows oxygen and nutrients to pass into the fetus from the mother's bloodstream and bodily wastes to pass out to the mother.

Pleasure principle According to Freud, the principle upon which the id operates, demanding immediate gratification of its urges.

Polygenic traits Characteristics that are influenced by more than one pair of genes.

Polygraph A device that records autonomic fluctuations while a subject is questioned, in an effort to determine whether the subject is telling the truth.

Population The larger collection of animals or people from which a sample is drawn and that researchers want to generalize about.

Positive psychology Approach to psychology that uses theory and research to better understand the positive, adaptive, creative, and fulfilling aspects of human existence.

Positive reinforcement Reinforcement that occurs when a response is strengthened because it is followed by the presentation of a rewarding stimulus.

Positively skewed distribution A distribution in which scores pile up at the low end of the scale.

Postsynaptic potential (PSP) A voltage change at the receptor site on a postsynaptic cell membrane.

Posttraumatic stress disorder (PTSD) Disturbed behavior that is attributed to a major stressful event but that emerges after the stress is over.

Preconscious According to Freud, the level of awareness that contains material just beneath the surface of conscious awareness that can easily be retrieved.

Prejudice A negative attitude held toward members of a group.

Premises The reasons presented to persuade someone that a conclusion is true or probably true.

Prenatal period The period from conception to birth, usually encompassing nine months of pregnancy.

Preparedness Species-specific predisposition to be conditioned in certain ways and not others.

Pressure Expectations or demands that one behave in a certain way.

Primary appraisal An initial evaluation of whether an event is (1) irrelevant to you, (2) relevant but not threatening, or (3) stressful.

Primary reinforcers Events that are inherently reinforcing because they satisfy biological needs.

Primary sex characteristics The sexual structures necessary for reproduction.

Proactive interference A memory problem that occurs when previously learned information interferes with the retention of new information.

Problem solving Active efforts to discover what must be done to achieve a goal that is not readily available.

Procedural memory system See *Nondeclarative memory system*.

Prognosis A forecast about the probable course of an illness.

Projection Attributing one's own thoughts, feelings, or motives to another.

Projective tests Psychological tests that ask subjects to respond to vague, ambiguous stimuli in ways that may reveal the subjects' needs, feelings, and personality traits.

Prospective memory The ability to remember to perform actions in the future.

Psychiatrists Physicians who specialize in the diagnosis and treatment of psychological disorders.

Psychiatry A branch of medicine concerned with the diagnosis and treatment of psychological problems and disorders.

Psychoactive drugs Chemical substances that modify mental, emotional, or behavioral functioning.

Psychoanalysis An insight therapy that emphasizes the recovery of unconscious conflicts, motives, and defenses through techniques such as free association and transference.

Psychoanalytic theory A theory developed by Freud that attempts to explain personality, motivation, and mental disorders by focusing on unconscious determinants of behavior.

Psychological dependence The condition that exists when a person must continue to take a drug in order to satisfy intense mental and emotional craving for the drug.

Psychological test A standardized measure of a sample of a person's behavior.

Psychology The science that studies behavior and the physiological and cognitive processes that underlie it, and the profession that applies the accumulated knowledge of this science to practical problems.

Psychosexual stages According to Freud, developmental periods with a characteristic sexual focus that leave their mark on a person's adult personality.

Puberty The period of early adolescence marked by rapid physical growth and the development of sexual (reproductive) maturity.

Punishment An event that follows a response that weakens or suppresses the tendency to make that response.

Pupil The opening in the center of the iris that helps regulate the amount of light passing into the rear chamber of the eye.

R

Random assignment The design of a study such that all subjects have an equal chance of being assigned to any group or condition.

Rationalization Creating false but plausible excuses to justify unacceptable behavior.

Reaction formation Behaving in a way that's exactly the opposite of one's true feelings.

Reaction range Genetically determined limits on IQ or other traits.

Reactivity Alteration of a subject's behavior due to the presence of an observer.

Reality principle According to Freud, the principle on which the ego operates, which seeks to delay gratification of the id's urges until appropriate outlets and situations can be found.

Recall measure A memory test that requires subjects to reproduce information on their own without any cues.

Receiver The person to whom a message is sent.

Receptive field of a visual cell The retinal area that, when stimulated, affects the firing of that cell.

Reciprocity Liking those who show that they like you.

Reciprocity norm The rule that people should pay back in kind what they receive from others.

Recognition measure A memory test that requires subjects to select previously learned information from an array of options.

Regression A reversion to immature patterns of behavior.

Regression toward the mean Effect that occurs when people who score extremely high or low on some trait are measured a second time and their new score falls closer to the mean (average).

Rehearsal The process of repetitively verbalizing or thinking about information to be stored in memory.

Reinforcement An event following a response that strengthens the tendency to make that response.

Reinforcement contingencies The circumstances or rules that determine whether responses lead to the presentation of reinforcers.

Relearning measure A memory test that requires a subject to memorize information a second time to determine how much time or effort is saved by having learned it before.

Reliability The measurement consistency of a test (or of other kinds of measurement techniques).

REM sleep A deep stage of sleep marked by rapid eye movements, high-frequency brain waves, and dreaming.

Renewal effect Referring to the phenomenon that occurs if a response is extinguished in a different environment than it was acquired; the extinguished response will reappear if the animal is returned to the original environment where acquisition took place.

Replication The repetition of a study to see whether the earlier results are duplicated.

Representativeness heuristic Basing the estimated probability of an event on how similar it is to the typical prototype of that event.

Repression Keeping distressing thoughts and feelings buried in the unconscious.

Research methods Differing approaches to the observation, measurement, and manipulation and control of variables in empirical studies.

Resistance Largely unconscious defensive maneuvers a client uses to hinder the progress of therapy.

Resistance to extinction In operant conditioning, the phenomenon that occurs when an organism continues to make a response after delivery of the reinforcer for it has been terminated.

Response. See *Conditioned response, Unconditioned response*.

Resting potential The stable, negative charge of a neuron when it is inactive.

Retention The proportion of material retained (remembered).

Retina The neural tissue lining the inside back surface of the eye; it absorbs light, processes images, and sends visual information to the brain.

Retinal disparity A cue to the depth based on the fact that objects within 25 feet project images to slightly different locations on the left and right retinas, so the right and left eyes see slightly different views of the object.

Retrieval Recovering information from memory stores.

Retroactive interference A memory problem that occurs when new information impairs the retention of previously learned information.

Retrograde amnesia Loss of memories for events that occurred prior to a head injury.

Retrospective memory The ability to remember events from the past or previously learned information.

Reuptake A process in which neurotransmitters are sponged up from the synaptic cleft by the presynaptic membrane.

Reversible figure A drawing that is compatible with two different interpretations that can shift back and forth.

Risky decision making Making choices under conditions of uncertainty.

Rods Specialized visual receptors that play a key role in night vision and peripheral vision.

S

Sample The collection of subjects selected for observation in an empirical study.

Sampling bias A problem that occurs when a sample is not representative of the population from which it is drawn.

Scatter diagram A graph in which paired X and Y scores for each subject are plotted as single points.

Schedule of reinforcement A specific presentation of reinforcers over time.

Schema An organized cluster of knowledge about a particular object or sequence of events.

Schizophrenic disorders A class of psychological disorders marked by disturbances in thought that spill over to affect perceptual, social, and emotional processes.

Secondary appraisal An evaluation of your coping resources and options for dealing with the stress.

Secondary (conditioned) reinforcers Stimulus events that acquire reinforcing qualities by being associated with primary reinforcers.

Secondary sex characteristics Physical features that are associated with gender but that are not directly involved in reproduction.

Sedatives Sleep-inducing drugs that tend to decrease central nervous system activation and behavioral activity.

Self-actualizing persons People with exceptionally healthy personalities, marked by continued personal growth.

Self-concept A collection of beliefs about one's own nature, unique qualities, and typical behavior.

Self-efficacy One's belief about one's ability to perform behaviors that should lead to expected outcomes.

Self-report inventories Personality tests that ask individuals to answer a series of questions about their characteristic behavior.

Self-serving bias The tendency to attribute one's successes to personal factors and one's failures to situational factors.

Semantic memory system General knowledge that is not tied to the time when the information was learned.

Semantic network Concepts joined together by links that show how the concepts are related.

Sensation The stimulation of sense organs.

Sensory adaptation A gradual decline in sensitivity to prolonged stimulation.

Sensory memory The preservation of information in its original sensory form for a brief time, usually only a fraction of a second.

Separation anxiety Emotional distress seen in many infants when they are separated from people with whom they have formed an attachment.

Serial-position effect In memory tests, the fact that subjects show better recall for items at the beginning and end of a list than for items in the middle.

Sex The biologically based categories of male and female.

Sexual orientation A person's preference for emotional and sexual relationships with individuals of the same sex, the other sex, or either sex.

Shaping The reinforcement of closer and closer approximations of a desired response.

Short-term memory (STM) A limited-capacity store that can maintain unrehearsed information for about 20 to 30 seconds.

Skinner box A small enclosure in which an animal can make a specific response that is systematically recorded while the consequences of the response are controlled.

Sleep apnea A sleep disorder characterized by frequent reflexive gasping for air that awakens the sleeper and disrupts sleep.

Slow-wave sleep Sleep stages 3 and 4, during which low-frequency delta waves become prominent in EEG recordings.

Social desirability bias A tendency to give socially approved answers to questions about oneself.

Social loafing A reduction in effort by individuals when they work in groups as compared to when they work by themselves.

Social psychology The branch of psychology concerned with the way individuals' thoughts, feelings, and behaviors are influenced by others.

Social roles Widely shared expectations about how people in certain positions are supposed to behave.

Social skills training A behavior therapy designed to improve interpersonal skills that emphasizes shaping, modeling, and behavioral rehearsal.

Social support Various types of aid and succor provided by members of one's social networks.

Socialization The acquisition of the norms, roles, and behaviors expected of people in a particular society.

Soma The cell body of a neuron; it contains the nucleus and much of the chemical machinery common to most cells.

Somatic nervous system The system of nerves that connect to voluntary skeletal muscles and to sensory receptors.

Somnambulism Arising and walking about while remaining asleep; sleepwalking.

Source The person who sends a communication.

Source monitoring The process of making attributions about the origins of memories.

Source-monitoring error An error that occurs when a memory derived from one source is misattributed to another source.

Spermarche The first occurrence of ejaculation.

Split-brain surgery A procedure in which the bundle of fibers that connects the cerebral hemispheres (the corpus callosum) is cut to reduce the severity of epileptic seizures.

Spontaneous recovery In classical conditioning, the reappearance of an extinguished response after a period of nonexposure to the conditioned stimulus.

Stage A developmental period during which characteristic patterns of behavior are exhibited and certain capacities become established.

Standard deviation An index of the amount of variability in a set of data.

Standardization The uniform procedures used in the administration and scoring of a test.

Statistical significance The condition that exists when the probability that the observed findings are due to chance is very low.

Statistics The use of mathematics to organize, summarize, and interpret numerical data. See also *Descriptive statistics, Inferential statistics*.

Stereotypes Widely held beliefs that people have certain characteristics because of their membership in a particular group.

Stimulants Drugs that tend to increase central nervous system activation and behavioral activity.

Stimulus See *conditioned stimulus, Unconditioned stimulus*.

Stimulus discrimination The phenomenon that occurs when an organism that has learned a response to a specific stimulus does not respond in the same way to stimuli that are similar to the original stimulus.

Stimulus generalization The phenomenon that occurs when an organism that has learned a response to a specific stimulus responds in the same way to new stimuli that are similar to the original stimulus.

Storage Maintaining encoded information in memory over time.

Stress Any circumstances that threaten or are perceived to threaten one's well-being and that thereby tax one's coping abilities.

Striving for superiority According to Adler, the universal drive to adapt, improve oneself, and master life's challenges.

Structuralism A school of psychology based on the notion that the task of psychology is to analyze consciousness into its basic elements and to investigate how these elements are related.

Subjective well-being Individuals' perceptions of their overall happiness and life satisfaction.

Subjects See *participants*.

Sublimation A defense mechanism in which unconscious, unacceptable impulses are channeled into socially acceptable, perhaps even admirable, behaviors.

Subtractive color mixing Formation of colors by removing some wavelengths of light, leaving less light than was originally there.

Superego According to Freud, the moral component of personality that incorporates social standards about what represents right and wrong.

Survey A descriptive research method in which researchers use questionnaires or interviews to gather information about specific aspects of subjects' behavior.

Sustainable world A world in which human activities and needs are balanced with those of other species and future generations, taking into account ecological as well as social and economic factors.

Sympathetic division The branch of the autonomic nervous system that mobilizes the body's resources for emergencies.

Synapse A junction where information is transmitted from one neuron to the next.

Synaptic cleft A microscopic gap between the terminal button of a neuron and the cell membrane of another neuron.

Systematic desensitization A behavior therapy used to reduce clients' anxiety responses through counterconditioning.

T

Tardive dyskinesia A neurological disorder marked by chronic tremors and involuntary spastic movements.

Telegraphic speech Referring to a child's early sentences, which consist mainly of content words; articles, prepositions, and other less critical words are omitted.

Terminal buttons Small knobs at the end of axons that secrete chemicals called neurotransmitters.

Thalamus A structure in the forebrain through which all sensory information (except smell) must pass to get to the cerebral cortex.

Theory A system of interrelated ideas that is used to explain a set of observations.

Theory of bounded rationality The idea that people tend to use simple strategies in decision making that focus on only a few facets of available options and often result in "irrational" decisions that are less than optimal.

Tip-of-the-tongue phenomenon The temporary inability to remember something you know, accompanied by a feeling that it's just out of reach.

Tolerance A progressive decrease in a person's responsiveness to a drug.

Top-down processing In form perception, a progression from the whole to the elements.

Transference In therapy, the phenomenon that occurs when clients start relating to their therapists in ways that mimic critical relationships in their lives.

Trial In classical conditioning, any presentation of a stimulus or pair of stimuli.

Trial and error Trying possible solutions sequentially and discarding those that are in error until one works.

Trichromatic theory The idea that the human eye has three types of receptors with differing sensitivities to different light wavelengths.

Twin studies A research design in which hereditary influence is assessed by comparing the resemblance of identical twins and fraternal twins with respect to a trait.

Type A personality Personality characterized by (1) a strong competitive orientation, (2) impatience and time urgency, and (3) anger and hostility.

Type B personality Personality characterized by relatively relaxed, patient, easygoing, amicable behavior.

U

Unconditioned response (UCR) An unlearned reaction to an unconditioned stimulus that occurs without previous conditioning.

Unconditioned stimulus (UCS) A stimulus that evokes an unconditioned response without previous conditioning.

Unconscious According to Freud, thoughts, memories, and desires that are well below the surface of conscious awareness but that nonetheless exert great influence on behavior.

Underextensions Mistake that occurs when a child incorrectly uses a word to describe a narrower set of objects or actions than it is meant to.

Undifferentiated schizophrenia A type of schizophrenia marked by idiosyncratic mixtures of schizophrenic symptoms.

V

Validity The ability of a test to measure what it was designed to measure.

Variability The extent to which the scores in a data set tend to vary from one another and from the mean.

Variable-interval (VI) schedule A reinforcement schedule in which the reinforcer is given for the first response after a variable time interval has elapsed.

Variable-ratio (VR) schedule A reinforcement schedule in which the reinforcer is given after a variable number of nonreinforced responses.

Variables Any measurable conditions, events, characteristics, or behaviors that are controlled or observed in a study.

Visual illusion An apparently inexplicable discrepancy between the appearance of a visual stimulus and its physical reality.

W

working memory A modular system for temporary storage and manipulation of information.

working memory capacity (WMC) One's ability to hold and manipulate information in conscious attention.

Z

Zygote A one-celled organism formed by the union of a sperm and an egg.

References

Abe, T., Komada, Y., Nishida, Y., Hayashida, K., & Inoue, Y. (2010). Short sleep duration and long spells of driving are associated with the occurrence of Japanese drivers' rear-end collisions and single-car accidents. *Journal of Sleep Research, 19*(2), 310–316. doi:10.1111/j.1365-2869.2009.00806.x

Abel, E. L. (1998). *Fetal alcohol abuse syndrome.* New York, NY: Plenum.

Abel, E. L., & Kruger, M. L. (2010). Smile intensity in photographs predicts longevity. *Psychological Science, 21*(4), 542–544.

Abel, M. H. (2002). Humor, stress, and coping strategies. *Humor: International Journal of Humor Research, 15,* 365–381.

Aboud, F. E., & Amato, M. (2001). Developmental and socialization influences on intergroup bias. In R. Brown & S. L. Gaertner (Eds.), *Blackwell handbook of social psychology: Intergroup processes.* Malden, MA: Blackwell.

Abramson, L. Y., Alloy, L. B., & Metalsky, J. I. (1995). Hopelessness depression. In J. N. Buchanan & M. E. P. Seligman (Eds.), *Explanatory style.* Hillsdale, NJ: Erlbaum.

Abramson, L. Y., Seligman, M. E. P., & Teasdale, J. (1978). Learned helplessness in humans: Critique and reformulation. *Journal of Abnormal Psychology, 87,* 32–48.

Adam, T. C., & Epel, E. (2007). Stress, eating and the reward system. *Physiology and Behavior, 91,* 449–458.

Adams, J. L. (1980). *Conceptual blockbusting.* San Francisco, CA: W. H. Freeman.

Adams, R. L., & Culbertson, J. L. (2005). Personality assessment: Adults and children. In B. J. Sadock & V. A. Sadock (Eds.), *Kaplan & Sadock's comprehensive textbook of psychiatry.* Philadelphia, PA: Lippincott Williams & Wilkins.

Ader, R. (2001). Psychoneuroimmunology. *Current Directions in Psychological Science, 10*(3), 94–98.

Ader, R. (2003). Conditioned immunomodulation: Research needs and directions. *Brain, Behavior, and Immunity, 17*(1), S51–S57.

Ader, R., & Cohen, N. (1984). Behavior and the immune system. In W. D. Gentry (Ed.), *Handbook of behavioral medicine.* New York, NY: Guilford.

Ader, R., & Cohen, N. (1993). Psychoneuroimmunology: Conditioning and stress. *Annual Review of Psychology, 44,* 53–85.

Adler, A. (1917). *Study of organ inferiority and its psychical compensation.* New York, NY: Nervous and Mental Diseases Publishing Co.

Adler, A. (1927). *Practice and theory of individual psychology.* New York, NY: Harcourt, Brace & World.

Adler, L. L. (Ed.). (1993). *International handbook on gender roles.* Westport, CT: Greenwood.

Adolph, K. E., & Berger, S. E. (2011). Physical and motor development. In M. H. Bornstein & M. E. Lamb (Eds.), *Developmental science: An advanced textbook* (pp. 109–198). New York, NY: Psychology Press.

Adolph, K. E., Karasik, L. B., & Tamis-Lemonda, C. S. (2010). Motor skills. In M. H. Bornstein (Ed.), *Handbook of cultural developmental science* (pp. 61–88). New York, NY: Psychology Press.

Affleck, G., Tennen, H., Urrows, S., & Higgins, P. (1994). Person and contextual features of daily stress reactivity: Individual differences in relations of undesirable daily events with mood disturbance and chronic pain intensity. *Journal of Personality and Social Psychology, 66,* 329–340.

Agarwal, P. K., Karpicke, J. D., Kang, S. K., Roediger, H., & McDermott, K. B. (2008). Examining the testing effect with open- and closed-book tests. *Applied Cognitive Psychology, 22*(7), 861–876. doi:10.1002/acp.1391

Ahima, R. S., & Osei, S. Y. (2004). Leptin signaling. *Physiology & Behavior, 81,* 223–241.

Ahlgren, M., Wohlfahrt, J., Olsen, L. W., Sorensen, T. L., & Melbye, M. (2007). Birth weight and risk of cancer. *Cancer, 110*(2), 412–419. doi:10.1002/cncr.22773

Aikins, D. E., & Craske, M. G. (2001). Cognitive theories of generalized anxiety disorder. *Psychiatric Clinics of North America, 24*(1), 57–74.

Ainsworth, M. D. S., Blehar, M. C., Waters, E., & Wall, S. (1978). *Patterns of attachment: A psychological study of the strange situation.* Hillsdale, NJ: Erlbaum.

Ajzen, I., & Fishbein, M. (2000). Attitudes and the attitude-behavior relation: Reasoned and automatic processes. In W. Stroebe & M. Hewstone (Eds.), *European review of social psychology* (Vol. 11). Chichester, UK: Wiley.

Ajzen, I., & Fishbein, M. (2005). The influence of attitudes on behavior. In D. Albarracin, B. T. Johnson, & M. P. Zanna (Eds.), *The handbook of attitudes.* Mahwah, NJ: Erlbaum.

Akerstedt, T., Hume, K., Minors, D., & Waterhouse, J. (1997). Good sleep—its timing and physiological sleep characteristics. *Journal of Sleep Research, 6,* 221–229.

Akimoto, S. A., & Sanbonmatsu, D. M. (1999). Differences in self-effacing behavior between European and Japanese Americans: Effect on competence evaluations. *Journal of Cross-Cultural Psychology, 30,* 159–177.

Akiskal, H. S. (2000). Mood disorders: Clinical features. In B. J. Sadock & V. A. Sadock (Eds.), *Kaplan and Sadock's comprehensive textbook of psychiatry* (7th ed., Vol. 1, pp. 1338–1376). Philadelphia, PA: Lippincott Williams & Wilkins.

Akiskal, H. S. (2009). Mood disorders: Clinical features. In B. J. Sadock, V. A. Sadock, & P. Ruiz (Eds.), *Kaplan & Sadock's comprehensive textbook of psychiatry* (9th ed., pp. 1693–1733). Philadelphia, PA: Lippincott Williams & Wilkins.

Albarracin, D., & Vargas, P. (2010). Attitudes and persuasion: From biology to social responses to persuasive intent. In S. T. Fiske, D. T. Gilbert, G. Lindzey, & S. T. Fiske (Eds.), *Handbook of social psychology,* (5th ed., Vol. 1, pp. 353–393). Hoboken, NJ: Wiley.

Albert M. A. (2008). Neuropsychology of the development of Alzheimer's disease. In F. I. M. Craik & T. A. Salthouse (Eds.), *Handbook of aging and cognition* (2nd ed., pp. 97–132). New York, NY: Psychology Press.

Albert, M. S., & Killiany, R. J. (2001). Age-related cognitive change and brain-behavior relationships. In J. E. Birren & K. W. Schaie (Eds.), *Handbook of the psychology of aging* (5th ed., pp. 160–184). San Diego, CA: Academic Press.

Alcock, J. (2005). *Animal behavior.* Sunderland, MA: Sinauer Associates.

Aldington, S., Harwood, M., Cox, B., Weatherall, M., Beckert, L., Hansell, A., et al. (2008). Cannabis use and risk of lung cancer: A case-control study. *European Respiratory Journal, 31,* 280–286.

Aldington, S., Williams, M., Nowitz, M., Weatherall, M., Pritchard, A., McNaughton, A., et al. (2007). Effects of cannabis on pulmonary structure, function and symptoms. *Thorax, 62,* 1058–1063.

Aldrich, M. S. (2000). Cardinal manifestations of sleep disorders. In M. H. Kryger, T. Roth, & W. C. Dement (Eds.), *Principles and practice of sleep medicine.* Philadelphia, PA: Saunders.

Aldwin, C. M., & Gilmer, D. F. (2004). *Health, illness, and optimal aging: Biological and psychosocial perspectives.* Thousand Oaks, CA: Sage Publications.

Alhakami, A. S., & Slovic, P. (1994). A psychological study of the inverse relationship between perceived risk and perceived benefit. *Risk Analysis, 14,* 1085–1096.

Allan, R. W. (1998). Operant-respondent interactions. In W. O'Donohue (Ed.), *Learning and behavior therapy.* Boston, MA: Allyn & Bacon.

Alloy, L. B., Abramson, L. Y., Whitehouse, W. G., Hogan, M. E., Tashman, N. A., Steinberg, D. L., Rose, D. T., & Donovan, P. (1999). Depressogenic cognitive styles: Predictive validity, information processing and personality characteristics, and developmental origins. *Behavioral Research and Therapy, 37,* 503–531.

Allport, G. W. (1937). *Personality: A psychological interpretation.* New York, NY: Holt.

Allport, G. W. (1961). *Pattern and growth in personality.* New York, NY: Holt.

Altman, I. (1990). Centripetal and centrifugal trends in psychology. In L. Brickman & H. Ellis (Eds.), *Preparing psychologists for the 21st century: Proceedings of the National Conference on Graduate Education in Psychology.* Hillsdale, NJ: Erlbaum.

Altshuler, L. L., Suppes, T., Black, D. O., Nolen, W. A., Leverich, G., Keck, P. E., Jr., et al. (2006). Lower switch rate in depressed patients with Bipolar II than Bipolar I disorder treated adjunctively with second-generation antidepressants. *American Journal of Psychiatry, 163,* 313–315.

Amabile, T. M. (1996). *Creativity in context.* Boulder, CO: Westview.

Amato, P. R. (2006). Marital discord, divorce, and children's well-being: Results from a 20-year longitudinal study of two generations. In A. Clarke-Stewart & J. Dunn (Eds.), *Families count: Effects on child and adolescent development* (pp. 179–202). New York, NY: Cambridge University Press.

Amato, P. R., & Dorius, C. (2010). Fathers, children, and divorce. In M. Lamb (Ed.), *The role of the father in child development* (5th ed., pp. 177–200). Hoboken, NJ: Wiley.

Ambady, N., & Rosenthal, R. (1993). Half a minute: Predicting teacher evaluations from thin slices of nonverbal behavior and physical attractiveness. *Journal of Personality and Social Psychology, 64*(3), 431–441. doi:10.1037/0022-3514.64.3.431

Ambady, N., Hallahan, M., & Conner, B. (1999). Accuracy of judgments of sexual orientation from thin slices of behavior. *Journal of Personality and Social Psychology, 77*(3), 538–547. doi:10.1037/0022-3514.77.3.538

Ambady, N., & Weisbuch, M. (2010). Nonverbal behavior. In S. T. Fiske, D. T. Gilbert, & G. Lindzey (Eds.), *Handbook of social psychology* (5th ed., Vol. 1, pp. 353–393). Hoboken, NJ: Wiley.

Amedi, A., Floel, A., Knecht, S., Zohary, E., & Cohen, L. G. (2004). Transcranial magnetic stimulation of the occipital pole interferes with verbal processing in blind subjects. *Nature Neuroscience, 7,* 1266–1270.

American Psychiatric Association Task Force on Electroconvulsive Therapy. (2001). *The practice of electroconvulsive therapy: Recommendations for treatment* (2nd ed.). Washington, DC: American Psychiatric Association.

American Psychiatric Association. (1994). *Diagnostic and statistical manual of mental disorders* (4th ed.). Washington, DC: Author.

American Psychiatric Association. (2000). *Diagnostic and statistical manual of mental disorders* (4th ed. Text revision). Washington, DC: Author.

American Psychological Association. (1984). *Behavioral research with animals.* Washington, DC: Author.

American Psychological Association. (2002). Ethical principles of psychologists and code of conduct. *American Psychologist, 57,* 1060–1073.

Amodio, D. M., & Devine, P. G. (2006). Stereotyping and evaluation in implicit race bias: Evidence for independent constructs and unique effects on behavior. *Journal of Personality and Social Psychology, 91*(4), 652–661. doi:10.1037/0022-3514.91.4.652

Amodio, D. M., Harmon-Jones, E., Devine, P. G., Curtin, J. J., Hartley, S. L., & Covert, A. E. (2004). Neural signals for the detection of unintentional race bias. *Psychological Science, 15*(2), 88–93.

Amyx, D., & Alford, B. L. (2005). The effects of salesperson need for achievement and sales manager leader reward behavior. *Journal of Personal Selling & Sales Management, 25*(4), 345–359.

Anand, B. K., & Brobeck, J. R. (1951). Hypothalamic control of food intake in rats and cats. *Yale Journal of Biology and Medicine, 24,* 123–140.

Anderluh, M. B., Tchanturia, K., & Rabe-Hesketh, S. (2003). Childhood obsessive-compulsive personality traits in adult women with eating disorders: Defining a broader eating disorder phenotype. *American Journal of Psychiatry, 160,* 242–247.

Anderson, A. E., & Yager, J. (2005). Eating disorders. In B. J. Sadock & V. A. Sadock (Eds.), *Kaplan & Sadock's comprehensive textbook of psychiatry.* Philadelphia, PA: Lippincott Williams & Wilkins.

Anderson, B. (2003). Brain imaging and *g.* In H. Nyborg (Ed.), *The scientific study of general intelligence: Tribute to Arthur R. Jensen.* Oxford, UK: Pergamon.

Anderson, C., Keltner, D., & John, O. P. (2003). Emotional convergence between people over time. *Journal of Personality and Social Psychology, 84,* 1054–1068.

Anderson, C. A., Berkowitz, L., Donnerstein, E., Huesman, L. R., Johnson, J. D., Linz, D., Malamuth, N. M. , & Wartella, E. (2003). The influence of media violence on youth. *Psychological Science in the Public Interest, 4*(3), 81–110.

Anderson, E. A., Kohler, J. K., & Letiecq, B. L. (2002). Low-income fathers and "Responsible Fatherhood" programs: A qualitative investigation of participants' experiences. *Family Relations, 51,* 148–155.

Anderson, K. J. (1990). Arousal and the inverted-U hypothesis: A critique of Neiss's "reconceptualizing arousal." *Psychological Bulletin, 107,* 96–100.

Anderson, M. C., & Neely, J. H. (1996). Interference and inhibition in memory retrieval. In E. L. Bjork & R. A. Bjork (Eds.), *Memory.* San Diego, CA: Academic Press.

Anderson-Fye, E. P., & Becker, A. E. (2004). Sociocultural aspects of eating disorders and obesity. In J. K. Thompson (Ed.), *Handbook of eating disorders and obesity.* New York, NY: Wiley.

Andreasen, N. C. (1990). Positive and negative symptoms: Historical and conceptual aspects. In N. C. Andreasen (Ed.), *Modern problems of pharmacopsychiatry: Positive and negative symptoms and syndromes.* Basel: Karger.

Andreasen, N. C. (2005). *The creating brain: The neuroscience of genius.* New York, NY: Dana Press.

Andrews, G., Charney, D., Sirovatka, P., & Regier, D. (Eds.). (2009). *Stress-induced and fear circuitry disorders: Advancing the research agenda for DSM-V.* Arlington, VA: American Psychiatric Publishing.

Angell, M. (2004). *The truth about the drug companies: How they deceive us and what to do about it.* New York, NY: Random House.

Anglin, J. M. (1993). Vocabulary development: A morphological analysis. *Monographs of the Society for Research in Child Development, 58.*

Angrosino, M. V. (2007). *Naturalistic observation: Qualitative essentials.* Walnut Creek, CA: Left Coast Press.

Ansbacher, H. (1970, February). Alfred Adler, individual psychology. *Psychology Today,* pp. 42–44, 66.

Anthony, I. C., & Bell, J. E. (2008). The neuropathology of HIV/AIDS. *International Review of Psychiatry, 20*(1), 15–24.

Antonuccio, D. O., Danton, W. G., & McClanahan, T. M. (2003). Psychology in the prescription era: Building a firewall between marketing and science. *American Psychologist, 58,* 1028–1043.

Antony, M. M., & McCabe, R. E. (2003). Anxiety disorders: Social and specific phobias. In A. Tasman, J. Kay, & J. A. Lieberman (Eds.), *Psychiatry.* New York, NY: Wiley.

Apkarian, A. V., Bushnell, M. C., Treede, R., & Zubieta, J. (2005). Human brain mechanisms of pain perception and regulation in health and disease. *European Journal of Pain, 9,* 463–484.

Appelbaum, P. S. (2002). Responses to the presidential debate—The systematic defunding of psychiatric care: A crisis at our doorstep. *American Journal of Psychiatry, 159,* 1638–1640.

Appleton, K. M., Gentry, R. C., & Shepherd, R. (2006). Evidence of a role for conditioning in the development of liking for flavours in humans in everyday life. *Physiology & Behavior, 87,* 478–486.

Aquilino, W. S. (2006). Family relationships and support systems in emerging adulthood. In J. J. Arnett & J. L. Tanner (Eds.), *Emerging adults in America: Coming of age in the 21st century.* Washington, DC: American Psychological Association.

Arcelus, J., Whight, D., Langham, C., Baggott, J., McGrain, L., Meadows, L., & Meyer, C. (2009). A case series evaluation of the modified version of interpersonal psychotherapy (IPT) for the treatment of bulimic eating disorders: A pilot study. *European Eating Disorders Review, 17*(4), 260–268. doi:10.1002/(ISSN)1099-096810.1002/erv.v17:410.1002/erv.932.

Archer, J. (1996). Sex differences in social behavior: Are the social role and evolutionary explanations compatible? *American Psychologist, 51,* 909–917.

Archer, J. (2005). Are women or men the more aggressive sex? In S. Fein, G. R. Goethals, & M. J.

Sansdtrom (Eds.), *Gender and aggression: Inter-disciplinary perspectives.* Mahwah, NJ: Erlbaum.

Archibald, A. B., Graber, J. A., & Brooks-Gunn, J. (2003). Pubertal processes and physiological growth in adolescence. In G. R. Adams & M. D. Berzonsky (Eds.), *Blackwell handbook of adolescence.* Malden, MA: Blackwell Publishing.

Arden, R., Gottfredson, L. S., & Miller, G. (2009). Does a fitness factor contribute to the association between intelligence and health outcomes? Evidence from medical abnormality counts among 3654 U.S. veterans. *Intelligence, 37*(6), 581–591. doi:10.1016/j.intell.2009.03.008

Arendt, J. (2009). Managing jet lag: Some of the problems and possible new solutions. *Sleep Medicine Reviews, 13*(4), 249–256. doi:10.1016/j.smrv.2008.07.011

Arendt, J. (2010). Shift work: Coping with the biological clock. *Occupational Medicine, 60*(1), 10–20. doi:10.1093/occmed/kqp162

Arendt, J., & Skene, D. J. (2005). Melatonin as a chronobiotic. *Sleep Medicine Review, 9*(1), 25–39.

Arendt, J., Stone, B., & Skene, D. J. (2000). Jet lag and sleep disruption. In M. H. Kryger, T. Roth, & W. C. Dement (Eds.), *Principles and practice of sleep medicine.* Philadelphia, PA: Saunders.

Arendt, J., Stone, B., & Skene, D. J. (2005). Sleep disruption in jet lag and other circadian rhythm-related disorders. In M. H. Kryger, T. Roth, & W. C. Dement (Eds.). *Principles and practice of sleep medicine.* Philadelphia, PA: Elsevier Saunders.

Argyle, M. (1987). *The psychology of happiness.* London: Metheun.

Argyle, M. (1999). Causes and correlates of happiness. In D. Kahneman, E. Diener, & N. Schwarz (Eds.), *Well-being: The foundations of hedonic psychology.* New York, NY: Russell Sage Foundation.

Argyle, M. (2001). *The psychology of happiness.* New York, NY: Routledge.

Arkes, H. R., Wortmann, R. L., Saville, P. D., & Harkness, A. R. (1981). Hindsight bias among physicians weighing the likelihood of diagnoses. *Journal of Applied Psychology, 66,* 252–254.

Arkowitz, H., & Lilienfeld, S. O. (2007). The best medicine? How drugs stack up against talk therapy for the treatment of depression. *Scientific American Mind, 18*(5), 80–83.

Armbruster, B. B. (2000). Taking notes from lectures. In R. F. Flippo & D. C. Caverly (Eds.), *Handbook of college reading and study strategy research.* Mahwah, NJ: Erlbaum.

Arndt, J., & Vess, M. (2008). Tales from existential oceans: Terror management theory and how the awareness of our mortality affects us all. *Social and Personality Psychology Compass, 2*(2), 909–928. doi:10.1111/j.1751-9004.2008.00079.x

Arnett, J. J. (2000). Emerging adulthood: A theory of development from the late teens through the twenties. *American Psychologist, 55,* 469–480.

Arnett, J. J. (2001). Conceptions of the transition to adulthood: Perspectives from adolescence

to midlife. *Journal of Adult Development, 8,* 133–143.

Arnett, J. J. (2004). *Emerging adulthood: The winding road from the late teens through the twenties.* New York, NY: Oxford University Press.

Arnett, J. J. (2006). Emerging adulthood: Understanding the new way of coming of age. In J. J. Arnett & J. L. Tanner (Eds.), *Emerging adults in America: Coming of age in the 21st century.* Washington, DC: American Psychological Association.

Arnett, J. J. (2008). The neglected 95%: Why American psychology needs to become less American. *American Psychologist, 63*(7), 602–614. doi:10.1037/0003-066X.63.7.602.

Aron, A., Fisher, H., & Mashek, D. J. (2005). Reward, motivation, and emotion systems associated with early-stage intense romantic love. *Journal of Neurophysiology, 94*(1), 327–337.

Aronson, E., & Mills, J. (1959). The effect of severity of initiation on liking for a group. *Journal of Abnormal and Social Psychology, 59,* 177–181.

Arrigo, J. M., & Pezdek, K. (1997). Lessons from the study of psychogenic amnesia. *Current Directions in Psychological Science, 6,* 148–152.

Asch, S. E. (1951). Effects of group pressure on the modification and distortion of judgments. In H. Guetzkow (Ed.), *Groups, leadership and men.* Pittsburgh: Carnegie Press.

Asch, S. E. (1955). Opinions and social pressures. *Scientific American, 193*(5), 31–35.

Asch, S. E. (1956). Studies of independence and conformity: A minority of one against a unanimous majority. *Psychological Monographs, 70*(9, Whole No. 416).

Aserinsky, E., & Kleitman, N. (1953). Regularly occurring periods of eye mobility and concomitant phenomena during sleep. *Science, 118,* 273–274.

Assefi, S. L., & Garry, M. (2003). Absolut® memory distortions: Alcohol placebos influence the misinformation effect. *Psychological Science, 14*(1), 77–80.

Associated Press. (2010, March 30). U.K. panel calls climate data valid. *New York Times.* Retrieved from http://www.nytimes.com/2010/03/31/science/earth/31climate.html

Atkinson, J. W. (1974). The mainsprings of achievement-oriented activity. In J. W. Atkinson & J. O. Raynor (Eds.), *Motivation and achievement.* New York, NY: Wiley.

Atkinson, J. W. (1981). Studying personality in the context of an advanced motivational psychology. *American Psychologist, 36,* 117–128.

Atkinson, J. W. (1992). Motivational determinants of thematic appercetion. In C. P. Smith (Ed.), *Motivation and personality: Handbook of thematic content analysis.* New York, NY: Cambridge University Press.

Atkinson, J. W., & Litwin, G. H. (1960). Achievement motive and test anxiety conceived as motive to approach success and to avoid

failure. *Journal of Abnormal and Social Psychology, 60,* 52–63.

Atkinson, R. C., & Shiffrin, R. M. (1968). Human memory: A proposed system and its control processes. In K. W. Spence & J. T. Spence (Eds.), *The psychology of learning and motivation* (Vol. 2). New York, NY: Academic Press.

Atkinson, R. C., & Shiffrin, R. M. (1971). The control of short-term memory. *Scientific American, 225,* 82–90.

Ator, N. A. (2005). Conducting behavioral research: Methodological and laboratory animal welfare issues. In C. K. Akins, S. Panicker, & C. L. Cunningham (Eds.), *Laboratory animals in research and teaching: Ethics, care and methods.* Washington, DC: American Psychological Association.

Auyeung, B., Baron-Cohen, S., Ashwin, E., Knickmeyer, R., Taylor, K., Hackett, G., & Hines, M. (2009). Fetal testosterone predicts sexually differentiated childhood behavior in girls and in boys. *Psychological Science, 20*(2), 144–148. doi:10.1111/j.1467-9280.2009.02279.x

Ax, R. K., Bigelow, B. J., Harowski, K., Meredith, J. M., Nussbaum, D. & Taylor, R. R. (2008). Prescriptive authority for psychologists and the public sector: Serving underserved health care consumers. *Psychological Services, 5*(2), 184–197.

Ayanian, J. Z., & Cleary, P. D. (1999). Perceived risks of heart disease and cancer among cigarette smokers. *Journal of the American Medical Association, 281,* 1019–1021.

Ayotte, B. J., Margrett, J. A., & Hicks-Patrick, J. (2010). Physical activity in middle-aged and young-old adults: The roles of self-efficacy, barriers, outcome expectancies, self-regulatory behaviors and social support. *Journal of Health Psychology, 15*(2), 173–185. doi:10.1177/1359105309342283

Baars, B. J. (1986). *The cognitive revolution in psychology.* New York, NY: Guilford.

Back, M. D., Schmukle, S. C., & Egloff, B. (2010). Why are narcissists so charming at first sight? Decoding the narcissism-popularity link at zero acquaintance. *Journal of Personality and Social Psychology, 98*(1), 132–145. doi:10.1037/a0016338

Baddeley, A. D. (1986). *Working memory.* New York, NY: Oxford University Press.

Baddeley, A. D. (1989). The uses of working memory. In P. R. Soloman, G. R. Goethals, C. M. Kelley, & B. R. Stephens (Eds.), *Memory: Interdisciplinary approaches.* New York, NY: Springer-Verlag.

Baddeley, A. D. (1992). Working memory. *Science, 255,* 556–559.

Baddeley, A. D. (2001). Is working memory still working? *American Psychologist, 56,* 851–864.

Baddeley, A. D. (2003). Working memory: Looking back and looking forward. *Nature Reviews Neuroscience, 4,* 829–839.

Baddeley, A. D. (2007). *Working memory, thought, and action.* New York, NY: Oxford University Press.

Baddeley, A. D., & Hitch, G. (1974). Working memory. In G. H. Bower (Ed.), *The psychology of learning and motivation* (Vol. 8). New York, NY: Academic Press.

Bahrick, H. P. (2000). Long-term maintenance of knowledge. In E. Tulving & F. I. M. Craik (Eds.), *The Oxford handbook of memory* (pp. 347–362). New York, NY: Oxford University Press.

Bailey, C. H., & Kandel, E. R. (2009). Synaptic and cellular basis of learning. In G. G. Berntson & J. T. Cacioppo (Eds.), *Handbook of neuroscience for the behavioral sciences* (Vol. 1, pp. 528–551). Hoboken, NJ: Wiley.

Bailey, J. M. (2003). Biological perspectives on sexual orientation. In L. D. Garnets & D. C. Kimmel (Eds.), *Psychological perspectives on lesbian, gay, and bisexual experiences*. New York, NY: Columbia University Press.

Bailey, J. M., & Pillard, R. C. (1991). A genetic study of male homosexual orientation. *Archives of General Psychology, 48,* 1089–1097.

Bailey, J. M., Pillard, R. C., Neale, M. C. I., & Agyei, Y. (1993). Heritable factors influence sexual orientation in women. *Archives of General Psychiatry, 50,* 217–223.

Bailey, J. M., & Zucker, K. J. (1995). Childhood sex-typed behavior and sexual orientation: A conceptual analysis and quantitative review. *Developmental Psychology, 31,* 43–55.

Baillargeon, R. (2002). The acquisition of physical knowledge in infancy: A summary in eight lessons. In U. Goswami (Ed.), *Blackwell handbook of childhood cognitive development*. Malden, MA: Blackwell Publishing.

Baillargeon, R. (2004). Infants' physical world. *Current Directions in Psychological Science, 13*(3), 89–94.

Baillargeon, R. (2008). Innate ideas revisited: For a principle of persistence in infants' physical reasoning. *Perspectives on Psychological Science, 3*(1), 2–13.

Bains, J. S., & Oliet, S. H. R. (2007). Glia: They make your memories stick! *Trends in Neuroscience, 30,* 417–424.

Baker, G. J., Suchday, S., & Krantz, D. S. (2007). Heart disease/attack. In G. Fink (Ed.), *Encyclopedia of stress*. San Diego, CA: Elsevier.

Balcetis, E., & Dunning, D. A. (2010). Wishful seeing: More desired objects are seen as closer. *Psychological Science, 21*(1), 147–152. doi:10.1177/0956797609356283.

Baldessarini, R. J., Tondo, L., Strombom, I. M., Dominguez, S., Fawcett, J., Licinio, J., Oquendo, M. A., Tollefson, G. D., Valuck, R. J., & Tohen, M. (2007). Ecological studies of antidepressant treatment and suicidal risks. *Harvard Review of Psychiatry, 15,* 133–145.

Baldwin, E. (1993). The case for animal research in psychology. *Journal of Social Issues, 49*(1), 121–131.

Baldwin, W. (2000). Information no one else knows: The value of self-report. In A. A. Stone, J. S. Turkkan, C. A. Bachrach, J. B. Jobe, H. S. Kurtzman, & V. Cain (Eds.), *The science of self-report: Implications for research and practice*. Mahwah, NJ: Erlbaum.

Bale, T. L., Baram, T. Z., Brown, A. S., Goldstein, J. M., Insel, T. R., McCarthy, M. M., et al. (2010). Early life programming and neurodevelopmental disorders. *Biological Psychiatry, 68*(4), 314–319. doi:10.1016/j.biopsych.2010.05.028

Ball, K., Edwards, J. D., & Ross, L. A. (2007). The impact of speed of processing training on cognitive and everyday functions. *Journals of Gerontology: Series B, 62B* (Special Issue 1), 19–31.

Balter, M. (2010). Did working memory spark creative culture? *Science, 328*(5975), 160–163. doi:10.1126/science.328.5975.160

Banaji, M. R., & Heiphetz, L. (2010). Attitudes. In S. T. Fiske, D. T. Gilbert, & G. Lindzey (Eds.), *Handbook of social psychology* (Vol. 1, 5th ed., pp. 353–393). Hoboken, NJ: Wiley.

Bandura, A. (1977). *Social learning theory.* Englewood Cliffs, NJ: Prentice-Hall.

Bandura, A. (1982). The psychology of chance encounters and life paths. *American Psychologist, 37,* 747–755.

Bandura, A. (1986). *Social foundations of thought and action: A social-cognitive theory.* Englewood Cliffs, NJ: Prentice-Hall.

Bandura, A. (1990). Perceived self-efficacy in the exercise of personal agency. *Journal of Applied Sport Psychology, 2*(2), 128–163.

Bandura, A. (1993). Perceived self-efficacy in cognitive development and functioning. *Educational Psychologist, 28*(2), 117–148.

Bandura, A. (1995). Exercise of personal and collective efficacy in changing societies. In A. Bandura (Ed.), *Self-efficacy in changing societies.* New York, NY: Cambridge University Press.

Bandura, A. (1999a). Social cognitive theory of personality. In L. A. Pervin & O. P. John (Eds.), *Handbook of personality: Theory and research.* New York, NY: Guilford.

Bandura, A. (1999b). A sociocognitive analysis of substance abuse: An agentic perspective. *Psychological Science, 10*(3), 214–217.

Bandura, A. (2006). Toward a psychology of human agency. *Perspectives on Psychological Science, 1,* 164–180.

Bandura, A., Ross, D., & Ross, S. A. (1963a). Imitation of film-mediated aggressive models. *Journal of Abnormal and Social Psychology, 66,* 3–11.

Bandura, A., Ross, D., & Ross. S. A. (1963b). Vicarious reinforcement and imitative learning. *Journal of Abnormal and Social Psychology, 67*(6), 6011–607.

Banich, M. T., & Heller, W. (1998). Evolving perspectives on lateralization of function. *Current Directions in Psychological Science, 7,* 1.

Banks, S., & Dinges, D. F. (2007). Behavioral and physiological consequences of sleep restriction. *Journal of Clinical Sleep Medicine, 3*(5), 519–528.

Banks, W. A., & Watkins, L. R. (2006). Mediation of chronic pain: Not by neurons alone. *Pain, 124,* 1–2.

Banks, W. P., & Krajicek, D. (1991). Perception. *Annual Review of Psychology, 42,* 305–331.

Banyard, V. L., & Williams, L. M. (1999). Memories for child sexual abuse and mental health functioning: Findings on a sample of women and implications for future research. In L. M. Williams & V. L. Banyard (Eds.), *Trauma & memory.* Thousand Oaks, CA: Sage Publications.

Baral, B. D., & Das, J. P. (2004). Intelligence: What is indigenous to India and what is shared? In R. J. Sternberg (Ed.), *International handbook of intelligence.* New York, NY: Cambridge University Press.

Barber, L., Munz, D., Bagsby, P., & Powell, E. (2010). Sleep consistency and sufficiency: Are both necessary for less psychological strain? *Stress & Health: Journal of the International Society for the Investigation of Stress, 26*(3), 186–193.

Barber, T. X. (1979). Suggested ("hypnotic") behavior: The trance paradigm versus an alternative paradigm. In E. Fromm & R. E. Shor (Eds.), *Hypnosis: Developments in research and new perspectives.* New York, NY: Aldine.

Barber, T. X. (1986). Realities of stage hypnosis. In B. Zilbergeld, M. G. Edelstien, & D. L. Araoz (Eds.), *Hypnosis: Questions and answers.* New York, NY: Norton.

Barch, D. M. (2003). Cognition in schizophrenia: Does working memory work? *Current Directions in Psychological Science, 12*(4), 146–150.

Bard, P. (1934). On emotional experience after decortication with some remarks on theoretical views. *Psychological Review, 41,* 309–329.

Bargh, J. A., Gollwitzer, P. M., & Oettingen, G. (2010). Motivation. In S. T. Fiske, D. T. Gilbert, & G. Lindzey (Eds.), *Handbook of social psychology* (5th ed., Vol. 1, pp. 268–316). New York, NY: Wiley.

Bargh, J. A., & McKenna, K. Y. A. (2004). The Internet and social life. *Annual Review of Psychology, 55,* 573–590.

Bargh, J. A., McKenna, K. Y. A., & Fitzsimons, G. M. (2002). Can you see the real me? Activation and expression of the "true self" on the Internet. *Journal of Social Issues, 58,* 33–48.

Barlett, D. L., & Steele, J. B. (1979). *Empire: The life, legend and madness of Howard Hughes.* New York, NY: Norton.

Barlow, D. H., Pincus, D. B., Heinrichs, N., & Choate, M. L. (2003). Anxiety disorders. In G. Stricker & T. A. Widiger (Eds.), *Handbook of psychology, Vol. 8: Clinical psychology.* New York, NY: Wiley.

Barnes, V. A., Treiber, F., & Davis, H. (2001). The impact of Transcendental Meditation on cardiovascular function at rest and during acute stress in adolescents with high normal blood pressure. *Journal of Psychosomatic Research, 51,* 597–605.

Barnett, S. W. (2004). Does Head Start have lasting cognitive effects? The myth of fade-out. In E. Zigler & S. J. Styfco (Eds.), *The Head Start debates.* Baltimore, MD: Paul H. Brooks Publishing.

Barrett, L. F., Mesquita, B., Ochsner, K. N., & Gross, J. J. (2007). The experience of emotion. *Annual Review of Psychology, 58,* 373–403.

Barry-Walsh, J. (2005). Dissociative identity disorder. *Australian & New Zealand Journal of Psychiatry, 39*(1-2), 109–110.

Barsky, A. J. (1988). The paradox of health. *New England Journal of Medicine, 318,* 414–418.

Bartels, M., Rietveld, M. J. H., Van Baal, G. C. M., & Boomsma, D. I. (2002). Genetic and environmental influences on the development of intelligence. *Behavior Genetics, 32*(4), 237–249.

Bartoshuk, L. M. (1988). Taste. In R. C. Atkinson, R. J. Herrnstein, G. Lindzey, & R. D. Luce (Eds.), *Stevens' handbook of experimental psychology: Perception and motivation* (Vol. 1). New York, NY: Wiley.

Bartoshuk, L. M. (1993a). Genetic and pathological taste variation: What can we learn from animal models and human disease? In D. Chadwick, J. Marsh, & J. Goode (Eds.), *The molecular basis of smell and taste transduction*. New York, NY: Wiley.

Bartoshuk, L. M. (1993b). The biological basis of food perception and acceptance. *Food Quality and Preference, 4,* 21–32.

Bartoshuk, L. M., & Beauchamp, G. K. (1994). Chemical senses. *Annual Review of Psychology, 45,* 419–449.

Bartoshuk, L. M., Duffy, V. B., & Miller, I. J. (1994). PTC/PROP taste: Anatomy, psychophysics, and sex effects. *Physiology & Behavior, 56,* 1165–1171.

Bartz, J. A., & Hollander, E. (2006). The neuroscience of affiliation: Forging links between basic and clinical research on neuropeptides and social behavior. *Hormones and Behavior, 50*(4), 518–528. doi:10.1016/j.yhbeh.2006.06.018

Basbaum, A. I., & Jessel, T. M. (2000). The perception of pain. In E. R. Kandel, J. H. Schwartz, & T. M. Jessell (Eds.), *Principles of neural science*. New York, NY: McGraw-Hill.

Basow, S. A. (1992). *Gender: Stereotypes and roles*. Pacific Grove, CA: Brooks/Cole.

Bassok, M. (2003). Analogical transfer in problem solving. In J. E. Davidson & R. J. Sternberg (Eds.), *The psychology of problem solving*. New York, NY: Cambridge University Press.

Basson, M. D., Bartoshuk, L. M., Dichello, S. Z., Panzini, L., Weiffenbach, J. M., & Duffy, V. B. (2005). Association between 6-n-propylthiouracil (PROP) bitterness and colonic neoplasms. *Digestive Diseases Sciences, 50,* 483–489.

Bassuk, E. L., Buckner, J. C., Perloff, J. N., & Bassuk, S. S. (1998). Prevalence of mental health and substance use disorders among homeless and low-income housed mothers. *American Journal of Psychiatry, 155,* 1561–1564.

Batterham, P. J., Christensen, H., & Mackinnon, A. J. (2009). Fluid intelligence is independently associated with all-cause mortality over 17 years in an elderly community sample: An investigation of potential mechanisms. *Intelligence, 37*(6), 551–560. doi:10.1016/j.intell.2008.10.004

Batty, G., Deary, I., & Gottfredson, L. (2007). Premorbid (early life) IQ and later mortality risk: Systematic review. *Annals of Epidemiology, 17*(4), 278–288.

Baum, A., Grunberg, N. E., & Singer, J. E. (1992). Biochemical measurements in the study of emotion. *Psychological Science, 3,* 56–60.

Baumeister, R. F. (1989). The optimal margin of illusion. *Journal of Social and Clinical Psychology, 8,* 176–189.

Baumeister, R. F. (2000). Gender differences in erotic plasticity: The female sex drive as socially flexible and responsive. *Psychological Bulletin, 126,* 347–374.

Baumeister, R. F. (2004). Gender and erotic plasticity: Sociocultural influences on the sex drive. *Sexual and Relationship Therapy, 19,* 133–139.

Baumeister, R. F., & Leary, M. R. (1995). The need to belong: Desire for interpersonal attachments as a fundamental human motivation. *Psychological Bulletin, 117,* 497–529.

Baumeister, R. F., & Twenge, J. M. (2002). Cultural suppression of female sexuality. *Review of General Psychology, 6,* 166–203.

Baumeister, R. F., & Vohs, K. D. (2001). Narcissism as addiction to esteem. *Psychological Inquiry, 12*(4), 206–210.

Baumrind, D. (1964). Some thoughts on the ethics of reading Milgram's "Behavioral study of obedience." *American Psychologist, 19,* 421–423.

Baumrind, D. (1985). Research using intentional deception: Ethical issues revisited. *American Psychologist, 40,* 165–174.

Baylis, G. C., & Driver, J. (1995). One-sided edge assignment in vision: 1. Figure-ground segmentation and attention to objects. *Current Directions in Psychological Science, 4,* 140–146.

Beck, A. T. (1976). *Cognitive therapy and the emotional disorders*. New York, NY: International Universities Press.

Beck, A. T. (1987). Cognitive therapy. In J. K. Zeig (Ed.), *The evolution of psychotherapy*. New York, NY: Brunner/Mazel.

Beck, A. T. (1991). Cognitive therapy: A 30-year retrospective. *American Psychologist, 46,* 368–375.

Beck, A. T. (1997). Cognitive therapy: Reflections. In J. K. Zeig (Ed.), *The evolution of psychotherapy: The third conference*. New York, NY: Brunner/Mazel.

Beck, A. T. (2008). The evolution of the cognitive model of depression and its neurobiological correlates. *American Journal of Psychiatry, 165*(8), 969–977. doi:10.1176/appi.ajp.2008.08050721

Beck, A. T., & Weishaar, M. E. (2011). Cognitive therapy. In R. J. Corsini & D. Wedding (Eds.), *Current psychotherapies* (9th ed.). Belmont, CA: Brooks/Cole.

Beck, H. P., Levinson, S., & Irons, G. (2009). Finding Little Albert: A journey to John B. Watson's infant laboratory. *American Psychologist, 64*(7), 605–614. doi:10.1037/a0017234.

Becker, A., & Fay, K. (2006). Sociocultural issues and eating disorders. In S. Wonderlich, J. Mitchell, M. de Zwaan, & H. Steiger (Eds.), *Annual review of eating disorders*. Oxon, England: Radcliffe.

Becker, A. L. (2009, November 29). Science of memory: Researchers to study pieces of unique brain. *The Hartford Courant*. Retrieved from http://www.courant.com

Beckers, T., Miller, R. R., DeHouwer, J., & Urushihara, K. (2006). Reasoning rats: Forward blocking in Pavlovian animal conditioning is sensitive to constraints of causal inference. *Journal of Experimental Psychology: General, 135,* 92–102.

Becskei, C., Lutz, T. A., & Riediger, T. (2008). Glucose reverses fasting-induced activation in the arcuate nucleus of mice. *Neuroreport: For Rapid Communication of Neuroscience Research, 19*(1), 105–109.

Beddoe, R., Costanza, R., Farley, JU., Garza, E., Kent, J., Kubiszewski, I., Martinez, L., McCowen, T., Murphy, KI., Myers, N., Ogden, Z., Stapleton, K., & Woodward, J. (2009). Overcoming systematic roadblocks to sustainability: The evolutionary redesign of worldviews, institutions, and technologies. *Proceedings from the National Academy of Science (PNAS), 106,* 2483–2489.

Beeman, M. J., & Chiarello, C. (1998). Complementary right and left hemisphere language comprehension. *Current Directions in Psychological Science, 7,* 2–7.

Beer, J. M., Arnold, R. D., & Loehlin, J. C. (1998). Genetic and environmental influences on MMPI Factor Scales: Joint model fitting to twin and adoption data. *Journal of Personality and Social Psychology, 74,* 818–827.

Beer, J. S., Shimamura, A. P., & Knight, R. T. (2004). Frontal lobe contributions to executive control of cognitive and social behavior. In M. S. Gazzaniga (Ed.), *The cognitive neurosciences*. Cambridge, MA: MIT Press.

Beidel, D. C., & Stipelman, B. (2007). Anxiety disorders. In M. Hersen, S. M. Turner, & D. C. Beidel (Eds.), *Adult psychopathology and diagnosis*. New York, NY: Wiley.

Beilin, H. (1992). Piaget's enduring contribution to developmental psychology. *Developmental Psychology, 28,* 191–204.

Bekelman, J. E., Li, Y., & Gross, C. P. (2003). Scope and impact of financial conflicts of interest in biomedical research. *Journal of the American Medical Association, 289,* 454–465.

Békésy, G. von. (1947). The variation of phase along the basilar membrane with sinusoidal vibrations. *Journal of the Acoustical Society of America, 19,* 452–460.

Bekkouche, N. S., Holmes, S., Whittaker, K. S., & Krantz, D. S. (2011). Stress and the heart: Psychosocial stress and coronary heart disease. In R. J. Contrada & A. Baum (Eds.), *The handbook of stress science: Biology, psychology, and health* (pp. 111–121). New York, NY: Springer Publishing.

Belger, A., & Barch, D. M. (2009). Cognitive neuroscience and neuroimaging in schizophrenia. In D. S. Charney & E. J. Nestler (Eds.), *Neurobiology of mental illness* (3rd ed., pp. 303–320). New York, NY: Oxford University Press.

Bell, A. P., Weinberg, M. S., & Hammersmith, S. K. (1981). *Sexual preference: Its development in men and women.* Bloomington: Indiana University Press.

Bellis, M. A., Downing, J., & Ashton, J. R. (2006). Adults at 12? Trends in puberty and their public health consequences. *Journal of Epidemiology and Community Health, 60,* 910–911.

Bem, D. J. (1996). Exotic becomes erotic: A developmental theory of sexual orientation. *Psychological Review, 103,* 320–335.

Bem, S. L. (1985). Androgyny and gender schema theory: A conceptual and empirical integration. In T. B. Sonderegger (Ed.), *Nebraska symposium on motivation, 1984: Psychology and gender* (Vol. 32). Lincoln: University of Nebraska Press.

Ben-Porath, Y. S. (2003). Assessing personality and psychopathology with self-report inventories. In J. R. Graham & J. A. Naglieri (Eds.), *Handbook of psychology, Vol. 10: Assessment psychology.* New York, NY: Wiley.

Bender, D. S., Skodol, A. E., Dyck, I. R., Markowitz, J. C., Shea, M. T., Yen, S., et al. (2007). Ethnicity and mental health treatment utilization by patients with personality disorders. *Journal of Consulting and Clinical Psychology, 75,* 992–999.

Benedetti, F. (2008). *Placebo effects: Understanding the mechanisms in health and disease.* New York, NY: Oxford University Press.

Benham, G. (2010). Sleep: An important factor in stress-health models. *Stress & Health: Journal of the International Society for the Investigation of Stress, 26*(3), 204–214.

Benjamin, L. R., & Simpson, J. A. (2009). The power of the situation: The impact of Milgram's obedience studies on personality and social psychology. *American Psychologist, 64*(1), 12–19.

Benjamin, L. T., Jr. (2000). The psychology laboratory at the turn of the 20th century. *American Psychologist, 55,* 318–321.

Benjamin, L. T., Jr., & Baker, D. B. (2004). *From seance to science: A history of the profession of psychology in America.* Belmont, CA: Wadsworth.

Benoît, M., & Norton, M. I. (2003). Perceptions of a fluid consensus: Uniqueness bias, false consensus, false polarization, and pluralistic ignorance in a water conservation crisis. *Personality and Social Psychology Bulletin, 29,* 559–567.

Benson, H. (1975). *The relaxation response.* New York, NY: Morrow.

Benson, H., & Klipper, M. Z. (1988). *The relaxation response.* New York, NY: Avon.

Bentall, R. P. (2009). *Doctoring the mind: Is our current treatment of mental illness really any good?* New York, NY: New York University Press.

Benton, D. (2004). Role of parents in the determination of the food preferences of children and the development of obesity. *International Journal of Obesity, 28,* 858–869.

Berenbaum, S. A., Martin, C. L., & Ruble, D. N. (2008). Gender development. In W. Damon & R. M. Lerner (Eds.), *Child and adolescent development: An advanced course* (pp. 647–681). New York, NY: Wiley.

Berenbaum, S. A., & Snyder, E. (1995). Early hormonal influences on childhood sex-typed activity and playmate preferences: Implications for the development of sexual orientation. *Developmental Psychology, 31,* 31–42.

Berghmans, R. L. P. (2007). Misleading research participants: Moral aspects of deception in psychological research. *Netherlands Journal of Psychology, 63*(1), 14–20.

Bergner, S., Monk, C., & Werner, E. A. (2008). Dyadic intervention during pregnancy? Treating pregnant women and possibly reaching the future baby. *Infant Mental Health Journal, 29*(5), 399–419. doi:10.1002/imhj.20190

Berkowitz, L. (1989). Frustration-aggression hypothesis: Examination and reformulation. *Psychological Bulletin, 106,* 59–73.

Berlin, L. J., Ispa, J. M., Fine, M. A., Brooks-Gunn, J., Brady-Smith, C., Ayoub, C., & Bai, Y. (2009). Correlates and consequences of spanking and verbal punishment for low-income White, African American, and Mexican American toddlers. *Child Development, 80*(5), 1403–1420. doi:10.1111/j.1467-8624.2009.01341.x.

Berman, A. L. (2009). Depression and suicide. In I. H. Gotlib & C. L. Hammen (Eds.), *Handbook of depression* (2nd ed.). New York, NY: Guilford.

Berman, M. G., Jonides, J., & Kaplan, S. (2008). The cognitive benefits of interacting with nature. *Psychological Science, 19,* 1207–1212.

Berman, R. M., Sporn, J., Charney, D. S., & Mathew, S. J. (2009). Principles of the pharmacotherapy of depression. In D. S. Charney & E. J. Nestler (Eds.), *Neurobiology of mental illness* (pp. 491–515). New York, NY: Guilford.

Bernstein, D. M., & Loftus, E. F. (2009). The consequences of false memories for food preferences and choices. *Perspectives on Psychological Science, 4*(2), 135–139. doi:10.1111/j.1745-6924.2009.01113.x

Bernstein, H. (2007). Maternal and perinatal infection-viral. In S. G. Gabbe, J. R. Niebyl, & J. L. Simpson (Eds.) *Obstetrics: Normal and problem pregnancies* (5th ed., pp. 1203–1232). Philadelphia, PA: Elsevier.

Berridge, K. C. (2004). Motivation concepts in behavioral neuroscience. *Physiology and Behavior, 81*(2), 179–209.

Berry, C. M., & Sackett, P. R. (2009). Individual differences in course choice result in underestimation of the validity of college admissions systems. *Psychological Science, 20*(7), 822–830. doi:10.1111/j.1467-9280.2009.02368.x.

Berry, D. T. R., Wetter, M. W., & Baer, R. A. (1995). Assessment of malingering. In J. N. Butcher (Ed.), *Clinical personality assessment: Practical approaches.* New York, NY: Oxford University Press.

Berry, J. W. (1994). Cross-cultural variations in intelligence. In R. J. Sternberg (Ed.), *Encyclopedia of human intelligence.* New York, NY: Macmillan.

Berry, J. W., Poortinga, Y., Segall, M., & Dasen, P. (1992). *Cross-cultural psychology.* New York, NY: Cambridge University Press.

Berscheid, E. (1988). Some comments on love's anatomy: Or, whatever happened to old-fashioned lust. In R. J. Sternberg & M. L. Barnes (Eds.), *The psychology of love.* New Haven: Yale University Press.

Berscheid, E. (2006). Searching for the meaning of "love." In R. J. Sternberg & K. Weis (Eds.), *The new psychology of love.* New Haven, CT: Yale University Press.

Bertenthal, B. I., & Clifton, R. K. (1998). Perception and action. In W. Damon (Ed.), *Handbook of child psychology, Vol. 2: Cognition, perception, and language.* New York, NY: Wiley.

Berto, R. (2005). Exposure to restorative environments helps restore attentional capacity. *Journal of Environmental Psychology, 25,* 249–259.

Bertram, L., & Tanzi, R. E. (2008). Thirty years of Alzheimer's disease genetics: The implications of systematic meta-analyses. *Nature Reviews Neuroscience, 9*(10), 768–778. doi:10.1038/nrn2494

Bertrand, R. M., & Lachman, M. E. (2003). Personality development in adulthood and old age. In R. M. Lerner, M. A. Easterbrooks, & J. Mistry (Eds.), *Handbook of psychology, Vol. 6: Developmental psychology.* New York, NY: Wiley.

Bettelheim, B. (1967). *The empty fortress.* New York, NY: Free Press.

Bettmann, J. E., & Jasperson, R. A. (2008). Adults in wilderness treatment: A unique application of attachment theory and research. *Clinical Social Work Journal, 36,* 51–61.

Beumont, P. J. V. (2002). Clinical presentation of anorexia nervosa and bulimia nervosa. In C. G. Fairburn & K. D. Brownell (Eds.), *Eating disorders and obesity: A comprehensive handbook.* New York, NY: Guilford.

Beusterien, K. M., Davis, E. A., Flood, R., Howard, K., & Jordan, J. (2008). HIV patient insight on adhering to medication: A qualitative analysis. *AIDS Care, 20,* 251–259.

Beutler, L. E. (2002). The dodo bird is extinct. *Clinical Psychology: Science & Practice, 9*(1), 30–34.

Beutler, L. E., Bongar, B., & Shurkin, J. N. (2001). *A consumer's guide to psychotherapy.* New York, NY: Oxford University Press.

Beutler, L. E., Malik, M., Alimohamed, S., Harwood, T. M., Talebi, H., Noble, S., & Wong, E. (2004). Therapist variables. In M. J. Lambert (Ed.), *Bergin and Garfield's handbook of psychotherapy and behavior change.* New York, NY: Wiley.

Bhasin, T., & Schendel, D. (2007). Sociodemographic risk factors for autism in a U.S. metropolitan area. *Journal of Autism and Developmental Disorders, 37,* 667–677.

Bhaskaran, K., Hamouda, O., Sannes, M., Boufassa, F., Johnson, A., Lambert, P., & Porter, K. (2008). Changes in the risk of death after HIV seroconversion compared with mortality in the general population. *Journal of the American Medical Association, 300*(1), 51–59.

Biblarz, T. J., & Stacey, J. (2010). How does the gender of parents matter? *Journal of Marriage and Family, 72*(1), 3–22. doi:10.1111/j.1741-3737 .2009.00678.x

Biederman, I., Hilton, H. J., & Hummel, J. E. (1991). Pattern goodness and pattern recognition. In G. R. Lockhead & J. R. Pomerantz (Eds.), *The perception of structure.* Washington, DC: American Psychological Association.

Biermann, T., Estel, D., Sperling, W., Bleich, S., Kornhuber, J., & Reulbach, U. (2005). Influence of lunar phases on suicide: The end of a myth? A population-based study. *Chronobiology International, 22*, 1137–1143.

Bigelow, B. J. (2006). There's an elephant in the room: The impact of early poverty and neglect on intelligence and common learning disorders in children, adolescents, and their parents. *Developmental Disabilities Bulletin, 34*(1–2), 177–215.

Birkeland, S. A., Manson, T. M., Kisamore, J. L., Brannick, M. T., & Smith, M. A. (2006). A meta-analytic investigation of job applicant faking on personality measures. *International Journal of Selection and Assessment, 14*, 317–335.

Birney, D. P., Citron-Pousty, J. H., Lutz, D. J., & Sternberg, R. J. (2005). The development of cognitive and intellectual abilities. In M. H. Bornstein & M. E. Lamb (Eds.), *Developmental science: An advanced textbook.* Mahwah, NJ: Erlbaum.

Birney, D. P., & Sternberg, R. J. (2011). The development of cognitive abilities. In M. H. Bornstein & M. E. Lamb (Eds.), *Developmental science: An advanced textbook* (pp. 353–388). New York, NY: Psychology Press.

Bishop, S. R. (2002). What do we really know about mindfulness-based stress reduction? *Psychosomatic Medicine, 64*(1), 71–83.

Bittman, M. (2008, January 27). Rethinking the meat guzzler. *The New York Times.* Retrieved from http://www.nytimes.com/2008/01/27/weekinreview/27bittman.html

Bjork, R. A. (1992). Interference and forgetting. In L. R. Squire (Ed.), *Encyclopedia of learning and memory.* New York, NY: Macmillan.

Bjorkland, D. E. (2005). *Children's thinking: Cognitive development and individual differences* (4th ed.). Belmont, CA: Wadsworth.

Blair, C., Gamson, D., Thorne, S., & Baker, D. (2005). Rising mean IQ: Cognitive demand of mathematics education for young children, population exposure to formal schooling, and the neurobiology of the prefrontal cortex. *Intelligence, 33*, 93–106.

Blair, S. N., Kohl, H. W., Paffenbarger, R. S., Clark, D. G., Cooper, K. H., & Gibbons, L. W. (1989). Physical fitness and all-cause mortality: A prospective study of healthy men and women. *Journal of the American Medical Association, 262*, 2395–2401.

Blakemore, S. (2008). Development of the social brain during adolescence. *The Quarterly Journal of Experimental Psychology, 61*(1), 40–49. doi:10.1080/17470210701508715

Blanchard, E. B., & Keefer, L. (2003). Irritable bowel syndrome. In A. M. Nezu, C. M. Nezu, & P. A. Geller (Eds.), *Handbook of psychology, Vol. 9: Health psychology.* New York, NY: Wiley.

Blanchard, F. A., Lilly, T., & Vaughn, L. A. (1991). Reducing the expression of racial prejudice. *Psychological Science, 2*, 101–105.

Blank, H., Musch, J., & Pohl, R. F. (2007). Hindsight bias: On being wise after the event. *Social Cognition, 25*(1), 1–9.

Blankenhorn, D. (1995). *Fatherless America: Confronting our most urgent social problem.* New York, NY: Basic Books.

Blass, T. (1999). The Milgram paradigm after 35 years: Some things we now know about obedience to authority. *Journal of Applied Social Psychology, 29*, 955–978.

Blass, T. (2009). From New Haven to Santa Clara: A historical perspective on the Milgram obedience experiments. *American Psychologist, 64*(1), 37–45. doi:10.1037/a0014434

Bleak, J., & Frederick, C. M. (1998). Superstitious behavior in sport: Levels of effectiveness and determinants of use in three collegiate sports. *Journal of Sport Behavior, 21*, 1-15.

Bleuler, E. (1911). *Dementia praecox or the group F schizophrenias.* New York, NY: International Universities Press.

Block, J. R., & Yuker, H. E. (1992). *Can you believe your eyes?: Over 250 illusions and other visual oddities.* New York, NY: Brunner/Mazel.

Block, N. (2002). How heritability misleads us about race. In J. Fish (Ed.), *Race and intelligence: Separating science from myth.* Mahwah, NJ: Erlbaum.

Boase, J., & Wellman, B. (2006). Personal relationships: On and off the Internet. In A. L. Vangelisti & D. Perlman (Eds.), *The Cambridge handbook of personal relationships.* New York, NY: Cambridge University Press.

Bobo, W. V., Rapoport, J. L., Abi-Dargham, A., Fatemi, H., & Meltzer, H. Y. (2008). The neurobiology of schizophrenia. In A. Tasman, J. Kay, J. A. Lieberman, M. B. First, & M. Maj (Eds.), *Psychiatry* (3rd ed.). New York, NY: Wiley-Blackwell.

Bochner, S., & Jones, J. (2003). *Child language development: Learning to talk.* London: Whurr Publishers.

Bodenhausen, G. V., Todd, A. R., & Richeson, J. A. (2009). Controlling prejudice and stereotyping: Antecedents, mechanisms, and contexts. In T. D. Nelson (Ed.), *Handbook of prejudice, stereotyping, and discrimination* (pp. 1–22). New York, NY: Psychology Press.

Bodenheimer, T. (2000). Uneasy alliance: Clinical investigators and the pharmaceutical industry. *New England Journal of Medicine, 342*, 1539–1544.

Boecker, H., Sprenger, T., Spilker, M. E., Henriksen, G., Koppenhoefer, M., & Wagner, K. J., et al. (2008). The runner's high: Opioidergic mechanisms in the human brain. *Cerebral Cortex, 18*(11), 2523–2531. doi:10.1093/cercor/bhn013

Bögels, S. M., & Voncken, M. (2008). Social skills training versus cognitive therapy for social anxiety disorder characterized by fear of blushing, trembling, or sweating. *International Journal of Cognitive Therapy, 1*(2), 138–150. doi:10.1521/ijct.2008.1.2.138

Bogg, T., & Roberts, B. W. (2004). Conscientiousness and health-related behaviors: A meta-analysis of the leading behavioral contributors to mortality. *Psychological Bulletin, 130*, 887–919.

Bohner, G., & Dickel, N. (2011). Attitudes and attitude change. *Annual Review of Psychology, 62*, 391–417.

Bohner, G., & Schwarz, N. (2001). Attitudes, persuasion, and behavior. In A. Tesser & N. Schwarz (Eds.), *Blackwell handbook of social psychology: Intraindividual processes.* Malden, MA: Blackwell.

Boland, R. J., & Keller, M. B. (2008). Antidepressants. In A. Tasman, J. Kay, J. A. Lieberman, M. B. First, & M. Maj (Eds.), *Psychiatry* (3rd ed.). New York, NY: Wiley-Blackwell.

Boldry, J. G., Gaertner, L., & Quinn, J. (2007). Measuring the measures: A meta-analytic investigation of the measures of outgroup homogeneity. *Group Processes & Intergroup Relations, 10*, 157–178.

Boles, D. B. (2005). A large-sample study of sex differences in functional cerebral lateralization. *Journal of Clinical and Experimental Neuropsychology, 27*(6), 759–768. doi:10.1081/13803390590954263

Bolger, N. (1990). Coping as a personality process: A prospective study. *Journal of Personality and Social Psychology, 59*, 525–537.

Bolles, R. C. (1975). *Theory of motivation.* New York, NY: Harper & Row.

Bolling, M. Y., Terry, C. M., & Kohlenberg, R. J. (2006). Behavioral theories. In J. C. Thomas & D. L. Segal (Eds.), *Comprehensive handbook of personality and psychopathology.* New York, NY: Wiley.

Boly, M., Faymonville, M.-E., Vogt, B. A., Maquet, P., & Laureys, S. (2007). Hypnotic regulation of consciousness and the pain neuromatrix. In G. A. Jamieson (Ed.), *Hypnosis and conscious states: The cognitive neuroscience perspective.* New York, NY: Oxford University Press.

Bonanno, G. A. (2005). Resilience in the face of potential trauma. *Current Directions in Psychological Science, 14*(3), 135–138.

Bond, R., & Smith, P. B. (1996). Culture and conformity: A meta-analysis of studies using Asch's line judgment task. *Psychological Bulletin, 119*, 111–137.

Bonnet, M. H. (2005). Acute sleep deprivation. In M. H. Kryger, T. Roth, & W. C. Dement (Eds.), *Principles and practice of sleep medicine.* Philadelphia, PA: Elsevier Saunders.

Bono, G., McCullough, M. E., & Root, L. M. (2008). Forgiveness, feeling connected to others, and well-being: Two longitudinal studies. *Personality and Social Psychology Bulletin, 34,* 182–195.

Bootzin, R. R., Manber, R., Loewy, D. H., Kuo, T. F., & Franzen, P. L. (2001). Sleep disorders. In P. B. Sutker & H. E. Adams (Eds.), *Comprehensive handbook of psychopathology.* New York, NY: Kluwer Academic/Plenum.

Borbely, A. A., & Achermann, P. (2005). Sleep homeostasis and models of sleep regulation. In M. H. Kryger, T. Roth, & W. C. Dement (Eds.), *Principles and practice of sleep medicine.* Philadelphia, PA: Elsevier Saunders.

Bordnick, P. S., Elkins, R. L., Orr, T. E., Walters, P., & Thyer, B. A. (2004). Evaluating the relative effectiveness of three aversion therapies designed to reduce craving among cocaine abusers. *Behavioral Interventions, 19*(1), 1–24.

Borgida, E., & Nisbett, R. E. (1977). The differential impact of abstract vs. concrete information on decisions. *Journal of Applied Social Psychology, 7,* 258–271.

Boring, E. G. (1966). A note on the origin of the word *psychology. Journal of the History of the Behavioral Sciences, 2,* 167.

Borkenau, P., Mauer, N., Riemann, R., Spinath, F. M., & Angleitner, A. (2004). Thin slices of behavior as cues of personality and intelligence. *Journal of Personality and Social Psychology, 86*(4), 599–614. doi:10.1037/0022-3514.86.4.599

Bornstein, R. F. (1989). Exposure and affect: Overview and meta-analysis of research, 1968–1987. *Psychological Bulletin, 106*(2), 265–289. doi:10.1037/0033-2909.106.2.265

Bornstein, R. F. (2003). Psychodynamic models of personality. In T. Millon & M. J. Lerner (Eds.), *Handbook of psychology, Vol. 5: Personality and social psychology.* New York, NY: Wiley.

Bosma, H., van Boxtel, M. P. J., Ponds, R. W. H. M., Houx, P. J., Burdorf, A., & Jolles, J. (2002). Mental work demands protect against cognitive impairment: MAAS prospective cohort study. *Experimental Aging Research, 29*(1), 33–45.

Bost, K. K., Cox, M. J., Burchinal, M. R., & Payne, C. (2002). Structural and supporting changes in couples' family and friendship networks across the transition to parenthood. *Journal of Marriage and the Family, 64,* 517–531.

Bouchard, T. J., Jr. (1997). IQ similarity in twins reared apart: Findings and responses to critics. In R. J. Sternberg, & E. L. Grigorenko (Eds.), *Intelligence, heredity, and environment.* New York, NY: Cambridge University Press.

Bouchard, T. J., Jr. (1998). Genetic and environmental influences on adult intelligence and special mental abilities. *Human Biology, 70,* 257–279.

Bouchard, T. J., Jr. (2004). Genetic influence on human psychological traits: A survey. *Current Directions in Psychological Science, 13*(4), 148–151.

Bouchard, T. J., Jr., Lykken, D. T., McGue, M., Segal, N. L., & Tellegen, A. (1990). Sources of human psychological differences: The Minnesota study of twins reared apart. *Science, 250,* 223–228.

Bourgeois, J. A., Seaman, J. S., & Servis, M. E. (2003). Delirium, dementia, and amnestic disorders. In R. E. Hales & S. C. Yudofsky (Eds.), *Textbook of clinical Psychiatry.* Washington, DC: American Psychiatric Publishing.

Bourguignon, E. (1972). Dreams and altered states of consciousness in anthropological research. In F. L. K. Hsu (Ed.), *Psychological anthropology* (2nd ed.). Cambridge, MA: Schenkman.

Bouton, M. E. (2000). A learning theory perspective on lapse, relapse, and the maintenance of behavior change. *Health Psychology, 19,* 57–63.

Bouton, M. E., & Woods, A. M. (2009). Extinction: Behavioral mechanisms and their implications. In J. H. Byrne (Ed.), *Concise learning and memory: The editor's selection.* San Diego, CA: Elsevier.

Bowd, A. D., & Shapiro, K. J. (1993). The case against laboratory animal research in psychology. *Journal of Social Issues, 49*(1), 133–142.

Bower, G. H. (1970). Organizational factors in memory. *Cognitive Psychology, 1,* 18–46.

Bower, G. H., & Springston, F. (1970). Pauses as recoding points in letter series. *Journal of Experimental Psychology, 83,* 421–430.

Bower, J. E., Moskowitz, J., & Epel, E. (2009). Is benefit finding good for your health? Pathways linking positive life changes after stress and physical health outcomes. *Current Directions in Psychological Science, 18*(6), 337–341.

Bowers, M. (2007, July/August). The making of the MFT profession: Standards, regulation. *Family Therapy Magazine,* pp. 12–18.

Bowlby, J. (1969). *Attachment and loss: Vol. 1. Attachment.* New York, NY: Basic Books.

Bowlby, J. (1973). *Attachment and loss: Vol. 2. Separation, anxiety and anger.* New York, NY: Basic Books.

Bowlby, J. (1980). *Attachment and loss: Vol. 3. Sadness and depression.* New York, NY: Basic Books.

Boyce, C. J., Brown, G. A., & Moore, S. C. (2010). Money and happiness: Rank of income, not income, affects life satisfaction. *Psychological Science, 21*(4), 471–475.

Boyle, G. J. (2008). Critique of the five-factor model of personality. In G. J. Boyle, G. Matthews, & D. H. Saklofske (Eds.), *The Sage handbook of personality theory and assessment: Personality theories and models* (Vol. 1, pp. 295–312). Los Angles, CA: Sage.

Boyle, M. (2007). The problem with diagnosis. *The Psychologist, 20,* 290–292.

Bradshaw, J. L. (1989). *Hemispheric specialization and psychological function.* New York, NY: Wiley.

Bragg, E. A. (1996). Towards ecological self: Deep ecology meets constructionist self-theory. *Journal of Environmental Psychology, 16,* 93–108.

Brainerd, C. J. (1996). Piaget: A centennial celebration. *Psychological Science, 7,* 191–195.

Brainerd, C. J., & Reyna, V. F. (2005). *The science of false memory.* New York, NY: Oxford University Press.

Branaman, T. F., & Gallagher, S. N. (2005). Polygraph testing in sex offender treatment: A review of limitations. *American Journal of Forensic Psychology, 23*(1), 45–64.

Brannon, L., & Feist, J. (2007). *Health psychology: An introduction to behavior and health.* Belmont, CA: Wadsworth.

Branson, R. (2005). *Losing my virginity: The autobiography.* London: Virgin.

Branson, R. (2006). *Screw it, let's do it: Lessons in life.* London: Virgin.

Braun, M., Lewin-Epstein, N., Stier, H., & Baumgärtner, M. K. (2008). Perceived equity in the gendered division of household labor. *Journal of Marriage and Family, 70*(5), 1145–1156. doi:10.1111/j.1741-3737.2008.00556.x

Bravo, M. (2010). Context effects in perception. In E. B. Goldstein (Ed.), *Encyclopedia of perception.* Thousand Oaks, CA: Sage.

Bredt, B. M., Higuera-Alhino, D., Hebert, S. J., McCune, J. M., & Abrams, D. I. (2002). Short-term effects of cannabinoids on immune phenotype and function in HIV-1-infected patients. *Journal of Clinical Pharmacology, 42,* 90S–96S.

Breedlove, S. M. (1994). Sexual differentiation of the human nervous system. *Annual Review of Psychology, 45,* 389–418.

Breggin, P. R. (1991). *Toxic psychiatry.* New York, NY: St. Martin's Press.

Breggin, P. R. (2008). *Medication madness: A psychiatrist exposes the dangers of mood-altering medications.* New York, NY: St. Martin's Press.

Brehm, J. W. (1966). *A theory of psychological reactance.* New York, NY: Academic Press.

Breland, K., & Breland, M. (1961). The misbehavior of organisms. *American Psychologist, 16,* 681–684.

Bretherton, I., & Munholland, K. A. (2008). Internal working models in attachment relationships: Conceptual and empirical aspects of security. In J. Cassidy & P. R. Shaver (Eds.), *Handbook of attachment: Theory, research, and clinical applications* (2nd ed., pp. 102–130). New York, NY: Guilford.

Breugelmans, S. M., Poortinga, Y. H., Ambadar, Z., Setiadi, B., Vaca, J. B., Widiyanto, P., et al. (2005). Body sensations associated with emotions in Raramuri Indians, rural Javanese, and three student samples. *Emotion, 5,* 166–174.

Brewer, C. L. (1991). Perspectives on John B. Watson. In G. A. Kimble, M. Wertheimer, & C. White (Eds.), *Portraits of pioneers in psychology.* Hillside, NJ: Erlbaum.

Brewer, W. F. (2000). Bartlett, functionalism, and modern schema theories. *Journal of Mind and Behavior, 21,* 37–44.

Brewer, W. F., & Treyens, J. C. (1981). Role of schemata in memory for places. *Cognitive Psychology, 13,* 207–230.

Brewin, C. R. (2007). Autobiographical memory for trauma: Update on four controversies. *Memory, 15,* 227–248.

Bridge, J. A., & Barbe, R. P. (2004). Reducing hospital readmission in depression and schizophrenia: Current evidence. *Current Opinion in Psychiatry, 17,* 505–511.

Bridge, J. A., Iyengar, S., Salary, C. B., Barbe, R. P., Birmaher, B., Pincus, H. A., et al. (2007). Clinical response and risk for reported suicidal ideation and suicide attempts in pediatric antidepressant treatment: A meta-analysis of randomized controlled trials. *Journal of the American Medical Association, 297,* 1683–1969.

Brien, S. E., Ronksley, P. E., Turner, B. J., Mukamal, K. J., & Ghali, W. A. (2011). Effect of alcohol consumption on biological markers associated with risk of coronary heart disease: Systematic review and meta-analysis of interventional studies. *BMJ: British Medical Journal, 342*(7795), 480.

Briere, J., & Conte, J. R. (1993). Self-reported amnesia for abuse in adults molested as children. *Journal of Traumatic Stress, 6*(1), 21–31.

Brislin, R. (2000). *Understanding culture's influence on behavior.* Belmont, CA: Wadsworth.

Broadbent, D. E. (1958). *Perception and communication.* New York, NY: Pergamon Press.

Brobeck, J. R., Tepperman, T., & Long, C. N. (1943). Experimental hypothalamic hyperphagia in the albino rat. *Yale Journal of Biology and Medicine, 15,* 831–853.

Bröder, A. (1998). Deception can be acceptable. *American Psychologist, 53,* 805–806.

Brody, N. (1992). *Intelligence* (2nd ed.). San Diego, CA: Academic Press.

Brody, N. (2003). Jensen's genetic interpretation of racial differences in intelligence: Critical evaluation. In H. Nyborg (Ed.), *The scientific study of general intelligence: Tribute to Arthur R. Jensen.* Oxford, UK: Pergamon.

Broida, J., Tingley, L., Kimball, R., & Miele, J. (1993). Personality differences between pro- and anti-vivisectionists. *Society and Animals, 1,* 129–144.

Broughton, R. (1994). Important underemphasized aspects of sleep onset. In R. D. Ogilvie & J. R. Harsh (Eds.), *Sleep onset: Normal and abnormal processes.* Washington, DC: American Psychological Association.

Brown, A. S. (1991). A review of the tip-of-the-tongue experience. *Psychological Bulletin, 109,* 204–223.

Brown, A. S., & Derkits, E. J. (2010). Prenatal infection and schizophrenia: A review of epidemiologic and translational studies. *American Journal of Psychiatry, 167*(3), 261–280. doi:10.1176/appi.ajp.2009.09030361

Brown, A. S., & Susser, E. S. (2008). Prenatal nutritional deficiency and risk of adult schizophrenia. *Schizophrenia Bulletin, 34*(6), 1054–1063. doi:10.1093/schbul/sbn096

Brown, E. J., Juster, H. R., Heimberg, R. G., & Winning, C. D. (1998). Stressful life events and personality styles: Relation to impairment and treatment outcome in patients with social phobia. *Journal of Anxiety Disorders, 12,* 233–251.

Brown, H. D., & Kosslyn, S. M. (1993). Cerebral lateralization. *Current Opinion in Neurobiology, 3,* 183–186.

Brown, M. (1974). Some determinants of persistence and initiation of achievement-related activities. In J. W. Atkinson & J. O. Raynor (Eds.), *Motivation and achievement.* Washington, DC: Halsted.

Brown, M. (1998). *Richard Branson: The inside story.* London: Headline.

Brown, R., & Kulik, J. (1977). Flashbulb memories. *Cognition, 5,* 73–79.

Brown, R., & McNeill, D. (1966). The "tip-of-the-tongue" phenomenon. *Journal of Verbal Learning and Verbal Behavior, 5*(4), 325–337.

Brown, R. D., Goldstein, E., & Bjorklund, D. F. (2000). The history and zeitgeist of the repressed–false-memory debate: Scientific and sociological perspectives on suggestibility and childhood memory. In D. F. Bjorklund (Ed.), *False-memory creation in children and adults* (pp. 1–30). Mahwah, NJ: Erlbaum.

Brown, R. T. (1989). Creativity: What are we to measure? In J. A. Glover, R. R. Ronning, & C. R. Reynolds (Eds.), *Handbook of creativity.* New York, NY: Plenum.

Brown, S. C., & Craik, F. I. M. (2000). Encoding and retrieval of information. In E. Tulving & F. I. M. Craik (Eds.), *The Oxford handbook of memory* (pp. 93–108). New York, NY: Oxford University Press.

Brown, W. D. (2006). Insomnia: Prevalence and daytime consequences. In T. Lee-Chiong (Ed.), *Sleep: A comprehensive handbook.* Hoboken, NJ: Wiley-Liss.

Brownell, H. H., & Gardner, H. (1981). Hemisphere specialization: Definitions not incantations. *Behavioral and Brain Sciences, 4,* 64–65.

Bruce, D., Dolan, A., & Phillips-Grant, K. (2000). On the transition from childhood amnesia to the recall of personal memories. *Psychological Science, 11,* 360–364.

Bruckner-Gordon, F., Gangi, B. K., & Wallman, G. U. (1988). *Making therapy work: Your guide to choosing, using, and ending therapy.* New York, NY: Harper & Row.

Bruer, J. T. (1999). *The myth of the first three years: A new understanding of early brain development and life-long learning.* New York, NY: Free Press.

Bruer, J. T. (2002). Avoiding the pediatricians error: How neuroscientists can help educators (and themselves). *Nature Neuroscience, 5,* 1031–1033.

Brugha, T. S., McManus, S., Bankart, J., Scott, F., Purdon, S., Smith, J., Bebbington, P., Jenkins, R., & Meltzer, H. (2011). Epidemiology of autism spectrum disorders in adults in the community in England. *Archives of General Psychiatry, 68*(5), 459–466. doi:10.1001/archgenpsychiatry.2011.38

Brumbaugh, C. C., & Fraley, R. C. (2006). Transference and attachment: How do attachment patterns get carried forward from one relationship to the next? *Personality and Social Psychology Bulletin, 32,* 552–560.

Bryden, M. P. (1982). *Laterality: Functional asymmetry in the intact brain.* New York, NY: Academic Press.

Buccino, G., & Riggio, L. (2006). The role of the mirror neuron system in motor learning. *Kinesiology, 38*(1), 5–15.

Buck, L. B. (2000). Smell and taste: The chemical senses. In E. R. Kandel, J. H. Schwartz, & T. M. Jessell (Eds.), *Principles of neural science.* New York, NY: McGraw-Hill.

Buck, L. B. (2004). Olfactory receptors and coding in mammals. *Nutrition Reviews, 62,* S184–S188.

Buckley, K. W. (1982). The selling of a psychologist: John Broadus Watson and the application of behavioral techniques to advertising. *Journal of the History of Behavioral Sciences, 18*(3), 207–221. doi:10.1002/1520-6696(198207)18: 3<207::AID-JHBS2300180302.3.0.CO;2–8

Buckley, K. W. (1994). Misbehaviorism: The case of John B. Watson's dismissal from Johns Hopkins University. In J. T. Todd & E. K. Morris (Eds.), *Modern perspectives on John B. Watson and classical behaviorism.* Westport, CT: Greenwood Press.

Buckman, R. (2002). Communications and emotions: Skills and effort are key. *British Medical Journal, 325,* 672.

Bufe, B., Breslin, P. A. S., Kuhn, C., Reed, D. R., Tharp, C. D., Slack, J. P., Kim, U., Drayna, D., & Meyerhof, W. (2005). The molecular basis of individual differences in phenylthiocarbamide and propylthiouracil bitterness perception. *Current Biology, 15,* 322–327.

Buffardi, L. E., & Campbell, W. (2008). Narcissism and social networking web sites. *Personality and Social Psychology Bulletin, 34*(10), 1303–1314. doi:10.1177/0146167208320061

Bühler, C., & Allen, M. (1972). *Introduction to humanistic psychology.* Pacific Grove, CA: Brooks/Cole.

Bulik, C. M. (2004). Genetic and biological risk factors. In J. K. Thompson (Ed.), *Handbook of eating disorders and obesity.* New York, NY: Wiley.

Buller, D. J. (2009, January 1). Four fallacies of pop evolutionary psychology. *Scientific American,* pp. 74–81. doi:10.1038/scientificamerican0109-74

Bumpass, L., & Lu, H. (2000). Trends in cohabitation and implications for children's family contexts in the United States. *Population Studies, 54*(1), 29–41.

Burger, J. M. (1986). Temporal effects on attributions: Actor and observer differences. *Social Cognition, 4,* 377–387.

Burger, J. M. (1997). *Personality.* Pacific Grove: Brooks/Cole.

Burger, J. M. (1999). The foot-in-the-door compliance procedure: A multiple process analysis review. *Personality and Social Psychology Review, 3,* 303–325.

Burger, J. M. (2008). *Personality*. Belmont, CA: Wadsworth.

Burger, J. M. (2009). Replicating Milgram: Would people still obey today? *American Psychologist, 64*(1), 1–11. doi:10.1037/a0010932

Burgess, A. (2007). On the contribution of neurophysiology to hypnosis research: Current state and future directions. In G. A. Jamieson (Ed.), *Hypnosis and conscious states: The cognitive neuroscience perspective.* New York, NY: Oxford University Press.

Burke, B. L., Martens, A., & Faucher, E. H. (2010). Two decades of terror management theory: A meta-analysis of mortality salience research. *Personality and Social Psychology Review, 14*(2), 155–195. doi:10.1177/1088868309352321

Burke, D. M., & Shafto, M. A. (2004). Aging and language production. *Current Directions in Psychological Science, 13*(1), 21–24.

Burkhardt, D. A. (2010). Visual processing: Retinal. In E. B. Goldstein (Ed.), *Encyclopedia of perception.* Thousand Oaks, CA: Sage.

Burlingame, G. M., & Baldwin, S. (2011). Group therapy. In J. C. Norcross, G. R. Vandenbos, & D. K. Freedheim (Eds.), *History of psychotherapy: Continuity and change* (2nd ed.). Washington, DC: American Psychological Association.

Burns, B. D., & Corpus, B. (2004). Randomness and inductions from streaks: "Gambler's fallacy" versus "hot hand." *Psychonomic Bulletin & Review, 11*(1), 179–184.

Bushman, B. J. (2002). Does venting anger feed or extinguish the flame? Catharsis, rumination, distraction, anger, and aggressive responding. *Personality and Social Psychology Bulletin, 28,* 724–731.

Bushman, B. J., & Anderson, C. A. (2009). Comfortably numb: Desensitizing effects of violent media on helping others. *Psychological Science, 20*(3), 273–277. doi:10.1111/j.1467-9280.2009.02287.x.

Bushman, B. J., & Huesmann, L. R. (2001). Effects of televised violence on aggression. In D. G. Singer & J. L. Singer (Eds.), *Handbook of children and the media.* Thousand Oaks, CA: Sage.

Buss, D. M. (1985). Human mate selection. *American Scientist, 73,* 47–51.

Buss, D. M. (1988). The evolution of human intrasexual competition: Tactics of mate attraction. *Journal of Personality and Social Psychology, 54,* 616–628.

Buss, D. M. (1989). Sex differences in human mate preferences: Evolutionary hypotheses tested in 37 cultures. *Behavioral and Brain Sciences, 12,* 1–49.

Buss, D. M. (1991). Evolutionary personality psychology. *Annual Review of Psychology, 42,* 459–491.

Buss, D. M. (1994a). *The evolution of desire: Strategies of human mating.* New York, NY: Basic Books.

Buss, D. M. (1994b). Mate preferences in 37 cultures. In W. J. Lonner & R. S. Malpass (Eds.), *Psychology and culture.* Boston, MA: Allyn & Bacon.

Buss, D. M. (1995). Evolutionary psychology: A new paradigm for psychological science. *Psychological Inquiry, 6,* 1–30.

Buss, D. M. (1996). The evolutionary psychology of human social strategies. In E. T. Higgins & A. W. Kruglanski (Eds.), *Social psychology: Handbook of basic principles.* New York, NY: Guilford.

Buss, D. M. (1997). Evolutionary foundation of personality. In R. Hogan, J. Johnson, & S. Briggs (Eds.), *Handbook of personality psychology.* San Diego, CA: Academic Press.

Buss, D. M. (1999). *Evolutionary psychology: The new science of the mind.* Boston, MA: Allyn & Bacon.

Buss, D. M. (2006). The evolution of love. In R. J. Sternberg & K. Weis (Eds.), *The new psychology of love.* New Haven, CT: Yale University Press.

Buss, D. M. (2009). The great struggles of life: Darwin and the emergence of evolutionary psychology. *American Psychologist, 64*(2), 140–148. doi:10.1037/a0013207

Buss, D. M., & Schmitt, D. P. (1993). Sexual strategies theory: A contextual evolutionary analysis of human mating. *Psychological Review, 100,* 204–232.

Buss, D. M., & Shackelford, T. K. (2008). Attractive women want it all: Good genes, economic investment, parenting proclivities, and emotional commitment. *Evolutionary Psychology, 6*(1), 134–146.

Bussey, K., & Bandura, A. (1984). Influence of gender constancy and social power on sex-linked modeling. *Journal of Personality and Social Psychology, 47,* 1292–1302.

Bussey, K., & Bandura, A. (1999). Social cognitive theory of gender development and differentiation. *Psychological Review, 106,* 676–713.

Bussey, K., & Bandura, A. (2004). Social cognitive theory of gender development and functioning. In A. H. Eagly, A. E. Beall, & R. J. Sternberg (Eds.), *The psychology of gender.* New York, NY: Guilford.

Buster, J. E., & Carson, S. A. (2002). Endocrinology and diagnosis of pregnancy. In S. G. Gabbe, J. R. Niebyl, & J. L. Simpson (Eds.), *Obstetrics: Normal and problem pregnancies.* New York, NY: Churchill Livingstone.

Butcher, J. N. (1990). *The MMPI-2 in psychological treatment.* New York, NY: Oxford University Press.

Butcher, J. N. (2005). *A beginner's guide to the MMPI-2.* Washington, DC: American Psychological Association.

Butcher, J. N. (2006). *MMPI-2: A practitioner's guide.* Washington, DC: American Psychological Association.

Butler, A. C., & Roediger, H. (2008). Feedback enhances the positive effects and reduces the negative effects of multiple-choice testing. *Memory & Cognition, 36*(3), 604–616. doi:10.3758/MC.36.3.604

Button, T. M. M., Maughan, B., & McGuffin, P. (2007). The relationship of maternal smoking to psychological problems in the offspring. *Early Human Development, 83,* 727–732.

Buzan, D. S. (2004, March 12). I was not a lab rat. *The Guardian.* Retrieved from www.guardian.co.uk/education/2004/mar/12/highereducation.uk

Buzzell, L., & Chalquist, C. (2009). *Ecotherapy: Healing with nature in mind.* San Francisco, CA: Sierra Club Books.

Byne, W., Kemether, E., Jones, L., Haroutunian, V., & Davis, K. L. (1999). The neurochemistry of schizophrenia. In D. S. Charney, E. J. Nestler & B. S. Bunney (Eds.), *Neurobiology of mental illness* (pp. 236–245). New York, NY: Oxford University Press.

Byrne, D. (1997). An overview (and underview) of research and theory within the attraction paradigm. *Journal of Social and Personal Relationships, 14,* 417–431.

Cacioppo, J. T., Hawkley, L. C., Kalil, A., Hughes, M. E., Waite, L., & Thisted, R. A. (2008). Happiness and the invisible threads of social connection: The Chicago health, aging, and social relations study. In M. Eid & R. J. Larsen (Eds.), *The science of subjective well-being.* New York, NY: Guilford.

Cahn, B. R., & Polich, J. (2006). Meditation states and traits: EEG, ERP, and neuroimaging studies. *Psychological Bulletin, 132,* 180–211.

Cai, D. J., Mednick, S. A., Harrison, E. M., Kanady, J. C., & Mednick, S. C. (2009). REM, not incubation, improves creativity by priming associative networks. *PNAS Proceedings of the National Academy of Sciences of the United States of America, 106*(25), 10130–10134. doi:10.1073/pnas.0900271106

Cain, W. S. (1988). Olfaction. In R. C. Atkinson, R. J. Herrnstein, G. Lindzey, & R. D. Luce (Eds.), *Stevens' handbook of experimental psychology: Perception and motivation* (Vol. 1). New York, NY: Wiley.

Caine, E. D., & Lyness, J. M. (2000). Delirium, dementia, and amnestic and other cognitive disorders. In B. J. Sadock & V. A. Sadock (Eds.), *Kaplan and Sadock's comprehensive textbook of psychiatry.* Philadelphia, PA: Lippincott Williams & Wilkins.

Calhoun, L. G., & Tedeschi, R. G. (2006). The foundations of posttraumatic growth: An expanded framework. In L. G. Calhoun & R. G. Tedeschi (Eds.), *Handbook of posttraumatic growth: Research & practice.* Mahwah, NJ: Erlbaum.

Calhoun, L. G., & Tedeschi, R. G. (2008). The paradox of struggling with trauma: Guidelines for practice and directions for research. In S. Joseph & P. A. Linley (Eds.), *Trauma, recovery, and growth: Positive psychological perspectives on posttraumatic stress.* Hoboken, NJ: Wiley.

Callicutt, J. W. (2006). Homeless shelters: An uneasy component of the de facto mental health system. In J. Rosenberg & S. Rosenberg (Eds.), *Community mental health: Challenges for the 21st century.* New York, NY: Routledge.

Camaioni, L. (2001). Early language. In G. Bremner & A. Fogel (Eds.), *Blackwell handbook of infant development.* Malden, MA: Blackwell.

Cami, J., & Farre, M. (2003). Mechanisms of disease: Drug addiction. *New England Journal of Medicine, 349,* 975–986.

Campbell, A. (2005). Aggression. In D. M. Buss (Ed.), *The handbook of evolutionary psychology.* New York, NY: Wiley.

Campbell, J. (1971). *Hero with a thousand faces.* New York, NY: Harcourt Brace Jovanovich.

Campbell, K. B. (2000). Introduction to the special section: Information processing during sleep onset and sleep. *Canadian Journal of Experimental Psychology, 54*(4), 209–218.

Campbell, L., Simpson, J. A., Boldry, J., & Kashy, D. A. (2005). Perceptions of conflict and support in romantic relationships: The role of attachment anxiety. *Journal of Personality and Social Psychology, 88,* 510–531.

Campbell, W. K., & Foster, J. D. (2007). The narcissistic self: Background, an extended-agency model, and ongoing controversies. In C. Sedikides & S. J. Spencer (Eds.), *The self* (pp. 115–138). New York, NY: Psychology Press.

Campfield, L. A. (2002). Leptin and body weight regulation. In C. G. Fairburn & K. D. Brownell (Eds.), *Eating disorders and obesity: A comprehensive handbook* (pp. 32–36). New York, NY: Guilford.

Cannon, W. B. (1927). The James-Lange theory of emotions: A critical examination and an alternate theory. *American Journal of Psychology, 39,* 106–124.

Cannon, W. B. (1932). *The wisdom of the body.* New York, NY: Norton.

Cannon, W. B., & Washburn, A. L. (1912). An explanation of hunger. *American Journal of Physiology, 29,* 444–454.

Canter, P. H. (2003). The therapeutic effects of meditation. *British Medical Journal, 326,* 1049–1050.

Cappadocia, M., & Weiss, J. A. (2011). Review of social skills training groups for youth with Asperger syndrome and high functioning autism. *Research in Autism Spectrum Disorders, 5*(1), 70–78. doi:10.1016/j.rasd.2010.04.001

Card, J. P., Swanson, L. W., & Moore, R. (2008). The hypothalamus: An overview of regulatory systems. In L. Squire, D. Berg, F. Bloom, S. Du Lac, A. Ghosh, & N. Spitzer (Eds.), *Fundamental neuroscience* (3rd ed., pp. 795–808). San Diego, CA: Elsevier.

Cardeña, E., & Gleaves, D. H. (2007). Dissociative disorders. In M. Hersen, S. M. Turner, & D. C. Beidel (Eds.), *Adult psychopathology and diagnosis.* New York, NY: Wiley.

Carey, B. (2009, December 21). Building a search engine of the brain, slice by slice. *The New York Times.* Retrieved from www.newyorktimes.com

Carey, S. (2010). Beyond fast mapping. *Language Learning and Development, 6*(3), 184–205. doi:10.1080/15475441.2010.484379

Carli, L. L. (1999). Cognitive, reconstruction, hindsight, and reactions to victims and perpetrators. *Personality & Social Psychology Bulletin, 25,* 966–979.

Carlo, G. (2006). Care-based and altruistically based morality. In M. Killen & J. G. Smetana (Eds.), *Handbook of moral development.* Mahwah, NJ: Erlbaum.

Carlson, S. A., Fulton, J. E., Schoenborn, C. A., & Loustalot, F. (2010). Trend and prevalence estimates based on the 2008 Physical Activity Guidelines for Americans. *American Journal of Preventive Medicine, 39*(4), 305–313.

Carnagey, N. L., & Anderson, C. A. (2004). Violent video game exposure and aggression: A literature review. *Minerva Psichiatrica, 45,* 1–18.

Carpenter, W. T. (2002). From clinical trial to prescription. *Archives of General Psychology, 59,* 282–285.

Carrillo, M., Ricci, L. A., Coppersmith, G. A., & Melloni, R. R. (2009). The effect of increased serotonergic neurotransmission on aggression: A critical meta-analytical review of preclinical studies. *Psychopharmacology, 205*(3), 349–368. doi:10.1007/s00213-009-1543-2

Carroll, M. E., & Overmier, J. B. (2001). *Animal research and human health.* Washington, DC: American Psychological Association.

Carroll-Ghosh, T., Victor, B. S., & Bourgeois, J. A. (2003). Suicide. In R. E. Hales & S. C. Yudofsky (Eds.), *Textbook of clinical psychiatry.* Washington, DC: American Psychiatric Publishing.

Carskadon, M. A., & Dement, W. C. (2005). Normal human sleep: An overview. In M. H. Kryger, T. Roth, & W. C. Dement (Eds.), *Principles and practice of sleep medicine.* Philadelphia, PA: Elsevier Saunders.

Carskadon, M. A., & Rechtschaffen, A. (2005). Monitoring and staging human sleep. In M. H. Kryger, T. Roth, & W. C. Dement (Eds.). *Principles and practice of sleep medicine.* Philadelphia, PA: Elsevier Saunders.

Cartwright, R. D. (1977). *Night life: Explorations in dreaming.* Englewood Cliffs, NJ: Prentice-Hall.

Cartwright, R. D. (2004). The role of sleep in changing our minds: A psychologist's discussion of papers on memory reactivation and consolidation in sleep. *Learning & Memory, 11,* 660–663.

Cartwright, R. D. (2006). Sleepwalking. In T. Lee-Chiong (Ed.), *Sleep: A comprehensive handbook.* Hoboken, NJ: Wiley-Liss.

Cartwright, R. D., & Lamberg, L. (1992). *Crisis dreaming.* New York, NY: HarperCollins.

Carver, C. S., & Scheier, M. F. (1999). Optimism. In C. R. Snyder (Ed.), *Coping: The psychology of what works.* New York, NY: Oxford University Press.

Carver, C. S., Scheier, M. F., & Segerstrom, S. C. (2010). Optimism. *Clinical Psychology Review, 30*(7), 879–889.

Casanova, C., Merabet, L., Desautels, A., & Minville, K. (2001). Higher-order motion processing in the pulvinar. *Progress in Brain Research, 134,* 71–82.

Casey, B. J., Tottenham, N., Listen, C., & Durston, S. (2005). Imaging the developing brain: What have we learned about cognitive development? *Trends in Cognitive Sciences, 9*(3), 104–110. doi:10.1016/j.tics.2005.01.011

Caspi, A., & Herbener, E. S. (1990). Continuity and change: Assortative marriage and the consistency of personality in adulthood. *Journal of Personality and Social Psychology, 58*(2), 250–258.

Caspi, A., Roberts, B. W., & Shiner, R. L. (2005). Personality development: Stability and change. *Annual Review of Psychology, 56,* 453–484.

Caspi, O., & Burleson, K. O. (2005). Methodological challenges in meditation research. *Advances in Mind-Body Medicine, 21*(1), 4–11.

Cassel, R. N. (2000). Third force psychology and person-centered theory: From ego-status to ego-ideal. *Psychology: A Journal of Human Behavior, 37*(3), 44–48.

Cassidy, J. (2008). The nature of the child's ties. In J. Cassidy & P. R. Shaver (Eds.), *Handbook of attachment: Theory, research, and clinical applications* (2nd ed., pp. 3–22). New York, NY: Guilford.

Castle, D. (2008). Drawing conclusions about cannabis and psychosis. *Psychological Medicine, 38*(3), 459–460.

Castonguay, L. G., Reid, J. J., Jr., Halperin, G. S., & Goldfried, M. R. (2003). Psychotherapy integration. In G. Stricker & T. A. Widiger (Eds.), *Handbook of psychology, Vol. 8: Clinical psychology.* New York, NY: Wiley.

Catania, A. C. (1992). Reinforcement. In L. R. Squire (Ed.), *Encyclopedia of learning and memory.* New York, NY: Macmillan.

Catania, A. C., & Laties, V. G. (1999). Pavlov and Skinner: Two lives in science (an introduction to B. F. Skinner's "Some responses to the stimulus 'Pavlov'"). *Journal of the Experimental Analysis of Behavior, 72,* 455–461.

Catrambone, R. (1998). The subgoal learning model: Creating better examples so that students can solve novel problems. *Journal of Experimental Psychology: General, 127,* 355–376.

Cattell, R. B., Eber, H. W., & Tatsuoka, M. M. (1970). *Handbook of the Sixteen Personality Factor Questionnaire (16PF).* Champaign, IL: Institute for Personality and Ability Testing.

Caverly, D. C., Orlando, V. P., & Mullen, J. L. (2000). Textbook study reading. In R. F. Flippo & D. C. Caverly (Eds.), *Handbook of college reading and study strategy research.* Mahwah, NJ: Erlbaum.

Cepeda, N. J., Pashler, H., Vul, E., Wixted, J. T., & Roher, D. (2006). Distributed practice in verbal recall tasks: A review and quantitative synthesis. *Psychological Bulletin, 132,* 354–380.

Cerletti, U., & Bini, L. (1938). Un nuevo metodo di shockterapie "L'elettro-shock." *Boll. Acad. Med. Roma, 64,* 136–138.

Cetinkaya, H., & Domjan, M. (2006). Sexual fetishism in a quail (*Coturnix japonica*) model system: Test of reproductive success. *Journal of Comparative Psychology, 120*(4), 427–432. doi:10.1037/0735-7036.120.4.427

Cha, Y. (2010). Reinforcing separate spheres: The effect of spousal overwork on men's and women's employment in dual-earner households. *American Sociological Review, 75*(2), 303–329. doi:10.1177/000312241036530

Chaiken, S., & Maheswaran, D. (1994). Heuristic processing can bias systematic processing: Effects of source credibility, argument ambiguity, and task importance on attitude judgment. *Journal of Personality and Social Psychology, 66,* 460–473.

Chalquist, C. (2009). A look at the ecotherapy research evidence. *Ecopsychology, 1*(2), 64–74.

Chan, J. K., Thomas, A. K., & Bulevich, J. B. (2009). Recalling a witnessed event increases eyewitness suggestibility: The reversed testing effect. *Psychological Science, 20*(1), 66–73. doi:10.1111/j.1467-9280.2008.02245.x

Chan, J. W. C., & Vernon, P. E. (1988). Individual differences among the peoples of China. In S. H. Irvine & J. W. Berry (Eds.), *Human abilities in cultural context.* New York, NY: Cambridge University Press.

Chance, P. (2001, September/October). The brain goes to school: Why neuroscience research is going to the head of the class. *Psychology Today,* p. 72.

Chapman, P. D. (1988). *Schools as sorters: Lewis M. Terman, applied psychology, and the intelligence testing movement.* New York, NY: New York University Press.

Charrier, I., Pitcher, B. J., & Harcourt, R. G. (2009). Vocal recognition of mothers by Australian sea lion pups: Individual signature and environmental constraints. *Animal Behavior, 78*(5), 1127–1134. doi:10.1016/j.anbehav.2009 .07.032

Chawla, L. (1988). Children's concern for the natural environment. *Children's Environments Quarterly, 5*(3), 13–20.

Cheng, Y., Chen, C., Lin, C., Chou, K., & Decety, J. (2010). Love hurts: An fMRI study. *NeuroImage, 51*(2), 923–929. doi:10.1016/j .neuroimage.2010.02.047

Chess, S., & Thomas, A. (1996). *Temperament: Theory and practice.* New York, NY: Brunner/Mazel.

Chida, Y., & Steptoe, A. (2009). The association of anger and hostility with future coronary heart disease: A meta-analytic review of prospective evidence. *Journal of the American College of Cardiology, 53*(11), 936–946.

Chien, K., Che, P., Hsu, H., Su, T., Sung, F., Chen, M., & Lee, Y. (2010). Habitual sleep duration and insomnia and the risk of cardiovascular events and all-cause death: Report from a community-based cohort. *Sleep: Journal of Sleep and Sleep Disorders Research, 33*(2), 177–184.

Chiu, C., Kim, Y., & Wan, W. W. N. (2008). Personality: Cross-cultural perspectives. In G. J. Boyles, G. Matthews, & D. H. Saklofske (Eds.), *The Sage handbook of personality theory and assessment: Personality theories and models* (Vol. 1, pp. 124–144). Los Angles, CA: Sage.

Choi, I., Nisbett, R. E., & Norenzayan, A. (1999). Causal attribution across cultures: Variation and universality. *Psychological Bulletin, 125,* 47–63.

Cholewiak, R. W., & Cholewiak, S. A. (2010). Pain: Physiological mechanisms. In E. B. Goldstein (Ed.), *Encyclopedia of perception.* Thousand Oaks, CA: Sage.

Chomsky, N. (1957). *Syntactic structures.* The Hague: Mouton.

Chopra, S. S. (2003). Industry funding of clinical trials: Benefit of bias? *Journal of the American Medical Association, 290,* 113–114.

Christensen, B. K., Carney, C. E., & Segal, Z. V. (2006). Cognitive processing models of depression. In D. J. Stein, D. J. Kupfer, & A. F. Schatzberg (Eds.), *Textbook of mood disorders.* Washington, DC: American Psychiatric Publishing.

Christensen, B. T., & Schunn, C. D. (2007). The relationship of analogical distance to analogical function and preinventive structure: The case of engineering design. *Memory & Cognition, 35*(1), 29–38.

Christensen, C. C. (2005). Preferences for descriptors of hypnosis: A brief communication. *International Journal of Clinical and Experimental Hypnosis, 53,* 281–289.

Christensen, L. (1988). Deception in psychological research: When is its use justified? *Personality and Social Psychology Bulletin, 14,* 664–675.

Christian, L. M., Deichert, N. T., Gouin, J., Graham, J. E., & Kiecolt-Glaser, J. K. (2009). Psychological influences on neuroendocrine and immune outcomes. In G. G. Berntson & J. T. Cacioppo (Eds.), *Handbook of neuroscience for the behavioral sciences,* (Vol. 2, pp. 1260–1279). Hoboken, NJ: Wiley.

Chu, J. A., Frey, L. M., Ganzel, B. L., & Matthews, J. A. (1999). Memories of childhood abuse: Dissociation, amnesia, and corroboration. *American Journal of Psychiatry, 156,* 749–755.

Chudler, E. H. (2007). The power of the full moon. Running on empty? In S. Della Sala (Ed.), *Tall tales about the mind & brain: Separating fact from fiction* (pp. 401–410). New York, NY: Oxford University Press.

Chun, M. M., & Wolfe, J. M. (2001). Visual attention. In E. B. Goldstein (Ed.), *Blackwell handbook of perception.* Malden, MA: Blackwell.

Church, A. (2010). Current perspectives in the study of personality across cultures. *Perspectives on Psychological Science, 5*(4), 441–449. doi:10.1177/1745691610375559

Churchland, P. S., & Ramachandran, V. S. (1996). Filling in: Why Dennett is wrong. In K. Atkins (Ed.), *Perception.* Oxford, England: Oxford University Press.

Cialdini, R. B. (2007). *Influence: Science and practice.* New York, NY: HarperCollins.

Cialdini, R. B. (2008). *Influence: Science and practice* (5th ed.). Boston, MA: Allyn & Bacon.

Cialdini, R. B., & Griskevicius, V. (2010). Social influence. In R. F. Baumeister & E. J. Finkel (Eds.), *Advanced social psychology: The state of the science* (pp. 385–417). New York, NY: Oxford University Press.

Cialdini, R. B., Reno, R. R., & Kallgren, C. A. (1990). A focus theory of normative conduct: Recycling the concept of norms to reduce littering in public places. *Journal of Personality and Social Psychology, 58,* 1015–1026.

Cialdini, R. B., & Trost, M. R. (1998). Social influence: Social norms, conformity, and compliance. In D. T. Gilbert, S. T. Fiske, & G. Lindzey (Eds.), *The handbook of social psychology.* New York, NY: McGraw-Hill.

Ciborowski, T. (1997). "Superstition" in the collegiate baseball player. *Sport Psychologist, 11,* 305–317.

Cicero, T. J., Inciardi, J. A., & Muñoz, A. (2005). Trends in abuse of OxyContin and other opioid analgesics in the United States: 2002–2004. *The Journal of Pain, 6,* 662–672.

Clark, R. D., & Hatfield, E. (1989). Gender differences in receptivity to sexual offers. *Journal of Psychology & Human Sexuality, 2*(1), 39–55.

Clark, R. E. (2004). The classical origins of Pavlov's conditioning. *Integrative Physiological & Behavioral Science, 39,* 279–294.

Clayton, S. (2003). Environmental identity: A conceptual and an operational definition. In S. Clayton & S. Opotow (Eds.), *Identity and the natural environment.* Cambridge, MA: MIT Press.

Clayton, S., & Myers, G. (2009). *Conservation psychology: Understanding and promoting human care for nature.* Oxford, UK: Wiley-Blackwell.

Clements, A. M., Rimrodt, S. L., Abel, J. R., Blankner, J. G., Mostofsky, S. H., Pekar, J. J., et al. (2006). Sex differences in cerebral laterality of language and visuospatial processing. *Brain and Language, 98*(2), 150–158. doi:10.1016/j.bandl .2006.04.007

Clore, G. L., & Ortony, A. (2008). Appraisal theories: How cognition shapes affect into emotion. In M. Lewis, J. M. Haviland-Jones, & L. F. Barrett, *Handbook of emotions* (3rd ed.). New York, NY: Guilford.

Clow, A. (2001). The physiology of stress. In F. Jones & J. Bright (Eds.), *Stress: Myth, theory, and research.* Harlow, UK: Pearson, Education.

Coderre, T. J., Mogil, J. S., & Bushnell, M. C. (2003). The biological psychology of pain. In M. Gallagher & R. J. Nelson (Eds.), *Handbook of psychology, Vol. 3: Biological psychology.* New York, NY: Wiley.

Coenen, A. (1998). Neuronal phenomena associated with vigilance and consciousness: From cellular mechanisms to electroencephalographic patterns. *Consciousness & Cognition: An International Journal, 7,* 42–53.

Cohan, C. L., & Kleinbaum, S. (2002). Toward a greater understanding of the cohabitation effect: Premarital cohabitation and marital communication. *Journal of Marriage and Family, 64*(1), 180–192. doi:10.1111/j.1741-3737.2002.00180.x

Cohen, C. E. (1981). Person categories and social perception: Testing some boundaries of the processing effects of prior knowledge. *Journal of Personality and Social Psychology, 40,* 441–452.

Cohen, D. B. (1999). *Stranger in the nest: Do parents really shape their child's personality, intelligence, or character?* New York, NY: Wiley.

Cohen, S. (2005). Pittsburgh common cold studies: Psychosocial predictors of susceptibility to respiratory infectious illness. *International Journal of Behavioral Medicine, 12*(3), 123–131.

Cohen, S., Janicki-Deverts, D., & Miller, G. E. (2007). Psychological stress and disease. *Journal of the American Medical Association, 298,* 1685–1687.

Cohen, S., Kessler, R. C., & Gordon, L. U. (1995). Strategies for measuring stress in studies of psychiatric and physical disorders. In S. Cohen, R. C. Kessler, & L. U. Gordon (Eds.), *Measuring stress: A guide for health and social scientists* (pp. 3–28). New York, NY: Oxford University Press.

Cohen, S., & Pressman, S. D. (2006). Positive affect and health. *Current Directions in Psychological Science, 15*(3), 122–125.

Cohen, S., Tyrrell, D. A. J., & Smith, A. P. (1993). Negative life events, perceived stress, negative affect, and susceptibility to the common cold. *Journal of Personality and Social Psychology, 64,* 131–140.

Colaguiri, B., & Boakes, R. A. (2010). Perceived treatment, feedback, and placebo effects in double-blind RCTs: An experimental analysis. *Psychopharmacology, 208*(3), 433–441. doi: 10.1007/s00213-009-1743-9.

Colby, A., & Kohlberg, L. (1987). *The measurement of moral judgment* (Vols. 1–2). New York, NY: Cambridge University Press.

Cole, E., Erdman, E., & Rothblum, E. (Eds.). (1994). *Wilderness therapy for women: The power of adventure.* New York, NY: Haworth Press.

Collins, C. J., Hanges, P. J., & Locke, E. A. (2004). The relationship of achievement motivation to entrepreneurial behavior: A meta-analysis. *Human Performance, 17*(1), 95–117. doi:10 .1207/S15327043HUP1701_5

Collins, M. A., & Zebrowitz, L. A. (1995). The contributions of appearance to occupational outcomes in civilian and military settings. *Journal of Applied Social Psychology, 25,* 129–163.

Collins, W. A., & Laursen, B. (2006). Parent-adolescent relationships. In P. Noller & J. A. Feeney (Eds.), *Close relationships: Functions, forms and processes.* Hove, England: Psychology Press.

Collop, N. A. (2006). Polysomnography. In T. Lee-Chiong (Ed.), *Sleep: A comprehensive handbook.* Hoboken, NJ: Wiley-Liss.

Colom, R., Haier, R. J., Head, K., Álvarez-Linera, J., Quiroga, M., Shih, P., & Jung, R. E. (2009). Gray matter correlates of fluid, crystallized, and spatial intelligence: Testing the P-FIT model. *Intelligence, 37*(2), 124–135. doi:10.1016/j .intell.2008.07.007

Colom, R., Lluis-Font, J. M., & Andres-Pueyo, A. (2005). The generational intelligence gains are caused by decreasing variance in the lower half of the distribution: Supporting evidence for the nutrition hypothesis. *Intelligence, 33,* 83–91.

Coltrane, S. (2001). Research on household labor: Modeling and measuring the social embeddedness of routine family work. In R. M. Milardo (Ed.), *Understanding families into the new millennium: A decade in review* (pp. 427–452). Minneapolis, MN: National Council on Family Relations.

Colwill, R. M. (1993). An associative analysis of instrumental learning. *Current Directions in Psychological Science, 2*(4), 111–116.

Comas-Diaz, L. (2006). Cultural variation in the therapeutic relationship. In C. D. Goodheart, A. E. Kazdin, & R. J. Sternberg (Eds.), *Evidence-based psychotherapy: Where practice and research meet.* Washington, DC: American Psychological Association.

Combs, D. R., & Mueser, K. T. (2007). Schizophrenia. In M. Hersen, S. M. Turner, & D. C. Beidel (Eds.), *Adult psychopathology and diagnosis.* New York, NY: Wiley.

Comer, D. R. (1995). A model of social loafing in real work groups. *Human Relations, 48,* 647–667.

Compas, B. E. (2004). Processes of risk and resilience during adolescence: Linking contexts and individuals. In R. M. Lerner & L. Steinberg (Eds.), *Handbook of adolescent psychology.* New York, NY: Wiley.

Compton, D. M., Dietrich, K. L., & Smith, J. S. (1995). Animal rights activism and animal welfare concerns in the academic setting: Levels of activism and perceived importance of research with animals. *Psychological Reports, 76,* 23–31.

Confer, J. C., Easton, J. A., Fleischman, D. S., Goetz, C. D., Lewis, D. M. G., Perilloux, C., & Buss, D. M. (2010). Evolutionary psychology: Controversies, questions, prospects, and limitations. *American Psychologist, 65*(2), 110–126. doi: 10.1037/a0018413

Connor, C. E., Pasupathy, A., Brincat, S., & Yamane, Y. (2009). Neural transformation of object information by ventral pathway visual cortex. In M. S. Gazzaniga (Ed.), *The cognitive neurosciences.* Cambridge, MA: MIT Press.

Conway, A. R. A., Kane, M. J., & Engle, R. W. (2003). Working memory capacity and its relation to general intelligence. *Trends in Cognitive Sciences, 7,* 547–552.

Cooke, L. (2007). The importance of exposure for healthy eating in childhood: A review. *Journal of Human Nutrition and Dietetics, 20,* 294–301.

Coolidge, F. L., & Wynn, T. (2009). *The rise of homo sapiens: The evolution of modern thinking.* Malden, MA: Wiley-Blackwell. doi:10.1002/9781444308297

Coon, D. J. (1994). "Not a creature of reason": The alleged impact of Watsonian behaviorism on advertising in the 1920s. In J. T. Todd & E. K. Morris (Eds.), *Modern perspectives on John B. Watson and classical behaviorism.* Westport, CT: Greenwood Press.

Cooper, H. M. (1990). Meta-analysis and the integrative research review. In C. Hendrick & M. S. Clark (Eds.), *Research methods in personality and social psychology: Review of personality and social psychology* (Vol. 11, pp. 142–163). Thousand Oaks, CA: Sage Publications.

Cooper, H. M. (2010). *Research synthesis and meta-analysis: A step-by-step approach* (4th ed.). Thousand Oaks, CA: Sage.

Cooper, L., & Bright, J. (2001). Individual differences in reactions to stress. In F. Jones & J. Bright (Eds.), *Stress: Myth, theory and research.* Harlow, UK: Pearson Education.

Corballis, M. C. (1991). *The lopsided ape.* New York, NY: Oxford University Press.

Corballis, M. C. (2007). The dual-brain myth. In S. Della Sala (Ed.), *Tall tales about the mind & brain: Separating fact from fiction* (pp. 291–313). New York, NY: Oxford University Press.

Corballis, M. C., Hattie, J., & Fletcher, R. (2008). Handedness and intellectual achievement: An even-handed look. *Neuropsychologia, 46*(1), 374–378. doi:10.1016/j.neuropsychologia .2007.09.009

Corballis, P. M. (2003). Visuospatial processing and the right-hemisphere interpreter. *Brain & Cognition, 53*(2), 171–176.

Coren, S. (1992). *The left-hander syndrome: The causes and consequences of left-handedness.* New York, NY: Free Press.

Coren, S., & Aks, D. J. (1990). Moon illusion in pictures: A multimechanism approach. *Journal of Experimental Psychology: Human Perception and Performance, 16,* 365–380.

Coren, S., & Girgus, J. S. (1978). *Seeing is deceiving: The psychology of visual illusions.* Hillsdale, NJ: Erlbaum.

Corkin, S. (1984). Lasting consequences of bilateral medial temporal lobectomy: Clinical course and experimental findings in H. M. *Seminars in Neurology, 4,* 249–259.

Corkin, S. (2002). What's new with the amnesic patient H. M.? *Nature Reviews Neuroscience, 3,* 153–159.

Cornblatt, B. A., Green, M. F., Walker, E. F., & Mittal, V. A. (2009). Schizophrenia: Etiology and neurocognition. In P. H. Blaney & T. Millon (Eds.), *Oxford textbook of psychopathology* (2nd ed., pp. 298–332). New York, NY: Oxford University Press.

Corrigan, P. W., & Larson, J. E. (2008). Stigma. In K. T. Mueser & D. V. Jeste (Eds.), *Clinical handbook of schizophrenia* (pp. 533–540). New York, NY: Guilford.

Corsica, J. A., & Perri, M. G. (2003). Obesity. In A. M. Nezu, C. M. Nezu, & P. A. Geller (Eds.), *Handbook of psychology, Vol. 9: Health psychology.* New York, NY: Wiley.

Cosmides, L. L., & Tooby, J. (1989). Evolutionary psychology and the generation of culture. Part II. Case study: A computational theory of social exchange. *Ethology and Sociobiology, 10,* 51–97.

Cosmides, L. L., & Tooby, J. (1996). Are humans good intuitive statisticians after all? Rethinking some conclusions from the literature on judgment under uncertainty. *Cognition, 58*, 1–73.

Costa, P. T., Jr., & McCrae, R. R. (1985). *NEO Personality Inventory*. Odessa, FL: Psychological Assessment Resources.

Costa, P. T., Jr., & McCrae, R. R. (1992). *Revised NEO Personality Inventory: NEO PI and NEO Five-Factor Inventory* (Professional Manual). Odessa, FL: Psychological Assessment Resources.

Costa, P. T., Jr., & McCrae, R. R. (1994). Set like plaster? Evidence for the stability of adult personality. In T. F. Heatherton & J. L. Weinberger (Eds.), *Can personality change?* Washington, DC: American Psychological Association.

Costa, P. T., Jr., & McCrae, R. R. (1997). Longitudinal stability of adult personality. In R. Hogan, J. Johnson, & S. Briggs (Eds.), *Handbook of personality psychology*. San Diego, CA: Academic Press.

Costa, P. T., Jr., & McCrae, R. R. (2008). The revised NEO Personality Inventory (NEO-PR-R). In G. J. Boyle, G. Matthews, & D. H. Saklofske (Eds.), *The Sage handbook of personality theory and assessment: Personality measurement and testing* (Vol. 2, pp. 179–198). Los Angeles, CA: Sage.

Côté, J. E. (2006). Emerging adulthood as an institutionalized moratorium: Risks and benefits to identity formation. In J. J. Arnett & J. L. Tanner (Eds.), *Emerging adults in America: Coming of age in the 21st century*. Washington, DC: American Psychological Association.

Cotman, C. W., Berchtold, N. C., & Christie, L.-A. (2007). Exercise builds brain health: Key roles of growth factor cascades and inflammation. *Trends in Neurosciences, 30*, 464–472.

Cotter, A., & Potter, J. E. (2006). Mother to child transmission. In J. Beal, J. J. Orrick, & K. Alfonso (Eds.), *HIV/AIDS: Primary care guide*. Norwalk, CT: Crown House.

Coutts, A. (2000). Nutrition and the life cycle. 1: Maternal nutrition and pregnancy. *British Journal of Nursing, 9*, 1133–1138.

Covino, N. A., & Pinnell, C. M. (2010). In S. J. Lynn, J. W. Rhue, & I. Kirsch (Eds.), *Handbook of clinical hypnosis* (2nd ed., pp. 551–574). Washington, DC: American Psychological Association.

Cowan, N. (2005). *Working memory capacity*. New York, NY: Psychology Press.

Cowan, N. (2010). The magical mystery four: How is working memory capacity limited, and why? *Current Directions in Psychological Science, 19*(1), 51–57. doi:10.1177/0963721409359277

Cowart, B. J. (2005). Taste, our body's gustatory gatekeeper. *Cerebrum, 7*(2), 7–22.

Cox, D., Meyers, E., & Sinha, P. (2004). Contextually evoked object-specific responses in human visual cortex. *Science, 304*, 115–117.

Cox, P. D., Vinogradov, S., & Yalom, I. D. (2008). Group therapy. In R. E. Hales, S. C. Yudofsky, & G. O. Gabbard (Eds.), *The American psychiatric publishing textbook of psychiatry* (pp. 1329–1376). Washington, DC: American Psychiatric Publishing.

Cox, R. E., & Bryant, R. A. (2008). Advances in hypnosis research: Methods, designs and contributions of intrinsic and instrumental hypnosis. In M. R. Nash & A. J. Barnier (Eds.). *The Oxford Handbook of Hypnosis: Theory, research and practice* (pp. 311–336). New York, NY: Oxford University Press.

Craig, J. C., & Rollman, G. B. (1999). Somesthesis. *Annual Review of Psychology, 50*, 305–331.

Craighead, W. E., Ritschel, L. A., Arnarson, E. O., & Gillespie, C. F. (2008). Major depressive disorder. In W. E. Craighead, D. J. Miklowitz, & L. W. Craighead (Eds.), *Psychopathology: History, diagnosis, and empirical foundations*. New York, NY: Wiley.

Craik, F. I. M. (2002). Levels of processing: Past, present . . . and future? *Memory, 10*(5–6), 305–318.

Craik, F. I. M., & Kester, J. D. (2000). Divided attention and memory: Impairment of processing or consolidation? In E. Tulving (Ed.), *Memory, consciousness, and the brain: The Tallinn conference* (pp. 38–51). Philadelphia, PA: Psychology Press.

Craik, F. I. M., & Lockhart, R. S. (1972). Levels of processing: A framework for memory research. *Journal of Verbal Learning and Verbal Behavior, 11*, 671–684.

Craik, F. I. M., & Tulving, E. (1975). Depth of processing and the retention of words in episodic memory. *Journal of Experimental Psychology: General, 104*, 268–294.

Cramer, P. (2000). Defense mechanisms in psychology today: Further processes for adaptation. *American Psychologist, 55*(6), 637–646.

Cramer, P. (2001). The unconscious status of defense mechanisms. *American Psychologist, 56*, 762–763.

Craske, M. G., & Waters, A. M. (2005). Panic disorders, phobias, and generalized anxiety disorder. *Annual Review of Clinical Psychology, 1*, 197–225.

Cravens, H. (1992). A scientific project locked in time: The Terman Genetic Studies of Genius, 1920s–1950s. *American Psychologist, 47*, 183–189.

Crede, M., & Kuncel, N. R. (2008). Study habits, skills, and attitudes: The third pillar supporting collegiate academic performance. *Perspectives on Psychological Science, 3*(6), 425–453. doi: 10.1111/j.1745-6924.2008.00089.x

Crews, F. (2006). *Follies of the wise: Dissenting essays*. Emeryville, CA: Shoemaker Hoard.

Crits-Christoph, P. (1997). Limitations of the dodo bird verdict and the role of clinical trials in psychotherapy research: Comment on Wampold et al. (1997). *Psychological Bulletin, 122*, 216–220.

Crits-Christoph, P., & Gibbons, M. B. C. (2009). The evaluation of psychological treatment. In M. C. Gelder, N. C. Andreasen, J. J. López-Ibor, Jr., & J. R. Geddes (Eds.), *New Oxford textbook of psychiatry* (2nd ed., Vol. 1). New York, NY: Oxford University Press.

Cross, S. E., & Markus, H. R. (1993). Gender in thought, belief, and action: A cognitive approach. In A. E. Beall & R. J. Sternberg (Eds.), *The psychology of gender*. New York, NY: Guilford.

Crow, S. J., Peterson, C. B., Swanson, S. A., Raymond, N. C., Specker, S., Eckert, E. D., & Mitchell, J. E. (2009). Increased mortality in bulimia nervosa and other eating disorders. *American Journal of Psychiatry, 166*(12), 1342–1346. doi:10.1176/appi.ajp.2009.09020247

Crowder, R. G., & Greene, R. L. (2000). Serial learning: Cognition and behavior. In E. Tulving & F. I. M. Craik (Eds.), *The Oxford handbook of memory* (pp. 125–136). New York, NY: Oxford University Press.

Cruz, C., della Rocco, P., & Hackworth, C. (2000). Effects of quick rotating schedules on the health and adjustment of air traffic controllers. *Aviation, Space, & Environmental Medicine, 71*, 400–407.

Cuban, L. (2004). Assessing the 20-year impact of multiple intelligences on schooling. *Teachers College Record, 106*(1), 140–146.

Cubelli, R., & Della Sala, S. (2008). Flashbulb memories: Special but not iconic. *Cortex: A Journal Devoted to the Study of the Nervous System and Behavior, 44*(7), 908–909. doi:10.1016/j.cortex.2008.03.003

Cullum, J., & Harton, H. C. (2007). Cultural evolution: Interpersonal influence, issue importance, and the development of shared attitudes in college residence halls. *Personality and Social Psychology Bulletin, 33*, 1327–1339.

Culpepper, L., Davidson, J. R. T., Dietrich, A. J., Goodman, W. K., Kroenke, K., & Schwenk, T. L. (2004). Suicidality as a possible effect of antidepressant treatment. *Journal of Clinical Psychiatry, 65*, 742–749.

Cummings, D. E. (2006). Ghrelin and the short-and long-term regulation of appetite and body weight. *Physiology & Behavior, 89*, 71–84.

Cummins, D. (2005). Dominance, status, and social hierarchies. In D. M. Buss (Ed.), *The handbook of evolutionary psychology*. New York, NY: Wiley.

Cunningham, C. O., & Selwyn, P. A. (2005). HIV-related medical complications and treatment. In J. H. Lowinson, P. Ruiz, R. B. Millman, & J. G. Langrod (Eds.), *Substance abuse: A comprehensive textbook*. Philadelphia, PA: Lippincott Williams & Williams.

Cunningham, F., Leveno, K., Bloom, S., Hauth, J., Rouse, D., & Spong, C. (2010). *Williams obstetrics* (23rd ed.). New York, NY: McGraw-Hill.

Cunningham, M. (2001). The influence of parental attitudes and behaviors on children's attitudes toward gender and household labor in early adulthood. *Journal of Marriage and the Family, 63*, 111–122.

Curtis, G. C., Magee, W. J., Eaton, W. W., Wittchen, H., & Kessler, R. C. (1998). Specific fears and phobias: Epidemiology and classification. *British Journal of Psychiatry, 173*, 212–217. doi:10.1192/bjp.173.3.212

Cushman, P. (1992). Psychotherapy to 1992: A historically situated interpretation. In

D. K. Freedheim (Ed.), *History of psychotherapy: A century of change.* Washington, DC: American Psychological Association.

Cutting, L. P., & Docherty, N. M. (2000). Schizophrenia outpatients' perceptions of their parents: Is expressed emotion a factor? *Journal of Abnormal Psychology, 109,* 266–272.

D'Souza, D. C. (2007). Cannabinoids and psychosis. *International Review of Neurobiology, 78,* 289–326.

Daiek, D. B., & Anter, N. M. (2004). *Critical reading for college and beyond.* New York, NY: McGraw Hill.

Dallman, M. F., Bhatnagar, S., & Viau, V. (2007). Hypothalamic-pituitary-adrenal axis. In G. Fink (Ed.), *Encyclopedia of stress.* San Diego, CA: Elsevier.

Daly, M., & Wilson, M. (1985). Child abuse and other risks of not living with both parents. *Ethology and Sociobiology, 6,* 197–210.

Damisch, L., Stoberock, B., & Mussweiler, T. (2010). Keep your fingers crossed! How superstition improves performance. *Psychological Science, 21*(7), 1014-1020.

Dang-Vu, T. T., Schabus, M., Cologan, V., & Maquet, P. (2009). Sleep: Implications for theories of dreaming and consciousness. In W. P. Banks (Ed.), *Encyclopedia of Consciousness* (pp. 357–374). San Diego, CA: Academic Press.

Daniel, E. (2007). Noise and hearing loss: A review. *Journal of School Health, 77*(5), 225–231. doi:10.1111/j.1746-1561.2007.00197.x.

Danziger, K. (1990). *Constructing the subject: Historical origins of psychological research.* Cambridge, England: Cambridge University Press.

Dapretto, M., & Bjork, E. (2000). The development of word retrieval abilities in the second year and its relation to early vocabulary growth. *Child Development, 71,* 635–648.

Darley, J. M., & Latané, B. (1968). Bystander intervention in emergencies: Diffusion of responsibility. *Journal of Personality and Social Psychology, 8,* 377–383.

Darwin, C. (1859). *The origin of species.* London: Murray.

Darwin, C. (1871). *Descent of man.* London: Murray.

Darwin, C. (1872). *The expression of emotions in man and animals.* New York, NY: Philosophical Library.

Das, H. H. J., de Wit, J. B. F., & Stroebe, W. (2005). Fear appeals motivate acceptance of action recommendations: Evidence for a positive bias in the processing of persuasive messages. *Personality and Social Psychology Bulletin, 29,* 650–664.

Dasen, P. R. (1994). Culture and cognitive development from a Piagetian perspective. In W. J. Lonner & R. Malpass (Eds.), *Psychology and Culture.* Boston, MA: Allyn & Bacon.

Davidson, K. W., Mostofsky, E., & Whang, W. (2010). Don't worry, be happy: Positive affect and reduced 10-year incident coronary heart disease:

The Canadian Nova Scotia Health Survey. *European Heart Journal, 31,* 1065–1070.

Davidson, R. J., Kabat-Zinn, J., Schumacher, J., Rosenkranz, M., Muller, D., Santorelli, S. F., Urbanowski, F., Harrington, A., Bonus, K., & Sheridan, J. F. (2003a). Alterations in brain and immune function produced by mindfulness meditation. *Psychosomatic Medicine, 65,* 564–570.

Davidson, R. J., Pizzagalli, D. A., & Nitschke, J. B. (2009). Representation and regulation of emotion in depression: Perspectives from affective neuroscience. In I. H. Gotlib & C. L. Hammen (Eds.), *Handbook of Depression* (2nd ed., pp. 218–248). New York, NY: Guilford.

Davidson, R. J., Pizzagalli, D., Nitschke, J. B., & Kalin, N. H. (2003b). Parsing the subcomponents of emotion and disorders of emotion: Perspectives from affective neuroscience. In R. J. Davidson, K. R. Scherer, & H. H. Goldsmith (Eds.), *Handbook of affective sciences.* New York, NY: Oxford University Press.

Davis, A., & Bremner, G. (2006). The experimental method in psychology. In G. M. Breakwell, S. Hammond, C. Fife-Schaw, & J. A. Smith (Eds.), *Research methods in psychology* (3rd ed.). London: Sage.

Davis, A. S., & Dean, R. S. (2005). Lateralization of cerebral functions and hemispheric specialization: Linking behavior, structure, and neuroimaging. In R. C. D'Amato, E. Fletcher-Janzen, & C. R. Reynolds (Eds.), *Handbook of school neuropsychology.* Hoboken, NJ: Wiley.

Davis, D., & Loftus, E. F. (2007). Internal and external sources of misinformation in adult witness memory. In M. P. Toglia, J. D. Read, D. F. Ross, & R. C. L. Lindsay (Eds.), *Handbook of eyewitness psychology: Vol. 1. Memory for events.* Mahwah, NJ: Erlbaum.

Davis, M. C., Zautra, A. J., Younger, J., Motivala, S. J., Attrep, J., & Irwin, M. R. (2008). Chronic stress and regulation of cellular markers of inflammation in rheumatoid arthritis: Implications for fatigue. *Brain, Behavior, and Immunity, 22*(1), 24–32. doi:10.1016/j.bbi.2007.06.01

Davis, O. S. P., Arden, R., & Plomin, R. (2008). g in middle childhood: Moderate genetic and shared environmental influence using diverse measures of general cognitive ability at 7, 9 and 10 years in a large population sample of twins. *Intelligence, 36,* 68–80.

Dawes, R. M. (1980). Social dilemmas. *Annual Review of Psychology, 31,* 169–193.

Dawes, R. M. (2001). *Everyday irrationality: How pseudo-scientists, lunatics, and the rest of us systematically fail to think rationally.* Boulder, CO: Westview Press.

Day, R. H. (1965). Inappropriate constancy explanation of spatial distortions. *Nature, 207,* 891–893.

de Castro, J. M. (2010). The control of food intake of free-living humans: Putting the pieces back together. *Physiology & Behavior, 100*(5), 446–453. doi:10.1016/j.physbeh.2010.04.028

de Castro, J. M., Bellisle, F., Dalix, A., & Pearcey, S. M. (2000). Palatability and intake relationships in free-living humans: Characterization and independence of influence in North Americans. *Physiology & Behavior, 70,* 343–350.

De Koninck, J. (2000). Waking experiences and dreaming. In M. H. Kryger, T. Roth, & W. C. Dement (Eds.), *Principles and practice of sleep medicine.* Philadelphia, PA: Saunders.

De Neys, W. (2006). Dual processing in reasoning: Two systems but one reasoner. *Psychological Science, 17,* 428–433.

de Vaus, D. A., Qu, L., & Weston, R. (2005). The disappearing link between premarital cohabitation and subsequent marital stability. *Journal of Population Research, 22*(2), 99–118.

de Villiers, J. G., & de Villiers, P. A. (1999). Language development. In M. H. Bornstein & M. E. Lamb (Eds.), *Developmental psychology: An advanced textbook.* Mahwah, NJ: Erlbaum.

De Villiers, P. (1977). Choice in concurrent schedules and a quantitative formulation of the law of effect. In W. K. Honig & J. E. R. Staddon (Eds.), *Handbook of operant behavior.* Englewood Cliffs, NJ: Prentice-Hall.

De Waal, F. (2001). *The ape and the sushi master: Cultural reflections of a primatologist.* New York, NY: Basic Books.

de Wit, J. B. F., Das, E., & Vet, R. (2008). What works best: Objective statistics or a personal testimonial? An assessment of the persuasive effects of different types of message evidence on risk perception. *Health Psychology, 27*(1), 110–115. doi:10.1037/0278-6133.27.1.110.

Deary, I. J., Strand, S., Smith, P., & Fernandes, C. (2007). Intelligence and educational achievement. *Intelligence, 35,* 13–21.

Deary, I. J., Whalley, L. J., & Starr, J. M. (2009). *A lifetime of intelligence: Follow-up studies of the Scottish mental surveys of 1932 and 1947.* Washington, DC: American Psychological Association. doi:10.1037/11857-000

Deary, I. J., Whiteman, M. C., Starr, J. M., Whalley, L. J., & Fox, H. C. (2004). The impact of childhood intelligence on later life: Following up the Scottish mental surveys of 1932 and 1947. *Journal of Personality and Social Psychology, 86,* 130–147.

Deaux, K. (1993). Commentary: Sorry, wrong number—A reply to Gentile's call. *Psychological Science, 4,* 125–126.

DeCarvalho, R. J. (1991). *The founders of humanistic psychology.* New York, NY: Praeger.

Dechêne, A., Stahl, C., Hansen, J., & Wänke, M. (2010). The truth about the truth: A meta-analytic review of the truth effect. *Personality and Social Psychology Review, 14*(2), 238–257. doi:10.1177/1088868309352251

Deer, B. (2011). How the case against MMR vaccine was fixed. *BMJ, 342,* 77–82.

Deese, J. (1959). On the prediction of occurrence of particular verbal intrusions in immediate recall. *Journal of Experimental Psychology, 58,* 17–22.

Defeyter, M. A., & German, T. P. (2003). Acquiring an understanding of design: Evidence from children's insight problem solving. *Cognition, 89*(2), 133–155.

Degenhardt, L., & Hall, W. (2006). Is cannabis use a contributory cause of psychosis? *Canadian Journal of Psychiatry, 51*, 556–565.

Deitmer, J. W., & Rose, C. R. (2010). Ion changes and signaling in perisynaptic glia. *Brain Research Reviews, 63*(1–2), 113–129. doi:10.1016/j.brainresrev.2009.10.006

Del Monte, M. M. (2000). Retrieved memories of childhood sexual abuse. *British Journal of Medical Psychology, 73*, 1–13.

Delis, D. C., & Lucas, J. A. (1996). Memory. In B. S. Fogel, R. B. Schiffer, & S. M. Rao (Eds.), *Neuropsychiatry*. Baltimore, MD: Williams & Wilkins.

DeLisi, L. E. (2008). The effect of cannabis on the brain: Can it cause brain anomalies that lead to increased risk for schizophrenia? *Current Opinion in Psychiatry, 21*, 140–150.

DeLong, M. R. (2000). The basal ganglia. In E. R. Kandel, J. H. Schwartz, & T. M. Jessell (Eds.), *Principles of neural science* (pp. 853–872). New York, NY: McGraw-Hill.

DeLongis, A., Folkman, S., & Lazarus, R. S. (1988). The impact of daily stress on health and mood: Psychological and social resources as mediators. *Journal of Personality and Social Psychology, 54*, 486–495.

Dement, W. C. (1978). *Some must watch while some must sleep*. New York, NY: Norton.

Dement, W. C. (1992). *The sleepwatchers*. Stanford, CA: Stanford Alumni Association.

Dement, W. C. (2003). Knocking on Kleitman's door: The view from 50 years later. *Sleep Medicine Reviews, 7*(4), 289–292.

Dement, W. C. (2005). History of sleep psychology. In M. H. Kryger, T. Roth, & W. C. Dement (Eds.), *Principles and practice of sleep medicine*. Philadelphia, PA: Elsevier Saunders.

Dement, W. C., & Vaughan, G. (1999). *The promise of sleep*. New York, NY: Delacorte Press.

Dement, W. C., & Wolpert, E. (1958). The relation of eye movements, bodily motility, and external stimuli to dream content. *Journal of Experimental Psychology, 53*, 543–553.

Dempster, F. N. (1996). Distributing and managing the conditions of encoding and practice. In E. L. Bjork & R. A. Bjork (Eds.), *Memory*. San Diego, CA: Academic Press.

Derevensky, J. L., & Gupta, R. (2004). Preface. In J. L. Derevensky & R. Gupta (Eds.), *Gambling problems in youth: Theoretical and applied perspectives* (pp. xxi–xxiv). New York, NY: Kluwer/Plenum.

Derogatis, L. R., & Coons, H. L. (1993). Self-report measures of stress. In L. Goldberger & S. Breznitz (Eds.), *Handbook of stress: Theoretical and clinical aspects* (2nd ed.). New York, NY: Free Press.

Des Jarlais, D. C., Hagan, H., & Friedman, S. R. (2005). Epidemiology and emerging public health perspectives. In J. H. Lowinson, P. Ruiz, R. B. Millman, & J. G. Langrod (Eds.), *Substance abuse: A comprehensive textbook*. Philadelphia, PA: Lippincott Williams & Wilkins.

Deutch, A. Y., & Roth, R. H. (2008). Neurotransmitters. In L. Squire, D. Berg, F. Bloom, S. Du Lac, A. Ghosh, & N. Spitzer (Eds.), *Fundamental neuroscience* (3rd ed., pp. 133–156). San Diego, CA: Elsevier.

Devine, P. G., & Sharp, L. B. (2009). Automaticity and control in stereotyping and prejudice. In T. D. Nelson (Ed.), *Handbook of prejudice, stereotyping, and discrimination* (pp. 1–22). New York, NY: Psychology Press.

Devine, P. G., Tauer, J. M., Barron, K. E., Elliot, A. J., & Vance, K. M. (1999). Moving beyond attitude change in the study of dissonance-related processes. In E. Harmon-Jones & J. Mills (Eds.), *Cognitive dissonance: Progress on a pivotal theory in social psychology*. Washington, DC: American Psychological Association.

Devlin, B., Fienberg, S. E., Resnick, D. P., & Roeder, K. (2002). Intelligence and success: Is it all in the genes? In J. M. Fish (Ed.), *Race and intelligence: Separating science from myth* (pp. 355–368). Mahwah, NJ: Erlbaum.

Devos, T. (2008). Implicit attitudes 101: Theoretical and empirical insights. In W. D. Crano, & R. Prislin (Eds.), *Attitudes and attitude change* (pp. 61–84). New York, NY: Psychology Press

Dew, M. A., Bromet, E. J., & Switzer, G. E. (2000). Epidemiology. In M. Hersen & A. S. Bellack (Eds.), *Psychopathology in adulthood*. Boston, MA: Allyn & Bacon.

Dewsbury, D. A. (2009). Charles Darwin and psychology at the bicentennial and sesquicentennial: An introduction. *American Psychologist, 64*(2), 67–74. doi:10.1037/a0013205

Di Forti, M., Morrison, P. D., Butt, A., & Murray, R. M. (2007). Cannabis use and psychiatric and cognitive disorders: The chicken or the egg? *Current Opinion in Psychiatry, 20*, 228–234.

Di Lorenzo, P. M., & Rosen, A. M. (2010). Taste. In E. B. Goldstein (Ed.), *Encyclopedia of perception*. Thousand Oaks, CA: Sage.

Di Lorenzo, P. M., & Youngentob, S. L. (2003). Olfaction and taste. In M. Gallagher & R. J. Nelson (Eds.), *Handbook of psychology, Vol. 3: Biological psychology*. New York, NY: Wiley.

Diamond, L. M. (2003). Was it a phase? Young women's relinquishment of lesbian/bisexual identities over a 5-year period. *Journal of Personality and Social Psychology, 84*, 352–364.

Diamond, L. M. (2007). The evolution of plasticity in female-female desire. *Journal of Psychology & Human Sexuality, 18*, 245–274.

Diamond, L. M. (2008). Female bisexuality from adolescence to adulthood: Results from a 10-year longitudinal study. *Developmental Psychology, 44*(1), 5–14. doi:10.1037/0012-1649.44.1.5

DiCicco-Bloom, E., & Falluel-Morel, A. (2009). Neural development & neurogenesis. In B. J. Sadock, V. A. Sadock, & P. Ruiz (Eds.), *Kaplan & Sadock's comprehensive textbook of psychiatry* (9th ed., Vol. 1, pp. 42–64). Philadelphia, PA: Lippincott Williams & Wilkins.

Dick, D. M., & Rose, R. J. (2002). Behavior genetics: What's new? What's next? *Current Directions in Psychological Science, 11*(2), 70–74.

Dickens, W. T., & Flynn, J. R. (2001). Heritability estimates versus large environmental effects: The IQ paradox resolved. *Psychological Review, 108*, 346–369.

Dickens, W. T., & Flynn, J. R. (2006). Black Americans reduce the racial IQ gap: Evidence from standardization samples. *Psychological Science, 17*, 913–920.

Dickerson, C. A., Thibodeau, R., Aronson, E., & Miller , D. (1992) Using cognitive dissonance to encourage water conservation. *Journal of Applied Social Psychology, 22*, 841–854.

Diekman, A. B., & Murnen, S. K. (2004). Learning to be little women and little men: The inequitable gender equality of nonsexist children's literature. *Sex Roles, 50*, 373–385.

Diener, E., & Biswas-Diener, R. (2002). Will money increase subjective well-being? *Social Indicators Research, 57*(2), 119–169. doi:10.1023/A:1014411319119

Diener, E., & Diener, C. (1996). Most people are happy. *Psyhological Science, 7*, 181–185.

Diener, E., Gohm, C. L., Suh, E., & Oishi, S. (2000). Similarity of the relations between marital status and subjective well-being across cultures. *Journal of Cross-Cultural Psychology, 31*, 419–436.

Diener, E., Kesebir, P., & Tov, W. (2009). Happiness. In M. R. Leary & R. H. Hoyle (Eds.), *Handbook of individual differences in social behavior* (pp. 147–160). New York, NY: Guilford.

Diener, E., & Seligman, M. E. P. (2004). Beyond money: Toward an economy of well-being. *Psychological Science in the Public Interest, 5*(1), 1–31.

Diener, E., Wolsic, B., & Fujita, F. (1995). Physical attractiveness and subjective well-being. *Journal of Personality and Social Psychology, 69*, 120–129.

Dijksterhuis, A. (2010). Automaticity and the unconscious. In S. T. Fiske, D. T. Gilbert, & G. Lindzey (Eds.), *Handbook of social psychology* (5th ed., Vol. 1, pp. 228–267). New York, NY: Wiley.

Dijksterhuis, A., Bos, M. W., Nordgren, L. F., & van Baaren, R. B. (2006). On making the right choice: The deliberation-without-attention effect. *Science, 311*, 1005–1007.

Dijksterhuis, A., & Nordgren, L. F. (2006). A theory of unconscious thought. *Perspectives on Psychological Science, 1*(2), 95–109.

Dijksterhuis, A., & van Olden, Z. (2006). On the benefits of thinking unconsciously: Unconscious thought can increase post-choice satisfaction. *Journal of Experimental Social Psychology, 42*, 627–631.

Dillbeck, M. C., & Orme-Johnson, D. W. (1987). Physiological differences between transcendental meditation and rest. *American Psychologist, 42*, 879–881.

DiMatteo, M. R. (1991). *The psychology of health, illness, and medical care: An individual perspective*. Pacific Grove, CA: Brooks/Cole.

DiMatteo, M. R. (1997). Health behaviors and care decisions: An overview of professional-patient communication. In D. S. Gochman (Ed.), *Handbook of health behavior research II: Provider determinants.* New York, NY: Plenum.

DiMatteo, M. R. (2004a). Social support and patient adherence to medical treatment: A meta analysis. *Health Psychology, 23,* 207–218.

DiMatteo, M. R. (2004b). Variations in patients' adherence to medical recommendations: A quantitative review of 50 years of research. *Medical Care, 42,* 200–209.

DiMatteo, M. R., Giordani, P. J., Lepper, H. S., & Croghan, T. W. (2002). Patient adherence and medical treatment outcomes: A meta-analysis. *Medical Care, 40,* 794–811.

Dimsdale, J. E. (2008). Psychological stress and cardiovascular disease. *Journal of the American College of Cardiology, 51*(13), 1237–1246.

Dimsdale, J. E., Irwin, M., Keefe, F. J., & Stein, M. B. (2005). Stress and anxiety. In B. J. Sadock & V. A. Sadock (Eds.), *Kaplan & Sadock's comprehensive textbook of psychiatry.* Philadelphia, PA: Lippincott Williams & Wilkins.

Dinehart, M. E., Hayes, J. E., Bartoshuk, L. M., Lanier, S. L., & Duffy, V. B. (2006). Bitter taste markers explain variability in vegetable sweetness, bitterness, and intake. *Physiology & Behavior, 87,* 304–313.

Dinges, D. F. (1993). Napping. In M.A. Carskadon (Ed.), *Encyclopedia of sleep and dreaming.* New York, NY: Macmillan.

Dinges, D. F., Rogers, N. L., & Baynard, M. D. (2005). Chronic sleep deprivation. In M. H. Kryger, T. Roth, & W. C. Dement (Eds.), *Principles and practice of sleep medicine.* Philadelphia, PA: Elsevier Saunders.

Dinsmoor, J. A. (1998). Punishment. In W. O'Donohue (Ed.), *Learning and behavior therapy.* Boston, MA: Allyn & Bacon.

Dinsmoor, J. A. (2004). The etymology of basic concepts in the experimental analysis of behavior. *Journal of the Experimental Analysis of Behavior, 82,* 311–316.

Dion, K. K., & Dion, K. L. (2006). Individualism, collectivism, and the psychology of love. In R. J. Sternberg & K. Weis (Eds.), *The new psychology of love.* New Haven, CT: Yale University Press.

Dissell, R. (2005, December 14). Student from Ohio robbed bank to feed gambling habit, lawyer says. *The Plain Dealer.*

Dixon, L., & Goldman, H. (2004). Forty years of progress in community mental health: The role of evidence-based practices. *Administration & Policy in Mental Health, 31*(5), 381–392.

Dixon, M., & Laurence, J. R. (1992). Two hundred years of hypnosis research: Questions resolved? Questions unanswered! In E. Fromm & M. R. Nash (Eds.), *Contemporary hypnosis research.* New York, NY: Guilford.

Dixon, R. A., & Cohen, A. (2003). Cognitive development in adulthood. In R. M. Lerner, M. A. Easterbrooks, & J. Mistry (Eds.), *Handbook of psychology, Vol. 6: Developmental psychology.* New York, NY: Wiley.

Dobzhansky, T. (1937). *Genetics and the origin of species.* New York, NY: Columbia University Press.

Dodds, R. A., Ward, T. B., & Smith, S. M. (2011). A review of experimental literature on incubation in problem solving and creativity. In M. A. Runco (Ed.), *Creativity research handbook* (Vol. 3). Cresskill, NJ: Hampton. doi:10.1016/j.neuroimage.2010.01.021

Dohrenwend, B. P. (2006). Inventorying stressful life events as risk factors for psychopathology: Toward resolution of the problem of intracategory variability. *Psychological Bulletin, 132,* 477–495.

Doja, A., & Roberts, W. (2006). Immunizations and autism: A review of the literature. *Canadian Journal of Neurological Sciences, 33*(4), 341–346.

Dolder, C. R. (2008). Side effects of antipsychotics. In K. T. Mueser & D. V. Jeste (Eds.), *Clinical handbook of schizophrenia* (pp. 168–177). New York, NY: Guilford.

Dollard, J., Doob, L. W., Miller, N. E., Mowrer, O. H., & Sears, R. R. (1939). *Frustration and aggression.* New Haven: Yale University Press.

Domes, G., Heinrichs, M., Michel, A., Berger, C., & Herpertz, S. C. (2007). Oxytocin improves "mind-reading" in humans. *Biological Psychiatry, 61*(6), 731–733. doi:10.1016/j.biopsych.2006.07.015

Domhoff, G. W. (2005a). The content of dreams: Methodologic and theoretical implications. In M. H. Kryger, T. Roth, & W. C. Dement (Eds.), *Principles and practice of sleep medicine.* Philadelphia, PA: Elsevier Saunders.

Domhoff, G. W. (2005b). Refocusing the neurocognitive approach to dreams: A critique of the Hobson versus Solms debate. *Dreaming, 15*(1), 3–20.

Dominowski, R. L., & Bourne, L. E., Jr. (1994). History of research on thinking and problem solving. In R. J. Sternberg (Ed.), *Thinking and problem solving.* San Diego, CA: Academic Press.

Domjan, M. (1992). Adult learning and mate choice: Possibilities and experimental evidence. *American Zoologist, 32,* 48–61.

Domjan, M. (1994). Formulation of a behavior system for sexual conditioning. *Psychonomic Bulletin & Review, 1,* 421–428.

Domjan, M. (1998). *The principles of learning and behavior.* Pacific Grove: Brooks/Cole.

Domjan, M., & Purdy, J. E. (1995). Animal research in psychology: More than meets the eye of the general psychology student. *American Psychologist, 50,* 496–503.

Donaldson, Z. R., & Young, L. J. (2008). Oxytocin, vasopressin, and the neurogenetics of sociality. *Science, 322*(5903), 900–904. doi:10.1126/science.1158668

Doty, R. L. (1991). Olfactory system. In T. V. Getchell, R. L. Doty, L. M. Bartoshuk, & J. B. Snow, Jr. (Eds.), *Smell and taste in health and disease.* New York, NY: Raven.

Doty, R. L. (2001). Olfaction. *Annual Review of Psychology, 52,* 423–452.

Doty, R. L. (2010). Olfaction. In E. B. Goldstein (Ed.), *Encyclopedia of perception.* Thousand Oaks, CA: Sage.

Dougall, A. L., & Baum, A. (2001). Stress, health, and illness. In A. Baum, T. A. Revenson, & J. E. Singer (Eds.), *Handbook of health psychology* (pp. 321–338). Mahwah, NJ: Erlbaum.

Douglas, A. J. (2010). Baby on board: Do responses to stress in the maternal brain mediate adverse pregnancy outcome? *Frontiers in Neuroendocrinology, 31*(3), 359–376. doi:10.1016/j.yfrne.2010.05.002

Dovidio, J. F., & Gaertner, S. L. (2008). New directions in aversive racism research: Persistence and pervasiveness. In C. Willis-Esqueda (Ed.), *Motivational aspects of prejudice and racism* (pp. 43–67). New York, NY: Springer Science & Business Media. doi:10.1007/978-0-387-73233-6_3

Dovidio, J. F., & Gaertner, S. L. (2010). Intergroup bias. In S. T. Fiske, D. T. Gilbert, & G. Lindzey (Eds.), *Handbook of social psychology* (5th ed., Vol. 1, pp. 353–393). Hoboken, NJ: Wiley.

Dovidio, J. F., Gaertner, S. L., & Kawakami, K. (2010). Racism. In J. F. Dovidio, M. Hewstone, P. Glick, & V. M. Esses (Eds.), *The Sage handbook of prejudice, stereotyping, and discrimination.* Los Angeles, CA: Sage.

Dowling, K. W. (2005). The effect of lunar phases on domestic violence incident rates. *The Forensic Examiner, 14*(4), 13–18.

Downar, J., & Kapur, S. (2008). Biological theories. In K. T. Mueser & D. V. Jeste (Eds.), *Clinical handbook of schizophrenia* (pp. 25–34). New York, NY: Guilford.

Draganski, B., Gaser, C., Busch, V., Schuierer, G., Bogdahn, U., & May, A. (2004). Changes in grey matter induced by training. *Nature, 427,* 311–312.

Dranovsky, A., & Hen, R. (2006). Hippocampal neurogenesis: Regulation by stress and antidepressants. *Biological Psychiatry, 59,* 1136–1143.

Draycott, S., & Dabbs, A. (1998). Cognitive dissonance 1: An overview of the literature and its integration into theory and practice of clinical psychology. *British Journal of Clinical Psychology, 37,* 341–353.

Drewnowski, A. (1995). Standards for the treatment of obesity. In K. D. Brownell, & C. G. Fairburn (Eds.), *Eating disorders and obesity: A comprehensive handbook.* New York, NY: Guilford.

Drews, F. A., Pasupathi, M., & Strayer, D. L. (2008). Passenger and cell phone conversations in simulated driving. *Journal of Experimental Psychology: Applied, 14*(4), 392–400. doi:10.1037/a0013119

Drews, F. A., Yazdani, H., Godfrey, C. N., Cooper, J. M., & Strayer, D. L. (2009). Text messaging during simulated driving. *Human Factors, 51*(5), 762–770. doi:10.1177/0018720809353319

Dubicka, B., Hadley, S., & Roberts, C. (2006). Suicidal behaviour in youths with depression treated with new-generation antidepressants—Meta-analysis. *British Journal of Psychiatry, 189,* 393–398.

Dubno, J. R. (2010). Aging and hearing. In E. B. Goldstein (Ed.), *Encyclopedia of perception.* Thousand Oaks, CA: Sage.

DuBois, G. E. (2010). Taste stimuli: Chemicals and food. In E. B. Goldstein (Ed.), *Encyclopedia of perception.* Thousand Oaks, CA: Sage.

Dubovsky, S. L. (2009). Benzodiazepine receptor agonists and antagonists. In B. J. Sadock, V. A. Sadock, & P. Ruiz (Eds.), *Kaplan & Sadock's comprehensive textbook of psychiatry* (pp. 3044–3055). Philadelphia, PA: Lippincott Williams & Wilkins.

Duckworth, A. L., & Seligman, M. E. P. (2005). Self-discipline outdoes IQ in predicting academic performance of adolescents. *Psychological Science, 16,* 939–944.

Duckworth, K., & Borus, J. F. (1999). Population-based psychiatry in the public sector and managed care. In A. M. Nicholi (Ed.), *The Harvard guide to psychiatry.* Cambridge, MA: Harvard University Press.

Dudai, Y. (2004). The neurobiology of consolidation, or, how stable is the engram? *Annual Review of Psychology, 55,* 51–86.

Dudley, M., Hadzi-Pavlovic, D., Andrews, D., & Perich, T. (2008). New-generation antidepressants, suicide and depressed adolescents: How should clinicians respond to changing evidence? *Australian and New Zealand Journal of Psychiatry, 42*(6), 456–466. doi:10.1080/00048670802050538

Duffy, J. F., Willson, H. J., Wang, W., & Czeisler, C. A. (2009). Healthy older adults better tolerate sleep deprivation than young adults. *Journal of the American Geriatrics Society, 57*(7), 1245–1251. doi:10.1111/j.1532-5415.2009.02303.x

Duffy, V. B. (2004). Associations between oral sensation, dietary behaviors and risk of cardiovascular disease (CVD). *Appetite, 43*(1), 5–9.

Duffy, V. B., Lucchina, L. A., & Bartoshuk, L. M. (2004). Genetic variation in taste: Potential biomarker for cardiovascular disease risk? In J. Prescott & B. J. Tepper (Eds.), *Genetic variations in taste sensitivity: Measurement, significance and implications* (pp. 195–228), New York, NY: Dekker.

Duffy, V. B., Peterson, J. M., & Bartoshuk, L. M. (2004). Associations between taste genetics, oral sensations and alcohol intake. *Physiology & Behavior, 82,* 435–445.

Dum, R. P., & Strick, P. L. (2009). Basal ganglia and cerebellar circuits with the cerebral cortex. In M. S. Gazzangia (Ed.), *The cognitive neurosciences* (4th ed., pp. 553–564). Cambridge, MA: MIT Press.

Duman, R. S., & Monteggia, L. M. (2006). A neurotrophic model for stress-related mood disorders. *Biological Psychiatry, 59,* 1116–1127.

Duman, R. S., Polan, H. J., & Schatzberg, A. (2008). Neurobiologic foundations of mood disorders. In A. Tasman, J. Kay, J. A. Lieberman, M. B. First, & M. Maj (Eds.), *Psychiatry* (3rd ed.). New York, NY: Wiley-Blackwell.

Dunbar, K., & Blanchette, I. (2001). The in vivo/in vitro approach to cognition: The case of analogy. *Trends in Cognitive Sciences, 5,* 334–339.

Dunbar-Jacob, J., & Schlenk, E. (2001). Patient adherence to treatment regimen. In A. Baum, T. A. Revenson, & J. E. Singer (Eds.), *Handbook of health psychology.* Mahwah, NJ: Erlbaum.

Duncan, B. L. (1976). Differential social perception and attribution of intergroup violence: Testing the lower limits of stereotyping of blacks. *Journal of Personality and Social Psychology, 34,* 590–598.

Duncan, E., Boshoven, W., Harenski, K., Fiallos, A., Tracy, H., Jovanovic, T., et al. (2007). An fMRI study of the interaction of stress and cocaine cues on cocaine craving in cocaine-dependent users. *The American Journal on Addictions, 16*(3), 174–182. doi:10.1080/10550490701375285

Dunlop, B. W., Garlow, S. J., & Nemeroff, C. B. (2009). The neurochemistry of depressive disorders: Clinical studies. In D. S. Charney & E. J. Nestler (Eds.), *Neurobiology of mental illness* (3rd ed., pp. 435–460). New York, NY: Oxford University Press.

Dunn, E. W., Wilson, T. D., & Gilbert, D. T. (2003). Location, location, location: The misprediction of satisfaction in housing lotteries. *Personality and Social Psychology Bulletin, 29*(11), 1421–1432. doi:10.1177/0146167203256867

Durlak, J. A. (2003). Basic principles of meta-analysis. In M. C. Roberts and S. S. Ilardi (Eds.), *Handbook of research methods in clinical psychology.* Malden, MA: Blackwell.

Dutton, D. G., & Aron, A. P. (1974). Some evidence for heightened sexual attraction under conditions of high anxiety. *Journal of Personality and Social Psychology, 30,* 510–517. doi:10.1037/h0037031

Dwyer, J. (1995). Popular diets. In K. D. Brownell & C. G. Fairburn (Eds.), *Eating disorders and obesity.* New York, NY: Guilford.

Eagly, A. H. (1995). The science and politics of comparing women and men. *American Psychologist, 50,* 145–158.

Eagly, A. H., & Chaiken, S. (1995). Attitude strength, attitude structure, and resistance to change. In R. E. Petty & J. A. Krosnick (Eds.), *Attitude strength: Antecedents and consequences.* Mahwah, NJ: Erlbaum.

Eagly, A. H., & Wood, W. (1999). The origins of sex differences in human behavior: Evolved dispositions versus social roles. *American Psychologist, 54,* 408–423.

Easterlin, B. L., & Cardena, E. (1999). Cognitive and emotional differences between short- and long-term Vipassana meditators. *Imagination, Cognition and Personality, 18*(1), 68–81.

Ebbinghaus, H. (1885/1964). *Memory: A contribution to experimental psychology* (H. A. Ruger & E. R. Bussemius, Trans.). New York, NY: Dover.

Edwards, D. M., Hale, K. L., Maddux, R. E., & Rapaport, M. H. (2008). Anxiolytic drugs. In A. Tasman, J. Kay, J. A. Lieberman, M. B. First, & M. Maj (Eds.), *Psychiatry* (3rd ed.). New York, NY: Wiley-Blackwell.

Edwards, S., Jedrychowski, W., Butscher, M., Camann, D., Kieltyka, A., Mroz, E., et al. (2010). Prenatal exposure to airborne polycyclic aromatic hydrocarbons and children's intelligence at 5 years of age in a prospective cohort study in Poland. *Environmental Health Perspectives, 118*(9), 1326–1331. doi:10.1289/ehp.0901070

Efron, R. (1990). *The decline and fall of hemispheric specialization.* Hillsdale, NJ: Erlbaum.

Ehrenberg, O., & Ehrenberg, M. (1994). *The psychotherapy maze: A consumer's guide to getting in and out of therapy.* Northvale, NJ: Jason Aronson.

Eibl-Eibesfeldt, I. (1975). *Ethology: The biology of behavior.* New York, NY: Holt, Rinehart, & Winston.

Eich, E., Macaulay, D., Loewenstein, R. J., & Dihle, P. H. (1997). Memory, amnesia, and dissociative identity disorder. *Psychological Science, 8,* 417–422.

Eichenbaum, H. (2004). An information processing framework for memory representation by the hippocampus. In M. S. Gazzaniga (Ed.), *The cognitive neurosciences.* Cambridge, MA: MIT Press.

Eichenwald, E., & Stark, A. (2008). Management and outcomes of very low birth weight. *New England Journal of Medicine, 358*(16), 1700–1711.

Eid, M., & Diener, E. (2001). Norms for experiencing emotions in different cultures: Inter- and intranational differences. *Journal of Personality and Social Psychology, 81,* 869–885.

Einstein, G. O., & McDaniel, M. A. (2004). *Memory fitness: A guide for successful aging.* New Haven, CT: Yale University Press.

Einstein, G. O., McDaniel, M. A., Williford, C. L., Pagan, J. L., & Dismukes, R. K. (2003). Forgetting of intentions in demanding situations is rapid. *Journal of Experimental Psychology: Applied, 9*(3), 147–162.

Eippert, F., Bingel, U., Schoell, E. D., Yacubian, J., Klinger, R., Lorenz, J., & Büchel, C. (2009). Activation of the opioidergic descending pain control system underlies placebo analgesia. *Neuron, 63*(4), 533–543.

Eisenberg, N., Spinrad, T., & Sadovsky, A. (2006). Empathy-related responding in children. In M. Killen & J. G. Smetana (Eds.), *Handbook of moral development.* Mahwah, NJ: Erlbaum.

Eisner, E. W. (2004). Multiple intelligences. *Teachers College Record, 106*(1), 31–39.

Ekman, P. (1992). Facial expressions of emotion: New findings, new questions. *Psychological Science, 3,* 34–38.

Ekman, P., & Friesen, W. V. (1975). *Unmasking the face.* Englewood Cliffs, NJ: Prentice-Hall.

Ekman, P., & Friesen, W. V. (1984). *Unmasking the face.* Palo Alto: Consulting Psychologists Press.

Elbogen, E. B., & Johnson, S. C. (2009). The intricate link between violence and mental disorder: Results from the national epidemiologic survey on alcohol and related conditions. *Archives of General Psychiatry, 66*(2), 152–161. doi:10.1001/archgenpsychiatry.2008.537

Elliot, A. J., & Maier, M. A. (2007). Color and psychological functioning. *Current Directions in Psychological Science, 16*(5), 250–254. doi:10.1111/j.1467-8721.2007.00514.x

Elliot, A. J., Maier, M. A., Binser, M. J., Friedman, R., & Pekrun, R. (2009). The effect of red on avoidance behavior in achievement contexts. *Personality and Social Psychology Bulletin, 35*(3), 365–375. doi:10.1177/0146167208328330

Elliot, A. J., Maier, M. A., Moller, A. C., Friedman, R., & Meinhardt, J. (2007). Color and psychological functioning: The effect of red on performance attainment. *Journal of Experimental Psychology: General, 136*(1), 154–168. doi:10.1037/0096-3445.136.1.154

Elliot, A. J., & Niesta, D. (2008). Romantic red: Red enhances men's attraction to women. *Journal of Personality and Social Psychology, 95*(5), 1150–1164. doi:10.1037/0022-3514.95.5.1150

Ellis, A. (1973). *Humanistic psychotherapy: The rational-emotive approach.* New York, NY: Julian Press.

Ellis, A. (1977). *Reason and emotion in psychotherapy.* Seacaucus, NJ: Lyle Stuart.

Ellis, A. (1985). *How to live with and without anger.* New York, NY: Citadel Press.

Ellis, A. (1987). The evolution of rational-emotive therapy (RET) and cognitive behavior therapy (CBT). In J. K. Zeig (Ed.), *The evolution of psychotherapy.* New York, NY: Brunner/Mazel.

Ellis, A. (1999). *How to make yourself happy and remarkably less disturbable.* Atascadero, CA: Impact Publishers.

Ellis, A. (2001). *Feeling better, getting better: Profound self-help therapy for your emotions.* Atascadero, CA: Impact Publishers.

Ellis, H. H. (1898). Autoerotism: A psychological study. *Alienist and Neurologist, 19,* 260–299.

Ellsworth, P. C., & Scherer, K. R. (2003). Appraisal processes in emotion. In R. J. Davidson, K. R. Scherer, & H. H. Goldsmith (Ed.), *Handbook of affective sciences.* New York, NY: Oxford University Press.

Ellwood, S., Pallier, G., Snyder, A., & Gallate, J. (2009). The incubation effect: Hatching a solution? *Creativity Research Journal, 21*(1), 6–14. doi:10.1080/10400410802633368

Elmitiny, N., Yan, X., Radwan, E., Russo, C., & Nashar, D. (2010). Classification analysis of driver's stop/go decision and red-light running violation. *Accident Analysis and Prevention, 42*(1), 101–111. doi:10.1016/j.aap.2009.07.007

Elms, A. C. (2009). Obedience lite. *American Psychologist, 64*(1), 32–36. doi:10.1037/a0014473

Elpers, J. R. (2000). Public psychiatry. In B. J. Sadock & V. A. Sadock (Eds.), *Kaplan and Sadock's comprehensive textbook of psychiatry* (7th ed., Vol. 2). Philadelphia, PA: Lippincott Williams & Wilkins.

Elpers, J. R. (2001). Public psychiatry. In B. J. Sadock & V. A. Sadock (Eds.), *Kaplan and Sadock's comprehensive textbook of psychiatry* (7th ed., Vol. 2). Philadelphia, PA: Lippincott Williams & Wilkins.

Else-Quest, N. M., Hyde, J., & Linn, M. C. (2010). Cross-national patterns of gender differences in mathematics: A meta-analysis. *Psychological Bulletin, 136*(1), 103–127. doi:10.1037/a0018053

Emavardhana, T., & Tori, C. D. (1997). Changes in self-concept, ego defense mechanisms, and religiosity following seven-day Vipassana meditation retreats. *Journal for the Scientific Study of Religion, 36,* 194–206.

Emmelkamp, P. M. G. (1994). Behavior therapy with adults. In A. E. Bergin & S. L. Garfield (Eds.), *Handbook of psychotherapy and behavior change* (4th ed.). New York, NY: Wiley.

Emmelkamp, P. M. G. (2004). Behavior therapy with adults. In M. J. Lambert (Ed.), *Bergin and Garfield's handbook of psychotherapy and behavior change.* New York, NY: Wiley.

Engemann, K. M., & Owyang, M. T. (2005, April). So much for that merit raise: The link between wages and appearance. *The Regional Economist,* pp. 10–11.

Engle, R. W. (2001). What is working memory capacity? In H. L. Roediger III, J. S. Nairne, I. Neath, & A. M. Surprenant (Eds.), *The nature of remembering: Essays in honor of Robert G. Crowder.* Washington, DC: American Psychological Association.

Epley, N., & Huff, C. (1998). Suspicion, affective response, and educational benefit as a result of deception in psychology research. *Personality and Social Psychology Bulletin, 24,* 759–768.

Epstein, S., Donovan, S., & Denes-Raj, V. (1999). The missing link in the paradox of the Linda conjunction problem: Beyond knowing and thinking of the conjunction rule, the intrinsic appeal of heuristic processing. *Personality and Social Psychology Bulletin, 25,* 204–214.

Erber, M. W., Hodges, S. D., & Wilson, T. D. (1995). Attitude strength, attitude stability, and the effects of analyzing reasons. In R. E. Petty & J. A. Krosnick (Eds.), *Attitude strength: Antecedents and consequences.* Mahwah, NJ: Erlbaum.

Erdelyi, M. H. (2001). Defense processes can be conscious or unconscious. *American Psychologist, 56,* 761–762.

Erdfelder, E., Brandt, M., & Bröder, A. (2007). Recollection biases in hindsight judgments. *Social Cognition, 25,* 114–131.

Erikson, E. (1963). *Childhood and society.* New York, NY: Norton.

Erikson, E. (1968). *Identity: Youth and crisis.* New York, NY: Norton.

Espejo, E., Ferriter, C., Hazel, N., Keenan-Miller, D., Hoffman, L., & Hammen, C. (2011). Predictors of subjective ratings of stressor severity: The effects of current mood and neuroticism. *Stress & Health: Journal of the International Society for the Investigation of Stress, 27*(1), 23–33.

Esses, V. M., Jackson, L. M., & Bennett-AbuAyyash, C. (2010). Intergroup competition. In J. F. Dovidio, M. Hewstone, P. Glick, & V. M. Esses (Eds.), *The Sage handbook of prejudice, stereotyping, and discrimination.* Los Angeles, CA: Sage.

Esterson, A. (2001). The mythologizing of psychoanalytic history: Deception and self-deception in Freud's accounts of the seduction theory episode. *History of Psychiatry, 7,* 329–352.

Estes, W. K. (1999). Models of human memory: A 30-year retrospective. In C. Izawa (Ed.), *On human memory: Evolution, progress, and reflections on the 30th anniversary of the Atkinson-Shiffrin model.* Mahwah, NJ: Erlbaum.

Evans, G. W. (2004). The environment of childhood poverty. *American Psychologist, 59*(2), 77–92.

Evans, G. W., & Wener, R. E. (2006). Rail commuting duration and passenger stress. *Health Psychology, 25,* 408–412.

Evans, J. T. (2007). *Hypothetical thinking: Dual processes in reasoning and judgment.* New York, NY: Psychology Press.

Everett, P. B., Hayward, S. C., & Meyers, A. W. (1974). The effects of a token reinforcement procedure on bus ridership. *Journal of Applied Behavior Analysis, 7,* 1–9.

Eysenck, H. J. (1967). *The biological basis of personality.* Springfield, IL: Charles C. Thomas.

Eysenck, H. J. (1982). *Personality, genetics and behavior: Selected papers.* New York, NY: Praeger.

Eysenck, H. J. (1990a). Biological dimensions of personality. In L. A. Pervin (Ed.), *Handbook of personality: Theory and research.* New York, NY: Guilford.

Eysenck, H. J. (1990b). *Decline and fall of the Freudian empire.* Washington, DC: Scott-Townsend.

Eysenck, H. J., & Kamin, L. (1981). *The intelligence controversy.* New York, NY: Wiley.

Eysenck, M. W., Mogg, K., May, J., Richards, A., & Mathews, A. (1991). Bias in interpretation of ambiguous sentences related to threat in anxiety. *Journal of Abnormal Psychology, 100,* 144–150.

Faber Taylor, A. & Kuo, F. E. (2009). Children with attention deficits concentrate better after walk in the park. *Journal of Attention Disorders, 12,* 402–409.

Fabrigar, L. R., MacDonald, T. K., & Wegener, D. T. (2005). The structure of attitudes. In D. Albarracin, B. T. Johnson, & M. P. Zanna (Eds.), *The handbook of attitudes.* Mahwah, NJ: Erlbaum.

Fabrigar, L. R., & Wegener, D. T. (2010). Attitude structure. In R. F. Baumeister & E. J. Finkel (Eds.), *Advanced social psychology: The state of the science* (pp. 177–216). New York, NY: Oxford University Press.

Fagot, B. I., Hagan, R., Leinbach, M. D., & Kronsberg, S. (1985). Differential reactions to assertive and communicative acts of toddler boys and girls. *Child Development, 56,* 1499–1505.

Fairburn, C. G., Cooper, Z., & Murphy, R. (2009). Bulimia nervosa. In M. C. Gelder, N. C. Andreasen, J. J. López-Ibor, Jr., & J. R. Geddes (Eds.). *New Oxford textbook of psychiatry* (2nd ed., Vol. 1). New York, NY: Oxford University Press.

Fakhoury, W., & Priebe, S. (2002). The process of deinstitutionalization: An international overview. *Current Opinion in Psychiatry, 15*(2), 187–192.

Falls, W. A. (1998). Extinction: A review of therapy and the evidence suggesting that memories are not erased with nonreinforcement. In W. O'Donohue (Ed.), *Learning and behavior therapy.* Boston, MA: Allyn & Bacon.

Faraday, A. (1974). *The dream game.* New York, NY: Harper & Row.

Farah, A. (1997). An overview of ECT. *Primary Psychiatry, 4,* 58–62.

Faravelli, C., & Pallanti, S. (1989). Recent life events and panic disorders. *American Journal of Psychiatry, 146,* 622–626.

Fatemi, S., & Folsom, T. D. (2009). The neurodevelopmental hypothesis of schizophrenia, revisited. *Schizophrenia Bulletin, 35*(3), 528–548. doi:10.1093/schbul/sbn187

Fausto-Sterling, A. (1992). *Myths of gender.* New York, NY: Basic Books.

Fazio, R. H., & Olson, M. A. (2003). Attitudes: Foundations, functions, and consequences. In M. A. Hogg & J. Cooper (Eds.), *The Sage handbook of social psychology.* Thousand Oaks, CA: Sage.

Fearon, R., Bakermans-Kranenburg, M. J., van IJzendoorn, M. H., Lapsley, A., & Roisman, G. I. (2010). The significance of insecure attachment and disorganization in the development of children's externalizing behavior: A meta-analytic study. *Child Development, 81*(2), 435–456. doi:10.1111/j.1467-8624.2009.01405.x

Feeney, D. M. (1987). Human rights and animal welfare. *American Psychologist, 42,* 593–599.

Feeney, J. A. (2008). Adult romantic attachment: Developments in the study of couple relationships. In J. Cassidy & P. R. Shaver (Eds.), *Handbook of attachment: Theory, research, and clinical applications* (2nd ed., pp. 456–481). New York, NY: Guilford.

Fehr, B. (2001). The status of theory and research on love and commitment. In G. J. O. Fletcher & M. S. Clark (Eds.), *Blackwell handbook of social psychology: Interpersonal processes.* Malden, MA: Blackwell Publishing.

Fehr, B. (2008). Friendship formation. In S. Sprecher, A. Wenzel, & J. Harvey (Eds.), *Handbook of relationship initiation* (pp. 235–247). New York, NY: Psychology Press.

Feingold, A. (1992). Good-looking people are not what we think. *Psychological Bulletin, 111,* 304–341.

Feinstein, J. S., Adolphs, R., Damasio, A., & Tranel, D. (2011). The human amygdala and the induction and experience of fear. *Current Biology, 21,* 34–38. doi:10.1016/j.cub.2010.11.042

Feist, G. J. (1998). A meta-analysis of personality in scientific and artistic creativity. *Personality and Social Psychology Review, 2,* 290-309.

Feist, G. J. (2004). The evolved fluid specificity of human creativity talent. In R. J. Sternberg, E. L. Grigorenko, & J. L. Singer (Eds.), *Creativity: From potential to realization.* Washington, DC: American Psychological Association.

Feist, G. J. (2010). The function of personality in creativity: The nature and nurture of the creative personality. In J. C. Kaufman & R. J. Sternberg (Eds.), *The Cambridge handbook of creativity* (pp. 113–130). New York, NY: Cambridge University Press.

Feldman, D. H. (1988). Creativity: Dreams, insights, and transformations. In R. J. Sternberg (Ed.), *The nature of creativity: Contemporary psychological perspectives.* Cambridge: Cambridge University Press.

Feldman, D. H. (2003). Cognitive development in childhood. In R. M. Lerner, M. A. Easterbrooks, & J. Mistry (Eds.), *Handbook of psychology, Vol. 6: Developmental psychology.* New York, NY: Wiley.

Feng, J., Spence, I., & Pratt, J. (2007). Playing an action video game reduces gender differences in spatial cognition. *Psychological Science, 18*(10), 850–855. doi:10.1111/j.1467-9280.2007.01990.x

Fenwick, P. (1987). Meditation and the EEG. In M. A. West (Ed.), *The psychology of meditation.* Oxford: Clarendon Press.

Ferguson, M. J., & Bargh, J. A. (2004). Liking is for doing: The effects of goal pursuit on automatic evaluation. *Journal of Personality and Social Psychology, 87,* 557–572.

Ferguson, T. (1993). Working with your doctor. In D. Goleman & J. Gurin (Eds.), *Mind-body medicine: How to use your mind for better health.* Yonkers, NY: Consumer Reports Books.

Ferster, C. S., & Skinner, B. F. (1957). *Schedules of reinforcement.* New York, NY: Appleton-Century-Crofts.

Festinger, L. (1957). *A theory of cognitive dissonance.* Stanford, CA: Stanford University Press.

Festinger, L., & Carlsmith, J. M. (1959). Cognitive consequences of forced compliance. *Journal of Abnormal and Social Psychology, 58,* 203–210.

Feuerstein, G. Z., Ruffolo, R. R., Coughlin, C., Wang, J., & Miller, D. (2007). Inflammation. In G. Fink (Ed.), *Encyclopedia of stress.* San Diego, CA: Elsevier.

Ficca, G., Axelsson, J., Mollicone, D. J., Muto, V., & Vitiello, M. V. (2010). Naps, cognition and performance. *Sleep Medicine Reviews, 14*(4), 249–258. doi:10.1016/j.smrv.2009.09.005

Fields, R. D. (2004). The other half of the brain. *Scientific American, 290*(4), 54–61.

Fife-Schaw, C. (2006). Questionnaire design. In G. M. Breakwell, S. Hammond, C. Fife-Schaw, & J. A. Smith (Eds.), *Research methods in psychology* (3rd ed.). London, England: Sage.

Fifer, W. P., Monk, C. E., & Grose-Fifer, J. (2001). Prenatal development and risk. In G. Bremner & A. Fogel (Eds.), *Blackwell handbook of infant development* (pp. 505–542). Malden, MA: Blackwell.

Figueredo, A. J., Gladden, P., Vásquez, G., Wolf, P. S. A., & Jones, D. N. (2009). Evolutionary theories of personality. In P. J. Corr & G. Matthews (Eds.), *Cambridge handbook of personality psychology* (pp. 265–274). New York, NY: Cambridge University Press.

Figueredo, A. J., Sefcek, J. A., Vasquez, G., Brumbach, B. H., King, J. E., & Jacobs, W. J. (2005). Evolutionary personality psychology. In D. M. Buss (Ed.), *The handbook of evolutionary psychology.* New York, NY: Wiley.

Finan, P. H., Zautra, A. J., & Wershba, R. (2011). The dynamics of emotion in adaptation to stress. In R. J. Contrada & A. Baum (Eds.), *The handbook of stress science: Biology, psychology, and health* (pp. 111–121). New York, NY: Springer.

Fine, C. (2010). From scanner to sound bite: Issues in interpreting and reporting sex differences in the brain. *Current Directions in Psychological Science, 19*(5), 280–283. doi:10.1177/0963721410383248

Fink, B., Neave, N., Manning, J. T., & Grammer, K. (2006). Facial symmetry and judgments of attractiveness, health and personality. *Personality and Individual Differences, 41,* 1253–1262.

Fink, B., & Penton-Voak, I. (2002). Evolutionary psychology of facial attractiveness. *Current Directions in Psychological Science, 11*(5), 154–158.

Fink, M. F. (2009). Non-pharmacological somatic treatments: Electroconvulsive therapy. In M. C. Gelder, N. C. Andreasen, J. J. López-Ibor, Jr., & J. R. Geddes (Eds.), *New Oxford textbook of psychiatry* (2nd ed., Vol. 1). New York, NY: Oxford University Press.

Finnegan, L. P., & Kandall, S. R. (2005). Maternal and neonatal effects of alcohol and drugs. In J. H. Lowinson, P. Ruiz, R. B. Millman, & J. G. Langrod (Eds.), *Substance abuse: A comprehensive textbook.* Baltimore, MD: Williams & Wilkins.

Finucane, M. L., Alhakami, A. S., Slovic, P., & Johnson, S. M. (2000). The affect heuristic in judgments of risks and benefits. *Journal of Behavioral Decision Making, 13,* 1–17.

First, M. B. (2008). Psychiatric classification. In A. Tasman, J. Kay, J. A. Lieberman, M. B. First, & M. Maj (Eds.), *Psychiatry* (3rd ed.). New York, NY: Wiley-Blackwell.

Fischer, K. W., & Hencke, R. W. (1996). Infants' construction of actions in context: Piaget's contribution to research on early development. *Psychological Science, 7,* 204–210.

Fischhoff, B. (2007). An early history of hindsight research. *Social Cognition, 25*(1), 10–13.

Fisher, S., & Greenberg, R. P. (1996). *Freud scientifically reappraised: Testing the theories and therapy.* New York, NY: Wiley.

Fisher, S., & Greenberg, R. P. (1997). The curse of the placebo: Fanciful pursuit of a pure biological therapy. In S. Fisher & R. P. Greenberg (Eds.), *From placebo to panacea: Putting psychiatric drugs to the test.* New York, NY: Wiley.

Fishman, D. B., & Franks, C. M. (1992). Evolution and differentiation within behavior therapy: A theoretical epistemological review. In D. K. Freedheim (Ed.), *History of psychotherapy: A century of change*. Washington, DC: American Psychological Association.

Fiske, S. T. (1998). Stereotyping, prejudice, and discrimination. In D. T. Gilbert, S. T. Fiske, & G. Lindzey (Eds.), *The handbook of social psychology*. New York, NY: McGraw-Hill.

Fiske, S. T. (2004). Mind the gap: In praise of informal sources of formal theory. *Personality and Social Psychology Review, 8*(2), 132–137.

Fiske, S. T., & Russell, A. M. (2010). Cognitive processes. In J. F. Dovidio, M. Hewstone, P. Glick, & V. M. Esses (Eds.), *The Sage handbook of prejudice, stereotyping, and discrimination*. Los Angeles, CA: Sage.

Fitness, J., Fletcher, G., & Overall, N. (2003). Interpersonal attraction and intimate relationships. In M. A. Hogg & J. Cooper (Eds.), *The Sage handbook of social psychology*. Thousand Oaks, CA: Sage.

Fitzgerald, P. B. (2009). Repetitive transcranial magnetic stimulation treatment for depression: Lots of promise but still lots of questions. *Brain Stimulation, 2*(4), 185–187. doi:10.1016/j.brs.2009.08.005

Flavell, J. H. (1996). Piaget's legacy. *Psychological Science, 7*, 200–203.

Fleeson, W. (2004). Moving personality beyond the person-situation debate: The challenge and the opportunity of within-person variability. *Current Directions in Psychological Science, 13*(2), 83–87.

Fleeson, W., Malanos, A. B., & Achille, N. M. (2002). An intraindividual process approach to the relationship between extraversion and positive affect: Is acting extraverted as "good" as being extraverted? *Journal of Personality and Social Psychology, 83*, 1409–1422.

Flett, G. L., Vredenburg, K., & Krames, L. (1995). The stability of depressive symptoms in college students: An empirical demonstration of regression to the mean. *Journal of Psychopathology & Behavioral Assessment, 17*, 403–415.

Florentine, M., & Heinz, M. (2010). Audition: Loudness. In E. B. Goldstein (Ed.), *Encyclopedia of perception*. Thousand Oaks, CA: Sage.

Flores, B. H., Musselman, D. L., DeBattista, C., Garlow, S. J., Schatzberg, A. F., & Nemeroff, C. B. (2004). Biology of mood disorders. In A. F. Schatzberg & C. B. Nemeroff (Eds.), *Textbook of psychopharmacology*. Washington, DC: American Psychiatric Publishing.

Floyd, J. A., Janisse, J. J., Jenuwine, E. S., & Ager, J. W. (2007). Changes in REM-sleep percentage over the adult lifespan. *Sleep, 30*, 829–836.

Flynn, J. R. (1987). Massive IQ gains in 14 nations: What IQ tests really measure. *Psychological Bulletin, 101*, 171–191.

Flynn, J. R. (1999). Searching for justice: The discovery of IQ gains over time. *American Psychologist, 54*, 5–20.

Flynn, J. R. (2003). Movies about intelligence: The limitations of *g. Current Directions in Psychological Science, 12*(3), 95–99.

Flynn, J. R. (2007). *What is intelligence? Beyond the Flynn effect*. New York, NY: Cambridge University Press.

Flynn, M. G., McFarlin, B. K., & Markofski, M. M. (2007). The anti-inflammatory actions of exercise training. *American Journal of Lifestyle Medicine, 1*, 220–235.

Fodor, E. M., & Carver, R. A. (2000). Achievement and power motives, performance feedback, and creativity. *Journal of Research in Personality, 34*, 380–396.

Foldvary-Schaefer, N. (2006). *Getting a good night's sleep*. Cleveland: Cleveland Clinic Press.

Folkman, S. (2008). The case for positive emotions in the stress process. *Anxiety, Stress & Coping: An International Journal, 21*(1), 3–14.

Folkman, S., & Moskowitz, J. T. (2000). Positive affect and the other side of coping. *American Psychologist, 55*, 647–654.

Folkman, S., & Moskowitz, J. T. (2004). Coping: Pitfalls and promise. *Annual Review of Psychology, 55*, 745–774.

Folkman, S., Moskowitz, J. T., Ozer, E. M., & Park, C. L. (1997). Positive meaningful events and coping in the context of HIV/AIDS. In B. H. Gottlieb (Ed.), *Coping with chronic stress* (pp. 293–314). New York, NY: Plenum.

Follette, W. C., & Davis, D. (2009). Clinical practice and the issue of repressed memories: Avoiding an ice patch on the slippery slope. In W. O'Donohue & S. R. Graybar (Eds.), *Handbook of contemporary psychotherapy: Toward an improved understanding of effective psychotherapy* (pp. 47–73). Thousand Oaks, CA: Sage.

Folsom, D. P., Gilmer, T., Barrio, C., Moore, D. J., Bucardo, J., Lindamer, L. A., et al. (2007). A longitudinal study of the use of mental health services by persons with serious mental illness: Do Spanish-speaking Latinos differ from English-speaking Latinos and Caucasians? *American Journal Psychiatry, 164*, 1173–1180.

Folsom, D. P., Hawthorne, W., Lindamer, L., Gilmer, T., Bailey, A., Golsham, S., Garcia, P., Unutzer, J., Hough, R., & Jeste, D. V. (2005). Prevalence and risk factors for homelessness and utilization of mental health services among 10,340 patients with serious mental illness in a large public mental health system. *American Journal Psychiatry, 162*, 370–376.

Food and Agriculture Organization of the United Nations. (2006). Livestock's long shadow: Environmental issues and options. Retrieved from http://www.fao.org/docrep/010/a0701e/a0701e00.htm

Foote, B., Smolin, Y., Kaplan M., Legatt, M. E., & Lipschitz, D. (2006). Prevalence of dissociative disorders in psychiatric outpatients. *American Journal of Psychiatry, 163*, 623–629.

Forcier, K., Stroud, L. R., Papandonatos, G. D., Hitsman, B., Reiches, M., Krishnamoorthy, J., et al. (2006). Links between physical fitness and cardiovascular reactivity and recovery to psychological stressors: A meta-analysis. *Health Psychology, 25*, 723–739.

Forsyth, D. R. (2004). Inferences about actions performed in constraining contexts: Correspondence bias or correspondent inference? *Current Psychology: Developmental, Learning, Personality, Social, 23*(1), 41–51.

Forsyth, D. R., & Strong, S. R. (1986). The scientific study of counseling and psychotherapy: A unificationist view. *American Psychologist, 41*, 113–119.

Foster, R. G. (2004). Are we trying to banish biological time? *Cerebrum, 6*, 7–26.

Foulkes, D. (1985). *Dreaming: A cognitive-psychological analysis*. Hillsdale, NJ: Erlbaum.

Foulkes, D. (1996). Dream research: 1953–1993. *Sleep, 19*, 609–624.

Fournier, J. C., DeRubeis, R. J., Hollon, S. D., Dimidjian, S., Amsterdam, J. D., Shelton, R. C., & Fawcett, J. (2010). Antidepressant drug effects and depression severity: A patient-level meta-analysis. *Journal of the American Medical Association, 303*(1), 47–53.

Fowers, B. J., & Davidov, B. J. (2006). The virtue of multiculturalism: Personal transformation, character, and openness to the other. *American Psychologist, 61*, 581–594.

Fox, G. L., Bruce, C., & Combs-Orme, T. (2000). Parenting expectations and concerns of fathers and mothers of newborn infants. *Family Relations, 49*(2), 123–131.

Francis, G. (1999). Spatial frequency and visual persistence: Cortical reset. *Spatial Vision, 12*, 31–50.

Francis, L. A., & Birch, L. L. (2005). Maternal influences on daughters' restrained eating behavior. *Health Psychology, 24*, 548–554.

Frank, J. D. (1961). *Persuasion and healing*. Baltimore, MD: Johns Hopkins University Press.

Frank, L. K. (1939). Projective methods for the study of personality. *Journal of Psychology, 8*, 343–389.

Frank, L. R. (1990). Electroshock: Death, brain damage, memory loss, and brainwashing. *The Journal of Mind and Behavior, 11*(3/4), 489–512.

Frankland, P. W., & Bontempi, B. (2005). The organization of recent and remote memories. *Nature Reviews Neuroscience, 6*(2), 119–130.

Frantz, C. M., & Mayer, F. S. (2009). The emergency of climate change: Why are we failing to take action? *Analyses of Social Issues & Public Policy, 9*, 205–222.

Frasure-Smith, N., & Lesperance, F. (2005). Depression and coronary heart disease: Complex synergism of mind, body, and environment. *Current Directions in Psychological Science, 14*(1), 39–43.

Frederick, S., & Loewenstein, G. (1999). Hedonic adaptation. In D. Kahneman, E. Diener, & N. Schwarz (Eds.), *Well-being: The foundations of hedonic psychology*. New York, NY: Russell Sage Foundation.

Fredrickson, B. L. (2001). The role of positive emotions in positive psychology: The broaden-and-build theory of positive emotions. *American Psychologist, 56*, 218–226.

Fredrickson, B. L. (2005). The broaden-and-build theory of positive emotions. In F. A. Huppert, N. Baylis, & B. Keverne (Eds.), *The science of well-being.* New York, NY: Oxford University Press.

Fredrickson, B. L. (2006). The broaden-and-build theory of positive emotions. In M. Csikszentmihalyi, & I. S. Csikszentmihalyi (Eds.), *A life worth living: Contributions to positive psychology.* New York, NY: Oxford University Press.

Fredrickson, B. L., & Losada, M. F. (2005). Positive affect and the complex dynamics of human flourishing. *American Psychologist, 60,* 678–686.

Fredrickson, B. L., Tugade, M. M., Waugh, C. E., & Larkin, G. R. (2003). What good are positive emotions in crises? A prospective study of resilience and emotions following the terrorist attacks on the United States on September 11, 2001. *Journal of Personality and Social Psychology, 84,* 365–376.

Freedman, J. L., & Fraser, S. C. (1966). Compliance without pressure: The foot-in-the-door technique. *Journal of Personality and Social Psychology, 4,* 195–202.

Freedman, R., Ross, R., Michels, R., Appelbaum, P., Siever, L., Binder, R., et al. (2007). Psychiatrists, mental illness, and violence. *American Journal of Psychiatry, 164*(9), 1315–1317. doi:10.1176/appi.ajp.2007.07061013

Freeman, N. K. (2007). Preschoolers' perceptions of gender appropriate toys and their parents' beliefs about genderized behaviors: Miscommunication, mixed messages, or hidden truths? *Early Childhood Education Journal, 34*(5), 357–366. doi:10.1007/s10643-006-0123-x

Freud, A. (1936). *The ego and the mechanisms of defense.* London: Hogarth Press and Institute of Psycho-Analysis.

Freud, S. (1900/1953). *The interpretation of dreams.* In J. Strachey (Ed.), *The standard edition of the complete psychological works of Sigmund Freud* (Vols. 4 and 5). London: Hogarth. (original work published 1900)

Freud, S. (1901/1960). *The psychopathology of everyday life.* In J. Strachey (Ed.), *The standard edition of the complete psychological works of Sigmund Freud* (Vol. 6). London: Hogarth. (original work published 1900)

Freud, S. (1910/1957). *Leonardo da Vinci: A study in psychosexuality* (Vol. 11). London, England: Hogarth Press. (original work published 1910)

Freud, S. (1914/1953). On narcissism: An introduction. In J. Strachey (Ed., Trans.), *The standard edition of the complete psychological works of Sigmund Freud* (Vol. 1). London, England: Hogarth Press. (original work published 1914)

Freud, S. (1924). *A general introduction to psychoanalysis.* New York, NY: Boni & Liveright.

Freud, S. (1933/1964). *New introductory lectures on psychoanalysis.* In J. Strachey (Ed.), *The standard edition of the complete psychological works of Sigmund Freud* (Vol. 22). London: Hogarth.

Freud, S. (1940). An outline of psychoanalysis. *International Journal of Psychoanalysis, 21,* 27–84.

Frey, B. S., & Stutzer, A. (2002). What can economists learn from happiness research? *Journal of Economic Literature, 40,* 402–435.

Frey, K. S., & Ruble, D. N. (1992). Gender constancy and the cost of sex-typed behavior: A test of the conflict hypothesis. *Developmental Psychology, 28,* 714–721.

Friedkin, N. E. (1999). Choice shift and group polarization. *American Sociological Review, 64,* 856–875.

Friedman, H. S. (2007). Personality, disease, and self-healing. In H. S. Friedman & R. C. Silver (Eds.), *Foundations of health psychology.* New York, NY: Oxford University Press.

Friedman, H. S., & Adler, N. E. (2007). The history and background of health psychology. In H. S. Friedman & R. C. Silver (Eds.), *Foundations of health psychology.* New York, NY: Oxford University Press.

Friedman, M., & Rosenman, R. F. (1974). *Type A behavior and your heart.* New York, NY: Knopf.

Frijda, N. H. (1999). Emotions and hedonic experience. In D. Kahneman, E. Diener, & N. Schwarz (Eds.), *Well-being: The foundations of hedonic psychology.* New York, NY: Russell Sage Foundation.

Frishman, L. J. (2001). Basic visual processes. In E. B. Goldstein (Ed.), *Blackwell handbook of perception.* Malden, MA: Blackwell.

Fritze, J. G., Blashki, G. A., Burke, S., and Wiseman, J. (2008). Hope, despair and transformation: Climate change and the promotion of mental health and well-being. *International Journal of Mental Health Systems, 2.*

Frumkin, H. (2001). Beyond toxicity: Human health and the natural environment. *American Journal of Preventive Medicine, 20,* 234–240.

Fullana, M. A., Mataix-Cols, D., Caspi, A., Harrington, H., Grisham, J. R., Moffitt, T. E., & Poulton, R. (2009). Obsessions and compulsions in the community: Prevalence, interference, help-seeking, developmental stability, and co-occurring psychiatric conditions. *American Journal of Psychiatry, 166*(3), 329–336. doi:10.1176/appi.ajp.2008.08071006

Funder, D. C. (2001). Personality. *Annual Review of Psychology, 52,* 197–221.

Furnham, A., McManus, C., & Scott, D. (2004). Personality, empathy, and attitudes to animal welfare. *Anthrozoos, 16,* 135–146.

Furumoto, L., & Scarborough, E. (1986). Placing women in the history of psychology: The first American women psychologists. *American Psychologist, 41,* 35–42.

Fyer, A. J. (2009). Anxiety disorders: Genetics. In B. J. Sadock, V. A. Sadock, & P. Ruiz (Eds.), *Kaplan & Sadock's comprehensive textbook of psychiatry* (9th ed., pp. 1898–1905). Philadelphia, PA: Lippincott Williams & Wilkins.

Gabbard, G. O. (2005). Major modalities: Psychoanalytic/psychodynamic. In G. O. Gabbard, J. S. Beck, & J. Holmes (Eds.), *Oxford textbook of psychotherapy.* New York, NY: Oxford University Press.

Gaddis, C. (1999, August 8). A Boggs life. *Tampa Tribune.* Retrieved from http://rays.tbo.com/rays/MGBWZ4RSL3E.html.

Gaeth, G. J., & Shanteau, J. (2000). Reducing the influence of irrelevant information on experienced decision makers. In T. Connolly, H. R. Arkes, & K. R. Hammond (Eds.), *Judgment and decision making: An interdisciplinary reader* (2nd ed., pp. 305–323). New York, NY: Cambridge University Press.

Gage, F. H. (2002). Neurogenesis in the adult brain. *Journal of Neuroscience, 22,* 612–613.

Gais, S., & Born, J. (2004). Declarative memory consolidation: Mechanisms acting during human sleep. *Learning & Memory, 11,* 679–685.

Galambos, N. L. (2004). Gender and gender role development in adolescence. In R. M. Lerner & L. Steinberg (Eds.), *Handbook of adolescent psychology.* New York, NY: Wiley.

Galati, D., Scherer, K. R., & Ricci-Bitti, P. E. (1997). Voluntary facial expression of emotion: Comparing congenitally blind with normally sighted encoders. *Journal of Personality and Social Psychology, 73*(6), 1363–1379. doi:10.1037/0022-3514.73.6.1363

Gallese, V., Fadiga, L., Fogassi, L. , & Rizzolatti, G. (1996). Action recognition in the premotor cortex. *Brain, 119,* 593–609.

Gallup, G. G., Jr., & Frederick, D. A. (2010). The science of sex appeal: An evolutionary perspective. *Review of General Psychology, 14*(3), 240–250.

Gangwisch, J. E., Heymsfield, S. B., Boden-Albala, B., et al. (2006). Short sleep duration as a risk factor for hypertension: Analyses of the first National Health and Nutrition Examination Survey. *Hypertension, 5,* 833–839.

Garakani, A., Murrough, J. W., Charney, D. S., & Bremner, J. D. (2009). The neurobiology of anxiety disorders. In D. S. Charney & E. J. Nestler (Eds.). *Neurobiology of mental illness* (3rd ed., pp. 655–691). New York, NY: Oxford University Press.

Garb, H. N., Florio, C. M., & Grove, W. M. (1998). The validity of the Rorschach and the Minnesota Multiphasic Personality Inventory: Results form meta-analysis. *Psychological Science, 9,* 402–404.

Garcia, J. (1989). Food for Tolman: Cognition and cathexis in concert. In T. Archer & L. G. Nilsson (Eds.), *Aversion, avoidance, and anxiety: Perspectives on aversively motivated behavior.* Hillsdale, NJ: Erlbaum.

Garcia, J., Clarke, J. C., & Hankins, W. G. (1973). Natural responses to scheduled rewards. In P. P. G. Bateson & P. Klopfer (Eds.), *Perspectives in ethology.* New York, NY: Plenum.

Garcia, J., & Koelling, R. A. (1966). Learning with prolonged delay of reinforcement. *Psychonomic Science, 5,* 121–122.

Garcia, J., & Rusiniak, K. W. (1980). What the nose learns from the mouth. In D. Muller-Schwarze & R. M. Silverstein (Eds.), *Chemical signals.* New York, NY: Plenum.

Gardner, E. (1975). *Fundamentals of neurology.* Philadelphia, PA: Saunders.

Gardner, G., & Prugh, T. (2008). Seeding the sustainable economy. In L. Starke (Ed.), *2008 State of the World: Innovations for a sustainable economy.* New York, NY: Norton.

Gardner, G.. & Stern, P. C. (2002). Human reactions to environmental hazards: Perceptual and cognitive processes. In *Environmental problems and human behavior* (2nd ed.). Boston, MA: Allyn & Bacon.

Gardner, G., & Stern, P. C. (2008). The short list: The most effective actions U.S. households can take to curb climate change. *Environment, 50*(5), 12–24.

Gardner, H. (1983). *Frames of mind: The theory of multiple intelligences.* New York, NY: Basic Books.

Gardner, H. (1985). *The mind's new science: A history of the cognitive revolution.* New York, NY: Basic Books.

Gardner, H. (1993). *Multiple intelligences: The theory in practice.* New York, NY: Basic Books.

Gardner, H. (1999). *Intelligence reframed: Multiple intelligences for the 21st century.* New York, NY: Basic Books.

Gardner, H. (2004). Audiences for the theory of multiple intelligences. *Teachers College Record, 106*(1), 212–220.

Gardner, H. (2006). *Multiple intelligences: New horizons.* New York, NY: Basic Books.

Gardner, H., & Hatch, T. (1989). Multiple intelligences go to school: Educational implications of the theory of multiple intelligences. *Educational Researcher, 18* (8), 4–10.

Gardner, M., & Steinberg, L. (2005). Peer influence on risk-taking, risk preference, and risky decision-making in adolescence and adulthood: An experimental study. *Developmental Psychology, 41*, 625–635.

Garnett, N. (2005). Laws, regulations, and guidelines. In C. K. Akins, S. Panicker, & C. L. Cunningham (Eds.), *Laboratory animals in research and teaching: Ethics, care and methods.* Washington, DC: American Psychological Association.

Garvey, C. R. (1929). List of American psychology laboratories. *Psychological Bulletin, 26*, 652–660.

Gassmann, O., & Zeschky, M. (2008). Opening up the solution space: The role of analogical thinking for breakthrough product innovation. *Creativity & Innovation Management, 17*(2), 97–106. doi:10.1111/j.1467-8691.2008.00475.x

Gattig, A., & Hendrickx, L. (2007). Judgmental discounting and environmental risk perception: Dimensional similarities, domain differences, and implications for sustainability. *Journal of Social Issues, 63*, 21–39.

Gazzaniga, M. S. (1970). *The bisected brain.* New York, NY: Appleton-Century-Crofts.

Gazzaniga, M. S. (2005). Forty-five years of split-brain research and still going strong. *Nature Reviews Neuroscience, 6*, 653–659.

Gazzaniga, M. S. (2008). Spheres of influence. *Scientific American Mind, 19*(2), 32–39.

Gazzaniga, M. S., Bogen, J. E., & Sperry, R. W. (1965). Observations on visual perception after disconnection of the cerebral hemispheres in man. *Brain, 88,* 221–236.

Gazzaniga, M. S., Ivry, R. B., & Mangun, G. R. (2009). *Cognitive neuroscience: The biology of the mind* (3rd ed.). New York, NY: Norton.

Geary, D. C. (2007). An evolutionary perspective on sex difference in mathematics and the sciences. In S. J. Ceci & W. M. Williams (Eds.), *Why aren't more women in science?* (pp. 173–188). Washington, DC: American Psychological Association.

Gebhard, U., Nevers, P., & Billmann-Mahecha, E. (2003). Moralizing trees: Anthropomorphism and identity in children's relationships to nature. In S. Clayton & S. Opotow (Eds.), *Identity and the natural environment: The psychological significance of nature.* Cambridge, MA: MIT Press.

Gegenfurtner, K. (2010). Color perception: Physiological. In E. B. Goldstein (Ed.), *Encyclopedia of perception.* Thousand Oaks, CA: Sage.

Geller, E. S., Winett, R. A., & Everett, P. B. (1982). *Environmental preservation: New strategies for behavior change.* New York, NY: Pergamon Press.

Geller, J. L. (2009). The role of the hospital in the care of the mentally ill. In B. J. Sadock, V. A. Sadock, & P. Ruiz (Eds.), *Kaplan & Sadock's comprehensive textbook of psychiatry* (9th ed., pp. 4299–4314). Philadelphia, PA: Lippincott Williams & Wilkins.

Gentile, B., Grabe, S., Dolan-Pascoe, B., Twenge, J. M., Wells, B. E., & Maitino, A. (2009). Gender differences in domain-specific self-esteem: A meta-analysis. *Review of General Psychology, 13*(1), 34–45. doi:10.1037/a0013689

George, S. A. (2002). The menopause experience: A woman's perspective. *Journal of Obstetric, Gynecologic, and Neonatal Nursing, 31*, 71–85.

Ger, G., & Belk, R. W. (1996). Cross-cultural differences in materialism. *Journal of Economic Psychology, 17*, 55–77.

Geraerts, E., Raymaekers, L., & Merckelbach, H. (2008). Recovered memories of childhood sexual abuse: Current findings and their legal implications. *Legal and Criminological Psychology, 13*(2), 165–176. doi:10.1348/135532508X298559

Geraerts, E., Schooler, J. W., Merckelbach, H., Jelicic, M., Hauer, B. A., & Ambadar, Z. (2007). The reality of recovered memories: Corroborating continuous and discontinuous memories of childhood sexual abuse. *Psychological Science, 18*(7), 564–568. doi:10.1111/j.1467-9280.2007.01940.x

Gergen, K. J., Gulerce, A., Lock, A., & Misra, G. (1996). Psychological science in cultural context. *American Psychologist, 51*, 496–503.

Gershkoff-Stowe, L., & Hahn, E. R. (2007). Fast mapping skills in the developing lexicon. *Journal of Speech, Language, and Hearing Research, 50*, 682–696.

Gershoff, E. T. (2002). Parental corporal punishment and associated child behaviors and experiences: A meta-analytic and theoretical review. *Psychological Bulletin, 128*, 539–579.

Gershon, E. S., Berrettini, W. H., & Goldin, L. R. (1989). Mood disorders: Genetic aspects. In H. I. Kaplan & B. J. Sadock (Eds.), *Comprehensive textbook of psychiatry* (Vol. 5). Baltimore, MD: Williams & Wilkins.

Getchell, T. Y., & Getchell, M. L. (1991). Physiology of olfactory reception and transduction: General principles. In D. G. Laing, R. L. Doty, & W. Breipohl (Eds.), *The human sense of smell.* Berlin: Springer-Verlag.

Gibbons, D. E., & Lynn, S. J. (2010). Hypnotic inductions: A primer. In S. J. Lynn, J. W. Rhue, & I. Kirsch (Eds.), *Handbook of Clinical Hypnosis* (2nd ed., pp. 267–292). Washington, DC: American Psychological Association.

Gibbons, M. B. C., Crits-Christoph, P., & Hearon, B. (2008). The empirical status of psychodynamic therapies. *Annual Review of Clinical Psychology, 4*, 93–108.

Gibson, C., Folley, B. S., & Park, S. (2009). Enhanced divergent thinking and creativity in musicians: A behavioral and near-infrared spectroscopy study. *Brain and Cognition, 69*(1), 162–169. doi:10.1016/j.bandc.2008.07.009

Giedd, J. N. (2008). The teen brain: Insights from neuroimaging. *Journal of Adolescent Health, 42*, 335–343.

Gigerenzer, G. (2000). *Adaptive thinking: Rationality in the real world.* New York, NY: Oxford University Press.

Gigerenzer, G. (2004). Fast and frugal heuristics: The tools of bounded rationality. In D. J. Koehler & N. Harvey (Eds.), *Blackwell handbook of judgment and decision making.* Malden, MA: Blackwell Publishing.

Gigerenzer, G. (2008). Why heuristics work. *Perspective on Psychological Science, 3*(1), 20–29.

Gigerenzer, G., Gaissmaier, W., Kurz-Milcke, E., Schwartz, L. M., & Woloshin, S. (2007). Helping doctors and patients make sense of health statistics. *Psychological Science in the Public Interest, 8*(2), 53–96. doi:10.1111/j.1539-6053.2008.00033.x

Gigerenzer, G., & Todd, P. M. (1999). Fast and frugal heuristics: The adaptive toolbox. In G. Gigerenzer, P. M. Todd, & ABC Research Group (Eds.), *Simple heuristics that make us smart* (pp. 3–36). New York, NY: Oxford University Press.

Gilad, Y., Wiebe, V., Przeworski, M., Lancet, D., & Paabo, S. (2004). Loss of olfactory receptor genes coincides with the acquisition of full trichromatic vision in primates. *PLoS Biology, 5*(6), e148. doi:10.1371/journal.pbio.0020005

Gilbert, D. (2008). Daniel Gilbert at Pop!Tech: Gilbert speaks about the psychology of global warming. Retrieved from http://poptech.org/popcasts/dan_gilbert__poptech_2007

Gilbert, D. T. (1989). Thinking lightly about others: Automatic components of the social inference process. In J. S. Uleman & J. A. Bargh (Eds.), *Unintended thought: Limits of awareness, intention, and control.* New York, NY: Guilford.

Gilbert, D. T. (1998). Speeding with Ned: A personal view of the correspondence bias. In J. M. Darley & J. Cooper (Ed.), *Attribution and social interaction: The legacy of Edward E. Jones.* Washington, DC: American Psychological Association.

Gilbert, D. T. (2006). *Stumbling on happiness.* New York, NY: Alfred A. Knopf.

Gilbert, D. T., Driver-Linn, E., & Wilson, T. D. (2002). The trouble with Vronsky: Impact bias in the forecasting of future affective states. In L. F. Barrett & S. P (Eds.), *The wisdom in feeling: Psychological processes in emotional intelligence* (pp. 114–143). New York, NY: Guilford.

Gilbert, D. T., Pinel, E. C., Wilson, T. D., Blumberg, S. J., & Wheatley, T. P. (1998). Immune neglect: A source of durability bias in affective forecasting. *Journal of Personality and Social Psychology, 75*(3), 617–638. doi:10.1037/0022-3514.75.3.617

Gilgen, A. R. (1982). *American psychology since World War II: A profile of the discipline.* Westport, CT: Greenwood Press.

Gilovich, T. D., & Griffin, D. W. (2010). Judgment and decision making. In S. T. Fiske, D. T. Gilbert, & G. Lindzey (Eds.), *Handbook of social psychology* (5th ed., Vol. 1, pp. 542–588). Hoboken, NJ: Wiley.

Gilovich, T. D., Griffin, D., & Kahneman, D. (2002). *Heuristics and biases: The psychology of intuitive judgment.* New York, NY: Cambridge University Press.

Gimmig, D., Huguet, P., Caverni, J., & Cury, F. (2006). Choking under pressure and working memory capacity: When performance pressure reduces fluid intelligence. *Psychonomic Bulletin & Review, 13*(6), 1005–1010.

Gitlin, M. J. (2009). Pharmacotherapy and other somatic treatments for depression. In I. H. Gotlib & C. L. Hammen (Eds.), *Handbook of depression* (pp. 554–585). New York, NY: Guilford.

Gittelman, M. (2005). The neglected disaster. *International Journal of Mental Health, 34*(2), 9–21.

Gladue, B. A. (1994). The biopsychology of sexual orientation. *Current Directions in Psychological Science, 3,* 150–154.

Gladwell, M. (2005). *Blink: The power of thinking without thinking.* New York, NY: Little, Brown.

Glass, R. M. (2001). Electroconvulsive therapy. *Journal of the American Medical Association, 285,* 1346–1348.

Glass, R. M. (2004). Treatment of adolescents with major depression: Contributions of a major trial. *Journal of the American Medical Association, 292,* 861–863.

Glatt, S. J. (2008). Genetics. In K. T. Mueser & D. V. Jeste (Eds.), *Clinical handbook of schizophrenia* (pp. 55–64). New York, NY: Guilford.

Gleitman, L., & Newport, E. (1996). *The invention of language by children.* Cambridge, MA: MIT Press.

Gmelch, G. (1978). Baseball magic. *Human Nature, 1*(8), 32–39.

Gneezy, U., List, J. A., & Wu, G. (2006). The uncertainty effect: When a risky prospect is valued less than its worst possible outcome. *Quarterly Journal of Economics, 121*(4), 1283–1309.

Godlee, F., Smith, J., & Marcovitch, H. (2011). Wakefield's article linking MMR vaccine and autism was fraudulent. *BMJ, 342,* 64–66.

Goff, D. C., & Gudeman, J. E. (1999). The person with chronic mental illness. In A. M. Nicholi (Ed.), *The Harvard guide to psychiatry.* Cambridge, MA: Harvard University Press.

Gogtay, N., Giedd, J. N., Lusk, L., Hayashi, K. M., Rapoport, J. L., Thompson, P. M., et al. (2004). Dynamic mapping of human cortical development during childhood through early adulthood. *Proceedings of the National Academy of Sciences, 101,* 8174–8179.

Gold, M. S., & Jacobs, W. S. (2005). Cocaine and crack: Clinical aspects. In J. H. Lowinson, P. Ruiz, R. B. Millman, & J. G. Langrod (Eds.), *Substance abuse: A comprehensive textbook.* Philadelphia, PA: Lippincott Williams & Wilkins.

Golden, C. J., Sawicki, R. F., & Franzen, M. D. (1990). Test construction. In G. Goldstein & M. Hersen (Eds.), *Handbook of psychological assessment.* New York, NY: Pergamon Press.

Goldenberg, H. (1983). *Contemporary clinical psychology.* Pacific Grove, CA: Brooks/Cole.

Goldenberg, I., Goldenberg, H., & Pelavin, E. G. (2011). Family therapy. In R. J. Corsini & D. Wedding (Eds.), *Current psychotherapies* (9th ed.). Belmont, CA: Brooks/Cole.

Goldstein, D. G., & Gigerenzer, G. (1999). The recognition heuristic: How ignorance makes us smart. In G. Gigerenzer, P. M. Todd, & ABC Research Group (Eds.), *Simple heuristics that make us smart* (pp. 37–58). New York, NY: Oxford University Press.

Goldstein, D. G., & Gigerenzer, G. (2002). Models of ecological rationality: The recognition heuristic. *Psychological Review, 109,* 75–90.

Goldstein, E. B. (2001). Pictorial perception and art. In E. B. Goldstein (Ed.), *Blackwell handbook of perception.* Malden, MA: Blackwell.

Goldstein, E. B. (2010). Constancy. In E. B. Goldstein (Ed.), *Encyclopedia of perception.* Thousand Oaks, CA: Sage.

Goldstein, H. W., Zedeck, S., & Goldstein, I. L. (2002). g: Is this your final answer. *Human Performance, 15,* 123–142.

Goldstein, W. M., & Hogarth, R. M. (1997). Judgement and decision research: Some historical context. In W. M. Goldstein, & R. M. Hogarth (Eds.), *Research on judgement and decision making.* New York, NY: Cambridge University Press.

Goldston, K., & Baillie, A. J. (2008). Depression and coronary heart disease: A review of the epidemiological evidence, explanatory mechanisms and management approaches. *Clinical Psychology Review, 28,* 288–306.

González, H. M., Vega, W. A., Williams, D. R., Tarraf, W., West, B. T., & Neighbors, H. W. (2010). Depression care in the United States: Too little for too few. *Archives of General Psychiatry, 67*(1), 37–46.

Goodall, J. (1986). Social rejection, exclusion, and shunning among the Gombe chimpanzees. *Ethology & Sociobiology, 7,* 227–236.

Goodall, J. (1990). *Through a window: My thirty years with the chimpanzees of Gombe.* Boston, MA: Houghton, Mifflin.

Goodheart, C. D. (2006). Evidence, endeavor, and expertise in psychology practice. In C. D. Goodheart, A. E. Kazdin, & R. J. Sternberg (Eds.), *Evidence-based psychotherapy: Where practice and research meet* (pp. 37–62). Washington, DC: American Psychological Association.

Goodwin, C. J. (1991). Misportraying Pavlov's apparatus. *American Journal of Psychology, 104*(1), 135–141.

Goodwin, F. K., & Jamison, K. R. (2007). *Manic-depressive illness: Bipolar disorders and recurrent depression.* New York, NY: Oxford University Press.

Gopnik, A., Meltzoff, A. N., & Kuhl, P. K. (1999). *The scientist in the crib: Minds, brains, and how children learn.* New York, NY: Morrow.

Gorchoff, S. M., John, O. P., & Helson, R. (2008). Contextualizing change in marital satisfaction during middle age: An 18-year longitudinal study. *Psychological Science, 19*(11), 1194–1200. doi:10.1111/j.1467-9280.2008.02222.x

Gordon, H. W. (1990). The neurobiological basis of hemisphericity. In C. Trevarthen (Ed.), *Brain circuits and functions of the mind. Essays in honor of Roger W. Sperry.* Cambridge, MA: Cambridge University Press.

Gordon, J., & Abramov, I. (2001). Color vision. In E. B. Goldstein (Ed.), *Blackwell handbook of perception.* Malden, MA: Blackwell.

Goswami, U. (2006). Neuroscience and education: From research to practice? *Nature Reviews Neuroscience, 7*(5), 2–7.

Gottesmann, C. (2009). Discovery of the dreaming sleep stage: A recollection. *Sleep: Journal of Sleep and Sleep Disorders Research, 32*(1), 15–16.

Gottesman, I. I. (1991). *Schizophrenia genesis: The origins of madness.* New York, NY: W. H. Freeman.

Gottesman, I. I. (2001). Psychopathology through a life span-genetic prism. *American Psychologist, 56,* 867–878.

Gottesman, I. I., & Hanson, D. R. (2005). Human development: Biological and genetic processes. *Annual Review of Psychology, 56,* 263–86.

Gottfredson, L. S. (2002). Where and why g matters: Not a mystery. *Human Performance, 15,* 25–46.

Gottfredson, L. S. (2003a). Dissecting practical intelligence theory: Its claims and evidence. *Intelligence, 31,* 343–397.

Gottfredson, L. S. (2003b). G, jobs and life. In H. Nyborg (Ed.), *The scientific study of general intelligence: Tribute to Arthur R. Jensen.* Oxford, UK: Pergamon.

Gottfredson, L. S., & Deary, I. J. (2004). Intelligence predicts health and longevity, but why?

Current Directions in Psychological Science, 13(1), 1–4.

Gottschall, J. (2007). Greater emphasis on female attractiveness in *Homo sapiens:* A revised solution to an old evolutionary riddle. *Evolutionary Psychology, 5*(1), 347–357.

Gould, E. (2004). Stress, deprivation, and adult neurogenesis. In M. S. Gazzaniga (Ed.), *The cognitive neurosciences* (pp. 139–148). Cambridge, MA: MIT Press.

Gould, S. J., & Eldredge, N. (1977). Punctuated equilibria: The tempo and mode of evolution reconsidered. *Paleobiology, 3,* 115–151.

Gourevitch, M. N., & Arnsten, J. H. (2005). Medical complications of drug use. In J. H. Lowinson, P. Ruiz, R. B. Millman, & J. G. Langrod (Eds.), *Substance abuse: A comprehensive textbook.* Philadelphia, PA: Lippincott Williams & Wilkins.

Grady, D. (2006). Management of menopausal symptoms. *New England Journal of Medicine, 355,* 2338–2347.

Graham-Bermann, S. A. (2009, May). *Growing opposition to physical punishment: Empirical, human rights, and ethical arguments against an age-old practice.* Paper presented at the American Psychological Association's annual convention, Toronto, Ontario.

Granberg, G., & Holmberg, S. (1991). Self-reported turnout and voter validation. *American Journal of Political Science, 35,* 448–459.

Grandner, M. A., Hale, L., Moore, M., & Patel, N. P. (2010). Mortality associated with short sleep duration: The evidence, the possible mechanisms, and the future. *Sleep Medicine Reviews, 14*(3), 191–203. doi:10.1016/j.smrv.2009.07.006

Grandner, M. A., Patel, N. P., Gehrman, P. R., Perlis, M. L., & Pack, A. I. (2010a). Problems associated with short sleep: Bridging the gap between laboratory and epidemiological studies. *Sleep Medicine Reviews, 14*(4), 239–247. doi:10.1016/j.smrv.2009.08.001

Grandner, M. A., Patel, N. P., Gehrman, P. R., Xie, D., Sha, D., Weaver, T., & Gooneratne, N. (2010b). Who gets the best sleep? Ethnic and socioeconomic factors related to sleep complaints. *Sleep Medicine, 11*(5), 470–478. doi:10.1016/j.sleep.2009.10.006

Grant, J. A., Courtemanche, J., Duerden, E. G., Duncan, G. H., & Rainville, P. (2010). Cortical thickness and pain sensitivity in zen meditators. *Emotion, 10*(1), 43–53. doi:10.1037/a0018334

Grant, J. A., & Rainville, P. (2009). Pain sensitivity and analgesic effects of mindful states in Zen meditators: A cross-sectional study. *Psychosomatic Medicine, 71*(1), 106–114. doi:10.1097/PSY.0b013e31818f52ee

Grau, R., Salanova, M., & Peiro, J. M. (2001). Moderator effects of self-efficacy on occupational stress. *Psychology in Spain, 5*(1), 63–74.

Gray, C., & Della Sala, S. (2007). The Mozart effect: It's time to face the music! In S. Della Sala (Ed.), *Tall tales about the mind & brain: Separating fact from fiction* (pp. 148–157). New York, NY: Oxford University Press.

Gray, K., & Wegner, D. M. (2008). The sting of intentional pain. *Psychological Science, 19*(12), 1260–1262. doi:10.1111/j.1467-9280.2008.02208.x

Graziano, W. G., & Tobin, R. M. (2009). Agreeableness. In M. R. Leary & R. H. Hoyle (Eds.), *Handbook of individual differences in social behavior* (pp. 46–61). New York, NY: Guilford.

Green, C. D. (2009). Darwinian theory, functionalism, and the first American psychological revolution. *American Psychologist, 64*(2), 75–83. doi:10.1037/a0013338

Green, J. P. (1999). Hypnosis, context effects, and recall of early autobiographical memories. *International Journal of Clinical & Experimental Hypnosis, 47,* 284–300.

Green, J. P. (2003). Beliefs about hypnosis: Popular beliefs, misconceptions, and the importance of experience. *International Journal of Clinical and Experimental Hypnosis, 51*(4), 369–381. doi:10.1076/iceh.51.4.369.16408

Greenberg, J., Landau, M., Kosloff, S., & Solomon, S. (2009). How our dreams of death transcendence breed prejudice, stereotyping, and conflict: Terror management theory. In T. D. Nelson (Ed.), *Handbook of prejudice, stereotyping, and discrimination* (pp. 309–332). New York, NY: Psychology Press.

Greenberg, J. S. (2002). *Comprehensive stress management: Health and human performance.* New York, NY: McGraw-Hill.

Greene, R. L. (1992). *Human memory: Paradigms and paradoxes.* Hillsdale, NJ: Erlbaum.

Greenfield, P. M. (1998). The cultural evolution of IQ. In U. Neisser (Ed.), *The rising curve: Long-term gains in IQ and related measures.* Washington, DC: American Psychological Association.

Greenough, W. T. (1975). Experiential modification of the developing brain. *American Scientist, 63,* 37–46.

Greenough, W. T., & Volkmar, F. R. (1973). Pattern of dendritic branching in occipital cortex of rats reared in complex environments. *Experimental Neurology, 40,* 491–504.

Greenson, R. R. (1967). *The technique and practice of psychoanalysis* (Vol. 1). New York, NY: International Universities Press.

Greenstein, T. N. (2009). National context, family satisfaction, and fairness in the division of household labor. *Journal of Marriage and Family, 71*(4), 1039–1051. doi:10.1111/j.1741-3737.2009.00651.x

Greenwald, A. G., & Banaji, M. R. (1995). Implicit social cognition: Attitudes, self-esteem, and stereotypes. *Psychological Review, 102*(1), 4–27. doi:10.1037/0033-295X.102.1.4

Greenwald, A. G., McGhee, D. E., & Schwartz, J. K. (1998). Measuring individual differences in implicit cognition: The Implicit Association Test. *Journal of Personality and Social Psychology, 74*(6), 1464–1480. doi:10.1037/0022-3514.74.6.1464

Greenwald, A. G., Poehlman, T., Uhlmann, E., & Banaji, M. R. (2009). Understanding and using the Implicit Association Test: III. Meta-analysis of predictive validity. *Journal of Personality and Social Psychology, 97*(1), 17–41. doi:10.1037/a0015575

Greenway, R. (1995). The wilderness effect and ecopsychology. In T. Roszak, M. E. Gomes, & A. D. Kanner (Eds.), *Eco-psychology: Restoring the earth, healing the mind.* San Francisco, CA: Sierra Club Books.

Gregory, R. L. (1973). *Eye and brain.* New York, NY: McGraw-Hill.

Gregory, R. L. (1978). *Eye and brain* (2nd ed.). New York, NY: McGraw-Hill.

Greven, C. U., Harlaar, N., Kovas, Y., Chamorro-Premuzic, T., & Plomin, R. (2009). More than just IQ: School achievement is predicted by self-perceived abilities—But for genetic rather than environmental reasons. *Psychological Science, 20*(6), 753–762. doi:10.1111/j.1467-9280.2009.02366.x

Grigorenko, E. L. (2000). Heritability and intelligence. In R. J. Sternberg (Ed.), *Handbook of intelligence* (pp. 53–91). New York, NY: Cambridge University Press.

Grigorenko, E. L., & Sternberg, R. J. (2001). Analytical, creative, and practical intelligence as predictors of self-reported adaptive functioning: A case study in Russia. *Intelligence, 29,* 57–73.

Grigorenko, E. L., & Sternberg, R. J. (2003). The nature-nurture issue. In A. Slater & G. Bremner (Eds.), *An introduction to development psychology.* Malden, MA: Blackwell Publishers.

Griner, D., & Smith, T. B. (2006). Culturally adapted mental health intervention: A meta-analytic review. *Psychotherapy: Theory, Research, Practice, Training, 43,* 531–548.

Grinspoon, L., Bakalar, J. B., & Russo, E. (2005). Marihuana: Clinical aspects. In J. H. Lowinson, P. Ruiz, R. B. Millman, & J. G. Langrod (Eds.), *Substance abuse: A comprehensive textbook.* Philadelphia, PA: Lippincott Williams & Wilkins.

Griskevicius, V., Tybur, J. M., & Van den Bergh, B. (2010). Going green to be seen: Status, reputation, and conspicuous conservation. *Journal of Personality and Social Psychology, 98*(3), 392-404. doi:10.1037/a0017346

Gross, C. G. (2000). Neurogenesis in the adult brain: Death of a dogma. *Nature Reviews Neuroscience, 1,* 67–73.

Grossman, J. B., & Ruiz, P. (2004). Shall we make a leap-of-faith to disulfiram (Antabuse)? *Addictive Disorders & Their Treatment, 3*(3), 129–132.

Grossman, P., Niemann, L., Schmidt, S., & Walach, H. (2004). Mindfulness-based stress reduction and health benefits: A meta-analysis. *Journal of Psychosomatic Research, 57,* 35–43.

Grossman, R. P., & Till, B. D. (1998). The persistence of classically conditioned brand attitudes. *Journal of Advertising, 27,* 23–31.

Grossmann, K. E., & Grossmann, K. (1990). The wider concept of attachment in cross-cultural research. *Human Development, 33,* 31–47.

Groth-Marnat, G. (1997). *Handbook of psychological assessment*. New York, NY: Wiley.

Grubin, D., & Madsen, L. (2005). Lie detection and the polygraph: A historical review. *Journal of Forensic Psychiatry & Psychology, 16*, 357–369.

Grunberg, N. E., Berger, S. S., & Hamilton, K. R. (2011). Stress and drug use. In R. J. Contrada & A. Baum (Eds.), *The handbook of stress science: Biology, psychology, and health* (pp. 111–121). New York, NY: Springer Publishing.

Grunberg, N. E., Faraday, M. M., & Rahman, M. A. (2001). The psychobiology of nicotine self-administration. In A. Baum, T. A. Revenson, & J. E. Singer (Eds.), *Handbook of health psychology* (pp. 249–262). Mahwah, NJ: Erlbaum.

Grusec, J. E. (2006). The development of moral behavior and conscience from a socialization perspective. In M. Killen & J. G. Smetana (Eds.), *Handbook of moral development*. Mahwah, NJ: Erlbaum.

Guarda, A. S., Pinto, A. M., Coughlin, J. W., Hussain, S., Haug, N. A., & Heinberg, L. J. (2007). Perceived coercion and change in perceived need for admission in patients hospitalized for eating disorders. *American Journal of Psychiatry, 164*, 108–114.

Guenther, K. (1988). Mood and memory. In G. M. Davies & D. M. Thomson (Eds.), *Memory in context: Context in memory*. New York, NY: Wiley.

Guerrini, I., Thomson, A. D., & Gurling, H. D. (2007). The importance of alcohol misuse, malnutrition, and genetic susceptibility on brain growth and plasticity. *Neuroscience & Biobehavioral Reviews, 31*, 212–220.

Guilbault, R. L., Bryant, F. B., Brockway, J. H., & Posavac, E. J. (2004). A meta-analysis of research on hindsight bias. *Basic & Applied Social Psychology, 26*(2–3), 103–117.

Guilford, J. P. (1959). Three faces of intellect. *American Psychologist, 14*, 469–479.

Guilleminault, C., & Fromherz, S. (2005). Narcolepsy: Diagnosis and management. In M. H. Kryger, T. Roth, & W. C. Dement (Eds.). *Principles and practice of sleep medicine*. Philadelphia, PA: Elsevier Saunders.

Guiney, M. S., & Oberhauser, K. S. (2009). Conservation volunteers' connection to nature. *Ecopsychology, 1*(4), 187–197.

Gunn, S. R., & Gunn, W. S. (2006). Are we in the dark about sleepwalking's dangers? *Cerebrum*, 1–12.

Gur, R. C., & Gur, R. E. (2007). Neural substrates for sex differences in cognition. In S. J. Ceci & W. M. Williams (Eds.), *Why aren't more women in science?* (pp. 189–198). Washington, DC: American Psychological Association.

Guyton, A. C. (1991). *Textbook of medical physiology*. Philadelphia, PA: Saunders.

Guzman-Marin, R., Suntsova, N., Bashir, T., Nienhuis, R., Szymusiak, R., & McGinty, D. (2008). Rapid eye movement sleep deprivation contributes to reduction of neurogenesis in the hippocampal dentate gyrus of the adult rat. *Sleep: Journal of Sleep and Sleep Disorders Research, 31*(2), 167–175.

Haas, L. (1999). Families and work. In M. B. Sussman, S. K. Steinmetz, & G. W. Peterson (Eds.), *Handbook of marriage and the family* (pp. 571–612). New York, NY: Plenum.

Hackman, J. R., & Katz, N. (2010). Attitudes. In S. T. Fiske, D. T. Gilbert, & G. Lindzey (Eds.), *Handbook of social psychology* (5th ed., Vol. 1, pp. 353–393). Hoboken, NJ: Wiley.

Hadaway, C. K., Marler, P. L., & Chaves, M. (1993). What the polls don't show: A closer look at U.S. church attendance. *American Sociological Review, 58*, 741–752.

Hadjistavropoulos, H., Dash, H., Hadjistavropoulos, T., & Sullivan, T. (2007). Recurrent pain among university students: Contributions of self-efficacy and perfectionism to the pain experience. *Personality and Individual Differences, 42*, 1081–1091.

Hagerty, M. R. (2000). Social comparisons of income in one's community: Evidence from national surveys of income and happiness. *Journal of Personality and Social Psychology, 78*, 764–771.

Hahn, P. Y., Olson, L. J., & Somers, V. K. (2006). Cardiovascular complications of obstructive sleep apnea. In T. Lee-Chiong (Ed.), *Sleep: A comprehensive handbook*. Hoboken, NJ: Wiley-Liss.

Haier, R. J. (2009). Neuro-intelligence, neurometrics and the next phase of brain imaging studies. *Intelligence, 37*(2), 121–123. doi:10.1016/j.intell.2008.12.006

Hales, D. (1987). *How to sleep like a baby*. New York, NY: Ballantine.

Hall, C. B., Lipton, R. B., Sliwinski, M. M., Katz, M. J., Derby, C. A., & Verghese, J. J. (2009). Cognitive activities delay onset of memory decline in persons who develop dementia. *Neurology, 73*(5), 356–361. doi:10.1212/WNL.0b013e3181b04ae3

Hall, C. S. (1966). *The meaning of dreams*. New York, NY: McGraw-Hill.

Hall, C. S. (1979). The meaning of dreams. In D. Goleman & R. J. Davidson (Eds.), *Consciousness: Brain, states of awareness, and mysticism*. New York, NY: Harper & Row.

Hall, J. A., & Mast, M. S. (2008). Are women always more interpersonally sensitive than men? Impact of goals and content domain. *Personality and Social Psychology Bulletin, 34*, 144–155.

Hall, J. A., Carter, J. D., & Horgan, T. G. (2000). Gender differences in the nonverbal communication of emotion. In A. Fischer (Ed.), *Gender and emotion*. Cambridge, UK: Cambridge University Press.

Halmi, K. A. (2002). Physiology of anorexia nervosa and bulimia nervosa. In C. G. Fairburn & K. D. Brownell (Eds.), *Eating disorders and obesity: A comprehensive handbook*. New York, NY: Guilford.

Halmi, K. A. (2003). Eating disorders: Anorexia nervosa, bulimia nervosa, and obesity. In R. E. Hales & S. C. Yudofsky (Eds.), *Textbook of Clinical Psychiatry*. Washington, DC: American Psychiatric Publishing.

Halmi, K. A. (2008). Eating disorders: Anorexia nervosa, bulimia nervosa, and obesity. In R. E. Hales, S. C. Yudofsky, & G. O. Gabbard (Eds.), *The American Psychiatric Publishing textbook of psychiatry* (5th ed., pp. 921–970). Washington, DC: American Psychiatric Publishing.

Halpern, C., Hurtig, H., Jaggi, J., Grossman, M., Won, M., & Baltuch, G. (2007). Deep brain stimulation in neurologic disorders. *Parkinsonism & Related Disorders, 13*(1), 1–16.

Halpern, D. F. (1997). Sex differences in intellegence: Implications for education. *American Psychologist, 52*, 1091–1102.

Halpern, D. F. (1998). Teaching critical thinking for transfer across domains: Dispositions, skills, structure training, and metacognitive monitoring. *American Psychologist, 53*, 449–455.

Halpern, D. F. (2000). *Sex differences in cognitive abilities*. Mahwah, NJ: Erlbaum.

Halpern, D. F. (2003). *Thought and knowledge: An introduction to critical thinking*. Mahwah, NJ: Erlbaum.

Halpern, D. F. (2004). A cognitive-process taxonomy for sex differences in cognitive abilities. *Current Directions in Psychological Science, 13*(4), 135–139.

Halpern, D. F., Benbow, C. P., Geary, D. C., Gur, R. C., Hyde, J. S., & Gernsbacher, M. A. (2007). The science of sex differences in science and mathematics. *Psychological Science in the Public Interest, 8*, 1–51.

Hammad, T. A., Laughren, T., & Racoosin, J. (2006). Suicidality in pediatric patients treated with antidepressant drugs. *Archives of General Psychiatry, 63*, 332–339.

Hammen, C. (2003). Mood disorders. In G. Stricker & T. A. Widiger (Eds.), *Handbook of psychology, Vol. 8: Clinical psychology*. New York, NY: Wiley.

Hampson, E., van Anders, S. M., & Mullin, L. I. (2006). A female advantage in the recognition of emotional facial expressions: Test of an evolutionary hypothesis. *Evolution and Human Behavior, 27*, 401–416.

Haney, C., & Zimbardo, P. G. (1998). The past and future of U.S. prison policy: Twenty-five years after the Stanford Prison Experiment. *American Psychologist, 53*, 709–727.

Haney, C., Banks, W. C., & Zimbardo, P. G. (1973). Interpersonal dynamics in a simulated prison. *International Journal of Criminology and Penology, 1*, 69–97.

Hannigan, J. H., & Armant, D. R. (2000). Alcohol in pregnancy and neonatal outcome. *Seminars in Neonatology, 5*, 243–254.

Harley, E. M. (2007). Hindsight bias in legal decision making. *Social Cognition, 25*, 48–63.

Harley, T. A. (2008). *The psychology of language: From data to theory*. New York, NY: Psychology Press.

Harlow, H. F. (1958). The nature of love. *American Psychologist, 13,* 673–685.

Harlow, H. F. (1959). Love in infant monkeys. *Scientific American, 200*(6), 68–74.

Haroutunian, V., & Davis, K. L. (2003). Psychiatric pathophysiology. In A. Tasman, J. Kay, & J. A. Lieberman (Eds.), *Psychiatry*. New York, NY: Wiley.

Harris, J. E. (1984). Remembering to do things: A forgotten topic. In J. E. Harris & P. E. Morris (Eds.), *Everyday memory, actions, and absent-mindedness*. New York, NY: Academic Press.

Harris, J. L., Bargh, J. A., & Brownell, K. D. (2009). Priming effects of television food advertising on eating behavior. *Health Psychology, 28*(4), 404–413. doi:10.1037/a0014399

Harris, J. R. (1998). *The nurture assumption: Why children turn out the way they do*. New York, NY: Free Press.

Harte, J. L., & Eifert, G. H. (1995). The effects of running, environment, and attentional focus on athletes' catecholamine and cortisol levels and mood. *Psychophysiology, 32*(1), 49–54. doi:10.1111/j.1469-8986.1995.tb03405.x

Harte, J. L., Eifert, G. H., & Smith, R. (1995). The effects of running and meditation on beta-endorphin, corticotropin-releasing hormone and cortisol in plasma, and on mood. *Biological Psychology, 40*(3), 251–265. doi:10.1016/0301-0511(95)05118-T

Hartley, A. (2006). Changing role of the speed of processing construct in the cognitive psychology of human aging. In J. E. Birren & K. W. Schaie (Eds.), *Handbook of the psychology of aging*. San Diego, CA: Academic Press.

Harvey, P. D. (2010). Cognitive functioning and disability in schizophrenia. *Current Directions in Psychological Science, 19*(4), 249–254. doi:10.1177/0963721410378033

Haselton, M. G., Buss, D. M., Oubaid, V., & Angleitner, A. (2005). Sex, lies, and strategic interference: The psychology of deception between the sexes. *Personality and Social Psychology Bulletin, 31,* 3–23.

Haskard, K. B., Williams, S. L., DiMatteo, M., Rosenthal, R., White, M., & Goldstein, M. G. (2008). Physician and patient communication training in primary care: Effects on participation and satisfaction. *Health Psychology, 27*(5), 513–522. doi:10.1037/0278-6133.27.5.513

Haslam, N. (1997). Evidence that male sexual orientation is a matter of degree. *Journal of Personality and Social Psychology, 73,* 862–870.

Hastorf, A., & Cantril, H. (1954). They saw a game: A case study. *Journal of Abnormal and Social Psychology, 49,* 129–134.

Hatfield, E., & Rapson, R. L. (1993). *Love, sex, and intimacy: Their psychology, biology, and history*. New York, NY: HarperCollins.

Hatfield, E., Rapson, R. L., & Martel, L. D. (2007). Passionate love. In S. Kitayama &

D. Cohen (Eds.), *Handbook of cultural psychology*. New York, NY: Guilford.

Haugland, G., Siegel, C., Hopper, K., & Alexander, M. J. (1997). Mental illness among homeless individuals in a suburban county. *Psychiatric Services, 48,* 504–509.

Hauser, M., & Carey, S. (1998). Building a cognitive creature from a set of primitives: Evolutionary and developmental insights. In D. D. Cummins & C. Allen (Eds.), *The evolution of mind*. New York, NY: Oxford University Press.

Havermans, R. C., Siep, N., & Jansen, A. (2010). Sensory-specific satiety is impervious to the tasting of other foods with its assessment. *Appetite, 55*(2), 196–200. doi:10.1016/j.appet.2010.05.088

Haworth-Hoeppner, S. (2000). The critical shapes of body image: The role of culture and family in the production of eating disorders. *Journal of Marriage and the Family, 62,* 212–227.

Hayes, S., Hirsch, C., & Mathews, A. (2008). Restriction of working memory capacity during worry. *Journal of Abnormal Psychology, 117*(3), 712–717. doi:10.1037/a0012908

Hayne, H. (2007). Verbal recall of preverbal memories: Implications for the clinic and the courtroom. In M. Garry & H. Hayne (Eds.), *Do justice and let the sky fall: Elizabeth F. Lotus and her contributions to science, law, and academic freedom*. Mahwah, NJ: Erlbaum.

Haywood, T. W., Kravitz, H. M., Grossman, L. S., Cavanaugh, J. L., Jr., Davis, J. M., & Lewis, D. A. (1995). Predicting the "revolving door" phenomenon among patients with schizophrenic, schizoaffective, and affective disorders. *American Journal of Psychiatry, 152,* 861–956.

Hazan, C., & Shaver, P. (1986). *Parental caregiving style questionnaire*. Unpublished questionnaire.

Hazan, C., & Shaver, P. (1987). Romantic love conceptualized as an attachment process. *Journal of Personality and Social Psychology, 52,* 511–524.

He, J., Ogden, L. G., Vupputuri, S., Bazzano, L. A., Loria, C., & Whelton, P. K. (1999). Dietary sodium intake and subsequent risk of cardiovascular disease in overweight adults. *Journal of the American Medical Association, 282,* 2027–2034.

Healy, D. (2004). *Let them eat Prozac: The unhealthy relationship between the pharmaceutical industry and depression*. New York, NY: NYU Press.

Healy, D., & Whitaker, C. (2003). Antidepressants and suicide: Risk-benefit conundrums. *Journal of Psychiatry & Neuroscience, 28*(5), 28.

Heaps, C. M., & Nash, M. (2001). Comparing recollective experience in true and false autobiographical memories. *Journal of Experimental Psychology: Learning, Memory, and Cognition, 27,* 920–930.

Hearst, E. (1988). Fundamentals of learning and conditioning. In R. C. Atkinson, R. J. Herrnstein, G. Lindzey, & R. D. Luce (Eds.), *Stevens' handbook of experimental psychology*. New York, NY: Wiley.

Heider, F. (1958). *The psychology of interpersonal relations*. New York, NY: Wiley.

Heilman, M. E., & Haynes, M. C. (2005). No credit where credit is due: Attributional rationalization of women's success in male-female teams. *Journal of Applied Psychology, 90,* 905–916.

Heinrichs, R. W. (2005). The primacy of cognition in schizophrenia. *American Psychologist, 60,* 229–242.

Helgeson, V. S., Reynolds, K. A., & Tomich, P. L. (2006). A meta-analytic review of benefit finding and growth. *Journal of Consulting and Clinical Psychology, 74,* 797–816.

Hélie, S., & Sun, R. (2010). Incubation, insight, and creative problem solving: A unified theory and a connectionist model. *Psychological Review, 117*(3), 994–1024. doi:10.1037/a0019532

Hellige, J. B. (1990). Hemispheric asymmetry. *Annual Review of Psychology, 41,* 55–80.

Helmes, E. (2008). Modern applications of the MMPI/MMPI-2 in assessment. In G. J. Boyle, G. Matthews, & D. H. Saklofske (Eds.), *The Sage handbook of personality theory and assessment: Personality measurement and testing* (Vol. 2, pp. 589–607). Los Angeles, CA: Sage.

Helmholtz, H. von. (1852). On the theory of compound colors. *Philosophical Magazine, 4,* 519–534.

Helmholtz, H. von. (1863). *On the sensations of tone as a physiological basis for the theory of music* (A. J. Ellis, Trans.). New York, NY: Dover.

Helson, R., Jones, C., & Kwan, V. S. Y. (2002). Personality change over 40 years of adulthood: Hierarchical linear modeling analyses of two longitudinal studies. *Journal of Personality & Social Psychology, 83,* 752–766.

Helzer, J. E., Wittchen, H.–U., Krueger, R. F., & Kraemer, H. C. (2008a). Dimensional options for DSM-V: The way forward. In J. E. Helzer, H. C. Kraemer, R. F. Krueger, H.–U, Wittchen, P. J. Sirovatka, et al. (Eds.), *Dimensional approaches in diagnostic classification: Refining the research agenda for DSM-V* (pp. 115–127). Washington, DC: American Psychiatric Association.

Helzer, J., Kraemer, H., Krueger, R., Wittchen, H., Sirovatka, P., & Regier, D. (Eds.). (2008b). *Dimensional approaches in diagnostic classification: Refining the research agenda for DSM-V*. Washington, DC: American Psychiatric Association.

Hendrick, S. S., & Hendrick, C. (2000). Romantic love. In S. S. Hendrick & C. Hendrick (Eds.), *Close relationships*. Thousand Oaks, CA: Sage.

Heneka, M. T., O'Banion, M., Terwel, D., & Kummer, M. (2010). Neuroinflammatory processes in Alzheimer's disease. *Journal of Neural Transmission, 117*(8), 919–947. doi:10.1007/s00702-010-0438-z

Henriksson, M. M., Aro, H. M., Marttunen, M. J., Heikkinen, M. E., Isometsa, E. T., Kuoppasalmi, K. I., & Lonnqvist, J. K. (1993). Mental disorders and commorbidity of suicide. *American Journal of Psychiatry, 150,* 935–940.

Henry, P. J., Sternberg, R. J., & Grigorenko, E. L. (2005). Capturing successful intelligence through measures of analytic, creative, and practical skills. In O. Wilhelm & R. W. Engle (Eds.), *Handbook of understanding and measuring intelligence.* Thousand Oaks, CA: Sage.

Hepper, P. (2003). *Prenatal psychological and behavioural development.* Thousand Oaks, CA: Sage.

Herbenick, D., Reece, M., Schick, V., Sanders, S. A., Dodge, B., & Fortenberry, J. (2010). An event-level analysis of the sexual characteristics and composition among adults ages 18 to 59: Results from a national probability sample in the United States. *Journal of Sexual Medicine, 7*(Suppl 5), 346–361. doi:10.1111/j.1743-6109.2010.02020.x

Herbst, S., Pietrzak, R. H., Wagner, J., White, W. B., & Petry, N. M. (2007). Lifetime major depression is associated with coronary heart disease in older adults: Results from the national epidemiologic survey on alcohol and related conditions. *Psychosomatic Medicine, 69,* 729–734.

Herbstman, J., Sjodin, A., Kurzon, M., Lederman, S., Jones, R., Rauh, V., et al. (2010). Prenatal exposure to PBDEs and neurodevelopment. *Environmental Health Perspectives, 118*(5), 712–719. doi:10.1289/ehp.0901340

Herek, G. M. (2000). The psychology of sexual prejudice. *Current Directions in Psychological Science, 9,* 19–22.

Herek, G. M. (2009). Sexual prejudice. In T. D. Nelson (Ed.), *Handbook of prejudice, stereotyping, and discrimination* (pp. 441–467). New York, NY: Psychology Press.

Hermann, D., Raybeck, D., & Gruneberg, M. (2002). *Improving memory and study skills: Advances in theory and practice.* Ashland, OH: Hogrefe & Huber.

Hermann, R. C., Dorwart, R. A., Hoover, C. W., & Brody, J. (1995). Variation in ECT use in the United States. *American Journal of Psychiatry, 152,* 869–875.

Hermann, R. C., Ettner, S. L., Dorwart, R. A., Hoover, C. W., & Yeung, E. (1998). Characteristics of psychiatrists who perform ECT. *American Journal of Psychiatry, 155,* 889–894.

Hermans, H. J. M., & Kempen, H. J. G. (1998). Moving cultures: The perilous problems of cultural dichotomies in a globalizing society. *American Psychologist, 53,* 1111–1120.

Herrnstein, R. J., & Murray, C. (1994). *The bell curve: Intelligence and class structure in American life.* New York, NY: Free Press.

Hertzog, C., Kramer, A. F., Wilson, R. S., Lindenberger, U. (2009). Enrichment effects on adult cognitive development: Can the functional capacity of older adults be preserved and enhanced? *Psychological Science in the Public Interest, 9*(1), 1–65.

Herzog, D. B., & Delinski, S. S. (2001). Classification of eating disorders. In R. H. Striegel-Moore & L. Smolak (Eds.), *Eating disorders* (pp. 31–50). Washington, DC: American Psychological Association.

Hespos, S. J., Ferry, A. L., & Rips, L. J. (2009). Five-month-old infants have different expectations for solids and liquids. *Psychological Science, 20*(5), 603–611. doi:10.1111/j.1467-9280.2009.02331.x

Hetherington, E. M. (1999). Should we stay together for the sake of the children? In E. M. Hetherington (Ed.), *Coping with divorce, single parenting, and remarriage.* Mahwah, NJ: Erlbaum.

Hetherington, E. M. (2003). Intimate pathways: Changing patterns in close personal relationships across time. *Family Relations: Interdisciplinary Journal of Applied Family Studies, 52,* 318–331.

Hetherington, M. M., & Rolls, B. J. (1996). Sensory-specific satiety: Theoretical frameworks and central characteristics. In E. D. Capaldi (Ed.), *Why we eat what we eat: The psychology of eating* (pp. 267–290). Washington, DC: American Psychological Association.

Hewitt, B., & de Vaus, D. (2009). Change in the association between premarital cohabitation and separation, Australia 1945–2000. *Journal of Marriage and Family, 71*(2), 353–361. doi:10.1111/j.1741-3737.2009.00604.x

Hewstone, M. (1990). The "ultimate attribution error"? A review of the literature on intergroup causal attribution. *European Journal of Social Psychology, 20,* 311–335.

Higgins, E. T. (2004). Making a theory useful: Lessons handed down. *Personality and Social Psychology Review, 8*(2), 138–145.

Hilgard, E. R. (1965). *Hypnotic susceptibility.* New York, NY: Harcourt, Brace & World.

Hilgard, E. R. (1986). *Divided consciousness: Multiple controls in human thought and action.* New York, NY: Wiley.

Hilgard, E. R. (1992). Dissociation and theories of hypnosis. In E. Fromm & M. R. Nash (Eds.), *Contemporary hypnosis research.* New York, NY: Guilford.

Hill, C. E., & Lambert, M. J. (2004). Methodological issues in studying psychotherapy processes and outcomes. In M. J. Lambert (Ed.), *Bergin and Garfield's handbook of psychotherapy and behavior change.* New York, NY: Wiley.

Hilmert, C. J., Kulik, J. A., & Christenfeld, N. J. S. (2006). Positive and negative opinion modeling: The influence of another's similarity and dissimilarity. *Journal of Personality and Social Psychology, 90,* 440–452.

Hilton, J. L., & von Hippel, W. (1996). Stereotypes. *Annual Review of Psychology, 47,* 237–271.

Hines, M. (2004). Androgen, estrogen, and gender: Contributions of the early hormone environment to gender-related behavior. In A. H. Eagly, A. E. Beall, & R. J. Sternberg (Eds.), *The psychology of gender.* New York, NY: Guilford.

Hingson, R., & Sleet, D. A. (2006). Modifying alcohol use to reduce motor vehicle injury. In A. C. Gielen, D. A. Sleet, & R. J. DiClemente (Eds.), *Injury and violence prevention: Behavioral science theories, methods, and applications.* San Francisco, CA: Jossey-Bass.

Hinshaw, S. P. (2007). *The mark of shame: Stigma of mental illness and an agenda for change.* New York, NY: Oxford University Press.

Hinshaw, S. P., & Stier, A. (2008). Stigma as related to mental disorders. *Annual Review of Clinical Psychology, 4,* 367–393.

Hirsh, I. J., & Watson, C. S. (1996). Auditory psychophysics and perception. *Annual Review of Psychology, 47,* 461–484.

Hirsh, J. B. (2010). Personality and environmental concern. *Journal of Environmental Psychology, 30*(2), 245–248.

Hirshkowitz, M., Seplowitz-Hafkin, R. G., & Sharafkhaneh, A. (2009). Sleep disorders. In B. J. Sadock, V. A. Sadock, & P. Ruiz (Eds.), *Kaplan & Sadock's comprehensive textbook of psychiatry* (9th ed., Vol. 1, pp. 2150–2177). Philadelphia, PA: Lippincott Williams & Wilkins.

Hirst, W., Phelps, E. A., Buckner, R. L., Budson, A. E., Cuc, A., Gabrieli, J. E., et al. (2009). Long-term memory for the terrorist attack of September 11: Flashbulb memories, event memories, and the factors that influence their retention. *Journal of Experimental Psychology: General, 138*(2), 161–176. doi:10.1037/a0015527

Hobson, J. A. (1989). *Sleep.* New York, NY: Scientific American Library.

Hobson, J. A. (2007). Current understanding of cellular models of REM expression. In D. Barrett & P. McNamara (Eds.), *The new science of dreaming.* Westport, CT: Praeger.

Hobson, J. A., & McCarley, R. W. (1977). The brain as a dream state generator: An activation-synthesis hypothesis of the dream process. *American Journal of Psychiatry, 134,* 1335–1348.

Hobson, J. A., Pace-Schott, E. F., & Stickgold, R. (2000). Dreaming and the brain: Toward a cognitive neuroscience of conscious states. *Behavioral and Brain Sciences, 23,* 793–842; 904–1018; 1083–1121.

Hocevar, D., & Bachelor, P. (1989). A taxonomy and critique of measurements used in the study of creativity. In J. A. Glover, R. R. Ronning, & C. R. Reynolds (Eds.), *Handbook of creativity.* New York, NY: Plenum.

Hochberg, J. (1988). Visual perception. In R. C. Atkinson, R. J. Herrnstein, G. Lindzey, & R. D. Luce (Eds.), *Stevens' handbook of experimental psychology* (2nd ed., Vol. 1). New York, NY: Wiley.

Hodges, B. H., & Geyer, A. (2006). A nonconformist account of the Asch experiments: Values, pragmatics, and moral dilemmas. *Personality and Social Psychology Review, 10*(1), 2–19. doi:10.1207/s15327957pspr1001_1

Hodgkin, A. L., & Huxley, A. F. (1952). Currents carried by sodium and potassium ions through the membrane of the giant axon of Loligo. *Journal of Physiology, 116,* 449–472.

Hoek, H. W. (2002). Distribution of eating disorders. In C. G. Fairburn & K. D. Brownell (Eds.), *Eating disorders and obesity: A comprehensive handbook.* New York, NY: Guilford.

Hoerger, M., Quirk, S. W., Lucas, R. E., & Carr, T. H. (2009). Immune neglect in affective forecasting. *Journal of Research in Personality, 43*(1), 91–94. doi:10.1016/j.jrp.2008.10.001

Hoff, E. (2005). *Language development.* Belmont, CA: Wadsworth.

Hoffstein, V. (2005). Snoring and upper airway resistance. In M. H. Kryger, T. Roth, & W. C. Dement (Eds.). *Principles and practice of sleep medicine.* Philadelphia, PA: Elsevier Saunders.

Hofstede, G. (1980). *Culture's consequences: International differences in work-related values.* Beverly Hills, CA: Sage.

Hofstede, G. (1983). Dimensions of national cultures in fifty countries and three regions. In J. Deregowski, S. Dzuirawiec, & R. Annis (Eds.), *Explications in cross-cultural psychology.* Lisse: Swets and Zeitlinger.

Hofstede, G. (2001). *Culture's consequences: Comparing values, behaviors, institutions, and organizations across nations.* Thousand Oaks, CA: Sage.

Hogan, J., Barrett, P., & Hogan, R. (2007). Personality measurement, faking, and employment selection. *Journal of Applied Psychology, 92,* 1270–1285.

Hogan, M. F., & Morrison, A. K. (2008). Organization and economics of mental health treatment. In A. Tasman, J. Kay, J. A. Lieberman, M. B. First, & M. Maj (Eds.), *Psychiatry* (3rd ed.). New York, NY: Wiley-Blackwell.

Høglend, P., Bøgwald, K.-P., Amlo, S., Marble, A., Ulberg, R., Sjaastad, M. C., et al. (2008). Transference interpretations in dynamic psychotherapy: Do they really yield sustained effects? *American Journal of Psychiatry, 165,* 763–771.

Hoigaard, R., & Ingvaldsen, R. P. (2006). Social loafing in interactive groups: The effects of identifiability on effort and individual performance in floorball. *Athletic Insight: Online Journal of Sport Psychology, 8*(2).

Hoigaard, R., Säfvenbom, R., & Tonnessen, F. E. (2006). The relationship between group cohesion, group norms, and perceived social loafing in soccer teams. *Small Group Research, 37,* 217–232.

Holahan, C. J., & Moos, R. H. (1990). Life stressors, resistance factors, and improved psychological functioning: An extension of the stress resistance paradigm. *Journal of Personality and Social Psychology, 58,* 909–917.

Holahan, C. J., & Moos, R. H. (1994). Life stressors and mental health: Advances in conceptualizing stress resistance. In W. R. Avison & J. H. Gotlib (Eds.), *Stress and mental health: Contemporary issues and prospects for the future.* New York, NY: Plenum.

Holden, C. (1986, October). The rational optimist. *Psychology Today,* pp. 55–60.

Holden, C. (2004). FDA weighs suicide risk in children on antidepressants. *Science, 303,* 745.

Hollander, E., & Simeon, D. (2008). Anxiety disorders. In R. E. Hales, S. C. Yudofsky, &

G. O. Gabbard (Eds.), *The American Psychiatric Publishing textbook of psychiatry.* Washington, DC: American Psychiatric Publishing.

Hollands, C. (1989). Trivial and questionable research on animals. In G. Langley (Ed.), *Animal experimentation: The consensus changes.* New York, NY: Chapman & Hall.

Hollingworth, L. S. (1914). *Functional periodicity: An experimental study of the mental and motor abilities of women during menstruation.* New York, NY: Teachers College, Columbia University.

Hollingworth, L. S. (1916). Sex differences in mental tests. *Psychological Bulletin, 13,* 377–383.

Hollon, S. D., & DiGiuseppe, R. (2011). Cognitive theories of psychotherapy. In J. C. Norcross, G. R. Vandenbos, & D. K. Freedheim (Eds.), *History of psychotherapy: Continuity and change* (2nd ed.). Washington, DC: American Psychological Association.

Hollon, S. D., & Dimidjian, S. (2009). Cognitive and behavioral treatment of depression. In I. H. Gotlib & C. L. Hammen (Eds.), *Handbook of depression* (pp. 586–603). New York, NY: Guilford.

Hollon, S. D., Stewart, M. O., & Strunk, D. (2006). Enduring effects for cognitive behavior therapy in the treatment of depression and anxiety. *Annual Review of Psychology, 57,* 285–315.

Holmes, D. S. (1987). The influence of meditation versus rest on physiological arousal: A second examination. In M. A. West (Ed.), *The psychology of meditation.* Oxford: Clarendon Press.

Holmes, T. H., & Rahe, R. H. (1967). The Social Readjustment Rating Scale. *Journal of Psychosomatic Research, 11,* 213–218.

Holtgraves, T. (2004). Social desirability and self-reports: Testing models of socially desirable responding. *Personality and Social Psychology Bulletin, 30,* 161–172.

Holt-Lunstad, J., Smith, T. B., & Layton, J. B. (2010). Social relationships and mortality risk: A meta-analytic review. *PLoS Medicine, 7*(7), 1–20.

Holyoak, K. J. (2005). Analogy. In K. J. Holyoak & R. G. Morrison (Eds.), *The Cambridge handbook of thinking and reasoning.* New York, NY: Cambridge University Press.

Hong, G. K., Garcia, M., & Soriano, M. (2000). Responding to the challenge: Preparing mental health professionals for the new millennium. In I. Cuellar & F. A. Paniagua (Eds.), *Handbook of multicultural mental health: Assessment and treatment of diverse populations.* San Diego, CA: Academic Press.

Honig, W. K., & Alsop, B. (1992). Operant behavior. In L. R. Squire (Ed.), *Encyclopedia of learning and memory.* New York, NY: Macmillan.

Hooley, J. M. (2004). Do psychiatric patients do better clinically if they live with certain kinds of families? *Current Directions in Psychological Science, 13*(5), 202–205.

Hooley, J. M. (2007). Expressed emotion and relapse of psychopathology. *Annual Review of Clinical Psychology, 3,* 329–352.

Hooley, J. M. (2009). Schizophrenia: Interpersonal functioning. In P. H. Blaney & T. Millon (Eds.), *Oxford textbook of psychopathology* (2nd ed., pp. 333–360). New York, NY: Oxford University Press.

Hooley, J. M., & Candela, S. F. (1999). Interpersonal functioning in schizophrenia. In T. Millon, P. H. Blaney, & R. D. Davis (Eds.), *Oxford textbook of psychopathology* (pp. 311–338). New York, NY: Oxford University Press.

Hooper, J., & Teresi, D. (1986). *The 3-pound universe—brain.* New York, NY: Laurel.

Hopkins, W. D., & Cantalupo, C. (2008). Theoretical speculations on the evolutionary origins of hemispheric specialization. *Current Directions in Psychological Science, 17*(3), 233–237. doi:10.1111/j.1467-8721.2008.00581.x

Hopko, D. R., Crittendon, J. A., Grant, E., & Wilson, S. A. (2005). The impact of anxiety on performance IQ. *Anxiety, Stress, & Coping: An International Journal, 18*(1), 17–35.

Hopper, K., Harrison, G., Janca, A., & Satorius, N. (2007). *Recovery from schizophrenia: An international perspective—A report from the WHO Collaborative Project, the international study of schizophrenia.* New York, NY: Oxford University Press.

Horn, J. L. (2002). Selections of evidence, misleading assumptions, and oversimplifications: The political message of *The Bell Curve.* In J. M. Fish (Ed.), *Race and intelligence: Separating science from myth* (pp. 297–326). Mahwah, NJ: Erlbaum.

Horowitz, F. D. (1992). John B. Watson's legacy: Learning and environment. *Developmental Psychology, 28,* 360–367.

Horrey, W. J., & Wickens, C. D. (2006). Examining the impact of cell phone on driving using meta-analytic techniques. *Human Factors, 48,* 196–205.

Houlihan, J., Kropp, T., Wiles, R., Gray, S., & Campbell, C. (2005). *Body burden: The pollution in newborns.* Washington, DC: Environmental Working Group.

Houston, D. M., Santelmann, L. M., & Jusczyk, P. W. (2004). English-learning infants' segmentation of trisyllabic words from fluent speech. *Language and Cognitive Processes, 19*(1), 97–136.

Howard, D. J. (1995). "Chaining" the use of influence strategies for producing compliance behavior. *Journal of Social Behavior and Personality, 10,* 169–185.

Howes, O. D., & Kapur, S. (2009). The dopamine hypothesis of schizophrenia: Version III—The final common pathway. *Schizophrenia Bulletin, 35*(3), 549–562. doi:10.1093/schbul/sbp006

Hoyer, W. J., & Verhaeghen, P. (2006). Memory aging. In J. E. Birren & K. W. Schaie (Eds.), *Handbook of the psychology of aging.* San Diego, CA: Academic Press.

Hrdy, S. B. (1997). Raising Darwin's consciousness: Female sexuality and the prehominid origins of patriarchy. *Human Nature: An Interdiciplinary Biosocial Perspective, 8,* 1–49.

Hsu, L. K. G. (1990). *Eating disorders.* New York, NY: Guilford.

Hsu, L. K. G. (1995). Outcome of bulimia nervosa. In K. D. Brownell, & C. G. Fairburn (Eds.), *Eating disorders and obesity: A comprehensive handbook.* New York, NY: Guilford.

Hu, Y., Zhang, R., & Li, W. (2005). Relationships among jealousy, self-esteem and self-efficacy. *Chinese Journal of Clinical Psychology, 13,* 165–166, 172.

Hua, J. Y., & Smith, S. J. (2004). Neural activity and the dynamics of central nervous system development. *Nature Neuroscience, 7,* 327–332.

Huang, J., Lee, T., & Lu, M. (2007). Prenatal programming of childhood overweight and obesity. *Maternal & Child Health Journal, 11*(5), 461–473.

Hubel, D. H., & Wiesel, T. N. (1962). Receptive fields, binocular interaction and functional architecture in the cat's visual cortex. *Journal of Physiology, 160,* 106–154.

Hubel, D. H., & Wiesel, T. N. (1963). Receptive fields of cells in striate cortex of very young visually inexperienced kittens. *Journal of Neurophysiology, 26,* 994–1002.

Hubel, D. H., & Wiesel, T. N. (1979). Brain mechanisms of vision. In Scientific American (Eds.), *The brain.* San Franciso: W. H. Freeman.

Huber, R., & Tononi, G. (2009). Sleep and waking across the lifespan. In G. G. Berntson & J. T. Cacioppo (Eds.), *Handbook of neuroscience for the behavioral sciences* (Vol. 1, pp. 461–481). New York, NY: Wiley.

Hudson, J. I., Hiripi, E., Pope Jr., Harrison, G., & Kessler, R. C. (2007). The prevalence and correlates of eating disorders in the national comorbidity survey replication. *Biological Psychiatry, 61,* 348–358.

Hudson, W. (1960). Pictorial depth perception in sub-cultural groups in Africa. *Journal of Social Psychology, 52,* 183–208.

Hudson, W. (1967). The study of the problem of pictorial perception among unacculturated groups. *International Journal of Psychology, 2,* 89–107.

Hudspeth, A. J. (2000). Sensory transduction in the ear. In E. R. Kandel, J. H. Schwartz, & T. M. Jessell (Eds.), *Principles of neural science.* New York, NY: McGraw-Hill.

Huesmann, L. R. (1986). Psychological processes promoting the relation between exposure to media violence and aggressive behavior by the viewer. *Journal of Social Issues, 42,* 125–139.

Huesmann, L. R., & Miller, L. S. (1994). Long-term effects of repeated exposure to media violence in childhood. In L. R. Huesmann (Ed.), *Aggressive behavior: Current perspectives.* New York, NY: Plenum Press.

Huesmann, L. R., Moise-Titus, J., Podolski, C. L., & Eron, L. D. (2003). Longitudinal relations between children's exposure to TV violence and their aggressive and violent behavior in young adulthood: 1977–1992. *Developmental Psychology, 39,* 201–221.

Huey, E. D., Krueger, F., & Grafman, J. (2006). Representations in the human prefrontal cortex. *Current Directions in Psychological Science, 15,* 167–171.

Huey, L. Y., Cole, S., Cole, R. F., Daniels, A. S. & Katzelnick, D. J. (2009). Health care reform. In B. J. Sadock, V. A. Sadock, & P. Ruiz (Eds.), *Kaplan & Sadock's comprehensive textbook of psychiatry* (pp. 4282–4298). Philadelphia, PA: Lippincott Williams & Wilkins.

Hughes, J., Smith, T. W., Kosterlitz, H. W., Fothergill, L. A., Morgan, B. A., & Morris, H. R. (1975). Identification of two related pentapeptides from the brain with the potent opiate agonist activity. *Nature, 258,* 577–579.

Hunsley, J., Lee, C. M., & Wood, J. M. (2003). Controversial and questionable assessment techniques. In S. O. Lilienfeld, S. J. Lynn, & J. M. Lohr (Eds.), *Science and pseudoscience in clinical psychology.* New York, NY: Guilford.

Hunt, E. (2001). Multiple views of multiple intelligence [Review of the book *Intelligence reframed: Multiple intelligence in the 21st century*]. *Contemporary Psychology, 46,* 5–7.

Hunt, E., & Carlson, J. (2007). Considerations relating to the study of group differences in intelligence. *Perspectives on Psychological Science, 2*(2), 194–213. doi:10.1111/j.1745-6916 .2007.00037.x

Hunt, H. (1989). *The multiplicity of dreams: Memory, imagination and consciousness.* New Haven: Yale University Press.

Hunt, J. M., Smith, M. F., & Kernan, J. B. (1985). The effects of expectancy disconfirmation and argument strength on message processing level: An application to personal selling. In E. C. Hirschman & M. B. Holbrook (Eds.), *Advances in consumer research* (Vol. 12). Provo, UT: Association for Consumer Research.

Hurlemann, R., Patin, A., Onur, O. A., Cohen, M. X., Baumgartner, T., Metzler, S., et al. (2010). Oxytocin enhances amygdala-dependent, socially reinforced learning and emotional empathy in humans. *Journal of Neuroscience, 30*(14), 4999–5007. doi:10.1523/JNEUROSCI .5538-09.2010

Hurvich, L. M. (1981). *Color vision.* Sunderland, MA: Sinnauer Associates.

Hustinx, P. J., Kuyper, H., van der Werf, M. C., & Dijkstra, P. (2009). Achievement motivation revisited: New longitudinal data to demonstrate its predictive power. *Educational Psychology, 29*(5), 561–582. doi:10.1080/01443410903132128

Hutchinson, A. (2007, February). Watering holes: Las Vegas tries to prevent a water shortage. *Popular Mechanics,* p. 20.

Huttenlocher, P. R. (1994). Synaptogenesis in human cerebral cortex. In G. Dawson & K. W. Fischer (Eds.), *Human behavior and the developing brain.* New York, NY: Guilford.

Huttenlocher, P. R. (2002). *Neural plasticity: The effects of environment on the development of the cerebral cortex.* Cambridge, MA: Harvard University Press.

Hwang, W. C. (2006). The psychotherapy adaptation and modification framework: Application to Asian Americans. *American Psychologist, 61,* 702–715.

Hyde, J. S. (2005a). The gender similarities hypothesis. *American Psychologist, 60,* 581–892.

Hyde, J. S. (2005b). The genetics of sexual orientation. In J. S. Hyde (Ed.), *Biological substrates of human sexuality* (pp. 9–20). Washington, DC: American Psychological Association.

Hyde, J. S. (2007). New directions in the study of gender similarities and differences. *Current Directions in Psychological Science, 16*(5), 259–263. doi:10.1111/j.1467-8721.2007.00516.x

Hyde, J. S., & Mertz, J. E. (2009). Gender, culture, and mathematics performance. *Proceedings of the National Academy of Sciences of the United States of America, 106*(22), 8801–8807. doi:10.1073/ pnas.0901265106

Hyman, I. E., Jr., & Kleinknecht, E. E. (1999). False childhood memories: Research, theory, and applications. In L. M. Williams, & V. L. Banyard (Eds.), *Trauma & memory.* Thousand Oaks, CA: Sage Publications.

Hyman, I. E., Jr., Husband, T. H., & Billings, J. F. (1995). False memories of childhood experiences. *Applied Cognitive Psychology, 9,* 181–197.

Iacoboni, M. (2007). Face to face: The neural basis of social mirroring and empathy. *Psychiatric Annals, 37*(4), 236–241.

Iacoboni, M. (2009). Imitation, empathy, and mirror neurons. *Annual Review of Psychology, 60,* 653–670. doi:10.1146/annurev.psych.60 .110707.163604

Iacoboni, M., & Dapretto, M. (2006). The mirror neuron system and the consequences of its dysfunction. *Nature Reviews Neuroscience, 7,* 942–951.

Iacono, W. G., & Lykken, D. T. (1997). The validity of the lie detector: Two surveys of scientific opinion. *Journal of Applied Psychology, 82,* 426–433.

Iacono, W. G., & Patrick, C. J. (1999). Polygraph ("lie detector") testing: The state of the art. In A. K. Hess & I. B. Weiner (Eds.), *The handbook of forensic psychology* (pp. 440–473). New York, NY: Wiley.

Iams, J. D. (2002). Preterm birth. In S. G. Gabbe, J. R. Niebyl, & J. L. Simpson (Eds.), *Obstetrics: Normal and problem pregnancies.* New York, NY: Churchill Livingstone.

Iams, J. D., & Romero, R. (2007). Preterm birth. In S. G. Gabbe, J. R. Niebyl, & J. L. Simpson (Eds.), *Obstetrics: Normal and problem pregnancies* (5th ed., pp. 668–712). Philadelphia, PA: Elsevier.

Ickovics, J. R., Thayaparan, B., & Ethier, K. A. (2001). Women and AIDS: A contextual analysis. In A. Baum, T. A. Revenson, & J. E. Singer (Eds.), *Handbook of health psychology* (pp. 817–840). Mahwah, NJ: Erlbaum.

Inagaki, K., & Hatano, G. (2004). Vitalistic causality in young children's naive biology. *Trends in Cognitive Sciences, 8,* 356–362.

Infante, J. R., Torres-Avisbal, M., Pinel, P., Vallejo. J. A., Peran, F., Gonzalez, F., Contreras, P., Pacheco, C., Roldan, A., & Latre, J. M. (2001). Catecholamine levels in practitioners of the transcendental meditation technique. *Physiology & Behavior, 72*(1-2), 141–146.

Inglehart, R. (1990). *Culture shift in advanced industrial society.* Princeton, NJ: Princeton University Press.

Ingram, R. E., Scott, W. D., & Hamill, S. (2009). Depression: Social and cognitive aspects. In P. H. Blaney & T. Millon (Eds.), *Oxford textbook of psychopathology* (2nd ed., pp. 230–252). New York, NY: Oxford University Press.

Innocenti, G. M. (1994). Some new trends in the study of the corpus callosum. *Behavioral and Brain Research, 64,* 1–8.

Insel, T. R. (2010). Psychiatrists' relationships with pharmaceutical companies: Part of the problem or part of the solution? *Journal of the American Medical Association, 303*(12), 1192–1193. doi:10.1001/jama.2010.317

Intergovernmental Panel on Climate Change. (2007). *Climate change 2007: Synthesis report.* Retrieved 9/3/08 from http://www.ipcc.ch/pdf/assessment-report/ar4/syr/ar4_syr.pdf

Inzlicht, M., & Kang, S. K. (2010). Stereotype threat spillover: How coping with threats to social identity affects aggression, eating, decision making, and attention. *Journal of Personality and Social Psychology, 99*(3), 467–481. doi:10.1037/a0018951

Iredale, S. K., Nevill, C. H., & Lutz, C. K. (2010). The influence of observer presence on baboon (*Papio spp.*) and rhesus macaque (*Macaca mulatta*) behavior. *Applied Animal Behaviour Science, 122*(1), 53–57. doi:10.1016/j.applanim.2009.11.002.

Irvine, S. H., & Berry, J. W. (1988). *Human abilities in cultural context.* New York, NY: Cambridge University Press.

Isacsson, G. G., Holmgren, A. A., Ösby, U. U., & Ahlner, J. J. (2009). Decrease in suicide among the individuals treated with antidepressants: A controlled study of antidepressants in suicide, Sweden 1995–2005. *Acta Psychiatrica Scandinavica, 120*(1), 37–44. doi:10.1111/j.1600-0447.2009.01344.x

Isometsa, E. T., Heikkinen, M. E., Marttunen, M. J., Henriksson, M. M., Aro, H. M., & Lonnqvist, J. K. (1995). The last appointment before suicide: Is suicide intent communicated? *American Journal of Psychiatry, 152,* 919–922.

Iwawaki, S., & Vernon, P. E. (1988). Japanese abilities and achievements. In S. H. Irvine & J. W. Berry (Eds.), *Human abilities in cultural context.* New York, NY: Cambridge University Press.

Izard, C. E. (1984). Emotion-cognition relationships and human development. In C. E. Izard, J. Kagan, & R. B. Zajonc (Eds.), *Emotions, cognition and behavior.* Cambridge, England: Cambridge University Press.

Izard, C. E. (1990). Facial expressions and the regulation of emotions. *Journal of Personality and Social Psychology, 58,* 487–498.

Izard, C. E. (1991). *The psychology of emotions.* New York, NY: Plenum.

Izard, C. E. (1994). Innate and universal facial expressions: Evidence from developmental and cross-cultural research. *Psychological Bulletin, 115,* 288–299.

Izard, C. E., & Saxton, P. M. (1988). Emotions. In R. C. Atkinson, R. J. Herrnstein, G. Lindzey, & R. D. Luce (Eds.), *Stevens' handbook of experimental psychology* (Vol. 1). New York, NY: Wiley.

Jablensky, A. (2009). Course and outcome of schizophrenia and their prediction. In M. C. Gelder, N. C. Andreasen, J. J. López-Ibor, Jr., & J. R. Geddes (Eds.). *New Oxford textbook of psychiatry* (2nd ed., Vol. 1). New York, NY: Oxford University Press.

Jacob, R. G., & Pelham, W. (2005). Behavior therapy. In B. J. Sadock & V. A. Sadock (Eds.), *Kaplan and Sadock's comprehensive textbook of psychiatry* (pp. 2498–2547). Philadelphia, PA: Lippincott Williams & Wilkins.

Jacobs, B. L. (2004). Depression: The brain finally gets into the act. *Current Directions in Psychological Science, 13*(3), 103–106.

Jacobs, D. F. (2004). Youth gambling in North America: Long-term trends and future prospects. In J. L. Derevensky & R. Gupta (Eds.), *Gambling problems in youth: Theoretical and applied perspectives* (pp. 1-24). New York, NY: Kluwer/Plenum.

Jacobson, E. (1938). *Progressive relaxation.* Chicago: University of Chicago Press.

Jacoby, L. L., Hessels, S., & Bopp, K. (2001). Proactive and retroactive effects in memory performance: Dissociating recollection and accessibility bias. In H. L. Roediger, J. S. Nairne, I. Neath, & A. M. Surprenant (Eds.), *The nature of remembering: Essays in honor of Robert G. Crowder* (pp. 35–54). Washington, DC: American Psychological Association.

James, W. (1884). What is emotion? *Mind, 19,* 188–205.

James, W. (1890). *The principles of psychology.* New York, NY: Holt.

James, W. (1902). *The varieties of religious experience.* New York, NY: Modern Library.

James, W. H. (2005). Biological and psychosocial determinants of male and female human sexual orientation. *Journal of Biosocial Science, 37,* 555–567.

Jamison, K. R. (1988). Manic-depressive illness and accomplishment: Creativity, leadership, and social class. In F. K. Goodwin & K. R. Jamison (Eds.), *Manic-depressive illness.* Oxford, England: Oxford University Press.

Janig, W. (2003). The autonomic nervous system and its coordination by the brain. In R. J. Davidson, K. R. Scherer, & H. H. Goldsmith (Eds.), *Handbook of affective sciences.* New York, NY: Oxford University Press.

Janis, I. L. (1958). *Psychological stress.* New York, NY: Wiley.

Janis, I. L. (1972). *Victims of groupthink.* Boston, MA: Houghton Mifflin.

Janis, I. L., & Mann, L. (1977). *Decision making: A psychological analysis of conflict, choice, and commitment.* New York, NY: Free Press.

Janssen, L., Fennis, B. M., & Pruyn, A. H. (2010). Forewarned is forearmed: Conserving self-control strength to resist social influence. *Journal of Experimental Social Psychology, 46*(6), 911–921. doi:10.1016/j.jesp.2010.06.008

Javitt, D. C., & Laruelle, M. (2006). Neurochemical theories. In J. A. Lieberman, T. S. Stroup, & D. O. Perkins (Eds.), *Textbook of schizophrenia* (pp. 85–116). Washington, DC: American Psychiatric Publishing.

Jefferson, J. W., & Greist, J. H. (2009). Lithium. In B. J. Sadock, V. A. Sadock, & P. Ruiz (Eds.), *Kaplan & Sadock's comprehensive textbook of psychiatry* (pp. 3132–3144). Philadelphia, PA: Lippincott Williams & Wilkins.

Jensen, A. R. (1969). How much can we boost IQ and scholastic achievement? *Harvard Educational Review, 39,* 1–23.

Jensen, A. R. (1980). *Bias in mental testing.* New York, NY: Free Press.

Jensen, A. R. (1998). *The g factor: The science of mental ability.* Westport, CT: Praeger.

Jensen, M. P., & Patterson, D. R. (2008). Hypnosis in the relief of pain and pain disorders. In M. R. Nash & A. J. Barnier (Eds.). *The Oxford handbook of hypnosis: Theory, research and practice* (pp. 503–534). New York, NY: Oxford University Press.

Jessberger, S., Aimone, J. B., & Gage, F. H. (2009). Neurogenesis. In J. H. Byrne (Ed.), *Concise learning and memory: The editor's selection.* San Diego, CA: Elsevier.

Jessup, R. K., Veinott, E. S., Todd, P. M., & Busemeyer, J. R. (2009). Leaving the store empty-handed: Testing explanations for the too-much-choice effect using decision field theory. *Psychology & Marketing, 26*(3), 299–320. doi:10.1002/mar.20274

Jick, H., & Kaye, J. A. (2004). Autism and DPT vaccination in the United Kingdom. *New England Journal of Medicine, 350*(26), 2722–2723.

Jick, H., Kaye, J. A., & Jick, S. S. (2004). Antidepressants and the risk of suicidal behaviors. *Journal of The American Medical Association, 292,* 338–343.

Joffe, R. T. (2009). Neuropsychiatric aspects of multiple sclerosis and other demyelinating disorders. In B. J. Sadock, V. A. Sadock, & P. Ruiz (Eds.), *Kaplan & Sadock's comprehensive textbook of psychiatry* (9th ed., Vol. 1, pp. 248–272). Philadelphia, PA: Lippincott Williams & Wilkins.

John, O. P., Naumann, L. P., & Soto, C. J. (2008). Paradigm shift to the integrative Big Five trait taxonomy: History, measurement, and conceptual issues. In O. P. John, R. W. Robbins, & L. A. Pervin (Eds.), *Handbook of personality: Theory and research* (Vol. 3, pp. 114–158). New York, NY: Guilford.

Johnson, A. (2003). Procedural memory and skill acquisition. In A. F. Healy & R. W. Proctor (Eds.), *Handbook of psychology, Vol. 4: Experimental psychology.* New York, NY: Wiley.

Johnson, B. A., & Ait-Daoud, N. (2005). Alcohol: Clinical aspects. In J. H. Lowinson, P. Ruiz, R. B. Millman, & J. G. Langrod (Eds.), *Substance abuse: A comprehensive textbook*. Philadelphia, PA: Lippincott Williams & Wilkins.

Johnson, B. T., Maio, G. R., & Smith-McLallen, A. (2005). Communication and attitude change: Causes, processes, and effects. In D. Albarracin, B. T. Johnson, & M. P. Zanna (Eds.), *The handbook of attitudes*. Mahwah, NJ: Erlbaum.

Johnson, C., & Mullen, B. (1994). Evidence for the accessibility of paired distinctiveness in distinctiveness-based illusory correlation in stereotyping. *Personality and Social Psychology Bulletin, 20*, 65–70.

Johnson, E. O., & Breslau, N. (2006). Is the association of smoking and depression a recent phenomenon? *Nicotine & Tobacco Research, 8*, 257–262.

Johnson, J. G., & Sherman, M. F. (1997). Daily hassles mediate the relationship between major life events and psychiatric symptomatology: Longitudinal findings from an adolescent sample. *Journal of Social and Clinical Psychology, 16*, 389–404.

Johnson, M. K. (1996). Fact, fantasy, and public policy. In D. J. Herrmann, C. McEvoy, C. Hertzog, P. Hertel, & M. K. Johnson (Eds.), *Basic and applied memory research: Theory in context* (Vol. 1). Mahwah, NJ: Erlbaum.

Johnson, M. K. (2006). Memory and reality. *American Psychologist, 61*, 760–771.

Johnson, M. K., Hashtroudi, S., & Lindsay, D. S. (1993). Source monitoring. *Psychological Bulletin, 114*, 3–28.

Johnson, S. B., & Carlson, D. N. (2004). Medical regimen adherence: Concepts assessment, and interventions. In J. M. Raczynski & L. C. Leviton (Eds.), *Handbook of clinical health psychology: Vol 2. Disorders of behavior and health*. Washington, DC: American Psychological Association.

Johnson, S. C., Dweck, C. S., & Chen, F. S. (2007). Evidence for infants' internal working models of attachment. *Psychological Science, 18*(6), 501–502. doi:10.1111/j.1467-9280.2007.01929.x

Johnson, S. L., Joormann, J., LeMoult, & Miller, C. (2009). Mood disorders: Biological bases. In P. H. Blaney & T. Millon (Eds.), *Oxford textbook of psychopathology* (2nd ed., pp. 198–229). New York, NY: Oxford University Press.

Johnson, W. (2010). Understanding the genetics of intelligence: Can height help? Can corn oil? *Current Directions in Psychological Science, 19*(3), 177–182. doi:10.1177/0963721410370136

Johnson, W., & Krueger, R. F. (2006). How money buys happiness: Genetic and environmental processes linking finances and life satisfaction. *Journal of Personality and Social Psychology, 90*, 680–691.

Johnson, W., Turkheimer, E., Gottesman, I. I., & Bouchard, T. R. (2009). Beyond heritability: Twin studies in behavioral research. *Current Directions in Psychological Science, 18*(4), 217–220. doi:10.1111/j.1467-8721.2009.01639.x

Johnston, J. C., & McClelland, J. L. (1974). Perception of letters in words: Seek not and ye shall find. *Science, 184*, 1192–1194.

Joiner, T. E., Jr., & Timmons, K. A. (2009). Depression in its interpersonal context. In I. H. Gotlib & C. L. Hammen (Eds.), *Handbook of Depression* (2nd ed., pp. 322–339). New York, NY: Guilford.

Jones, E. E., & Davis, K. E. (1965). From acts to dispositions: The attribution process in person perception. In L. Berkowitz (Ed.), *Advances in experimental social psychology* (Vol. 2). New York, NY: Academic Press.

Jones, E. E., & Nisbett, R. E. (1971). The actor and the observer: Divergent perceptions of the causes of behavior. In E. E. Jones, D. E. Kanouse, H. H. Kelley, R. E. Nisbett, S. Valins, & B. Weiner (Eds.), *Attribution: Perceiving the causes of behavior*. Morristown, NJ: General Learning Press.

Jones, G. V. (1990). Misremembering a common object: When left is not right. *Memory & Cognition, 18*(2), 174–182.

Jordan, M., & Marshall, H. (2010). Taking counseling and psychotherapy outside: Destruction or enrichment of the therapeutic frame? *European Journal of Psychotherapy & Counseling, 12*(4), 345–359.

Jordan-Young, R. M. (2010). *Brainstorm: The flaws in the science of sex differences*. Cambridge, MA: Harvard University Press.

Joska, J. A., & Stein, D. J. (2008). Mood disorders. In R. E. Hales, S. C. Yudofsky, & G. O. Gabbard (Eds.), *The American Psychiatric Publishing textbook of psychiatry* (5th ed., pp. 457–504). Washington, DC: American Psychiatric Publishing.

Josse, G., & Tzourio-Mazoyer, N. (2004). Hemispheric specialization for language. *Brain Research Reviews, 44*, 1–12.

Judge, T. A., Hurst, C., & Simon, L. S. (2009). Does it pay to be smart, attractive, or confident (or all three)? Relationships among general mental ability, physical attractiveness, core self-evaluations, and income. *Journal of Applied Psychology, 94*(3), 742–755. doi:10.1037/a0015497

Judge, T. A., & Klinger, R. (2008). Job satisfaction: Subjective well-being at work. In M. Eid & R. J. Larsen (Eds.), *The science of subjective well-being*. New York, NY: Guilford.

Julien, R. M., Advokat, C. D., & Comaty, J. E. (2008). *A primer of drug action: A comprehensive guide to the actions, uses, and side effects of psychoactive drugs*. New York, NY: Worth.

Jung, C. G. (1917/1953). *On the psychology of the unconscious*. In H. Read, M. Fordham, & G. Adler (Eds.), *Collected works of C. G. Jung* (Vol. 7). Princeton, NJ: Princeton University Press.

Jung, C. G. (1921/1960). *Psychological types*. In H. Read, M. Fordham, & G. Adler (Eds.), *Collected works of C. G. Jung* (Vol. 6). Princeton, NJ: Princeton University Press.

Jung, C. G. (1933). *Modern man in search of a soul*. New York, NY: Harcourt, Brace & World.

Jung, R. E., & Haier, R. J. (2007). The Parieto-Frontal Integration Theory (P-FIT) of intelligence: Converging neuroimaging evidence. *Behavioral and Brain Sciences, 30*(2), 135–154. doi:10.1017/S0140525X07001185

Kaas, J. H. (2000). The reorganization of sensory and motor maps after injury in adult mammals. In M. S. Gazzaniga (Ed.), *The new cognitive neurosciences*. Cambridge, MA: MIT Press.

Kabat-Zinn, J. (2003). Mindfulness-based stress reduction (MBSR). *Constructivism in the Human Sciences, 8*, 73–107.

Kagan, J. (1998, November/December). A parent's influence is peerless. *Harvard Education Letter*.

Kagan, J., & Fox, A. (2006). Biology, culture, and temperamental biases. In N. Eisenberg, W. Damon, & R. M. Lerner (Eds.), *Handbook of child psychology: Social, emotional, and personality development*. Hoboken, NJ: Wiley.

Kahn, D. (2007). Metacognition, recognition, and reflection while dreaming. In D. Barrett & P. McNamara (Eds.), *The new science of dreaming*. Westport, CT: Praeger.

Kahn, P. H., Jr. (2003). The development of environmental moral identity. In S. Clayton & S. Opotow (Eds.), *Identity and the natural environment: The psychological significance of nature*. Cambridge, MA: MIT Press.

Kahn, P. H., Jr. (2007). The child's environmental amnesia—it's ours. *Children, Youth and Environments 17*, 199–207.

Kahn, P. H., Jr., & Kellert, S. R. (2002). *Children and nature: Psychological, sociocultural, and evolutionary investigations*. Cambridge MA: MIT Press.

Kahneman, D. (1999). Objective happiness. In D. Kahneman, E. Diener, & N. Schwarz (Eds.), *Well-being: The foundations of hedonic psychology*. New York, NY: Russell Sage Foundation.

Kahneman, D. (2003). A perspective on judgment and choice: Mapping bounded rationality. *American Psychologist, 58*, 697–720.

Kahneman, D., & Deaton, A. (2010). High income improves evaluation of life but not emotional well-being. *Proceedings of the National Academy of Sciences of the United States of America, 107*(38), 16489–16493. doi:10.1073/pnas.1011492107

Kahneman, D., & Tversky, A. (1973). On the psychology of prediction. *Psychological Review, 80*, 237–251.

Kahneman, D., & Tversky, A. (1979). Prospect theory: An analysis of decision under risk. *Econometrica, 47*, 263–292.

Kahneman, D., & Tversky, A. (1982). Subjective probability: A judgment of representativeness. In D. Kahneman, P. Slovic, & A. Tversky (Eds.), *Judgment under uncertainty: Heuristics and biases*. Cambridge: Cambridge University Press.

Kahneman, D., & Tversky, A. (2000). *Choices, values, and frames*. New York, NY: Cambridge University Press.

Kaiser, A., Haller, S., Schmitz, S., & Nitsch, C. (2009). On sex/gender related similarities and differences in fMRI language research. *Brain Research Reviews, 61*(2), 49–59. doi:10.1016/j.brainresrev.2009.03.005

Kajantie, E. (2008). Physiological stress response, estrogen, and the male-female mortality gap. *Current Directions in Psychological Science, 17*(5), 348–352. doi:10.1111/j.1467-8721.2008.00604.x

Kajantie, E., & Phillips, D. W. (2006). The effects of sex and hormonal status on the physiological response to acute psychosocial stress. *Psychoneuroendocrinology, 31*(2), 151–178. doi:10.1016/j.psyneuen.2005.07.002

Kales, J. D., Kales, A., Bixler, E. O., Soldatos, C. R., Cadieux, R. J., Kashurba, G. J., & Vela-Bueno, A. (1984). Biopsychobehavioral correlates of insomnia: V. Clinical characteristics and behavioral correlates. *American Journal of Psychiatry, 141*, 1371–1376.

Kalichman, S. C. (1995). *Understanding AIDS: A guide for mental health professionals.* Washington, DC: American Psychological Association.

Kalmijn, M. (1998). Intermarriage and homogamy: Causes, patterns, trends. *Annual Review of Sociology, 24*, 395–421.

Kanazawa, S. (2006). Mind the gap . . . in intelligence: Reexamining the relationship between inequality and health. *British Journal of Health Psychology, 11*, 623–642.

Kandel, E. R. (2000). Nerve cells and behavior. In E. R. Kandel, J. H. Schwartz, & T. M. Jessell (Eds.), *Principles of neural science* (pp. 19–35). New York, NY: McGraw-Hill.

Kandel, E. R. (2001). The molecular biology of memory storage: A dialogue between genes and synapses. *Science, 294*, 1030–1038.

Kandel, E. R., & Siegelbaum, S. A. (2000). Synaptic integration. In E. R. Kandel, J. H. Schwartz & T. M. Jessell (Eds.), *Principles of neural science* (pp. 207–228). New York, NY: McGraw-Hill.

Kandler, C., Bleidorn, W., Riemann, R., Spinath, F. M., Thiel, W., & Angleitner, A. (2010). Sources of cumulative continuity in personality: A longitudinal multiple-rater twin study. *Journal of Personality and Social Psychology, 98*(6), 995–1008. doi:10.1037/a0019558

Kane, J. (1991). *Be sick well: A healthy approach to chronic illness.* Oakland, CA: New Harbinger Publications.

Kane, J. M., Stroup, T. S., & Marder, S. R. (2009). Schizophrenia: Pharmacological treatment. In B. J. Sadock, V. A. Sadock, & P. Ruiz (Eds.), *Kaplan & Sadock's comprehensive textbook of psychiatry* (pp. 1547–1555). Philadelphia, PA: Lippincott Williams & Wilkins.

Kane, M. J., & Engle, R. W. (2002). The role of prefrontal cortex in working-memory capacity, executive attention, and general fluid intelligence: An individual-differences perspective. *Psychonomic Bulletin & Review, 9*, 637–671.

Kane, M. J., Brown, L. H., McVay, J. C., Silivia, P. J., Myin-Germeys, I., & Kwapil, T. R. (2007). For whom the mind wanders, and when: An experience-sampling study of working memory and executive control in daily life. *Psychological Science, 18*, 614–621.

Kane, T. D., Marks, M. A., Zaccaro, S. J., & Blair, V. (1996). Self-efficacy, personal goals, and wrestlers' self-regulation. *Journal of Sport & Exercise Psychology, 18*, 36–48.

Kanwisher, N., & Yovel, G. (2009). Face perception. In G. G. Berntson & J. T. Cacioppo (Eds.), *Handbook of neuroscience for the behavioral sciences.* New York, NY: Wiley.

Kaplan, J. T., & Iacoboni, M. (2006). Getting a grip on other minds: Mirror neurons, intention understanding, and cognitive empathy. *Social Neuroscience, 1*, 175–183.

Kaplan, K. A., Itoi, A., & Dement, W. C. (2007). Awareness of sleepiness and ability to predict sleep onset: Can drivers avoid falling asleep at the wheel? *Sleep Medicine, 9*(1), 71–79. doi:10.1016/j.sleep.2007.02.001

Kaplan, R., & Kaplan, S. (1989). *The experience of nature: A psychological perspective.* Cambridge, MA: Cambridge University Press.

Kaplan, S. (1995). The restorative benefits of nature: Toward an integrative framework. *Journal of Environmental Psychology, 15*, 169–182.

Karasu, T. B. (2005). Psychoanalysis and psychoanalytic psychotherapy. In B. J. Sadock & V. A. Sadock (Eds.), *Kaplan and Sadock's comprehensive textbook of psychiatry.* Philadelphia, PA: Lippincott Williams & Wilkins.

Karau, S. J., & Williams, K. D. (1993). Social loafing: A meta-analytic review and theoretical integration. *Journal of Personality and Social Psychology, 65*, 681–706.

Karlsgodt, K. H., Sun, D., & Cannon, T. D. (2010). Structural and functional brain abnormalities in schizophrenia. *Current Directions in Psychological Science, 19*(4), 226–231. doi:10.1177/0963721410377601

Karp, A., Andel, R., Parker, M. G., Wang, H., Winblad, B., & Fratiglioni, L. (2009). Mentally stimulating activities at work during midlife and dementia risk after age 75: Follow-up study from the Kungsholmen Project. *American Journal of Geriatric Psychiatry, 17*(3), 227–236. doi:10.1097/JGP.0b013e318190b691

Karpicke, J. D., Butler, A. C., & Roediger, H. (2009). Metacognitive strategies in student learning: Do students practise retrieval when they study on their own? *Memory, 17*(4), 471–479. doi:10.1080/09658210802647009

Karpicke, J. D., & Roediger, H. (2008). The critical importance of retrieval for learning. *Science, 319*(5865), 966–968. doi:10.1126/science.1152408

Kass, S. J., Cole, K. S., & Stanny, C. J. (2007). Effects of distraction and experience on situation awareness and simulated driving. *Transportation Research Part F: Traffic Psychology and Behaviour, 10*, 321–329.

Kassam, K. S., Gilbert, D. T., Swencionis, J. K., & Wilson, T. D. (2009). Misconceptions of memory: The Scooter Libby effect. *Psychological Science, 20*(5), 551–552. doi:10.1111/j.1467-9280.2009.02334.x

Kasser, T. (2002). *The high price of materialism.* Cambridge, MA: MIT Press.

Kasser, T., & Kanner, A.D. (2004). *Psychology and consumer culture: The struggle for a good life in a materialistic world.* Washington DC: American Psychological Association.

Kasser, T., Ryan, R. M., Couchman, C. E., & Sheldon, K. M. (2004). Materialistic values: Their causes and consequences. In T. Kasser & A. D. Kanner (Eds.), *Psychology and consumer culture: The struggle for a good life in a materialistic world.* Washington, DC: American Psychological Association.

Kasser, T., & Sharma, Y. S. (1999). Reproductive freedom, educational equality, and females' preference for resource-aquisition characteristics in mates. *Psychological Science, 10*, 374–377.

Kassin, S. M., Tubb, V. A., Hosch, H. M., & Memon, A. (2001). On the "general acceptance" of eyewitness testimony research: A new survey of the experts. *American Psychologist, 56*, 405–416.

Katigbak, M. S., Church, A. T., Guanzon-Lapena, M. A., Carlota, A. J. & del Pilar, G. H. (2002). Are indigenous personality dimensions culture specific? Philippine inventories and the five-factor model. *Journal of Personality and Social Psychology, 82*, 89–101.

Kaufman, A. S. (2000). Tests of intelligence. In R. J. Sternberg (Ed.), *Handbook of intelligence* (pp. 445–476). New York, NY: Cambridge University Press.

Kaufman, J. C., & Baer, J. (2002). Could Steven Spielberg manage the Yankees?: Creative thinking in different domains. *Korean Journal of Thinking & Problem Solving, 12*(2), 5–14.

Kaufman, J. C., & Baer, J. (2004). Hawking's haiku, Madonna's math: Why it is hard to be creative in every room of the house. In R. J. Sternberg, E. L. Grigorenko, & J. L. Singer (Eds.), *Creativity: From potential to realization.* Washington, DC: American Psychological Association.

Kaufman, L., Vassiliades, V., Noble, R., Alexander, R., Kaufman, J., & Edlund, S. (2007). Perceptual distance and the moon illusion. *Spatial Vision, 20*, 155–175. doi:10.1163/156856807779369698

Kay, J., & Kay, R. L. (2008). Individual psychoanalytic psychotherapy. In A. Tasman, J. Kay, J. A. Lieberman, M. B. First, & M. Maj (Eds.), *Psychiatry* (3rd ed.). New York, NY: Wiley-Blackwell.

Kazdin, A. (1994). Methodology, design, and evaluation in psychotherapy research. In A. E. Bergin & S. L. Garfield (Eds.), *Handbook of psychotherapy and behavior change* (4th ed.). New York, NY: Wiley.

Kazdin, A. (2001). *Behavior modification in applied settings.* Belmont: Wadsworth.

Kazdin, A., & Benjet, C. (2003). Spanking children: Evidence and issues. *Current Directions in Psychological Science, 12*(3), 99–103.

Keane, T. M., Marshall, A. D., & Taft, C. T. (2006). Posttraumatic stress disorder: Etiology, epidemiology, and treatment outcome. *Annual Review of Clinical Psychology, 2*, 161–197.

Keating, D. P. (2004). Cognitive and brain development. In R. M. Lerner & L. Steinberg (Eds.), *Handbook of adolescent psychology*. New York, NY: Wiley.

Keefauver, S. P., & Guilleminault, C. (1994). Sleep terrors and sleepwalking. In M. H. Kryger, T. Roth, & W. C. Dement (Eds.), *Principles and practice of sleep medicine* (2nd ed.). Philadelphia, PA: Saunders.

Kefalov, V. J. (2010). Visual receptors and transduction. In E. B. Goldstein (Ed.), *Encyclopedia of perception*. Thousand Oaks, CA: Sage.

Kehoe, E. J., & Macrae, M. (1998). Classical conditioning. In W. O'Donohue (Ed.), *Learning and behavior therapy*. Boston, Allyn & Bacon.

Keller, P. A., & Block, L. G. (1999). The effect of affect-based dissonance versus cognition-based dissonance on motivated reasoning and health-related persuasion. *Journal of Experimental Psychology: Applied, 5*, 302–313.

Kellert, S. R. (1993). The biological basis for human values of nature. In S. R. Kellert & E. O. Wilson (Eds.), *The biophilia hypothesis*. Washington, DC: Island Press.

Kelley, H. H. (1950). The warm-cold variable in first impressions of persons. *Journal of Personality, 18*, 431–439.

Kelley, H. H. (1967). Attributional theory in social psychology. *Nebraska Symposium on Motivation, 15*, 192–241.

Kellogg, S. H., & Young, J. E. (2008). Cognitive Therapy. In J. L. Lebow (Ed.), *Twenty-first century psychotherapies: Contemporary approaches to theory and practice*. New York, NY: Wiley.

Kelly, B. D., Feeney, L., O'Callaghan, E., Browne, R., Byrne, M., Mulryan, N., Scully, A., Morris, M., Kinsella, A., Takei, N., McNeil, T., Walsh, D., & Larkin, C. (2004). Obstetric adversity and age at first presentation with schizophrenia: Evidence of a dose-response relationship. *American Journal of Psychiatry, 161*, 920–922.

Kelman, H. C. (1967). Human use of human subjects: The problem of deception in social psychological experiments. *Psychological Bulletin, 67*, 1–11.

Kelman, H. C. (1982). Ethical issues in different social science methods. In T. L. Beauchamp, R. R. Faden, R. J. Wallace, Jr., & L. Walters (Eds.), *Ethical issues in social science research*. Baltimore, MD: Johns Hopkins University Press.

Kelsoe, J. R. (2009). Mood disorders: Genetics. In B. J. Sadock, V. A. Sadock, & P. Ruiz (Eds.), *Kaplan & Sadock's comprehensive textbook of psychiatry* (9th ed., pp. 1653–1663). Philadelphia, PA: Lippincott Williams & Wilkins.

Kendler, K. S., Myers, J., & Prescott, C. A. (2005). Sex differences in the relationship between social support and risk for major depression: A longitudinal study of opposite-sex twin pairs. *American Journal of Psychiatry, 162*, 250–256.

Kenfield, S. A., Stampfer, M. J., Rosner, B. A., & Colditz, G. A. (2008). Smoking and smoking cessation in relation to mortality in women. *Journal of the American Medical Association, 299*, 2037–2047.

Kennedy, T. E., Hawkins, R. D., & Kandel, E. R. (1992). Molecular interrelationships between short- and long-term memory. In L. R. Squire & N. Butters (Eds.), *Neuropsychology of Memory* (2nd ed.). New York, NY: Wiley.

Kenrick, D. T., & Gutierres, S. E. (1980). Contrast effects and judgments of physical attractiveness: When beauty becomes a social problem. *Journal of Personality and Social Psychology, 38*, 131–140.

Kenrick, D. T., Griskevicius, V., Neuberg, S. L., & Schaller, M. (2010). Renovating the pyramid of needs: Contemporary extensions built upon ancient foundations. *Perspectives on Psychological Science, 5*(3), 292–314. doi:10.1177/1745691610369469

Kenrick, D. T., Trost, M. R., & Sundie, J. M. (2004). Sex roles as adaptations: An evolutionary perspective on gender differences and similarities. In A. H. Eagly, A. E. Beall, & R. J. Sternberg (Eds.), *The psychology of gender*. New York, NY: Guilford.

Kermer, D. A., Driver-Linn, E., Wilson, T. D., & Gilbert, D. T. (2006). Loss aversion is an affective forecasting error. *Psychological Science, 17*, 649–653.

Kern, M. L., & Friedman, H. S. (2008). Do conscientious individuals live longer? A quantitative review. *Health Psychology, 27*(5), 505–512. doi:10.1037/0278-6133.27.5.505

Kerns, K. A., Abraham, M. M., Schlegelmilch, A., & Morgan, T. A. (2007). Mother-child attachment in later middle-childhood: Assessment approaches and associations with mood and emotion. *Attachment & Human Development, 9*(1), 33–53.

Kesebir, S., Graham, J., & Oishi, S. (2010). A theory of human needs should be human-centered, not animal-centered: Commentary on Kenrick et al. (2010). *Perspectives on Psychological Science, 5*(3), 315–319. doi:10.1177/1745691610369470

Kessen, W. (1996). American psychology just before Piaget. *Psychological Science, 7*, 196–199.

Kessler, R. C., Berglund, P., Demler, O., Jin, R., Koretz, D., Merikangas, K. R., Rush, A. J., Walters, E. E., & Wang, P. S. (2003). The epidemiology of major depressive disorder: Results from the national comorbidity survey replication (NCS-R). *Journal of the American Medical Association, 189*, 3095–3105.

Kiecolt-Glaser, J. K., Garner, W., Speicher, C., Penn, G. M., Holliday, J., & Glaser, R. (1984). Psychosocial modifiers of immunocompetence in medical students. *Psychosomatic Medicine, 46*(1), 7–14.

Kiecolt-Glaser, J. K., & Glaser, R. (1995). Measurement of immune response. In S. Cohen, R. C. Kessler, & L. U. Gordon (Eds.), *Measuring stress: A guide for health and social scientists*. New York, NY: Oxford University Press.

Kieseppa, T., Partonen, T., Huakka, J., Kaprio, J., & Lonnqvist, J. (2004). High concordance of bipolar 1 disorder in a nationwide sample of twins. *American Journal of Psychiatry, 161*, 1814–1821.

Kiesler, D. J. (1999). *Beyond the disease model of mental disorders*. New York, NY: Praeger Publishers.

Kihlstrom, J. F. (2001). Dissociative disorders. In P. B. Sutker & H. E. Adams (Eds.), *Comprehensive handbook of psychopathology* (3rd ed., pp. 259–276). New York, NY: Kluwer Academic/Plenum Publishers.

Kihlstrom, J. F. (2004). An unbalanced balancing act: Blocked, recovered, and false memories in the laboratory and clinic. *Clinical Psychology: Science & Practice, 11*(1), 34–41.

Kihlstrom, J. F., & Cork, R. C. (2007). Consciousness and anesthesia. In M. Velmans & S. Schneider (Eds.), *The Blackwell companion to consciousness*. Malden, MA: Blackwell Publishing.

Killeen, P. R. (1981). Learning as causal inference. In M. L. Commons & J. A. Nevin (Eds.), *Quantitative analyses of behavior, Vol. 1: Discriminative properties of reinforcement schedules*. Cambridge, MA: Ballinger.

Killen, M., Richardson, C. B., & Kelly, M. C. (2010). Developmental perspectives. In J. F. Dovidio, M. Hewstone, P. Glick, & V. M. Esses (Eds.), *The Sage handbook of prejudice, stereotyping, and discrimination*. Los Angeles, CA: Sage.

Kim, H., & Markus, H. R. (1999). Deviance or uniqueness, harmony or conformity? A cultural analysis. *Journal of Personality and Social Psychology, 77*, 785–800.

Kim, H. S., Sherman, D. K., Ko, D., & Taylor, S. E. (2006). Pursuit of comfort and pursuit of harmony: Culture, relationships, and social support seeking. *Personality and Social Psychology Bulletin, 32*(12), 1595–1607. doi:10.1177/0146167206291991

Kim, H. S., Sherman, D. K., & Taylor, S. E. (2008). Culture and social support. *American Psychologist, 63*(6), 518–526. doi:10.1037/0003-066X

Kim, K. H. (2005). Can only intelligent people be creative? *Journal of Secondary Gifted Education, 16*, 57–66.

Kim, S., Plumb, R., Gredig, Q., Rankin, L., & Taylor, B. (2008). Medium-term post-Katrina health sequelae among New Orleans residents: Predictors of poor mental and physical health. *Journal of Clinical Nursing, 17*(17), 2335–2342

Kimmel, A. J. (1996). *Ethical issues in behavioral research: A survey*. Cambridge, MA: Blackwell.

Kimura, D. (1973). The asymmetry of the human brain. *Scientific American, 228*, 70–78.

King, A. C., Oman, R. F., Brassington, G. S., Bliwise, D. L., & Haskell, W. L. (1997). Moderate-intensity exercise and self-rated quality of sleep in older adults: A randomized controlled trial. *Journal of the American Medical Association, 277*, 32–37.

King, B. M. (2006). The rise, fall, and resurrection of the ventromedial hypothalamus in the regulation of feeding behavior and body weight. *Physiology & Behavior, 87*, 221–244.

King, G. R., & Ellinwood Jr., E. H. (2005). Amphetamines and other stimulants. In J. H. Lowinson, P. Ruiz, R. B. Millman, & J. G. Langrod (Eds.), *Substance abuse: A comprehensive textbook*. Philadelphia, PA: Lippincott Williams & Wilkins.

King, S., St-Hilaire, A., & Heidkamp, D. (2010). Prenatal factors in schizophrenia. *Current Directions in Psychological Science, 19*(4), 209–213. doi:10.1177/0963721410378360

Kinnunen, T., Haukkala, A., Korhonen, T., Quiles, Z. N., Spiro, A. I., & Garvey, A. J. (2006). Depression and smoking across 25 years of the normative aging study. *International Journal of Psychiatry in Medicine, 36*, 413–426.

Kinsbourne, M. (1997). What qualifies a representation for a role in consciousness? In J. D. Cohen & J. W. Schooler (Eds.), *Scientific approaches to consciousness*. Mahwah, NJ: Erlbaum.

Kinsey, A. C., Pomeroy, W. B., & Martin, C. E. (1948). *Sexual behavior in the human male*. Philadelphia, PA: Saunders.

Kinsey, A. C., Pomeroy, W. B., Martin, C. E., & Gebhard, P. H. (1953). *Sexual behavior in the human female*. Philadelphia, PA: Saunders.

Kirby, D. (2005). *Evidence of harm: Mercury in vaccines and the autism epidemic: A medical controversy*. New York, NY: St. Martin's Press.

Kirov, G., & Owen, M. J. (2009). Genetics of schizophrenia. In B. J. Sadock, V. A. Sadock, & P. Ruiz (Eds.), *Kaplan & Sadock's comprehensive textbook of psychiatry* (9th ed., Vol. 1, pp. 1462–1472). Philadelphia, PA: Lippincott Williams & Wilkins.

Kirsch, I. (1997). Response expectancy theory and application: A decennial review. *Applied and Preventive Psychology, 6*, 69–79.

Kirsch, I. (2000). The response set theory of hypnosis. *American Journal of Clinical Hypnosis, 42*, 274–292.

Kirsch, I. (2010). *The emperor's new drugs: Exploding the antidepressant myth*. New York, NY: Basic Books.

Kirsch, I., Mazzoni, G., & Montgomery, G. H. (2007). Remembrance of hypnosis past. *American Journal of Clinical Hypnosis, 49*, 171–178.

Kitzes, J., Wackernagel, M., Loh, J., Peller, A., Goldfinger, S., Cheng, D., & Tea, K. (2008). Shrink and share: Humanity's present and future Ecological Footprint. *Philosophical Transactions of the Royal Society of London*, Series B, Biological Sciences, 363, 467–475.

Klein, D. N. (2010). Chronic depression: Diagnosis and classification. *Current Directions in Psychological Science, 19*(2), 96–100. doi:10.1177/0963721410366007

Klein, P. D. (1997). Multiplying the problems of intelligence by eight: A critique of Gardner's theory. *Canadian Journal of Education, 22*, 377–394.

Klein, T. W., Friedman, H., & Specter, S. (1998). Marijuana, immunity and infection. *Journal of Neuroimmunology, 83*, 102–115.

Kleinke, C. L. (2007). What does it mean to cope? In A. Monat, R. S. Lazarus, & G. Reevy (Eds.), *The Praeger handbook on stress and coping*. Westport, CT: Praeger.

Kleinke, C. L., Peterson, T. R., & Rutledge, T. R. (1998). Effects of self-generated facial expressions on mood. *Journal of Personality and Social Psychology, 74*, 272–279.

Kleinmuntz, B. (1980). *Essentials of abnormal psychology*. San Francisco, CA: Harper & Row.

Kleinmuntz, B., & Szucko, J. J. (1984). Lie detection in ancient and modern times: A call for contemporary scientific study. *American Psychologist, 39*(7), 766–776. doi:10.1037/0003-066X.39.7.766

Kleinspehn-Ammerlahn, A., Kotter-Grühn, D., & Smith, J. (2008). Self-perceptions of aging: Do subjective age and satisfaction with aging change during old age?. *The Journals of Gerontology: Series B: Psychological Sciences and Social Sciences, 63B*(6), 377–385.

Klerman, E. B., & Dijk, D. J. (2008). Age-related reduction in the maximal capacity for sleep-implications for insomnia. *Current Biology, 18*, 1118–1123.

Klerman, E. B., Davis, J. B., Duffy, J. F., Dijk, D., & Kronauer, R. E. (2004). Older people awaken more frequently but fall back asleep at the same rate as younger people. *Sleep: Journal of Sleep & Sleep Disorders Research, 27*, 793–798.

Kliegel, M., Zimprich, D., & Rott, C. (2004). Life-long intellectual activities mediate the predictive effect of early education on cognitive impairment in centenarians: A retrospective study. *Aging & Mental Health, 8*, 430–437.

Kline, P. (1991). *Intelligence: The psychometric view*. New York, NY: Routledge, Chapman, & Hall.

Kline, P. (1995). A critical review of the measurement of personality and intelligence. In D. H. Saklofske & M. Zeidner (Eds.), *International handbook of personality and intelligence*. New York, NY: Plenum.

Klosch, G., & Kraft, U. (2005). Sweet dreams are made of this. *Scientific American Mind, 16*(2), 38–45.

Kluft, R. P. (1996). Dissociative identity disorder. In L. K. Michelson & W. J. Ray (Eds.), *Handbook of dissociation: Theoretical, empirical, and clinical perspectives*. New York, NY: Plenum.

Klump, K. L., & Culbert, K. M. (2007). Molecular genetic studies of eating disorders: Current status and future directions. *Current Directions in Psychological Science, 16*, 37–41.

Knapp, C. M., & Kornetsky, C. (2009). Neural basis of pleasure and reward. In G. G. Berntson & J. T. Cacioppo (Eds.), *Handbook of neuroscience for the behavioral sciences* (Vol. 1, pp. 781–806). New York, NY: Wiley.

Knauss, W. (2005). Group psychotherapy. In G. O. Gabbard, J. S. Beck, & J. Holmes (Eds.), *Oxford textbook of psychotherapy*. New York, NY: Oxford University Press.

Knecht, S., Drager, B., Floel, A., Lohmann, H., Breitenstein, C., Henningsen, H., & Ringelstein, E. B. (2001). Behavioural relevance of atypical language lateralization in healthy subjects. *Brain, 124*, 1657–1665.

Knecht, S., Fioel, A., Drager, B., Breitenstein, C., Sommer, J., Henningsen, H., Ringelstein, E. B., & Pascual-Leone, A. (2002). Degree of language lateralization determines susceptibility to unilateral brain lesions. *Nature Neuroscience, 5*, 695–699.

Knight, J. (2004). The truth about lying. *Nature, 428*, 692–694.

Knutson, K. L., & Van Cauter, E. (2008). Associations between sleep loss and increased risk of obesity and diabetes. In D. W. Pfaff, & B. L. Kieffer (Eds.), *Annals of the New York Academy of Sciences. Molecular and biophysical mechanisms of arousal, alertness, and attention* (pp. 287–304). Malden, MA: Blackwell Publishing.

Kobrin, J. L., Patterson, B. F., Shaw, E. J., Mattern, K. D., & Barbuti, S. M. (2008). *Validity of the SAT for predicting first-year college grade point average* (College Board research report no. 2008-5). New York, NY: College Board.

Kodama, S., Saito, K., Tanaka, S., Maki, M., Yachi, Y., Asumi, M., et al. (2009). Cardiorespiratory fitness as a quantitative predictor of all-cause mortality and cardiovascular events in healthy men and women: a meta-analysis. *Journal of the American Medical Association, 301*(19), 2024–2035.

Koger, S. M. & Winter, D. D. (2010). *The Psychology of environmental problems: Psychology for Sustainability* (3rd ed.). New York, NY: Psychology Press.

Koger, S. M., Schettler, T. & Weiss, B. (2005). Environmental toxicants and developmental disabilities: A challenge for psychologists. *American Psychologist, 60*, 243–255.

Kohlberg, L. (1963). The development of children's orientations toward a moral order: I. Sequence in the development of moral thought. *Vita Humana, 6*, 11–33.

Kohlberg, L. (1969). Stage and sequence: The cognitive-developmental approach to socialization. In D. A. Goslin (Ed.), *Handbook of socialization theory and research*. Chicago: Rand McNally.

Kohlberg, L. (1976). Moral stages and moralization: Cognitive-developmental approach. In T. Lickona (Ed.), *Moral development and behavior: Theory, research and social issues*. New York, NY: Holt, Rinehart & Winston.

Kohlberg, L. (1984). *Essays on moral development, Vol. 2: The psychology of moral development*. San Francisco, CA: Harper & Row.

Kokkinos, P., Myers, J., Kokkinos, J. P., Pittaras, A., Narayan, P., Manolis, A., et al. (2007). Exercise capacity and mortality in black and white men. *Circulation, 117*, 614–622.

Koksal, F., Domjan, M., Kurt, A., Sertel, O., Orung, S., Bowers, R., & Kumru, G. (2004). An animal model of fetishism. *Behaviour Research and Therapy, 42*(12), 1421–1434. doi:10.1016/j.brat.2003.10.001

Kollmuss, A. & Agyeman, J. (2002). Mind the gap: Why do people act environmentally and what are the barriers to pro-environmental behaviour? *Environmental Education Research, 8*, 239–260.

Koob, G. F., & Le Moal, M. (2006). *Neurobiology of addiction*. San Diego, CA: Academic Press.

Koob, G. F., Everitt, B. J., & Robbins, T. W. (2008). Reward, motivation, and addiction. In L. Squire, D. Berg, F. Bloom, S. Du Lac, A. Ghosh, N. Spitzer (Eds.), *Fundamental neuroscience* (3rd ed., pp. 87–111). San Diego, CA: Elsevier.

Koordeman, R., Anschutz, D. J., van Baaren, R. B., & Engels, R. E. (2010). Exposure to soda commercials affects sugar-sweetened soda consumption in young women. An observational experimental study. *Appetite, 54,* 619–622. doi:10.1016/j.appet.2010.03.008

Kop, W. J., Gottdiener, J. S., & Krantz, D. S. (2001). Stress and silent ischemia. In A. Baum, T. A. Revenson, & J. E. Singer (Eds.), *Handbook of health psychology* (pp. 669–682). Mahwah, NJ: Erlbaum.

Kop, W. J., Weissman, N. J., Zhu, J., Bonsall, R. W., Doyle, M., Stretch, M. R., Glaes, S. B., Krantz, D. S., Gottdiener, J. S., & Tracy, R. P. (2008). Effect of acute mental stress and exercise on inflammatory markers in patients with coronary artery disease and healthy controls. *American Journal of Cardiology, 101,* 767–773.

Koriat, A., & Bjork, R. A. (2005). Illusions of competence in monitoring one's knowledge during study. *Journal of Experimental Psychology: Learning, Memory, and Cognition, 31*(2), 187–194.

Koriat, A., Goldsmith, M., & Pansky, A. (2000). Toward a psychology of memory accuracy. *Annual Review of Psychology, 51,* 481–537.

Koriat, A., Lichtenstein, S., & Fischhoff, B. (1980). Reasons for confidence. *Journal of Experimental Psychology, 6,* 107–118.

Korn, J. H. (1997). *Illusions of reality: A history of deception in social psychology.* Albany: State University of New York Press.

Kornell, N., Castel, A. D., Eich, T. S., & Bjork, R. A. (2010). Spacing as the friend of both memory and induction in young and older adults. *Psychology and Aging, 25*(2), 498–503. doi:10.1037/a0017807

Kornell, N., Hays, M., & Bjork, R. A. (2009). Unsuccessful retrieval attempts enhance subsequent learning. *Journal of Experimental Psychology: Learning, Memory, and Cognition, 35*(4), 989–998. doi:10.1037/a0015729

Kornhaber, M. L. (2004). Multiple intelligences: From the ivory tower to the dusty classroom—But why? *Teachers College Record, 106*(1), 57–76.

Kosfeld, M., Heinrichs, M., Zak, P. J., Fischbacher, U., & Fehr, E. (2005). Oxytocin increases trust in humans. *Nature, 435*(7042), 673–676. doi:10.1038/nature03701

Kotovsky, K., Hayes, J. R., & Simon, H. A. (1985). Why are some problems hard? Evidence from Tower of Hanoi. *Cognitive Psychology, 17,* 248–294.

Kotter-Grühn, D., Kleinspehn-Ammerlahn, A., Gerstorf, D., & Smith, J. (2009). Self-perceptions of aging predict mortality and change with approaching death: 16-year longitudinal results from the Berlin Aging Study. *Psychology and Aging, 24*(3), 654–667. doi:10.1037/a0016510

Kotulak, R. (1996). *Inside the brain: Revolutionary discoveries of how the mind works.* Kansas City: Andrews McMeel.

Kouzma, N. M., & Kennedy, G. A. (2004). Self-reported sources of stress in senior high school students. *Psychological Reports, 94,* 314–316.

Kowalski, P., & Taylor, A. K. (2009). The effect of refuting misconceptions in the introductory psychology class. *Teaching of Psychology, 36*(3), 153-159. doi:10.1080/00986280902959986

Kozorovitskiy, Y., & Gould, E. (2007). Adult neurogenesis and regeneration in the brain. In Y. Sern (Ed.), *Cognitive reserve: Theory and applications.* Philadelphia, PA: Taylor and Francis.

Kracke, W. (1991). Myths in dreams, thought in images: An Amazonian contribution to the psychoanalytic theory of primary process. In B. Tedlock (Ed.), *Dreaming: Anthropological and psychological interpretations.* Santa Fe, NM: School of American Research Press.

Kraemer, H. C. (2008). DSM categories and dimensions in clinical and research contexts. In J. E. Helzer, H. C. Kraemer, R. F. Krueger, H.-U. Wittchen, P. J. Sirovatka, et al. (Eds.), *Dimensional approaches in diagnostic classification: Refining the research agenda for DSM-V* (pp. 5–17). Washington, DC: American Psychiatric Association.

Krakauer, D., & Dallenbach, K. M. (1937). Gustatory adaptation to sweet, sour, and bitter. *American Journal of Psychology, 49,* 469–475.

Krakauer, J. (1998). *Into thin air: A personal account of the Mount Everest disaster.* New York, NY: Villard.

Kramer, P. D. (2006). *Freud: Inventor of the modern mind.* New York, NY: HarperCollins.

Krebs, D. L., & Denton, K. (1997). Social illusions and self-deception: The evolution of biases in person perception. In J. A. Simpson & D. T. Kenrick (Eds.), *Evolutionary social psychology.* Mahwah, NJ: Erlbaum.

Kremen, W. S., Jacobsen, K. C., Xian, H., Eisen, S. A., Eaves, L. J., Tsuang, M. T., & Lyons, M. J. (2007). Genetics of verbal working memory processes: A twin study of middle-aged men. *Neuropsychology, 21*(5), 569–580. doi:10.1037/0894-4105.21.5.569

Kriegsfeld, L. J., & Nelson, R. J. (2009). Biological rhythms. In G. G. Berntson & J. T. Cacioppo (Eds.), *Handbook of neuroscience for the behavioral sciences* (Vol. 1, pp. 56–81). New York, NY: Wiley.

Krieth, M. (1991). Water inputs in California food production. University of California Agricultural Issues Center. Retrieved June 4, 2009 from http://www.sakia.org/cms/fileadmin/content/irrig/general/kreith_1991_water_inputs_in_ca_food_production–excerpt.pdf

Kristeller, J. L., Baer, R. A., & Quillian-Wolever, R. (2006). Mindfulness-based approaches to eating disorders. In R. A. Baer (Ed.), *Mindfulness-based treatment approaches: Clinician's guide to evidence base and applications* (pp. 75–91). San Diego, CA: Elsevier.

Kroger, J. (2003). Identity development during adolescence. In G. R. Adams & M. D. Berzonsky (Eds.), *Blackwell handbook of adolescence.* Malden, MA: Blackwell Publishing.

Krojgaard, P. (2005). Continuity and discontinuity in developmental psychology. *Psyke & Logos, 26*(2), 377–394.

Krosnick, J. A. (1999). Survey research. *Annual Review Psychology, 50,* 537–567.

Krosnick, J. A., & Fabrigar, L. R. (1998). *Designing good questionnaires: Insights from psychology.* New York, NY: Oxford University Press.

Krueger, J., Ham, J. J., & Linford, K. M. (1996). Perceptions of behavioral consistency: Are people aware of the actor-observer effect? *Psychological Science, 7,* 259–264.

Krueger, K. R., Wilson, R. S., Kamenetsky, J. M., Barnes, L. L., Bienias, J. L., & Bennett, D. A. (2009). Social engagement and cognitive function in old age. *Experimental Aging Research, 35*(1), 45–60. doi:10.1080/03610730802545028

Krueger, R. F., & Johnson, W. (2008). Behavioral genetics and personality: A new look at the integration of nature and nurture. In O. P. John, R. W. Robbins, & L. A. Pervin (Eds.), *Handbook of personality: Theory and research* (Vol. 3, pp. 287–310). New York, NY: Guilford.

Kruglanski, A. W., & Stroebe, W. (2005). The influence of beliefs and goals on attitudes: Issues of structure, function, and dynamics. In D. Albarracin, B. T. Johnson, & M. P. Zanna (Eds.), *The handbook of attitudes.* Mahwah, NJ: Erlbaum.

Krull, D. S. (2001). On partitioning the fundamental attribution error: Dispositionalism and the correspondence bias. In G. B. Moskowitz (Ed.), *Cognitive social psychology: The Princeton Symposium on the legacy and future of social cognition.* Mahwah, NJ: Erlbaum.

Krull, D. S., & Erickson, D. J. (1995). Inferential hopscotch: How people draw social inferences from behavior. *Current Directions in Psychological Science, 4,* 35–38.

Kryger, M. H. (1993). Snoring. In M. A. Carskadon (Ed.), *Encyclopedia of sleep and dreaming.* New York, NY: Macmillan.

Kryger, M. H., Roth, T., & Dement, W. C. (2005). *Principles and practice of sleep medicine.* Philadelphia, PA: Elsevier Saunders.

Kudielka, B. M., & Kirschbaum, C. (2005). Sex differences in HPA axis responses to stress: A review. *Biological Pschology, 69,* 113–132.

Kuepper, R., Morrison, P. D., van Os, J., Murray, R. M., Kenis, G., & Henquet, C. (2010). Does dopamine mediate the psychosis-inducing effects of cannabis? A review and integration of findings across disciplines. *Schizophrenia Research, 121*(1–3), 107–117. doi:10.1016/j.schres.2010.05.031

Kuepper, R., van Os, J., Lieb, R., Wittchen, H., Höfler, M., & Henquet, C. (2011). Continued cannabis use and risk of incidence and persistence of psychotic symptoms: 10 year follow-up cohort study. *BMJ: British Medical Journal, 342*(7796). Retrieved from http://www.bmj.com/content/342/bmj.d738.full

Kuhn, D. (2006). Do cognitive changes accompany developments in the adolescent brain? *Perspectives on Psychological Science, 1*(1), 59–67.

Kulick, A. R., Pope, H. G., & Keck, P. E. (1990). Lycanthropy and self-identification. *Journal of Nervous & Mental Disease, 178*(2), 134–137.

Kung, S., & Mrazek, D. A. (2005). Psychiatric emergency department visits on full-moon nights. *Psychiatric Services, 56,* 221–222.

Kunstler, J. H. (2005). *The long emergency: Surviving the end of oil, climate change, and other converging catastrophes of the twenty-first century.* New York, NY: Grove Press.

Kuo, F. E., & Sullivan, W. C. (2001). Aggression and violence in the inner city: Effects of environment via mental fatigue. *Environment and Behavior, 33*(4), 543–571.

Kuo, Y. T., Parkinson, J. R. C., Chaudhri, O. B., Herlihy, A. H., So, P. W., Dhillo, W. S., et al. (2007). The temporal sequence of gut peptide-CNS interactions tracked in vivo by magnetic resonance imaging. *Journal of Neuroscience, 27,* 12341–12348.

Kurtz, K. J., & Loewenstein, J. (2007). Converging on a new role for analogy in problem solving and retrieval: When two problems are better than one. *Memory & Cognition, 35,* 334–342.

Kurtz, M. M., & Mueser, K. T. (2008). A meta-analysis of controlled research on social skills training for schizophrenia. *Journal of Consulting and Clinical Psychology, 76*(3), 491–504. doi:10.1037/0022-006X.76.3.491

Kutchins, H., & Kirk, S. A. (1997). *Making us crazy: DSM—The psychiatric Bible and the creation of mental disorders.* New York, NY: Free Press.

Kyle, S. D., Morgan, K., & Espie, C. A. (2010). Insomnia and health-related quality of life. *Sleep Medicine Reviews, 14*(1), 69–82. doi:10.1016/j.smrv.2009.07.004

LaBine, S. J., & LaBine, G. (1996). Determinations of negligence and the hindsight bias. *Law & Human Behavior, 20,* 501–516.

Labouvie-Vief, G. (2006). Emerging structures of adult thought. In J. J. Arnett & J. L. Tanner (Eds.), *Emerging adults in America: Coming of age in the 21st century.* Washington, DC: American Psychological Association.

Lachman, S. J. (1996). Processes in perception: Psychological transformations of highly structured stimulus material. *Perceptual and Motor Skills, 83,* 411–418.

Lachter, J., Forster, K. I., & Ruthruff, E. (2004). Forty-five years after Broadbent (1958): Still no identification without attention. *Psychological Review, 111,* 880–913.

Lader, M. H. (2002). Managing dependence and withdrawal with newer hypnotic medications in the treatment of insomnia. *Journal of Clinical Psychiatry, 4*(suppl 1), 33–37.

Lagopoulos, J., Xu, J., Rasmussen, I., Vik, A., Malhi, G., Eliassen, C. F., et al. (2009). Increased theta and alpha EEG activity during nondirective meditation. *The Journal of Alternative and Complementary Medicine, 15*(11), 1187–1192.

Lahey, B. B. (2009). Public health significance of neuroticism. *American Psychologist, 64*(4), 241–256. doi:10.1037/a0015309

Lakein, A. (1996). *How to get control of your time and your life.* New York, NY: New American Library.

Lakey, B., & Cronin, A. (2008). Low social support and major depression: Research, theory and methodological issues. In K. S. Dobson & D. A. Dozois (Eds.), *Risk factors in depression* (pp. 385–408). San Diego, CA: Academic Press. doi:10.1016/B978-0-08-045078-0.00017-4

Lamb, H. R. (1998). Deinstitutionalization at the beginning of the new millenium. *Harvard Review of Psychiatry, 6,* 1–10.

Lamb, M. E., & Lewis, C. (2011). The role of parent-child relationships in child development. In M. H. Bornstein & M. E. Lamb (Eds.), *Developmental science: An advanced textbook* (pp. 469–518). New York, NY: Psychology Press.

Lamb, M. E., Ketterlinus, R. D., & Fracasso, M. P. (1992). Parent-child relationships. In M. H. Bornstein & M. E. Lamb (Eds.), *Developmental psychology: An advanced textbook* (3rd ed.). Hillsdale, NJ: Erlbaum.

Lambert, M. J. (2011). Psychotherapy research and its achievements. In J. C. Norcross, G. R. Vandenbos, & D. K. Freedheim (Eds.), *History of psychotherapy: Continuity and change* (2nd ed.). Washington, DC: American Psychological Association.

Lambert, M. J., & Archer, A. (2006). Research findings on the effects of psychotherapy and their implications for practice. In C. D. Goodheart, A. E. Kazdin, & R. J. Sternberg (Eds.), *Evidence-based psychotherapy: Where practice and research meet* (pp. 111–130). Washington, DC: American Psychological Association.

Lambert, M. J., Bergin, A. E., & Garfield, S. L. (2004). Introduction and historical overview. In M. J. Lambert (Ed.), *Bergin and Garfield's handbook of psychotherapy and behavior change.* New York, NY: Wiley.

Lambert, M. J., & Ogles, B. M. (2004). The efficacy and effectiveness of psychotherapy. In M. J. Lambert (Ed.), *Bergin and Garfield's handbook of psychotherapy and behavior change.* New York, NY: Wiley.

Lampert, R., Shusterman, V., Burg, M., McPherson, C., Batsford, W., Goldberg, A., & Soufer, R. (2009). Anger-induced T-wave alternans predicts future ventricular arrhythmias in patients with implantable cardioverter-defibrillators. *Journal of the American College of Cardiology, 53*(9), 774–778.

Lampinen, J. M., Neuschatz, J. S., & Payne, D. G. (1999). Source attributions and false memories: A test of the demand characteristics account. *Psychonomic Bulletin & Review, 6,* 130–135.

Landabaso, M. A., Iraurgi, I., Sanz, J., Calle, R., Ruiz de Apodaka, J., Jimenez-Lerma, J. M., & Gutierrez-Fraile, M. (1999). Naltrexone in the treatment of alcoholism. Two-year follow up results. *European Journal of Psychiatry, 13,* 97–105.

Landel-Graham, J., Yount, S. E., & Rudnicki, S. R. (2003). Diabetes mellitus. In A. M. Nezu, C. M. Nezu, & P. A. Geller (Eds.). *Handbook of psychology, Vol. 9: Health psychology.* New York, NY: Wiley.

Lange, C. (1885). One leuds beveegelser. In K. Dunlap (Ed.), *The emotions.* Baltimore, MD: Williams & Wilkins.

Langlois, J. H., Kalakanis, L., Rubenstein, A. J., Larson, A., Hallam, M., & Smoot, M. (2000). Maxims or myths of beauty? A meta-analytic and theoretical review. *Psychological Bulletin, 126,* 390–423.

Lanyon, R. I., & Goodstein, L. D. (1997). *Personality assessment.* New York, NY: Wiley.

Lapierre, Y. D. (2003). Suicidality with selective serotonin reuptake inhibitors: Valid claim? *Journal of Psychiatry & Neuroscience, 28,* 340–347.

Larsen, D. P., Butler, A. C., & Roediger, H. L., III. (2009). Repeated testing improves long-term retention relative to repeated study: A randomised controlled trial. *Medical Education, 43*(12), 1174–1181. doi:10.1111/j.1365-2923.2009.03518.x

Larsen, J. T., Berntson, G. G., Poehlmann, K. M., Ito, T. A., & Cacioppo, J. T. (2008). The psychophysiology of emotion. In M. Lewis, J. M. Haviland-Jones, & L. F. Barrett (Eds.), *Handbook of emotions* (3rd ed., pp. 180–195). New York, NY: Guilford.

Laska, M., Seibt, A., & Weber, A. (2000). "Microsmatic" primates revisited: Olfactory sensitivity in the squirrel monkey. *Chemical Senses, 25,* 47–53. doi:10.1093/chemse/25.1.47

Latané, B. (1981). The psychology of social impact. *American Psychologist, 36,* 343–356.

Latané, B., & Nida, S. A. (1981). Ten years of research on group size and helping. *Psychological Bulletin, 89,* 308–324.

Latané, B., Williams, K., & Harkins, S. (1979). Many hands make light the work: The causes and consequences of social loafing. *Journal of Personality and Social Psychology, 37,* 822–832.

Laughlin, H. (1967). *The neuroses.* Washington, DC: Butterworth.

Laughlin, H. (1979). *The ego and its defenses.* New York, NY: Aronson.

Laumann, E. O., Gagnon, J. H., Michael, R. T., & Michaels, S. (1994). *The social organization of sexuality: Sexual practices in the United States.* Chicago: University of Chicago Press.

Lauriello, J., Bustillo, J. R., & Keith, J. (2005). Schizophrenia: Scope of the problem. In B. J. Sadock & V. A. Sadock (Eds.), *Kaplan & Sadock's comprehensive textbook of psychiatry.* Philadelphia, PA: Lippincott Williams & Wilkins.

Laursen, B., Coy, K. C., & Collins, W. A. (1998). Reconsidering changes in parent-child conflict across adolescence: A meta-analysis. *Child Development, 69,* 817–832.

Lazarus, A. A. (1995). Different types of eclecticism and integration: Let's be aware of the dangers. *Journal of Psychotherapy Integration, 5,* 27–39.

Lazarus, A. A. (2008). Technical eclecticism and multimodal therapy. In J. L. Lebow (Ed.), *Twenty-first century psychotherapies: Contemporary approaches to theory and practice.* New York, NY: Wiley.

Lazarus, R. S. (1993). Why we should think of stress as a subset of emotion. In L. Goldberger & S. Breznitz (Eds.), *Handbook of stress: Theoretical and clinical aspects* (2nd ed.). New York, NY: Free Press.

Lazarus, R. S., & Folkman, S. (1984). *Stress, appraisal, and coping.* New York, NY: Springer.

Leavitt, F. (1995). *Drugs and behavior* (3rd ed.). Thousand Oaks, CA: Sage.

LeBoeuf, R. A., & Shafir, E. B. (2005). Decision making. In K. J. Holyoak & R. G. Morrison (Eds.), *The Cambridge handbook of thinking and reasoning.* New York, NY: Cambridge University Press.

Lebow, J. L. (2008). Couple and family therapy. In J. L Lebow (Ed.), *Twenty-first century psychotherapies: Contemporary approaches to theory and practice* (pp. 307–346). New York, NY: Wiley.

Ledbetter, A. M., Griffin, E., & Sparks, G. G. (2007). Forecasting "friends forever": A longitudinal investigation of sustained closeness between best friends. *Personal Relationships, 14*(2), 343–350. doi:10.1111/j.1475-6811.2007.00158.x

LeDoux, J. E. (1994). Emotion, memory and the brain. *Scientific American, 270,* 50–57.

LeDoux, J. E. (1995). Emotion: Clues from the brain. *Annual Review of Psychology, 46,* 209–235.

LeDoux, J. E. (1996). *The emotional brain.* New York, NY: Simon & Schuster.

LeDoux, J. E. (2000). Emotion circuits in the brain. *Annual Review of Neuroscience, 23,* 155–184.

LeDoux, J. E., & Phelps, E. A. (2008). Emotional networks in the brain. In M. Lewis, J. M. Haviland-Jones, & L. F. Barrett, *Handbook of emotions* (3rd ed.). New York, NY: Guilford.

LeDoux, J. E., Schiller, D., & Cain, C. (2009). Emotional reaction and action: From threat processing to goal-directed behavior. In M. S. Gazzangia (Ed.), *The cognitive neurosciences* (4th ed., pp. 905–924). Cambridge, MA: MIT Press.

Lee, K., & Ashton, M. C. (2008). The HEXACO personality factors in the indigenous personality lexicons of English and 11 other languages. *Journal of Personality, 76*(5), 1001–1053. doi:10.1111/j.1467-6494.2008.00512.x

Lee, L., Loewenstein, G., Ariely, D., Hong, J., & Young, J. (2008). If I'm not hot, are you hot or not? Physical-attractiveness evaluations and dating preferences as a function of one's own attractiveness. *Psychological Science, 19*(7), 669–677. doi:10.1111/j.1467-9280.2008.02141.x

Lee, I.-M., & Skerrett, P. J. (2001). Physical activity and all-cause mortality: What is the dose-response relation? *Medicine and Science in Sports and Exercise, 33,* S459–S471.

Lee, R. M., & Ramirez, M. (2000). The history, current status, and future of multicultural psychotherapy. In I. Cuellar & F. A. Paniagua (Eds.), *Handbook of multicultural mental health: Assessment and treatment of diverse populations.* San Diego, CA: Academic Press.

Lee, S., & Katzman, M. A. (2002). Cross-cultural perspectives on eating disorders. In C. G. Fairburn & K. D. Brownell (Eds.), *Eating disorders and obesity: A comprehensive handbook.* New York, NY: Guilford.

Lee-Chiong, T., & Sateia, M. (2006). Pharmacologic therapy of insomnia. In T. Lee-Chiong (Ed.), *Sleep: A comprehensive handbook.* Hoboken, NJ: Wiley-Liss.

Leeper, R. W. (1935). A study of a neglected portion of the field of learning: The development of sensory organization. *Journal of Genetic Psychology, 46,* 41–75.

Lefcourt, H. M. (2001). The humor solution. In C. R. Snyder (Ed.), *Coping with stress: Effective people and processes* (pp. 68–92). New York, NY: Oxford University Press.

Lefcourt, H. M. (2005). Humor. In C. R. Snyder & S. J. Lopez (Eds.), *Handbook of positive psychology.* New York, NY: Oxford University Press.

Lefcourt, H. M., Davidson, K., Shepherd, R., Phillips, M., Prkachin, K., & Mills, D. (1995). Perspective-taking humor: Accounting for stress moderation. *Journal of Social and Clinical Psychology, 14,* 373–391.

Leff, J. (2006). Whose life is it anyway? Quality of life for long-stay patients discharged from psychiatric hospitals. In H. Katschnig, H. Freeman, & N. Sartorius (Eds.), *Quality of life in mental disorders.* New York, NY: Wiley.

Leff, J., & Vaughn, C. (1985). *Expressed emotion in families.* New York, NY: Guilford.

Legault, E., & Laurence, J.-R. (2007). Recovered memories of childhood sexual abuse: Social worker, psychologist, and psychiatrist reports of beliefs, practices, and cases. *Australian Journal of Clinical & Experimental Hypnosis, 35,* 111–133.

Lehman, P. K. & Geller, E. S. (2004). Behavior analysis and environmental protection: Accomplishments and potential for more. *Behavior and Social Issues, 13,* 13–32.

Leichsenring, F. & Rabung, S. (2008). Effectiveness of long-term psychodynamic psychotherapy: A meta-analysis. *Journal of the American Medical Association, 13,* 1551–1565.

Leighton, J. P., & Sternberg, R. J. (2003). Reasoning and problem solving. In A. F. Healy & R. W. Proctor (Eds.), *Handbook of psychology, Vol. 4: Experimental psychology.* New York, NY: Wiley.

Lemay, E. P., Jr., Clark, M. S., & Greenberg, A. (2010). What is beautiful is good because what is beautiful is desired: Physical attractiveness stereotyping as projection of interpersonal goals. *Personality and Social Psychology Bulletin, 36*(3), 339-353. doi:10.1177/0146167209359700

Leon, D. A., Lawlor, D. A., Clark, H. H., Batty, G. D., & Macintyre, S. S. (2009). The association of childhood intelligence with mortality risk from adolescence to middle age: Findings from the Aberdeen Children of the 1950s cohort study. *Intelligence, 37*(6), 520–528. doi:10.1016/j.intell.2008.11.00

Lepine, R., Barrouillet, P., & Camos, V. (2005). What makes working memory spans so predictive of high-level cognition? *Psychonomic Bulletin & Review, 12*(1), 165–170.

Lerman, H. (1986). *A mote in Freud's eye: From psychoanalysis to the psychology of women.* New York, NY: Springer.

Lett, H. S., Blumenthal, J. A., Babyak, M. A., Sherwood, A., Strauman, T., Robbins, C., & Newman, M. F. (2004). Depression as a risk factor for coronary artery disease: Evidence, mechanisms, and treatment. *Psychosomatic Medicine, 66,* 305–315.

Leuner, B., & Gould, E. (2010). Structural plasticity and hippocampal function. *Annual Review of Psychology, 61,* 111–140. doi:10.1146/annurev.psych.093008.100359

Leuner, B., Gould, E., & Shors, T. J. (2006). Is there a link between adult neurogenesis and learning? *Hippocampus, 16,* 216–224.

LeVay, S. (1996). *Queer science: The use and abuse of research into homosexuality.* Cambridge, MA: MIT Press.

Levenson, R. W. (1992). Autonomic nervous system differences among emotions. *Psychological Science, 3,* 23–27.

Levenson, R. W. (2003). Autonomic specificity and emotion. In R. J. Davidson, K. R. Scherer, & H. H. Goldsmith (Eds.), *Handbook of affective sciences.* New York, NY: Oxford University Press.

Levine, M. P., & Harrison, K. (2004). Media's role in the perpetuation and prevention of negative body image and disordered eating. In J. K. Thompson (Ed.), *Handbook of eating disorders and obesity.* New York, NY: Wiley.

Levine, R., & Norenzayan, A. (1999). The pace of life in 31 countries. *Journal of Cross-Cultural Psychology, 30,* 178–205.

Levinthal, C. F. (2008). *Drugs, behavior, and modern society.* Boston, MA: Pearson.

Levis, D. J. (1989). The case for a return to a two-factor theory of avoidance: The failure of non-fear interpretations. In S. B. Klein & R. R. Bowrer (Eds.), *Contemporary learning theories: Pavlovian conditioning and the status of traditional learning theory.* Hillsdale, NJ: Erlbaum.

Levitt, J. B. (2010). Receptive fields. In E. B. Goldstein (Ed.), *Encyclopedia of perception.* Thousand Oaks, CA: Sage.

Levy, G. D., Taylor, M. G., & Gelman, S. A. (1995). Traditional and evaluative aspects of flexibility in gender roles, social conventions, moral rules, and physical laws. *Child Development, 66,* 515–531.

Levy, J., Trevarthen, C., & Sperry, R. W. (1972). Perception of bilateral chimeric figures following hemispheric disconnection. *Brain, 95,* 61–78.

Lewandowsky, S., Duncan, M., & Brown, G. D. A. (2004). Time does not cause forgetting in short-term serial recall. *Psychonomic Bulletin & Review, 11*(5), 771–790.

Lewin, K. (1935). *A dynamic theory of personality.* New York, NY: McGraw-Hill.

Lewis, S., Escalona, P. R., & Keith, S. J. (2009). Phenomenology of schizophrenia. In B. J. Sadock, V. A. Sadock, & P. Ruiz (Eds.), *Kaplan & Sadock's comprehensive textbook of psychiatry* (9th ed., pp. 1433–1450). Philadelphia, PA: Lippincott Williams & Wilkins.

Li, N. P., Bailey, J. M., Kenrick, D. T., & Linsenmeier, J. A. W. (2002). The necessities and luxuries of mate preferences: Testing the tradeoffs. *Journal of Personality and Social Psychology, 82,* 947–955.

Li, N. P., & Kenrick, D. T. (2006). Sex similarities and differences in preferences for short-term mates: What, whether, and why. *Journal of Personality and Social Psychology, 90,* 468–489.

Liberman, R. P., & Kopelowicz, A. (2005). Recovery from schizophrenia: A concept in search of research. *Psychiatric Services, 56,* 735–742.

Lichtenstein, S., Fischhoff, B., & Phillips, L. (1982). Calibration of probabilities: The state of the art to 1980. In D. Kahneman, P. Slovic, & A. Tversky (Eds.), *Judgment under uncertainty: Heuristics and biases.* Cambridge, England: Cambridge University Press.

Lickliter, R. (2009). The fallacy of partitioning: Epigenetics' validation of the organism-environment system. *Ecological Psychology, 21*(2), 138-146. doi:10.1080/10407410902877157

Liddle, P. F. (2009). Descriptive clinical features of schizophrenia. In M. C. Gelder, N. C. Andreasen, J. J. López-Ibor, Jr., & J. R. Geddes (Eds.). *New Oxford textbook of psychiatry* (2nd ed., Vol. 1). New York, NY: Oxford University Press.

Lieberman, D., & Hatfield, E. (2006). Passionate love: Cross-cultural and evolutionary perspectives. In R. J. Sternberg & K. Weis (Eds.), *The new psychology of love.* New Haven, CT: Yale University Press.

Liebert, R. M., & Liebert, L. L. (1998). *Liebert & Spiegler's personality strategies and issues.* Pacific Grove: Brooks/Cole.

Liefbroer, A. C., & Dourleijn, E. (2006). Unmarried cohabitation and union stability: Testing the role of diffusion using data from 16 European countries. *Demography, 43,* 203–221.

Lien, M.-C., Ruthruff, E., & Johnston, J. C. (2006). Attentional limitations in doing two tasks at once. *Current Directions in Psychological Science, 15,* 89–93.

Lilienfeld, S. O. (2007). Psychological treatments that cause harm. *Perspectives on Psychological Science, 2,* 53–70.

Lilienfeld, S. O., Ammirati, R., & Landfield, K. (2009). Giving debiasing away: Can psychological research on correcting cognitive errors promote human welfare? *Perspectives on Psychological Science, 4*(4), 390–398. doi:10.1111/j.1745-6924.2009.01144.x

Lilienfeld, S. O., & Lynn, S. J. (2003). Dissociative identity disorder: Multiple personalities, multiple controversies. In S. O. Lilienfeld, S. J. Lynn, & J. M. Lohr (Eds.), *Science and pseudoscience in clinical psychology.* New York, NY: Guilford.

Lilienfeld, S. O., Lynn, S. J., Kirsch, I., Chaves, J. F., Sarbin, T. R., Ganaway, G. K., & Powell, R. A. (1999). Dissociative identity disorder and the sociocognitive model: Recalling the lessons of the past. *Psychological Bulletin, 125,* 507–523.

Lilienfeld, S. O., Lynn, S. J., Ruscio, J., & Beyerstein, B. L. (2010). *50 great myths of popular psychology: Shattering widespread misconceptions about human behavior.* Malden, MA: Wiley-Blackwell.

Lilienfeld, S. O., Wood, J. M., & Garb, H. N. (2000). The scientific status of projective tests. *Psychological Science in the Public Interest, 1*(2), 27–66.

Lim, M. M., & Young, L. J. (2006). Neuropeptidergic regulation of affiliative behavior and social bonding in animals. *Hormones and Behavior, 50*(4), 506–517.

Lin, S. W., & Anthnelli, R. M. (2005). Genetic factors in the risk for substance use disorders. In J. H. Lowinson, P. Ruiz, R. B. Millman, & J. G. Langrod (Eds.), *Substance abuse: A comprehensive textbook.* Philadelphia, PA: Lippincott Williams & Wilkins.

Lindau, S., & Gavrilova, N. (2010). Sex, health, and years of sexually active life gained due to good health: Evidence from two U.S. population based cross sectional surveys of ageing. *BMJ: British Medical Journal, 340,* c810. doi:10.1136/bmj.c810

Linde, J. A., Rothman, A. J., Baldwin, A. S., & Jeffery, R. W. (2006). The impact of self-efficacy on behavior change and weight change among overweight participants in a weight loss trial. *Health Psychology, 25,* 282–291.

Lindgren, H. C. (1969). *The psychology of college success: A dynamic approach.* New York, NY: Wiley.

Lindsay, M., & Lester, D. (2004). *Suicide by cop: Committing suicide by provoking police to shoot you (death, value and meaning).* Amityville, NY: Baywood Publishing.

Lindsay, P. H., & Norman, D. A. (1977). *Human information processing.* New York, NY: Academic Press.

Lindsay, S. D., Allen, B. P., Chan, J. C. K., & Dahl, L. C. (2004). Eyewitness suggestibility and source similarity: Intrusions of details from one event into memory reports of another event. *Journal of Memory & Language, 50*(1), 96–111.

Lindsay, S. D., & Read, J. D. (2001). The recovered memories controversy: Where do we go from here? In G. M. Davies & T. Dalgleish (Eds.), *Recovered memories: Seeking the middle ground.* Chichester, England: Wiley.

Lindshield, S. M., & Rodrigues, M. A. (2009). Tool use in wild spider monkeys (*Ateles geoffroyi*). *Primates, 50*(3), 269–272. doi:10.1007/s10329-009-0144-3

Linn, S. (2008). Commercializing childhood: The corporate takeover of kids' lives. (interview by the Multinational Monitor). Retrieved from http://towardfreedom.com/home/content/view/1389/1/

Lippa, R. A. (1994). *Introduction to social psychology.* Pacific Grove, CA: Brooks/Cole.

Lippa, R. A. (2005). *Gender, nature, and nurture.* Mahwah, NJ: Erlbaum.

Lipton, J. S., & Spelke, E. S. (2004). Discrimination of large and small numerosities by human infants. *Infancy, 5,* 271–290.

Liptzin, B., Gottlieb, G. L., & Summergrad, P. (2007). The future of psychiatric services in general hospitals. *American Journal of Psychiatry, 164*(10), 1468–1472.

Lissek, S., Rabin, S., Heller, R. E., Lukenbaugh, D., Geraci, M., Pine, D. S., & Grillon, C. (2010). Overgeneralization of conditioned fear as a pathogenic marker of panic disorder. *American Journal of Psychiatry, 167*(1), 47–55. doi:10.1176/appi.ajp.2009.09030410

Little, A. C., & Mannion, H. (2006). Viewing attractive or unattractive same-sex individuals changes self-rated attractiveness and face preferences in women. *Animal Behaviour, 72,* 981–987.

Liu, M., Siefferman, L., Mays, H., Jr., Steffen, J. E., & Hill, G. E. (2009). A field test of female mate preference for male plumage coloration in eastern bluebirds. *Animal Behaviour, 78*(4), 879–885. doi:10.1016/j.anbehav.2009.07.012

Livesley, W. J., Jang, K. L., & Vernon, P. A. (2003). Genetic basis of personality structure. In T. Millon & M. J. Lerner (Eds.), *Handbook of psychology, Vol. 5: Personality and social psychology.* New York, NY: Wiley.

Lizarraga, M. L. S., & Ganuza, J. M. G. (2003). Improvement of mental rotation in girls and boys. *Sex Roles, 40,* 277–286.

Lockhart, R. S. (1992). Measurement of memory. In L. R. Squire (Ed.), *Encyclopedia of learning and memory.* New York, NY: Macmillan.

Lockhart, R. S. (2000). Methods of memory research. In E. Tulving & F. I. M. Craik (Eds.), *The Oxford handbook of memory* (pp. 45–58). New York, NY: Oxford University Press.

Lockhart, R. S., & Craik, F. I. (1990). Levels of processing: A retrospective commentary on a framework for memory research. *Canadian Journal of Psychology, 44*(1), 87–112.

Locurto, C. (1990). The malleability of IQ as judged from adoption studies. *Intelligence, 14,* 275–292.

Loehlin, J. C. (1992). *Genes and environment in personality development.* Newbury Park, CA: Sage.

Loehlin, J. C. (2000). Group differences in intelligence. In R. J. Sternberg (Ed.), *Handbook of intelligence* (pp. 176–195). New York, NY: Cambridge University Press.

Loehlin, J. C., Horn, J. M., & Willerman, L. (1997). Heredity, environment, and IQ in the Texas Adoption Project. In R. J. Sternberg & E. L. Grigorenko (Eds.), *Intelligence, heredity, and environment.* New York, NY: Cambridge University Press.

Loftus, E. F. (1979). *Eyewitness testimony.* Cambridge, MA: Harvard University Press.

Loftus, E. F. (1992). When a lie becomes memory's truth: Memory distortion after exposure to misinformation. *Current Directions in Psychological Science, 1,* 121–123.

Loftus, E. F. (1994). The repressed memory controversy. *American Psychologist, 49,* 443–445.

Loftus, E. F. (1998). Remembering dangerously. In R. A. Baker (Ed.), *Child sexual abuse and false memory syndrome.* Amherst, NY: Prometheus Books.

Loftus, E. F. (2003). Make believe memories. *American Psychologist, 58,* 864–873.

Loftus, E. F. (2004). Memories of things unseen. *Current Directions in Psychological Science, 13*(4), 145–147.

Loftus, E. F. (2005). Planting misinformation in the human mind: A 30-year investigation of the malleability of memory. *Learning & Memory, 12,* 361–366.

Loftus, E. F., & Bernstein, D. M. (2005). Rich false memories: The royal road to success. In A. F. Healy (Ed.), *Experimental cognitive psychology and its applications.* Washington, DC: American Psychological Association.

Loftus, E. F., & Cahill, L. (2007). Memory distortion: From misinformation to rich false memory. In J. S. Nairne (Ed.), *The foundations of remembering: Essays in honor of Henry L. Roediger III.* New York, NY: Psychology Press.

Loftus, E. F., & Davis, D. (2006). Recovered memories. *Annual Review of Clinical Psychology, 2,* 469–498.

Loftus, E. F., & Palmer, J. C. (1974). Reconstruction of automobile destruction: An example of the interaction between language and memory. *Journal of Verbal Learning and Verbal Behavior, 13,* 585–589.

Logue, A. W. (1991). *The psychology of eating and drinking* (2nd ed.). New York, NY: W. H. Freeman.

Lohmann, R. I. (2007). Dreams and ethnography. In D. Barrett & P. McNamara (Eds.), *The new science of dreaming.* Westport, CT: Praeger.

Lohoff, F. W., & Berrettini, W. H. (2009). Genetics of mood disorders. In D. S. Charney & E. J. Nestler (Eds.), *Neurobiology of mental illness* (3rd ed., pp. 360–377). New York, NY: Oxford University Press.

Lohr, J. M., Olatunji, B. O., Baumeister, R. F., & Bushman, B. J. (2007). The psychology of anger venting and empirically supported alternatives that do no harm. *The Scientific Review of Mental Health Practice: Objective Investigations of Controversial and Unorthodox Claims in Clinical Psychology, Psychiatry, and Social Work, 5*(1), 53–64.

Long, J. E., Jr. (2005). Power to prescribe: The debate over prescription privileges for psychologists and the legal issues implicated. *Law & Psychology, 29,* 243–260.

Longman, D. G., & Atkinson, R. H. (2005). *College learning and study skills.* Belmont, CA: Wadsworth.

Lonner, W. J. (2009). A retrospective on the beginnings of JCCP and IACCP. *Journal of Cross-Cultural Psychology, 40*(2), 167–169. doi:10.1177/0022022109332406

Lorenzo, G. L., Biesanz, J. C., & Human, L. J. (2010). What is beautiful is good and more accurately understood: Physical attractiveness and accuracy in first impressions of personality. *Psychological Science, 21*(12), 1777–1782. doi:10.1177/0956797610388048

Lothane, Z. (2006). Freud's legacy—Is it still with us? *Psychoanalytic Psychology, 23*(2), 285–301. doi:10.1037/0736-9735.23.2.285

Lott, B. (1987). *Women's lives.* Pacific Grove, CA: Brooks/Cole.

Lott, B. (2002). Cognitive and behavioral distancing from the poor. *American Psychologist, 57,* 100–110.

Lovejoy, T. E., & Hannah, L. (2005). *Climate change and biodiversity.* New Haven, CT: Yale University Press.

Lowinson, J. H., Ruiz, P., Millman, R. B., & Langrod, J. G. (2005). *Substance abuse: A comprehensive textbook.* Philadelphia, PA: Lippincott Williams & Wilkins.

Luborsky, E. B., O'Reilly-Landry, M., & Arlow, J. A. (2011). Psychoanalysis. In R. J. Corsini & D. Wedding (Eds.), *Current psychotherapies* (9th ed.). Belmont, CA: Brooks/Cole.

Luborsky, L., & Barrett, M. S. (2006). The history and empirical status of key psychoanalytic concepts. *Annual Review Clinical Psychology, 2,* 1–19.

Luborsky, L., Rosenthal, R., Diguer, L., Andrusyna, T. P., Berman, J. S., Levitt, J. T., Seligman, D. A., & Krause, E. D. (2002). The dodo bird verdict is alive and well—mostly. *Clinical Psychology: Science & Practice, 9,* 2–12.

Luborsky, L., Singer, B., & Luborsky, L. (1975). Comparative studies of psychotherapies: Is it true that everyone has won and all must have prizes? *Archives of General Psychiatry, 32,* 995–1008.

Lucas, A. R., Beard, C. M., O'Fallon, W. M., & Kurland, L. T. (1991). 50-year trends in the incidence of anorexia nervosa in Rochester, Minn.: A population-based study. *American Journal of Psychiatry, 148,* 917–922.

Lucas, R. E. (2007). Adaptation and the set-point model of subjective well-being: Does happiness change after major life events? *Current Directions in Psychological Science, 16,* 75–79.

Lucas, R. E. (2008). Personality and subjective well-being. In M. Eid & R. J. Larsen (Eds.), *The science of subjective well-being.* New York, NY: Guilford.

Lucas, R. E., Clark, A. E., Georgellis, Y., & Diener, E. (2004). Unemployment alters the set point for life satisfaction. *Psychological Science, 15*(1), 8–13.

Lucas, R. E., & Diener, E. (2008). Personality and subjective well-being. In O. P. John, R. W. Robins, & L. A. Pervin (Eds.), *Handbook of personality psychology: Theory and research* (3rd ed., pp. 795–814). New York, NY: Guilford.

Luchins, A. S. (1942). Mechanization in problem solving. *Psychological Monographs, 54* (6, Whole No. 248).

Luders, E., Narr, K. L., Thompson, P. M., & Toga, A. W. (2009). Neuroanatomical correlates of intelligence. *Intelligence, 37*(2), 156–163. doi:10.1016/j.intell.2008.07.002

Ludwig, A. M. (1994). Mental illness and creative activity in female writers. *American Journal of Psychiatry, 151,* 1650–1656.

Ludwig, A. M. (1995). *The price of greatness: Resolving the creativity and madness controversy.* New York, NY: Guilford.

Ludwig, A. M. (1998). Method and madness in the arts and sciences. *Creativity Research Journal, 11,* 93–101.

Lugaresi, E., Cirignotta, F., Montagna, P., & Sforza, E. (1994). Snoring: Pathogenic, clinical, and therapeutic aspects. In M. H. Kryger, T. Roth, & W. C. Dement (Eds.), *Principles and practice of sleep medicine* (2nd ed.). Philadelphia, PA: Saunders.

Luh, C. W. (1922). The conditions of retention. *Psychological Monographs, 31.*

Lundberg, A. (1998). Environmental change and human health. In A. Lundberg (Ed.), *The Environment and Mental Health: A Guide for Clinicians* (pp. 5–23). Mahwah, NJ: Erlbaum.

Lundberg, U. (2007). Catecholamines. In G. Fink (Ed.), *Encyclopedia of stress.* San Diego, CA: Elsevier.

Lupien, S. J., & Maheu, F. S. (2007). Memory and stress. In G. Fink (Ed.), *Encyclopedia of stress.* San Diego, CA: Elsevier.

Lurie, P., Almeida, C. M., Stine, N. , Stine, A. R., & Wolfe, S. M. (2006). Financial conflict of interest disclosure and voting patterns at Food and Drug Administration Drug Advisory Committee meetings. *Journal of the American Medical Association, 295,* 1921–1928.

Lustig, C., Berman, M. G., Nee, D., Lewis, R. L., Sledge Moore, K., & Jonides, J. (2009). Psychological and neural mechanisms of short-term memory. In G. G. Berntson & J. T. Cacioppo (Eds.), *Handbook of neuroscience for the behavioral sciences* (Vol 1, pp. 567–585). Hoboken, NJ: Wiley.

Lutz, C. (1987). Goals, events and understanding in Ifaluk emotion theory. In N. Quinn & D. Holland (Eds.), *Cultural models in language and thought.* Cambridge, England: Cambridge University Press.

Lykken, D. T. (1998). *A tremor in the blood: Uses and abuses of the lie detector.* New York, NY: Plenum Press.

Lynch, S. K., Turkheimer, E., D'Onofrio, B. M., Mendle, J., Emery, R. E., Slutske, W. S., et al. (2006). A genetically informed study of the association between harsh punishment and offspring behavioral problems. *Journal of Family Psychology, 20,* 190–198.

Lynn, D. J., & Vaillant, G. E. (1998). Anonymity, neutrality, and confidentiality in the actual methods of Sigmund Freud: A review of 43 cases, 1907–1939. *American Journal of Psychiatry, 155,* 163–171.

Lynn, S. J., Kirsch, I., & Hallquist, M. N. (2008). Social cognitive theories of hypnosis. In M. R. Nash & A. J. Barnier (Eds.). *Oxford handbook of hypnosis: Theory, research and practice* (pp. 111–140). New York, NY: Oxford University Press.

Lynn, S. J., Kirsch, I., Knox, J., Fassler, O., & Lilienfeld, S. O. (2007). Hypnotic regulation of consciousness and the pain neuromatrix. In G. A. Jamieson (Ed.), *Hypnosis and conscious states: The cognitive neuroscience perspective.* New York, NY: Oxford University Press.

Lynn, S. J., Lock, T., Loftus, E. F. , Krackow, E., & Lilienfeld, S. O. (2003). The remembrance of things past: Problematic memory recovery techniques in psychotherapy. In S. O. Lilienfeld, S. J. Lynn, & J. M. Lohr (Eds.), *Science and pseudoscience in clinical psychology*. New York, NY: Guilford.

Lynn, S. J., Neuschatz, J., & Fite, R. (2002). Hypnosis and memory: Implications for the courtroom and psychotherapy. In M. L. Eisen (Ed.), *Memory and suggestibility in the forensic interview*. Mahwah, NJ: Erlbaum.

Lynne, S. D., Graber, J. A., Nichols, T. R., & Brooks-Gunn, J., & Botwin, G. J. (2007). Links between pubertal timing, peer influences, and externalizing behaviors among urban students followed through middle school. *Journal of Adolescent Health, 40*(2).

Lyubomirsky, S., Sheldon, K. M., & Schkade, D. (2005). Pursuing happiness: The architecture of sustainable change. *Review of General Psychology, 9*, 111–131.

Lyubomirsky, S., Sousa, L., & Dickerhoof, R. (2006). The costs and benefits of writing, talking, and thinking about life's triumphs and defeats. *Journal of Personality and Social Psychology, 90*, 692–708.

Lyubomirsky, S., Tkach, C., & DiMatteo, R. M. (2006). What are the differences between happiness and self-esteem? *Social Indicators Research, 78*, 363–404.

Maas, J. B. (1998). *Power sleep*. New York, NY: Harper Perennial.

Maccoby, E. E. (2000). Parenting and its effects on children: On reading and misreading behavior genetics. *Annual Review of Psychology, 51*, 1–27.

MacCoun, R. J. (1998). Biases in the interpretation and use of research results. *Annual Review Psychology, 49*, 259–287.

MacDonald, K. (1998). Evolution, culture, and the five-factor model. *Journal of Cross-Cultural Psychology, 29*, 119–149.

MacGregor, J. N., Ormerod, T. C., & Chronicle, E. P. (2001). Information-processing and insight: A process model of performance on the nine-dot and related problems. *Journal of Experimental Psychology: Learning, Memory, and Cognition, 27*, 176–201.

Mack, A. (2003). Inattentional blindness: Looking without seeing. *Current Directions in Psychological Science, 12*(5), 180–184.

Mack, A. H., Franklin Jr., J. E., & Frances, R. J. (2003). Substance use disorders. In R. E. Hales & S. C. Yudofsky (Eds.), *Textbook of clinical psychiatry*. Washington, DC: American Psychiatric Publishing.

MacKellar, D. A., Valleroy, L. A., Secura, G. M., Behel, S., Bingham, T., Celentano, D. D., Koblin, B. A., LaLota, M., McFarland, W., Shehan, D., Thiede, H., Torian, L. V., & Janssen, R. S., & Young Men's Survey Study Group. (2005). Unrecognized HIV infection, risk behaviors, and perceptions of risk among young men who have sex with men: Opportunities for advancing HIV prevention in the third

decade of HIV/AIDS. *Journal of Acquired Immune Deficiency Syndromes, 38*, 603–614.

Mackintosh, N. J. (1998). *IQ and human intelligence*. Oxford: Oxford University Press.

MacLean, P. D. (1954). Studies on limbic system ("viosceal brain") and their bearing on psychosomatic problems. In E. D. Wittkower & R. A. Cleghorn (Eds.), *Recent developments in psychosomatic medicine*. Philadelphia, PA: Lippincott.

MacLean, P. D. (1993). Cerebral evolution of emotion. In M. Lewis & J. M. Haviland (Eds.), *Handbook of emotions*. New York, NY: Guilford.

MacMillan, H. L., Fleming, J. E., Streiner, D. L., Lin, E., Boyle, M. H., Jamieson, E., Duku, E. K., Walsh, C. A., Wong, M. Y. Y., & Beardslee, W. R. (2001). Childhood abuse and lifetime psychopathology in a community sample. *American Journal of Psychiatry, 158*, 1878–1883.

MacMillan, H. L., Fleming, J. E., Trocme, N., Boyle, M. H., Wong, M., Racine, Y. A., Beardslee, W. R., & Offord, D. R. (1997). Prevalence of child physical and sexual abuse in the community: Results from the Ontario health supplement. *Journal of the American Medical Association, 278*, 131–135.

Macrae, C. N., & Quadflieg, S. (2010). Perceiving people. In S. T. Fiske, D. T. Gilbert, & G. Lindzey (Eds.), *Handbook of social psychology* (5th ed., Vol. 1, pp. 353–393). Hoboken, NJ: Wiley.

Macy, J. R. (1995). Working through environmental despair. In T. Roszak, M. E. Gomes, & A. D. Kanner (Eds.), *Ecopsychology: Restoring the earth, healing the mind* (pp. 240–259). San Francisco, CA: Sierra Club.

Maddi, S. R. (1989). *Personality theories: A comparative analysis*. Chicago, IL: Dorsey Press.

Maddux, W. W., Adam, H., & Galinsky, A. D. (2010). When in Rome . . . Learn why the Romans do what they do: How multicultural learning experiences facilitate creativity. *Personality and Social Psychology Bulletin, 36*(6), 731–741. doi:10.1177/0146167210367786

Maddux, W. W., & Galinsky, A. D. (2009). Cultural borders and mental barriers: The relationship between living abroad and creativity. *Journal of Personality and Social Psychology, 96*(5), 1047–1061. doi:10.1037/a0014861

Madsen, K. M., Hviid, A., Vestergaard, M., Schendel, D., Wohlfahrt, J., Thorsen, P., et al. (2002). A population-based study of measles, mumps, and rubella vaccination and autism. *New England Journal of Medicine, 347*, 1477–1482.

Magnavita, J. J. (2008). Psychoanalytic psychotherapy. In J. L. Lebow (Ed.), *Twenty-first century psychotherapies: Contemporary approaches to theory and practice*. New York, NY: Wiley.

Maguire, W., Weisstein, N., & Klymenko, V. (1990). From visual structure to perceptual function. In K. N. Leibovic (Ed.), *Science of vision*. New York, NY: Springer-Verlag.

Maher, B. A. (2001). Delusions. In P. B. Sutker & H. E. Adams (Eds.), *Comprehensive handbook of psychopathology* (3rd ed., pp. 309–370). New York, NY: Kluwer Academic/Plenum Publishers.

Mahncke, H. W., Connor, B. B., Appelman, J., Ahsanuddin, O. N., Hardy, J. L., Wood, R. A., et al. (2006). Memory enhancement in healthy older adults using a brain plasticity-based training program: A randomized, controlled study. *Proceedings of the National Academy of Sciences of the United States of America, 103*(33), 12523–12528. doi:10.1073/pnas.0605194103

Mahoney, M. J. (1974). *Cognition and behavior modification*. Cambridge, MA: Ballinger.

Mahowald, M. W. (1993). Sleepwalking. In M. A. Carskadon (Ed.), *Encyclopedia of sleep and dreaming*. New York, NY: Macmillan.

Mahowald, M. W., & Schenck, C. H. (2005). Insights from studying human sleep disorders. *Nature, 437*, 1279–1285.

Maier, M. A., Elliot, A. J., & Lichtenfeld, S. (2008). Mediation of the negative effect of red on intellectual performance. *Personality and Social Psychology Bulletin, 34*(11), 1530–1540. doi:10.1177/0146167208323104

Maier, N. R. F. (1931). Reasoning and learning. *Psychological Review, 38*, 332–346.

Major, B., & Townsend, S. S. M. (2010). Coping with bias. In J. F. Dovidio, M. Hewstone, P. Glick, & V. M. Esses (Eds.), *The Sage handbook of prejudice, stereotyping, and discrimination*. Los Angeles, CA: Sage.

Malcolm, J. (1980: Pt. 1 Nov. 24; Pt. 2 Dec. 1). The impossible profession. *The New Yorker*, pp. 55–133, 54–152.

Maldonado, J. R., & Spiegel, D. (2008). Dissociative disorders. In R. E. Hales, S. C. Yudofsky, & G. O. Gabbard (Eds.), *The American Psychiatric Publishing textbook of psychiatry* (5th ed., pp. 665–710). Washington, DC: American Psychiatric Publishing.

Maletzky, B. M. (2002). The paraphilias: Research and treatment. In P. E. Nathan & J. M. Gorman (Eds.), *A guide to treatments that work*. London: Oxford University Press.

Maltzman, I. (1994). Why alcoholism is a disease. *Journal of Psychoactive Drugs, 26*, 13–31.

Mandel, H. & Young, J. (2009). *Here's the deal: Don't touch me*. New York, NY: Bantam Books.

Mandler, G. (1984). *Mind and body*. New York, NY: Norton.

Mandler, G. (1993). Thought, memory, and learning: Effects of emotional stress. In L. Goldberger & S. Breznitz (Eds.), *Handbook of stress: Theoretical and clinical aspects* (2nd ed.). New York, NY: Free Press.

Mandler, G. (2002). Origins of the cognitive revolution. *Journal of the History of the Behavioral Sciences, 38*, 339–353.

Maner, J. K., Gailliot, M. T., Rouby, D. A., & Miller, S. L. (2007). Can't take my eyes off you: Attentional adhesion to mates and rivals. *Journal of Personality and Social Psychology, 93*, 389–401.

Mann, J. J., & Currier, D. (2006). Understanding and preventing suicide. In D. J. Stein, D. J. Kupfer, & A. F. Schatzberg (Eds.), *Textbook of mood disorders*. Washington, DC: American Psychiatric Publishing.

Manna, A., Raffone, A., Perrucci, M., Nardo, D., Ferretti, A., Tartaro, A., et al. (2010). Neural correlates of focused attention and cognitive monitoring in meditation. *Brain Research Bulletin, 82*(1–2), 46–56. doi:10.1016/j.brainresbull.2010.03.001

Maratsos, M. P. (2007). Commentary. *Monographs of the Society for Research in Child Development, 72*, 121–126.

Marcia, J. E. (1966). Development and validation of ego identity status. *Journal of Personality and Social Psychology, 3*, 551–558.

Marcia, J. E. (1980). Identity in adolescence. In J. Adelson (Ed.), *Handbook of adolescent psychology.* New York, NY: Wiley.

Marcia, J. E. (1994). The empirical study of ego identity. In H. A. Bosma, T. L. G. Graafsma, H. D. Grotevant, & D. J. de Levita (Eds.), *Identity and development: An interdisciplinary approach.* Thousand Oaks, CA: Sage.

Marcus, G. F. (1996). Why do children say "breaked"? *Current Directions in Psychological Science, 5*, 81–85.

Marder, S. R., Hurford, I. M., & van Kammen, D. P. (2009). Second-generation antipsychotics. In B. J. Sadock, V. A. Sadock, & P. Ruiz (Eds.), *Kaplan & Sadock's comprehensive textbook of psychiatry* (pp. 3206–3240). Philadelphia, PA: Lippincott Williams & Wilkins.

Marewski, J. N., Gaissmaier, W., & Gigerenzer, G. (2010). Good judgments do not require complex cognition. *Cognitive Processing, 11*(2), 103–121. doi:10.1007/s10339-009-0337-0

Markowitsch, H. J. (2000). Neuroanatomy of memory. In E. Tulving & F. I. M. Craik (Eds.), *The Oxford handbook of memory* (pp. 465–484). New York, NY: Oxford University Press.

Markowitz, E. M., Goldberg, L. R., Ashton, M. C., & Lee, K. (2012). Profiling the "pro-environmental individual": A personality perspective. *Journal of Personality, 80*, 81–111.

Markus, H. R., & Hamedani, M. G. (2007). Sociocultural psychology: The dynamic interdependence among self systems and social systems. In S. Kitayama & D. Cohen (Eds.), *Handbook of cultural psychology.* New York, NY: Guilford.

Markus, H. R., & Kitayama, S. (1991). Culture and the self: Implications for cognition, emotion, and motivation. *Psychological Review, 98*, 224–253.

Markus, H. R., & Kitayama, S. (1994). The cultural construction of self and emotion: Implications for social behavior. In S. Kitayama & H. R. Markus (Eds.), *Emotions and culture: Empirical studies of mutual influence.* Washington, DC: American Psychological Association.

Markus, H. R., & Kitayama, S. (2003). Culture, self, and the reality of the social. *Psychological Inquiry, 14*(3–4), 277–283.

Marsh, E. J. (2007). Retelling is not the same as recalling: Implications for memory. *Current Directions in Psychological Science, 16*(1), 16–20.

Marsh, E. J., & Tversky, B. (2004). Spinning the stories of our lives. *Applied Cognitive Psychology, 18*, 491–503.

Marteau, T. M., & Weinman, J. (2004). Communicating about health threats and treatments. In S. Sutton, A. Baum, & M. Johnston (Ed), *The Sage handbook of health psychology.* Thousand Oaks, CA: Sage.

Martin, C. L., & Ruble, D. (2004). Children's search for gender cues: Cognitive perspectives on gender development. *Current Directions in Psychological Science, 13*(2), 67–70.

Martin, L. R., Friedman, H. S., & Schwartz, J. E. (2007). Personality and mortality risk across the life span: The importance of conscientiousness as a biopsychosocial attribute. *Health Psychology, 26*, 428–436.

Martin, R., & Leventhal, H. (2004). Symptom perception and health care-seeking behavior. In J. M. Raczynski & L. C. Leviton (Eds.), *Handbook of clinical health psychology, Vol. 2: Disorders of behavior and health.* Washington, DC: American Psychological Association.

Martin, R. A. (2002). Is laughter the best medicine? Humor, laughter, and physical health. *Current Directions in Psychological Science, 11*(6), 216–220.

Martinez, M., Marangell, L. B., & Martinez, J. M. (2008). Psychopharmacology. In R. E. Hales, S. C. Yudofsky, & G. O. Gabbard (Eds.), *The American psychiatric publishing textbook of psychiatry* (pp. 1053–1132). Washington, DC: American Psychiatric Publishing.

Maslow, A. H. (1954). *Motivation and personality.* New York, NY: Harper & Row.

Maslow, A. H. (1968). *Toward a psychology of being.* New York, NY: Van Nostrand.

Maslow, A. H. (1970). *Motivation and personality.* New York, NY: Harper & Row.

Mason, G. F., Krystal, J. H., & Sanacora, G. (2009). Nuclear magnetic resonance imaging and spectroscopy: Basic principles and recent findings in neuropsychiatric disorder. In B. J. Sadock, V. A. Sadock, & P. Ruiz (Eds.), *Kaplan & Sadock's comprehensive textbook of psychiatry* (9th ed., Vol. 1, pp. 248–272). Philadelphia, PA: Lippincott Williams & Wilkins.

Massen, C., & Vaterrodt-Plünnecke, B. (2006). The role of proactive interference in mnemonic techniques. *Memory, 14*, 189–196.

Massen, C., Vaterrodt-Plünnecke, B., Krings, L., & Hilbig, B. E. (2009). Effects of instruction on learners' ability to generate an effective pathway in the method of loci. *Memory, 17*(7), 724–731. doi:10.1080/09658210903012442

Master, S. L., Eisenberger, N. I., Taylor, S. E., Naliboff, B. D., Shirinyan, D., & Lieberman, M. D. (2009). A picture's worth: Partner photographs reduce experimentally induced pain. *Psychological Science, 20*(11), 1316–1318. doi:10.1111/j.14679280.2009.02444.x

Masterpasqua, F. (2009). Psychology and epigenetics. *Review of General Psychology, 13*(3), 194–201. doi:10.1037/a0016301

Masters, W. H., & Johnson, V. E. (1966). *Human sexual response.* Boston, MA: Little, Brown.

Masters, W. H., & Johnson, V. E. (1970). *Human sexual inadequacy.* Boston, MA: Little, Brown.

Mastro, D. E., Behm-Morawitz, E., & Kopacz, M. A. (2008). Exposure to television portrayals of Latinos: The implications of aversive racism and social identity theory. *Human Communication Research, 34*, 1–27.

Masuda, T. (2010). Cultural effects on visual perception. In E. B. Goldstein (Ed.), *Encyclopedia of perception.* Thousand Oaks, CA: Sage.

Masuda, T., & Nisbett, R. E. (2001). Attending holistically versus analytically: Comparing the context sensitivity of Japanese and Americans. *Journal of Personality and Social Psychology, 81*, 922–934.

Mathews, S., & Herzog, H. A. (1997). Personality and attitudes toward the treatment of animals. *Society and Animals, 5*, 169–175.

Matlin, M. W. (2008). *The psychology of women.* Belmont, CA: Wadsworth.

Matsumoto, D. (1994). *People: Psychology from a cultural perspective.* Pacific Grove, CA: Brooks/Cole.

Matsumoto, D. (2003). Cross-cultural research. In S. F. Davis (Ed.), *Handbook of research methods in experimental psychology.* Malden, MA: Blackwell Publishers.

Matsumoto, D., & Juang, L. (2008). *Culture and psychology.* Belmont, CA: Wadsworth.

Matsumoto, D., Nezlek, J. B., & Koopmann, B. (2007). Evidence for universality in phenomenological emotion response system coherence. *Emotion, 7*, 57–67.

Matsumoto, D., & Willingham, B. (2009). Spontaneous facial expressions of emotion of congenitally and noncongenitally blind individuals. *Journal of Personality and Social Psychology, 96*(1), 1–10. doi:10.1037/a0014037

Matsumoto, D., & Yoo, S. (2006). Toward a new generation of cross-cultural research. *Perspectives on Psychological Science, 1*, 234–250.

Matthey, S. (1998). P<.05—But is it clinically significant?: Practical examples for clinicians. *Behaviour Change, 15*, 140–146.

Maugh, T. H., II. (2008, December 9). Henry M. dies at 82: Victim of brain surgery accident offered doctors key insights into memory. *Los Angeles Times.* Retrieved from http://latimes.com

Mauk, M. D., & Thach, W. T. (2008). Cerebellum. In L. Squire, D. Berg, F. Bloom, S. Du Lac, A. Ghosh, N. Spitzer (Eds.), *Fundamental neuroscience* (3rd ed., pp. 751–774). San Diego, CA: Elsevier.

Mayer, F. S., & Frantz, C. M. (2004). The connectedness to nature scale: A measure of individuals' feeling in community with nature. *Journal of Environmental Psychology, 24*, 503–515.

Mays, V. M., Rubin, J., Sabourin, M., & Walker, L. (1996). Moving toward a global psychology: Changing theories and practice to meet the needs of a changing world. *American Psychologist, 51*, 485–487.

Mazur, J. E. (1993). Predicting the strength of a conditioned reinforcer: Effects of delay and uncertainty. *Current Directions in Psychological Science, 2*(3), 70–74. doi:10.1111/1467-8721.ep10770907

Mazzoni, G., Heap, M., & Scoboria, A. (2010). Hypnosis and memory: Theory, laboratory research, and applications. In S. Lynn, J. W. Rhue, & I. Kirsch (Eds.), *Handbook of clinical hypnosis* (2nd ed., pp. 709–741). Washington, DC: American Psychological Association.

Mazzoni, G., & Lynn, S. J. (2007). Using hypnosis in eyewitness memory: Past and current issues. In M. P. Toglia, J. D. Read, D. F. Ross, & R. C. Lindsay (Eds.), *Handbook of eyewitness psychology: Vol. 1. Memory for events.* Mahwah, NJ: Erlbaum.

McAnarney, E. R. (2008). Adolescent brain development: Forging new links? *Journal of Adolescent Health, 42*(4), 321–323.

McBride, D. L. & Korell, G. (2005). Wilderness therapy for abused women. *Canadian Journal of Counseling, 39,* 3–14.

McBride-Chang, C., & Jacklin, C. N. (1993). Early play arousal, sex-typed play, and activity level as precursors to later rough-and-tumble play. *Early Education & Development, 4,* 99–108.

McBurney, D. H. (1996). *How to think like a psychologist: Critical thinking in psychology.* Upper Saddle River, NJ: Prentice-Hall.

McBurney, D. H., Zapp, D. J., & Streeter. S. A. (2005). Preferred number of sexual partners: Tails of distributions and tales of mating systems. *Evolution and Human Behavior, 26,* 271–278.

McCabe, R. E., & Antony, M. M. (2008). Anxiety disorders: Social and specific phobias. In A. Tasman, J. Kay, J. A. Lieberman, M. B. First, & M. Maj (Eds.), *Psychiatry* (3rd ed.). New York, NY: Wiley-Blackwell.

McCarley, R. W. (1994). Dreams and the biology of sleep. In M. H. Kryger, T. Roth, & W. C. Dement (Eds.), *Principles and practice of sleep medicine* (2nd ed.). Philadelphia, PA: Saunders.

McCauley, M. E., Eskes, G., & Moscovitch, M. (1996). The effect of imagery on explicit and implicit tests of memory in young and old people: A double dissociation. *Canadian Journal of Experimental Psychology, 50,* 34–41.

McClelland, D. C. (1975). *Power: The inner experience.* New York, NY: Irvington.

McClelland, D. C. (1985). How motives, skills and values determine what people do. *American Psychologist, 40,* 812–825.

McClelland, D. C., Atkinson, J. W., Clark, R. A., & Lowell, E. L. (1953). *The achievement motive.* New York, NY: Appleton-Century-Crofts.

McClelland, D. C., & Koestner, R. (1992). The achievement motive. In C. P. Smith (Ed.), *Motivation and personality: Handbook of thematic content analysis.* New York, NY: Cambridge University Press.

McClernon, F. J., & Gilbert, D. G. (2007). Smoking and stress. In G. Fink (Ed.), *Encyclopedia of stress* (2nd ed.). San Diego, CA: Academic Press.

McClure-Tone, E. B., & Pine, D. S. (2009). Clinical features of the anxiety disorders. In B. J. Sadock, V. A. Sadock, & P. Ruiz (Eds.), *Kaplan & Sadock's comprehensive textbook of psychiatry* (9th ed., pp. 1844–1855). Philadelphia, PA: Lippincott Williams & Wilkins.

McCord, J. (2005). Unintended consequences of punishment. In M. Donnelly & M. A. Straus (Eds.), *Corporal punishment of children in theoretical perspective* New Haven, CT: Yale University Press.

McCormick, D. A. (2008). Membrane potential and action potential. In L. Squire, D. Berg, F. Bloom, S. Du Lac, A. Ghosh, & N. Spitzer (Eds.), *Fundamental neuroscience* (3rd ed., pp. 112–132). San Diego, CA: Elsevier.

McCrae, R. R. (1984). Situational determinants of coping responses: Loss, threat and challenge. *Journal of Personality and Social Psychology, 46,* 919–928.

McCrae, R. R. (2005). Personality structure. In V. A. Derlega, B. A. Winstead, & W. H. Jones (Eds.), *Personality: Contemporary theory and research.* Belmont, CA: Wadsworth.

McCrae, R. R., & Costa, P. T., Jr. (1985). Updating Norman's "adequate taxonomy": Intelligence and personality dimensions in natural language and in questionnaires. *Journal of Personality and Social Psychology, 49,* 710–721.

McCrae, R. R., & Costa, P. T., Jr. (1987). Validation of the five-factor model of personality across instruments and observers. *Journal of Personality and Social Psychology, 52,* 81–90.

McCrae, R. R., & Costa, P. T., Jr. (1997). Personality trait structure as a human universal. *American Psychologist, 52,* 509–516.

McCrae, R. R., & Costa, P. T., Jr. (1999). A five-factor theory of personality. In L. A. Pervin & O. P. John (Eds.), *Handbook of personality: Theory and research.* New York, NY: Guilford.

McCrae, R. R., & Costa, P. T., Jr. (2003). *Personality in adulthood: A five factor theory perspective.* New York, NY: Guilford.

McCrae, R. R., & Costa, P. T., Jr. (2007). Brief versions of the NEO-PI-3. *Journal of Individual Differences, 28,* 116–128.

McCrae, R. R., & Costa, P. T., Jr. (2008). The five-factor theory of personality. In O. P. John, R. W. Robbins, & L. A. Pervin (Eds.), *Handbook of personality: Theory and research* (Vol. 3, pp. 159–181). New York, NY: Guilford.

McCrae, R. R., & Sutin, A. R. (2009). Openness to experience. In M. R. Leary & R. H. Hoyle (Eds.), *Handbook of individual differences in social behavior* (pp. 257–273). New York, NY: Guilford.

McCrae, R. R., & Terracciano, A. (2006). National character and personality. *Current Directions in Psychological Science, 15,* 156–161.

McCrae, R. R., & Terracciano, A., & Personality Profiles of Cultures Project. (2005a). Personality profiles of cultures: Aggregate personality traits. *Journal of Personality and Social Psychology, 89,* 407–425.

McCrae, R. R., Terracciano, A., & 78 members of the Personality Profiles of Cultures Project. (2005b). Universal features of personality traits from the observer's perspective: Data from 50 cultures. *Journal of Personality and Social Psychology, 88,* 547–561.

McCrink, K., & Wynn, K. (2004). Large-number addition and subtraction by 9-month-old infants. *Psychological Science, 15,* 776–781.

McCullough, M. E. (2001). Forgiving. In C. R. Snyder (Ed.), *Coping with stress: Effective people and processes* (pp. 93–113). New York, NY: Oxford University Press.

McCullough, M. E., & Witvliet, C. V. (2002). The psychology of forgiveness. In C. R. Synder & S. J. Lopez (Eds.), *Handbook of positive psychology.* New York, NY: Oxford University Press.

McDaniel, M. A. (2005). Big-brained people are smarter: A meta-analysis of the relationship between *in vivo* brain volume and intelligence. *Intelligence, 33,* 337–346.

McDaniel, M. A., & Einstein, G. O. (1986). Bizarre imagery as an effective memory aid: The importance of distinctiveness. *Journal of Experimental Psychology: Learning, Memory & Cognition, 12,* 54–65.

McDaniel, M. A., Einstein, G. O., Stout, A. C., & Morgan, Z. (2003). Aging and maintaining intentions over delays: Do it or lose it. *Psychology and Aging, 18,* 823–835.

McDaniel, M. A., Waddill, P. J., & Shakesby, P. S. (1996). Study strategies, interest, and learning from text: The application of material appropriate processing. In D. J. Herrmann, C. McEvoy, C. Hertzog, P. Hertel, & M. K. Johnson (Eds.), *Basic and applied memory research: Theory in context* (Vol. 1). Mahwah, NJ: Erlbaum.

McDermott, K. B. (2007). Inducing false memories through associated lists: A window onto everyday false memories? In J. S. Nairne (Ed.), *The foundations of remembering: Essays in honor of Henry L. Roediger III.* New York, NY: Psychology Press.

McDevitt, M. A., & Williams, B. A. (2001). Effects of signaled versus unsignaled delay of reinforcement on choice. *Journal of the Experimental Analysis of Behavior, 75,* 165–182. doi:10.1901/jeab.2001.75-165

McDonald, C., & Murphy, K. C. (2003). The new genetics of schizophrenia. *Psychiatric Clinics of North America, 26*(1), 41–63.

McDonald, W. M., Thompson, T. R., McCall W. V., & Zormuski, C. F. (2004). Electroconvulsive therapy. In A. F. Schatzberg & C. B. Nemeroff (Eds.), *Textbook of psychopharmacology.* Washington, DC: American Psychiatric Publishing.

McEwen, B. S. (2009). Stress and coping. In G. G. Berntson & J. T. Cacioppo (Eds.), *Handbook of neuroscience for the behavioral sciences* (Vol. 2, pp. 1220–1235). Hoboken, NJ: Wiley.

McGeoch, J. A., & McDonald, W. T. (1931). Meaningful relation and retroactive inhibition. *American Journal of Psychology, 43,* 579–588.

McGlashan, T. H., & Hoffman, R. E. (2000). Schizophrenia: Psychodynamic to neurodynamic theories. In B. J. Sadock & V. A. Sadock (Eds.), *Kaplan and Sadock's comprehensive textbook of psychiatry* (7th ed., Vol. 1, pp. 1159–1168). Philadelphia, PA: Lippincott Williams & Wilkins.

McGowan, P. O., Meaney, M. J., & Szyf, M. (2008). Diet and the epigenetic (re)programming of phenotypic differences in behavior. *Brain Research, 1237,* 12–24. doi:10.1016/j.brainres.2008.07.074

McGrath, J., Welham, J., Scott, J., Varghese, D., Degenhardt, L., Hayatbakhsh, M., et al. (2010). Association between cannabis use and psychosis-related outcomes using sibling pair analysis in a cohort of young adults. *Archives of General Psychiatry, 67*(5), 440–447. doi:10.1001/archgenpsychiatry.2010.6

McGrew, J. H., Wright, E. R., Pescosolido, B. A., & McDonel, E. C. (1999). The closing of Central State Hospital: Long-term outcomes for persons with severe mental illness. *Journal of Behavioral Health Services & Research, 26,* 246–261.

McGue, M., Bouchard, T. J., Jr., Iacono, W. G., & Lykken, D. T. (1993). Behavioral genetics of cognitive ability: A life-span perspective. In R. Plomin & G. E. McClearn (Eds.), *Nature, nurture and psychology.* Washington, DC: American Psychological Association.

McGuigan, F. J., & Lehrer, P. M. (2007). Progressive relaxation: Origins, principles, and clinical applications. In P. M. Lehrer, R. L. Woolfolk, & W. E. Sime (Eds.), *Principles and practice of stress management.* New York, NY: Guilford.

McHugh, P. R. (1995). Dissociative identity disorder as a socially constructed artifact. *Journal of Practical Psychiatry and Behavioral Health, 1,* 158–166.

McKenna, K. Y. A. (2008). MySpace or your place: Relationship initiation and development in the wired and wireless world. In S. Sprecher, A. Wenzel, & J. Harvey (Eds.), *Handbook of relationship initiation* (pp. 235–247). New York, NY: Psychology Press.

McKenna, K. Y. A., & Bargh, J. A. (2000). Plan 9 from cyberspace: The implications of the Internet for personality and social psychology. *Personality and Social Psychology Review, 4,* 57–75.

McKenna, K. Y. A., Green, A., & Gleason, M. (2002). Relationship formation on the Internet: What's the big attraction? *Journal of Social Issues, 58,* 9–31.

McKone, E., Crookes, K., & Kanwisher, N. (2009). The cognitive and neural development of face recognition in humans. In M. S. Gazzaniga (Ed.), *The cognitive neurosciences.* Cambridge, MA: MIT Press.

McLay, R. N., Daylo, A. A., & Hammer, P. S. (2006). No effect of lunar cycle on psychiatric admissions or emergency evaluations. *Military Medicine, 171,* 1239–1242.

McLean, D. E., & Link, B. G. (1994). Unraveling complexity: Strategies to refine concepts, measures, and research designs in the study of life events and mental health. In W. R. Avison & I. H. Gotlib (Eds.), *Stress and mental health: Contemporary issues and prospects for the future.* New York, NY: Plenum.

McLellan, A. T., Lewis, D. C., O'Brien, C. P., & Kleber, H. D. (2000). Drug dependence, a chronic mental illness: Implications for treatment, insurance, and outcome evaluation. *Journal of the American Medical Association, 284,* 1689–1695.

McLoughlin, K., & Paquet, M. (2005, December 14). Gambling led Hogan to robbery, lawyer says. *Lehigh University's The Brown and White.* Retrieved March 21, 2006 from http://www.bw.lehigh.edu/story.asp?ID=19313.

McLoyd, V. C. (1998). Socioeconomic disadvantage and child development. *American Psychologist, 53,* 185–204.

McNally, R. J. (1994). Cognitive bias in panic disorder. *Current Directions in Psychological Science, 3,* 129–132.

McNally, R. J. (1996). *Panic disorder: A critical analysis.* New York, NY: Guilford.

McNally, R. J. (2003). *Remembering trauma.* Cambridge, MA: Belknap Press/Harvard University Press.

McNally, R. J. (2007). Betrayal trauma theory: A critical appraisal. *Memory, 15,* 280–294.

McNally, R. J. (2009). Posttraumatic stress disorder. In P. H. Blaney & T. Millon (Eds.), *Oxford textbook of psychopathology* (2nd ed., pp. 176–197). New York, NY: Oxford University Press.

McNally, R. J., & Geraerts, E. (2009). A new solution to the recovered memory debate. *Perspectives on Psychological Science, 4*(2), 126–134. doi:10.1111/j.1745-6924.2009.01112.x

McNeil, T. F., Cantor-Graae, E., & Ismail, B. (2000). Obstetrics complications and congenital malformation in schizophrenia. *Brain Research Reviews, 31,* 166–178.

McNulty, J. K., Neff, L. A., & Karney, B. R. (2008). Beyond initial attraction: Physical attractiveness in newlywed marriage. *Journal of Family Psychology, 22*(4), 135–143.

McPartland, J. Klin, A., Westphal, A., & Volkmar, F. R. (2008). Childhood disorders: The pervasive developmental disorders. In In A. Tasman, J. Kay, J. A. Lieberman, M. B. First, & M. Maj (Eds.), *Psychiatry* (3rd ed.). New York, NY: John Wiley.

McQueen, M. B., & Blacker, D. (2008). Genetics of Alzheimer's disease. In J. W. Smoller, B. R. Sheidley, & M. T. Tsuang (Eds.). *Psychiatric genetics: Applications in clinical practice* (pp. 177–193). Arlington, VA: American Psychiatric Publishing.

McWhorter, K. T. (2007). *College reading & study skills.* New York, NY: Pearson Longman.

Mechanic, D. (1980). *Mental health and social policy.* Englewood Cliffs, NJ: Prentice-Hall.

Mechanic, D. (1999). Mental health and mental illness. In A. V. Horvitz & T. L. Scheid (Eds.), *A handbook for the study of mental health: Social contexts, theories, and systems.* New York, NY: Cambridge University Press.

Mednick, S. A., Machon, R. A., Huttunen, M. O., & Bonett, D. (1988). Adult schizophrenia following prenatal exposure to an influenza epidemic. *Archives of General Psychiatry, 45,* 189–192.

Mednick, S. C., Cali, D. J., Kanady, J., & Drummond, S. A. (2008). Comparing the benefits of caffeine, naps and placebo on verbal, motor and perceptual memory. *Behavioural Brain Research, 193*(1), 79–86. doi:10.1016/j.bbr.2008.04.028

Mednick, S. C., & Drummond, S. P. A. (2009). Napping. In R. Stickgold & M. P. Walker (Eds.), *The neuroscience of sleep* (pp. 254–262). San Diego, CA: Academic Press.

Meerlo, P., Mistlberger, R. E., Jacobs, B. L., Heller, H., & McGinty, D. (2009). New neurons in the adult brain: The role of sleep and consequences of sleep loss. *Sleep Medicine Reviews, 13*(3), 187–194. doi:10.1016/j.smrv.2008.07.004

Meeus, W., van de Schoot, R., Keijsers, L., Schwartz, S. J., & Branje, S. (2010). On the progression and stability of adolescent identity formation: A five-wave longitudinal study in early-to-middle and middle-to-late adolescence. *Child Development, 81*(5), 1565–1581. doi:10.1111/j.1467-8624.2010.01492.x

Mehdizadeh, S. (2010). Self-presentation 2.0: Narcissism and self-esteem on Facebook. *Cyberpsychology, Behavior, and Social Networking, 13*(4), 357–364. doi:10.1089/cyber.2009.0257

Mehl, M. R. (2007). Eavesdropping on health: A naturalistic observation approach for social health research. *Social and Personality Psychology Compass, 1*(1), 359–380. doi:10.1111/j.1751-9004.2007.00034.x

Mehl, M. R., Vazire, S., Holleran, S. E., & Clark, C. (2010). Eavesdropping on happiness: Well-being is related to having less small talk and more substantive conversations. *Psychological Science, 21*(4), 539–541.

Mehra, R., Moore, B. A., Crothers, K., Tetrault, J., & Fiellin, D. A. (2006). The association between marijuana smoking and lung cancer: A systematic review. *Archives of Internal Medicine, 166,* 1359–1367.

Meichenbaum, D. H. (1977). *Cognitive-behavior modification.* New York, NY: Plenum.

Meinz, E. J., & Hambrick, D. Z. (2010). Deliberate practice is necessary but not sufficient to explain individual differences in piano sight-reading skill: The role of working memory capacity. *Psychological Science, 21*(7), 914–919.

Meister, B. (2007). Neurotransmitters in key neurons of the hypothalamus that regulate feeding behavior and body weight. *Physiology & Behavior, 92,* 263–271.

Melson, G. F. (2001). *Why the wild things are: Animals in the lives of children.* Cambridge, MA: Harvard University Press.

Melson, G. F. (2003). Child development and the human-companion animal bond. *American Behavioral Scientist, 47,* 31–39.

Meltzer, H. Y., & Bobo, W. V. (2009). Antipsychotic and anticholinergic drugs. In M. C. Gelder, N. C. Andreasen, J. J. López-Ibor, Jr., & J. R. Geddes (Eds.), *New Oxford textbook of psychiatry* (2nd ed., Vol. 1). New York, NY: Oxford University Press.

Melvin, G. A., Posner, K., Standley, B. H., & Oquendo, M. A. (2008). Management of the suicidal patient. In A. Tasman, J. Kay, J. A. Lieberman, M. B. First, & M. Maj (Eds.), *Psychiatry* (3rd ed.). New York, NY: Wiley-Blackwell.

Melzack, R., & Wall, P. D. (1965). Pain mechanisms: A new theory. *Science, 150*, 971–979.

Mendelson, W. B. (2005). Hypnotic medications: Mechanisms of action and pharmacologic effects. In M. H. Kryger, T. Roth, & W. C. Dement (Eds.), *Principles and practice of sleep medicine*. Philadelphia, PA: Elsevier Saunders.

Menninger, W. W. (2005). Role of the psychiatric hospital in the treatment of mental illness. In B. J. Sadock & V. A. Sadock (Eds.), *Kaplan & Sadock's comprehensive textbook of psychiatry*. Philadelphia, PA: Lippincott Williams & Wilkins.

Merikangas, K. R., & Kalaydjian, A. E. (2009). Epidemiology of anxiety disorders. In B. J. Sadock, V. A. Sadock, & P. Ruiz (Eds.), *Kaplan & Sadock's comprehensive textbook of psychiatry* (9th ed., pp. 1856–1863). Philadelphia, PA: Lippincott Williams & Wilkins.

Merikangas, K. R., & Pato, M. (2009). Recent developments in the epidemiology of bipolar disorder in adults and children: Magnitude, correlates, and future directions. *Clinical Psychology: Science and Practice, 16*(2), 121–133. doi:10.1111/j.1468-2850.2009.01152.x

Merikangas, K. R., & Risch, N. (2003). Will the genomics revolution revolutionize psychiatry? *American Journal of Psychiatry, 160*, 625–635.

Merikle, P. M. (2007). Preconscious processing. In M. Velmans & S. Schneider (Eds.), *The Blackwell companion to consciousness*. Malden, MA: Blackwell Publishing.

Mesquita, B. (2003). Emotions as dynamic cultural phenomena. In R. J. Davidson, K. R. Scherer, & H. H. Goldsmith (Eds.), *Handbook of affective sciences*. New York, NY: Oxford University Press.

Mesquita, B., & Leu, J. (2007). The cultural psychology of emotion. In S. Kitayama & D. Cohen (Eds.), *Handbook of cultural psychology*. New York, NY: Guilford.

Metzger, E. D. (1999). Electroconvulsive therapy. In A. M. Nicholi (Ed.), *The Harvard guide to psychiatry*. Cambridge, MA: Harvard University Press.

Meyer, R. E. (1996). The disease called addiction: Emerging evidence in a 200-year debate. *The Lancet, 347*, 162–166.

Meyer, R. G. (1992). *Practical clinical hypnosis: Techniques and applications*. New York, NY: Lexington Books.

Meyer-Bahlburg, H. F. L., Ehrhardt, A. A., Rosen, L. R., Gruen, R. S., Veridiano, N. P., Vann, F. H., & Neuwalder, H. F. (1995). Prenatal estrogens and the development of homosexual orientation. *Developmental Psychology, 31*, 12–21.

Meyerbröker, K., & Emmelkamp, P. G. (2010). Virtual reality exposure therapy in anxiety disorders: A systematic review of process-and-outcome studies. *Depression and Anxiety, 27*(10), 933–944. doi:10.1002/da.20734

Mezulis, A. H., Abramson, L. Y., Hyde, J. S., & Hankin, B. L. (2004). Is there a universal positivity bias in attributions? A meta-analytic review of individual, developmental and cultural differences in the self-serving attributional bias. *Psychological Bulletin, 130*, 711–747.

Michaels, S. (1996). The prevalence of homosexuality in the United States. In R. P. Cabaj & T. S. Stein (Eds.), *Textbook of homosexuality and mental health*. Washington, DC: American Psychiatric Press.

Mignot, E. (2005). Narcolepsy: Diagnosis and management. In M. H. Kryger, T. Roth, & W. C. Dement (Eds.), *Principles and practice of sleep medicine*. Philadelphia, PA: Elsevier Saunders.

Mikulincer, M., & Shaver, P. R. (2007). *Attachment in adulthood: Structure, dynamics, and change*. New York, NY: Guilford.

Mikulincer, M., & Shaver, P. R. (2008). Adult attachment and affect regulation. In J. Cassidy & P. R. Shaver (Eds.), *Handbook of attachment: Theory, research, and clinical applications* (2nd ed., pp. 456–481). New York, NY: Guilford.

Milar, K. S. (2000). The first generation of women psychologists and the psychology of women. *American Psychologist, 55*, 616–619.

Milgram, S. (1963). Behavioral study of obedience. *Journal of Abnormal and Social Psychology, 67*, 371–378.

Milgram, S. (1964). Issues in the study of obedience. *American Psychologist, 19*, 848–852.

Milgram, S. (1968). Reply to the critics. *International Journal of Psychiatry, 6*, 294–295.

Milgram, S. (1974). *Obedience to authority*. New York, NY: Harper & Row.

Milinski, M., Sommerfeld, R. D., Krambeck, H. J., Reed, F. A., & Marotzke, J. (2008). The collective-risk social dilemma and the prevention of simulated dangerous climate change. *Proceedings of the National Academy of Sciences, 105*, 2291–2294.

Milkman, K. L., Chugh, D., & Bazerman, M. H. (2009). How can decision making be improved? *Perspectives on Psychological Science, 4*(4), 379–383. doi:10.1111/j.1745-6924.2009.01142.x

Miller, A. G. (1986). *The obedience experiments: A case study of controversy in social science*. New York, NY: Praeger.

Miller, E., & Wallis, J. (2008). The prefrontal cortex and executive brain functions. In L. Squire, D. Berg, F. Bloom, S. Du Lac, A. Ghosh, & N. Spitzer (Eds.), *Fundamental neuroscience* (3rd ed., pp. 1199–1222). San Diego, CA: Elsevier.

Miller, G. (2009). The brain collector. *Science, 324*(5935), 1634–1636.

Miller, G. A. (1956). The magical number seven, plus or minus two: Some limits on our capacity for processing information. *Psychological Review, 63*, 81–97.

Miller, G. A. (2003). The cognitive revolution: A historical perspective. *Trends in Cognitive Sciences, 7*(3), 141–144.

Miller, G. E., & Blackwell, E. (2006). Turning up the heat: Inflammation as a mechanism linking chronic stress, depression, and heart disease. *Current Directions in Psychological Science, 15*, 269–272.

Miller, G. T. (2007). *Living in the environment: Principles, connections and solutions* (14th ed.). Belmont, CA: Wadsworth/Thompson Learning.

Miller, I. J., & Reedy, F. E. Jr. (1990). Variations in human taste-bud density and taste intensity perception. *Physiological Behavior, 47*, 1213–1219.

Miller, J. G. (2006). Insights into moral development from cultural psychology. In M. Killen & J. G. Smetana (Eds.), *Handbook of moral development*. Mahwah, NJ: Erlbaum.

Miller, J. M., & Peterson, D. A. M. (2004). Theoretical and empirical implications of attitude strength. *Journal of Politics, 66*, 847–867.

Miller, N. E. (1944). Experimental studies of conflict. In J. M. Hunt (Ed.), *Personality and the behavior disorders* (Vol. 1). New York, NY: Ronald.

Miller, N. E. (1959). Liberalization of basic S-R concepts: Extension to conflict behavior, motivation, and social learning. In S. Koch (Ed.), *Psychology: A study of a science* (Vol. 2). New York, NY: McGraw-Hill.

Miller, N. E. (1985). The value of behavioral research on animals. *American Psychologist, 40*, 423–440.

Miller, R. R., & Grace, R. C. (2003). Conditioning and learning. In A. F. Healy & R. W. Proctor (Eds.), *Handbook of psychology, Vol. 4: Experimental psychology*. New York, NY: Wiley.

Milligan, E. D., & Watkins, L. R. (2009). Pathological and protective roles of glia in chronic pain. *Nature Reviews Neuroscience, 10*(1), 23–36. doi:10.1038/nrn2533

Millstone, E. (1989). Methods and practices of animal experimentation. In G. Langley (Ed.), *Animal experimentation: The consensus changes*. New York, NY: Chapman & Hall.

Mineka, S., & Öhman, A. (2002). Phobias and preparedness: The selective, automatic and encapsulated nature of fear. *Biological Psychiatry, 52*, 927–937.

Mineka, S., & Zinbarg, R. E. (2006). A contemporary learning theory perspective on the etiology of anxiety disorders: It's not what you thought it was. *American Psychologist, 61*, 10–26.

Minkel, J. D., & Dinges, D. F. (2009). Circadian rhythms in sleepiness, alertness, and performance. In R. Stickgold & M. P. Walker (Eds.), *The neuroscience of sleep* (pp. 183–190). San Diego, CA: Academic Press.

Minton, H. L. (2000). Lewis Madison Terman. In A. E. Kazdin (Ed.), *Encyclopedia of psychology*. Washington, DC: American Psychological Association.

Minzenberg, M. J., Yoon, J. H., & Carter, C. S. (2008). Schizophrenia. In R. E. Hales, S. C. Yudofsky, & G. O. Gabbard (Eds.), *The American Psychiatric Publishing textbook of psychiatry* (5th ed., pp. 407–456). Washington, DC: American Psychiatric Publishing.

Miranda, J., Bernal, G., Lau, A., Kohn, L., Hwang, W., & LaFromboise, T. (2005). State of the science on psychosocial interventions for ethnic minorities. *Annual Review of Clinical Psychology, 1*, 113–42.

Mirescu, C., & Gould, E. (2006). Stress and adult neurogenesis. *Hippocampus, 16*, 233–238.

Mischel, W. (1961). Delay of gratification, need for achievement, and acquiescence in another culture. *Journal of Abnormal and Social Psychology, 62,* 543–552.

Mischel, W. (1968). *Personality and assessment.* New York, NY: Wiley.

Mischel, W. (1973). Toward a cognitive social learning conceptualization of personality. *Psychological Review, 80,* 252–283.

Mischel, W. (1984). Convergences and challenges in the search for consistency. *American Psychologist, 39,* 351–364.

Misra, R., & Castillo, L. G. (2004). Academic stress among college students: Comparison of American and international students. *International Journal of Stress Management, 11,* 132–148.

Mitchell, K. J., & Johnson, M. K. (2000). Source monitoring: Attributing mental experiences. In E. Tulving & F. I. M. Craik (Eds.), *The Oxford handbook of memory* (pp. 179–196). New York, NY: Oxford University Press.

Miyamoto, S., Lieberman, J. A., Fleishhacker, W. W., Aoba, A., & Marder, S. R. (2003). Antipsychotic drugs. In A. Tasman, J. Kay, & J. A. Lieberman (Eds.), *Psychiatry.* New York, NY: Wiley.

Miyamoto, S., Merrill, D. B., Lieberman, J. A., Fleischacker, W. W., & Marder, S. R. (2008). Antipsychotic drugs. In A. Tasman, J. Kay, J. A. Lieberman, M. B. First, & M. Maj (Eds.), *Psychiatry* (3rd ed.). New York, NY: Wiley-Blackwell.

Modestin, J. (1992). Multiple personality disorder in Switzerland. *American Journal of Psychiatry, 149,* 88–92.

Moe, A., & De Bini, R. (2004). Studying passages with the loci method: Are subject-generated more effective than experimenter-supplied loci pathways? *Journal of Mental Imagery, 28* (3–4), 75–86.

Mojtabai, R., & Olfson, M. (2010). National trends in psychotropic medication polypharmacy in office-based psychiatry. *Archives of General Psychiatry, 67*(1), 26–36.

Moller, A. C., Elliot, A. J., & Maier, M. A. (2009). Basic hue-meaning associations. *Emotion, 9*(6), 898–902. doi:10.1037/a0017811

Monastra, V. J. (2008). Social skills training for children and teens with ADHD: The neuroeducational life skills program. In V. J. Monastra (Ed.), *Unlocking the potential of patients with ADHD: A model for clinical practice.* Washington, DC: American Psychological Association.

Moncrieff, J. (2001). Are antidepressants overrated? A review of methodological problems in antidepressant trials. *Journal of Nervous and Mental Disorders, 189,* 288–295.

Monk, T. H. (2000). Shift work. In M. H. Kryger, T. Roth, & W. C. Dement (Eds.), *Principles and practice of sleep medicine.* Philadelphia, PA: Saunders.

Monk, T. H. (2005). Aging human circadian rhythms: Conventional wisdom may not always be right. *Journal of Biological Rhythms, 20*(4), 366–374. doi:10.1177/0748730405277378

Monk, T. H. (2006). Jet lag. In T. Lee-Chiong (Ed.), *Sleep: A comprehensive handbook.* Hoboken, NJ: Wiley-Liss.

Monroe, S. M. (2008). Modern approaches to conceptualizing and measuring human life stress. *Annual Review of Clinical Psychology, 4,* 33–52.

Monroe, S. M., & Hadjiyannakis, K. (2002). The social environment and depression: Focusing on severe life stress. In I. H. Gotlib & C. L. Hammen (Eds.), *Handbook of depression.* New York, NY: Guilford.

Monroe, S. M., & Slavich, G. M. (2007). Psychological stressors overview. In G. Fink (Ed.), *Encyclopedia of stress* (2nd ed.). San Diego, CA: Academic Press.

Monroe, S. M., Slavich, G. M., & Georgiades, K. (2009). The social environment and life stress in depression. In I. H. Gotlib & C. L. Hammen (Eds.), *Handbook of depression* (2nd ed., pp. 340–360). New York, NY: Guilford.

Monti, J. M., Jantos, H., & Monti, D. (2008). Serotonin and sleep-wake regulation. Neurochemistry of sleep and wakefulness. In J. M. Monti, S. R. Pandi-Perumal, & C. M. Sinton (Eds.), *Neurochemistry of sleep and wakefulness* (pp. 244–279). New York, NY: Cambridge University Press.

Montoya, R. (2008). I'm hot, so I'd say you're not: The influence of objective physical attractiveness on mate selection. *Personality and Social Psychology Bulletin, 34*(10), 1315–1331. doi:10.1177/0146167208320387

Moore, B. C. J. (2001). Basic auditory processes. In E. B. Goldstein (Ed.), *Blackwell handbook of perception.* Malden, MA: Blackwell.

Moore, B. C. J. (2010). Audition. In E. B. Goldstein (Ed.), *Encyclopedia of perception.* Thousand Oaks, CA: Sage.

Moore, K. L., & Persaud, T. V. N. (2008). *Before we are born* (7th ed.). Philadelphia, PA: Saunders.

Moore, R. Y. (2006). Biological rythms and sleep. In T. Lee-Chiong (Ed.), *Sleep: A comprehensive handbook.* Hoboken, NJ: Wiley-Liss.

Moran, T. H. (2004). Gut peptides in the control of food intake: 30 years of ideas. *Physiology & Behavior, 82,* 175–180.

Morata, T. C. (2007). Young people: Their noise and music exposures and the risk of hearing loss. *International Journal of Audiology, 46*(3), 111–112. doi:10.1080/14992020601103079

Morewedge, C. K., & Norton, M. I. (2009). When dreaming is believing: The (motivated) interpretation of dreams. *Journal of Personality and Social Psychology, 96*(2), 249–264. doi:10.1037/a0013264

Morgan, H. (1996). An analysis of Gardner's theory of multiple intelligence. *Roeper Review, 18,* 263–269.

Morgan, R. D. & Cohen, L. M. (2008). Clinical and counseling psychology: Can differences be gleaned from printed recruiting materials?

Training and Education in Professional Psychology, 2(3), 156–164.

Morhenn, V. B., Park, J., Piper, E., & Zak, P. J. (2008). Monetary sacrifice among strangers is mediated by endogenous oxytocin release after physical contact. *Evolution and Human Behavior, 29*(6), 375–383. doi:10.1016/j.evolhumbehav.2008.04.004

Morokoff, P. J., Quina, K., Harlow, L. L., Whitmire, L., Grimley, D. M., Gibson, P. R., & Burkholder, G. J. (1997). Sexual assertiveness scale (SAS) for women: Development and validation. *Journal of Personality and Social Psychology, 73,* 790–804.

Morrison, A. R. (2003). The brain on night shift. *Cerebrum, 5*(3), 23–36.

Morry, M. M. (2007). The attraction-similarity hypothesis among cross-sex friends: Relationship satisfaction, perceived similarities, and self-serving perceptions. *Journal of Social and Personal Relationships, 24*(1), 117–138. doi:10.1177/0265407507072615

Morry, M. M. (2009). Similarity principle of attraction. In H. T. Reis & S. Sprecher (Eds.), *Encyclopedia of human relationships* (pp. 1500–1504). Los Angeles, CA: Sage.

Morton, A. (2010). *Angelina: An unauthorized biography.* New York, NY: St. Martin's Press.

Most, S. B., Scholl, B. J., Clifford, E. R., & Simons, D. J. (2005). What you see is what you set: Sustained inattentional blindness and the capture of awareness. *Psychological Review, 112,* 217–242.

Most, S. B., Simons, D. J., Scholl, B. J., Jimenez, R., Clifford, E., & Chabris, C. F. (2001). How not to be seen: The contribution of similarity and selective ignoring to sustained inattentional blindness. *Psychological Science, 12*(1), 9–17.

Motivala, S. J., & Irwin, M. R. (2007). Sleep and immunity: Cytokine pathways linking sleep and health outcomes. *Current Directions in Psychological Science, 16,* 21–25.

Mowrer, O. H. (1947). On the dual nature of learning: A reinterpretation of "conditioning" and "problem-solving." *Harvard Educational Review, 17,* 102–150.

Mrdjenovic, G., & Levitsky, D. A. (2005). Children eat what they are served: The imprecise regulation of energy intake. *Appetite, 3,* 273–282.

Muench, J., & Hamer, A. M. (2010). Adverse effects of antipsychotic medications. *American Family Physician, 81*(5), 617–622.

Mulligan, N. W. (1998). The role of attention during encoding in implicit and explicit memory. *Journal of Experimental Psychology: Learning, Memory, & Cognition, 24,* 27–47.

Mulvaney, M. K., & Mebert, C. J. (2007). Parental corporal punishment predicts behavior problems in early childhood. *Journal of Family Psychology, 21,* 389–397.

Munck, A. (2007). Corticosteroids and stress. In G. Fink (Ed.), *Encyclopedia of stress.* San Diego, CA: Elsevier.

Munk-Jorgensen, P. (1999). Has deinstitutionalization gone too far? *European Archives of Psychiatry & Clinical Neuroscience, 249*(3), 136–143.

Munsey, C. (2008). Prescriptive authority in the states: A look at which states allow RxP and which have considered it. *Monitor on Psychology, 39*(2).

Murdock, B. (2001). Analysis of the serial position curve. In H. L. Roediger III, J. S. Nairne, I. Neath, & A. M. Surprenant (Eds.), *The nature of remembering: Essays in honor of Robert G. Crowder* (pp. 151–170). Washington, DC: American Psychological Association.

Muris, P. (2002). Relationships between self-efficacy and symptoms of anxiety disorders and depression in a normal adolescent sample. *Personality and Individual Differences, 32,* 337–348.

Muris, P., & Merckelbach, H. (2001). The etiology of childhood specific phobia: A multifactorial model. In M. W. Vasey, & M. R. Dadds (Eds.), *The developmental psychopathology of anxiety.* (pp. 355-385). New York, NY: Oxford University Press.

Murphy, K. R. (2002). Can conflicting perspectives on the role of *g* in personnel selection be resolved? *Human Performance, 15,* 173–186.

Murray, E. A. (2007). The amygdala, reward and emotion. *Trends in Cognitive Sciences, 11,* 489–497.

Murray, R. M., & Bramon, E. (2005). Developmental model of schizophrenia. In B. J. Sadock & V. A. Sadock (Eds.), *Kaplan & Sadock's comprehensive textbook of psychiatry* (pp. 1381–1395). Philadelphia, PA: Lippincott Williams & Wilkins.

Murray, R. M., Morrison, P. D., Henquet, C., & Di Forti, M. (2007). Cannabis, the mind and society: The hash realities. *Nature Reviews: Neuroscience, 8,* 885–895.

Murstein, B. I., & Fontaine, P. A. (1993). The public's knowledge about psychologists and other mental health professionals. *American Psychologist, 48,* 839–845.

Mustanski, B. S., Chivers, M. L., & Bailey, J. M. (2002). A critical review of recent biological research on human sexual orientation. *Annual Review of Sex Research, 12,* 89–140.

Mutz, D. C., & Goldman, S. K. (2010). Mass media. In J. F. Dovidio, M. Hewstone, P. Glick, & V. M. Esses (Eds.), *The Sage handbook of prejudice, stereotyping, and discrimination.* Los Angeles, CA: Sage.

Muzina, D. J., Kemp, D. E., & Calabrese, J. R. (2008). Mood stabilizers. In A. Tasman, J. Kay, J. A. Lieberman, M. B. First, & M. Maj (Eds.), *Psychiatry* (3rd ed.). New York, NY: Wiley-Blackwell.

Myers, D. (2010). *Social psychology* (10th Ed.). New York, NY: McGraw-Hill.

Myers, D. G. (1992). *The pursuit of happiness: Who is happy—and why.* New York, NY: Morrow.

Myers, D. G. (1999). Close relationships and quality of life. In D. Kahneman, E. Diener, & N. Schwarz (Eds.), *Well-being: The foundations of hedonic psychology.* New York, NY: Russell Sage Foundation.

Myers, D. G. (2002). *Intuition: Its powers and perils.* New Haven, CT: Yale University Press.

Myers, D. G., & Diener, E. (1995). Who is happy? *Psychological Science, 6,* 10–19.

Myers, D. G., & Diener, E. (1997). The pursuit of happiness. *Scientific American Special Issue, 7,* 40–43.

Myers, D. G., & Lamm, H. (1976). The group polarization phenomenon. *Psychological Bulletin, 83,* 602–627.

Myers, G. (2007). *The significance of children and animals: Social development and our connections to other species.* West Lafayette, IN: Purdue University Press.

Mynatt, C. R., Doherty, M. E., & Tweney, R. D. (1978). Consequences of confirmation and disconfirmation in a simulated research environment. *Quarterly Journal of Experimental Psychology, 30,* 395–406.

Myrtek, M. (2007). Type A behavior and hostility as independent risk factors for coronary heart disease. In J. Jordan, B. Bardé, & A. M. Zeiher (Eds.), *Contributions toward evidence-based psychocardiology: A systematic review of the literature.* Washington, DC: American Psychological Association.

Nabi, H., Singh-Manoux, A., Shipley, M., Gimeno, D., Marmot, M. G., & Kivimaki, M. (2008). Do psychological factors affect inflammation and incident coronary heart disease? The Whitehall II study. *Arteriosclerosis, Thrombosis, and Vascular Biology, 24.* 1398-1406.

Nadelson, C. C., Notman, M. T., & McCarthy, M. K. (2005). Gender issues in psychotherapy. In G. O. Gabbard, J. S. Beck, & J. Holmes (Eds.), *Oxford textbook of psychotherapy.* New York, NY: Oxford University Press.

Nairne, J. S. (2002). Remembering over the short-term: The case against the standard model. *Annual Review of Psychology, 53,* 53–81.

Nairne, J. S. (2003). Sensory and working memory. In A. F. Healy & R. W. Proctor (Eds.), *Handbook of psychology, Vol. 4: Experimental psychology.* New York, NY: Wiley.

Naish, P. L. N. (2006). Time to explain the nature of hypnosis? *Contemporary Hypnosis, 23,*, 33–46.

Narr, K. L., Woods, R. P., Thompson, P. M., Szeszko, P., Robinson, D., Dimtcheva, T., et al. (2007). Relationships between IQ and regional cortical gray matter thickness in healthy adults. *Cerebral Cortex, 17*(9), 2163–2171. doi:10.1093/cercor/bhl125

Nash, M., Perez, N., Tasso, A., & Levy, J. (2009). Clinical research on the utility of hypnosis in the prevention, diagnosis, and treatment of medical and psychiatric disorders. *International Journal of Clinical & Experimental Hypnosis, 57*(4), 443–450.

Näslund, E., & Hellström, P. M. (2007). Appetite signaling: From gut peptides and enteric nerves to brain. *Physiology & Behavior, 92,* 256–262.

National Oceanic and Atmospheric Administration. (2012). State of the Climate Global Analysis. *NOAA Satellite and Information Services; National Climatic Data Center.* Available from http://www.ncdc.noaa.gov/sotc/global/

National Sleep Foundation. (2010). *Sleep in America poll: Summary of findings.* Retrieved from http://www.sleepfoundation.org/sites/default/files/nsaw/NSF%20Sleep%20in%20%20America%20Poll%20-%20Summary%20of%20Findings%20.pdf

Naumann, L. P., Vazire, S., Rentfrow, P. J., & Gosling, S. D. (2009). Personality judgments based on physical appearance. *Personality and Social Psychology Bulletin, 35*(12), 1661–1671. doi:10.1177/0146167209346309

Neighbors, H. W., Caldwell, C., Williams, D. R., Nesse, R., Taylor, R. J., Bullard, K. M., et al. (2007). Race, ethnicity, and the use of services for mental disorders: Results from the National Survey of American Life. *Archives of General Psychiatry, 64,* 485–494.

Neisser, U. (1967). *Cognitive psychology.* New York, NY: Appleton-Century-Crofts.

Neisser, U. (1998). Introduction: Rising test scores and what they mean. In U. Neisser (Ed.), *The rising curve: Long-term gains in IQ and related measures.* Washington, DC: American Psychological Association.

Neisser, U., Boodoo, G., Bouchard, T. J., Jr., Boykin, A. W., Brody, N., Ceci, S. J., Halpern, D. F., Loehlin, J. C., Perloff, R., Sternberg, R. J., & Urbina, S. (1996). Intelligence: Knowns and unknowns. *American Psychologist, 51,* 77–101.

Nemeroff, C. B., Kalali, A., Keller, M. B., Charney, D. S., Lenderts, S. E., Cascade, E. F., et al. (2007). Impact of publicity concerning pediatric suicidality data on physician practice patterns in the United States. *Archives of General Psychiatry, 64,* 466–472.

Nemeth, C., & Chiles, C. (1988). Modelling courage: The role of dissent in fostering independence. *European Journal of Social Psychology, 18,* 275–280.

Nesse, R. M., & Ellsworth, P. C. (2009). Evolution, emotions, and emotional disorders. *American Psychologist, 64*(2), 129–139. doi:10.1037/a0013503

Nestler, E. J., & Malenka, R. C. (2004). The addicted brain. *Scientific American, 290*(3), 78–85.

Nettle, D. (2006). The evolution of personality variation in humans and other animals. *American Psychologist, 61,* 622–631.

Neuberg, S. L., Kenrick, D. T., & Schaller, M. (2010). Evolutionary social psychology. In S. T. Fiske, D. T. Gilbert, & G. Lindzey (Eds.), *Handbook of social psychology,*(5th ed., Vol. 2, pp. 761–796). Hoboken, NJ: Wiley.

Neugroschl, J. A., Kolevzon, A., Samuels, S. C., & Marin, D. B. (2005). Dementia. In B. J. Sadock & V. A. Sadock (Eds.), *Kaplan & Sadock's comprehensive textbook of psychiatry.* Philadelphia, PA: Lippincott Williams & Wilkins.

Neuschatz, J. S., Lampinen, J. M., Preston, E. L., Hawkins, E. R., & Toglia, M. P. (2002). The effect of memory schemata on memory and the phenomenological experience of naturalistic situations. *Applied Cognitive Psychology, 16,* 687–708.

Neuschatz, J. S., Lampinen, J. M., Toglia, M. P., Payne, D. G., & Cisneros, E. P. (2007). False memory research: History, theory, and applied implications. In M. P. Toglia, J. D. Read, D. F. Ross, & R. C. L. Lindsay (Eds.), *Handbook of eyewitness psychology: Volume 1. Memory for events.* Mahwah, NJ: Erlbaum.

Newcombe, N. S. (2007). Taking science seriously: Straight thinking about spatial sex differences. In S. J. Ceci & W. M. Williams (Eds.), *Why aren't more women in science?* (pp. 69–78). Washington, DC: American Psychological Association.

Newman, C. F., & Beck, A. T. (2009). Cognitive therapy. In B. J. Sadock, V. A. Sadock, & P. Ruiz (Eds.), *Kaplan & Sadock's comprehensive textbook of psychiatry* (pp. 2857–2872). Philadelphia, PA: Lippincott Williams & Wilkins.

Newschaffer, C. J., Croen, L. A., Daniels, J., Giarelli, E., Grether, J. K., Levy, & S. E., et al. (2007). The epidemiology of autism spectrum disorders. *Annual Review of Public Health, 28,* 235–258.

Niccols, A. (2007). Fetal alcohol syndrome and the developing socio-emotional brain. *Brain and Cognition, 65,* 135–142.

Nickerson, R. S., & Adams, M. J. (1979). Long-term memory for a common object. *Cognitive Psychology, 11,* 287–307.

Niebyl, J. R., & Simpson, J. L. (2007). Drugs and environmental agents in pregnancy and lactation: Embryology, teratology, epidemiology. In S. G. Gabbe, J. R. Niebyl, & J. L. Simpson (Eds.) *Obstetrics: Normal and problem pregnancies* (5th ed., pp. 184–214). Philadelphia, PA: Elsevier.

Nielsen, T. A., & Stenstrom, P. (2005). What are the memory sources of dreaming? *Nature, 437,* 1286–1289.

Nielsen, T. A., Zadra, A. L., Simard, V., Saucier, S., Stenstrom, P., Smith, C., & Kuiken, D. (2003). The typical dreams of Canadian university students. *Dreaming, 13*(4), 211–235.

Nievar, M. A., & Becker, B. J. (2008). Sensitivity as a privileged predictor of attachment: A second perspective on De Wolff and Van IJzendoorn's meta-analysis. *Social Development, 17,* 102–114.

Nikelly, A. G. (1994). Alcoholism: Social as well as psycho-medical problem—The missing "big picture." *Journal of Alcohol & Drug Education, 39,* 1–12.

Nir, Y., & Tononi, G. (2010). Dreaming and the brain: From phenomenology to neurophysiology. *Trends in Cognitive Sciences, 14*(2), 88–100. doi:10.1016/j.tics.2009.12.001

Nisbet, E. K., Zelenski, J. M., & Murphy, S. A. (2009). The Nature Relatedness Scale: Linking individuals' connection with nature to environmental concern and behavior. *Environment and Behavior, 41*(5), 715–740.

Nisbett, R. E. (Ed.). (1993). *Rules for reasoning.* Hillsdale, NJ: Erlbaum.

Nisbett, R. E. (2005). Heredity, environment, and race differences in IQ: A commentary on Rushton and Jensen. *Psychology, Public Policy, and the Law, 11,* 302–310.

Nisbett, R. E. (2009). *Intelligence and how to get it: Why schools and cultures count.* New York, NY: Norton.

Nisbett, R. E., & Miyamoto, Y. (2005). The influence of culture: Holistic versus analytic perception. *Trends in Cognitive Sciences, 9,* 467–473.

Nisbett, R. E., Peng, K., Choi, I., & Norenzayan, A. (2001). Culture and systems of thought: Holistic versus analytic cognition. *Psychological Review, 108,* 291–310.

Nist, S. L., & Holschuh, J. L. (2000). Comprehension strategies at the college level. In R. F. Flippo & D. C. Caverly (Eds.), *Handbook of college reading and study strategy research.* Mahwah, NJ: Erlbaum.

Nithianantharajah, J., & Hannan, A. J. (2006). Enriched environments, experience–dependent plasticity and disorders of the nervous system. *Nature Reviews Neuroscience, 7,* 697–709.

Noble, K. G., McCandliss, B. D., & Farah, M. J. (2007). Socioeconomic gradients predict individual differences in neurocognitive abilities. *Developmental Science, 10,* 464–480.

Noftle, E. E., & Robins, R. W. (2007). Personality predictors of academic outcomes: Big Five correlates of GPA and SAT scores. *Journal of Personality and Social Psychology, 93,* 116–130.

Nolen-Hoeksema, S. (1991). Responses to depression and their effects on the duration of depressive episodes. *Journal of Abnormal Psychology, 100,* 569–582.

Nolen-Hoeksema, S. (2000). The role of rumination in depressive disorders and mixed anxiety/depressive symptoms. *Journal of Abnormal Psychology, 109,* 504–511.

Nolen-Hoeksema, S. (2001). Gender differences in depression. *Current Directions in Psychological Science, 10,* 173–176.

Nolen-Hoeksema, S., & Hilt, L. M. (2009). Gender differences in depression. In I. H. Gotlib & C. L. Hammen (Eds.), *Handbook of Depression* (2nd ed., pp. 386–404). New York, NY: Guilford.

Nolen-Hoeksema, S., Wisco, B. E., & Lyubomirsky, S. (2008). Rethinking rumination. *Perspectives on Psychological Science, 3*(5), 400–424. doi:10.1111/j.1745-6924.2008.00088.x

Nomaguchi, K. M., & Milkie, M. A. (2003). Costs and rewards of children: The effects of becoming a parent on adults' lives. *Journal of Marriage and the Family, 65,* 356–374.

Norcross, J. C. (1995). Dispelling the dodo bird verdict and the exclusivity myth in psychotherapy. *Psychotherapy, 32,* 500–504.

Norcross, J. C., Hedges, M., & Castle, P. H. (2002). Psychologists conducting psychotherapy in 2001: A study of the Division 29 membership. *Psychotherapy: Theory, Research, Practice, Training, 39,* 97–102.

Norenzayan, A., & Heine, S. J. (2005). Psychological universals: What are they and how can we know? *Psychological Bulletin, 131,* 763–784.

Norman, T. R. (2009). Melatonin: Hormone of the night. *Acta Neuropsychiatrica, 21*(5), 263–265. doi:10.1111/acn.2009.21.issue-510.1111/j.1601-5215.2009.00411.x

Norris, F. H., & Slone, L. B. (2007). The epidemiology of trauma and PTSD. In M. J. Friedman, T. M. Keane, & P. A. Resick (Eds.), *Handbook of PTSD: Science and practice* (pp. 78–98). New York, NY: Guilford.

North, C. S., Eyrich, K. M., Pollio, D. E., & Spitznagel, E. L. (2004). Are rates of psychiatric disorders in the homeless population changing? *American Journal of Public Health, 94*(1), 103–108.

Norton, C. (2005). Animal experiments—A cardinal sin? *The Psychologist, 18*(2), 69.

Nosek, B. A., Banaji, M., & Greenwald, A. G. (2002). Harvesting implicit group attitudes and beliefs from a demonstration web site. *Group Dynamics: Theory, Research, and Practice, 6*(1), 101–115. doi:10.1037/1089-2699.6.1.101

Nosek, B. A., Greenwald, A. G., & Banaji, M. R. (2007). The Implicit Association Test at age 7: A Methodological and conceptual review. In J. A. Bargh (Ed.), *Social psychology and the unconscious: The automaticity of higher mental processes* (pp. 265–292). New York, NY: Psychology Press.

Novemsky, N., & Kahneman, D. (2005). The boundaries of loss aversion. *Journal of Marketing Research, 42,* 119–128.

Novick, L. R., & Bassok, M. (2005). Problem solving. In K. J. Holyoak & R. G. Morrison (Eds.), *The Cambridge handbook of thinking and reasoning.* New York, NY: Cambridge University Press.

Noyes, R., Clarkson, C., Crowe, R. R., Yates, W. R., & McChesney, C. M. (1987). A family study of generalized anxiety disorder. *American Journal of Psychiatry, 144,* 1019–1024.

Nucci, L. P. (2002). The development of moral reasoning. In U. Goswami (Eds.), *Blackwell handbook of childhood cognitive development.* Malden, MA: Blackwell Publishing.

O'Brien, C. P., Volkow, N., & Li, T.-K. (2006). What's in a word? Addiction versus dependence in DSM-V. *American Journal of Psychiatry, 163,* 764–765.

O'Connor, D. B., & Conner, M. (2011). Effects of stress on eating behavior. In R. J. Contrada & A. Baum (Eds.), *The handbook of stress science: Biology, psychology, and health* (pp. 111–121). New York, NY: Springer.

O'Donohue, W. (1998). Conditioning and third generation behavior therapy. In W. O'Donohue (Ed.), *Learning and behavior therapy.* Boston, MA: Allyn & Bacon.

O'Leary, K. D., Kent, R. N., & Kanowitz, J. (1975). Shaping data collection congruent with experimental hypotheses. *Journal of Applied Behavior Analysis, 8,* 43–51.

O'Leary, M. B., & Cummings, J. N. (2007). The spatial, temporal, and configurational characteristics of geographic dispersion in teams. *MIS Quarterly, 31,* 433–452.

O'Sullivan, D. (2006). Meta-analysis. In G. M. Breakwell, S. Hammond, C. Fife-Schaw, & J. A. Smith (Eds.), *Research methods in psychology* (3rd ed.). London: Sage.

Ohayon, M. M., Carskadon, M. A., Guilleminault, C., & Vitiello, M. V. (2004). Meta-analysis of quantitative sleep parameters from childhood to old age in healthy individuals: Developing normative sleep values across the human lifespan. *Sleep: Journal of Sleep & Sleep Disorders Research, 27,* 1255–1273.

Öhman, A. (1979). Fear relevance, autonomic conditioning, and phobias: A laboratory model. In P-O Sjödén, S. Bates & W. S. Dockens III (Eds.), *Trends in behavior therapy.* New York, NY: Academic Press.

Öhman, A., Dimberg, U., & Öst, L.-G. (1985). Animal and social phobias: Biological constraints on learned fear responses. In S. Reiss, & R. R. Bootzin (Eds.), *Theoretical issues in behavior therapy.* New York, NY: Academic Press.

Öhman, A., & Mineka, S. (2001). Fears, phobias, and preparedness: Toward an evolved module of fear and fear learning. *Psychological Review, 108,* 483–522.

Öhman, A., & Wiens, S. (2003). On the automaticity of autonomic responses in emotion: An evolutionary perspective. In R. J. Davidson, K. R. Scherer, & H. H. Goldsmith (Eds.), *Handbook of affective sciences.* New York, NY: Oxford University Press.

Okami, P., & Shackelford, T. K. (2001). Human sex differences in sexual psychology and behavior. *Annual Review of Sex Research, 12,* 186–241.

Oken, B. S. (2008). Placebo effects: Clinical aspects and neurobiology. *Brain: A Journal of Neurology, 131*(11), 2812–2823. doi:10.1093/brain/awn116

Olds, J. (1956). Pleasure centers in the brain. *Scientific American, 193,* 105–116.

Olds, J., & Milner, P. (1954). Positive reinforcement produced by electrical stimulation of the septal area and other regions of the rat brain. *Journal of Comparative and Physiological Psychology, 47,* 419–427.

Olds, M. E., & Fobe, J. L. (1981). The central basis of motivation: Intracranial self-stimulation studies. *Annual Review of Psychology, 32,* 523–574.

Olfson, M., Cherry, D. K., & Lewis-Fernández, R. (2009). Racial differences in visit duration of outpatient psychiatric visits. *Archives of General Psychiatry, 66*(2), 214–221.

Olfson, M., & Marcus, S. C. (2009). National patterns in antidepressant medication treatment. *Archives of General Psychiatry, 66*(8), 848–856.

Olfson, M., & Marcus, S. C. (2010). National trends in outpatient psychotherapy. *The American Journal of Psychiatry, 167*(12), 1456–1463. doi:10.1176/appi.ajp.2010.10040570

Olson, E. J., & Park, J. G. (2006). Snoring. In T. Lee-Chiong (Ed.), *Sleep: A comprehensive handbook.* Hoboken, NJ: Wiley-Liss.

Olson, J. M., & Maio, G. R. (2003). Persuasion and attitude change. In T. Millon & M. J. Lerner (Eds.), *Handbook of psychology, Vol. 5: Personality and social psychology.* New York, NY: Wiley.

Olson, J. M., Roese, N. J., & Zanna, M. P. (1996). Expectancies. In E. T. Higgins & A. W. Kruglanski (Eds.), *Social psychology: Handbook of basic principles.* New York, NY: Guilford.

Olson, M. A., & Fazio, R. H. (2001). Implicit attitude formation through classical conditioning. *Psychological Science, 12,* 413–417.

Olson, M. A., & Fazio, R. H. (2002). Implicit acquisition and manifestation of classically conditioned attitudes. *Social Cognition, 20*(2), 89–104.

Ondeck, D. M. (2003). Impact of culture on pain. *Home Health Care Management & Practice, 15,* 255–257.

Ones, D. S., Viswesvaran, C., & Dilchert, S. (2005). Cognitive ability in selection decisions. In O. Wilhelm & R. W. Engle (Eds.), *Handbook of understanding and measuring intelligence.* Thousand Oaks, CA: Sage.

Ong, A. D. (2010). Pathways linking positive emotion and health in later life. *Current Directions in Psychological Science, 19*(6), 358–362. doi:10.1177/0963721410388805

Ono, K. (1987). Supersitious behavior in humans. *Journal of the Experimental Analysis of Behavior, 47*(3), 261–271. doi:10.1901/jeab.1987.47-261

Opotow, S. & Weiss, L. (2000). Denial and the process of moral exclusion in environmental conflict. *Journal of Social Issues, 56,* 475–490.

Oppliger, P. A. (2007). Effects of gender stereotyping on socialization. In R. W. Preiss, B. M. Gayle, N. Burrell, M. Allen, & J. Bryant (Eds.), *Mass media effects research: Advances through meta-analysis* (pp. 192–214). Mahwah, NJ: Erlbaum.

Orne, M. T. (1951). The mechanisms of hypnotic age regression: An experimental study. *Journal of Abnormal and Social Psychology, 46,* 213–225.

Orne, M. T., & Holland, C. C. (1968). On the ecological validity of laboratory deceptions. *International Journal of Psychiatry, 6,* 282–293.

Ornstein, R. E. (1977). *The psychology of consciousness.* New York, NY: Harcourt Brace Jovanovich.

Orth, U., Trzesniewski, K. H., & Robins, R. W. (2010). Self-esteem development from young adulthood to old age: A cohort-sequential longitudinal study. *Journal of Personality and Social Psychology, 98*(4), 645–658. doi:10.1037/a0018769

Ortmann, A., & Hertwig, R. (1997). Is deception acceptable? *American Psychologist, 52,* 746–747.

Osbaldiston, R., & Sheldon, K. M. (2002). Social dilemmas and sustainability: Promoting peoples' motivation to "cooperate with the future." In P. Schmuck & W. P. Schultz (Eds.), *Psychology of sustainable development* (pp. 37–58). Boston, MA: Kluwer Academic Press.

Ostovich, J. M., & Sabini, J. (2004). How are sociosexuality, sex drive, and lifetime number of sexual partners related? *Personality and Social Psychology Bulletin, 30,* 1255–1266.

Outtz, J. L. (2002). The role of cognitive ability tests in employment selection. *Human Performance, 15,* 161–171.

Overton, S. L., & Medina, S. L. (2008). The stigma of mental illness. *Journal of Counseling & Development, 86*(2), 143–151.

Owley, T., Leventhal, B. L., & Cook, E. H. (2005). Childhood disorders: The autism spectrum disorders. In A. Tasman, J. Kay, & J. A. Lieberman (Eds.), *Psychiatry* (2nd ed., Vol 1, pp. 757–778). New York, NY: Wiley.

Ozer, D. J., & Benet-Martínez, V. (2006). Personality and the prediction of consequential outcomes. *Annual Review of Psychology, 57,* 401–421.

Ozer, E. J., Best, S. R., Lipsey, T. L., & Weiss, D. S. (2003). Predictors of posttraumatic stress disorder and symptoms in adults: A meta-analysis. *Psychological Bulletin, 129,* 52–73.

Pace-Schott, E. F. (2005). The neurobiology of dreaming. In M. H. Kryger, T. Roth, & W. C. Dement (Eds.). *Principles and practice of sleep medicine.* Philadelphia, PA: Elsevier Saunders.

Pace-Schott, E. F. (2009). Sleep architecture. In R. Stickgold & M. P. Walker (Eds.), *The neuroscience of sleep* (pp. 11–17). San Diego, CA: Academic Press.

Pachter, W. S., Fox, R. E., Zimbardo, P., & Antonuccio, D. O. (2007). Corporate funding and conflicts of interest: A primer for psychologists. *American Psychologist, 62*(9), 1005–1015.

Padgett, D. A., & Sheridan, J. F. (2000). Herpesviruses. In G. Fink (Ed.), *Encyclopedia of stress* (pp. 357–363). San Diego, CA: Academic Press.

Pahl, S., Harris, P. R., Todd, H. A., & Rutter, D. R. (2005). Comparative optimism for environmental risks. *Journal of Environmental Psychology, 25,* 1–11.

Paivio, A. (1986). *Mental representations: A dual coding approach.* New York, NY: Oxford University Press.

Paivio, A. (2007). *Mind and its evolution: A dual coding theoretical approach.* Mahwah, NJ: Erlbaum.

Paivio, A., Khan, M., & Begg, I. (2000). Concreteness of relational effects on recall of adjective-noun pairs. *Canadian Journal of Experimental Psychology, 54*(3), 149–160.

Paivio, A., Smythe, P. E., & Yuille, J. C. (1968). Imagery versus meaningfulness of nouns in paired-associate learning. *Canadian Journal of Psychology, 22,* 427–441.

Palmer, S. E. (2003). Visual perception of objects. In A. F. Healy & R. W. Proctor (Eds.), *Handbook of psychology, Vol. 4: Experimental psychology.* New York, NY: Wiley.

Pan, B. A., & Uccelli, P. (2009). Semantic development: Learning the meaning of words. In J. B. Gleason & N. B. Ratner (Eds.), *The development of language.* Boston, MA: Pearson.

Panksepp, J. (1991). Affective neuroscience: A conceptual framework for the neurobiological study of emotions. In K. T. Strongman (Ed.), *International review of studies on emotion*. Chichester, England: Wiley.

Papp, K. V., Walsh, S. J., & Snyder, P. J. (2009). Immediate and delayed effects of cognitive interventions in healthy elderly: A review of current literature and future directions. *Alzheimer's & Dementia, 5*(1), 50–60. doi:10.1016/j.jalz.2008.10.008

Park, D. C., & Huang, C. (2010). Culture wires the brain: A cognitive neuroscience perspective. *Perspectives on Psychological Science, 5*(4), 391–400. doi:10.1177/1745691610374591

Partinen, M., & Hublin, C. (2005). Epidemiology of sleep disorders. In M. H. Kryger, T. Roth, & W. C. Dement (Eds.). *Principles and practice of sleep medicine*. Philadelphia, PA: Elsevier Saunders.

Pascual-Leone, A. (2009). Characterizing and modulating neuroplasticity of the adult human brain. In M. S. Gazzangia (Ed.), *The cognitive neurosciences* (4th ed., pp. 141–152). Cambridge, MA: MIT Press.

Pashler, H., Johnston, J. C., & Ruthruff, E. (2001). Attention and performance. *Annual Review of Psychology, 52,* 629–651.

Pasternak, T., Bisley, J. W., & Calkins, D. (2003). Visual processing in the primate brain. In M. Gallagher & R. J. Nelson (Eds.), *Handbook of psychology: Biological psychology*. New York, NY: Wiley.

Patel, J. K., Pinals, D. A., & Breier, A. (2008). Schizophrenia and other psychoses. In A. Tasman, J. Kay, J. A. Lieberman, M. B. First, & M. Maj (Eds.), *Psychiatry* (3rd ed.). New York, NY: Wiley-Blackwell.

Patel, S. R., Ayas, N. T., Malhotra, M. R., White, D. P., Schernhammer, E. S., Speizer, F. E., et al. (2004). A prospective study of sleep duration and mortality risk in women. *Sleep: Journal of Sleep and Sleep Disorders Research, 27,* 440–444.

Patel, S. R., Malhotra, A., Gottlieb, D. J., White, P., & Hu, F. B. (2006). Correlates of long sleep deprivation. *Sleep: Journal of Sleep and Sleep Disorders Research, 29,* 881–889.

Patel, S. R., Zhu, X., Storfer-Isser, A., Mehra, R., Jenny, N. S., Tracy, R., & Redline, S. (2009). Sleep duration and biomarkers of inflammation. *Sleep: Journal of Sleep and Sleep Disorders Research, 32*(2), 200–204.

Pato, M. T., Fanous, A., Eisen, J. L., & Phillips, K. A. (2008). Anxiety disorders: Obsessive-compulsive disorder. In A. Tasman, J. Kay, J. A. Lieberman, M. B. First, & M. Maj (Eds.), *Psychiatry* (3rd ed.). New York, NY: Wiley-Blackwell.

Patston, L. M., Kirk, I. J., Rolfe, M. S., Corballis, M. C., & Tippett, L. J. (2007). The unusual symmetry of musicians: Musicians have equilateral interhemispheric transfer for visual information. *Neuropsychologia, 45*(9), 2059–2065. doi:10.1016/j.neuropsychologia.2007.02.001

Pattanashetty, R., Sathiamma, S., Talakkad, S., Nityananda, P., Trichur, R., & Kutty, B. M. (2010). Practitioners of vipassana meditation exhibit enhanced slow wave sleep and REM sleep states across different age groups. *Sleep and Biological Rhythms, 8*(1), 34–41. doi:10.1111/j.1479-8425.2009.00416.x

Patterson, C. J. (2003). Children of lesbian and gay parents. In L. D. Garnets & D. C. Kimmel (Eds.), *Psychological perspectives on lesbian, gay, and bisexual experiences* (2nd ed., pp. 497–548). New York, NY: Columbia University Press.

Patzer, G. L. (2006). *The power and paradox of physical attractiveness*. Boca Raton, FL: Brown Walker Press.

Paul, R. (2009). Parents ask: Am I risking autism if I vaccinate my children? *Journal of Autism and Developmental Disorders, 39*(6), 962-963.

Paulhus, D. L. (1991). Measurement and control of response bias. In J. P. Robinson, P. Shaver, & L. S. Wrightsman (Eds.), *Measures of personality and social psychological attitudes*. San Diego, CA: Academic Press.

Paulhus, D. L. (1998). Interpersonal and intrapsychic adaptiveness of trait self-enhancement: A mixed blessing? *Journal of Personality and Social Psychology, 74*(5), 1197–1208. doi:10.1037/0022-3514.74.5.1197

Paulos, J. A. (1995). *A mathematician reads the newspaper*. New York, NY: Doubleday.

Pavlov, I. P. (1906). The scientific investigation of psychical faculties or processes in the higher animals. *Science, 24,* 613–619.

Pavlov, I. P. (1927). *Conditioned reflexes* (G. V. Anrep, Trans.). London: Oxford University Press.

Payne, D. G., & Blackwell, J. M. (1998). Truth in memory: Caveat emptor. In S. J. Lynn & K. M. McConkey (Eds.), *Truth in memory*. New York, NY: Guilford.

Pearce, M. S., Deary, I. J., Young, A. H., & Parker, L. L. (2006). Childhood IQ and deaths up to middle age: The Newcastle Thousand Families Study. *Public Health, 120*(11), 1020–1026. doi:10.1016/j.puhe.2006.06.01

Pedersen, A. F., Bovbjerg, D. H., & Zachariae, R. (2011). Stress and susceptibility to infectious disease. In R. J. Contrada & A. Baum (Eds.), *The handbook of stress science: Biology, psychology, and health* (pp. 111–121). New York, NY: Springer.

Pedersen, P. (1994). A culture-centered approach to counseling. In W. J. Lonner & R. Malpass (Eds.), *Psychology and culture*. Boston, MA: Allyn & Bacon.

Peele, S. (1989). *Diseasing of America: Addiction treatment out of control*. Lexington, MA: Lexington Books.

Peele, S. (2000). What addiction is and is not: The impact of mistaken notions of addiction. *Addiction Research, 8,* 599–607.

Pelayo, R., & Lopes, M. C. (2006). Narcolepsy. In T. Lee-Chiong (Ed.), *Sleep: A comprehensive handbook*. Hoboken, NJ: Wiley-Liss.

Pellegrino, J. E., & Pellegrino, L. (2008). Fetal alcohol syndrome and related disorders. In P. J. Accardo (Eds.), *Capture and Accardo's neurodevelopment disabilities in infancy and childhood: Neurodevelopmental diagnosis and treatment*. Baltimore, MD: Paul H. Brookes Publishing.

Peng, J. H., Tao, Z. Z., & Huang, Z. W. (2007). Risk of damage to hearing from personal listening devices in young adults. *Journal of Otolaryngology, 36*(3), 181–185. doi:10.2310/7070.2007.0032

Penn, D. C., & Povinelli, D. J. (2007). Causal cognition in human and nonhuman animals: A comparative, critical review. *Annual Review of Psychology, 58,* 97–118.

Pennebaker, J. W., Colder, M., & Sharp, L. K. (1990). Accelerating the coping process. *Journal of Personality and Social Psychology, 58,* 528–537.

Peplau, L. A. (2003). Human sexuality: How do men and women differ? *Current Directions in Psychological Science, 12*(2), 37–40.

Peplau, L., & Fingerhut, A. W. (2007). The close relationships of lesbian and gay men. *Annual Review of Psychology, 58,* 405–424. doi:10.1146/annurev.psych.58.110405.085701

Pereira, A. C., Huddleston, D. E., Brickman, A. M., Sosunov, A. A., Hen, R., McKhann, G. M., et al. (2007). An in vivo correlate of exercise-induced neurogenesis in the adult dentate gyrus. *Proceedings of the National Academy of Sciences, 104,* 5638–5643.

Perkins, D. O., Miller-Anderson, L., & Lieberman, J. A. (2006). Natural history and predictors of clinical course. In J. A. Lieberman, T. S. Stroup, & D. O. Perkins (Eds.), *Textbook of schizophrenia*. Washington, DC: American Psychiatric Publishing.

Perlis, R. H., Perlis, C. S., Wu, Y., Hwang, C., Joseph, M., & Nierenberg, A. A. (2005). Industry sponsorship and financial conflict of interest in the reporting of clinical trials in psychiatry. *American Journal of Psychiatry, 162,* 1957–1960.

Perone, M., Galizio, M., & Baron, A. (1988). The relevance of animal-based principles in the laboratory study of human operant conditioning. In G. Davey & C. Cullen (Eds.), *Human operant conditioning and behavior modification*. New York, NY: Wiley.

Perry, W., & Braff, D. L. (1994). Information-processing deficits and thought disorder in schizophrenia. *American Journal of Psychiatry, 151,* 363–367.

Person, E. S. (1990). The influence of values in psychoanalysis: The case of female psychology. In C. Zanardi (Ed.), *Essential papers in psychoanalysis*. New York, NY: New York University Press.

Pert, C. B. (2002). The wisdom of the receptors: Neuropeptides, the emotions, and bodymind. *Advances in Mind-Body Medicine, 18*(1), 30–35.

Pert, C. B., & Snyder, S. H. (1973). Opiate receptor: Demonstration in the nervous tissue. *Science, 179,* 1011–1014.

Perugini, E. M., Kirsch, I., Allen, S. T., Coldwell, E., Meredith, J. M., Montgomery, G. H., & Sheehan, J. (1998). Surreptitious observation of response to hypnotically suggested hallucinations: A test of the compliance hypothesis. *International Journal of Clinical & Experimental Hypnosis, 46,* 191–203.

Pescosolido, B. A., Martin, J. K., Long, J., Medina, T. R., Phelan, J. C., & Link, B. G. (2010). "A disease like any other"? A decade of change in public reactions to schizophrenia, depression, and alcohol dependence. *American Journal of Psychiatry, 167*(11), 1321–1330. doi:10.1176/appi.ajp.2010.09121743

Peterson, C., & Park, N. (2009). Positive psychology. In B. J. Sadock, V. A. Sadock, & P. Ruiz (Eds.), *Kaplan & Sadock's comprehensive textbook of psychiatry* (pp. 2939–2951). Philadelphia, PA: Lippincott Williams & Wilkins.

Peterson, C., Seligman, M. E. P., Yurko, K. H., Martin, L. R., & Friedman, H. S. (1998). Catastrophizing and untimely death. *Psychological Science, 9,* 127–130.

Peterson, L. R., & Peterson, M. J. (1959). Short-term retention of individual verbal items. *Journal of Experimental Psychology, 58,* 193–198.

Petrie, K. J., & Pennebaker, J. W. (2004). Health-related cognitions. In S. Sutton, A. Baum, & M. Johnston (Eds.), *The Sage handbook of health psychology.* Thousand Oaks, CA: Sage.

Petrill, S. A. (2005). Behavioral genetics and intelligence. In O. Wilhelm & R. W. Engle (Eds.), *Handbook of understanding and measuring intelligence.* Thousand Oaks, CA: Sage.

Petry, N. M. (2005). *Pathological gambling: Etiology, comorbidity, and treatment.* Washington, D.C.: American Psychological Association.

Petry, N. M. (2010). Pathological gambling and the DSM-V. *International Gambling Studies, 10*(2), 113–115. doi:10.1080/14459795.2010.501086

Petty, R. E., & Briñol, P. (2008). Persuasion: From single to multiple to metacognitive processes. *Perspectives on Psychological Science, 3,* 137–147.

Petty, R. E., & Briñol, P. (2010). Attitude change. In R. F. Baumeister & E. J. Finkel (Eds.), *Advanced social psychology: The state of the science* (pp. 217–259). New York, NY: Oxford University Press.

Petty, R. E., & Cacioppo, J. T. (1986). *Communication and persuasion: Central and peripheral routes to attitude change.* New York, NY: Springer-Verlag.

Petty, R. E., & Wegener, D. T. (1998). Attitude change: Multiple roles for persuasion variables. In D. T. Gilbert, S. T. Fiske, & G. Lindzey (Eds.), *The handbook of social psychology.* New York, NY: McGraw-Hill.

Petty, R. E., & Wegener, D. T. (1999). The elaboration likelihood model: Current status and controversies. In S. Chaiken & Y. Trope (Eds.), *Dual-process theories in social psychology.* New York, NY: Guilford.

Petty, R. E., Wheeler, S. C., & Tormala, Z. L. (2003). Persuasion and attitude change. In T. Millon & M. J. Lerner (Eds.), *Handbook of Psychology, Vol. 5: Personality and social psychology.* New York, NY: Wiley.

Petty, S. C., Sachs-Ericsson, N., & Joiner, T. E., Jr. (2004). Interpersonal functioning deficits: Temporary or stable characteristics of depressed individuals. *Journal of Affective Disorders, 81,* 115–122.

Pezdek, K. (2003). Event memory and autobiographical memory for the events of September 11, 2001. *Applied Cognitive Psychology, 17,* 1033–1045.

Pfau, M., Kenski, H. C., Nitz, M., & Sorenson, J. (1990). Efficacy of inoculation strategies in promoting resistance to political attack messages: Application to direct mail. *Communication Monographs, 57,* 25–43.

Pfaus, J. G., Kippin, T. E., & Centeno, S. (2001). Conditioning and sexual behavior: A review. *Hormones & Behavior, 40,* 291–321.

Phares, V. (1996). *Fathers and developmental psychopathology.* New York, NY: Wiley.

Phelps, E. A. (2005). The interaction of emotion and cognition: The relation between the human amygdala and cognitive awareness. In R. R. Hassin, J. S. Uleman, & J. A. Bargh (Eds.), *The new unconcious: Oxford series in social cognition and social neuroscience.* New York, NY: Oxford University Press.

Phelps, E. A. (2006). Emotion and cognition: Insights from studies of the human amygdala. *Annual Review of Psychology, 57,* 27–53.

Phillips, B., & Kryger, M. H. (2005). Management of obstructive sleep apnea-hypopnea syndrome. In M. H. Kryger, T. Roth, & W. C. Dement (Eds.), *Principles and practice of sleep medicine.* Philadelphia, PA: Saunders.

Pi, E. H., & Simpson, G. M. (2001). Medication-induced movement disorders. In B. J. Sadock & V. A. Sadock (Eds.), *Kaplan and Sadock's comprehensive textbook of psychiatry* (7th ed., Vol. 2). Philadelphia, PA: Lippincott Williams & Wilkins.

Piaget, J. (1929). *The child's conception of world* (J. Tomlinson, Trans.). New York, NY: Harcourt Brace. (Original work published in 1926)

Piaget, J. (1932). *The moral judgment of the child* (M. Gabain, Trans.). Glencoe, IL: Free Press.

Piaget, J. (1952). *The origins of intelligence in children* (M. Cook, Trans.). New York, NY: International Universities Press. (Original work published in 1933)

Piaget, J. (1954). *The construction of reality in the child* (M. Cook, Trans.). New York, NY: Basic Books. (Original work published in 1937)

Piaget, J. (1983). Piaget's theory (G. Cellerier & J. Langer, Trans.). In P. H. Mussen (Series Ed.) & W. Kessen (Volume Ed.), *Handbook of child psychology: History, theory, and methods* (4th ed., Vol. 1, pp. 103–126). New York, NY: Wiley. (Original work published in 1970)

Pierce, R. C., & Kumaresan, V. (2006). The mesolimbic dopamine system: The final common pathway for the reinforcing effect of drugs of abuse? *Neuroscience Biobehavioral Reviews, 30,* 215–238.

Pies, R. (2009). Should DSM-V designate "Internet addiction" a mental disorder? *Psychiatry, 6*(2), 31–37.

Pietschnig, J., Voracek, M., & Formann, A. K. (2010). Mozart effect–Shmozart effect: A meta-analysis. *Intelligence, 38*(3), 314–323. doi:10.1016/j.intell.2010.03.001

Pillow, D. R., Zautra, A. J., & Sandler, I. (1996). Major life events and minor stressors: Identifying mediational links in the stress process. *Journal of Personality and Social Psychology, 70,* 381–394.

Pincus, D. (2006). Who is Freud and what does the new century behold? *Psychoanalytic Psychology, 23*(2), 367–372. doi:10.1037/0736-9735.23.2.367

Pink, D. H. (2005). *A whole new mind: Why right-brainers will rule the future.* New York, NY: Penguin.

Pinquart, M., Duberstein, P. R., & Lyness, J. M. (2006). Treatments for later-life depressive conditions: A meta-analytic comparison of pharmacotherapy and psychotherapy. *American Journal of Psychiatry, 163,* 1493–1501.

Pintar, J. (2010). Il n'y a pas d'hypnotisme: A history of hypnosis in theory and practice. In S. J. Lynn, J. W. Rhue, & I. Kirsch (Eds.), *Handbook of Clinical Hypnosis* (2nd ed., pp. 19–46). Washington, DC: American Psychological Association.

Pinyerd, B., & Zipf, W. B. (2005). Puberty—Timing is everything! *Journal of Pediatric Nursing, 20,* 75–82.

Pirog, R., & Benjamin, A. (2003). *Checking the food odometer: Comparing food miles for local versus conventional produce sales to Iowa institutions.* Leopold Center for Sustainable Agriculture, Iowa State University.

Pittman, F., III. (1994, January/February). A buyer's guide to psychotherapy. *Psychology Today,* 50–53, 74–81.

Plante, T. G., Caputo, D., & Chizmar, L. (2000). Perceived fitness and responses to laboratory-induced stress. *International Journal of Stress Management, 7*(1), 61–73.

Plomin, R. (1993). Nature and nurture: Perspective and prospective. In R. Plomin & G. E. McClearn (Eds.), *Nature, nurture and psychology.* Washington, DC: American Psychological Association.

Plomin, R. (1994). Nature, nurture, and development. In R. J. Sternberg (Ed.), *Encyclopedia of human intelligence.* New York, NY: Macmillan.

Plomin, R. (2003). General cognitive ability. In R. Plomin & J. C. DeFries (Eds.), *Behavioral genetics in the postgenomic era.* Washinton, DC: American Psychological Association.

Plomin, R. (2004). Genetics and developmental psychology. *Merrill-Palmer Quarterly: Journal of Developmental Psychology, 50*(3), 341–352. doi:10.1353/mpq.2004.0024

Plomin, R., DeFries, J. C., McClearn, G. E., & McGuffin, P. (2001). *Behavioral genetics.* New York, NY: Freeman.

Plomin, R., DeFries, J. C., McClearn, G. E., & McGuffin, P. (2008). *Behavioral genetics*. New York, NY: Worth.

Plomin, R., & Spinath, F. M. (2004). Intelligence: Genetics, genes, and genomics. *Journal of Personality & Social Psychology, 86*, 112–129.

Plucker, J. A., & Makel, M. C. (2010). Assessment of creativity. In J. C. Kaufman & R. J. Sternberg (Eds.), *The Cambridge handbook of creativity* (pp. 48–73). New York, NY: Cambridge University Press.

Plucker, J. A., & Renzulli, J. S. (1999). Psychometric approaches to the study of human creativity. In R. J. Sternberg (Ed.), *Handbook of creativity*. New York, NY: Cambridge University Press.

Plutchik, R. (1984). Emotions: A general psychoevolutionary theory. In K. R. Scherer & P. Ekman (Eds.), *Approaches to emotion*. Hillsdale, NJ: Erlbaum.

Plutchik, R. (1993). Emotions and their vicissitudes: Emotions and psychopathology. In M. Lewis & J. M. Haviland (Eds.), *Handbook of emotions*. New York, NY: Guilford.

Pogue-Geile, M. F., & Yokley, J. L. (2010). Current research on the genetic contributors to schizophrenia. *Current Directions in Psychological Science, 19*(4), 214–219. doi:10.1177/0963721410378490

Policastro, E., & Gardner, H. (1999). From case studies to robust generalizations: An approach to the study of creativity. In R. J. Sternberg (Ed.), *Handbook of creativity*. New York, NY: Cambridge University Press.

Pomerantz, E. M., Ng, F. F. Y., & Wang, Q. (2004). Gender socialization: A parent X child model. In A. H. Eagly, A. E. Beall, & R. J. Sternberg (Eds.), *The psychology of gender*. New York, NY: Guilford.

Popenoe, D. (2009). *Families without fathers: Fathers, marriage, and children in American society*. Piscataway, NJ: Transaction.

Porcerelli, J. H., Cogan, R., Kamoo, R., & Miller, K. (2010). Convergent validity of the Defense Mechanisms Manual and the Defensive Functioning Scale. *Journal of Personality Assessment, 92*(5), 432–438. doi:10.1080/00223891.2010.497421

Porter, J., Craven, B., Khan, R. M., Chang, S., Kang, I., Judkewitz, B., Volpe, J., et al. (2007). Mechanisms of scent-tracking in humans. *Nature Neuroscience, 10*(1), 27–29. doi:10.1038/nn1819

Porter, S., Yuille, J. C., & Lehman, D. R. (1999). The nature of real, implanted, and fabricated memories for emotional childhood events: Implications for the recovered memory debate. *Law and Human Behavior, 23*, 517–537.

Posada, G., Kaloustian, G., Richmond, K., & Moreno, A. J. (2007). Maternal secure base support and preschoolers' secure base behavior in natural environments. *Attachment & Human Development, 9*, 393–411.

Post, F. (1996). Verbal creativity, depression and alcoholism: An investigation of one hundred American and British writers. *British Journal of Psychiatry, 168*, 545–555.

Post, R. M. & Altshuler, L. L. (2009). Mood disorders: Treatment of bipolar disorders. In B. J. Sadock, V. A. Sadock, & P. Ruiz (Eds.), *Kaplan & Sadock's comprehensive textbook of psychiatry* (pp. 1743–1812). Philadelphia, PA: Lippincott Williams & Wilkins.

Postman, L. (1985). Human learning and memory. In G. A. Kimble & K. Schlesinger (Eds.), *Topics in the history of psychology*. Hillsdale, NJ: Erlbaum.

Poulin-Dubois, D., & Graham, S. A. (2007). Cognitive processes in early word learning. In E. Hoff & M. Shatz (Eds.), *Blackwell handbook of language development*. Malden, MA: Blackwell.

Powell, L. H., & Williams, K. (2007). Hostility. In G. Fink (Ed.), *Encyclopedia of stress*. San Diego, CA: Elsevier.

Powell, R. A., & Boer, D. P. (1995). Did Freud misinterpret reported memories of sexual abuse as fantasies? *Psychological Reports, 77*, 563–570.

Powell, R. A., & Gee, T. L. (1999). The effects of hypnosis on dissociative identity disorder: A reexamination of the evidence. *Canadian Journal of Psychiatry, 44*, 914–916.

Powley, T. L. (2008). Central control of autonomic functions: Organization of the autonomic nervous system. In L. Squire, D. Berg, F. Bloom, S. Du Lac, A. Ghosh, & N. Spitzer (Eds.), *Fundamental neuroscience* (3rd ed., pp. 809–828). San Diego, CA: Elsevier.

Powley, T. L. (2009). Hunger. In G. G. Berntson & J. T. Cacioppo (Eds.), *Handbook of neuroscience for the behavioral sciences*, (Vol. 2, pp. 659–679). Hoboken, NJ: Wiley.

Prat-Sala, M., & Redford, P. (2010). The interplay between motivation, self-efficacy, and approaches to studying. *British Journal of Educational Psychology, 80*(2), 283–305. doi:10.1348/000709909X480563

Prescott, J. (2010). Taste: Supertasters. In E. B. Goldstein (Ed.), *Encyclopedia of perception*. Thousand Oaks, CA: Sage.

Pressman, S. D., Cohen, S., Miller, G. E., Barkin, A., Rabin, B. S., & Treanor, J. J. (2005). Loneliness, social network size, and immune response to influenza vaccination in college freshman. *Health Psychology, 24*, 297–306.

Price, D. D., Finniss, D. G., & Benedetti, F. (2008). A comprehensive review of the placebo effect: Recent advances and current thought. *Annual Review of Psychology, 59*, 565–590. doi:10.1146/annurev.psych.59.113006.095941u

Price, M. (2008). Div. 55's drive for RxP: The American Society for the Advancement of Pharmacotherapy pushes for prescriptive authority. *Monitor on Psychology, 39*(2).

Priester, J. R., & Petty, R. E. (1995). Source attributions and persuasion; Perceived honesty as a determinant of message scrutiny. *Personality and Social Psychology Bulletin, 21*, 637–654.

Priester, J. R., & Petty, R. E. (2001). Extending the bases of subjective attitudinal ambivalence: Interpersonal and intrapersonal antecedents of evaluative tension. *Journal of Personality and Social Psychology, 80*, 19–34.

Priester, J. R., & Petty, R. E. (2003). The influence of spokesperson trustworthiness on message elaboration, attitude strength, and advertising. *Journal of Consumer Psychology, 13*, 408–421.

Prifitera, A. (1994). Wechsler scales of intelligence. In R. J. Sternberg (Ed.), *Encyclopedia of human intelligence*. New York, NY: Macmillan.

Pritchard, J. (2010). Virtual rewards for driving green. *The Behavior Analyst, 33*, 185-187.

Prochaska, J. O. (1994). Strong and weak principles for progressing from precontemplation to action on the basis of twelve problem behaviors. *Health Psychology, 13*, 47–51.

Prochaska, J. O., Velicer, W. F., Prochaska, J. M., & Johnson, J. L. (2004). Size, consistency, and stability of stage effects for smoking cessation. *Addictive Behaviors, 29*, 207–213.

Proffitt, D. R., & Caudek, C. (2003). Depth perception and the perception of events. In A. F. Healy & R. W. Proctor (Eds.), *Handbook of psychology, Vol. 4: Experimental psychology*. New York, NY: Wiley.

Prolo, P., & Chiappelli, F. (2007). Immune suppression. In G. Fink (Ed.), *Encyclopedia of stress*. San Diego, CA: Elsevier.

Pronin, E., Wegner, D. M., McCarthy, K., & Rodriguez, S. (2006). Everyday magical powers: The role of apparent mental causation in the overestimation of personal influence. *Journal of Personality and Social Psychology, 91*, 218–231. doi:10.1037/0022-3514.91.2.218

Proulx, C. M., Helms, H. M., & Buehler, C. (2007). Marital quality and personal well-being: A meta-analysis. *Journal of Marriage and Family, 69*(3), 576–593. doi:10.1111/j.1741-3737.2007.00393

Prudic, J. (2009). Electroconvulsive therapy. In B. J. Sadock, V. A. Sadock, & P. Ruiz (Eds.), *Kaplan & Sadock's comprehensive textbook of psychiatry* (pp. 3285–3300). Philadelphia, PA: Lippincott Williams & Wilkins.

Prudic, J., Olfson, M., Marcus, S. C., Fuller, R. B., & Sackeim, H. A. (2004). Effectiveness of electroconvulsive therapy in community settings. *Biological Psychiatry, 55*, 301–312.

Pruitt, D. G. (1971). Choice shifts in group discussion: An introductory review. *Journal of Personality and Social Psychology, 20*, 339–360.

Purves, D. (2009). Vision. In G. G. Berntson & J. T. Cacioppo (Eds.), *Handbook of neuroscience for the behavioral sciences*. New York, NY: Wiley.

Pyszczynski, T., Greenberg, J., Solomon, S., Arndt, J., & Schimel, J. (2004). Why do people need self-esteem? A theoretical and empirical review. *Psychological Bulletin, 130*, 435–468.

Pyszczynski, T., Solomon, S., & Greenberg, J. (2003). *In the wake of 9/11: The psychology of terror*. Washington, DC: American Psychological Association.

Qui, C., De Ronchi, D., & Fratiglioni, L. (2007). The epidemiology of the dementias: An update. *Current Opinion in Psychiatry, 20*(4), 380–385. doi:10.1097/YCO.0b013e32816ebc7b

Quinn, K. A., Macrae, C. N., & Bodenhausen, G. V. (2003). Stereotyping and impression formation: How categorical thinking shapes person perception. In M. A. Hogg & J. Cooper (Eds.), *The Sage handbook of social psychology*. Thousand Oaks, CA: Sage.

Quoidbach, J., Dunn, E. W., Petrides, K. V., & Mikolajczak, M. (2010). Money giveth, money taketh away: The dual effect of wealth on happiness. *Psychological Science, 21*(6), 759–763.

Rachman, S. J. (1992). Behavior therapy. In L. R. Squire (Ed.), *Encyclopedia of learning and memory*. New York, NY: Macmillan.

Rachman, S. J. (2009). Psychological treatment of anxiety: The evolution of behavior therapy and cognitive behavior therapy. *Annual Review of Clinical Psychology, 5*, 97–119.

Radak, Z., Hart, N., Sarga, L., Koltai, E., Atalay, M., Ohno, H., & Boldogh, I. (2010). Exercise plays a preventive role against Alzheimer's disease. *Journal of Alzheimer's Disease, 20*(3), 777–783.

Raichle, M. E. (2006). Functional neuroimaging: A historical and physiological perspective. In R. Cabeza & A. Kingstone (Eds.), *Handbook of functional neuroimaging of cognition*. Cambridge, MA: MIT Press.

Rains, G. D. (2002). *Principles of human neuropsychology*. New York, NY: McGraw-Hill.

Rakic, P., Bourgeois, J. P., & Goldman-Rakic, P. S. (1994). Synaptic development of the cerebral cortex: Implications for learning, memory, and mental illness. *Progress in brain research, 102*, 227–243.

Rama, A. N., Cho, S. C., & Kushida, C. A. (2006). Normal human sleep. In T. Lee-Chiong (Ed.), *Sleep: A comprehensive handbook*. Hoboken, NJ: Wiley-Liss.

Ramaekers, J. G., Berghaus, G., van Laar, M., & Drummer, O. H. (2004). Dose related risk of motor vehicle crashes after cannabis use. *Drug and Alcohol Dependence, 73*, 109–119.

Ramchand, R., Schell, T. L., Karney, B. R., Osilla, K., Burns, R. M., & Caldarone, L. (2010). Disparate prevalence estimates of PTSD among service members who served in Iraq and Afghanistan: Possible explanations. *Journal of Traumatic Stress, 23*(1), 59–68.

Ramey, C. T., & Ramey, S. L. (2004). Early educational interventions and intelligence. In E. Zigler & S. J. Styfco (Eds.), *The Head Start debate*. Baltimore, MD: Paul H. Brookes Publishing.

Ramey, S. L. (1999). Head Start and preschool education: Toward continued improvement. *American Psychologist, 54*, 344–346.

Ramirez-Esparza, N., Mehl, M. R., Alvarez-Bermudez, J., & Pennebaker, J. W. (2009). Are Mexicans more or less sociable than Americans? Insights from a naturalistic observation study. *Journal of Research in Personality, 43*(1), 1–7. doi:10.1016/j.jrp.2008.09.002

Ramsay, D. S., Seeley, R. J., Bolles, R. C., & Woods, S. C. (1996). Ingestive homeostasis: The primacy of learning. In E. D. Capaldi (Ed.), *Why we eat what we eat: The psychology of eating* (pp. 11–29). Washington, DC: American Psychological Association.

Ranson, K. E., & Urichuk, L. J. (2008). The effect of parent-child attachment relationships on child biopsychosocial outcomes: A review. *Early Child Development and Care, 178*, 129–152.

Rasch, B., & Born, J. (2008). Reactivation and consolidation of memory during sleep. *Current Directions in Psychological Science, 17*(3), 188–192. doi:10.1111/j.1467-8721.2008.00572.x

Raskin, N. J., Rogers, C. R., & Witty, M. C. (2011). Client-centered therapy. In R. J. Corsini & D. Wedding (Eds.), *Current psychotherapies* (9th ed.). Belmont, CA: Brooks/Cole.

Raskin, R. N., & Hall, C. S. (1979). A narcissistic personality inventory. *Psychological Reports, 45*(2), 590.

Raskin, R. N., & Hall, C. S. (1981). The Narcissistic Personality Inventory: Alternate form reliability and further evidence of construct validity. *Journal of Personality Assessment, 45*(2), 159–162. doi:10.1207/s15327752jpa4502_10

Raskin, R. N., & Terry, H. (1988). A principal-components analysis of the Narcissistic Personality Inventory and further evidence of its construct validity. *Journal of Personality and Social Psychology, 54*(5), 890–902. doi:10.1037/0022-3514.54.5.890

Rasmussen, H. N., Scheier, M. F., & Greenhouse, J. B. (2009). Optimism and physical health: A Meta-analytic review. *Annals of Behavioral Medicine, 37*(3), 239–256. doi:10.1007/s12160-009-9111-x

Rauscher, F. H., Shaw, G. L., & Ky, K. N. (1993). Music and spatial task performance. *Nature, 365*, 611.

Rauscher, F. H., Shaw, G. L., & Ky, K. N. (1995). Listening to Mozart enhances spatial-temporal reasoning: Towards a neurophysiological basis. *Neuroscience Letters, 185*, 44–47.

Raynor, H. A., & Epstein, L. H. (2001). Dietary variety, energy regulation, and obesity. *Psychological Bulletin, 127*, 325–341.

Raynor, J. O., & Entin, E. E. (1982). Future orientation and achievement motivation. In J. O. Raynor & E. E. Entin (Eds.), *Motivation, career striving, and aging*. New York, NY: Hemisphere.

Reber, R. (2004). Availability. In F. P. Rudiger (Ed.), *Cognitive illusions*. New York, NY: Psychology Press.

Recht, L. D., Lew, R. A., & Schwartz, W. J. (1995). Baseball teams beaten by jet lag. *Nature, 377*, 583.

Rechtschaffen, A. (1994). Sleep onset: Conceptual issues. In R. D. Ogilvie & J. R. Harsh (Eds.), *Sleep onset: Normal and abnormal processes*. Washington, DC: American Psychological Association.

Redker, C. M., & Gibson, B. (2009). Music as an unconditioned stimulus: Positive and negative effects of country music on implicit attitudes, explicit attitudes, and brand choice. *Journal of Applied Social Psychology, 31*, 2689–2705. doi:10.1111/j.1559-1816.2009.00544.x

Rees, C. J., & Metcalfe, B. (2003). The faking of personality questionnaire results: Who's kidding whom? *Journal of Managerial Psychology, 18*(2), 156–165.

Reeve, C. L., & Hakel, M. D. (2002). Asking the right questions about g. *Human Performance, 15*, 47–74.

Reeves, A. J. (2010). Visual light- and dark-adaptation. In E. B. Goldstein (Ed.), *Encyclopedia of perception*. Thousand Oaks, CA: Sage.

Refinetti, R. (2006). *Circadian physiology*. Boca Raton, FL: Taylor & Francis.

Regan, P. C. (1998). What if you can't get what you want? Willingness to compromise ideal mate selection standards as a function of sex, mate value, and relationship context. *Personality and Social Psychology Bulletin, 24*, 1294–1303.

Regan, P. C. (2008). *The mating game: A primer on love, sex, and marriage* (2nd ed.). Thousand Oaks, CA: Sage.

Regan, T. (1997). The rights of humans and other animals. *Ethics & Behavior, 7*(2), 103–111.

Reger, G. M., Holloway, K. M., Candy, C., Rothbaum, B. O., Difede, J., Rizzo, A. A., & Gahm, G. A. (2011). Effectiveness of virtual reality exposure therapy for active duty soldiers in a military mental health clinic. *Journal of Traumatic Stress, 24*(1), 93–96. doi:10.1002/jts.20574

Regier, D. A., & Burke, J. D. (2000). Epidemiology. In B. J. Sadock & V. A. Sadock (Eds.), *Kaplan and Sadock's comprehensive textbook of psychiatry*. Philadelphia, PA: Lippincott Williams & Wilkins.

Regier, D. A., Narrow, W. E., Kuhl, E. A., & Kupfer, D. J. (2009). The conceptual development of DSM-V. *American Journal of Psychiatry, 166*(6), 645–650. doi:10.1176/appi.ajp.2009.09020279

Rehm, L. P., Wagner, A., & Ivens-Tyndal, Co. (2001). Mood disorders: Unipolar and bipolar. In P. B. Sutker & H. E. Adams (Eds.), *Comprehensive handbook of psychopathology* (pp. 277–308). New York, NY: Kluwer Academic/Plenum.

Reichert, T. (2003). The prevalence of sexual imagery in ads targeted to young adults. *Journal of Consumer Affairs, 37*, 403–412.

Reichert, T., Heckler, S. E., & Jackson, S. (2001). The effects of sexual social marketing appeals on cognitive processing and persuasion. *Journal of Advertising, 30*(1), 13–27.

Reichert, T., & Lambiase, J. (2003). How to get "kissably close": Examining how advertisers appeal to consumers' sexual needs and desires. *Sexuality & Culture: An Interdisciplinary Quarterly, 7*(3), 120–136.

Reid, R. C., & Usrey, W. M. (2008). Vision. In L. Squire, D. Berg, F. Bloom, S. du Lac, A. Ghosh, & N. Spitzer (Eds.), *Fundamental neuroscience*. San Diego, CA: Elsevier.

Reimer, T., Mata, R., & Stoecklin, M. (2004). The use of heuristics in persuasion: Deriving cues on source expertise from argument quality. *Current Research in Social Psychology, 10*(6).

Reinharz, D., Lesage, A. D., & Contandriopoulos, A. P. (2000). Cost-effectiveness analysis of psychiatric deinstitutionalization. *Canadian Journal of Psychiatry, 45*, 533–538.

Reis, H. T., & Aron, A. (2008). Love: What is it, why does it matter, and how does it operate? *Perspectives on Psychological Science, 3*, 80–86.

Reisner, A. D. (1998). Repressed memories: True and false. In R. A. Baker (Ed.), *Child sexual abuse and false memory syndrome.* Amherst, NY: Prometheus Books.

Repetto, M., & Gold, M. S. (2005). Cocaine and crack: Neurobiology. In J. H. Lowinson, P. Ruiz, R. B. Millman, & J. G. Langrod (Eds.), *Substance abuse: A comprehensive textbook.* Philadelphia, PA: Lippincott Williams & Wilkins.

Rescorla, R. A. (1978). Some implications of a cognitive perspective on Pavlovian conditioning. In S. H. Hulse, H. Fowler, & W. K. Honig (Eds.), *Cognitive processes in animal behavior.* Hillsdale, NJ: Erlbaum.

Rescorla, R. A. (1980). *Pavlovian second-order conditioning.* Hillsdale, NJ: Erlbaum.

Rescorla, R. A., & Wagner, A. R. (1972). A theory of Pavlovian conditioning: Variations in the effectiveness of reinforcement and nonreinforcement. In A. H. Black & W. F. Prokasky (Eds.), *Classical conditioning: II. Current research and theory.* New York, NY: Appleton-Century-Crofts.

Resick, P. A., Monson, C. M., & Rizvi, S. L. (2008). Posttraumatic stress disorder. In W. E. Craighead, D. J. Miklowitz, & L. W. Craighead (Eds.), *Psychopathology: History, diagnosis, and empirical foundations.* New York, NY: Wiley.

Resnick, S. M. (2006). Sex differences in regional brain structure and function. In P. W. Kapan (Ed.), *Neurologic disease in women* (2nd ed., pp. 15–26). New York, NY: Demos Medical.

Reuter-Lorenz, P. A., & Miller, A. C. (1998). The cognitive neuroscience of human laterality: Lessons from the bisected brain. *Current Directions in Psychological Science, 7*, 15–20.

Reutskaja, E., & Hogarth, R. M. (2009). Satisfaction in choice as a function of the number of alternatives: When "goods satiate." *Psychology & Marketing, 26*(3), 197–203. doi:10.1002/mar.20268

Reynolds, A. J., Temple, J. T., Robertson, D. L., & Mann, E. A. (2001). Long-term effects of an early childhood intervention on educational achievement and juvenile arrest: A 15-year follow-up of low-income children in public schools. *Journal of the American Medical Association, 285*, 2339–2346.

Reynolds, E. H. (2002). Benefits and risks of folic acid to the nervous system. *Journal of Neurology, Neurosurgery & Psychiatry, 72*(5), 567–571. doi:10.1136/jnnp.72.5.567

Reynolds, K. J., Turner, J. C., & Haslam, S. A. (2000). When are we better than them and they worse than us? A closer look at social discrimination in positive and negative domains. *Journal of Personality and Social Psychology, 78*, 64–80.

Rhodes, G., Simmons, L. W., & Peters, M. (2005). Attractiveness and sexual behavior: Does attractivness enhance mating success? *Evolution and Human Behavior, 26*, 186–201.

Rhodewalt, F., & Peterson, B. (2009). Narcissism. In M. R. Leary & R. H. Hoyle (Eds.), *Handbook of individual differences in social behavior* (pp. 547–560). New York, NY: Guilford.

Richards, S. S., & Sweet, R. A. (2009). Dementia. In B. J. Sadock, V. A. Sadock, & P. Ruiz (Eds.), *Kaplan & Sadock's comprehensive textbook of psychiatry* (9th ed., Vol. 1, pp. 1167–1197). Philadelphia, PA: Lippincott Williams & Wilkins.

Richardson, C. R., Kriska, A. M., Lantz, P. M., & Hayword, R. A. (2004). Physical activity and mortality across cardiovascular disease risk groups. *Medicine and Science in Sports and Exercise, 36*, 1923–1929.

Richardson, G. S. (1993). Circadian rhythms. In M. A. Carskadon (Ed.), *Encyclopedia of sleep and dreaming.* New York, NY: Macmillan.

Richardson, G. S. (2006). Shift work sleep disorder. In T. Lee-Chiong (Ed.), *Sleep: A comprehensive handbook.* Hoboken, NJ: Wiley-Liss.

Richardson, R. C. (2007). *Evolutionary psychology as maladapted psychology.* Cambridge, MA: MIT Press.

Rieger, G., Linsenmeier, J. W., Gygax, L., & Bailey, J. (2008). Sexual orientation and childhood gender nonconformity: Evidence from home videos. *Developmental Psychology, 44*(1), 46–58. doi:10.1037/0012-1649.44.1.46

Rieskamp, J., & Hoffrage, U. (1999). When do people use simple heuristics, and how can we tell? In G. Gigerenzer, P. M. Todd, & ABC Research Group (Eds.), *Simple heuristics that make us smart* (pp. 141–168). New York, NY: Oxford University Press.

Riggio, H. R., & Halpern, D. F. (2006). Understanding human thought: Educating students as critical thinkers. In W. Buskist & S. F. Davis (Eds.), *Handbook of the teaching of psychology.* Malden, MA: Blackwell Publishing.

Rihmer, Z., & Angst, J. (2009). Mood disorders: Epidemiology. In B. J. Sadock, V. A. Sadock, & P. Ruiz (Eds.), *Kaplan & Sadock's comprehensive textbook of psychiatry* (9th ed., pp. 1645–1652). Philadelphia, PA: Lippincott Williams & Wilkins.

Riis, J., Loewenstein, G., Baron, J., Jepson, C., Fagerlin, A., & Ubel, P. A. (2005). Ignorance of hedonic adaptation to hemodialysis: A study using ecological momentary assessment. *Journal of Experimental Psychology: General, 134*(1), 3–9.

Risen, J. L., & Gilovich, T. (2007). Informal logical fallacies. In R. J. Sternberg, H. L. Roediger III, & D. F. Halpern (Eds.), *Critical thinking in psychology.* New York, NY: Cambridge University Press.

Risen, J. L., & Gilovich, T. (2008). Why people are reluctant to tempt fate. *Journal of Personality and Social Psychology, 95*, 293–307. doi:10.1037/0022-3514.95.2.293

Rising, K., Bacchetti, P., & Bero, L. (2008). Reporting bias in drug trials submitted to the Food and Drug Administration: Review of publication and presentation. *PLoS Medicine, 5*(11), e217.

Riskind, J. H. (2005). Cognitive mechanisms in generalized anxiety disorder: A second generation of theoretical perspectives. *Cognitive Therapy & Research, 29*(1), 1–5.

Rissling, M., & Ancoli-Israel, S. (2009). Sleep in aging. In R. Stickgold & M. P. Walker (Eds.), *The neuroscience of sleep* (pp. 78–86). San Diego, CA: Academic Press.

Ritter, K. (2011). New report confirms Arctic melt accelerating. Associated Press, May 3. Retrieved from http://hosted2.ap.org/APDEFAULT/terms/Article_2011-05-03-EU-Arctic-Climate-Change/id-bb2a142692274df4a51b3ae347b0f797

Ritter, R. C. (2004). Gastrointestinal mechanisms of satiation for food. *Physiology & Behavior, 81*, 249–273.

Rizzolatti, G. (2005). The mirror neuron system and imitation. In S. Hurley & N. Chater (Eds.), *Perspectives on imitation: From neuroscience to social science: Vol. 1. Mechanisms of imitation and imitation in animals.* Cambridge, MA: MIT Press.

Rizzolatti, G., & Craighero, L. (2004). The mirror-neuron system. *Annual Review of Neuroscience, 27*, 169–192.

Robelia, B. A., Greenhow, C., & Burton, L. (2011). Environmental learning in online social networks: Adopting environmentally responsible behaviors. *Environmental Education Research, 17*, 553–575. doi:10.1080/13504622.2011.565118

Roberts, B. W., Caspi, A., & Moffitt, T. (2003). Work experiences and personality development in young adulthood. *Journal of Personality and Social Psychology, 84*, 582–593.

Roberts, B. W., & DelVecchio, W. F. (2000). The rank-order consistency of personality traits from childhood to old age: A quantitative review of longitudinal studies. *Psychological Bulletin, 126*, 3–25.

Roberts, B. W., Jackson, J. J., Fayard, J. V., Edmonds, G., & Meints, J. (2009). Conscientiousness. In M. R. Leary & R. H. Hoyle (Eds.), *Handbook of individual differences in social behavior* (pp. 257–273). New York, NY: Guilford.

Roberts, B. W., Kuncel, N. R., Shiner, R., Caspi, A., & Goldberg, L. R. (2007). The power of personality: The comparative validity of personality traits, socioeconomic status, and cognitive ability for predicting important life outcomes. *Perspectives on Psychological Science, 2*, 313–345.

Roberts, B. W., & Pomerantz, E. M. (2004). On traits, situations, and their integration: A developmental perspective. *Personality and Social Psychology Review, 8*, 402–416.

Roberts, B. W., Walton, K. E., & Bogg, T. (2005). Conscientiousness and health across the life course. *Review of General Psychology, 9*(2), 156–168.

Roberts, B. W., Wood, D., & Caspi, A. (2008). The development of personality traits in adulthood. In O. P. John, R. W. Robins, & L. A. Pervin (Eds.), *Handbook of personality: Theory and research* (3rd ed., pp. 375–398). New York, NY: Guilford.

Roberts, D. F., Foehr, U. G., & Rideout, V. (2005). Generation M: Media in the lives of 8–18 year olds (Publication No. 7251). Menlo Park, CA: Henry J. Kaiser Family Foundation.

Roberts, J. E., & Ciesla, J. A. (2007). Stress generation. In G. Fink (Ed.), *Encyclopedia of stress*. San Diego, CA: Elsevier.

Roberts, M. C., Brown, K. J., & Smith-Boydston, J. M. (2003). The scientific process and publishing research. In M. C. Roberts and S. S. Ilardi (Eds.), *Handbook of research methods in clinical psychology*. Malden, MA: Blackwell.

Robiner, W. N., Bearman, D. L., Berman, M., Grove, W. M., Colon, E., Armstrong, J., Mareck, S., & Tanenbaum, R. L. (2003). Prescriptive authority for psychologists: Despite deficits in education and knowledge. *Journal of Clinical Psychology in Medical Settings, 10*(3), 211–212.

Robins, R. W., Gosling, S. D., & Craik, K. H. (1999). An empirical analysis of trends in psychology. *American Psychologist, 54*, 117–128.

Robinson, D. G., Woerner, M. G., McMeniman, M., Mendelowitz, A., & Bilder, R. M. (2004). Symptomatic and functional recovery from a first episode of schizophrenia or schizoaffective disorder. *American Journal of Psychiatry, 161*, 473–479.

Robles, T. F., Glaser, R., & Kiecolt-Glaser, J. K. (2005). Out of balance: A new look at chronic stress, depression, and immunity. *Current Directions in Psychological Science, 14*, 111–115.

Rockey, D. L., Jr., Beason, K. R., Howington, E. B., Rockey, C. M., & Gilbert, J. D. (2005). Gambling by Greek-affiliated college students: An association between affiliation and gambling. *Journal of College Student Development, 46*, 75-87.

Rodgers, J. E. (1982). The malleable memory of eyewitnesses. *Science Digest, 3*, 32–35.

Rodieck, R. W. (1998). *The first steps in seeing.* Sunderland, MA: Sinauer.

Roediger, H. L., III. (1980). Memory metaphors in cognitive psychology. *Memory & Cognition, 8*, 231–246.

Roediger, H. L., III, Agarwal, P. K., Kang, S. K., & Marsh, E. J. (2010). Benefits of testing memory: Best practices and boundary conditions. In G. M. Davies & D. B. Wright, (Eds.), *Current issues in applied memory research* (pp. 13–49). New York, NY: Psychology Press.

Roediger, H. L., III, Gallo, D. A., & Geraci, L. (2002). Processing approaches to cognition: The impetus from the levels-of-processing framework. *Memory, 10*, 319–332.

Roediger, H. L., III, & Karpicke, J. D. (2006a). Test-enhanced learning: Taking memory tests improves long-term retention. *Psychological Science, 17*, 249–255.

Roediger, H. L., III, & Karpicke, J. D. (2006b). The power of testing memory: Basic research and implications for educational practice. *Perspectives on Psychological Science, 1*(3), 181–210.

Roediger, H. L., III, & McDermott, K. B. (1995). Creating false memories: Remembering words not presented in lists. *Journal of Experimental Psychology: Learning, Memory, and Cognition, 21*, 803–814.

Roediger, H. L., III, & McDermott, K. B. (2000). Tricks of memory. *Current Directions in Psychological Science, 9*, 123–127.

Roediger, H. L., III, Wheeler, M. A., & Rajaram, S. (1993). Remembering, knowing, and reconstructing the past. In D. L. Medin (Ed.), *The psychology of learning and motivation: Advances in research and theory*. San Diego, CA: Academic Press.

Roehrs, T., & Roth, T. (2000). Hypnotics: Efficacy and adverse effects. In M. H. Kryger, T. Roth, & W. C. Dement (Eds.), *Principles and practice of sleep medicine*. Philadelphia, PA: Saunders.

Roffwarg, H. P., Muzio, J. N., & Dement, W. C. (1966). Ontogenetic development of the human sleep-dream cycle. *Science, 152*, 604–619.

Rogers, C. R. (1951). *Client-centered therapy: Its current practice, implications, and theory.* Boston, MA: Houghton Mifflin.

Rogers, C. R. (1961). *On becoming a person: A therapist's view of psychotherapy.* Boston, MA: Houghton Mifflin.

Rogers, C. R. (1980). *A way of being.* Boston, MA: Houghton Mifflin.

Rogers, C. R. (1986). Client-centered therapy. In I. L. Kutash & A. Wolf (Eds.), *Psychotherapist's casebook*. San Francisco, CA: Jossey-Bass.

Rogoff, B. (2003). *The cultural nature of human development.* New York, NY: Oxford University Press.

Rohner, R. P., & Veneziano, R. A. (2001). The importance of father love: History and contemporary evidence. *Review of General Psychology, 5*, 382–405.

Rohrer, D., & Taylor, K. (2006). The effects of overlearning and distributed practice on the retention of mathematics knowledge. *Applied Cognitive Psychology, 20*, 1209–1224.

Rollman, G. B. (2010). Pain: Cognitive and contextual influences. In E. B. Goldstein (Ed.), *Encyclopedia of perception*. Thousand Oaks, CA: Sage.

Rolls, E. T. (1990). A theory of emotion, and its application to understanding the neural basis of emotion. *Cognition and Emotion, 4*, 161–190.

Ronksley, P. E., Brien, S. E., Turner, B. J., Mukamal, K. J., & Ghali, W. A. (2011). Association of alcohol consumption with selected cardiovascular disease outcomes: a systematic review and meta-analysis. *BMJ: British Medical Journal, 342*(7795), 479.

Rose, D., Wykes, T., Leese, M., Bindman, J., & Fleischmann, P. (2003). Patient's perspectives on electroconvulsive therapy: Systematic review. *British Medical Journal, 326*, 1363–1365.

Rose, N. R. (2007). Neuroimmunomodulation. In G. Fink (Ed.), *Encyclopedia of stress*. San Diego, CA: Elsevier.

Roseboom, T., de Rooij, S., & Painter, R. (2006). The Dutch famine and its long-term consequences for adult health. *Early Human Development, 82*, 485–491.

Rosenblum, K. (2009). Conditioned taste aversion and taste learning: Molecular mechanisms. In J. H. Byrne (Ed.), *Concise learning and memory: The editor's selection*. San Diego, CA: Elsevier.

Rosenthal, R. (1976). *Experimenter effects in behavioral research.* New York, NY: Halsted.

Rosenthal, R. (1994). Interpersonal expectancy effects: A 30–year perspective. *Current Directions in Psychological Science, 3*, 176–179.

Rosenthal, R. (2002). Experimenter and clinical effects in scientific inquiry and clinical practice. *Prevention & Treatment, 5*(38).

Rosenthal, R., & Fode, K. L. (1963). Three experiments in experimenter bias. *Psychological Reports, 12*, 491–511.

Rosenzweig, M. R., & Bennet, E. L. (1996). Psychobiology of plasticity: Effects of training and experience on brain and behavior. *Behavioural Brain Research, 78*(5), 57–65.

Rosenzweig, M. R., Krech, D., & Bennett, E. L. (1961). Heredity, environment, brain biochemistry, and learning. In *Current trends in psychological theory*. Pittsburgh: University of Pittsburgh Press.

Rosenzweig, M. R., Krech, D., Bennett, E. L., & Diamond, M. (1962). Effects of environmental complexity and training on brain chemistry and anatomy: A replication and extension. *Journal of Comparative and Physiological Psychology, 55*, 429–437.

Ross, H., & Plug, C. (2002). *The mystery of the moon illusion: Exploring the size perception.* New York, NY: Oxford.

Ross, L., & Nisbett, R. E. (1991). *The person and the situation: Perspectives of social psychology.* New York, NY: McGraw-Hill.

Roszak, T., Gomes, M. E., & Kanner, A. D. (Eds.). (1995). *Ecopsychology: Restoring the earth, healing the mind.* San Francisco, CA: Sierra Club.

Rothbart, M. (2001). Category dynamics and the modification of outgroup stereotypes. In R. Brown & S. L. Gaertner (Eds.), *Blackwell handbook of social psychology: Intergroup processes*. Malden, MA: Blackwell.

Rowa, K., & Antony, M. M. (2008). Generalized anxiety disorders. In W. E. Craighead, D. J. Miklowitz, & L. W. Craighead (Eds.), *Psychopathology: History, diagnosis, and empirical foundations*. New York, NY: Wiley.

Rowatt, W. C., Cunningham, M. R., & Druen, P. B. (1999). Lying to get a date: The effect of facial physical attractiveness on the willingness to deceive prospective dating partners. *Journal of Social & Personal Relationships, 16*, 209–223.

Rowe, D., & van den Oord, E. J. C. G. (2005). Genetic and environmental influences. In V. A. Derlega, B. A. Winstead, & W. H. Jones (Eds.), *Personality: Contemporary theory and research*. Belmont, CA: Wadsworth.

Rowny, S., & Lisanby, S. H. (2008). Brain stimulation in psychiatry. In A. Tasman, J. Kay, J. A. Lieberman, M. B. First, & M. Maj (Eds.), *Psychiatry* (3rd ed.). New York, NY: Wiley-Blackwell.

Roy, M., Piche, M., Chen, J., Peretz, I., & Rainville, P. (2009). Cerebral and spinal modulation of pain by emotions. *PNAS Proceedings of the National Academy of Sciences of the United States of America, 106*(49), 20900-20905. doi:10.1073/pnas.0904706106

Rozin, P. (2007). Food and eating. In S. Kitayama & D. Cohen (Eds.), *Handbook of cultural psychology.* New York, NY: Guilford.

Rozin, P., Kabnick, K., Pete, E., Fischler, C., & Shields, C. (2003). The ecology of eating: Smaller portion sizes in France than in the United States help explain the French paradox. *Psychological Science, 14,* 450-454.

Ruble, D. N., & Martin, C. L. (1998). Gender development. In W. Damon (Ed.), *Handbook of child psychology (Vol. 3): Social, emotional, and personality development.* New York, NY: Wiley.

Ruble, T. L. (1983). Sex stereotypes: Issues of change in the 70s. *Sex Roles, 9,* 397-402.

Ruiter, R. A., Abraham, C., & Kok, G. (2001). Scary warnings and rational precautions: A review of the psychology of fear appeals. *Psychology & Health, 16,* 613-630.

Runyan, W. M. (2006). Psychobiography and the psychology of science: Understanding relations between the life and work of individual psychologists. *Review of General Psychology, 10,* 147-162.

Ruscio, J. (2006). *Clear thinking with psychology: Separating sense from nonsense.* Belmont, CA: Wadsworth.

Rushton, J. P. (2003). Race differences in *g* and the "Jensen effect." In H. Nyborg (Ed.), *The scientific study of general intelligence: Tribute to Arthur R. Jensen.* Oxford, UK: Pergamon.

Rushton, J. P., & Ankney, C. D. (2007). The evolution of brain size and intelligence. In S. M. Platek, J. P. Keenan, & T. K. Shackleford (Eds.), *Evolutionary cognitive neuroscience.* Cambridge: MIT Press.

Rushton, J. P., & Jensen, A. R. (2005). Thirty years of research on race differences in cognitive ability. *Psychology, Public Policy, and Law, 11,* 235-294.

Rushton, J. P., & Jensen, A. R. (2010). The rise and fall of the Flynn effect as a reason to expect a narrowing of the black-white IQ gap. *Intelligence, 38*(2), 213-219. doi:10.1016/j.intell.2009 .12.002

Russell, G. F. M. (1995). Anorexia nervosa through time. In G. Szmukler, C. Dare, & J. Treasure (Eds.), *Handbook of eating disorders: Theory, treatment, and research.* New York, NY: Wiley.

Russell, G. F. M. (2009). Anorexia nervosa. In M. C. Gelder, N. C. Andreasen, J. J. López-Ibor, Jr., & J. R. Geddes (Eds.). *New Oxford textbook of psychiatry* (2nd ed., Vol. 1). New York, NY: Oxford University Press.

Russell, J. A. (1991). Culture and the categorization of emotions. *Psychological Bulletin, 110,* 426-450.

Russell, J. A. (2007). Stress milestones. *Stress: The International Journal on the Biology of Stress, 10*(1), 1-2.

Russell, K. C. (2005). Two years later: A qualitative assessment of youth well-being and the role of aftercare in outdoor behavioral healthcare treatment. *Child and Youth Care Forum, 34*(3), 209-239.

Russo, N. F., & Denmark, F. L. (1987). Contributions of women to psychology. *Annual Review of Psychology, 38,* 279-298.

Rutherford, A. (2000). Radical behaviorism and psychology's public: B. F. Skinner in the popular press, 1934-1990. *History of Psychology, 3,* 371-395.

Rutherford, W. (1886). A new theory of hearing. *Journal of Anatomy and Physiology, 21,* 166-168.

Rutter, M. (2006). *Genes and behavior: Nature-nurture interplay explained.* Maiden, MA: Blackwell Publishing.

Rutter, M. (2007). Gene-environment interdependence. *Developmental Science, 10*(1), 12-18. doi:10.1111/j.1467-7687.2007.00557.x

Ryder, R. D. (2006). Speciesism in the laboratory. In P. Singer (Ed.), *In defense of animals: The second wave.* Malden, MA: Blackwell Publishing.

Sabanayagam, C., & Shankar, A. (2010). Sleep duration and cardiovascular disease: Results from the National Health Interview Survey. *Sleep: Journal of Sleep and Sleep Disorders Research, 33*(8), 1037-1042.

Sackeim, H. A., Dillingham, E. M., Prudic, J., Cooper, T., McCall, W. V., Rosenquist, P., et al. (2009). Effect of concomitant pharmacotherapy on electroconvulsive therapy outcomes: Short-term efficacy and adverse effects. *Archives of General Psychiatry, 66*(7), 729-737.

Sackeim, H. A., Haskett, R. F., Mulsant, B. H., Thase, M. E., Mann, J. J., Pettinati, H. M., Greenberg, R. M., Crowe, R. R., Cooper, T. B., & Prudic, J. (2001). Continuation pharmacotherapy in the prevention of relapse following electroconvulsive therapy: A randomized controlled trial. *Journal of the American Medical Association, 285,* 1299-1307.

Sackeim, H. A., Prudic, J., Fuller, R., Keilp, J., Lavori, P. W., & Olfson, M. (2007). The cognitive effects of electroconvulsive therapy in community settings. *Neuropsychopharmacology, 32,* 244-254.

Sacks, O. (1987). *The man who mistook his wife for a hat.* New York, NY: Harper & Row.

Sadker, M., & Sadker, D. (1994). *Failing at fairness: How America's schools cheat girls.* New York, NY: Scribners.

Sadler, J. Z. (2005). *Values and psychiatric diagnosis.* New York, NY: Oxford University Press.

Saks, A. M. (2006). Multiple predictions and criteria of job search success. *Journal of Vocational Behavior, 68,* 400-415.

Salthouse, T. A. (1996). The processing-speed theory of adult age differences in cognition. *Psychological Review, 103,* 403-428.

Salthouse, T. A. (2000). Aging and measures of processing speed. *Biological Psychology, 54,* 35-54.

Salthouse, T. A. (2003). Memory aging from 18-80. *Alzheimer Disease & Associated Disorders, 17*(3), 162-167.

Salthouse, T. A. (2004). What and when of cognitive aging. *Current Directions in Psychological Science, 13*(4), 140-144.

Salthouse, T. A. (2006). Mental exercise and mental aging. *Perspectives on Psychological Science, 1,* 68-87.

Salvy, S., Jarrin, D., Paluch, R., Irfan, N., & Pliner, P. (2007). Effects of social influence on eating in couples, friends and strangers. *Appetite, 49*(1), 92-99. doi:10.1016/j.appet.2006.12.004

Samberg, E., & Marcus, E. R. (2005). Process, resistance, and interpretation. In E. S. Person, A. M. Cooper, & G. O. Gabbard (Eds.), *Textbook of psychoanalysis.* Washington, DC: American Psychiatric Publishing.

Samnaliev, M., & Clark, R. E. (2008). The economics of schizophrenia. In K. T. Mueser & D. V. Jeste (Eds.), *Clinical handbook of schizophrenia* (pp. 25-34). New York, NY: Guilford.

Sanders, M. H., & Givelber, R. J. (2006). Overview of obstructive sleep apnea in adults. In T. Lee-Chiong (Ed.), *Sleep: A comprehensive handbook.* Hoboken, NJ: Wiley-Liss.

Sandin, B., Chorot, P., Santed, M. A., & Valiente, R. M. (2004). Differences in negative life events between patients with anxiety disorders, depression and hypochondriasis. *Anxiety, Stress & Coping: An International Journal, 17*(1), 37-47.

Sanger, D. J. (2004). The pharmacology and mechanisms of action of new generation, non-benzodiazepine hypnotic agents. *CNS Drugs, 18*(Suppl1), 9-15.

Sanna, L. J., & Schwarz, N. (2006). Metacognitive experiences and human judgment: The case of hindsight bias and its debiasing. *Current Directions in Psychological Science, 15,* 172-176.

Saper, C. B. (2000). Brain stem, reflexive behavior, and the cranial nerves. In E. R. Kandel, J. H. Schwartz, & T. M. Jessell (Eds.), *Principles of neural science* (pp. 873-888). New York, NY: McGraw-Hill.

Sapolsky, R. M. (2007). Stress, stress-related disease, and emotion regulation. In J. J. Gross (Ed.), *Handbook of emotion regulation.* New York, NY: Guilford.

Saunders, C. D. (2003). The emerging field of conservation psychology. *Human Ecology Review, 10,* 137-149.

Savin-Williams, R. C. (2006). Who's gay? Does it matter? *Current Directions in Psychological Science, 15,* 40-44.

Saxe, L., & Ben-Shakhar, G. (1999). Admissibility of polygraph tests: The application of scientific standards post-Daubert. *Psychology, Public Policy, and Law, 5,* 203-223.

Sayer, L. C. (2005). Gender, time, and inequality: Trends in women's and men's paid work, unpaid work, and free time. *Social Forces, 84,* 285–303.

Scarr, S., & Weinberg, R. A. (1977). Intellectual similarities within families of both adopted and biological children. *Intelligence, 32,* 170–190.

Scarr, S., & Weinberg, R. A. (1983). The Minnesota adoption studies: Genetic differences and malleability. *Child Development, 54,* 260–267.

Schachter, S. (1959). *The psychology of affiliation.* Stanford, CA: Stanford University Press.

Schachter, S. (1964). The interaction of cognitive and physiological determinants of emotional state. In L. Berkowitz (Ed.), *Advances in experimental social psychology* (Vol. 1). New York, NY: Academic Press.

Schachter, S., & Singer, J. E. (1962). Cognitive, social and physiological determinants of emotional state. *Psychological Review, 69,* 379–399.

Schachter, S., & Singer, J. E. (1979). Comments on the Maslach and Marshall-Zimbardo experiments. *Journal of Personality and Social Psychology, 37,* 989–995.

Schacter, D. L. (1996). *Searching for memory: The brain, the mind, and the past.* New York, NY: Basic Books.

Schacter, D. L. (1999). The seven sins of memory: Insights from psychology and cognitive neuroscience. *American Psychologist, 54,* 182–203.

Schacter, D. L. (2001). *The seven sins of memory: How the mind forgets and remembers.* Boston, MA: Houghton Mifflin.

Schaefer, A. (2005). Commuting takes its toll. *Scientific American Mind, 16*(3), 14–15.

Schaeffer, N. C. (2000). Asking questions about threatening topics: A selective overview. In A. A. Stone, J. S. Turkkan, C. A. Bachrach, J. B. Jobe, H. S. Kurtzman, & V. Cain (Eds.), *The science of self-report: Implications for research and practice.* Mahwah, NJ: Erlbaum.

Schafe, G. E., & Bernstein, I. E. (1996). Taste aversion learning. In E. D. Capaldi (Ed.), *Why we eat what we eat: The psychology of eating* (pp. 31–52). Washington, DC: American Psychological Association.

Schellenberg, E. (2004). Music lessons enhance IQ. *Psychological Science, 15*(8), 511–514. doi:10.1111/j.0956-7976.2004.00711.x

Schellenberg, E. (2005). Music and cognitive abilities. *Current Directions in Psychological Science, 14*(6), 317–320. doi:10.1111/j.0963-7214.2005.00389.x

Schellenberg, E. (2006). Long-term positive associations between music lessons and IQ. *Journal of Educational Psychology, 98*(2), 457–468. doi:10.1037/0022-0663.98.2.457

Schieber, F. (2006). Vision and aging. In J. E. Birren & K. W. Schaie (Eds.), *Handbook of the psychology of aging.* San Diego, CA: Academic Press.

Schiffman, J., Ekstrom, M., LaBrie, J., Schulsinger, F., Sorenson, H., & Mednick, S. (2002). Minor physical anomalies and schizophrenia spectrum disorders: A prospective investigation. *American Journal of Psychiatry, 159,* 238–243.

Schimmack, U., & Crites, S. L. (2005). The structure of affect. In D. Albarracin, B. T. Johnson, & M. P. Zanna (Eds.), *The handbook of attitudes.* Mahwah, NJ: Erlbaum.

Schirillo, J. A. (2010). Gestalt approach. In E. B. Goldstein (Ed.), *Encyclopedia of perception.* Thousand Oaks, CA: Sage.

Schlapobersky, J., & Pines, M. (2009). Group methods in adult psychiatry. In M. C. Gelder, N. C. Andreasen, J. J. López-Ibor, Jr., & J. R. Geddes (Eds.), *New Oxford textbook of psychiatry* (2nd ed., Vol. 1). New York, NY: Oxford University Press.

Schmeichel, B. J., Gailliot, M. T., Filardo, E., McGregor, I., Gitter, S., & Baumeister, R. F. (2009). Terror management theory and self-esteem revisited: The roles of implicit and explicit self-esteem in mortality salience effects. *Journal of Personality and Social Psychology, 96*(5), 1077–1087. doi:10.1037/a0015091

Schmidt, F. L. (2002). The role of general cognitive ability and job performance: Why there cannot be a debate. *Human Performance, 15,* 187–210.

Schmidt, F. L., & Hunter, J. (2004). General mental ability in the world of work: Occupational attainment and job performance. *Journal of Personality and Social Psychology, 86,* 162–173.

Schmitt, D. P. (2005). Fundamentals of human mating strategies. In D. M. Buss (Ed.), *The handbook of evolutionary psychology.* New York, NY: Wiley.

Schmitt, D. P., & International Sexuality Description Project. (2003). Universal sex differences in the desire for sexual variety: Tests from 52 nations, 6 continents, and 13 islands. *Journal of Personality and Social Psychology, 85,* 85–104.

Schmitz, J. M., & DeLaune, K. A. (2005). Nicotine. In J. H. Lowinson, P. Ruiz, R. B. Millman, & J. G. Langrod (Eds.), *Substance abuse: A comprehensive textbook.* Philadelphia, PA: Lippincott Williams & Williams.

Schmolck, H., Buffalo, E. A., & Squire, L. R. (2000). Memory distortions develop over time: Recollections of the O. J. Simpson trial verdict after 15 and 32 months. *Psychological Science, 11,* 39–45.

Schmuck, P. & Schultz, P. W. (2002). Sustainable development as a challenge for psychology. In P. Schmuck & P. W. Schultz (Eds.), *Psychology of Sustainable Development* (pp. 3–17). Boston, MA: Kluwer Academic Publishers.

Schnittker, J. (2008). An uncertain revolution: Why the rise of a genetic model of mental illness has not increased tolerance. *Social Science & Medicine, 67*(9), 1370–1381. doi:10.1016/j.socscimed.2008.07.007

Schnoll, R., Martinez, E., Tatum, K., Glass, M., Bernath, A., Ferris, D., & Reynolds, P. (2011). Increased self-efficacy to quit and perceived control over withdrawal symptoms predict smoking cessation following nicotine dependence treatment. *Addictive Behaviors, 36*(1–2), 144–147.

Schooler, C. (2007). Use it—and keep it, longer, probably: A reply to Salthouse. *Perspectives on Psychological Science, 2,* 24–29.

Schramm, D. G., Marshall, J. P., Harris, V. W., & Lee, T. R. (2005). After "I do": The newlywed transition. *Marriage and Family Review, 38,* 45–67.

Schultz, J. H., & Luthe, W. (1959). *Autogenic training.* New York, NY: Grune & Stratton.

Schultz, P. W. (2000). Empathizing with nature: The effects of perspective taking on concern for environmental issues. *Journal of Social Issues, 56,* 391406.

Schultz, P. W. (2001). The structure of environmental concern: Concern for self, other people, and the biosphere. *Journal of Environmental Psychology, 21,* 1–13.

Schultz, P. W., Gouveia, V. V., Cameron, L. D., Tankha, G., Schmuck, P., & Franek, M. (2005). Values and their relationship to environmental concern and conservation behavior. *Journal of Cross-Cultural Psychology, 36,* 457–475.

Schulz-Hardt, S., Frey, D., Luethgens, C., & Moscovici, S. (2000). Biased information search in group decision making. *Journal of Personality & Social Psychology, 78,* 655–669.

Schuman, H., & Kalton, G. (1985). Survey methods. In G. Lindzey & E. Aronson (Eds.), *Handbook of social psychology* (3rd ed.). New York, NY: Random House.

Schumann, C. M., & Amaral, D. G. (2006). Stereological analysis of amygdale neuron number in autism. *Journal of Neuroscience, 26,* 7674–7679.

Schwartz, B. (2004). *The paradox of choice: Why more is less.* New York, NY: Ecco.

Schwartz, B., & Robbins, S. J. (1995). *Psychology of learning and behavior* (4th ed.). New York, NY: Norton.

Schwartz, B. L. (1999). Sparkling at the end of the tongue: The etiology of tip-of-the-tongue phenomenology. *Psychonomic Bulletin & Review, 6,* 379–393.

Schwartz, B. L. (2002). *Tip-of-the-tongue states: Phenomenology, mechanism, and lexical retrieval.* Mahwah, NJ: Erlbaum.

Schwartz, G. L., & Azzara, A. V. (2004). Sensory neurobiological analysis of neuropeptide modulation of meal size. *Physiology & Behavior, 82,* 81–87.

Schwartz, L., Slater, M. A., & Birchler, G. R. (1994). Interpersonal stress and pain behaviors in patients with chronic pain. *Journal of Consulting and Clinical Psychology, 62,* 861–864.

Schwartz, M. W., Woods, S. C., Porte, D., Seeley, R. J., & Baskin, D. G. (2000). Central nervous system control of food intake. *Nature, 404,* 661–671.

Schwarz, N. (1999). Self-reports: How the questions shape the answers. *American Psychologist, 54,* 93–105.

Schwarz, N., & Strack, F. (1999). Reports of subjective well-being: Judgmental processes and their methodological implications. In D. Kahneman, E. Diener, & N. Schwarz (Eds.), *Well-being: The foundations of hedonic psychology.* New York, NY: Russell Sage Foundation.

Schwarz, T. L. (2008). Release of neurotransmitters. In L. Squire, D. Berg, F. Bloom, S. Du Lac, A. Ghosh, & N. Spitzer (Eds.), *Fundamental neuroscience* (3rd ed., pp. 157–180). San Diego, CA: Elsevier.

Scoboria, A., Mazzoni, G., Kirsch, I., & Milling, L. S. (2002). Immediate and persisting effects of misleading questions and hypnosis on memory reports. *Journal of Experimental Psychology: Applied, 8*(1), 26–32. doi:10.1037/1076-898X.8.1.26

Scott, K. (2008). Chemical senses: Taste and olfaction. In L. Squire, D. Berg, F. Bloom, S. du Lac, A. Ghosh, & N. Spitzer (Eds.), *Fundamental Neuroscience.* San Diego, CA: Elsevier.

Scott, V., McDade, D. M., & Luckman, S. M. (2007). Rapid changes in the sensitivity of arcuate nucleus neurons to central ghrelin in relation to feeding status. *Physiology & Behavior, 90,* 180–185.

Scoville, W. B., & Milner, B. (1957). Loss of recent memory after bilateral hippocampal lesions. *Journal of Neurology, Neurosurgery & Psychiatry, 20,* 11–21.

Scull, A. (1990). Deinstitutionalization: Cycles of despair. *The Journal of Mind and Behavior, 11*(3/4), 301–312.

Scully, J. A., Tosi, H., & Banning, K. (2000). Life event checklists: Revisiting the social readjustment rating scale after 30 years. *Educational & Psychological Measurement, 60,* 864–876.

Searleman, A. (1996). Personality variables and prospective memory performance. In D. J. Herrmann, C. McEvoy, C. Hertzog, P. Hertel, & M. K. Johnson (Eds.), *Basic and applied memory research: Practical applications* (Vol. 2). Mahwah, NJ: Erlbaum.

Searleman, A., & Herrmann, D. (1994). *Memory from a broader perspective.* New York, NY: McGraw-Hill.

Sears, D. O. (1975). Political socialization. In F. I. Greenstein & N. W. Polsby (Eds.), *Handbook of political science* (Vol. 2). Reading, MA: Addison-Wesley.

Sedikides, C., & Strube, M. J. (1997). Self-evaluation: To thine own self be good, to thine own self be sure, to thine own self be true, and to thine own self be better. In M. P. Zanna (Ed.), *Advances in experimental social psychology.* New York, NY: Academic Press.

Seery, M. D., Holman, E., & Silver, R. (2010). Whatever does not kill us: Cumulative lifetime adversity, vulnerability, and resilience. *Journal of Personality and Social Psychology, 99*(6), 1025–1041. doi:10.1037/a0021344

Segall, M. H., Campbell, D. T., Herskovits, M. J. (1966). *The influence of culture on visual perception.* Indianapolis: Bobbs-Merrill.

Segall, M. H., Dasen, P. R., Berry, J. W., & Poortinga, Y. H. (1990). *Human behavior in global perspective: An introduction to cross-cultural psychology.* New York, NY: Pergamon Press.

Segerstrom, S. C., & Sephton, S. E. (2010). Optimistic expectancies and cell-mediated immunity: The role of positive affect. *Psychological Science, 21*(3), 448–455. doi:10.1177/0956797610362061

Seifer, R. (2001). Socioeconomic status, multiple risks, and development of intelligence. In R. J. Sternberg & E. L. Grigorenko (Eds.), *Environmental effects on cognitive abilities* (pp. 59–82). Mahwah, NJ: Erlbaum.

Seligman, M. E. P. (1971). Phobias and preparedness. *Behavior Therapy, 2,* 307–321.

Seligman, M. E. P. (1974). Depression and learned helplessness. In R. J. Friedman & M. M. Katz (Eds.), *The psychology of depression: Contemporary theory and research.* New York, NY: Wiley.

Seligman, M. E. P. (1990). *Learned optimism.* New York, NY: Pocket Books.

Seligman, M. E. P. (1992). *Helplessness: On depression, development, and death.* New York, NY: Freeman.

Seligman, M. E. P. (1995). The effectiveness of psychotherapy. *American Psychologist, 50,* 965–974.

Seligman, M. E. P. (2003). The past and future of positive psychology. In C. L. M. Keyes & J. Haidt (Eds.), *Flourishing: Positive psychology and the life well-lived.* Washington, DC: American Psychological Association.

Seligman, M. E. P., & Csikszentmihalyi, M. (2000). Positive psychology: An introduction. *American Psychologist, 55,* 5–14.

Seligman, M. E. P., & Hager, J. L. (1972, August). Biological boundaries of learning (the sauce béarnaise syndrome). *Psychology Today,* pp. 59–61, 84–87.

Selye, H. (1936). A syndrome produced by diverse nocuous agents. *Nature, 138,* 32.

Selye, H. (1956). *The stress of life.* New York, NY: McGraw-Hill.

Selye, H. (1973). The evolution of the stress concept. *American Scientist, 61*(6), 672–699.

Selye, H. (1974). *Stress without distress.* New York, NY: Lippincott.

Selye, H. (1982). History and present status of the stress concept. In L. Goldberger & S. Breznitz (Eds.), *Handbook of stress: Theoretical and clinical aspects.* New York, NY: Free Press.

Senior, C., Thomson, K., Badger, J., & Butler, M. J. R. (2007). Interviewing strategies in the face of beauty: A psychophysiological investigation into the job negotiation process. *Annals of the New York Academy of Sciences, 1118,* 142–162.

Serper, M. R. (2011). Aggression in schizophrenia. *Schizophrenia Bulletin, 37*(Suppl 5), 897–898. doi:10.1093/schbul/sbr090

Seta, J. J., Seta, C. E., & McElroy, T. (2002). Strategies for reducing the stress of negative life experiences: An average/summation analysis. *Personality and Social Psychology Bulletin, 28,* 1574–1585.

Shackelford, T. K., Schmitt, D. P., & Buss, D. M. (2005). Universal dimensions of human mate preferences. *Personality & Individual Differences, 39,* 447–458.

Shafir, E., & LeBoeuf, R. A. (2002). Rationality. *Annual Review of Psychology, 53,* 491–517.

Shank, R. P., Smith-Swintosky, V. L., & Twyman, R. E. (2000). Amino acid neurotransmitters. In B. J. Sadock & V. A. Sadock (Eds.), *Kaplan & Sadock's comprehensive textbook of psychiatry* (Vol. 1). New York, NY: Lippincott Williams & Wilkins.

Shapiro, D. H., Jr. (1984). Overview: Clinical and physiological comparison of meditation with other self-control strategies. In D. H. Shapiro, Jr., & R. N. Walsh (Eds.), *Meditation: Classic and contemporary perspectives.* New York, NY: Aldine.

Sharpe, D., Adair, J. G., & Roese, N. J. (1992). Twenty years of deception research: A decline in subjects' trust? *Personality and Social Psychology Bulletin, 18,* 585–590.

Sharps, M. J., & Wertheimer, M. (2000). Gestalt perspectives on cognitive science and on experimental psychology. *Review of General Psychology, 4,* 315–336.

Shattuck, P. T. (2006). The contribution of diagnostic substitution to the growing administrative prevalence of autism in U.S. special education. *Pediatrics, 117,* 1028–1037.

Shatz, C. J. (1992, September). The developing brain. *Scientific American,* 60–67.

Shaver, P. R., & Mikulincer, M. (2006). A behavioral systems approach to romantic love relationships: Attachment, caregiving, and sex. In R. J. Sternberg & K. Weis (Eds.), *The new psychology of love.* New Haven, CT: Yale University Press.

Shaver, P. R., Schachner, D. A., & Mikulincer, M. (2005). Attachment style, excessive reassurance seeking, relationship processes, and depression. *Personality and Social Psychology Bulletin, 31*(3), 343–359.

Shavitt, S., Sanbonmatsu, D. M., Smittipatana, S., & Posavac, S. S. (1999). Broadening the conditions for illusory correlation formation: Implications for judging minority groups. *Basic & Applied Social Psychology, 21,* 263–279.

Shaw, J. S. I., McClure, K. A., & Dykstra, J. A. (2007). Eyewitness confidence from the witnessed event through trial. In M. P. Toglia, J. D. Read, D. F. Ross, & R. C. L. Lindsay (Eds.), *Handbook of eyewitness psychology: Vol. 1. Memory for events.* Mahwah, NJ: Erlbaum.

Shea, A. K., & Steiner, M. (2008). Cigarette smoking during pregnancy. *Nicotine & Tobacco Research, 10,* 267–278.

Shear, J., & Jevning, R. (1999). Pure consciousness: Scientific exploration of meditation techniques. *Journal of Consciousness Studies, 6,* 189–209.

Shearer, B. (2004). Multiple intelligences theory after 20 years. *Teachers College Record, 106*(1), 2–16.

Shedler, J. (2010). The efficacy of psychodynamic psychotherapy. *American Psychologist, 65*(2), 98–109. doi:10.1037/a0018378

Sheehan, S. (1982). *Is there no place on earth for me?* Boston, MA: Houghton Mifflin.

Sheldon, K. M., & Kasser, T. (2001). Goals, congruence, and positive well-being: New empirical support for humanistic theories. *Journal of Humanistic Psychology, 41*(1), 30–50.

Shelton, J. T., Elliott, E. M., Hill, B. D., Calamia, M. R., & Gouvier, W. (2009). A comparison of laboratory and clinical working memory tests and their prediction of fluid intelligence. *Intelligence, 37*(3), 283–293. doi:10.1016/j.intell.2008.11.005

Shelton, J. T., Elliott, E. M., Matthews, R. A., Hill, B. D., & Gouvier, W. (2010). The relationships of working memory, secondary memory, and general fluid intelligence: Working memory is special. *Journal of Experimental Psychology: Learning, Memory, and Cognition, 36*(3), 813–820. doi:10.1037/a0019046

Shenton, M. E., & Kubicki, M. (2009). Structural brain imaging in schizophrenia. In B. J. Sadock, V. A. Sadock, & P. Ruiz (Eds.), *Kaplan & Sadock's comprehensive textbook of psychiatry* (9th ed., Vol. 1, pp. 1494–1506). Philadelphia, PA: Lippincott Williams & Wilkins.

Shepard, R. N. (1990). *Mind sights.* New York, NY: W. H. Freeman.

Shepherd, G. M. (2004). The human sense of smell: Are we better than we think? *PLoS Biology, 2*(5), 0572–0575. doi:10.1371/journal.pbio.0020146

Shepperd, J., Malone, W., & Sweeny, K. (2008). Exploring causes of the self-serving bias. *Social and Personality Psychology Compass, 2,* 895–908.

Sherif, M., Harvey, O., White, B., Hood, W., & Sherif, C. (1961). *Intergroup conflict and cooperation: The Robber's Cave experiment.* Norman: University of Oklahoma, Institute of Group Behavior.

Sherman, D. K., Nelson, L. D., & Ross, L. D. (2003). Naive realism and affirmative action: Adversaries are more similar than they think. *Basic and Applied Social Psychology, 25,* 275–289.

Sherman, M., & Key, C. B. (1932). The intelligence of isolated mountain children. *Child Development, 3,* 279–290.

Shermer, M. (2004, March). None so blind. *Scientific American,* p. 42.

Shimamura, A. P., Berry, J. M., Mangels, J. A., Rusting, C. L., & Jurica, P. J. (1995). Memory and cognitive abilities in university professors: Evidence for successful aging. *Psychological Science, 6,* 271–277.

Shimp, T. A., Stuart, E. W., & Engle, R. W. (1991). A program of classical conditioning experiments testing variations in the conditioned stimulus and context. *Journal of Consumer Research, 18,* 1–12.

Shiue, Y., Chiu, C., & Chang, C. (2010). Exploring and mitigating social loafing in online communities. *Computers in Human Behavior, 26*(4), 768–777. doi:10.1016/j.chb.2010.01.014

Shobe, K. K., & Schooler, J. W. (2001). Discovering fact and fiction: Case-based analyses of authentic and fabricated discovered memories of abuse. In G. M. Davies & T. Dalgleish (Eds.), *Recovered memories: Seeking the middle ground.* Chichester, England: Wiley.

Shrager, Y. & Squire, L. R. (2009). Medial temporal lobe function and human memory. In M. S. Gazzaniga (Ed.) The cognitive neurosciences (4th ed., pp. 675–690). Cambridge, MA: MIT Press.

Siegel, J. M. (2004). The neurotransmitters of sleep. *Journal of Clinical Psychiatry, 65*(Suppl16), 4–7.

Siegel, M. (2007, August, 28). New Orleans still facing a psychiatric emergency. *The Globe and Mail (Canada),* A17.

Siegler, R. S. (1992). The other Alfred Binet. *Developmental Psychology, 28,* 179–190.

Sigel, I. E. (2004). Head Start—Revisiting a historical psychoeducational intervention: A revisionist perspective. In E. Zigler & S. J. Styfco (Eds.), *The Head Start debate.* Baltimore, MD: Paul H. Brookes Publishing.

Sigman, M., & Whaley, S. E. (1998). The role of nutrition in the development of intelligence. In U. Neisser (Ed.), *The rising curve: Long-term gains in IQ and related measures.* Washington, DC: American Psychological Association.

Signorielli, N. (2001). Television's gender role images and contribution to stereotyping: Past present future. In D. G. Singer & J. L. Singer (Eds.), *Handbook of children and the media.* Thousand Oaks, CA: Sage.

Signorielli, N., McLeod, D., & Healy, E. (1994). Gender stereotypes in MTV commercials: The beat goes on. *Journal of Broadcasting & Electronic Media, 38,* 91–101.

Silver, E., Cirincion, C., & Steadman, H. J. (1994). Demythologizing inaccurate perceptions of the insanity defense. *Law & Human Behavior, 18,* 63–70.

Silverman, I., & Choi, J. (2005). Locating places. In D. M. Buss (Ed.), *The handbook of evolutionary psychology.* New York, NY: Wiley.

Silverman, I., Choi, J., Mackewn, A., Fisher, M., Moro, J., & Olshansky, E. (2000). Evolved mechanisms underlying wayfinding: Further studies on the hunter-gatherer theory of spatial sex differences. *Evolution and Human Behavior, 21,* 201–213.

Silverman, I., & Eals, M. (1992). Sex differences in spatial ability: Evolutionary theory and data. In J. Barkow, L. Cosmides, & J. Tooby (Eds.), *The adapted mind.* New York, NY: Oxford University Press.

Silverman, I., & Phillips, K. (1998). The evolutionary psychology of spatial sex differences. In C. Crawford & D.L. Krebs (Eds.), *Handbook of evolutionary psychology: Ideas, issues, and applications.* Mahwah, NJ: Erlbaum.

Silverstein, L. B., & Auerbach, C. F. (1999). Deconstructing the essential father. *American Psychologist, 54,* 397–407.

Silvia, P. J. (2008). Another look at creativity and intelligence: Exploring higher-order models and probable confounds. *Personality and Individual Differences, 44,* 1012–1021.

Silvia, P. J., & Kaufman, J. C. (2010). Creativity and mental illness. In J. C. Kaufman & R. J. Sternberg (Eds.), *The Cambridge handbook of creativity* (pp. 381–394). New York, NY: Cambridge University Press.

Simeon, D., Loewenstein, R. J. (2009). Dissociative disorders. In B. J. Sadock, V. A. Sadock, & P. Ruiz (Eds.), *Kaplan & Sadock's comprehensive textbook of psychiatry* (9th ed., pp. 1965–2026). Philadelphia, PA: Lippincott Williams & Wilkins.

Simon, G. E., & Savarino, J. (2007). Suicide attempts among patients starting depression treatment with medications or psychotherapy. *American Journal of Psychiatry, 164,* 1029–1034.

Simon, G. E., Savarino, J., Operskalski, B., & Wang, P. S. (2006). Suicide risk during antidepressant treatment. *American Journal of Psychiatry, 163,* 41–47.

Simon, H. A. (1957). *Models of man.* New York, NY: Wiley.

Simon, H. A. (1974). How big is a chunk? *Science, 183,* 482–488.

Simons, D. K., & Chabris, C. F. (1999). Gorillas in our midst: Sustained inattentional blindness for dynamic events. *Perception, 28,* 1059–1074.

Simonsohn, U. (2009). Direct risk aversion: Evidence from risky prospects valued below their worst outcome. *Psychological Science, 20*(6), 686–692. doi:10.1111/j.1467-9280.2009.02349.x

Simpson, J. L., & Jauniaux, E. (2007). Pregnancy loss. In S. G. Gabbe, J. R. Niebyl, & J. L. Simpson (Eds.) *Obstetrics: Normal and problem pregnancies* (5th ed., pp. 628–649). Philadelphia, PA: Elsevier.

Sinclair, D. (1981). *Mechanisms of cutaneous stimulation.* Oxford, England: Oxford University Press.

Sinclair, S., Dunn, R., & Lowery, B. S. (2005). The relationship between parental racial attitudes and children's implicit prejudice. *Journal of Experimental Social Psychology, 41,* 283–289.

Singer, L. T., Arendt, R., Minnes, S., Farkas, K., Salvator, A., Kirchner, H. L., & Kliegman, R. (2002). Cognitive and motor outcomes of cocaine-exposed infants. *Journal of the American Medical Association, 287,* 1952–1960.

Singer, W. (2007). Large-scale temporal coordination of cortical activity as a prerequisite for conscious experience. In M. Velmans & S. Schneider (Eds.), *The Blackwell companion to consciousness.* Malden, MA: Blackwell Publishing.

Sinha, D. (1983). Human assessment in the Indian context. In S. H. Irvine & J. W. Berry (Eds.), *Human assessment and cultural factors.* New York, NY: Plenum.

Sio, U., & Ormerod, T. C. (2009). Does incubation enhance problem solving? A meta-analytic review. *Psychological Bulletin, 135*(1), 94–120. doi:10.1037/a0014212

Sivertsen, B., Omvik, S., Pallesen, S., Bjorvatn, B., Havik, O. E., Kvale, G., et al. (2006). Cognitive behavioral therapy vs. Zopiclone for treatment of chronic primary insomnia in older adults: A randomized controlled trial. *Journal of the American Medical Association, 295,* 2851–2858.

SJB. (2006, March 6). Overcoming problem gambling [Why?]. Message posted to http://www .gamcare.org.uk/forum/index.php?tid=7193.

Skinner, A. E. G. (2001). Recovered memories of abuse: Effects on the individual. In G. M. Davies & T. Dalgleish (Eds.), *Recovered memories: Seeking the middle ground.* Chichester, England: Wiley & Sons.

Skinner, B. F. (1938). *The behavior of organisms.* New York, NY: Appleton-Century-Crofts.

Skinner, B. F. (1945, October). Baby in a box: The mechanical baby-tender. *Ladies' Home Journal,* pp. 30–31, 135–136, 138.

Skinner, B. F. (1948). Superstition in the pigeon. *Journal of Experimental Psychology, 38,* 168–172. doi:10.1037/0096-3445.121.3.273

Skinner, B. F. (1953). *Science and human behavior.* New York, NY: Macmillan.

Skinner, B. F. (1957). *Verbal behavior.* New York, NY: Appleton-Century-Crofts.

Skinner, B. F. (1969). *Contingencies of reinforcement.* New York, NY: Appleton-Century-Crofts.

Skinner, B. F. (1971). *Beyond freedom and dignity.* New York, NY: Knopf.

Skinner, B. F. (1984). Selection by consequences. *Behavioral and Brain Sciences, 7*(4), 477–510.

Skinner, B. F. (1987). *Upon further reflection.* Englewood Cliffs, NJ: Prentice-Hall.

Slamecka, N. J. (1985). Ebbinghaus: Some associations. *Journal of Experimental Psychology: Learning, Memory and Cognition, 11,* 414–435.

Slamecka, N. J. (1992). Forgetting. In L. R. Squire (Ed.), *Encyclopedia of learning and memory.* New York, NY: Macmillan.

Slatcher, R. B., & Pennebaker, J. W. (2005). Emotional processing of traumatic events. In C. L. Cooper (Ed.), *Handbook of stress medicine and health.* Boca Raton, FL: CRC Press.

Slater, E., & Shields, J. (1969). Genetical aspects of anxiety. In M. H. Lader (Ed.), *Studies of anxiety.* Ashford, England: Headley Brothers.

Slaughter, M. (1990). The vertebrate retina. In K. N. Leibovic (Ed.), *Science of vision.* New York, NY: Springer-Verlag.

Slobin, D. I. (1985). *A cross-linguistic study of language acquisition.* Hillsdale, NJ: Erlbaum.

Slobin, D. I. (1992). *The crosslinguistic study of language acquisition.* Hillsdale, NJ: Erlbaum.

Sloman, S. A. (2002). Two systems of reasoning. In T. Gilovich, D. Griffin, & D. Kahneman (Eds.), *Heuristics and biases.* New York, NY: Cambridge University Press.

Slovic, P., & Fischhoff, B. (1977). On the psychology of experimental surprises. *Journal of Experimental Psychology: Human Perception and Performance, 3,* 544–551.

Slovic, P., Finucane, M. L., Peters, E., & MacGregor, D. G. (2004). Risk as analysis and risk as feelings: Some thoughts about affect, reason, risk, and rationality. *Risk Analysis, 24,* 311–322.

Slovic, P., Fischhoff, B., & Lichtenstein, S. (1982). Facts versus fears: Understanding perceived risk. In D. Kahneman, P. Slovic, &

A. Tversky (Eds.), *Judgment under uncertainty: Heuristics and biases.* Cambridge, England: Cambridge University Press.

Smedley, S. R., & Eisner, T. (1996). Sodium: A male moth's gift to its offspring. *Proceedings of the National Academy of Sciences, 93,* 809–813.

Smetana, J. G., Campione, B. N., & Metzger, A. (2006). Adolescent development in interpersonal and societal contexts. *Annual Review of Psychology, 57,* 255–284.

Smith, C. A., & Lazarus, R. S. (1993). Appraisal components, core relational themes, and the emotions. *Cognition and Emotion, 7,* 233–269.

Smith, C. P. (1992). Reliability issues. In C. P. Smith (Ed.), *Motivation and personality: Handbook of thematic content analysis.* New York, NY: Cambridge University Press.

Smith, D. A. (1999). The end of theoretical orientations? *Applied & Preventative Psychology, 8,* 269–280.

Smith, F. J., & Campfield, L. A. (1993). Meal initiation occurs after experimental induction of transient declines in blood glucose. *American Journal of Physiology, 265,* 1423–1429.

Smith, G., Housen, P., Yaffe, K., Ruff, R., Kennison, R., Mahncke, H., & Zelinski, E. (2009). A cognitive training program based on principles of brain plasticity: Results from the Improvement in Memory with Plasticity-based Adaptive Cognitive Training (IMPACT) study. *Journal of the American Geriatrics Society, 57*(4), 594–603. doi:10.1111/j.1532-5415.2008.02167.x

Smith, G. T., Spillane, N. S., & Annus, A. M. (2006). Implications of an emerging integration of universal and culturally specific psychologies. *Perspectives on Psychological Science, 1,* 211–233.

Smith, J. C. (1975). Meditation and psychotherapy: A review of the literature. *Psychological Bulletin, 32,* 553–564.

Smith, J. C. (2007). The psychology of relaxation. In P. M. Lehrer, R. L. Woolfolk, & W. E. Sime (Eds.), *Principles and practice of stress management.* New York, NY: Guilford.

Smith, M. L., & Glass, G. V. (1977). Meta-analysis of psychotherapy outcome studies. *American Psychologist, 32,* 752–760.

Smith, M. R., Fogg, L. F., & Eastman, C. I. (2009). A compromise circadian phase position for permanent night work improves mood, fatigue, and performance. *Sleep: Journal of Sleep and Sleep Disorders Research, 32*(11), 1481–1489.

Smith, P. B. (2001). Cross-cultural studies of social influence. In D. Matsumoto (Ed.), *The handbook of culture and psychology.* New York, NY: Oxford University Press.

Smith, P. B., & Bond, M. H. (1994). *Social psychology across cultures: Analysis and perspectives.* Boston, MA: Allyn & Bacon.

Smith, S. (1988). Environmental context-dependent memory. In G. M. Davies & D. M. Thomson (Eds.), *Memory in context: Context in memory.* New York, NY: Wiley.

Smith, S. M. (1995). Getting into and out of mental ruts: A theory of fixation, incubation, and insight. In R. J. Sternberg & J. E. Davidson

(Eds.), *The nature of insight* (pp. 229–251). Cambridge, MA: MIT Press.

Smith, S. M., & Gleaves, D. H. (2007). Recovered memories. In M. P. Toglia, J. D. Read, D. F. Ross, & R. C. L. Lindsay (Eds.), *Handbook of eyewitness psychology: Volume 1. Memory for events.* Mahwah, NJ: Erlbaum.

Smith, S. M., McIntosh, W. D., & Bazzini, D. G. (1999). Are the beautiful good in Hollywood? An investigation of the beauty-and-goodness stereotype on film. *Basic & Applied Social Psychology, 21,* 69–80.

Smith, T. W., & Gallo, L. C. (2001). Personality traits as risk factors for physical illness. In A. Baum, T. A. Revenson, & J. E. Singer (Eds.), *Handbook of health psychology* (pp. 139–174). Mahwah, NJ: Erlbaum.

Smolak, L., & Murnen, S. K. (2001). Gender and eating problems. In R. H. Striegel-Moore & L. Smolak (Eds.), *Eating disorders: Innovative directions in research and practice* (pp. 91–110). Washington, DC: American Psychological Association.

Smyth, J. M., & Pennebaker, J. W. (1999). Sharing one's story: Translating emotional experiences into words as a coping tool. In C. R. Snyder (Ed.), *Coping: The psychology of what works.* New York, NY: Oxford University Press.

Smyth, J. M., & Pennebaker, J. W. (2001). What are the health effects of disclosure? In A. Baum, T. A. Revenson & J. E. Singer (Eds.), *Handbook of health psychology* (pp. 339–348). Mahwah, NJ: Erlbaum.

Snedecor, S. M., Pomerleau, C. S., Mehringer, A. M., Ninowski, R., & Pomerleau, O. F. (2006). Differences in smoking-related variables based on phenylthiocabamide "taster" status. *Addictive Behaviors, 31,* 2309–2312.

Snow, R. E. (1986). Individual differences in the design of educational programs. *American Psychologist, 41,* 1029–1039.

Snowden, L. R., & Hu, T. W. (1996). Outpatient service use in minority-serving mental health programs. *Administration and Policy in Mental Health, 24,* 149–159.

Snowden, L. R., & Yamada, A. (2005). Cultural differences in access to care. *Annual Review of Clinical Psychology, 1,* 143–166.

Solberg, E. C., Diener, E., Wirtz, D., Lucas, R. E., & Oishi, S. (2002). Wanting, having, and satisfaction: Examining the role of desire discrepancies in satisfaction with income. *Journal of Personality and Social Psychology, 83,* 725–734.

Soldatos, C. R., Allaert, F. A., Ohta, T., & Dikeos, D. G. (2005). How do individuals sleep around the world? Results from a single-day survey in ten countries. *Sleep Medicine, 6,* 5–13.

Solms, M. (2004). Freud returns. *Scientific American, 290*(5), 83–88.

Solomon, S., Greenberg, J., & Pyszczynski, T. (1991). A terror management theory of social behavior: The psychological functions of self-esteem and cultural worldviews. In M. Zanna (Ed.), *Advances in experimental social psychology* (Vol. 24). Orlando, FL: Academic Press.

Solomon, S., Greenberg, J., & Pyszczynski, T. (2004a). Lethal consumption: Death-denying materialism. In T. Kasser & A. D. Kanner (Eds.), *Psychology and consumer culture: The struggle for a good life in a materialistic world.* Washington, DC: American Psychological Association.

Solomon, S., Greenberg, J., & Pyszczynski, T. (2004b). The cultural animal: Twenty years of terror management. In J. Greenberg, S. L. Koole, & T. Pyszczynski (Eds.), *Handbook of experimental existential psychology.* New York, NY: Guilford.

Solso, R. L. (1994). *Cognition and the visual arts.* Cambridge, MA: MIT Press.

Sommer, I. E., Aleman, A., Somers, M., Boks, M. P., & Kahn, R. S. (2008). Sex differences in handedness, asymmetry of the planum temporale and functional language lateralization. *Brain Research, 1206*, 76–88. doi:10.1016/j.brainres.2008.01.003

Song, S., Sjostrom, P. J., Reigl, M., Nelson, S., & Chklovskii, D. B. (2005). Highly nonrandom features of synaptic connectivity in local cortical circuits. *PLoS Biol, 3*(3), 1–13.

Spangler, W. D. (1992). Validity of questionnaire and TAT measures of need for achievement: Two meta-analyses. *Psychological Bulletin, 112*, 140–154.

Spanos, N. P. (1991). A sociocognitive approach to hypnosis. In S. J. Lynn & J. W. Rhue (Eds.), *Theories of hypnosis: Current models and perspectives* (pp. 324–361). New York, NY: Guilford.

Spanos, N. P. (1994). Multiple identity enactments and multiple personality disorder: A sociocognitive perspective. *Psychological Bulletin, 116*, 143–165.

Spanos, N. P. (1996). *Multiple identities and false memories.* Washington, DC: American Psychological Association.

Spear, J. H. (2007). Prominent schools or other active specialties? A fresh look at some trends in psychology. *Review of General Psychology, 11*(4), 363–380. doi:10.1037/1089-2680.11.4.363

Speed, A., & Gangestad, S. W. (1997). Romantic popularity and mate preferences: A peer-nomination study. *Personality and Social Psychology Bulletin, 23*, 928–936.

Spelke, E. S., & Kinzler, K. D. (2007). Core knowledge. *Developmental Science, 10*(1), 89–96.

Spelke, E. S., & Newport, E. L. (1998). Nativism, empiricism, and the development of knowledge. In W. Damon (Ed.), *Handbook of child psychology (Vol. 1): Theoretical models of human development.* New York, NY: Wiley.

Spence, I., Wong, P., Rusan, M., & Rastegar, N. (2006). How color enhances visual memory for natural scenes. *Psychological Science, 14*(1), 1–6.

Sperling, G. (1960). The information available in brief visual presentations. *Psychological Monographs, 74*(11, Whole No. 498).

Sperry, R. W. (1982). Some effects of disconnecting the cerebral hemispheres. *Science, 217*, 1223–1226, 1250.

Spiegel, D. (2003a). Hypnosis and traumatic dissociation: Therapeutic opportunities. *Journal of Trauma & Dissociation, 4*(3), 73–90.

Spiegel, D. (2003b). Negative and positive visual hypnotic hallucinations: Attending inside and out. *International Journal of Clinical & Experimental Hypnosis, 51*(2), 130–146.

Spiegel, D., Cutcomb, S., Ren, C., & Pribram, K. (1985). Hypnotic hallucination alters evoked potentials. *Journal of Abnormal Psychology, 94*, 249–255.

Spiegler, M. D., & Guevremont, D. C. (2010). *Contemporary behavior therapy* (5th ed.). Belmont, CA: Wadsworth.

Spinath, B., Spinath, F. M., Harlaar, N., & Plomin, R. (2006). Predicting school achievement from general cognitive ability, self-perceived ability, and intrinsic value. *Intelligence, 34*(4), 363–374. doi:10.1016/j.intell.2005.11.004

Spironelli, C., Angrilli, A., & Stegagno, L. (2008). Failure of language lateralization in schizophrenia patients: An ERP study on early linguistic components. *Journal of Psychiatry & Neuroscience, 33*(3), 235–243.

Spitz, H. I. (2009). Group psychotherapy. In B. J. Sadock, V. A. Sadock, & P. Ruiz (Eds.), *Kaplan & Sadock's comprehensive textbook of psychiatry* (pp. 2832–2856). Philadelphia, PA: Lippincott Williams & Wilkins.

Sprecher, S. (1998). Insiders' perspectives on reasons for attraction to a close other. *Social Psychology Quarterly, 61*, 287–300.

Sprecher, S., & Duck, S. (1994). Sweet talk: The importance of perceived communication for romantic and friendship attraction experienced during a get-acquainted date. *Personality and Social Psychology Bulletin, 20*, 391–400.

Sprecher, S., Schwartz, P., Harvey, J., & Hatfield, E. (2008). Thebusinessoflove.com: Relationship initiation at Internet matchmaking services. In S. Sprecher, A. Wenzel, & J. Harvey (Eds.), *Handbook of relationship initiation* (pp. 235–247). New York, NY: Psychology Press.

Springer, S. P., & Deutsch, G. (1998). *Left brain, right brain.* New York, NY: W. H. Freeman.

Squire, L. R. (2004). Memory systems of the brain: A brief history and current perspective. *Neurobiology of Learning & Memory, 82*(3), 171–177.

Squire, L. R. (2009). Memory and brain systems: 1969–2009. *The Journal of Neuroscience, 29*(41), 12711–12716. doi:10.1523/JNEUROSCI.3575-09.2009

Squire, L. R., & Shrager, Y. (2009). Declarative memory systems: Amnesia. In J. H. Byrne (Ed.), *Concise learning and memory: The editor's selection.* San Diego, CA: Elsevier.

Squire, L. R., Knowlton, B., & Musen, G. (1993). The structure and organization of memory. *Annual Review of Psychology, 44*, 453–495.

Staddon, J. E. R., & Simmelhag, V. L. (1971). The "superstition" experiment: A reexamination of its implications for the principles of adaptive behavior. *Psychological Review, 78*, 3–43. doi:10.1037/h0030305

Staines, G. L. (2008). The relative efficacy of psychotherapy: Reassessing the methods-based paradigm. *Review of General Psychology, 12*(4), 330–343.

Stajkovic, A. D., & Luthans, F. (1998). Self-efficacy and work-related performance: A meta-analysis. *Psychological Bulletin, 124*, 240–261.

Staley, J. K., & Krystal, J. H. (2009). Radiotracer imaging and positron emission topography and single photon emission computer topography. In B. J. Sadock, V. A. Sadock, & P. Ruiz (Eds.), *Kaplan & Sadock's comprehensive textbook of psychiatry* (9th ed., Vol. 1, pp. 42–64). Philadelphia, PA: Lippincott Williams & Wilkins.

Stamatakis, E., Hillsdon, M., Mishra, G., Hamer, M., & Marmot, M. (2009). Television viewing and other screen-based entertainment in relation to multiple socioeconomic status indicators and area deprivation: The Scottish Health Survey 2003. *Journal of Epidemiology and Community Health, 63*, 734–740. doi:10.1136/jech.2008.085902

Stangor, C. (2009). The study of stereotyping, prejudice, and discrimination within social psychology: A quick history of theory and research. In T. D. Nelson (Ed.), *Handbook of prejudice, stereotyping, and discrimination* (pp. 1–22). New York, NY: Psychology Press.

Stanley, M. A., & Beidel, D. C. (2009). Behavior therapy. In B. J. Sadock, V. A. Sadock, & P. Ruiz (Eds.), *Kaplan & Sadock's comprehensive textbook of psychiatry* (pp. 2781–2803). Philadelphia, PA: Lippincott Williams & Wilkins.

Stanovich, K. E. (2003). The fundamental computational biases of human cognition: Heuristics that (sometimes) impair decision making and problem solving. In J. E. Davidson & R. J. Sternberg (Eds.), *The psychology of problem solving.* New York, NY: Cambridge University Press.

Stanovich, K. E. (2004). *How to think straight about psychology.* Boston, MA: Allyn & Bacon.

Stanovich, K. E. (2009). *What intelligence tests miss: The psychology of rational thought.* New Haven, CT: Yale University Press.

Stanovich, K. E., & West, R. F. (2008). On the relative independence of thinking biases and cognitive ability. *Journal of Personality and Social Psychology, 94*(4), 672–695. doi:10.1037/0022-3514.94.4.672

Steel, P. (2007). The nature of procrastination: A meta-analytic and theoretical review of quintessential self-regulatory failure. *Psychological Bulletin, 133*, 65–94.

Steele, K. M. (2003). Do rats show a Mozart effect? *Music Perception, 21*, 251–265.

Steiger, H., & Bruce, K. R. (2009). Eating disorders. In P. H. Blaney & T. Millon (Eds.), *Oxford textbook of psychopathology* (2nd ed., pp. 431–451). New York, NY: Oxford University Press.

Steiger, H., Bruce, K. R., & Israel, M. (2003). Eating disorders. In G. Stricker & T. A. Widiger (Eds.), *Handbook of psychology, Vol. 8: Clinical psychology.* New York, NY: Wiley.

Stein, B. E., & Meredith, M. A. (1993). *Vision, touch, and audition: Making sense of it all.* Cambridge, MA: MIT Press.

Stein, B. E., Wallace, M. T., & Stanford, T. R. (2000). Brain mechanisms for synthesizing information from different sensory modalities. In E. B. Goldstein (Ed.), *Blackwell handbook of perception*. Malden, MA: Blackwell.

Steinberg, L. (2007). Risk taking in adolescence: New perspectives from brain and behavioral science. *Perspectives on Psychological Science, 16*, 55–59.

Steinberg, L. (2008). A social neuroscience perspective on adolescent risk-taking. *Developmental Review, 28*(1), 78–106. doi:10.1016/j.dr.2007.08.002

Steinberg, L., & Morris, A. S. (2001). Adolescent development. *Annual Review of Psychology, 52*, 83–110.

Steinhausen, H. (2002). The outcome of anorexia nervosa in the 20th century. *American Journal of Psychiatry, 159*, 1284–1293.

Stellar, E. (1954). The physiology of motivation. *Psychological Review, 61*, 5–22.

Stepanski, E. J., & Wyatt, J. K. (2003). Use of sleep hygiene in the treatment of insomnia. *Sleep Medicine Reviews, 7*(3), 215–225.

Steptoe, A. (2007). Stress effects: Overview. In G. Fink (Ed.), *Encyclopedia of stress*. San Diego, CA: Elsevier.

Steptoe, A., Gibson, E. L., Hamer, M., & Wardle, J. (2007). Neuroendocrine and cardiovascular correlates of positive affect measured by ecological momentary assessment and by questionnaire. *Psychoneuroendocrinology, 32*, 56–64.

Sternberg, R. J. (1985). *Beyond IQ: A triarchic theory of human intelligence*. New York, NY: Cambridge University Press.

Sternberg, R. J. (1986). *Intelligence applied: Understanding and increasing your intellectual skills*. New York, NY: Harcourt Brace Jovanovich.

Sternberg, R. J. (1988a). A three-facet model of creativity. In R. J. Sternberg (Ed.), *The nature of creativity: Contemporary psychological perspectives*. Cambridge, England: Cambridge University Press.

Sternberg, R. J. (1988b). *The triarchic mind: A new theory of human intelligence*. New York, NY: Viking.

Sternberg, R. J. (1991). Theory-based testing of intellectual abilities: Rationale for the triarchic abilities test. In H. A. H. Rowe (Ed.), *Intelligence: Reconceptualization and measurement*. Hillsdale, NJ: Erlbaum.

Sternberg, R. J. (1998). How intelligent is intelligence testing? *Scientific American Presents Exploring Intelligence, 9*, 12–17.

Sternberg, R. J. (1999). The theory of successful intelligence. *Review of General Psychology, 3*, 292–316.

Sternberg, R. J. (2000a). Creativity is a decision. In A. L. Costa (Ed.), *Teaching for intelligence II* (pp. 85–106). Arlington Heights, IL: Skylight Training.

Sternberg, R. J. (2000b). Successful intelligence: A unified view of giftedness. In C. F. M. van Lieshout & P. G. Heymans (Eds.), *Developing talent across the life span* (pp. 43–65). Philadelphia, PA: Psychology Press.

Sternberg, R. J. (2003a). Construct validity of the theory of successful intelligence. In R. J. Sternberg, J. Lautrey, & T. I. Lubart (Eds.), *Models of intelligence: International perspectives*. Washington, DC: American Psychological Association.

Sternberg, R. J. (2003b). My house is a very, very, very fine house—But it is not the only house. In H. Nyborg (Ed.), *The scientific study of general intelligence: Tribute to Arthur R. Jensen*. Oxford, UK: Pergamon.

Sternberg, R. J. (2004). Culture and Intelligence. *American Psychologist, 59*, 325–338.

Sternberg, R. J. (2005a). There are no public policy implications: A reply to Rushton and Jensen. *Psychology, Public Policy, and the Law, 11*, 295–301.

Sternberg, R. J. (2005b). The triarchic theory of successful intelligence. In D. P. Flanagan & P. L. Harrison (Eds.), *Contemporary intellectual assessment: Theories, tests and issues* (pp. 103–119). New York, NY: Guilford.

Sternberg, R. J. (2007). Intelligence and culture. In S. Kitayama & D. Cohen (Eds.), *Handbook of cultural psychology* (pp. 547–568). New York, NY: Guilford.

Sternberg, R. J. (2009). Component processes in analogical reasoning. In J. C. Kaufman & E. L. Grigorenko (Eds.), *The essential Sternberg: Essays on intelligence, psychology, and education* (pp. 145–179). New York, NY: Springer.

Sternberg, R. J., Conway, B. E., Ketron, J. L., & Bernstein, M. (1981). People's conceptions of intelligence. *Journal of Personality and Social Psychology, 41*, 37–55.

Sternberg, R. J., Grigorenko, E. L., & Kidd, K. K. (2005). Intelligence, race, and genetics. *American Psychologist, 60*, 45–69.

Sternberg, R. J., & Hedlund, J. (2002). Practical intelligence, g, and work psychology. *Human Performance, 15*, 143–160.

Sternberg, R. J., & O'Hara, L. A. (1999). Creativity and intelligence. In R. J. Sternberg (Ed.), *Handbook of creativity*. New York, NY: Cambridge University Press.

Stewart, W. H., Jr., & Roth, P. L. (2007). A meta-analysis of achievement motivation differences between entrepreneurs and managers. *Journal of Small Business Management, 45*, 401–421.

Stewart-Williams, S. (2004). The placebo puzzle: Putting the pieces together. *Health Psychology, 23*, 198–206.

Stickgold, R. (2001). Toward a cognitive neuroscience of sleep. *Sleep Medicine Reviews, 5*, 417–421.

Stickgold, R. (2005). Why we dream. In M. H. Kryger, T. Roth, & W. C. Dement (Eds.). *Principles and practice of sleep medicine*. Philadelphia, PA: Elsevier Saunders.

Stickgold, R., & Walker, M. P. (2004). To sleep, perchance to gain creative insight. *Trends in Cognitive Sciences, 8*(5), 191–192.

Stickgold, R., & Walker, M. P. (2005). Memory consolidation and reconsolidation: What is the role of sleep? *Trends in Neurosciences, 28*(8), 408–415.

Stockman, A. (2010). Color mixing. In E. B. Goldstein (Ed.), *Encyclopedia of perception*. Thousand Oaks, CA: Sage.

Stoddard, G. (1943). *The meaning of intelligence*. New York, NY: Macmillan.

Stokstad, E. (2009, November 25). Americans' eating habits more wasteful than ever. *ScienceNOW*. Retrieved from http://news.sciencemag.org/sciencenow/2009/11/25-01.html?ref=hp

Stone, L. (1977). *The family, sex and marriage in England 1500–1800*. New York, NY: Harper & Row.

Stone, W. N. (2008). Group psychotherapy. In A. Tasman, J. Kay, J. A. Lieberman, M. B. First, & M. Maj (Eds.), *Psychiatry* (3rd ed.). New York, NY: Wiley-Blackwell.

Stoner, J. A. F. (1961). *A comparison of individual and group decisions involving risk*. Unpublished master's thesis, Massachusetts Institute of Technology.

Stoohs, R. A., Blum, H. C., Haselhorst, M., Duchna, H. W., Guilleminault, C., & Dement, W. C. (1998). Normative data on snoring: A comparison between younger and older adults. *European Respiratory Journal, 11*, 451–457.

Storandt, M. (2008). Cognitive deficits in the early stages of Alzheimer's disease. *Current Directions in Psychological Science, 17*(3), 198–202. doi:10.1111/j.1467-8721.2008.00574.x

Strahan, E. J., Lafrance, A., Wilson, A. E., Ethier, N., Spencer, S. J., & Zanna, M. P. (2008). Victoria's dirty secret: How sociocultural norms influence adolescent girls and women. *Personality and Social Psychology Bulletin, 34*(2), 288–301.

Strange, D., Clifasefi, S., & Garry, M. (2007). False memories. In M. Garry & H. Hayne (Eds.), *Do justice and let the sky fall: Elizabeth F. Lotus and her contributions to science, law, and academic freedom*. Mahwah, NJ: Erlbaum.

Straus, M. A. (2000). Corporal punishment and primary prevention of physical abuse. *Child Abuse & Neglect, 24*, 1109–1114.

Straus, M. A., & Paschall, M. J. (2009). Corporal punishment by mothers and development of children's cognitive ability: A longitudinal study of two nationally representative age cohorts. *Journal of Aggression, Maltreatment, & Trauma, 18*(5), 459–483. doi:10.1080/10926770903035168

Strayer, D. L., Drews, F. A., & Crouch, D. J. (2006). A comparison of the cell phone driver and the drunk driver. *Human Factors, 48*, 381–391.

Streissguth, A. (2007). Offspring effects of prenatal alcohol exposure from birth to 25 years: The Seattle prospective longitudinal study. *Journal of Clinical Psychology in Medical Settings, 14*, 81–101.

Streit, W. J. (2005). Microglia and neuroprotection: Implications for Alzheimer's disease. *Brain Research Reviews, 48*, 234–239.

Strenze, T. (2007). Intelligence and socioeconomic success: A meta-analytic review of longitudinal research. *Intelligence, 35*, 401–426.

Strick, M., Holland, R. W., & van Knippenberg, A. (2008). Seductive eyes: Attractiveness and direct gaze increase desire for associated objects. *Cognition, 106*, 1487–1496. doi:10.1016/j.cognition.2007.05.008

Strick, M., van Baaren, R. B., Holland, R. W., & van Knippenberg, A. (2009). Humor in advertisements enhances product liking by mere association. *Journal of Experimental Psychology: Applied, 15*, 35–45.

Striegel-Moore, R. H., & Bulik, C. M. (2007). Risk factors for eating disorders. *American Psychologist, 62*, 181–198.

Stubbe, J. H., Posthuma, D., Boomsma, D. I., & de Geus, E. J. C. (2005). Heritability of life satisfaction in adults: A twin study. *Psychological Medicine, 35*, 1581–1588.

Sturgis, P. (2006). Surveys and sampling. In G. M. Breakwell, S. Hammond, C. Fife-Schaw, & J. A. Smith (Eds.), *Research methods in psychology* (3rd ed.). London: Sage.

Stylianou-Korsnes, M., Reiner, M., Magnussen, S. J., & Feldman, M. W. (2010). Visual recognition of shapes and textures: An fMRI study. *Brain Structure & Function, 214*(4), 355–359. doi:10.1007/s00429-010-0241-5

Subotnik, K. L., Nuechterlein, K. H., Ventura, J., Gitlin, M. J., Marder, S., Mintz, J., et al. (2010). Risperidone nonadherence and return of positive symptoms in the early course of schizophrenia. *American Journal of Psychiatry, 168*(3), 286–292.

Sudak, H. S. (2009). Suicide. In B. J. Sadock, V. A. Sadock, & P. Ruiz (Eds.), *Kaplan & Sadock's comprehensive textbook of psychiatry* (9th ed., pp. 2717–2731). Philadelphia, PA: Lippincott Williams & Wilkins.

Sue, D. W., & Sue, D. (1999). *Counseling the culturally different: Theory and practice.* New York, NY: Wiley.

Sue, S. (2003). In defense of cultural competency in psychotherapy and treatment. *American Psychologist, 58*, 964–970.

Sue, S., Zane, N., Hall, G., & Berger, L. K. (2009). The case for cultural competency in psychotherapeutic interventions. *Annual Review of Psychology, 60*, 525–548. doi:10.1146/annurev.psych.60.110707.163651

Sue, S., Zane, N., & Young, K. (1994). Research on psychotherapy with culturally diverse populations. In A. E. Bergin & S. L. Garfield (Eds.), *Handbook of psychotherapy and behavior change* (4th ed.). New York, NY: Wiley.

Sufka, K. J., & Price, D. D. (2002). Gate control theory reconsidered. *Brain & Mind, 3*, 277–290.

Sugita, Y. (2009). Innate face processing. *Current Opinion in Neurobiology, 19*(1), 39–44. doi:10.1016/j.conb.2009.03.001

Suls, J. M., Luger, T., & Martin, R. (2010). The biopsychosocial model and the use of theory in health psychology. In J. M. Suls, K. W. Davidson, & R. M. Kaplan (Eds.), *Handbook of health psychology and behavioral medicine* (pp. 15–27). New York, NY: Guilford.

Summerfield, C., & Koechlin, E. (2009). Decision making and prefrontal executive function. In M. S. Gazzangia (Ed.), *The cognitive neurosciences* (4th ed., pp. 1019–1030). Cambridge, MA: MIT Press.

Sundin, J. J., Fear, N. T., Iversen, A. A., Rona, R. J., & Wessely, S. S. (2010). PTSD after deployment to Iraq: Conflicting rates, conflicting claims. *Psychological Medicine: A Journal of Research in Psychiatry and the Allied Sciences, 40*(3), 367–382. doi:10.1017/S0033291709990791

Super, C. M. (1976). Environmental effects on motor development: A case of African infant precocity. *Developmental Medicine and Child Neurology, 18*, 561–567.

Surra, C. A., Gray, C. R., Boettcher, T. J., Cottle, N. R., & West, A. R. (2006). From courtship to universal properties: Research on dating and mate selection, 1950 to 2003. In A. L. Vangelisti & D. Perlman (Eds.), *The Cambridge handbook of personal relationships* (pp. 113–130). New York, NY: Cambridge University Press.

Surtees, P., & Wainwright, N. (2007). Life events and health. In G. Fink (Ed.), *Encyclopedia of stress*. San Diego, CA: Elsevier.

Surtees, P., Wainwright, N., Luben, R., Wareham, N., Bingham, S., & Khaw, K. (2008). Depression and ischemic heart disease mortality: Evidence from the EPIC-Norfolk United Kingdom Prospective Cohort Study. *American Journal of Psychiatry, 165*(4), 515–523.

Susman, E. J., Dorn, L. D., & Schiefelbein, V. L. (2003). Puberty, sexuality, and health. In R. M. Lerner, M. A. Easterbrooks, & J. Mistry (Eds.), *Handbook of psychology, Vol. 6: Developmental psychology*. New York, NY: Wiley.

Susman, E. J., & Rogol, A. (2004). Puberty and psychological development. In R. M. Lerner & L. Steinberg (Eds.), *Handbook of adolescent psychology*. New York, NY: Wiley.

Susser, E. B., Neugebauer, R., Hoek, H. W., Brown, A. S., Lin, S., Labovitz, D., & Gorman, J. M. (1996). Schizophrenia after prenatal famine: Further evidence. *Archives of General Psychiatry, 53*, 25–31.

Sussman, N. (2009). Selective serotonin reuptake inhibitors. In B. J. Sadock, V. A. Sadock, & P. Ruiz (Eds.), *Kaplan & Sadock's comprehensive textbook of psychiatry* (pp. 3190–3205). Philadelphia, PA: Lippincott Williams & Wilkins.

Swan, G. E., Hudmon, K. S., & Khroyan, T. V. (2003). Tobacco dependence. In A. M. Nezu, C. M. Nezu, & P. A. Geller (Eds.), *Handbook of psychology, Vol. 9: Health Psychology*. New York, NY: Wiley.

Swank, J. M., & Daire, A. P. (2010). Multiple family adventure-based therapy groups: An innovative integration of two approaches. *The Family Journal: Counseling and Therapy for Couples and Families, 18*(3), 241–247.

Swibel, M. (2006, July 3). Bad girl interrupted. *Forbes*. Retrieved from http://www.forbes.com/forbes/2006/0703/118.html

Swim, J. K. (1994). Perceived versus meta-analytic effect sizes: An assessment of the accuracy of gender stereotypes. *Journal of Personality and Social Psychology, 66*, 21–36.

Swim, J. K., & Sanna, L. J. (1996). He's skilled, she's lucky: A meta-analysis of observers' attributions for women's and men's successes and failures. *Personality and Social Psychology Bulletin, 22*, 507–519.

Swingley, D. (2008). The roots of the early vocabulary in infants' learning from speech. *Current Directions in Psychological Science, 17*(5), 308–312. doi:10.1111/j.1467-8721.2008.00596.x

Szasz, T. (1974). *The myth of mental illness*. New York, NY: Harper & Row.

Szasz, T. (1990). Law and psychiatry: The problems that will not go away. *The Journal of Mind and Behavior, 11*(3/4), 557–564.

Szegedy-Maszak, M. (2005, August 8). In gambling's grip. *Los Angeles Times*. Retrieved March 10, 2006, from http://www.latimes.com/features/printedition/health/la-he-gamble8aug08,1,3002368.story?coll=la-headlines-pe-health

Szigethy, E. M. & Friedman, E. S. (2009). Combined psychotherapy and pharmacology. In B. J. Sadock, V. A. Sadock, & P. Ruiz (Eds.), *Kaplan & Sadock's comprehensive textbook of psychiatry* (pp. 2923–2931). Philadelphia, PA: Lippincott Williams & Wilkins.

Szmukler, G. I., & Patton, G. (1995). Sociocultural models of eating disorders. In G. Szmukler, C. Dare, & J. Treasure (Eds.), *Handbook of eating disorders: Theory, treatment, and research*. New York, NY: Wiley.

Szpunar, K. K., & McDermott, K. B. (2009). Episodic memory: An evolving concept. In J. H. Byrne (Ed.), *Concise learning and memory: The editor's selection*. San Diego, CA: Elsevier.

Szymusiak, R. (2009). Thermoregulation during sleep and sleep deprivation. In R. Stickgold & M. P. Walker (Eds.), *The neuroscience of sleep* (pp. 218–222). San Diego, CA: Academic Press.

Tach, L., & Halpern-Meekin, S. (2009). How does premarital cohabitation affect trajectories of marital quality? *Journal of Marriage and Family, 71*(2), 298–317. doi:10.1111/j.1741-3737.2009.00600.x

Tait, D. M., & Carroll, J. (2010). Color deficiency. In E. B. Goldstein (Ed.), *Encyclopedia of perception*. Thousand Oaks, CA: Sage.

Takarangi, M. T., Polaschek, D. L., Garry, M., & Loftus, E. F. (2008). Psychological science, victim advocates, and the problem of recovered memories. *International Review of Victimology, 15*(2), 147–163.

Talarico, J. M., & Rubin, D. C. (2003). Confidence, not consistency, characterizes flashbulb memories. *Psychological Science, 14*, 455–461.

Talarico, J. M., & Rubin, D. C. (2007). Flashbulb memories are special after all; in phenomenology, not accuracy. *Applied Cognitive Psychology, 21*, 557–578.

Talarico, J. M., & Rubin, D. C. (2009). Flashbulb memories result from ordinary memory processes and extraordinary event characteristics. In O. Luminet & A. Curci (Eds.), *Flashbulb memories: New issues and new perspectives* (pp. 79–97). New York, NY: Psychology Press.

Talbott, J. A. (2004). Deinstitutionalization: Avoiding the disasters of the past. *Psychiatric Services, 55,* 1112–1115.

Tamakoshi, A., Ohno, Y., & JACC Study Group. (2004). Self-reported sleep duration as a predictor of all-cause mortality: Results from JACC study, Japan. *Sleep: A Journal of Sleep and Sleep Disorders Research, 27,* 51–54.

Tanaka, J., Weiskopf, D., & Williams, P. (2001). The role of color in high-level vision. *Trends in Cognitive Sciences, 5,* 211–215.

Tanner, J. L. (2006). Recentering during emerging adulthood: A critical turning point in life span human development. In J. J. Arnett & J. L. Tanner (Eds.), *Emerging adults in America: Coming of age in the 21st century.* Washington, DC: American Psychological Association.

Tapia, J. C., & Lichtman, J. W. (2008). Synapse elimination. In L. Squire, D. Berg, F. Bloom, S. Du Lac, A. Ghosh, & N. Spitzer (Eds.), *Fundamental neuroscience* (3rd ed., pp. 469–490). San Diego, CA: Elsevier.

Tart, C. T. (1988). From spontaneous event to lucidity: A review of attempts to consciously control nocturnal dreaming. In J. Gackenbach & S. LaBerge (Eds.), *Conscious mind, sleeping brain: Perspectives on lucid dreaming.* New York, NY: Plenum.

Tashkin, D. P., Baldwin, G. C., Sarafian, T., Dubinett, S., & Roth, M. D. (2002). Respiratory and immunologic consequences of marijuana smoking. *Journal of Clinical Pharmacology, 42,* 71S–81S.

Tavris, C. (1998, September 13). Peer pressure (Review of *The Nurture Assumption). The New York Times Book Review, 103,* p. 14.

Taylor, C. A., Manganello, J. A., Lee, S. J., & Rice, J. C. (2010). Mothers' spanking of 3-year-old children and subsequent risk of children's aggressive behavior. *Pediatrics, 125*(5), 1057–1065. doi:10.1542/peds.2009-2678

Taylor, E. (2001). Positive psychology and humanistic psychology: A reply to Seligman. *Journal of Humanistic Psychology, 41*(1), 13–29.

Taylor, S., Cox, B. J., & Asmundson, G. J. G. (2009). Anxiety disorders: Panic and phobias. In P. H. Blaney & T. Millon (Eds.), *Oxford textbook of psychopathology* (2nd ed., pp. 119–145). New York, NY: Oxford University Press.

Taylor, S. E. (2007). Social support. In H. S. Friedman & R. C. Silver (Eds.), *Foundations of health psychology.* New York, NY: Oxford University Press.

Taylor, S. E., & Brown, J. D. (1988). Illusion and well-being: A social psychological perspective on mental health. *Psychological Bulletin, 103,* 193–210.

Taylor, S. E., & Brown, J. D. (1994). Positive illusions and well-being revisited: Separating fact from fiction. *Psychological Bulletin, 116,* 21–27.

Taylor, S. E., Sherman, D. K., Kim, H. S., Jarcho, J., Takagi, K., & Dunagan, M. S. (2004). Culture and social support: Who seeks it and why? *Journal of Personality and Social Psychology, 87*(3), 354–362. doi:10.1037/0022-3514.87.3.354

Taylor, S. E., Welch, W. T., Kim, H. S., & Sherman, D. K. (2007). Cultural differences in the impact of social support on psychological and biological stress responses. *Psychological Science, 18*(9), 831–837. doi:10.1111/j.1467-9280.2007.01987.x

Teachman, J. (2003). Premarital sex, premarital cohabitation and the risk of subsequent marital dissolution among women. *Journal of Marriage and Family, 65*(2), 444–455. doi:10.1111/j.1741-3737.2003.00444.x

Tedlock, L. B. (1992). Zuni and Quiche dream sharing and interpreting. In B. Tedlock (Ed.), *Dreaming: Anthropoligical and psychological interpretations.* Santa Fe, NM: School of American Research Press.

Teigen, K. H. (2004). Judgments by representativeness. In F. P. Rudiger (Ed.), *Cognitive illusions.* New York, NY: Psychology Press.

Tellegen, A., Lykken, D. T., Bouchard, T. J., Jr., Wilcox, K. J., Segal, N. L., & Rich, S. (1988). Personality similarity in twins reared apart and together. *Journal of Personality and Social Psychology, 54,* 1031–1039.

Temple, J. L., Giacomelli, A. M., Roemmich, J. N., & Epstein, L. H. (2008). Dietary variety impairs habituation in children. *Health Psychology, 27,* S10–S19.

Tennen, H., & Affleck, G. (1999). Finding benefits in adversity. In C. R. Snyder (Ed.), *Coping: The psychology of what works.* New York, NY: Oxford University Press.

Terman, L. (1916). *The measurement of intelligence: An explanation of and a complete guide for the use of the Stanford revision and extension of the Binet-Simon Intelligence Scale.* Boston, MA: Houghton Mifflin.

Terr, L. (1994). *Unchained memories.* New York, NY: Basic Books.

Terracciano, A., Abdel-Khalak, A. M., Adam, N., Adamovova, L., Ahn, C. K., Ahn, H. N., et al. (2005). National character does not reflect mean personality trait levels in 49 cultures. *Science, 310,* 96–100.

Thase, M. E. (2009). Selective serotonin-norepinephrine reuptake inhibitors. In B. J. Sadock, V. A. Sadock, & P. Ruiz (Eds.), *Kaplan & Sadock's comprehensive textbook of psychiatry* (pp. 3184–3189). Philadelphia, PA: Lippincott Williams & Wilkins.

Thayer, A., & Lynn, S. J. (2006). Guided imagery and recovered memory therapy: Considerations and cautions. *Journal of Forensic Psychology Practice, 6,* 63–73.

Thelen, E. (1995). Motor development: A new synthesis. *American Psychologist, 50,* 79–95.

Thomas, A., & Chess, S. (1977). *Temperament and development.* New York, NY: Brunner/Mazel.

Thomas, D. R. (1992). Discrimination and generalization. In L. R. Squire (Ed.), *Encyclopedia of learning and memory.* New York, NY: Macmillan.

Thompson, J. K., & Kinder, B. (2003). Eating disorders. In M. Hersen & S. Turner (Eds.), *Handbook of adult psychopathology.* New York, NY: Plenum Press.

Thompson, J. K., Roehrig, M., & Kinder, B. N. (2007). Eating disorders. In M. Hersen, S. M. Turner, & D. C. Beidel (Eds.), *Adult psychopathology and diagnosis.* New York, NY: Wiley.

Thompson, J. K., & Stice, E. (2001). Thin-ideal internalization: Mounting evidence for a new risk factor for body-image disturbance and eating pathology. *Current Directions in Psychological Science, 10*(5), 181–183.

Thompson, R. A. (2008). Early attachment and later development: Familiar questions, new answers. In J. Cassidy & P. R. Shaver (Eds.), *Handbook of attachment: Theory, research, and clinical applications* (2nd ed., pp. 348–365). New York, NY: Guilford.

Thompson, R. A., & Nelson, C. A. (2001). Developmental science and the media: Early brain development. *American Psychologist, 56,* 5–15.

Thompson, R. F. (1989). A model system approach to memory. In P. R. Solomon, G. R. Goethals, C. M. Kelley, & B. R. Stephens (Eds.), *Memory: Interdisciplinary approaches.* New York, NY: Springer-Verlag.

Thompson, R. F. (1992). Memory. *Current Opinion in Neurobiology, 2,* 203–208.

Thompson, R. F. (2005). In search of memory traces. *Annual Review of Psychology, 56,* 1–23.

Thompson, R. F., & Zola, S. M. (2003). In D. K. Freedheim (Ed.), *Handbook of psychology* (Vol. 2): New York, NY: Wiley.

Thornhill, R. (1976). Sexual selection and nuptial feeding behavior in *Bittacus apicalis* (Insecta: Mecoptera). *American Naturalist, 110,* 529–548.

Thornton, B., & Maurice, J. K. (1999). Physical attractiveness contrast effect and the moderating influence of self-consciousness. *Sex Roles, 40,* 379–392.

Thornton, B., & Moore, S. (1993). Physical attractiveness contrast effect: Implications for self-esteem and evaluations of the social self. *Personality and Social Psychology Bulletin, 19,* 474–480.

Thornton, L. M., Mazzeo, S. E., & Bulik, C. M. (2011). The heritability of eating disorders: Methods and current findings. In R. H. Adan & W. H. Kaye (Eds.), *Behavioral neurobiology of eating disorders* (pp. 141–156). New York, NY: Springer-Verlag.

Thun, M. J., Apicella, L. F., & Henley, S. J. (2000). Smoking vs. other risk factors as the cause of smoking-attributable deaths: Confounding in the courtroom. *Journal of the American Medical Association, 284,* 706–712.

Tice, D. M., Bratslavsky, E., & Baumeister, R. F. (2001). Emotional distress regulation takes precedence over impulse control: If you feel bad, do it! *Journal of Personality and Social Psychology, 80,* 53–67.

Till, B. D., & Priluck, R. L. (2000). Stimulus generalization in classical conditioning: An initial investigation and extension. *Psychology and Marketing, 17,* 55–72.

Timm, D. A., & Slavin, J. L. (2008). Dietary fiber and the relationship to chronic diseases. *American Journal of Lifestyle Medicine, 2,*, 233–240.

Titsworth, B. S., & Kiewra, K. A. (2004). Spoken organizational lecture cues and student notetaking as facilitators of student learning. *Contemporary Educational Psychology, 29,* 447–461.

Todd, J. T., & Morris, E. K. (1992). Case histories in the great power of steady misrepresentation. *American Psychologist, 47,* 1441–1453.

Todd, P. M., & Gigerenzer, G. (2000). Precis of simple heuristics that make us smart. *Behavioral & Brain Sciences, 23,* 727–780.

Todd, P. M., & Gigerenzer, G. (2007). Environments that make us smart: Ecological rationality. *Current Directions in Psychological Science, 16,* 167–171.

Toga, A. W., Thompson, P. M., & Sowell, E. R. (2006). Mapping brain maturation. *Trends in Neurosciences, 29,* 148–159.

Tolman, D. L., & Diamond, L. M. (2001). Desegregating sexuality research: Cultural and biological perspectives on gender and desire. *Annual Review of Sex Research, 12,* 33–74.

Tom, S. M., Fox, C. R., Trepel, C., & Poldrack, R. A. (2007). The neural basis of loss aversion in decision-making under risk. *Science, 315,* 515–518.

Tomkins, S. S. (1980). Affect as amplification: Some modifications in theory. In R. Plutchik & H. Kellerman (Eds.), *Emotion: Theory, research and experience* (Vol. 1). New York, NY: Academic Press.

Tomkins, S. S. (1991). *Affect, imagery, consciousness: 3. Anger and fear.* New York, NY: Springer-Verlag.

Torgersen, S. (1979). The nature and origin of common phobic fears. *British Journal of Psychiatry, 119,* 343–351.

Torgersen, S. (1983). Genetic factors in anxiety disorders. *Archives of General Psychiatry, 40,* 1085–1089.

Tormala, Z. L., & Petty, R. E. (2002). What doesn't kill me makes me stronger: The effects of resisting persuasion on attitude certainty. *Journal of Personality and Social Psychology, 83,* 1298–1313.

Tormala, Z. L., & Petty, R. E. (2004). Resistance to persuasion and attitude certainty: The moderating role of elaboration. *Personality and Social Psychology Bulletin, 30,* 1446–1457.

Torres, A. R., Prince, M. J., Bebbington, P. E., Bhugra, D., Brugha, T. S., & Farrell, M. et al. (2006). Obsessive-compulsive disorder: Prevalence, comorbidity, impact, and help-seeking in the British national psychiatric morbidity survey of 2000. *American Journal of Psychiatry, 163,* 1978–1985.

Torres, L., & Saunders, S. M. (2009). Evaluation of psychotherapy. In B. J. Sadock, V. A. Sadock, & P. Ruiz (Eds.), *Kaplan & Sadock's comprehensive textbook of psychiatry* (9th ed.). Philadelphia, PA: Lippincott Williams & Wilkins.

Torrey, E. F. (1992). *Freudian fraud: The malignant effect of Freud's theory on American thought and culture.* New York, NY: Harper Perennial.

Torrey, E. F. (1996). *Out of the shadows.* New York, NY: Wiley.

Toufexis, A. (1990, December 17). Drowsy America. *Time,* pp. 78–85.

Tourangeau, R. (2004). Survey research and societal change. *Annual Review of Psychology, 55,* 775–801.

Tourangeau, R., & Yan, T. (2007). Sensitive questions in surveys. *Psychological Bulletin, 133,* 859–883.

Tov, W., & Diener, E. (2007). Culture and subjective well-being. In S. Kitayama & D. Cohen (Eds.), *Handbook of cultural psychology.* New York, NY: Guilford.

Toyota, H., & Kikuchi, Y. (2004). Self-generated elaboration and spacing effects on incidental memory. *Perceptual and Motor Skills, 99,* 1193–1200.

Toyota, H., & Kikuchi, Y. (2005). Encoding richness of self-generated elaboration and spacing effects on incidental memory. *Perceptual and Motor Skills, 101,* 621–627.

Tracy, J. L., & Robins, R. W. (2008). The automaticity of emotion recognition. *Emotion, 8,* 81–95.

Travis, F. (2001). Autonomic and EEG patterns distinguish transcending from other experiences during Transcendental Meditation practice. *International Journal of Psychophysiology, 42,* 1–9.

Travis, F., & Pearson, C. (2000). Pure consciousness: Distinct phenomenological and physiological correlates of "consciousness itself." *International Journal of Neuroscience, 100*(1-4), 77–89.

Triandis, H. C. (1989). Self and social behavior in differing cultural contexts. *Psychological Review, 96,* 269–289.

Triandis, H. C. (1994). *Culture and social behavior.* New York, NY: McGraw-Hill.

Triandis, H. C. (2001). Individualism and collectivism: Past, present, and future. In D. Matsumoto (Ed.), *The handbook of culture and psychology.* New York, NY: Oxford University Press.

Triandis, H. C. (2007). Culture and psychology: A history of the study of their relationship. In S. Kitayama & D. Cohen (Eds.), *Handbook of cultural psychology.* New York, NY: Guilford.

Trivers, R. L. (1972). Parental investment and sexual selection. In B. Campbell (Ed.), *Sexual selection and the descent of man.* Chicago: Aldine.

Trotter, R. J. (1986, September). The three faces of love. *Psychology Today,* pp. 46–54.

Trujillo, M. (2005). Culture-bound syndromes. In B. J. Sadock & V. A. Sadock (Eds.), *Kaplan & Sadock's comprehensive textbook of psychiatry.*

Philadelphia, PA: Lippincott Williams & Wilkins.

Tsankova, N., Renthal, W., Kumar, A., & Nestler, E. J. (2007). Epigenetic regulation in psychiatric disorders. *Nature Reviews Neuroscience, 8*(5), 355–367.

Tsigos, C., Kyrou, I., & Chrousos, G. P. (2005). Stress, endocrine manifestations and diseases. In C. L. Cooper (Ed.), *Handbook of stress medicine and health.* Boca Raton, FL: CRC Press.

Tucker, A. M., Dinges, D. F., & Van Dongen, H. P. A. (2007). Trait interindividual differences in the sleep physiology of healthy young adults. *Journal of Sleep Research, 16,* 170–180.

Tuckey, M. R., & Brewer, N. (2003). The influence of schemas, stimulus ambiguity, and interview schedule on eyewitness memory over time. *Journal of Experimental Psychology: Applied, 9,* 101–118.

Tugade, M. M., & Fredrickson, B. L. (2004). Resilient individuals use positive emotions to bounce back from negative emotional experiences. *Journal of Personality and Social Psychology, 86,* 320–333.

Tulving, E. (1986). What kind of a hypothesis is the distinction between episodic and semantic memory? *Journal of Experimental Psychology: Learning, Memory and Cognition, 12,* 307–311.

Tulving, E. (1993). What is episodic memory? *Current Directions in Psychological Science, 2*(3), 67–70.

Tulving, E. (2001). Origin of autonoesis in episodic memory. In H. L. Roediger III, J. S. Nairne, I. Neath, & A. M. Surprenant (Eds.), *The nature of remembering: Essays in honor of Robert G. Crowder* (pp. 17–34). Washington, DC: American Psychological Association.

Tulving, E. (2002). Episodic memory: From mind to brain. *Annual Review of Psychology, 53,* 1–25.

Tulving, E., & Thomson, D. M. (1973). Encoding specificity and retrieval processes in episodic memory. *Psychological Review, 80,* 352–373.

Tunnell, K. D. (2005). The Oxycontin epidemic and crime panic in rural Kentucky. *Contemporary Drug Problems, 32,* 225–258.

Turk, D. C., & Okifuji, A. (2003). Pain management. In A. M. Nezu, C. M. Nezu, & P. A. Geller (Eds.), *Handbook of psychology, Vol. 9: Health psychology.* New York, NY: Wiley.

Turkheimer, E., Haley, A., Waldron, M., D'Onofrio, B., & Gottesman, I. I. (2003). Socioeconomic status modifies heritability of IQ in young children. *Psychological Science, 14,* 623–628.

Turkkan, J. S. (1989). Classical conditioning: The new hegemony. *Behavioral and Brain Sciences, 12,* 121–179.

Turkle, S. (2011). *Alone together.* New York, NY: Basic Books,

Turner, E. H., Matthews, A. M., Linardos, E., Tell, R. A., & Rosenthal, R. (2008). Selective publication of antidepressant trials and its influence on apparent efficacy. *New England Journal of Medicine, 358,* 252–260.

Turner, J. R., & Wheaton, B. (1995). Checklist measurement of stressful life events. In S. Cohen, R. C. Kessler, & L. U. Gordon (Eds.), *Measuring stress: A guide for health and social scientists.* New York, NY: Oxford University Press.

Tversky, A., & Kahneman, D. (1973). Availability: A heuristic for judging frequency and probability. *Cognitive Psychology, 5,* 207–232.

Tversky, A., & Kahneman, D. (1974). Judgments under uncertainty: Heuristics and biases. *Science, 185,* 1124–1131.

Tversky, A., & Kahneman, D. (1982). Judgment under uncertainty: Heuristics and biases. In D. Kahneman, P. Slovic, & A. Tversky (Eds.), *Judgment under uncertainty: Heuristics and biases.* New York, NY: Cambridge University Press.

Tversky, A., & Kahneman, D. (1983). Extensional versus intuitive reasoning: The conjunction fallacy in probability judgment. *Psychological Review, 90,* 283–315.

Twenge, J. M., & Campbell, W. (2009). *The narcissism epidemic: Living in the age of enlightenment.* New York, NY: Free Press.

Twenge, J. M., Campbell, W. K., & Foster, C. A. (2003). Parenthood and marital satisfaction: A meta-analytic review. *Journal of Marriage and the Family, 65,* 574–583.

Twenge, J. M., & Foster, J. D. (2010). Birth cohort increases in narcissistic personality traits among American college students, 1982–2009. *Social Psychological and Personality Science, 1,* 99–106.

Twenge, J. M., Konrath, S., Foster, J. D., Campbell, W., & Bushman, B. J. (2008). Egos inflating over time: A cross-temporal meta-analysis of the Narcissistic Personality Inventory. *Journal of Personality, 76*(4), 875–902. doi:10.1111/j.1467-6494.2008.00507.x

Uchino, B. N., & Birmingham, W. (2011). Stress and support processes. In R. J. Contrada & A. Baum (Eds.), *The handbook of stress science: Biology, psychology, and health* (pp. 111–121). New York, NY: Springer Publishing.

Uchino, B. N., Uno, D., & Holt-Lunstad, J. (1999). Social support, physiological processes, and health. *Current Directions in Psychological Science, 8,* 145–148.

UNAIDS (Joint United Nations Programme on HIV/AIDS). (2009). *AIDS epidemic update.* Geneva, Switzerland: World Health Organization. Retrived from http://data.unaids.org/pub/Report/2009/jc1700_epi_update_2009_en.pdf

Underwood, B. J. (1961). Ten years of massed practice on distributed practice. *Psychological Review, 68,* 229–247.

Unger, R. K., & Crawford, M. (1992). *Women and gender: A feminist psychology.* New York, NY: McGraw-Hill.

Ursano, A. M., Kartheiser, P. H., & Barnhill, L. J. (2008). Disorders usually first diagnosed in infancy, childhood, or adolescence. In R. E. Hales, S. C. Yudofsky, & G. O. Gabbard (Eds.), *The American Psychiatric Publishing textbook of psychiatry* (5th ed., pp. 861–920). Washington, DC: American Psychiatric Publishing.

Ursano, R. J., & Silberman, E. K. (1999). Psychoanalysis, psychoanalytic psychotherapy, and supportive psychotherapy. In R. E. Hales, S. C. Yudofsky, & J. A. Talbott (Eds.), *American Psychiatric Press textbook of psychiatry.* Washington, DC: American Psychiatric Press.

Ursano, R. J., & Silberman, E. K. (2003). Psychoanalysis, psychoanalytic psychotherapy, and supportive psychotherapy. In R. E. Hales & S. C. Yudofsky (Eds.), *Textbook of clinical psychiatry.* Washington, DC: American Psychiatric Publishing.

Ursano, R. J., Sonnenberg, S. M., & Lazar, S. G. (2008). Psychodynamic psychotherapy. In R. E. Hales, S. C. Yudofsky, & G. O. Gabbard (Eds.), *The American Psychiatric Publishing textbook of psychiatry* (pp. 1171–1190). Washington, DC: American Psychiatric Publishing.

U.S. Centers for Disease Control and Prevention. (2009). Climate change and public health. Retrieved from http://www.cdc.gov/climatechange/policy.htm

U.S. Centers for Disease Control and Prevention (CDC) (2011). Diagnoses of HIV infection and AIDS in the United States and dependent areas, 2009. *HIV Surveillance Report, 21.* Retrieved from www.cdc.gov/hiv/surveillance/resources/reports/2009report/

U.S. Department of Health and Human Services. (1999). *Mental health: A report of the Surgeon General.* Washington, DC: U.S. Government Printing Office.

U.S. Department of Health and Human Services. (2006). *The health consequences of involuntary exposure to tobacco smoke: A report of the Surgeon General.* Atlanta, GA: H.H.S.

U.S. Energy Information Administration. (2010). Oil: Crude and petroleum products explained. Petroleum statistics. Retrieved from http://www.eia.doe.gov/energyexplained/index.cfm?page=oil_home#tab2

U.S. Environmental Protection Agency. (2006). Climate change. Retrieved electronically June 4, 2009 at http://epa.gov/climatechange/index.html

U.S. Environmental Protection Agency. (2008). About air toxics. Technology transfer network air toxics web site. Retrieved from http://www.epa.gov/ttn/atw/allabout.html

U.S. Environmental Protection Agency. (2011). Basic information about food waste. Retrieved from http://www.epa.gov/wastes/conserve/materials/organics/food/fd-basic.htm

Väänänen, A. (2010). Psychosocial work environment and risk of ischaemic heart disease in women. *Occupational & Environmental Medicine, 67*(5), 291–292.

Vaillant, G. E. (1994). Ego mechanisms of defense and personality psychopathology. *Journal of Abnormal Psychology, 103,* 44–50.

Valenstein, E. S. (1973). *Brain control.* New York, NY: Wiley.

Valli, K., & Revonsuo, A. (2009). Sleep: Dreaming data and theories. In W. P. Banks (Ed.), *Encyclopedia of Consciousness* (pp. 341–356). San Diego, CA: Academic Press.

Vallortigara, G., & Rogers, L. J. (2005). Survival with an asymmetrical brain: Advantages and disadvantages of cerebral lateralization. *Behavioral and Brain Sciences, 28*(4), 575–633. doi:10.1017/S0140525X05000105

Van Blerkom, D. L. (2006). *College study skills: Becoming a strategic learner.* Belmont, CA: Wadsworth.

Van Boven, L. (2005). Experientialism, materialism, and the pursuit of happiness. *Review of General Psychology, 9,* 132–142.

Van de Castle, R. L. (1994). *Our dreaming mind.* New York, NY: Ballantine Books.

van den Berg, A. E., Hartig, T., & Staats, H. (2007). Preference for Nature in Urbanized Societies: Stress, Restoration, and the Pursuit of Sustainability. *Journal of Social Issues, 63,* 79–96.

van den Berg, A. E. & van den Berg C. G. (2011). A comparison of children with ADHD in a natural and built setting. *Child Care, Health and Development, 37,* 430–439. doi:10.1111/j.1365-2214.2010.01172.x

van den Boom, D. (2001). First attachments: Theory and research. In G. Bremner & A. Fogel (Eds.), *Blackwell handbook of infant development* (pp. 296–325). Malden, MA: Blackwell Publishing.

Van der Hart, O., & Nijenhuis, E. R. S. (2009). Dissociative disorders. In P. H. Blaney & T. Millon (Eds.), *Oxford textbook of psychopathology* (2nd ed., pp. 452–481). New York, NY: Oxford University Press.

Van Dongen, H. P. A., & Dinges, D. F. (2005). Circadian rhythms in sleepiness, alertness, and performance. In M. H. Kryger, T. Roth, & W. C. Dement (Eds.), *Principles and practice of sleep medicine.* Philadelphia, PA: Elsevier Saunders.

van Eck, M., Nicolson, N. A., & Berkhof, J. (1998). Effects of stressful daily events on mood states: Relationship to global perceived stress. *Journal of Personality and Social Psychology, 75,* 1572–1585.

van Griensven, F., Chakkraband, M. L. S., Thienkrua, W., Pengjuntr, W., Cardozo, B. L., & Tantipiwatanaskul, P. et al. (2007). Mental health problems among adults in tsunami-affected areas in Southern Thailand. *Journal of the American Medical Association, 296,* 537–548.

van Ijzendoorn, M. H., & Bakermans-Kranenburg, M. J. (2004). Maternal sensitivity and infant temperament in the formation of attachment. In G. Bremner & A. Slater (Eds.), *Theories of infant development.* Malden, MA: Blackwell Publishing.

van Ijzendoorn, M. H., & Juffer, F. (2005). Adoption is a successful natural intervention enhancing adopted children's IQ and school performance. *Current Directions in Psychological Science, 14,* 326–330.

van Ijzendoorn, M. H., & Kroonenberg, P. M. (1988). Cross-cultural patterns of attachment: A meta-analysis of the strange situation. *Child Development, 59,* 147–156.

van Ijzendoorn, M. H., & Sagi, A. (1999). Cross-cultural patterns of attachment: Universal and contextual dimensions. In J. Cassidy & P. R. Shaver (Eds.), *Handbook of attachment: Theory, research, and clinical applications.* New York, NY: Guilford.

van IJzendoorn, M. H., & Sagi-Schwartz, A. (2008). Cross-cultural patterns of attachment: Universal and contextual dimensions. In J. Cassidy & P. R. Shaver (Eds.), *Handbook of attachment: Theory, research, and clinical applications* (2nd ed., pp. 3–22). New York, NY: Guilford.

Van Kammen, D. P., Hurford, I., & Marder, S. R. (2009). First-generation antipsychotics. In B. J. Sadock, V. A. Sadock, & P. Ruiz (Eds.), *Kaplan & Sadock's comprehensive textbook of psychiatry* (pp. 3105–3126). Philadelphia, PA: Lippincott Williams & Wilkins.

van Leeuwen, M. L., Matthijs, L, & Macrae, C. N. (2004). Is beautiful always good? Implicit benefits of facial attractiveness. *Social Cognition, 22,* 637–649.

van Swol, L. M. (2009). Extreme members and group polarization. *Social Influence, 4*(3), 185–199. doi:10.1080/15534510802584368

Van Vugt, M. (2002). Central, individual, or collective control? Social dilemma strategies for natural resource management. *American Behavioral Scientist, 45*(5), 783–800.

Vandenbroucke, J. P., & Psaty, B. M. (2008). Benefits and risks of drug treatments: How to combine the best evidence on benefits with the best data about adverse effects. *Journal of the American Medical Association, 300*(20), 2417–2419.

Vandereycken, W. (2002). History of anorexia nervosa and bulimia nervosa. In C. G. Fairburn, & K. D. Brownell (Eds.), *Eating disorders and obesity.* New York, NY: Guilford.

Varnum, M. W., Grossmann, I., Kitayama, S., & Nisbett, R. E. (2010). The origin of cultural differences in cognition: The social orientation hypothesis. *Current Directions in Psychological Science, 19*(1), 9–13. doi:10.1177/0963721409359301

Vartanian, L. R., Herman, C., & Wansink, B. (2008). Are we aware of the external factors that influence our food intake? *Health Psychology, 27*(5), 533–538. doi:10.1037/0278-6133.27.5.533

Vazquez, C., Munoz, M., & Sanz, J. (1997). Lifetime and 12-month prevalence of DSM-III-R mental disorders among the homeless in Madrid: A European study using the CIDI. *Acta Psychiatrica Scandinavica, 95,* 523–530.

Veasey, S. C. (2009). Sleep apnea. In R. Stickgold & M. P. Walker (Eds.), *The neuroscience of sleep* (pp. 263–269). San Diego, CA: Academic Press.

Vecera, S. P., & Palmer, S. E. (2006). Grounding the figure: Surface attachment influences figure-ground organization. *Psychonmic Bulletin & Review, 13,* 563–569.

Vecera, S. P., Vogel, E. K., & Woodman, G. F. (2002). Lower region: A new cue for figure-ground assignment. *Journal of Experimental Psychology: General, 131,* 194–205.

Veenhoven, R. R. (2008). Healthy happiness: Effects of happiness on physical health and the consequences for preventive health care. *Journal of Happiness Studies, 9*(3), 449–469. doi:10.1007/s10902-006-9042-1

Venn, A., & Britton, J. (2007). Exposure to secondhand smoke and biomarkers of cardiovascular disease risk in never-smoking adults. *Circulation, 115*(8), 990–995.

Vermeeren, A. (2004). Residual effects of hypnotics: Epidemiology and clinical implications. *CNS Drugs, 18*(5), 297–328.

Vernon, P. A., Wickett, J. C., Bazana, G. P., & Stelmack, R. M. (2000). The neuropsychology and psychophysiology of human intelligence. In R. J. Sternberg (Ed.), *Handbook of intelligence.* Cambridge, UK: Cambridge University Press.

Vgontzas, A. N., Liao, D., Bixler, E. O., Chrousos, G. P., & Vela-Bueno, A. (2009). Insomnia with objective short sleep duration is associated with a high risk for hypertension. *Sleep: Journal of Sleep and Sleep Disorders Research, 32*(4), 491–497.

Victoroff, J. (2005). Central nervous system changes with normal aging. In B. J. Sadock & V. A. Sadock (Eds.), *Kaplan & Sadock's comprehensive textbook of psychiatry.* Philadelphia, PA: Lippincott Williams & Wilkins.

Videbech, P. (2006). Hippocampus and unipolar depression. *Directions in Psychiatry, 26,* 183–194.

Videbech, P., & Ravnkilde, B. (2004). Hippocampal volume and depression: A meta-analysis of MRI studies. *American Journal of Psychiatry, 161,* 1957–1966.

Viglione, D. J., & Rivera, B. (2003). Assessing personality and psychopathology with projective methods. In J. R. Graham & J. A. Naglieri (Eds.), *Handbook of psychology, Vol. 10: Assessment psychology.* New York, NY: Wiley.

Visser, P. S., & Cooper, J. (2003). Attitude change. In M. A. Hogg & J. Cooper (Eds.), *The Sage handbook of social psychology.* Thousand Oaks, CA: Sage.

Vitiello, M. V. (2009). Recent advances in understanding sleep and sleep disturbances in older adults: Growing older does not mean sleeping poorly. *Current Directions in Psychological Science, 18*(6), 316–320. doi:10.1111/j.1467-8721.2009.01659.x

Vogel, I., Brug, J., Hosli, E. J., van der Ploeg, C. P. B., & Raat, H. (2008). MP3 players and hearing loss: Adolescents' perceptions of loud music and hearing conservation. *Journal of Pediatrics, 152*(3), 400–404. doi:10.1016/j.jpeds.2007.07.009

Vogel, I., Brug, J., van der Ploeg, C. P. B., & Raat, H. (2007). Young people's exposure to loud music: A summary of the literature. *American Journal of Preventative Medicine, 33*(2), 124–133. doi:10.1016/j.amepre.2007.03.016.

Vohs, K. D., Baumeister, R. F., Schmeichel, B. J., Twenge, J. M., Nelson, N. M., & Tice, D. M. (2008). Making choices impairs subsequent self-control: A limited-resource account of decision making, self-regulation, and active initiative. *Journal of Personality and Social Psychology, 94*(5), 883–898. doi:10.1037/0022-3514.94.5.883

Volkmar, F. R., Klin, A., Schultz, R. T., & State, M. W. (2009). Pervasive developmental disorders. In B. J. Sadock, V. A. Sadock, & P. Ruiz (Eds.), *Kaplan & Sadock's comprehensive textbook of psychiatry* (9th ed., pp. 3540–3559). Philadelphia, PA: Lippincott Williams & Wilkins.

Volkow, N. D., Fowler, J. S., & Wang, G. J. (2004). The addicted human brain viewed in the light of imaging studies: Brain circuits and treatment strategies. *Neuropharmacology, 47,* 3–13.

Voyer, D. (1996). On the magnitude of laterality effects and sex differences in functional lateralities. *Laterality, 1,* 51–83.

Voyer, D., Nolan, C., & Voyer, S. (2000). The relation between experience and spatial performance in men and women. *Sex Roles, 43,* 891–915.

Vyse, S. A. (1997). *Believing in magic: The psychology of superstition.* New York, NY: Oxford University Press.

Vyse, S. A. (2000). *Believing in magic: The psychology of superstition.* New York, NY: Oxford University Press.

Vythilingam, M., Shen, J., Drevets, W. C., & Innis, R. B. (2005). Nuclear magnetic resonance imaging: Basic principles and recent findings in neuropsychiatric disorders. In B. J. Sadock & V. A. Sadock (Eds.), *Kaplan & Sadock's comprehensive textbook of psychiatry.* Philadelphia, PA: Lippincott Williams & Wilkins.

Waage, S., Moen, B., Pallesen, S., Eriksen, H. R., Ursin, H., Åkerstedt, T., & Bjorvatn, B. (2009). Shift work disorder among oil rig workers in the North Sea. *Sleep: Journal of Sleep and Sleep Disorders Research, 32*(4), 558–565.

Wager, T. D., Hernandez, L., & Lindquist, M. A. (2009). Essentials of functional neuroimaging. In G. G. Bernston & J. T. Cacioppo (Eds.), *Handbook of neuroscience for the behavioral sciences* (Vol. 1, pp. 152–197). New York, NY: Wiley.

Wager, T. D., Scott, D. J., & Zubieta, J. (2007). Placebo effects on human μ-opioid activity during pain. *PNAS Proceedings of the National Academy of Sciences of the United States of America, 104*(26), 11056–11061. doi:10.1073/pnas.0702413104

Wagner, H. (1989). The physiological differentiation of emotions. In H. Wagner & A. Manstead (Eds.), *Handbook of social psychophysiology.* New York, NY: Wiley.

Wagstaff, G. F., David, D., Kirsch, I., & Lynn, S. J. (2010). The cognitive-behavioral model of hypnotherapy. In S. J. Lynn, J. W. Rhue, & I. Kirsch (Eds.), *Handbook of clinical hypnosis* (2nd ed., pp. 179–208). Washington, DC: American Psychological Association.

Wai, J., Cacchio, M., Putallaz, M., & Makel, M. C. (2010). Sex differences in the right tail of cognitive abilities: A 30-year examination. *Intelligence, 38*(4), 412–423. doi:10.1016/j.intell.2010.04.006

Wald, G. (1964). The receptors of human color vision. *Science, 145,* 1007–1017.

Walker, E., Kestler, L., Bollini, A., & Hochman, K. M. (2004). Schizophrenia: Etiology and course. *Annual Review of Psychology, 55,* 401–430.

Walker, E., Mittal, V., & Tessner, K. (2008). Stress and the hypothalamic pituitary adrenal axis in the developmental course of schizophrenia. *Annual Review of Clinical Psychology, 4,* 189–216.

Walker, E., & Tessner, K. (2008). Schizophrenia. *Perspectives on Psychological Science, 3,* 30–37.

Walker, L. J. (1988). The development of moral reasoning. In R. Vasta (Ed.), *Annals of child development* (Vol. 5). Greenwich, CT: JAI Press.

Walker, L. J. (1989). A longitudinal study of moral reasoning. *Child Development, 60,* 157–166.

Walker, L. J. (2007). Progress and prospects in the psychology of moral development. In G. W. Ladd (Ed.), *Appraising the human developmental sciences: Essays in honor of Merrill-Palmer Quarterly.* Detroit: Wayne State University Press.

Walker, L. J., & Taylor, J. H. (1991). Strange transitions in moral reasoning: A longitudinal study of developmental processes. *Developmental Psychology, 27,* 330–337.

Walker, M. P. (2009). Sleep-dependent memory processing. In R. Stickgold & M. P. Walker (Eds.), *The neuroscience of sleep* (pp. 230–240). San Diego, CA: Academic Press.

Walker, M. P., Brakefield, T., Morgan, A., Hobson, J. A., & Stickgold, R. (2002). Practice with sleep makes perfect: Sleep dependent motor skill learning. *Neuron, 35,* 205–211.

Walker, M. P., & Stickgold, R. (2004). Sleep-dependent learning and memory consolidation. *Neuron, 44,* 121–133.

Walker, M. P., & Stickgold, R. (2006). Sleep, memory, and plasticity. *Annual Review of Psychology, 57,* 139–166.

Wallace, B., & Fisher, L. E. (1999). *Consciousness and behavior.* Boston, MA: Allyn & Bacon.

Wallace, D. S., Paulson, R. M., Lord, C. G., & Bond, C. F. Jr. (2005). Which behaviors do attitudes predict? Meta-analyzing the effects of social pressure and perceived difficulty. *Review of General Psychology, 9,* 214–227.

Wallner, B., & Machatschke, I. H. (2009). The evolution of violence in men: The function of central cholesterol and serotonin. *Progress in Neuro-Psychopharmacology & Biological Psychiatry, 33*(3), 391–397. doi:10.1016/j.pnpbp .2009.02.006

Walsh, B. T. (2003). Eating disorders. In A. Tasman, J. Kay, & J. A. Lieberman (Eds.), *Psychiatry.* New York, NY: Wiley.

Walsh, B. T., Seidman, S. N., Sysko, R., & Gould, M. (2002). Placebo response studies of major depression: Variable, substantial and growing. *Journal of the American Medical Association, 287,* 1840–1847.

Walsh, J. K., Dement, W. C., & Dinges, D. F. (2005). Sleep medicine, public policy, and public health. In M. H. Kryger, T. Roth, & W. C. Dement (Eds.). *Principles and practice of sleep medicine.* Philadelphia, PA: Elsevier Saunders.

Walsh, R., & Shapiro, S. L. (2006). The meeting of meditative disciplines and Western psychology: A mutually enriching dialogue. *American Psychologist, 61,* 227–239.

Walter, C. A. (2000). The psychological meaning of menopause: Women's experiences. *Journal of Women and Aging, 12*(3–4), 117–131.

Walther, E., & Grigoriadis, S. (2003). Why sad people like shoes better: The influence of mood on the evaluative conditioning of consumer attitudes. *Psychology & Marketing, 10,* 755–775.

Walther, E., & Langer, T. (2008). Attitude formation and change through association: An evaluative conditioning account. In W. D. Crano & R. Prislin (Eds.), *Attitudes and attitude change* (pp. 61–84). New York, NY: Psychology Press.

Walther, E., Nagengast, B., & Trasselli, C. (2005). Evaluative conditioning in social psychology: Facts and speculations. *Cognition and Emotion, 19*(2), 175–196.

Wampold, B. E. (2001). *The great psychotherapy debate.* Mahwah, NJ: Erlbaum.

Wampold, B. E., Imel, Z. E., & Minami, T. (2007). The story of placebo effects in medicine: Evidence in context. *Journal of Clinical Psychology, 63*(4), 379–390. doi:10.1002/jclp.20354

Wampold, B. E., Minami, T., Tierney, S. C., Baskin, T. W., & Bhati, K. S. (2005). The placebo is powerful: Estimating placebo effects in medicine and psychotherapy from randomized clinical trials. *Journal of Clinical Psychology , 61*(7), 835–854. doi:10.1002/jclp.20129

Wamsley, E. J., & Stickgold, R. (2009). Incorporation of waking events into dreams. In R. Stickgold & M. P. Walker (Eds.), *The neuroscience of sleep* (pp. 330–337). San Diego, CA: Academic Press.

Wang, P. S., Berglund, P., Olfson, M., Pincus, H. A., Wells, K. B., & Kessler, R. C. (2005). Failure and delay in initial treatment contact after first onset of mental disorders in the National Comorbidity Survey Replication. *Archives of General Psychiatry, 62,* 603–613.

Wang, P. S., Lane, M., Olfson, M., Pincus, H. A., Wells, K. B., & Kessler, R. C. (2005). Twelve-month use of mental health services in the United States: Results from the National Comorbidity Survey Replication. *Archives of General Psychiatry, 62,* 629–640.

Wangensteen, O. H., & Carlson, A. J. (1931). Hunger sensation after total gastrectomy. *Proceedings of the Society for Experimental Biology, 28,* 545–547.

Wansink, B. (2010). From mindless eating to mindlessly eating better. *Physiology & Behavior, 100*(5), 454–463. doi:10.1016/j.physbeh.2010 .05.003

Wansink, B., & Kim, J. (2005). Bad popcorn in big buckets: Portion size can influence intake as much as taste. *Journal of Nutrition Education and Behavior, 37*(5), 242–245. doi:10.1016/ S1499-4046(06)60278-9

Wansink, B., Painter, J. E., & North, J. (2005). Bottomless bowls: Why visual cues of portion size may influence intake. *Obesity Research, 13*(1), 93–100. doi:10.1038/oby.2005.12

Wargo, E. (2008). The many lives of superstition. *APS Observer, 21*(9), 18–24.

Warr, P. (1999). Well-being and the workplace. In D. Kahneman, E. Diener, & N. Schwarz (Eds.), *Well-being: The foundations of hedonic psychology.* New York, NY: Russell Sage Foundation.

Watanabe, M., Kikuchi, H., Tanaka, K., & Takahashi, M. (2010). Association of short sleep duration with weight gain and obesity at 1-year follow-up: A large-scale prospective study. *Sleep: Journal of Sleep and Sleep Disorders Research, 33*(2), 161–167.

Waterhouse, L. (2006). Multiple intelligences, the Mozart effect, and emotional intelligence: A critical review. *Educational Psychologist, 41,* 207–225.

Watkins, L. R. (2007). Immune and glial regulation of pain. *Brain, Behavior, and Immunity, 21,* 519–521.

Watson, D. L., & Tharp, R. G. (2007). *Self-directed behavior: Self-modification for personal adjustment.* Belmont, CA: Wadsworth.

Watson, D., Klohen, E. C., Casillas, A., Nus Simms, E., Haig, J., & Berry, D. S. (2004). Match makers and deal breakers: Analyses of assortative mating in newlywed couples. *Journal of Personality, 72,* 1029–1068.

Watson, J. B. (1913). Psychology as the behaviorist views it. *Psychological Review, 20,* 158–177.

Watson, J. B. (1919). *Psychology from the standpoint of a behaviorist.* Philadelphia, PA: Lippincott.

Watson, J. B. (1924). *Behaviorism.* New York, NY: Norton.

Watson, J. B., & Rayner, R. (1920). Conditioned emotional reactions. *Journal of Experimental Psychology, 3,* 1–14.

Waugh, N. C., & Norman, D. A. (1965). Primary memory. *Psychological Review, 72,* 89–104.

Waxman, S. (2002). Early word-learning and conceptual development: Everything had a name and each name gave birth to a new thought. In U. Goswami (Ed.), *Blackwell handbook of childhood cognitive development* (pp. 102–126). Malden, MA: Blackwell.

Waxman, S. (2005). Why is the concept "living thing" so elusive? Concepts, languages, and the development of folkbiology. In W. Ahn, R. L. Goldstone, B. C. Love, A. B. Markman, & P. Woolf (Eds.), *Categorization inside and outside the laboratory: Essays in honor of Douglas L. Medin* (pp. 49–67). Washington, DC: American Psychological Association.

Weaver, D. R., & Reppert, S. M. (2008). Circadian timekeeping. In L. Squire, D. Berg, F. Bloom, S. Du Lac, A. Ghosh, & N. Spitzer (Eds.), *Fundamental neuroscience* (3rd ed., pp. 931–958). San Diego, CA: Academic Press.

Webb, W. B., & Dinges, D. F. (1989). Cultural perspectives on napping and the siesta. In D. F. Dinges & R. J. Broughton (Eds.), *Sleep and* alertness: *Chronobiological, behavioral, and medical aspects of napping*. New York, NY: Raven.

Weber, L. J. (2006). *Profits before people?* Bloomington, IN: Indiana University Press.

Webster, G. D. (2009). Parental investment theory. In H. T. Reis & S. Sprecher (Eds.), *Encyclopedia of human relationships* (Vol. 3, pp. 1194–1197). Los Angeles, CA: Sage.

Webster, M. (2010). Color perception. In E. B. Goldstein (Ed.), *Encyclopedia of perception*. Thousand Oaks, CA: Sage.

Wechsler, D. (1939). *The measurement of adult intelligence*. Baltimore, MD: Williams & Wilkins.

Wegner, D. M. (1997). Why the mind wanders. In J. D. Cohen & J. W. Schooler (Eds.), *Scientific approaches to consciousness*. Mahwah, NJ: Erlbaum.

Wegner, D. M., & Wheatley, T. (1999). Apparent mental causation: Sources of the experience of will. *American Psychologist, 54*, 480–492. doi:10.1037/0003-066X.54.7.480

Wehring, H. J., & Carpenter, W. T. (2011). Violence and schizophrenia. *Schizophrenia Bulletin, 37*(Suppl 5), 877–878. doi:10.1093/schbul/sbr094

Weinberg, R. A. (1989). Intelligence and IQ: Landmark issues and great debates. *American Psychologist, 44*, 98–104.

Weiner, B. (Ed.). (1974). *Achievement motivation and attribution theory*. Morristown, NJ: General Learning Press.

Weiner, B. (1980). *Human motivation*. New York, NY: Holt, Rinehart & Winston.

Weiner, B. (1986). *An attributional theory of motivation and emotion*. New York, NY: Springer-Verlag.

Weiner, B. (1994). Integrating social and personal theories of achievement striving. *Review of Educational Research, 64*, 557–573.

Weinfeld, N. S., Sroufe, L. A., Egeland, B., & Carlson, E. (2008). Individual differences in infant-caregiver attachment: Conceptual and empirical aspects of security. In J. Cassidy & P. R. Shaver (Eds.), *Handbook of attachment: Theory, research, and clinical applications* (2nd ed., pp. 78–101). New York, NY: Guilford.

Weintraub, K. (2011). Autism counts. *Nature, 479*(7371), 22–24. doi:10.1038/479022a

Weisberg, R. W. (1986). *Creativity: Genius and other myths*. New York, NY: W. H. Freeman.

Weisberg, R. W. (1993). *Creativity: Beyond the myth of genius*. New York, NY: W. H. Freeman.

Weisberg, R. W. (1999). Creativity and knowledge: A challenge to theories. In R. J. Sternberg (Ed.), *Handbook of creativity*. New York, NY: Cambridge University Press.

Weisberg, R. W. (2006). *Creativity: Understanding innovation in problem solving, science, invention, and the arts*. New York, NY: Wiley.

Weiser, D. A., & Riggio, H. R. (2010). Family background and academic achievement: Does self-efficacy mediate outcomes? *Social Psychol-*

ogy *of Education, 13*(3), 367–383. doi:10.1007/s11218-010-9115-1

Weisler, R. H., Barbee, J. G., & Townsend, M. H. (2007). Mental health and recovery in the Gulf Coast after Hurricanes Katrina and Rita. *Journal of the American Medical Association, 296*, 585–588.

Weiss, A., Bates, T. C., & Luciano, M. (2008). Happiness is a personal(ity) thing. *Psychological Science, 19*, 205–210.

Weiss, J. L., Overpeck, J. T., & Strauss, B. (2011). Implications of recent sea level rise science for low-elevation areas in coastal cities of the conterminous U.S.A. *Climatic Change 105*, 635–645.

Weiten, W. (1998). Pressure, major life events, and psychological symptoms. *Journal of Social Behavior and Personality, 13*, 51–68.

Weiten, W., & Diamond, S. S. (1979). A critical review of the jury-simulation paradigm: The case of defendant characteristics. *Law and Human Behavior, 3*, 71–93.

Weiten, W., Guadagno, R. E., & Beck, C. A. (1996). Students' perceptions of textbook pedagogical aids. *Teaching of Psychology, 23*, 105–107.

Wells, G. L., & Bradfield, A. L. (1998). "Good, you identified the suspect": Feedback to eyewitnesses disorts their reports of the witnessing experience. *Journal of Applied Psychology, 83*, 360–376.

Wells, G. L., Memon, A., & Penrod, S. D. (2006). Eyewitness evidence: Improving its probative value. *Psychological Science in the Public Interest, 7*, 45–75.

Wells, G. L., Olson, E. A., & Charman, S. D. (2002). The confidence of eyewitnesses in their identifications from lineups. *Current Directions in Psychological Science, 11*(5), 151–154.

Wells, N. M., & Evans, G. W. (2003). Nearby nature: A buffer of life stress among rural children. *Environment and Behavior, 35*, 311–330.

Wertheimer, M. (1912). Experiment-elle studien über das sehen von bewegung. *Zeitschrift für Psychologie, 60*, 312–378.

Wesson, D. R., Smith, D. E., Ling, W., & Seymour, R. B. (2005). Sedative-hypnotics. In M. H. Kryger, T. Roth, & W. C. Dement (Eds.). *Principles and practice of sleep medicine*. Philadelphia, PA: Elsevier Saunders.

Westen, D. Gabbard, G. O., & Ortigo, K. M. (2008). Psychoanalytic approaches to personality. In O. P. John, R. W. Robins, & L. A. Pervin (Eds.), *Handbook of personality psychology: Theory and research*. New York, NY: Guilford.

Wetherby, A. M., & Prizant, B. M. (2005). Enhancing language and communication development in autism spectrum disorders: Assessment and intervention guidelines. In D. Zager (Ed.), *Autism spectrum disorders: Identification, education, and treatment* (3rd ed., pp. 327–365). Hillside, NJ: Lawrence Erlbaum Associates.

Wethington, E. (2007). Life events scale. In G. Fink (Ed.), *Encyclopedia of stress*. San Diego, CA: Elsevier.

Whincup, P., Kaye, S., Owen, C., Huxley, R., Cook, D., Anazawa, S., et al. (2008). Birth weight and risk of type 2 diabetes: A systematic review. *Journal of the American Medical Association, 300*(24), 2886–2897.

Whitaker, R. (2002). *Mad in America: Bad science, bad medicine, and the enduring mistreatment of the mentally ill*. New York, NY: Perseus Publishing.

Whitbourne, S. K., Zuschlag, M. K., Elliot, L. B., & Waterman, A. S. (1992). Psychosocial development in adulthood: A 22-year sequential study. *Journal of Personality and Social Psychology, 63*, 260–271.

White, C. M., & Hoffrage, U. (2009). Testing the tyranny of too much choice against the allure of more choice. *Psychology & Marketing, 26*(3), 280–298. doi:10.1002/mar.20273

White, S. H. (2000). Conceptual foundations of IQ testing. *Psychology, Public Policy, and Law, 6*, 33–43.

Whitfield, C. L. (1995). *Memory and abuse: Remembering and healing the effects of trauma*. Deerfield Beach, FL: Health Communications.

Whitty, M. T. (2008). Liberating or debilitating? An examination of romantic relationships, sexual relationships and friendships on the net. *Computers in Human Behavior, 24*, 1837–1850.

Widiger, T. A. (2009). Neuroticism. In M. R. Leary & R. H. Hoyle (Eds.), *Handbook of individual differences in social behavior* (pp. 129–146). New York, NY: Guilford.

Widiger, T. A., Livesley, W., & Clark, L. (2009). An integrative dimensional classification of personality disorder. *Psychological Assessment, 21*(3), 243–255. doi:10.1037/a0016606

Widiger, T. A., & Sankis, L. M. (2000). Adult psychopathology: Issues and controversies. *Annual Review of Psychology, 51*, 377–404.

Widiger, T. A., & Trull, T. J. (2007). Plate tectonics in the classification of personality disorder: Shifting to a dimensional model. *American Psychologist, 62*(2), 71–83. doi:10.1037/0003-066X.62.2.71

Wilding, J., & Valentine, E. (1996). Memory expertise. In D. J. Herrmann, C. McEvoy, C. Hertzog, P. Hertel, & M. K. Johnson (Eds.), *Basic and applied memory research: Theory in context* (Vol. 1). Mahwah, NJ: Erlbaum.

Willford, J. A., Leech, S. L., & Day, N. L. (2006). Moderate prenatal alcohol exposure and cognitive status of children at age 10. *Alcoholism: Clinical and Experimental Research, 30*, 1051–1059.

Williams, B. A. (1988). Reinforcement, choice, and response strength. In R. C. Atkinson, R. J. Herrnstein, G. Lindzey, & R. D. Luce (Eds.), *Stevens' handbook of experimental psychology*. New York, NY: Wiley.

Williams, C. G., Gagne, M., Ryan, R. M., & Deci, E. L. (2002). Facilitating autonomous motivation for smoking cessation. *Health Psychology, 21*, 40–50.

Williams, J. E., Paton, C. C., Siegler, I. C., Eigenbrodt, M. L., Neito, F. J., & Tyroler, H. A. (2000). Anger proneness predicts coronary heart disease risk. *Circulation, 101*, 2034–2039.

Williams, P. (2005). What is psychoanalysis? What is a psychoanalyst? In E. S. Person, A. M. Cooper, & G. O. Gabbard (Eds.), *Textbook of psychoanalysis*. Washington, DC: American Psychiatric Publishing.

Williams, R. E., Kaliani, L., DiBenedetti, D. B., Zhou, X., Fehnel, S. E., & Clark, R. V. (2007). Healthcare seeking and treatment for menopausal symptoms in the United States. *Maturitas, 58*, 348–358.

Williams, R. L., & Eggert, A. (2002). Notetaking predictors of test performance. *Teaching of Psychology, 29*(3), 234–237.

Williams, W. M. (1998). Are we raising smarter children today? School-and-home-related infuences on IQ. In U. Neisser (Ed.), *The rising curve: Long-term gains in IQ and related measures*. Washington, DC: American Psychological Association.

Williams, W. M., & Ceci, S. J. (1997). Are Americans becoming more or less alike?: Trends in race, class, and ability differences in intelligence. *American Psychologist, 52*, 1226–1235.

Williamson, D. A., Zucker, N. L., Martin, C. K., & Smeets, M. A. M. (2001). Etiology and management of eating disorders. In P. B. Sutker & H. E. Adams (Eds.), *Comprehensive handbook of psychopathology*. New York, NY: Kluwer Academic/Plenum.

Willis, S. L., Tennstedt, S. L., Marsiske, M., Ball, K., Elias, J., Koepke, K. M., Morris, J. N., et al. (2006). Long-term effects of cognitive training on everyday functional outcomes in older adults. *Journal of American Medical Association, 296*, 2805–2814.

Willoughby, T., Motz, M., & Wood, E. (1997). The impact of interest and strategy use on memory performance for child, adolescent, and adult learners. *Alberta Journal of Educational Research, 43*, 127–141.

Wills, T. A., & Fegan, M. (2001). Social networks and social support. In A. Baum, T. A. Revenson, & J. E. Singer (Eds.), *Handbook of health psychology* (pp. 209–234). Mahwah, NJ: Erlbaum.

Wilsnack, S. C., Wonderlich, S. A., Kristjanson, A. F., Vogeltanz-Holm, N. D., & Wilsnack, R. W. (2002). Self-reports of forgetting and remembering childhood sexual abuse in a nationally representative sample of U.S. women. *Child Abuse and Neglect, 26*(2), 139–147.

Wilson, G. T. (2011). Behavior therapy. In R. J. Corsini & D. Wedding (Eds.), *Current psychotherapies* (9th ed.). Belmont, CA: Brooks/Cole.

Wilson, T. D., & Gilbert, D. T. (2003). Affective forecasting. In M. P. Zanna (Ed.), *Advances in experimental social psychology* (Vol. 35, pp. 345–411). San Diego, CA: Academic Press. doi:10.1016/S0065-2601(03)01006-2

Wilson, T. D., & Gilbert, D. T. (2005). Affective forecasting: Knowing what to want. *Current Directions in Psychological Science, 14*, 131–134.

Wilt, J., & Revelle, W. (2009). Extraversion. In M. R. Leary & R. H. Hoyle (Eds.), *Handbook of individual differences in social behavior* (pp. 257–273). New York, NY: Guilford.

Windholz, G. (1997). Ivan P. Pavlov: An overview of his life and psychological work. *American Psychologist, 52*, 941–946.

Winett, R. A., Hatcher, J. W., Fort, T. R., Leckliter, I. N., Love, S. Q., Riley, A. W., & Fishback, J. F. (1982). The effects of videotape modeling and daily feedback on residential electricity conservation, home temperature and humidity, perceived comfort, and clothing worn: Winter and summer. *Journal of Applied Behavior Analysis, 15*, 381–402.

Wing, L., & Potter, D. (2009). The epidemiology of autism spectrum disorders: Is the prevalence rising? In S. Goldstein, J. A. Naglieri, & S. Ozonoff (Eds.), *Assessment of autism spectrum disorders* (pp. 18–54). New York, NY: Guilford.

Wingfield, A., Tun, P. A., & McCoy, S. L. (2005). Hearing loss in older adulthood: What it is and how it interacts with cognitive performance. *Current Directions in Psychological Science, 14*, 144–148.

Winn, P. (1995). The lateral hypothalmus and motivated behavior: An old syndrome reassessed and a new perspective gained. *Current Directions in Psychological Science, 4*, 182–187.

Winter, D. D. & Cava, M. M. (2006) The psycho-ecology of armed conflict. *Journal of Social Issues, 62*, 19–40.

Winter, D. G. (2010). Why achievement motivation predicts success in business but failure in politics: The importance of personal control. *Journal of Personality, 78*(6), 1637–1667. doi:10.1111/j.1467-6494.2010.00665.x

Winters, K. C., Arthur, N., Leitten, W., & Botzet, A. (2004). Gambling and drug abuse in adolescence. In In J. L. Derevensky & R. Gupta (Eds.), *Gambling problems in youth: Theoretical and applied perspectives* (pp. 57-80). New York, NY: Kluwer/Plenum.

Wise, R. A. (1999). Animal models of addiction. In D. S. Charney, E. J. Nestler, & B. S. Bunney (Eds.), *Neurobiology of mental illness*. New York, NY: Oxford University Press.

Wise, R. A. (2002). Brain reward circuitry: Insights from unsensed incentives. *Neuron, 36*, 229–240.

Wittkower, E. D., & Warnes, H. (1984). Cultural aspects of psychotherapy. In J. E. Mezzich & C. E. Berganza (Eds.), *Culture and psychopathology*. New York, NY: Columbia University Press.

Wolfe, J. M., Kluender, K. R., Levi, D. M., Bartoshuk, L. M., Herz, R. S., Klatzky, R. L., & Lederman, S. J. (2006). *Sensation and perception*. Sunderland, MA: Sinauer Associates.

Wolford, G., Miller, M. B., & Gazzaniga, M. S. (2004). Split decisions. In M. S. Gazzaniga (Ed.), *The cognitive neurosciences*. Cambridge, MA: MIT Press.

Wolitzky, D. L. (2006). Psychodynamic theories. In J. C. Thomas & D. L. Segal (Eds.), *Comprehensive handbook of personality and psychopathology*. New York, NY: Wiley.

Wolpe, J. (1958). *Psychotherapy by reciprocal inhibition*. Stanford, CA: Stanford University Press.

Wolpe, J. (1990). *The practice of behavior therapy*. Elmsford, NY: Pergamon Press.

Wonderlich, S. A. (2002). Personality and eating disorders. In C. G. Fairburn & K. D. Brownell (Eds.), *Eating disorders and obesity: A comprehensive handbook*. New York, NY: Guilford.

Wong, L. A. (2006). *Essential study skills*. Boston, MA: Houghton Mifflin.

Wong, P. T. P. (2006). Existential and humanistic theories. In J. C. Thomas & D. L. Segal (Eds.), *Comprehensive handbook of personality and psychopathology*. New York, NY: Wiley.

Wood, E., Desmarais, S., & Gugula, S. (2002). The impact of parenting experience on gender stereotyped toy play of children. *Sex Roles, 47*(1–2), 39–49.

Wood, J. N., & Spelke, E. S. (2005). Chronometric studies of numerical cognition in five-month-old infants. *Cognition, 97*, 23–39.

Wood, P. B. (2007). Fibromyalgia. In G. Fink (Ed.), *Encyclopedia of stress*. San Diego, CA: Elsevier.

Wood, R. A., & Griffiths, M. D. (2007). A qualitative investigation of problem gambling as an escape-based coping strategy. *Psychology & Psychotherapy: Theory, Research & Practice, 80*(1), 107–125.

Woodhead, M. (2004). When psychology informs public policy: The case. In E. Zigler & S. J. Styfco (Eds.), *The Head Start debate*. Baltimore, MD: Paul H. Brookes Publishing.

Woods, S. C., & Stricker, E. M. (2008). Food intake and metabolism. In L. Squire, D. Berg, F. Bloom, S. du Lac, A. Ghosh, & N. Spitzer, *Fundamental neuroscience* (3rd ed.). San Diego, CA: Academic Press.

Woody, E. Z., & Sadler, P. (2008). In M. R. Nash & A. J. Barnier (Eds.). *Oxford handbook of hypnosis: Theory, research and practice* (pp. 81–110). New York, NY: Oxford University Press.

Woolfolk, R. L., & Richardson, F. C. (1978). *Stress, sanity and survival*. New York, NY: Sovereign/Monarch.

World Resources Institute. (2001). *Facts and figures: Environmental data tables, energy and resource use*. Table ERC.5: Resource Consumption. [Data file]. Available from World Resources Institute website, http://www.wri.org/trends/index.html

Worthen, J. B., & Wade, C. E. (1999). Direction of travel and visiting team athletic performance: Support for a circadian dysrhythmia hypothesis. *Journal of Sport Behavior, 22*, 279–287.

Worthington, R. L., Soth-McNett, A. M., & Moreno, M. V. (2007). Multicultural counseling competencies research: A 20-year content analysis. *Journal of Counseling Psychology, 54*, 351–361.

Wrosch, C., & Scheier, M. F. (2003). Personality and quality of life: The importance of optimism and goal adjustment. *Quality of Life Research: An International Journal of Quality of Life As-*

pects of Treatment, Care & Rehabilitation, 12, 59–72.

Wrosch, C., Miller, G. E., Scheier, M. F., & de Pontet, S. B. (2007). Giving up on unattainable goals: Benefits for health? *Personality and Social Psychology Bulletin, 33,* 251–265.

Wundt, W. (1874/1904). *Principles of physiological psychology.* Leipzig: Engelmann.

Wynn, K. (1992). Addition and subtraction by human infants. *Nature, 358,* 749–750.

Wynn, K. (1996). Infants' individuation and enumeration of sequential actions. *Psychological Science, 7,* 164–169.

Wynn, K. (1998). An evolved capacity for number. In D. D. Cummins & C. Allen (Eds.), *The evolution of mind.* New York, NY: Oxford University Press.

Xu, J., & Roberts, R. E. (2010). The power of positive emotions: It's a matter of life or death—Subjective well-being and longevity over 28 years in a general population. *Health Psychology, 29*(1), 9–19. doi:10.1037/a0016767

Yaffe, K. K., Fiocco, A. J., Lindquist, K. K., Vittinghoff, E. E., Simonsick, E. M., Newman, A. B., et al. (2009). Predictors of maintaining cognitive function in older adults: The Health ABC Study. *Neurology, 72*(23), 2029–2035. doi:10.1212/WNL.0b013e3181a92c36

Yamamoto, J., Silva, J. A., Justice, L. R., Chang, C. Y., & Leong, G. B. (1993). Cross-cultural psychotherapy. In A. C. Gaw (Ed.), *Culture, ethnicity, and mental illness.* Washington, DC: American Psychiatric Press.

Yates, F. A. (1966). *The art of memory.* London: Routledge & Kegan Paul.

Yeomans, M. R., Tepper, B. J., Rietzschel, J., & Prescott, J. (2007). Human hedonic responses to sweetness: Role of taste genetics and anatomy. *Physiology & Behavior, 91,* 264–273.

Yerkes, R. M., & Morgulis, S. (1909). The method of Pavlov in animal psychology. *Psychological Bulletin, 6,* 257–273.

Yost, W. A. (2000). *Fundamentals of hearing: An introduction.* San Diego, CA: Academic Press.

Yost, W. A. (2010). Audition: Pitch perception. In E. B. Goldstein (Ed.), *Encyclopedia of perception.* Thousand Oaks, CA: Sage.

Young, K. S. (2009). Internet addiction: Diagnosis and treatment considerations. *Journal of Contemporary Psychotherapy, 39*(4), 241–246. doi:10.1007/s10879-009-9120-x

Young, T. B. (2004). Epidemiology of daytime sleepiness: Definitions, symptomatology, and prevalence. *Journal of Clinical Psychiatry, 65*(Suppl16), 12–16.

Zajonc, R. B. (1968). Attitudinal effects of mere exposure. *Journal of Personality and Social Psychology, 9,* 1–29.

Zak, P. J., Kurzban, R., & Matzner, W. T. (2005). Oxytocin is associated with human trustworthiness. *Hormones and Behavior, 48*(5), 522–527. doi:10.1016/j.yhbeh.2005.07.009

Zane, N., Hall, G. C. N., Sue, S., Young, K., & Nunez, J. (2004). Research on psychotherapy with culturally diverse populations. In M. J. Lambert (Ed.), *Bergin and Garfield's handbook of psychotherapy and behavior change.* New York, NY: Wiley.

Zaragoza, M. S., Belli, R. F., & Payment, K. E. (2007). Misinformation effects and the suggestibility of eyewitness memory. In M. Garry & H. Hayne (Eds.), *Do justice and let the sky fall: Elizabeth F. Lotus and her contributions to science, law, and academic freedom.* Mahwah, NJ: Erlbaum.

Zárate, M. A. (2009). Racism in the 21st century. In T. D. Nelson (Ed.), *Handbook of prejudice, stereotyping, and discrimination* (pp. 1–22). New York, NY: Psychology Press.

Zatzick, D. F., & Dimsdale, J. E. (1990). Cultural variations in response to painful stimuli. *Psychosomatic Medicine, 52*(5), 544–557.

Zechmeister, E. B., & Nyberg, S. E. (1982). *Human memory: An introduction to research and theory.* Pacific Grove, CA: Brooks/Cole.

Zeidan, F., Gordon, N. S., Merchant, J., & Goolkasian, P. (2010). The effects of brief mindfulness meditation training on experimentally induced pain. *The Journal of Pain, 11*(3), 199–209. doi:10.1016/j.jpain.2009.07.015

Zeiler, M. (1977). Schedules of reinforcement: The controlling variables. In W. K. Honig & J. E. R. Staddon (Eds.), *Handbook of operant behavior.* Englewood Cliffs, NJ: Prentice-Hall.

Zenhausen, R. (1978). Imagery, cerebral dominance and style of thinking: A unified field model. *Bulletin of the Psychonomic Society, 12,* 381–384.

Zhang, T., & Meaney, M. J. (2010). Epigenetics and the environmental regulation of the genome and its function. *Annual Review of Psychology, 61,* 439–466. doi:10.1146/annurev.psych.60 .110707.163625

Zillmer, E. A., Spiers, M. V., & Culbertson, W. C. (2008). *Principles of neuropsychology.* Belmont, CA: Wadsworth.

Zimbardo, P. G. (2004, May 9). Power turns good soldiers into "bad apples." *Boston Globe.* Retrieved from http://www.boston.com/news/ globe/editorial_opinion/oped/ articles/2004/05/09

Zimbardo, P. G., Haney, C., & Banks, W. C. (1973, April 8). The mind is a formidable jailer: A Pirandellian prison. *New York Times Magazine,* Section 6, p. 36.

Zimmerman, I. L., & Woo-Sam, J. M. (1984). Intellectual assessment of children. In G. Goldstein & M. Hersen (Eds.), *Handbook of psychological assessment.* New York, NY: Pergamon Press.

Zimmerman, M., & Spitzer, R. L. (2009). Psychiatric classification. In B. J. Sadock, V. A. Sadock, & P. Ruiz (Eds.), *Kaplan & Sadock's comprehensive textbook of psychiatry* (9th ed., pp. 1108–1138). Philadelphia, PA: Lippincott Williams & Wilkins.

Zinbarg, R. E., & Griffith, J. W. (2008). Behavior Therapy. In J. L. Lebow (Ed.), *Twenty-first century psychotherapies: Contemporary approaches to theory and practice.* New York, NY: Wiley.

Zohar, J., Fostick, L., & Juven-Wetzler, E. (2009). Obsessive-compulsive disorder. In M. C. Gelder, N. C. Andreasen, J. J. López-Ibor, Jr., & J. R. Geddes (Eds.). *New Oxford textbook of psychiatry* (2nd ed., Vol. 1). New York, NY: Oxford University Press.

Zola, S. M., & Squire, L. R. (2000). The medial temporal lobe and the hippocampus. In E. Tulving & F. I. M. Craik (Eds.), *The Oxford handbook of memory* (pp. 485–500). New York, NY: Oxford University Press.

Zorick, F. J., & Walsh, J. K. (2000). Evaluation and management of insomnia: An overview. In M. H. Kryger, T. Roth, & W. C. Dement (Eds.), *Principles and practice of sleep medicine.* Philadelphia, PA: Saunders.

Zorumski, C. F., Isenberg, K. E., & Mennerick, S. (2009). Cellular and synaptic electrophysiology. In B. J. Sadock, V. A. Sadock, & P. Ruiz (Eds.), *Kaplan & Sadock's comprehensive textbook of psychiatry* (9th ed., Vol. 1, pp. 129–146). Philadelphia, PA: Lippincott Williams & Wilkins.

Zrenner, E., Abramov, I., Akita, M., Cowey, A., Livingstone, M., & Valberg, A. (1990). Color perception: Retina to cortex. In L. Spillman & J. S. Werner (Eds.), *Visual perception: The neurophysiological foundations.* San Diego, CA: Academic Press.

Zubieta, J., Bueller, J. A., Jackson, L. R., Scott, D. J., Xu, Y., Koeppe, R. A., Nichols, T. E., et al. (2005). Placebo effects mediated by endogenous opioid activity on m-opioid receptors. *The Journal of Neuroscience, 25*(34), 7754–7762. doi:10.1523/JNEUROSCI.0439-05.2005

Zuckerman, M. (1971). Dimensions of sensation seeking. *Journal of Consulting and Clinical Psychology, 36,* 45–52.

Zurbriggen, E. L., & Sturman, T. S. (2002). Linking motives and emotions: A test of McClelland's hypothesis. *Personality & Social Psychology Bulletin, 28,* 521–535.

Name Index

Yamamoto, J., 525
Yan, T., 51
Yates, F. A., 240
Yeomans, M. R., 126
Yerkes, R. M., 178
Yoo, S., 13, 21
Yoon, J. H., 70, 486
Yost, W. A., 124, 348
Young, J. E., 516
Young, K., 446, 525
Young, L. J., 85
Young, T., 109
Young, T. B., 150
Youngentob, S. L., 126

Yount, S. E., 449
Yovel, G., 108
Yuille, J. C., 218, 219, 233
Yuker, H. E., 113

Z

Zachariae, R., 450
Zajonc, R., 413
Zak, P. J., 86
Zane, N., 525
Zanna, M. P., 399
Zapp, D. J., 298
Zaragoza, M. S., 226
Zárate, M. A., 427

Zatzick, D. F., 128
Zautra, A. J., 435, 441
Zebrowski, L. A., 398
Zechmeister, E. B., 23
Zedeck, S., 269
Zeidan, F., 162
Zeiler, M., 193
Zelenski, J. M., A-29
Zenhausen, R., 94
Zeschky, M., 254
Zhang, R., 374
Zhang, T., 89
Zillmer, E. A., 72, 81
Zimbardo, P. G., 375, 420–421

Zimmerman, I. L., 267
Zimmerman, M., 470
Zimprich, D., 350
Zinbarg, R., 181, 475, 516
Zipf, W. B., 342
Zoeller, R. F., Jr., 454
Zohar, J., 473
Zola, S. M., 12, 236
Zorick, F. J., 154
Zorumski, C. F., 64
Zrenner, E., 111
Zubieta, J., 51
Zucker, K. J., 300
Zurbriggen, E. L., 303

Subject Index

children (continued)
    language development in, 331–332
    media violence and, 203, 206
    moral development in, 338–340
    motor development in, 328
    parental investment in, 297
    parental love for, 376
    personality development in, 368–370
    physical punishment of, 197–198
    sleep cycle of, 148, 150
chimpanzees, Goodall's study of, 44
China, A-33
chloride ions, 65
chlorpromazine, 517
choice overload, 257
choices
    conflict and, 437
    factors in, 257–258
cholesterol, 448
chromosomes, 86, 87, 324
chronic pain, self-efficacy and, 374
chunks, in short-term memory, 221–222
cigarettes, 210, 453
circadian rhythms, 143–144
circular reasoning, 173, 319
clarification, in client-centered therapy, 511
Clark University, 7
classical conditioning, 177–186
    acquisition in, 182, 191
    in advertising, 210
    of anxiety responses, 475, 514
    of attitudes, 413
    avoidance learning and, 195–196
    basic processes in, 182–186
    in business negotiations, 211
    discrimination in, 185, 191
    of emotions, 180–181
    in everyday life, 180–182
    extinction in, 182, 191
    of food preferences, 295
    generalization in, 184–185, 191
    interaction with operant conditioning, 195–196
    observational learning and, 201
    overview of, 204–205
    Pavlov's formulation of, 178–180
    of physiological responses, 181
    in politics, 211
    signal relations in, 200
    spontaneous recovery in, 183
    of taste aversion, 199
    terminology and procedures for, 179
classical music, for infants, 96, 97
claustrophobia, 472
client-centered therapy, 510–511, 523–524, 530
climate change, A-31–A-32
clinical psychologists, 45, 506
clinical psychology, 11–12, 17, 18
clinical social workers, 506
clitoris, 295
closure, as Gestalt principle, 115
Clouser, Ronald, 244
CNS depressants. See depressants
CNS stimulants. See stimulants
cocaine, 163, 164
    brain activity and, 75
    health effects of, 167
    neurotransmitters and, 70
    prenatal development and, 326
    synapses and, 166
cochlea, 123, 124
coefficient of determination, A-27
cognition, 12, 249
cognitive abilities
    aging and, 349–350
    gender differences in, 27, 351

cognitive appraisal, of stressful events, 441
cognitive development, 334–337
    moral development and, 339
    Piaget's stage theory of, 334–337
cognitive dissonance, 415–416, A-36
cognitive performance, sleep deprivation and, 151
cognitive perspective, 10, 12, 249
    on conditioning, 200–201
    on dreaming, 157, 158
    on emotion, 311–312
    on gender-role learning, 354
    on intelligence, 279
cognitive psychology, 16, 17
cognitive revolution, 249
cognitive style, 95
    culture and, 256
    depression and, 483
cognitive tasks, hemispheres and, 93, 94
cognitive therapy, 515, 523–524, 531
cognitive-behavioral therapy, 515–516, 523–524
cohabitation, 346–347
collective unconscious, 370
collectivism, 403, 423
    conformity and, 420
    marriage and, 407
college admissions tests, 42, 46
college students
    gambling by, 1–2
    increase in narcissism among, 383
    as research subjects, 50
colleges, psychology laboratories at, 4
color, effect on behavior, 111–112
color blindness, 110
color circle, 111
color mixing, 109, 110
color vision, 105, 109–111
    opponent process theory of, 110–111
    trichromatic theory of, 109–110, 111
Columbia University, 5
commitment, 343, 406
common sense, versus scientific approach, 35
commons dilemmas, A-36
communication
    with health providers, 456
    nonverbal, 308, 309
    persuasive, 411–412
communities, positive, 14
community mental health centers, 525, 529, 530
community mental health movement, 526
comorbidity, 498
companionate love, 406
comparative optimism, A-39
comparators, 136–137
compensation, 371
competence, attractiveness and, 399
competition
    between groups, 428
    individualism and, 403
complementary colors, 110, 111
compliance
    with authority, 418–420
    with medical advice, 456–457
composers, mental illness and, 283
compulsions, 473
computerized tomography (CT) scans, 75
conclusions, 34, 40, 318
concordance rates
    for anxiety disorders, 475
    for mood disorders, 482
    for schizophrenia, 488
concrete operational period, 335, 336–337

conditionability, 380
conditioned reinforcers, 191
conditioned response (CR), 179, 180, 181, 183, 184, 185, 186, 195, 199, 210, 413–414, 475, 514
conditioned stimulus (CS), 179, 180, 181, 182, 183, 184, 185, 186, 195, 199, 200–201, 210, 413–414, 475, 514
conditioning
    biological constraints on, 198–200
    cognitive processes in, 200–201
    contingencies and, 201
    defined, 177
    evaluative, 181–182, 210, 413
    personality and, 373
    rapid, 199
    see also classical conditioning; operant conditioning
cones, 104–105, 111
confirmatory biases, 399, 425
conflict(s)
    between groups, 428–429
    internal, 365–366
    parent-child, 347
    in romantic relationships, 407
    as source of stress, 437
    types of, 437
    unconscious, 365–366
conformity, 417–418
conformity pressure, 439
confounding of variables, 39
congruence, 376, 510
conjunction fallacy, 260, 499
conjunctive probabilities, 498, 499
conscientiousness, 345, 363, 381, 390, 451
conscious, 365, 366
consciousness
    altered, 160–161
    altering with drugs, 163–167
    brain activity and, 142
    contents of, 141
    divided, 160
    in meditation, 161
    nature of, 141–142
    states of, 142
    stream of, 5, 141
    study of, 3–4
consensus, false, A-39
conservation, 335–336
conservation psychology, A-29
conservatism, 33, 34
consistency, cross-situational, 362, 375
consolidation, of memory, 152, 236
conspicuous consumption, A-35
constancies, perceptual, 118
constraints, unnecessary, 252–253
construct validity, 278
constructive coping, 447, 458–461
consumers, choice overload and, 257
consumption, conspicuous, A-35
contact comfort, 329–330
context, perceptual hypotheses and, 116
context cues, 224–225
contingencies, conditioning and, 201, 208
continuity, as Gestalt principle, 115, 116
contradictory evidence, 27, 97, 285
control, as goal of scientific approach, 32
control group, 36, 37
conventional level, 339
convergent thinking, 282
coping, 458–461
    constructive, 447, 458–461
    defensive, 446–447

problem-focused, 451, 452, A-41
    with stress, 444–445
cornea, 103
coronary disease, sleep loss and, 153
coronary heart disease, 448
corporal punishment, 197–198
corpus callosum, 79, 82, 83, 353
correlation(s), 41–43, A-25–A-26
    causation and, 42–43, 46–47, 462, 366–367
    of IQ scores, 271
    positive and negative, 41, 267
    prediction and, 42, A-26–A-27
    reliability and, 267
    strength of, 42, A-25
    between stress and illness, 450
correlation coefficient, 42, 267, A-25
    calculating, A-26
correlational research, 41–47
    advantages of, 46, 49
    disadvantages of, 46–47, 49
    on media violence, 206
corticosteroids, 444
counseling psychologists, 506
counseling psychology, 17, 18
counselors, 507
counterarguments, 318
counterattitudinal behavior, 415
couples therapy, 512
courtship behavior, 92
crack cocaine, 164, 167
cramming, 241
creative intelligence, 279
creativity, 282–283
    Freud's view of, 368
    REM sleep and, 152
credibility, of sources, 412, 416, 430–431
critical periods, 96, 97
critical thinking, defined, 26
cross-cultural research, 13
    on close relationships, 407
    on emotion, 308–309
    on motor development, 328
    on personality, 403–404
    on social behavior, 426
cross-situational consistency, 375
crystal meth, 164
Crystal, Billy, 503
CT (computerized tomography) scans, 75
Cuba, 424
Cubism, 134
cues, to depth perception, 116–118
cultural differences
    in attachment patterns, 330–331
    in attributional processes, 403
    in close relationships, 407
    in depth perception, 118
    in dreaming, 157
    in intelligence, 281
    in intelligence testing, 269
    in IQ scores, 274
    in moral reasoning, 340
    in motor development, 328
    in perception, 139, 132
    in perception of visual illusions, 119–120
    in sleep patterns, 150–151
    in sociability, 43–44
    see also culture
cultural diversity, psychology and, 13
cultural worldviews, 386
culture, 21–22
    archetypes and, 370–371
    cognitive development and, 338
    cognitive style and, 256
    conformity and, 420
    eating disorders and, 497

marital therapy, 512
marketing, Watson's contributions to, 8
marriage, 346–347
  arranged, 407
  cultural differences in, 407
  median age at first, 346
marriage and family counselors, 506, 507
masculinity, 351
Massachusetts General Hospital, 236
massed practice, 241, 242
matching hypothesis, 405
matching websites, 408
matchstick problem, 253, 254
mate preferences
  gender differences in, 298–299, 408–409
  parental investment and, 297, 298
mate selection, in animals, 297
material goods, happiness and, 315
materialism, 384, 387, A-34–A-35
materialistic values, A-36
mathematical ability, gender differences in, 351
mathematics, infants and, 338
maturation, 328
  sexual, 341–342
McCain, John, 211
me-first attitude, 384
Me, Myself, and Irene, 478
mean, A-22
  regression toward, 532, 533
meaning, memory and, 242
measurement, as goal of scientific approach, 31–32
meat consumption, A-34
media
  as source of gender-role socialization, 355
  as source of prejudicial attitudes, 428
  violence in, 203, 206
medial forebrain bundle, 78, 166
medial temporal lobe memory system, 236
median, A-22
medical advice, adhering to, 456–457
medical diagnoses, hindsight bias and, 393
medical model, of abnormal behavior, 467–468
medical services, using, 456
medical statistics, 462
medical students' disease, 498
medical treatment, seeking, 455–456
meditation, 161–162
medulla, 76, 77
melatonin, 144, 154
memorization, 242
memory
  aging and, 349, 350
  biological basis of, 234–237
  brain areas for, 236
  consolidation of, 152, 236
  distortions in, 226
  for dreams, 170–171
  false, 231–234
  glial cells and, 65
  hypnosis and, 160
  improving, 240–243
  information processing approach to, 220
  key processes in, 215
  levels-of-processing theory, 217–218
  limbic system and, 78
  long-term, 222–223
  loss of, 235–246
  napping and, 169
  reconstructive nature of, 227–228, 244

sensory, 220
short-term, 220–222
training programs for, 350
memory loss, 477
memory systems, 237–239
memory trace, 220
  decay of, 229–230
menarche, 342
menopause, 348
menstruation, 342
mental ability, tests of, 264–265
mental age, calculation of, 264–265
mental health services, use of, 505, 525
mental hospitals, 526–527
mental illness. *See* psychological disorders
mental processes, study of, 12
mental retardation, 285, 326, 470
mental rotation, 27
mental set, 252
mental speed, 349
mere exposure effect, 413
mescaline, 164
Mesmer, Franz Anton, 158
mesmerism, 158
mesolimbic dopamine pathway, 166
message factors, in persuasion, 412–413
meta-analysis, 47
methadone, 163
methamphetamine, 164
method of loci, 240, 243
Mexican Americans, mental health services and, 525
microcephaly, 338
microelectrodes, 65
midbrain, 76, 77
middle ear, 123
military returnees, 474
Miller, Johnny Lee, 323
Miller, Zell, 96
mindfulness meditation, 161
Minnesota Multiphasic Personality Inventory (MMPI), 390
minorities
  IQ scores of, 274–277
  mental health services for, 525
  stereotyping of, 387
  see also specific minorities
mirror neurons, 79–80
miscarriage, 325
misinformation effect, 226, 233, 244
MMPI, 390
mnemonic devices, 240, 243
mode, A-22
models, 201, 202, 354, 374, 515
  for pro-environment behavior, A-38–A-39
Molaison, Henry, 235
monamine neurotransmitters, 70
money, happiness and, 315
monocular cues to depth perception, 117–118
Monroe, Marilyn, 371
mood disorders, 470, 478–484, 492–493
  biological factors in, 482–483, 493
  cognitive factors in, 483, 493
  creativity and, 283
  drug therapy for, 518–519
  electroconvulsive therapy for, 521
  etiology of, 482–484, 493
  interpersonal roots of, 483–484, 493
  neurochemical factors in, 482
  prenatal development and, 327
  prevalence of, 480, 481, 498
  stress and, 484, 493
  types of, 478–481, 492
  vulnerability to, 494

mood stabilizers, 519–520
mood swings, 481
moon illusion, 119
moral development, 338–340, 365
morphine, 71, 163, 164
mortality, 261–262
  awareness of, 386–387
  Big Five traits and, 363
  childhood IQ and, 278
  exercise and, 461
  sleep duration and, 153
  smoking and, 453
  social support and, 451
mortality salience, 386
mother-infant attachment, 328–330
mothers. *See* parents
motivated forgetting, 231, 367
motivation
  achievement, 302–303
  Adler's view of, 371
  defined, 290
  distance estimates and, 118
  drive theories of, 290
  emotion and, 303
  evolutionary theories of, 291
  incentive theories of, 290–291
  observational learning and, 202
  sexual, 295–302
motivation to remember (MTR), 218–219
motives, 290–291
motor cortex, 79, 80
motor development, 328, 329
motor neurons, 69
motor skills, mirror neurons and, 79–80
Mount Everest, 289
movement
  coordination of, 77
  illusion of, 114
  motor cortex and, 79
Mozart effect, 97
MRI (magnetic resonance imaging) scans, 75
Müller-Lyer illusion, 118–119, 120
multiaxial system, 470–471
multicultural sensitivity, in psychotherapy, 524–525
multiculturalism, 13
multifactorial causation, 20–21, 93, 165, 168–169, 457, 494
multimodal therapy, 531
multiple-choice tests, 229
multiple personality disorder, 477–478
multiple sclerosis, 64
multitasking, 216–217
muscles
  nerves and, 73
  neurotransmitters and, 69
music, ability to read, 222
musical training, cognition and, 97
musicians, cerebral specialization and, 94
myelin sheath, 64
myelinization, 278, 342, 489
Myers-Briggs Type Inventory, A-37

N

naive realism, 33
names, remembering, 216
napping, 151, 169
narcissism, 383, 386
narcissistic personality disorder, 383
Narcissistic Personality Inventory (NPI), 383
narcolepsy, 154
narcotics, 163, 164, 165, 326
narrative methods, 242

Nash, John, 486
national character, 403, 404
National Comorbidity Study, 498
Native Americans, IQ scores of, 274
natural selection, 14, 90, 91, 291, 352
  face recognition and, 109
  of personality traits, 381
naturalistic observation, 43–44, 48–49
nature
  children and, A-40–A-41
  connection to, A-29
  stress reduction and, A-41
nature-immersion therapy, A-41–A-42
nature versus nurture, 7–8, 22
  in intelligence, 269–277, 281
  in learning, 206
  see also heredity; environment
Nazi Germany, 211, 418
nearsightedness, 103, 104
Necker cube, 116, 134, 135
need for achievement, 302–303
need for affiliation, 302
need for self-actualization, 378
needs
  biological, 291
  gratification of, 369
  Maslow's hierarchy of, 377
negative correlation, 41, 267, A-25
negative emotionality, 363
negative reinforcement, 194-195, 196–197
negative self-talk, 459
negative thinking, 445, 446
  depressive disorder and, 483
NEO Personality Inventory, 390
nerves, 72–73
nervous system
  autonomic, 73, 305–306
  cells in, 64–65
  information processing in, 63–71
  organization of, 71–74
  peripheral, 72–73
neural circuits, for memory, 236–237
neural impulse, 65–66
neural networks, 68
neuritic plaques, 348
neurodevelopmental hypothesis, 489–490
neurofibrillary tangles, 348
neurogenesis, 81–82, 237, 444
  exercise and, 454
  sleep and, 152
  suppression of, 482–483
neurons, 64–65
  aging and, 348
  as feature detectors, 108
  mirror, 79–80
  motor, 69
  myelinization of, 278, 342, 489
  new, 81, 482
  number of in brain, 71
  resting potential of, 65
  in visual cortex, 108
neuroscience perspective, 13
neuroses, 507
neuroticism, 345, 363, 382, 390, 450
neurotransmitters, 64, 67, 68
  anxiety disorders and, 475
  hormones and, 85
  in hunger, 292, 293
  memory and, 237
  monamine, 70
  mood disorders and, 482
  psychoactive drug action and, 165–166
  in schizophrenia, 488
  see also specific neurotransmitters
newborns, sleep cycle of, 148, 150
nicotine, 163

night vision, 105
nightmares, 474
nine-dot problem, 252–253, 254
nominal fallacy, 173
non-REM (NREM) sleep, 147, 148–149
non sequitur, 319
nondeclarative memory system, 237
nonsense syllables, 227
nonverbal behavior, 308, 309
nonverbal communication, gender differences in, 352
nonverbal expressiveness, impression formation and, 399
norepinephrine (NE), 69, 70, 166, 482
normal distribution, 265–267, A-23–A-24
normality, versus abnormality, 468–469
norms, social, 364, 468, A-35
nose, smell and, 126
note taking, during lectures, 25
nucleus accumbens, 166
null hypothesis, A-28
Nurture Assumption, The (Harris), 393
nutrition, prenatal development and, 326

O

obedience, 418–420
obesity, 454
   fear of, 495
   sleep loss and, 153
   sleep problems and, 154
   snoring and, 169
   taste preferences and, 91
   television viewing and, 46
object permanence, 335
objectivity, as research goal, 51
observation
   direct, 34
   naturalistic, 43–44, 48–49
observational learning, 201–203, 206
   of attitudes, 414
   eating behavior and, 295
   of gender roles, 354
   overview of, 204–205
   personality and, 374
   of prejudice, 428
observers, biases of, 402
obsessions, 473
obsessive-compulsive disorder (OCD), 471, 473, 474
   etiology of, 475
   neurotransmitters and, 70
   therapy for, 531
occipital lobe, 79, 80, 81, 107, 108
occupational attainment
   Big Five traits and, 363
   IQ scores and, 268–269
occupational stereotypes, 399
odors, types of, 127
Oedipal complex, 369–370, 509
oil supply, world's, A-33
olfactory bulb, 81, 126
olfactory cilia, 126
olfactory system, 126–127, 130–111
open monitoring, 161
openness to experience, 345, 363, 382, 390
operant chamber, 187
operant conditioning, 9, 186–198
   acquisition in, 188, 191
   of anxiety responses, 475
   of attitudes, 414
   basic processes in, 188–190
   discrimination in, 190
   extinction in, 189–190, 191
   of gender roles, 354
   generalization in, 191

interaction with classical conditioning, 195–196
   observational learning and, 201
   overview of, 204–205
   personality and, 388–389
   of prejudice, 428
   shaping in, 189
   Skinner's conception of, 186–188
   of sustainable lifestyles, A-38
   terminology and procedures for, 187–188
operational definitions, 33
operations, mental, 336
opiates, 78, 163, 164, 165
   endogenous, 71
opponent process theory, of color vision, 110–111
opposites, attraction of, 405
optic chiasm, 107
optic disk, 103, 104, 105
optic nerve, 83, 103, 105, 107
optical illusions, 118–119, 134, 135
optimal level of arousal, 442–443
optimal marginal of illusion, 447
optimism, 317
   comparative, A-39
   stress reduction and, 451
oral stage, 369
orders, obeying, 418–420
organic mental disorders, 470
orgasm phase, of sexual response cycle, 296
Origin of Species (Darwin), 90
ossicles, of ear, 123
osteoporosis, 495
outcomes, reinforcement and, 200–201
Outdoor Behavioral Health Industry Council, A-42
outgroups, 400, 429
outlining, 242
ovaries, 342, 343
overconfidence, 245
overconsumption, A-34–A-35
overdose, drug, 165, 166–167
overeating, 495
   behavior modification for, 208
overextension, 331–332
overextrapolations, 97
overregularization, 332
Oxycontin, 163
oxytocin, 85

P

Pagano, Bernard, 244
pain
   endorphins and, 71
   glia and, 65
   perception of, 127–129
   tolerance for, 128, 162
paintings, perceptual principles and, 132–135
palatability, of food, 293
Paltrow, Gyyneth, 479
pancreas, 293
panic disorder, 472
   etiology of, 476
   therapy for, 531
papillae, on tongue, 125
Pappenheim, Bertha, 504
parallel processing, in regulating hunger, 292
paralysis, spinal cord and, 74
paranoid schizophrenia, 486
parasympathetic nervous system, 73, 74, 306, A-41
paraventricular nucleus (PVN), 292, 293
parent-child attachment, 330

parental investment, 297
parenting/parenthood, 347
   as a fundamental human need, 378
   happiness and, 315
   psychology and, 20
parents
   caregiving styles of, 406
   children's personality and, 381, 393
   disciplinary procedures of, 197–198
   as source of prejudicial attitudes, 428
   unconditional love from, 376
parietal lobe, 79, 80, 107, 127
Parkinson's disease, 70, 77, 348
paroxetine, 519
participants, 33, 53
   deception of, 419
passionate love, 406
patterns, perception of, 112–120
Pavlovian conditioning, 178
Paxil, 519
peak experiences, 379
Pearson product-moment correlation, A-26
peer influence, in adolescence, 343
peer modeling, A-39
peer review process, 35
penis, 295
penis envy, 369
pennies, 215
percentile scores, 267, 345, A-24–A-25
perception, 101
   auditory, 124
   of color, 109–111
   of depth, 116–118
   of forms and patterns, 112–120
   Gestalt principles of, 114–116
   of pain, 128–199
   of taste, 125–126
   person, 398–400
   subjectivity of, 22, 112, 120, 129, 168, 399–400, 426
perceptual asymmetries, 83–84, 94
perceptual constancies, 118
perceptual hypotheses, 116
perceptual set, 112, 113, 116
perfectionism, 497
performance
   academic, 23
   individual versus group, 423
   see also task performance
performance pressure, 438–439
Pergament, Moshe, 1
peripheral nervous system, 72–73
peripheral route to, 416
peripheral vision, 105
persecution, delusions of, 486
person-centered theory, of personality, 376–377, 384–385
person perception, 398–400
   evolutionary perspective on, 400
   expectations and, 22
   subjectivity in, 399–400
person-situation controversy, 374–375
personal distress, as criterion for abnormality, 469
personal unconscious, 370
personality
   Adler's theory of, 371
   attractiveness and, 520
   behavioral perspectives on, 372–375, 384–385
   biological perspectives on, 379–382, 384–385
   consistency of, 362
   culture and, 403–404
   distinctiveness of, 362
   five-factor model of, 362–363
   Freud's psychoanalytic theory of, 364–372
   genetic basis for, 381

happiness and, 316–317
health and, 451–452
healthy, 379
heart disease and, 448–449
heredity and, 88
hindsight and, 392–393
humanistic perspectives on, 375–379, 384–385
impressions of, 399
Jung's theory of, 370–371
Maslow's view of, 377–379
multiple, 477–478
nature of, 362–363
observational learning and, 374
persuasability and, 413
psychodynamic perspectives on, 364–372
Rogers's person-centered theory of, 376–377, 384–385
social loafing and, 423
stability of, 345
personality, "split," 484, 485
personality development
   in adulthood, 344–346
   in childhood, 332–334
   Freud's stages of, 368–370, 385
   operant conditioning and, 373
   Rogers's view of, 376, 385
   Skinner's view of, 372–373, 385
personality disorders, 470
personality psychology, 16, 17
personality structure
   Eysenck's view of, 379–380, 385
   Freud's view of, 364–365, 366, 385
   Skinner's view of, 372–373, 385
personality tests, 302, 345, 389–391
personality traits, 362
   basic, 363, 385
   creativity and, 283
   culture and, 403–404
   eating disorders and, 496–497
   evolution and, 381
   heritability of, 381
   pro-environmental values and, A-37–A-38
   testing of, 390–391
persuasion, 411–412
   central route to, 416
   classical conditioning and, 210–211
   peripheral route to, 416
   resistance to, 413
   susceptibility to, 413
   techniques of, 136, 430–431
pessimism, 451–452, 484
pessimistic explanatory style, 483
pesticides, A-44
PET (positron emission tomography) scans, 75
phallic stage, 369
pharmaceutical industry, 520
phi phenomenon, 114
philosophy, psychology and, 3
phobias, 177–178, 180, 472
   conditioning of, 196, 475
   preparedness and, 199–200
   treatment for, 514, 515, 531
phobic disorder, 472–472
phonemic encoding, 217, 218, 229
phonological loop, 222
physical appearance, person perception and, 398
physical attractiveness. *See* attractiveness
physical dependence, on drugs, 154, 165, 166
physical fitness, 454, 461
physiological arousal, 73, 305–306
physiological needs, 377
physiological psychology, 16, 17

physiological recording, as data collection method, 34
physiology, psychology and, 3
Picasso, Pablo, 134
pictorial depth cues, 117–118, 132
pigeons
    operant condition of, 187, 189, 190, 200
    research on, 9
pineal gland, 144
pinna, 122, 123
pitch, 121, 124
pituitary gland, 98, 100, 85, 444
place theory, of hearing, 124
placebo effects, 50–51, 128, 129
    in therapy, 532, 533
placenta, 324, 326
plastics, A-44
plateau phase, of sexual response cycle, 295
Plato, 219
pleasure centers, in brain, 78, 166
pleasure principle, 364, 366
Poggendorff illusion, 119
pointillism, 133
poker, Internet, 1
poliarization, false, A-39
political agenda, 367
political debates, 33, 34
politics, classical conditioning and, 211
pollution, A-34
polygenic traits, 87
polygraph, 305–307
pons, 76, 77, 158, 170
Ponzo illusion, 119
population, 47, 50 , A-27
positive correlation, 41, 267, A-25
positive emotionality, 363
positive psychology, 452
positive psychology movement, 14, 379
postconventional level, 339
posthypnotic suggestion, 159
postsynaptic neuron, 66, 67
postsynaptic potential (PSP), 68
posttraumatic stress disorder (PTSD), 232, 474, A-36–A-37, A-41
potassium ions, 65
poverty 272, 367
    happiness and, 315
    use of mental health services and, 525
practical intelligence, 268, 279
Pragnanz, 116
preconscious, 365, 366
preconventional level, 339
predators, avoiding, 92
prediction, as goal of scientific approach, 32
preferences
    classical conditioning of, 210
    making choices about, 257–258
prefrontal cortex, 80, 166, 342, 343
pregnancy, 324–327
    drinking during, 326–327
    illness during, 489–490
    nutrition during, 326
prejudice, 410, 411, 426–429
    cultural worldviews and, 387
    defined, 427
    learning, 428
premature births, 338
premises, 318
prenatal development, 324–327
    environmental factors in, 326–327
    hormones in, 301, 352–353
    maternal drug use and, 326
    maternal illness and, 327
    maternal nutrition and, 326
    schizophrenia and, 489–490
preoperational period, 335, 336

preparedness, 199–209, 475
prescriptions, drug, 523
pressure, as source of stress, 438–439
presynaptic neuron, 66, 67
prevalence, lifetime, 498–499
primary appraisal, 436
primary auditory cortex, 79
primary colors, 110
primary motor cortex, 79, 80
primary-process thinking, 364, 366
primary sex characteristics, 342
primary somatosensory cortex, 79, 80
primary visual cortex, 79, 80, 107, 108, 109
Principles of Psychology (James), 5
Priscilla the Fastidious Pig, 189
prison guards, 420–421
proactive interference, 230, 231
probabilities
    evaluating, 462–463
    judging, 258–259
    in prevalence of psychological disorders, 498–499
    reasoning about, 498–499
    statistics and, A-28
problem solving, 250–256
    approaches to, 253–255
    barriers to, 250–253
    in childhood, 336
    culture and, 256
problems
    confronting, 447
    representation of, 255
    types of, 250, 251
"problems in living," 468
procedural memory system, 237, 238
procrastination, 456
productive vocabulary, 331
productivity, group, 422–423
prognosis, 468
progressive relaxation, 461
projection, 367, A-37
projective tests, 302, 391
prompts, A-38
PROP (propylthiouracil), 125
propaganda, 211
prosocial behavior, 340
prospective memory, 239
prototypes, 498, 499
provider-patient communications, 456
proximity, as Gestalt principle, 115
Prozac, 519
psilocybin, 164
psuedoforgetting, 229
psyche, 3
psychiatric nurses, 506
psychiatrists, 504, 506, 529
psychiatry, 18
psychic reflexes, 178
PsychINFO, 61–62
psychoactive drugs, 163–167
    dependence on, 165, 166
    effects of, 165
    medical uses of, 163
    neurochemical action of, 165–166
    principal types of, 163–165
    side effects of, 163
psychoanalysis, 6, 364, 504, 507–509, 523–524
psychoanalytic theory, 6–7, 13, 364–371, 393
    criticism of, 9, 371–372
psychodynamic theories, 364–372
    Adler's, 371
    evaluation of, 371–372
    Freud's, 364–370, 384–385
    Jung's, 370–371
psychodynamic therapies, 509–510
    effectiveness of, 530–531

psychological autopsies, 45
psychological dependence, on drugs, 165, 166
psychological disorders
    Big Five traits and, 363
    classification of, 470–471
    creativity and, 283
    medical model of, 467–468
    prevalence of, 498
    recovery from, 513
    suicide and, 45
    testing for, 390
    treatment of, 503–531
    see also specific disorders
psychological tests/testing, 20, 389–391
    of creativity, 282–283
    as data collection method, 34
    normal distribution on, A-24
    projective, 302
psychologists, 506
    environmental, A-29
    settings for, 16, 17
    see also therapists
psychology
    applied, 11–12, 17
    clinical, 11–12
    as college major, 15
    defined, 15
    degrees in, 17–18
    early history of, 3–11
    empiricism in, 19, 31
    ethics in, 52–54
    first formal laboratory for, 3
    myths about, 2
    origin of word, 3
    positive, 14
    as practical, 1
    as profession, 11–12, 16–18
    professional specialties in, 17–18
    research areas in, 16–17
    as science, 3–4
    scientific approach in, 31–36
    sociohistorical context for, 20
    theoretical diversity in, 19–20
    as way of thinking, 1
psychometrics psychology, 16, 17
psychosexual stages, 368–370
psychosocial crises, 333
psychosomatic diseases, 448
psychotherapy, 503–531
    behavioral approaches to, 513–516, 523–524
    benefits of, 513
    client-centered, 510–511, 523–524
    clients for, 505
    cognitive-behavioral approaches to, 515–516, 523–524
    cost of, 530
    eclecticism in, 524
    effectiveness of, 513, 516, 530–533
    group, 511–512
    multicultural sensitivity in, 524–525
    placebo effects in, 532
    practitioners of, 505–506
    process of, 531
    psychoanalytic approach to, 507–509, 523–524
    psychodynamic approaches to, 509–510
    quack, 533
    settings for, 529
    stigma associated with, 505
    types of, 504
    utilization rates for, 505
    willingness to seek, 505
    see also specific therapies; therapists
PTC (phenylthiocarbamide), 125
puberty, 341, 342, 370
public goods dilemmas, A-37

pulmonary diseases, 453
pulsatile hormone release, 85
punishment, 196–198
    aggression in children and, 203
    in behavior modification programs, 209
    personality development and, 373
    physical, 197–198
    toilet training and, 369
pupil, 103–104
purity
    of light, 102
    of sounds, 121, 122

Q

quail, 191
questionnaires, 46
    as data collection method, 34
    problems with, 51
Quichua (Ecuador), 310

R

racial stereotypes, 427
racism, 411
    modern, 427
random assignment, 39
random sampling, 39
rapid eye movements, 141, 146, 148–149
ratio schedules of reinforcement, 192, 193
rational-emotive behavior therapy, 459, 515, 530
rational thinking, 459
rationality, bounded, 257
rationalization, 367
rats
    enriched environments for, 96, 97
    operant conditioning of, 187, 188
reaction formation, 367
reaction range, 274, 275
reaction time, sleep deprivation and, 151
reactivity, 44
reading, improving, 24
reality principle, 364–365, 366
reasoning
    circular, 173, 319
    errors in, 263
    fallacies in, 284, 319
    in health decisions, 463
    moral, 338–340
reassurance seeking, 407
recall measures of retention, 228
receiver factors, in persuasion, 412, 413
receptive field
    of cells in visual cortex, 108–109
    of retinal cells, 106
    for skin cells, 127
receptive vocabulary, 331
receptor sites, 67, 68
receptors
    for hearing, 123, 124, 131
    for smell, 126, 131
    for taste, 125–126, 131
    visual, 104–105, 106, 131
reciprocity effects, 405
reciprocity norm, 211, 431
recognition heuristic, 263
recognition measures of retention, 288–229
reconstructive memory, 227–228, 244
recovered memories controversy, 231–234
recreational drugs, 163–167
recycling, A-35, A-44
red color, psychological effects of, 112
reflex, conditioned, 179
reflex learning, 237
reflex responses, 515

shuttle box, 194–195
siblings
  heredity and, 87–88
  personality differences in, 381
  see also genetic relatedness; twin studies
siesta cultures, 151
sight. *See* vision
signal relations, 200
similarity
  attraction and, 405, 408
  as Gestalt principle, 115
  of persuasive sources, 412
simplicity, as Gestalt principle, 115, 116
Sixteen Personality Factor Inventory, A-38
size constancy, 118, 119
size perception, 137
skepticism, 19, 35, 55
skewed distributions, A-22, A-23
skills
  memory for, 238
  motor, 328
skin, receptors in, 127, 131
Skinner box, 187, 188, 189–190, 193, 196
Slave Market with Disappearing Bust of Voltaire (Dali), 134
sleep, 145–155
  age trends in, 148, 150
  amount of, 150
  awareness during, 142
  brain centers for, 77
  common questions about, 169–170
  consolidation theory of, 236
  culture and, 150–151
  duration of, 153
  eye movements in, 141, 146–147, 148–149
  need for, 169
  onset of, 145
  problem solving during, 255
  quality of, 144, 461
  serotonin and, 70
  stages of, 145–151
sleep apnea, 154–155, 169
sleep deprivation, 151–155
sleep disorders, 153–155
sleep laboratories, 145
sleep problems, 169–170
sleep restriction, 151
sleep spindles, 146
sleepiness, 150, 155
sleeping pills, 154
sleepwalking, 155
slippery slope, 319, 367
slips of the tongue, 6, 365
slot machines, 192
slow-wave sleep (SWS), 146
  deprivation of, 152
  napping and, 169
SM, case study, 63
smell, sense of, 126–127, 130–131
smoking, 453–454
  depression and, 43
  heart disease and, 448
  prenatal development and, 326
  prevalence of, 453
  quitting, 453–454
  self-efficacy and, 374
snoring, 154, 169
sociability, ethnic differences in, 43–44
social activity happiness and, 316
social behavior, hormones and, 85
social class
  IQ scores and, 277
  sleep habits and, 150
  television viewing and, 46
social cognitive theory, 373–374, 375

social desirability bias, 51, 59, 391
social dilemmas, environmental, A-36–A-37
social identity, A-37
social influence, strategies of, 431
social intelligence, 268
social isolation, 451
social learning theory, 373, 375
social loafing, 423
social modeling, A-38
social motives, 291
social networking, 383, 407
social norms, 364, A-35
  deviation from, 468
social phobias, 476
social pressure, 417–421
social psychology, 16, 17, 397
Social Readjustment Rating Scale (SRRS), 438, 439
social roles, 421
social service agencies, 529, 530
social skills, poor, 484
social skills training, 515
social stigma, of mental illness, 468
social support
  adherence to medical advice and, 457
  implicit versus explicit, 451
  lack of, 484
  stress and, 451–452, 459
social workers, 506
socialization, 404
  cultural differences in, 403
  gender-role, 354–355
socioeconomic status
  longevity and, 376
  father absence and, 367
  IQ scores and, 275–276
  television viewing and, 46
sociohistorical context, 20, 168, 281, 314, 389
sodium ions, 65
soma, of neuron, 64
somatic nervous system, 73
somatoform disorders, 470
somatosensory cortex, 79, 127, 128
somnambulism, 155
Sonata, 154
sound, 121
source factors, in persuasion, 412, 430
source monitoring, 226–227
source-monitoring error, 227, 233, 244
spanking, 197
spatial ability, gender differences in, 27
special education, 270
specialization, in psychology, 17–18
species, evolution of, 14, 90–91
species-specific predispositions, 209
spectrum, 102, 109
speech, brain centers for, 82
sperm, 86, 324
sperm release, classical conditioning of, 181
spermarche, 342
spider monkeys, studies of, 44
spinal cord, 74, 76
  pain and, 129
split-brain research, 82–83
spontaneous recovery, in classical conditioning, 183
spontaneous remission, 513
sports teams, travel effects on, 144
sprachiasmatic nucleus (SCN), 144
SRRS, 438, 439
stage theories, 333
  Erikson's, 333–334, 343, 345–346
  Freud's, 368–370
  Kohlberg's, 338–340
  Piaget's, 334–337

standard deviation (SD), 266, A-23, A-24
Stanford-Binet Intelligence Scale, 265
Stanford Prison Simulation, 420–421
statistical methods, A-21–A-28
statistical significance, 462, A-28
statistics, 34, A-21
  descriptive, A-22–A-27
  empiricism and, A-28
  health-related, 462–463
  inferential, A-27–A-28
  probabilities and, 498–499
stereotypes, 387, 399
  ethnic, 44
  gender, 351
  implicit attitudes and, 410–411
  of mental illness, 468
  prejudice and, 427
stimulants, 70, 78, 163, 164, 165 167, 170
stimulus
  aversive, 194, 195, 196
  for color vision, 109
  conditioned, 179, 180, 181, 182, 183, 184, 185, 186, 195, 199, 200, 210, 413–414, 475
  discriminative, 190, A-38
  for hearing, 121
  neutral, 178–179
  for touch, 127
  unconditioned, 179, 180, 181, 182, 183, 184, 185, 186, 195, 199, 413–414
stimulus contiguity, 182
stimulus control, 190
stimulus discrimination, 185, 191
stimulus generalization, 183–184, 191
stimulus-response associations, 179
stomach contractions, hunger and, 291–292
storage, memory, 215, 219–225
strategies, decision making, 264
stream of consciousness, 5, 141
stress
  anxiety disorders and, 476, 493
  autonomic arousal and, 73
  behavioral response to, 441, 444–447
  brain-body pathways in, 443–444
  chronic, 443
  coining of term, 443
  coping with, 458–461
  defined, 435
  depression and, 481
  dissociative disorders and, 478
  emotional responses to, 441–443
  as everyday effect, 435
  exercise and, 454
  factors moderating, 451–452
  illness and, 449–450
  immune functioning and, 449–450
  as inevitable, 459
  meditation and, 162
  mood disorders and, 484, 493
  physiological response to, 305–306, 441, 443–444
  positive effects of, 452
  relaxation and, 461
  resistance to, self-efficacy and, 374
  schizophrenia and, 490
  self-imposed, 440
  types of, 436–440
  urban setting and, A-36–A-37, A-41–A-42
stress management, 458–461
stress-vulnerability models, 494
stressful events, appraisal of, 435–436, 459
string problem, 250, 251
structural encoding, 217, 218

structuralism, 4–5
study habits, 23–24, 241–242
subgoals, in problem solving, 253
subjective experiences, positive, 14
subjective well-being, 314–317
subjectivity
  of experience, 55, 165, 240, 458
  of perception, 22, 112, 120, 129, 168, 399–400, 426
  of person perception, 426
subjects
  deception of, 53
  in experiments, 36
  random assignment of, 39
  research, 8, 33, 50
sublimation, 367, 368
substance abuse treatment, 374
substance-related disorders, 470, 498
subtractive color mixing, 109, 110
success
  attributions for, 401–402, 408
  incentive value of, 303
sudden infant death syndrome, 326
suggestibility, 158
  of eyewitnesses, 227
suicide
  case studies of, 45
  mood disorders and, 481–482
  SSRIs and, 519
suicide by cop, 1
Sunday Afternoon on the Island of La Grande Jatte (Seurat), 133, 134
superego, 365, 366
superior colliculus, 107–108
superiority, striving for, 371
superstition, 177, 200–201, 467
supertasters, 125–126
Surrealists, 134
survey research, 33, 46, 48–49, 51
susceptibility, to persuasion, 413
sustainability, environmental, A-29–A-44
symbolism, in dreams, 171, 508
symbols, archetypes and, 370–371
sympathetic nervous system, 73–74, 306, 519
symptoms, interpretation of, 456
synapatic cleft, 166
synapses, 64–65, 66–68
  action of neurotransmitters at, 68–71
  creation of new, 68
  density of, 97
  dopamine, 488
  drug effects at, 165–166
  formation of, 96, 97
  for memory, 236–237
  new, 81
  number of, in brain, 71
synaptic cleft, 66, 67, 68
synaptic pruning, 68, 97, 342–343
synaptic vesicles, 67
systematic desensitization, 514, 515, 523–524, 531

T

tactile stimulation, 127
Tahiti, 309
tardive dyskinesia, 517
task performance
  achievement need and, 302
  arousal and, 442–443
  color and, 112
taste, sense of, 125–126, 130–131
taste aversions, 199, 295
taste buds, 125, 126
taste preferences, 91, 295
taste sensitivity, 126
tastes, primary, 125

MindTap Student User Guide

Welcome to MindTap's Student User Guide! This guide will help you get started with MindTap by providing in depth, step-by-step instructions, created specifically for the student user.

Contents

Benefits of Using MindTap

MindTap from Cengage Learning represents a new approach to a highly personalized, online learning platform. A cloud-based learning solution, MindTap combines all of your learning tools - readings, multimedia, activities and assessments into a singular Learning Path that guides you through the curriculum. Instructors personalize the experience by customizing the presentation of these learning tools to their students; even seamlessly introducing their own content into the Learning Path via "apps" that integrate into the MindTap platform.

Where to Buy

- Bookstore: **MindTap is available bundled with your textbook for a valuable savings at the bookstore.**

First Time Login

To get started, navigate to: login.cengagebrain.com.
➔ If this is your first time using a Cengage Learning Product, you will need to create a new account.

Create Profile

➔ Now you will need to enter the MindTap access code which came with your text.

➔ Follow the directions and create a Cengage Learning student account.

CENGAGE LEARNING
DIGITAL COURSE SUPPORT

→ Once completed, you will be directed to your dashboard.

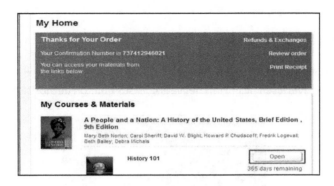

Enter Your Course Key

→ To access the MindTap product which you just registered, press

→ Enter your instructor-provided MindTap CourseKey.

→ Confirm that the Course Key corresponds to the correct course.

→ Choose Continue and you are bought directly into your MindTap Course!

Returning User

To get started, navigate to: login.cengagebrain.com. Please log in to your CengageBrain account to activate your product. If you have forgotten your password please select the "Forgot Password" link to retrieve your password.

CENGAGE Learning
ENGAGEMENT SERVICES

Walkthrough

Home Page – The Personal Learning Experience

→ MindTap is a customizable, complete solution that is more than an eBook and different from any learning management system you've ever used. MindTap delivers courses built on authoritative Cengage Learning content.

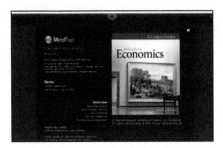

Learning Path

→ The MindTap experience begins with the **Learning Path**, which lists Pre-Lecture and Post-Lecture resources for every chapter. For example, click on Chapter 2 for examples of both resources.

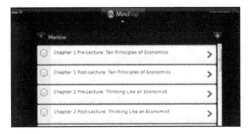

Pre-Lecture

Overview

→ Each chapter presents the same consistent set of **Pre-Lecture** resources.

Introduction Video

→ Every MindTap Pre-Lecture section begins with a relevant **Introduction Video** that highlights key topics—and engages interest.

Learning Objectives

→ After watching the video, you can review chapter **Learning Objectives**, which capture essential concepts in an easy-to-read format.

Chapter Overview

→ Next, read the **Overview**. It provides a breakdown of major topic areas and includes illustrations and examples that students can review before class.

Chapter Quiz

→ The **Pre-Lecture Quiz** provides you with a clear understanding of their strong and weak areas with respect to the topic, so you can tailor your studying accordingly.

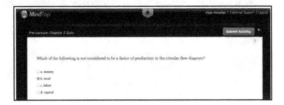

Post-Lecture

Overview

→ Within the **Post-Lecture**, students easily access their reading and homework assignments.

Reading Activity

→ An interactive learning resource, the **MindTap Reader** was built from the ground up to create a unique digital reading experience.

Homework

→ After completing the Reading Activity, move on to your **Homework**. You can complete and submit homework online—and receive instant feedback.

➜ When you answered incorrectly, you can read an explanation that clarifies the correct response.

Features

Easy Navigation

➜ Within the reader, users can navigate from section to section or page to page with guidance from page thumbnails and arrows.

Convenient Tools

➜ The robust functionality of the MindTap Reader allows students to make notes, highlight text, and even find a definition right from the page.

Learning Apps

Overview

➔ A comprehensive library of **Learning Apps** gives students what they need to prepare for a course or exam—all from a single platform.

Notebook

➔ By clicking the **My Notes** icon, students can access the **Notebook**, which allows them to write, print, and share their notes. They can also access their notes outside the MindTap environment if they have an EverNote account.

Dictionary

➔ The **Merriam-Webster dictionary app** makes it easy for students to find definitions of new or unfamiliar words. In addition, a click on a word that appears in bold font delivers the definition via the same app.

Flashcards

➔ Students can either click through MindTap Reader's **Flashcard app** or create their own flashcards to review key terms and concepts.

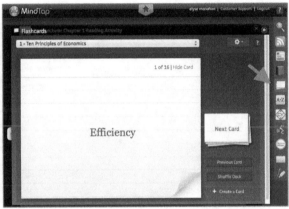

Text-to-Speech ReadSpeaker

➔ If students retain more information by hearing instead of reading, they can select a portion of the assignment and listen to it using the **ReadSpeaker text-to-speech app**.

ConnectYard

➔ MindTaps boosts engagement by encouraging students to interact with their content, as well as with their peers, instructors, and tutors via the **ConnectYard social app**.

View Progress

➔ The **View Progress App** archives grades and makes them easily available to you, keeping you apprised of personal and current class standings.

Product Support

Questions with your CengageBrain account?	Questions regarding MindTap?
• Check the FAQs in the Support area of your CengageBrain home. • Write to cengagebrain.support@cengage.com • Call 866.994.2427 Mon. through Fri. from 8 AM to 6 PM EST	• Go to www.cengage.com/support for 24/7 live chat! • Call 800.354.9706 Mon. through Thurs. 8:30 AM to 9 PM EST and Fri. 8:30 AM to 6 PM EST